HANDBOOK OF MEDICAL IMAGE COMPUTING AND COMPUTER ASSISTED INTERVENTION

THE ELSEVIER AND MICCAI SOCIETY BOOK SERIES

Advisory Board

Titles:

Balocco, A., et al., Computing and Visualization for Intravascular Imaging and Computer Assisted Stenting, 9780128110188

Dalca, A.V., et al., Imaging Genetics, 9780128139684

Depeursinge, A., et al., Biomedical Texture Analysis, 9780128121337

Munsell, B., et al., Connectomics, 9780128138380

Pennec, X., et al., Riemannian Geometric Statistics in Medical Image Analysis, 9780128147252

Wu, G., and Sabuncu, M., Machine Learning and Medical Imaging, 9780128040768

Zhou S.K., Medical Image Recognition, Segmentation and Parsing, 9780128025819

Zhou, S.K., et al., Deep Learning for Medical Image Analysis, 9780128104088

Zhou, S.K., et al., Handbook of Medical Image Computing and Computer Assisted Intervention, 9780128161760

MICCAI

HANDBOOK OF MEDICAL IMAGE COMPUTING AND COMPUTER ASSISTED INTERVENTION

Edited by

S. KEVIN ZHOU
Institute of Computing Technology
Chinese Academy of Sciences
Beijing, China

DANIEL RUECKERT
Imperial College London
London, United Kingdom

GABOR FICHTINGER
Queen's University
Kingston, ON, Canada

ACADEMIC PRESS
An imprint of Elsevier

Academic Press is an imprint of Elsevier
125 London Wall, London EC2Y 5AS, United Kingdom
525 B Street, Suite 1650, San Diego, CA 92101, United States
50 Hampshire Street, 5th Floor, Cambridge, MA 02139, United States
The Boulevard, Langford Lane, Kidlington, Oxford OX5 1GB, United Kingdom

Library of Congress Cataloging-in-Publication Data
A catalog record for this book is available from the Library of Congress

British Library Cataloguing-in-Publication Data
A catalogue record for this book is available from the British Library

ISBN: 978-0-12-816176-0

For information on all Academic Press publications
visit our website at https://www.elsevier.com/books-and-journals

Publisher: Mara Conner
Acquisition Editor: Tim Pitts
Editorial Project Manager: Leticia M. Lima
Production Project Manager: Selvaraj Raviraj
Designer: Christian J. Bilbow

Typeset by VTeX

Working together
to grow libraries in
developing countries

www.elsevier.com • www.bookaid.org

Contents

Contributors   *xvii*

Acknowledgment   *xxvii*

1. Image synthesis and superresolution in medical imaging   **1**

Jerry L. Prince, Aaron Carass, Can Zhao, Blake E. Dewey, Snehashis Roy, Dzung L. Pham

1.1.	Introduction	1
1.2.	Image synthesis	2
1.3.	Superresolution	12
1.4.	Conclusion	18
	References	19

2. Machine learning for image reconstruction   **25**

Kerstin Hammernik, Florian Knoll

2.1.	Inverse problems in imaging	26
2.2.	Unsupervised learning in image reconstruction	30
2.3.	Supervised learning in image reconstruction	32
2.4.	Training data	48
2.5.	Loss functions and evaluation of image quality	49
2.6.	Discussion	53
	Acknowledgments	54
	References	54

3. Liver lesion detection in CT using deep learning techniques   **65**

Avi Ben-Cohen, Hayit Greenspan

3.1.	Introduction	65
3.2.	Fully convolutional network for liver lesion detection in CT examinations	68
3.3.	Fully convolutional network for CT to PET synthesis to augment malignant liver lesion detection	77
3.4.	Discussion and conclusions	84
	Acknowledgments	87
	References	87

4. CAD in lung   **91**

Kensaku Mori

4.1.	Overview	91
4.2.	Origin of lung CAD	92
4.3.	Lung CAD systems	92
4.4.	Localized disease	93

4.5.   Diffuse lung disease   96
4.6.   Anatomical structure extraction   98
References   104

5.   Text mining and deep learning for disease classification   **109**

Yifan Peng, Zizhao Zhang, Xiaosong Wang, Lin Yang, Le Lu

5.1.   Introduction   109
5.2.   Literature review   110
5.3.   Case study 1: text mining in radiology reports and images   114
5.4.   Case study 2: text mining in pathology reports and images   122
5.5.   Conclusion and future work   129
Acknowledgments   130
References   130

6.   Multiatlas segmentation   **137**

Bennett A. Landman, Ilwoo Lyu, Yuankai Huo, Andrew J. Asman

6.1.   Introduction   138
6.2.   History of atlas-based segmentation   139
6.3.   Mathematical framework   146
6.4.   Connection between multiatlas segmentation and machine learning 154
6.5.   Multiatlas segmentation using machine learning   154
6.6.   Machine learning using multiatlas segmentation   155
6.7.   Integrating multiatlas segmentation and machine learning   155
6.8.   Challenges and applications   155
6.9.   Unsolved problems   156
Glossary   157
References   158

7.   Segmentation using adversarial image-to-image networks   **165**

Dong Yang, Tao Xiong, Daguang Xu, S. Kevin Zhou

7.1.   Introduction   165
7.2.   Segmentation using an adversarial image-to-image network   169
7.3.   Volumetric domain adaptation with intrinsic semantic cycle consistency   172
References   181

8.   Multimodal medical volumes translation and segmentation with generative adversarial network   **183**

Zizhao Zhang, Lin Yang, Yefeng Zheng

8.1.   Introduction   183
8.2.   Literature review   186
8.3.   Preliminary   188
8.4.   Method   190

8.5. Network architecture and training details 192
8.6. Experimental results 194
8.7. Conclusions 200
References 201

9. Landmark detection and multiorgan segmentation: Representations and supervised approaches **205**

S. Kevin Zhou, Zhoubing Xu

9.1. Introduction 205
9.2. Landmark detection 207
9.3. Multiorgan segmentation 217
9.4. Conclusion 227
References 227

10. Deep multilevel contextual networks for biomedical image segmentation **231**

Hao Chen, Qi Dou, Xiaojuan Qi, Jie-Zhi Cheng, Pheng-Ann Heng

10.1. Introduction 231
10.2. Related work 233
10.3. Method 235
10.4. Experiments and results 237
10.5. Discussion and conclusion 244
Acknowledgment 244
References 245

11. LOGISMOS-JEI: Segmentation using optimal graph search and just-enough interaction **249**

Honghai Zhang, Kyungmoo Lee, Zhi Chen, Satyananda Kashyap, Milan Sonka

11.1. Introduction 249
11.2. LOGISMOS 251
11.3. Just-enough interaction 256
11.4. Retinal OCT segmentation 257
11.5. Coronary OCT segmentation 260
11.6. Knee MR segmentation 265
11.7. Modular application design 268
11.8. Conclusion 269
Acknowledgments 270
References 270

12. Deformable models, sparsity and learning-based segmentation for cardiac MRI based analytics **273**

Dimitris N. Metaxas, Zhennan Yan

12.1. Introduction 273

12.2. Deep learning based segmentation of ventricles   277
12.3. Shape refinement by sparse shape composition   283
12.4. 3D modeling   285
12.5. Conclusion and future directions   288
References   288

13. Image registration with sliding motion   293
Mattias P. Heinrich, Bartłomiej W. Papież

13.1. Challenges of motion discontinuities in medical imaging   293
13.2. Sliding preserving regularization for Demons   296
13.3. Discrete optimization for displacements   303
13.4. Image registration for cancer applications   311
13.5. Conclusions   313
References   314

14. Image registration using machine and deep learning   319
Xiaohuan Cao, Jingfan Fan, Pei Dong, Sahar Ahmad, Pew-Thian Yap, Dinggang Shen

14.1. Introduction   319
14.2. Machine-learning-based registration   322
14.3. Machine-learning-based multimodal registration   326
14.4. Deep-learning-based registration   332
References   338

15. Imaging biomarkers in Alzheimer's disease   343
Carole H. Sudre, M. Jorge Cardoso, Marc Modat, Sebastien Ourselin

15.1. Introduction   344
15.2. Range of imaging modalities and associated biomarkers   345
15.3. Biomarker extraction evolution   349
15.4. Biomarkers in practice   353
15.5. Biomarkers' strategies: practical examples   356
15.6. Future avenues of image analysis for biomarkers in Alzheimer's disease   360
References   363

16. Machine learning based imaging biomarkers in large scale population studies: A neuroimaging perspective   379
Guray Erus, Mohamad Habes, Christos Davatzikos

16.1. Introduction   379
16.2. Large scale population studies in neuroimage analysis: steps towards dimensional neuroimaging; harmonization challenges   382
16.3. Unsupervised pattern learning for dimensionality reduction of neuroimaging data   385
16.4. Supervised classification based imaging biomarkers for disease diagnosis   387
16.5. Multivariate pattern regression for brain age prediction   389

16.6.   Deep learning in neuroimaging analysis   392
16.7.   Revealing heterogeneity of imaging patterns of brain diseases   393
16.8.   Conclusions   394
References   395

17. Imaging biomarkers for cardiovascular diseases   **401**

Avan Suinesiaputra, Kathleen Gilbert, Beau Pontre, Alistair A. Young

17.1.   Introduction   401
17.2.   Cardiac imaging   402
17.3.   Cardiac shape and function   404
17.4.   Cardiac motion   409
17.5.   Coronary and vascular function   412
17.6.   Myocardial structure   416
17.7.   Population-based cardiac image biomarkers   419
References   420

18. Radiomics   **429**

Martijn P.A. Starmans, Sebastian R. van der Voort, Jose M. Castillo Tovar, Jifke F. Veenland,
    Stefan Klein, Wiro J. Niessen

18.1.   Introduction   430
18.2.   Data acquisition & preparation   431
18.3.   Segmentation   434
18.4.   Features   437
18.5.   Data mining   441
18.6.   Study design   444
18.7.   Infrastructure   447
18.8.   Conclusion   451
Acknowledgment   452
References   452

19. Random forests in medical image computing   **457**

Ender Konukoglu, Ben Glocker

19.1.   A different way to use context   457
19.2.   Feature selection and ensembling   459
19.3.   Algorithm basics   460
19.4.   Applications   467
19.5.   Conclusions   476
References   476

20. Convolutional neural networks   **481**

Jonas Teuwen, Nikita Moriakov

20.1.   Introduction   481

20.2.   Neural networks   482
20.3.   Convolutional neural networks   487
20.4.   CNN architectures for classification   492
20.5.   Practical methodology   495
20.6.   Future challenges   499
References   500

21. Deep learning: RNNs and LSTM   **503**

Robert DiPietro, Gregory D. Hager

21.1.   From feedforward to recurrent   503
21.2.   Modeling with RNNs   507
21.3.   Training RNNs (and why simple RNNs aren't enough)   510
21.4.   Long short-term memory and gated recurrent units   514
21.5.   Example applications of RNNs at MICCAI   517
References   518

22. Deep multiple instance learning for digital histopathology   **521**

Maximilian Ilse, Jakub M. Tomczak, Max Welling

22.1.   Multiple instance learning   522
22.2.   Deep multiple instance learning   524
22.3.   Methodology   525
22.4.   MIL approaches   526
22.5.   MIL pooling functions   528
22.6.   Application to histopathology   533
References   545

23. Deep learning: Generative adversarial networks and adversarial methods   **547**

Jelmer M. Wolterink, Konstantinos Kamnitsas, Christian Ledig, Ivana Išgum

23.1.   Introduction   547
23.2.   Generative adversarial networks   549
23.3.   Adversarial methods for image domain translation   554
23.4.   Domain adaptation via adversarial training   558
23.5.   Applications in biomedical image analysis   559
23.6.   Discussion and conclusion   568
References   570

24. Linear statistical shape models and landmark location   **575**

T.F. Cootes

24.1.   Introduction   576
24.2.   Shape models   576
24.3.   Automated landmark location strategies   586
24.4.   Discussion   595

Appendix 24.A 595
References 597

25. Computer-integrated interventional medicine: A 30 year perspective 599

Russell H. Taylor

25.1. Introduction: a three-way partnership between humans, technology, and information to improve patient care 599
25.2. The information flow in computer-integrated interventional medicine 603
25.3. Intraoperative systems for CIIM 608
25.4. Emerging research themes 615
References 616

26. Technology and applications in interventional imaging: 2D X-ray radiography/fluoroscopy and 3D cone-beam CT 625

Sebastian Schafer, Jeffrey H. Siewerdsen

26.1. The 2D imaging chain 626
26.2. The 3D imaging chain 635
26.3. System embodiments 649
26.4. Applications 654
References 664

27. Interventional imaging: MR 673

Eva Rothgang, William S. Anderson, Elodie Breton, Afshin Gangi, Julien Garnon, Bennet Hensen, Brendan F. Judy, Urte Kägebein, Frank K. Wacker

27.1. Motivation 674
27.2. Technical background 675
27.3. Clinical applications 684
References 692

28. Interventional imaging: Ultrasound 701

Ilker Hacihaliloglu, Elvis C.S. Chen, Parvin Mousavi, Purang Abolmaesumi, Emad Boctor, Cristian A. Linte

28.1. Introduction: ultrasound imaging 702
28.2. Ultrasound-guided cardiac interventions 702
28.3. Ultrasound data manipulation and image fusion for cardiac applications 705
28.4. Ultrasound imaging in orthopedics 708
28.5. Image-guided therapeutic applications 711
28.6. Summary and future perspectives 715
Acknowledgments 715
References 716

29. Interventional imaging: Vision — 721

Stefanie Speidel, Sebastian Bodenstedt, Francisco Vasconcelos, Danail Stoyanov

29.1. Vision-based interventional imaging modalities — 722
29.2. Geometric scene analysis — 725
29.3. Visual scene interpretation — 732
29.4. Clinical applications — 734
29.5. Discussion — 736
Acknowledgments — 738
References — 738

30. Interventional imaging: Biophotonics — 747

Daniel S. Elson

30.1. A brief introduction to light–tissue interactions and white light imaging — 748
30.2. Summary of chapter structure — 749
30.3. Fluorescence imaging — 750
30.4. Multispectral imaging — 753
30.5. Microscopy techniques — 756
30.6. Optical coherence tomography — 760
30.7. Photoacoustic methods — 761
30.8. Optical perfusion imaging — 764
30.9. Macroscopic scanning of optical systems and visualization — 765
30.10. Summary — 767
References — 767

31. External tracking devices and tracked tool calibration — 777

Elvis C.S. Chen, Andras Lasso, Gabor Fichtinger

31.1. Introduction — 777
31.2. Target registration error estimation for paired measurements — 778
31.3. External spatial measurement devices — 780
31.4. Stylus calibration — 782
31.5. Template-based calibration — 784
31.6. Ultrasound probe calibration — 785
31.7. Camera hand–eye calibration — 787
31.8. Conclusion and resources — 790
References — 791

32. Image-based surgery planning — 795

Caroline Essert, Leo Joskowicz

32.1. Background and motivation — 795
32.2. General concepts — 796
32.3. Treatment planning for bone fracture in orthopaedic surgery — 798
32.4. Treatment planning for keyhole neurosurgery and percutaneous ablation — 804

32.5. Future challenges 811
References 813

33. Human–machine interfaces for medical imaging and clinical interventions 817

Roy Eagleson, Sandrine de Ribaupierre

33.1. HCI for medical imaging vs clinical interventions 817
33.2. Human–computer interfaces: design and evaluation 820
33.3. What is an interface? 821
33.4. Human outputs are computer inputs 822
33.5. Position inputs (free-space pointing and navigation interactions) 822
33.6. Direct manipulation vs proxy-based interactions (cursors) 823
33.7. Control of viewpoint 824
33.8. Selection (object-based interactions) 824
33.9. Quantification (object-based position setting) 825
33.10. User interactions: selection vs position, object-based vs free-space 826
33.11. Text inputs (strings encoded/parsed as formal and informal language) 828
33.12. Language-based control (text commands or spoken language) 828
33.13. Image-based and workspace-based interactions: movement and selection events 830
33.14. Task representations for image-based and intervention-based interfaces 833
33.15. Design and evaluation guidelines for human–computer interfaces: human inputs are computer outputs – the system design must respect perceptual capacities and constraints 834
33.16. Objective evaluation of performance on a task mediated by an interface 836
References 838

34. Robotic interventions 841

Pradipta Biswas, Sakura Sikander, Pankaj Pramod Kulkarni, Marilu Ortiz, Sang-Eun Song

34.1. Introduction 841
34.2. Precision positioning 842
34.3. Master–slave system 844
34.4. Image guided robotic tool guide 846
34.5. Interactive manipulation 848
34.6. Articulated access 850
34.7. Untethered microrobots 852
34.8. Soft robotics 853
34.9. Summary 855
References 855

35. System integration 861

Andras Lasso, Peter Kazanzides

35.1. Introduction 862
35.2. System design 862
35.3. Frameworks and middleware 864

35.4.	Development process	871
35.5.	Example integrated systems	875
35.6.	Conclusions	888
References		889

36. Clinical translation

893

Aaron Fenster

36.1.	Introduction	893
36.2.	Definitions	894
36.3.	Useful researcher characteristics for clinical translation	896
36.4.	Example of clinical translation: 3D ultrasound-guided prostate biopsy	901
36.5.	Conclusions	905
References		906

37. Interventional procedures training

909

Tamas Ungi, Matthew Holden, Boris Zevin, Gabor Fichtinger

37.1.	Introduction	909
37.2.	Assessment	911
37.3.	Feedback	917
37.4.	Simulated environments	919
37.5.	Shared resources	924
37.6.	Summary	925
References		925

38. Surgical data science

931

Gregory D. Hager, Lena Maier-Hein, S. Swaroop Vedula

38.1.	Concept of surgical data science (SDS)	931
38.2.	Clinical context for SDS and its applications	934
38.3.	Technical approaches for SDS	938
38.4.	Future challenges for SDS	942
38.5.	Conclusion	945
Acknowledgments		945
References		945

39. Computational biomechanics for medical image analysis

953

Adam Wittek, Karol Miller

39.1.	Introduction	953
39.2.	Image analysis informs biomechanics: patient-specific computational biomechanics model from medical images	955
39.3.	Biomechanics informs image analysis: computational biomechanics model as image registration tool	961
39.4.	Discussion	969

Acknowledgments 972
References 972

40. Challenges in Computer Assisted Interventions 979

P. Stefan, J. Traub, C. Hennersperger, M. Esposito, N. Navab

40.1. Introduction to computer assisted interventions 979
40.2. Advanced technology in computer assisted interventions 984
40.3. Translational challenge 991
40.4. Simulation 994
40.5. Summary 1004
References 1004

Index *1013*

Contributors

Purang Abolmaesumi
University of British Columbia, Vancouver, BC, Canada

Sahar Ahmad
Department of Radiology and BRIC, University of North Carolina, Chapel Hill, NC, United States

William S. Anderson
Department of Neurosurgery, Johns Hopkins Hospital, Baltimore, MD, United States

Andrew J. Asman
Pandora Media Inc., Oakland, CA, United States

Avi Ben-Cohen
Tel Aviv University, Faculty of Engineering, Department of Biomedical Engineering, Medical Image Processing Laboratory, Tel Aviv, Israel

Pradipta Biswas
Mechanical and Aerospace Engineering, University of Central Florida, Orlando, FL, United States

Emad Boctor
Johns Hopkins University, Baltimore, MD, United States

Sebastian Bodenstedt
National Center for Tumor Diseases (NCT), Partner Site Dresden, Division of Translational Surgical Oncology (TSO), Dresden, Germany

Elodie Breton
ICube UMR7357, University of Strasbourg, CNRS, Strasbourg, France

Xiaohuan Cao
Shanghai United Imaging Intelligence Co., Ltd., Shanghai, China

Aaron Carass
Dept. of Electrical and Computer Engineering, The Johns Hopkins University, Baltimore, MD, United States
Dept. of Computer Science, The Johns Hopkins University, Baltimore, MD, United States

M. Jorge Cardoso
School of Biomedical Engineering & Imaging Sciences, King's College London, London, United Kingdom

Jose M. Castillo Tovar

Erasmus MC, Department of Radiology and Nuclear Medicine, Rotterdam, the Netherlands

Erasmus MC, Department of Medical Informatics, Rotterdam, the Netherlands

Elvis C.S. Chen

Western University, London, ON, Canada

Robarts Research Institute, Western University, London, ON, Canada

Hao Chen

The Chinese University of Hong Kong, Department of Computer Science and Engineering, Hong Kong, China

Zhi Chen

The Iowa Institute for Biomedical Imaging, The University of Iowa, Iowa City, IA, United States

Jie-Zhi Cheng

Shenzhen University, School of Medicine, Shenzhen, China

T.F. Cootes

The University of Manchester, Manchester, United Kingdom

Christos Davatzikos

Artificial Intelligence in Biomedical Imaging Lab (AIBIL), Center for Biomedical Image Computing and Analytics (CBICA), Perelman School of Medicine, University of Pennsylvania, Philadelphia, PA, United States

Sandrine de Ribaupierre

Clinical Neurological Sciences, University of Western Ontario, London, ON, Canada

Blake E. Dewey

Dept. of Electrical and Computer Engineering, The Johns Hopkins University, Baltimore, MD, United States

Robert DiPietro

Johns Hopkins University, Department of Computer Science, Baltimore, MD, United States

Pei Dong

Shanghai United Imaging Intelligence Co., Ltd., Shanghai, China

Qi Dou

The Chinese University of Hong Kong, Department of Computer Science and Engineering, Hong Kong, China

Roy Eagleson

Software Engineering, University of Western Ontario, London, ON, Canada

Daniel S. Elson

Hamlyn Centre for Robotic Surgery, Institute of Global Health Innovation and Department of Surgery and Cancer, Imperial College London, London, United Kingdom

Guray Erus

Artificial Intelligence in Biomedical Imaging Lab (AIBIL), Center for Biomedical Image Computing and Analytics (CBICA), Perelman School of Medicine, University of Pennsylvania, Philadelphia, PA, United States

M. Esposito

Technische Universität München, Computer Aided Medical Procedures, Munich, Germany

Caroline Essert

ICube / Université de Strasbourg, Illkirch, France

Jingfan Fan

Department of Radiology and BRIC, University of North Carolina, Chapel Hill, NC, United States

Aaron Fenster

Robarts Research Institute, Western University, London, ON, Canada

Gabor Fichtinger

Queen's University, Kingston, ON, Canada

School of Computing, Queen's University, Kingston, ON, Canada

Afshin Gangi

Department of Interventional Imaging, Strasbourg University Hospital (HUS), Strasbourg, France

ICube UMR7357, University of Strasbourg, CNRS, Strasbourg, France

Julien Garnon

Department of Interventional Imaging, Strasbourg University Hospital (HUS), Strasbourg, France

ICube UMR7357, University of Strasbourg, CNRS, Strasbourg, France

Kathleen Gilbert

Department of Anatomy and Medical Imaging, University of Auckland, Auckland, New Zealand

Ben Glocker

Department of Computing, Imperial College London, London, United Kingdom

Hayit Greenspan

Tel Aviv University, Faculty of Engineering, Department of Biomedical Engineering, Medical Image Processing Laboratory, Tel Aviv, Israel

Mohamad Habes

Artificial Intelligence in Biomedical Imaging Lab (AIBIL), Center for Biomedical Image Computing and Analytics (CBICA), Perelman School of Medicine, University of Pennsylvania, Philadelphia, PA, United States

Ilker Hacihaliloglu

Rutgers University, Piscataway, NJ, United States

Gregory D. Hager

Johns Hopkins University, Department of Computer Science, Baltimore, MD, United States

Johns Hopkins University, Malone Center for Engineering in Healthcare, Baltimore, MD, United States

Kerstin Hammernik

Graz University of Technology, Institute of Computer Graphics and Vision, Graz, Austria

Department of Computing, Imperial College London, London, United Kingdom

Mattias P. Heinrich

Institute of Medical Informatics, University of Lübeck, Lübeck, Germany

Pheng-Ann Heng

The Chinese University of Hong Kong, Department of Computer Science and Engineering, Hong Kong, China

C. Hennersperger

Technische Universität München, Computer Aided Medical Procedures, Munich, Germany

Bennet Hensen

Department of Diagnostical and Interventional Radiology, Hannover Medical School, Hannover, Germany

Matthew Holden

School of Computing, Queen's University, Kingston, ON, Canada

Yuankai Huo

Vanderbilt University, Electrical Engineering, Nashville, TN, United States

Maximilian Ilse

University of Amsterdam, Amsterdam Machine Learning Lab, Amsterdam, the Netherlands

Ivana Išgum

Image Sciences Institute, University Medical Center Utrecht, Utrecht, the Netherlands

Leo Joskowicz

The Hebrew University of Jerusalem, Jerusalem, Israel

Brendan F. Judy
Department of Neurosurgery, Johns Hopkins Hospital, Baltimore, MD, United States

Urte Kägebein
Department of Diagnostical and Interventional Radiology, Hannover Medical School, Hannover, Germany

Konstantinos Kamnitsas
Imperial College London, London, United Kingdom

Satyananda Kashyap
The Iowa Institute for Biomedical Imaging, The University of Iowa, Iowa City, IA, United States

Peter Kazanzides
Computer Science, Johns Hopkins University, Baltimore, MD, United States

Stefan Klein
Erasmus MC, Department of Radiology and Nuclear Medicine, Rotterdam, the Netherlands
Erasmus MC, Department of Medical Informatics, Rotterdam, the Netherlands

Florian Knoll
New York University, Radiology, Center for Biomedical Imaging and Center for Advanced Imaging Innovation and Research, New York, NY, United States

Ender Konukoglu
Computer Vision Laboratory, ETH Zürich, Zürich, Switzerland

Pankaj Pramod Kulkarni
Mechanical and Aerospace Engineering, University of Central Florida, Orlando, FL, United States

Bennett A. Landman
Vanderbilt University, Electrical Engineering, Nashville, TN, United States

Andras Lasso
Queen's University, Kingston, ON, Canada
School of Computing, Queen's University, Kingston, Ontario, Canada

Christian Ledig
Imagen Technologies, New York, NY, United States

Kyungmoo Lee
The Iowa Institute for Biomedical Imaging, The University of Iowa, Iowa City, IA, United States

Cristian A. Linte

Rochester Institute of Technology, Rochester, NY, United States

Le Lu

Department of Radiology and Imaging Sciences, Clinical Center, National Institutes of Health, Bethesda, MD, United States

Ilwoo Lyu

Vanderbilt University, Electrical Engineering, Nashville, TN, United States

Lena Maier-Hein

German Cancer Research Center (DKFZ), Div. Computer Assisted Medical Interventions (CAMI), Heidelberg, Germany

Dimitris N. Metaxas

Rutgers University, Department of Computer Science, Piscataway, NJ, United States

Karol Miller

Intelligent Systems for Medicine Laboratory, Department of Mechanical Engineering, The University of Western Australia, Perth, WA, Australia

Marc Modat

School of Biomedical Engineering & Imaging Sciences, King's College London, London, United Kingdom

Kensaku Mori

Nagoya University, Nagoya, Japan

Nikita Moriakov

Radboud University Medical Center, Department of Radiology and Nuclear Medicine, Nijmegen, the Netherlands

Parvin Mousavi

Queen's University, Kingston, ON, Canada

N. Navab

Technische Universität München, Computer Aided Medical Procedures, Munich, Germany
Johns Hopkins University, Computer Aided Medical Procedures, Baltimore, MD, United States

Wiro J. Niessen

Erasmus MC, Department of Radiology and Nuclear Medicine, Rotterdam, the Netherlands
Erasmus MC, Department of Medical Informatics, Rotterdam, the Netherlands
Delft University of Technology, Faculty of Applied Sciences, Delft, the Netherlands

Marilu Ortiz

Mechanical and Aerospace Engineering, University of Central Florida, Orlando, FL, United States

Sebastien Ourselin

School of Biomedical Engineering & Imaging Sciences, King's College London, London, United Kingdom

Bartłomiej W. Papież

Big Data Institute, University of Oxford, Oxford, United Kingdom

Yifan Peng

National Center for Biotechnology Information, National Library of Medicine, National Institutes of Health, Bethesda, MD, United States

Dzung L. Pham

CNRM, Henry M. Jackson Foundation for the Advancement of Military Medicine, Bethesda, MD, United States

Beau Pontre

Department of Anatomy and Medical Imaging, University of Auckland, Auckland, New Zealand

Jerry L. Prince

Dept. of Electrical and Computer Engineering, The Johns Hopkins University, Baltimore, MD, United States

Dept. of Computer Science, The Johns Hopkins University, Baltimore, MD, United States

Xiaojuan Qi

The Chinese University of Hong Kong, Department of Computer Science and Engineering, Hong Kong, China

Eva Rothgang

Department of Medical Engineering, Technical University of Applied Sciences Amberg-Weiden, Weiden, Germany

Snehashis Roy

CNRM, Henry M. Jackson Foundation for the Advancement of Military Medicine, Bethesda, MD, United States

Sebastian Schafer

Advanced Therapies, Siemens Healthineers, Forchheim, Germany

Dinggang Shen

Department of Radiology and BRIC, University of North Carolina, Chapel Hill, NC, United States

Sakura Sikander

Mechanical and Aerospace Engineering, University of Central Florida, Orlando, FL, United States

Jeffrey H. Siewerdsen

Department of Biomedical Engineering, Johns Hopkins University, Baltimore, MD, United States

Sang-Eun Song

Mechanical and Aerospace Engineering, University of Central Florida, Orlando, FL, United States

Milan Sonka

The Iowa Institute for Biomedical Imaging, The University of Iowa, Iowa City, IA, United States

Stefanie Speidel

National Center for Tumor Diseases (NCT), Partner Site Dresden, Division of Translational Surgical Oncology (TSO), Dresden, Germany

Martijn P.A. Starmans

Erasmus MC, Department of Radiology and Nuclear Medicine, Rotterdam, the Netherlands
Erasmus MC, Department of Medical Informatics, Rotterdam, the Netherlands

P. Stefan

Technische Universität München, Computer Aided Medical Procedures, Munich, Germany

Danail Stoyanov

Wellcome/EPSRC Centre for Interventional and Surgical Sciences (WEISS), UCL Computer Sciences, London, United Kingdom

Carole H. Sudre

School of Biomedical Engineering & Imaging Sciences, King's College London, London, United Kingdom

Avan Suinesiaputra

Department of Anatomy and Medical Imaging, University of Auckland, Auckland, New Zealand

Russell H. Taylor

Department of Computer Science, Johns Hopkins University, Baltimore, MD, United States

Jonas Teuwen

Radboud University Medical Center, Department of Radiology and Nuclear Medicine, Nijmegen, the Netherlands
Netherlands Cancer Institute, Department of Radiation Oncology, Amsterdam, the Netherlands

Jakub M. Tomczak

University of Amsterdam, Amsterdam Machine Learning Lab, Amsterdam, the Netherlands

J. Traub

Technische Universität München, Computer Aided Medical Procedures, Munich, Germany
SurgicEye GmbH, Munich, Germany

Tamas Ungi

School of Computing, Queen's University, Kingston, ON, Canada

Sebastian R. van der Voort

Erasmus MC, Department of Radiology and Nuclear Medicine, Rotterdam, the Netherlands
Erasmus MC, Department of Medical Informatics, Rotterdam, the Netherlands

Francisco Vasconcelos

Wellcome/EPSRC Centre for Interventional and Surgical Sciences (WEISS), UCL Computer
Sciences, London, United Kingdom

S. Swaroop Vedula

Johns Hopkins University, Malone Center for Engineering in Healthcare, Baltimore, MD,
United States

Jifke F. Veenland

Erasmus MC, Department of Radiology and Nuclear Medicine, Rotterdam, the Netherlands
Erasmus MC, Department of Medical Informatics, Rotterdam, the Netherlands

Frank K. Wacker

Department of Diagnostical and Interventional Radiology, Hannover Medical School,
Hannover, Germany

Xiaosong Wang

Department of Radiology and Imaging Sciences, Clinical Center, National Institutes of Health,
Bethesda, MD, United States

Max Welling

University of Amsterdam, Amsterdam Machine Learning Lab, Amsterdam, the Netherlands

Adam Wittek

Intelligent Systems for Medicine Laboratory, Department of Mechanical Engineering, The
University of Western Australia, Perth, WA, Australia

Jelmer M. Wolterink

Image Sciences Institute, University Medical Center Utrecht, Utrecht, the Netherlands

Tao Xiong

Electrical and Computer Engineering, Johns Hopkins University, Baltimore, MD, United States

Daguang Xu

NVIDIA, Santa Clara, CA, United States

Zhoubing Xu

Siemens Healthineers, Princeton, NJ, United States

Zhennan Yan

SenseBrain, Princeton, NJ, United States

Dong Yang

Computer Science, Rutgers University, Piscataway, NJ, United States

Lin Yang

Department of Computer Information and Science Engineering (CISE), University of Florida, Gainesville, FL, United States

University of Florida, Biomedical Engineering, Gainesville, FL, United States

Pew-Thian Yap

Department of Radiology and BRIC, University of North Carolina, Chapel Hill, NC, United States

Alistair A. Young

Department of Anatomy and Medical Imaging, University of Auckland, Auckland, New Zealand

Boris Zevin

Department of Surgery, Queen's University, Kingston, ON, Canada

Honghai Zhang

The Iowa Institute for Biomedical Imaging, The University of Iowa, Iowa City, IA, United States

Zizhao Zhang

Department of Computer Information and Science Engineering (CISE), University of Florida, Gainesville, FL, United States

Can Zhao

Dept. of Electrical and Computer Engineering, The Johns Hopkins University, Baltimore, MD, United States

Yefeng Zheng

Tencent

S. Kevin Zhou

Institute of Computing Technology, Chinese Academy of Sciences, Beijing, China

Acknowledgment

We are deeply indebted to numerous people who made this book possible.

We thank all chapter authors who diligently finished their chapters and provided reviews on time and with quality. We extend our gratitude to the Elsevier team, especially the editor, Tim Pitts, and editorial project manager, Leticia M. Lima, who exhibited patience and provided help when needed while keeping the book production on schedule.

Kevin is grateful to his colleagues and friends, especially at the Institute of Computing Technology, Chinese Academy of Sciences (in particular, those at his MIRACLE group), including Dr. Xilin Chen, Ms. Xiaohong Wang, Dr. Hu Han, Dr. Li Xiao, Dr. Ruiping Wang, Dr. Shiguang Shan, Han Li, Ruocheng Gao, Qingsong Yao, Jun Li, Jiuwen Zhu, Zhiying Ke, Chao Huang, Zheju Li, etc., and at Z^2Sky Technologies, Inc., including Dr. Yuanyuan Lv, Zhiwei Cheng, Dr. Jingdan Zhang, Mr. Bo Wu, Haofu Liao, Wei-An Lin, Xiaohang Sun, Cheng Peng, Jiarui Zhang, Dr. Hai Su, Kara Luo, Yefeng Jiang, Xinwei Yu, etc., for their support and help. Kevin really appreciates Rama's mentoring and support for almost 20 years.

Finally, thanks to our families who shared the burden of this work.

S. Kevin Zhou, Daniel Reuckert, Gabor Fichtinger

August 28, 2019

CHAPTER 1

Image synthesis and superresolution in medical imaging

Jerry L. Prince[a,b]**, Aaron Carass**[a,b]**, Can Zhao**[a]**, Blake E. Dewey**[a]**, Snehashis Roy**[c]**, Dzung L. Pham**[c]

[a]Dept. of Electrical and Computer Engineering, The Johns Hopkins University, Baltimore, MD, United States
[b]Dept. of Computer Science, The Johns Hopkins University, Baltimore, MD, United States
[c]CNRM, Henry M. Jackson Foundation for the Advancement of Military Medicine, Bethesda, MD, United States

Contents

1.1. Introduction	1
1.2. Image synthesis	2
1.2.1 Physics-based image synthesis	2
1.2.2 Classification-based synthesis	3
1.2.3 Registration-based synthesis	5
1.2.4 Example-based synthesis	6
1.2.5 Scan normalization in MRI	9
1.3. Superresolution	12
1.3.1 Superresolution reconstruction	12
1.3.2 Single-image deconvolution	14
1.3.3 Example-based superresolution	15
1.4. Conclusion	18
References	19

1.1. Introduction

Two of the most common classes of image processing algorithms are image restoration and image enhancement. *Image restoration* is a process that seeks to recover an image that has been corrupted in some way. Unlike image reconstruction, which recovers images from observations in a different space, image restoration is an image–to–image operation. *Image enhancement* is an image–to–image process that creates new characteristics in images that were not present in the original or the observed image. Image enhancement is generally used to generate more visually pleasant images. In the context of medical imaging, both of these general processes are used either to improve images for visualization or to facilitate further analysis for either clinical or scientific applications.

Image synthesis and superresolution are special cases of image restoration and enhancement. *Image synthesis*, where one creates new images whose acquisition contrast or modality had not been acquired, can be thought of as belonging to either category, restoration or enhancement, depending on its use. *Superresolution*, where one creates images whose resolution is better than that which was observed, falls into the category of image enhancement and can be implemented using image synthesis techniques. Since image synthesis has become a very general approach, offering broad applications in medical imaging, including its application to superresolution, we begin this chapter by describing image synthesis. With this background in hand, we move on to describe superresolution.

1.2. Image synthesis

In its most general form, image synthesis is the process of creating new images that had not been acquired from an image description or observed data. In the medical imaging context, this has usually meant an *image-to-image* [33,39] transformation wherein a set of input images depicts the anatomy under specified acquisition conditions, and the output image depicts the same anatomy under different acquisition conditions. Examples include synthesizing a computed tomography (CT) image from one or more magnetic resonance (MR) images [29] and synthesizing a T2-weighted (T_2w) MR image from a T1-weighted (T_1w) MR image [45]. Important applications of this basic idea include direct synthesis of image segmentations [37], synthesis for reducing noise or artifacts in images [15], and synthesis for superresolution [96]. To illustrate the power of image synthesis and because it is an important emerging capability in medical imaging, we describe superresolution in the second part of this chapter.

Before proceeding, we note that *image synthesis* has other names. Hofmann et al. [35, 36] and others [13,17] have used the prefix *pseudo* to mean synthetic—e.g., pseudo-CT. The phrase *image quality transfer* has also been used for synthesis [1]. The words *normalization*, *data harmonization*, and *homogenization* typically have narrower meanings but are often carried out by synthesis methods. Our use of the term image synthesis is fairly well accepted and is also used in the computer vision community, though we note that the term *image translation* can also be considered a synonym for image synthesis and is in increasingly common use.

1.2.1 Physics-based image synthesis

In *physics-based image synthesis* (in MR imaging), several images are acquired of the same anatomy with different pulse sequences and pulse sequence parameters so that one or more underlying physical parameters—e.g., T_1, T_2, and P_D (proton density)—can be computed by inverting the so-called *imaging equations* [61,68]. Given the underlying physical parameters, these same imaging equations can then be used to synthesize new images of the anatomy as if they had been acquired with different pulse sequence parameters or even entirely different pulse sequences. One advantage of generating images

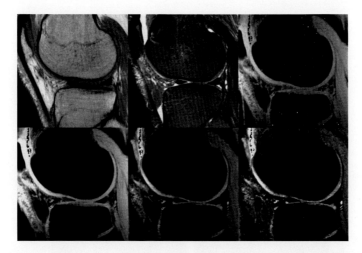

Figure 1.1 Sagittal images of a normal knee. Top left: Standard intermediate-weighted fast SE MR image. Top middle: Fat-saturated T2-weighted fast SE MR image. Four additional images were acquired with variable T2-weighted image contrasts to generate a T2 map of the tissue. Synthetic images with arbitrary TE can then be created and four examples are shown here: top right, TE = 0 ms; bottom left, TE = 6 ms; bottom middle, TE = 30 ms; bottom right, TE = 60 ms. (Credit: Andreisek et al. [3].)

this way is that because the synthetic images are produced mathematically, they need not correspond to physically realizable pulse sequences. This early work was extended to *pulse sequence extrapolation* [6,52], synthesis in which multiple acquired spin–echo images were used to generate inversion-recovery images with arbitrary inversion times. With this approach, one could carry out retrospective optimization of the MR image contrast between one or more tissues. An illustration of this approach using sagittal images of a normal male knee is shown in Fig. 1.1.

1.2.2 Classification-based synthesis

Physics-based synthesis requires knowledge of the underlying tissue parameters at each voxel. *Classification-based synthesis* is a relaxed version of this method, wherein only the *type* of tissue that makes up each voxel is required. In this case, nominal physical parameter values corresponding to that tissue type are used in imaging equations to synthesize an image with an arbitrary contrast. For example, if an image containing just the brain is classified into gray matter (GM), white matter (WM), and cerebrospinal fluid (CSF), then the T_1, T_2, and P_D values that have been previously measured for these types of tissues can be used to synthesize a new image having the same anatomy.

Classification-based synthesis has the advantage of cross–modality synthesis using physics and mathematical imaging equations. For example, an MR image segmented into different tissue classes can use the linear attenuation coefficients of those classes to synthesize a CT image of the subject. This approach has been used with a Dixon pulse

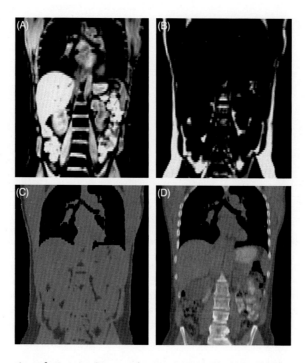

Figure 1.2 Segmentation of a 2-point Dixon pulse sequence with derived (A) water and (B) fat images producing the (C) linear attenuation map; (D) the linear attenuation map derived from CT shows bone that cannot be observed from the Dixon pulse sequence. (From Martinez-Moller A., Souvatzoglou M., Delso G., et al., Tissue classification as a potential approach for attenuation correction in whole-body PET/MRI: evaluation with PET/CT data, J. Nucl. Med. 50 (4) (2009) 520–526, Figure 3, © SNMMI.)

sequence [55] to synthesize CT images for attenuation correction in PET-MR scanners [57]; this pulse sequence allows easy classification of background, watery tissues, and fatty tissues where approximate X-ray linear attenuation coefficients are known. Direct physics-based synthesis cannot be used for this application since there is no way to directly estimate (i.e., via imaging equations) the linear attenuation coefficient for X-rays from multiple MR image acquisitions. A fundamental problem with this application of classification-based synthesis is that the accuracy of the approach depends on the capability of the segmentation algorithm. Since the Dixon pulse sequence cannot visualize bone, bone is not among the tissues that are labeled, leading to problematic results in man body regions. Fig. 1.2 illustrates this method, as well as its inability to synthesize bone.

Classification-based synthesis is at the core of BrainWeb [12], an important MR neuroimage simulation package that has been used extensively in the evaluation of image processing algorithms. BrainWeb goes four steps further than what is described above in that: (i) it uses hand-guided segmentations for tissue classification, (ii) it includes a relatively large number of tissue types, (iii) it uses soft classification—so-called *membership functions*—to describe the partial volume contributions of the tissue types that comprise each voxel, and (iv) images are synthesized from the classification using physics-based models which includes the application of random noise and intensity inhomogeneities (if directed to do so) in order to produce very realistic neuroimages. The BrainWeb approach is limited in that the image can only be synthesized on the available anatomies (around two dozen) that have been carefully prepared for this purpose.

1.2.3 Registration-based synthesis

Registration-based image synthesis was first proposed in the seminal paper of Miller et al. [58]. This approach requires a *textbook* or *atlas* (in today's preferred vernacular), which is a collection of multiple images of a given subject (or multiple subjects). When the atlas is deformed into alignment with the subject (or target) anatomy, typically using deformable registration, then all of the atlas images can be carried by the same transformation into alignment with the subject. Since (ideally) the atlas images now match the anatomy of the subject, these transformed images can be considered as synthetic subject images. Miller et al. considered the case where alternate MR tissue contrasts are present in the atlas as well as different modalities such as CT and positron emission tomography (PET). Miller et al. [58] also envisioned synthesis through the combination of registration and classification-based synthesis. Here, they suggested that an atlas containing tissue classifications could be registered to the subject and then used with imaging equations to synthesize a new modality or contrast.

Hofmann et al. [35,36] explored registration based synthesis by having anatomical textbooks, or rather *atlas pairs*, of MR and CT images. They registered the atlas MR image and a subject MR image, and then applied the deformation to the atlas CT image to generate a subject pseudo-CT image. However, instead of working with just a single image pair as an atlas, they used n MR/CT atlas pairs ($n = 17$ [36]) with all image pairs being registered to the subject MR image, yielding n predictions of the subject's CT values. The use of multiple registrations made the method more robust to the potentially poor alignments that can result from large differences in anatomy or poor convergence of the algorithm. The outputs from the multiple registrations were combined to determine the subject's CT image. Various combination strategies have been proposed. Hofmann et al. [35] used a patch similarity index, where a voxel-wise similarity between a registered MR atlas and the subject MR was computed based on the ℓ_2 distance between patches obtained from atlas and subject MR images, as well as their (5-class) segmentations at that voxel, with a weight giving more importance to the center voxel of patches. Once the similarity image was computed for each registered atlas, the corresponding atlas CTs were weighted by the similarity index and linearly combined.

Burgos et al. [8,9] proposed a different similarity index based on blurring the registered MR images and computing voxel-wise correlations. However, instead of directly using correlations as the similarity, they used weighted ranks of correlations for a more

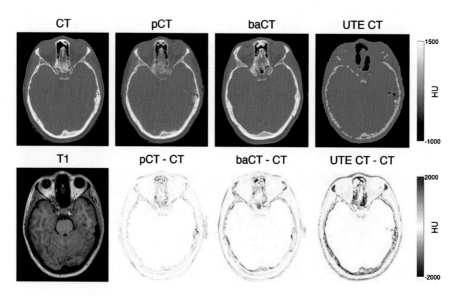

Figure 1.3 Top left to right: the acquired CT, the pseudo-CT obtained using multiple atlases, the pseudo-CT obtained using the best atlas, and the pseudo-CT obtained using a pair of ultrafast echo-time (UTE) MR images. Bottom left to right: the acquired T1-weighted image and three differences between the pseudo-CTs (top row) and the true acquired CT. (Credit: Burgos et al. [8].)

robust measure, because MR intensities are inherently prone to inhomogeneity and noise. An example result using this method is shown in Fig. 1.3. A similar strategy was described by Lee et al. [51], where local correlations were replaced by a structural similarity index (SSIM), which is less sensitive to contrast stretching and noise.

Wu et al. [90] used a dictionary-based approach where more accurate and time consuming deformable registration was not required; instead, an affine registration was sufficient to align the subject and atlas images. They proposed local patch dictionaries from multi-contrast (T_1w and T_2w) atlas MR images, which were used to find weights for a subject MR patch. The weights were assumed to be nonnegative and sparse, leading to only very similar atlas patches from the dictionary having nonzero weights. The corresponding atlas CT patches were combined with the sparse weights to generate a synthetic subject CT patch. A similar strategy was used by Degen et al. [13], where the dictionary was comprised of MIND features of the images [32] instead of raw MR intensities.

1.2.4 Example-based synthesis

Example-based synthesis methods use atlases or training data to help estimate the synthetic output but, unlike registration-based synthesis methods, are not dependent on the spatial alignment of the subject image and the atlases. One of the early examples of this approach was by Hertzmann et al. [33], who proposed—in the context of computer vision—the concept of *image analogies*, which looks for image B' that is analogous to image B in the same way that image A' is analogous to image A. Here, $\mathcal{A} = \{A, A'\}$ is an atlas (or textbook) in the same way that registration-based synthesis had an atlas. But rather than using deformable registration to register A (and A') to B, this method finds a mapping (or regression) between features in A and intensities in A' and then applies that same mapping to features in B in order to generate B'. Here, the atlas features provide examples that are used to determine the mapping used for synthesis, which is the reason for calling this basic approach *example-based synthesis*. Emerging from this fundamental notion, there are a host of methods that have been proposed for image synthesis in medical imaging, differing in the nature of the atlas images, how the features are defined, and how the regression is learned.

Sparse reconstruction synthesis. Roy et al. [72,73] used $m \times m \times m$ patches surrounding a given voxel as the features in A. This choice acknowledges that a one-to-one relationship between the voxels in A and those in A' is unlikely to exist, but the context surrounding a given voxel in A will provide additional information about the desired value in A' to synthesize. In this paper, the principle of sparse reconstruction is used to form the desired mapping. Given a patch $\mathbf{b}$, a collection of N patches in A that resemble $\mathbf{s}$ are found and arranged as a matrix $\mathbf{A} = [\mathbf{a}_1, \ldots, \mathbf{a}_N]$—i.e., a patch dictionary. Then the following sparse reconstruction problem is solved for each voxel

$$\hat{x} = \arg\min_{x}\{\|\mathbf{b} - \mathbf{A}x\|_2^2 + \lambda\|x\|_1\}, \tag{1.1}$$

where λ is a regularization constant that determines the sparsity of x. The corresponding patches from the desired atlas image A' is arranged as matrix $\mathbf{A}' = [\mathbf{a}'_1, \ldots, \mathbf{a}'_N]$ and the new contrast is computed as

$$\hat{\mathbf{b}}' = \mathbf{A}'\hat{x}. \tag{1.2}$$

The interpretation of (1.1) is that it finds a sparse collection of patches in atlas image A that *reconstructs* (approximately) the desired patch in B. When these discovered coefficients are used in (1.2), the desired contrast is reconstructed in a parsimonious manner from an optimal matching set of patches. Typically only the center voxel is used in the reconstruction of the whole image so these two steps must be repeated for each voxel, which is a time-consuming process. An example result of this method—known as "MR Image Example-based Contrast Synthesis" or MIMECS–from Roy et al. [73] is shown in Fig. 1.4.

Random forest regression synthesis. Rather than defining an explicit mapping between features in the atlas, the previous approach defines an implicit mapping that is computed for each subject patch "on the fly." Machine learning methods, on the other

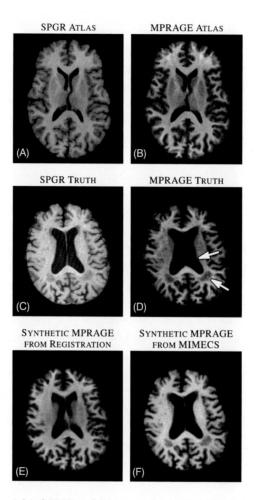

Figure 1.4 (A) Atlas T1-weighted SPGR and (B) its corresponding T1-weighted MPRAGE; (C) Subject T1-weighted SPGR scan and (D) its T1-weighted MPRAGE image (only used for comparison). Atlas SPGR is deformably registered to the subject SPGR. This deformation is applied to the atlas MPRAGE to obtain (E) a synthetic subject MPRAGE; (F) Synthetic MPRAGE image generated by MIMECS. (Credit: Roy et al. [73].)

hand, focus on finding an explicit mapping—i.e., a regression $\mathcal{R}$—between patches **a** in the A image in the atlas and corresponding intensities a' in the A' image in the atlas. Given this mapping, synthetic images are created by running subject patches through this trained regression: $b' = \mathcal{R}\{\mathbf{b}\}$.

Jog et al. [40,41,45,46] and others [1,2,93] find the desired mapping using random forests (RF) [7]. One benefit of using random forests is that they tend to require a relatively small amount of training data (than, for example, deep networks) and they can easily use any available features besides simple patches. In particular, Jog et al. [45]

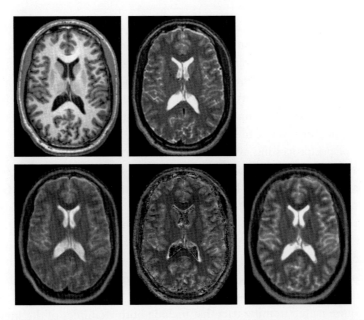

Figure 1.5 Top left to right: the input MPRAGE image and the real T2-weighted image (shown only for comparison). Bottom left to right: a registration fusion result (similar to Burgos et al. [8]), the MIMECS result (see [73]), and the REPLICA synthetic T2-weighted image. (Credit: Jog et al. [45].)

showed that just three paired subject 3D images provided sufficient training data. It was also shown that patches with an additional "constellation" of average image values taken from three image scales provided improved performance when data from outside the brain (skin, fat, muscle) were synthesized. Jog et al. [45] also demonstrated how data from multiple acquisitions—e.g., T_1w, T_2w, and P_Dw—could be used within the same framework to lead to improved synthesis of fluid attenuated inversion recovery (FLAIR) images, readily revealing the white matter lesions that are usually present in multiple sclerosis (MS) patients. An example result from Jog et al. [45] (the method called REPLICA) is shown in Fig. 1.5.

1.2.5 Scan normalization in MRI

Unlike some modalities such as CT, MRI is not inherently a quantitative imaging technique, particularly with respect to common structural T_1w and T_2w sequences. This issue is compounded by the fact that the intensity properties of the acquisition are affected by a wide variety of pulse sequence parameters. Differences in intensity properties have been shown to cause substantial discrepancies in the results of automated image segmentation algorithms and other quantitative analyses [5,20,48,49,77,82]. Biberacher et al. [5] examined brain volume variations across acquisitions from different scanner manufacturers, and showed that interscanner variation on a number of different brain and lesion volume measures were found to be significantly larger than the intrascanner variation. One common approach to address this issue is to perform harmonized acquisitions by restricting the field strength, scanner manufacturer, and pulse sequence protocol. However, Shinohara et al. [82] imaged a multiple sclerosis patient at seven different sites across North America, and even with careful matching of the MRI pulse sequences, brain volume variations across sites derived from several different segmentation algorithms were still significant.

A number of postprocessing approaches have been proposed for dealing with scan intensity differences, including statistical modeling [11,47], and alignment of image histograms using linear or piecewise linear transformations [31,59,60,79,83]. Because the transformations alter the global histogram, local contrast differences are not addressed by this approach. Furthermore, there is an inherent assumption that the global histogram is similar in the two images being matched. In the case where one image possesses pathology and the other does not or when the extent of pathology differs markedly, this assumption is violated and can lead to inaccurate results. Example-based image synthesis approaches have also been proposed for contrast normalization [15,45,73]. Most approaches require paired training data that include both examples of the input acquisition and the output acquisition.

Fig. 1.6 shows an example of an example-based deep learning technique for paired harmonization [15]. In this work, scans from the same set of patients before and after a scanner hardware and software upgrade were acquired and used as training data. Because scans took place within a short time span, anatomical changes were assumed to be negligible. The differing appearance of ventricular size is primarily due to partial volume averaging caused by thicker sections in the prior FLAIR sequence. The synthesis was based on a modified 2D U-net architecture [69] applied to three orthogonal views. Overall the harmonized images show remarkable consistency and this was further corroborated by significantly improved stability in segmentation volumes [15].

In performing scan normalization, the requirement that the atlas images have the same scan properties as the input data can be difficult to fulfill, particularly in retrospective analyses where such paired data may have never been acquired. The PSI-CLONE (Pulse Sequence Information-based Contrast Learning On Neighborhood Ensemble) synthesis method [43] addresses this problem by first performing a pulse sequence regression step that adjusts for these differences. This is accomplished by combining physics-based synthesis with example-based synthesis. PSI-CLONE uses imaging equations to model the sequences, and aligns the image intensities in the parameter space of the equations. A flow chart depicting the steps of PSI-CLONE is provided in Fig. 1.7. Rather than include a specific type of MRI scan, quantitative maps (denoted A_q in the figure) of the underlying nuclear magnetic resonance (NMR) parameters, T_1, T_2, and P_D are included within its atlas images, along with a set of desired output atlases. By estimating the pulse sequence parameters P of the input image, the NMR

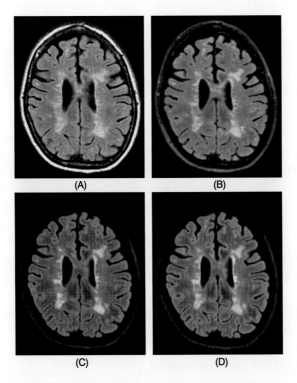

Figure 1.6 Paired harmonization: (A) scan before acquisition upgrade, (B) scan after upgrade, (C) harmonized scan before upgrade, (D) harmonized scan after upgrade. (Credit: Dewey et al. [15].)

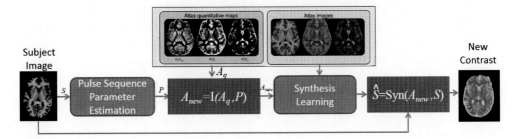

Figure 1.7 Flow chart for Ψ-CLONE synthesis. An input subject image has its pulse sequence parameters estimated, which are used to create a customized atlas, A_{new}, from the Atlas quantitative maps. This A_{new} is used to train a regression between pulse sequence of the input subject image and the desired contrast. See the text for complete details. (Credit: Jog et al. [44].)

parameters can be used to synthesize an atlas contrast that is similar to the subject image, denoted A_{new}. A patch–based regression [43,45] is then applied to map the original image to the desired output contrast. Because synthesis offers greater flexibility in that the transformation can be based on local properties of the images, and be non-parametric, PSI-CLONE was shown to outperform global histogram normalization methods [43].

1.3. Superresolution

Superresolution can be thought of as resolution enhancement (when image acquisition limits the resolution) or resolution restoration (when image transmission has led to a loss of data and consequently degraded resolution). To be clear, it refers to improvement of the underlying (physics-based) resolution, not the digital resolution of the image voxels. Zero-padding Fourier space (as is often done on the MR scanner itself), for example, is not superresolution since it only affects the spacing between the voxels that represent the image. Superresolution can be an approach that combines acquisition strategies with postprocessing, as in *superresolution reconstruction* [63], or an approach that is strictly limited to postprocessing, as in *image deconvolution* [50]. Computer vision researchers tend to refer to these processes as *multiimage superresolution* [30] and *single-image superresolution*, respectively. In this section, we consider superresolution developments from both historical and technical points of view and provide a few examples of the most important developments related to medical imaging.

1.3.1 Superresolution reconstruction

Superresolution reconstruction (SRR) involves the acquisition of multiple low-resolution (LR) scans that are combined in postprocessing to achieve a single high-resolution (HR) scan. SRR has been well-developed and validated in simulations, phantoms, and human studies [26,63,87]. Nearly all approaches have focused on improving through-plane resolution using multiple image volumes acquired with poor resolution in one direction (the through-plane direction). Early efforts considered the acquisition of shifted image stacks [26,27]; however, it has been shown that these methods can reduce the effects of through-plane aliasing but can only improve resolution through deconvolution since all images have precisely the same Fourier information in them [75].

The most common method for SRR is to combine multiple acquisitions of rotated image stacks (so-called multiorientation scans), which have different Fourier information among the scans [4,24,76,87,89]. An illustration of the Fourier content of three hypothetical image stacks acquired in the axial, coronal, and sagittal orientations is shown in Fig. 1.8. It is clear that any one acquisition is lacking Fourier content in their through plane direction, but by combining the three acquisitions, some of the missing Fourier information is recovered. An example of a superresolution reconstruction using six rotated orientations is shown in Fig. 1.9.

All of these early approaches are model-based and typically incorporate a geometric transformation, a blur operator (the PSF), a downsampling operator, and a noise term to model each acquired LR image. Given such a model, a classical SRR algorithm has

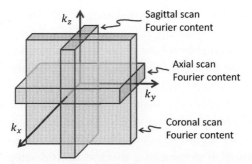

Figure 1.8 Illustration of the Fourier content for three hypothetical scans acquired in the axial, sagittal, and coronal directions.

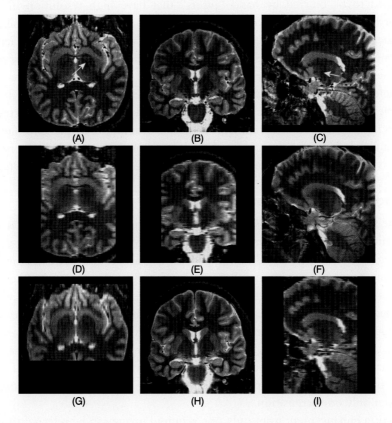

Figure 1.9 Example of superresolution reconstruction from multiple orientations: (A)–(C) axial, coronal, and sagittal views of the superresolution result (voxel size $0.5 \times 0.5 \times 0.5$ mm) that used six rotated multislice image stacks and algebraic reconstruction technique (ART) reconstruction; (D)–(F) axial, coronal, and sagittal views of one sagittal multislice stack (voxel size $3 \times 0.46875 \times 0.46875$ mm); (G)–(I) axial, coronal, and sagittal views of one coronal multislice stack (voxel size $0.46786 \times 3 \times 0.46875$ mm) (Credit: Shilling et al. [81].)

three steps [63]: (i) registration of the acquired images; (ii) interpolation of these images onto an HR grid; and (iii) deconvolution to remove blur and noise. Because of the size of the problems, iterative algorithms have generally been required, and several variants have been reported [19,38,64,65,84,97]. Plenge et al. [64] carried out a comparison and extensive evaluation of these methods, extending a previous comparison in [27]. They demonstrated that, with equal image acquisition time and signal-to-noise ratio, SRR can indeed improve resolution over direct HR acquisition (given equal acquisition time). They also noted that slightly regularized solutions achieved the best results.

Delbracio and Sapiro [14] developed a method to "side-step" the requirement to know the PSF and therefore avoid the ill-posed deconvolution step. Their method, called *Fourier burst accumulation* (FBA), exploits the fact that acquisitions by hand-held cameras tend to be blurred by hand "jitters" that have high resolution in one direction (orthogonal to the jitter direction) and lower resolution in the other. When multiple snapshots are acquired, each acquired image will preserve the Fourier coefficients in one dominant direction and degrade them in the other directions (by reducing their Fourier magnitudes). Therefore, combination of all acquired images is conceptually simple: take the Fourier transform of all images, pick the maximum value at each Fourier frequency, and inverse transform the result. Two recent superresolution approaches for magnetic resonance images acquired with higher in-plane resolution and lower through-plane resolution have exploited this approach in a hybrid approach that also exploits example-based superresolution (see descriptions below) [42,95,96].

1.3.2 Single-image deconvolution

One of the key problems in SRR methods is registration of the acquired LR images. This is particularly problematic in diffusion weighted SRR, where Scherrer et al. [76] required registration to be carried out in q-space. It is also problematic in conventional T_1w imaging simply due to the small geometric irregularities caused by the different orientations of the phase encode directions of the acquired images [4,66,67,87]. Such irregularities, though small, cause blurring of the combined images which leads to artifacts and inadequate resolution recovery. Irregularities in image alignment are further compounded in cases where imaging of motion is desired, such as cardiac imaging [66, 67] and imaging of tongue motion [88,89]. Because of this and because of the time penalty incurred to acquire multiple images, it is highly desirable to carry out superresolution from only one acquisition.

Resolution enhancement from only one acquired image can be referred to as image deconvolution, image restoration, single-frame image zooming, image upscaling, single-image superresolution, or self-superresolution [18,21–23,25,28,42,50,62,80,91,94,95]. Deconvolution has a long history in signal and image processing. It has had limited use in medical imaging, however, largely because it is an extremely ill-posed problem and therefore highly susceptible to increasing noise. Also, when the PSF is not known precisely, deconvolution efforts can produce severe artifacts, most notably so-called ringing artifacts.

In MR imaging applications, the PSF is generally assumed to be known since it can be inferred in the in-plane directions by the Fourier resolutions implied by the read-out and phase-encode extents and in the through-plane direction by the slice-selection pulse in 2D MRI or by the three Fourier extents in 3D MRI. Note, however, that the Fourier extents of phase encodes and readouts cause a complete absence of Fourier content outside of these ranges. In this case, deconvolution as it is conventionally thought of is impossible as Fourier content is not just attenuated but is entirely suppressed. As a result, while deconvolution might be theoretically possible in MRI (because of some apodization due to $T2^*$ effects), it is truly applicable only to restore through-plane resolution in 2D MRI—and even then aliasing is the major problem, not resolution [27,96].

1.3.3 Example-based superresolution

Example-based methods for all kinds of image processing goals including noise reduction and superresolution, largely originating from the machine learning community [22, 92]. These methods have been enjoying great success in the image processing, computer vision, and medical imaging communities. In the most prominent type of superresolution method, examples of both LR and HR images of the same scene—so-called atlas images—can be used as training data to inform us about the likely appearance of the HR image given only the LR image [10,74,78,85,86]. This use of the image analogies [34] framework (described above) in superresolution applications is straightforward. The atlas, in this case, will contain a low-resolution (LR) image A and a high-resolution (HR) image A'. Features from A will be used to predict the intensities (or patches) in A' to synthesize an HR image B' from an input LR image B. The use of external atlases (exemplars) is extremely common in the example-based superresolution literature [16,34, 53]. The use of external atlases may be problematic, however, because the image contrast and signal-to-noise of the subject image may not be quite the same as that of the atlas. As well, it may not be possible to acquire an HR image of suitable quality for an atlas because of the tradeoffs in MR acquisition.

Three approaches to avoid the use of external atlases have emerged in the literature: (i) assume that the images are self-similar across scales [25,56]; (ii) use intermodality priors, [70,71]; and (iii) exploit the presence of both high-resolution and low-resolution information that is present in images acquired with elongated voxels [42,95,96].

The use of scale-space self-similarity is straightforward given the "image analogies" framework described above. Take the subject image and degrade its resolution by low-pass filtering, creating a pair of images, one LR and one OR (original resolution). These become A and A', respectively, in the notation of image analogies. Then features from both the LR image and the OR image are computed and a mapping from the LR features to the OR features is learned by regression (using a machine learning method).

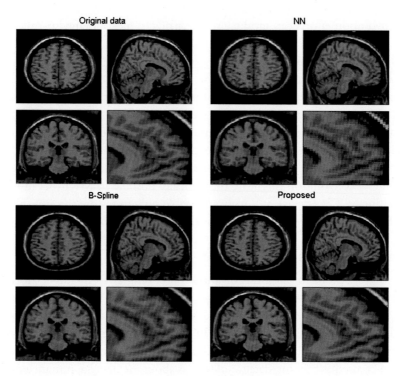

Figure 1.10 Results of isotropic voxel upsampling. LR data (voxel resolution = 2 × 2 × 2 mm) was up sampled to have a 1 × 1 × 1 mm voxel resolution using nearest neighbor (NN) (upper right), B-splines (lower left), and nonlocal means superresolution (lower right). (Credit: Manjon et al. [56].)

This learnt mapping is then applied to the original subject image features—serving as image B here—creating features and image B' at (presumably) yet even higher resolution than the original image. The nonlocal MRI upsampling method of Manjon et al. [56] uses, at its core, the same philosophy though it exploits a nonlocal approach to identifying the features that are used to map the original image to a higher-resolution version. An example of the results of this approach is shown in Fig. 1.10. The problem with these methods is that the learnt mappings do not truly describe the relationship between the acquired image and a higher resolution image; they just assume that the same relationship between features exists at multiple scales, which may not be true in general.

A method called *brain hallucination* has been proposed as an alternative to the methods that assume scale–space invariance [70,71]. This approach exploits the fact that it is common in MR imaging protocols to acquire both an LR T_2w image and an HR T_1w image. T_2-weighted images have a tissue contrast that depends largely on the transverse magnetization while T_1w images have a tissue contrast that depends largely on the longitudinal magnetization. This dichotomy in resolutions exists because T_1w images

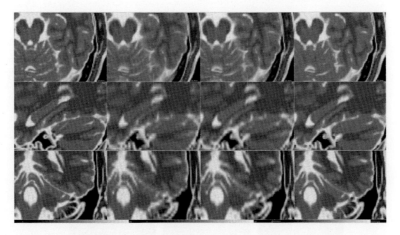

Figure 1.11 Example of "brain hallucination" reconstruction results. Left to right: ground truth, trilinear interpolation, cubic B-spline, brain hallucination. (Credit: Rousseau [71].)

can, in general, be acquired at higher resolution, higher SNR, and shorter time than either $P_D w$ or $T_2 w$ images.

Brain hallucination runs the HR $T_1 w$ image through a low pass filter and learns a mapping—also using a nonlocal approach—between the LR features and the original image; this forms the A and A' image pair in the notation of image analogies. The learnt mapping is then applied to the $T_2 w$ image to find an HR version of this image; these two form the B and B' images in the notation of image analogies. An example showing a close-up of a superresolution $T_2 w$ image is shown in Fig. 1.11. This approach might arguably be better since it uses an actual HR image, but it might not be accurate because it assumes that the relationship between $T_1 w$ features is the same as that for $T_2 w$ features (across scales). Thus, it may introduce features that are intrinsic to one modality and not to the other.

The final approach we consider here is the synthetic multiorientation resolution enhancement (SMORE) approach described in [42,95,96]. This approach exploits the fact that many scans are acquired with elongated voxels having better resolutions in the in-plane than through-plane direction. The method first applies a low-pass filter in one of the in-plane directions and learns a regression between that LR image and the original OR image. Anchored adaptive neighborhood (patch-based) regression [85] was used in [42] while the deep network EDSR [54] was used in [95,96] to carry out this regression. This regression is then applied to the original image *in the through-plane direction* to enhance its resolution. Multiple orientations—i.e., rotations about the through-plane axis—are used to establish additional training data for the regressions as well as more complete Fourier coverage and the resulting Fourier volumes are combined using Fourier burst accumulation [14]. When 2D MR images are acquired and

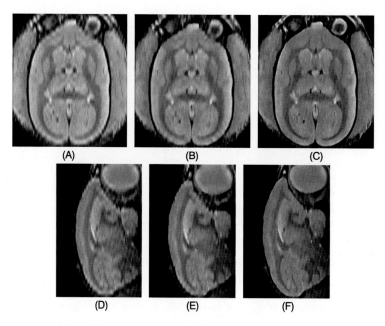

Figure 1.12 Experiment on a 0.15 × 0.15 × 1 mm LR marmoset PD MRI, showing axial views of (A) cubic B-spline interpolated image, (B) SMORE without antialiasing, (C) SMORE with antialiasing, and (D)–(F) sagittal views of the same. (Credit: Zhao et al. [96].)

the slice thickness is equal to the slice separation, aliasing is also present [27]. The SMORE method is also able to learn a relationship between an aliased and nonaliased version of itself and run an antialiasing process as well as superresolution [96]. An example demonstrating the performance of SMORE is shown in Fig. 1.12. One limitation of this method is that the final resolution is limited by the in–plane resolution.

1.4. Conclusion

Both image synthesis and superresolution have improved dramatically since the incorporation of machine learning methods and the use of examples to drive the methods. Significant questions remain, however, about the limits of their ultimate capability and their validity in any given untested scenario, particularly in the case of pathological data, where examples of representative training data may be sparse or nonexistent. Methods to compute and display measures of reliability are being developed, and these developments will help to provide additional confidence in the use of these approaches for both scientific and clinical use. It is truly an exciting time to join the medical imaging research community as new methods are emerging and new capabilities previously thought impossible are now becoming possible.

References

[1] D.C. Alexander, D. Zikic, A. Ghosh, R. Tanno, V. Wottschel, J. Zhang, E. Kaden, T.B. Dyrby, S.N. Sotiropoulos, H. Zhang, A. Criminisi, Image quality transfer and applications in diffusion MRI, NeuroImage 152 (2017) 283–298.

[2] D.C. Alexander, D. Zikic, J. Zhang, H. Zhang, A. Criminisi, Image quality transfer via random forest regression: applications in diffusion MRI, in: 17th International Conference on Medical Image Computing and Computer Assisted Intervention (MICCAI 2014), in: Lecture Notes in Computer Science, vol. 8675, Springer, Berlin Heidelberg, 2014, pp. 225–232.

[3] G. Andreisek, L.M. White, J.S. Theodoropoulos, A. Naraghi, N. Young, C.Y. Zhao, T.C. Mamisch, M.S. Sussman, Synthetic–echo time postprocessing technique for generating images with variable T2-weighted contrast: diagnosis of meniscal and cartilage abnormalities of the knee, Radiology 254 (1) (2009) 188–199.

[4] Y. Bai, X. Han, J.L. Prince, Super-resolution reconstruction of MR brain images, in: Proc. of 38th Annual Conference on Information Sciences and Systems, Princeton, New Jersey, 2004, pp. 1358–1363.

[5] V. Biberacher, P. Schmidt, A. Keshavan, C.C. Boucard, R. Righart, P. Sämann, C. Preibisch, D. Fröbel, L. Aly, B. Hemmer, C. Zimmer, R.G. Henry, M. Mühlau, Intra- and interscanner variability of magnetic resonance imaging based volumetry in multiple sclerosis, NeuroImage 142 (2016) 188–197.

[6] S.A. Bobman, S.J. Riederer, J.N. Lee, T. Tasciyan, F. Farzaneh, H.Z. Wang, Pulse sequence extrapolation with MR image synthesis, Radiology 159 (1) (1986) 253–258.

[7] L. Breiman, Random forests, Mach. Learn. 45 (1) (2001) 5–32.

[8] N. Burgos, M.J. Cardoso, K. Thielemans, M. Modat, S. Pedemonte, J. Dickson, A. Barnes, R. Ahmed, C.J. Mahoney, J.M. Schott, J.S. Duncan, D. Atkinson, S.R. Arridge, B.F. Hutton, S. Ourselin, Attenuation correction synthesis for hybrid PET-MR scanners: application to brain studies, IEEE Trans. Med. Imaging 33 (12) (2014) 2332–2341.

[9] N. Burgos, M.J. Cardoso, K. Thielemans, M. Modat, S. Pedemonte, J. Dickson, A. Barnes, J.S. Duncan, D. Atkinson, S.R. Arridge, B.F. Hutton, S. Ourselin, Attenuation correction synthesis for hybrid PET-MR scanners, in: 16th International Conference on Medical Image Computing and Computer Assisted Intervention (MICCAI 2013), in: Lecture Notes in Computer Science, vol. 8149, Springer, Berlin Heidelberg, 2013, pp. 147–154.

[10] H. Chang, D.Y. Yeung, Y. Xiong, Super-resolution through neighbor embedding, in: Proceedings of the 2004 IEEE Computer Society Conference on Computer Vision and Pattern Recognition, 2004, CVPR 2004, vol. 1, IEEE, 2004, pp. 1–8.

[11] A.S. Chua, S. Egorova, M.C. Anderson, M. Polgar-Turcsanyi, T. Chitnis, H.L. Weiner, C.R. Guttmann, R. Bakshi, B.C. Healy, Handling changes in MRI acquisition parameters in modeling whole brain lesion volume and atrophy data in multiple sclerosis subjects: comparison of linear mixed-effect models, NeuroImage Clin. 8 (2015) 606–610.

[12] C. Cocosco, V. Kollokian, R.S. Kwan, A. Evans, Brainweb: Online interface to a 3D MRI simulated brain database, NeuroImage 5 (4) (1997) S425.

[13] J. Degen, M.P. Heinrich, Multi-atlas based pseudo-CT synthesis using multimodal image registration and local atlas fusion strategies, in: 2016 IEEE Conference on Computer Vision and Pattern Recognition Workshops (CVPRW), 2016, pp. 600–608.

[14] M. Delbracio, G. Sapiro, Removing camera shake via weighted Fourier burst accumulation, IEEE Trans. Image Process. 24 (11) (2015).

[15] B.E. Dewey, C. Zhao, A. Carass, J. Oh, P.A. Calabresi, P.C. van Zijl, J.L. Prince, Deep harmonization of inconsistent MR data for consistent volume segmentation, in: Proceedings of the International Workshop on Simulation and Synthesis in Medical Imaging, Springer, 2018, pp. 20–30.

[16] C. Dong, C.C. Loy, K. He, X. Tang, Image super-resolution using deep convolutional networks, IEEE Trans. Pattern Anal. Mach. Intell. 38 (2) (2016) 295–307.

[17] J.A. Dowling, J. Lambert, J. Parker, O. Salvado, J. Fripp, A. Capp, C. Wratten, J.W. Denham, P.B. Greer, An atlas-based electron density mapping method for magnetic resonance imaging (MRI)-alone treatment planning and adaptive MRI-based prostate radiation therapy, Int. J. Radiat. Oncol. Biol. Phys. 83 (1) (2012) e5–e11.

[18] M. Ebrahimi, E.R. Vrscay, Solving the inverse problem of image zooming using "self-examples", in: International Conference Image Analysis and Recognition, Springer, 2007, pp. 117–130.

[19] M. Elad, A. Feuer, Restoration of a single superresolution image from several blurred, noisy, and undersampled measured images, IEEE Trans. Image Process. 6 (12) (1997) 1646–1658.

[20] C. Fennema-Notestine, A.C. Gamst, B.T. Quinn, J. Pacheco, T.L. Jernigan, L. Thal, R. Buckner, R. Killiany, D. Blacker, A.M. Dale, et al., Feasibility of multi-site clinical structural neuroimaging studies of aging using legacy data, Neuroinformatics 5 (4) (2007) 235–245.

[21] G. Freedman, R. Fattal, Image and video upscaling from local self-examples, ACM Trans. Graph. 30 (2) (2011) 12.

[22] W.T. Freeman, T.R. Jones, E.C. Pasztor, Example-based super-resolution, IEEE Comput. Graph. Appl. 22 (2) (2002) 56–65.

[23] W.T. Freeman, E.C. Pasztor, O.T. Carmichael, Learning low-level vision, Int. J. Comput. Vis. 40 (1) (2000) 25–47.

[24] A. Gholipour, J.A. Estroff, S.K. Warfield, Robust super-resolution volume reconstruction from slice acquisitions: application to fetal brain MRI, IEEE Trans. Med. Imaging 29 (10) (2010) 1739–1758.

[25] D. Glasner, S. Bagon, M. Irani, Super-resolution from a single image, in: 2009 IEEE 12th International Conference on Computer Vision, IEEE, 2009, pp. 349–356.

[26] H. Greenspan, Super-resolution in medical imaging, Comput. J. 52 (1) (2009) 43–63.

[27] H. Greenspan, G. Oz, N. Kiryati, S. Peled, MRI inter-slice reconstruction using super-resolution, Magn. Reson. Imaging 20 (5) (2002) 437–446.

[28] R. Gruner, T. Taxt, Iterative blind deconvolution in magnetic resonance brain perfusion imaging, Magn. Reson. Med. 55 (4) (2006) 805–815.

[29] X. Han, MR-based synthetic CT generation using a deep convolutional neural network method, Med. Phys. 44 (4) (2017) 1408–1419.

[30] G. Harikumar, Y. Bresler, Exact image deconvolution from multiple fir blurs, IEEE Trans. Image Process. 8 (6) (1999) 846–862.

[31] Q. He, N. Shiee, D.S. Reich, P.A. Calabresi, D.L. Pham, Intensity standardization of longitudinal images using 4D clustering, in: 10th International Symposium on Biomedical Imaging (ISBI 2013), 2013, pp. 1388–1391.

[32] M.P. Heinrich, M. Jenkinson, M. Bhushan, T. Matin, F.V. Gleeson, S.M. Brady, J.A. Schnabel, Mind: modality independent neighbourhood descriptor for multi-modal deformable registration, Med. Image Anal. 16 (7) (2012) 1423–1435.

[33] A. Hertzmann, C.E. Jacobs, N. Oliver, B. Curless, D.H. Salesin, Image analogies, in: Proceedings of the 28th Annual Conference on Computer Graphics and Interactive Techniques, SIGGRAPH '01, 2001, pp. 327–340.

[34] W.T. Freeman, T.R. Jones, E.C. Pasztor, Example-based super-resolution, IEEE Comput. Graph. Appl. 22 (2) (2002 Mar.) 56–65.

[35] M. Hofmann, I. Bezrukov, F. Mantlik, P. Aschoff, F. Steinke, T. Beyer, B.J. Pichler, B. Schölkopf, MRI-based attenuation correction for whole-body PET/MRI: quantitative evaluation of segmentation- and atlas-based methods, J. Nucl. Med. 52 (9) (2011) 1392–1399.

[36] M. Hofmann, F. Steinke, V. Scheel, G. Charpiat, J. Farquhar, P. Aschoff, M. Brady, B. Schölkopf, B.J. Pichler, MRI-based attenuation correction for PET/MRI: a novel approach combining pattern recognition and atlas registration, J. Nucl. Med. 49 (11) (2008) 1875–1883.

[37] Y. Huo, Z. Xu, K. Aboud, P. Parvathaneni, S. Bao, C. Bermudez, S.M. Resnick, L.E. Cutting, B.A. Landman, Spatially localized atlas network tiles enables 3D whole brain segmentation from limited

data, in: Proceedings of International Conference on Medical Image Computing and Computer-Assisted Intervention, MICCAI Society, Springer, 2018, pp. 698–705.

[38] M. Irani, S. Peleg, Improving resolution by image registration, CVGIP, Graph. Models Image Process. 53 (3) (1991) 231–239.

[39] P. Isola, J.Y. Zhu, T. Zhou, A.A. Efros, Image-to-image translation with conditional adversarial networks, in: 2017 IEEE Conference on Computer Vision and Pattern Recognition (CVPR), 2018, pp. 5967–5976.

[40] A. Jog, A. Carass, D.L. Pham, J.L. Prince, Random forest FLAIR reconstruction from T1, T2, and PD-weighted MRI, in: 11th International Symposium on Biomedical Imaging (ISBI 2014), 2014, pp. 1079–1082.

[41] A. Jog, A. Carass, J.L. Prince, Improving magnetic resonance resolution with supervised learning, in: 11th International Symposium on Biomedical Imaging (ISBI 2014), 2014, pp. 987–990.

[42] A. Jog, A. Carass, J.L. Prince, Self super-resolution for magnetic resonance images, in: International Conference on Medical Image Computing and Computer-Assisted Intervention, Springer, 2016, pp. 553–560.

[43] A. Jog, A. Carass, S. Roy, D.L. Pham, J.L. Prince, MR image synthesis by contrast learning on neighborhood ensembles, Med. Image Anal. 24 (1) (2015) 63–76.

[44] A.S. Jog, Image Synthesis in Magnetic Resonance Neuroimaging, Doctoral dissertation, Johns Hopkins University.

[45] A. Jog, A. Carass, S. Roy, D.L. Pham, J.L. Prince, Random forest regression for magnetic resonance image synthesis, Med. Image Anal. 35 (2017) 475–488.

[46] A. Jog, S. Roy, A. Carass, J.L. Prince, Magnetic resonance image synthesis through patch regression, in: 10th International Symposium on Biomedical Imaging (ISBI 2013), 2013, pp. 350–353.

[47] B.C. Jones, G. Nair, C.D. Shea, C.M. Crainiceanu, I.C. Cortese, D.S. Reich, Quantification of multiple-sclerosis-related brain atrophy in two heterogeneous MRI datasets using mixed-effects modeling, NeuroImage Clin. 3 (2013) 171–179.

[48] J. Jovicich, M. Marizzoni, R. Sala-Llonch, B. Bosch, D. Bartrés-Faz, J. Arnold, J. Benninghoff, J. Wiltfang, L. Roccatagliata, F. Nobili, et al., Brain morphometry reproducibility in multi-center 3 T MRI studies: a comparison of cross-sectional and longitudinal segmentations, NeuroImage 83 (2013) 472–484.

[49] A. Keshavan, F. Paul, M.K. Beyer, A.H. Zhu, N. Papinutto, R.T. Shinohara, W. Stern, M. Amann, R. Bakshi, A. Bischof, et al., Power estimation for non-standardized multisite studies, NeuroImage 134 (2016) 281–294.

[50] J. Kotera, F. Sroubek, P. Milanfar, Blind deconvolution using alternating maximum a posteriori estimation with heavy-tailed priors, in: International Conference on Computer Analysis of Images and Patterns, Springer, 2013, pp. 59–66.

[51] J. Lee, A. Carass, A. Jog, C. Zhao, J.L. Prince, Multi-atlas-based CT synthesis from conventional MRI with patch-based refinement for MRI-based radiotherapy planning, in: Medical Imaging 2017: Image Processing, Orlando, FL, February 11–16, 2017, in: Proceedings SPIE, vol. 10133, 2017.

[52] J.N. Lee, S.J. Riederer, S.A. Bobman, F. Farzaneh, H.Z. Wang, Instrumentation for rapid MR image synthesis, Magn. Reson. Med. 3 (1) (1986) 33–43.

[53] Y. Liang, J. Wang, S. Zhou, Y. Gong, N. Zheng, Incorporating image priors with deep convolutional neural networks for image super-resolution, Neurocomputing 194 (2016) 340–347.

[54] B. Lim, S. Son, H. Kim, S. Nah, K.M. Lee, Enhanced deep residual networks for single image super-resolution, in: The IEEE Conference on Computer Vision and Pattern Recognition (CVPR) Workshops, 2017, p. 4.

[55] J. Ma, Dixon techniques for water and fat imaging, J. Magn. Reson. Imaging 28 (3) (2008) 543–558.

[56] J.V. Manjon, P. Coupe, A. Buades, V. Fonov, D. Louis Collins, M. Robles, Non-local MRI upsampling, Med. Image Anal. 14 (6) (2010) 784–792.

[57] A. Martinez-Moller, M. Souvatzoglou, G. Delso, R.A. Bundschuh, C. Chefd'hotel, S.I. Ziegler, N. Navab, M. Schwaiger, S.G. Nekolla, Tissue classification as a potential approach for attenuation correction in whole-body PET/MRI: evaluation with PET/CT data, J. Nucl. Med. 50 (4) (2009) 520.

[58] M.I. Miller, G.E. Christensen, Y. Amit, U. Grenander, Mathematical textbook of deformable neuroanatomies, Proc. Natl. Acad. Sci. 90 (24) (1993) 11,944–11,948.

[59] L.G. Nyúl, J.K. Udupa, New variants of a method of MRI scale normalization, in: 16th Inf. Proc. in Med. Imaging (IPMI 1999), in: Lecture Notes in Computer Science, vol. 1613, Springer, Berlin Heidelberg, 1999, pp. 490–495.

[60] L.G. Nyúl, J.K. Udupa, On standardizing the MR image intensity scale, Magn. Reson. Med. 42 (6) (1999) 1072–1081.

[61] D. Ortendahl, N. Hylton, L. Kaufman, L. Crook, R. Cannon, J. Watts, Calculated NMR images, in: Second Annual Meeting of the Society of Magnetic Resonance in Medicine, 1983, pp. 272–273.

[62] L. Pan, W. Yan, H. Zheng, Super-resolution from a single image based on local self-similarity, Multimed. Tools Appl. 75 (18) (2016) 11,037–11,057.

[63] S.C. Park, M.K. Park, M.G. Kang, Super-resolution image reconstruction: a technical overview, IEEE Signal Process. Mag. 20 (3) (2003) 21–36.

[64] E. Plenge, D.H. Poot, M. Bernsen, G. Kotek, G. Houston, P. Wielopolski, L. van der Weerd, W.J. Niessen, E. Meijering, Super-resolution methods in MRI: can they improve the trade-off between resolution, signal-to-noise ratio, and acquisition time?, Magn. Reson. Med. 68 (6) (2012) 1983–1993.

[65] D.H. Poot, V. Van Meir, J. Sijbers, General and efficient super-resolution method for multi-slice MRI, in: International Conference on Medical Image Computing and Computer-Assisted Intervention, Springer, 2010, pp. 615–622.

[66] S.U. Rahman, S. Wesarg, Combining short-axis and long-axis cardiac MR images by applying a super-resolution reconstruction algorithm, in: Medical Imaging: Image Processing, 2010, p. 76230I.

[67] S.U. Rahman, S. Wesarg, Upsampling of cardiac MR images: comparison of averaging and super-resolution for the combination of multiple views, in: 2010 10th IEEE International Conference on Information Technology and Applications in Biomedicine (ITAB), IEEE, 2010, pp. 1–4.

[68] S.J. Riederer, S.A. Suddarth, S.A. Bobman, J.N. Lee, H.Z. Wang, J.R. MacFall, Automated MR image synthesis: feasibility studies, Radiology 153 (1) (1984) 203–206.

[69] O. Ronneberger, P. Fischer, T. Brox, U-net: convolutional networks for biomedical image segmentation, in: International Conference on Medical Image Computing and Computer-Assisted Intervention, Springer, 2015, pp. 234–241.

[70] F. Rousseau, Brain hallucination, in: 2008 European Conference on Computer Vision (ECCV 2008), 2008, pp. 497–508.

[71] F. Rousseau, The Alzheimer's disease neuroimaging initiative: a non-local approach for image super-resolution using intermodality priors, Med. Image Anal. 14 (4) (2010) 594–605.

[72] S. Roy, A. Carass, J.L. Prince, A compressed sensing approach for MR tissue contrast synthesis, in: 22nd Inf. Proc. in Med. Imaging (IPMI 2011), in: Lecture Notes in Computer Science, vol. 6801, Springer, Berlin Heidelberg, 2011, pp. 371–383.

[73] S. Roy, A. Carass, J.L. Prince, Magnetic resonance image example based contrast synthesis, IEEE Trans. Med. Imaging 32 (12) (2013) 2348–2363.

[74] J. Salvador, E. Pérez-Pellitero, Naive Bayes super-resolution forest, in: Proceedings of the IEEE International Conference on Computer Vision, 2015, pp. 325–333.

[75] K. Scheffler, Superresolution in MRI?, Magn. Reson. Med. 48 (2) (2002) 408.

[76] B. Scherrer, A. Gholipour, S.K. Warfield, Super-resolution reconstruction to increase the spatial resolution of diffusion weighted images from orthogonal anisotropic acquisitions, Med. Image Anal. 16 (7) (2012) 1465–1476.

[77] H.G. Schnack, N.E. van Haren, R.M. Brouwer, G.C.M. van Baal, M. Picchioni, M. Weisbrod, H. Sauer, T.D. Cannon, M. Huttunen, C. Lepage, D.L. Collins, A. Evans, R.M. Murray, R.S. Kahn,

H.E. Hulshoff Pol, Mapping reliability in multicenter MRI: voxel-based morphometry and cortical thickness, Hum. Brain Mapp. 31 (12) (2010) 1967–1982.

[78] S. Schulter, C. Leistner, H. Bischof, Fast and accurate image upscaling with super-resolution forests, in: Proceedings of the IEEE Conference on Computer Vision and Pattern Recognition, 2015, pp. 3791–3799.

[79] M. Shah, Y. Xiao, N. Subbanna, S. Francis, D.L. Arnold, D.L. Collins, T. Arbel, Evaluating intensity normalization on MRIs of human brain with multiple sclerosis, Med. Image Anal. 15 (2) (2011) 267–282.

[80] F. Shi, J. Cheng, L. Wang, P.T. Yap, D. Shen, LRTV: MR image super-resolution with low-rank and total variation regularizations, IEEE Trans. Med. Imaging 34 (12) (2015) 2459–2466.

[81] R.Z. Shilling, T.Q. Robbie, T. Bailloeul, K. Mewes, R.M. Mersereau, M.E. Brummer, A super-resolution framework for 3-D high-resolution and high-contrast imaging using 2-D multislice MRI, IEEE Trans. Med. Imaging 28 (5) (2009) 633–644.

[82] R.T. Shinohara, J. Oh, G. Nair, P.A. Calabresi, C. Davatzikos, J. Doshi, R.G. Henry, G. Kim, K.L. Linn, N. Papinutto, D. Pelletier, D.L. Pham, D.S. Reich, W. Rooney, S. Roy, W. Stern, S. Tummala, F. Yousuf, A. Zhu, N.L. Sicotte, R. Bakshi, Volumetric analysis from a harmonized multisite brain MRI study of a single subject with multiple sclerosis, Am. J. Neuroradiol. 38 (8) (2017) 1501–1509.

[83] R.T. Shinohara, E.M. Sweeney, J. Goldsmith, N. Shiee, F.J. Marteen, P.A. Calabresi, S. Jarso, D.L. Pham, D.S. Reich, C.M. Crainiceanu, Statistical normalization techniques for magnetic resonance imaging, NeuroImage Clin. 6 (2014) 9–19.

[84] H. Stark, P. Oskoui, High-resolution image recovery from image-plane arrays, using convex projections, J. Opt. Soc. Am. A 6 (11) (1989) 1715–1726.

[85] R. Timofte, V. De Smet, L. Van Gool, Anchored neighborhood regression for fast example-based super-resolution, in: 2013 IEEE International Conference on Computer Vision (ICCV), 2013, pp. 1920–1927.

[86] R. Timofte, V. De Smet, L. Van Gool, A plus: adjusted anchored neighborhood regression for fast super-resolution, in: Asian Conference on Computer Vision, 2015, pp. 111–126.

[87] E. Van Reeth, I.W. Tham, C.H. Tan, C.L. Poh, Super-resolution in magnetic resonance imaging: a review, Concepts Magn. Reson., Part A 40 (6) (2012) 306–325.

[88] J. Woo, Y. Bai, S. Roy, E.Z. Murano, M. Stone, J.L. Prince, Super-resolution reconstruction for tongue MR images, in: Proceedings of SPIE – the International Society for Optical Engineering, vol. 8314, NIH Public Access, 2012.

[89] J. Woo, E.Z. Murano, M. Stone, J.L. Prince, Reconstruction of high-resolution tongue volumes from MRI, IEEE Trans. Biomed. Eng. 59 (12) (2012) 3511–3524, https://doi.org/10.1109/TBME.2012.2218246, URL http://www.ncbi.nlm.nih.gov/pubmed/23033324.

[90] Y. Wu, W. Yang, L. Lu, Z. Lu, L. Zhong, M. Huang, Y. Feng, Q. Feng, W. Chen, Prediction of CT substitutes from MR images based on local diffeomorphic mapping for brain pet attenuation correction, J. Nucl. Med. 57 (2016) 1635–1641.

[91] J. Xiong, Q. Liu, Y. Wang, X. Xu, A two-stage convolutional sparse prior model for image restoration, J. Vis. Commun. Image Represent. 48 (2017) 268–280.

[92] J. Yang, J. Wright, T.S. Huang, Y. Ma, Image super-resolution via sparse representation, IEEE Trans. Image Process. 19 (11) (2010) 2861–2873.

[93] D.H. Ye, D. Zikic, B. Glocker, A. Criminisi, E. Konukoglu, Modality propagation: coherent synthesis of subject-specific scans with data-driven regularization, in: 16th International Conference on Medical Image Computing and Computer Assisted Intervention (MICCAI 2013), in: Lecture Notes in Computer Science, vol. 8149, Springer, Berlin Heidelberg, 2013, pp. 606–613.

[94] K. Zhang, X. Gao, D. Tao, X. Li, Single image super-resolution with non-local means and steering kernel regression, IEEE Trans. Image Process. 21 (11) (2012) 4544–4556.

[95] C. Zhao, A. Carass, B.E. Dewey, J.L. Prince, Self super-resolution for magnetic resonance images using deep networks, in: 2018 IEEE 15th International Symposium on Biomedical Imaging (ISBI 2018), IEEE, 2018, pp. 365–368.

[96] C. Zhao, A. Carass, B.E. Dewey, J. Woo, J. Oh, P.A. Calabresi, D.S. Reich, P. Sati, D.L. Pham, J.L. Prince, A deep learning based anti-aliasing self super-resolution algorithm for MRI, in: International Conference on Medical Image Computing and Computer-Assisted Intervention, Springer, 2018, pp. 100–108.

[97] A. Zomet, A. Rav-Acha, S. Peleg, Robust super-resolution, in: Proceedings of the 2001 IEEE Computer Society Conference on Computer Vision and Pattern Recognition, 2001, CVPR 2001, IEEE, 2001, pp. I-645–I-650.

CHAPTER 2

Machine learning for image reconstruction

Kerstin Hammernik[a,b], Florian Knoll[c]
[a]Graz University of Technology, Institute of Computer Graphics and Vision, Graz, Austria
[b]Department of Computing, Imperial College London, London, United Kingdom
[c]New York University, Radiology, Center for Biomedical Imaging and Center for Advanced Imaging Innovation and Research, New York, NY, United States

Contents

2.1.	Inverse problems in imaging	26
2.2.	Unsupervised learning in image reconstruction	30
2.3.	Supervised learning in image reconstruction	32
	2.3.1 Learning an improved regularization function	34
	2.3.2 Learning an iterative reconstruction model	37
	2.3.3 Deep learning for image and data enhancement	44
	2.3.4 Learning a direct mapping	46
	2.3.5 Example: Comparison between learned iterative reconstruction and learned postprocessing	47
2.4.	Training data	48
2.5.	Loss functions and evaluation of image quality	49
2.6.	Discussion	53
	Acknowledgments	54
	References	54

During the past years, deep learning [1,2] has caused a paradigm shift in computer vision from using handcrafted features and statistical classifiers to data-driven and learning-based approaches which are able to learn both the feature representations and classifiers from suitable training data. Impressive improvements in image quality and accuracy have been achieved for various applications in computer vision such as image classification [3], semantic segmentation [4], optical flow [5], and image restoration [6]. In medical imaging, the deep learning techniques have mostly focused on image classification [7] and segmentations tasks [8], while the application to image reconstruction is rather new [9–11]. First results in using Artificial Neural Networks (ANNs) for reconstruction in Magnetic Resonance Imaging (MRI) [12], Computed Tomography (CT) [13] and Single Photon Emission Computed Tomography (SPECT) [14–17] have been already shown in the 1990s. The major reason for today's success of deep learning methods for medical image reconstruction is that the training data and computational power has increased by an enormous margin over the past years.

Handbook of Medical Image Computing and Computer Assisted Intervention
https://doi.org/10.1016/B978-0-12-816176-0.00007-7

This chapter introduces how machine learning is able to improve upon the state-of-the-art in medical image reconstruction of high-quality images from incomplete data. We present a general overview over existing techniques in computer vision and medical imaging in order to give an intuition of how machine learning can be applied to image reconstruction. Furthermore, this chapter provides a deeper mathematical understanding of how machine learning techniques can be employed for image reconstruction tasks. Therefore, we draw connections to traditional approaches of solving inverse problems, rather than presenting details about the used neural network architectures. Approaches for both unsupervised, such as dictionary learning, and supervised learning are covered in this chapter. The reviewed approaches for supervised learning range from learning of hyperparameters and more general regularizers in a variational model to replace steps in an iterative reconstruction algorithm with Convolutional Neural Networks (CNNs), to learning image enhancement and learning a full mapping between measured data and reconstructed images. With the major focus on supervised learning, this chapter also includes key challenges such as suitable training data, transfer learning, selection of the loss function for training and evaluation of image quality.

2.1. Inverse problems in imaging

Inverse problems arise in various applications ranging from medicine over geophysics to economics. In the area of computer vision, this includes, but is not limited to, image segmentation, motion correction, image registration, object detection, and image reconstruction. Considering medical image reconstruction, the goal is to reconstruct an image $x \in \mathbb{K}^{N_x}$ from measurement data $y \in \mathbb{K}^{N_y}$ given the following system of equations

$$y = A(x) + \nu, \tag{2.1}$$

where $\nu \in \mathbb{K}^{N_y}$ is an additive random noise variable and the field $\mathbb{K} = \mathbb{R}, \mathbb{C}$ is the set of either the real numbers $\mathbb{R}$ or complex numbers $\mathbb{C}$. The dimensions of the vector space of the image x and data y is denoted by N_x and N_y, respectively. The forward operator $A : \mathbb{K}^{N_x} \to \mathbb{K}^{N_y}$ defines a mapping between the normed vector spaces of the image data and the measurement data. We mainly consider the ℓ_p-norm for $p \geq 1$ of a vector $z \in \mathbb{K}^N$ which is defined for an N-dimensional field $\mathbb{K}^N$ as

$$\|z\|_p = \left(\sum_{i=1}^{N} |z_i|^p \right)^{\frac{1}{p}}.$$

The forward operator A describes the acquisition process to measure y given the physical and technical conditions and limitations, which often involves approximations of the real physics. In *MRI*, the forward operator includes the Fourier Transform (FT)

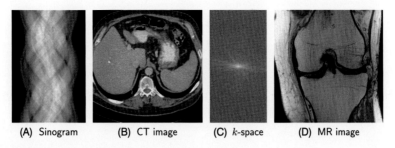

(A) Sinogram   (B) CT image   (C) k-space   (D) MR image

Figure 2.1 *Example measurement spaces and image spaces for CT and MRI.* A *CT* image (B) is reconstructed from a sinogram (A) based on the Radon transform. For *MR* images (D), the data are acquired in Fourier domain, termed k-space (C).

to map an image to the measurement space (k-space), while the fundamental relationship to map images to sinograms in CT is mainly described by the Radon transform. Fig. 2.1 illustrates examples for image and measurement data for MRI and CT. Typical examples for medical image reconstruction problems are the reconstruction from Cartesian or non-Cartesian undersampled k-space data in MRI from single or multiple receiver channels, where the latter is commonly termed Parallel Imaging (PI). In CT typical applications are low-dose, sparse-view and limited-angle CT, which are based on parallel-beam, cone-beam, fan-beam, or spiral acquisitions. In Positron Emission Tomography (PET), typical applications are dose reduction, improved resolution, attenuation correction, and motion correction. In Photoacoustic Tomography (PAT), one aims at recovering the initial pressure distribution which is related to the optical absorption of biological tissue. Common techniques here are sparse sampling or limited-angle acquisitions. Generally speaking, one often seeks to acquire as few measurements as possible. This reduces acquisition time, ionizing radiation dose for CT or PET and decreases motion artifacts, which greatly increases patient comfort, reduces risks for patients and lowers overall healthcare costs.

Recovering x from the measurement data y is often an ill-posed problem: A solution might not exist, the solution might not be unique, or the solution might be unstable with respect to small variations in the data [18]. Obtaining a solution for x in Eq. (2.1) is ill-posed in most practical cases, because of uncertainties due to measurement errors, low Signal-to-Noise Ratio (SNR), incomplete data, and hardware limitations. Hence, no explicit solution can be obtained for x. A natural approach is to minimize the data-misfit using

$$x^* \in \arg\min_{x \in \mathbb{K}^{N_x}} \mathcal{D}\big[A(x), y\big], \qquad (2.2)$$

where $\mathcal{D} : \mathbb{K}^{N_y} \times \mathbb{K}^{N_y} \to \mathbb{R}$ is a mapping representing the statistical properties of the data. For normally distributed noise, an assumption that is true for MRI k-space data, a common approach here is to estimate a least-squares solution

$$x^* \in \arg\min_{x \in \mathbb{K}^{N_x}} \frac{1}{2} \|A(x) - y\|_2^2.$$ (2.3)

For different noise statistics, e.g., Poisson distributed samples encountered in *PET* and to some degree in *CT*, the Kullback–Leibler divergence is commonly used

$$x^* \in \arg\min_{x \in \mathbb{K}^{N_x}} \sum_{i=1}^{N_y} \left(A(x)_i - y_i \log(A(x))_i \right),$$

where i denotes discrete sampling locations. Calculating the minimizer of these problems often leads to over-fitting the noisy measurement data. There exist several methods to restrict the solution space and search for an approximate solution in order to avoid solutions that are dominated by noise. One possibility is to perform early stopping [19], which acts as regularization. Another possibility is to impose additional constraints on x and add a regularization term to Eq. (2.2), leading to the variational model

$$x^* \in \arg\min_{x \in \mathbb{K}^{N_x}} \lambda \mathcal{D}\left[A(x), y\right] + \mathcal{R}\left[x\right],$$ (2.4)

where $\lambda > 0$ is a weight parameter that controls the influence of the regularization term $\mathcal{R}$ and the data consistency term $\mathcal{D}$. In traditional optimization, simple generic and robust image priors are used. In the context of imaging, a common choice for the regularization term is a discrete approximation of the Total Variation (TV) semi-norm [20], which reads as

$$\mathcal{R}\left[x\right] = \|\mathrm{D}x\|_{2,1} = \sum_{i=1}^{N_x} \sqrt{\sum_d \left(|\mathrm{D}x|_i^{(d)}\right)^2},$$ (2.5)

where the operator $\mathrm{D} : \mathbb{K}^{N_x} \to \mathbb{K}^{N_x \cdot d}$ approximates the image gradient by finite differences [21], the index i indicates the discrete pixel locations in image domain and d denotes the dimension of the image space. Due to the convexity of the *TV* semi-norm and, hence, the entire variational model in Eq. (2.4), it allows for efficient global optimization. One particular feature of the *TV* semi-norm is that it approximates sparsity in the image edges, hence, it allows for sharp discontinuities in the reconstruction. However, it favors piecewise constant solutions which are often not a suitable regularization to describe the content of natural and medical images. Especially when it comes to the acceleration of the image acquisition process, the choice of the regularization part and thus the weight parameter has a strong influence on how the final solution appears.

In the context of medical image reconstruction, Compressed Sensing (CS) [22–25] is a widely used technique to reconstruct images from only a few measurements, sampled below the Nyquist rate [26,27]. *CS* requires three conditions to be fulfilled. The first condition is the incoherence of artifacts arising due to the encoding of the under-sampled measurements γ [23,24]. In *MRI* this can be achieved by non-Cartesian [22] or pseudorandom [25] sampling trajectories. The second condition states that the image has to be represented sparsely in a certain transform domain, which can be achieved by Wavelets [25,28] or the *TV* semi-norm including extensions to higher-order Total Generalized Variation (TGV) [20,22,29,30] as presented in Eq. (2.5). To enforce sparsity and additionally allow for efficient global optimization, the ℓ_1 norm is used to approx-imate sparsity of the transformed image in the convex setting. Finally, both conditions, i.e., the consistency to the measured data and the sparsity in the transform domain, are combined in a nonlinear reconstruction given in Eq. (2.4), defining the third *CS* condition.

CS approaches show highly promising results for various imaging applications, how-ever, the translation to clinical practice is not trivial. In the case of *MRI*, Cartesian sampling schemes, which violate the incoherence assumption of artifacts, form the majority of clinical examinations [31]. Another observation is that the sparsifying trans-forms used in *CS* are too simple to capture the complex image content and structure of artifacts of medical images. Images reconstructed with the simple, handcrafted priors are often criticized by radiologists because the reconstructions can appear unnatural or blocky [31]. Another drawback, not only for *CS*-based approaches but also for many other iterative approaches, is the computational complexity and long reconstruction times for many of the algorithms used to solve the nonlinear optimization problems. Finally, the sensitivity of hyperparameters to the final reconstruction results makes it challenging to translate *CS* to clinical examinations, where imaging situations might vary. If the hyperparameters are selected poorly, the reconstruction might be either un-derregularized and still show artifacts or it might be overregularized and thus biased. The latter case often results in a loss of details, which could be pathologies in the worst case, and an unnatural appearance of the images.

If we take a closer look at iterative reconstruction approaches, we observe that every new task is treated as a new optimization problem and no prior knowledge of the known structure of artifacts and the image content is taken into account. However, this contradicts how human radiologists read images, as they are trained throughout their careers to recognize certain patterns and read through diagnostic irrelevant patterns as residual artifacts [31]. When translating this observation to machine learning, this means that the optimization task can be transferred to an off-line training task where the key parameters are learned from undersampled data and clean images instead of solving an online optimization task for each new dataset based on handcrafted features. In the following sections, we will see how machine learning strategies in unsupervised and supervised learning improve upon the regularizer and overcome other challenges of *CS*-based approaches.

2.2. Unsupervised learning in image reconstruction

We briefly review unsupervised learning strategies such as dictionary and sparsifying transform learning along with a K-sparse Autoencoder (KSAE). The dictionary or the sparsifying transform can either be pretrained from a set of distorted training data or learned simultaneously with the reconstruction, which is termed *blind compressed sensing*.

Dictionary learning works at the level of image patches $x_p \in \mathbb{K}^{N_p}$ of size $p \times p$. The dimension of the patch is defined by $N_p = p^2$. An arbitrary path $x_{p,i} \in \mathbb{K}^{N_p}$ can be extracted from an image x for the ith patch location using a patch extraction matrix $P_i : \mathbb{K}^{N_p \times N_x}$. This patch extraction matrix P_i is defined for all N_s possible patch locations i in the image and considers the correct boundary conditions, e.g., symmetric or zero boundary conditions. The aim of synthesis dictionary learning is that an image patch can be approximated by a sparse linear combination of a dictionary $D \in \mathbb{K}^{N_p \times N_\alpha}$ with a sparse N_α-dimensional vector $\alpha_i \in \mathbb{K}^{N_\alpha}$. The dictionary $D = [d_1, \dots, d_{N_\alpha}]$ consists of a normalized set of basis vectors d_j, $j = 1, \dots, N_\alpha$, called atoms. The according optimization problem for blind CS is formulated as [32]

$$\min_{\substack{x \in \mathbb{K}^{N_x} \\ D \in \mathbb{K}^{N_p \times N_\alpha}}} \sum_{i=1}^{N_s} \frac{1}{2} \|P_i x - D\alpha_i\|_2^2 + \frac{\lambda}{2} \|Ax - y\|_2^2 \quad \text{s.t.} \quad \|\alpha_i\|_0 \leq K_0 \ \forall i, \ \|d_j\|_2 \leq 1 \ \forall j,$$

where $\lambda > 0$ and the parameter K_0 defines the sparsity level. However, the above problem is NP-hard, even if the ℓ_0 quasinorm is replaced by the convex ℓ_1 norm. Ravishankar et al. [32] proposed to solve this problem using an alternating minimization scheme. In the first step, the dictionary is learned using a K-Singular Value Decomposition (SVD) [33] algorithm. Due to the high computational requirement, only a fraction of all patches is used for this step. The sparse codes α_i for all image patches are then estimated using the Orthogonal Matching Pursuit (OMP) algorithm [34]. In the second step, the reconstruction is updated, while the dictionary D and sparse codes α_i are fixed. The reconstruction quality highly depends on the sparsity level K_0 and the size of the dictionary. Promising results using dictionary learning have been shown for *MRI* [32,35] and *CT* [36].

Instead of learning a synthesis dictionary, Ravishankar et al. [37] also proposed to learn the sparsifying transform, which can be seen as a generalization of the analysis model. Applied to blind CS, the corresponding model reads [38,39]

$$\min_{\substack{x \in \mathbb{K}^{N_x} \\ W \in \mathbb{K}^{N_p \times N_p} \\ \alpha \in \mathbb{K}^{N_\alpha \times N_s}}} \sum_{i=1}^{N_s} \left(\frac{1}{2} \|WP_i x - \alpha_i\|_2^2 + \beta \|\alpha_i\|_0 \right) + \frac{\lambda}{2} \|Ax - y\|_2^2 \quad \text{s.t.} \quad W^* W = I,$$

where $\beta > 0$, $\lambda > 0$ and $\alpha = [\alpha_1, \dots, \alpha_{N_s}]$ is a matrix of all sparse vectors α_i. The sparsifying transform is represented by the matrix $W \in \mathbb{K}^{N_p \times N_p}$. Similar to dictionary learning, this problem can be solved by alternating minimization of the sparsifying transform W, the sparse codes $\alpha_i \forall i$ and the reconstruction x [38,39]. In general, learning of the sparsifying transform is computationally inexpensive compared to dictionary learning, because a closed-form solution based on thresholding exists for the sparse codes. In medical imaging, transform-based learning has led to promising results for both *MRI* and *CT* [38–41]. Recently, the dictionary, transform and thresholding operators for *MRI* reconstruction were learned based on a supervised learning scheme [42] (see Sect. 2.3.2 for more details).

In both dictionary learning and sparsifying transform learning, patches are approximated by a sparse combination of dictionary atoms. To incorporate the whole image, an alternative approach is to learn a convolutional sparse representation [43,44], where an image is approximated by convolving a number of K dictionary filters $\zeta_k \in \mathbb{K}^{N_\zeta}$ with sparse coefficient maps $c_k \in \mathbb{K}^{N_x}$. The convolutional dictionary problem in synthesis form is formulated as

$$\min_{\substack{\zeta_k \in \mathbb{K}^{N_\zeta} \\ c_k \in \mathbb{K}^{N_x}}} \frac{1}{2} \sum_{s=1}^{S} \left(\left\| x_s - \sum_{k=1}^{K} \zeta_k * c_{k,s} \right\|_2^2 + \lambda \sum_{k=1}^{K} \| c_{k,s} \|_1 \right) \quad \text{s.t.} \quad \| \zeta_k \|_2 \leq 1 \; \forall k,$$

where $\lambda > 0$ and x_s is the sth of S training samples. To reconstruct a new image, the filters ζ_k are fixed and the sparse coefficient maps c_k are learned. The final image is reconstructed by computing $x^* = \sum_{k=1}^{K} \zeta_k * c_k$.

A very recent approach for unsupervised learning learns a nonlinear sparse prior based on *KSAE* [45] with application to iterative low-dose *CT* reconstruction. The goal of the *KSAE* is [46] to train an encoder f_{enc} and decoder f_{dec}

$$(\theta_{\text{enc}}^*, \theta_{\text{dec}}^*) \in \arg\min_{\theta_{\text{enc}}, \theta_{\text{dec}}} \sum_{i=1}^{N_s} \frac{1}{2} \| x_i - f_{\text{dec}}(f_{\text{enc}}(x_i)) \|_2^2 \quad \text{s.t.} \quad \| f_{\text{enc}}(x_i) \|_0 \leq K_0 \; \forall i,$$

where K_0 defines the sparsity level and θ_{enc}^* and θ_{dec}^* denote the optimal parameters for the encoder f_{enc} and decoder f_{dec}, respectively. Here, x_i denotes the ith of N_s training patches of clean reference images, i.e., normal-dose *CT* images. The encoder and decoder are realized using fully-connected networks and Rectified Linear Unit (ReLU) activations. Once the encoder and decoder networks are learned, a new image can be reconstructed according to the following unconstrained optimization problem

$$\min_{\substack{x \in \mathbb{K}^{N_x} \\ \hat{x} \in \mathbb{K}^{N_x \times N_s}}} \frac{1}{2} \sum_{i=1}^{N_s} \| P_i x - f_{\text{dec}}(f_{\text{enc}}(\hat{x}_i)) \|_2^2 + \frac{\lambda}{2} \| Ax - y \|_2^2,$$

where $\lambda > 0$, P_i is the patch-extraction matrix as defined for dictionary and transform learning, and $\hat{x} = [\hat{x}_1, \dots, \hat{x}_{N_s}]$ are the patches projected on the set trained by the au-

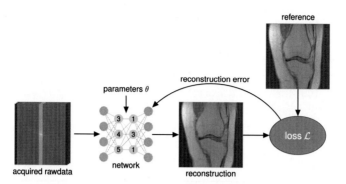

Figure 2.2 *Schematic illustration of the training process.* The corrupted data are propagated through a network with parameters θ that should be learned to obtain an artifact-free reconstruction. The quality corresponds to the selected loss function $\mathcal{L}$ that measures the similarity between the reconstructed image and the reference image. The reconstruction error is propagated back through the network to achieve a new set of parameters. Once the training has converged, new images can be reconstructed efficiently by simply forward-propagating the new data through the network using the fixed learned parameters.

toencoder. Wu et al. [45] propose to solve this optimization problem in an alternating manner using the Separable Quadratic Surrogate (SQS) algorithm.

2.3. Supervised learning in image reconstruction

Supervised learning approaches require three major ingredients for successful learning: a network architecture f_θ, suitable training data and an appropriate loss function $\mathcal{L}$. In an off-line training procedure as depicted in Fig. 2.2, the corrupted data are fed to a network parametrized by the parameters θ that are optimized during training. The output of the network is compared to a reference image using a loss function $\mathcal{L}$ that measures the similarity between the two images. This determines the reconstruction error that is back-propagated [47] through the network to obtain a new set of updated parameters. This process is repeated until the training has converged. Once all the parameters are learned, new images can be reconstructed efficiently as a simple application of f_θ.

Fig. 2.3 illustrates different strategies of how neural networks can be employed in image reconstruction. In the first method, a data–driven regularizer is learned from pairs of corrupted and clean images. This includes learning optimal weight parameters using bi–level optimization or learning an improved denoiser, which replaces fixed proximal steps in an iterative reconstruction scheme involving operations that ensure consistency to the given measurement data. The second approach focuses on learning an unrolled iterative optimization scheme, involving data consistency term operations in every single unrolled step. These two approaches ensure data consistency to the measured data, which is not ensured by the following two approaches. The third approach defines im-

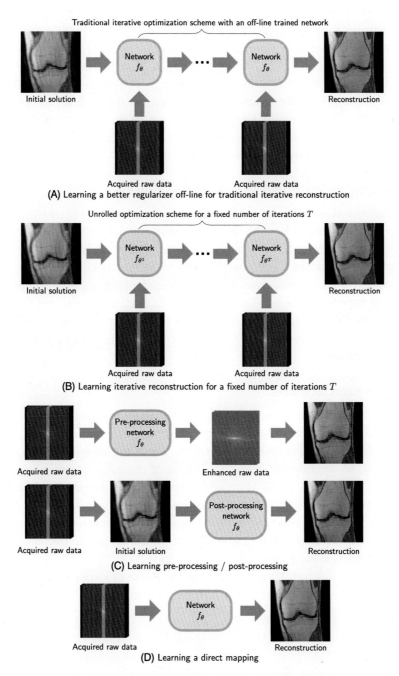

Figure 2.3 *Overview of how image reconstruction can be defined as deep learning-based problem.*
(A) Data-driven regularization in a traditional optimization problem with an off-line trained denoising network; (B) Learning an unrolled optimization scheme for a fixed number of iterations T; (C) Image enhancement in data or image domain; (D) Direct Mapping.

age reconstruction as an image enhancement problem, which tries to improve upon an initial corrupted reconstruction from the measured data without including the measured data in the learning process itself. This approach also includes improvements upon the measured data directly in the measurement domain and performs, e.g., artifact correction before the image is finally reconstructed. The fourth approach focuses on mapping the measured data directly to the image domain, where the whole transform or parts of the image formation process can be learned. The four different approaches will be reviewed in detail in the following subsections.

2.3.1 Learning an improved regularization function

Given the variational model in Eq. (2.4), a natural question is how to select not only the correct weight parameter λ, but also the regularization function $\mathcal{R}$ itself. While *bi-level optimization* [48–54] addresses the first question, the underlying handcrafted regularizer might still be too weak for more complex reconstruction tasks. Thus, developments have focused on the use of nonconvex regularizers, embedded in a bi-level optimization approach. An overview over modern regularization techniques for inverse problems can be found in [55]. In recent publications, *CNNs* are trained to act as additional regularization in a variational model or to replace a proximal mapping in a Proximal Gradient (PG) scheme.

Nonconvex regularization

Simple convex regularizers such as the *TV* semi-norm as defined in Eq. (2.5) enable efficient global optimization where a unique solution exists. The used ℓ_1 norm is a convex approximation to the sparsity-inducing l_0 norm. However, the ℓ_1 norm is not a suitable model to describe the prior distribution of natural and medical images. The quasiconvex ℓ_q norm with $q \in (0, 1)$ approximates the prior distribution better and already yields superior results [56]. However, when leaving convexity assumptions behind and moving to nonconvex optimization, finding a good solution is even more challenging and highly sophisticated optimization algorithms are needed to overcome spurious local minima while allowing for efficient computation.

An example for nonconvex regularization is the Fields of Experts (FoE) model [57], which can be seen as an extension of the *TV* semi-norm

$$\mathcal{R}[x] = \sum_{i=1}^{N_k} \langle \rho_i(K_i x), \mathbf{1} \rangle . \qquad (2.6)$$

Here, the single term of the *TV* semi-norm is extended to N_k terms consisting of nonlinear potential functions $\rho_i(z) = (\rho_{i,1}(z_1), \dots, \rho_{i,N}(z_N)) \in \mathbb{K}^{N_x}$ and linear convolution operators $K_i : \mathbb{K}^{N_x} \to \mathbb{K}^{N_x}$. The symbol $\mathbf{1} \in \mathbb{K}^{N_x}$ indicates a vector of ones. The free parameters of the *FoE* model are the convolution operators and the parametrization of the nonlinear potential functions, which are both learned from data [53,57]. The selected potential functions are associated with the statistics of natural images [58]. An example are the log-Student-t functions $\rho_{i,j}(z_j) = \alpha_{i,j} \log(\beta_{i,j} z_j^2 + 1)$, applied in a pointwise manner, where j represents the discrete pixel locations in image domain. Learning strategies of the *FoE* model such as bi-level optimization [53,59,60] and learned iterative reconstructions, termed Variational Networks (VNs) [61–63], will be presented in this chapter.

Bi-level optimization

One natural question that arises when solving Eq. (2.4) is how to select the weight parameter λ. Different approaches exist to tackle this problem such as reinforcement learning [64] and bi-level optimization. Bi-level optimization problems consist of two problems: (i) A higher-level problem which defines the goal of the optimization, e.g., minimizing the Mean Squared Error (MSE). The outcome of this problem depends on (ii) the solution of the lower-level problem, which could be the solution to Eq. (2.4). Mathematically speaking, bi-level optimization reads as

$$\min_{\theta \geq 0} \mathcal{L}\left(x^*(\theta), x_{\text{ref}}\right) \quad \text{s.t.} \quad x^*(\theta) \in \arg\min_{x \in \mathbb{K}^{N_x}} E(x, \theta),$$

where x^* is a solution to the lower-level problem $\arg\min_{x \in \mathbb{K}^{N_x}} E(x, \theta)$, depending on trainable parameters θ, and minimizing $\mathcal{L}$ defines the higher-level problem that compares x^* with a reference x_{ref} using a certain mapping $\mathcal{L}$. To solve this bi-level optimization problem, the lower-level problem needs to be solved with high accuracy and is in general required to be twice differentiable in order to compute the gradient of the higher-level problem

$$\frac{\partial \mathcal{L}}{\partial \theta} = -\frac{\partial^2 E}{\partial x^* \partial \theta} \left(\frac{\partial^2 E}{(\partial x^*)^2}\right)^{-1} \frac{\partial \mathcal{L}}{\partial x^*},$$

where $\beta > 0$ and $\lambda > 0$. In [65], a way to consider nonsmooth functions as lower-level problems in bi-level optimization is proposed. Bi-level optimization helps to tune the reconstruction results, as the right weight parameters are learned as shown for analysis prior learning [52] and various image restoration problems [48–51,54]. However, the underlying regularizers are often still too simple to capture the characteristics of natural and medical images. Hence, the focus moved from learning single parameters to learning function parametrizations and filters from data [53,59,60,66] which fit the statistics of natural images better [58]. However, the major drawbacks of bi-level optimization problems are the huge computational effort and the requirement to solve the lower-level problem exactly, which is especially critical in the context of medical image reconstruction due to, e.g., large-scale problems or the expensive computations of the forward operator A and the adjoint operator A^*.

Convolutional neural networks as regularization

There are different ways to include *CNNs* in existing models. The earliest example in the context of *MR* image reconstruction trains a *CNN* that maps artifact-corrupted images $A^*(y)$ to artifact-free images x_{ref} [67]. The trained *CNN* is then embedded in a *CS* formulation, where the *CNN* output acts as a reference image for the new optimization problem

$$x^* \in \arg\min_{x \in \mathbb{K}^{N_x}} \frac{\beta}{2} \left\| f_\theta(A^*(y)) - x \right\|_2^2 + \frac{\lambda}{2} \left\| A(x) - y \right\|_2^2 + \mathcal{R}\,[x].$$

The parameters $\beta > 0$ and $\lambda > 0$ are weight parameters that have to be selected individually for this optimization problem and $\mathcal{R}\,[x]$ is an arbitrary fixed regularization function. The operators A and A^* define the forward and adjoint operator, respectively.

Another possibility how *CNNs* can improve the reconstruction quality is to replace existing proximal mappings in iterative reconstruction procedures to estimate a solution for the variational model in Eq. (2.4). In many iterative reconstruction algorithms such as the *PG* method, the proximal mapping $\text{prox}_{\tau\mathcal{R}}$ is employed to fulfill the regularization constraint while a gradient step is performed w.r.t. the data consistency term $\mathcal{D}$. This leads to the following iterative scheme:

$$x^{t+1} = \text{prox}_{\tau\mathcal{R}} \left(x^t - \tau \nabla_x \mathcal{D}\left[A(x^t), y \right] \right),$$

where the proximal operator is defined as

$$\text{prox}_{\tau\mathcal{R}}(\hat{x}) = \arg\min_{x \in \mathbb{K}^{N_x}} \frac{1}{2\tau} \left\| x - \hat{x} \right\|_2^2 + \mathcal{R}\,[x]. \qquad (2.7)$$

Heide et al. [68] and Venkatakrishnan et al. [69] observed that the proximal mapping in Eq. (2.7) coincides with the Maximum-A-Posteriori (MAP) estimation of a Gaussian denoiser. It was suggested to replace the proximal operator by more sophisticated denoising algorithms such as BM3D [70] and Non-Local Means (NLM) [71]. In fact, this does not have to be necessarily done for the projected gradient method, but can also be achieved with any first-order method such as the Alternating Direction Method of Multipliers (ADMM) [72], used in the plug-and-play priors framework by [69], or the Primal–Dual (PD) algorithm [73], as shown in [68]. Replacing the denoising steps by BM3D and *NLM* denoising steps in medical image reconstruction has been successfully applied to *MRI* [74–76] and *CT* [77,78].

Inspired by [68,69], Meinhardt et al. [79] replaced the proximal operator by a learned denoising *CNN*

$$x^{t+1} = f_\theta \left(x^t - \tau \nabla_x \mathcal{D}\left[A(x^t), y \right] \right).$$

As before, this is not only restricted to a single *PG* method, but can also be used for other methods like *ADMM* or *PD*. The training of the used *CNN* is based on pairs of corrupted and clean reference images. The *CNN* can be trained more effectively by additionally feeding pairs of intermediate reconstruction results and reference images to the *CNN* [80,81]. Promising results towards learning a proximal operator were shown for *CT* [80–82] and *PET* [83]. Obviously, learning a proximal operator has the advantage that it can be trained offline, meaning that the content of natural or medical images is reflected in the *CNN*. Once the denoiser is learned, it offers flexible usage for any new optimization problem with arbitrary data consistency terms. The learned denoiser, i.e., the proximal operator, remains the same in every single step of the optimization procedure.

2.3.2 Learning an iterative reconstruction model

Instead of solving a new optimization problem for each task, the whole iterative reconstruction procedure itself can be learned. This can be motivated by the Landweber method [84]. Given an iteration-dependent step size τ^t and an initial solution x^0, the Landweber method performs a gradient descent on the least-squares problem Eq. (2.3), leading to the following iterative algorithm:

$$x^{t+1} = x^t - \tau^t \nabla_x \mathcal{D}\left[A(x^t), y\right].$$

In order to prevent over-fitting to the measurement data y, it is beneficial to stop the Landweber method after a finite number of iterations T [19], which is known as early stopping. When including the regularization term, this idea can be extended to unroll a (proximal) gradient algorithm for a finite number of iterations T, where the data consistency term and regularization term are applied in an alternating manner

$$x^{t+\frac{1}{2}} = f_1(x^t), \tag{2.8}$$

$$x^{t+1} = f_2(x^{t+\frac{1}{2}}). \tag{2.9}$$

Here, the functions f_1 and f_2 consider the prior term and the data term, or vice versa, depending on the algorithm. The goal is now to learn this optimization scheme for a fixed number of T iterations, including step sizes, the prior model and weight parameters. We also see that this formulation enforces data consistency steps in every iteration. In 2005, Gregor and LeCun made first attempts towards learning an unrolled scheme by proposing the Learned Iterative Shrinkage and Thresholding Algorithm (LISTA) algorithm [85], which learns an encoder network to approximate the sparse codes in Iterative Shrinkage and Thresholding Algorithm (ISTA) [86,87]. As stated in the previous section, this scheme is not only restricted to (proximal) gradient methods [61,62,88,89], but can be also extended to a broader class of optimization algorithms [90–94].

Algorithm 1 Learned Proximal Gradient, gradient in $\mathcal{R}$ [91,89].

Input: $x_0 \in \mathbb{K}^{N_x}$

 for $t = 0, \ldots, T - 1$ **do**

  $x^{t+\frac{1}{2}} = x^t - f_{\theta^t}$

  $x^{t+1} = \text{prox}_{\lambda^t \mathcal{D}[A(\cdot), y]} \left(x^{t+\frac{1}{2}} \right) = \underset{x \in \mathbb{K}^{N_x}}{\arg\min} \frac{1}{2} \left\| x - x^{t+\frac{1}{2}} \right\|_2^2 + \lambda^t \mathcal{D}\left[A(x), y \right]$

 end for

The first possibility to solve Eqs. (2.8) and (2.9) is with a *PG* method where f_1 computes the gradient w.r.t. $\mathcal{R}$ and f_2 models the proximal operator on $\mathcal{D}$. This results in

$$x^{t+\frac{1}{2}} = x^t - \tau^t \nabla_x \mathcal{R}\left[x^t \right], \tag{2.10}$$

$$x^{t+1} = \text{prox}_{\tau^t \lambda \mathcal{D}[A(\cdot), y]} \left(x^{t+\frac{1}{2}} \right) = \underset{x \in \mathbb{K}^{N_x}}{\arg\min} \frac{1}{2\tau^t} \left\| x - x^{t+\frac{1}{2}} \right\|_2^2 + \lambda \mathcal{D}\left[A(x), y \right]. \tag{2.11}$$

Diamond et al. [91] and Schlemper et al. [89] suggest to replace the gradient update in Eq. (2.10) by a trainable function f_{θ^t} representing a *CNN*, which is allowed to change in every iteration t, or the weights θ can be shared across the different iterations [95–97]. Then, Eq. (2.10) naturally turns into a residual neural network [98]. The step size in Eq. (2.11) can be neglected as it is implicitly contained in the weight parameter λ and the *CNN*, which are both allowed to change in every iteration. This version of the learned *PG* with the gradient in $\mathcal{R}$ is depicted in Algorithm 1. To train Algorithm 1 end-to-end, a closed-form solution of the proximal operator has to exist.

Example: Single-coil MRI reconstruction [89]

An example in medical imaging for which the proximal operator has a closed-form solution is single-receive-coil MRI reconstruction. The data consistency term reads as $\mathcal{D}\left[A(x), y \right] = \frac{1}{2} \left\| Ax - y \right\|_2^2$ with $A = PF$, where $\mathcal{F}$ is the Fourier transform and P models the encoding matrix, filling the missing k-space lines with zeros. The proximal mapping to this data consistency term is computed as

$$x^{t+1} = \mathcal{F}^* \Lambda^t \mathcal{F} x^{t+\frac{1}{2}} + \frac{\lambda^t}{1 + \lambda^t} \mathcal{F}^* P^* y,$$

$$\Lambda_{ii}^t = \begin{cases} 1 & \text{if } i \notin \Omega, \\ \frac{1}{1+\lambda^t} & \text{if } i \in \Omega, \end{cases}$$

where Λ is a diagonal matrix and Ω defines the index set of acquired k-space samples. As this proximal mapping enforces data consistency, this step is also termed *data consistency layer* in [89,97].

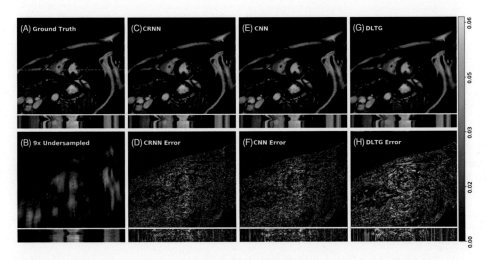

Figure 2.4 *Cardiac reconstructions for 9-fold accelerated MRI data along with their error maps.* The recurrent *CNN* approach [97] and *CNN* approach [89] outperform dictionary learning [35].

Various applications in *MRI* exist to solve Eq. (2.4) with algorithms like Algorithm 1. Schlemper et al. [89] proposed a deep cascaded *CNN* with the focus on dynamic *MRI* in a single-coil setting. This approach was improved by Qin et al. [97] who introduced a recurrent neural network architecture that shares weights over layers and considers additional memory in both spatial and time domain. An example cardiac reconstruction comparing the *CNN* architecture of [89], the recurrent *CNN* architecture of [97] and dictionary learning [35] is depicted in Fig. 2.4 for 9-fold accelerated *MRI* data. The recurrent architecture performs on similar lines in the spatial domain and shows improved results in the temporal direction, indicated by the error maps. Both approaches outperform dictionary learning by a substantial margin.

Aggarwal et al. [95,96] proposed an approach for both single-coil and multi-coil *MRI* for static and dynamic imaging. A similar idea was used by [99], which consists of a single iteration of *CNN* regularization and data consistency step. An improved version using a recurrent architecture was presented in [100]. Fig. 2.5 shows an example sagittal brain reconstruction for 6-fold accelerated *MRI* data from [95]. The qualitative inspection and quantitative Peak Signal-To-Noise Ratio (PSNR) values indicate that the learning-based reconstruction outperforms the *CS* approach using the *TV* semi-norm.

A second possibility to solve Eqs. (2.8) and (2.9) is a variant of the *PG* method where f_1 now computes the gradient w.r.t. $\mathcal{D}$ and f_2 models the proximal operator on $\mathcal{R}$, resulting in

$$x^{t+\frac{1}{2}} = x^t - \tau^t \nabla_x \mathcal{D}\left[A(x^t), y\right],$$
$$x^{t+1} = \text{prox}_{\tau^t \mathcal{R}}\left(x^{t+\frac{1}{2}}\right).$$

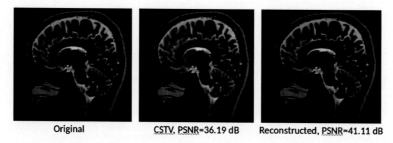

Original   CSTV, PSNR=36.19 dB   Reconstructed, PSNR=41.11 dB

Figure 2.5 *Sagittal brain reconstructions for 6-fold accelerated MRI data along with their error maps.* The learning-based approach [95] outperforms the CS-based approach qualitatively and quantitatively.

Algorithm 2 Learned Proximal Gradient, gradient in $\mathcal{D}$ [101].

Input: $x_0 \in \mathbb{K}^{N_x}$
  for $t = 0, \ldots, T-1$ **do**
    $x^{t+1} = f_{\theta^t}\left(x^t, \nabla_x \mathcal{D}\left[A(x^t), y\right]\right)$
  end for

Algorithm 3 Learned Proximal Gradient with memory, gradient in $\mathcal{D}$ [88].

Input: $x_0 \in \mathbb{K}^{N_x}$, $x_{\mathrm{mem}}^0 \in \mathbb{K}^{N_{x,\mathrm{mem}}}$
  for $t = 0, \ldots, T-1$ **do**
    $\left(x^{t+1}, x_{\mathrm{mem}}^{t+1}\right) = f_{\theta^t}\left(x^t, \nabla_x \mathcal{D}\left[A(x^t), y\right], x_{\mathrm{mem}}^t\right)$
  end for

In principle, the proximal operator can be replaced by a trainable function f_{θ^t}, however, it is challenging to define the correct step size τ^t. Therefore, Adler et al. [88,90] and Hauptmann et al. [101] proposed to let the CNN learn how to combine x^t with the gradient of the data consistency term $\nabla_x \mathcal{D}\left[A(x^t), y\right]$. Hence, f_{θ^t} takes x^t stacked with $\nabla_x \mathcal{D}\left[A(x^t), y\right]$ as an input, such that the update x^{t+1} can be reformulated as shown in Algorithm 2. Motivated by accelerated gradient methods, information of earlier iterates can be used by extending the formulation with an additional memory variable $x_{\mathrm{mem}} \in \mathbb{K}^{N_{x,\mathrm{mem}}}$, leading to Algorithm 3, where $N_{x,\mathrm{mem}}$ defines the dimension of the memory.

To introduce another class of optimizers, let us first go back to traditional optimization. For this purpose, we formulate the variational model in Eq. (2.4) as a general model

$$\min_{x \in \mathbb{K}^{N_x}} F(H(x)) + G(x), \tag{2.12}$$

where $F : \mathbb{K}^{N_p} \to \mathbb{R}$ is a proper convex lower-semicontinuous (l.s.c.) and possibly nonsmooth function, the function $G : \mathbb{K}^{N_x} \to \mathbb{R}$ is smooth and proper convex *l.s.c.*, and

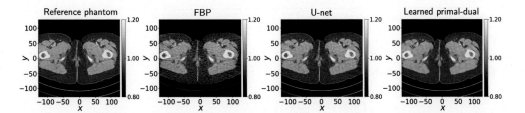

Figure 2.6 *Example CT reconstruction of the Mayo Low-Dose CT dataset.* The learned *PD* reconstruction method of [90] yields substantially improved image quality compared to the *FBP* reconstruction and a purely image-based U-net reconstruction.

$H : \mathbb{K}^{N_x} \to \mathbb{K}^{N_p}$ is a differentiable, possibly nonlinear operator. In some cases, the proximal mapping on F does not have a closed–form solution, so *PD* methods [73,21], which were extended to nonlinear operators [102], offer a possibility to tackle this problem. By introducing a dual variable $p \in \mathbb{K}^{N_p}$, the primal problem in Eq. (2.12) can be cast to a *PD* saddle-point problem with the following structure

$$\min_{x \in \mathbb{K}^{N_x}} \max_{p \in \mathbb{K}^{N_p}} \langle H(x), p \rangle + G(x) - F^*(p),$$

where F^* is the Fenchel conjugate of F. An approximate solution can be estimated using the (nonlinear) *PD* hybrid gradient method depicted in Algorithm 4, where τ and σ are the primal and dual step sizes, and the expression $\left[\partial H(x^t) \right]^* : \mathbb{K}^{N_p} \to \mathbb{K}^{N_x}$ denotes the adjoint of the derivative of H, evaluated in x^t. When inspecting Algorithm 4, we observe two proximal operators in the primal and dual space, as well as an over-relaxation step. This is the motivation of Adler et al. [90] to learn the proximal operators along with the update steps, resulting in the learned *PD* Algorithm 5, where the parameters that are learned during training are $\theta = \left[\theta_{\mathrm{primal}}, \theta_{\mathrm{dual}} \right]$.

The learned *PG* methods have been applied to different medical inverse problems. Adler et al. [88,90] showcase Algorithms 3 and 5 on a 2D *CT* problem, including a discussion on the performance using linear and nonlinear operators. A comparison between the learned *PD* method of [90] to a Filtered Back-Projection (FBP) and U-net reconstruction is illustrated in Fig. 2.6 for an example from the Mayo Low-Dose *CT* dataset[1]. The learned *PD* method clearly outperforms the purely image-enhancement U-net method and *FBP* reconstruction. Hauptmann et al. [101] used Algorithm 2 for *PAT* reconstruction. An extension to a multiscale U-net architecture was presented in [103].

Another possibility to tackle the problem defined in Eq. (2.4) is to take gradient steps in the direction of the prior term and the data consistency term, either in an alternated way or in a single combined step. This concept was initially used in learning

---

[1] https://www.aapm.org/GrandChallenge/LowDoseCT/.

Algorithm 4 Nonlinear Primal–Dual Hybrid Gradient [73,102].

Input: $x^0 \in \mathbb{K}^{N_x}$, $p^0 \in \mathbb{K}^{N_p}$

Choose: $\sigma, \tau > 0$ s.t. $\sigma\tau \|H\|_2^2 \leq 1$, $\vartheta \in [0, 1]$

    for $t = 0, \ldots, T-1$ **do**

        $p^{t+1} = \text{prox}_{\sigma F^*}\left(p^t + \sigma H(\tilde{x}^t)\right)$

        $x^{t+1} = \text{prox}_{\tau G}\left(x^t - \tau\left[\partial H(x^t)\right]^*(p^{t+1})\right)$

        $\tilde{x}^{t+1} = x^{t+1} + \vartheta\left(x^{t+1} - x^t\right)$

    end for

Algorithm 5 Learned Primal–Dual [90].

Input: $x_0 \in \mathbb{K}^{N_x}$, $p_0 \in \mathbb{K}^{N_p}$, $x_{\text{mem}}^0 \in \mathbb{K}^{N_{x,\text{mem}}}$, $p_{\text{mem}}^0 \in \mathbb{K}^{N_{p,\text{mem}}}$

    for $t = 0, \ldots, T-1$ **do**

        $\left(p^{t+1}, p_{\text{mem}}^{t+1}\right) = f_{\theta_{\text{dual}}^t}\left(p^t, p_{\text{mem}}^t, H(x_{\text{mem}}^{(1),t}), y\right)$

        $\left(x^{t+1}, x_{\text{mem}}^{t+1}\right) = f_{\theta_{\text{primal}}^t}\left(x^t, x_{\text{mem}}^t, \left[\partial H(x^t)\right]^*(p^{t+1})\right)$

    end for

---

an optimized reaction–diffusion process for image restoration [61], and further led to the formulation of *Variational Networks* [62,63], which have a strong connection to both variational models and deep learning. The basic concept of *VNs* relies on unrolling a gradient descent step for a finite number of iterations T in direction of the gradient of a smooth variational model defined in Eq. (2.4)

$$x^{t+1} = x^t - \tau^t\left(\nabla_x\mathcal{R}\left[x^t\right] + \nabla_x\mathcal{D}\left[A(x^t), y\right]\right). \tag{2.13}$$

The step size τ^t can be neglected during learning as it is implicitly contained in $\mathcal{R}$ and $\mathcal{D}$. *VNs* are characterized by the special structure of the regularization term and data consistency term which is related to variational models as depicted in Algorithm 6. For the regularization part, this relation is typically fulfilled by the *FoE* model. Plugging in the gradient of the *FoE* model Eq. (2.6) and the gradient of a simple data consistency term that is weighted by a parameter λ into Eq. (2.13) yields

$$x^{t+1} = x^t - \sum_{i=1}^{N_k}(K_i^t)^\top\phi_i^t(K_i^t x) - \lambda^t A^*\nabla\mathcal{D}\left[A(x^t), y\right], \quad \theta^t = \left[K_i^t, \phi_i^t, \lambda^t\right], \tag{2.14}$$

where the activation functions $\phi_i^t(z) = \text{diag}(\phi_{i,1}^t(z_1), \ldots, \phi_{i,N}^t(z_N)) : \mathbb{K}^{N_x} \to \mathbb{K}^{N_x}$ are defined by the first derivative of potential functions $\phi_{i,j}^t = \rho_{i,j}^{',t}$. The term $(K_i^t)^\top : \mathbb{K}^{N_x} \to \mathbb{K}^{N_x}$ defines the adjoint convolution operator. The parameters θ that are learned in a *VN* are the filters defined in K_i^t, parametrized activation functions ϕ_i^t and additional parameters such as the weight parameter λ^t. In case the exact data consistency term is not known, it can be replaced by a trainable data consistency term, e.g.,

---

Algorithm 6 Variational Networks [61–63].

Input: $x^0 \in \mathbb{K}^{N_x}$

    for $t = 0, \ldots, T - 1$ **do**

        $x^{t+1} = x^t - f_{\theta^t_{\mathcal{R}}}(x^t) - f_{\theta^t_{\mathcal{D}}}(x^t, y)$ s.t. $f_{\theta^t_{\mathcal{R}}} = \nabla_x \mathcal{R}_{\theta^t_{\mathcal{R}}}, f_{\theta^t_{\mathcal{D}}} = \nabla_x \mathcal{D}_{\theta^t_{\mathcal{D}}}$

    end for

Algorithm 7 Recurrent Inference Machines [110].

Input: $x^0 \in \mathbb{K}^{N_x}, x^0_{\text{mem}} = 0$

    for $t = 0, \ldots, T - 1$ **do**

        $x^{t+1}_{\text{mem}} = \hat{f}_\theta(\nabla_x \log p(y|x)(x^t), x^t, x^{t+1}_{\text{mem}})$

        $x^{t+1} = x^t + f_\theta(\nabla_x \log p(y|x)(x^t), x^t, x^{t+1}_{\text{mem}})$

    end for

$\mathcal{D}[A(x^t), y] = \rho^t_D(Ax^t - y)$ [92,104] where ρ_D are potential functions defined in the same way as ρ. Due to the strong connection to variational models, *VNs* allow us to gain some insights into what is learned by the model, as filters and activation/potential functions can be visualized. The first works on restricting the potential functions to convex functions and studies on the relation to energy minimization were shown in [63]. Furthermore, *VNs* are a versatile architecture that have shown state-of-the-art results not only in image restoration tasks, including image denoising [61], JPEG deblocking [61], demosaicing [104], and image inpainting [105], but also in *MRI* reconstruction [62,106] and low-dose *CT* reconstruction [107]. In Real-Time Hand-Held Sound-Speed Imaging [92], an unrolled gradient descent scheme with momentum is learned along with an additional parametrization of the data consistency term. Inspired by the idea of *VNs*, Chen et al. [108] replaced the gradient of the regularization function by a *CNN* part for sparse-view *CT* reconstruction. In a similar approach, a *CNN* with trainable activation functions was used for joint denoising and segmentation of tumor cells [109].

A different approach for learned iterative *MR* reconstruction using Recurrent Inference Machines [110] was shown in [111] and is stated in Algorithm 7. An aliased image along with the gradient of its log-likelihood $\nabla_x \log p(y|x)(x^t)$ is fed to a recurrent neural network f_θ, where weights are shared across iterations. This produces an incremental update of the input x and the latent memory variable x_{mem}, where $\hat{f}_\theta$ in Algorithm 7 is the part of f_θ generating the update for x_{mem}.

There are also other approaches that fall into the class of learning an iterative reconstruction. Dictionary-transform learning has been presented in Sect. 2.2, where alternating updates w.r.t. to data consistency term and dictionary/transform update steps are performed. Recently, Ravishanker et al. [42] proposed to unroll this scheme and learn the regularizer layer-by-layer in a supervised way, involving the dictionary, transforms and thresholds using a neural network approach. For *MRI* reconstruction, Eo et al. [112] proposed the KIKI-net that performs iterative updates in the k-space and image domain which are both trained with *CNNs*, with intermediate data consistency layers.

The presented unrolled model-based iterative approaches were defined in a very generic way which makes them convenient to adapt to a new model when the forward and adjoint operators A and A^* are known. Thus, data consistency to the measured data y is ensured in every single iteration. However, the complexity of some operators in medical image reconstruction such as *PAT* [101] makes it infeasible to train the whole algorithm end-to-end. In this case, the algorithm has to be trained in a greedy manner iteration-by-iteration, although end-to-end training would result in a performance increase [61]. Hence, a trade-off between tractable computation time and quality of the output has to be made. If the parameters in every iteration vary, the model is more flexible to adapt to training data [63]. Special recurrent architectures share the weights across iterations and additionally transport information through the iterative procedure via a memory state variable, which greatly reduces the number of parameters while still being flexible.

2.3.3 Deep learning for image and data enhancement

In contrast to iterative reconstruction methods, where the measured raw data are accounted in every reconstruction step, enhancement methods do not include the physical model. Enhancement can be performed in the data domain as preprocessing $y^* = f_\theta(y)$ or in the image domain as postprocessing $x^* = f_\theta(x^0)$. In the case of preprocessing, the reconstruction is performed on the enhanced measurement data y^*, while in the case of postprocessing an initial solution x^0 is first reconstructed and then enhanced to obtain x^*. An obvious advantage is that the training is highly efficient as the physical model, which is often heavily time consuming to evaluate numerically, is not considered. The drawback is that the used network architecture can only work on information that is provided in the initial guess and the information that is extracted from the training data. Consequently, consistency to measured raw data is not maintained for postprocessing methods. As the algorithms solely work in the image domain, various types of postprocessing methods such as image denoising, artifact removal and image superresolution fall into this class of problems. These algorithms are either applied after reconstruction of x_0 or on top of other correction methods.

In *MR* imaging, the input to the used algorithms are mainly coil-combined or sum-of-squares-combined images. In [113,114], MR images were reconstructed from aliased single-coil images using a U-net architecture. Extensions to 3D [115] and dynamic *MRI* [116] were made using similar approaches. Jin et al. [115] additionally suggest to provide input and reference images that underwent a Wavelet transform to suppress image modality-specific noise, similar to [117]. Instead of learning the mapping from the aliased input image to the artifact-free reference image, residual learning [98] provides a way to learn the aliasing artifacts instead, which are then subtracted from the aliased input image as presented in [118,119]. Using a similar approach, Lee et al. [120] included both image magnitude and phase information and showed that this acts as iterative k-space interpolation. While the aforementioned algorithms mainly work on single-coil images, Kwon et al. [121] introduced a Multi Layer Perceptron (MLP) that unfolds the single coil images of Cartesian undersampled data line-by-line, similar to classical Sensitivity Encoding (SENSE) [122]. However, this architecture has to be adapted and retrained for different matrix sizes and sampling patterns. Besides undersampled MR image reconstruction, a residual CNN approach was used for single-shot T_2 mapping using overlapping-echo detachment planar imaging [123]. Another research area for postprocessing methods is image superresolution. Deep learning approaches offer a way to directly learn the mapping from low-resolution to high-resolution images, where learning-based results generally outperform conventional interpolation approaches such as cubic interpolation. This topic was studied in the context of dynamic MRI [124], static MRI [125–127], fetal MRI [128], and Diffusion Tensor Imaging (DTI) [129].

Image denoising of low-dose CT data is a well studied example for the application of CNNs in medical image reconstruction [130–135]. Low-dose CT has been also studied within the framework of deep convolutional framelets [117,136,137], which draws a mathematical connection between CNNs and framelet representations where the underlying encoder–decoder structure originates from the Hankel matrix decomposition. Within this framework, the input to the used U-net underwent a wavelet transform. A similar wavelet residual learning approach was proposed for limited-angle CT [138]. VNs [61,63] provide another alternative for both low-dose CT [107] and limited-angle CT [139]. To account for the structured streaking artifacts in sparse-view CT, opposed to an increase in unstructured noise that arise from low-dose CT, algorithms such as residual learning using a U-net architecture [140–142], deep convolutional framelets [143], or a combination of DenseNet and deconvolution [144] were proposed. Image superresolution was also studied in the context of CT to map thick slices to thin slices [145]. Another application of image enhancement methods is CNN-based Metal Artifact Correction (MAR) in CT [146]. Here, a CNN is trained to generate an image with reduced artifacts from uncorrected and precorrected images. The forward projections of the predicted image are then used to correct the projections which are affected by metals such that the FBP yields an artifact-reduced image.

Image enhancement in PET imaging has been studied in [147]. Here, an enhanced PET image was generated from multiple MAP solutions with different regularization weights using an MLP. Xu et al. [148] proposed to map a set of adjacent low-dose PET slices to a standard-dose PET image using a U-net architecture. Xiang et al. [149] fed both a low-dose PET and a T_1-weighted MR image in a CNN to obtain a standard-dose PET image.

In the area of PAT, Antholzer et al. [150] presented a CNN approach to improve the quality of sparsely sampled reconstructions. Schwab et al. [151] first reconstructed limited-view *PAT* data and applied a dynamic aperture length correction algorithm, before a U-net is applied to improve the final reconstruction quality.

Instead of performing postprocessing to enhance reconstructions in the image domain, another approach is to perform preprocessing to enhance the measurement data itself. Examples here are artifact detection and removal, such as *MAR* in *CT*. While Claus et al. [152] used an *MLP* to inpaint the missing data in the sinogram on patches, Park et al. [153] learned a U-net to correct the areas affected by metals on the whole sinogram. In *PAT*, reflection artifacts are created by waves due to echogenic structures, which might appear as a true signal. Allman et al. [154] locate and classify wave sources and artifacts and correct the measurement data before reconstruction.

2.3.4 Learning a direct mapping

Up to now, the presented methods train a neural network in the image domain. Image reconstruction can be also seen from a different perspective where the complete or partial mapping from the measured data to the image is learned. Learning the complete mapping means that no information of the underlying physics is incorporated, i.e.,

$$x^* = f_\theta(y).$$

To be able to realize this mapping, a high dimensional parameter space as well as diverse training data that account for all kinds of different data are required. However, this is typically infeasible in medical imaging due to the limited amount of training data. Besides the high memory requirements of full direct mappings, there is also no guarantee that the final reconstruction is consistent to the measured data. Furthermore, it is a challenging question if the valid and well known operations such as *FT* or Radon transform should be replaced by a neural network, although efficient implementations exist.

An example for a full direct mapping from the measured data to the image is Automated Transform by Manifold Approximation (AUTOMAP) [155] which was proposed for a broad range of applications. The key of the network architecture is that fully connected layers are used as first layers, followed by a *CNN*, similar to ReconNet [156] which acts on sparsely sampled image patches. In the context of *MRI*, the inverse *FT* is learned. Although results for small image sizes in [155] demonstrate this to be a promising research direction, a major practical challenge of *AUTOMAP* is that the algorithm does not scale to large problems due to the huge memory requirements of fully connected layers.

Another example that falls into this class of problems is learning a transform from a small number of Digitally Reconstructed Radiograph (DDR) projections to a *CT* reconstruction using a *CNN* [157–159]. In [157,158], images are generated from 1D sum projections *DDRs* which are repeated in the direction of the acquisition angle.

The images of the different acquisition angles are stacked and form the input to a U-net architecture, whose output is the final CT image. Similarly, sinograms can be directly mapped to image space using a CNN architecture. This direct reconstruction approach using an encoder–decoder network was proposed by Häggström et al. [160] for PET reconstruction.

Instead of learning the entire model, only parts of the reconstruction process can be replaced by deep neural networks, while known mathematical transforms contained in A^* are fixed and fully connected layers become needless

$$x^* = A^*(f_\theta(y)).$$

Hence, parts such as the ramp filter for Backprojection (BP) could be learned [14]. A similar approach was proposed for limited-angle CT, where projection-domain weights are learned to account for missing data for different geometries [161,162]. The backprojection layer is mapped to a neural network with fixed weights corresponding to the true mathematical transform, enabling full end-to-end training of the architecture.

Motivated by the k-space interpolation by the Annihilating Filter-Based Low-Rank Hankel Structured Matrix Completion Approach (ALOHA), Ye et al. [137] drew connections between the Hankel matrix decomposition and deep neural networks by convolutional framelets, which have been presented for image enhancement problems in Sect. 2.3.3. Similar U-net architectures and residual learning strategies were used to inpaint the missing k-space data while the loss function itself is defined in image domain, with application to accelerated MRI [163], MR angiography [164], and Echo Planar Imaging (EPI) ghost correction [165].

2.3.5 Example: Comparison between learned iterative reconstruction and learned postprocessing

An important question that arises is if the acquired measurement data have to be included in the learning-based reconstruction pipeline. To get a first answer to this question, we performed an experiment with variational networks for accelerated MR image reconstruction. We trained one reconstruction network according to [62]. For the second network, we set the data consistency term to a denoising data term $\mathcal{D}[x^t, y] = \|x^t - x^0\|_2^2$ where x^0 corresponds to the initial zero-filled solution. The two networks have the same number of parameters and structure of the regularizer to handle complex numbers, the only difference is in the data consistency term. Fig. 2.7 shows the results for the reconstruction VN and denoising VN on four times undersampled Cartesian data. It clearly demonstrates that the reconstruction VN outperforms the denoising VN for this specific setup in terms of visual impression and quantitative measures Root-Mean-Squared-Error (RMSE) and Structural Similarity Index (SSIM). In the presence of more training data and more complex networks, the denoising network might also

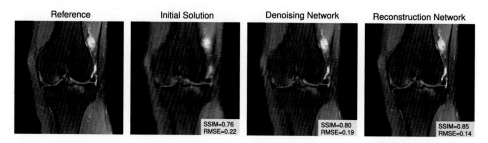

Figure 2.7 *Comparison of a reconstruction VN and denoising VN for the reconstruction of four times Cartesian undersampled MRI data.* The two *VNs* were trained with the same configuration [62] and only differed in the data consistency term. The denoising results show a lot of remaining artifacts which can be fully suppressed using the reconstruction variational network. The quantitative measures *RMSE* and *SSIM* support the observations in image quality.

learn the appearance of certain structures in the image domain, and lead to improved results. However, the information content of the measurement data can in the best case only stay the same for orthogonal transformations and otherwise can only decrease with every processing step. These results also suggest that it is beneficial to include the data consistency term in reconstruction to decrease the complexity of the regularizer.

2.4. Training data

The existence of the ImageNet database [166], which currently contains roughly 14 million labeled images from 1000 different classes in 2012 itself is often credited as a major enabler in training deep neural networks. It does not only provide access to data for the development of new methods, but it also serves as a standardized test benchmark that allows for objective comparison of new developments to existing approaches in the literature. There is an increasing number of ongoing projects with the goal of providing public data repositories with a continuously increasing number of cases that reaches up to several hundred thousands. Examples are the UK-Biobank[2], the human connectome project[3], the Montreal Neurological Institute's Brain Images of Tumors for Evaluation database[4], the National Alzheimer's Coordinating Center (NACC)[5] or the Alzheimer's disease Neuroimaging Initiative (ADNI)[6]. However, these projects only archive reconstructed images and not the raw measurement data that were measured to obtain the images. At this stage, public data repositories largely consist of fragmented

---

[2] http://www.ukbiobank.ac.uk/.

[3] http://www.humanconnectomeproject.org/.

[4] http://www.bic.mni.mcgill.ca/~laurence/data/.

[5] https://www.alz.washington.edu/WEB/researcher_home.html.

[6] http://adni.loni.usc.edu/.

collections of data provided by individual groups in connection with specific research papers (e.g., [139]) or data associated with dedicated research challenges, like the Low Dose CT challenge organized by Mayo Clinic[7]. Two data sharing endeavor were recently started ([8] and [9]) with the goal to provide raw k-space data from multiple vendors in the standardized ISMRMD rawdata format [167]. At the time of writing, the number of provided raw datasets still only ranges in the order of hundreds. In summary, in medical image reconstruction, the current lack of a standardized raw data archive makes it challenging to both train models from really large datasets, and validate the performances of new approaches.

Transfer learning

Current network architectures consist of a large number of free parameters and require extensive computations, training time, and large datasets. Especially in cases where it is challenging or impossible to acquire large-scale datasets, a common scenario in medical imaging, the concept of transfer learning [168] provides a way to still be able to obtain reasonable results for learning-based approaches. The idea of transfer learning [168] is that networks are pretrained on large available datasets such as ImageNet [166] or simulated data. Afterwards, the network is fine-tuned on a limited amount of application-dependent data such that the networks adapt on the current application. Transfer learning was recently investigated for MR image reconstruction of neurological data [169] with a cascaded CNN architecture proposed in [89], and for musculoskeletal data [106] using a VN [139] where the architectures were pretrained on natural images. Learning destreaking on CT images and fine-tune on radially undersampled MR data was presented in [118].

2.5. Loss functions and evaluation of image quality

The performance of supervised learning-based approaches does not only depend on the network architecture and training data, but also on the loss functions used during training. The loss function measures the similarity between the reconstructed image x and a reference image x_{ref} during training. Consequently, the loss function has a huge impact on the final image quality of the reconstructions. A common choice in learning-based approaches is the MSE

$$\mathcal{L}_{\text{mse}}(x, x_{\text{ref}}) = \frac{1}{2N} \left\| x^T(\theta) - x_{\text{ref}} \right\|_2^2,$$

[7] https://www.aapm.org/GrandChallenge/LowDoseCT/.
[8] http://mridata.org/.
[9] https://fastmri.med.nyu.edu/.

where N denotes the number of pixels. Although the *MSE* is easy to optimize, it is known to be not robust against outliers and to result in blurred reconstructions [170] due to its averaging behavior. This effect is particularly prominent if the training data are noisy. There are also a number of evaluation measures that are commonly used for quantitative evaluation, which are related to the *MSE*. The Normalized Root Mean Squared Error (NRMSE) allows for comparison between data that differ in terms of scaling

$$\mathcal{L}_{\mathrm{nrmse}}(x, x_{\mathrm{ref}}) = \frac{\left\| x^T(\theta) - x_{\mathrm{ref}} \right\|_2}{\left\| x_{\mathrm{ref}} \right\|_2}.$$

The *PSNR* involves the maximum possible intensity value I_{max} of the image and is a common measure used for quantitative evaluation

$$\mathcal{L}_{\mathrm{psnr}}(x, x_{\mathrm{ref}}) = 20 \log_{10} \frac{I_{\mathrm{max}} \sqrt{N}}{\left\| x^T(\theta) - x_{\mathrm{ref}} \right\|_2}.$$

Obviously, all these measures compare images pixel-by-pixel, however, it is known that these measures represent the human perceptual system poorly [171,170].

Instead of comparing pixel-wise intensity values, the perceptual-motivated *SSIM* [171] considers local patch statistics. The variant of *SSIM* which is commonly used in literature consists of a luminance term l and contrast term c defined as follows

$$\mathrm{SSIM}(x, x_{\mathrm{ref}}) = \frac{1}{N} \sum_{i \in \Omega} l(x(i), x_{\mathrm{ref}}(i))^{\alpha} c(x(i), x_{\mathrm{ref}}(i))^{\beta}$$

$$= \frac{1}{N} \sum_{i \in \Omega} \left(\frac{2 \mu_{x(i)} \mu_{x_{\mathrm{ref}}(i)} + c_1}{\mu_{x(i)}^2 + \mu_{x_{\mathrm{ref}}(i)}^2 + c_1} \right)^{\alpha} \left(\frac{2 \sigma_{x(i)} \sigma_{x_{\mathrm{ref}}(i)} + c_2}{\sigma_{x(i)}^2 + \sigma_{x_{\mathrm{ref}}(i)}^2 + c_2} \right)^{\beta}.$$

The means $\mu_{\cdot(i)}$ and standard deviations $\sigma_{\cdot(i)}$ for each patch around the pixel position i defined in the domain Ω can be modeled by convolving the whole image with a Gaussian filter with standard deviation σ_G or an average filter of a predefined window size, according to the implementation. The parameters c_1 and c_2 are user-defined constants and the exponents α and β are commonly set to 1. Common settings for the *SSIM* are a Gaussian filter of size 11 along with standard deviation σ_G and $c_1 = (0.01L)^2$, $c_2 = (0.03L)^2$ where L denotes the dynamic range of the underlying images. As the *SSIM* is defined in the interval $[-1, 1]$ the final loss function can be written as

$$\mathcal{L}_{\mathrm{ssim}}(x^t(\theta), x_{\mathrm{ref}}) = 1 - \mathrm{SSIM}(x^T(\theta), x_{\mathrm{ref}}).$$

As the formulation shows, the outcome of the measure depends on the chosen Gaussian kernel with standard deviation σ_G. Wang et al. [172] proposed a Multi-Scale Structural

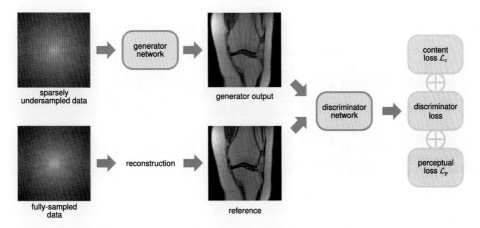

Figure 2.8 *Conceptual illustration of GANs for image reconstruction.* For image reconstruction, *GANs* are combined with a content loss $\mathcal{L}_c$ such as *MSE* to stabilize the training. Various authors showed that using a perceptual loss $\mathcal{L}_p$ based on features from the VGG network [182] results in even more improved reconstructions.

Similarity Index (MS-SSIM), which evaluates and combines the *SSIM* values across different resolutions. Although there exist more complex quantitative error measures such as Feature Similarity Index (FSIM) [173] or HaarPsi [174], not every quantitative similarity measure can be used as a loss function, because differentiability is required for network training, which might not be the case for more complex quantitative measures.

Generative Adversarial Networks (GANs) [175] have shown a great potential in increasing the perceptual image quality by training a loss function from data. Fig. 2.8 shows the basic architecture of *GANs* for image reconstruction. *GANs* consist of two networks, a generator network and a discriminator network, that try to compete with each other: The generator generates images from a source distribution, whereas the discriminator tries to distinguish the generated images from a clean reference distribution. However, *GANs* are inherently difficult to train. The initial formulation involves a sigmoid cross-entropy loss which often leads to mode collapse, vanishing gradients and thus unstable training. Many other strategies have been proposed to stabilize the training such as Wasserstein Generative Adversarial Networks (wGANs) [176], which were further stabilized with gradient penalty [177], or least-squares *GANs* [178].

While *GANs* are capable to generate images that appear with a similar texture to the target distribution, this does not necessarily conclude that the resulting images are anatomically correct. Especially, if only few data are available, *GANs* might introduce new artificial structures, an effect commonly known as hallucination. While this behavior can be desirable in the context of natural images, when the goal is only to create images that appear sharp and natural, it must be avoided in medical imaging and diagnosis. Therefore, pixel-based content losses such as ℓ_2 or ℓ_1 norms are added to the

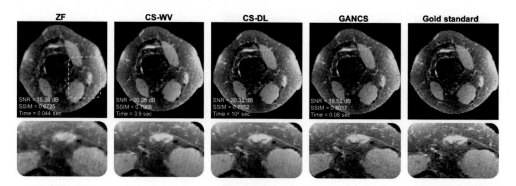

Figure 2.9 *Example comparison of GAN-based MR image reconstruction.* Test case reconstructions of axial knee images from *k*-space data acquired with 5-fold accelerated variable density sampling with radial view ordering. The *GAN* approach from [99] is compared against *CS* using Wavelets (CS-WV) and dictionary learning (CS-DL). Quantitative metrics in comparison to the ground truth are shown next to the images.

GAN loss to guide the reconstruction and thus provide general information about the image content [179,180]. This idea was further extended by introducing a perceptual loss [180,181], which is based on feature responses of the VGG network [182].

Wolterink et al. [134] used a *GAN* together with an ℓ_2 loss for noise reduction in low-dose *CT*. In another approach for low-dose *CT* image denoising, a *wGAN* architecture with gradient penalty was combined with *MSE* as content loss and a perceptual VGG loss [135]. Thaler et al. [157] included an ℓ_1 content loss in a *wGAN* architecture with gradient penalty for *CT* reconstruction from *DDR* projections. They also provide first insights in the importance of the content loss to guide the reconstruction process and the limits for data acquisition to obtain reasonable results.

A classical *GAN* approach combined with stabilizing content losses for enhancing *MRI* reconstructions was proposed in [114,183,184]. Least-squares *GANs* were studied in [99,100] in combination with an ℓ_2 loss for accelerated *MR*. An example reconstruction where the *GAN* approach from [99] is compared against CS using wavelets (CS-WV) [25] and dictionary learning (CS-DL) [32] is shown in Fig. 2.9. The combination of the two loss terms was 0.99 times ℓ_2 loss and 0.01 times *GAN* loss. The *GAN* reconstructions seem to better retain the high-frequency details, and obtain reconstructions that contain more realistic texture with sharper edges. Quan et al. [185] adopted a *GAN* with cyclic loss [186] that ensures that the generated images are similar to the input distribution using a second generator. In another approach for *MRI*, Seitzer et al. [187] refined reconstructions trained with *MSE* by learning a residual image using a *GAN* architecture with additional feature matching loss [188] and VGG loss.

Currently, most research studies that develop new machine learning methods for image reconstruction use a quantitative, objective metric to evaluate the performance of their approach defined in the previous beginning of this section. While these criteria are essential and the most objective way to evaluate results, they only give limited insight into the real diagnostic value of the reconstructed images, which is sometimes determined by the presence or absence of very small and subtle structures in the images, and usually not captured well by these metrics. Therefore, it is still an open question in the context of machine learning for image reconstruction to what degree these approaches are robust and general enough such that they can be translated successfully to clinical practice. This requires the assessment of generalization in light of intersubject anatomical and pathological variations encountered in a typical patient population in large scale prospective clinical evaluation studies. A radiologists' reader study of the visual image quality of the reconstructions regarding criteria like image sharpness, residual aliasing artifacts and apparent SNR was performed in the initial publication on VNs for 20 knee exams [139]. In [189], the performance of this architecture was evaluated with similar criteria in 157 abdominal patients. In both studies, learned image reconstruction was found to outperform conventional PI and CS with respect to these criteria. While these studies are examples of evaluations that go beyond objective quantitative metrics, they are still limited to some degree because they also do not specifically consider the diagnostic information of a medical imaging dataset. Some artifacts decrease the visual appearance of the images, while still allowing to make the correct diagnosis. On the other hand, those artifacts that lead to an incorrect diagnosis and therefore an incorrect patient management decision need to be considered truly failed imaging exams. A small-scale prospective study of the diagnostic content of learned image reconstruction was performed in [190] for 25 knee MRI patients. The reconstructions were assessed for the presence or absence of typical pathologies like meniscal tears or ligament tears and the diagnostic outcome was compared to a clinical gold standard data acquisition and for some cases was followed up with a scope exam to obtain a true ground truth. Excellent agreement between the two acquisitions was found in this study, demonstrating that an accelerated acquisition with a learned reconstruction had the same diagnostic content and therefore led to the same clinical decision as the existing gold standard. However, this study is still limited by its comparably small sample size, the restriction to a very specific type of exam and the analysis of only one contrast out of a usually more diverse MR acquisition.

2.6. Discussion

Motivated by promising initial research results, novel and exciting developments happened in machine learning for medical image reconstruction over the last 3 years. This chapter provides an overview of these developments in computer vision and medical imaging, and a classification in different categories based on their mathematical properties. While the focus is given on medical image reconstruction, the goal of this chapter was not to compare the performance against each other. In many cases, this is not even possible because some of the approaches were designed for very different applications and boundary conditions. For example, the approaches that learn a direct mapping have great potential in applications where the forward imaging model is only known with some degree of uncertainty. In contrast, in applications where the forward model is known explicitly from the imaging physics, inclusion of the knowledge from the physics as nontrainable elements of the reconstruction leads to a substantial reduction of model parameters which reduces Graphics Processing Unit (GPU) memory requirements, number of required training data and risk of overfitting. Considering the architecture, this is clearly visible when comparing learned–iterative reconstruction and learned image enhancement. While the focus for learned–iterative reconstruction is to gain much of the iterative nature of the algorithm while having smaller network architectures, the expressive power is gained by using larger architectures for image enhancement, such as the U–net [191]. As a consequence, because of the large variety in applications, it cannot be expected that a single approach will emerge as the "default" method for machine learning based image reconstruction.

GANs provide a promising research direction, they also carry a potential risk with them such as creating new, artificial structures which is critical in diagnosis. Hence, an important research direction is to study the application potential of GANs for clinical routine and also the limits for sparse data acquisition, which greatly depends on the research question. The observation in this chapter also suggests that the used quantitative error measures represent the image quality poorly.

The current focus of research is mainly on network architectures, the selection of the loss functions, numerical and algorithmical developments, as well as the use of high performance computing for efficient training procedures. Further focus will direct to improve on quantitative error measures used during validation, as well as to support the clinical impact of current research findings with large-scale clinical reader studies. Finally, it is expected that the performance of machine learning methods in image reconstruction will continue to increase with the increasing public availability of large, clean, and diverse datasets.

Acknowledgments

We acknowledge grant support from the Austrian Science Fund (FWF) under the START project BIVISION, No. Y729, the European Research Council under the Horizon 2020 program, ERC starting grant "HOMOVIS", No. 640156, and from the US National Institutes of Health (NIH P41EB017183 and R01EB024532), as well as hardware support from Nvidia corporation.

References

[1] I. Goodfellow, Y. Bengio, A. Courville, Deep Learning, MIT Press, 2016.
[2] Y. LeCun, Y. Bengio, G. Hinton, Deep learning, Nature 521 (7553) (2015) 436–444.

[3] A. Krizhevsky, I. Sutskever, E.H. Geoffrey, ImageNet classification with deep convolutional neural networks, in: Advances in Neural Information Processing Systems, 2012, pp. 1097–1105.

[4] L.C. Chen, G. Papandreou, I. Kokkinos, K. Murphy, A.L. Yuille, Semantic image segmentation with deep convolutional nets and fully connected CRFs, in: International Conference on Learning Representations, 2015, pp. 1–14.

[5] A. Dosovitskiy, P. Fischer, E. Ilg, P. Häusser, C. Hazirbas, V. Golkov, et al., FlowNet: learning optical flow with convolutional networks, in: IEEE International Conference on Computer Vision, 2015, pp. 2758–2766.

[6] K. Zhang, W. Zuo, Y. Chen, D. Meng, L. Zhang, Beyond a Gaussian denoiser: residual learning of deep CNN for image denoising, IEEE Transactions on Image Processing 26 (7) (2017) 3142–3155.

[7] Y. Liu, K.K. Gadepalli, M. Norouzi, G. Dahl, T. Kohlberger, S. Venugopalan, et al., Detecting cancer metastases on gigapixel pathology images, preprint, arXiv:1703.02442, 2017.

[8] K. Kamnitsas, C. Ledig, V.F.J. Newcombe, J.P. Simpson, A.D. Kane, D.K. Menon, et al., Efficient multi-scale 3D CNN with fully connected CRF for accurate brain lesion segmentation, Medical Image Analysis 36 (2017) 61–78, URL https://github.com/Kamnitsask/deepmedic.

[9] M.T. McCann, K.H. Jin, M. Unser, Convolutional neural networks for inverse problems in imaging: a review, IEEE Signal Processing Magazine 34 (6) (2017) 85–95.

[10] G. Wang, A perspective on deep imaging, IEEE Access 4 (2016) 8914–8924.

[11] G. Wang, J.C. Ye, K. Mueller, J.A. Fessler, Image reconstruction is a new frontier of machine learning, IEEE Transactions on Medical Imaging 37 (6) (2018) 1289–1296.

[12] D. Karras, M. Reczko, V. Mertzios, D. Graveron-Demilly, D. van Ormondt, R. Papademetriou, Neural network reconstruction of MR images from noisy and sparse k-space samples, in: Proceedings of the International Conference on Signal Processing, 2000, pp. 2115–2118.

[13] X.F. Ma, M. Fukuhara, T. Takeda, Neural network CT image reconstruction method for small amount of projection data, Nuclear Instruments & Methods in Physics Research. Section A, Accelerators, Spectrometers, Detectors and Associated Equipment 449 (1–2) (2000) 366–377.

[14] C.R. Floyd, An artificial neural network for SPECT image reconstruction, IEEE Transactions on Medical Imaging 10 (3) (1991) 485–487.

[15] J.P. Kerr, E.B. Bartlett, Neural network reconstruction of single-photon emission computed tomography images, Journal of Digital Imaging 8 (3) (1995) 116–126.

[16] P. Knoll, S. Mirzaei, A. Müllner, T. Leitha, K. Koriska, H. Köhn, et al., An artificial neural net and error backpropagation to reconstruct single photon emission computerized tomography data, Medical Physics 26 (2) (1999) 244–248.

[17] P. Paschalis, N.D. Giokaris, A. Karabarbounis, G.K. Loudos, D. Maintas, C.N. Papanicolas, et al., Tomographic image reconstruction using Artificial Neural Networks, Nuclear Instruments & Methods in Physics Research. Section A, Accelerators, Spectrometers, Detectors and Associated Equipment 527 (1–2) (2004) 211–215.

[18] J. Hadamard, Sur les problemes aux derivees partielles et leur signification physique, Princeton University Bulletin 13 (13) (1902) 49–52.

[19] M. Hanke, A. Neubauer, O. Scherzer, A convergence analysis of the Landweber iteration for non-linear ill-posed problems, Numerische Mathematik 72 (1) (1995) 21–37.

[20] L.I. Rudin, S. Osher, E. Fatemi, Nonlinear total variation based noise removal algorithms, Physica D 60 (1–4) (1992) 259–268.

[21] A. Chambolle, T. Pock, An introduction to continuous optimization for imaging, Acta Numerica 25 (2016) 161–319.

[22] K.T. Block, M. Uecker, J. Frahm, Undersampled radial MRI with multiple coils. Iterative image reconstruction using a total variation constraint, Magnetic Resonance in Medicine 57 (6) (2007) 1086–1098.

[23] E.J. Candès, J. Romberg, T. Tao, Robust uncertainty principles: exact signal reconstruction from highly incomplete frequency information, IEEE Transactions on Information Theory 52 (2) (2006) 489–509.

[24] D.L. Donoho, Compressed sensing, IEEE Transactions on Information Theory 52 (4) (2006) 1289–1306.

[25] M. Lustig, D. Donoho, J.M. Pauly, Sparse MRI: the application of compressed sensing for rapid MR imaging, Magnetic Resonance in Medicine 58 (6) (2007) 1182–1195.

[26] H. Nyquist, Certain topics in telegraph transmission theory, Transactions of the American Institute of Electrical Engineers 47 (2) (1928) 617–644.

[27] C.E. Shannon, Communication in the presence of noise, Proceedings of the Institute of Radio Engineers 37 (1) (1949) 10–21.

[28] I. Daubechies, The wavelet transform, time-frequency localization and signal analysis, IEEE Transactions on Information Theory 36 (5) (1990) 961–1005.

[29] K. Bredies, K. Kunisch, T. Pock, Total generalized variation, SIAM Journal on Imaging Sciences 3 (3) (2010) 492–526.

[30] F. Knoll, K. Bredies, T. Pock, R. Stollberger, Second order total generalized variation (TGV) for MRI, Magnetic Resonance in Medicine 65 (2) (2011) 480–491.

[31] K.G. Hollingsworth, Reducing acquisition time in clinical MRI by data undersampling and compressed sensing reconstruction, Physics in Medicine and Biology 60 (21) (2015) R297–R322.

[32] S. Ravishankar, Y. Bresler, MR image reconstruction from highly undersampled k-space data by dictionary learning, IEEE Transactions on Medical Imaging 30 (5) (2011) 1028–1041.

[33] M. Aharon, M. Elad, A. Bruckstein, K-SVD: an algorithm for designing overcomplete dictionaries for sparse representation, IEEE Transactions on Signal Processing 54 (11) (2006) 4311–4322.

[34] T.T. Cai, L. Wang, Orthogonal matching pursuit for sparse signal recovery with noise, IEEE Transactions on Information Theory 57 (7) (2011) 4680–4688.

[35] J. Caballero, A.N. Price, D. Rueckert, J.V. Hajnal, Dictionary learning and time sparsity for dynamic MR data reconstruction, IEEE Transactions on Medical Imaging 33 (4) (2014) 979–994, https://doi.org/10.1109/TMI.2014.2301271.

[36] Q. Xu, H. Yu, X. Mou, L. Zhang, J. Hsieh, G. Wang, Low-dose X-ray CT reconstruction via dictionary learning, IEEE Transactions on Medical Imaging 31 (9) (2012) 1682–1697.

[37] S. Ravishankar, Y. Bresler, Learning sparsifying transforms, IEEE Transactions on Signal Processing 61 (5) (2013) 1072–1086.

[38] S. Ravishankar, Y. Bresler, Data-Driven learning of a union of sparsifying transforms model for blind compressed sensing, IEEE Transactions on Computational Imaging 2 (3) (2016) 294–309.

[39] S. Ravishankar, Y. Bresler, Efficient blind compressed sensing using sparsifying transforms with convergence guarantees and application to magnetic resonance imaging, SIAM Journal on Imaging Sciences 8 (4) (2015) 2519–2557, arXiv:1501.02923.

[40] S. Ravishankar, B. Wen, Y. Bresler, Online sparsifying transform learning – Part I: algorithms, IEEE Journal of Selected Topics in Signal Processing 9 (4) (2015) 625–636.

[41] X. Zheng, S. Ravishankar, Y. Long, J.A. Fessler, PWLS-ULTRA: an efficient clustering and learning-based approach for low-dose 3D CT image reconstruction, IEEE Transactions on Medical Imaging 37 (6) (2018) 1498–1510.

[42] S. Ravishankar, A. Lahiri, C. Blocker, J.A. Fessler, Deep dictionary-transform learning for image reconstruction, in: IEEE International Symposium on Biomedical Imaging, 2018, pp. 1208–1212.

[43] B. Wohlberg, Efficient algorithms for convolutional sparse representations, IEEE Transactions on Image Processing 25 (1) (2016) 301–315.

[44] I.Y. Chun, J.A. Fessler, Convolutional dictionary learning: acceleration and convergence, IEEE Transactions on Image Processing 27 (4) (2018) 1697–1712.

[45] D. Wu, K. Kim, G. El Fakhri, Q. Li, Iterative low-dose CT reconstruction with priors trained by artificial neural network, IEEE Transactions on Medical Imaging 36 (12) (2017) 2479–2486, URL https://github.com/wudufan/KSAERecon.

[46] A. Makhzani, B. Frey, Winner-take-all autoencoders, in: Advances in Neural Information Processing Systems, 2015, pp. 2791–2799.

[47] Y. LeCun, L. Bottou, G. Orr, K.R. Müller, Efficient BackProp, in: Lecture Notes in Computer Science, vol. 1524, 1998, pp. 5–50.

[48] L. Calatroni, C. Cao, J. Carlos De los Reyes, C.B. Schönlieb, T. Valkonen, Bilevel approaches for learning of variational imaging models, in: M. Bergounioux, G. Peyré, C. Schnörr, J.B. Caillau, T. Haberkorn (Eds.), Variational Methods: In Imaging and Geometric Control, De Gruyter, Berlin, Boston, 2016, pp. 252–290.

[49] J.C. De Los Reyes, C.B. Schönlieb, T. Valkonen, The structure of optimal parameters for image restoration problems, Journal of Mathematical Analysis and Applications 434 (1) (2016) 464–500.

[50] J.C. De los Reyes, C.B. Schönlieb, T. Valkonen, Bilevel parameter learning for higher-order total variation regularisation models, Journal of Mathematical Imaging and Vision 57 (1) (2017) 1–25.

[51] J.C. De Los Reyes, C.B. Schönlieb, Image denoising: learning the noise model via nonsmooth PDE-constrained optimization, Inverse Problems and Imaging 7 (4) (2013) 1183–1214.

[52] G. Peyré, J.M. Fadili, Learning analysis sparsity priors, in: Sampta'11, 2011.

[53] K.G. Samuel, M.F. Tappen, Learning optimized MAP estimates in continuously-valued MRF models, in: IEEE Conference on Computer Vision and Pattern Recognition Workshops, 2009, pp. 477–484.

[54] C. Van Chung, J.C. De los Reyes, C.B. Schönlieb, Learning optimal spatially-dependent regularization parameters in total variation image denoising, Inverse Problems 33 (7) (2017) 074005.

[55] M. Benning, M. Burger, Modern regularization methods for inverse problems, Acta Numerica 27 (2018) 1–111.

[56] M. Nikolova, M.K. Ng, S. Zhang, W.K. Ching, Efficient reconstruction of piecewise constant images using nonsmooth nonconvex minimization, SIAM Journal on Imaging Sciences 1 (1) (2008) 2–25.

[57] S. Roth, M.J. Black, Fields of experts, International Journal of Computer Vision 82 (2) (2009) 205–229.

[58] Jinggang Huang, D. Mumford, Statistics of natural images and models, in: IEEE Conference on Computer Vision and Pattern Recognition, 1999, pp. 541–547.

[59] Y. Chen, T. Pock, R. Ranftl, H. Bischof, Revisiting loss-specific training of filter-based MRFs for image restoration, in: German Conference on Pattern Recognition, 2013, pp. 271–281.

[60] Y. Chen, R. Ranftl, T. Pock, Insights into analysis operator learning: from patch-based sparse models to higher order MRFs, IEEE Transactions on Image Processing 23 (3) (2014) 1060–1072.

[61] Y. Chen, W. Yu, T. Pock, On learning optimized reaction diffusion processes for effective image restoration, in: IEEE Conference on Computer Vision and Pattern Recognition, 2015, pp. 5261–5269.

[62] K. Hammernik, T. Klatzer, E. Kobler, M.P. Recht, D.K. Sodickson, T. Pock, et al., Learning a variational network for reconstruction of accelerated MRI data, Magnetic Resonance in Medicine 79 (6) (2018) 3055–3071, https://github.com/VLOGroup/mri-variationalnetwork.

[63] E. Kobler, T. Klatzer, K. Hammernik, T. Pock, Variational networks: connecting variational methods and deep learning, in: German Conference on Pattern Recognition, 2017, pp. 281–293, URL https://github.com/VLOGroup/denoising-variationalnetwork.

[64] C. Shen, Y. Gonzalez, L. Chen, S.B. Jiang, X. Jia, Intelligent parameter tuning in optimization-based iterative CT reconstruction via deep reinforcement learning, IEEE Transactions on Medical Imaging 37 (6) (2018) 1430–1439.

[65] P. Ochs, R. Ranftl, T. Brox, T. Pock, Techniques for gradient based bilevel optimization with nonsmooth lower level problems, Journal of Mathematical Imaging and Vision 56 (2) (2016) 175–194.

[66] K. Kunisch, T. Pock, A bilevel optimization approach for parameter learning in variational models, SIAM Journal on Imaging Sciences 6 (2) (2013) 938–983.

[67] S. Wang, Z. Su, L. Ying, X. Peng, S. Zhu, F. Liang, et al., Accelerating magnetic resonance imaging via deep learning, in: IEEE International Symposium on Biomedical Imaging, 2016, pp. 514–517.

[68] F. Heide, M. Steinberger, Yt Tsai, O. Gallo, W. Heidrich, K. Egiazarian, et al., FlexISP: a flexible camera image processing framework, ACM Transactions on Graphics 33 (6) (2014) 1–13.

[69] S.V. Venkatakrishnan, C.A. Bouman, B. Wohlberg, Plug-and-play priors for model based reconstruction, in: IEEE Global Conference on Signal and Information Processing, 2013, pp. 945–948.

[70] K. Dabov, A. Foi, V. Katkovnik, K. Egiazarian, Image denoising with block-matching and 3D filtering, in: SPIE Electronic Imaging, 2006, p. 606414.

[71] A. Buades, B. Coll, J.M. Morel, Non-local means denoising, Image Processing On Line 1 (2011) 208–212.

[72] S. Boyd, N. Parikh, E. Chu, B. Peleato, J. Eckstein, Distributed optimization and statistical learning via the alternating direction method of multipliers, Foundations and Trends in Machine Learning 3 (1) (2011) 1–122.

[73] A. Chambolle, T. Pock, A first-order primal–dual algorithm for convex problems with applications to imaging, Journal of Mathematical Imaging and Vision 40 (1) (2011) 120–145.

[74] G. Adluru, T. Tasdizen, M.C. Schabel, E.V. Dibella, Reconstruction of 3D dynamic contrast-enhanced magnetic resonance imaging using nonlocal means, Journal of Magnetic Resonance Imaging 32 (5) (2010) 1217–1227.

[75] G. Adluru, T. Tasdizen, R. Whitaker, E. DiBella, Improving undersampled MRI reconstruction using non-local means, in: IEEE International Conference on Pattern Recognition, 2010, pp. 4000–4003.

[76] E.M. Eksioglu, Decoupled algorithm for MRI reconstruction using nonlocal block matching model: BM3D-MRI, Journal of Mathematical Imaging and Vision 56 (3) (2016) 430–440, URL http://web.itu.edu.tr/eksioglue/pubs/BM3D_MRI_toolbox.zip.

[77] Z. Chen, H. Qi, S. Wu, Y. Xu, L. Zhou, Few-view CT reconstruction via a novel non-local means algorithm, Physica Medica 32 (10) (2016) 1276–1283.

[78] H. Qi, Z. Chen, S. Wu, Y. Xu, L. Zhou, Iterative image reconstruction using modified non-local means filtering for limited-angle computed tomography, Physica Medica 32 (9) (2016) 1041–1051.

[79] T. Meinhardt, M. Moeller, C. Hazirbas, D. Cremers, Learning proximal operators: using denoising networks for regularizing inverse imaging problems, in: IEEE International Conference on Computer Vision, 2017, pp. 1799–1808.

[80] H. Gupta, K.H. Jin, H.Q. Nguyen, M.T. McCann, M. Unser, CNN-based projected gradient descent for consistent CT image reconstruction, IEEE Transactions on Medical Imaging 37 (6) (2018) 1440–1453, URL https://github.com/harshit-gupta-epfl/CNN-RPGD.

[81] B. Kelly, T.P. Matthews, M.A. Anastasio, Deep Learning-Guided Image Reconstruction from Incomplete Data, preprint, arXiv:1709.00584, 2017.

[82] B. Chen, K. Xiang, Z. Gong, J. Wang, S. Tan, Statistical iterative CBCT reconstruction based on neural network, IEEE Transactions on Medical Imaging 37 (6) (2018) 1511–1521, URL https://github.com/HUST-Tan/Deblur-CBCT.

[83] K. Gong, J. Guan, K. Kim, X. Zhang, J. Yang, Y. Seo, et al., Iterative PET image reconstruction using convolutional neural network representation, IEEE Transactions on Medical Imaging 38 (3) (2018) 675–685, https://doi.org/10.1109/TMI.2018.2869871, URL https://github.com/guanjiahui/IterativeCNN, arXiv:1710.03344.

[84] L. Landweber, An iteration formula for Fredholm integral equations of the first kind, American Journal of Mathematics 73 (3) (1951) 615–624.

[85] K. Gregor, Y. Lecun, Learning fast approximations of sparse coding, in: Proceedings of the International Conference on Machine Learning, 2010, pp. 399–406.

[86] A. Chambolle, R. De Vore, Nam-Yong Lee, B. Lucier, Nonlinear wavelet image processing: variational problems, compression, and noise removal through wavelet shrinkage, IEEE Transactions on Image Processing 7 (3) (1998) 319–335.

[87] I. Daubechies, M. Defrise, C. De Mol, An iterative thresholding algorithm for linear inverse problems with a sparsity constraint, Communications on Pure and Applied Mathematics 57 (11) (2004) 1413–1457.

[88] J. Adler, O. Öktem, Solving ill-posed inverse problems using iterative deep neural networks, Inverse Problems 33 (12) (2017) 1–24, URL https://github.com/adler-j/learned_gradient_tomography.

[89] J. Schlemper, J. Caballero, J.V. Hajnal, A.N. Price, D. Rueckert, A deep cascade of convolutional neural networks for dynamic MR image reconstruction, IEEE Transactions on Medical Imaging 37 (2) (2018) 491–503, URL https://github.com/js3611/Deep-MRI-Reconstruction.

[90] J. Adler, O. Öktem, Learned primal-dual reconstruction, IEEE Transactions on Medical Imaging 37 (6) (2018) 1322–1332, URL https://github.com/adler-j/learned_primal_dual.

[91] S. Diamond, V. Sitzmann, F. Heide, G. Wetzstein, Unrolled optimization with deep priors, preprint, arXiv:1705.08041, 2017, pp. 1–11.

[92] V. Vishnevskiy, S.J. Sanabria, O. Goksel, Image reconstruction via variational network for real-time hand-held sound-speed imaging, in: Machine Learning for Medical Image Reconstruction (MLMIR), 2018.

[93] S. Wang, S. Fidler, R. Urtasun, Proximal deep structured models, in: Advances in Neural Information Processing Systems (NIPS), 2016, pp. 865–873.

[94] Y. Yang, J. Sun, H. Li, Z. Xu, ADMM-Net: a deep learning approach for compressive sensing MRI, in: Advances in Neural Information Processing Systems, 2017, pp. 10–18, URL https://github.com/yangyan92/Deep-ADMM-Net.

[95] H.K. Aggarwal, M.P. Mani, Jacob M. Model, Based image reconstruction using deep learned priors (modl), in: IEEE International Symposium on Biomedical Imaging, 2018, pp. 671–674.

[96] H.K. Aggarwal, M.P. Mani, Jacob M. MoDL, Model based deep learning architecture for inverse problems, IEEE Transactions on Medical Imaging 38 (2) (2019) 394–405, URL https://github.com/hkaggarwal/modl.

[97] C. Qin, J. Schlemper, J. Caballero, A.N. Price, J.V. Hajnal, D. Rueckert, Convolutional recurrent neural networks for dynamic MR image reconstruction, IEEE Transactions on Medical Imaging 38 (1) (2019) 280–290, https://doi.org/10.1109/TMI.2018.2863670, arXiv:1712.01751v3.

[98] K. He, X. Zhang, S. Ren, J. Sun, Deep residual learning for image recognition, in: IEEE Conference on Computer Vision and Pattern Recognition, 2016, pp. 770–778.

[99] M. Mardani, E. Gong, J.Y. Cheng, S.S. Vasanawala, G. Zaharchuk, L. Xing, et al., Deep generative adversarial neural networks for compressive sensing (GANCS) MRI, IEEE Transactions on Medical Imaging 38 (1) (2019) 167–179, URL https://github.com/gongenhao/GANCS.

[100] M. Mardani, E. Gong, J.Y. Cheng, J. Pauly, L. Xing, Recurrent generative adversarial neural networks for compressive imaging, in: IEEE International Workshop on Computational Advances in Multi-Sensor Adaptive Processing (CAMSAP), 2017, pp. 1–5.

[101] A. Hauptmann, F. Lucka, M. Betcke, N. Huynh, J. Adler, B. Cox, et al., Model-based learning for accelerated, limited-view 3-D photoacoustic tomography, IEEE Transactions on Medical Imaging 37 (6) (2018) 1382–1393, URL https://github.com/asHauptmann/3DPAT_DGD.

[102] T. Valkonen, A primal–dual hybrid gradient method for nonlinear operators with applications to MRI, Inverse Problems 30 (5) (2014) 055012.

[103] A. Hauptmann, B. Cox, F. Lucka, N. Huynh, M. Betcke, P. Beard, et al., Approximate k-space models and deep learning for fast photoacoustic reconstruction, in: Proceedings of International Workshop on Machine Learning for Medical Image Reconstruction, 2018, pp. 103–111.

[104] T. Klatzer, K. Hammernik, P. Knöbelreiter, T. Pock, Learning joint demosaicing and denoising based on sequential energy minimization, in: IEEE International Conference on Computational Photography, 2016, pp. 1–11.

[105] W. Yu, S. Heber, T. Pock, Learning reaction–diffusion models for image inpainting, in: German Conference on Pattern Recognition, Springer, 2015, pp. 356–367.

[106] F. Knoll, K. Hammernik, E. Kobler, T. Pock, M.P. Recht, D.K. Sodickson, Assessment of the generalization of learned image reconstruction and the potential for transfer learning, Magnetic Resonance in Medicine 81 (1) (2019) 116–128.

[107] E. Kobler, M. Muckley, B. Chen, F. Knoll, K. Hammernik, T. Pock, et al., Variational deep learning for low-dose computed tomography, in: IEEE International Conference on Acoustics, Speech and Signal Processing, 2018, pp. 6687–6691.

[108] H. Chen, Y. Zhang, Y. Chen, J. Zhang, W. Zhang, H. Sun, et al., LEARN: learned experts' assessment-based reconstruction network for sparse-data CT, IEEE Transactions on Medical Imaging 37 (6) (2018) 1333–1347, URL https://github.com/maybe198376/LEARN.

[109] A. Effland, M. Hölzel, T. Klatzer, E. Kobler, J. Landsberg, L. Neuhäuser, et al., Variational networks for joint image reconstruction and classification of tumor immune cell interactions in melanoma tissue sections, in: Bildverarbeitung Für die Medizin 2018, 2018, pp. 334–340.

[110] P. Putzky, M. Welling, Recurrent inference machines for solving inverse problems, preprint, arXiv: 1706.04008, 2017.

[111] K. Lønning, P. Putzky, M. Welling, Recurrent inference machines for accelerated MRI reconstruction, in: International Conference on Medical Imaging With Deep Learning, 2018, pp. 1–11.

[112] T. Eo, Y. Jun, T. Kim, J. Jang, H.J. Lee, D. Hwang, KIKI-net: cross-domain convolutional neural networks for reconstructing undersampled magnetic resonance images, Magnetic Resonance in Medicine 80 (5) (2018) 2188–2201.

[113] C.M. Hyun, H.P. Kim, S.M. Lee, S. Lee, J.K. Seo, Deep learning for undersampled MRI reconstruction, Physics in Medicine and Biology 63 (13) (2018), URL https://github.com/hpkim0512/Deep_MRI_Unet.

[114] G. Yang, S. Yu, H. Dong, G. Slabaugh, P.L. Dragotti, X. Ye, et al., DAGAN: deep de-aliasing generative adversarial networks for fast compressed sensing MRI reconstruction, IEEE Transactions on Medical Imaging 37 (6) (2017) 1310–1321, https://doi.org/10.1109/tmi.2017.2785879.

[115] K.H. Jin, M. Unser, 3D BPConvNet to reconstruct parallel MRI, in: IEEE International Symposium on Biomedical Imaging, 2018, pp. 361–364, URL https://github.com/panakino/3dbpconv.

[116] C.M. Sandino, J.Y. Cheng, Deep convolutional neural networks for accelerated dynamic magnetic resonance imaging, In: Stanford University CS231N, Course project.

[117] E. Kang, J. Min, J.C. Ye, A deep convolutional neural network using directional wavelets for low-dose X-ray CT reconstruction, Medical Physics 44 (10) (2017) e360–e375, URL https://github.com/eunh/low_dose_CT.

[118] Y. Han, J. Yoo, H.H. Kim, H.J. Shin, K. Sung, J.C. Ye, Deep learning with domain adaptation for accelerated projection-reconstruction MR, Magnetic Resonance in Medicine 80 (3) (2018) 1189–1205.

[119] D. Lee, J. Yoo, J.C. Ye, Deep artifact learning for compressed sensing and parallel MRI, preprint, arXiv:1703.01120, 2017.

[120] D. Lee, J. Yoo, S. Tak, J. Ye, Deep residual learning for accelerated MRI using magnitude and phase networks, IEEE Transactions on Biomedical Engineering 65 (9) (2018) 1985–1995, arXiv: 1804.00432.

[121] K. Kwon, D. Kim, H. Park, A parallel MR imaging method using multilayer perceptron, Medical Physics 44 (12) (2017) 6209–6224.

[122] K.P. Pruessmann, M. Weiger, M.B. Scheidegger, P. Boesiger, SENSE: sensitivity encoding for fast MRI, Magnetic Resonance in Medicine 42 (5) (1999) 952–962.

[123] C. Cai, C. Wang, Y. Zeng, S. Cai, D. Liang, Y. Wu, et al., Single-shot T2 mapping using overlapping-echo detachment planar imaging and a deep convolutional neural network, Magnetic Resonance in Medicine 80 (5) (2018) 2202–2214.

[124] O. Oktay, W. Bai, M. Lee, R. Guerrero, K. Kamnitsas, J. Caballero, et al., Multi-input cardiac image super-resolution using convolutional neural networks, in: International Conference on Medical Image Computing and Computer-Assisted Intervention, 2016, pp. 246–254.

[125] A.S. Chaudhari, Z. Fang, F. Kogan, J. Wood, K.J. Stevens, E.K. Gibbons, et al., Super-resolution musculoskeletal MRI using deep learning, Magnetic Resonance in Medicine 80 (5) (2018) 2139–2154.

[126] C.H. Pham, A. Ducournau, R. Fablet, F. Rousseau, Brain MRI super-resolution using deep 3D convolutional networks, in: IEEE International Symposium on Biomedical Imaging, 2017, pp. 197–200.

[127] J. Shi, Q. Liu, C. Wang, Q. Zhang, S. Ying, H. Xu, Super-resolution reconstruction of MR image with a novel residual learning network algorithm, Physics in Medicine and Biology 63 (8) (2018) 085011.

[128] S. McDonagh, B. Hou, A. Alansary, O. Oktay, K. Kamnitsas, M. Rutherford, et al., Context-sensitive super-resolution for fast fetal magnetic resonance imaging, in: Lecture Notes in Computer Science (including subseries Lecture Notes in Artificial Intelligence and Lecture Notes in Bioinformatics), vol. 10555, 2017, pp. 116–126.

[129] R. Tanno, D.E. Worrall, A. Gosh, E. Kaden, S.N. Sotiropoulos, A. Criminisi, et al., Bayesian image quality transfer with CNNs: exploring uncertainty in dMRI super-resolution, in: International Conference on Medical Image Computing and Computer Assisted Intervention, 2017.

[130] H. Chen, Y. Zhang, M.K. Kalra, F. Lin, Y. Chen, P. Liao, et al., Low-dose CT with a residual encoder–decoder convolutional neural network, IEEE Transactions on Medical Imaging 36 (12) (2017) 2524–2535, URL https://github.com/maybe198376/Low-Dose-CT-With-a-Residual-Encoder-Decoder-Convolutional-Neural-Network.

[131] H. Chen, Y. Zhang, W. Zhang, P. Liao, K. Li, J. Zhou, Low-dose CT denoising with convolutional neural network, in: IEEE International Symposium on Biomedical Imaging, 2017, pp. 2–5.

[132] H. Li, K. Mueller, Low-dose CT streak artifacts removal using deep residual neural network, in: Proceedings of the International Meeting on Fully Three-Dimensional Image Reconstruction in Radiology and Nuclear Medicine, 2017, pp. 3–6.

[133] H. Shan, Y. Zhang, Q. Yang, U. Kruger, M.K. Kalra, L. Sun, et al., 3-D convolutional encoder–decoder network for low-dose CT via transfer learning from a 2-D trained network, IEEE Transactions on Medical Imaging 37 (6) (2018) 1522–1534, URL https://github.com/hmshan/CPCE-3D.

[134] J.M. Wolterink, T. Leiner, M.A. Viergever, Isgum I, generative adversarial networks for noise reduction in low-dose CT, IEEE Transactions on Medical Imaging 36 (12) (2017) 2536–2545.

[135] Q. Yang, P. Yan, Y. Zhang, H. Yu, Y. Shi, X. Mou, et al., Low-dose CT image denoising using a generative adversarial network with Wasserstein distance and perceptual loss, IEEE Transactions on Medical Imaging 37 (6) (2018) 1348–1357.

[136] E. Kang, W. Chang, J. Yoo, J.C. Ye, Deep convolutional framelet denosing for low-dose CT via wavelet residual network, IEEE Transactions on Medical Imaging 37 (6) (2018) 1358–1369, URL https://github.com/eunh/low_dose_CT.

[137] J.C. Ye, Y. Han, E. Cha, Deep convolutional framelets: a general deep learning framework for inverse problems, SIAM Journal on Imaging Sciences 11 (2) (2018) 991–1048.

[138] J. Gu, J.C. Ye, Multi-scale wavelet domain residual learning for limited-angle CT reconstruction, preprint, arXiv:1703.01382, 2017.

[139] K. Hammernik, T. Würfl, T. Pock, A. Maier, A deep learning architecture for limited-angle computed tomography reconstruction, in: Bildverarbeitung Für die Medizin 2017, 2017, pp. 92–97.

[140] Y.S. Han, J. Yoo, J.C. Ye, Deep residual learning for compressed sensing CT reconstruction via persistent homology analysis, preprint, arXiv:1611.06391, 2016.

[141] K.H. Jin, M.T. McCann, E. Froustey, M. Unser, Deep convolutional neural network for inverse problems in imaging, IEEE Transactions on Image Processing 26 (9) (2017) 4509–4522, URL https://github.com/panakino/FBPConvNet.

[142] S. Xie, X. Zheng, Y. Chen, L. Xie, J. Liu, Y. Zhang, et al., Artifact removal using improved GoogLeNet for sparse-view CT reconstruction, Scientific Reports 8 (1) (2018) 6700.

[143] Y. Han, J.C. Ye, Framing u-net via deep convolutional framelets: application to sparse-view CT, IEEE Transactions on Medical Imaging 37 (6) (2018) 1418–1429, URL https://github.com/hanyoseob/framing-u-net.

[144] Z. Zhang, X. Liang, X. Dong, Y. Xie, G. Cao, A sparse-view CT reconstruction method based on combination of DenseNet and deconvolution, IEEE Transactions on Medical Imaging 37 (6) (2018) 1407–1417.

[145] J. Park, D. Hwang, K.Y. Kim, S.K. Kang, Y.K. Kim, J.S. Lee, Computed tomography super-resolution using deep convolutional neural network, Physics in Medicine and Biology 63 (14) (2018) 145011.

[146] Y. Zhang, H. Yu, Convolutional neural network based metal artifact reduction in X-ray computed tomography, IEEE Transactions on Medical Imaging 37 (6) (2018) 1370–1381, URL https://github.com/yanbozhang007/CNN-MAR.git.

[147] B. Yang, L. Ying, J. Tang, Artificial neural network enhanced Bayesian PET image reconstruction, IEEE Transactions on Medical Imaging 37 (6) (2018) 1297–1309.

[148] J. Xu, E. Gong, J. Pauly, G. Zaharchuk, 200x low-dose PET reconstruction using deep learning, preprint, arXiv:1712.04119, 2017.

[149] L. Xiang, Y. Qiao, D. Nie, L. An, W. Lin, Q. Wang, et al., Deep auto-context convolutional neural networks for standard-dose PET image estimation from low-dose PET/MRI, Neurocomputing 267 (2017) 406–416.

[150] S. Antholzer, M. Haltmeier, J. Schwab, Deep learning for photoacoustic tomography from sparse data, Inverse Problems in Science & Engineering (2018) 1–19, arXiv:1704.04587, 2017.

[151] J. Schwab, S. Antholzer, R. Nuster, M. Haltmeier, DALnet: high-resolution photoacoustic projection imaging using deep learning, preprint, arXiv:1801.06693, 2018.

[152] B. Claus, Y. Jin, L. Gjesteby, G. Wang, B. De Man, Metal-artifact reduction using deep-learning based sinogram completion: initial results, in: International Conference on Fully 3D Image Reconstruction, 2017, pp. 631–635.

[153] H.S. Park, S.M. Lee, H.P. Kim, J.K. Seo, CT sinogram-consistency learning for metal-induced beam hardening correction, Medical Physics 45 (12) (2018) 5376–5384, arXiv:1708.00607.

[154] D. Allman, A. Reiter, M.A. Bell, Photoacoustic source detection and reflection artifact removal enabled by deep learning, IEEE Transactions on Medical Imaging 37 (6) (2018) 1464–1477, URL https://github.com/derekallman/Photoacoustic-FasterRCNN.

[155] B. Zhu, J.Z. Liu, S.F. Cauley, B.R. Rosen, M.S. Rosen, Image reconstruction by domain-transform manifold learning, Nature 555 (7697) (2018) 487–492.

[156] K. Kulkarni, S. Lohit, P. Turaga, R. Kerviche, A. Ashok, ReconNet: non-iterative reconstruction of images from compressively sensed measurements, in: IEEE Conference on Computer Vision and Pattern Recognition, 2016, pp. 449–458.

[157] F. Thaler, K. Hammernik, C. Payer, M. Urschler, D. Stern, Computed tomography slice reconstruction from a limited number of digitally reconstructed radiographs using Wasserstein generative adversarial networks, in: Machine Learning for Medical Image Reconstruction, 2018.

[158] F. Thaler, C. Payer, D. Stern, Volumetric reconstruction from a limited number of digitally reconstructed radiographs using CNNs, in: Proceedings of the OAGM Workshop 2018, 2018, pp. 13–19.

[159] D.H. Ye, G.T. Buzzard, M. Ruby, C.A. Bouman, Deep back projection for sparse-view CT reconstruction, preprint, arXiv:1807.02370, 2018.

[160] I. Häggström, C.R. Schmidtlein, G. Campanella, T.J. Fuchs, DeepPET: a deep encoder–decoder network for directly solving the PET reconstruction inverse problem, preprint, arXiv:1804.07851, 2018.

[161] T. Würfl, F.C. Ghesu, V. Christlein, A. Maier, Deep learning computed tomography, in: International Conference on Medical Image Computing and Computer Assisted Intervention (MICCAI), 2016, pp. 432–440.

[162] T. Würfl, M. Hoffmann, V. Christlein, K. Breininger, Y. Huang, M. Unberath, et al., Deep learning computed tomography: learning projection-domain weights from image domain in limited angle problems, IEEE Transactions on Medical Imaging 37 (6) (2018) 1454–1463, URL https://github.com/ma0ho/Deep-Learning-Cone-Beam-CT.

[163] Y. Han, J.C. Ye, K-space deep learning for accelerated MRI, preprint, arXiv:1805.03779, 2018, pp. 1–11.

[164] E. Cha, E.Y. Kim, J.C. Ye, *k*-space deep learning for parallel MRI: application to time-resolved MR angiography, preprint, arXiv:1806.00806, 2018, pp. 1–11.

[165] J. Lee, Y. Han, J.C. Ye, K-space deep learning for reference-free EPI ghost correction, preprint, arXiv:1806.00153, 2018.

[166] Jia Deng, Wei Dong, R. Socher, Li-Jia Li, Kai Li, Li Fei-Fei, ImageNet: a large-scale hierarchical image database, in: IEEE Conference on Computer Vision and Pattern Recognition, 2009, pp. 248–255.

[167] S.J. Inati, J.D. Naegele, N.R. Zwart, V. Roopchansingh, M.J. Lizak, D.C. Hansen, et al., ISMRM raw data format: a proposed standard for MRI raw datasets, Magnetic Resonance in Medicine 77 (1) (2017) 411–421.

[168] C.B. Do, A.Y. Ng, Transfer learning for text classification, in: Advances in Neural Information Processing Systems, 2005, pp. 299–306.

[169] S.U.H. Dar, T. Çukur, A transfer-learning approach for accelerated MRI using deep neural networks, preprint, arXiv:1710.02615, 2017.

[170] H. Zhao, O. Gallo, I. Frosio, J. Kautz, Loss functions for image restoration with neural networks, IEEE Transactions on Computational Imaging 3 (1) (2016) 47–57, arXiv:1511.08861.

[171] Z. Wang, A.C. Bovik, H.R. Sheikh, E.P. Simoncelli, Image quality assessment: from error visibility to structural similarity, IEEE Transactions on Image Processing 13 (4) (2004) 600–612.

[172] Z. Wang, E.P. Simoncelli, A.C. Bovik, Multi-scale structural similarity for image quality assessment, in: IEEE Asilomar Conference on Signals, Systems and Computers, vol. 2, 2003, pp. 9–13.

[173] Lin Zhang, Lei Zhang, Xuanqin Mou, D. Zhang, FSIM: a feature similarity index for image quality assessment, IEEE Transactions on Image Processing 20 (8) (2011) 2378–2386.

[174] R. Reisenhofer, S. Bosse, G. Kutyniok, T. Wiegand, A Haar wavelet-based perceptual similarity index for image quality assessment, Signal Processing. Image Communication 61 (2018) 33–43.

[175] I. Goodfellow, J. Pouget-Abadie, M. Mirza, B. Xu, D. Warde-Farley, S. Ozair, et al., Generative adversarial nets, in: Advances in Neural Information Processing Systems, 2014, pp. 2672–2680.

[176] M. Arjovsky, S. Chintala, L. Bottou, Wasserstein generative adversarial networks, in: Proceedings of the International Conference on Machine Learning, 2017, pp. 214–223.

[177] I. Gulrajani, F. Ahmed, M. Arjovsky, V. Dumoulin, A. Courville, Improved training of Wasserstein GANs, preprint, arXiv:1704.00028, 2017.

[178] X. Mao, Q. Li, H. Xie, R.Y.K. Lau, Z. Wang, S.P. Smolley, Least squares generative adversarial networks, in: IEEE International Conference on Computer Vision, 2017, pp. 2794–2802.

[179] P. Isola, J.Y. Zhu, T. Zhou, A.A. Efros, Image-to-image translation with conditional adversarial networks, in: IEEE Conference on Computer Vision and Pattern Recognition, vol. 2017-Janua, ISBN 9781538604571, 2017, pp. 5967–5976, arXiv:1611.07004.

[180] C. Ledig, L. Theis, F. Huszár, J. Caballero, A. Cunningham, A. Acosta, et al., Photo-realistic single image super-resolution using a generative adversarial network, in: IEEE Conference on Computer Vision and Pattern Recognition, 2017, pp. 4681–4690.

[181] S.M. Assari, H. Idrees, M. Shah, Perceptual losses for real-time style transfer and super-resolution, in: Proceedings of the European Conference on Computer Vision, 2016, pp. 694–711.

[182] K. Simonyan, A. Zisserman, Very deep convolutional networks for large-scale image recognition, in: International Conference for Learning Representations, 2015, pp. 1–14.

[183] K. Kim, D. Wu, K. Gong, J. Dutta, J.H. Kim, Y.D. Son, et al., Penalized PET reconstruction using deep learning prior and local linear fitting, IEEE Transactions on Medical Imaging 37 (6) (2018) 1478–1487.

[184] O. Shitrit, T. Riklin Raviv, Accelerated Magnetic Resonance Imaging by Adversarial Neural Network, Lecture Notes in Computer Science (including subseries Lecture Notes in Artificial Intelligence and Lecture Notes in Bioinformatics, vol. 10553, Springer, Cham, 2017, pp. 30–38.

[185] T.M. Quan, T. Nguyen-Duc, W.K. Jeong, Compressed sensing MRI reconstruction using a generative adversarial network with a cyclic loss, IEEE Transactions on Medical Imaging 37 (6) (2018) 1488–1497, URL https://github.com/tmquan/RefineGAN.

[186] J.Y. Zhu, T. Park, P. Isola, A.A. Efros, Unpaired image-to-image translation using cycle-consistent adversarial networks, in: IEEE International Conference on Computer Vision, 2017, pp. 2223–2232, URL https://junyanz.github.io/CycleGAN/.

[187] M. Seitzer, G. Yang, J. Schlemper, O. Oktay, T. Würfl, V. Christlein, et al., Adversarial and perceptual refinement for compressed sensing MRI reconstruction, in: Machine Learning for Medical Image Reconstruction, 2018.

[188] T. Salimans, I. Goodfellow, W. Zaremba, V. Cheung, A. Radford, X. Chen, Improved techniques for training GANs, in: Advances in Neural Information Processing Systems, 2016, pp. 2234–2242.

[189] F. Chen, V. Taviani, I. Malkiel, J.Y. Cheng, J.I. Tamir, J. Shaikh, et al., Variable-density single-shot fast spin-echo MRI with deep learning reconstruction by using variational networks, Radiology (2018) 1–8.

[190] F. Knoll, K. Hammernik, E. Garwood, A. Hirschmann, L. Rybak, M. Bruno, et al., Accelerated knee imaging using a deep learning based reconstruction, in: Proceedings of the International Society of Magnetic Resonance in Medicine, 2017, p. 645.

[191] O. Ronneberger, P. Fischer, T. Brox, U-Net: convolutional networks for biomedical image segmentation, in: International Conference on Medical Image Computing and Computer Assisted Intervention, 2015, pp. 234–241.

CHAPTER 3

Liver lesion detection in CT using deep learning techniques

Avi Ben-Cohen, Hayit Greenspan

Tel Aviv University, Faculty of Engineering, Department of Biomedical Engineering, Medical Image Processing Laboratory, Tel Aviv, Israel

Contents

3.1. Introduction	65
3.1.1 Prior work: segmentation vs. detection	66
3.1.2 FCN for pixel-to-pixel transformations	67
3.2. Fully convolutional network for liver lesion detection in CT examinations	68
3.2.1 Lesion candidate detection via a fully convolutional network architecture	68
3.2.1.1 FCN candidate generation results	*70*
3.2.2 Superpixel sparse-based classification for false-positives reduction	71
3.2.3 Experiments and results	73
3.2.3.1 Data	*73*
3.2.3.2 Comparative system performance	*74*
3.3. Fully convolutional network for CT to PET synthesis to augment malignant liver lesion detection	77
3.3.1 Related work	78
3.3.2 Deep learning-based virtual-PET generation	79
3.3.2.1 Training data preparation	*79*
3.3.2.2 The networks	*80*
3.3.2.3 SUV-adapted loss function	*81*
3.3.3 Experiments and results	82
3.3.3.1 Dataset	*82*
3.3.3.2 Experimental setting	*82*
3.3.3.3 Liver lesion detection using the virtual-PET	*83*
3.4. Discussion and conclusions	84
Acknowledgments	87
References	87

3.1. Introduction

In this chapter we focus on liver analysis using deep learning tools. Specifically we focus on liver lesion detection. CT is the most important imaging tool for diagnosis and follow-up of oncological patients. For example, in 2007, over 70 million CT scans were performed in the United States [1]. CT images are widely used by clinicians for detection, diagnosis, and monitoring of liver lesions [2]. Images are acquired before and after intravenous injection of a contrast agent. Radiologists usually detect and diagnose liver

Handbook of Medical Image Computing and Computer Assisted Intervention
https://doi.org/10.1016/B978-0-12-816176-0.00008-9

lesions based on the different density of the lesions which are expressed in Hounsfield units (HU) with different scan timing and an optimal detection in the portal phase (60 seconds post injection) [3].

A variety of lesions, both benign and malignant, can be found in the liver. Among them, metastasis are the major cause of death from cancer [4]. The liver is frequently affected by metastatic disease, arising commonly from primary sites in the colon, breast, lung, pancreas, and stomach [5]. There is a large variability in the number, size, and general appearance of metastatic liver lesions, making computerized metastatic liver lesion detection a challenging task. Fig. 3.1 presents a few liver examples with metastasis.

Current radiological practice is to manually analyze the liver. This is a time-consuming task requiring the radiologist to search through a 3D CT scan which may include hundreds of slices and multiple lesions. For early detection purposes, it is of particular importance to detect what are known as "too small to characterize" lesions. This requires additional radiologist time and focus, and is considered a difficult challenge. Given the advances in artificial intelligence capabilities in recent years and more specifically deep learning methods, the integration of these tools in clinical practice can lead to a much more efficient and accurate diagnosis and treatment. Thus, developing computational tools for CT interpretations has a high clinical value, as well as economic potential.

3.1.1 Prior work: segmentation vs. detection

Automated computerized analysis tools are starting to emerge for the detection, segmentation, and characterization of liver lesions. One important distinction to note is the difference in definitions and in the objectives for a segmentation vs. detection task. In the *detection task* the objective is to find *all lesions*. This includes very small lesions, as finding those can support the radiologist's diagnosis to an even greater extent than detecting large obvious lesions. Therefore, in evaluating automated detection system performance, we need to use an evaluation measure that penalizes a miss of a small and large lesion equally. This often implies increasing the sensitivity – so as to catch all possible lesion candidates. The challenge is then to achieve the high sensitivity goal without increasing the detection of false-positive candidates. It is common practice to aim for a false-positive rate of between 1–3 lesions per case, in order to provide a tool that will be useful in actual clinical practice.

The objective of the *segmentation* task is to output a lesion segmentation mask similar to the one manually circumscribed by experts. A segmentation result can miss one or two small lesions and still get a high segmentation score if the larger lesions were correctly segmented. Fig. 3.1 demonstrated the difference in the output provided by a detection versus segmentation mask. The liver lesion segmentation task has attracted a great deal of attention in recent years, including the MICCAI 2008 Grand Challenge [6], ISBI 2017, and MICCAI 2017 LiTS challenge [7].

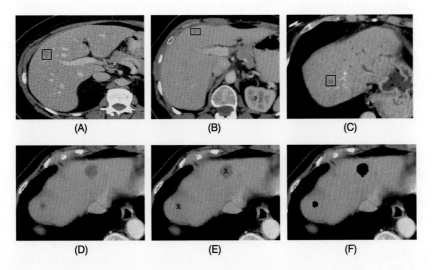

Figure 3.1 Liver lesion examples: (A)–(C) include a cropped CT image with lesions marked by a blue rectangle. Detection and segmentation examples: (D) cropped CT including two liver lesions; (E) lesion detection; (F) lesion segmentation masks. The segmentation mask includes every voxel inside the lesion (in blue). The detection includes a marked point inside the lesion.

In this chapter we focus on the liver lesion *detection* task. Prior work in the detection task involves region-based approaches (e.g., [8]) as well as patch-based approaches (e.g., [9]). In the work presented herein, we focused on a global analysis scheme via a fully-convolutional network (FCN), along with a localized refining stage. We also use cross-modality analysis to augment the system performance further. The use of the FCN as a tool for global image analysis will be introduced next. Section 3.2 presents our FCN-based combined global and local scheme for the lesion detection task. In Sect. 3.3 we describe the combined PET and CT solution we developed.

3.1.2 FCN for pixel-to-pixel transformations

The Fully Convolutional Network (FCN) [10] has been increasingly used in different medical image segmentation problems. In recent years we also see its use in liver tumor segmentation and detection tasks [11–14]. The FCN was introduced in the image segmentation domain, as an alternative to using image patches. Using FCN, the image could be analyzed globally instead of using localized patches. Thus, there is no need to select representative patches, eliminate redundant calculations where patches overlap, and scale up more efficiently with image resolution. Moreover, there can be a fusion of different scales by adding links that combine the final prediction layer with lower layers with finer strides. Since all the fully connected layers are replaced by convolution layers, the FCN can take inputs of arbitrary sizes and produce correspondingly-sized outputs with efficient inference and learning. Unlike patch based methods, the loss function using this architecture is computed over the entire image segmentation result. The most common FCN used in medical imaging applications is the U–Net [15]. The U–Net architecture consists of a contracting path to capture context and a symmetric expanding path that enables precise localization. In general, the FCN architectures can be used for tasks that involve a pixel-wise loss function such as reconstruction, synthesis, and other image-to-image tasks.

3.2. Fully convolutional network for liver lesion detection in CT examinations

We describe next a fully automated system that can analyze an input CT examination, and detect liver metastases with high accuracy, specifically by exploring detection performance of small lesions. The system comprises two main stages: In the first stage, lesion candidates are generated from the input CT volume. The focus of this stage is on high sensitivity – so as not to miss lesions. In the second stage, each lesion candidate is further reviewed, to validate its categorization as a lesion. The goal of this stage is to fine-tune the original detection by removing false-positives from the system. In most of this chapter, we will assume that the liver has been segmented, and we focus on detecting lesions within it. Experimental results for a complete system that automatically segments the liver as one of its tasks, will be provided as well. The described system is based on several of our published works [16,14,17].

3.2.1 Lesion candidate detection via a fully convolutional network architecture

In their reading routine, radiologists scan axial slices of the liver. Following that routine, the input to the system consists of axial slices from the CT volume. In a classical network-based solution, these slices are input to the network sequentially, with the slice of interest copied three times in order to utilize the standard networks that are commonly pretrained on color images and expect three channels as input. When considering the context of lesions, we note that the lesions are present in several sequential slices. In the regular screening routine, radiologists scan across the slices in order to detect and verify findings. Following this, it was suggested in [18] to provide three slices to the network simultaneously: the target slice in the center and two adjacent slices above and below. Using an FCN-based analysis, this module learns to output a lesion probability map.

In the following we provide details about the FCN architecture used: The proposed network architecture is based on that proposed by Long et al. [10]. It uses the VGG-16 architecture [19] by discarding the final classifier layer and converting all fully connected layers to convolutions. We appended a 1×1 convolution with channel dimension 2 to predict scores for lesion or liver at each of the coarse output locations, followed by a

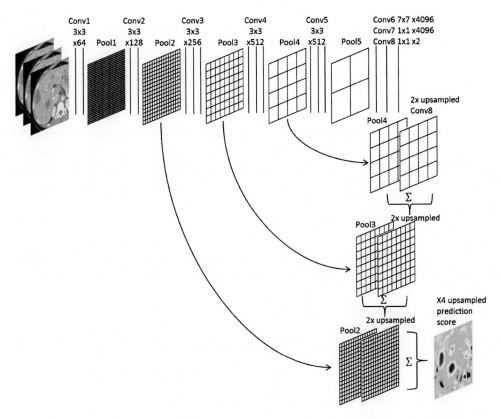

Figure 3.2 FCN-4s network architecture. Each convolution layer is illustrated by a straight line with the receptive field size and number of channels denoted above. The ReLU activation function and drop-out are not shown for brevity.

deconvolution layer to upsample the coarse outputs to pixel-dense outputs. The up-sampling was performed in-network for end-to-end learning by backpropagation from the pixelwise loss. However, since small lesions require higher resolution for detection, we used an additional lower level linking, which make use of higher resolution for the final output. This is done by linking the second max-pool layer in a similar way to the linking of the third and fourth max-pool layers. The final FCN network architecture, termed FCN-4s net, is presented in Fig. 3.2. The fusion steps within the FCN architecture were shown to support the analysis of different lesion sizes. The output of the network is a lesion probability map.

Additional network implementation details are provided next: To achieve fixed in-slice resolution across all patient data, as well as fixed slice spacing in the network input, we resized (using linear interpolation) to obtain a fixed pixel spacing of 0.71 mm and a fixed slice spacing between adjacent slices of 1 mm. In this work, we focus on liver metastases that vary considerably in size. To reflect this in the training data, we applied different scale transformations to the available training images in each batch. For each input image in each batch, two numerical values between 0.9 to 1.1 were randomly selected (uniform distribution). Two corresponding scale transformations were applied to the image (3 adjacent slices), using nearest-neighbor for resampling, to generate two training images.

Training of the network was conducted as follows: Input images along with the corresponding liver and lesion segmentation masks provided by the human expert were used to train the network. Examples of masks are shown in Fig. 3.4. We used the stochastic gradient descent with GPU acceleration (Nvidia GTX 1080). Regions surrounding the liver, including the different organs and tissues, were ignored during training. The softmax log-loss function was computed pixel-wise with different weights for each class of pixels to overcome class imbalance: Most of the pixels in each image belonged to the liver, and a much smaller number belonged to the lesions. The learning process was therefore balanced using fixed weights that were inversely proportional to the population ratios. The learning rate was chosen to be 0.0005 for the first 30 epochs and 0.0001 for the last 40 epochs (a total of 70 epochs). The weight decay was chosen to be 0.0005 and the momentum parameter was 0.9.

3.2.1.1 FCN candidate generation results

Experiments were conducted to evaluate the FCN across several architecture variations. We start with the well-known FCN architecture, termed FCN-8s [10], as the baseline architecture. To that we add the proposed usage of adjacent slices as input as well as the additional lower level linking. In this initial experiment, we used CT scans from the Sheba medical center, taken during the period from 2009 to 2015. Different CT scanners were used with 0.71–1.17 mm pixel spacing and 1.25–5 mm slice thickness. Markings of the entire liver and hepatic metastases' boundaries were conducted by a board certified radiologist (E.K. with eight years of experience) and a radiology resident (A.K. with one year of experience), in consensus. Each CT image was resized to obtain a fixed pixel spacing of 0.71 mm. They included 20 patients with 1–3 CT examinations per patient and overall 68 lesion segmentation masks and 43 liver segmentation masks. The data included a variety of liver metastatic lesions derived from different primary cancers. Each lesion was defined based on the radiologist's annotations. In case of overlapping lesions they were considered as one.

In assessing the automated system performance, certain definitions and measures are needed: We defined a lesion as detected when a certain connected component (CC) in the system output overlapped with the radiologist's marked lesion mask. Two detection measures were used here:

- *TPR* – number of correctly detected lesions divided by the total number of lesions.
- *FPC* – defined as the total number of false detections divided by the number of patients.

Table 3.1 Testing the FCN using additional adjacent slices (3 slices) and linking lower level pooling layer (FCN-4s).

Method	TPR	FPC
FCN-4s 3 slices	0.88	0.74
FCN-8s 3 slices	0.86	1.1
FCN-8s	0.85	1.1

A 3-fold cross validation (CV) was used (each group containing different patients) using the lesion detection dataset.

Results are presented in Table 3.1. We note that the FCN-4s with the addition of neighbor slices performed better than the other methods, with better TPR and better FPC. Intuitively, we believe that in our task of lesion detection, the FCN-4s is more appropriate than the FCN-8s due to the fact that lesions are inherently smaller in size than general objects in natural scenery or other real-world domains.

3.2.2 Superpixel sparse-based classification for false-positives reduction

We next propose to combine the global FCN-based system, with local patch level analysis for false-positive reduction. The proposed liver lesion detection framework is comprised of two main modules, as shown in Fig. 3.3. The first module is an FCN. Based on the high-probability candidate lesion regions from the first module, the second module follows with localized patch level analysis using superpixel sparse based classification. This module's objective is to classify each localized superpixel as a lesion or not. Thus it provides a fine-tuning step, with the objective of increasing sensitivity to lesions while removing false-positives (FPs). This work was published in [17].

The combination of global and local analysis for false-positive reduction has been shown to be a promising approach in a range of medical applications [20–22]. In this particular work, we represent the local patch information using superpixels to extract homogeneous localized regions and a sparse representation to represent the content of those localized regions. Superpixels provide an efficient way to select patches of interest and to avoid the redundancy of densely extracted patches. We divided each liver in each CT examination into a set of homogeneous superpixels. Each image was clustered into N superpixels using the well-known SLIC algorithm [23], where N is chosen so that each superpixel will be approximately of size 25 mm^2. The SLIC algorithm is known to preserve strong edges. This ensures that the superpixels align to preserve the overall liver boundary and the lesion boundaries. As in our network training, non-liver superpixels were not included in the classification.

For each candidate region a superpixel map is generated, and for each superpixel, a representative feature vector is extracted. Using a pre-learned dictionary, a sparse-code representation is computed and classified. The rationale for using superpixels as well as

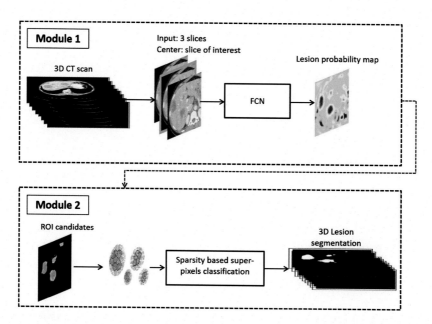

Figure 3.3 The proposed lesion detection framework.

the generation of the superpixel representation are described in detail in [16,17]. The LC-KSVD method was used here [24]. This method aims to leverage the supervised information of input signals or feature vectors to learn a reconstructive and discriminative dictionary. The dictionary items were chosen so that each one represented a subset of the training feature vectors ideally from a single class. Hence, each dictionary item could be associated with a single label. Thus there was an explicit correspondence between dictionary items and the appropriate labels. This connection was created using a label consistency regularization term and a joint classification error in the objective function for learning a dictionary with more balanced reconstructive and discriminative power. The learned classifier was used to classify superpixel representation as lesion or non-lesion.

An additional fine-tuning was conducted next, using the FCN output to enable dictionary and classifier personalization. A selection of superpixels was made, from each given test case, based on the corresponding FCN probability map. This was done as follows: Superpixels with an average probability above a high-value threshold (0.98) were labeled "lesion" and those with an average probability below a low-threshold (0.2) of were labeled "non-lesion". Using this set of selected superpixels (in cases where the number of lesion superpixels was at least half the dictionary size), the sparsity based dictionary and the linear classifier parameters were fine-tuned.

Following the fine-tuning stage, all candidate superpixels from the first module were classified as lesion or non-lesion using the jointly learned linear classifier, to provide a

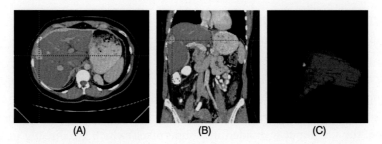

Figure 3.4 Experts' segmentation masks: (A) axial view; (B) coronal view; (C) 3D segmentation mask; liver mask in red and lesion mask in green.

binary detection map for the input CT scan. Next we used a connected-component labeling algorithm to transform the binary detection map to a lesion detection map, where each connected-component represented a lesion detected by our system.

3.2.3 Experiments and results

To evaluate the performance of the system, we conducted several sets of experiments. These included evaluations of a development set followed by the results of an independent testing set. We focused on the lesion detection within the liver to evaluate the detection performance independent of automated liver segmentation capabilities. Thus, the majority of the experiments and evaluations were constrained to the manually circumscribed liver area. As a final experiment, we included our own liver segmentation algorithm in a fully automated liver segmentation and lesion detection framework.

3.2.3.1 Data

The data used in the current work included CT scans from the Sheba Medical Center. Algorithms were developed using the set described in Sect. 3.2.1.1 as a development dataset (20 patients and 68 lesions) and were tested on an additional testing set that included CT examinations from 14 patients with a total of 55 lesions, out of which 35% were considered small lesions. In the development set, we obtained 1–3 marked slices per patient. In the testing set, we obtained marked slices in the entire CT volume (multislice). Fig. 3.4 shows examples of the segmentation masks provided by the radiologists.

We defined a lesion as a small lesion if its longest diameter (LD) was less than 1.5 cm [25]. In our testing set we had 19 small lesions out of the 55 lesions (35%). The mean LD of all lesions in the development set was 39.2 ± 17.3 mm (7.1–55.3 mm) and 39.3 ± 28.4 mm (9.3–91.2 mm) for the lesions in the testing set. The data included various liver metastatic lesions derived from different primary cancers.

3.2.3.2 *Comparative system performance*

We used the FPC and TPR detection measurements as described in Sect. 3.2.1. Note that due to the data available in our study, we extracted a 2D CC in the development set whereas for the testing set, the CC and corresponding overlap measures were in 3D.

We compared the proposed system to five alternative analysis schemes:

1. A *superpixel sparse dictionary learning and classification – sparsity based scheme*. In this scheme, the CT input is divided into superpixels which are directly input to the superpixel dictionary learning, and classified using superpixel sparse-based classification [16]. This is a local patch based analysis method that uses the smart selection of patches based on super pixels.

2. *Patch-based CNN* based on Li et al. [26], which used patches of 17 × 17 pixels which are fed to the CNN for classification into lesion/normal area. A CNN model with seven hidden layers was used, which included three convolutional layers, two max-pooling layers, a fully connected layer, ReLU, and a softmax classifier. This is also a local patch based analysis with no special selection of the patches but using a CNN architecture for the final classification.

3. The *U-Net* scheme. Here, the proposed FCN architecture is replaced by the well-known U-Net architecture [15] with no use of localized analysis. The U-Net includes several skip connections with additional convolution filters in the expansion path compared to the FCN-4s used in this study. This makes the U-Net more sensitive to different changes in the image in low and high scales.

4. FCN-4s. The first module described in this work with no use of localized analysis.

5. *FCN-4s + Sparsity based scheme*. Our proposed system, combining the FCN global analysis with a sparsity-based superpixel analysis.

A 3-fold CV was used (each group containing different patients) for both the development set and the testing set using the experts' defined masks as the gold standard. Each test fold included approximately 7 patients in the development set and 5 patients in the testing set. Average results are presented for all patients (20 in the development set and 14 in the testing set) using CV.

Table 3.2 presents the results for the development and testing set. Using the development set, the sparsity-based superpixel analysis scheme on its own generated the lowest TPR, at a reasonable FPC. Comparison of the two global analysis schemes that we compare (FCN-4s and U-Net) indicated that the FCN-4s had a higher TPR with a lower FPC. Combining the global FCN-4s with the sparsity-based superpixel analysis maintained a high detection performance of more than 88%, with a reduction in the FPC.

Using the testing set, a trend similar to performance on the development set was observed. The FCN-4s with the sparsity based false-positive reduction had the highest detection performance compared to other methods with a TPR of 94.6% and a

Table 3.2 Performance evaluation on the development and testing sets.

Method	Development		Testing	
	TPR [%]	FPC	TPR [%]	FPC
Patch-based CNN	85.3	1.9	78.2	9.7
Sparsity based	82.4	1.1	83.6	9.2
U-Net	83.8	3.0	92.7	7.6
FCN-4s	88.2	0.74	92.7	4.2
FCN-4s + sparsity based	**88.2**	**0.53**	**94.6**	**2.9**

Table 3.3 Detection performance for small and normal sized lesions on the testing set.

Method	TPR [%] All	FPC All	TPR [%] Normal	TPR [%] Small
Patch-based CNN	78.2	9.7	88.9	63.2
Sparsity based	83.6	9.2	91.7	68.4
U-Net	92.7	7.6	91.7	94.7
FCN-4s	92.7	4.2	91.7	94.7
FCN-4s + sparsity	**94.6**	**2.9**	**94.4**	**94.7**

significant improvement (P–value < 0.001) in the number of false-positives with a 2.9 FPC.

Fig. 3.5 shows sample results using our method: (A) the CT input slices, (B) the output results, and (C) the results using patch based CNN, sparsity based classification, and U-Net. The results show the per-pixel labels as true-positive (TP), false-positive (FP), and false-negative (FN). Using this visualization, blobs including blue regions (true-positive) represent correctly detected lesions; blobs that only include a red region are defined as false-positives, and blobs that only include a green region are defined as false-negatives.

Table 3.3 depicts the results for small sized lesions with a lesion–diameter of less than 1.5 cm and normal sized lesions with a lesion–diameter above 1.5 cm. When adding the small candidate detection, the best results were obtained using the FCN-4s with the sparsity based false-positives reduction which yielded 2.9 FPC and 94.6% TPR. A TPR of 94.4% was obtained for the normal sized lesions and 94.7% for the small lesions. The sparsity based false-positives reduction increased the TPR, which occurred in cases where two correctly detected candidates were connected by a false classification of some voxels. In these cases we obtained one connected component instead of two. The reduction of the connecting voxels added another correct detection of a lesion and increased the TPR.

Analyzing the average runtime per-slice of each method, we get the following results: FCN-4s, 0.178 s; FCN-4s + sparsity, 0.489 s; U-Net, 0.578 s; Sparsity based, 2.023 s; Patch-based CNN, 5.321 s.

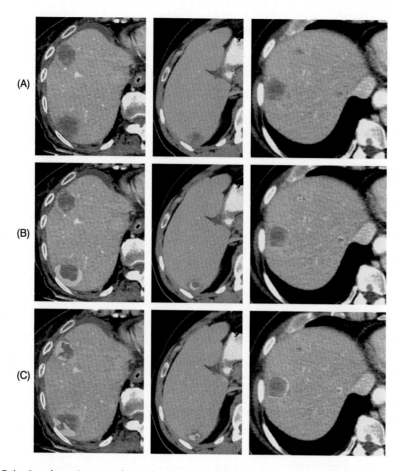

Figure 3.5 Lesion detection sample results: (A) input-CT slices (cropped); (B) detection candidates using our method; (C) detection candidates using different methods from left to right: patch-based CNN, sparsity based, and U-Net method. For each connected component the following conventions were used: false-positive pixels are in red, false-negative pixels are in green, and true-positive pixels are in blue.

In the final experiment, we tested a clinically viable scenario, in which the automated system needs to first localize the liver, following which it can detect the lesions within it. For this experiment, we used our previously developed liver segmentation network which is based on the FCN-8s architecture (for details see [14]). Following the liver segmentation output, we used our lesion detection framework to automatically detect the lesions in the liver segmentation results. We achieved a TPR of 90.9% and an FPC of 3.0 using the fully automatic algorithm. These results are comparable to the detection results achieved using the manual segmentation of the liver with a lower TPR and slightly higher FPC.

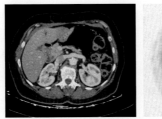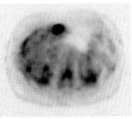

Figure 3.6 An axial CT slice (left) with its corresponding PET slice (right). Dark regions in the PET image indicate high FDG uptake.

3.3. Fully convolutional network for CT to PET synthesis to augment malignant liver lesion detection

CT scans provide anatomical information. This information includes liver lesions, which need to be detected by the human expert as well as by automated systems. However, in some cases malignant tumors can have low contrast with the liver parenchyma or are small in size – and this introduces a detection challenge for the expert radiologist as well as for the automated system. Additional modalities exist which acquire information on the *functional* state of the body. One such modality is the Positron Emission Tomography (PET).

PET images provide metabolic information; thus they show images with augmented response in a malignant tumor region. The combination of PET and CT scanners has become a standard component of diagnosis and staging in oncology [27,28]. An increased accumulation of fluoro-D-glucose (FDG) in PET relative to normal tissue is a useful marker for many cancers and can help in detection and localization of malignant lesions [28]. Additionally, PET/CT imaging is becoming an important evaluation tool for new drug therapies [29]. An example of an axial slice taken from a CT scan and its corresponding PET slice is shown in Fig. 3.6. It can be seen that the PET image resolution is lower than the CT image resolution showing less anatomical details. However, there is a malignant liver lesion that is less visible in the CT image and can be easily detected in the PET image as a large dark blob.

Although PET imaging has many advantages and its use is steadily increasing, it has a few disadvantages. PET/CT entails added radiation exposure in comparison to CT-only scans. Moreover, PET/CT is relatively expensive compared to CT. Hence, it is still not offered in a large proportion of medical centers in the world. The clinical importance of PET in the management of cancer patients and, on the other hand, the difficulty in providing PET imaging as part of standard imaging raises a potential need for an alternative, less expensive, fast, and easy to use PET-like imaging.

In this section we show our work on using deep learning capabilities for image synthesis to enable the generation of PET-like images, and the ability to use these images similar to the clinical PET input, to mask-out false candidates. We have explored several variations on the FCN-based network, for the image synthesis [30,31]. Here, we will present a system that combines advantages of FCN and Generative Adversarial Network (GAN) based networks for the generation of PET-like images from CT volumes. The strengths of both methods are used to create realistic looking virtual PET images. We focus our attention to hepatic malignant lesions.

3.3.1 Related work

Cross modality synthesis is the process in which one image modality source enables the generation of another, possibly less available modality. Several studies in the medical imaging field have shown cross-modality synthesis: Roy et al. [32] proposed an example based approach relying on sparse reconstruction from image patches for Magnetic Resonance (MR) image contrast synthesis. Similar work was proposed in [33]. Bahrami et al. [34] proposed a multilevel Canonical Correlation Analysis (CCA) method and group sparsity as a hierarchical framework to reconstruct 7T-like from 3T MR imaging (MRI). Van Nguyen et al. proposed [35] a location-sensitive deep network by integrating intensity feature from image voxels and spatial information for synthesizing MR images across domains.

The deep learning field has enabled a new approach to this task, as seen by many new works that have recently come out. In [36–38] different CNN based methods and architectures were explored to learn an end-to-end nonlinear mapping from MR images to CT images. For the case of unpaired data, a CycleGAN model was used to synthesize brain CT images from brain MR by Wolterink et al. [39]. Chartsias et al. [40] demonstrated a similar concept for synthesizing cardiac MR images from CT images.

In the case of PET/CT pairs, the PET study can be used to highlight malignant lesions and improve the detection compared to the use of CT data alone. In a study conducted in parallel to ours, Bi et al. [41] used a multichannel generative adversarial network to synthesize PET images from CT images with manually annotated lung tumors. Their model learns the integration from both CT and a given annotated label, to synthesize the high uptake and the anatomical background. They demonstrated that using the synthesized PET images a comparable detection performance to that achieved using the original PET data. We note that manual labeling of the tumors is needed in their work.

In the current work our objective is to use information from CT data to estimate PET-like images with an emphasis on malignant lesions in the liver. The suggested system is fully automated, with no manual labeling needed. Similar to the radiologists, who have an easier time identifying malignant liver lesions in a PET/CT scan (vs only a CT scan) we want to make use of the estimated PET-like images to improve the detection of malignant lesions using an automated lesion detection software. The overview of the advanced detection methodology is depicted in Fig. 3.7, and will be described in detail below.

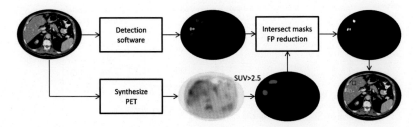

Figure 3.7 Overview of proposed system: combining synthesized PET image with a lesion detection software. The output of the detection software includes true-positives (in green) along with false-positives (in red). Thresholding over the synthesized PET image to extract high-response regions (in blue) can help reduce the false-positives by intersecting the detection mask with the thresholding mask.

3.3.2 Deep learning-based virtual-PET generation

The proposed framework includes two main modules: a training module which includes data preparation, and a testing module which accepts CT images as input and predicts synthesized PET images. We use an FCN to generate initial PET-like images given the input CT images. We next use a conditional GAN (cGAN) to improve and refine the FCN output. Fig. 3.8 shows a diagram of our general framework. High SUV uptake values are shown as dark regions in the output images, similar to the PET scans that are used by radiologists today. In the following subsections we describe the training data preparation, the FCN and cGAN architectures, and the proposed loss functions.

3.3.2.1 Training data preparation

In the training phase a source, CT image, and a target, PET image, are input to the network. The images need to be similar in size in order to be simultaneously introduced. Hence, a preprocessing step is needed to align the lower–resolution PET images with the CT scans. The alignment step uses the given offset provided for each scan and the voxel size (in mm) ratio between both scans.

CT and PET studies include a large value range. In CT imagery, Hounsfield units (HUs) are used. In PET, the standardized uptake value (SUV) is commonly used as a relative measure of FDG uptake [42] defined as

$$SUV = \frac{r}{d'/w}, \tag{3.1}$$

where r is the radioactivity concentration [kBq/ml] measured by the PET scanner within a region of interest (ROI), d' is the decay–corrected amount of injected radiolabeled FDG [kBq], and w is the weight of the patient [g], which is used as a surrogate for a distribution volume of tracer. It was found experimentally that contrast adjustment was a useful step in translating between the SUV and CT HU values: contrast adjustment was done by clipping extreme values and by scaling, to adjust the PET images into

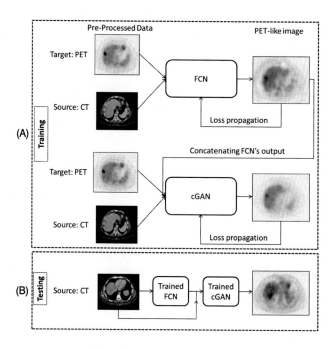

Figure 3.8 The proposed virtual PET system.

the SUV range of 0 to 20. This range includes most of the interesting SUV values of malignant lesions. Similarly, CT image values were adjusted to be within −160 to 240 HU, which is the standard HU windowing used by the radiologists when evaluating the liver parenchyma.

3.3.2.2 The networks

I. Fully convolutional network architecture

The FCN architecture used is similar to that shown in Fig. 3.2. Here, the CT image serves as input and the estimated PET image as output. In this case only one CT slice was used as input, we empirically found that using adjacent slices did not improve the quality of the results.

II. Conditional-GAN architecture

Generative Adversarial Networks (GANs) have been highly popular in the computer vision community ever since they were introduced by Goodfellow et al. [43]. Different variations of GANs were recently proposed to generate high quality realistic natural images [44–47]. Interesting applications of GAN include generating images of one style from another style (image-to–image translation) [48] and image inpainting using GAN [49].

GANs are generative models that learn a mapping from random noise vector z to output image y. cGANs [48] learn a mapping from observed image x and random noise vector z to y. The generator G is trained to produce outputs that cannot be distinguished from "real" images by an adversely trained discriminator, D, which is trained to detect real vs. fake images.

Recently, several medical imaging applications have applied the GAN framework [50–55,30,36–38]. Most studies have employed the image-to-image GAN technique to create label-to-segmentation translation, segmentation-to-image translation or medical cross modality translations, and recently GANs were used for data augmentation purposes [56].

III. Combined network

The output from the FCN was found experimentally to have a satisfactory response in regions with high SUV but to be less accurate and blurry in regions with low contrast. We therefore introduced the cGAN network to refine the FCN's output. The input to the cGAN includes two channels, one with the CT image and the second with the corresponding FCN output (simple concatenation). We adapt a similar cGAN architecture as in [48] with a few modifications. In the original cGAN the objective can be expressed as

$$\mathcal{L}_{cGAN}(G, D) = \mathbb{E}_{ct,pet}[\log D(ct, pet)] + \mathbb{E}_{ct,z}[\log(1 - D(ct, G(ct, z)))], \quad (3.2)$$

where G tries to minimize this objective against an adversarial D that tries to maximize it, ct is the CT input slice, pet is the corresponding PET slice, and z is random noise. In our objective we embed the FCN's output (*fcn*) as in

$$\mathcal{L}_{Modified-cGAN}(G, D) = \mathbb{E}_{fcn,ct,pet}[\log D(fcn, ct, pet)] +$$
$$\mathbb{E}_{fcn,ct,z}[\log(1 - D(fcn, ct, G(fcn, ct, z)))]. \quad (3.3)$$

We tried both *L1* and *L2* distance measures for the generator G. No noticeable difference was observed using the different distance measures, and we chose to use the *L2* distance in our experiments. The final optimization process is as follows:

$$G^* = \arg\min_G \max_D L_{Modified-cGAN}(G, D) + \lambda \mathbb{E}_{fcn,ct,z,pet}\|pet - G(fcn, ct, z)\|_2, \quad (3.4)$$

where G^* is the optimal setting and λ balances the contribution of the two terms.

We used a "U–Net" [15] based generator (encoder and decoder) and a 5–layer discriminator (architecture specifications can be found in [31]).

3.3.2.3 SUV-adapted loss function

Malignant lesions in PET scans are usually observed with high SUV values (> 2.5) [57]. We note that most of the SUV values in PET scans are low and only a minority include high SUVs. Hence, we used the SUV value in each pixel as a weight for the pixel-wise loss function, as shown in Eq. (3.5) (N is the number of samples). With this additional term in the loss function, the network focuses on high SUV valued pixels, even though most pixels include lower values:

$$L = \frac{1}{N} \sum_{i=1}^{N} I_{PET}(i)(Syn_{PET}(i) - I_{PET}(i))^2. \qquad (3.5)$$

While this approach helped the FCN learn the malignant tumor appearance and provide a better response in the synthesized PET images, it did not help when training the cGAN. Hence, we modified the loss function by computing the weighted average reconstruction loss (Eq. (3.5)) for high SUVs (> 2.5) and for low SUVs (≤ 2.5) as in

$$L_{cGAN} = L_{lowSUV} + L_{highSUV}. \qquad (3.6)$$

This way the cGAN training was able to achieve better response in regions with high SUV while not substantially reducing the quality of reconstruction in other regions.

3.3.3 Experiments and results

To evaluate the performance of the system, we conducted several sets of experiments. A development set was used for training and validation. The final results are presented for an independent testing set. We demonstrate the applicability of the system to augment performance of a liver lesion detection system.

3.3.3.1 Dataset

The data used in this work includes PET/CT scans (pairs of contrast-enhanced portal phase CT scans with their corresponding PET scans) from the Sheba Medical Center, obtained from 2014 to 2015. An institutional review board (IRB) approval was granted for this retrospective study. The dataset contains 60 CT (with 0.97 mm pixel spacing and 4 mm slice thickness) and PET (with 3 mm pixel spacing and 4 mm slice thickness) pairs, from 60 different patients. We constrained the analysis to slices in the region of the liver for our study. Not all PET/CT scans in our dataset included liver lesions. The data was collected in two phases. In the first phase the collected data included PET/CT scans that were used for the development and validation of the explored methods. In the second phase new data was collected for testing with no additional modifications of the algorithms. The training set included 23 PET/CT pairs (6 with malignant liver lesions) and the testing was performed on 37 pairs (9 with malignant liver lesions).

3.3.3.2 Experimental setting

The networks were implemented and trained using Keras framework [58] on a PC with a single Nvidia 1080 Ti GPU. The following hyperparameters were used for all

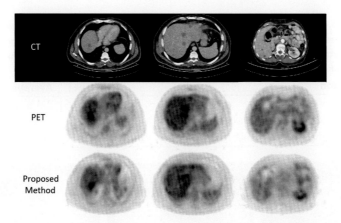

Figure 3.9 Sample results of the predicted PET using our method compared to the real PET with the corresponding CT images.

networks: the learning rate of 0.00001 with a batch size of 4. Adam optimizer [59] was used with $\beta = 0.5$. For the cGAN, we used $\lambda = 20$ in the optimization process presented in Eq. (3.4). To make the network model more robust to variability in location and scaling, online data transformations were performed with uniform sampling of scale $[-0.9, 1.1]$ and translations $[-25, 25]$ in each epoch. We randomly chose 20% of the training images for validation which were used to optimize the training process.

The proposed method reconstruction performance was compared with several method variations and was demonstrated to most-strongly emphasize malignant lesions for the detection task [31]. Qualitative results are shown in Fig. 3.9. It compares the method's virtual PET images with the original PET study images. The virtual PET provided a very similar response to the real PET in the presented cases. The left column includes one malignant lesion, the second column includes three liver metastases (malignant lesions), and the right column includes two cysts (benign lesions).

3.3.3.3 Liver lesion detection using the virtual-PET

In the following experiment, we used the synthesized (virtual) PET images as an additional false-positive reduction layer for an existing lesion detection software. Since high SUV values can be indicative of malignant lesions, thresholding the PET using a high SUV threshold ($th = 2.5$) can reduce irrelevant regions for lesion detection.

We suggest the following scheme for improving a given lesion detection software: Given an input CT scan, the detection software outputs lesion candidates as a binary mask. This mask may include false detections. Give the same CT scan, a virtual PET image is generated. It is next thresholded, as described above. The two generated binary masks are next intersected. This step results in the removal of false detections. A block

Table 3.4 Detection measurements using the FCN and sparsity based detection software presented in Sect. 3.2 with and without SUV thresholding on the synthesized PET. In bold we show the results obtained using the proposed method including the FCN and cGAN.

Method	TPR [%]	Average FPC
Detection soft.	94.6	2.9 ± 2.1
Detection soft. & virtual PET (FCN)	90.9	2.2 ± 1.7
Detection soft. & virtual PET (FCN+cGAN)	**94.6**	**2.1 ± 1.7**

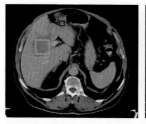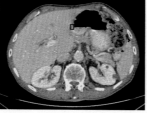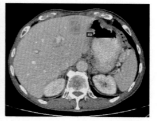

Figure 3.10 Sample results using the FCN and sparsity based detection software presented in Sect. 3.2: correctly detected lesions (green); false-positives (red) that were removed by combining the virtual PET (FCN+cGAN) using SUV thresholding.

diagram of the proposed framework is shown in Fig. 3.7. This, rather naïve approach, shows the clinical relevance of using the virtual PET to improve existing software.

We use the same lesion detection system that was presented in Sect. 3.2 [17]. The test set includes 14 CT scans with 55 lesions, as presented in Sect. 3.2.3.1. Two evaluation measurements were computed, the TPR and the FPC for each case, as in Sect. 3.2.1. Table 3.4 shows the performance with and without the proposed false-positive reduction layer. In this scenario, results were constrained to the manually annotated liver. Using the proposed method, the average FPC decreased from 2.9 to 2.1; an improvement of 28% (with P-value < 0.05) with a similar TPR. Fig. 3.10 shows examples of cases with false-positives that were removed (in red) by combining the proposed virtual PET method with the detection software presented in Sect. 3.2.

As a final experiment, we tested a fully automatic framework with an automatic liver segmentation scheme, as in [17]. Thus, we use an automatic liver segmentation instead of the manually circumscribed liver. Using our method the average FPC decreased from 3.0 to 2.3; an improvement of 23% (with P-value < 0.05) with a slight, not significant decrease of the TPR from 90.9% to 89.1%.

3.4. Discussion and conclusions

In this chapter we introduced the liver lesion detection task and presented two deep learning based methods as a clinical relevant solution. In Sect. 3.2 we presented a computer-aided detection system to detect liver lesions in CT images using an FCN with a sparsity based online fine-tuning for false-positive reduction. The FCN-4s architecture was shown to successfully detect lesions in both the development as well as the testing sets, as shown in Table 3.2. The sparsity based classification scheme was shown to significantly reduce the FPC. We note a difference in the range of the results in the two sets. This is due to the difference in the data settings: The data we obtained in the testing set had multi-slice lesion segmentation masks with only 1–2 slices marked in the development set. Given the additional data per patient, most lesions appeared on several slices in the test set, and thus had a higher likelihood of being detected. We therefore expected an overall increase in the TPR as well as in the FPC. Both these trends were present in the results.

The experimental results listed in Table 3.3 demonstrate that the FCN-4s method with the sparsity based fine-tuning is robust to lesion size, detecting 94.7% of the small lesions. Fig. 3.5 shows the detection results for several patients with different lesion sizes. Although all the lesions were detected, in some cases the overlap with the experts' segmentation mask was smaller than in others. However, as we discuss shortly, we believe that the output of the detection system can serve as an initial lesion segmentation mask.

We compared our FCN architecture to the U–Net architecture in Table 3.2. In both the development and testing sets the U–Net had a higher FPC than the FCN-4s. Thus, whereas the U–Net architecture exhibited superior segmentation performance in several medical applications, in the detection task the FCN-4s showed superiority.

Most of the experiments in our study were designed for detection performance evaluation, and concentrated on a manually circumscribed liver region. As a final experiment, we evaluated the proposed method using an automated liver segmentation tool. In our initial experiment, we achieved clinically relevant results of 90.9% TPR with 3.0 FPC.

In this work we focused on lesion detection. To further enhance the system to provide accurate segmentation, these detection results can be used as an initial mask for the lesions, following which additional segmentation algorithms can be implemented for expansion and refinement. Note that no significant pre- or postprocessing was implemented in the suggested method. Adding these steps could increase lesion detection accuracy and enable more accurate segmentation as well.

The FCN-4s in our system uses 3 adjacent slices as input. In examinations with large slice spacing, the images were interpolated to have a fixed slice spacing of 1 mm. For very small lesions, this means that a lesion will be present on a single slice alone which results in a lower TPR. It is clear that higher resolution in acquisitions will increase the overall detection rate. Moreover, using the automatic liver segmentation, a slight decrease in TPR was observed. A more accurate liver segmentation could improve the results of our fully automatic algorithm. The data augmentation in our training only included scale transformations. Additional augmentation techniques such as gray level transformations and deformations could make the system more robust to these changes.

In Sect. 3.3, a novel system for PET synthesis using only CT scans was presented. The system includes an FCN model and a cGAN model that refines the synthesized output extracted from the FCN. The proposed methodology is an extension to an earlier work [30], in which we used a pyramid based image blending step to combine the advantages of an FCN and a cGAN network. The proposed framework was shown to provide realistic PET estimation with special attention to malignant lesions using a custom loss function for each model. Not using an image blending step provided savings in time and reduced the need for manually defining a threshold for the blending mask, while improving the system performance.

We wanted to see if the proposed method can be used to improve the proposed automatic liver lesion detection software. Our system was easily integrated into the lesion detection software. Using a pathological SUV threshold of 2.5 we achieved a decrease in false-positive from an average of 2.9 per case to 2.1 (28% improvement). This experiment shows the benefit of using the proposed system to improve a given liver lesion analysis software. Since this method was trained on a dataset that was not seen by the existing detection software it improved its results. However, no manual labeling was conducted in this experiment since our method uses only PET/CT pairs for training.

One possible application could be to use the virtual PET to improve lesion segmentation. However, the PET images are quite blurry and so is the virtual PET, making it hard to assess the segmentation process. Hence, we believe that detection approaches are more relevant for this method.

We used a rather naïve approach by thresholding the virtual PET to reduce the amount of false-positives per case in an existing lesion detection software. However, the proposed system can be easily integrated into the training process of different networks for different tasks such as detection (as shown here) and classification.

Our proposed framework with the FCN–cGAN combination and the custom loss function has shown promising results in terms of reconstruction measures as well as detection measures by integrating it with the lesion detection software presented in Sect. 3.2. A major strength of this framework is that no manual labeling was used to train the system to synthesize PET images. As we well know, the task of manually labeling and annotating medical data is hard, and contributes to the usually small data sets that are used in todays' medical imaging research. Each year millions of PET/CT studies are conducted worldwide, and utilizing the current method, the CT and PET pairing can be used as "free" labeled and annotated data, with potential for big data, approaching millions of studies. This work can be expanded by obtaining a larger dataset with vast experiments using the entire CT and not just the liver region as well as integrating it into the training process of deep learning based detection and classification networks. The presented system can be used for many applications in which PET examination is needed such as evaluation of drug therapies and detection of malignant lesions.

There are additional possible directions for future work. In order to transition the work to a clinically-viable tool, large scale validation should be conducted in a real clinical environment. Preliminary steps in this direction have already been initiated by deploying stand-alone executables for each system presented in this chapter. The integration of our automated analysis tools with user interface applications for radiologists' decision support systems will enable us to conduct clinical studies at the Sheba Medical Center, get feedback, and further improve the current systems.

To conclude, the proposed methods aim to provide a solution to several key areas of concern in healthcare today: (i) *Data overload*: Advances in technology have resulted in the availability of higher resolution scanners that generate large amounts of imagery which are now available to the physician. However, no tools have been developed to support the analysis of these data, and thus much of the data available is not used efficiently or correctly; (ii) *Subjective medical analysis and cross-physician variability*: The analysis of image data is highly subjective and based on the experience of the expert. There is a general consensus that two physicians can differ considerably in their diagnosis; (iii) Low-resource countries lack basic healthcare: there is a lack of advanced imaging systems as well as experts.

The tools presented in this chapter can contribute to the ongoing improvement of healthcare by responding to the issues mentioned above, improving physicians' workflow and decision making process while increasing objectivity in the process, enhancing accuracy and saving time.

Acknowledgments

We thank Dr. Eyal Klang, Prof. Michal M. Amitai, Prof. Simona Ben-Haim, Prof. Eli Konen, and Dr. Stephen P. Raskin from the Sheba Medical Center for providing the clinical knowledge and guidance as well as relevant data used in this study.

This research was supported by the Israel Science Foundation (grant No. 1918/16).

References

[1] A. Sarma, M.E. Heilbrun, K.E. Conner, S.M. Stevens, S.C. Woller, C.G. Elliott, Radiation and chest ct scan examinations: what do we know? Chest 142 (3) (2012) 750–760.

[2] H.M. Taylor, P.R. Ros, Hepatic imaging: an overview, Radiologic Clinics 36 (2) (1998) 237–245.

[3] K.D. Hopper, K. Singapuri, A. Finkel, Body CT and oncologic imaging 1, Radiology 215 (1) (2000) 27–40.

[4] W.H. Organization, Fact sheet n 297, February 2006, available online at: http://www.who.int/cancer/en/index.html.

[5] G.T. Sica, H. Ji, P.R. Ros, CT and MR imaging of hepatic metastases, American Journal of Roentgenology 174 (3) (2000) 691–698.

[6] X. Deng, G. Du, Editorial: 3D segmentation in the clinic: a grand challenge II-liver tumor segmentation, in: International Conference on Medical Image Computing and Computer-Assisted Intervention 2008, Springer, 2008.

[7] P.F. Christ, LiTS – Liver Tumor Segmentation Challenge, URL https://competitions.codalab.org/competitions/15595, 2017.

[8] L. Ruskó, Á. Perényi, Automated liver lesion detection in CT images based on multi-level geometric features, International Journal of Computer Assisted Radiology and Surgery 9 (4) (2014) 577–593, https://doi.org/10.1007/s11548-013-0949-9.

[9] M. Frid-Adar, I. Diamant, E. Klang, M. Amitai, J. Goldberger, H. Greenspan, Modeling the intra-class variability for liver lesion detection using a multi-class patch-based CNN, in: International Workshop on Patch-Based Techniques in Medical Imaging, Springer, 2017, pp. 129–137.

[10] J. Long, E. Shelhamer, T. Darrell, Fully convolutional networks for semantic segmentation, in: Proceedings of the IEEE Conference on Computer Vision and Pattern Recognition, 2015, pp. 3431–3440.

[11] P.F. Christ, M.E.A. Elshaer, F. Ettlinger, S. Tatavarty, et al., Automatic liver and lesion segmentation in ct using cascaded fully convolutional neural networks and 3D conditional random fields, in: International Conference on Medical Image Computing and Computer-Assisted Intervention, Springer, 2016, pp. 415–423.

[12] Q. Dou, H. Chen, Y. Jin, L. Yu, J. Qin, P.-A. Heng, 3D deeply supervised network for automatic liver segmentation from CT volumes, in: International Conference on Medical Image Computing and Computer-Assisted Intervention, Springer, 2016, pp. 149–157.

[13] X. Li, H. Chen, X. Qi, Q. Dou, C.-W. Fu, P.A. Heng, H-DenseUNet: hybrid densely connected UNet for liver and liver tumor segmentation from CT volumes, preprint, arXiv:1709.07330.

[14] A. Ben-Cohen, I. Diamant, E. Klang, M. Amitai, H. Greenspan, Fully convolutional network for liver segmentation and lesions detection, in: Deep Learning and Data Labeling for Medical Applications, Springer, 2016, pp. 77–85.

[15] O. Ronneberger, P. Fischer, T. Brox, U-Net: convolutional networks for biomedical image segmentation, in: International Conference on Medical Image Computing and Computer-Assisted Intervention, Springer, 2015, pp. 234–241.

[16] A. Ben-Cohen, E. Klang, M. Amitai, H. Greenspan, Sparsity-based liver metastases detection using learned dictionaries, in: 2016 IEEE 13th International Symposium on Biomedical Imaging (ISBI), IEEE, 2016, pp. 1195–1198.

[17] A. Ben-Cohen, E. Klang, A. Kerpel, E. Konen, M.M. Amitai, H. Greenspan, Fully convolutional network and sparsity-based dictionary learning for liver lesion detection in CT examinations, Neurocomputing 275 (2017) 1585–1594.

[18] A. Ben-Cohen, I. Diamant, E. Klang, M. Amitai, H. Greenspan, Fully convolutional network for liver segmentation and lesions detection, in: International Workshop on Large-Scale Annotation of Biomedical Data and Expert Label Synthesis, Springer, 2016, pp. 77–85.

[19] K. Simonyan, A. Zisserman, Very deep convolutional networks for large-scale image recognition, preprint, arXiv:1409.1556.

[20] L. Lu, P. Devarakota, S. Vikal, D. Wu, Y. Zheng, M. Wolf, Computer aided diagnosis using multilevel image features on large-scale evaluation, in: International MICCAI Workshop on Medical Computer Vision, Springer, 2013, pp. 161–174.

[21] H.R. Roth, L. Lu, J. Liu, J. Yao, A. Seff, K. Cherry, R.M. Summers, Improving computer-aided detection using convolutional neural networks and random view aggregation, IEEE Transactions on Medical Imaging 35 (5) (2016) 1170–1181.

[22] A.A.A. Setio, F. Ciompi, G. Litjens, P. Gerke, C. Jacobs, S.J. van Riel, M.M.W. Wille, M. Naqibullah, C.I. Sánchez, B. van Ginneken, Pulmonary nodule detection in CT images: false positive reduction using multi-view convolutional networks, IEEE Transactions on Medical Imaging 35 (5) (2016) 1160–1169.

[23] R. Achanta, A. Shaji, K. Smith, A. Lucchi, P. Fua, S. Süsstrunk, SLIC superpixels compared to state-of-the-art superpixel methods, IEEE Transactions on Pattern Analysis and Machine Intelligence 34 (11) (2012) 2274–2282, https://doi.org/10.1109/TPAMI.2012.120.

[24] Z. Jiang, Z. Lin, L.S. Davis, Learning a discriminative dictionary for sparse coding via label consistent k-SVD, in: 2011 IEEE Conference on Computer Vision and Pattern Recognition (CVPR), IEEE, 2011, pp. 1697–1704.

[25] H.I. Khalil, S.A. Patterson, D.M. Panicek, Hepatic lesions deemed too small to characterize at CT: prevalence and importance in women with breast cancer, Radiology 235 (3) (2005) 872–878, https://doi.org/10.1148/radiol.2353041099.

[26] W. Li, F. Jia, Q. Hu, Automatic segmentation of liver tumor in CT images with deep convolutional neural networks, Journal of Computer and Communications 3 (11) (2015) 146, https://doi.org/10.4236/jcc.2015.311023.

[27] W.A. Weber, Assessing tumor response to therapy, Journal of Nuclear Medicine 50 (Suppl. 1) (2009) 1S–10S.

[28] G.J. Kelloff, J.M. Hoffman, B. Johnson, H.I. Scher, B.A. Siegel, E.Y. Cheng, B.D. Cheson, J. O'Shaughnessy, K.Z. Guyton, D.A. Mankoff, et al., Progress and promise of FDG-PET imaging for cancer patient management and oncologic drug development, Clinical Cancer Research 11 (8) (2005) 2785–2808.

[29] W.A. Weber, A.L. Grosu, J. Czernin, Technology insight: advances in molecular imaging and an appraisal of PET/CT scanning, Nature Reviews. Clinical Oncology 5 (3) (2008) 160.

[30] A. Ben-Cohen, E. Klang, S.P. Raskin, M.M. Amitai, H. Greenspan, Virtual PET images from CT data using deep convolutional networks: initial results, in: International Workshop on Simulation and Synthesis in Medical Imaging, Springer, 2017, pp. 49–57.

[31] A. Ben-Cohen, E. Klang, S.P. Raskin, S. Soffer, S. Ben-Haim, E. Konen, M.M. Amitai, H. Greenspan, Cross-modality synthesis from CT to PET using FCN and GAN networks for improved automated lesion detection, Engineering Applications of Artificial Intelligence 78 (2019) 186–194.

[32] S. Roy, A. Carass, J.L. Prince, Magnetic resonance image example-based contrast synthesis, IEEE Transactions on Medical Imaging 32 (12) (2013) 2348–2363.

[33] J.E. Iglesias, E. Konukoglu, D. Zikic, B. Glocker, K. Van Leemput, B. Fischl, Is synthesizing MRI contrast useful for inter-modality analysis? in: International Conference on Medical Image Computing and Computer-Assisted Intervention, Springer, 2013, pp. 631–638.

[34] K. Bahrami, F. Shi, X. Zong, H.W. Shin, H. An, D. Shen, Hierarchical reconstruction of 7T-like images from 3T MRI using multi-level CCA and group sparsity, in: International Conference on Medical Image Computing and Computer-Assisted Intervention, Springer, 2015, pp. 659–666.

[35] H. Van Nguyen, K. Zhou, R. Vemulapalli, Cross-domain synthesis of medical images using efficient location-sensitive deep network, in: International Conference on Medical Image Computing and Computer-Assisted Intervention, Springer, 2015, pp. 677–684.

[36] D. Nie, X. Cao, Y. Gao, L. Wang, D. Shen, Estimating CT image from MRI data using 3D fully convolutional networks, in: Deep Learning and Data Labeling for Medical Applications, Springer, 2016, pp. 170–178.

[37] X. Han, MR-based synthetic CT generation using a deep convolutional neural network method, Medical Physics 44 (4) (2017) 1408–1419.

[38] L. Xiang, Q. Wang, D. Nie, Y. Qiao, D. Shen, Deep embedding convolutional neural network for synthesizing CT image from T1-weighted MR image, preprint, arXiv:1709.02073.

[39] J.M. Wolterink, A.M. Dinkla, M.H. Savenije, P.R. Seevinck, C.A. van den Berg, I. Išgum, Deep MR to CT synthesis using unpaired data, in: International Workshop on Simulation and Synthesis in Medical Imaging, Springer, 2017, pp. 14–23.

[40] A. Chartsias, T. Joyce, R. Dharmakumar, S.A. Tsaftaris, Adversarial image synthesis for unpaired multi-modal cardiac data, in: International Workshop on Simulation and Synthesis in Medical Imaging, Springer, 2017, pp. 3–13.

[41] L. Bi, J. Kim, A. Kumar, D. Feng, M. Fulham, Synthesis of positron emission tomography (PET) images via multi-channel generative adversarial networks (GANs), in: Molecular Imaging, Reconstruction and Analysis of Moving Body Organs, and Stroke Imaging and Treatment, Springer, 2017, pp. 43–51.

[42] K. Higashi, A.C. Clavo, R.L. Wahl, Does FDG uptake measure proliferative activity of human cancer cells? In vitro comparison with DNA flow cytometry and tritiated thymidine uptake, Journal of Nuclear Medicine 34 (3) (1993) 414–419.

[43] I. Goodfellow, J. Pouget-Abadie, M. Mirza, B. Xu, D. Warde-Farley, S. Ozair, A. Courville, Y. Bengio, Generative adversarial nets, in: Advances in Neural Information Processing Systems, 2014, pp. 2672–2680.

[44] A. Radford, L. Metz, S. Chintala, Unsupervised representation learning with deep convolutional generative adversarial networks, preprint, arXiv:1511.06434.

[45] E.L. Denton, S. Chintala, R. Fergus, et al., Deep generative image models using a Laplacian pyramid of adversarial networks, in: Advances in Neural Information Processing Systems, 2015, pp. 1486–1494.

[46] M. Mirza, S. Osindero, Conditional generative adversarial nets, preprint, arXiv:1411.1784.

[47] A. Odena, C. Olah, J. Shlens, Conditional image synthesis with auxiliary classifier GANs, preprint, arXiv:1610.09585.

[48] P. Isola, J.-Y. Zhu, T. Zhou, A.A. Efros, Image-to-image translation with conditional adversarial networks, arXiv preprint.

[49] R. Yeh, C. Chen, T.Y. Lim, M. Hasegawa-Johnson, M.N. Do, Semantic image inpainting with perceptual and contextual losses, preprint, arXiv:1607.07539.

[50] P. Costa, A. Galdran, M.I. Meyer, M.D. Abràmoff, M. Niemeijer, A.M. Mendonça, A. Campilho, Towards adversarial retinal image synthesis, preprint, arXiv:1701.08974.

[51] W. Dai, J. Doyle, X. Liang, H. Zhang, N. Dong, Y. Li, E.P. Xing, SCAN: structure correcting adversarial network for chest X-rays organ segmentation, preprint, arXiv:1703.08770.

[52] Y. Xue, T. Xu, H. Zhang, R. Long, X. Huang Segan, Adversarial network with multi-scale l_1 loss for medical image segmentation, preprint, arXiv:1706.01805.

[53] D. Nie, R. Trullo, C. Petitjean, S. Ruan, D. Shen, Medical image synthesis with context-aware generative adversarial networks, preprint, arXiv:1612.05362.

[54] T. Schlegl, P. Seeböck, S.M. Waldstein, U. Schmidt-Erfurth, G. Langs, Unsupervised anomaly detection with generative adversarial networks to guide marker discovery, in: International Conference on Information Processing in Medical Imaging, Springer, 2017, pp. 146–157.

[55] V. Alex, M.S. KP, S.S. Chennamsetty, G. Krishnamurthi, Generative adversarial networks for brain lesion detection, in: SPIE Medical Imaging, International Society for Optics and Photonics, 2017, p. 101330G.

[56] M. Frid-Adar, E. Klang, M. Amitai, J. Goldberger, H. Greenspan, Synthetic data augmentation using GAN for improved liver lesion classification, preprint, arXiv:1801.02385.

[57] L. Kostakoglu, H. Agress Jr, S.J. Goldsmith, Clinical role of FDG pet in evaluation of cancer patients, Radiographics 23 (2) (2003) 315–340.

[58] F. Chollet, et al., Keras, 2015.

[59] D.P. Kingma, J. Ba Adam, A method for stochastic optimization, preprint, arXiv:1412.6980.

CHAPTER 4

CAD in lung

Kensaku Mori
Nagoya University, Nagoya, Japan

Contents

4.1. Overview		91
4.2. Origin of lung CAD		92
4.3. Lung CAD systems		92
4.4. Localized disease		93
	4.4.1 Lung nodule	93
	4.4.1.1 Nodule detection and segmentation	*94*
	4.4.2 Ground Glass Opacity (GGO) nodule	95
	4.4.3 Enlarged lymph node	96
4.5. Diffuse lung disease		96
	4.5.1 Emphysema	97
4.6. Anatomical structure extraction		98
	4.6.1 Airway	98
	4.6.2 Blood vessel segmentation in the lung	100
	4.6.3 Lung area extraction	102
	4.6.4 Lung lobe segmentation	102
References		104

4.1. Overview

The lung is a major target organ in medical image computing and computer-assisted surgery [30]. The lung, whose major function is the exchange of gas between the air and the blood, has many anatomical structures including lobes, blood vessels, and airways. Recognition of this anatomical structure is important in the creation of a computer-aided diagnosis (CAD) system for the lung.

The American Cancer Society has reported that lung cancer is the leading cause of cancer-related deaths in the United States. In Japan, lung cancer is the most prevalent cancer and the leading cause of cancer-related deaths. Detecting lung cancers from chest X-ray or chest computed tomography (CT) images is a primary focus of lung CAD. Lung CAD is also one of the pioneering research areas in CAD's development history. In this chapter, we introduce several applications of lung CAD, including lung cancer detection and qualitative lung cancer diagnosis.

Handbook of Medical Image Computing and Computer Assisted Intervention
https://doi.org/10.1016/B978-0-12-816176-0.00009-0

4.2. Origin of lung CAD

Lung CAD research began in the 1960s. Very early lung CAD work consisted of lung cancer detection from chest X-ray films. Chest X-ray films were digitized by a film scanner, transformed to a mainframe computer, and then analyzed. Toriwaki et al. presented very early research in lung cancer detection from chest X-ray images. In Japan, annual chest X-ray screening is performed for tuberculosis prevention. Lung cancer is also detectible from X-ray films, and Toriwaki et al.'s research work was therefore performed for such purposes. They enhanced lung cancer regions using differential filtering techniques. Anatomical structures including the rib cage were also extracted.

Chest X-ray images (chest radiographs) are commonly used in the clinical field because they are convenient. Chest X-ray systems are simpler than X-ray CT imaging systems and have lower imaging costs. CAD systems for chest X-ray radiography have been investigated since the late 1960s or early 1970s [35], and automated lung nodule detection has also been developed. Toriwaki et al. introduced a system that recognizes the lung structure and outputs diagnostic results of abnormal shadows and heart diseases [33]. Computerized analysis of chest X-ray radiography is difficult due to the overlapping of anatomical structures on images. Recent progress in deep layer neural networks has begun to resolve such issues [32]. Although much research has been done on chest X-ray radiography processing, this chapter focuses on chest CAD for chest CT images.

Chest CT became very common in the early 1990s. The chest X-ray CT was considered a replacement for chest X-rays. CT screening trials were performed in early 1990 in Japan. These trials were conducted in relatively small medical communities including the Tokyo Health Service Association [13]. Lung CT screening trials were also performed in the US beginning in 2002, the primary results of which were presented in 2011 [27]. Since radiologists need to read many chest CT images in a short time, computer-assisted technology support is needed. Computer-assisted reading has become a core technology to support lung screening. The Lung Image Database Consortium (LIDC) should be noted as the activating force behind the promotion of chest CT CAD research [1]. The National Lung Screening Trial (NLST) and LIDC provide a chest CT image database for CAD researchers. These images are widely used as benchmark data in the development of chest CT CAD.

4.3. Lung CAD systems

Lung CAD systems can be classified into several categories: (a) detection, (b) segmentation, (c) classification, (d) qualification, (e) quantification, and (f) anatomical structure extraction. Their targets are: (i) lung cancer (or nodule), (ii) diffuse lung disease (pneumonia, tuberculosis, or asthma), and (iii) pneumothorax.

In the detection process, suspicious regions are detected from input images. Lung nodules or emphysema regions are typical targets. Segmentation is the segmentation of suspicious regions. Qualification applies an abnormality measure. Quantification quantitatively measures a disease. Anatomical segmentation is the extraction of anatomical structures from the input images. In the lung, anatomical structure segmentation includes the rib cage, airway, lung field, blood vessels, and mediastinum structures.

There are many types of lung disease which can be classified into localized or diffuse. Lung cancer is the most popular target in medical image computing. Localized disease includes lung cancer and lymph node enlargement in the hilar area. Diffuse lung disease includes emphysema, pneumonia, asthma, and fibrosis. In the medical image computing area, many methods have been investigated to detect, segment, quantify, qualify, or classify such lung diseases, and there are several approaches to processing lung images. Recent advances in deep neural networks (DNN) are drastically changing lung image processing methods [9].

4.4. Localized disease

A typical localized lung disease case is a lung nodule. A lung nodule is a blob-like structure observed on chest CT images. The average lung nodule size is around 30 mm. If it exceeds 30 mm, it is typically called a mass. Since lung nodules are possible precursors to lung cancer, they must be detected in lung cancer screenings for early diagnosis and treatment. They are sometimes observed as nodules attached to the lung pleura or vessel. These lung nodules are called juxta-pleural or juxta-vessel lung nodules. In strict classification, lung nodules can be classified as solitary, juxta-pleural, or juxta-vessel. This section treats these nodules as solitary lung nodules.

Solitary lung nodule detection is a major focus of lung CAD systems. Lung nodules are detected using a filtering technique or deep convolutional neural network (CNN). In the detection of juxta-pleural or juxta-vessel nodules, separation of the lung nodule from the pleura or the vessel is important in constructing a detection algorithm. With the deep CNN approach, the DNN is trained to detect and segment lung nodules via training data. CNNs, such as a residual neural network (ResNet) or dense convolutional network (DenseNet) [8], can be utilized for the detection process [9].

4.4.1 Lung nodule

Lung nodules are actively studied in chest medical image processing. Automated lung nodule detection can be used for processing lung cancer screening or daily clinical routine work. Chest X-ray images or chest CT images are typically used. Because chest X-ray images are easily taken and inexpensive, some countries including Japan use them for lung cancer screening. A chest CT image can provide volumetric information about the lung. Although it is hard to find lung nodules or other disease on a chest X-ray image due to overlapping of the anatomical structure (a chest X-ray is a simple projection image and, therefore, for example, lung nodule detection is difficult behind the heart or where the ribs overlap), but chest CT images do not have such issues.

Medical image computing of lung nodules can be classified into (a) lung nodule detection and segmentation, and (b) lung nodule qualification. In lung nodule detection and segmentation, lung nodule locations are identified or segmented on the input images. This process is sometimes called computer-aided detection (CADe). In this process, mass regions are identified, but the malignancy of lung nodules is not considered. In lung nodule qualification, the malignancy of the lung nodules is qualified or quantified [29] and the lung tumor growth rate is measured. This process is called computer-aided diagnosis (CADx).

4.4.1.1 Nodule detection and segmentation

In lung image processing, lung nodule detection is a primary target of medical image computing [34,39]. As mentioned above, a lung nodule is a precursor marker of lung cancer. Lung nodules are typically spherical; therefore, some shape-oriented enhancement filters have been created to emphasize lung nodules. A deep learning-based approach can also be used for lung nodule detection [31]. With the filter-based approach, a Laplacian-based method or Hessian matrix-based approach is used. These approaches primarily emphasize blob-like regions on a given CT volume. The second difference filter (Laplacian filter) is designed to emphasize lung nodules of target sizes (normally 5 mm or larger). The Hessian-based approach is also designed to emphasize lung nodules. A multiscale approach with varying σ of the Gaussian smoothing filter is utilized for detecting lung nodules of various sizes.

The typical lung nodule detection process consists of the following steps: (1) preprocessing, (2) lung area extraction, (3) blob structure enhancement inside the lung area, and (4) false-positive reduction. The lung area extraction process commonly uses a simple thresholding technique followed by connected component analysis. A statistical shape model or deep learning-based procedure also can be employed. The blob structure enhancement filter is used to enhance lung nodule regions. Directional difference filtering or intensity analysis (Hessian-based intensity structure analysis) can also be used. Candidate regions of lung nodules can be located by deep CNN. After obtaining candidate regions, false-positives are reduced using computed features of the candidate regions. These features include average intensity, variation of intensities, and circularity (sphericalness), and are fed into a shallow neural network or support vector machine. Each candidate region is classified as either true or false.

Hessian-based approach

Frangi and Sato proposed filters to enhance lines, sheets, or blob structures on a volumetric image using the second derivative features. They used eigenvalues of the Hessian matrix, which consist of the second derivative of intensity values from the input volumetric images. The Hessian-matrix is a matrix of the second derivatives of a given image I and is defined as

$$H = \begin{pmatrix} I_{xx} & I_{xy} & I_{xz} \\ I_{yx} & I_{yy} & I_{yz} \\ I_{zx} & I_{zy} & I_{zz} \end{pmatrix}$$

for a three-dimensional case. A derivative of I can be obtained by subtraction of the intensity values after Gaussian kernel smoothing of a given σ. The three eigenvalues calculated from H are represented by λ_1, λ_2, λ_3 ($\lambda_3 < \lambda_2 < \lambda_1 < 0$). Blobness can be measured as

$$\mathrm{BSE}\left(x, y, z\right) = \frac{\|\lambda_1\|^2}{\hat{\lambda}},$$

where $\hat{\lambda} = |\lambda_1 + \lambda_1 + \lambda_1|/3$. This enhancement process is applied to all voxels of the input images. After enhancing the input image using Hessian-based analysis, the lung nodule regions are obtained by thresholding the enhanced image. However, the initial results of the lung nodule detection process contain many false-positive regions. These regions are typically blood vessels. A false-positive reduction process including connected component and feature value-based analyses is typically employed for reducing false-positive regions. Alternatively, Chen et al. employed the fast marching method (FMM), a simplified level-set method, to separate lung nodule regions and other regions. They defined the speed function from the output of the blobness enhancement filter and the lineness filter for separation. An example of Hessian-based lung nodule detection results is shown in Fig. 4.1.

Deep learning-based approach

This approach extracts lung nodule regions by training a CNN [28,38]. One method defines a volume of interest (VOI) (i.e., $32 \times 32 \times 32$ voxels) and trains a classifier to output whether or not a lung nodule can be observed in the VOI. Because a typical chest CT volume size is $512 \times 512 \times 320$ voxels for high resolution (HR) CT images, a sliding window approach is used to cover all lung regions. As CNN classifiers, AlexNet, DenseNet, or ResNet and their 3D extensions are used.

4.4.2 Ground Glass Opacity (GGO) nodule

Solid nodules show almost uniform and high intensity values inside of them. In contrast, ground glass opacity (GGO) nodules are nonuniform and exhibit moderate intensity values. This causes thickening of the alveoli and macroscopic increase in the intensity values of the lung nodules. Typical GGO nodules have a solid part and a ground glass opacity part. Simple thresholding and following morphological operation is not possible

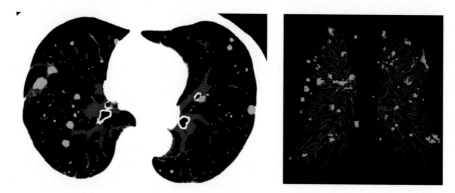

Figure 4.1 Example of lung nodule segmentation from chest X-ray CT images (green regions). Pulmonary blood vessels are simultaneously extracted (red).

to segment GGO nodules while maintaining both good sensitivity and specificity. It is a little bit harder to extract GGO nodules in a fully automated way from chest CT images. One method is to manually specify the GGO nodule region on the CT image to define a VOI and segment the GGO nodule inside the manually specified VOI. Multithresholds are automatically calculated using an expectation-maximization (EM) algorithm to calculate the thresholds for a solid nodule region, GGO region, and other regions.

4.4.3 Enlarged lymph node

Diagnosis of enlarged lymph nodes is essential in chest CT diagnosis. When a patient has disease in the lung, pulmonary or mediastinum lymph nodes enlarge. Diagnosing enlarged pulmonary or mediastinum lymph nodes is thus an important task for a chest CT CAD system. Enlarged lymph nodes are typically blob shaped and can be enhanced by a blobness filter based on the Hessian matrix. Since these enhancement filters detect many false-positive regions whose shapes resemble enlarged lymph nodes, a false-positive (FP) reduction process is executed after candidate lymph node region extraction. Furthermore, station numbers are assigned to each lymph node of the mediastinum area. Feuerstein et al. proposed the atlas-based segmentation of the mediastinum lymph node [7]. The mediastinum atlas is utilized for segmentation, FP reduction, and station number assignment.

Another approach for mediastinum lymph node extraction is to use a CNN. The U-net, V-net, or similar architecture of a full CNN is used for mediastinum lymph node segmentation.

4.5. Diffuse lung disease

Diffuse lung disease means the spread of disease through a part of or the entire lung. Emphysema is an example of a diffuse lung disease actively investigated by MICCAI

(The Medical Image Computing and Computer Assisted Intervention Society). Because diffuse lung disease progresses along with the lung microstructure, including the alveoli, interlobular septa, or inter lobules, diffuse lung disease image processing is mainly based on texture analysis.

4.5.1 Emphysema

Chronic obstructive pulmonary disease (COPD) is a chronic inflammatory lung disease that obstructs airflow in the lungs. Pulmonary emphysema is a COPD disease. The primary treatment for emphysema is to reduce its progress. Since the lung structures are obstructed, a dark region will appear on chest CT images. This dark region is called a low attenuation area (LAA). An LAA% (low attenuation area percentage ratio) measure is used to quantify these low attenuation areas. Although there are several definitions, LAA is defined as a region whose CT values are less than 900 HU (Hounsfield Unit). Hence, LAA% is defined as

$$LAA\% = \frac{LAA}{Lung\ area},$$

where *Lung area* is the specific area of the lung and LAA is the area of measurement. *Lung area* can be obtained by simple thresholding with the morphological operation for connected component analysis. For precise LAA extraction, Nagao et al. used a region growing method in emphysema region extraction [24,26]. Their method considers voxels whose intensity values are less than or equal to the threshold value t_a as the emphysema voxels. Furthermore, emphysema regions with voxels whose intensity values range from t_a and t_b are extracted by the region growing method. The growing conditions can be described as

Condition A: $E^{[6]}(p_i) < a$, and
Condition B: $\left(a \leq E^{[6]}(p_i) < b\right) \wedge \left(V^{[6]}(p_i) \leq c\frac{E^{[6]}(p_i)-a}{b-a} + d\right),$

where $E^{[6]}(p_i)$ and $V^{[6]}(p_i)$ are the mean and the variance of the intensities of 6-neighbor voxels of the voxel p_i. Variables a, b, c, and d are manually adjusted constants. Voxels whose intensities are $s = \frac{a+b}{2}$ are used as seed points for region growing. An example of LAA area extraction is shown in Fig. 4.2.

A pulmonary function test is also performed in emphysema diagnosis. Nimura et al. used pulmonary function test results in CT-based COPD diagnosis for better COPD severity assessment [26].

As will be discussed in the following sections, the right lung has three lobes and the left has two. LAA% is computed for each lung lobe [17].

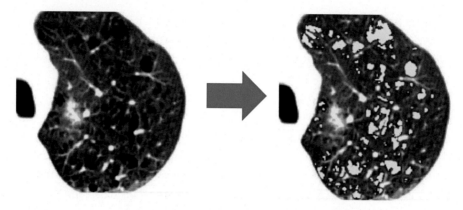

Figure 4.2 Example of emphysema region extraction from chest CT images. Yellow regions indicate LAA.

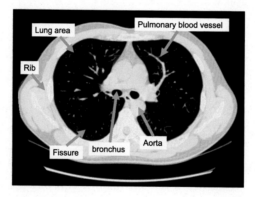

Figure 4.3 Anatomical structure of chest area.

4.6. Anatomical structure extraction

It is important to consider anatomical structure recognition of the lung when developing a chest CAD system [36]. The representative anatomical structures are the lung parenchyma (the lung area), airway, and blood vessels (Fig. 4.3).

4.6.1 Airway

Airway segmentation from chest CT images is an important task in chest CT image analysis [10]. The lung's anatomical structure can be analyzed based on the airway structures, including lung lobe classification or blood vessel separation for either the pulmonary arteries or veins. The lung airway has hollow-tube structures filled with air and is recognized as dark regions on CT images. This airway has a tree-like structure, so it can be segmented from CT images by following the dark regions from the trachea when there is no heavy stenosis. The region growing-based approach or VOI-based approach has been proposed for this purpose. Another strategy for airway region extraction is to classify a voxel as inside the airway (inside the luminal region) or outside the airway, which can be done with a machine learning technique. Hand-crafted features or a CNN can also be used. A deep learning-based approach can be used for a voxel-by-voxel classification method. Although the region growing approach can segment airway regions as a connected component, the voxel-based approach can detect airway regions basically voxel-by-voxel, making it possible to detect airway trees with severe stenosis. However, the voxel-based approach needs to reconstruct the airway tree regions from the classification results. Thus, this process must be carefully designed to avoid inadvertently missing some bronchial branches.

The region growing-based airway segmentation approach is basically performed by tracing the voxels that are connected from a seed point [18,19]. Since the trachea can be clearly identified on CT images from both an anatomical point of view and image intensity, a point inside the trachea is often utilized as the seed point for region growing in airway segmentation. As mentioned above, because the airway has small CT values on the inside, region growing is performed to trace voxels with lower intensity values. If we set a threshold value that distinguishes the inside and outside of the airway as a higher value, we can capture more bronchial branches. However, if we increase the threshold value, we extract more bronchus regions with excessive areas that are outside of the bronchus area. This is called an explosion. If we use a simple threshold value, it is important to adjust the threshold value. Mori et al. proposed a method to find the optimum threshold value in region growing-based bronchus extraction. They proposed using a threshold value that is just before the extraction explosion occurs [19]. A deep learning-based leakage detection process was also proposed by Charbonnier et al. [3].

Region growing-based bronchus region extraction is limited when extracting thinner bronchial branches. A partial volume effect increases the CT values inside the luminal region of the bronchus. This phenomenon is obvious in thin airway regions. If we increase the threshold value to extract thinner bronchial branches, it causes an explosion. Kitasaka et al. introduced a VOI-based bronchus region algorithm to solve this problem [11] using VOI, which covers a bronchial branch, to adjust the threshold values for each bronchial branch. They placed a cuboid VOI that gradually extends in the running direction of a bronchial branch for the trachea and then performed threshold adjustment and VOI extension. If a bifurcation is encountered, two VOIs are placed for each branch. Inside the VOI, region growing is applied to extract the bronchial regions, and then threshold adjustment and VOI extension is performed in the same manner. This process allows us to set different threshold values for each branch. Laplacian-based image enhancement is also applied to extract thinner branches. The fully convolutional network (FCN)-based method can be used to extract bronchial branch regions in a VOI [16].

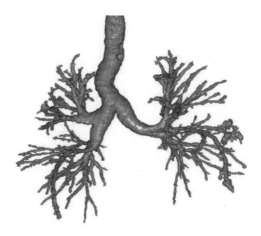

Figure 4.4 Example of airway extraction from CT images.

Another airway segmentation approach, called voxel classification, is to classify a voxel as either of the airway or not [14]. Kitasaka et al. proposed a bronchus region extraction method from CT images based on the voxel-based classification approach [12]. This method emphasizes the voxels of line parts by a Hessian-based filter and then determines whether the voxels are inside the bronchial luminal region by using a tube extraction filter based on a radial reach filter. Since the outputs contain many false-positives, we eliminate such voxels by checking coincident running directions obtained from the Hessian-based line enhancement filter (eigenvectors that correspond to the largest eigenvalues) and tube extraction filter. This extended approach can be found in [15]. An example of airway extraction results is shown in Fig. 4.4.

Anatomical labeling of bronchial branches is also an extended application of airway segmentation. The bronchial branches have their own anatomical names. These names are closely related to the lung's anatomy. One approach for assigning anatomical labels is graph matching of the airway structures extracted from CT images with reference to tree structures. Tree (graph) structures are sequentially matched from the trachea side. Anatomical names assigned with reference to tree structure are used for assigning anatomical labels to input tree structures. Graph matching is based on the features of bronchial branches [20,21]. Machine learning-based anatomical labeling has also been developed. With this labeling, features extracted from each bronchial branch are used to determine their anatomical names [23]. An example of anatomical labeling is shown in Fig. 4.5.

4.6.2 Blood vessel segmentation in the lung

The lung exchanges CO_2 and O_2 gases with the blood. Arteries transport CO_2-rich blood into the lung and veins transport the blood out after gas exchange. Pulmonary

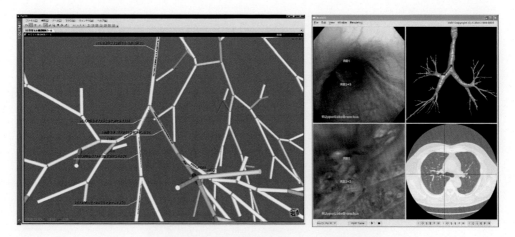

Figure 4.5 Automated anatomical labeling of bronchial branches and its application to bronchoscopy CAD.

blood vessels inside the lung have a tree-like structure. These blood vessels bifurcate into very tiny blood vessels and thus cannot be observed on chest CT images due to the resolution limitation of CT scanners.

Extraction of pulmonary blood vessels can be categorized into (a) simple thresholding and (b) utilization of a blood vessel enhancement filter. Since the lung area has lower intensity (CT) values due to the air inside of it and blood vessels have higher values due to the blood inside of them, simple thresholding can extract pulmonary blood vessels. However, this approach also extracts bronchial walls that also have higher intensity values. Furthermore, the posterior side of the lung has higher intensities than the anterior side when CT images are taken in the supine position, which is due to gravity causing differences in blood pressure. We need to remove this CT value bias of the lung field in order to extract pulmonary blood vessels by simple thresholding.

Another way to extract pulmonary blood vessels is to use the line enhancement filters based on the Sato or Frangi filters. Chen et al. used the level set approach to extract pulmonary blood vessels and lung nodules separately [5]. They defined the speed function of the fast-marching method, a simplified implementation of the level set method, based on the line filter enhancement and blob-structure enhancement filters. Since different wave propagation speeds are calculated in the blood vessel regions (line) and the lung nodule regions (blob), it is possible to separately extract blood vessel regions from other structures. An example of pulmonary blood vessel extraction is shown in Fig. 4.6.

Pulmonary artery and vein separation is also important in recognizing lung structure. Pulmonary arteries run parallel to the bronchus while pulmonary veins do not. A deep learning-based approach to separating the pulmonary arteries and veins can be found in [4,25].

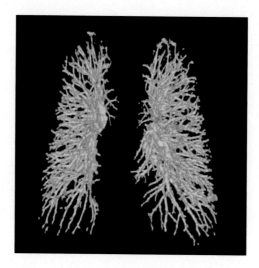

Figure 4.6 Example of pulmonary blood vessel extraction from chest CT images.

4.6.3 Lung area extraction

Lung area segmentation is a fundamental technique in chest image processing. In chest X-ray imaging, the lung area is depicted as dark regions because of the air contained in the lungs. Simple thresholding followed by connected component analysis is a good solution. However, such a simple method does not work well in cases of pathology. For example, if there are large high-intensity regions caused by lung disease, these regions are excluded from the lung area by simple thresholding. A morphological operation such as a closing operation cannot fill such large defect regions. This problem also applies to chest X-ray images.

Shape model-based approaches have been proposed to solve this problem. A statistical shape model or active shape models are used to extract the lung region for pathological cases. Shape models are fit to an input image and the lung regions are extracted using shape model information to compensate for the shape information around the pathological areas.

Deep learning is also a good approach for extracting lung areas on chest CT images. An FCN like U-net or V-net can be employed for lung region extraction. Original CT images and manually annotated lung regions are fed in to train the network to output a lung area segmentation result. Including pathological cases in the training dataset will allow this method to correctly extract lung regions in disease cases.

4.6.4 Lung lobe segmentation

As mentioned earlier, the lungs consist of five lobes (the upper, middle, and lower lobes in the right lung and the upper and lower lobes in the left lung) (Fig. 4.7). The lungs

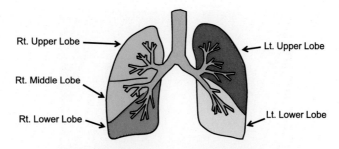

Figure 4.7 Structure of lung lobe.

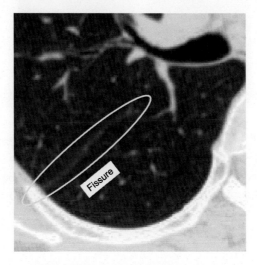

Figure 4.8 Pulmonary fissure observed on chest CT images.

can be considered as a set of three balloons in the right lung and two balloons in the left lung. The contacting areas of each lung lobe are curves called fissures [37]. On CT slice images, these fissures appear as curves. Lung lobes directly relate to lung function and airway bifurcation, and lung lobe segmentation is a research area in chest image analysis [6,2,36,22].

Lung lobe segmentation can be classified into two major approaches: (a) fissure curve detection followed by lung lobe division (Fig. 4.8) and (b) lung area division based on airway branches. Both methods assume that the lung area has already been extracted from the input CT image as stated previously. With approach (a), lung fissure regions are first extracted by a sheet structure enhancement filter. Then, the fissure region is subtracted from the lung area. After this process, figure decomposition is conducted to obtain the lung lobe region [22]. Method (b) uses the anatomical knowledge of each lobe bronchus (right upper lobe bronchus, right middle lobe bronchus, left upper

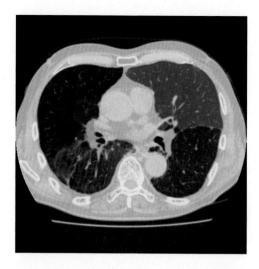

Figure 4.9 Example of lung lobe segmentation result.

lobe bronchus, and left lower lobe bronchus). Each lung lobe area can be obtained by performing Voronoi division by considering each lobe bronchus and their peripheral branches as seed points. Same seed labels are assigned to each lobe bronchus and their peripheral branches. The Voronoi division process is executed to divide the lung area into lobe regions. Fig. 4.9 shows an example of lung lobe division.

References

[1] S.G. Armato, G. McLennan, L. Bidaut, M.F. McNitt-Gray, C.R. Meyer, A.P. Reeves, et al., The Lung Image Database Consortium (LIDC) and Image Database Resource Initiative (IDRI): a completed reference database of lung nodules on CT scans, Medical Physics 38 (2) (2011) 915–931, https://doi.org/10.1118/1.3528204.

[2] F.J.S. Bragman, J.R. McClelland, J. Jacob, J.R. Hurst, D.J. Hawkes, Pulmonary lobe segmentation with probabilistic segmentation of the fissures and a groupwise fissure prior, IEEE Transactions on Medical Imaging 36 (8) (2017) 1650–1663, https://doi.org/10.1109/TMI.2017.2688377.

[3] J.-P. Charbonnier, E.M. van Rikxoort, A.A.A. Setio, C.M. Schaefer-Prokop, B. van Ginneken, F. Ciompi, Improving airway segmentation in computed tomography using leak detection with convolutional networks, Medical Image Analysis 36 (2017) 52–60, https://doi.org/10.1016/j.media.2016.11.001.

[4] J.P. Charbonnier, M. Brink, F. Ciompi, E.T. Scholten, C.M. Schaefer-Prokop, E.M. van Rikxoort, Automatic pulmonary artery-vein separation and classification in computed tomography using tree partitioning and peripheral vessel matching, IEEE Transactions on Medical Imaging 35 (3) (2016) 882–892, https://doi.org/10.1109/TMI.2015.2500279.

[5] B. Chen, T. Kitasaka, H. Honma, H. Takabatake, M. Mori, H. Natori, K. Mori, Automatic segmentation of pulmonary blood vessels and nodules based on local intensity structure analysis and surface propagation in 3D chest CT images, International Journal of Computer Assisted Radiology and Surgery 7 (3) (2012) 465–482, https://doi.org/10.1007/s11548-011-0638-5.

[6] T. Doel, D.J. Gavaghan, V. Grau, Review of automatic pulmonary lobe segmentation methods from CT, Computerized Medical Imaging and Graphics 40 (2015) 13–29, https://doi.org/10.1016/j.compmedimag.2014.10.008.

[7] M. Feuerstein, B. Glocker, T. Kitasaka, Y. Nakamura, S. Iwano, K. Mori, Mediastinal atlas creation from 3-D chest computed tomography images: application to automated detection and station mapping of lymph nodes, Medical Image Analysis 16 (1) (2012) 63–74, https://doi.org/10.1016/j.media.2011.05.005.

[8] G. Huang, Z. Liu, L. Van Der Maaten, K.Q. Weinberger, Densely connected convolutional networks, in: Proceedings – 30th IEEE Conference on Computer Vision and Pattern Recognition, CVPR 2017, 2017 January, pp. 2261–2269.

[9] G. Litjens, T. Kooi, B.E. Bejnordi, A.A.A. Setio, F. Ciompi, M. Ghafoorian, J.A.W.M. van der Laak, B. van Ginneken, C.I. Sánchez, A survey on deep learning in medical image analysis, Medical Image Analysis 42 (2017) 60–88, https://doi.org/10.1016/j.media.2017.07.005.

[10] P. Lo, B. van Ginneken, J.M. Reinhardt, T. Yavarna, P.A. de Jong, B. Irving, et al., Extraction of airways from CT (EXACT'09), IEEE Transactions on Medical Imaging 31 (11) (2012) 2093–2107, https://doi.org/10.1109/TMI.2012.2209674.

[11] T. Kitasaka, K. Mori, Y. Suenaga, J. Hasegawa, J. Toriwaki, A method for segmenting bronchial trees from 3D chest X-ray CT images, in: Lecture Notes in Computer Science, vol. 2879, 2003, pp. 603–610.

[12] T. Kitasaka, H. Yano, M. Feuerstein, K. Mori, Bronchial region extraction from 3D chest CT image by voxel classification based on local, in: The Third International Workshop on Pulmonary Image Analysis, January 2010, pp. 21–29.

[13] R. Kakinuma, K. Ashizawa, T. Kobayashi, A. Fukushima, H. Hayashi, T. Kondo, et al., Comparison of sensitivity of lung nodule detection between radiologists and technologists on low-dose CT lung cancer screening images, British Journal of Radiology 85 (1017) (2012) 603–608, https://doi.org/10.1259/bjr/75768386.

[14] P. Lo, J. Sporring, H. Ashraf, J.J.H. Pedersen, M. de Bruijne Marleen, Vessel-guided airway tree segmentation: a voxel classification approach, Medical Image Analysis 14 (4) (2010) 527–538, https://doi.org/10.1016/j.media.2010.03.004.

[15] Q. Meng, T. Kitasaka, Y. Nimura, M. Oda, J. Ueno, K. Mori, Automatic segmentation of airway tree based on local intensity filter and machine learning technique in 3D chest CT volume, International Journal of Computer Assisted Radiology and Surgery 12 (2) (2017) 245–261, https://doi.org/10.1007/s11548-016-1492-2.

[16] Q. Meng, H.R. Roth, T. Kitasaka, M. Oda, J. Ueno, K. Mori, Tracking and segmentation of the airways in chest CT using a fully convolutional network, in: Lecture Notes in Computer Science (including subseries Lecture Notes in Artificial Intelligence and Lecture Notes in Bioinformatics), vol. 10434, 2017, pp. 198–207.

[17] F.A.A. Mohamed Hoesein, E. van Rikxoort, B. van Ginneken, P.A. de Jong, M. Prokop, J.-W.J. Lammers, P. Zanen, Computed tomography-quantified emphysema distribution is associated with lung function decline, The European Respiratory Journal 40 (4) (2012) 844–850, https://doi.org/10.1183/09031936.00186311.

[18] K. Mori, J.-I. Hasegawa, J.-I. Toriwaki, H. Anno, K. Katada, Automated extraction and visualization of bronchus from 3D CT images of lung, in: Lecture Notes in Computer Science (including subseries Lecture Notes in Artificial Intelligence and Lecture Notes in Bioinformatics), vol. 905, 1995.

[19] K. Mori, J. Hasegawa, J. Toriwaki, H. Anno, K. Katada, Recognition of bronchus in three-dimensional X-ray CT images with applications to virtualized bronchoscopy system, in: Proceedings – International Conference on Pattern Recognition, 3, 1996.

[20] K. Mori, J. Hasegawa, Y. Suenaga, J. Toriwaki, Automated anatomical labeling of the bronchial branch and its application to the virtual bronchoscopy system, IEEE Transactions on Medical Imaging 19 (2) (2000) 103–114, https://doi.org/10.1109/42.836370.

[21] K. Mori, S. Ema, T. Kitasaka, Y. Mekada, I. Ide, H. Murase, et al., Automated nomenclature of bronchial branches extracted from CT images and its application to biopsy path planning in virtual bronchoscopy, in: Medical Image Computing and Computer-Assisted Intervention: MICCAI, International Conference on Medical Image Computing and Computer-Assisted Intervention, 8(Pt 2), 2005, pp. 854–861, retrieved from http://www.ncbi.nlm.nih.gov/pubmed/16686040.

[22] K. Mori, Y. Nakada, T. Kitasaka, Y. Suenaga, H. Takabatake, M. Mori, H. Natori, Lung lobe and segmental lobe extraction from 3D chest CT datasets based on figure decomposition and Voronoi division, in: Medical Imaging 2008: Image Processing, in: Proc. SPIE, vol. 6914, March 2008.

[23] K. Mori, S. Ota, D. Deguchi, T. Kitasaka, Y. Suenaga, S. Iwano, et al., Automated anatomical labeling of bronchial branches extracted from CT datasets based on machine learning and combination optimization and its application to bronchoscope guidance, in: Medical Image Computing and Computer-Assisted Intervention: MICCAI, International Conference on Medical Image Computing and Computer-Assisted Intervention, 12(Pt 2), 2009, pp. 707–714, retrieved from http://www.ncbi.nlm.nih.gov/pubmed/20426174.

[24] J. Nagao, T. Aiguchi, K. Mori, Y. Suenaga, J. Toriwaki, M. Mori, H. Natori, A CAD system for quantifying COPD based on 3-D CT images, https://doi.org/10.1007/978-3-540-39899-8_89, 2003.

[25] P. Nardelli, D. Jimenez-Carretero, D. Bermejo-Pelaez, G.R. Washko, F.N. Rahaghi, M.J. Ledesma-Carbayo, R. San Jose Estepar, Pulmonary artery–vein classification in CT images using deep learning, IEEE Transactions on Medical Imaging 37 (11) (2018) 2428–2440, https://doi.org/10.1109/TMI.2018.2833385.

[26] Y. Nimura, T. Kitasaka, H. Honma, H. Takabatake, M. Mori, H. Natori, K. Mori, Assessment of COPD severity by combining pulmonary function tests and chest CT images, International Journal of Computer Assisted Radiology and Surgery 8 (3) (2013), https://doi.org/10.1007/s11548-012-0798-y.

[27] National Lung Screening Trial Research Team, D.R. Aberle, A.M. Adams, C.D. Berg, W.C. Black, J.D. Clapp, et al., Reduced lung-cancer mortality with low-dose computed tomographic screening, The New England Journal of Medicine 365 (5) (2011) 395–409, https://doi.org/10.1056/NEJMoa1102873.

[28] A.A.A. Setio, F. Ciompi, G. Litjens, P. Gerke, C. Jacobs, S.J. van Riel, et al., Pulmonary nodule detection in CT images: false positive reduction using multi-view convolutional networks, IEEE Transactions on Medical Imaging 35 (5) (2016) 1160–1169, https://doi.org/10.1109/TMI.2016.2536809.

[29] E. Shakibapour, A. Cunha, G. Aresta, A.M. Mendonça, A. Campilho, An unsupervised metaheuristic search approach for segmentation and volume measurement of pulmonary nodules in lung CT scans, Expert Systems with Applications 119 (2019) 415–428, https://doi.org/10.1016/j.eswa.2018.11.010s.

[30] I. Sluimer, A. Schilham, M. Prokop, B. van Ginneken, Computer analysis of computed tomography scans of the lung: a survey, IEEE Transactions on Medical Imaging 25 (4) (2006) 385–405, https://doi.org/10.1109/TMI.2005.862753.

[31] K. Suzuki, Feng Li, S. Sone, K. Doi, Computer-aided diagnostic scheme for distinction between benign and malignant nodules in thoracic low-dose CT by use of massive training artificial neural network, IEEE Transactions on Medical Imaging 24 (9) (2005) 1138–1150, https://doi.org/10.1109/TMI.2005.852048.

[32] K. Suzuki, H. Yoshida, J. Nappi, A.H. Dachman, Massive-training artificial neural network (MTANN) for reduction of false positives in computer-aided detection of polyps: suppression of rectal tubes, Medical Physics 33 (10) (2006) 3814–3824.

[33] J.-I. Toriwaki, Y. Suenaga, T. Negoro, T. Fukumura, Pattern recognition of chest X-ray images, Computer Graphics and Image Processing 2 (3–4) (1973) 252–271, https://doi.org/10.1016/0146-664x(73)90005-1.

[34] I.R.S. Valente, P.C. Cortez, E.C. Neto, J.M. Soares, V.H.C. de Albuquerque, J.M.R.S. Tavares, Automatic 3D pulmonary nodule detection in CT images: a survey, Computer Methods and Programs in Biomedicine 124 (2016) 91–107, https://doi.org/10.1016/j.cmpb.2015.10.006.

[35] B. Van Ginneken, B.M. Ter Haar Romeny, M.A. Viergever, Computer-aided diagnosis in chest radiography: a survey, IEEE Transactions on Medical Imaging 20 (12) (2001) 1228–1241, https://doi.org/10.1109/42.974918.

[36] E.M. van Rikxoort, B. van Ginneken, Automated segmentation of pulmonary structures in thoracic computed tomography scans: a review, Physics in Medicine and Biology 58 (17) (2013) R187–R220, https://doi.org/10.1088/0031-9155/58/17/R187.

[37] J. Wang, M. Betke, J.P. Ko, Pulmonary fissure segmentation on CT, Medical Image Analysis 10 (4) (2006) 530–547, https://doi.org/10.1016/j.media.2006.05.003.

[38] M. Winkels, T.S. Cohen, 3D G-CNNs for pulmonary nodule detection, (Midl), 1–11, retrieved from http://arxiv.org/abs/1804.04656, 2018.

[39] J. Zhang, Y. Xia, H. Cui, Y. Zhang, Pulmonary nodule detection in medical images: a survey, Biomedical Signal Processing and Control 43 (2018) 138–147, https://doi.org/10.1016/j.bspc.2018.01.011.

CHAPTER 5

Text mining and deep learning for disease classification

Yifan Peng[a]**, Zizhao Zhang**[b]**, Xiaosong Wang**[c]**, Lin Yang**[b]**, Le Lu**[c]

[a]National Center for Biotechnology Information, National Library of Medicine, National Institutes of Health, Bethesda, MD, United States
[b]Department of Computer Information and Science Engineering (CISE), University of Florida, Gainesville, FL, United States
[c]Department of Radiology and Imaging Sciences, Clinical Center, National Institutes of Health, Bethesda, MD, United States

Contents

5.1. Introduction	109
5.2. Literature review	110
5.2.1 Text mining	110
5.2.2 Disease classification	111
5.3. Case study 1: text mining in radiology reports and images	114
5.3.1 Text mining radiology reports	114
5.3.1.1 Architecture	114
5.3.1.2 Evaluation of NegBio	116
5.3.2 ChestX-ray 14 construction	117
5.3.3 Common thoracic disease detection and localization	117
5.3.3.1 Architecture	117
5.3.3.2 Evaluation	120
5.4. Case study 2: text mining in pathology reports and images	122
5.4.1 Image model	123
5.4.2 Language model	123
5.4.3 Dual-attention model	124
5.4.4 Image prediction	125
5.4.5 Evaluation	126
5.5. Conclusion and future work	129
Acknowledgments	130
References	130

5.1. Introduction

Medical imaging has been a common examination in daily clinical routine for screening and diagnosis of a variety of diseases. Although hospitals have accumulated a large number of image exams and associated reports, it is not yet challenging to effectively use them to build high precision computer-aided diagnosis systems. Recently, deep learning algorithms, a class of machine learning methods based on deep neural networks, have quickly become the state-of-the-art in computer vision [69,35,75]. However, they have not yet realized their full potentials on medical imaging, mainly because large-scale images with quality labels that are needed to train complex deep learning systems are not available [38,13,21].

In this chapter, we first present an overview of cutting-edge techniques for mining existing images and free-text report data for the machine learning purpose and then demonstrate two case studies in radiological and pathological images, respectively. In the first case study, we present a method to text-mine disease image labels (where each image can have multilabels) from the associated radiological reports using natural language processing. Using such a text-mining approach, we construct and release a new dataset, ChestX-ray14, consisting of 112,120 frontal-view X-ray images with 14 text-mined disease labels [71]. To the best of our knowledge, ChestX-ray14 is currently the largest publicly available medical image dataset in the scientific community. Given such a large-scale dataset, we further proposed a deep learning model to detect and locate commonly occurring thoracic diseases. We demonstrated that these diseases can be detected and even spatially-located via a unified weakly-supervised multilabel image classification and disease localization formulation. Our initial quantitative results are promising. However, developing fully-automated deep learning based "reading chest X-rays" systems is still an arduous journey to be exploited.

In the second case study, we introduce the semantic knowledge of medical images from their diagnostic reports to provide inspirational network training and an interpretable prediction mechanism with our proposed novel multimodal neural network, namely TandemNet. Inside TandemNet, a language model is used to represent report text, which cooperates with the image model in a tandem scheme. We propose a novel dual-attention model that facilitates high-level interactions between visual and semantic information and effectively distills useful features for prediction. In the testing stage, TandemNet can make accurate image prediction with an optional report text input. It also interprets its prediction by producing attention on the image and text informative feature pieces, and further generating diagnostic report paragraphs. Based on a pathological bladder cancer images and their diagnostic reports (BCIDR) dataset, sufficient experiments demonstrate that our method effectively learns and integrates knowledge from multimodalities and obtains significantly improved performance than comparing baselines.

5.2. Literature review

5.2.1 Text mining

In radiology, findings are observations regarding each area of the body examined in the imaging study and their mentions in radiology reports can be positive, negative or uncertain. Here, we call a finding negative if it is ruled out by the radiologist (e.g., "effusion" in "No infiltrate or effusion"), and uncertain if it is in an equivocal or hypothetical statement (e.g., "pneumothorax" in "suspicious pneumothorax").

Negative and uncertain findings are frequent in radiology reports [10]. Since they may indicate the absence of findings mentioned within the radiology report, identifying them is as important as identifying positive findings. Otherwise, downstream information–extraction or image–classification algorithms may return many irrelevant results.

Discriminating between positive, negative, and uncertain findings remains challenging [75,23,46,73]. Previous studies of negation detection include both rule-based and machine-learning approaches. Rule-based systems rely on negation keywords and rules to determine the negation [23,46,73]. The rules can either utilize regular expression [11, 26,9], parse tree, or dependency graph to capture long distance information between negation keywords and the target [47,62,44]. Among others, NegEx is a widely used algorithm that utilizes regular expressions. In its early version, NegEx limited the scope by hard-coded word windows size ($n = 5$). For example, NegEx cannot detect negative "effusion" in "clear of focal airspace disease, pneumothorax, or pleural effusion" because "effusion" is beyond the scope of "clear". In its later versions, the algorithm extended scope to the end of the sentence or allowed the user to set a window size. To further overcome the limitation of a fixed windows size, Sohn et al. [62] proposed to use regular expressions on the dependency path, and Mehrabi et al. [44] used dependency patterns as a post-processing step after NegEx to remove false positives of negative findings.

Alternatively, machine learning offers another approach to extract negations [75, 31,14,24]. These approaches need manually annotated in-domain data to ensure their performance. Unfortunately, such data are generally not publicly available [48,66,63,1]. Furthermore, machine learning based approaches often suffer in generalizability – the ability to perform well on text previously unseen.

5.2.2 Disease classification

The rapid and tremendous progress has been evidenced in a range of computer vision problems via deep learning and large-scale annotated image datasets [37,56,39,22]. Drastically improved quantitative performances in object recognition, detection, and segmentation are demonstrated in comparison to previous shallow methodologies built upon hand-crafted image features. Deep neural network representations further make the joint language and vision learning tasks more feasible to solve, in image captioning [69,35,51,34,67], visual question answering [2,65,74,82], knowledge-guided transfer learning [52,5], and so on. However, the intriguing and strongly observable performance gaps of the current state-of-the-art object detection and segmentation methods demonstrate that there is still significant room for performance improvement when underlying challenges (represented by different datasets) become greater. For example, MS COCO [39] is composed of 80 object categories from 200k images, with 1.2M instances (350k are people) where every instance is segmented and many instances are small objects. Comparing to PASCAL VOC [22] of only 20 classes and 11,530 images containing 27,450 annotated objects with bounding-boxes (B-Box), the top competing object detection approaches achieve in 0.413 in MS COCO versus 0.884 in PASCAL VOC under mean Average Precision (mAP).

Deep learning yields similar rises in performance in the medical image analysis domain for object (often human anatomical or pathological structures in radiology imaging) detection and segmentation tasks. Recent notable work includes (but is not limited to) a brief review on the future promise of deep learning [25] and a collection of important medical applications on lymph node and interstitial lung disease detection and classification [55,60], cerebral microbleed detection [18], pulmonary nodule detection in CT images [57], automated pancreas segmentation [54], cell image segmentation and tracking [53], predicting spinal radiological scores [33], and extensions of multimodal imaging segmentation [45,27]. The main limitation is that all proposed methods are evaluated on some small-to-middle scale problems of (at most) several hundred patients. It remains unclear how well the current deep learning techniques will scale up to tens of thousands of patient studies.

In the era of deep learning in computer vision, research efforts on building various annotated image datasets [56,22,39,2,51,82,34,36] with different characteristics play indispensably important roles on the better definition of the forthcoming problems, challenges, and subsequently possible technological progresses. Particularly, here we focus on the relationship and joint learning of image (chest X-rays) and text (X-ray reports). The previous representative image caption generation work [69,35] utilize Flickr8K, Flickr30K [50] and MS COCO [39] datasets that hold 8000, 31,000, and 123,000 images, respectively, and every image is annotated by five sentences via Amazon Mechanical Turk (AMT). The text generally describes annotator's attention of objects and activity occurring on an image in a straightforward manner. Region-level ImageNet pretrained convolutional neural networks (CNN) based detectors are used to parse an input image and output a list of attributes or "visually-grounded high-level concepts" (including objects, actions, scenes, and so on) in [35,74]. Visual question answering (VQA) requires more detailed parsing and complex reasoning on the image contents to answer the paired natural language questions. A new dataset containing 250k natural images, 760k questions, and 10M text answers [2] is provided to address this new challenge. Additionally, databases such as "Flickr30k Entities" [51], "Visual7W" [82], and "Visual Genome" [36,34] are introduced to construct and learn the spatially-dense and increasingly difficult semantic links between textual descriptions and image regions through the object-level grounding.

Though one could argue that the high-level analogy exists between image caption generation, visual question answering and imaging based disease diagnosis [59,58], there are three factors making truly large-scale medical image based diagnosis (e.g., involving tens of thousands of patients) tremendously more formidable.

1. Generic, open-ended image-level anatomy and pathology labels cannot be obtained through crowd-sourcing, such as Amazon Mechanical Turk (AMT), which is prohibitively implausible for non-medically trained annotators. Therefore, we exploit to mine the per-image (possibly multiple) common thoracic pathology labels from the image-attached chest X-ray radiological reports using Natural Language Processing techniques. Radiologists tend to write more abstract and complex logical reasoning sentences than the plain describing texts in [79,39].

2. The spatial dimensions of a chest X-ray are usually 2000×3000 pixels. Local pathological image regions can show hugely varying sizes or extents but often very small comparing to the full image scale. Fully dense annotation of region-level bounding boxes (for grounding the pathological findings) would normally be needed in computer vision datasets [51,82,36] but may be completely nonviable for the time being. Consequently, we formulate and verify a weakly-supervised multilabel image classification and disease localization framework to address this difficulty.

3. So far, all image captioning and VQA techniques in computer vision strongly depend on the ImageNet pretrained deep CNN models which already perform very well in a large number of object classes and serves a good baseline for further model fine-tuning. However, this situation does not apply to the medical image diagnosis domain. Thus, we must learn the deep image recognition and localization models while constructing the weakly-labeled medical image database.

There have been recent efforts on creating openly available annotated medical image databases [54,72,77,55] with the studied patient numbers ranging from a few hundreds to two thousands. Particularly for chest X-rays, the largest public dataset is OpenI that contains 3955 radiology reports from the Indiana Network for Patient Care and 7470 associated chest X-rays from the hospitals picture archiving and communication system (PACS). This database is utilized in [59] as a problem of caption generation but no quantitative disease detection results are reported. Our newly proposed chest X-ray database is at least one order of magnitude larger than OpenI. To achieve the better clinical relevance, we focus to exploit the quantitative performance on weakly-supervised multilabel image classification and disease localization of common thoracic diseases, in analogy to the intermediate step of "detecting attributes" in [74] or "visual grounding" for [51,82,34].

Diagnostic pathology image prediction has been widely investigated recently, such as breast cancer tissue image classification [3,20] and colorectal biopsy [78]. Liu et al. [41] train a deep neural network (i.e., Inception model) to detect cancer metastases. Most existing methods utilize disease labels or tumor pixel annotations. There is a growing interest on how to make use of richer clinical information to guide CNNs training. The two case studies shown here are pioneer studies to make use of diagnostic reports to train CNNs for image disease classification.

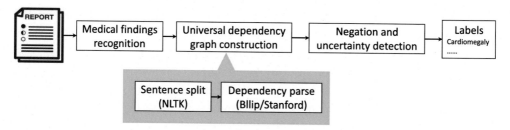

Figure 5.1 The pipeline of NegBio.

In computer vision, visual language models are studied to learn a joint embedding of both modalities. For example, He and Peng [29] combine image and captions to perform image classification. Wang et al. [70] learn a two-branch network to match images and text for various multimodal tasks (e.g., caption-based image retrieval). However, these methods require image and paired text to be available in both training and testing data. In the second case study, we present TandemNet that only needs text input during the training stage, which thereby makes the method applicable to real world settings. In the testing stage, the model can make prediction with optional text input.

5.3. Case study 1: text mining in radiology reports and images

In this study, we first introduced a text-mining algorithm to extract disease labels from the radiology reports. We then applied the algorithm on the PACS database at National Institutes of Health Clinical Center to construct a weakly-labeled image dataset. Using this dataset, we further investigated a deep learning model for image disease classification and localization.

5.3.1 Text mining radiology reports

We propose NegBio, a new and open-source rule-based tool for negation and uncertain detection in radiology reports [49]. Unlike previous methods, NegBio utilizes universal dependencies for pattern definition and subgraph matching for graph traversal search so that the scope for negation/uncertainty is not limited to fixed word distance [15,40]. In addition to negation, NegBio also detects uncertainty, a useful feature that is not well studied before.

5.3.1.1 Architecture

NegBio takes as inputting a sentence with pre-tagged mentions of medical findings and checks whether a specific finding is negative or uncertain. Fig. 5.1 shows the overall pipeline of NegBio. Detailed steps are described in the following subsections.

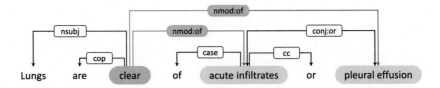

Figure 5.2 The dependency graph of "Lungs are clear of acute infiltrates or pleural effusion".

5.3.1.1.1 Medical findings recognition

Our approach labeled the reports in two passes. We first detected all the findings and their corresponding UMLS concepts using MetaMap [4]. Here we only focused on 14 common disease finding types: *Atelectasis, Cardiomegaly, Consolidation, Edema, Effusion, Emphysema, Fibrosis, Hernia, Infiltration, Mass, Nodule, Pleural Thickening, Pneumonia, and Pneumothorax*. These 14 finding types are most common in our institute, which are selected by radiologists from a clinical perspective. The next steps involved applying NegBio to all identified findings and subsequently ruling out those that are negative and uncertain.

5.3.1.1.2 Universal dependency graph construction

NegBio utilized the universal dependency graph (UDG) to extract negative and uncertain findings. UDG is a directed graph of one sentence designed to provide a simple description of the grammatical relationships in this sentence that can be easily understood by nonlinguists and effectively used by downstream language understanding tasks [15]. The nodes in a UDG are words of a sentence with information such as the part-of-speech and the lemma. The edges in a UDG represent typed dependencies from the governor to its dependent and are labeled with dependency type such as "nsubj" (nominal subject) or "conj" (conjunction). As an example, Fig. 5.2 shows a UDG of sentence "Lungs are clear of acute infiltrates or pleural effusion." where "Lung" is the subject and "acute infiltrates" and "pleural effusion" are two coordinating findings.

To obtain the UDG of a sentence, we first split and tokenized each report into sentences using NLTK [7]. Next, we parsed each sentence with the Bllip parser trained with the biomedical model [12,43]. The universal dependencies were then obtained by applying the Stanford dependencies converter on the parse tree with the CCProcessed and Universal option.

5.3.1.1.3 Negation and uncertainty detection

In NegBio, we defined rules on the UDG by utilizing the dependency label and direction information. We searched the UDG from the head word of a finding mention (e.g., "effusion" in Fig. 5.2). If the word node matches one of our pre-defined patterns, we treated it as negative/uncertain. For example, the finding "pleural effusion" in Fig. 5.2

Table 5.1 Descriptions of ChestX-ray and BioScope.

Dataset	Reports	Findings
ChestX-ray	900	2131
BioScope test set	977	466

is negated because it matches the rule "{disease} <nmod:of {lemma:/clear/}". The rule indicates that "clear" is the governor of "effusion" with a dependency "nmod:of". In NegBio, we use "Semgrex", a pattern language, for rapid development of dependency rules [8].

Since our patterns are defined on the graph, the negation/uncertainty scope is thus not limited to word distance. Instead, it is based on syntactic context. Specifically, we converted each rule to a subgraph for matching nodes/edges in the dependency graph. Here, we applied a subgraph matching algorithm to search the patterns in the graph [40]. Therefore, the negation/uncertainty scope is all vertices covered in the subgraph. The computational complexity of the Bllip parser and subgraph-matching algorithm is $O(m^3)$ and $O(m^2 k^m)$, respectively, where m is the length of an input sentence and k is the vertex degree.

5.3.1.2 Evaluation of NegBio

We evaluated NegBio on two public datasets (Table 5.1). One is **ChestX-ray**, a newly constructed gold-standard dataset to assess the robustness of NegBio. We randomly selected 900 reports from a larger radiology dataset collected from a national hospital and asked two annotators to mark the above 14 types of findings. A trial set of 30 reports was first used to help us better understand the annotation task. Then, each report was independently annotated by two experts. In this paper, we used the interrater agreement to measure the level of agreement between two experts. The Cohen's kappa is 84.3%. The second corpus is **BioScope**, which consists of medical and biological texts annotated for negation, speculation, and their linguistic scope [68]. Here, we considered only negation annotations in BioScope for our purpose. Hence, the test set of medical free-texts consists of 977 radiology reports with 466 negative scopes. To set the ground truth for negations, we followed the lead of [16] in our evaluation. We used the MetaMap to annotate the findings in the negative scopes and treat them as ground truth. As a result, we obtained 233 findings within the 466 annotated negative scopes.

Table 5.2 compares NegBio with the widely-used NegEx system [26] as measured by precision (P), recall (R), and F1-score (F). It shows that our tool achieved precision and F-score improvements on both corpora. We observed that on ChestX-ray, the overall precision with NegBio was substantially higher (11.6% improvement) than that of NegEx and overall higher F1-score (94.4%). On BioScope we observed that the overall performance of NegBio was higher than that of NegEx with a substantial 25.5% increase in precision and 13.6% increase in F1-score.

Table 5.2 Evaluation results using NegEx and NegBio.

	NegEx			NegBio		
	P	R	F	P	R	F
ChestX–ray	82.8	95.5	88.7	94.4	94.4	94.4
BioScope	70.6	98.7	82.3	96.1	95.7	95.9

5.3.2 ChestX-ray 14 construction

Using such a text-mining approach, we constructed and released a new dataset, ChestX-ray14 (https://nihcc.app.box.com/v/ChestXray-NIHCC/), consisting of 108,948 frontal-view X-ray images with 14 text-mined disease labels from the associated radiological reports [49,71]. Our dataset is extracted from the clinical PACS database at National Institutes of Health Clinical Center and consists of ~60% of all frontal chest X-rays in the hospital. Therefore we expect this dataset is significantly more representative to the real patient population distributions and realistic clinical diagnosis challenges, than any previous chest X-ray datasets. To the best of our knowledge, ChestX-ray14 is the largest publicly available medical image dataset in the scientific community.

5.3.3 Common thoracic disease detection and localization

Reading and diagnosing chest X-ray images may be an entry-level task for radiologists, but, in fact, it is a complex reasoning problem which often requires careful observation and good knowledge of anatomical principles, physiology, and pathology. Such factors increase the difficulty of developing a consistent and automated technique for reading chest X-ray images while simultaneously considering all common thoracic diseases.

As the main application of ChestX-ray14 dataset, we present a unified weakly-supervised multilabel image classification and pathology localization framework (Fig. 5.3), which can detect the presence of multiple pathologies and subsequently generate bounding boxes around the corresponding pathologies. In details, we tailor Deep Convolutional Neural Network (DCNN) architectures for weakly-supervised object localization, by considering large image capacity, various multilabel CNN losses and different pooling strategies.

5.3.3.1 Architecture

5.3.3.1.1 Unified DCNN framework

Our goal is to first detect if one or multiple pathologies are presented in each X-ray image and later we can locate them using the activation and weights extracted from the network. We tackle this problem by training a multilabel DCNN classification model. Fig. 5.3 illustrates the DCNN architecture we adapted, with similarity to several previous weakly-supervised object localization methods [6,81,19,32]. Specifically, we perform the network surgery on the pretrained models using ImageNet [17,56], e.g.,

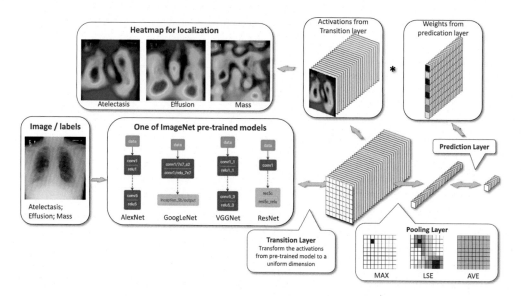

Figure 5.3 The overall flow-chart of our unified DCNN framework and disease localization process.

AlexNet [64], GoogLeNet [64], VGGNet-16 [61], and ResNet-50 [28], by leaving out the fully-connected layers and the final classification layers. We insert a transition layer, a global pooling layer, a prediction layer and a loss layer after the last convolutional layer. In a similar fashion as described in [81], a combination of deep activations from transition layer (a set of spatial image features) and the weights of prediction inner-product layer (trained feature weighting) can enable us to find the plausible spatial locations of diseases.

Multi-label setup. There are several options of image label representation and the choices of multilabel classification loss functions. Here, we define a 14-dimensional label vector $\mathbf{y}$, where each element indicates the presence with respect to according pathology in the image while an all-zero vector represents the status of "non-14 finding" (no pathology is found in the scope of any of 14 disease categories as listed). This definition transits the multilabel classification problem into a regression-like loss setting.

Transition layer. Due to the large variety of pretrained DCNN architectures we adopt, a transition layer is usually required to transform the activations from previous layers into a uniform dimension of output, $S \times S \times D$, $S \in \{8, 16, 32\}$; D represents the dimension of features at spatial location (i, j), $i, j \in \{1, \ldots, S\}$, which can be varied in different model settings, e.g., $D = 1024$ for GoogLeNet and $D = 2048$ for ResNet. The transition layer helps pass down the weights from pretrained DCNN models in a standard form, which is critical for using this layer's activations to further generate the heatmap in pathology localization step.

Multilabel classification loss layer. We first experiment 3 standard loss functions for the regression task instead of using the softmax loss for traditional multiclass classification model, i.e., Hinge Loss (HL), Euclidean Loss (EL), and Cross–Entropy Loss (CEL). We find that the model has difficulty learning positive instances (images with pathologies) and the image labels are rather sparse, meaning there are extensively more "0"s than "1"s. This is due to our one-hot-like image labeling strategy and the unbalanced numbers of pathology and "non-14 finding" classes. Therefore, we introduce the positive/negative balancing factor β_P, to enforce the learning of positive examples.

5.3.3.1.2 Weakly-supervised pathology localization

Global pooling layer and prediction layer. In our multilabel image classification network, the global pooling and the predication layer are designed not only to be part of the DCNN for classification but also to generate the likelihood map of pathologies, namely a heatmap. The location with a peak in the heatmap generally corresponds to the presence of disease pattern with a high probability. The upper part of Fig. 5.3 demonstrates the process of producing this heatmap. By performing a global pooling after the transition layer, the weights learned in the prediction layer can function as the weights of spatial maps from the transition layer. Therefore, we can produce weighted spatial activation maps for each disease class (with a size of $S \times S \times C$) by multiplying the activation from transition layer (with a size of $S \times S \times D$) and the weights of prediction layer (with a size of $D \times C$).

The pooling layer plays an important role that chooses what information is to be passed down. Besides the conventional max pooling and average pooling, we also utilize the Log–Sum–Exp (LSE) pooling proposed in [50]. The LSE pooled value x_p is defined as

$$x_p = \frac{1}{r} \log \left[\frac{1}{S} \sum_{(i,j) \in S} \exp(r \cdot x_{ij}) \right]$$

where x_{ij} is the activation value at (i, j), (i, j) is one location in the pooling region S, and $S = s \times s$ is the total number of locations in S. By controlling the hyperparameter r, the pooled value ranges from the maximum in S (when $r \to \infty$) to average ($r \to 0$). It serves as an adjustable option between max pooling and average pooling. Since the LSE function suffers from overflow/underflow problems, the following equivalent is used while implementing the LSE pooling layer in our own DCNN architecture,

$$x_p = x^* + \frac{1}{r} \log \left[\frac{1}{S} \sum_{(i,j) \in S} \exp(r \cdot (x_{ij} - x^*)) \right]$$

where $x^* = \max\{|x_{ij}|, (i, j) \in S\}$.

Bounding box generation. The heatmap produced from our multilabel classification framework indicates the approximate spatial location of one thoracic disease class each time. Due to the simplicity of intensity distributions in these resulting heatmaps, applying an ad-hoc thresholding based B-Box generation method for this task is found to be sufficient. The intensities in heatmaps are first normalized to 0–255 and then thresholded by 60 and 80 individually. Finally, B-Boxes are generated to cover the isolated regions in the resulting binary maps.

5.3.3.2 Evaluation

CNN setting. Our multilabel CNN architecture is implemented using Caffe framework [50]. The ImageNet pretrained models are obtained from the Caffe model zoo. Our unified DCNN takes the weights from those models and only the transition layers and prediction layers are trained from scratch. Due to the large image size and the limit of GPU memory, it is necessary to reduce the image batch size to load the entire model and keep activations in GPU while we increase the iteration size to accumulate the gradients for more iterations. The combination of both may vary in different CNN models but we set *batch size* × *iter size* = 80 as a constant. Furthermore, the total training iterations are customized for different CNN models to prevent overfitting. More complex models like ResNet-50 take less iterations (e.g., 10,000 iterations) to converge. The DCNN models are trained using a Dev-Box Linux server with 4 Titan X GPUs.

Multilabel disease classification. Fig. 5.4 demonstrates the multilabel classification ROC curves on 8 pathology classes by initializing the DCNN framework with 4 different pretrained models of AlexNet, GoogLeNet, VGG, and ResNet-50. The corresponding Area-Under-Curve (AUC) values of ResNet-50 are given in Table 5.3. The quantitative performance varies greatly, in which the model based on ResNet-50 achieves the best results. The "Cardiomegaly" (AUC = 0.8065) and "Pneumothorax" (AUC = 0.8055) classes are consistently well-recognized compared to other groups while the detection ratios can be relatively lower for pathologies which contain small objects, e.g., "Infiltration" and "Nodule" classes. Mass is difficult to detect due to its huge within-class appearance variation. The lower performance on "Pneumonia" (AUC = 0.6326) is probably because of lack of total instances in our patient population (less than 1% X-rays labeled as Pneumonia). This finding is consistent with the comparison on object detection performance.

Next, we demonstrate the performance improvement by using the positive/negative instances balanced loss functions. As shown in Table 5.4, the weighted loss (WCEL) provides better overall performance than CEL, especially for those classes with relative fewer positive instances, e.g., AUC for "Cardiomegaly" is increased from 0.7262 to 0.8141, and from 0.5164 to 0.6333 for "Pneumonia".

Disease localization. Leveraging the fine-tuned DCNN models for multilabel disease classification, we can calculate the disease heatmaps using the activations of the

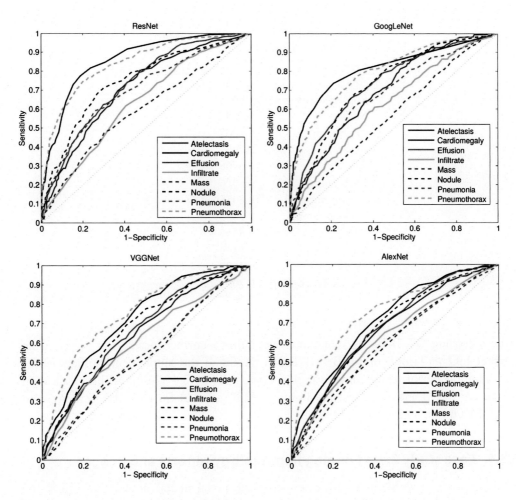

Figure 5.4 Comparison of multilabel classification performance with different model initializations.

transition layer and the weights from the prediction layer, and even generate the B-Boxes for each pathology candidate. The computed bounding boxes are evaluated against the hand annotated ground truth (GT) boxes (included in ChestX-ray14). Although the total number of B-Box annotations (1600 instances) is relatively small compared to the entire dataset, it may be still sufficient to get a reasonable estimate on how the proposed framework performs on the weakly-supervised disease localization task. To examine the accuracy of computerized B-Boxes versus the GT B-Boxes, two types of measurement are used, i.e., the standard Intersection over Union ratio (IoU) or the Intersection over the detected B-Box area ratio (IoBB) (like Area of Precision or Purity). Due to the relatively low spatial resolution of heatmaps (32 × 32) in contrast to the original image dimensions (1024 × 1024), the computed B-Boxes are often larger than

Table 5.3 AUCs of ROC curves for multilabel classification for ChestX-ray14.

ResNet-50	ChestX-ray14
Atelectasis	0.7158
Cardiomegaly	0.8065
Effusion	0.7843
Infiltration	0.6089
Mass	0.7057
Nodule	0.6706
Pneumonia	0.6326
Pneumothorax	0.8055
Consolidation	0.7078
Edema	0.8345
Emphysema	0.8149
Fibrosis	0.7688
Pleural Thickening	0.7082
Hernia	0.7667

the according GT B-Boxes. Therefore, we define a correct localization by requiring either $IoU > T(IoU)$ or $IoBB > T(IoBB)$. Refer to the supplementary material for localization performance under varying $T(IoU)$. Table 5.4 illustrates the localization accuracy (Acc.) and Average False-Positive (AFP) number for each disease type, with $T(IoBB)$ in $\{0.1, 0.25, 0.5, 0.75, 0.9\}$.

5.4. Case study 2: text mining in pathology reports and images

In this section, we demonstrate a unified multimodal neural network to utilize the diagnostic reports (i.e., pathology images in this study) to guide CNN training to distill visual features and make accurate image disease classification.

In medical image understanding, CNNs gradually become the prominent paradigm for various computational vision problems. Training CNNs to diagnose medical images primarily follows pure engineering trends in an end-to-end fashion. However, the principles of CNNs during training and testing are difficult to interpret and justify. In clinical practice, domain experts teach learners by explaining findings and observations to make a disease decision rather than leaving learners to find clues from images themselves. Inspired by this fact, in this paper, we explore the usage of semantic knowledge of medical images from their diagnostic reports to provide explanatory supports for CNN-based image understanding. The proposed network learns to provide interpretable diagnostic predictions in the form of attention and natural language descriptions. The diagnostic report is a common type of medical record in clinics, which is comprised of semantic descriptions about the observations of biological features.

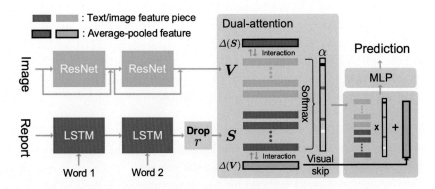

Figure 5.5 An illustration of the TandemNet.

TandemNet takes images and associated reports as training data (Fig. 5.5). In this section, we demonstrate a unified multimodal neural network to utilize the diagnostic reports (i.e., pathology images in this study) to guide CNN training to distill visual features and make accurate image disease classification. The advantage of this method is that the text information is not necessary to be available in the inference stage. It satisfies the face in the real-world setting that the reports of test images may not be available. Moreover, it enables attention based interpretable prediction that can visually justify its prediction.

5.4.1 Image model

We adopt the (new preactivated) residual network (ResNet) as our image model. The identity mapping in ResNet significantly improves the network generalization ability. There are many architecture variants of ResNet. We adopt the wide ResNet (WRN) which has shown better performance and higher efficiency with much less layers. It also offers scalability of the network (number of parameters) by adjusting a widen factor (i.e., the channel of feature maps) and depth. Transferring learning is widely used in medical image classification. Beside WRN, we also use and compare a ResNet18 which is pretrained on the ImageNet dataset. We extract the output of the layer before average pooling as our image representation, denoted as V with dimension $C \times G$. The input image size is 224×224, so $G = 14 \times 14$; C depends on the widening factor.

5.4.2 Language model

We adopt Long Short-Term Memory (LSTM) to model diagnostic report sentences. LSTM improves vanilla recurrent neural networks (RNNs) for natural language processing and is also widely used for multimodal applications, such as image captioning. It has a sophisticated unit design, which enables long-term dependency and greatly reduces the gradient vanishing problem in RNNs. Given a sequence of words $\{x_1, x_2, \ldots, x_n\}$,

LSTM reads the words one at a time and maintains a memory state m_t in D dimensions and a hidden state h_t in D dimensions. At each time step, LSTM updates them by computing the following equations

$$m_t, h_t = \text{LSTM}(x_t, m_t, h_t)$$

where x_t is the input word embedding vector. To compute the embedding vector, we first encode it as a one-hot vector with the length equal to the vocabulary size. Only the position corresponding to the word is 1 and the rest are 0. Then, the one-hot vector is multiplied by a learned word embedding matrix together with the LSTM.

The hidden state is a vector encoding of sentences. The treatment of it varies from problems. For example, in image captioning, a multilayer perceptron (MLP) is used to decode it as a predicted word at each time step. In machine translation [42], all hidden states could be used. A medical report is more formal than a natural image caption. It usually describes multiple types of biological features structured by a series of sentences. It is important to represent all feature descriptions but maintain the variety and independence among them. To this end, we extract the hidden state of every feature description (in our implementation, it is achieved by adding a special token at the end of each sentence beforehand and extracting the hidden states at all the placed tokens). In this way, we obtain a text representation matrix $S = [h_1, \ldots, h_N]$ for N feature descriptions (in a whole pathology reports). This strategy has more advantages: it enables the network to adaptively select useful semantic features and determine respective feature importance to disease labels.

5.4.3 Dual-attention model

The attention mechanism is an active topic in both computer vision and natural language communities [76]. Briefly, it gives networks the ability to generate attention on parts of the inputs (like visual attention in the brain cortex), which is achieved by computing a context vector with attended information preserved.

Different from most existing approaches that study attention on images or text, given the image representation and the report representation, our dual-attention model can generate attention on important image regions and sentence parts simultaneously. Specifically, we define the attention function f_a to compute a piecewise weight vector α as

$$e = f_a(V, S), \qquad \alpha_i = \frac{\exp(e_i)}{\sum_i \exp(e_i)}$$

The function to convert e to α is called the softmax function. It normalizes the elements in α so that they are summed to 1. Also α in $G + N$ dimensional space has individual weights for visual and semantic features (i.e., V and S). Each weight decides the importance of a feature pieces. Furthermore, f_a is specifically defined as

$$z_v = \tanh(W_V V + W_s \Delta (S) \mathbb{I}^T),$$
$$z_s = \tanh(W_s S + W_v \Delta (V) \mathbb{I}^T),$$
$$e = w^T [z_v; z_s] + b.$$

Before the input of f_a, the two matrices, V and S, are firstly embedded through a 1×1 convolutional layer, followed by tanh to embed them into the same dimension; W_V, W_s, w, and b are model parameters to be learned; Δ denotes the global average-pooling operator on the last dimension of the input; [;] denotes the concatenation operator. Finally, we obtain a context vector c by

$$c = O\alpha = \sum_{i=1}^{G} \alpha_i V + \sum_{i=G+1}^{N} \alpha_i S, \quad \text{where } O = [V; S].$$

In our formulation, the computation of image and text attention is mutually dependent and involves high-level interactions. The image attention is conditioned on the global text vector $\Delta (S)$ and the text attention is conditioned on the global image vector $\Delta (V)$. When computing the weight vector α, both contribute through z_v and z_s. We also consider extra configurations: computing two e by two w, and then concatenating them to compute α with one softmax or computing two α with two softmax functions. Both configurations underperform ours. We conclude that our configuration is optimal for the visual and semantic information to interact with each other.

Intuitively, our dual-attention mechanism encourages better alignment of visual information with semantic information piecewise, which thereby improves the ability of TandemNet to discriminate useful features for attention computation. We will validate this experimentally.

5.4.4 Image prediction

To improve the model generalization, we propose two effective techniques for the prediction module of the dual-attention model.

Visual skip-connection. The probability of a disease label p is computed as

$$p = MLP(c + \Delta (V)).$$

The image feature $\Delta (V)$ skips the dual-model and is directly added onto c (see Fig. 5.7). During backpropagation, this skip-connection attention directly passes gradients for the loss layer to the CNN, which prevents possible gradient vanishing in the dual-attention model from obstructing CNN training.

Stochastic modality adaptation. We propose to stochastically "abandon" text information during training. This strategy generalizes TandemNet to make accurate prediction with absent text. Our proposed strategy is inspired by Dropout and the stochastic depth network [30], which are effective for model generalization. Specifically, we define a drop rate r as the probability to remove (zero-out) the text part S during the entire network training stage. Thus, based to the principle of dropout, S will be scaled by 1 r if text is given in testing.

The effectiveness of these two techniques is validated below.

5.4.5 Evaluation

Our implementation is based on Torch7. We use a small WRN with depth $= 16$ and widening-factor $= 4$ (denoted as WRN16-4), resulting in 2.7M parameters and $C = 256$. We use dropout with 0.3 after each convolution. We use $D = 256$ for LSTM, $M = 256$, and $K = 128$. We use SGD with a learning rate 0.01 for the CNN (used likewise for standard CNN training for comparison) and Adam with 1e 4 for the dual-attention model, which are multiplied by 0.9 per epoch. We also limit the gradient magnitude of the dual-attention model to 0.1 by normalization. The source code of this method is available at https://github.com/zizhaozhang/tandemnet.

The pathology image dataset we used here is collected by [80]. Please refer to the original paper for more details. It is an H&E stained pathology images dataset of bladder cancer. There are 1000 500 500 RGB images were extracted randomly close to urothelial regions of corresponding patients' whole slides. For each image, there are five pathology reports are provided by domain experts. Each report addresses five types of cell appearance features, namely the state of *nuclear pleomorphism*, *cell crowding*, *cell polarity*, *mitosis*, and *prominence of nucleoli*. Then a conclusion is decided for each image-text pair, which comprises four classes, i.e., *normal* tissue, *low-grade* (papillary urothelial neoplasm of low malignant potential) carcinoma, *high-grade* carcinoma, and *insufficient information*. Thus, there are five ground-truth reports per image and 5000 image-text pairs in total. We randomly split 20% (6/32) of patients including 1000 samples as the testing set and the remaining 80% of patients including 4000 samples (20% as the validation set for model selection) for training and validation. We subtract the data RGB mean and augment through clip, mirror, and rotation.

We firstly evaluate Tandem on pathology image classification tasks. Recall that a trained model can classify image with (w/) or without (w/o) report text input. Table 5.4 and Fig. 5.6 show the quantitative evaluation of TandemNet. For comparison with CNNs, we train a WRN16-4 and also an ResNet18 (which has 11M parameters) pretrained on ImageNet2. We found transfer learning is beneficial. To test this effect in TandemNet, we replace WRN16-4 with a pretrained ResNet18 (TandemNet-TL). As can be observed, TandemNet and TandemNet-TL significantly improve WRN16-4 and ResNet18-TL when only images are provided. We observe TandemNet-TL slightly underperforms TandemNet when text is provided with multiple trails. We hypothesize that it is because fine-tuning a model pretrained on a completely different natural image

Table 5.4 The quantitative evaluation. The first block shows standard CNNs so text is irrelevant. TL indicates transfer learning, i.e., the CNN is pretrained on ImageNet.

Method	Accuracy (%)	
	w/o text	w/ text
WRN16-4	75.4	–
ResNet18-RL	79.4	–
TandemNet-WVS	79.4	**85.6**
TandemNet	82.4	**89.9**
TandemNet-TL	**84.9**	88.6

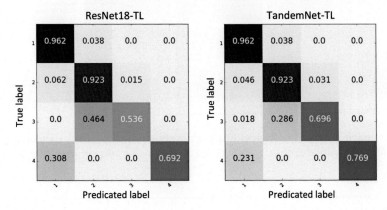

Figure 5.6 The confusion matrices of two compared methods ResNet18-TL and TandemNet-TL (w/o text) in Table 5.4.

domain is relatively hard to get aligned with medical reports in the proposed dual-attention model. From Fig. 5.6, high grade (label id 3) is more likely to be misclassified as low grade (2), and some insufficient information (4) is confused with normal (1).

In the equation of visual-skip connection, one question that may arise is that, when testing without text, whether it is merely $\Delta(V)$ from the CNN that produces useful features rather than c from the dual-attention model (since the removal (zero-out) of S could possibly destroy the attention ability). To validate the actual role of c, we remove the visual skip-connection and train the model (denoted as TandemNet-WVS in Table 5.4), and it improves ResNet16-4 by 4% without text. The qualitative evaluation below also validates the effectiveness of the dual-attention model.

We analyze the text drop rate in Fig. 5.8. When the drop rate is low, the model obsessively uses text information, so it achieves low accuracy without text. When the drop rate is high, the text cannot be well adapted, resulting in decreased accuracy with or without text. The drop rate of 0.5 performs best and thereby is used in this paper. As illustrated in Fig. 5.8, we found that the classification of text is easier than that of images,

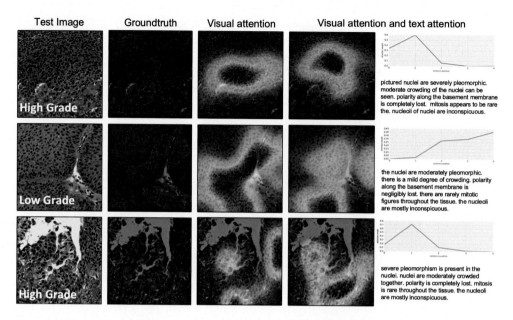

Figure 5.7 From left to right: Test images (the bottom shows disease labels), pathologist's annotations, visual attention w/o text; visual attention and corresponding text attention (the bottom shows text inputs).

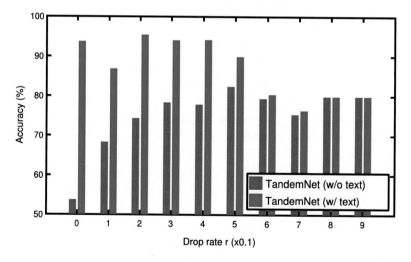

Figure 5.8 The accuracy with varying drop rates.

therefore its accuracy is much higher. However, please note that the primary aim of this paper is to use text information only at the training stage. While at the testing stage, the goal is to accurately classify images without text.

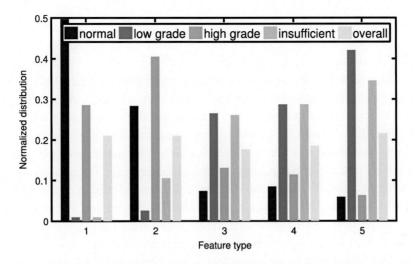

Figure 5.9 The averaged text attention per feature type (and overall) to each disease label.

We visualize the attention weights to show how TandemNet captures image and text information to support its prediction (the image attention map is computed by upsampling the $G = 14 \times 14$ weights of α to the image space). To validate the visual attention, without notifying our results beforehand, we ask a pathologist to highlight regions of some test images he/she thinks are important. Fig. 5.9 illustrates the performance. Our attention maps show surprisingly high consistency with pathologist's annotations. The attention without text is also promising, although it is less accurate than the results with text. Therefore, we can conclude that TandemNet effectively uses semantic information to improve visual attention and substantially maintains such attention capability though the semantic information is not provided. The text attention is shown in the last column of Fig. 5.9. We can see that our text attention result is quite selective in only picking up useful semantic features.

Furthermore, the text attention statistics over the dataset provides insights into the pathologists' diagnosis. We can investigate which feature contributes the most to which disease label (see Fig. 5.9). For example, nuclear pleomorphism (feature type 1) shows small effects on the low-grade disease label. Cell crowding (2) has large effects on high-grade. We can justify the reason of text attention by closely looking at images of Fig. 5.9: high grade images have obvious high cell crowding degree. Moreover, this result strongly demonstrates the successful image–text alignment of our dual-attention model.

5.5. Conclusion and future work

Constructing hospital-scale medical image databases with computerized diagnostic performance benchmarks has not been fully addressed. We attempt to build "machine–

human annotated" comprehensive databases that present realistic clinical and methodological challenges of handling at least tens of thousands of patients (somewhat like "ImageNet" in natural images). The main goal is to initiate future efforts by promoting public datasets in this important domain. Building truly large-scale, fully-automated high precision medical diagnosis systems remains a strenuous task. As an example, the constructed ChestX-ray14 can enable the data-hungry deep neural network paradigms to create clinically meaningful applications, including common disease pattern mining, disease correlation analysis, automated radiological report generation, etc. As another example, this chapter also presents a novel multimodal network, TandemNet, which can jointly learn from medical images and diagnostic reports and predict in an interpretable scheme through a novel dual-attention mechanism. Sufficient and comprehensive experiments on BCIDR demonstrate that TandemNet is favorable for more intelligent computer-aided medical image diagnosis. Possible future work includes exploring their applicability in clinical texts beyond radiological and pathological, by coping with larger datasets crossing different modalities. Taken together, we expect presented works will contribute to the advancement in understanding of the radiological and pathological world and enhancing the clinical decision-making.

Acknowledgments

This work was supported by the Intramural Research Programs of the National Institutes of Health, National Library of Medicine and Clinical Center.

References

[1] D. Albright, A. Lanfranchi, A. Fredriksen, W.F. Styler, C. Warner, J.D. Hwang, J.D. Choi, D. Dligach, R.D. Nielsen, J. Martin, et al., Towards comprehensive syntactic and semantic annotations of the clinical narrative, Journal of the American Medical Informatics Association 20 (2013) 922–930.

[2] S. Antol, A. Agrawal, J. Lu, M. Mitchell, D. Batra, C. Lawrence Zitnick, D. Parikh, Vqa: visual question answering, in: Proceedings of the IEEE International Conference on Computer Vision, 2015, pp. 2425–2433.

[3] T. Araujo, G. Aresta, E. Castro, J. Rouco, P. Aguiar, C. Eloy, A. Polonia, A. Campilho, Classification of breast cancer histology images using Convolutional Neural Networks, PLoS ONE 12 (2017) e0177544.

[4] A.R. Aronson, F.M. Lang, An overview of MetaMap: historical perspective and recent advances, Journal of the American Medical Informatics Association 17 (2010) 229–236.

[5] L.J. Ba, K. Swersky, S. Fidler, R. Salakhutdinov, Predicting deep zero-shot convolutional neural networks using textual descriptions, in: ICCV, 2015, pp. 4247–4255.

[6] S. Banerjee, A. Lavie, METEOR: an automatic metric for MT evaluation with improved correlation with human judgments, in: Proceedings of the ACL Workshop on Intrinsic and Extrinsic Evaluation Measures for Machine Translation and/or Summarization, 2005, pp. 65–72.

[7] S. Bird, E. Klein, E. Loper, Natural Language Processing with Python: Analyzing Text with the Natural Language Toolkit, O'Reilly Media, Inc., 2009.

[8] N. Chambers, D. Cer, T. Grenager, D. Hall, C. Kiddon, B. Maccartney, M.-C. De Marneffe, D. Ramage, E. Yeh, C.D. Manning, Learning alignments and leveraging natural logic, in: Proceedings of the ACL-PASCAL Workshop on Textual Entailment and Paraphrasing, 2007, pp. 165–170.

[9] B.E. Chapman, S. Lee, H.P. Kang, W.W. Chapman, Document-level classification of CT pulmonary angiography reports based on an extension of the ConText algorithm, Journal of Biomedical Informatics 44 (2011) 728–737.

[10] W.W. Chapman, W. Bridewell, P. Hanbury, G.F. Cooper, B.G. Buchanan, Evaluation of negation phrases in narrative clinical reports, in: Proc. AMIA Symp., 2001, pp. 105–109.

[11] W.W. Chapman, W. Bridewell, P. Hanbury, G.F. Cooper, B.G. Buchanan, A simple algorithm for identifying negated findings and diseases in discharge summaries, Journal of Biomedical Informatics 34 (2001) 301–310.

[12] E. Charniak, M. Johnson, Coarse-to-fine n-best parsing and MaxEnt discriminative reranking, in: Proceedings of the 43rd Annual Meeting on Association for Computational Linguistics (ACL), 2005, pp. 173–180.

[13] G. Chartrand, P.M. Cheng, E. Vorontsov, M. Drozdzal, S. Turcotte, C.J. Pal, S. Kadoury, A. Tang, Deep learning: a primer for radiologists, Radiographics 37 (2017) 2113–2131.

[14] C. Clark, J. Aberdeen, M. Coarr, D. Tresner-Kirsch, B. Wellner, A. Yeh, L. Hirschman, MITRE system for clinical assertion status classification, Journal of the American Medical Informatics Association 18 (2011) 563–567.

[15] M.-C. De Marneffe, T. Dozat, N. Silveira, K. Haverinen, F. Ginter, J. Nivre, C.D. Manning, Universal Stanford dependencies: a cross-linguistic typology, in: Proceedings of 9th International Conference on Language Resources and Evaluation (LREC), 2014, pp. 4585–4592.

[16] D. Demner-Fushman, W.J. Rogers, A.R. Aronson, MetaMap Lite: an evaluation of a new Java implementation of MetaMap, Journal of the American Medical Informatics Association 24 (2017) 1–5.

[17] J. Deng, W. Dong, R. Socher, L.-J. Li, L. Kai, F.-F. Li, ImageNet: A Large-Scale Hierarchical Image Database, 2009, pp. 248–255.

[18] Q. Dou, H. Chen, L. Yu, L. Zhao, J. Qin, D. Wang, V.C. Mok, L. Shi, P.-A. Heng, Automatic detection of cerebral microbleeds from MR images via 3D convolutional neural networks, IEEE Transactions on Medical Imaging 35 (2016) 1182–1195.

[19] T. Durand, N. Thome, M. Cord, Weldon: weakly supervised learning of deep convolutional neural networks, in: Proceedings of the IEEE Conference on Computer Vision and Pattern Recognition, 2016, pp. 4743–4752.

[20] B. Ehteshami Bejnordi, M. Veta, P. Johannes Van Diest, B. Van Ginneken, N. Karssemeijer, G. Litjens, J. Van Der Laak, C.C. The, M. Hermsen, Q.F. Manson, M. Balkenhol, O. Geessink, N. Stathonikos, M.C. Van Dijk, P. Bult, F. Beca, A.H. Beck, D. Wang, A. Khosla, R. Gargeya, H. Irshad, A. Zhong, Q. Dou, Q. Li, H. Chen, H.J. Lin, P.A. Heng, C. Hass, E. Bruni, Q. Wong, U. Halici, M.U. Oner, R. Cetin-Atalay, M. Berseth, V. Khvatkov, A. Vylegzhanin, O. Kraus, M. Shaban, N. Rajpoot, R. Awan, K. Sirinukunwattana, T. Qaiser, Y.W. Tsang, D. Tellez, J. Annuscheit, P. Hufnagl, M. Valkonen, K. Kartasalo, L. Latonen, P. Ruusuvuori, K. Liimatainen, S. Albarqouni, B. Mungal, A. George, S. Demirci, N. Navab, S. Watanabe, S. Seno, Y. Takenaka, H. Matsuda, H. Ahmady Phoulady, V. Kovalev, A. Kalinovsky, V. Liauchuk, G. Bueno, M.M. Fernandez-Carrobles, I. Serrano, O. Deniz, D. Racoceanu, R. Venancio, Diagnostic assessment of deep learning algorithms for detection of lymph node metastases in women with breast cancer, JAMA 318 (2017) 2199–2210.

[21] A. Esteva, B. Kuprel, R.A. Novoa, J. Ko, S.M. Swetter, H.M. Blau, S. Thrun, Dermatologist-level classification of skin cancer with deep neural networks, Nature 542 (2017) 115–118.

[22] M. Everingham, S.A. Eslami, L. Van Gool, C.K. Williams, J. Winn, A. Zisserman, The Pascal visual object classes challenge: a retrospective, International Journal of Computer Vision 111 (2015) 98–136.

[23] G. Gkotsis, S. Velupillai, A. Oellrich, H. Dean, M. Liakata, R. Dutta, Don't let notes be misunderstood: a negation detection method for assessing risk of suicide in mental health records,

in: Proceedings of the 3rd Workshop on Computational Linguistics and Clinical Psychology: From Linguistic Signal to Clinical Reality, San Diego, California, June 2016, pp. 95–105, D:\Acronis\latex\texmf\bibtex\bib\pdf\gkotsis2016dont.pdf.

[24] S. Goryachev, M. Sordo, Q.T. Zeng, L. Ngo, Implementation and Evaluation of Four Different Methods of Negation Detection, DSG, Brigham and Women's Hospital, Harvard Medical School, 2006.

[25] H. Greenspan, B. Van Ginneken, R.M. Summers, Guest editorial deep learning in medical imaging: overview and future promise of an exciting new technique, IEEE Transactions on Medical Imaging 35 (2016) 1153–1159.

[26] H. Harkema, J.N. Dowling, T. Thornblade, W.W. Chapman, ConText: an algorithm for determining negation, experiencer, and temporal status from clinical reports, Journal of Biomedical Informatics 42 (2009) 839–851.

[27] M. Havaei, N. Guizard, N. Chapados, Y. Bengio, HeMIS: hetero-modal image segmentation, vol. 9901, 2016, pp. 469–477.

[28] K. He, X. Zhang, S. Ren, J. Sun, Deep residual learning for image recognition, in: Proceedings of the IEEE Conference on Computer Vision and Pattern Recognition, 2016, pp. 770–778.

[29] X. He, Y. Peng, Fine-Grained Image Classification via Combining Vision and Language, 2017, pp. 7332–7340.

[30] G. Huang, Y. Sun, Z. Liu, D. Sedra, K.Q. Weinberger, Deep networks with stochastic depth, in: European Conference on Computer Vision, Springer, 2016, pp. 646–661.

[31] Y. Huang, H.J. Lowe, A novel hybrid approach to automated negation detection in clinical radiology reports, Journal of the American Medical Informatics Association 14 (2007) 304–311.

[32] S. Hwang, H.-E. Kim, Self-transfer learning for weakly supervised lesion localization, in: International Conference on Medical Image Computing and Computer-Assisted Intervention, Springer, 2016, pp. 239–246.

[33] A. Jamaludin, T. Kadir, A. Zisserman, SpineNet: automatically pinpointing classification evidence in spinal MRIs, vol. 9901, 2016, pp. 166–175.

[34] J. Johnson, A. Karpathy, L. Fei-Fei, Densecap: fully convolutional localization networks for dense captioning, in: Proceedings of the IEEE Conference on Computer Vision and Pattern Recognition, 2016, pp. 4565–4574.

[35] A. Karpathy, L. Fei-Fei, Deep visual-semantic alignments for generating image descriptions, IEEE Transactions on Pattern Analysis and Machine Intelligence 39 (2017) 664–676.

[36] R. Krishna, Y. Zhu, O. Groth, J. Johnson, K. Hata, J. Kravitz, S. Chen, Y. Kalantidis, L.-J. Li, D.A. Shamma, M.S. Bernstein, L. Fei-Fei, Visual genome: connecting language and vision using crowdsourced dense image annotations, International Journal of Computer Vision 123 (2017) 32–73.

[37] A. Krizhevsky, I. Sutskever, G.E. Hinton, Imagenet classification with deep convolutional neural networks, Advances in Neural Information Processing Systems (2012) 1097–1105.

[38] J.G. Lee, S. Jun, Y.W. Cho, H. Lee, G.B. Kim, J.B. Seo, N. Kim, Deep learning in medical imaging: general overview, Korean Journal of Radiology 18 (2017) 570–584.

[39] T.-Y. Lin, M. Maire, S. Belongie, J. Hays, P. Perona, D. Ramanan, P. Dollár, C.L. Zitnick, Microsoft coco: common objects in context, in: European Conference on Computer Vision, Springer, 2014, pp. 740–755.

[40] H. Liu, L. Hunter, V. Keselj, K. Verspoor, Approximate subgraph matching-based literature mining for biomedical events and relations, PLoS ONE 8 (2013) e60954.

[41] Y. Liu, K. Gadepalli, M. Norouzi, G.E. Dahl, T. Kohlberger, A. Boyko, S. Venugopalan, A. Timofeev, P.Q. Nelson, G.S. Corrado, Detecting cancer metastases on gigapixel pathology images, preprint, arXiv:1703.02442, 2017.

[42] T. Luong, H. Pham, C.D. Manning, Effective approaches to attention-based neural machine translation, in: Proceedings of the 2015 Conference on Empirical Methods in Natural Language Processing, 2015, pp. 1412–1421.

[43] D. Mcclosky, Any Domain Parsing: Automatic Domain Adaptation for Natural Language Parsing, Thesis, Department of Computer Science, Brown University, 2009.

[44] S. Mehrabi, A. Krishnan, S. Sohn, A.M. Roch, H. Schmidt, J. Kesterson, C. Beesley, P. Dexter, C.M. Schmidt, H. Liu, M. Palakal, DEEPEN: a negation detection system for clinical text incorporating dependency relation into NegEx, Journal of Biomedical Informatics 54 (2015) 213–219.

[45] P. Moeskops, J.M. Wolterink, B.H.M. Van Der Velden, K.G.A. Gilhuijs, T. Leiner, M.A. Viergever, I. Išgum, Deep learning for multi-task medical image segmentation in multiple modalities, vol. 9901, 2016, pp. 478–486.

[46] R. Morante, Descriptive analysis of negation cues in biomedical texts, in: International Conference on Language Resources and Evaluation (LREC), 2010, pp. 1429–1436, morante2010descriptive.pdf.

[47] P.G. Mutalik, A. Deshpande, P.M. Nadkarni, Use of general-purpose negation detection to augment concept indexing of medical documents: a quantitative study using the UMLS, Journal of the American Medical Informatics Association 8 (2001) 598–609.

[48] P.V. Ogren, G.K. Savova, C.G. Chute, Constructing evaluation corpora for automated clinical named entity recognition, in: N. Calzolari, K. Choukri, B. Maegaard, J. Mariani, J. Odijk, S. Piperidis, D. Tapias (Eds.), Proceedings of the Sixth International Conference on Language Resources and Evaluation (LREC), May 2008, Marrakesh, Morocco, European Language Resources Association (ELRA), May 2008, pp. 28–30, ogren2008constructing.pdf.

[49] Y. Peng, X. Wang, L. Lu, M. Bagheri, R. Summers, Z. Lu, NegBio: a high-performance tool for negation and uncertainty detection in radiology reports, preprint, arXiv:1712.05898, 2017.

[50] P.O. Pinheiro, R. Collobert, From image-level to pixel-level labeling with convolutional networks, in: Proceedings of the IEEE Conference on Computer Vision and Pattern Recognition, 2015, pp. 1713–1721.

[51] B.A. Plummer, L. Wang, C.M. Cervantes, J.C. Caicedo, J. Hockenmaier, S. Lazebnik, Flickr30k entities: collecting region-to-phrase correspondences for richer image-to-sentence models, in: 2015 IEEE International Conference on Computer Vision (ICCV), IEEE, 2015, pp. 2641–2649.

[52] R. Qiao, L. Liu, C. Shen, A. Van Den Hengel, Less is more: zero-shot learning from online textual documents with noise suppression, in: Proceedings of the IEEE Conference on Computer Vision and Pattern Recognition, 2016, pp. 2249–2257.

[53] O. Ronneberger, P. Fischer, T. Brox, U-net: convolutional networks for biomedical image segmentation 9351 (2015) 234–241.

[54] H.R. Roth, L. Lu, A. Farag, H.-C. Shin, J. Liu, E.B. Turkbey, R.M. Summers, DeepOrgan: multilevel deep convolutional networks for automated pancreas segmentation 9349 (2015) 556–564.

[55] H.R. Roth, L. Lu, A. Seff, K.M. Cherry, J. Hoffman, S. Wang, J. Liu, E. Turkbey, R.M. Summers, A new 2.5 D representation for lymph node detection using random sets of deep convolutional neural network observations, in: International Conference on Medical Image Computing and Computer-Assisted Intervention, Springer, 2014, pp. 520–527.

[56] O. Russakovsky, J. Deng, H. Su, J. Krause, S. Satheesh, S. Ma, Z. Huang, A. Karpathy, A. Khosla, M. Bernstein, Imagenet large scale visual recognition challenge, International Journal of Computer Vision 115 (2015) 211–252.

[57] A.A.A. Setio, F. Ciompi, G. Litjens, P. Gerke, C. Jacobs, S.J. Van Riel, M.M.W. Wille, M. Naqibullah, C.I. Sanchez, B. Van Ginneken, Pulmonary nodule detection in CT images: false positive reduction using multi-view convolutional networks, IEEE Transactions on Medical Imaging 35 (2016) 1160–1169.

[58] H.-C. Shin, L. Lu, L. Kim, A. Seff, J. Yao, R. Summers, Interleaved text/image deep mining on a large-scale radiology database for automated image interpretation, Journal of Machine Learning Research 17 (2016) 2.

[59] H.-C. Shin, K. Roberts, L. Lu, D. Demner-Fushman, J. Yao, R.M. Summers, Learning to read chest x-rays: recurrent neural cascade model for automated image annotation, in: Proceedings of the IEEE Conference on Computer Vision and Pattern Recognition, 2016, pp. 2497–2506.

[60] H.-C. Shin, H.R. Roth, M. Gao, L. Lu, Z. Xu, I. Nogues, J. Yao, D. Mollura, R.M. Summers, Deep convolutional neural networks for computer-aided detection: CNN architectures, dataset characteristics and transfer learning, IEEE Transactions on Medical Imaging 35 (2016) 1285–1298.

[61] K. Simonyan, A. Zisserman, Very deep convolutional networks for large-scale image recognition, preprint, arXiv:1409.1556, 2014.

[62] S. Sohn, S. Wu, C.G. Chute, Dependency parser-based negation detection in clinical narratives, in: AMIA Summits on Translational Science Proceedings, 2012, pp. 1–8.

[63] H. Suominen, Overview of the ShARe/CLEF eHealth evaluation lab 2013, in: International Conference of the Cross-Language Evaluation Forum for European Languages, 2013, pp. 212–231.

[64] C. Szegedy, W. Liu, Y. Jia, P. Sermanet, S. Reed, D. Anguelov, D. Erhan, V. Vanhoucke, A. Rabinovich, Going deeper with convolutions, in: 2015 IEEE Conference on Computer Vision and Pattern Recognition (CVPR), 2015.

[65] M. Tapaswi, Y. Zhu, R. Stiefelhagen, A. Torralba, R. Urtasun, S. Fidler, Movieqa: understanding stories in movies through question-answering, in: Proceedings of the IEEE Conference on Computer Vision and Pattern Recognition, 2016, pp. 4631–4640.

[66] O. Uzuner, B.R. South, S. Shen, S.L. Duvall, 2010 I2b2/VA challenge on concepts, assertions, and relations in clinical text, Journal of the American Medical Informatics Association 18 (2011) 552–556.

[67] I. Vendrov, R. Kiros, S. Fidler, R. Urtasun, Order-embeddings of images and language, preprint, arXiv:1511.06361, 2015.

[68] V. Vincze, Speculation and negation annotation in natural language texts: what the case of BioScope might (not) reveal, in: Proceedings of the Workshop on Negation and Speculation in Natural Language Processing, Association for Computational Linguistics, 2010, pp. 28–31.

[69] O. Vinyals, A. Toshev, S. Bengio, D. Erhan, Show and tell: a neural image caption generator, in: 2015 IEEE Conference on Computer Vision and Pattern Recognition (CVPR), IEEE, 2015, pp. 3156–3164.

[70] L. Wang, Y. Li, J. Huang, S. Lazebnik, Learning two-branch neural networks for image-text matching tasks, IEEE Transactions on Pattern Analysis and Machine Intelligence 41 (2019) 394–407.

[71] X. Wang, Y. Peng, L. Lu, Z. Lu, M. Bagheri, R.M. Summers, Chestx-ray8: hospital-scale chest x-ray database and benchmarks on weakly-supervised classification and localization of common thorax diseases, in: 2017 IEEE Conference on Computer Vision and Pattern Recognition (CVPR), IEEE, 2017.

[72] H.-J. Wilke, J. Urban, M. KÜMin, The benefits of multi-disciplinary research on intervertebral disc degeneration, European Spine Journal 23 (2014) 303–304.

[73] A.S. Wu, B.H. Do, J. Kim, D.L. Rubin, Evaluation of negation and uncertainty detection and its impact on precision and recall in search, Journal of Digital Imaging 24 (2011) 234–242.

[74] Q. Wu, P. Wang, C. Shen, A. Dick, A. Van Den Hengel, Ask me anything: free-form visual question answering based on knowledge from external sources, in: Proceedings of the IEEE Conference on Computer Vision and Pattern Recognition, 2016, pp. 4622–4630.

[75] S. Wu, T. Miller, J. Masanz, M. Coarr, S. Halgrim, D. Carrell, C. Clark, Negation's not solved: generalizability versus optimizability in clinical natural language processing, PLoS ONE 9 (2014) e112774.

[76] K. Xu, J. Ba, R. Kiros, K. Cho, A. Courville, R. Salakhudinov, R. Zemel, Y. Bengio, Show, attend and tell: neural image caption generation with visual attention, in: International Conference on Machine Learning, 2015, pp. 2048–2057.

[77] J. Yao, J.E. Burns, D. Forsberg, A. Seitel, A. Rasoulian, P. Abolmaesumi, K. Hammernik, M. Urschler, B. Ibragimov, R. Korez, T. Vrtovec, I. Castro-Mateos, J.M. Pozo, A.F. Frangi, R.M. Summers, S. Li, A multi-center milestone study of clinical vertebral CT segmentation, Computerized Medical Imaging and Graphics 49 (2016) 16–28.

[78] H. Yoshida, Y. Yamashita, T. Shimazu, E. Cosatto, T. Kiyuna, H. Taniguchi, S. Sekine, A. Ochiai, Automated histological classification of whole slide images of colorectal biopsy specimens, Oncotarget 8 (2017) 90719–90729.

[79] P. Young, A. Lai, M. Hodosh, J. Hockenmaier, From image descriptions to visual denotations: new similarity metrics for semantic inference over event descriptions, Transactions of the Association for Computational Linguistics 2 (2014) 67–78.

[80] Z. Zhang, Y. Xie, F. Xing, M. Mcgough, L. Yang, MDNet: A Semantically and Visually Interpretable Medical Image Diagnosis Network, 2017, pp. 3549–3557.

[81] B. Zhou, A. Khosla, A. Lapedriza, A. Oliva, A. Torralba, Learning deep features for discriminative localization, in: 2016 IEEE Conference on Computer Vision and Pattern Recognition (CVPR), IEEE, 2016, pp. 2921–2929.

[82] Y. Zhu, O. Groth, M. Bernstein, L. Fei-Fei, Visual7w: grounded question answering in images, in: Proceedings of the IEEE Conference on Computer Vision and Pattern Recognition, 2016, pp. 4995–5004.

CHAPTER 6

Multiatlas segmentation

Bennett A. Landman[a], **Ilwoo Lyu**[a], **Yuankai Huo**[a], **Andrew J. Asman**[b]

[a]Vanderbilt University, Electrical Engineering, Nashville, TN, United States
[b]Pandora Media Inc., Oakland, CA, United States

Contents

6.1.	Introduction	138
6.2.	History of atlas-based segmentation	139
	6.2.1 Atlas generation	140
	6.2.2 Preprocessing	141
	6.2.3 Registration	141
	6.2.3.1 Linear	*142*
	6.2.3.2 Nonlinear	*142*
	6.2.3.3 Label propagation	*142*
	6.2.4 Atlas selection	142
	6.2.5 Label fusion	143
	6.2.5.1 Voting	*143*
	6.2.5.2 Rater modeling	*143*
	6.2.5.3 Bayesian / generative models	*144*
	6.2.6 Post hoc analysis	145
	6.2.6.1 Corrective learning	*145*
	6.2.6.2 EM-refinement	*145*
	6.2.6.3 Markov Random Field (MRF)	*145*
	6.2.6.4 Morphology correction	*146*
6.3.	Mathematical framework	146
	6.3.1 Problem definition	146
	6.3.2 Voting label fusion	147
	6.3.3 Statistical label fusion	148
	6.3.4 Spatially varying performance and nonlocal STAPLE	150
	6.3.5 Spatial STAPLE	150
	6.3.6 Nonlocal STAPLE	151
	6.3.7 Nonlocal spatial STAPLE	151
	6.3.8 E-step: estimation of the voxel-wise label probability	152
	6.3.9 M-step: estimation of the performance level parameters	153
6.4.	Connection between multiatlas segmentation and machine learning	154
6.5.	Multiatlas segmentation using machine learning	154
6.6.	Machine learning using multiatlas segmentation	155
6.7.	Integrating multiatlas segmentation and machine learning	155
6.8.	Challenges and applications	155
	6.8.1 Multiatlas labeling on cortical surfaces and sulcal landmarks	156
6.9.	Unsolved problems	156

Handbook of Medical Image Computing and Computer Assisted Intervention
https://doi.org/10.1016/B978-0-12-816176-0.00011-9
137

Glossary   157
References   158

6.1. Introduction

Annotated spatial representations of human anatomy (*atlases*) have served essential functions in the communication, development, and evaluation of knowledge involving biological mechanisms since at least the Egyptian Edwin Smith Surgical Papyrus (circa 1600 BCE) [13]. Modern, visual atlases came into prevalence in the late 16th century in Italy and reemerged in Europe with the legalization of cadaver dissections in the 19th century [92]. These anatomical drawings with spatial contextual information form the foundation of modern medical anatomy education and physiological understanding.

Since the cyto-architectural studies of Korbinian Brodmann [20], standardized coordinate systems have proven essential in enabling structured investigation and characterization of the relationship between the structure and function of the human mind. For more than a century, Brodmann's cortical cytoarchitectural labels persisted as the de facto standard for comparing brain functional areas. In 1988, Talairach and Tournoux enabled direct access to this resource through presentation of normalized coordinates and anatomical regions for a single cadaver brain [109,67]. The "Talairach atlas" provided for systematic three-dimensional inquiry into the rich knowledge base surrounding Brodmann's regions. Despite this breakthrough, accessing Talairach information on individual basis or in a study-specific manner was highly problematic as this atlas (1) did not capture anatomical variability or (2) provide a systematic manner in which to transfer meta-information from one patient to another or from one cohort to another. In a transformative development, Collins et al. coregistered 305 MRI studies to the Talairach atlas and averaged these data to form population templates (e.g., the *MNI space*) [26,83]. The MNI space enabled quantitative description and correlation of brain structure, function, metabolism, and architecture across disciplines and scales (e.g., from cellular pathology to whole brain patterns of activation).

The pioneering efforts in brain atlas development compensated for head size and simple shape changes using affine registration to define an "average space" best match to the postmortem Talairach atlas [26]. With this method, consistent features are preserved (e.g., the brain's white matter core) while more variable features appear blurred (e.g., cortical gyral regions). This averaged representation is highly amenable as an image registration target because numerical methods are rarely trapped by local minima. Hence, approximate correspondence can be robustly determined with respect to variations in image quality, image features, and relatively major anatomical changes (e.g., tumors, surgical interventions, etc.). This robust framework enabled automated, systematic localization of findings and provided a framework for metaanalyses.

Nevertheless, it would be quite surprising to find an exact correspondence between the underlying structures, — let alone the radiological images themselves, — from any living patient to either a "representative" subject (e.g., Talairach) or to a statistical average (e.g., MNI). This issue of homology (i.e., image correspondence) has been forefront in structural neuroimaging and intersubject analysis [32]. In terms of registration (e.g., the process of aligning images), one can:

- compensate for a minimal amount of "uninteresting" variation and analyze the residual variation left in the resulting registered image intensities;
- explain all "interesting" variation in the registration process and examine the deformation field used to match the images; or
- choose from a continuum of possible registration models that lie between the two extremes and classify either (or both) the residuals or deformations as "interesting."

The core concept of *multiatlas* segmentation is that a single best/perfect/ideal match is not necessary because registration between atlases and an unlabeled medical image is a random process. Within this context, registration errors can be thought of in terms of algorithmic error (e.g., search failures, local minima, or noise) and homology errors. With a "successful" registration method, the search process and influence of noise on failures can be modeled as unbiased (zero-mean). Meanwhile, with careful selection/weighting of atlases, the set of homology errors can also be modeled as unbiased (zero mean). If both conditions hold, then constructing an *appropriate* average with an increasing number of atlases will yield consistently reduced expected error. The field of multiatlas segmentation is focused on understanding and optimizing the processing decisions that lead up to the registration processing, selection of an appropriate registration philosophy (as noted above) with a corresponding method, statistical fusion of the resulting registered atlas pairs, and postprocessing to achieve sufficiently accurate and precise segmentation results given limited training data.

6.2. History of atlas-based segmentation

Atlas-based segmentation approaches are an example-based segmentation method, whose aim is to encode the intensity–label relationship in the atlases to assign labels to an unlabeled intensity image [57,89]. An atlas is typically referred as a pair of intensity image and its corresponding labeled image, in which every voxel in the intensity image is assigned with a tissue type (label) from manual delineation, histology, or localization experiments. Since such atlas generation procedure is time and/or resource consuming, atlases were rare resources and even a single atlas is available in many studies. Herein, single atlas segmentation methods (SAS) were introduced as early efforts in atlas-based segmentation, which treats segmentation as an one-to-one image registration and label propagation [36,27,66]. A nonrigid registration is commonly performed between the atlas image and target image to map the atlas labels onto the coordinate system of the test image [14,61,98,85]. The quality of SAS is insufficient when the pairwise registration failed to capture wide anatomical variation.

Due to the inherent bias of using a single atlas, an alternative strategy that utilizes multiple atlases has been proposed to leverage the atlas-based segmentation performance. Early works of utilizing multiple atlases constructed a probabilistic atlas by coregistering individual training atlases to a precomputed atlas space (e.g., a population intensity atlas). Then, an unlabeled test image is registered to the atlas space and the segmentation is obtained by employing the probabilistic atlas as a spatial prior [5,43,86]. The probabilistic atlas-based segmentation alleviates the bias from the perspective of statistical inference across the population. However, the capability of modeling intersubject variation is still limited since the probabilistic model typically learned the "average" prior, which might yield inferior performance for unusual/alternative anatomical variations.

Since 2003, a new perspective of using multiple atlases has been proposed, in which each atlas is employed in the segmentation directly rather than forming a summarized (probabilistic) atlas. We refer to the methods in such perspective as multi-atlas segmentation (MAS) [95,48,65]. In MAS, each atlas plays the role as a rater, who provides a reference segmentation for a target image (as SAS). The principle of MAS is to integrate the information from multiple atlases (raters) to the final segmentation, which is similar to the boosting idea in machine learning that creates a single strong learner from a set of weak learners [102]. There are three major advantages of MAS compared with SAS: (1) more intersubject variations can be captured from multiple atlases; (2) The robustness of segmentation is leveraged by tolerating occasional registration failures; (3) The bias of atlas selection in SAS is alleviated.

Since multiple atlases are used in MAS, a decade of efforts has been spent to enable the MAS as a segmentation pipeline [57]. The key techniques can be categorized as including atlas generation, preprocessing, registration, atlas selection, label propagation, and corrective learning.

6.2.1 Atlas generation

Atlases are referred as pairs of intensity images (intensity atlases) and the corresponding labeled images (label atlases), which are typically obtained by resource consuming manual delineation by experts [90]. Therefore, it is costly for any individual research lab to obtain a large number of atlases. Then, two questions become important when preparing the atlases: (1) Which atlases should we label? (2) How many atlases do we need for a segmentation problem? For the first question, it is essential to preselect representative atlases to capture more variabilities and reduce the bias. The aim is to maximize the performance when segmenting new data. For such a purpose, many strategies have been proposed. The most straightforward way is to select atlases using prior knowledge via visual inspection [128] and feature selection [59]. Another option is to perform more quantitative investigation. For instance, we can cluster the intensity of potential atlases using k-means on the L_2 norm to identify a representative set of atlases to label [38].

More recent efforts used the "active learning" methods when large pool of unlabeled candidate atlases are available [15].

For the second question, in practice, 10–20 atlases are typically sufficient for a good multiatlas segmentation [2]. More atlases would leverage the segmentation performance, yet, the computational cost will also be increased. Therefore, a common strategy is to acquire a larger number of atlases (e.g., >30 atlases), and select a subset (e.g., 15 atlases) for multiatlas segmentation. This strategy is called atlas selection, which will be introduced later.

When we are not able to locate enough decent atlases or the available atlases are not sufficiently representative, we could employ atlas augmentation techniques to use (1) nonexpert/low quality segmentations [19,124], (2) portion of atlases [69], (3) unlabeled atlases [123], (4) automatic segmentation [24], etc., as atlases in MAS.

6.2.2 Preprocessing

Another major challenge of deploying MAS is to improve the ability of generalization when segmenting a testing image, which has very different image intensities or was acquired from different sites. To address such challenge, preprocessing steps are typically employed to minimize the differences between atlases and testing data. The preprocessing can be done for both atlases and testing data.

For both atlases and testing data, the preprocessing typically includes the bias field correction [115] and intensity harmonization [17]. Moreover, the learning techniques have also been integrated in preprocessing. For example, we could localize the target organs and crop the atlases to contain only organs' regions [125,117]. Then, the MAS methods can be robust and computationally more efficient. On the other hand, ranking the atlases with different weights in MAS is another important technique can be deployed in preprocessing [103,107,101].

The deployment of preprocessing depends on the applications. If the target imaging modalities have the scaled intensities (like CT), the bias field correction and intensity harmonizations are typically not necessary. However, for imaging modalities without scaled intensities (like MRI), the bias field correction [115], and intensity harmonization [17] are typically included.

6.2.3 Registration

Image registration, a key technique in medical image processing, is the process to transform different images into a common coordinate system [108]. In MAS, registration determines the pairwise correspondence between each individual atlas to testing image [81,51]. In practice, consecutive linear and nonlinear registration are performed when registering an atlas to testing image. The registration could be applied directly from the atlas to testing image, or an intermediate template (e.g., MNI305 template) was used to perform a two steps registration.

6.2.3.1 Linear

Rigid [60] and affine [60] registration are the most prevalent linear registration methods in MAS. The purpose is to roughly align two images in the same coordinate system.

6.2.3.2 Nonlinear

Various nonlinear registration methods are available for MAS [33]. The choice of non-linear registration methods is based on the applications and the similarity between source and target images. For brain registration, ANTs (Advanced Normalization Tools) [14], NiftyReg [85], IRTK (Image Registration Toolkit) [98], FSL (FMRIB Software Library) [61], and SPM [47] all provide decent performance for nonlinear registration without a variety of choices on deformation models, objective functions, and optimization algorithms. For abdominal organ segmentation, DEEDs (DEnsE Displacement Sampling) [49] registration provides a superior and fast solution to capture the large deformation in human abdomen.

6.2.3.3 Label propagation

Label propagation is a key technique for propagating the labels from one coordinate system to another learned from registration. In practice, the most convenient and efficient way is to perform nearest neighbor interpolation, where each voxel in target space only has a single label from source space [4,70,99]. To leverage the performance of label propagation, machine learning methods have been proposed beyond the nearest neighbor interpolation by introducing learning procedures [130,12].

6.2.4 Atlas selection

MAS employs multiple atlases to reduce the bias and capture more variations [95]. However, it does not mean more atlases will ensure the better segmentation performance. The authors of [1,54] showed that the performance of using a carefully selected set of atlases yields better performance compared with using all available atlases. This selection process is called "atlas selection" [70,95,123], which is a key technique in MAS. Moreover, another obvious advantage of performing atlas selection is to reduce the computational time. For example, selecting half of the atlases would reduce at least half of the total registration time.

The core idea of atlas selection is to rank the atlases from image-based similarity measures or nonimage metrics [3,28] from the hypothesis that the atlases with higher rank will lead to better segmentation performance. In practice, image-based similarity measures are the most widely used atlas selection strategy [2], which calculate the sum of squared differences, correlation, or mutual information between atlases and target images.

6.2.5 Label fusion

Given the target image and the registered atlas information (consisting of both intensities and labels), label fusion attempts to estimate the underlying segmentation. The concept of label fusion arose in the context of statistical machine learning. Kearns and Valiant [63] suggested that a collection of "weak learners" (i.e., raters that are only slightly better than chance) could be fused (or "boosted") to form a "strong learner" (i.e., a single rater with arbitrarily high accuracy). This proposal was first proven a year later [102], and, with the introduction of AdaBoost [46] in 1995, the process of "boosting" multiple classifiers became widely practical and popular. Perhaps surprisingly, it was not until approximately 2004 that the boosting literature was successfully translated to the medical imaging analysis context for the fusion of image labels [121,96]. Today, label fusion is an extremely popular topic for ongoing research. Below, we delve into the details of label fusion and discuss the different perspectives on the optimal ways to fuse image labels.

6.2.5.1 Voting

The first, and simplest way to perform label fusion is to utilize a voting-based framework. In voting label fusion there are generally two primary assumptions: (1) the prior distribution is unnecessary as all of the registered atlases provide accurate and consistent spatial information, and (2) the model probability density functions can be approximated using Parzen's window density approach [87]. Perhaps surprisingly, a majority vote, the simplest voting-based fusion strategy, has been consistently shown to result in highly robust and accurate segmentations [96,48,2]. In a majority vote, all atlases are weighted equally. Later, weighted voting strategies that use global [4], local [59,99], semilocal [120], and nonlocal [31] intensity similarity metrics have demonstrated consistent improvement segmentation accuracy.

There are many ways to estimate these weighting functions (e.g., Gaussian intensity differences [59,99,120], correlation coefficients [22], or mutual information [4]). One of the more common weighting schemes is to use a Gaussian distribution to model the intensity differences between the target and the atlas images.

A typical weighted voting MAS pipeline can be summarized as follows. First, the registered atlases and target images are compared using a predefined similarity metric. The results of this comparison lead to a voxelwise weighting for each of the registered atlases. These weights are then combined with the observed labels in order to construct the probability of each label at all voxels. Finally, the fused segmentation is constructed by taking the maximum likelihood label at each voxel.

6.2.5.2 Rater modeling

In stark contrast to ad hoc voting, statistical fusion strategies (e.g., Simultaneous Truth and Performance Level Estimation, STAPLE [121]) directly integrate a stochastic model of rater behavior into the estimation process. Mathematically, this model of rater behavior manifests itself by augmenting the conditional distribution. However, unlike voting-based label fusion frameworks, statistical fusion attempts to simultaneously estimate both (1) the underlying segmentation probabilities and (2) the rater performance level parameters.

To accomplish this, statistical fusion strategies use the Expectation Maximization (EM) formulation [37]. In an EM framework, the desired model parameters are iteratively estimated using two subsequent steps (referred to as the E-step and the M-step, respectively). In the E-step, the voxelwise label probabilities are estimated using the current estimate of the rater performance level parameters. In the M-step, the performance level parameters are updated by finding the parameters that maximize the expected value of the conditional log-likelihood function (i.e., using the results of the previous E-step). This iterative process is then repeated until the algorithm converges (i.e., until the estimated performance level parameters cease to change beyond a pre-defined threshold).

Nevertheless, despite elegant theory and success on human raters, applications of the statistical fusion framework to the multiatlas context has proven problematic [6]. In response, a myriad of advancements to the statistical fusion framework have been proposed to account for (1) spatially varying task difficulty [96,7], (2) spatially varying rater performance [6,8,30,122], (3) instabilities in the rater performance level parameters [69,29], and (4) models of hierarchical performance estimation [11]. While these advancements have been shown to dramatically improve segmentation accuracy, they still fail to incorporate useful intensity information that is critical for accurately modeling multiatlas segmentation behavior. As a result, alternative techniques that utilize intensity information have been proposed that account for (1) imperfect registration correspondence [9,53] and (2) ad hoc extensions that ignore voxels based upon a priori similarity measures [22,122,23] have been considered. Statistical fusion strategies represent a fascinating framework for estimating the underlying segmentation while simultaneously incorporating a model of registered atlas observation behavior. This theoretical consistency makes statistical fusion significantly more attractive than ad hoc voting-based approaches.

Given the target image, the registered atlas information and a priori label probabilities, the statistical fusion process estimates the final segmentation through an Expectation Maximization (EM) estimation process. The E- and M-steps of the EM framework are iterated until convergence of the algorithm. Lastly, given the final estimate the label probabilities, the fused segmentation is constructed by taking the maximum likelihood label at each voxel.

6.2.5.3 Bayesian / generative models

Statistical label fusion is one type of the generative model that is based on maximum likelihood estimation (MLE) by iteratively performing EM algorithm. Another perspective of performing multiatlas label fusion using the generative model is to maximize the posterior probability of labels using Bayesian inference [99]. The Bayesian inference model has been successfully applied to multimodal label fusion without assuming the relation between the intensities of atlases and the testing images [58].

6.2.6 Post hoc analysis

Several techniques have been considered for performing a postprocessing refinement of the estimated segmentation in order to improve the segmentation accuracy. While many errors in a multiatlas segmentation context can be corrected through more efficient modeling of the atlas observation behavior, there exists a different type of error in which consistent mistakes are to be expected due to (1) inconsistencies in the expected labels, and (2) pathological/morphological differences that are not present on the atlases. As a result, postprocessing refinement techniques have been considered that attempt to account for these types of errors.

6.2.6.1 Corrective learning

Machine learning techniques that construct classifiers (e.g., via AdaBoost) for correcting consistent segmentation errors are becoming increasingly popular in the segmentation literature [118,125]. These types of "wrapper" methods have been shown to provide the consistent improvement in segmentation accuracy; however, determining optimal techniques for feature selection criteria and initializing model parameters represent fascinating areas of continuing research.

6.2.6.2 EM-refinement

Another type of postprocessing refinement is to perform a metaanalysis framework in order to enforce desired constraints (i.e., consistency with the training data). For instance, the idea of applying the intensity-driven EM segmentation after a multiatlas segmentation is becoming increasingly popular [77,72]. However, this type of formulation is limited to scenarios where the intensity characteristics between the desired anatomical structures can be probabilistically separated. For example, in multiorgan abdomen segmentation, many of the desired organs have identical, or nearly identical, intensity characteristics on CT. As a result, EM refinement techniques are often unable to discover distributions that uniquely identify the individual organs, and the approach would rely on extremely accurate a priori structural context.

6.2.6.3 Markov Random Field (MRF)

Building upon the random field theory in imaging statistics [18], Markov Random Fields (MRFs) provide a mechanism for enforcing spatial consistency across images. In general, the idea behind MRF integration is to regularize the a priori distribution by simultaneously taking into account the previous estimate of the segmentation and the relationships between the neighboring voxels. Through careful design of the neighborhood (or clique) structure, MRFs provide a theoretically sound procedure for incorporating the complex interactions between voxels in an image. Particularly, for early intensity based segmentation algorithms, MRFs played in critical role in increasing the accuracy and consistency of the underlying segmentations [129,50]. For multiatlas segmentation, spatial consistency is typically maintained due to the smoothness constraints of typical registration algorithms. As a result, although MRFs have been shown to provide accuracy improvements for multiatlas segmentation [121], the observed improvement is typically minimal.

6.2.6.4 Morphology correction

Mathematical morphology is essential in regularizing the geometrical and anatomical structures of segmentation results [52,55]. For example, if we know that the segmenting organ has particular anatomical features (e.g., one-connected, convex, smooth, etc.) from prior knowledge, we could provide the several shift–invariant basic operations (e.g., open, close, erosion, dilation, etc.) to regularize the geometrical structures of segmentation. The morphological filters (e.g., a disk, square, diamond, etc., shape kernels) are typically required to perform the corresponding morphological operations.

6.3. Mathematical framework

Given the target image and the registered atlas information (consisting of both intensities and labels) label fusion attempts to estimate the underlying segmentation. This section provides a common mathematical framework to explain each of the methods. The derivation closely follows Spatial STAPLE [8] and NLS [9] that use an Expectation Maximization (EM) framework [37,84]. The notation follows STAPLE [121] throughout this chapter.

6.3.1 Problem definition

A target gray-level image with N voxels is represented as a one-dimensional vector $I \in \mathbb{R}^{N \times 1}$. Given L labels, let $T \in \{0, \ldots, L-1\}^{N \times 1}$ be the corresponding latent true segmentation to I. Since T is unknown, the goal is to estimate T using R atlases (raters) with their intensity values $A \in \mathbb{R}^{N \times R}$ and label decisions $D \in \{0, \ldots, L-1\}^{N \times R}$. For convenience, we denote true label at voxel i ($1 \le i \le N$) by $T_i \in \{0, \ldots, L-1\}$ in the remainder of this chapter.

The goal of any label fusion framework is to accurately estimate the following probability density function:

$$W_{si} = f(T_i = s | I, A, D), \tag{6.1}$$

where W_{si} can be directly interpreted as the probability that the true label at voxel i is equal to label s given the provided contextual information. Using a standard Bayesian expansion, Eq. (6.1) can be rewritten by

$$W_{si} = \frac{f(T_i = s)f(D, A|T_i = s, I)}{\sum_n f(T_i = n)f(D, A|T_i = n, I)}, \tag{6.2}$$

where $f(T_i = s)$ represents the prior distribution governing the underlying segmentation and represents distribution governing the relationships between the observed atlas information and the latent target segmentation. Lastly, one of the most common assumptions in the label fusion literature [99] is that the observed atlas labels and the observed atlas intensities are conditionally independent resulting in

$$W_{si} = \frac{f(T_i = s)f(D|T_i = s)f(A|I)}{\sum_n f(T_i = n)f(D|T_i = n)f(A|I)}. \tag{6.3}$$

While this might seem like it neglects the complex relationships between labels and intensity, the common assumption is that the information gained by direct incorporation of the target/atlas intensity relationships accurately approximates these complex relationships through the assumed conditional independence. With that said, further investigation into estimating the target label probabilities, using joint models of atlas performance is an active area of continuing research [119,120].

   Using this general framework, there are two primary fields-of-thought within the label fusion community. First, voting label fusion attempts to find optimal weights in order to determine which atlases are optimally representative in terms of some local/semilocal/global metric. Nevertheless, these techniques are primarily ad hoc and lack a consistent theoretical underpinning. In stark contrast, statistical fusion techniques attempt to model atlas performance using a statistically driven rater performance model. Significantly more detail on these two approaches is provided in the following sections.

6.3.2 Voting label fusion

The simplest way to perform label fusion is to utilize a voting-based framework. In voting label fusion there are generally two primary assumptions (1) the prior distribution is unnecessary as all of the registered atlases provide accurate and consistent spatial information (i.e., $f(T_i = s) = 1/L$) and (2) the model probability density functions can be approximated using Parzen's window density approach. As a result, a general voting-based fusion approach would simplify to

$$W_{si} = \frac{\sum_j f(D_{ij}|T_i = s)f(A_j|I)}{\sum_n \sum_j f(D_{ij}|T_i = n)f(A_j|I)}. \tag{6.4}$$

Perhaps surprisingly, a majority vote, the simplest voting-based fusion strategy, has been consistently shown to result in highly robust and accurate segmentations [96,48,2]. In a majority vote, all atlases are weighted equally and result in Eq. (6.4) simplifies to

$$W_{si} = \frac{\sum_j \delta(D_{ij}, s)}{\sum_n \sum_j \delta(D_{ij}, n)},\tag{6.5}$$

where $\delta(\cdot, \cdot)$ is the Kronecker delta function. More recently weighted voting strategies that use global [4,25], local [59,99,119], semilocal [99,120], and nonlocal [31] intensity similarity metrics have demonstrated consistent improvement in segmentation accuracy. Regardless of the type of weight, however, weighted voting strategies can typically be simplified to be of the general form:

$$\begin{aligned}W_{si} &= \frac{\sum_j \delta(D_{ij}, s)f(A_j|I)}{\sum_n \sum_j \delta(D_{ij}, n)f(A_j|I)}\\ &= \frac{\sum_j w_{ij}\delta(D_{ij}, s)}{\sum_n \sum_j w_{ij}\delta(D_{ij}, n)},\end{aligned}\tag{6.6}$$

where w_{ij} is simply a weighting function governing the likelihood that the correct answer at voxel i is obtained from atlas. Note that there are many ways to estimate these weighting functions (e.g., Gaussian intensity differences [59,99,120], correlation coefficients [4], or mutual information [4]). For example, one of the more common weighting schemes is to use a Gaussian distribution to model the intensity differences between the target and the atlas images. Particularly for high resolution MR images of the brain, using a strict intensity difference framework has been shown to be more accurate than many of the alternative weighting schemes [4]. Using a Gaussian distribution governing the intensity difference the weighting scheme could be constructed by

$$w_{ij} = \frac{1}{Z_w} \exp\left(-\frac{(A_{ij} - I_i)^2}{2\sigma^2}\right),\tag{6.7}$$

where σ is a standard deviation parameter for the Gaussian distribution. Nevertheless, regardless of the weighting metric, the general weighted voting fusion framework remains essentially identical. With that said, additional investigation into the optimal weighting metric for a given application remains an open problem.

6.3.3 Statistical label fusion

In stark contrast to ad hoc voting, statistical fusion strategies (e.g., Simultaneous Truth and Performance Level Estimation, STAPLE) directly integrate a stochastic model of rater behavior into the estimation process. In STAPLE family of approaches, the label fusion problem is regarded as a probabilistic estimation of hidden true segmentation based on the performance of multiple atlases. For atlas j ($1 \le j \le R$), we define the performance parameter $\theta_{js's}$ that indicates the probability of the observed label s' given that s is the true label. The performance parameters can be written as a matrix form $\theta \in [0, 1]^{R \times L \times L}$. In brief, unlike voting-based label fusion frameworks, statistical fusion attempts to simultaneously estimate both (1) the underlying segmentation probabilities and (2) the rater performance level parameters θ.

If both D and T are known, θ is solvable via maximum likelihood estimation (MLE) from the complete log-likelihood function:

$$\hat{\theta} = \arg\max_{\theta} \ln f(D, T|\theta), \tag{6.8}$$

where $f(D, T|\theta)$ is a probability mass function. Since T is unavailable, $f(D, T|\theta)$ cannot be solved analytically. This can be instead formulated by a conditional probability density function of true labels given D and θ. In this sense, the performance parameters are estimated via an Expectation and Maximization (EM) framework to maximize the following incomplete log-likelihood function:

$$\hat{\theta} = \arg\max_{\theta} \ln f(D|\theta). \tag{6.9}$$

In the E-step at the kth iteration, the weight variables $W_{s.}^{(k)} \in [0, 1]^{L \times N}$ are estimated from the performance parameters $\theta^{(k)}$. More precisely, $W_{si}^{(k)}$ encodes the probability of the latent true label at voxel i, i.e., $W_{si}^{(k)} = f(T_i = s|D, \theta^{(k)})$. We assume statistically conditional independence between atlases. Hence, by Bayes' rule, $W_{si}^{(k)}$ is expanded as follows:

$$W_{si}^{(k)} = \frac{f(T_i = s) \prod_j f(D_{ij} = s'|T_i = s, \theta_j^{(k)})}{\sum_n f(T_i = n) \prod_j f(D_{ij} = s'|T_i = n, \theta_j^{(k)})}, \tag{6.10}$$

where $f(T_i = s)$ is a prior of true segmentation. The denominator is a normalizing constant that forces $\sum_s W_{si}^{(k)} = 1$. Using $\theta_{js's}^{(k)}$, Eq. (6.10) has a simplified form

$$W_{si}^{(k)} = \frac{f(T_i = s) \prod_j \theta_{js's}^{(k)}}{\sum_n f(T_i = n) \prod_j \theta_{js'n}^{(k)}}. \tag{6.11}$$

In the M-step, we maximize the performance parameters at the $(k + 1)$th iteration:

$$\theta_j^{(k+1)} = \arg\max_{\theta_j} \sum_i E[\ln f(D_{ij}|T_i, \theta_j)|D, \theta_j^{(k)}]. \tag{6.12}$$

This is efficiently solved by

$$\theta_{js's}^{(k+1)} = \frac{\sum_{i:D_{ij}=s'} W_{si}^{(k)}}{\sum_i W_{si}^{(k)}}. \tag{6.13}$$

This process iteratively solves for the true data likelihood in the E-Step and updates the performance parameters in the M-Step.

6.3.4 Spatially varying performance and nonlocal STAPLE

The global performance parameters might not completely fit to the entire images. In recent years, several methods have been proposed to improve the performance as extensions of STAPLE such as Spatial STAPLE [8] and Nonlocal STAPLE (NLS) [9]. The main idea is to estimate locally defined performance rather than global parameters.

6.3.5 Spatial STAPLE

Spatial STAPLE reformats the global performance matrix $\theta_{js's}$ into a voxelwise form $\theta_{jis's} \in [0, 1]^{R \times N \times L \times L}$ that measures the performance of atlas j at voxel i, where $\theta_{jis's} = f(D_{ij} = s' | T_i = s, \theta_{ji})$. Given s' and s, we have

$$
\theta_{s's} = \begin{bmatrix}
\theta_{11s's} & \theta_{21s's} & \cdots & \theta_{R1s's} \\
\theta_{12s's} & \theta_{22s's} & \cdots & \theta_{R1s's} \\
\vdots & \vdots & \ddots & \vdots \\
\theta_{1Ns's} & \theta_{2Ns's} & \cdots & \theta_{RNs's}
\end{bmatrix}.
\tag{6.14}
$$

This assumes that the rating performance of each atlas is spatially varying on different parts of images. In this way, atlases more naturally estimate voxel–wise parameters than traditional global performance [8]. Specifically, Spatial STALE updates the weight variables W in the E-step by modifying Eq. (6.10):

$$
W_{si}^{(k)} = \frac{f(T_i = s) \prod_j \theta_{jis's}^{(k)}}{\sum_n f(T_i = n) \prod_j \theta_{jis'n}^{(k)}}.
\tag{6.15}
$$

The M-step follows the derivation of STAPLE. However, since the degrees of freedom increase by a factor of N, two extra steps are necessary to account for the increased complexity. First, the performance parameters are binned over small pooling regions instead of a strictly voxel-wise derivation. As discussed in [8], this can be addressed by defining spatial pooling regions B. Second, the performance is augmented by a nonparametric prior $\theta_j^{(0)}$ on the performance [8,68]. This augmentation improves the stability of the performance parameters. Thus the M-Step is given by

$$
\theta_{jis's}^{(k+1)} = \frac{\lambda_{ijs'} \theta_{js's}^{(0)} + \sum_{i' \in B_i : D_{i'j} = s'} W_{si'}^{(k)}}{\lambda_{ijs'} \sum_s \theta_{js's}^{(0)} + \sum_{i' \in B_i} W_{si'}^{(k)}},
\tag{6.16}
$$

where $\sum_{s'} \theta_{jis's} = 1$, and $\lambda_{ijs'}$ is a weighting parameter determined by the size of B. This balances the prior and the updated probability. We derive $\lambda_{ijs'}$ using the same definition in [8].

6.3.6 Nonlocal STAPLE

NLS modifies the performance by integrating intensity into the estimation process. Unlike STAPLE that only uses label information, NLS employs intensity of atlas images A and target image I into the STAPLE framework using a patch-based nonlocal correspondence manner [9]. Patch-based nonlocal correspondence was initially introduced to account for registration inaccuracy. NLS incorporates patch-based nonlocal correspondence into the STAPLE framework as follows. In the E-Step, the weight variables W is updated by

$$W_{si}^{(k)} = \frac{f(T_i = s) \prod_j \sum_{i' \in N(i)} \theta_{jis's}^{(k)} \alpha_{ji'i}}{\sum_n f(T_i = n) \prod_j \sum_{i' \in N(i)} \theta_{jis'n}^{(k)} \alpha_{ji'i}}, \tag{6.17}$$

where $N(i)$ is a search neighborhood around voxel i and $\alpha_{ji'i}$ is the nonlocal weighting between voxel i in the target image at voxel i' on the jth atlas within the search parameter $N(i)$,

$$\alpha_{ji'i} = \frac{1}{Z_\alpha} \exp\left(-\frac{\|\mathcal{G}(A_{i'j}) - \mathcal{G}(I_i)\|_2^2}{2\sigma_i^2}\right) \exp\left(-\frac{\mathcal{E}_{i'i}^2}{2\sigma_d^2}\right), \tag{6.18}$$

where $\mathcal{G}(\cdot)$ is the set of intensities within its patch neighborhood; σ_i and σ_d are the standard deviations of the intensity and distance weights, respectively; $\mathcal{E}_{i'i}$ is the canonical Euclidean distance in the physical space between voxels i and i'. Lastly, Z_α is a normalizing constant to ensure

$$\sum_{i' \in N(i)} \alpha_{ji'i} = 1, \tag{6.19}$$

where $\alpha_{ji'i}$ can be interpreted as the probability of nonlocal correspondence both taking the intensity similarity and spatial distance into account. In the M-step, the performance parameters θ are updated by

$$\theta_{jis's}^{(k+1)} = \frac{\sum_i \left(\sum_{i' \in N(i): D_{i'j}=s'} \alpha_{ji'i}\right) W_{si}^{(k)}}{\sum_i W_{si}^{(k)}}. \tag{6.20}$$

This essentially follows the original M-Step of STAPLE while allowing nonlocal correspondence.

6.3.7 Nonlocal spatial STAPLE

The Nonlocal Spatial STAPLE (NLSS) algorithm incorporates both Spatial STAPLE and Nonlocal STAPLE. The NLSS algorithm defines the following performance level function:

$$f(D_{i'j} = s', A_j | T_i = s, I_i, \theta_{jis's}), \tag{6.21}$$

where i' is the voxel on atlas j that corresponds to target voxel i. Unfortunately, such a correspondence is unknown. However, this can be approximated by calculating the expectation in the search neighborhood with the assumption that the intensities and labels are conditional independent. From Eq. (6.18), we have

$$
\begin{aligned}
f(D_{i'j} = s', A_j | T_i = s, I_i, \theta_{jis's}) &\approx E[f(D_j, A_j | T_i = s, I_i, \theta_{jis})] \\
&= E[f(D_j | T_i = s, \theta_{jis}) f(A_j I_i)] \\
&= \sum_{i' \in N(i)} f(D_{i'j} = s' | T_i = s, \theta_{jis's}) f(A_j I_i) \\
&= \sum_{i' \in N(i)} \theta_{jis's} \alpha_{ji'i}.
\end{aligned}
\tag{6.22}
$$

The EM framework is then used to iteratively solve W and θ.

6.3.8 E-step: estimation of the voxel-wise label probability

In the E-step of NLSS, the weight variable $W \in R^{L \times N}$ is given by

$$
W_{si}^{(k)} = f(T_i = s | D, A, I, \theta_i^{(k)}).
\tag{6.23}
$$

This is the conditional probability of the true label of voxel i is label s at the kth iteration. By Bayes' rule with the assumption of conditional independence of observations, $W_{si}^{(k)}$ can be rewritten by

$$
W_{si}^{(k)} = \frac{f(T_i = s) \prod_j f(D_{i'j} = s', A_j | T_i = s, I_i, \theta_{jis's}^{(k)})}{\sum_n f(T_i = n) \prod_j f(D_{i'j} = s', A_j | T_i = n, I_i, \theta_{jis'n}^{(k)})},
\tag{6.24}
$$

where $f(T_i = s)$ is a prior of true segmentation. We incorporate the spatially varying performance parameters derived in Spatial STAPLE and the nonlocal correspondence derived in Nonlocal STAPLE. This yields

$$
W_{si}^{(k)} = \frac{f(T_i = s) \prod_j \sum_{i' \in N(i)} \theta_{jis's}^{(k)} \alpha_{ji'i}}{\sum_n f(T_i = n) \prod_j \sum_{i' \in N(i)} \theta_{jis'n}^{(k)} \alpha_{ji'i}}.
\tag{6.25}
$$

6.3.9 M-step: estimation of the performance level parameters

In the M-step of NLSS, the previously calculated $W_{si}^{(k)}$ is used to update $\theta_{ji}^{(k+1)}$ by maximizing the expectation of the log–likelihood function as

$$
\begin{aligned}
\theta_{ji}^{(k+1)} &= \arg\max_{\theta_{ji}} \sum_{i' \in B_i} E[\ln f(D_{i'j}, A_j | T_{i'}, I_{i'}, \theta_{jis's}^{(k)}) | D, A, I, \theta^{(k)}] \\
&= \arg\max_{\theta_{ji}} \sum_{i' \in B_i} \sum_s W_{si'}^{(k)} \ln f(D_{i'j}, A_j | T_{i'} = s, I_{i'}, \theta_{jis's}^{(k)}) \\
&= \arg\max_{\theta_{ji}} \sum_{s'} \sum_{i' \in B_i} \sum_s W_{si'}^{(k)} \ln f(D_{i'j} = s', A_j | T_{i'} = s, I_{i'}, \theta_{jis's}^{(k)}) \qquad (6.26) \\
&= \arg\max_{\theta_{ji}} \sum_{i' \in B_i} \sum_s W_{si'}^{(k)} \ln \left(\sum_{i'' \in N(i'): D_{i''j}=s'} \theta_{jis's} \alpha_{ji''i'} \right).
\end{aligned}
$$

Using a Lagrange multiplier λ with a constraint $\sum_{s'} \theta_{jis's} = 1$, the problem becomes a constrained optimization

$$
\begin{aligned}
0 &= \frac{\partial}{\partial \theta_{jin'n}} \left[\sum_{i' \in B_i} \sum_s W_{si'}^{(k)} \ln \left(\sum_{i'' \in N(i'): D_{i''j}=s'} \theta_{jis's} \alpha_{ji''i'} \right) + \lambda \sum_{s'} \theta_{jis's}^{(k+1)} \right] \\
&= \frac{\sum_{i' \in B_i} W_{ni'}^{(k)} \frac{\partial}{\partial \theta_{jin'n}} \left[\sum_s \sum_{i'' \in N(i'): D_{i''j}=s'} \theta_{jis's} \alpha_{ji''i'} \right]}{\theta_{jin'n}} + \lambda \qquad (6.27) \\
&= \frac{\sum_{i' \in B_i} W_{ni'}^{(k)} \left(\sum_{i'' \in N(i'): D_{i''j}=n'} \alpha_{ji''i'} \right)}{\theta_{jin'n}} + \lambda.
\end{aligned}
$$

We have

$$
\theta_{jin'n} = \frac{\sum_{i' \in B_i} W_{ni'}^{(k)} \left(\sum_{i'' \in N(i'): D_{i''j}=n'} \alpha_{ji''i'} \right)}{-\lambda}. \qquad (6.28)
$$

Finally, the final solution is obtained by eliminating λ:

$$
\theta_{jis's}^{(k+1)} = \frac{\sum_{i' \in B_i} \left(\sum_{i'' \in N(i'): D_{i''j}=s'} \alpha_{ji''i'} \right) W_{si'}^{(k)}}{\sum_{i' \in B_i} W_{si'}^{(k)}}. \qquad (6.29)
$$

Like Spatial STAPLE, the same whole-image implicit prior $\theta_{jis's}^{(0)}$ is introduced for computational and stability concerns [8] number of approaches (e.g., STAPLE [121], majority vote, locally weighted vote [99], etc.). In the NLSS implementation, the majority vote without consensus voxels is employed as default [95]. Then, the final stable version of Eq. (6.29) is reformulated to

$$
\theta_{jis's}^{(k+1)} = \frac{\lambda_{ijs'}\theta_{js's}^{(0)} + \sum_{i' \in B_i} \left(\sum_{i'' \in N(i'):D_{i''j}=s'} \alpha_{ji''i'} \right) W_{si'}^{(k)}}{\lambda_{ijs'} \sum_s \theta_{js's}^{(0)} + \sum_{i' \in B_i} W_{si'}^{(k)}},
\tag{6.30}
$$

where $\lambda_{ijs'}$ is a weighting parameter which depends on the size of pooling region B_i, which balances the prior and the updated probability. We derive $\lambda_{ijs'}$ and B_i using the same way as in [8].

Notice that Eq. (6.29) is the theoretical expression of the M-step in the EM framework while Eq. (6.30) is an approximation for computational stability. The implementations of both cases have been provided in the publicly available open-source code, which enables the users to switch between each other by controlling $\lambda_{ijs'}$. In practice, Eq. (6.30) typically provides better performance than Eq. (6.29).

6.4. Connection between multiatlas segmentation and machine learning

A key similarity between multiatlas segmentation and machine learning is that the segmentation is a learning procedure using training data.

6.5. Multiatlas segmentation using machine learning

Machine learning techniques have been widely used in the multiatlas segmentation to leverage the segmentation accuracy and efficiency. The major purposes of preprocessing, atlas selection and post hoc analyses in multiatlas segmentation pipeline are to leverage the segmentation performance by (1) learning extra information from the atlases and target image, and (2) applying the prelearned knowledge from other resources. In preprocessing, the machine learning based label propagation can be used to replace the standard nearest neighbor interpolation. In atlas selection, the key step is to learn the similarity between atlases and the target image. As a result, prevalent feature extraction [130,126], manifold learning [123,12], and clustering [120] machine learning techniques have been widely used in atlas selection. In post hoc analyses, prior knowledge [118,125], spatial correspondence [129,50], and topological relationship [52,55] have typically considered to further refine the segmentation results. To achieve this aim, the corrective machine learning, random fields, and morphological correction have been broadly applied to ad hoc analyses.

6.6. Machine learning using multiatlas segmentation

In machine learning, boosting learning [102] has been regarded as one of the most successful learning strategies. Multiatlas segmentation contributes a new boosting learning strategy for machine learning community [41]. Meanwhile, the multiatlas segmentation is able to perform reasonable segmentation with limited number of atlases (e.g., less than 50 atlases), which is valuable in medical imaging community as the atlases are expensive commodity. Previous studies generate auxiliary labels on thousands of previously unlabeled images by performing multiatlas, which leverage the segmentation performance by using large-scale medical images [56,97].

6.7. Integrating multiatlas segmentation and machine learning

In recent years, one of the most significant innovations in machine learning is deep learning. Deep convolutional neural networks (CNN) have become a hot field in medical image segmentation. The key differences between CNN and other deep convolutional neural networks (DNN) are that the hierarchical patch-based convolution operations are used in CNN, which not only reduces computational cost, but abstracts images on different feature levels. Since the patch-based learning is the core operations for both CNN and multiatlas segmentation. It is natural to integrate multiatlas segmentation with deep learning. As a result, significant efforts have been made to proposed label fusion based CNN/DNN networks to leveraging the segmentation performance [127].

6.8. Challenges and applications

Variation in normal brain anatomy represents a microcosm of the anatomical variation which we need to address in segmentation more generally. Cranial and subcortical structures tend to be highly regular and can be reliably matched with limited deformation models, while cortical, vascular, muscular, soft tissue, and peripheral nerve courses exhibit a much higher degree of variability. In neuroscience, both the volumes and shapes of cerebral structures have been shown to be correlated with pathology and function. Hence, the clinical question dictates which aspects of correspondence are "interesting." In the body, skeletal anatomy is much more regular than organ or soft tissue structure. As with the pioneering efforts in brain atlasing, other communities have sought to establish robust, but approximate homologies throughout the body.

A central challenge of the effort to synthesize an atlas of in vivo, whole-body, adult anatomical variability will be to define appropriate homologies in a representative and meaningful context. In particular, we recognize the specific challenges in establishing homologies between (1) differing imaging perspectives of the same anatomy (i.e., intermodality correspondence), (2) differing positional and temporal anatomical conditions (i.e., intraindividual correspondence), (3) local images and whole-body structure (e.g., part-to-whole correspondence), (4) the same anatomy of different individuals (i.e., interindividual correspondence), (5) in vivo/postmortem correspondence, and (6) extreme imaging conditions, acquisitions, and hardware (i.e., robust imaging correspondence). These fundamental issues have not been addressed in a unified framework for body atlasing.

6.8.1 Multiatlas labeling on cortical surfaces and sulcal landmarks

The sulcal and gyral folding patterns are principle landmarks of a human cerebral cortex. These are related to brain functions and the organization of functional regions [40,45]. They have played key roles in many neuroimaging applications particularly in discovering cortical morphometry: brain development and degeneration [21,40,113,39,64,79] and shape variability [112,76,42,35,34]. In this sense, consistent labeling (parcellation) of cortical region of interests is key in cortical morphometry. However, a main challenge has arisen from the nature of the cortical folding patterns with its highly complex and variable shapes.

3D cortical regional parcellation is the most popular way in cortical morphometry [116,111,74,75,110]. Akin to image volume segmentation, a cortex can be subdivided into multiple local regions. Sandor and Leahy [100] used a manually labeled brain atlas. In this context, an atlas encodes neuroanatomical labeling conventions determined by knowledge on structure–function relationships and cytoarchitectronic or receptor labeling properties of regions. This approach warps the atlas to an individual subject's cortical surface to transfer the labels of cortical features from the atlas. In [74,93], watershed approach was used to segment regions, and then they are manually labeled by an expert. Later Fischl et al. [44] proposed cortical parcellation by maximizing likelihood that combines prior neuroanatomical information and cortical geometry.

In sulcal specific region detection, labeling process can be applied on automatically extracted sulcal curves (sulcal fundi) [62,105,104,73,80]. A graph-based approach was proposed in [71,82], where sulci and their relations are represented by nodes and edges. The detected sulci were labeled based on a training set. This approach was further extended to detection of major cortical sulci. Joint sulcal shape priors between neighboring sulci were used in the learning process [106]. General learning-based techniques were also proposed in [94,16,114,88]. Unlike learning techniques, sulcal curves were labeled by finding the similar curve shapes in atlases [78] via majority vote.

6.9. Unsolved problems

Despite its maturity and widespread use, multi-atlas segmentation is not a solved problem patiently awaiting tinkering for particular medical imaging applications. There are core theoretical problems that remain unsolved and present interesting avenues of contemplation:

How many atlases are enough? The general rule of thumb is that 30 seems to be enough. Perhaps not surprisingly, this wisdom of the crowd conveniently matches the approximate number of atlases that were publicly available in well-known grand challenges [68]. The number of required atlases is typically assessed via bootstrapping, and bootstrapping techniques for variance estimation are biased towards zero as the number samples approach the available population. A previous work with nearly 200 atlases [91] has shown continuous (but diminishing) improvement using well beyond 100 atlases. Improving our statistical procedures for variance estimation and reconciling statistically significant improvements versus clinically meaningful ones would be of substantial benefit for clinical translation of atlas-based methods.

Is it possible to generate reliable estimates of segmentation confidence? Statistical fusion approaches that estimate a rater performance model naturally yield confidence estimates, and voting based approaches can be assessed with atlas variance. Yet, when internal metrics of confidence are compared with withheld validation sets, the estimated accuracies tend to be exceedingly optimistic. One possible explanation is that the covariance structure between atlases is not currently well-modeled. While JLF [120] moves in this direction, the field has not been well explored from the perspective of accurate performance estimation.

When manual segmentation resources are available, which dataset should be included next? A related question is "Given the ability to label *n* atlases, which subset of images should be chosen?" The intuition behind atlas curation is that interpolation of labels to new targets that lie within an anatomical manifold is efficient, but extrapolation outside of the sampled areas is difficult. Hence, atlases should be chosen to *reasonably* sample the space of interest. Despite widespread empirical success with multiatlas methods, little traction has been found at creating a portable (nonapplication specific) definition of manifolds that leads to an efficient sampling procedure. Advancements that lead to systematic construction of data that underly the analysis approach (as opposed to samples of convenience) could lead to greater opportunities for generalization and clinical translation.

How can unexpected images or unexpected findings be handled? Consider an extreme case in which a set of atlases are of brains, while a target image contains a foot. Multiatlas segmentation approaches will find the most likely location of a brain in the foot. While the out-of-atlas framework [10] could be used to identify areas of anomalies, no standard multiatlas labeling pipeline would currently report anything out of the ordinary and quality assurance/quality control has not hitherto been considered a problem integral to segmentation theory. As automated image processing in radiology becomes necessary and algorithms experience the gestalt to clinical imaging (as opposed the comfort of well-controlled research data), we will need to find new ways to allow our algorithms to fail gracefully.

Glossary

JLF	joint label fusion
MAL	multiatlas labeling
STAPLE	simultaneous truth and performance level estimation

References

[1] P. Aljabar, R. Heckemann, A. Hammers, J.V. Hajnal, D. Rueckert, Classifier selection strategies for label fusion using large atlas databases, in: International Conference on Medical Image Computing and Computer-Assisted Intervention, Springer, 2007, pp. 523–531.

[2] P. Aljabar, R.A. Heckemann, A. Hammers, J.V. Hajnal, D. Rueckert, Multi-atlas based segmentation of brain images: atlas selection and its effect on accuracy, NeuroImage 46 (3) (2009) 726–738.

[3] B.S. Aribisala, S.R. Cox, K.J. Ferguson, S.E. MacPherson, A.M. MacLullich, N.A. Royle, M.V. Hernández, M.E. Bastin, I.J. Deary, J.M. Wardlaw, Assessing the performance of atlas-based prefrontal brain parcellation in an ageing cohort, Journal of Computer Assisted Tomography 37 (2) (2013).

[4] X. Artaechevarria, A. Munoz-Barrutia, C. Ortiz-de Solórzano, Combination strategies in multi-atlas image segmentation: application to brain MR data, IEEE Transactions on Medical Imaging 28 (8) (2009) 1266–1277.

[5] J. Ashburner, K.J. Friston, Unified segmentation, NeuroImage 26 (3) (2005) 839–851.

[6] A.J. Asman, B.A. Landman, Characterizing spatially varying performance to improve multi-atlas multi-label segmentation, in: Biennial International Conference on Information Processing in Medical Imaging, Springer, 2011, pp. 85–96.

[7] A.J. Asman, B.A. Landman, Robust statistical label fusion through consensus level, labeler accuracy, and truth estimation (collate), IEEE Transactions on Medical Imaging 30 (10) (2011) 1779–1794.

[8] A.J. Asman, B.A. Landman, Formulating spatially varying performance in the statistical fusion framework, IEEE Transactions on Medical Imaging 31 (6) (2012) 1326–1336.

[9] A.J. Asman, B.A. Landman, Non-local statistical label fusion for multi-atlas segmentation, Medical Image Analysis 17 (2) (2013) 194–208.

[10] A.J. Asman, L.B. Chambless, R.C. Thompson, B.A. Landman, Out-of-atlas likelihood estimation using multi-atlas segmentation, Medical Physics 40 (4) (2013).

[11] A.J. Asman, A.S. Dagley, B.A. Landman, Statistical label fusion with hierarchical performance models, in: Medical Imaging 2014: Image Processing, in: Proc. SPIE, vol. 9034, International Society for Optics and Photonics, 2014, p. 90341E.

[12] A.J. Asman, Y. Huo, A.J. Plassard, B.A. Landman, Multi-atlas learner fusion: an efficient segmentation approach for large-scale data, Medical Image Analysis 26 (1) (2015) 82–91.

[13] H.M. Atta Edwin, Smith surgical papyrus: the oldest known surgical treatise, The American Surgeon 65 (12) (1999) 1190.

[14] B.B. Avants, C.L. Epstein, M. Grossman, J.C. Gee, Symmetric diffeomorphic image registration with cross-correlation: evaluating automated labeling of elderly and neurodegenerative brain, Medical Image Analysis 12 (1) (2008) 26–41.

[15] S.P. Awate, R.T. Whitaker, Multiatlas segmentation as nonparametric regression, IEEE Transactions on Medical Imaging 33 (9) (2014) 1803–1817.

[16] K.J. Behnke, M.E. Rettmann, D.L. Pham, D. Shen, S.M. Resnick, C. Davatzikos, J.L. Prince, Automatic classification of sulcal regions of the human brain cortex using pattern recognition, in: Medical Imaging 2003, International Society for Optics and Photonics, 2003, pp. 1499–1510.

[17] J.-P. Bergeest, F. Jäger, A comparison of five methods for signal intensity standardization in MRI, in: Bildverarbeitung für die Medizin 2008, Springer, 2008, pp. 36–40.

[18] J. Besag, On the statistical analysis of dirty pictures, Journal of the Royal Statistical Society, Series B, Methodological (1986) 259–302.

[19] J.A. Bogovic, B. Jedynak, R. Rigg, A. Du, B.A. Landman, J.L. Prince, S.H. Ying, Approaching expert results using a hierarchical cerebellum parcellation protocol for multiple inexpert human raters, NeuroImage 64 (2013) 616–629.

[20] K. Brodmann, Beiträge zur histologischen Lokalisation der Grosshirnrinde, 1908.

[21] A. Cachia, M.-L. Paillère-Martinot, A. Galinowski, D. Januel, R. de Beaurepaire, F. Bellivier, E. Artiges, J. Andoh, D. Bartrés-Faz, E. Duchesnay, et al., Cortical folding abnormalities in schizophrenia patients with resistant auditory hallucinations, NeuroImage 39 (3) (2008) 927–935.

[22] M. Cardoso, K. Leung, M. Modat, J. Barnes, S. Ourselin, Locally ranked staple for template based segmentation propagation, 2011.

[23] M.J. Cardoso, K. Leung, M. Modat, S. Keihaninejad, D. Cash, J. Barnes, N.C. Fox, S. Ourselin, STEPS: similarity and truth estimation for propagated segmentations and its application to hippocampal segmentation and brain parcelation, Medical Image Analysis 17 (6) (2013) 671–684.

[24] M.M. Chakravarty, P. Steadman, M.C. Eede, R.D. Calcott, V. Gu, P. Shaw, A. Raznahan, D.L. Collins, J.P. Lerch, Performing label-fusion-based segmentation using multiple automatically generated templates, Human Brain Mapping 34 (10) (2013) 2635–2654.

[25] A. Chen, K.J. Niermann, M.A. Deeley, B.M. Dawant, Evaluation of multi atlas-based approaches for the segmentation of the thyroid gland in IMRT head-and-neck CT images, in: Medical Imaging 2011: Image Processing, in: Proc. SPIE, vol. 7962, International Society for Optics and Photonics, 2011, p. 796224.

[26] D.L. Collins, P. Neelin, T.M. Peters, A.C. Evans, Automatic 3D intersubject registration of MR volumetric data in standardized Talairach space, Journal of Computer Assisted Tomography 18 (2) (1994) 192–205.

[27] D.L. Collins, C.J. Holmes, T.M. Peters, A.C. Evans, Automatic 3-d model-based neuroanatomical segmentation, Human Brain Mapping 3 (3) (1995) 190–208.

[28] O. Commowick, G. Malandain, Efficient selection of the most similar image in a database for critical structures segmentation, in: International Conference on Medical Image Computing and Computer-Assisted Intervention, Springer, 2007, pp. 203–210.

[29] O. Commowick, S.K. Warfield, Incorporating priors on expert performance parameters for segmentation validation and label fusion: a maximum a posteriori staple, in: International Conference on Medical Image Computing and Computer-Assisted Intervention, Springer, 2010, pp. 25–32.

[30] O. Commowick, A. Akhondi-Asl, S.K. Warfield, Estimating a reference standard segmentation with spatially varying performance parameters: local map staple, IEEE Transactions on Medical Imaging 31 (8) (2012) 1593–1606.

[31] P. Coupé, J.V. Manjón, V. Fonov, J. Pruessner, M. Robles, D.L. Collins, Patch-based segmentation using expert priors: application to hippocampus and ventricle segmentation, NeuroImage 54 (2) (2011) 940–954.

[32] W. Crum, L. Griffin, D. Hill, D. Hawkes, Zen and the art of medical image registration: correspondence, homology, and quality, NeuroImage 20 (3) (2003) 1425–1437.

[33] W.R. Crum, T. Hartkens, D. Hill, Non-rigid image registration: theory and practice, British Journal of Radiology 77 (suppl_2) (2004) S140–S153.

[34] M.D. Cykowski, O. Coulon, P.V. Kochunov, K. Amunts, J.L. Lancaster, A.R. Laird, D.C. Glahn, P.T. Fox, The central sulcus: an observer-independent characterization of sulcal landmarks and depth asymmetry, Cerebral Cortex 18 (9) (2008) 1999–2009.

[35] M.D. Cykowski, P.V. Kochunov, R.J. Ingham, J.C. Ingham, J.-F. Mangin, D. Rivière, J.L. Lancaster, P.T. Fox, Perisylvian sulcal morphology and cerebral asymmetry patterns in adults who stutter, Cerebral Cortex 18 (3) (2008) 571–583.

[36] B.M. Dawant, S.L. Hartmann, J.-P. Thirion, F. Maes, D. Vandermeulen, P. Demaerel, Automatic 3-d segmentation of internal structures of the head in mr images using a combination of similarity and free-form transformations. I. Methodology and validation on normal subjects, IEEE Transactions on Medical Imaging 18 (10) (1999) 909–916.

[37] A.P. Dempster, N.M. Laird, D.B. Rubin, Maximum likelihood from incomplete data via the EM algorithm, Journal of the Royal Statistical Society, Series B, Methodological (1977) 1–38.

[38] J. Doshi, G. Erus, Y. Ou, B. Gaonkar, C. Davatzikos, Multi-atlas skull-stripping, Academic Radiology 20 (12) (2013) 1566–1576.

[39] G. Douaud, T.E. Behrens, C. Poupon, Y. Cointepas, S. Jbabdi, V. Gaura, N. Golestani, P. Krystkowiak, C. Verny, P. Damier, et al., In vivo evidence for the selective subcortical degeneration in Huntington's disease, NeuroImage 46 (4) (2009) 958–966.

[40] J. Dubois, M. Benders, C. Borradori-Tolsa, A. Cachia, F. Lazeyras, R.H.-V. Leuchter, S. Sizonenko, S. Warfield, J. Mangin, P.S. Hüppi, Primary cortical folding in the human newborn: an early marker of later functional development, Brain 131 (8) (2008) 2028–2041.

[41] L. Fang, L. Zhang, D. Nie, X. Cao, K. Bahrami, H. He, D. Shen, Brain image labeling using multi-atlas guided 3D fully convolutional networks, in: International Workshop on Patch-Based Techniques in Medical Imaging, Springer, 2017, pp. 12–19.

[42] P. Fillard, V. Arsigny, X. Pennec, K.M. Hayashi, P.M. Thompson, N. Ayache, Measuring brain variability by extrapolating sparse tensor fields measured on sulcal lines, NeuroImage 34 (2) (2007) 639–650.

[43] B. Fischl, D.H. Salat, E. Busa, M. Albert, M. Dieterich, C. Haselgrove, A. Van Der Kouwe, R. Killiany, D. Kennedy, S. Klaveness, et al., Whole brain segmentation: automated labeling of neuroanatomical structures in the human brain, Neuron 33 (3) (2002) 341–355.

[44] B. Fischl, A. van der Kouwe, C. Destrieux, E. Halgren, F. Ségonne, D.H. Salat, E. Busa, L.J. Seidman, J. Goldstein, D. Kennedy, et al., Automatically parcellating the human cerebral cortex, Cerebral Cortex 14 (1) (2004) 11–22.

[45] B. Fischl, N. Rajendran, E. Busa, J. Augustinack, O. Hinds, B.T. Yeo, H. Mohlberg, K. Amunts, K. Zilles, Cortical folding patterns and predicting cytoarchitecture, Cerebral Cortex 18 (8) (2007) 1973–1980.

[46] Y. Freund, R.E. Schapire, A decision-theoretic generalization of on-line learning and an application to boosting, Journal of Computer and System Sciences 55 (1) (1997) 119–139.

[47] K.J. Friston, A.P. Holmes, K.J. Worsley, J.-P. Poline, C.D. Frith, R.S. Frackowiak, Statistical parametric maps in functional imaging: a general linear approach, Human Brain Mapping 2 (4) (1994) 189–210.

[48] R.A. Heckemann, J.V. Hajnal, P. Aljabar, D. Rueckert, A. Hammers, Automatic anatomical brain mri segmentation combining label propagation and decision fusion, NeuroImage 33 (1) (2006) 115–126.

[49] M.P. Heinrich, M. Jenkinson, M. Brady, J.A. Schnabel, MRF-based deformable registration and ventilation estimation of lung CT, IEEE Transactions on Medical Imaging 32 (7) (2013) 1239–1248.

[50] K. Held, E.R. Kops, B.J. Krause, W.M. Wells, R. Kikinis, H.-W. Muller-Gartner, Markov random field segmentation of brain MR images, IEEE Transactions on Medical Imaging 16 (6) (1997) 878–886.

[51] D.L. Hill, P.G. Batchelor, M. Holden, D.J. Hawkes, Medical image registration, Physics in Medicine and Biology 46 (3) (2001) R1.

[52] S. Hu, E.A. Hoffman, J.M. Reinhardt, Automatic lung segmentation for accurate quantitation of volumetric X-ray CT images, IEEE Transactions on Medical Imaging 20 (6) (2001) 490–498.

[53] Y. Huo, A.J. Asman, A.J. Plassard, B.A. Landman, Simultaneous total intracranial volume and posterior fossa volume estimation using multi-atlas label fusion, Human Brain Mapping 38 (2) (2017) 599–616.

[54] Y. Huo, J. Liu, Z. Xu, R.L. Harrigan, A. Assad, R.G. Abramson, B.A. Landman, Robust multi-contrast MRI spleen segmentation for splenomegaly using multi-atlas segmentation, IEEE Transactions on Biomedical Engineering 65 (2018) 336–343.

[55] Y. Huo, J. Liu, Z. Xu, R.L. Harrigan, A. Assad, R.G. Abramson, B.A. Landman, Robust multicontrast MRI spleen segmentation for splenomegaly using multi-atlas segmentation, IEEE Transactions on Biomedical Engineering 65 (2) (2018) 336–343.

[56] Y. Huo, Z. Xu, K. Aboud, P. Parvathaneni, S. Bao, C. Bermudez, S.M. Resnick, L.E. Cutting, B.A. Landman, Spatially localized atlas network tiles enables 3D whole brain segmentation from limited data, preprint, arXiv:1806.00546, 2018.

[57] J.E. Iglesias, M.R. Sabuncu, Multi-atlas segmentation of biomedical images: a survey, Medical Image Analysis 24 (1) (2015) 205–219.

[58] J.E. Iglesias, M.R. Sabuncu, K. Van Leemput, A generative model for multi-atlas segmentation across modalities, in: 2012 9th IEEE International Symposium on Biomedical Imaging (ISBI), IEEE, 2012, pp. 888–891.

[59] I. Isgum, M. Staring, A. Rutten, M. Prokop, M.A. Viergever, B. Van Ginneken, Multi-atlas-based segmentation with local decision fusion—application to cardiac and aortic segmentation in CT scans, IEEE Transactions on Medical Imaging 28 (7) (2009) 1000–1010.

[60] M. Jenkinson, S. Smith, A global optimisation method for robust affine registration of brain images, Medical Image Analysis 5 (2) (2001) 143–156.

[61] M. Jenkinson, C.F. Beckmann, T.E. Behrens, M.W. Woolrich, S.M. Smith, FSL, NeuroImage 62 (2) (2012) 782–790.

[62] C.-Y. Kao, M. Hofer, G. Sapiro, J. Stern, K. Rehm, D.A. Rottenberg, A geometric method for automatic extraction of sulcal fundi, IEEE Transactions on Medical Imaging 26 (4) (2007) 530–540.

[63] M. Kearns, Learning Boolean Formulae or Finite Automata Is as Hard as Factoring, Technical Report TR-14-88, Harvard University Aikem Computation Laboratory, 1988.

[64] S.H. Kim, I. Lyu, V.S. Fonov, C. Vachet, H.C. Hazlett, R.G. Smith, J. Piven, S.R. Dager, R.C. Mckinstry, J.R. Pruett, et al., Development of cortical shape in the human brain from 6 to 24 months of age via a novel measure of shape complexity, NeuroImage 135 (2016) 163–176.

[65] A. Klein, B. Mensh, S. Ghosh, J. Tourville, J. Hirsch, Mindboggle: automated brain labeling with multiple atlases, BMC Medical Imaging 5 (1) (2005) 7.

[66] J. Lancaster, L. Rainey, J. Summerlin, C. Freitas, P. Fox, A. Evans, A. Toga, J. Mazziotta, Automated labeling of the human brain: a preliminary report on the development and evaluation of a forward-transform method, Human Brain Mapping 5 (4) (1997) 238.

[67] J.L. Lancaster, M.G. Woldorff, L.M. Parsons, M. Liotti, C.S. Freitas, L. Rainey, P.V. Kochunov, D. Nickerson, S.A. Mikiten, P.T. Fox, Automated Talairach atlas labels for functional brain mapping, Human Brain Mapping 10 (3) (2000) 120–131.

[68] B. Landman, S. Warfield, Miccai 2012 workshop on multi-atlas labeling, in: Medical Image Computing and Computer Assisted Intervention Conference, 2012.

[69] B.A. Landman, A.J. Asman, A.G. Scoggins, J.A. Bogovic, F. Xing, J.L. Prince, Robust statistical fusion of image labels, IEEE Transactions on Medical Imaging 31 (2) (2012) 512–522.

[70] T.R. Langerak, U.A. van der Heide, A.N. Kotte, M.A. Viergever, M. Van Vulpen, J.P. Pluim, Label fusion in atlas-based segmentation using a selective and iterative method for performance level estimation (simple), IEEE Transactions on Medical Imaging 29 (12) (2010) 2000–2008.

[71] G. Le Goualher, E. Procyk, D.L. Collins, R. Venugopal, C. Barillot, A.C. Evans, Automated extraction and variability analysis of sulcal neuroanatomy, IEEE Transactions on Medical Imaging 18 (3) (1999) 206–217.

[72] C. Ledig, R. Wolz, P. Aljabar, J. Lötjönen, R.A. Heckemann, A. Hammers, D. Rueckert, Multi-class brain segmentation using atlas propagation and EM-based refinement, in: 2012 9th IEEE International Symposium on Biomedical Imaging (ISBI), IEEE, 2012, pp. 896–899.

[73] G. Li, L. Guo, J. Nie, T. Liu, An automated pipeline for cortical sulcal fundi extraction, Medical Image Analysis 14 (3) (2010) 343–359.

[74] G. Lohmann, Extracting line representations of sulcal and gyral patterns in mr images of the human brain, IEEE Transactions on Medical Imaging 17 (6) (1998) 1040–1048.

[75] G. Lohmann, D. Von Cramon, Automatic labelling of the human cortical surface using sulcal basins, Medical Image Analysis 4 (3) (2000) 179–188.

[76] G. Lohmann, D.Y. von Cramon, H. Steinmetz, Sulcal variability of twins, Cerebral Cortex 9 (7) (1999) 754–763.

[77] J.M. Lötjönen, R. Wolz, J.R. Koikkalainen, L. Thurfjell, G. Waldemar, H. Soininen, D. Rueckert, A.D.N. Initiative, et al., Fast and robust multi-atlas segmentation of brain magnetic resonance images, NeuroImage 49 (3) (2010) 2352–2365.

[78] I. Lyu, J.-K. Seong, S.Y. Shin, K. Im, J.H. Roh, M.-J. Kim, G.H. Kim, J.H. Kim, A.C. Evans, D.L. Na, et al., Spectral-based automatic labeling and refining of human cortical sulcal curves using expert-provided examples, NeuroImage 52 (1) (2010) 142–157.

[79] I. Lyu, S.H. Kim, J. Bullins, J.H. Gilmore, M.A. Styner, Novel local shape-adaptive gyrification index with application to brain development, in: International Conference on Medical Image Computing and Computer-Assisted Intervention, Springer, 2017, pp. 31–39.

[80] I. Lyu, S.H. Kim, N.D. Woodward, M.A. Styner, B.A. Landman Trace, A topological graph representation for automatic sulcal curve extraction, IEEE Transactions on Medical Imaging 37 (7) (2018) 1653–1663.

[81] J.A. Maintz, M.A. Viergever, A survey of medical image registration, Medical Image Analysis 2 (1) (1998) 1–36.

[82] J.-F. Mangin, J. Régis, I. Bloch, V. Frouin, Y. Samson, J. López-Krahe, A mrf based random graph modelling the human cortical topography, in: Computer Vision, Virtual Reality and Robotics in Medicine, Springer, 1995, pp. 177–183.

[83] J.C. Mazziotta, A.W. Toga, A. Evans, P. Fox, J. Lancaster, et al., A probabilistic atlas of the human brain: theory and rationale for its development, NeuroImage 2 (2) (1995) 89–101.

[84] G. McLachlan, T. Krishnan, The EM Algorithm and Extensions, vol. 382, John Wiley & Sons, 2007.

[85] M. Modat, G.R. Ridgway, Z.A. Taylor, M. Lehmann, J. Barnes, D.J. Hawkes, N.C. Fox, S. Ourselin, Fast free-form deformation using graphics processing units, Computer Methods and Programs in Biomedicine 98 (3) (2010) 278–284.

[86] H. Park, P.H. Bland, C.R. Meyer, Construction of an abdominal probabilistic atlas and its application in segmentation, IEEE Transactions on Medical Imaging 22 (4) (2003) 483–492.

[87] E. Parzen, On estimation of a probability density function and mode, The Annals of Mathematical Statistics 33 (3) (1962) 1065–1076.

[88] M. Perrot, D. Riviere, J.-F. Mangin, Identifying cortical sulci from localization, shape and local organization, in: 2008 5th IEEE International Symposium on Biomedical Imaging: From Nano to Macro, IEEE, 2008, pp. 420–423.

[89] D.L. Pham, C. Xu, J.L. Prince, Current methods in medical image segmentation, Annual Review of Biomedical Engineering 2 (1) (2000) 315–337.

[90] S. Pieper, M. Halle, R. Kikinis, 3D slicer, in: IEEE International Symposium on Biomedical Imaging: Nano to Macro, 2004, IEEE, 2004, pp. 632–635.

[91] A.J. Plassard, M. McHugo, S. Heckers, B.A. Landman, Multi-scale hippocampal parcellation improves atlas-based segmentation accuracy, in: Medical Imaging 2017: Image Processing, in: Proc. SPIE, vol. 10133, International Society for Optics and Photonics, 2017, p. 101332D.

[92] Z.I. Pozeg, E.S. Flamm, Vesalius and the 1543 epitome of his "de humani corporis fabrica librorum": a uniquely illuminated copy, The Papers of the Bibliographical Society of America 103 (2) (2009) 199–220.

[93] M.E. Rettmann, X. Han, C. Xu, J.L. Prince, Automated sulcal segmentation using watersheds on the cortical surface, NeuroImage 15 (2) (2002) 329–344.

[94] D. Riviere, J.-F. Mangin, D. Papadopoulos-Orfanos, J.-M. Martinez, V. Frouin, J. Régis, Automatic recognition of cortical sulci of the human brain using a congregation of neural networks, Medical Image Analysis 6 (2) (2002) 77–92.

[95] T. Rohlfing, R. Brandt, R. Menzel, C.R. Maurer Jr., Evaluation of atlas selection strategies for atlas-based image segmentation with application to confocal microscopy images of bee brains, NeuroImage 21 (4) (2004) 1428–1442.

[96] T. Rohlfing, D.B. Russakoff, C.R. Maurer, Performance-based classifier combination in atlas-based image segmentation using expectation-maximization parameter estimation, IEEE Transactions on Medical Imaging 23 (8) (2004) 983–994.

[97] A.G. Roy, S. Conjeti, D. Sheet, A. Katouzian, N. Navab, C. Wachinger, Error corrective boosting for learning fully convolutional networks with limited data, in: International Conference on Medical Image Computing and Computer-Assisted Intervention, Springer, 2017, pp. 231–239.

[98] D. Rueckert, L.I. Sonoda, C. Hayes, D.L. Hill, M.O. Leach, D.J. Hawkes, Nonrigid registration using free-form deformations: application to breast MR images, IEEE Transactions on Medical Imaging 18 (8) (1999) 712–721.

[99] M.R. Sabuncu, B.T. Yeo, K. Van Leemput, B. Fischl, P. Golland, A generative model for image segmentation based on label fusion, IEEE Transactions on Medical Imaging 29 (10) (2010) 1714–1729.

[100] S. Sandor, R. Leahy, Surface-based labeling of cortical anatomy using a deformable atlas, IEEE Transactions on Medical Imaging 16 (1) (1997) 41–54.

[101] G. Sanroma, G. Wu, Y. Gao, D. Shen, Learning to rank atlases for multiple-atlas segmentation, IEEE Transactions on Medical Imaging 33 (10) (2014) 1939–1953.

[102] R.E. Schapire, The strength of weak learnability, Machine Learning 5 (2) (1990) 197–227.

[103] M. Sdika, Combining atlas based segmentation and intensity classification with nearest neighbor transform and accuracy weighted vote, Medical Image Analysis 14 (2) (2010) 219–226.

[104] J. Seong, K. Im, S. Yoo, S. Seo, D. Na, J. Lee, Automatic extraction of sulcal lines on cortical surfaces based on anisotropic geodesic distance, NeuroImage 49 (1) (2010) 293–302.

[105] Y. Shi, P.M. Thompson, I. Dinov, A.W. Toga, Hamilton–Jacobi skeleton on cortical surfaces, IEEE Transactions on Medical Imaging 27 (5) (2008) 664–673.

[106] Y. Shi, Z. Tu, A.L. Reiss, R.A. Dutton, A.D. Lee, A.M. Galaburda, I. Dinov, P.M. Thompson, A.W. Toga, Joint sulcal detection on cortical surfaces with graphical models and boosted priors, IEEE Transactions on Medical Imaging 28 (3) (2009) 361–373.

[107] C. Sjöberg, A. Ahnesjö, Multi-atlas based segmentation using probabilistic label fusion with adaptive weighting of image similarity measures, Computer Methods and Programs in Biomedicine 110 (3) (2013) 308–319.

[108] A. Sotiras, C. Davatzikos, N. Paragios, Deformable medical image registration: a survey, IEEE Transactions on Medical Imaging 32 (7) (2013) 1153–1190.

[109] J. Talairach, P. Tournoux, Co-Planar Stereotaxic Atlas of the Human Brain. 3-Dimensional Proportional System: An Approach to Cerebral Imaging, 1988.

[110] X. Tao, J.L. Prince, C. Davatzikos, Using a statistical shape model to extract sulcal curves on the outer cortex of the human brain, IEEE Transactions on Medical Imaging 21 (5) (2002) 513–524.

[111] P. Thompson, C. Schwartz, A. Toga, High-resolution random mesh algorithms for creating a probabilistic 3D surface atlas of the human brain, NeuroImage 3 (1) (1996) 19–34.

[112] P.M. Thompson, C. Schwartz, R.T. Lin, A.A. Khan, A.W. Toga, Three-dimensional statistical analysis of sulcal variability in the human brain, Journal of Neuroscience 16 (13) (1996) 4261–4274.

[113] P.M. Thompson, K.M. Hayashi, E.R. Sowell, N. Gogtay, J.N. Giedd, J.L. Rapoport, G.I. De Zubicaray, A.L. Janke, S.E. Rose, J. Semple, et al., Mapping cortical change in Alzheimer's disease, brain development, and schizophrenia, NeuroImage 23 (2004) S2–S18.

[114] Z. Tu, S. Zheng, A.L. Yuille, A.L. Reiss, R.A. Dutton, A.D. Lee, A.M. Galaburda, I. Dinov, P.M. Thompson, A.W. Toga, Automated extraction of the cortical sulci based on a supervised learning approach, IEEE Transactions on Medical Imaging 26 (4) (2007) 541–552.

[115] N.J. Tustison, B.B. Avants, P.A. Cook, Y. Zheng, A. Egan, P.A. Yushkevich, J.C. Gee, N4ITK: improved N3 bias correction, IEEE Transactions on Medical Imaging 29 (6) (2010) 1310–1320.

[116] M. Vaillant, C. Davatzikos, R.N. Bryan, Finding 3D parametric representations of the deep cortical folds, in: Proceedings of the Workshop on Mathematical Methods in Biomedical Image Analysis, 1996, IEEE, 1996, pp. 151–159.

[117] E.M. van Rikxoort, I. Isgum, Y. Arzhaeva, M. Staring, S. Klein, M.A. Viergever, J.P. Pluim, B. van Ginneken, Adaptive local multi-atlas segmentation: application to the heart and the caudate nucleus, Medical Image Analysis 14 (1) (2010) 39–49.

[118] H. Wang, S.R. Das, J.W. Suh, M. Altinay, J. Pluta, C. Craige, B. Avants, P.A. Yushkevich, A.D.N. Initiative, et al., A learning-based wrapper method to correct systematic errors in automatic image segmentation: consistently improved performance in hippocampus, cortex and brain segmentation, NeuroImage 55 (3) (2011) 968–985.

[119] H. Wang, J.W. Suh, J. Pluta, M. Altinay, P. Yushkevich, Optimal weights for multi-atlas label fusion, in: Biennial International Conference on Information Processing in Medical Imaging, Springer, 2011, pp. 73–84.

[120] H. Wang, J.W. Suh, S.R. Das, J.B. Pluta, C. Craige, P.A. Yushkevich, Multi-atlas segmentation with joint label fusion, IEEE Transactions on Pattern Analysis and Machine Intelligence 35 (3) (2013) 611–623.

[121] S.K. Warfield, K.H. Zou, W.M. Wells, Simultaneous truth and performance level estimation (STAPLE): an algorithm for the validation of image segmentation, IEEE Transactions on Medical Imaging 23 (7) (2004) 903–921.

[122] N.I. Weisenfeld, S.K. Warfield, Learning likelihoods for labeling (L3): a general multi-classifier segmentation algorithm, in: International Conference on Medical Image Computing and Computer-Assisted Intervention, Springer, 2011, pp. 322–329.

[123] R. Wolz, P. Aljabar, J.V. Hajnal, A. Hammers, D. Rueckert, A.D.N. Initiative, et al., LEAP: learning embeddings for atlas propagation, NeuroImage 49 (2) (2010) 1316–1325.

[124] Z. Xu, A.J. Asman, E. Singh, L. Chambless, R. Thompson, B.A. Landman, Segmentation of malignant gliomas through remote collaboration and statistical fusion, Medical Physics 39 (10) (2012) 5981–5989.

[125] Z. Xu, R.P. Burke, C.P. Lee, R.B. Baucom, B.K. Poulose, R.G. Abramson, B.A. Landman, Efficient multi-atlas abdominal segmentation on clinically acquired CT with simple context learning, Medical Image Analysis 24 (1) (2015) 18–27.

[126] H. Yang, J. Sun, H. Li, L. Wang, Z. Xu, Deep fusion net for multi-atlas segmentation: application to cardiac MR images, in: International Conference on Medical Image Computing and Computer-Assisted Intervention, Springer, 2016, pp. 521–528.

[127] H. Yang, J. Sun, H. Li, L. Wang, Z. Xu, Neural multi-atlas label fusion: application to cardiac MR images, preprint, arXiv:1709.09641, 2017.

[128] J. Yang, Y. Zhang, L. Zhang, L. Dong, Automatic segmentation of parotids from CT scans using multiple atlases, in: Medical Image Analysis for the Clinic: a Grand Challenge, 2010, pp. 323–330.

[129] Y. Zhang, M. Brady, S. Smith, Segmentation of brain MR images through a hidden Markov random field model and the expectation-maximization algorithm, IEEE Transactions on Medical Imaging 20 (1) (2001) 45–57.

[130] D. Zikic, B. Glocker, A. Criminisi, Encoding atlases by randomized classification forests for efficient multi-atlas label propagation, Medical Image Analysis 18 (8) (2014) 1262–1273.

CHAPTER 7

Segmentation using adversarial image-to-image networks

Dong Yang[a], Tao Xiong[b], Daguang Xu[c], S. Kevin Zhou[d]
[a]Computer Science, Rutgers University, Piscataway, NJ, United States
[b]Electrical and Computer Engineering, Johns Hopkins University, Baltimore, MD, United States
[c]NVIDIA, Santa Clara, CA, United States
[d]Institute of Computing Technology, Chinese Academy of Sciences, Beijing, China

Contents

7.1. Introduction		165
7.1.1 Generative adversarial network		165
7.1.2 Deep image-to-image network		167
7.2. Segmentation using an adversarial image-to-image network		169
7.2.1 Experiments		171
7.3. Volumetric domain adaptation with intrinsic semantic cycle consistency		172
7.3.1 Methodology		175
7.3.1.1 3D dense U-Net for left atrium segmentation		*176*
7.3.1.2 Volumetric domain adaptation with cycle consistency		*176*
7.3.2 Experiments		178
7.3.3 Conclusions		180
References		181

There are many interesting recent developments in deep learning. The most important one, in my opinion, is adversarial training (also called GAN for Generative Adversarial Networks). This, and the variations that are now being proposed, is the most interesting idea in the last 10 years in ML, in my opinion.

Yann LeCun

7.1. Introduction

7.1.1 Generative adversarial network

Generative adversarial network (GAN) is one class of deep neural network architectures designed for unsupervised machine learning in the fields such as computer vision, natural language processing, and medical image analysis. The idea of GAN is to enable two or more neural networks to compete with each other and eventually achieve balance during optimization. GAN is designed as a generative machine learning model that learns the distribution of data classes. It was introduced by Goodfellow et al. in 2014 to model the image representation with the latent vector space using multi-layer

Handbook of Medical Image Computing and Computer Assisted Intervention
https://doi.org/10.1016/B978-0-12-816176-0.00012-0

perceptrons (MLP) [22]. For general GAN, there are two subneural networks in the algorithm: a generator network and a discriminator network. The generator aims to generate a "fake" image from a random D-dimensional noise vector. Then, the discriminator network predicts the real/fake label for the input of the real images or the generated images, and acts as a binary classifier. During the optimization, the objective from the binary classification helps when updating parameters in both generator and discriminator via gradient descent. While the objective is being minimized, the generator continues to produce better and better images which are close to real image domain. Meanwhile, it is harder for discriminator to distinguish real or generated images.

Later, a Deep Convolutional Generative Adversarial Network (DCGAN) was proposed by Radford et al. for image generation with convolutional filters [1]. DCGAN adopted unsupervised learning setting to model image representations in both the generator and discriminator. After training, it generates synthetic images of high quality, from the learned underlying distribution of contextual appearance. The trained discriminator also performs as an image feature extractor for image classification tasks, comparing with other unsupervised learning algorithms.

Isola et al. proposed an image-to-image framework using generative adversarial networks for image translation, called *pix2pix* [29]. It can translate from labels to images, or from sketches to images. The design is inspired by DCGAN, in which the adversarial networks guarantee the quality of generated images, and the generator is a classic image-to-image network, e.g., U-net [5]. The discriminator is purely trained with small patches sampled from the original input. The framework is simple but very efficient to achieve very good image generation results.

Recently, Zhu et al. presented Cycle-Consistent Adversarial Networks (Cycle-GANs) for learning to translate an image from a source domain X to a target domain Y without having explicitly paired images in the training samples [2]. For example, CycleGAN is able to translate a painting with a style of Monet to another painting with a style of Van Gogh. In order to learn this mapping $G : X \rightarrow Y$, an adversarial loss is typically introduced so that the distribution of images from $G(X)$ is indistinguishable from the distribution Y. Because the task is designed for training on unpaired data that is highly under-constrained and not well aligned, CycleGAN incorporates an inverse mapping $F : Y \rightarrow X$ and a cycle consistency loss to enforce $F(G(X)) = X$ in the loss function. Compared to the normal GAN-based framework, ClycleGAN consists of two mapping functions G and F, and their associated adversarial discriminators D_Y and D_X. Intuitively, the discriminator D_Y enforces the mapping G to generate the outputs indistinguishable from domain Y, and vice versa for discriminator D_X and mapping F. Therefore, the cycle consistent adversarial learning sets CycleGAN apart from other GAN-based image-to-image translation works.

7.1.2 Deep image-to-image network

Recently, deep image-to-image networks have been wildly used in the computer vision tasks such as recognition, semantic segmentation, and landmark detection. Basically, deep image-to-image networks are designed in a fully convolutional manner and simply perform on arbitrary-sized inputs. They are trained end-to-end and output the spatial pixels-to-pixels classification map or heat maps. These deep image-to-image networks take advantage of the fully convolution and parallel computation, which is highly efficient in terms of training and inference compared to the patch-wise approaches. Furthermore, they simply and efficiently learn the global information from the whole image inputs as well as ground truths, which sets them apart from the conventional sliding window approaches.

Many published works have developed these deep image-to-image networks and demonstrated their state-of-the-art performance on the computer vision tasks. Long et al. proposed a fully convolutional network (FCN) for semantic segmentation by extending the conventional classification networks to segmentation [3]. It dramatically improved the state-of-the-art and the efficiency of learning and inference. Badrinarayanan et al. presented another novel deep fully convolutional neural network architecture named SegNet for semantic pixelwise segmentation in scene understanding [4]. SegNet is composed of an encoder network and a corresponding decoder network followed by a pixelwise classification layer. A significant contribution of SegNet focuses on the nonlinear upsampling using the indexes' information from the encoder. Such deep image-to-image networks are also quite commonly used in the community of medical imaging analysis. Ronneberger et al. proposed a U-Net for biomedical image segmentation and achieved the state-of-the-art performance on the ISBI cell tracking challenge 2015 [5]. The U-shaped architecture of U-Net consists of a contracting path, an expansive path, and a feature forward bridge, which enables the seamless segmentation on arbitrarily large images. Milletari et al. also designed a fully convolutional neural network called V-Net for volumeric medical image segmentation, which extended the fully convolutional neural networks from the applications of 2D images to 3D volumes [6]. The basic architecture is similar to that of U-Net. However, it is composed of 3D convolution layers instead of conventional 2D convolution layers and learns a residual function inspired by the work of ResNet. Furthermore, this work also introduced a novel objective function based on the Dice coefficient during training. Overall, it both improved the performance and efficiency compared to U-Net.

Recently, more sophisticated image-to-image networks have been proposed for many challenging clinical tasks such as automatic liver segmentation and vertebrae landmark localization and identification. Dou et al. presented a novel 3D deeply supervised network (3D DSN) for automatic liver segmentation in CT volumes [7]. The 3D DSN performs full convolution on the CT volumes to enable end-to-end training and inference. Furthermore, this framework has incorporated a deep supervision mechanism and

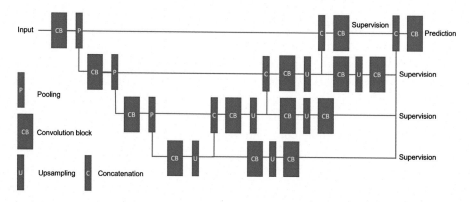

Figure 7.1 Architecture of Deep Image-to-Image Network (DI2IN). The DI2IN is composed of a convolutional encoder–decoder network with feature concatenation, while the backend is a multilevel deep supervision network. The convolution block consists of one-to-multiple convolution layers. The pooling layer usually uses convolution layer with stride larger than 1.

a conditional random field to achieve refined segmentation results. Yang et al. proposed an automatic and efficient deep image-to-image network (DI2IN) to localize and identify the vertebra centroids in 3D CT volumes [8,9]. The DI2IN as shown in Fig. 7.1, as a convolutional encoder–decoder network, directly performs on the 3D CT volumes and generates the multichannel probability maps for different vertebrae. Additionally, several advanced techniques such as feature layer concatenation and deep supervision are also introduced in the DI2IN to further improve the quality of probability maps. This work introduces a more complex deep supervision method to improve the performance. Multiple branches are separated from the middle layers of the decoder in the master network. They upsample each input feature map to the same size of the image, followed by several convolution layers to match the channel number of ground truth. The supervision happens at the end of each branch i and shares the same ground truth data in order to calculate the loss item l_i. The final output is determined by another convolution of the concatenation of all branches' outputs and the decoder output. The total loss l_{total} is a weighted sum of the loss from all branches and that from the final output, as shown in the following equation; w_i is the weight for each loss:

$$l_{total} = \sum_i w_i l_i + l_{final}. \qquad (7.1)$$

Li et al. proposed a high-resolution and compact convolutional network for MR images segmentation [10]. This work incorporates the recent efficient and flexible elements of modern convolutional network such as dilated convolution and residual connection for further reducing the complexity and improving the training efficiency of the network. Harrison et al. also presented a deep supervised learning framework with a progressive and multipath scheme for pathological lung segmentation, which is called a progressive holistically-nested network (P-HNN) [11]. Basically, P-HNN adopts the convolutional architecture of VGG-16 network as its base network and then uses deep supervision to guide the training in a progressive manner. To address the limitation in conventional 2D and 3D convolutions in medical imaging analysis, Li et al. designed a hybrid densely connected UNet (H-DenseUNet) for left atrium and tumor segmentation [12]. The 2D DenseUNet learns the intraslice features from the slices of the 3D input volume. Furthermore, the 3D network learns the interslice features from the 3D input volumes concatenated with the intraslice features. Eventually, a hybrid feature fusion layer integrates both intra- and interslice features for generating the accurate liver and lesion segmentation.

7.2. Segmentation using an adversarial image-to-image network

Semantic segmentation of various structures of the human body, such as organs, bones, tissues, vessels, etc., is an essential step in many clinical routines. It is usually formulated as a dense labeling problem where the goal is to predict a category label of each pixel in the input images. Most recent state-of-the-art methods are designed based on the deep image-to-image networks because of their superior performance in both accuracy and efficiency. However, these networks usually treat the prediction of each pixel independently from each other. Several works alleviated this problem by applying some postprocessing methods, such as connected component analysis, CRF analysis, etc. Connected component analysis usually assumes the predicted segmentation contains only one single connected component under some connected mechanism (4-connect and 8-connect in 2D, 6-connect and 26-connect in 3D). It has been shown to be very effective at alleviating the false-positive problems. On the other hand, CRF method enforces the spatial contiguity in the output maps. The prediction of DI2IN can be used to define its unary potentials. With some certain class of the pairwise potentials, the CRF problem can be solved using the filter-based techniques [13]. Lin et al. show that the CRF inference with CNN as the underlying unary potential can be trained in an end-to-end manner using a recurrent neural network formulation of the mean-field iterations [14]. It has also been shown that by replacing the fully-connected CRF with a locally connected CRF, more categories of pairwise potential can be trained using DNNs.

Despite these advantages, the CRF method only uses the unary potential and the pairwise potential. In the meantime, higher-order potentials have been shown to be very effective in achieving better consistency [15]. Arnab et al. integrate some specific classes of high order potential into the CNN segmentation network, despite its limited number of higher order parameters [16]. In 2016, Luc et al. combine CNN-based segmentation model with the GAN, aiming to enforce higher-order consistency without limiting to a

Figure 7.2 Architecture of the adversarial deep image-to-image network (DI2IN-AN). The generator shall generate the prediction, while the discriminator tries to distinguish between the prediction and the ground truth during the training process.

very specific class of high-order potential. The segmentation loss is optimized together with an adversarial term which encourages the model to produce predictions that are indistinguishable from the ground truth masks through the competition between the generator and the discriminator. Comparing with previous works, the discriminator uses a DNN which shall enforce higher-order potential by assessing the joint relation of many image labels.

In [18], Yang et al. presented an automatic liver segmentation approach using an adversarial image-to-image network (DI2IN-AN), as shown in Fig. 7.2. A DI2IN is served as the generator while a multilayer CNN is used as the discriminator. The discriminator shall try to push the distribution of the prediction towards that of the ground truth which can also be considered as a refinement of the generator's output. Comparing with those postprocessing refinement methods, the DI2IN-AN has better computation efficiency since the discriminator does not need to be executed during inference.

The segmentation loss, e.g., binary cross-entropy loss, Jaccard loss, or the Dice loss, is optimized alternatively with the adversarial loss. Denote by D and G the discriminator and generator, respectively. For the discriminator, $D\left(Y; \theta^D\right)$, the ground truth label Y_{gt} is assigned as one, and the prediction $Y_{pred} = G\left(X; \theta^G\right)$ is assigned as zero where X is the input volume. The discriminator is trained by optimizing the following functions:

$$l_D = -\mathbb{E}_{y \sim p_{gt}} \log\left(D\left(y; \theta^D\right)\right) - \mathbb{E}_{y' \sim p_{pred}} \log\left(1 - D\left(y'; \theta^D\right)\right)$$
$$= -\mathbb{E}_{y \sim p_{gt}} \log\left(D\left(y; \theta^D\right)\right) - \mathbb{E}_{x \sim p_{data}} \log\left(1 - D\left(G\left(x; \theta^G\right); \theta^D\right)\right). \quad (7.2)$$

During the training of the discriminator, the gradient of loss l_D is propagated back to update the parameters of the generator network G. At this stage, the generator loss l_G has two components. The first part is the conventional segmentation loss between ground truth and the prediction. Minimizing the second loss component enables the discriminator D to confuse the ground truth with the prediction from G:

$$l_G = \mathbb{E}_{y \sim p_{pred}, y' \sim p_{gt}} \left[l_{seg}\left(y, y'\right)\right] - \lambda \mathbb{E}_{y \sim p_{pred}} \log\left(1 - D\left(y; \theta^D\right)\right)$$
$$= \mathbb{E}_{y \sim p_{pred}, y' \sim p_{gt}} \left[l_{seg}\left(y, y'\right)\right] - \lambda \mathbb{E}_{x \sim p_{data}} \log\left(1 - D\left(G\left(x; \theta^G\right); \theta^D\right)\right). \quad (7.3)$$

As suggested in [17], $-\log\left(1 - D(G(x))\right)$ is replaced with $\log\left(D(G(X))\right)$. This will maximize the probability of the prediction to be the ground truth, instead of minimizing

---

Algorithm 1: Adversarial training of generator and discriminator.

Input : pretrained generator (DI2IN) with weights θ_0^G
Output: updated generator weights θ_1^G

1 **for** *number of training iterations* **do**
2   **for** k_D *steps* **do**
3   sample a mini–batch of training images $x \sim p_{data}$;
4   generate prediction y_{pred} for x with $G\left(x; \theta_0^G\right)$;
5        $\theta^D \leftarrow$ propagate back the stochastic gradient $\nabla l_D\left(y_{gt}, y_{pred}\right)$;
6   **end**
7   **for** k_G *steps* **do**
8   sample a mini–batch of training images $x' \sim p_{data}$;
9   generate y'_{pred} for x' with $G\left(x'; \theta_0^G\right)$ and compute $D\left(G\left(x'\right)\right)$;
10       $\theta_1^G \leftarrow$ propagate back the stochastic gradient $\nabla l_G\left(y'_{gt}, y'_{pred}\right)$;
11   **end**
12     $\theta_0^G \leftarrow \theta_1^G$
13 **end**

---

the probability that the prediction is not the generated label map. With this change, the gradient during the training of the generator will be stronger, which will also reduce the time for convergence:

$$l_G = \mathbb{E}_{y \sim p_{pred}, y' \sim p_{gt}} \left[l_{seg}\left(y, y'\right)\right] + \lambda \mathbb{E}_{x \sim p_{data}} \log D\left(G\left(x; \theta^G\right); \theta^D\right). \qquad (7.4)$$

The generator and discriminator are trained in an alternative way for several iterations, as shown in Algorithm 1. Finally, it will be very difficult for the discriminator to distinguish between the prediction output and the ground truth. In other words, the prediction becomes indistinguishable from the ground truth. After the training process, the discriminator is no longer needed during the inference time. Thus DI2IN-AN method can improve the quality of the generator's output without introducing extra computation burden at the inference time.

7.2.1 Experiments

Experiments were done using 1000+ CT volumes to demonstrate the effectiveness of adversarial mechanism. The liver of each volume was delineated by human experts. This data covers large variations in populations, contrast phases, scanning ranges, pathologies, field of view (FOV), etc. The interslice distance varies from 0.5 to 7.0 mm. All scans cover the abdominal regions but may extend to head and feet. Tumor can be found in multiple cases. The volumes may also have various other disease. For example, pleural

Table 7.1 Comparison of DI2IN and DI2IN-AN on 50 unseen CT data.

Method	ASD (mm)				Dice			
	Mean	Std	Max	Median	Mean	Std	Min	Median
DI2IN	2.15	0.81	6.51	1.95	0.94	0.02	0.87	0.95
DI2IN-AN	**1.90**	0.74	**6.32**	**1.74**	**0.95**	0.02	**0.88**	0.95

effusion, which brightens the lung region and changes the pattern of upper boundary of liver.

Then additional 50 volumes were collected from clinical sites for the independent testing. The livers from these data were also annotated by human experts for the purpose of evaluation. The dataset were downsampled to 3.0 mm resolution isotropically to speed up the processing and lower the consumption of computing memory without loss of accuracy. In the adversarial training, λ was set to 0.01, and the number of overall training iterations was 100. For training D, k_D was 10 and the mini-batch size was 8. For training G, k_G was 1 and the mini-batch size was 4.

The average symmetric surface distance (ASD) and Dice coefficients were compared. As shown in Table 7.1, DI2IN-AN achieved better performance in both evaluation metrics. Some experimental results of DI2IN-AN on test data are compared with ground truth in Fig. 7.3. We also compared with the CRF and graph cut as postprocessing methods. However, their results became worse because a large portion of the test data has no contrast and the boundary of the liver bottom of many cases is very fuzzy. CRF and graph cut algorithms both suffer from very serious leakage in these situations.

Fig. 7.4 shows a patient with severe pleural effusion, which brightens the lung region and changes the pattern of upper boundary of liver. It increases the difficulty for automatic liver segmentation a lot since in most CT volumes, the lung looks dark with a low intensity. As can be seen from the image, DI2IN-AN method can identify the shape of the liver and segment the upper boundary with high accuracy.

7.3. Volumetric domain adaptation with intrinsic semantic cycle consistency

As stated above, deep neural network (DNN) has demonstrated superior performance in solving various problems in medical imaging applications, such as classification, segmentation, localization, detection, etc. This is mainly attributed to its excellent ability at representing a large amount of labeled training data. However, DNN has an obvious drawback at generalization: the network trained using the annotations in one domain (the source domain, such as CT) does not perform well when applied directly to another domain (the target domain, such as cone beam CT, MRI, or CT from different scanning protocols). To address that, it requires lots of annotations in the target domain, which can be expensive and time consuming. Thus, it is desired to develop algorithms

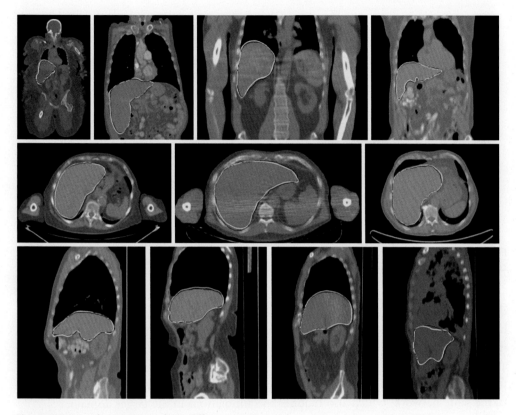

Figure 7.3 Visual comparison from different views. Yellow meshes are ground truth. Red ones are the prediction from DI2IN-AN.

that can transfer the knowledge of existing annotations in the source domain to solve the same problem in the target domain. This becomes more severe in some applications that does not have enough data.

In the past, many approaches had been developed to address these issues. The registration based algorithms, such as [19], try to learn an explicit transformation function that can best transfer the images from the source domain to the target domain. Such methods usually require multiple pairs of images in both domains. The landmark or segmentation mask in the target domain is then generated by applying the resulting transformation function to the existing annotations in source domain. This type of methods is usually time consuming at inference (several minutes) and relies heavily on the accuracy of the hand-designed transformation function. On the other hand, the transfer learning algorithms, such as [20], are also widely studied, which first train a model using the large number of images and annotations in the source domain, and then fine-tune the model using a smaller number of images and annotations in the target domain. The transfer learning methods became very popular in the tasks using the

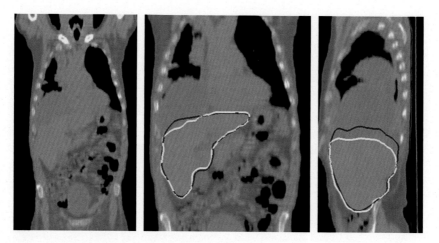

Figure 7.4 One challenging case with pleural effusion: left panel shows the image; middle and right compare DI2IN-AN result (red) with ground truth (yellow).

deep learning algorithms. In addition to the whole model, the transfer learning can also be applied to arbitrary intermediate features of the model. However, transfer learning methods still require annotations in the target domain, which may not always be available. Similarly, Moeskops et al. [21] learn a domain-invariant segmentation model by feeding the images and annotations from both the source domain and the target domain to the same network, which also requires the annotations in the target domain.

In contrast, the domain adaptation methods try to solve the problem by assuming no annotation available in the target domain. The generative adversarial network (GAN) [22] is widely used in these methods. In [23], the adversarial network is added to the segmentation network to distinguish the domain of the input data through the analysis of multiple intermediate features, which makes the segmentation network domain-invariant. In contrary, segmentation networks can also be added to GAN which are domain-invariant in synthesizing the images [24]. Recently, Huo et al. [25] synthesized 2D images from the source domain using CycleGAN and trained a segmentation model using the synthesized images in the target domain and the annotations from the source domain.

In this section, we presented a volumetric domain adaptation method (shown in Fig. 7.5) which takes the advantage of intrinsic semantic cycle consistency in the source and target domains. As a result, no paired images or annotations in the target domain is needed. In contrast to [25], we used a volumetric CycleGAN block to generate the synthesized target domain volume, which greatly preserves the image consistency between slices. We also added an adversarial network to distinguish the features generated using synthesized and real images in the target domain, which showed improvement in the segmentation accuracy. Meanwhile, other two adversarial networks in the volumetric

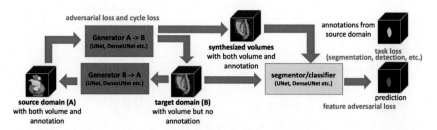

Figure 7.5 The proposed volumetric end-to-end domain adaptation (VeeDA) method. The CycleGAN block synthesizes the target domain images from the source domain. Feature adversarial loss is added to enforce the feature-level consistency in the target domain.

CycleGAN block improve its performance of volume-to-volume translation. Different from [26], our network is trained end-to-end from scratch, which improves the segmentation accuracy as well shown in the experiments. Our method is validated using the domain adaptation task of left atrium segmentation from the CT domain (source) to the MRI domain (target). Tens of millions of people would be affected by the cardiovascular diseases every year all over the world. And the accurate left atrium (LA) segmentation provides important visual guidance for cardiac intervention. Especially, the locations of pulmonary veins of LA are critical in catheter ablation for atrial fibrillation (AF). Automatic left atrium segmentation is a key component in both planning 3D CT and treatment 3D MRI procedure. However, automated segmentation of left atrium in MRI is complex and challenging. Because various image artifacts and noise, introduced during imaging, exists in the appearance of MRI. Thus, in our training steps of the experiments, we assume that CT data has both volumes and annotations while MRI data only has volumes and no annotation. The experimental results show that our proposed method preserves the intrinsic semantic information and generalizes well for left atrium segmentation of MRI. Attributed to the synthetic images from the source domain, the proposed method outperforms comparable to the models trained using the left atrium annotation of MRI volumes.

7.3.1 Methodology

In this section, we present the details of the proposed VeeDA method with intrinsic semantic cycle consistency. The 3D dense U-Net is introduced as the generative models and the segmentation model. The 3D dense U-Net has several advantages for both model training and inference, because of its architecture design. Using the proposed method, the unsupervised domain adaptation and the volumetric domain translation are well accomplished simultaneously.

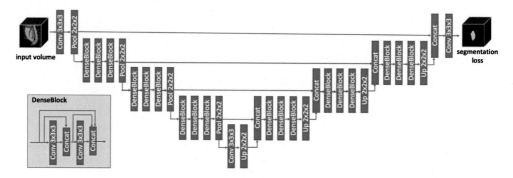

Figure 7.6 3D dense U-Net. Its each level consists of multiple dense blocks.

7.3.1.1 3D dense U-Net for left atrium segmentation

The main task in this study is left atrium segmentation, which is defined as binary classification for voxels, in 3D medical images. The input of the task model is the 3D CT/MRI volumes, and the output is the same-size likelihood maps for voxels belonging to the left atrium region. The left atrium region can be readily determined by thresholding with a constant (e.g., 0.5).

We propose a novel deep neural network structure, called 3D dense U-Net, as our base model for the segmentation and generation tasks, as shown in Fig. 7.6. The core component of 3D dense U-Net is densely connected block. The neural networks using densely connected blocks, introduced in [27], have demonstrated to be successful in several computer vision applications, such as image recognition. The complete connections between convolutional layers within a dense block provide multiple paths for gradient backpropagation, and implicitly add deep supervision for individual layers and multi-scale regularization to the network. We adopt multiple dense blocks in both encoder and decoder to capture the hierarchical features at different levels. Meanwhile, the 3D dense U-Net follows the design of the U-shape convolutional encoder–decoder. It has skip connections between the corresponding encoder layers and decoder layers, which passes the multiscale features from encoder to decoder, combining both the high and low level information for the final inference. 3D Dice loss l_{seg} is used in the training, which represent the statistics of the voxel prediction, to enforce the global constraint in the output [28].

7.3.1.2 Volumetric domain adaptation with cycle consistency

The objective of the unsupervised domain adaptation is to learn a task model (segmentation model) in the target domain B, given the source data X_A, the source label Y_A, and the target data X_B. No pair information between two domains A and B is further required. In order to transfer the volume–label mapping relationship in domain A, the mutual information between two domains A and B needs to be captured indirectly. The segmentation mapping entirely learned from domain A normally performs poorly in domain B.

First, we propose a cycle generative model to formulate the mapping between domain A and B. Two generative networks $G_{A \to B}$ and $G_{B \to A}$ are trained only with the data from each domain. The back-and-forth mapping mechanism encourages the comprehensive constraints for the models and helps improve domain-to-domain translation. Ideally, the data $x_A \in X_A$ should be consistent with the outcome of $G_{B \to A}(G_{A \to B}(x_A))$, and it is the same for x_B. We enforce the cycle-consistent loss in Eq. (7.5) with l_1-norm penalty for the generative model:

$$
\begin{aligned}
l_{cycle} = {}& E_{x_A \sim X_A}\left[\|x_A - G_{B \to A}(G_{A \to B}(x_A))\|_1\right] \\
& + E_{x_B \sim X_B}\left[\|x_B - G_{A \to B}(G_{B \to A}(x_B))\|_1\right].
\end{aligned}
\tag{7.5}
$$

To further make sure the generators G_A and G_B preserve the intensity distribution and appearance details, an additional identity mapping loss in Eq. (7.6) is adopted during the training. The assumption is that x_A has to be identical to $G_{B \to A}(x_A)$, which is same for x_B versus $G_{A \to B}(x_B)$:

$$
l_{idt} = E_{x_A \sim X_A}\left[\|x_A - G_{B \to A}(x_A)\|_1\right] + E_{x_B \sim X_B}\left[\|x_B - G_{A \to B}(x_B)\|_1\right].
\tag{7.6}
$$

We adopt two adversarial networks D_A and D_B as regularization for the generators, which try to distinguish between the real volumes and the generated ones. The penalty objective loss for D_A is the conventional cross-entropy shown in Eq. (7.7). The adversarial loss for D_B is similar:

$$
l_{adv,A} = -E_{x_A \sim X_A}\left[\log(D_A(x_A))\right] - E_{x_B \sim X_B}\left[\log(1 - D_A(G_{B \to A}(x_B)))\right].
\tag{7.7}
$$

To achieve the domain adaptation, we concatenate the current generative model and the proposed segmentation network H. The output of $G_{A \to B}(x_A)$ is the input of H. We use the corresponding label Y_A as the golden standard because ideally the fake $G_{A \to B}(x_A)$ is very close to the domain B. At inference, H is only applied in the domain B. Moreover, we add a feature-level discriminator D_F to distinguish the feature from x_B input or $G_{A \to B}(x_A)$ input shown in Eq. (7.8). The feature is from one intermediate layer of network H. This discriminator is beneficial for not only regularizing volume-to-volume translation in the high-dimensional space, but also improving the effectiveness of segmentation:

$$
\begin{aligned}
l_{adv,F} = {}& -E_{x_B \sim X_B}\left[\log\left(D_F\left(H_{feat}(x_B)\right)\right)\right] \\
& - E_{x_A \sim X_A}\left[\log\left(1 - D_F\left(H_{feat}(G_{A \to B}(x_A))\right)\right)\right].
\end{aligned}
\tag{7.8}
$$

All the aforementioned discriminators also provide additional losses (shown in Eqs. (7.9) and (7.10)) during the training process of generators. The main purpose of the losses is to make the discriminators confused about the real data and the fake data generated from the networks. The closer the fake data is from the real one, the better performance the segmentation network H would have:

$$l'_{adv,A} = -E_{x_A \sim X_A} \left[\log \left(1 - D_A \left(x_A\right)\right)\right] - E_{x_B \sim X_B} \left[\log \left(D_A \left(G_{B \to A} \left(x_B\right)\right)\right)\right] \tag{7.9}$$

$$\begin{aligned} l'_{adv,F} = &-E_{x_A \sim X_A} \left[\log \left(D_F \left(H_{feat} \left(G_{A \to B} \left(x_A\right)\right)\right)\right)\right] \\ &- E_{x_B \sim X_B} \left[\log \left(1 - D_F \left(H_{feat} \left(x_B\right)\right)\right)\right]. \end{aligned} \tag{7.10}$$

Overall, we train the generative and the segmentation networks by minimizing the loss in Eq. (7.11), and train the discriminators by minimizing the loss in Eq. (7.12). These two losses are optimized alternatively. We halt the training process when the segmentation loss in domain B is converged. Then, the generative model can be used for volume translation, while the segmentation network can be applied in domain B:

$$l_{total,G} = l_{cycle} + l_{idt} + l_{seg} + l'_{adv,A} + l'_{adv,B} + l'_{adv,F}, \tag{7.11}$$

$$l_{total,D} = l_{adv,A} + l_{adv,B} + l_{adv,F}. \tag{7.12}$$

We utilize the 3D dense U-net for both generative networks and segmentation networks $H_{X \to Y}$. The modified PatchGAN [29] for 3D input is used as our discriminators D_A, D_B, and D_F, which tells whether the small patch is real or generated. The patch inputs also benefit the training process and reduce the memory consumption. Moreover, because the layer, ahead of the last up-sampling layer in the 3D dense U–Net, contains both high-level and low-level features from the skip connection, we utilize it for computing adversarial losses for extra regularization.

7.3.2 Experiments

For our experiments, we use the dataset from the challenge of multimodality whole heart segmentation associated with MICCAI 2017 [30]; 20 MRI and 20 CT volumes with ground truth labels are utilized for domain adaptation. The MRI and CT datasets were acquired from independent groups of subjects. The CT volumes has the number of slices ranged from 177 to 363 with a typical resolution of $0.49 \times 0.49 \times 0.63 \, \mathrm{mm}^3$. Each slice has 512×512 pixels in general. The number of MRI slices also varied from patient to patient, ranging from 128 to 160 slices, with a typical resolution of $0.97 \times 0.97 \times 1.05 \, \mathrm{mm}^3$. Each slice has 288×288 pixels in general. Both CT images and MRI images were manually annotated and reviewed by experienced radiation oncologists. We resampled the dataset into 2.0 mm resolution isotropically to speed up the computation and lower the memory consumption. All the experiments were conducted using the PyTorch library and ran on a desktop with an NVIDIA K80 GPU. The run time for

Table 7.2 Performance comparison of different methods using Dice coefficients.

Method	Dice			
	Mean	Std	Max	Median
DenseUNet (CT)	0.19	0.03	0.24	0.20
Adversarial network in [23]	0.38	0.06	0.44	0.39
VeeDA w/o feature adversarial loss	0.61	0.05	0.66	0.62
VeeDA (not end-to-end)	0.59	0.04	0.65	0.60
DenseUNet (MRI, supervised)	0.67	0.07	0.76	0.68
VeeDA	**0.64**	0.05	**0.70**	**0.65**

the resulting segmentation network is less than one second for a whole MRI volume on GPU.

Table 7.2 compares the performance of the proposed VeeDA algorithm with the following five methods. For fair comparison, all the dense U-Nets and discriminator networks used had the same configuration. In order to show the generalizability of our proposed method, if not explicitly specified, we ran 3-fold cross-validation for the MRI volumes and the setting was the same across different experiments. In each fold, the testing MRI volumes were unseen during the training phase. Unless mentioned otherwise, all the networks were trained end-to-end from scratch. More details can be found in the supplementary material.

DenseUNet (CT). A dense U-Net was trained using all the CT volumes and annotations for segmentation. No MRI volumes were used in the training step. At testing, the resulting model was applied directly to all the MRI volumes. As shown in Table 7.2, the model generalized poorly due to the domain shift.

Adversarial network in [23]. We implemented the multiconnected adversarial network in [23] with a dense U-Net as the backbone network. For fair comparison, single resolution volume was used as the input. We tried different combinations of features for the multiconnected domain discriminator and reported the one with the best performance, which still underperformed compared to our proposed VeeDA method.

VeeDA w/o feature adversarial loss. This is the proposed VeeDA method but without the feature adversarial loss. It is similar to the EssNet in [25], but generates better synthesized MRI images than EssNet because the volumetric network can better preserve the image consistency between slices of the synthesized volume. The network performance could potentially be further improved by combining the feature-level adaptation with the cycle consistency, as reported in [26].

VeeDA (not end-to-end). Similar to [26], the network was trained piece-by-piece: first, the CycleGAN block was trained using the CT and MRI training images; then the rest of the network was added and trained with CycleGAN block frozen; finally, the whole network was fine-tuned altogether. It performs worse than VeeDA network,

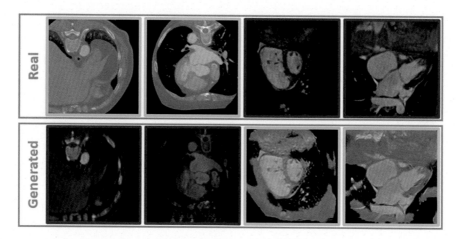

Figure 7.7 Visual results of the proposed generative model: (first row) input of generators; (second row) output from the generators. Red box indicates the real/generated samples in MRI domain. Green box indicates the real/generated samples in CT domain. The generative models are able to remove artifacts from MRI and add artifacts into CT.

suggesting that end-to-end training can boost the performance of our proposed network.

DenseUNet (MRI). A dense U-Net was trained using the MRI training images and annotations for segmentation. The resulting model was then applied to the MRI testing images. No CT image or annotations were used. This model is usually considered as the upper limit of domain adaptation network, as it assumes that annotations are available for the target domain [23]. Table 7.2 shows that the DenseUNet(MRI) performs better than the VeeDA model. It is considerable because the dense U-Net model has been trained on the real MRI dataset with labels. But our VeeDA model never sees any labels of the MRI dataset.

VeeDA. As shown in Figs. 7.7 and 7.8, our proposed volumetric end-to-end domain adaptation (VeeDA) method generates high quality synthesized images and achieves better segmentation accuracy than all the domain adaptation methods discussed above.

7.3.3 Conclusions

In this chapter, we briefly introduced the adversarial mechanism, deep image-to-image network, and how GAN can improve the segmentation prediction and solve the domain adaptation with intrinsic cycle consistency. As shown in the experiments, GAN is very powerful and efficient in various tasks. It will be very interesting topic to see if applying GAN with other types of representation, such as triangulation mesh and point set, can achieve similar or better performance.

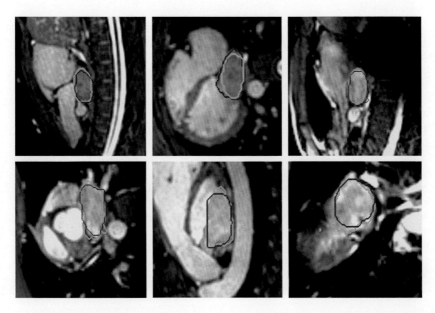

Figure 7.8 Sample results of the proposed segmentation model. Red contours are the prediction, and green contours are the ground truth.

References

[1] A. Radford, L. Metz, S. Chintala, Unsupervised representation learning with deep convolutional generative adversarial networks, in: ICLR, 2016.

[2] J.Y. Zhu, T. Park, P. Isola, A.A. Efros, Unpaired image-to-image translation using cycle-consistent adversarial networks, in: ICCV, 2017, pp. 2242–2251.

[3] J. Long, E. Shelhamer, T. Darrell, Fully convolutional networks for semantic segmentation, in: CVPR, 2015, pp. 3431–3440.

[4] V. Badrinarayanan, A. Kendall, R. Cipolla, Segnet: a deep convolutional encoder–decoder architecture for image segmentation, IEEE Trans. Pattern Anal. Mach. Intell. 39 (12) (2017) 2481–2495.

[5] O. Ronneberger, P. Fischer, T. Brox, U-Net: convolutional networks for biomedical image segmentation, in: MICCAI, 2015, pp. 234–241.

[6] F. Milletari, N. Navab, S. Ahmadi, V-Net: fully convolutional neural networks for volumetric medical image segmentation, in: 3D Vision, 2016, pp. 565–571.

[7] Q. Dou, H. Chen, Y. Jin, L. Yu, J. Qin, P.A. Heng, 3D deeply supervised network for automatic liver segmentation from CT volumes, in: MICCAI, 2016, pp. 149–157.

[8] D. Yang, T. Xiong, D. Xu, Q. Huang, D. Liu, S.K. Zhou, Z. Xu, J. Park, M. Chen, T. Tran, S. Chin, D. Metaxas, D. Comaniciu, Automatic vertebra labeling in large-scale 3D CT using deep image-to-image network with message passing and sparsity regularization, in: IPMI, 2017, pp. 633–644.

[9] D. Yang, T. Xiong, D. Xu, S.K. Zhou, Z. Xu, M. Chen, J. Park, J. Grbic, T. Tran, S. Chin, D. Metaxas, D. Comaniciu, Deep image-to-image recurrent network with shape basis learning for automatic vertebra labeling in large-scale 3D CT volumes, in: MICCAI, 2017, pp. 498–506.

[10] W. Li, G. Wang, L. Fidon, S. Ourselin, M.J. Cardoso, T. Vercauteren, On the compactness, efficiency, and representation of 3D convolutional networks: brain parcellation as a pretext task, in: IPMI, 2017, pp. 348–360.

[11] A.P. Harrison, Z. Xu, K. George, L. Lu, S.M. Summers, D.J. Mollura, Progressive and multi-path holistically nested neural networks for pathological lung segmentation from CT images, in: MICCAI, 2017, pp. 621–629.

[12] X. Li, H. Chen, X. Qi, Q. Dou, C. Fu, P.A. Heng, H-DenseUNet: hybrid densely connected U-Net for liver and liver tumor segmentation from CT volumes, arXiv:1709.07330, 2017.

[13] P. krahenbuhl, V. Koltun, Parameter learning and convergent inference for dense random fields, in: ICML, 2013.

[14] S. Zheng, S. Jayasumana, B. Romera-Paredes, V. Vineet, Z. Su, D. Du, C. Huang, P. Torr, Conditional random fields as recurrent neural networks, in: ICCV, 2015.

[15] P. Kohli, L. Ladicky, P. Torr, Robust higher order potentials for enforcing label consistency, Int. J. Comput. Vis. 82 (3) (2009) 302–324.

[16] A. Arnab, S. Jayasumana, S. Zheng, P. Torr, Higher order conditional random fields in deep neural networks, in: ECCV, 2016.

[17] P. Luc, C. Couprie, S. Chintala, Semantic segmentation using adversarial networks, in: Workshop on Adversarial Training, NIPS, 2016.

[18] D. Yang, D. Xu, S.K. Zhou, B. Georgescu, M. Chen, S. Grbic, D. Metaxas, D. Comaniciu, Automatic liver segmentation using an adversarial image-to-image network, in: MICCAI, 2017, pp. 507–515.

[19] R. Wolz, C. Chu, K. Misawa, M. Fujiwara, K. Mori, D. Rueckert, Automated abdominal multi-organ segmentation with subject-specific atlas generation, IEEE Trans. Med. Imaging 32 (9) (2013) 1723–1730.

[20] H.C. Shin, H.R. Roth, M. Gao, L. Lu, Z. Xu, I. Nogues, J. Yao, D. Mollura, R.M. Summers, Deep convolutional neural networks for computer-aided detection: CNN architectures, dataset characteristics and transfer learning, IEEE Trans. Med. Imaging 35 (5) (2016) 1285–1298.

[21] P. Moeskops, J.M. Wolterink, B.H. van der Velden, K.G. Gilhuijs, T. Leiner, M.A. Viergever, I. Isgum, Deep learning for multi-task medical image segmentation in multiple modalities, in: MICCAI, 2016.

[22] I. Goodfellow, J. Pouget-Abadie, M. Mirza, B. Xu, D. Warde-Farley, S. Ozair, A. Courville, Y. Bengio, Generative adversarial nets, in: NIPS, 2014, pp. 2672–2680.

[23] K. Kamnitsas, C. Baumgartner, C. Ledig, V. Newcombe, J. Simpson, A. Kane, D. Menon, A. Nori, D. Rueckert, B. Glocker, Unsupervised domain adaptation in brain lesion segmentation with adversarial networks, in: IPMI, 2017, pp. 597–609.

[24] S. Sankaranarayanan, Y. Balaji, A. Jain, S. Lim, R. Chellappa, Unsupervised domain adaptation for semantic segmentation with GANs, arXiv:1711.06969, 2017.

[25] Y. Huo, Z. Xu, S. Bao, A. Assad, R. Abramson, B. Landman, Adversarial synthesis learning enables segmentation without target modality ground truth, in: ISBI, 2018.

[26] J. Hoffman, E. Tzeng, T. Park, K. Saenko, A. Efros, T. Darrell, CyCADA: cycle-consistent adversarial domain adaptation, arXiv:1711.03213, 2017.

[27] G. Huang, Z. Liu, K.Q. Weinberger, L. van der Maaten, Densely connected convolutional networks, in: CVPR, 2017.

[28] F. Milletari, N. Navab, S.A. Ahmadi, V-Net: fully convolutional neural networks for volumetric medical image segmentation, in: Fourth International Conference in 3D Vision (3DV), IEEE, 2016.

[29] P. Isola, J.Y. Zhu, T. Zhou, A.A. Efros, Image-to-image translation with conditional adversarial networks, in: CVPR, 2017.

[30] X. Zhuang, J. Shen, Multi-scale patch and multi-modality atlases for whole heart segmentation of MRI, Med. Image Anal. 31 (2016) 77–87.

CHAPTER 8

Multimodal medical volumes translation and segmentation with generative adversarial network

Zizhao Zhang[a], Lin Yang[a,b], Yefeng Zheng[c]
[a]Department of Computer Information and Science Engineering (CISE), University of Florida, Gainesville, FL, United States
[b]University of Florida, Biomedical Engineering, Gainesville, FL, United States
[c]Tencent

Contents

8.1. Introduction	183
8.2. Literature review	186
8.2.1 Medical image synthesis	186
8.2.2 Image segmentation	187
8.3. Preliminary	188
8.3.1 CNN for segmentation	188
8.3.2 Generative adversarial network	188
8.3.3 Image-to-image translation for unpaired data	189
8.3.4 Problems in unpaired volume-to-volume translation	189
8.4. Method	190
8.4.1 Volume-to-volume cycle consistency	190
8.4.2 Volume-to-volume shape consistency	191
8.4.3 Multimodal volume segmentation	191
8.4.4 Method objective	192
8.5. Network architecture and training details	192
8.5.1 Architecture	192
8.5.2 Training details	194
8.6. Experimental results	194
8.6.1 Dataset	194
8.6.2 Cross-domain translation evaluation	195
8.6.3 Segmentation evaluation	196
8.6.4 Gap between synthetic and real data	199
8.6.5 Is more synthetic data better?	200
8.7. Conclusions	200
References	201

8.1. Introduction

In current clinical practice, multiple imaging modalities may be available for disease diagnosis and surgical planning [1]. For a specific patient group, a certain imaging modality

Handbook of Medical Image Computing and Computer Assisted Intervention
https://doi.org/10.1016/B978-0-12-816176-0.00013-2
183

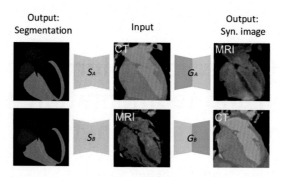

Figure 8.1 Our method learns two parallel sets of generators $G_{A/B}$ and segmentors $S_{A/B}$ for two modalities A and B to translate and segment holistic 3D volumes. Here we illustrate using CT and MRI cardiovascular 3D images.

might be more popular than others. Due to the proliferation of multiple imaging modalities, there is a strong clinical need to develop a cross-modality image transfer analysis system to assist clinical treatment, such as radiation therapy planning [2].

Machine learning (ML) based methods have been widely used for medical image analysis [3,4], including detection, segmentation, and tracking of an anatomical structure. Such methods are often generic and can be extended from one imaging modality to another by retraining on the target imaging modality. However, a sufficient number of representative training images are required to achieve enough robustness. In practice, it is often difficult to collect enough training images, especially for a new imaging modality not well established in clinical practice yet. Synthesized data are often used as supplementary training data in hope that they can boost the generalization capability of a trained ML model. However, the distribution gap between synthesized data and real data often determines the success of such an approach. This paper presents a novel method to address the above-mentioned two demanding tasks (Fig. 8.1).

In general scenarios, for one type of medical image (e.g., brain or cardiovascular images), researchers can obtain patient data from multiple modalities acquiring from different imaging protocols. However, most methods for different classification tasks (e.g., segmentation) are studied and investigated on respective modalities. The expensive and repeated labeling process is conducted on each individual domain. Taking advantage of labeled data from other modalities is quite challenging due to the large data distribution discrepancy. Assuming we have a mapping function that can arbitrarily translate data between two modalities, we can take advantage of translated synthetic data to help the training of various kinds of classification models, like segmentation. This problem contains two major tasks, the first is to synthesize realistic images and the second is to use synthetic data and make it beneficial for machine learning (ML) model generalization. It is a very appealing yet challenging problem in medical image analysis.

To synthesize medical images, recent advances [5–7] have used generative adversarial networks (GAN) [8] to formulate it as an image-to-image translation task. These methods require pixel-to-pixel correspondence between two domain data to build direct cross-modality reconstruction. However, in a more common scenario, multimodal medical images are in 3D and do not have cross-modality paired data. A method to learn from unpaired data is more general purpose. Furthermore, tomography structures (e.g., shape), in medical images/volumes, contain diagnostic information. Keeping their invariance in translation is critical. However, when using GANs without paired data, due to the lack of direct reconstruction, relying on discriminators to guarantee this requirement is not enough as we explain later.

Accurate medical volume segmentation provides quantitative evaluation that is critical for clinical diagnosis. Fully convolutional networks (FCN) [9] and U–Net [10] based networks are widely used to handle 2D or 3D medical image segmentation tasks. Adversarial learning can not only be used for synthesizing images, but also used to improve segmentation quality [11,12,5,13], which is achieved by adding an adversarial loss. However, adding adversarial losses on a segmentation network only incrementally refine the results. It cannot remedy the most important problem of insufficiency of labeled data. Augmenting the training data space is the most straightforward and effective way to improve segmentation or for domain adaptation. So generating high-quality synthetic data is a more promising way.

We present a general-purpose method to realize both medical volume translation as well as segmentation. In brief, given two sets of unpaired data in two modalities, we simultaneously learn generators for cross-domain volume-to-volume translation and stronger segmentors by taking advantage of synthetic data translated from the other domain. Our method is composed of several 3D CNNs. From the generator learning view, we propose to train adversarial networks with cycle-consistency [14] to solve the problem of data without correspondence. We then propose a novel shape-consistency scheme to guarantee the shape invariance of synthetic images, which is supported by another CNN, namely segmentor. From the segmentor learning view, segmentors directly take advantage of generators by using synthetic data to boost the segmentation performance in an online fashion. Both generator and segmentor can take benefits from each other in our end-to-end training fashion with one joint optimization objective.

On a dataset with 4496 cardiovascular 3D images in MRI and CT modalities, we conduct extensive experiments to demonstrate the effectiveness of our method qualitatively and quantitatively from both generator and segmentor views with our proposed auxiliary evaluation metrics. We show that using synthetic data as an isolated offline data augmentation process underperforms our end-to-end online approach. On the volume segmentation task, blindly using synthetic data with a small number of real data can even distract the optimization when trained in the offline fashion. However, our method does not have this problem and leads to consistent improvement.

8.2. Literature review

There are two demanding goals in medical image synthesis. The first is synthesizing realistic cross-modality images [15,5], and second is to use synthetic data from other modalities with sufficient labeled data to help classification tasks (e.g., domain adaptation [11]). The target of this method is to realize cross-modality translation of 3D medical images and segmentation simultaneously. We discuss related work about medical image synthesis and segmentation in the following.

8.2.1 Medical image synthesis

In computer vision, recent image-to-image translation is formulated as a pixel-to-pixel mapping using encoder–decoder CNNs [16,17,14,18,19,17,20,21]. The value of building such domain translation is very meaningful in medical imaging to help domain adaptation [11], and so on [22]. Several studies have explored cross-modality translation for medical images, using sparse coding [15,23], GANs [5,24], CNN [25], etc. GANs have attracted wide interests in helping addressing such tasks to generate high-quality, less blurry results [8,26–28]. More recent studies apply pixel-to-pixel GANs for brain MRI to CT image translation [5,11] and retinal vessel annotation to image translation [6]. However, these methods presume targeting images have paired cross-domain data. Learning from unpaired cross-domain data is an attractive yet not well explored problem [23,29].

While for many medical images (e.g., cardiovascular images), acquiring paired training data is difficult or even impossible. The ability of learning from totally unpaired data is critical. In addition, preserving the tomography structure (e.g., shape) is a necessary requirement for medical images. However, existing methods have not explicitly considered this problem.

Synthesizing medical data to overcome insufficient labeled data attracted wide interests recently [30–33]. Due to the diversity of medical modalities, learning an unsupervised translation between modalities is a promising direction [6]. Recently, GANs is used to improve the realism of synthetic data [30,34], thus reducing the gap between real and synthetic data for several natural image datasets. Furthermore, Kamnitsas et al. [11] demonstrate the benefits on brain (MRI and CT) images, by using synthetic data as augmented training data to help lesion segmentation.

Apart from synthesizing data, several studies [12,13,35,36] use adversarial learning as an extra supervision on the segmentation or detection networks. The adversarial loss plays a role of constraining the prediction to be close to the distribution of ground truth. However, such strategy is a refinement process, so it is less likely to remedy the cost of data insufficiency.

8.2.2 Image segmentation

Deep learning has become the mainstream of medical image segmentation methods [37–42]. Ciresan et al. [43] adopt the standard CNN as a patchwise pixel classifier to segment the neuronal membranes (EM) of electron microscopy images. This study is a pioneer work of using CNN for medical image segmentation. The majority of segmentation methods follows the structure of the FCN [44], HED [45] networks and U-Net [10]. In U-Net, to handle touching objects, a weighted loss is introduced to penalize the errors around the boundary margin between objects. The state-of-the-art segmentation performance on the EM dataset is achieved by a new deep contextual network proposed in [46]. The deep contextual network adopts an architecture that is similar to HED. The difference is that the final segmentation result is a combined version of the segmentation results derived from different layers through an auxiliary classification layer. In the forward propagation, such design can more efficiently exploit the contextual information from different layers for edge detection. In return, the lower layers can be deeply supervised through these auxiliary classification layers. This is because the classification layers provide a shortcut between the lower layers and final segmentation error. The authors of [47,48] propose a deep contour-aware network for gland image segmentation. This method uses side outputs as multitasking deep supervision. The detected contour map is merged with the segmented binary mask to prevent touching of glands, which is a special treatment to cell contours. In a followup work, Xu et al. [49] propose a multichannel side supervision CNN for gland segmentation. This network can be treated as a combination of HED and FCN for simultaneous segmentation and contour detection. Similarly, Nogues et al. [50] propose a lymph node cluster segmentation algorithm based on HED, FCN, and structured optimization to address the contour appearance variation. Cai et al. [51] propose a data fusion step using conditional random field (CRF) to adaptively consider the segmentation mask generated by FCN and the contour map generated by HED for pancreas segmentation.

CNN based methods for 3D medical image segmentation have been attracting attentions in recent two years. Most existing methods are extensions of known 2D CNNs. The authors of [52] propose a 3D deeply supervised network for liver segmentation. It can be viewed as a 3D extension of HED. Moreover, it uses a fully connected CRF to refine the object contours. 3D U-Net [53] is proposed by the same group with U-Net for 3D volumetric segmentation. Milletari et al. propose V-Net [54], which contains a new loss function based on Dice coefficient to resolve the strong imbalance between foreground and background. It uses the skip-connection strategy of U-Net to prevent the detail information loss which will affect fine contour prediction.

8.3. Preliminary

We begin by introducing the basics of GANs and segmentation. Then, we discuss the recent advances on image-to-image translation and clarify their existing problems when used for medical volume-to-volume translation as our motivation.

8.3.1 CNN for segmentation

CNN is widely used to perform dense (pixelwise) classification. In the family of CNN based segmentation, U-Net [10] is a very successful approach. Different from FCN or ResNet designs, it has a U-shape structure that each bottom layer will be connected to symmetric upper layers. This design has multiple advantages [55].

- It allows easy training and fast gradient backpropagation, which is similar to the blockwise skip-connection of ResNet.
- It in nature combines multiple level feature maps at different scales so as to capture both global and local information. This merit is quite useful for medical image segmentation.

Currently, U-Net is still used as a strong benchmark for various medical image segmentation tasks. Also, it is used as generators in GANs [16,14]. Our segmentation method utilizes U-Net to achieve segmentation as will be detailed in the method.

8.3.2 Generative adversarial network

The GAN has been recognized as a powerful generative model for unsupervised image generation [8]. The original generative model aims to model the distribution of real images by learning to transform a latent low-dimensional variable to the actual training image data distribution. Capturing the distribution of high-dimensional image space is very challenging. GAN is composed by a generator model and a discriminator model. The goal of generator is to learn an effective transformation from latent variables to images. The goal of discriminator, trained together with discriminator, is to distinguish (i.e., classify) the real images in the training data from the generated fake images from generator. The generator and discriminator compete each other and improve each other during the adversarial training until the models reach a balance (also called Nash equilibrium). Let's define the generator as G and discriminator as D, the adversarial objective is a min–max loss function

$$\min_G \max_D V(G, D) = \mathbb{E}_{x \sim p_{data}(x)}[\log D(x)] + \mathbb{E}_{x \sim p_z(z)}[1 - \log D(G(z))], \qquad (8.1)$$

where x is training data, z contains latent variables.

The above is the basic of general GANs. GAN has been generalized to solve variable kinds of problems. Image-to-image translation (where z becomes an image space) is an important topic. GAN has been widely used for image translation in the applications that need pixel-to-pixel mapping, such as image style transfer [56], image superresolution [15], or modality translation [33] (that we address here). In fact, most applications need paired data for training. While in many real world settings, acquiring paired data can be difficult or even impossible. For example, the paired cardiac volumes of CT and MRI cannot be acquired because hearts always beat. We will see in the next about how to train GANs without paired data.

8.3.3 Image-to-image translation for unpaired data

ConditionalGAN [16] shows a strategy to learn such translation mapping with a conditional setting to capture structure information. However, it needs paired cross-domain images for the pixelwise reconstruction loss. For some types of translation tasks, acquiring paired training data from two domains is difficult or even impossible. Recently, CycleGAN [14] and other similar methods [18,57] were proposed to generalize ConditionalGAN to address this issue. Here, we use CycleGAN to illustrate the key idea.

Given a set of unpaired data from two domains, A and B, CycleGAN learns two mappings, $G_B : A \rightarrow B$ and $G_A : B \rightarrow A$, with two generators G_A and G_B, at the same time. To bypass the infeasibility of pixelwise reconstruction with paired data, i.e., $G_B(A) \approx B$ or $G_A(B) \approx A$, CycleGAN introduces an effective cycle-consistency loss for $G_A(G_B(A)) \approx A$ and $G_B(G_A(B)) \approx B$. The idea is that the generated target domain data is able to return back to the exact data in the source domain it is generated from. To guarantee the fidelity of fake data $G_B(A)$ and $G_A(B)$, CycleGAN uses two discriminators D_A and D_B to distinguish real or synthetic data and thereby encourage generators to synthesize realistic data [8].

8.3.4 Problems in unpaired volume-to-volume translation

Lacking supervision with a direct reconstruction error between $G_B(A)$ and B or $G_A(B)$ and A brings some uncertainties and difficulties in achieving desired outputs in some tasks. And, it is even more challenging when training with 3D CNNs.

To be specific, cycle-consistency has an intrinsic ambiguity with respect to geometric transformations. For example, suppose generation functions, G_A and G_B, are cycle consistent, e.g., $G_A(G_B(A)) = A$. Let T be a bijective geometric transformation (e.g., translation, rotation, scaling, or even nonrigid transformation) with inverse transformation T^{-1}.

It is easy to show that

$$G'_A = G_A \circ T \text{ and } G'_B = G_B \circ T^{-1} \qquad (8.2)$$

are also cycle consistent. Here, $\circ$ denotes the concatenation operation of two transformations. That means, using CycleGAN, when an image is translated from one domain to the other it can be geometrically distorted. And the distortion can be recovered

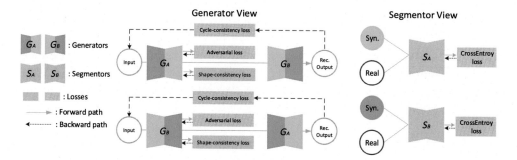

Figure 8.2 The illustration of our method from the generator view (left) and the segmentor view (right). **Generator view:** Two generators learn cross-domain translation between domain A and B, which are supervised by a cycle-consistency loss, a discriminative loss, and a shape-consistency loss (supported by segmentors), respectively. **Segmentor view:** Segmentors are trained by real data and extra synthetic data translated from domain-specific generators. Best viewed in color.

when it is translated back to the original domain without provoking any penalty in data fidelity cost. From the discriminator perspective, geometric transformation often does not change the realness of synthesized images since the shape of training data is arbitrary.

Such problem can destroy anatomical structures in synthetic medical volumes, which, however, has not been addressed by existing methods. In the following, we introduce our main method that uses a shape-consistency supervention to achieve realistic and shape-invariant cross-domain translation of 3D volumes, as well as dual-domain segmentation which are boosted by synthetic data from generators. We propose to couple these two actually highly-related tasks and encourage networks of respective tasks to take advantage of each other through a joint optimization objective.

8.4. Method

This section introduces our proposed medical volume-to-volume translation, with adversarial, cycle-consistency and shape-consistency losses, as well as dual-modality segmentation. Fig. 8.2 illustrates our method.

8.4.1 Volume-to-volume cycle consistency

To solve the task of learning generators with unpaired volumes from two domains, A and B, we adopt the idea of the cycle-consistency loss for generators G_A and G_B to force the reconstructed synthetic sample $G_A(G_B(x_A))$ and $G_B(G_A(x_B))$ to be identical to their inputs x_A and x_B:

$$\mathcal{L}_{cyc}(G_A, G_B) = \mathbb{E}_{x_A \sim p_d(x_A)}[||G_A(G_B(x_A)) - x_A||_1]$$
$$+ \mathbb{E}_{x_B \sim p_d(x_B)}[||G_B(G_A(x_B)) - x_B||_1], \quad (8.3)$$

where x_A is a sample from domain A and x_B is from domain B; $\mathcal{L}_{cyc}$ uses the L1 loss over all voxels, which shows better visual results than the L2 loss.

8.4.2 Volume-to-volume shape consistency

To solve the intrinsic ambiguity with respect to geometric transformations in cycle consistency as we pointed out above, our method introduces two auxiliary mappings, defined as $S_A : A \rightarrow Y$ and $S_B : B \rightarrow Y$, to constrain the geometric invariance of synthetic data. They map the translated data from respective domain generators into a shared shape space Y (i.e., a semantic label space) and compute pixelwise semantic ownership. The two mappings are represented by two CNNs, namely segmentors. We use them as extra supervision on the generators to support shape consistency (see Fig. 8.2) by optimizing

$$
\begin{aligned}
\mathcal{L}_{shape}(S_A,\ S_B,\ G_A,\ G_B) = {} & \mathbb{E}_{x_B \sim p_d(x_B)}[-\frac{1}{N}\sum_i y_B^i \log(S_A(G_A(x_B))_i)] \\
& + \mathbb{E}_{x_A \sim p_d(x_A)}[-\frac{1}{N}\sum_i y_A^i \log(S_B(G_B(x_A))_i)],
\end{aligned}
\tag{8.4}
$$

where $y_A, y_B \in Y$ denote the ground truth shape representation of sample volumes x_A and x_B, respectively; $y_A^i, y_B^i \in \{0, 1, \ldots, C\}$ represent one voxel with one out of C classes; N is the total number of voxels in a volume; $\mathcal{L}_{shape}$ is formulated as a standard multiclass cross-entropy loss. This objective is designed to update the generator G_A and G_B while keep S_A and S_B fixed. Intuitively, in the first term, a synthesized image x_A by generator G_A in domain A should result in the same shape representations y_B of its source image x_B in domain B when mapping to the shape space through S_A (the same for the second term).

Regularization. Shape consistency provides a level of regularization on generators. Recall that different from ConditionalGAN, since we have no paired data, the only supervision for $G_A(x_B)$ and $G_B(x_A)$ is the adversarial loss, which is not sufficient to preserve all types of information in synthetic images, such as the annotation correctness. Shrivastava et al. [30] introduce a self-regularization loss between an input image and an output image to force the annotations to be preserved. Our shape-consistency performs a similar role to preserve pixelwise semantic label ownership, as a way to regularize the generators and guarantee the anatomical structure invariance in medical volumes.

8.4.3 Multimodal volume segmentation

The second parallel task we address in our method is to make use of synthetic data for improving the generalization of segmentation network, which is trained together with generators. From the segmentor view (Fig. 8.2) of S_A and S_B, the synthetic volumes $\{G_B(x_A), y_A\}$ and $\{G_A(x_B), y_B\}$ provide extra training data to help improve the segmentors in an online manner. During training, S_A and S_B take both real data and synthetic data that are generated by generators online (see Fig. 8.2). By maximizing the usage of synthetic data, we also use reconstructed synthetic data, $\{G_A(G_B(x_A)), y_A\}$ and $\{G_B(G_A(x_B)), y_B\}$, as the inputs of segmentors.

Note that the most straightforward way to use synthetic data is fusing them with real data and then train a segmentation CNN. We denote this as an ad hoc offline data augmentation approach. In comparison, our method implicitly performs data augmentation in an online manner. Formulated in our optimization objective, our method can use synthetic data more adaptively, which thereby offers more stable training and thereby better performance than the offline approach. We will demonstrate this in experiments.

8.4.4 Method objective

Given the definitions of cycle- and shape-consistency losses above, we define our full objective as:

$$
\begin{aligned}
\mathcal{L}(G_A, G_B, D_A, D_B, S_A, S_B) = {} & \mathcal{L}_{GAN}(G_A, D_A) \\
& + \mathcal{L}_{GAN}(G_B, D_B) \\
& + \lambda \mathcal{L}_{cyc}(G_A, G_B) \\
& + \gamma \mathcal{L}_{shape}(S_A, S_B, G_A, G_B).
\end{aligned}
\tag{8.5}
$$

The adversarial loss $\mathcal{L}_{GAN}$ (defined in [14,16]) encourages local realism of synthetic data (see architecture details); λ is set to 10 and γ is set to 1 during training. To optimize $\mathcal{L}_{GAN}$, $\mathcal{L}_{cyc}$, and $\mathcal{L}_{shape}$, we update them alternatively: optimizing $G_{A/B}$ with $S_{A/B}$ and $D_{A/B}$ fixed and then optimizing $S_{A/B}$ and $D_{A/B}$ (they are independent), respectively, with $G_{A/B}$ fixed.

The generators and segmentors are mutually beneficial because, to make the full objective optimized, the generators have to generate synthetic data with lower shape-consistency loss, which, from another angle, indicates lower segmentation losses over synthetic training data.

8.5. Network architecture and training details

This section discusses necessary architecture and training details for generating high-quality 3D images.

8.5.1 Architecture

Training deep networks end-to-end on 3D images is much more difficult (from optimization and memory aspects) than 2D images. Instead of using 2.5D [58] or sub-

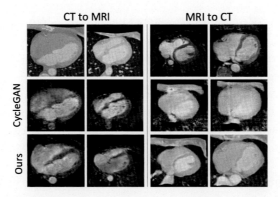

Figure 8.3 Example outputs on 2D slides of 3D cardiovascular CT and MRI images generated by 3D CycleGAN (second row) and ours (third row). The first row is the input samples. The original results of CycleGAN have severe artifacts, checkerboard effects, and missing anatomies (e.g., descending aorta and spine), while our method overcomes these issues and achieves significantly better quality.

volumes [11], our method directly deals with holistic volumes. There are several keys of network designs in order to achieve visually good results. The architecture of our method is composed of 3D fully convolutional layers with instance normalization [59] (performs better than batch normalization [60]) and ReLU for generators or LeakyReLU for discriminators. CycleGAN originally designs generators with multiple residual blocks [61]. Differently, in our generators, we make several critical modifications with justifications.

First, we find that using both bottom and top layer representations are critical to maintain the anatomical structures in medical images. We use long-range skip-connection in U-Net [10] as it achieves much faster convergence and locally smooth results. ConditionalGAN also uses U-Net generators, but we do not downsample feature maps as greedily as it does. We apply 3 times downsampling with stride-2 3×3×3 convolutions in total, so the maximum downsampling rate is 8. The upsampling part is symmetric. Two sequential convolutions are used for each resolution, as it performs better than using one. Second, we replace transpose-convolutions to stride 2 nearest upsampling followed by a 3×3×3 convolution to realize upsampling as well as channel changes. It is also observed in [62] that transpose-convolution can cause checkerboard artifacts due to the uneven overlapping of convolutional kernels. Actually, this effect is even severer for 3D transpose-convolutions as one pixel may be covered by 2^3 overlapping kernels (results in 8 times uneven overlapping). Fig. 8.3 compares the results with CycleGAN, demonstrating that our method can obtain significantly better visual quality.[1]

---

[1] We have experimented CycleGAN with many different configurations of generators and discriminators. All trials did not achieve desired visual results compared with our configuration.

For discriminators, we adopt the PatchGAN proposed by [30] to classify whether an overlapping subvolume is real or fake, rather than to classify the whole volume. Such approach limits discriminators to use unexpected information from arbitrary volume locations to make decisions.

For segmentors, we use another U-Net [10], but without any normalization layer. Totally, 3 times symmetric downsampling and upsampling are performed by stride 2 max-pooling and nearest upsampling. For each resolution, we use two sequential $3 \times 3 \times 3$ convolutions.

8.5.2 Training details

We use the Adam solver [63] for segmentors with a learning rate of $2e{-}4$ and closely follow the settings in CycleGAN to train generators with discriminators. In the next section, for the purpose of fast experimenting, we choose to pretrain the $G_{A/B}$ and $D_{A/B}$ separately first and then train the whole network jointly. We hypothesized that fine-tuning generators and segmentors first is supposed to have better performance because they only affect each other after they have the sense of reasonable outputs. Nevertheless, we observed that training all from scratch can also obtain similar results. It demonstrates the effectiveness to couple both tasks in an end-to-end network and make them converge harmonically. We pretrain segmentors for 100 epochs and generators for 60 epochs. After jointly training for 50 epochs, we decrease the learning rates for both generators and segmentors steadily for another 50 epochs till 0. We found that if the learning rate decreases to a certain small value, the synthetic images turn to show clear artifacts and the segmentors tend to overfit. We apply early stop when the segmentation loss no longer decreases for about 5 epochs (usually takes 40 epochs to reach a desired point). In training, the number of training data in two domains can be different. We go through all data in the domain with larger amount as one epoch.

8.6. Experimental results

This section evaluates and discusses our method. We introduce a 3D cardiovascular image dataset. Heart is a perfect example of the difficulty in getting paired cross-modality data as it is a nonrigid organ and it keeps beating. Even if there are CT and MRI scans from the same patient, they cannot be perfectly aligned. We evaluate the two tasks we addressed in our method, i.e., volume segmentation and synthesis, both qualitatively and quantitatively with our proposed auxiliary evaluation metrics.

8.6.1 Dataset

We collected 4354 contrasted cardiac CT scans from patients with various cardiovascular diseases (2–3 volumes per patients). The resolution inside an axial slice is isotropic and varies from 0.28 to 0.74 mm for different volumes. The slice thickness (distance between

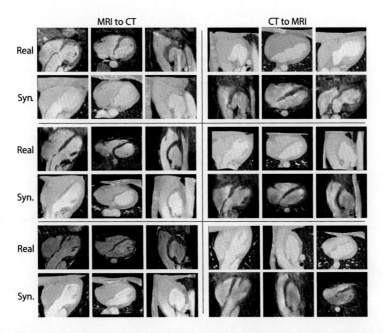

Figure 8.4 Qualitative results of our translation from MRI to CT (left columns) and from CT to MRI (right columns). For each sample (in one out of six grids), we show three orthogonal cuts through the center of 3D volumes.

neighboring slices) is larger than the in-slice resolution and varies from 0.4 to 2.0 mm. In addition, we collected 142 cardiac MRI scans with a new compressed sensing scanning protocol. The MRI volumes have a near isotropic resolution ranging from 0.75 to 2.0 mm. This true 3D MRI scan with isotropic voxel size is a new imaging modality, only available in handful top hospitals. All volumes are resampled to 1.5 mm for the following experiments. We crop sub-volumes of $112 \times 112 \times 86$ voxels around the heart center. The endocardium of all four cardiac chambers is annotated. The left ventricle epicardium is annotated too, resulting in five anatomical regions.

We denote CT as domain A data and MRI as domain B. We organize the dataset in two sets S_1 and S_2. For S_1, we randomly select 142 CT volumes from all CT images to match the number of MRI volumes. For both modalities, 50% data is used as training and validation and the rest 50% as test data. For S_2, we use all the rest 4212 CT volumes as an extra augmentation dataset, which is used to generate synthetic MRI volumes for segmentation. We fix the test data in S_1 for all experiments.

8.6.2 Cross-domain translation evaluation

We evaluate the generators both qualitatively and quantitatively. Fig. 8.4 shows some typical synthetic results of our method. As can be observed visually, the synthetic images

Table 8.1 Shape quality evaluation using S-score (see text for definition). The synthetic volumes using our method have much better shape quality on both modalities. SC denotes shape consistency.

Method	S-score (%)	
	CT	MRI
G w/o SC	66.8	67.5
G w/ SC (Ours)	**69.2**	**69.6**

are close to real images and no obvious geometric distortion is introduced during image translation. Our method preserves cardiac anatomies, like aorta and spine, very well.

Shape invariance evaluation. For methods of GANs to generate class–specific natural images, [64] proposes to use the Inception score to evaluate the diversity of generated images, by using an auxiliary trained classification network.

Inspired by this, we propose the S-core (segmentation score) to evaluate the shape invariance quality of synthetic images. We train two segmentation networks on the training data of respective modalities and compare the multiclass Dice score of synthetic volumes. For each synthetic volume, S-score is computed by comparing to the ground truth of the corresponding real volume it is translated from. Hence, higher score indicates better matched shape (i.e., less geometric distortion). Table 8.1 shows the S-score of synthetic data from CT and MRI for generators without the shape-consistency loss, denoted as "G w/o SC." Note that it is mostly similar with CycleGAN but using our optimized network designs. As can be seen, our method (G w/ SC) with shape-consistency achieves large improvement over the baseline on both modalities.

8.6.3 Segmentation evaluation

Here we show how well our method can use the synthetic data and help improve segmentation. We compare to an ad hoc approach as we mentioned above. Specifically, we individually train two segmentors, denoted as $\tilde{S}_A$ and $\tilde{S}_B$. We treat the segmentation performance of them as Baseline (R) in the following. Then we train generators $\tilde{G}_A$ and $\tilde{G}_B$ with the adversarial and cycle-consistency losses (setting the weight of the shape-consistency loss to 0). Then by adding synthetic data, we perform the following comparison:

1. Ad hoc approach (ADA). We use $\tilde{G}_A$ and $\tilde{G}_B$ to generate synthetic data (To make fair comparison, both synthetic data $G_{A/B}(x_{B/A})$ and reconstructed data

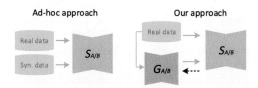

Figure 8.5 Illustration of the strategies to use synthetic data to improve segmentation. The left is the comparing ad hoc offline approach. The right is our approach that uses synthetic data from the generator in an online fashion.

$G_{A/B}(G_{B/A}(x_{A/B}))$ are used). We fine-tune $\tilde{S}_{A/B}$ using synthetic together with real data (Fig. 8.5, left).[2]

2. Our method. We join $\tilde{S}_A$, $\tilde{S}_B$, $\tilde{G}_A$, and $\tilde{G}_B$ (also with discriminators) and fine-tune the overall networks in an end-to-end fashion (Fig. 8.5, right), as specified in the training details.

Note that the backbone segmentation network is U–Net [10]. For medical image segmentation, U–Net is well recognized as one of the best end-to-end CNN. Its long-range skip connection performs usually better than or equally well to FCN or ResNet/DenseNet based architectures [55], especially for small-size medical datasets. Therefore, U–Net usually represents state-of-the-art in medical image segmentation.

We perform this experimental procedure on both S_1 and S_2. In the first experiment on S_1, we test the scenario that how well our method uses synthetic data to improve segmentation given only limited real data. Since we need to vary the number of data in one modality and fix another, we perform the experiments on both modalities, respectively.

By using 14% real data and all synthetic data from the counter modality, Table 8.2 compares the segmentation results. We use the standard multiclass Dice score as the evaluation metric [65]. As can be observed, our method achieves much better performance on both modalities. For CT segmentation, ADA even deteriorates the performance. We speculate that it is because the baseline model trained with very few real data has not been stabilized. Synthetic data distracts optimization when used for training offline. While our method adapts them fairly well and leads to significant improvement.

We also demonstrate the qualitative results of our method in Fig. 8.6. By only using extra synthetic data, our method largely corrects the segmentation errors. Furthermore, we show the results by varying the number of real volumes used in Fig. 8.7 (left and middle). Our method has consistently better performance than ADA. In addition, we notice the increment is growing slower as the number of real volumes increases. One reason is that more real data makes the segmentors get closer to its capacity, so the

---

[2] At each training batch, we take half real and half synthetic data to prevent possible distraction from low-quality synthetic data.

Table 8.2 The segmentation performance comparison. Initialized from the baseline model trained with only **R**eal data (Baseline (R)), the second and third rows show the boosted results by using **S**ynthetic data with the comparing ad hoc (ADA) method and our method, respectively.

Method	Dice score (%)	
	CT	MRI
Baseline (R)	67.8	70.3
ADA (R+S)	66.0	71.0
Ours (R+S)	**74.4**	**73.2**

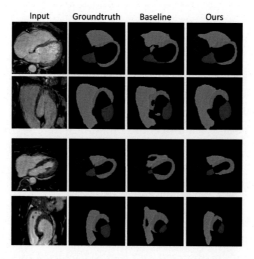

Figure 8.6 The qualitative evaluation of segmentation results on MRI. We show the axial and sagittal views of two samples. Our method boosts the baseline segmentation network with only extra synthetic data. As can be observed, the segmentation errors of the baseline are largely corrected.

benefit of extra synthetic data gets smaller. But this situation can be definitely balanced out by increasing the network size of segmentors.

The second experiment is applied on S_2, which has much more CT data, so we aim at boosting the MRI segmentor. We vary the number of used synthetic data and use all real MRI data. Fig. 8.7 (right) compares the results. Our method still shows better performance. As can be observed, our method uses 23% synthetic data to reach the accuracy of the ADA when it uses 100% synthetic data.

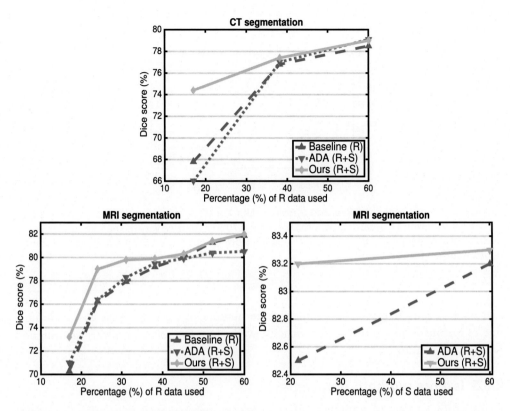

Figure 8.7 The segmentation accuracy (mean Dice score) comparison to demonstrate the effectiveness of our method of using **S**ynthetic data to boost segmentation. The top plot shows the segmentation accuracy by varying the percentage of **R**eal data used for training segmentation on CT using dataset S_1, using an equal number of synthetic data. Baseline (R) is trained with only real data. Others are trained from it, e.g., ADA (R+S) is trained by adding only **S** data. The bottom-left plot shows the same experiments on MRI. The bottom-right plot shows results by varying the number of synthetic data on MRI using dataset S_2 using an equal number of real data. Our method has consistently better performance. See text for details about comparing methods.

8.6.4 Gap between synthetic and real data

Reducing the distribution gap between real and synthetic data is the key to make synthetic data useful for segmentation. Here we show a way to interpret the gap between synthetic and real data by evaluating their effectiveness to improve segmentation. On dataset S_1, we train an MRI segmentor using 14% real data. Then we boost the segmentor by adding (1) pure MRI real data, (2) using ADA, and (3) using our method. As shown in Fig. 8.8, our method reduces the gap of the ADA significantly, i.e., by 61% given 14% real data, and 20.9% given 85% real data.

Moreover, we found that, when using the synthetic data as augmented data offline (our comparing baseline), too much synthetic data could diverge the network training.

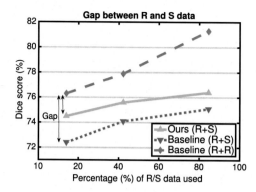

Figure 8.8 The gap analysis of **R**eal and **S**ynthetic data. For all comparing methods, we use one pre-trained network with 14% real data, whose Dice score is 70.3%. Then we vary the number of R or S data used to boost segmentation of Baseline (R+R), Baseline (R+S), and Ours (R+S). Our method significantly reduces the gap for all settings.

While in our method, we did not observe such situation. However, we also observe that the gap is more difficult to reduce as the number of read data increases. Although one of reasons is due to the modal capacity, we believe the solution of this *gap-reduction* worth further study.

8.6.5 Is more synthetic data better?

Using synthetic data to improve a neural network performance is an attractive topic. However, based on our results, we find stacking as many as synthetic data does not always improve the performance (here we do not consider the positive influence of increasing the model complexity). It is highly affected by the proportion between real and fake images. As shown in Fig. 8.7 (bottom-right), when transferring 100% domain A to improve the segmentation performance of domain B has only slight improvement compared with transferring 25% domain A. Moreover, we found that using the synthetic data as augmented data offline (our comparing baseline), too much synthetic data will diverge the network training. While in our method, we did not observe such situation, which means our online approach adapts synthetic data better.

8.7. Conclusions

In this paper, we present a method that can simultaneously learn to translate and segment 3D medical images, which are two significant tasks in medical imaging. Training generators for cross-domain volume-to-volume translation is more difficult than that on 2D images. We address three key problems that are important in synthesizing realistic 3D medical images: (1) learn from unpaired data, (2) keep anatomy (i.e., shape) consistency, and (3) use synthetic data to improve volume segmentation effectively. We demonstrate that our unified method that couples the two tasks is more effective than solving them exclusively. Extensive experiments on a 3D cardiovascular dataset validate the effectiveness and superiority of our method.

Deep neural networks are data ineffective. There is growing interest on how to generate synthesized images to augment training data. The proliferation of data modality provides a clear motivation for its application in medical image analysis. For future study, we will explore our method in different modalities with both 2D and 3D images. In addition, some further directions are open for study. For example, to achieve cross-modality translation, we currently need shape annotation, which is expensive to acquire? Keeping anatomy consistency without using shape annotation is a clearly valuable extension.

References

[1] X. Cao, J. Yang, Y. Gao, Y. Guo, G. Wu, D. Shen, Dual-core steered non-rigid registration for multi-modal images via bi-directional image synthesis, Medical Image Analysis 41 (2017) 18–31.

[2] N. Burgos, M.J. Cardoso, F. Guerreiro, C. Veiga, M. Modat, J. McClelland, et al., Robust CT synthesis for radiotherapy planning: application to the head and neck region, in: Proc. Int'l Conf. Medical Image Computing and Computer Assisted Intervention, 2015.

[3] Z. Zhang, Y. Xie, F. Xing, M. Mcgough, L. Yang, MDNet: a semantically and visually interpretable medical image diagnosis network, in: Proc. IEEE Conf. Computer Vision and Pattern Recognition, 2017.

[4] Z. Zhang, P. Chen, M. Sapkota, L. Yang, TandemNet: distilling knowledge from medical images using diagnostic reports as optional semantic references, in: Proc. Int'l Conf. Medical Image Computing and Computer Assisted Intervention, 2017.

[5] D. Nie, R. Trullo, C. Petitjean, S. Ruan, D. Shen, Medical image synthesis with context-aware generative adversarial networks, preprint, arXiv:1612.05362, 2016.

[6] P. Costa, A. Galdran, M.I. Meyer, M.D. Abràmoff, M. Niemeijer, A.M. Mendonça, et al., Towards adversarial retinal image synthesis, preprint, arXiv:1701.08974, 2017.

[7] Z. Zhang, L. Yang, Y. Zheng, Translating and segmenting multimodal medical volumes with cycle- and shape-consistency generative adversarial network, preprint, arXiv:1802.09655, 2018.

[8] I. Goodfellow, J. Pouget-Abadie, M. Mirza, B. Xu, D. Warde-Farley, S. Ozair, et al., Generative adversarial nets, in: Advances in Neural Information Processing Systems, 2014, pp. 2672–2680.

[9] E. Shelhamer, J. Long, T. Darrell, Fully convolutional networks for semantic segmentation, IEEE Transactions on Pattern Analysis and Machine Intelligence 39 (4) (2016) 640–651.

[10] O. Ronneberger, P. Fischer, T. Brox, U-Net: convolutional networks for biomedical image segmentation, in: International Conference on Medical Image Computing and Computer-Assisted Intervention, 2015, pp. 234–241.

[11] K. Kamnitsas, C. Baumgartner, C. Ledig, V. Newcombe, J. Simpson, A. Kane, et al., Unsupervised domain adaptation in brain lesion segmentation with adversarial networks, in: Proc. Information Processing in Medical Imaging, 2017.

[12] S. Kohl, D. Bonekamp, H.P. Schlemmer, K. Yaqubi, M. Hohenfellner, B. Hadaschik, et al., Adversarial networks for the detection of aggressive prostate cancer, preprint, arXiv:1702.08014, 2017.

[13] P. Luc, C. Couprie, S. Chintala, J. Verbeek, Semantic segmentation using adversarial networks, in: NIPS Workshop on Adversarial Training, 2016.

[14] J.Y. Zhu, T. Park, P. Isola, A.A. Efros, Unpaired image-to-image translation using cycle-consistent adversarial networks, in: Proc. Int'l Conf. Computer Vision, 2017.

[15] Y. Huang, L. Shao, A.F. Frangi, Simultaneous super-resolution and cross-modality synthesis of 3D medical images using weakly-supervised joint convolutional sparse coding, in: Proc. IEEE Conf. Computer Vision and Pattern Recognition, 2017.

[16] P. Isola, J.Y. Zhu, T. Zhou, A.A. Efros, Image-to-image translation with conditional adversarial networks, in: Proc. IEEE Conf. Computer Vision and Pattern Recognition, 2017.

[17] M.Y. Liu, T. Breuel, J. Kautz, Unsupervised image-to-image translation networks, preprint, arXiv:1703.00848, 2017.

[18] T. Kim, M. Cha, H. Kim, J. Lee, J. Kim, Learning to discover cross-domain relations with generative adversarial networks, in: Proc. Int'l Conf. Machine Learning, 2017.

[19] Y. Zhu, M. Elhoseiny, B. Liu, A. Elgammal, Imagine it for me: generative adversarial approach for zero-shot learning from noisy texts, preprint, arXiv:1712.01381, 2017.

[20] H. Zhang, V.M. Patel, Densely connected pyramid dehazing network, in: Proc. IEEE Conf. Computer Vision and Pattern Recognition, 2018.

[21] Y. Gong, S. Karanam, Z. Wu, K.C. Peng, J. Ernst, P.C. Doerschuk, Learning compositional visual concepts with mutual consistency, preprint, arXiv:1711.06148, 2017.

[22] Z. Zhang, A. Romero, M.J. Muckley, P. Vincent, L. Yang, M. Drozdzal, Reducing uncertainty in undersampled MRI reconstruction with active acquisition, preprint, arXiv:1902.03051, 2019.

[23] R. Vemulapalli, H. Van Nguyen, S. Kevin Zhou, Unsupervised cross-modal synthesis of subject-specific scans, in: Proc. Int'l Conf. Computer Vision, 2015.

[24] A. Osokin, A. Chessel, R.E.C. Salas, F. Vaggi, GANs for biological image synthesis, preprint, arXiv:1708.04692, 2017.

[25] H. Van Nguyen, K. Zhou, R. Vemulapalli, Cross-domain synthesis of medical images using efficient location-sensitive deep network, in: Proc. Int'l Conf. Medical Image Computing and Computer Assisted Intervention, 2015.

[26] M. Arjovsky, S. Chintala, L. Bottou, Wasserstein GAN, preprint, arXiv:1701.07875, 2017.

[27] D. Berthelot, T. Schumm, L. Metz, BEGAN: boundary equilibrium generative adversarial networks, preprint, arXiv:1703.10717, 2017.

[28] Z. Zhang, Y. Xie, L. Yang, Photographic text-to-image synthesis with a hierarchically-nested adversarial network, in: Proc. IEEE Conf. Computer Vision and Pattern Recognition, 2018.

[29] M.Y. Liu, O. Tuzel, Coupled generative adversarial networks, in: Advances in Neural Information Processing Systems, 2016.

[30] A. Shrivastava, T. Pfister, O. Tuzel, J. Susskind, W. Wang, R. Webb, Learning from simulated and unsupervised images through adversarial training, in: Proceedings – IEEE Computer Society Conference on Computer Vision and Pattern Recognition, 2017.

[31] J.E. Iglesias, E. Konukoglu, D. Zikic, B. Glocker, K. Van Leemput, B. Fischl, Is synthesizing MRI contrast useful for inter-modality analysis?, in: Proc. Int'l Conf. Medical Image Computing and Computer Assisted Intervention, 2013.

[32] J. Xue, H. Zhang, K. Dana, K. Nishino, Differential angular imaging for material recognition, in: Proc. IEEE Conf. Computer Vision and Pattern Recognition, 2017.

[33] Y. Huo, Z. Xu, S. Bao, A. Assad, R.G. Abramson, B.A. Landman, Adversarial synthesis learning enables segmentation without target modality ground truth, in: Proc IEEE Int'l Sym. Biomedical Imaging, 2018.

[34] K. Bousmalis, N. Silberman, D. Dohan, D. Erhan, D. Krishnan, Unsupervised pixel-level domain adaptation with generative adversarial networks, in: Proc. IEEE Conf. Computer Vision and Pattern Recognition, 2017.

[35] D. Yang, D. Xu, S.K. Zhou, B. Georgescu, M. Chen, S. Grbic, et al., Automatic liver segmentation using an adversarial image-to-image network, in: Proc. Int'l Conf. Medical Image Computing and Computer Assisted Intervention, 2017.

[36] Y. Xue, T. Xu, H. Zhang, R. Long, X. Huang, SegAN: adversarial network with multi-scale l_1 loss for medical image segmentation, preprint, arXiv:1706.01805, 2017.

[37] H.C. Shin, H.R. Roth, M. Gao, L. Lu, Z. Xu, I. Nogues, et al., Deep convolutional neural networks for computer-aided detection: CNN architectures, dataset characteristics and transfer learning, IEEE Transactions on Medical Imaging 35 (5) (2016) 1285–1298.

[38] H.R. Roth, L. Lu, J. Liu, J. Yao, A. Seff, K. Cherry, et al., Improving computer-aided detection using convolutional neural networks and random view aggregation, IEEE Transactions on Medical Imaging 35 (5) (2016) 1170–1181.

[39] Y. Xie, Z. Zhang, M. Sapkota, L. Yang, Spatial clockwork recurrent neural network for muscle perimysium segmentation, in: International Conference on Medical Image Computing and Computer-Assisted Intervention, Springer, 2016, pp. 185–193.

[40] A. BenTaieb, G. Hamarneh, Topology aware fully convolutional networks for histology gland segmentation, in: International Conference on Medical Image Computing and Computer-Assisted Intervention, Springer, 2016, pp. 460–468.

[41] J. Cai, L. Lu, Y. Xie, F. Xing, L. Yang, Improving deep pancreas segmentation in CT and MRI images via recurrent neural contextual learning and direct loss function, in: International Conference on Medical Image Computing and Computer-Assisted Intervention, 2017.

[42] Y. Huo, Z. Xu, S. Bao, C. Bermudez, A.J. Plassard, J. Liu, et al., Splenomegaly segmentation using global convolutional kernels and conditional generative adversarial networks, in: Medical Imaging: Image Processing, vol. 10574, International Society for Optics and Photonics, 2018, p. 1057409.

[43] D. Ciresan, A. Giusti, L.M. Gambardella, J. Schmidhuber, Deep neural networks segment neuronal membranes in electron microscopy images, in: Advances in Neural Information Processing Systems, 2012, pp. 2843–2851.

[44] J. Long, E. Shelhamer, T. Darrell, Fully convolutional networks for semantic segmentation, in: Proc. IEEE Conf. Computer Vision and Pattern Recognition, 2015, pp. 3431–3440.

[45] S. Xie, Z. Tu, Holistically-nested edge detection, in: Proceedings of the IEEE International Conference on Computer Vision, 2015, pp. 1395–1403.

[46] H. Chen, X.J. Qi, J.Z. Cheng, P.A. Heng, Deep contextual networks for neuronal structure segmentation, in: Thirtieth AAAI Conference on Artificial Intelligence, 2016.

[47] H. Chen, X. Qi, L. Yu, P.A. Heng Dcan, Deep contour-aware networks for accurate gland segmentation, in: Proc. IEEE Conf. Computer Vision and Pattern Recognition, 2016, pp. 2487–2496.

[48] H. Chen, X. Qi, L. Yu, Q. Dou, J. Qin, P.A. Heng, DCAN: deep contour-aware networks for object instance segmentation from histology images, Medical Image Analysis 36 (2017) 135–146.

[49] Y. Xu, Y. Li, M. Liu, Y. Wang, M. Lai, I. Eric, et al., Gland instance segmentation by deep multi-channel side supervision, in: International Conference on Medical Image Computing and Computer-Assisted Intervention, 2016, pp. 496–504.

[50] I. Nogues, L. Lu, X. Wang, H. Roth, G. Bertasius, N. Lay, et al., Automatic lymph node cluster segmentation using holistically-nested neural networks and structured optimization in CT images, in: Proc. Int'l Conf. Medical Image Computing and Computer Assisted Intervention, 2016, pp. 388–397.

[51] J. Cai, L. Lu, Z. Zhang, F. Xing, L. Yang, Q. Yin, Pancreas segmentation in MRI using graph-based decision fusion on convolutional neural networks, in: International Conference on Medical Image Computing and Computer-Assisted Intervention, 2016, pp. 442–450.

[52] Q. Dou, H. Chen, Y. Jin, L. Yu, J. Qin, P.A. Heng, 3D deeply supervised network for automatic liver segmentation from CT volumes, in: International Conference on Medical Image Computing and Computer-Assisted Intervention, 2016, pp. 149–157.

[53] Ö. Çiçek, A. Abdulkadir, S.S. Lienkamp, T. Brox, O. Ronneberger, 3D U-Net: learning dense volumetric segmentation from sparse annotation, in: International Conference on Medical Image Computing and Computer-Assisted Intervention, 2016, pp. 424–432.

[54] F. Milletari, N. Navab, V-Net Ahmadi SA, Fully convolutional neural networks for volumetric medical image segmentation, in: 2016 Fourth International Conference on 3D Vision (3DV), 2016, pp. 565–571.

[55] M. Drozdzal, E. Vorontsov, G. Chartrand, S. Kadoury, C. Pal, The importance of skip connections in biomedical image segmentation, in: Deep Learning and Data Labeling for Medical Applications, Springer, 2016, pp. 179–187.

[56] R. Zhang, P. Isola, A.A. Efros, Colorful image colorization, in: Proc. European Conf. Computer Vision, 2016.

[57] Z. Yi, H. Zhang, P.T. Gong, et al., DualGAN: unsupervised dual learning for image-to-image translation, preprint, arXiv:1704.02510, 2017.

[58] H.R. Roth, L. Lu, A. Seff, K.M. Cherry, J. Hoffman, S. Wang, et al., A new 2.5D representation for lymph node detection using random sets of deep convolutional neural network observations, in: Proc. Int'l Conf. Medical Image Computing and Computer Assisted Intervention, 2014, pp. 520–527.

[59] D. Ulyanov, A. Vedaldi, V. Lempitsky, Instance normalization: the missing ingredient for fast stylization, preprint, arXiv:1607.08022, 2016.

[60] S. Ioffe, C. Szegedy, Batch normalization: accelerating deep network training by reducing internal covariate shift, preprint, arXiv:1502.03167, 2015.

[61] K. He, X. Zhang, S. Ren, J. Sun, Deep residual learning for image recognition, in: Proc. IEEE Conf. Computer Vision and Pattern Recognition, 2016.

[62] A. Odena, V. Dumoulin, C. Olah, Deconvolution and checkerboard artifacts, Distill (2016).

[63] D. Kingma, J. Ba, Adam: a method for stochastic optimization, preprint, arXiv:1412.6980, 2014.

[64] T. Salimans, I. Goodfellow, W. Zaremba, V. Cheung, A. Radford, X. Chen, Improved techniques for training GANs, in: Advances in Neural Information Processing Systems, 2016.

[65] L.R. Dice, Measures of the amount of ecologic association between species, Ecology 26 (3) (1945) 297–302.

CHAPTER 9

Landmark detection and multiorgan segmentation: Representations and supervised approaches

S. Kevin Zhou[a], Zhoubing Xu[b]
[a]Institute of Computing Technology, Chinese Academy of Sciences, Beijing, China
[b]Siemens Healthineers, Princeton, NJ, United States

Contents

9.1. Introduction	205
9.2. Landmark detection	207
9.2.1 Landmark representation	207
9.2.1.1 Point-based representation	*207*
9.2.1.2 Relative offset representation	*208*
9.2.1.3 Identity map representation	*208*
9.2.1.4 Distance map representation	*209*
9.2.1.5 Heat map representation	*209*
9.2.1.6 Discrete action map representation	*210*
9.2.2 Action classification for landmark detection	211
9.2.2.1 Method	*212*
9.2.2.2 Dataset & experimental setup	*213*
9.2.2.3 Qualitative and quantitative results	*215*
9.3. Multiorgan segmentation	217
9.3.1 Shape representation	217
9.3.2 Context integration for multiorgan segmentation	219
9.3.2.1 Joint landmark detection using context integration	*219*
9.3.2.2 Organ shape initialization and refinement	*221*
9.3.2.3 Comparison with other methods	*222*
9.3.2.4 Experimental results	*223*
9.4. Conclusion	227
References	227

9.1. Introduction

Medical landmark detection and image segmentation are two crucial tasks in medical image analysis.

Medical landmarks are commonly used to represent distinct points in an image that likely coincide with anatomical structures. In clinical practices, landmarks play important roles in interpreting and navigating the images just like geographic landmarks that

Handbook of Medical Image Computing and Computer Assisted Intervention
https://doi.org/10.1016/B978-0-12-816176-0.00014-4

help travelers navigate the world. Also landmarks are used to derive measurements (e.g., width, length, size, etc.) of organs [1], and to trigger subsequent, computationally intensive medical image analysis applications. In multimodality image registration (such as PET-CT) or in registration of follow-up scans, the fusion of multiple images can be initialized or guided by the positions of such anatomical structures [2,3]. In vessel centerline tracing, vessel bifurcations can provide the start and end points of certain vessels to enable fully-automated tracing [4]. In organ segmentation, the center position of an organ can provide the initial seed points to initiate segmentation algorithms [5]. In seminar reporting, automatically found anatomical structures can be helpful in configuring the optimal intensity window for display [6,7], or offer the text tooltips for structures in the scan [8].

Medical image segmentation concerns finding the exact boundary of an (anatomical) object in a medical image. When there are multiple objects in the image, segmentation of multiple objects becomes medical image parsing, which in the most general form assigns semantic labels to pixels. By grouping the pixels with the same label, image segmentation is realized. From image segmentation, clinical measurements such as organ volume can be computed, disease such as enlarge liver can be diagnosed.

The holy grail of a medical anatomy parsing system is that its parsing complexity matches that of Foundation Model Anatomy (FMA) ontology [9], which is concerned with the representation of classes or types and relationships necessary for the symbolic representation of the phenotypic structure of the human body in a form that is understandable to human and is also navigable, parsable, and interpretable by machine-based systems. As one of the largest computer-based knowledge sources in the biomedical sciences, it contains approximately 75,000 classes and over 120,000 terms, and over 2.1 million relationship instances from over 160 relationship types that link FMA classes into a coherent symbolic model. A less complex representation is Terminologia Anatomica [10], which is the international standard of human anatomical terminology for about 7500 human gross (macroscopic) anatomical structures. The holy grail of a medical diagnosis system is that its diagnosis complexity matches that of Radiology Gamuts Ontology (RGO) [11], which offers such a knowledge resource for radiology diagnosis. RGO hosts thousands of differential-diagnosis listings for imaging findings in all body systems. Further, all of the causes of an finding and all of the findings that it causes are provided. In summary, RGO defines 16,912 entities with 12,878 "causes" (conditions that cause findings) and 4662 "effects" (e.g., imaging findings). Also, there are 1782 hierarchical ("is-a") links and 55,564 causal ("may-cause") links.

Current landmark detection and image segmentation methods are far behind the holy grail; however, there are state-of-the-art approaches, especially machine learning based, that are able to achieve good results especially for certain applications.

Any intelligent system starts from a sensible knowledge representation. The most fundamental role that a knowledge representation plays [12] is that "it is a surrogate, a substitute for the thing itself. This leads to the so-called fidelity question: how close is the surrogate to the real thing? The only completely accurate representation of an object is the object itself. All other representations are inaccurate; they inevitably contain simplifying assumptions and possibly artifacts."

This chapter aims to introduce landmark and shape representations and two associated state-of-the-art approaches, one for landmark detection and the other for segmentation. It is structured as follows. In Sect. 9.2, we first illustrate how to represent a landmark, starting from a single point, to a heat map and to a discrete action map, and demonstrate different supervised learning methods that utilize different landmark representation [1]. In Sect. 9.3, we address multi-organ segmentation in a similar fashion by starting with organ representations and then presenting a particular learning approach that fuses regression, which models global context, and classification, which models local context, for rapid multiorgan segmentation [7]. The chapter is concluded in Sect. 9.4.

9.2. Landmark detection

9.2.1 Landmark representation

In the most general form, an image[1] is a mapping function $\mathbf{I}(x, y) : R^2 \rightarrow R$. Practically, the image domain is a discrete grid Ω, say $[1 \ldots M] \times [1 \ldots N]$, and the image range is a discrete set, say $[0 \ldots 255]$. There are many ways to represent a landmark or a fiducial point in an image.

9.2.1.1 Point-based representation

A landmark $\mathbf{l}$ is a point $\mathbf{l} = (\hat{x}, \hat{y})$ often associated with certain anatomical structure or characteristic feature, which may or may not be present in the image $\mathbf{I}$. So, the point-based representation is the most straightforward.

Directly using the point-based representation, however, is not straightforward as modeling $p(\mathbf{l}|\mathbf{I})$ requires the full knowledge of the joint sample space $R^2 \times \mathbf{I}$ due to the absolute nature of the point-based representation. The landmark location $(\hat{x}, \hat{y})$ is image-dependent, that is, it varies depending on the image. To overcome this, relative representations are proposed.

---

[1] In this section we use an 2D gray-valued image as a working example. It is straightforward to extend from 2D to 3D and from gray to color.

9.2.1.2 Relative offset representation

To get rid of the absolute nature of point-based representation, one can utilize a *relative representation* such as relative offset [13]. It is defined as

$$\mathbf{r}(x, y) = (r_x(x, y), r_y(x, y)), \tag{9.1}$$

with

$$r_x(x, y) = x - \hat{x}, \quad r_y(x, y) = y - \hat{y}. \tag{9.2}$$

It seems that modeling $p(\mathbf{r}|\mathbf{I})$ is more complicated. But, the $\mathbf{r}(x, y)$ function has a special *self-centered property*:

$$\mathbf{r}(\hat{x}, \hat{y}) = (0, 0), \tag{9.3}$$

which makes the modeling easier as $(0, 0)$ corresponds to the landmark regardless of the image $\mathbf{I}$. In contrast, in the above-mentioned absolute point-based representation, the landmark location $(\hat{x}, \hat{y})$ varies depending on the image.

The relative offset representation possesses another *recovery property*:

$$(\hat{x}, \hat{y}) = (x, y) - r(x, y), \tag{9.4}$$

that is, it is easy to recover the landmark location with the knowledge of the current location (x, y) and the $\mathbf{r}(x, y)$ function, assuming that the latter is available (say via learning).

Because $\mathbf{r}$ and $\mathbf{I}$ share the same image grid Ω and with the assumption of conditional independence, we have

$$p(\mathbf{r}|\mathbf{I}) = \prod_{(u,v)} p(\mathbf{r}(u, v)|\mathbf{I}[u, v]), \tag{9.5}$$

where $\mathbf{I}[u, v]$ is the same image $\mathbf{I}$ but centered at (u, v) or an image patch cropped at (u, v). Now, modeling complexity becomes more manageable.

9.2.1.3 Identity map representation

An identity map $\pi(x, y)$ is defined as

$$\pi(x, y) = \delta(x - \hat{x}, y - \hat{y}), \tag{9.6}$$

where δ is a 2D Dirac function, taking a value of either 1 or 0. Note that the identity map is a relative representation too as it depends on the relative offset.

Following (9.5), we have

$$p(\pi | \mathbf{I}) = \prod_{(u,v)} p(\pi(u, v) | \mathbf{I}[u, v]), \tag{9.7}$$

where $p(\pi(u, v) | \mathbf{I}[u, v])$ is nothing but a *binary classification* function as $\pi(u, v)$ is either 0 or 1. Usually it is customary to learn a function F_W with its parameters denoted by W and the probability $p(\pi(u, v) | \mathbf{I}[u, v])$ is given as

$$p(+1 | \mathbf{I}[u, v]) = \frac{1}{1 + \exp(-2F_W(\mathbf{I}[u, v]))}. \tag{9.8}$$

9.2.1.4 Distance map representation

A distance map $d(x, y)$ is defined as

$$d(x, y) = \sqrt{|\mathbf{r}(x, y)|_2} \tag{9.9}$$

where $| \cdot |_2$ is a L_2 norm. The distance map $d(x, y)$ essentially summarizes the $\mathbf{r}(x, y)$ function using a distance operator. In reality, other norm functions or summary functions can be used, depending on need.

9.2.1.5 Heat map representation

A heat map $h(x, y)$ is defined as

$$h(x, y) = G \circ \pi(x, y) = G(x - \hat{x}, y - \hat{y}) \tag{9.10}$$

where $\circ$ denotes convolution and G is a convolution kernel. Typically, an isotropic 2D Gaussian kernel is used, that is,

$$h(x, y) = \frac{1}{2\pi\sigma^2} \exp\{-\frac{(x - \hat{x})^2 + (y - \hat{y})^2}{2\sigma^2}\} = \frac{1}{2\pi\sigma^2} \exp\{-\frac{d(x, y)^2}{2\sigma^2}\}. \tag{9.11}$$

This way, a heat map is directly connected with a distance map. This leads to another way of constructing a heat map via the use of distance map, that is,

$$h(x, y) = h(d(x, y)). \tag{9.12}$$

Using a heat map to represent a landmark is made popular by the work [14], in which a *regression* function is used for modeling, that is,

$$h(u, v) = F_W(\mathbf{I}[u, v]), \tag{9.13}$$

where F_W is the regression function with its parameters denoted by W.

9.2.1.6 Discrete action map representation

Most of the above-mentioned representations are continuous in nature and do not necessarily leverage the fact that the image grid Ω is discrete. As the name suggests, discrete action map representation is discrete; however, it is not as simple as discretizing a continuous value.

One perspective to interpret the recovery property of the relative offset representation $\mathbf{r}(x, y)$ is as follows: among all paths that traverse from a point (x, y) to the landmark $(\hat{x}, \hat{y})$, the relative offset vector $\mathbf{r}(x, y)$ helps define the shortest one as it characterizes a straight line. The discrete action map representation aims to "discretize" such a path.

Consider an agent that seeks an optimal action path from any location at (x, y) towards landmark $\mathbf{l} = (\hat{x}, \hat{y})$, which is composed of optimal action steps at pixels along the path on an image grid Ω. In other words, at each pixel the agent is allowed to take an action a with a unit movement $d_x^{(a)} \in \{-1, 0, 1\}$ and $d_y^{(a)} \in \{-1, 0, 1\}$. With the constraint of

$$\|d_x^{(a)}\|^2 + \|d_y^{(a)}\|^2 = 1, \tag{9.14}$$

we basically allow four possible action types $a \in \{0, 1, 2, 3\}$:

$$
\begin{aligned}
UP: & \quad (d_x^{(0)} = 0, \quad d_y^{(0)} = -1), \\
RIGHT: & \quad (d_x^{(1)} = 1, \quad d_y^{(1)} = 0), \\
DOWN: & \quad (d_x^{(2)} = 0, \quad d_y^{(2)} = 1), \\
LEFT: & \quad (d_x^{(3)} = -1, \quad d_y^{(3)} = 0).
\end{aligned}
$$

The optimal action step $\hat{a}$ is selected as the one with minimal Euclidean distance to the landmark $\mathbf{l}$ after its associated movement,

$$\hat{a} = \arg\min_a \sqrt{(x - \hat{x} + d_x^{(a)})^2 + (y - \hat{y} + d_y^{(a)})^2}. \tag{9.15}$$

After canceling out the common term $(x - \hat{x})^2 + (y - \hat{y})^2 + 1$, Eq. (9.15) becomes

$$\hat{a} = \arg\min_a (x - \hat{x})d_x^{(a)} + (y - \hat{y})d_y^{(a)}. \tag{9.16}$$

By replacing $d_x^{(a)}$ and $d_y^{(a)}$ with their actual values, the selection of $\hat{a}$ falls into four regions (one for each action type), where the regions are partitioned by two lines with slopes of ± 1 crossing the landmark (Fig. 9.1):

$$
\begin{aligned}
y &= x + (\hat{y} - \hat{x}), \\
y &= -x + (\hat{x} + \hat{y}).
\end{aligned}
$$

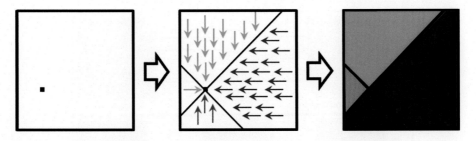

Figure 9.1 The discrete action map representation.

This generates a discrete action map $a(x, y)$ that represents the pixelwise optimal action step moving toward the target landmark location.

For example, suppose one starts searching the landmark at a random location, say in the red region as shown in Fig. 9.1, the optimal actions will keep moving up until hitting the line and then following the line to reach the target landmark. Using this discrete action map representation, the landmark detection problem is essentially converted into an image partitioning problem.

The potential benefit of adopting the discrete action map representation is as follows. Remember that the relative offset representation renders an attractive way of inferring the landmark location, but it is rather difficult to learn a continuous-valued function $\mathbf{r}(x, y)$ or $p(\mathbf{r}(u, v)|\mathbf{I}[u, v])$. The discrete action map representation "decomposes" a continuous value into a set of discrete actions, which collectively form the optimal path. With the aid of this "decomposition", it only needs to learn $p(a(u, v)|\mathbf{I}[u, v])$, which is a 4-class classification function. Therefore, the learning complexity is further reduced!

9.2.2 Action classification for landmark detection

The landmark detection problem has been studied using machine learning algorithms with good outcomes. A bootstrapped binary classifier, e.g., probabilistic boosting-tree (PBT [15]), can be trained to distinguish landmark and non-landmark locations [16]; this approach can be biased due to the highly unbalanced positive and negative samples. Alternatively, landmark locations can be learned in a regression manner through aggregating pixelwise relative distances to the landmark [17]; it provides more robustness, but less precision than the classification-based approach due to the complexity and variation of the image context. Recently, deep learning technologies have been adapted to medical imaging problems, and demonstrated promising performances by leveraging features trained from convolutional neural networks as opposed to hand-crafted features used in traditional machine learning approaches [18,19]. For landmark detection, a deep reinforcement learning (DRL) approach has been shown successful to detect annulus points in cardiac ultrasound images [20]. The DRL algorithm designs an artificial agent to search and learn the optimized path from any location towards target by maximizing

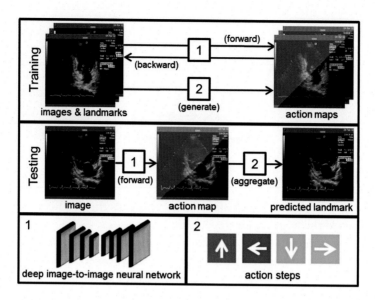

Figure 9.2 Training and testing pipeline.

an action-value function. Its greedy searching strategy allows the agent to walk through only a subset of the almost infinite paths across the image instead of scanning exhaustively; however, this may lead to major failures if not trained with adequate dataset variations. Here we focus on the discrete action map representation and its associated action classification approach for landmark detection (Fig. 9.2).

9.2.2.1 Method

During training to estimate the action map for a given image, a fully convolutional neural network can be employed given its efficient sampling scheme and large receptive field for comprehensive feature learning. Since both input (raw image) and output (action map) are images with the same size, we also call it a deep image-to-image network (DI2IN).

The landmark location needs to be derived from the estimated action map. However, the action map estimated by DI2IN may not always be in a perfect shape as how it is constructed. There can be uncertainties around the partition lines between action types. It is also possible that there are islands of different action types, which are false predictions, inside a particular action partition. This undermines the robustness of lots of possible approaches for landmark derivation. For example, starting from a random point and moving along with the estimated action steps like deep reinforcement learning may not guarantee the convergence at the target landmark. Similarly, linear regression of the two partition lines may be disrupted even though the slopes are known, while dynamic

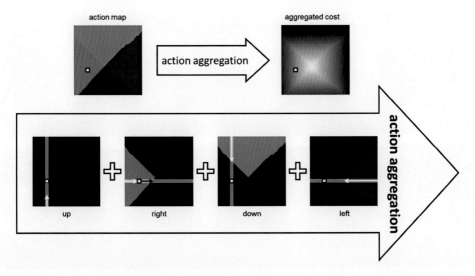

Figure 9.3 Illustration of action map aggregation on a single pixel. White arrow indicates increase of the objective function, while black arrow indicates value decrease.

programming based on the action flows can encounter dead locks. Here we propose an aggregate approach (Fig. 9.3). With the output action map $A(x, y)$ from DI2IN, the estimated landmark location coordinates (x', y') are determined by maximizing an objective function $C(\cdot)$ summed up with that of each action type $C_a(\cdot)$:

$$(x', y') = \arg\max_{(x,y)} C(x, y) = \arg\max_{(x,y)} \sum_a C_a(x, y), \tag{9.17}$$

where the action-wise objective function at pixel (x, y) is aggregated by the pixels with that specific action on the same row or column, specifically

$$C_a(x, y) = \begin{cases} d_x^{(a)}\{\sum_{i=x}^{\infty} \delta(A(i, y) == a) - \sum_{i=-\infty}^{x} \delta(A(i, y) == a)\} & \text{if } \|d_x^{(a)}\| = 1, \\ d_y^{(a)}\{\sum_{j=y}^{\infty} \delta(A(x, j) == a) - \sum_{j=-\infty}^{y} \delta(A(x, j) == a)\} & \text{if } \|d_y^{(a)}\| = 1. \end{cases} \tag{9.18}$$

Note that the objective function increments with pixels pointing towards (x, y), while decrements with pixels pointing away from (x, y) (Fig. 9.3). Such aggregation enables robust location coordinate derivation even with suboptimal action map from the DI2IN output.

9.2.2.2 Dataset & experimental setup

Ultrasound imaging is a widely used clinical procedure because it is safe, cost-effective, and non-invasive, where landmarks in a certain plane are used to provide diagnostic references. In cardiac ultrasound scans, landmarks are typically defined to measure the

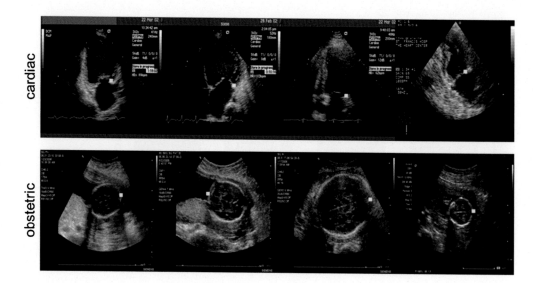

Figure 9.4 Example ultrasound images and associated landmarks.

width at the intersections between heart chambers, for example, the annulus points of mitral valves; in obstetric ultrasound scans, landmarks at the anterior and posterior end of the fetal head are considered important. Manual localization of the landmark points, however, is tedious and time consuming. In an ultrasound machine, user needs to use the track ball to adjust the caliper to the desirable location, which makes the work even more complex. Furthermore, the reliability of the measurements can be suffered from the subjective disagreement across users. Automating the landmark detection can substantially reduce the manual efforts, and make the clinical procedure more efficient; however, this is a very challenging task given the (1) noisy signal, (2) low contrast, and (3) variations in shapes, orientations, and respiration phases throughout ultrasound images (Fig. 9.4).

Two ultrasound datasets are used in this study including a cardiac and an obstetric dataset with 1353 and 1642 patients, respectively. Both datasets are collected and anonymized in the process of clinical routine. Landmarks of interest are annotated by clinical experts on each scan. There are 8892 frames in the cardiac dataset in total across the entire heart cycles rather than collect the images just around end–systole and end–diastole as in [20]. Therefore, the cardiac dataset in our experiment presents larger contextual variations and greater challenges for landmark detection. On an echocardiogram, landmarks are defined as the two annulus points, which are the roots of mitral valve in apical 2 chamber (A2C) view and apical 4 chamber (A4C) view. In the obstetric dataset, each patient has only one scanned image. On an obstetric scan, the first landmark is annotated at the anterior end of the fetal head, while the second is at the posterior end. Note that the orientations of fetal head can essentially cover 360 degrees across the ultrasound scans. Therefore, detecting these two landmarks on an obstetric scan is not an easy task even for humans. Careful identification of the internal brain structure is necessary for consistent manual annotation. For each dataset, 80% patients are randomly selected as training set, and the remaining 20% are used for testing. All images are normalized into 480×480 before further processing.

We apply the proposed approach to the cardiac and the obstetric ultrasound datasets individually. For each landmark, we train a DI2IN to learn its associated action map. The DI2IN is trained using the Caffe framework on a Linux workstation equipped with an Intel 3.50 GHz CPU and a 12 GB NVidia Titan X GPU. Specifically, we follow the symmetric network architecture of SegNet [21]. The network is constructed with an encoder using the same structure as the fully convolutional part of VGG-16 network [18], and a decoder that replaces the pooling layers with upsampling layers and then essentially reverses the encoder structure. Batch normalization is used for each convolutional layer, and the max-pooling indices are kept during pooling and restored during upsampling. A softmax layer is used to provide categorical outputs, while cross-entropy loss is calculated and weighted by precomputed class frequencies. The encoder part of DI2IN of is initialized with the weights of VGG-16 trained from ImageNet. During training, the minibatch size is set to 2, standard stochastic gradient descent is used for updates with learning rate as 1e–3 and momentum as 0.9 through 80,000 iterations. We compare the proposed SAC with other learning-based approaches on the same dataset including PBT, DRL, and a state-of-the-art regression-based approach using DI2IN [22] (we refer to it as I2I). Note that I2I and SAC uses similar network structure, while representing the landmark with heat map and discrete action map, respectively. For each method, we try our best to tune the configuration to provide reasonably good results. Distance error of landmark position in pixels is used for comparison since all images are in normalized space.

9.2.2.3 Qualitative and quantitative results

The discrete action maps estimated from SAC (Fig. 9.5) present sharp separations between regions of different action types with very few islands of false predictions. It turns out to be beneficial to keep the pooling indices in DI2IN, which enforcing the smoothness of the estimated action map. Overall, the estimated discrete action maps look very reasonable even though they are not exactly the same as the ground truth (the partitioning lines are not straight). The derived landmark locations from the estimated action maps are also close to those of the manual annotations.

For cardiac scans, it is not too hard to identify a rough location of the target landmarks in the middle of left ventricle and left atrium; however, it is challenging to have precise localization given that we include cardiac phases throughout heart cycles, where the relative locations vary a lot between the annulus points of mitral valves and the sur-

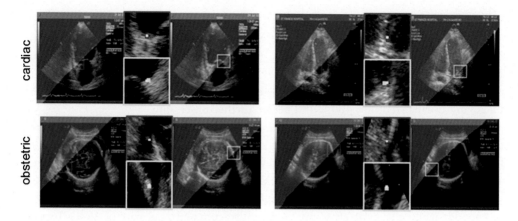

Figure 9.5 Example landmark detection results.

Table 9.1 Distance errors of landmark detection in pixels. Note that the best performance for each landmark is highlighted in bold. CA indicates cardiac scans, while OB indicates obstetric scans. Across all tests, our method presents significant improvements over other methods statistically ($p < 0.05$, t-test).

		PBT		DRL		I2I		SAC	
		lmk1	lmk2	lmk1	lmk2	lmk1	lmk2	lmk1	lmk2
CA	mean	10.45	13.85	7.69	10.02	6.73	9.02	**6.31**	**8.01**
	50%	5.74	8.11	5.43	7.63	5.00	6.40	**4.35**	**5.88**
	80%	11.11	16.18	9.33	13.73	8.54	11.40	**7.54**	**10.83**
OB	mean	59.23	130.66	29.99	32.45	30.07	21.97	**14.94**	**16.76**
	50%	35.31	139.49	11.69	13.17	5.39	6.08	**4.85**	**5.91**
	80%	109.84	193.64	43.98	45.76	13.34	15.54	**11.76**	**13.67**

rounding structures. Overall, SAC provides consistently better accuracy and robustness (Table 9.1) compared to the other benchmark methods.

For obstetric scans, it is challenging to identify the landmark location correctly without capturing the context in a large receptive field. Since the fetal head can be essentially oriented towards anywhere within the scan, huge ambiguities can be observed around the almost radially symmetric structure. It is very likely to make major failures, especially if only local context are used for feature modeling (PBT and DRL), while confusion of head orientation can be substantially prevented using DI2IN (I2I and SAC). SAC demonstrates the best performance among all tested methods.

9.3. Multiorgan segmentation

9.3.1 Shape representation

In the literature, there are many representations that approximate a medical object or anatomical structure using different simplifying assumptions. Fig. 9.6 shows a variety of shape representations commonly used in the literature.

- *Rigid representation.* The simplest representation is to translate a template to the object center $\mathbf{t} = [t_x, t_y]$ as shown in Fig. 9.6(A). In other words, only object center is considered. A complete rigid representation in Fig. 9.6(B) consists of translation, rotation, and scale parameters $\theta = [\mathbf{t}, \mathbf{r}, \mathbf{s}]$. When the scale parameter is isotropic, the above reduces to a similarity transformation. An extension of rigid representation is affine representation.

- *Free-form representation.* Common free-form representations, shown in Fig. 9.6(C)–(E), include point-based presentation (2D curve $\mathcal{S}$ or 3D mesh $\mathcal{M}$), mask function $\phi(x, y)$, level set function $\phi(x, y)$, etc.

- *Low-dimensional parametric representation.* The so-called statistical shape model (SSM) [23] shown in Fig. 9.6(F) is a common low-dimensional parametric representation based on principal component analysis (PCA) of a point-based free-form shape. Other low-dimensional parametric representations include M-rep [24], spherical harmonics (SPHARM) [25], spherical wavelets [26], etc.

A knowledge representation also is a medium for pragmatically efficient computation [12]. Therefore, it is beneficial to adopt a hierarchical, *rough-to-exact* representation that gradually approximates the object itself with increasing precision, which also makes computational reasoning more amenable and efficient as shown later.

A common rough-to-exact 3D object representation [13,27–29] consists of a rigid part fully specified by translation, rotation and scale parameters $\theta = [\mathbf{t}, \mathbf{r}, \mathbf{s}]$, a low-dimensional parametric part such as from the PCA shape space specified by the top PCA coefficients $\lambda = [\lambda_{1:m}]$ and a free-form nonrigid part such as a 3D shape $\mathcal{S}$, a 3D mesh $\mathcal{M}$, or a 3D mask or level set function ϕ.

$$\mathbf{O} = [\mathbf{t}, \mathbf{r}, \mathbf{s}; \lambda_{1:m}; \mathcal{S}] = [\theta; \lambda; \mathcal{S}], \quad \mathbf{O} = [\theta; \lambda; \mathcal{M}], \quad \mathbf{O} = [\theta; \lambda; \phi]. \qquad (9.19)$$

The PCA shape space characterizes a shape by a linear projection:

$$\mathcal{S} = \bar{\mathcal{S}}_0 + \sum_{m=1}^{M} \lambda_m \bar{\mathcal{S}}_m, \qquad (9.20)$$

where $\bar{\mathcal{S}}_0$ is the mean shape and $\bar{\mathcal{S}}_m$ is the mth top eigenshape. This PCA shape modeling forms the basis of famous Active Shape Model (ASM) [30]. In this hierarchical representation, the free-form part can be rough-to-exact, too. For a 3D mesh, the mesh

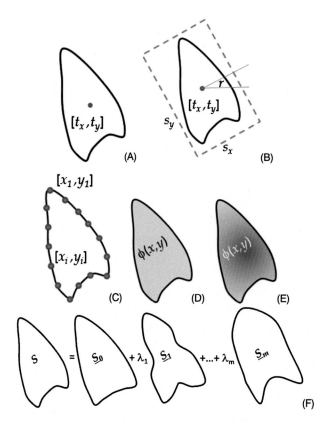

Figure 9.6 A graphical illustration of different shape representations using 2D shape as an example. (A) Rigid representation: translation only $\mathbf{t} = [t_x, t_y]$. (B) Rigid representation: $\theta = [t_x, t_y, r, s_x, s_y]$. (C) Free-form representation: $\mathcal{S} = [x_1, y_1, \ldots, x_n, y_n]$. (D) Free-form representation: a 2D binary mask function $\phi(x, y)$. (E) Free-form representation: a 2D real-valued level set function $\phi(x, y)$ (only the interior part is displayed). (F) Low-dimensional parametric representation: PCA projection $\mathcal{S} = \bar{\mathcal{S}}_0 + \sum_{m=1}^{M} \lambda_m \bar{\mathcal{S}}_m$. Source: S. Kevin Zhou, Introduction to medical image recognition, segmentation, and parsing, in: S. Kevin Zhou (Ed.), Medical Image Recognition, Segmentation, and Parsing, Academic Press, 2015.

vertex density can be a control parameter, from sparse to dense. For a level set function, it depends on the image resolution, from course to fine.

Recently, the free-form representation has gained prevalence due to deep learning that trains a deep neural network F_W. Especially a fully convolutional network (FCN) [19,22,31] allows efficient training of an image-to-image network, that is, the input to the network is an image and the output is also an image, sharing the same grid. In this chapter, we present a non–deep-learning based approach to multiorgan segmentation, which is both effective and efficient.

9.3.2 Context integration for multiorgan segmentation

We aim to segment C organ shapes, $\mathbf{S} = [\mathbf{S}_1, \ldots, \mathbf{S}_C]$, given a volumetric image $\mathbf{I}$. We denote the set of all voxels in the image $\mathbf{I}$ by Ω and its size by $|\Omega|$. We assume that there exists a set of D corresponding landmarks, $\mathbf{L} = [\mathbf{l}_1, \ldots, \mathbf{l}_D]$, on the multiple shapes $\mathbf{S}$ and decompose the problem into estimating (i) the landmarks given the image using the posterior $P(\mathbf{L}|\mathbf{I})$ defined in §9.3.2.1 and (ii) the shapes given the landmarks and the image using energy minimization in §9.3.2.2. We use the notation $[\mathbf{l}, \ldots, \mathbf{l}]_D$ to represent repeating $\mathbf{l}$ in D times.

9.3.2.1 Joint landmark detection using context integration

To jointly detect the landmarks, we integrate both local and global image context using a product rule into one posterior probability $P(\mathbf{L}|\mathbf{I})$:

$$P(\mathbf{L}|\mathbf{I}) = P^L(\mathbf{L}|\mathbf{I})P^G(\mathbf{X}|\mathbf{I}), \qquad (9.21)$$

where $P^L(\mathbf{L}|\mathbf{I})$ and $P^G(\mathbf{L}|\mathbf{I})$ are local and global context posteriors, respectively.

Local context posterior

Though not necessarily true, we assume that the landmarks are *locally independent*:

$$P^L(\mathbf{L}|\mathbf{I}) = \prod_{i=1}^{D} P^L(\mathbf{l}_i|\mathbf{I}). \qquad (9.22)$$

For modeling $P^L(\mathbf{l}_i|\mathbf{I})$, we exploit the local image context to learn a discriminative detector for landmark $\mathbf{l}_i$ (using, e.g., PBT [15]), that is,

$$P^L(\mathbf{l}_i|\mathbf{I}) = \omega_i^L(+1|\mathbf{I}[\mathbf{l}_i]), \qquad (9.23)$$

with $\mathbf{I}[\mathbf{l}_i]$ being the image or local image patch centered at $\mathbf{l}_i$ and $\omega_i^L(+1|\cdot)$ the local context detector for landmark $\mathbf{l}_i$.

Global context posterior

We integrate global evidence from all voxels in Ω:

$$P^G(\mathbf{L}|\mathbf{I}) = \sum_{\mathbf{y} \in \Omega} P^G(\mathbf{L}|\mathbf{I}, \mathbf{y})P(\mathbf{y}|\mathbf{I}) = |\Omega|^{-1} \sum_{\mathbf{y} \in \Omega} P^G(\mathbf{L}|\mathbf{I}[\mathbf{y}]). \qquad (9.24)$$

In (9.24), we assume a uniform prior probability $P(\mathbf{y}|\mathbf{I}) = |\Omega|^{-1}$ and $P^G(\mathbf{L}|\mathbf{I}[\mathbf{y}])$ is the probability of the landmarks at $\mathbf{L}$ when observing the image patch $\mathbf{I}[\mathbf{y}]$ at a location $\mathbf{y}$.

To learn $P^G(\mathbf{L}|\mathbf{I}[\mathbf{y}])$, we leverage annotated datasets and a "randomized" K-nearest neighbor approach. For a complete set of training images with annotated landmarks, we

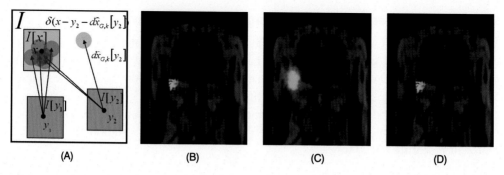

Figure 9.7 (A) An illustration of how image patches (green) predict the landmark location using global context and Eq. (9.25) and then these predictions are combined with local context at (blue) **x**. (B) Detection scores for a landmark on the top left of the liver in a low resolution MR FastView 3D volume, where local context gives spurious responses. (C) Global context gives a coarse localization. (D) The integration of local and global detection gives a fine scale density. Source: Lay et al., A context integration framework for rapid multiple organ parsing, in: S. Kevin Zhou (Ed.), Medical Image Recognition, Segmentation, and Parsing, Academic Press, 2015.

randomly form K subsets. From each subset of images with corresponding landmarks, we construct a training database $\{(\mathbf{J}_n, d\mathbf{L}_n)\}_{n=1}^{N}$ consisting of N pairs of image patch $\mathbf{J}$ and relative shift $d\mathbf{L}$ in an iterative fashion.

For a test image patch $\mathbf{I}[\mathbf{y}]$, we first find its NN $\hat{\mathbf{J}}_k$ from each subset; this way we find its K neighbors $\{\hat{\mathbf{J}}_1, \ldots, \hat{\mathbf{J}}_K\}$ along with their corresponding shift vectors $\{d\hat{\mathbf{L}}_1[\mathbf{y}], \ldots, d\hat{\mathbf{L}}_K[\mathbf{y}]\}$. We learn a random forest to efficiently finding the nearest neighbor. We then simply approximate $P^G(\mathbf{L}|\mathbf{I}[\mathbf{y}])$ as

$$P^G(\mathbf{L}|\mathbf{I}[\mathbf{y}]) = K^{-1} \sum_{k=1}^{K} \delta(\mathbf{L} - [\mathbf{y}, \ldots, \mathbf{y}]_D - d\hat{\mathbf{L}}_k[\mathbf{y}]). \tag{9.25}$$

Fig. 9.7 graphically illustrates how the approach works. It also gives an example of the local, global and joint posteriors. Even though the local detector may be inaccurate, it is only being applied at locations predicted from the global context, meaning it is possible to get a highly peaked posterior when integrating evidence from local and global context.

MMSE estimate for landmark location

The expected landmark location $\bar{\mathbf{L}}$, also the minimum mean square error (MMSE) estimate, is computed as

$$\bar{\mathbf{L}} = \sum_{\mathbf{L}} \mathbf{L} \, P(\mathbf{L}|\mathbf{I}) = \sum_{\mathbf{L}} \mathbf{L} \, P^L(\mathbf{L}|\mathbf{I}) P^G(\mathbf{L}|\mathbf{I}) \tag{9.26}$$

$$= \frac{1}{K|\Omega|} \sum_{\mathbf{L}} \sum_{\mathbf{y} \in \Omega} \sum_{k=1}^{K} \mathbf{L} \prod_{i=1}^{D} \omega_i^L(+1|\mathbf{I}[\mathbf{l}_i]) \delta(\mathbf{L} - [\mathbf{y}, \ldots, \mathbf{y}]_D - d\hat{\mathbf{L}}_k[\mathbf{y}]).$$

Using the local independence and vector decomposition, it can be shown that the expected location $\bar{\mathbf{l}}_i$ for a single landmark is computed as

$$\bar{\mathbf{l}}_i = K^{-1}|\Omega|^{-1} \sum_{\mathbf{y} \in \Omega} \sum_{k=1}^{K} (\mathbf{y} + \hat{d\mathbf{l}}_{k,i}[\mathbf{y}]) \omega_i^L(+1|\mathbf{I}[\mathbf{y} + \hat{d\mathbf{l}}_{k,i}[\mathbf{y}]]). \qquad (9.27)$$

Eq. (9.27) implies an efficient scheme − evaluating the local detector only for the locations predicted from the global context posterior instead of the whole image. Since the predicted locations are highly clustered around the true location, this brings the first significant reduction in computation.

Sparsity in global context

The global context from all voxels is highly redundant as neighboring patches tend to predict nearby landmark locations. Therefore, we can "sparsify" the global context by constructing the subset Ω_ℓ from the full voxel set Ω; for example, we can skip every other l voxels. This brings the second significant reduction in computation complexity by $O(l^3)$.

9.3.2.2 Organ shape initialization and refinement

Shape initialization using robust model alignment

An initial segmentation for each organ is then aligned to the sparse detected landmarks through the use of a statistical model of shape variation. Here we use a point distribution model, where each organ shape is represented as a mean shape or mesh with M mesh nodes, $\bar{\mathbf{V}} = [\bar{\mathbf{v}}_1, \bar{\mathbf{v}}_2, \ldots, \bar{\mathbf{v}}_M]$, plus a linear combination of a set of N eigenmodes, $\mathbf{U}_n = [\mathbf{u}_{1,n}, \mathbf{u}_{2,n}, \cdots \mathbf{u}_{M,n}]$, with $1 \leq n \leq N$.

As a complete organ shape is characterized by only a few coefficients that modulate the eigenmodes, the point distribution model can be used to infer a shape from a sparse set of landmark points. Given a set of detected landmarks, $\{\mathbf{l}_i\}$, the best fitting instance of the complete shape is found by minimizing the following robust energy function:

$$(\beta, \{a_n\}) = \operatorname{argmin}_{\beta, \{a_n\}} \sum_i \psi \left(\|\mathbf{l}_i - T_\beta\{\bar{\mathbf{v}}_{\pi(i)} + \sum_{n=1}^{N} a_n \mathbf{u}_{\pi(i),n}\}\|^2 \right) + \sum_{n=1}^{N} a_n^2/\lambda_n \qquad (9.28)$$

where the function $\pi(i)$ maps the landmark $\mathbf{l}_i$ to the corresponding mesh index in $\bar{\mathbf{V}}$, the function $T_\beta\{\cdot\}$ is a 9D similarity transform parameterized by the vector $\beta = [t_x, t_y, t_z, \theta_x, \theta_y, \theta_z, s_x, s_y, s_z]$, and λ_n are the corresponding eigenvalues. The first term measures the difference between a predicted shape point under a hypothesis transformation from the detected landmark, and the second term is a prior keeping the eigenmodes responsible for smaller variation closer to zero. As we typically only have a few landmarks, and have a PCA model for a larger number of vertices, using no prior term gives rise to an ill-posed problem. Finally, ψ is a robust norm, reducing the effect of outliers. We use $\psi(s^2) = s$.

Discriminative boundary refinement

Using the above initialization, a fine refinement of the points on the surface mesh is obtained by iteratively displacing each vertex along its surface normal, $\mathbf{v}_i \leftarrow \mathbf{v}_i + \mathbf{n}_i \hat{\tau}_i$. The best displacement for each point is obtained by maximizing the output of a discriminative classifier [32]:

$$\hat{\tau}_i = \text{argmax}_{\tau_i} \omega^B(+1 | \mathbf{v}_i + \mathbf{n}_i \tau_i). \tag{9.29}$$

Here, $\omega^B(+1|\cdot)$ is the boundary detector that scores whether the point, $\mathbf{v}_i + \mathbf{n}_i \tau_i$, is on the boundary of the organ being segmented. Regularity is incorporated in the previously independent estimated displacements by projecting the resulting mesh onto the linear subspace spanned by the linear shape model, as in the active shape model [30].

9.3.2.3 Comparison with other methods

Marginal space learning (MSL) is an effective learning-based approach to segmenting single organs in 3D volumes [27]. In MSL, the pose estimation problem is decomposed into subproblems of first estimating position, then orientation, then scale, and finally the coarse shape coefficients. The decomposition into subproblems keeps the learning-based parameter estimation at each phase tractable. Our proposed approach, the *Structured Sampling Machine*, also decomposes the shape estimation problem into more tractable components. However, instead of decomposing the problem into inhomogeneous components (e.g., position, orientation, scale), we subdivide the shape estimation problem into that of estimating a set of landmarks. The sequential estimation in MSL has been extended to multiple dependent structures in the Integrated Detection Network [33]. In this latter extension, the parameters (e.g., poses of organs) can be estimated by Monte Carlo or particle sampling methods. Other variants and use of MSL are in [34–36].

Detecting a set of landmarks to initialize the segmentation of organs has been proposed before in the medical imaging literature (e.g., [37,38]). Like these methods, our approach can utilize a sparse shape representation or a statistical point distribution model. However, the main difference is that we use local and global image context to simultaneously localize landmarks on multiple organs instead of using sliding window approaches to independently identify landmarks on a single organ. While detection-only approaches for landmark localization can be efficient (e.g., [39]), such efficient search strategies often give priority to certain landmarks. Thus a different ordering of the landmarks in the search can give different detection results. Our combination of local and global information can also achieve efficient detection and does not suffer from this limitation.

We indirectly infer the shape of multiple organs from image. Other approaches, such as the shape regression machine [13,40], propose to localize the shape using detection but to regress directly the low dimensional coefficients of a point distribution model from the image intensities. Instead, as learning-based detection is known to work well for keypoints, we pose the shape estimation problem as estimating multiple landmarks rather than shape coefficients directly. The shape regression machine approach also combines a classifier to aggregate the contribution of a regressor from multiple positions, but our detection strategy is founded as a sampling method to approximate the expectation of the landmark positions.

With regards of the use of regression to estimate multiple structures in medical image volumes, Criminisi et al. have used regression forests to identify the axis-aligned bounding box of multiple organs in CT volumes [41]. In contrast to their approach, where each voxel votes for the offset to the coordinates that define an axis aligned bounding box, our approach obtains landmarks on the shape of the object, meaning our method obtains not only a bounding box but also a segmentation. Further, our product of experts formulation leads to an effective way of sampling to estimate landmark positions. This means our approach only needs to be applied to a small subset of voxels during testing rather than every voxel in the volume.

9.3.2.4 Experimental results

Our system was implemented in C++ using OpenMP and compiled using Visual Studio 2008. In the experiments below, timing results are reported for an Intel Xeon 64-bit machine running Windows Server 2008 and using 16 threads.

We tested our approach on a challenging set of MR localizer scans acquired using a fast continuously moving table technique (syngo TimCT FastView, Siemens). Such scans are often used for MR examination planning to increase scan reproducibility and operator efficiency. A total of 185 volumes having 5 mm isotropic spacing were split into a training set of 135 and test set of 50. This data is challenging due to the low resolution, weak boundaries, inhomogeneous intensity within scan, and varying image contrast across scans. For this example, we used $K = 10$ NN. The local detectors were also trained on 5 mm resolution using a PBT [15] and a combination of Haar and image gradient features. A total of 33 landmarks were selected on the 6 organs, with 6 landmarks each on the liver and the lungs, and 5 landmarks each on the kidneys and heart.

First, we demonstrate the effectiveness of integrating local and global context with respect to accuracy and evaluation time. Table 9.2 illustrates median errors for all landmark positions averaged over the testing set. For the local context detector and local+global posterior, we used the MMSE estimate. While it is possible to get better speed-up with a sparse sampling of the global context when computing the expected value, we noticed that the MAP estimate gave better results as we reported in the ta-

Table 9.2 Accuracy (measured in mm) and timing results for the landmark detection using local, global, and local + global context posterior. Source: Lay et al., A context integration framework for rapid multiple organ parsing, in: S. Kevin Zhou (Ed.), Medical Image Recognition, Segmentation, and Parsing, Academic Press, 2015.

	Global		Local		Local + Global	
Spacing	**Time (s)**	**Median**	**Time (s)**	**Median**	**Time (s)**	**Median**
1 (5 mm)	2.76	**25.0 ± 17.4**	1.91	16.4 ± 10.6	–	–
5 (25 mm)	0.92	39.9 ± 33.4	–	–	2.11	**12.9 ± 7.52**
7 (35 mm)	0.91	54.1 ± 54.1	–	–	0.91	13.0 ± 7.56
15 (75 mm)	**0.89**	79.0 ± 85.6	–	–	**0.23**	14.1 ± 8.25

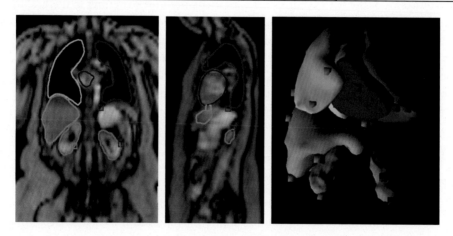

Figure 9.8 An illustration of the landmarks in 3D and automatic segmentation results. Our method is robust to a few failed landmarks. Source: Lay et al., A context integration framework for rapid multiple organ parsing, in: S. Kevin Zhou (Ed.), Medical Image Recognition, Segmentation, and Parsing, Academic Press, 2015.

ble. Obtaining the MAP estimate requires populating a probability image and scanning through the image to get the MAP estimate (this is proportional to the number of landmarks, which is why no speedup is reported in the table). Besides, the accuracy of the global context posterior suffers from sparse sampling, and even with dense sampling it still performs worse than the local + global method. On the other hand, it is evident that a sparser sampling of the volume has little impact on the accuracy of the local+global method. The local classifier is computed using a constrained search over the volume (e.g., using bounds for the landmark positions relative to the image [34]), but achieves worse accuracy and is still slower than our combined local+global posterior modeling.

The shape landmarks are used to infer the shape of all the organs (see Fig. 9.8). We compare the resulting segmentation results at several phases to a state-of-the-art hierarchical detection using marginal space learning (MSL) [34] that is known as both

Table 9.3 Accuracy (measured in mm) and timing for segmentation results using our approach compared to the MSL model on the MR FastView data. Source: Lay et al., A context integration framework for rapid multiple organ parsing, in: S. Kevin Zhou (Ed.), Medical Image Recognition, Segmentation, and Parsing, Academic Press, 2015.

	Skip (mm)	Time (s)	Liver	R. Kidney	L. Kidney	R. Lung	Heart	L. Lung
				Detection & Shape initialization				
MSL	–	5.50	9.21±1.82	**3.44±1.16**	**3.08±1.21**	7.29±1.64	5.98±1.59	7.42±1.71
Local+Global	25	2.21	**7.41±1.91**	4.10±1.34	4.31±1.81	**6.60±1.74**	**5.64±1.41**	**6.72±1.55**
	35	1.01	7.43±1.95	4.18±1.39	4.39±1.89	6.67±1.79	5.69±1.40	6.78±1.53
	50	0.55	7.55±2.03	4.36±1.43	4.57±1.93	6.77±1.86	5.78±1.48	6.83±1.64
	60	0.39	7.63±1.95	4.59±1.52	4.70±1.98	6.86±1.91	5.92±1.53	6.91±1.68
	75	**0.33**	7.94±2.21	5.13±1.77	5.38±2.90	6.97±1.95	5.98±1.57	6.88±1.75
				With boundary refinement				
MSL	–	6.36	4.87 ± 1.46	**2.26 ± 0.61**	**2.12 ± 0.68**	3.67 ± 0.95	**3.99 ± 1.36**	3.55 ± 0.97
(BSP)	25	2.89	**4.07±0.99**	2.33±0.68	2.41±1.61	**3.56±0.96**	4.02±1.50	**3.35±0.83**
	35	1.60	4.08±0.99	2.37±0.69	2.47±1.72	3.57±0.98	4.02±1.52	**3.35±0.83**
	50	1.13	4.09±1.01	2.37±0.73	2.48±1.66	3.57±0.95	4.06±1.62	3.36±0.83
	60	0.97	4.08±1.00	2.42±0.79	2.42±1.57	3.57±0.97	4.07±1.63	3.35±0.84
	75	**0.89**	4.17±1.14	2.51±1.00	2.84±2.51	3.57±0.95	4.11±1.64	3.37±0.83
Interuser variability			4.07±0.93	1.96±0.43	2.10±0.51	3.79±0.36	4.54±0.88	3.52±0.63

fast and accurate. For the MSL setup, the kidneys were predicted from the liver bounding box, meaning the kidney search range was more localized allowing the detection to be faster (the lungs were predicted relative to the heart in a similar manner). Table 9.3 illustrates the timing and accuracy results for the 50 unseen test cases using both MSL and our method. The accuracy is gauged by symmetric surface-to-surface distance. Fig. 9.9 illustrates two qualitative results.

The fast landmark detection and robust shape initialization can provide an approximate shape in as little as 0.33 s (for spacing of 75 mm, e.g., 15 voxels). The improvement of our initialization on the liver and lungs over the MSL approach is likely due to our use of more landmarks to capture more variations associated with complex anatomies than MSL that fits shapes of varying complexities into a rigid bounding box. On the other hand, for both kidneys with less variations in the shape but more in the appearance, MSL performs better as it considers kidney as a whole. The discriminative boundary deformation significantly improves the segmentation accuracy for both approaches, which yield comparable overall accuracy for all organs. Our approach is more efficient, e.g., over 5 times faster if we skip every 12th voxel (65 mm) in the global context. With a skipping factor of 75 mm, we achieved segmentation of 6 organs *within one second* and with accuracy almost as good as the best quality! Both methods perform fairly close to interuser variability.[2]

One potential concern with relying on far away global context information is that the reliability of the detection and segmentation may degrade or vary when given a subvolume. To investigate this, we evaluated the lung, liver, and heart segmentation

---

[2] The interuser variability was measured over 10 randomly selected unseen test cases.

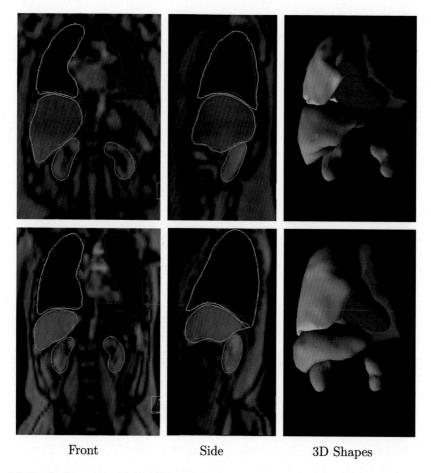

Front   Side   3D Shapes

Figure 9.9 Qualitative results of the MR FastView segmentation (solid) on unseen cases with ground truth (dotted). Source: Lay et al., A context integration framework for rapid multiple organ parsing, in: S. Kevin Zhou (Ed.), Medical Image Recognition, Segmentation, and Parsing, Academic Press, 2015.

accuracy on the same subset of unseen volumes, but this time we cropped the volumes 10 cm below the lung and heart, meaning that the kidneys and liver are not present. In these cropped volumes, using a spacing factor of 50 mm, we find the accuracy of our local+global method to be consistent with that in Table 9.3, where right lung accuracy was 3.57 ± 1.32, heart accuracy was slightly worse at 4.53 ± 2.39, and the left lung was 3.22 ± 1.02. Although the global model may predict instances of missing organs (e.g., the kidney and liver), these "false" detection can be pruned by thresholding the local classifier scores or by identifying missing organs as those with a low average boundary detector score.

9.4. Conclusion

In this chapter, we have offered a list of various representations to denote landmark and shape and discussed their pros and cons. Based on a discrete action map representation, we have presented a supervised action classification approach for landmark detection. Based on a progressive, rough-to-exact shape repression, we have presented a learning approach that fuses regression, which models global context, and classification, which models local context, for rapid multiple organ segmentation.

References

[1] Z. Xu, Q. Huang, J. Park, M. Chen, D. Xu, D. Yang, D. Liu, S.K. Zhou, Supervised action classifier: approaching landmark detection as image partitioning, in: International Conference on Medical Image Computing and Computer-Assisted Intervention, Springer, 2017, pp. 338–346.

[2] H.J. Johnson, G.E. Christensen, Consistent landmark and intensity-based image registration, IEEE Transactions on Medical Imaging 21 (5) (2002) 450–461.

[3] W.R. Crum, T. Hartkens, D. Hill, Non-rigid image registration: theory and practice, British Journal of Radiology 77 (suppl_2) (2004) S140–S153.

[4] T. Beck, D. Bernhardt, C. Biermann, R. Dillmann, Validation and detection of vessel landmarks by using anatomical knowledge, in: Medical Imaging 2010: Image Processing, vol. 7623, International Society for Optics and Photonics, 2010, 76234I.

[5] S. Banik, R.M. Rangayyan, G.S. Boag, Landmarking and segmentation of 3D CT images, Synthesis Lectures on Biomedical Engineering 4 (1) (2009) 1–170.

[6] O. Pauly, B. Glocker, A. Criminisi, D. Mateus, A.M. Möller, S. Nekolla, N. Navab, Fast multiple organ detection and localization in whole-body MR Dixon sequences, in: International Conference on Medical Image Computing and Computer-Assisted Intervention, Springer, 2011, pp. 239–247.

[7] N. Lay, N. Birkbeck, J. Zhang, S.K. Zhou, Rapid multi-organ segmentation using context integration and discriminative models, in: International Conference on Information Processing in Medical Imaging, Springer, 2013, pp. 450–462.

[8] S. Seifert, M. Kelm, M. Moeller, S. Mukherjee, A. Cavallaro, M. Huber, D. Comaniciu, Semantic annotation of medical images, in: Medical Imaging 2010: Advanced PACS-Based Imaging Informatics and Therapeutic Applications, vol. 7628, International Society for Optics and Photonics, 2010, p. 762808.

[9] C. Rosse, J.L. Mejino Jr, A reference ontology for biomedical informatics: the foundational model of anatomy, Journal of Biomedical Informatics 36 (6) (2003) 478–500.

[10] I. Whitmore, Terminologia anatomica: new terminology for the new anatomist, The Anatomical Record 257 (2) (1999) 50–53.

[11] J.J. Budovec, C.A. Lam, C.E. Kahn Jr, Informatics in radiology: radiology gamuts ontology: differential diagnosis for the semantic web, Radiographics 34 (1) (2014) 254–264.

[12] R. Davis, H. Shrobe, P. Szolovits, What is a knowledge representation?, AI Magazine 14 (1) (1993) 17.

[13] Shape regression machine and efficient segmentation of left ventricle endocardium from 2D b-mode echocardiogram, Medical Image Analysis 14 (4) (2010) 563–581.

[14] T. Pfister, J. Charles, A. Zisserman, Flowing convnets for human pose estimation in videos, in: IEEE International Conference on Computer Vision, 2015.

[15] Z. Tu, Probabilistic boosting-tree: learning discriminative models for classification, recognition, and clustering, in: ICCV, 2005, pp. 1589–1596.

[16] P. Viola, M. Jones, Fast and robust classification using asymmetric AdaBoost and a detector cascade, in: Advances in Neural Information Processing Systems, 2002, pp. 1311–1318.

[17] S.K. Zhou, D. Comaniciu, Shape regression machine, in: Biennial International Conference on Information Processing in Medical Imaging, Springer, 2007, pp. 13–25.

[18] K. Simonyan, A. Zisserman, Very deep convolutional networks for large-scale image recognition, preprint, arXiv:1409.1556.

[19] J. Long, E. Shelhamer, T. Darrell, Fully convolutional networks for semantic segmentation, in: Proceedings of the IEEE Conference on Computer Vision and Pattern Recognition, 2015, pp. 3431–3440.

[20] F.C. Ghesu, B. Georgescu, T. Mansi, D. Neumann, J. Hornegger, D. Comaniciu, An artificial agent for anatomical landmark detection in medical images, in: International Conference on Medical Image Computing and Computer-Assisted Intervention, Springer, 2016, pp. 229–237.

[21] V. Badrinarayanan, A. Kendall, R. Cipolla, Segnet: a deep convolutional encoder–decoder architecture for image segmentation, IEEE Transactions on Pattern Analysis and Machine Intelligence 12 (2017) 2481–2495.

[22] D. Yang, D. Xu, S.K. Zhou, B. Georgescu, M. Chen, S. Grbic, D. Metaxas, D. Comaniciu, Automatic liver segmentation using an adversarial image-to-image network, in: International Conference on Medical Image Computing and Computer-Assisted Intervention, Springer, 2017, pp. 507–515.

[23] T. Heimann, H.-P. Meinzer, Statistical shape models for 3D medical image segmentation: a review, Medical Image Analysis 13 (4) (2009) 543–563.

[24] S.M. Pizer, P.T. Fletcher, S. Joshi, A. Thall, J.Z. Chen, Y. Fridman, D.S. Fritsch, A.G. Gash, J.M. Glotzer, M.R. Jiroutek, et al., Deformable m-reps for 3D medical image segmentation, International Journal of Computer Vision 55 (2–3) (2003) 85–106.

[25] L. Shen, H. Farid, M.A. McPeek, Modeling three-dimensional morphological structures using spherical harmonics, Evolution: International Journal of Organic Evolution 63 (4) (2009) 1003–1016.

[26] D. Nain, S. Haker, A. Bobick, A. Tannenbaum, Shape-driven 3D segmentation using spherical wavelets, in: International Conference on Medical Image Computing and Computer-Assisted Intervention, Springer, 2006, pp. 66–74.

[27] Y. Zheng, A. Barbu, B. Georgescu, M. Scheuering, D. Comaniciu, Four-chamber heart modeling and automatic segmentation for 3D cardiac CT volumes using marginal space learning and steerable features, IEEE Transactions on Medical Imaging 27 (11) (2008) 1668–1681.

[28] T. Kohlberger, M. Sofka, J. Zhang, N. Birkbeck, J. Wetzl, J. Kaftan, J. Declerck, S.K. Zhou, Automatic multi-organ segmentation using learning-based segmentation and level set optimization, in: Medical Image Computing and Computer-Assisted Intervention – MICCAI 2011, Springer, Berlin Heidelberg, 2011, pp. 338–345.

[29] D. Wu, M. Sofka, N. Birkbeck, S.K. Zhou, Segmentation of multiple knee bones from ct for orthopedic knee surgery planning, in: International Conference on Medical Image Computing and Computer-Assisted Intervention, Springer, Cham, 2014, pp. 372–380.

[30] T.F. Cootes, C.J. Taylor, D.H. Cooper, J. Graham, Active shape models their training and application, Computer Vision and Image Understanding 61 (1995) 38–59.

[31] P. Isola, J.-Y. Zhu, T. Zhou, A.A. Efros, Image-to-image translation with conditional adversarial networks, preprint, arXiv:1611.07004.

[32] H. Ling, S.K. Zhou, Y. Zheng, B. Georgescu, M. Suehling, D. Comaniciu, Hierarchical, learning-based automatic liver segmentation, in: IEEE Conference on Computer Vision and Pattern Recognition, 2008, CVPR 2008, IEEE, 2008, pp. 1–8.

[33] M. Sofka, J. Zhang, S. Zhou, D. Comaniciu, Multiple object detection by sequential Monte Carlo and hierarchical detection network, in: CVPR, 2010.

[34] Y. Zheng, B. Georgescu, H. Ling, S.K. Zhou, M. Scheuering, D. Comaniciu, Constrained marginal space learning for efficient 3D anatomical structure detection in medical images, in: CVPR, 2009, pp. 194–201.

[35] B.M. Kelm, S.K. Zhou, M. Suehling, Y. Zheng, M. Wels, D. Comaniciu, Detection of 3D spinal geometry using iterated marginal space learning, in: MCV, Springer, 2010, pp. 96–105.

[36] J. Feulner, S.K. Zhou, M. Hammon, J. Hornegger, D. Comaniciu, Lymph node detection and segmentation in chest ct data using discriminative learning and a spatial prior, Medical Image Analysis 17 (2) (2013) 254–270.

[37] S. Zhang, Y. Zhan, M. Dewan, J. Huang, D.N. Metaxas, X.S. Zhou, Sparse shape composition: a new framework for shape prior modeling, in: CVPR, IEEE, 2011, pp. 1025–1032.

[38] M. Sofka, J. Wetzl, N. Birkbeck, J. Zhang, T. Kohlberger, J. Kaftan, J. Declerck, S. Zhou, Multi-stage learning for robust lung segmentation in challenging CT volumes, in: Proceedings of the 14th International Conference on Medical Image Computing and Computer-Assisted Intervention, MICCAI 2011, Toronto, Canada, 2011.

[39] D. Liu, K. Zhou, D. Bernhardt, D. Comaniciu, Search strategies for multiple landmark detection by submodular maximization, in: CVPR, IEEE, 2010.

[40] S.K. Zhou, J. Zhou, D. Comaniciu, A boosting regression approach to medical anatomy detection, in: IEEE Conference on Computer Vision and Pattern Recognition, CVPR'07, IEEE, 2007, pp. 1–8.

[41] A. Criminisi, J. Shotton, S. Bucciarelli, Decision forests with long-range spatial context for organ localization in CT volumes, in: MICCAI-PMMIA Workshop, 2009.

CHAPTER 10

Deep multilevel contextual networks for biomedical image segmentation

Hao Chen[a], Qi Dou[a], Xiaojuan Qi[a], Jie-Zhi Cheng[b], Pheng-Ann Heng[a]

[a]The Chinese University of Hong Kong, Department of Computer Science and Engineering, Hong Kong, China
[b]Shenzhen University, School of Medicine, Shenzhen, China

Contents

10.1.	Introduction	231
10.2.	Related work	233
	10.2.1 Electron microscopy image segmentation	233
	10.2.2 Nuclei segmentation	234
10.3.	Method	235
	10.3.1 Deep multilevel contextual network	235
	10.3.2 Regularization with auxiliary supervision	236
	10.3.3 Importance of receptive field	237
10.4.	Experiments and results	237
	10.4.1 Dataset and preprocessing	237
	10.4.1.1 2012 ISBI EM segmentation	237
	10.4.1.2 2015 MICCAI nuclei segmentation	238
	10.4.2 Details of training	238
	10.4.3 2012 ISBI neuronal structure segmentation challenge	238
	10.4.3.1 Qualitative evaluation	238
	10.4.3.2 Quantitative evaluation metrics	239
	10.4.3.3 Results comparison without postprocessing	240
	10.4.3.4 Results comparison with postprocessing	241
	10.4.3.5 Ablation studies of our method	242
	10.4.4 2015 MICCAI nuclei segmentation challenge	242
	10.4.4.1 Qualitative evaluation	242
	10.4.4.2 Quantitative evaluation metrics	242
	10.4.4.3 Quantitative results and comparison	243
	10.4.5 Computation time	244
10.5.	Discussion and conclusion	244
	Acknowledgment	244
	References	245

10.1. Introduction

Biomedical image segmentation has been a crucial, yet challenging topic in the field of medical image computing. It serves as one of the basic components for many biomedical related applications, such as medical disease diagnosis and biological interconnection

Handbook of Medical Image Computing and Computer Assisted Intervention
https://doi.org/10.1016/B978-0-12-816176-0.00015-6

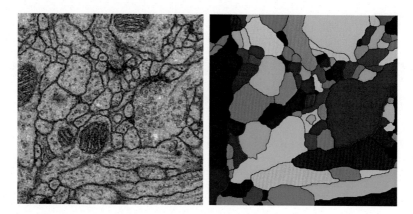

Figure 10.1 (Left) The original ssTEM image. (Right) The corresponding segmentation annotation (individual components are denoted by different colors).

interpretation. For example, the neuronal circuit reconstruction, also termed as connectome in neuroscience, from biological images can manifest the interconnections of neurons for more insightful functional analysis of the brain and other nervous systems [1, 2]. The 2D serial high resolution Electron Microscopy (EM) imaging is commonly used for the visualization of microneural circuits and hence is a very informative imaging tool for the connectome analysis. Fig. 10.1 illustrates a 2D example of serial section Transmission Electron Microscopy (ssTEM) images which are widely used for neuronal structure segmentation [3].

As can be observed in Fig. 10.1, the segmentation problem for the neuronal structures can be very challenging in three ways. First, the image deformation during the acquisition may blur the membrane boundaries between neighboring neurons as shown in Fig. 10.1 (left). Second, the variation of neuron membrane in terms of image contrast and membranal thickness can be very large. Particularly for the thickness, it can range from solid dark curves to grazed grey swaths [4]. Third, the presence of intracellular structures makes edge detection and region growing based methods ineffective for the identification of neuron membrane. Some confounding microstructures may also mislead the merging of regions or incorrect splitting of one region into several sections. Meanwhile, the imaging artifacts and image alignment errors can impose difficulties on the design of effective segmentation algorithms as well.

Recently, deep learning with hierarchical feature representations has achieved promising results in various applications, including image classification [5], object detection [6–8], and segmentation [9,10]. However, the performance gap between the computerized results and human annotations can be still perceivable. There are two main drawbacks of previous deep learning-based studies on this task. First, the operation of sliding window scanning imposes a heavy burden on the computational efficiency. This must be taken into consideration seriously regarding the large scale biomedical image segmentation. Second, the size of biological structures can be very diverse. Although, classification with single size subwindow can achieve good performance, it may produce unsatisfactory results in some regions where the size of contextual window is set inappropriately.

In order to tackle the aforementioned challenges, we propose a novel deep contextual segmentation network for biomedical image segmentation. This approach incorporates the multilevel contextual information with different receptive fields, thus it can remove the ambiguities of structural boundaries in essence that previous studies may fail to do. Inspired by previous studies [11,12], we further make the model deeper than in [11] and add auxiliary supervised classifiers to encourage the backpropagation flow. This augmented network can further unleash the power of deep neural networks for biomedical structure segmentation. Quantitative evaluation was extensively conducted on the public dataset of 2012 ISBI EM Segmentation Challenge [13] and 2015 MICCAI Nuclei Segmentation Challenge, with rich baseline results for comparison in terms of pixel- and object-level evaluation. Our method achieved the state-of-the-art results, which outperformed those of other methods on all evaluation measurements. It is also worth noting that our results surpassed the annotation by neuroanatomists when measuring the warping error in the EM Segmentation task. In addition, the superior performance on these two benchmarks demonstrated the generalization capability of our proposed method.

10.2. Related work

10.2.1 Electron microscopy image segmentation

The ssTEM images can depict more than tens of thousands of neurons where each neuron may have thousands of synaptic connections. Thus, the size of ssTEM images is usually formidably large and is on a terabyte scale. Accordingly, the extremely complicated interconnections of neuronal structures and sheer image volume are far beyond the human capability for annotation, as the manual labeling of all neuronal structures may take decades to finish [14–16]. In this case, automatic segmentation methods are highly demanded to assist the parsing of the ssTEM images into concrete neurological structures for further analysis [17].

Because of the anisotropic nature of ssTEM data, most previous methods were devised under the framework of initial 2D membrane detection and latter 3D linking process [4]. Although considerable progress has been made over the last decade, earlier studies achieved a limited accuracy of segmentation and often failed to suppress the intracellular structures effectively with the hand-crafted features, e.g., Radon and ray-like features [18,19,2,20].

Recently, Ciresan et al. employed the deep convolutional neural network as a pixelwise classifier by taking a square window centered on the pixel itself as input, which contains contextual appearance information [11]. This method achieved the best performance in 2012 ISBI neuronal structure segmentation challenge. A variant version with iterative refining process has been proposed to withstand the noise and recover the boundaries [16]. Besides, several methods worked on the probability maps produced by deep convolutional neural networks as a postprocessing step, such as learning based adaptive watershed [21], hierarchical merge tree with consistent constraints [22], and active learning approach for hierarchical agglomerative segmentation [23], to further improve the performance. These methods refined the segmentation results with respect to the measurements of Rand and warping errors [24] with significant performance boost in comparison to the results of [11].

10.2.2 Nuclei segmentation

With the advent of whole slide imaging scanners, tissue histopathology slides can be digitized and stored in the form of digital images. Meanwhile, histopathological analysis performed on these digital images has been demonstrated as an effective and reliable tool for cancer diagnosis and prognosis [25]. In the routine of histopathological examination, accurate detection and segmentation of certain histological structures, such as cancer nuclei, is one of crucial prerequisite steps to obtain reliable morphological statistics that characterize the aggressiveness of tumors. Specifically, counting of object instances such as cell nuclei has diagnostic significance for some cancerous diseases [26–28]. This requires an accurate detection and segmentation of cell nuclei. The nucleus morphism has an important diagnostic value for cancer grading [29–31].

For the nuclei detection and segmentation, various methods have been proposed to tackle this problem ranging from relatively simple approaches, such as thresholding and morphological operations [32,33], to more sophisticated methods based on hand-crafted features derived from boundaries/contours [26,34], gradients [35], Laplacian-of-Gaussian [36], cytological and textural features [37], etc. Then different classifiers (e.g., Support Vector Machine (SVM), Adaboost, and Bayesian) have been employed in the literature to detect and segment nuclei from histology images [38]. However, the hand-crafted features suffer from limited representation capabilities, and hence they can be vulnerable to different variations. Furthermore, the piecewise learning system separating feature extraction and classification may not be optimal or efficient for generating precise probability maps of histological structures.

Recently, stacked sparse autoencoders (SSAE) were exploited with unsupervised pretraining and following fine-tuning for nuclei detection from breast cancer histopathology images in [27]. Although along with merit of unsupervised pretraining, which can handle the situation of limited medical training data, the autoencoders usually achieved inferior performance on image recognition tasks compared to convolutional neural networks (CNNs). The success of the latter networks is mostly attributed to the more elegant structures for dealing with images. Regarding the convolutional neural networks, the authors of [39] employed deep convolutional neural networks for mitosis detection and achieved the best performance in two grand challenges [40,41]. To further improve the efficiency and effectiveness, Hao Chen et al. [42] developed a cascaded deep learning framework, i.e., a coarse model for retrieving candidates and a fine-discrimination model for singling out mitoses from hard mimics. A spatially constrained convolutional neural network was present in [43] incorporated with neighboring ensemble prediction, demonstrating the efficacy of deep learning based features from CNNs.

10.3. Method

10.3.1 Deep multilevel contextual network

In this section, we present a deeply supervised contextual network for biomedical image segmentation. Inspired by recent studies of fully convolutional networks (FCNs) [9, 44], which replace the fully connected layers with all convolutional kernels, the proposed network is a variant and takes full advantage of convolutional kernels for efficient and effective image segmentation. The architecture of the proposed method is illustrated in Fig. 10.2. It basically contains two modules, i.e., downsampling path with convolutional and max-pooling layers and upsampling path with convolutional and deconvolutional layers. Noting that we upsampled the feature maps with the backwards strided convolution in the upsampling path, thus we call them deconvolutional layers. The downsampling path aims at classifying the semantic meanings based on the high level abstract information, while the upsampling path is reconstructing the fine details such as boundaries. The upsampling layers are designed by taking full advantage of the different feature maps in hierarchical layers.

The basic idea behind this is that global or abstract information from higher layers helps to resolve the problem of what (i.e., classification capability), and local information from lower layers helps to resolve the problem of where (i.e., localization accuracy). Finally, this multilevel contextual information are fused together with a summing operation. The probability maps are generated by inputting the fused map into a softmax classification layer. Specifically, the architecture of neural network contains 16 convolutional layers, 3 max-pooling layers for downsampling, and 3 deconvolutional layers for upsampling. The convolutional layers along with convolutional kernels (3×3 or 1×1) perform linear mapping with shared parameters. The max-pooling layers downsample the size of feature maps by the max-pooling operation (kernel size 2×2 with a stride 2). The deconvolutional layers upsample the size of feature maps by the backwards strided convolution [9] ($2k \times 2k$ kernel with a stride k, $k = 2, 4$ and 8 for upsampling layers, respectively). A nonlinear mapping layer (elementwise rectified linear activations) is followed for each layer that contains parameters to be trained [5].

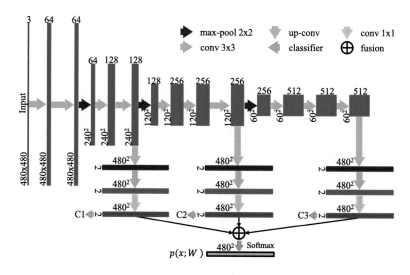

Figure 10.2 The architecture of the proposed deep contextual network.

10.3.2 Regularization with auxiliary supervision

In order to alleviate the problem of vanishing gradients and encourage the backpropagation of gradient flow in deep neural networks, the auxiliary classifiers C are injected for training the network. Furthermore, they can serve as regularization for reducing the overfitting and improve the discriminative capability of features in intermediate layers [45,12,46]. The classification layer after fusing multilevel contextual information produces the image segmentation results by leveraging the hierarchical feature representations. Finally, the training of whole network is formulated as a per-pixel classification problem with respect to the ground-truth segmentation masks as follows:

$$\mathcal{L}(\mathcal{X};\theta) = \frac{\lambda}{2}(\sum_c \|W_c\|_2^2 + \|W\|_2^2) - \sum_c \sum_{x \in \mathcal{X}} w_c \psi_c(x, \ell(x)) - \sum_{x \in \mathcal{X}} \psi(x, \ell(x)),$$

where the first part is the regularization term and latter one, including target and auxiliary classifiers, is the data loss term. The tradeoff between these two terms is controlled by the hyperparameter λ. Specifically, W denotes the parameters for inferring the target output $p(x; W)$, $\psi(x, \ell(x))$ denotes the cross-entropy loss regarding the true label $\ell(x)$ for pixel x in image space $\mathcal{X}$, similarly $\psi_c(x, \ell(x))$ is the loss from cth auxiliary classifier with parameters W_c for inferring the output, parameter w_c denotes the corresponding discount weight. Finally, parameters $\theta = \{W, W_c\}$ of deep contextual network are jointly optimized in an end-to-end way by minimizing the total loss function $\mathcal{L}$. For the testing data of biomedical images, the results are produced with an overlap–tile strategy to improve the robustness.

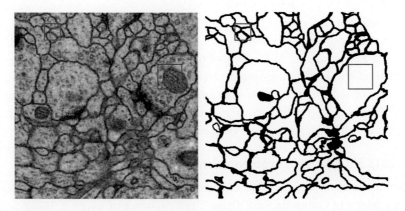

Figure 10.3 Illustration of contextual window size: (left) the original ssTEM image; (right) manual segmentation result by an expert human neuroanatomist (black and white pixels denote the membrane and nonmembrane, respectively).

10.3.3 Importance of receptive field

In the task of biomedical image segmentation, there is usually a large variation in the size of structures. Therefore, the size of a receptive field plays a key role in the pixel-wise classification given the corresponding contextual information. It's approximated as the size of object region with surrounding context, which is reflected as the intensity values within the window. As shown in Fig. 10.3, the accurate recognition of different regions from EM images may depend on different window sizes. For example, the cluttered neurons need a small window size for clearly separating the membranes between neighboring neurons, while a large size is required for neurons containing intracellular structures so as to suppress the false predictions. In the hierarchical structure of deep contextual networks, these upsampling layers have different receptive fields. With the depth increasing, the size of receptive field is becoming larger. Therefore, it can handle the variations of reception field size properly that different regions demand for correct segmentation while taking advantage of the hierarchical feature representations.

10.4. Experiments and results

10.4.1 Dataset and preprocessing
10.4.1.1 2012 ISBI EM segmentation

We evaluated our method on the public dataset of 2012 ISBI EM Segmentation Challenge [13], which is still open for submissions. The training dataset contains a stack of 30 slices from an ssTEM dataset of the Drosophila first instar larva ventral nerve cord (VNC), which measures approximately $2 \times 2 \times 1.5$ microns with a resolution of $4 \times 4 \times 50$ nm/voxel. The images were manually annotated in the pixel-level by a human neuroanatomist using the software tool TrakEm2 [47]. The ground truth masks of training data were provided while those of testing data with 30 slices were held out by the organizers for evaluation. We evaluated the performance of our method by submitting results to the online testing system. In order to improve the robustness of neural network, we utilized the strategy of data augmentation to enlarge the training dataset (about 10 times larger). The transformations of data augmentation include scaling, rotation, flipping, mirroring, and elastic distortion.

10.4.1.2 2015 MICCAI nuclei segmentation

We also evaluated our method on the challenge dataset on *Segmentation of Nuclei in Digital Pathology Images* of Computational Brain Tumor Cluster of Event (CBTC) workshop in conjunction with MICCAI 2015. The training data have at least 500 manually segmented nuclei in 15 image tiles and testing data include 18 images for evaluation (the ground truth is held out by the challenge organizers). Participants are asked to detect and segment all the nuclei of testing tiles, which are extracted from whole slide tissue images. The algorithm results are compared with consensus pathologist segmented subregions. We utilize the strategy of data augmentation to enlarge the training dataset. The transformations of data augmentation include translation and rotation.

10.4.2 Details of training

The proposed method was implemented with the mixed programming technology of Matlab[1] and C++ under the open-source framework of Caffe library [48]. We randomly cropped a region (size 480×480) from the original image as the input into the network and trained it with standard backpropagation using stochastic gradient descent (momentum = 0.9, weight decay = 0.0005, the learning rate was set as 0.01 initially and decreased by a factor of 10 every 2000 iterations). The parameter of corresponding discount weight w_c was set as 1 initially and decreased by a factor of 10 every 10000 iterations till a negligible value 0.01. The training time on the augmentation dataset took about three hours using a standard PC with a 2.50 GHz Intel(R) Xeon(R) E5–1620 CPU and an NVIDIA GeForce GTX Titan X GPU.

10.4.3 2012 ISBI neuronal structure segmentation challenge
10.4.3.1 Qualitative evaluation

Two examples of qualitative segmentation results without morphological boundary refinement are demonstrated in Fig. 10.4. We can see that our method can generate visually smooth and accurate segmentation results. As the red arrows show in the figure, it can successfully suppress the intracellular structures and produce good probability

---

[1] MATLAB® is a trademark of The MathWorks.

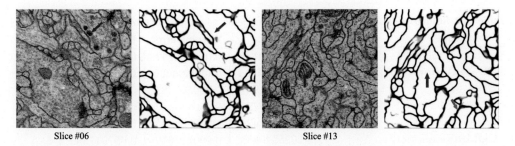

Slice #06   Slice #13

Figure 10.4 Examples of original EM images and segmentation results by our method (the darker color of pixels denotes the higher probability of being membrane in neuronal structure).

maps that classify the membrane and nonmembrane correctly. Furthermore, by utilizing multilevel representations of contextual information, our method can also close gaps (contour completion as the blue arrows shown in Fig. 10.4) in places where the contrast of membrane is low. Although there still exist ambiguous regions which are even hard for human experts, the results of our method are more accurate in comparison to those generated from previous deep learning studies [49,11]. This evidenced the efficacy of our proposed method qualitatively.

10.4.3.2 Quantitative evaluation metrics

In the 2012 ISBI EM Segmentation Challenge, the performance of different competing methods is ranked based on their pixel and object classification accuracy. Specifically, the 2D topology-based segmentation evaluation metrics include Rand, warping, and pixel errors [13,24], which are defined as follows:

Rand error: 1 − the maximal F-score of the foreground-restricted Rand index [50], a measure of similarity between two clusters or segmentations. For the EM segmentation evaluation, the zero component of the original labels (background pixels of the ground truth) is excluded.

Warping error: a segmentation metric that penalizes the topological disagreements (object splits and mergers).

Pixel error: 1 − the maximal F-score of pixel similarity, or squared Euclidean distance between the original and the result labels.

The evaluation system thresholds the probability maps with 9 different values (0.1–0.9 with an interval of 0.1) separately and return the minimum error for each segmentation metric. The quantitative comparison of different methods can be seen in Table 10.1. Note that the results show the best performance for each measurement across all submissions by each team individually. More details and results are available at

Table 10.1 Results of 2012 ISBI segmentation challenge on neuronal structures.

Group name	Rand error	Warping error	Pixel error	Rank
★★ human values ★★	0.002109173	0.000005341	0.001041591	
CUMedVision (Our)	**0.017334163**	**0.000000000**	**0.057953485**	**1**
DIVE-SCI	0.017841947	0.000307083	0.058436986	2
IDSIA-SCI	0.018919792	0.000616837	0.102692786	3
optree-idsia [21]	0.022777620	0.000807953	0.110460288	4
CUMedVision-motif	0.025540655	0.000321579	0.057912350	5
motif [16]	0.026326384	0.000426483	0.062739851	6
SCI [22]	0.028054308	0.000515747	0.063349324	7
Image Analysis Lab Freiburg [51]	0.038225781	0.000352859	0.061141279	8
Connectome	0.045905709	0.000478999	0.062029263	9
PyraMiD-LSTM [49]	0.046704591	0.000462341	0.061624006	10
DIVE	0.047680695	0.000374222	0.058205303	11
IDSIA [11]	0.048314096	0.000434367	0.060298549	12
INI	0.060110507	0.000495529	0.068537199	13
MLL-ETH [2]	0.063919883	0.000581741	0.079403258	14
CUMedVision-4 (C3)	0.043419035	0.000342178	0.060940140	
CUMedVision-4 (C2)	0.046058434	0.000421524	0.061248112	
CUMedVision-4 (C1)	0.258966855	0.001080322	0.102325669	
CUMedVision-4 (with C)	0.035134666	0.000334167	0.058372960	
CUMedVision-4 (w/o C)	0.040492503	0.000330353	0.062864362	
CUMedVision-6 (with C)	0.040406591	0.000000000	0.059902422	
CUMedVision-4 (with fusion)	0.017334163	0.000188446	0.057953485	

There are a total of 38 teams participating in this challenge.

the leader board.[2] We compared our method with the state-of-the-art methods with or without postprocessing separately. Furthermore, we conducted extensive experiments with ablation studies to probe the performance gain in our method and detail as follows.

10.4.3.3 Results comparison without postprocessing

Preliminary encouraging results were achieved by the *IDSIA* team [11], which utilized a deep convolutional neural network as a pixelwise classifier in a sliding window way. The best results were obtained by averaging the outputs from 4 deep neural network models. Different from this method by training the neural network with different window sizes (65 and 95) separately, our approach integrates multisize windows (i.e., different receptive fields in upsampling layers) into one unified framework. This can help to generate more accurate probability maps by leveraging multilevel contextual informa-

---

[2] Please refer to the leader board for more details: http://brainiac2.mit.edu/isbi_challenge/leaders-board.

tion. The *Image Analysis Lab Freiburg* team [51] designed a deep U-shaped network by concatenating features from lower layers and improved the results of [11]. This further demonstrated the effectiveness of contextual information for accurate segmentation. However, with such a deep network (i.e., 23 convolutional layers), the backpropagation of gradient flow may be a potential issue and training took a long time (about 10 hours). Instead of using the convolutional neural network, the *PyraMiD-LSTM* team employed a novel parallel multidimensional long short-term memory model for fast volumetric segmentation [49]. Unfortunately, a relatively inferior performance was achieved by this method. From Table 10.1, we can see that our deep segmentation network (with 6 model averaging results, i.e., *CUMedVision-6 (with C)*) without watershed fusion achieved the best performance in terms of warping error, which outperformed other methods by a large margin. Notably it's the only result that surpasses the performance of expert neuroanatomist annotation. Our submitted entry *CUMedVision-4 (with C)* averaging 4 models (the same number of models as in [11]) achieved much smaller Rand and warping errors than other teams also employing deep learning methods without sophisticated postprocessing steps, such as *DIVE*, *IDSIA*, and *Image Analysis Lab Freiburg*. This corroborates the superiority of our approach by exploring multilevel contextual information with auxiliary supervision.

10.4.3.4 Results comparison with postprocessing

Although the probability maps output from the deep contextual network are visually very good, we observe that the membrane of ambiguous regions can sometimes be discontinued. This is partially caused by the averaging effect of probability maps, which are generated by several trained models. Therefore, we utilized an off-the-shelf watershed algorithm [52] to refine the contour. The final fusion result $p_f(x)$ was produced by fusing the binary contour $p_w(x)$ and original probability map $p(x)$ with a linear combination

$$p_f(x) = w_f p(x) + (1 - w_f) p_w(x). \tag{10.1}$$

The parameter w_f is determined by obtaining the optimal result of Rand error on the training data in our experiments. After fusing the results from watershed method (i.e., CUMedVision-4 (with fusion)), the Rand error can be reduced dramatically while unfortunately increasing the warping error. This is reasonable since these two errors consider the segmentation evaluation metric from different aspects. The former could penalize even slightly misplaced boundaries while the latter disregards nontopological errors. Different from our simple postprocessing step, the *SCI* team postprocessed the probability maps generated by the team *DIVE* and *IDSIA* with a sophisticated postprocessing strategy [22]. The postprocessed results were evaluated under the team name of *DIVE-SCI* and *IDSIA-SCI*, respectively. Although it utilized a supervised way with hierarchical merge tree to achieve structure consistency, the performance is relatively inferior compared to ours, in which only an unsupervised watershed method was used for postprocessing. In addition, our method also outperformed other methods with sophisticated postprocessing techniques including *optree-idsia* and *motif* by a large margin. This further highlights the advantages of our method by exploring multilevel contextual information to generate probability maps with better likelihood. We released the probability maps including training and testing data of our method for enlightening further sophisticated postprocessing strategies.[3]

10.4.3.5 Ablation studies of our method

In order to probe the performance gain of our proposed method, extensive ablation studies were conducted to investigate the role of each component. As illustrated in Table 10.1, compared with methods using single contextual information including *CUMedVision-4 (C3/C2/C1)*, the deep contextual model harnessing the multilevel contextual cues achieved significantly better performance on all the measurements. Furthermore, we compared the performance with (*CUMedVision-4 (with C)*) and without (*CUMedVision-4 (w/o C)*) the injection of auxiliary classifiers C, the Rand and pixel errors from method with C were much smaller while the warping error with C is competitive compared to the method without C. This validated the efficacy of auxiliary classifiers with deep supervision for encouraging backpropagation of gradient flow. By fusing the results from the watershed method, we achieved the result with Rand error of 0.017334, warping error of 0.000188, and pixel error of 0.057953, outperforming those from other teams by a large margin. To sum up, our method achieved the best performance on different evaluation measurements, which demonstrates the promising possibility for real-world applications. Although there is a tradeoff with respect to different evaluation metrics, the neuroanatomists can choose the desirable results based on the specific neurological requirements.

10.4.4 2015 MICCAI nuclei segmentation challenge

10.4.4.1 Qualitative evaluation

Some segmentation examples of testing data from 2015 MICCAI nuclei segmentation challenge can be seen in Fig. 10.5. We can see that our method can accurately segment the nuclei from pathology images. Some touching nuclei can be further split with postprocessing steps such as a watershed algorithm.

10.4.4.2 Quantitative evaluation metrics

The nuclei segmentation challenge employed two metrics for evaluation: traditional Dice coefficient and object-level Dice coefficient. The Dice metric was applied to measure the amount of overlap between the results of algorithms and human annotations

---

[3] See http://appsrv.cse.cuhk.edu.hk%7Ehchen/research/2012isbi_seg.html.

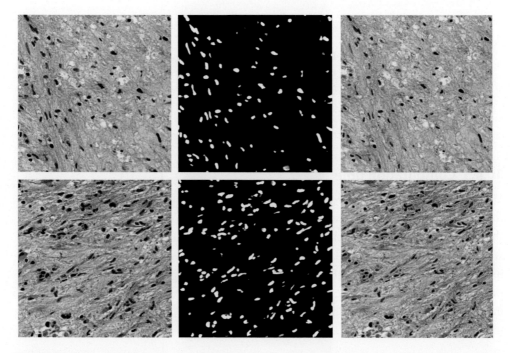

Figure 10.5 Examples of nuclei segmentation results: original images (left), probability maps (middle), and segmentation results by our method (right).

in terms of the nuclei regions that were detected and segmented. Dice metric does not take into account the cases of split and merge. A split is the case in which the human segments a region in a single nucleus, but the algorithm segments the same region in multiple nuclei. A merge is the case in which the algorithm segments a region into a single nucleus, but the human segments the same region into multiple nuclei. Object-level Dice coefficient is calculated based on the object-level segmentation, which provides a measure of splits and merges. Readers can refer to the challenge website[4] to learn more details of Dice and object-level Dice coefficients. The final ranking score was made by considering the average of Dice and object-level Dice coefficients.

10.4.4.3 Quantitative results and comparison

The quantitative results of our method and comparison with other methods can be seen in Table 10.2. Our method achieved the highest Dice score and outperformed other methods by a large margin, which demonstrates the efficacy and generalization capability of our proposed method quantitatively.

---

[4] 2015 MICCAI nuclei segmentation challenge: http://miccai.cloudapp.net:8000/competitions/37.

Table 10.2 Results of testing data in 2015 MICCAI nuclei segmentation challenge.

Team	Dice	Object-level dice	Score	Ranking
Our team	**0.877**	**0.722**	**0.799**	**1**
Team2	0.826	0.694	0.760	2
Team3	0.792	0.642	0.717	3
Team4	0.813	0.617	0.715	4

10.4.5 Computation time

Generally, it took about 0.4 seconds to process one test image with size 512×512 using the same configuration of training. Taking advantage of fully convolutional networks, the computation time is much less than in previous studies [11,16] utilizing a sliding window way, which caused a large number of redundant computations on neighboring pixels. With new imaging techniques producing much larger volumes (terabyte scale), the automatic methods with accurate and fast segmentation capabilities are of paramount importance. The fast speed and better accuracy of our method make it possible for large scale image analysis.

10.5. Discussion and conclusion

In this paper we have presented a deeply supervised contextual neural network for biomedical image segmentation. By harnessing the multilevel contextual information from the deep hierarchical feature representations, it can have better discrimination and localization abilities, which are key to biomedical image segmentation related tasks. The injected auxiliary classifiers can encourage the backpropagation of gradient flow in training the deep neural network, thus further improving the segmentation performance. Extensive experiments on the public dataset of 2012 ISBI EM Segmentation Challenge and 2015 MICCAI Nuclei Segmentation Challenge corroborated the effectiveness and generalization capability of our method. In addition, our approach is general and can be easily extended to other biomedical applications. Future work will include further refining of the segmentation results with other sophisticated postprocessing techniques [21–23] and more biomedical applications.

Acknowledgment

This work is supported by Hong Kong RGC General Research Fund (No. CUHK412513) and Shenzhen–Hong Kong Innovation Circle Funding Program (No. SGLH20131010151755080 and GHP/002/13SZ). The authors gratefully thank the challenge organizers for providing datasets and helping the evaluation.

References

[1] Olaf Sporns, Giulio Tononi, Rolf Kötter, The human connectome: a structural description of the human brain, PLoS Computational Biology 1 (4) (2005) e42.

[2] Dmitry Laptev, Alexander Vezhnevets, Sarvesh Dwivedi, Joachim M. Buhmann, Anisotropic ssTEM image segmentation using dense correspondence across sections, in: Medical Image Computing and Computer-Assisted Intervention – MICCAI 2012, Springer, 2012, pp. 323–330.

[3] Albert Cardona, Stephan Saalfeld, Stephan Preibisch, Benjamin Schmid, Anchi Cheng, Jim Pulokas, Pavel Tomancak, Volker Hartenstein, An integrated micro- and macroarchitectural analysis of the Drosophila brain by computer-assisted serial section electron microscopy, PLoS Biology 8 (10) (2010) 2564.

[4] Elizabeth Jurrus, Antonio R.C. Paiva, Shigeki Watanabe, James R. Anderson, Bryan W. Jones, Ross T. Whitaker, Erik M. Jorgensen, Robert E. Marc, Tolga Tasdizen, Detection of neuron membranes in electron microscopy images using a serial neural network architecture, Medical Image Analysis 14 (6) (2010) 770–783.

[5] Alex Krizhevsky, Ilya Sutskever, Geoffrey E. Hinton, Imagenet classification with deep convolutional neural networks, in: Advances in Neural Information Processing Systems, 2012, pp. 1097–1105.

[6] Karen Simonyan, Andrew Zisserman, Very deep convolutional networks for large-scale image recognition, preprint, arXiv:1409.1556, 2014.

[7] Hao Chen, Chiyao Shen, Jing Qin, Dong Ni, Lin Shi, Jack CY Cheng, Pheng-Ann Heng, Automatic localization and identification of vertebrae in spine CT via a joint learning model with deep neural networks, in: Medical Image Computing and Computer-Assisted Intervention – MICCAI 2015, Springer, 2015, pp. 515–522.

[8] Babak Ehteshami Bejnordi, Mitko Veta, Paul Johannes Van Diest, Bram Van Ginneken, Nico Karssemeijer, Geert Litjens, Jeroen A.W.M. Van Der Laak, Meyke Hermsen, Quirine F. Manson, Maschenka Balkenhol, et al., Diagnostic assessment of deep learning algorithms for detection of lymph node metastases in women with breast cancer, JAMA 318 (22) (2017) 2199–2210.

[9] Jonathan Long, Evan Shelhamer, Trevor Darrell, Fully convolutional networks for semantic segmentation, preprint, arXiv:1411.4038, 2014.

[10] Korsuk Sirinukunwattana, Josien P.W. Pluim, Hao Chen, Xiaojuan Qi, Pheng-Ann Heng, Yun Bo Gu, Li Yang Wang, Bogdan J. Matuszewski, Elia Bruni, Urko Sanchez, et al., Gland segmentation in colon histology images: the GlaS challenge contest, Medical Image Analysis 35 (2017) 489–502.

[11] Dan Ciresan, Alessandro Giusti, Luca M. Gambardella, Jürgen Schmidhuber, Deep neural networks segment neuronal membranes in electron microscopy images, in: Advances in Neural Information Processing Systems, 2012, pp. 2843–2851.

[12] Chen-Yu Lee, Saining Xie, Patrick Gallagher, Zhengyou Zhang, Zhuowen Tu, Deeply-supervised nets, preprint, arXiv:1409.5185, 2014.

[13] Arganda-Carreras Ignacio, Seung Sebastian, Cardona Albert, Schindelin Johannes, ISBI challenge: segmentation of neuronal structures in EM stacks, http://brainiac2.mit.edu/isbi_challenge/, 2012.

[14] J.G. White, E. Southgate, J.N. Thomson, S. Brenner, The structure of the nervous system of the nematode Caenorhabditis elegans: the mind of a worm, Philosophical Transactions of the Royal Society of London 314 (1986) 1–340.

[15] Davi D.Bock, Wei-Chung Allen Lee, Aaron M. Kerlin, Mark L. Andermann, Greg Hood, Arthur W. Wetzel, Sergey Yurgenson, Edward R. Soucy, Hyon Suk Kim, R. Clay Reid, Network anatomy and in vivo physiology of visual cortical neurons, Nature 471 (7337) (2011) 177–182.

[16] Xundong Wu, An iterative convolutional neural network algorithm improves electron microscopy image segmentation, preprint, arXiv:1506.05849, 2015.

[17] H. Sebastian Seung, Neuroscience: towards functional connectomics, Nature 471 (7337) (2011) 170–172.

[18] Ritwik Kumar, Amelio Vázquez-Reina, Hanspeter Pfister, Radon-like features and their application to connectomics, in: 2010 IEEE Computer Society Conference on Computer Vision and Pattern Recognition Workshops, CVPRW, IEEE, 2010, pp. 186–193.

[19] Yuriy Mishchenko, Automation of 3D reconstruction of neural tissue from large volume of conventional serial section transmission electron micrographs, Journal of Neuroscience Methods 176 (2) (2009) 276–289.

[20] Verena Kaynig, Thomas J. Fuchs, Joachim M. Buhmann, Geometrical consistent 3D tracing of neuronal processes in ssTEM data, in: Medical Image Computing and Computer-Assisted Intervention – MICCAI 2010, Springer, 2010, pp. 209–216.

[21] Mustafa Gökhan Uzunbaş, Chao Chen, Dimitris Metaxsas, Optree: a learning-based adaptive watershed algorithm for neuron segmentation, in: Medical Image Computing and Computer-Assisted Intervention – MICCAI 2014, Springer, 2014, pp. 97–105.

[22] TingLiu, Cory Jones, Mojtaba Seyedhosseini, Tolga Tasdizen, A modular hierarchical approach to 3D electron microscopy image segmentation, Journal of Neuroscience Methods 226 (2014) 88–102.

[23] Juan Nunez-Iglesias, Ryan Kennedy, Toufiq Parag, Jianbo Shi, Dmitri B. Chklovskii, Xi-Nian Zuo, Machine learning of hierarchical clustering to segment 2D and 3D images, PLoS ONE 8 (8) (2013) 08.

[24] VirenJain, Benjamin Bollmann, Mark Richardson, Daniel R. Berger, Moritz N. Helmstaedter, Kevin L. Briggman, Winfried Denk, Jared B. Bowden, John M. Mendenhall, Wickliffe C. Abraham, et al., Boundary learning by optimization with topological constraints, in: 2010 IEEE Conference on Computer Vision and Pattern Recognition, CVPR, IEEE, 2010, pp. 2488–2495.

[25] Metin N. Gurcan, Laura E. Boucheron, Ali Can, Anant Madabhushi, Nasir M. Rajpoot, Bulent Yener, Histopathological image analysis: a review, IEEE Reviews in Biomedical Engineering 2 (2009) 147–171.

[26] Shivang Naik, Scott Doyle, Shannon Agner, Anant Madabhushi, Michael Feldman, John Tomaszewski, Automated gland and nuclei segmentation for grading of prostate and breast cancer histopathology, in: 5th IEEE International Symposium on Biomedical Imaging, IEEE, 2008, pp. 284–287.

[27] Jun Xu, Lei Xiang, Qinshan Liu, Hannah Gilmore, Jianzhong Wu, Jinghai Tang, Anant Madabhushi, Stacked Sparse Autoencoder (SSAE) for nuclei detection on breast cancer histopathology images, IEEE Transactions on Medical Imaging 35 (2016) 119–130.

[28] Hao Chen, Xiaojuan Qi, Lequan Yu, Pheng-Ann Heng, DCAN: deep contour-aware networks for accurate gland segmentation, in: Proceedings of the IEEE conference on Computer Vision and Pattern Recognition, 2016, pp. 2487–2496.

[29] Michael Stierer, Harald Rosen, Renate Weber, Nuclear pleomorphism, a strong prognostic factor in axillary node-negative small invasive breast cancer, Breast Cancer Research and Treatment 20 (2) (1991) 109–116.

[30] B. Dunne, J.J. Going, Scoring nuclear pleomorphism in breast cancer, Histopathology 39 (3) (2001) 259–265.

[31] Christopher W. Elston, Ian O. Ellis, Pathological prognostic factors in breast cancer. I. The value of histological grade in breast cancer: experience from a large study with long-term follow-up, Histopathology 19 (5) (1991) 403–410.

[32] Humayun Irshad, et al., Automated mitosis detection in histopathology using morphological and multi-channel statistics features, Journal of Pathology Informatics 4 (1) (2013) 10.

[33] Chanho Jung, Changick Kim, Segmenting clustered nuclei using H-minima transform-based marker extraction and contour parameterization, IEEE Transactions on Biomedical Engineering 57 (10) (2010) 2600–2604.

[34] Stephan Wienert, Daniel Heim, Kai Saeger, Albrecht Stenzinger, Michael Beil, Peter Hufnagl, Manfred Dietel, Carsten Denkert, Frederick Klauschen, Detection and segmentation of cell nuclei in virtual microscopy images: a minimum-model approach, Scientific Reports 2 (2012).

[35] Mitko Veta, A. Huisman, Max A. Viergever, Paul J. van Diest, Josien P.W. Pluim, Marker-controlled watershed segmentation of nuclei in H&E stained breast cancer biopsy images, in: 2011 IEEE International Symposium on Biomedical Imaging: From Nano to Macro, IEEE, 2011, pp. 618–621.

[36] Yousef Al-Kofahi, Wiem Lassoued, William Lee, Badrinath Roysam, Improved automatic detection and segmentation of cell nuclei in histopathology images, IEEE Transactions on Bio-Medical Engineering 57 (4) (2010) 841–852.

[37] Kien Nguyen, Anil K. Jain, Bikash Sabata, et al., Prostate cancer detection: fusion of cytological and textural features, Journal of Pathology Informatics 2 (2) (2011) 3.

[38] Humayun Irshad, Antoine Veillard, Ludovic Roux, Daniel Racoceanu, Methods for nuclei detection, segmentation, and classification in digital histopathology: a review—current status and future potential, IEEE Reviews in Biomedical Engineering 7 (2014) 97–114.

[39] Dan C. Cireşan, Alessandro Giusti, Luca M. Gambardella, Jürgen Schmidhuber, Mitosis detection in breast cancer histology images with deep neural networks, in: Medical Image Computing and Computer-Assisted Intervention – MICCAI 2013, Springer, 2013, pp. 411–418.

[40] Ludovic Roux, Daniel Racoceanu, Nicolas Loménie, Maria Kulikova, Humayun Irshad, Jacques Klossa, Frédérique Capron, Catherine Genestie, Gilles Le Naour, Metin N. Gurcan, Mitosis detection in breast cancer histological images, an ICPR 2012 contest, Journal of Pathology Informatics 4 (2013).

[41] Mitko Veta, Paul J. Van Diest, Stefan M. Willems, Haibo Wang, Anant Madabhushi, Angel Cruz-Roa, Fabio Gonzalez, Anders B.L. Larsen, Jacob S. Vestergaard, Anders B. Dahl, et al., Assessment of algorithms for mitosis detection in breast cancer histopathology images, Medical Image Analysis 20 (1) (2015) 237–248.

[42] Hao Chen, Qi Dou, Xi Wang, Jing Qin, Pheng Ann Heng, Mitosis detection in breast cancer histology images via deep cascaded networks, in: Thirtieth AAAI Conference on Artificial Intelligence, 2016.

[43] Korsuk Sirinukunwattana, Shan Raza, Yee-Wah Tsang, David Snead, Ian Cree, Nasir Rajpoot, Locality sensitive deep learning for detection and classification of nuclei in routine colon cancer histology images, IEEE Transactions on Medical Imaging (2016) 1196–1206.

[44] Liang-Chieh Chen, George Papandreou, Iasonas Kokkinos, Kevin Murphy, Alan L. Yuille, Semantic image segmentation with deep convolutional nets and fully connected crfs, preprint, arXiv:1412.7062, 2014.

[45] Yoshua Bengio, Pascal Lamblin, Dan Popovici, Hugo Larochelle, et al., Greedy layer-wise training of deep networks, Advances in Neural Information Processing Systems 19 (2007) 153.

[46] Liwei Wang, Chen-Yu Lee, Zhuowen Tu, Svetlana Lazebnik, Training deeper convolutional networks with deep supervision, preprint, arXiv:1505.02496, 2015.

[47] Albert Cardona, Stephan Saalfeld, Johannes Schindelin, Ignacio Arganda-Carreras, Stephan Preibisch, Mark Longair, Pavel Tomancak, Volker Hartenstein, Rodney J. Douglas, TrakEM2 software for neural circuit reconstruction, PLoS ONE 7 (6) (2012) e38011.

[48] Yangqing Jia, Evan Shelhamer, Jeff Donahue, Sergey Karayev, Jonathan Long, Ross Girshick, Sergio Guadarrama, Trevor Darrell, Caffe: convolutional architecture for fast feature embedding, preprint, arXiv:1408.5093, 2014.

[49] Marijn F. Stollenga, Wonmin Byeon, Marcus Liwicki, Juergen Schmidhuber, Parallel multidimensional LSTM, with application to fast biomedical volumetric image segmentation, preprint, arXiv:1506.07452, 2015.

[50] William M. Rand, Objective criteria for the evaluation of clustering methods, Journal of the American Statistical Association 66 (336) (1971) 846–850.

[51] Olaf Ronneberger, Philipp Fischer, Thomas Brox, U-Net: convolutional networks for biomedical image segmentation, preprint, arXiv:1505.04597, 2015.

[52] S. Beucher, C. Lantuejoul, Use of watersheds in contour detection, in: International Conference on Image Processing, 1979.

CHAPTER 11

LOGISMOS-JEI: Segmentation using optimal graph search and just-enough interaction

Honghai Zhang, Kyungmoo Lee, Zhi Chen, Satyananda Kashyap, Milan Sonka

The Iowa Institute for Biomedical Imaging, The University of Iowa, Iowa City, IA, United States

Contents

11.1. Introduction	249
11.2. LOGISMOS	251
11.2.1 Initial mesh	251
11.2.2 Locations of graph nodes	252
11.2.3 Cost function design	252
11.2.4 Geometric constraints and priors	254
11.2.5 Graph optimization	255
11.3. Just-enough interaction	256
11.4. Retinal OCT segmentation	257
11.5. Coronary OCT segmentation	260
11.6. Knee MR segmentation	265
11.7. Modular application design	268
11.8. Conclusion	269
Acknowledgments	270
References	270

11.1. Introduction

Medical image acquisition capabilities have developed very rapidly in the past 30 years. In the meantime, the computer segmentation methods have also progressed rapidly to relieve the physicians from tedious and time-consuming manual tracing. However, no segmentation method is error-free especially in the presence of disease and/or in images of marginal quality. If automated segmentation fails, locally or otherwise, the analysts almost invariably have to manually correct errors by slice-by-slice retracing of all affected 2D slices. To a certain extent, the clinical acceptance of computer segmentation methods is hindered by the virtually guaranteed imperfections of current automated approaches in the presence of pathology or imaging artifacts, and – consequently – the lack of efficient correction methods.

Handbook of Medical Image Computing and Computer Assisted Intervention
https://doi.org/10.1016/B978-0-12-816176-0.00016-8

LOGISMOS (Layered Optimal Graph Image Segmentation for Multiple Objects and Surfaces) is a general approach for optimally segmenting multiple n-D surfaces that mutually interact within individual and/or between objects [1–4]. The search region for target surfaces is covered by *columns of interconnected graph nodes*, each of which is assigned a cost. Multisurface segmentation is achieved by finding the set of nodes, one per column, with globally minimal total cost. Additional context-specific graph arcs can be used to enforce geometric constraints that represent prior shape and anatomy knowledge.

Given node locations and geometric constraints, the segmentation result is solely determined by the employed cost function. The Just-Enough Interaction (JEI) extension [5] enables the user to modify segmentation by interactively specifying new surface locations. The underlying algorithm changes cost on affected nodes and finds a new optimal solution. Since only a small portion of the node costs are modified, the new solution can often be found and visualized in near real-time.

LOGISMOS has been continuously developed and improved since its introduction. So far, the method, its improvements, and applications have been reported in over 230 publications, in which many new techniques have been developed to improve various aspects of the framework. When employing LOGISMOS to solve a new segmentation problem, choosing the proper techniques becomes a daunting task especially when the best choices are originally developed for seemingly unrelated applications (e.g., different anatomical structures or another image modality). This chapter is aimed at both the conceptual designers of quantitative medical image analysis methods and developers adopting LOGISMOS-JEI to perform new segmentation tasks. In Section 11.2, we describe the essential principles of LOGISMOS and most frequently used graph construction methods.

The JEI extension of LOGISMOS has contributed to quantitative analysis success in many applications, enabling clinically appropriate results with a reasonable amount of intuitive and efficient user interventions [5–9]. In Section 11.3, we describe various cost modification strategies and discuss their suitability for different situations.

For any LOGISMOS-JEI application, the analysts – physicians or technologists – interact with the algorithm but are often oblivious to it. The developer must choose approaches to achieve the desired results with no or a few easy-to-understand settings. In addition, data visualization and the user interface also need to be carefully designed to fit the users' preference while maintaining efficient communication with the underlying algorithm. In Sections 11.4–11.6, we describe the design process of three clinical applications with a focus on how certain choices are made. The capability of JEI is demonstrated with respect to improvements in segmentation accuracy and the amount of human effort involved. In Section 11.7, a modular design environment is introduced to enable efficient development of clinical-oriented LOGISMOS-JEI applications.

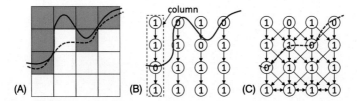

Figure 11.1 A 2D binary image segmentation using LOGISMOS: (A) binary image and the target paths with and without smoothness constraints (dashed and solid lines); (B) the corresponding graph with no smoothness constraints; (C) the corresponding graph for enforcing geometric constraints.

11.2. LOGISMOS

The basic ideas of LOGISMOS are illustrated on a simple example of segmenting 2D binary image with a left-to-right boundary that passes each column of pixels exactly once (Fig. 11.1(A)). In Fig. 11.1(B), a graph is constructed by: (1) associating each image pixel with a graph node, (2) assigning each node with a cost representing the unlikeness of the said node residing on the desired segmentation boundary, and (3) connecting nodes with intracolumn arcs. The segmentation problem is thus converted to finding the set of graph nodes, one per column, with minimum total cost and this graph problem can be solved with graph optimization. In addition, the smoothness of the result can be controlled by adding intercolumn arcs (Fig. 11.1(C)).

For general n-D surface segmentation, LOGISMOS inherently represents segmentation results as surface meshes with fixed numbers of vertices. The location of a vertex is chosen from a column of graph nodes associated with given costs. Various geometric constraints can be integrated into the graph to control the segmentation outcome. The segmentation-yielding graph optimization is guaranteed to find the set of nodes with globally optimal total cost while satisfying the geometric constraints. The basic steps of implementing n-D LOGISMOS are: (1) establishing the initial mesh, (2) determining the locations of graph nodes, (3) cost function design, (4) specifying geometric constraints and priors, and (5) graph optimization.

11.2.1 Initial mesh

The objective is to establish an initial mesh in the physical space to *approximately* represent the target surface. Fig. 11.2 shows three types of initial mesh. The grid-based rectangular mesh is suitable for terrain-like surfaces. The rectangular mesh built from cross-sectional slices with evenly distributed vertices is suitable for cylindrical or vessel-like surfaces. For any open or closed target surface, a generic mesh is used.

Various methods can be used to create the initial meshes. A flat plane can be used to define an initial mesh for terrain-like surfaces. Given an approximate centerline and a radius, an initial mesh for vessel-like surfaces can be constructed. For complex target shapes, an initial mesh can be derived from any available *presegmentation*.

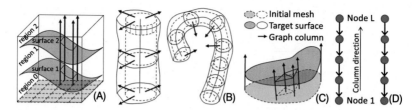

Figure 11.2 Initial meshes and graph columns for target surfaces that are (A) terrain-like, (B) cylindrical or vessel-like, and (C) generic. (D) Graph columns and nodes in 2D graph space.

The properties of the initial mesh affect design choices for the later steps and the segmentation quality. The densities of vertices determine the level of shape details that can be captured. The topology, how the vertices are interconnected to form the mesh, determines how geometric constraints are enforced. The distance to the target surface determines the length of the graph columns. The shape and smoothness of the initial mesh determine the physical shape (line or curve) of the graph columns.

11.2.2 Locations of graph nodes

Starting from the initial mesh, the search region of the target surface is covered with graph nodes. Each mesh vertex is associated with a column of nodes connected by directed arcs with infinite capacity as shown in Fig. 11.2(D).

For terrain-like target surfaces, the columns are constructed along one of the image axes. For cylindrical or vessel-like surfaces, the columns are along the lines connecting vertices and cross-section centers (Fig. 11.2(B)). For generic surfaces, constructing columns along surface normal directions is the common choice. The graph columns are *directional* with uniform orientation (e.g., pointing outward). When a *spatial* or *temporal* sequence of surfaces with similar shape are segmented simultaneously, each target surface is associated with a sub-graph as shown in Fig. 11.2. All subgraphs share the same set of node locations in the physical space thus forming a single higher-dimensional graph.

Depending on the shape of the initial mesh and desired column length, columns along straight lines may introduce topology error due to "crossing" columns. The general remedy is to use *curved* columns formed by electric line of force (ELF) [4] or gradient vector flow (GVF) [10], which are often expensive to compute but can be approximated with a reasonable quality.

11.2.3 Cost function design

The generic cost function for LOGISMOS uses *on-surface* costs that emulate the *unlikeness* of target surface passing thought a given node. Let the on-surface cost (denoted by subscript "s") of node k on column j of surface i be $c_s(i, j, k)$, the total on-surface cost for a given surface function $s(i, j)$ that chooses an on-surface node for each column is

$$C_s = \sum_{i=1}^{n} \sum_{j=1}^{m} c_s(i, j, s(i, j)). \tag{11.1}$$

The objective of segmentation is to find the optimal $s(i, j)$ that globally minimizes C_s. This minimum-cost-identifying problem is converted to finding a minimum closed set in a graph by defining on-surface terminal weight $w_s(i, j, k)$ as

$$w_s(i, j, k) = \begin{cases} -1, & \text{if } k = 1, \\ c_s(i, j, k) - c_s(i, j, k - 1), & \text{otherwise.} \end{cases} \tag{11.2}$$

If $w_s(i, j, k) < 0$, a directed arc from *source* to (i, j, k) with capacity $-w_s(i, j, k)$ is added to the graph, otherwise a directed arc from (i, j, k) to *sink* with capacity $w_s(i, j, k)$ is added to the graph. With these terminal arcs, the desired closed set can be found by any minimum *s–t* cut algorithm.

When the target surfaces are nonintersecting, the surface function $s(i, j)$ has an equivalent region function $r(j, k)$ that assigns image location for node (j, k) to one of the $n + 1$ regions (Fig. 11.2(A)). In-region cost $c_r(i, j, k)$ (denoted by subscript "r"), emulates the unlikeness of (j, k) belonging to region $i \in [0, n]$. The total in-region cost for a given $r(j, k)$ is

$$C_r = \sum_{j=1}^{m} \sum_{k=1}^{l} c_r(r(j, k), j, k). \tag{11.3}$$

The optimal $r(j, k)$ can be found by solving the equivalent minimum *s–t* cut problem using terminal arcs defined by in-region terminal weight $w_r(i, j, k)$, given by

$$w_r(i, j, k) = c_r(i - 1, j, k) - c_r(i, j, k). \tag{11.4}$$

The detailed information about utilizing in-region cost can be found in [11].

On-surface and in-region costs can be used individually or together. Since the total costs in Eqs. (11.1) and (11.3) are computed on different numbers of cost values, the combined total cost must be $C_s + \alpha C_r$, where α is used to control the relative contributions of the two types.

The cost function only needs to emulate unlikeness and therefore can be designed with various methods including gradient, intensity distribution, and/or machine learning. The cost value is not required to be nonnegative or normalized to a specific range. However, extra attention must be paid to surface-specific costs so that each such cost has a desired relative contribution to the total cost in multisurface segmentation tasks.

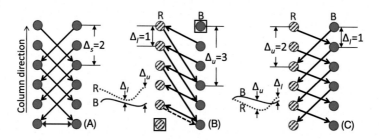

Figure 11.3 Setting geometric constraints. (A) Smoothness constraints Δ_s. The horizontal bi-directional arcs are not used for enforcing smoothness constraints but must be added to the graph. Separation constraints Δ_l and Δ_u for (B) noncrossing surfaces and (C) crossing surfaces. Deficient nodes are marked by squares. Dashed arc is required only if deficient nodes are excluded from the graph. The relative position of surfaces is defined with respect to the column direction.

11.2.4 Geometric constraints and priors

Minimizing total on-surface cost in graph in Fig. 11.2(D) can be achieved by choosing the node with minimal cost on each column without employing minimum s–t cut algorithm. However, the result is often far from clinically acceptable due to lack of embedded shape and anatomy knowledge. The real strength of LOGISMOS is that various geometric constraints can be incorporated into the graph as directed intercolumn arcs with *infinite* capacities (Fig. 11.3) to guarantee that only solutions satisfying the specified constraints will be considered during the graph optimization.

The smoothness constraint Δ_s determines the maximal allowed shape variation between neighboring columns of the same surface. If node k on a given column is the on-surface node, the on-surface nodes on the neighboring columns can only reside within $[k - \Delta_s, k + \Delta_s]$. Surface separation constraints, Δ_l and Δ_u, determine the bounds of distances between two surfaces on the corresponding columns. For the noncrossing case in Fig. 11.3(B), they are the minimum and maximum separation constraints. For the crossing case in Fig. 11.3(C), they represent the maximum distances one surface can vary above or below another. The motion of a temporal surface sequence can be controlled by Δ_l- and Δ_u-like arcs connecting corresponding columns from subgraphs representing neighboring time points. Note that the arc pattern for non-crossing separation is suitable for *uni-directional* motion and the arc pattern for crossing separation is suitable for *bi-directional* motion. Choosing proper values for the constraints must consider the following factors.

- All constraints are defined as number of nodes along the column direction.
- The mesh topology determines column pairs subject to the smoothness constraints.
- The smoothness is measured relatively to the initial mesh in the graph space.
- All constraints can be defined globally for all columns or locally if necessary.

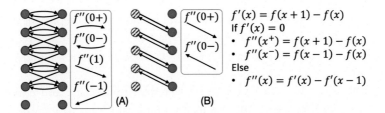

Figure 11.4 Incorporating shape and context priors as additional arcs with finite capacities: (A) shape priors of $|\delta - 0| \leq 2$; (B) context priors of $|\delta - 1| \leq 2$ after removing deficient nodes from the graph.

For multiple noncrossing surfaces with nonzero minimum surface separations, the number of nodes per column can be effectively reduced by excluding deficient nodes (Fig. 11.3(B)) that would not appear in any feasible solution.

The geometric constraints in Fig. 11.3 are also called *hard constraints* because they only set limits on the allowed shape variations without optimizing the total amount of shape variations. To provide better control of the resulting surfaces, shape and context priors (also called *soft constraints*) [12] can be employed.

Let δ represent shape variation between neighboring columns of a surface graph or distance between surfaces. The mean value of δ as $\bar{\delta}$ and distribution of δ may be derived from a known model and consequently represents the shape or content priors. The geometric constraints can be rewritten as $|\delta - \bar{\delta}| \leq \Delta$. Fig. 11.4 shows cases of $\bar{\delta} = 0$ and $\bar{\delta} = 1$, yielding $|\delta - 0| \leq 2$ and $|\delta - 1| \leq 2$, respectively. These shape and context priors can be incorporated into the graph by utilizing a convex function $f(\delta - \bar{\delta})$ that penalizes solutions with large values of $|\delta - \bar{\delta}|$. The additional penalties are added to the graph as intercolumn arcs with *finite* capacities as shown in Fig. 11.4, where the capacities of the arcs are defined based on first- and second-order derivatives of the convex function. Note that the convex function introduces additional penalty terms $\sum f(\delta - \bar{\delta})$ to the total cost to be minimized.

11.2.5 Graph optimization

The minimum s–t cut problem is solved by focusing on a dual problem of finding maximum flow, for which many algorithms are available and their performances were evaluated [13]. When LOGISMOS was first introduced, the Boykov–Kolmogorov (BK) algorithm [14] was used. The currently preferred algorithm is incremental breadth-first search (IBFS) [15] or Excesses IBFS (EIFBS) [16] because they are approximately 4 times faster than BK in LOGISMOS applications.

Clinical LOGISMOS applications often require graphs with millions of nodes, and certain design choices can substantially affect the optimization time the algorithm takes to find the maximum flow. The optimization time is linearly related to the number of columns but the relationship with the number of nodes per column is quadratic.

The absolute values of terminal weights in Eqs. (11.2) and (11.4) represent the amount of flow the graph will try to push through the network for each node. Reducing the number of nodes with nonzero terminal weight via the cost function design can reduce optimization time.

By comparing Figs. 11.3 and 11.4, it is clear that using shape and context priors substantially increases the number of arcs in the graph and leads to increased memory requirements. Therefore, shape and context priors should only be used when they can be accommodated by available memory resources.

Location-specific graph construction – choosing columns sizes and geometric constraints with respect to column location – can potentially reduce memory usage and optimization time of the graph, but it substantially increases the implementation complexity and thus should only be used when necessary and after comprehensive evaluation and testing.

11.3. Just-enough interaction

EIBFS or BK algorithm finds the maximum flow by dynamically pushing more flow into the network of graph nodes and arcs. Therefore, the algorithm inherently supports changing capacities of arcs in a saturated flow network (changing the underlying costs) to efficiently achieve new maximum flow [17,18]. If such changes only happen on a small portion of the graph, new solution can be quickly found without running the optimization from scratch. The JEI extension [5,6] utilizes the dynamic nature of the underlying algorithm to edit the segmentation result via interactive modification of local costs and their associated terminal weights. Since JEI modification is directly applied to the graph, the updated result is still globally optimal (with respect to the modified costs) and satisfies existing geometric constraints.

JEI utilizes user inputs about correct surface locations. Although certain visualization and interaction techniques such as volume rendering, stereo display, and motion tracking may help the user to quickly locate segmentation errors, the most efficient way for the user to accurately specify correct surface locations remains as drawing a *new contour* to replace an *old contour* on 2D slices. For each contour, two sets of affected graph nodes that are closest to and reside within a given distance range are located as the *on-surface* and *near-surface* nodes (Fig. 11.5(A)).

The general rule for cost modification is to lower the costs of nodes at desirable locations (those affected by the interactively determined new contour) and raise the costs of nodes associated with the old contour (surface). When JEI is expected to move surface to a specified location disregarding the existing node costs, constant extreme values should be used as the new node costs (Fig. 11.5(B)). Note that if the user-specified new contour violates the geometric constraints, the desired modification cannot be achieved since such a solution would not be allowed. When the new contour only indicates

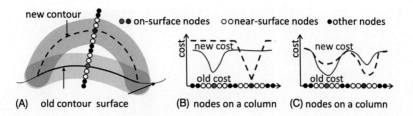

Figure 11.5 Basics of JEI: (A) on-surface and near-surface nodes associated with new and old contours; cost modifications using (B) extreme values and (C) multipliers.

an approximate location of the desired surface, the costs of the affected nodes should be lowered or raised using a cost offset or a cost multiplier that varies the node cost values with respect to the node's distance to the on-surface nodes (Fig. 11.5(C)). In this case, the pattern of the old node costs is still considered, the modification only makes the affected nodes more attractive or repulsive. Cost modification is also used to achieve *undo JEI* operation, during which the costs of affected nodes are restored to their previous values.

For any given application, the developer must consider the user's preferences on JEI operation to identify the proper cost modification strategies and fine-tune their parameters via comprehensive testing.

11.4. Retinal OCT segmentation

The retina is a light sensitive part of the back of the eye consisting of multiple cellular layers, where stimulation by light occurs, initiating the sensation of vision. The thickness of the individual retinal layers is an important clinical measure contributing to diagnosis and management of various eye diseases such as glaucoma, age-related macular degeneration (AMD), diabetic macular edema (DME), retinal vein occlusion (RVO), and others. Spectral-domain optical coherence tomography (OCT) produces high-resolution 3D images of the retinal layers. Fig. 11.6 shows an example of one central (foveal) slice from a 3D retinal OCT image; segmentation of its layer surfaces is given. Some typical sizes of OCT images acquired by various scanners are: $200 \times 1024 \times 200$, $768 \times 496 \times 61$, and $1024 \times 1536 \times 1024$ voxels (by the latest wide-field scanners).

A well-developed approach for this terrain-like segmentation task of simultaneously detecting multiple retinal layers is to use the LOGISMOS approach initialized with a flat mesh along the XZ-plane and forming columns along the Y-axis with graph nodes at original OCT image voxel locations. However, optimizing a graph with 500–1500 nodes per column is time-consuming because the running time is a quadratic function of the number of nodes per column. A multiresolution coarse-to-fine approach was therefore developed to reduce the effective column size by using 5 levels of increasing Y-axis resolutions starting from the lowest [19]. The segmentation result on each

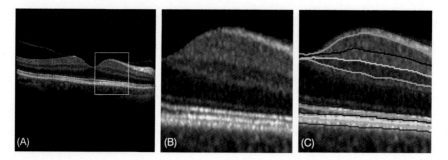

Figure 11.6 Example of normal retinal OCT: (A) the central XY-slice depicting fovea; details of the highlighted region are shown in (B) and the corresponding segmented retinal layer surfaces are shown in (C).

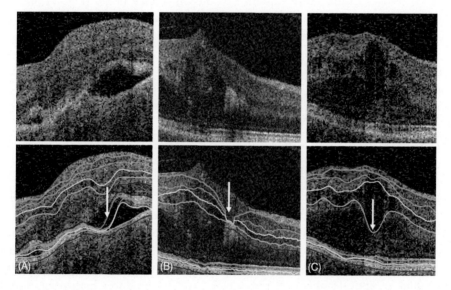

Figure 11.7 Examples of local segmentation errors caused by appearance-modifying retinal diseases: (A) AMD, (B) DME, and (C) RVO.

lower-resolution level serves as an initialization for the segmentation on the next higher-resolution level, using a narrow-band strategy. While the automated multilevel method performs well for normal or mild-disease OCT scans [19,11,20], it shows regional segmentation errors in severe retinal shape-changing diseases resulting in fluid-filled regions augmenting the retinal layer structure (Fig. 11.7). It is very difficult to design generally applicable cost functions to fit all image appearance scenarios of various pathologies. In reality of retinal disease variability, perfect performance of a fully automated segmentation technique is difficult if not impossible to achieve. In this case, the semiautomated

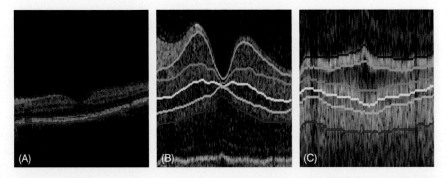

Figure 11.8 Two-stage retinal OCT layer segmentation: (A) presegmentation; final segmentations of (B) inner and (C) outer retinal surfaces.

JEI approach can be a valuable solution allowing the user to correct such locally or regionally missegmented surfaces.

Although the multilevel approach is run-time and memory-use efficient, it is not directly suitable for employing the JEI paradigm to correct segmentation errors such as those caused by layer-appearance-altering retinal diseases. The main problem of the multiscale/narrow-band strategy is that the user-specified corrections are sometimes quite dramatic, and may be positioned outside the narrow-band graph coverage at the full resolution level. If that happens, the cost modification must be applied to the lowest-resolution level for which the graph coverage is sufficient, followed by forming new graphs at all subsequent higher-resolution levels. This results in a substantial performance load when such a surface-modification case is encountered. Most importantly, subsequent resegmentation on multiple levels greatly increases the response time of user interactions and results in an unacceptable user experience.

To achieve acceptable balance between the efficiency of graph optimization and user experience when performing interactive JEI corrections, a two-stage approach was developed (Fig. 11.8) [9]. First, presegmentation of three selected surfaces is performed at 1/16 of the full Y-axis resolution. After visually checking the segmentation correctness and JEI-fixing the identified segmentation inaccuracies for these three surfaces, the presegmentation result (which is essentially correct after the presegmentation JEI step) is used to determine initial meshes and column sizes for the next-stage full-resolution segmentation steps. In this particular case, surfaces of the inner and outer retinal layers are segmented in two separate LOGISMOS-JEI segmentation runs – the inner retinal locate between the upper two presegmented surfaces and the outer retina between the lower two presegmented surfaces.

The employed cost function is primarily based on computing the first-order derivative along the Y-axis computed on Gaussian smoothed 3D image. The range of the costs is normalized with respect to the costs in the whole graph to [0,1]. When performing the JEI correction steps, the user specifies correct surface locations by drawing

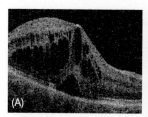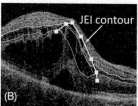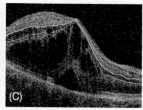

Figure 11.9 Example of JEI operations for RVO retinal OCT layer segmentation: (A) original image; (B) JEI contour intended for the bottom surface; (C) the resulting modified surfaces. Note that a single JEI contour introduces changes to 6 surfaces due to embedded separation constraints, and the errors on all neighboring slices are also corrected.

a JEI contour (Fig. 11.9) identifying the preferred locations of the modified surfaces to pass through the OCT image volume. Because each column of voxels along the Y-axis corresponds to a graph column, *new (preferred) on-surface nodes* can be easily located. For each new on-surface node, its cost is set to be highly attractive by assigning the value of -100, and the costs of all other nodes in the same column are set to 1. This cost modification scheme also raises the costs of all *old* on- and near-surface nodes without explicitly locating them, thus making the old contour less attractive.

In a testing set of 40 3D OCT scans from glaucoma, AMD, DME, and normal subjects, as judged by expert ophthalmologists, clinically acceptable segmentation results of 11 retinal layers defined by 12 surfaces were achieved using customized application as shown in Fig. 11.10 after 5.3 ± 1.4 minutes of JEI-based interactions per dataset consisting of 200 XY-slices. Compared with the JEI approach, a traditional slice-by-slice manual editing approach required at least 60 minutes per dataset to reach the same performance of clinically acceptable segmentation accuracy.

11.5. Coronary OCT segmentation

Optical coherence tomography (OCT) is capable of depicting close-to-the-lumen coronary artery wall layers at high resolution, facilitating precise measurement of their thickness. OCT is uniquely qualified for quantitative assessment of progressive and diffuse coronary artery disease, including quantification of plaque cap thickness in coronary atherosclerosis and/or status of early changes leading to cardiac allograft vasculopathy (CAV) in heart transplant patients. 3D coronary OCT images are acquired by placing an OCT catheter in the distal location of the coronary artery and pulling it back to a proximal location, acquiring image data along the pullback path. Since OCT imaging is an optical laser-beam imaging modality and thus light penetration is essential, blood must be temporarily replaced with a transparent fluid (saline or contrast liquid) for OCT imaging to be feasible. Consequently, the imaging must be performed very fast and the catheter is pulled back at a relatively high constant speed of 20 mm/s to produce 0.1 or

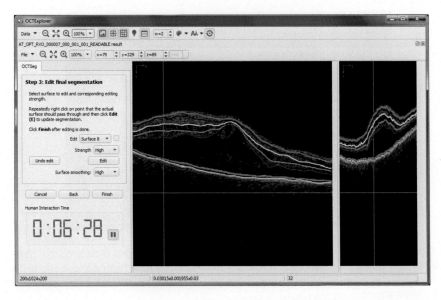

Figure 11.10 Retinal OCT LOGISMOS-JEI segmentation application. A timer is added to keep track of time spent while editing segmentation result.

0.2 mm frame-to-frame spacing. Typical OCT image pullback thus consists of 375–540 2D cross-sectional frames with 10 or 15 μm in-plane image resolution.

Resulting from the catheter-centric image acquisition, the catheter is always located in the image center. However, the catheter is not always located close to the center of the vessel lumen (Fig. 11.11). To achieve sufficiently accurate multisurface segmentation in all catheter positions, the graph construction must be lumen-centric rather than catheter-centric to avoid presence of long graph columns and unevenly distributed cross-sectional frame column vertices. As a result, presegmentation of the lumen and re-centering of the coordinate system must precede the multilayer segmentation that is attempted.

A two-stage segmentation method with JEI support was designed to produce accurate 3D segmentation of coronary wall layers and associated surfaces [21,22]. Following approximate detection of the lumen center for each OCT frame by computing the gray-level "mass" centroid, the lumen surface is approximated via its *presegmentation* (Fig. 11.11(A)). The initial approximate cylindrical mesh consists of 60 columns per frame and 30 μm in-column node spacing. Gaussian derivatives of intensities along the column direction are *quantized* and used as the cost function. The quantization reduces graph optimization time by removing subtle changes that have little influence on the presegmentation result. The presegmentation results are edited with JEI as needed to only fix substantial errors typically caused by strong OCT imaging artifacts. As a side note, presegmentation can also be performed without the above-described approximate

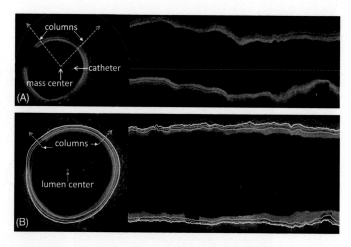

Figure 11.11 Example of coronary OCT image segmentation: (A) original cross-sectional frame and longitudinal view with presegmentation result; (B) lumen-center aligned frame and longitudinal view with final segmentation result.

lumen center identification – using the catheter location for forming the initial mesh. However, such approach yields less accurate presegmentation and consequently requires more involved JEI operations on frames where the catheter is very close to the vessel wall. Using the easy-to-derive mass center substantially reduces the amount of JEI operation required.

All frames are then aligned with respect to the more accurate lumen centers derived from the presegmented result (Fig. 11.11(B)). The approximate lumen surface, after being resampled with 120 vertices per frame with respect to the lumen center, is used as the initial mesh for the *final segmentation* (Fig. 11.11(B)) using 2.2 mm column length (2.0 mm tissue penetration and 0.2 mm lumen offset). The original in-frame OCT pixel spacing defines the in-column node spacing. The cost function is computed by passing the 3D lumen–unfolded image through 3×3 mean and median filters followed by a Sobel edge detector oriented along the column direction. Knowing the target edge pattern (dark-to-bright or bright-to-dark), the cost is further adjusted by setting a constant value to nodes with undesired edge direction and normalizing the cost range to $[-512, 0]$.

Following the multisurface segmentation of the wall layers, the user can perform JEI by defining so-called nudge-points on any frame or rotating longitudinal view (Figs. 11.12 and 11.13). New on-surface nodes are found as those that are closest to the intersections of graph columns and nudge-points contour in the physical space. For each new on-surface node, its cost is set to -512 and the costs of other nodes in the same column are set to 0. Note that – as described earlier in Section 11.4 – this

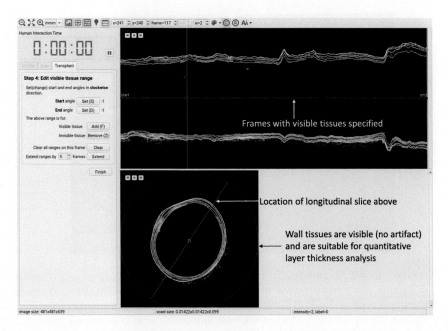

Figure 11.12 Coronary OCT LOGISMOS-JEI segmentation application showing the last step of the workflow – specifying visible wall tissues. OCT image is visualized with cross-sectional and rotating longitudinal views using sepia hue.

cost modification scheme raises the costs on *old* on- and near-surface nodes without explicitly locating them.

One hundred 3D coronary OCT images were acquired from 50 heart-transplant patients at 1 month and 12 months after a heart transplant surgery. In a randomly selected subset of 38 3D OCT pullback images, three surfaces that define intimal and medial layers were manually traced on 10 randomly selected frames per pullback by two expert cardiologists. The averaged manual tracings were used as the independent standard for validation.

The computation time of automated presegmentation was 19±3 seconds per 3D image. The automated final segmentation took 91±15 seconds. About 16 JEI operations on both pre- and final segmentations were performed on each 3D image on average, requiring 7.8±4.7 minutes of expert interaction time to reach visually correct solution for the entire pullback consisting of 375–540 OCT frames. Less than 1% of JEI time was spent on computing the new solution after JEI interaction by reoptimizing the maximum flow. In comparison, around 40 minutes were required for an expert to manually trace just 10 frames that were used for validation. It is unrealistic to expect an expert to trace the whole pullback of hundreds of frames to perform complete thickness assessment.

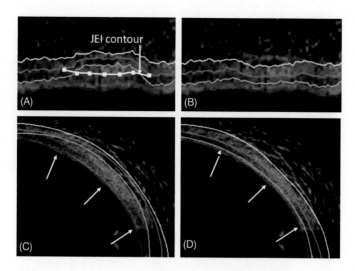

Figure 11.13 Examples of JEI operation for coronary OCT segmentation: (A, C) original LOGISMOS result with JEI contour modifying the outer media surface (orange); (B, D) JEI-modified segmentation. Note that a single JEI contour shown in (A) resulted in changes to all three surfaces three-dimensionally affecting multiple frames. Luminal surface in red, inner and outer media in green and orange. External support surface for improving algorithm robustness is shown in yellow.

Table 11.1 Surface positioning errors of coronary wall segmentation in comparison with the independent standard and inter-observer variability in $\mu \pm \sigma$ (µm).

	Signed			Unsigned		
	Lumen	**Intima**	**Media**	**Lumen**	**Intima**	**Media**
Auto	0.6±1.8	1.2±30.4	6.5±33.9	2.4±1.8	13.6±27.2	16.4±30.3
Auto+JEI	0.5±1.7	1.3±31.8	7.2±33.4	2.1±1.7	13.8±28.7	15.6±30.4
Inter-obs.	1.6±1.1	3.9±17.6	7.4±18.2	3.2±0.8	13.5±12.1	14.7±12.9

The surface positioning errors of the final segmentation are listed in Table 11.1. There was only a small subpixel bias in signed errors (in-frame pixel size of 10–15 µm). Statistical analysis showed that the efficient LOGISMOS-JEI analysis yielded analysis performance that was indistinguishable from that achieved by manual tracings. The capability of JEI is evident even more in Table 11.2 when thickness measures are considered. The decrease of maximum errors brought by JEI over the automated method is at the threshold of statistical significance ($p = 0.06$).

The coronary OCT segmentation approach reported above was employed to support a predictive CAV study in a heart-transplant population of 50 baseline-followup pullbacks [23], and provided highly detailed quantitative data on early CAV changes.

Table 11.2 Quality of intimal+medial thickness measures showing in distributions of errors ($\mu \pm \sigma$ μm) and regression analysis results.

	Error		Regression	
	Average	**Maximal**	R^2	**Equation**
Auto	5.0±31.2	63.7±66.1	0.93	$1.0x - 6.2$
Auto+JEI	5.4±28.5	55.5±56.7	0.96	$1.0x - 6.3$
Inter–obs.	6.8±10.6	58.3±29.0		

11.6. Knee MR segmentation

Magnetic resonance imaging (MRI) of the knee provides 3D information that enables reliable quantification of structural changes in osteoarthritic knees and the level of cartilage volume loss. The open-access Osteoarthritis Initiative (OAI) database[1] contains longitudinal (multiple annual scans) data of osteoarthritis (OA) patients. In our group's earlier work, 3D LOGISMOS was used in a fully automated knee segmentation method [4]. Electric line of force (ELF) was used to establish noncrossing curved graph columns and to identify graph column correspondence between objects (e.g., femur and tibia) via cross-surface mapping. Using simple gradient-based costs and interobject constraints, our 3D method produced very good results, especially for the bone surfaces. This 3D method was further improved to perform accurate 4D (3D+time) segmentation using graph cost derived from machine learning [24,7,8].

The progression of OA frequently introduces bone marrow lesions, cartilage surface thinning, mesical extrusion, and synovial fluid leakage, which make cartilage segmentation using gradient-based cost difficult. Our approach was to deal with the inherent variability of cartilage appearance on MR by introduction of machine learning to derive location-specific costs to further improve knee-cartilage segmentation performance. Since the OAI database only contains a limited number of datasets with manual tracings and since these tracings are only available for the regions of articular cartilage (Fig. 11.16(A)), additional sources of cartilage segmentation for machine learning of cost functions needed to be developed.

To overcome the problem of limited data sizes, the 3D JEI step was first used to edit the fully automated 3D LOGISMOS results produced by employing the gradient-based cost (Figs. 11.14 and 11.15) [7]. The JEI-edited results, requiring only a fraction of the time needed for fully-manual tracing in 3D, were verified by physicians and then considered a training set for the machine learning based cost definition. Expert-user provided JEI contours were up-sampled to obtain uniformly spaced points 0.5 mm apart, and a k-d tree nearest neighbor search was used to find new on-surface nodes. The cost modification assigned minimum cost to all new on-surface nodes and maximum cost to other nodes in the same columns.

---

[1] https://oai.epi-ucsf.org/datarelease/.

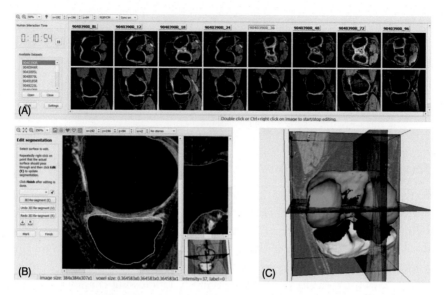

Figure 11.14 Knee MR LOGISMOS-JEI segmentation application: (A) main window showing thumbnail overview of the entire 4D (3D+time) dataset; (B) detail window with JEI controls on selected 3D dataset; and (C) complete view of 3D rendering of segmented surfaces.

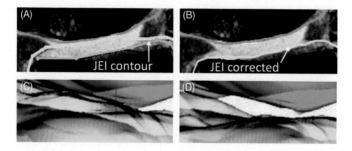

Figure 11.15 Example of JEI 3D surface editing shown by 2D slice image and 3D surface rendering: (A, C) original 3D LOGISMOS results, which were incorrectly affected by the presence of synovial fluid exhibiting similar brightness on MR images; (B, D) edited surfaces resulting from a single 2D JEI contour for tibia cartilage surface; (C, D) clearly show that a single 2D JEI operation opens the gap between the femur and tibia cartilage surfaces in 3D.

The gradient-based cost is capable of producing very accurate bone surface segmentation with -0.19 ± 0.07 and -0.13 ± 0.09 mm signed positioning errors and 0.40 ± 0.06 and 0.39 ± 0.09 mm unsigned errors for femur and tibia, respectively. The machine learning focused on deriving on–surface costs for the cartilage surfaces using a hierarchical approach. A neighborhood approximation forests (NAF) classifier [25] was trained on image patches and predicted whether a voxel or node is in the cartilage region. A random forest (RF) classifier then utilized 30 intensity-based and NAF–based features

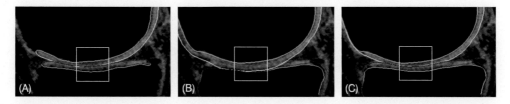

Figure 11.16 Example of segmentation accuracy improved by learned cost, especially within the highlighted rectangular region: (A) independent standard; (B) gradient cost; and (C) learned cost.

Table 11.3 Cartilage surface positioning errors (mm) achieved by costs from hierarchical classifier, gradient and single-stage RF classifier using 3D LOGISMOS.

N = 108	NAF+RF	Gradient	RF only
Femur signed	−0.01±0.18	−0.31±0.24	−0.10±0.17
Femur unsigned	0.55±0.11	0.69±0.13	0.56±0.10
Tibia signed	0.06±0.17	−0.11±0.35	0.11±0.22
Tibia unsigned	0.60±0.14	0.79±0.20	0.62±0.18

to provide the final on–surface location probability. The advantage of this hierarchical approach is that NAF explores global contextual features, which are combined with local contextual features derived by the RF. As shown in Fig. 11.16 and Table 11.3, the NAF+RF cost outperformed both the gradient and single-stage RF cost design, and the reduction in positioning errors was highly statistically significant (paired t-test, $p \ll 0.001$).

In addition to NAF+RF learning-based costs described above, 4D LOGISMOS was used to incorporate temporal context in the single 4D optimal segmentation process and yielded additional improvement of the overall accuracy, especially with respect to the intertime-point variation. In order to establish temporal correspondence of columns and define temporal constraints with proper reference surface, the initial 3D meshes must have the same topology and shape for all time points. This was achieved by the following steps.

1. Use 3D LOGISMOS to find bone surfaces on all time points, $S_1, \ldots, S_t$.
2. For $i = [2, t]$, find rigid transforms $\mathcal{T}_i$ such that $S_i \approx \mathcal{T}_i(S_1)$.
3. Use transformed S_1 on all time points as the initial mesh such that $S_i = \mathcal{T}_i(S_1)$.

Temporal constraints of $\Delta_l = \Delta_u = 0.6$ mm (twice the node spacing, roughly corresponding to in-plane MR image resolution), were applied using the crossing pattern shown in Fig. 11.3(C). When 4D-associated improvement was assessed using two time points for which fully-manual tracing was available and considering the accuracy in the whole cartilage regions, the improvement of 4D over 3D was subtle as shown in Table 11.4. When analyzing longer 4D sequences and focusing on cartilage thickness

Table 11.4 Cartilage surface positioning errors (mm) of 4D versus 3D LOGISMOS.

N=54	Baseline		12 months	
	4D	3D	4D	3D
Femur signed	**0.01±0.18**	0.01±0.19	−0.02±0.17	−0.04±0.17
Femur unsigned	**0.53±0.11**	0.54±0.11	0.55±0.11	0.55±0.11
Tibia signed	0.08±0.17	**0.07±0.16**	0.07±0.19	0.06±0.18
Tibia unsigned	0.59±0.14	0.60±0.14	0.60±0.16	0.60±0.14

Bold: statistically significant ($p < 0.05$) reduction in positioning errors.

Table 11.5 Unsigned cartilage subplate thickness errors (mm) of 5-time-point-4D versus 3D LOGISMOS within ranges defined with respect to maximum per patient.

	98–100% Max		95–100% Max		90–100% Max	
	4D	3D	4D	3D	4D	3D
cMF	**0.76±0.60**	1.11±0.63	**0.57±0.43**	0.87±0.41	**0.43±0.32**	0.68±0.29
cLF	1.46±2.36	1.67±1.82	1.07±1.73	1.16±1.02	0.74±0.95	0.84±0.55
cMT	**1.28±0.47**	1.78±1.36	**1.09±0.42**	1.48±1.00	**0.92±0.38**	1.19±0.63
cLT	**1.29±0.47**	1.40±0.49	**1.09±0.40**	1.17±0.41	**0.90±0.33**	0.98±0.34

cMF/cLF: central load-bearing medial/lateral femur.
cMT/cLT: central load-bearing medial/lateral tibia.
Bold: statistically significant ($p < 0.05$) reduction in thickness errors.

errors in clinically important load-bearing subplates, substantial local error reduction capability of 4D was achieved as is clearly shown in Table 11.5. As a related aspect, the temporal constraints incorporated in the 4D LOGISMOS-JEI approach also improved the efficiency of the JEI such that local/regional errors on multiple neighboring time points could often be fixed by JEI-interacting on a single time point 3D image only.

11.7. Modular application design

The development and efficient employment of the LOGISMOS-JEI method for a given segmentation problem is only possible if efficient, highly flexible graphical user interface (GUI) tools are available for data visualizations and user interactions. The end-users of the resulting application – expert analysts, physicians, technologists – require a GUI that is custom made for a specific clinical application and enables performing the quantitative LOGISMOS-JEI task time-efficiently and with a minimum effort possible. To streamline the development process of new LOGISMOS-JEI applications, a modular design environment was developed and employed for creating a number of quantitative image analysis tasks [26]. Each module in the LOGISMOS-JEI environment independently performs a specialized set of atomic tasks without an explicit knowledge of the implementation details of the other modules. The core modules of this environment and their tasks are as follows:

- *Data module* manages image and result data and provides "partial" data such as 2D slice image and result contours to be visualized upon receiving requests from other modules.
- *2D and 3D visualization modules* perform visualization of partial images and results and accept user interactions for visualization control and JEI.
- *Workflow module* provides GUI that guides the user through the segmentation and analysis workflow.
- *Segmentation module* performs the core task of LOGISMOS-JEI. It is the underlying segmentation engine of LOGISMOS-JEI and contains no GUI components.
- *Control module* coordinates the tasks of the above modules.

The inter-module communications and data exchanges are accomplished by a *signals and slots* mechanism that allows easy and flexible integration of modules into applications. Figs. 11.10, 11.12 and 11.14 show screen shots of LOGISMOS-JEI applications developed for tasks reported in Sections 11.4–11.6. Each of these task-specific applications includes various customizations. For each of these applications, adding clinical-task-specific functionality to existing modules and making customized workflow modules took less than two weeks of development effort. Subsequent system integration only required several hours.

11.8. Conclusion

LOGISMOS produces globally optimal results when segmenting n-dimensional multiple objects and/or surfaces utilizing highly customizable and flexible cost functions. The embedded geometric constraints explicitly incorporate a priori anatomical knowledge thus making LOGISMOS suitable for medical image segmentation.

The JEI extension enhances the capability and efficiency of LOGISMOS by dynamically integrating user inputs into the algorithm while maintaining the most important properties of the LOGISMOS result – global optimality and embedded constraints. The users of LOGISMOS-JEI applications can rely on the automated LOGISMOS method of the first stage to produce accurate results for the majority of the analyzed data. In cases when the automated LOGISMOS fails locally or regionally, analysts can utilize their problem-specific expertise to correct such errors introduced by disease-associated and/or image-artifact-caused ambiguities without turning to slice-by-slice manual tracing. Rather, the JEI stage of the analysis is based on the user interacting with the underlying segmentation algorithm. The results presented in Sections 11.4–11.6 show that LOGISMOS-JEI employed in various clinically-oriented applications not only produces accurate results but also achieves them with a substantially reduced human effort compared to the currently-necessary fully-manual tracing and editing of the automated results.

As shown in the MR knee segmentation application (Section 11.6), the results of LOGIMOS-JEI can be used as an independent standard to efficiently increase the training set sizes for machine-learning-based improvements of automated techniques. Furthermore, machine learning can be used to design data-specific cost functions further enhancing the capability of LOGISMOS when dealing with pathological image data. In all its stages and uses, the JEI reduces the human effort required. Such a feedback loop with automated segmentation, learning of cost functions, JEI-preparation of larger training datasets, and relearning on the resulting larger and larger data sizes brings LOGIMOS-JEI ever closer to a highly accurate performance when functioning in the fully automated LOGISMOS-only segmentation regime. Yet, it continues maintaining the capability of accepting human intervention due to the JEI functionality.

The development of the flexible and modular environment for development and employment of LOGISMOS-JEI image analysis applications is a major step toward reaching clinical acceptance of quantitative medical imaging and a step forward to acceptance of precision medicine principles in routine clinical practice.

More examples of LOGISMOS-JEI applications including animations and videos of JEI in action can be found at [27].

Acknowledgments

This work was supported in part by the grants from the National Institutes of Health (R01-EB004640, R01-EY019112, R01-EY018853), Ministry of Health of the Czech Republic (16-27465A, 16-28525A, 17-28784A – all rights reserved), and IKEM (MH-CZ-DRO-IKEM-IN 00023001). The OAI is a public-private partnership comprised of five contracts (N01-AR-2-2258; N01-AR-2-2259; N01-AR-2-2260; N01-AR-2-2261; N01-AR-2-2262) funded by the National Institutes of Health, a branch of the Department of Health and Human Services, and conducted by the OAI Study Investigators. Private funding partners include Merck Research Laboratories; Novartis Pharmaceuticals Corporation, GlaxoSmithKline; and Pfizer, Inc. Private sector funding for the OAI is managed by the Foundation for the National Institutes of Health. This manuscript was prepared using an OAI public use data set and does not necessarily reflect the opinions or views of the OAI investigators, the NIH, or the private funding partners.

References

[1] X. Wu, D.Z. Chen, Optimal net surface problems with applications, in: Automata, Languages and Programming, in: Lecture Notes in Computer Science, vol. 2380, Springer, 2002, pp. 1029–1042.

[2] K. Li, X. Wu, D.Z. Chen, M. Sonka, Globally optimal segmentation of interacting surfaces with geometric constraints, in: Proceedings of the 2004 IEEE Computer Society Conference on Computer Vision and Pattern Recognition (CVPR), Vol. 1, 2004, pp. 394–399.

[3] K. Li, X. Wu, D.Z. Chen, M. Sonka, Optimal surface segmentation in volumetric images — a graph-theoretic approach, IEEE Transactions on Pattern Analysis and Machine Intelligence 28 (1) (2006) 119–134.

[4] Y. Yin, X. Zhang, R. Williams, X. Wu, D.D. Anderson, M. Sonka, LOGISMOS — layered optimal graph image segmentation of multiple objects and surfaces: cartilage segmentation in the knee joint, IEEE Transactions on Medical Imaging 29 (12) (2010) 2023–2037.

[5] S. Sun, M. Sonka, R.R. Beichel, Graph-based IVUS segmentation with efficient computer-aided refinement, IEEE Transactions on Medical Imaging 32 (8) (2013) 1536–1549.

[6] S. Sun, M. Sonka, R.R. Beichel, Lung segmentation refinement based on optimal surface finding utilizing a hybrid desktop/virtual reality user interface, Computerized Medical Imaging and Graphics 37 (2013) 15–27.

[7] S. Kashyap, H. Zhang, M. Sonka, Just enough interaction for fast minimally interactive correction of 4D segmentation of knee MRI, Osteoarthritis and Cartilage (2017) S224–S225.

[8] S. Kashyap, H. Zhang, K. Rao, M. Sonka, Learning-based cost functions for 3-D and 4-D multi-surface multi-object segmentation of knee MRI: data from the osteoarthritis initiative, IEEE Transactions on Medical Imaging 37 (5) (2018) 1103–1113.

[9] K. Lee, H. Zhang, A. Wahle, M. Abramoff, M. Sonka, Multi-layer 3D simultaneous retinal OCT layer segmentation: just-enough interaction for routine clinical use, in: Lecture Notes in Computational Vision and Biomechanics, vol. 27, 2018, pp. 862–871.

[10] I. Oguz, M. Sonka, LOGISMOS-B: layered optimal graph image segmentation of multiple objects and surfaces for the brain, IEEE Transactions on Medical Imaging 33 (6) (2014) 1220–1235.

[11] M.K. Garvin, M.D. Abramoff, X. Wu, S.R. Russell, T.L. Burns, M. Sonka, Automated 3-D intraretinal layer segmentation of macular spectral-domain optical coherence tomography images, IEEE Transactions on Medical Imaging 28 (9) (2009) 1436–1447.

[12] Q. Song, J. Bai, M.K. Garvin, M. Sonka, J.M. Buatti, X. Wu, Optimal multiple surface segmentation with shape and context priors, IEEE Transactions on Medical Imaging 32 (2) (2013) 376–386.

[13] T. Verma, Maxflow revisited: an empirical comparison of maxflow algorithms for dense vision problems, in: Proceedings of the British Machine Vision Conference 2012, 2012.

[14] Y. Boykov, V. Kolmogorov, An experimental comparison of min-cut/max-flow algorithms for energy minimization in vision, IEEE Transactions on Pattern Analysis and Machine Intelligence 26 (9) (2004) 1124–1137.

[15] A.V. Goldberg, S. Hed, H. Kaplan, R.E. Tarjan, R.F. Werneck, Maximum flows by incremental breadth-first search, in: Algorithms – ESA 2011, in: Lecture Notes in Computer Science, vol. 6942, Springer, 2011, pp. 457–468.

[16] A.V. Goldberg, S. Hed, H. Kaplan, P. Kohli, R.E. Tarjan, R.F. Werneck, Faster and more dynamic maximum flow by incremental breadth-first search, in: Algorithms – ESA 2015, in: Lecture Notes in Computer Science, vol. 9294, Springer, 2015, pp. 619–630.

[17] Y. Boykov, M.P. Jolly, Interactive graph cuts for optimal boundary & region segmentation of objects in N-D images, in: Proc. Eighth IEEE Int. Conf. Computer Vision, ICCV 2001, Vol. 1, 2001, pp. 105–112.

[18] P. Kohli, P.H.S. Torr, Dynamic graph cuts for efficient inference in Markov random fields, IEEE Transactions on Pattern Analysis and Machine Intelligence 29 (12) (2007) 2079–2088.

[19] K. Lee, M. Niemeijer, M.K. Garvin, Y.H. Kwon, M. Sonka, M.D. Abramoff, Segmentation of the optic disc in 3-D OCT scans of the optic nerve head, IEEE Transactions on Medical Imaging 29 (1) (2010) 159–168.

[20] H. Bogunovic, M. Sonka, Y.H. Kwon, P. Kemp, M.D. Abramoff, X. Wu, Multi-surface and multi-field co-segmentation of 3-D retinal optical coherence tomography, IEEE Transactions on Medical Imaging 33 (12) (2014) 2242–2253.

[21] Z. Chen, Novel Quantitative Description Approaches Assessing Coronary Morphology and Development, Ph.D. thesis, The University of Iowa, 2016.

[22] Z. Chen, M. Pazdernik, H. Zhang, A. Wahle, Z. Guo, H. Bedanova, et al., Quantitative 3D analysis of coronary wall morphology in heart transplant patients: OCT-assessed cardiac allograft vasculopathy progression, Medical Image Analysis 50 (12) (2018) 95–105.

[23] M. Pazdernik, Z. Chen, H. Bedanova, J. Kautzner, V. Melenovsky, V. Karmazin, et al., Early detection of cardiac allograft vasculopathy using highly automated 3-dimensional optical coherence tomography analysis, The Journal of Heart and Lung Transplantation 37 (8) (2018) 992–1000.

[24] S. Kashyap, I. Oguz, H. Zhang, M. Sonka, Automated segmentation of knee MRI using hierarchical classifiers and just enough interaction based learning: data from osteoarthritis initiative, in: International Conference on Medical Image Computing and Computer-Assisted Intervention, Springer, 2016, pp. 344–351.

[25] E. Konukoglu, B. Glocker, D. Zikic, A. Criminisi, Neighbourhood approximation using randomized forests, Medical Image Analysis 17 (7) (2013) 790–804.

[26] H. Zhang, S. Kashyap, A. Wahle, M. Sonka, Highly modular multi-platform development environment for automated segmentation and just enough interaction, in: Interactive Medical Image Computing: 3rd International Workshop, IMIC 2016, held in conjunction with MICCAI 2016, Athens, Greece, October 2016, 2016.

[27] IIBI LOGISMOS, URL: http://www.iibi.uiowa.edu/logismos.

CHAPTER 12

Deformable models, sparsity and learning-based segmentation for cardiac MRI based analytics

Dimitris N. Metaxas[a], Zhennan Yan[b]
[a]Rutgers University, Department of Computer Science, Piscataway, NJ, United States
[b]SenseBrain, Princeton, NJ, United States

Contents

12.1. Introduction	273
12.1.1 Deformable models for cardiac modeling	274
12.1.2 Learning based cardiac segmentation	275
12.2. Deep learning based segmentation of ventricles	277
12.3. Shape refinement by sparse shape composition	283
12.4. 3D modeling	285
12.5. Conclusion and future directions	288
References	288

12.1. Introduction

Cardiovascular diseases (CVD), such as heart attack, stroke, heart failure (HF), arrhythmia, and coronary disease, are the most common cause of death globally, accounting for 31% of all global deaths in 2016. Of these deaths, 85% are due to heart attack and stroke [1]. In the US, CVD accounted for 30.8% of all deaths in 2013, and about half of people diagnosed with HF die within 5 years [2]. Consequently, the improved early diagnosis and accurate treatment of cardiac diseases is an open and important field of research.

A comprehensive analysis of patient-specific cardiac structure and motion is fundamental for understanding cardiac function, and essential for early detection and accurate treatment of CVDs. In classical diagnosis, electrocardiogram (ECG), echocardiography (echo), and chest X-ray are used to analyze cardiac function. However, they are not able to provide sufficient information for 3D or 4D heart modeling. Recent cardiac research based on high spatiotemporal resolution imaging, such as cardiac magnetic resonance (CMR) and computational tomography (CCT), aim to design comprehensive methods to accurately characterize the complex shape and motion of the heart. The primary hypothesis is that it would further enable the identification of subtle disease-evoked changes in cardiac anatomy and function, and thus lead to a refined evaluation

Handbook of Medical Image Computing and Computer Assisted Intervention
https://doi.org/10.1016/B978-0-12-816176-0.00017-X

and prediction of cardiac diseases for specific patient. In particular, CMR is preferable to CCT because it avoids exposure to ionizing radiation and can provide a wealth of functional information, especially for the evaluation of the extracardiac thoracic vasculature, ventricular function, and flow measurements [3].

The quantitative analysis of cardiac function in MRI requires the detection and delineation of multiple related structures in both end diastolic (ED) and end systolic (ES) phases, such as right ventricular cavity (RVC), left ventricular myocardium (LVM), and left ventricular cavity (LVC). In clinical diagnosis, identification of ED & ES phases, and delineation of related structures require doctors carefully examining tens to hundreds of MRI slices, which is time-consuming and labor intensive. Current automated cardiac function analysis methods depend heavily on having accurately annotated cardiac wall boundaries which is expensive and time consuming. Despite vigorous researches on automated or semiautomated image segmentation and analysis [4], the segmentation of cardiac chamber boundaries still remains challenging due to issues, such as wall irregularity, cluttered objects, high noise-to-signal ratio, and intensity inhomogeneity. Among the various types of approaches, deformable models and machine-learning based algorithms are two of the methods mostly used, besides the registration based frameworks [5–8].

Despite the progress in cardiac wall segmentation, there is still a lack of a robust and accurate automated segmentation algorithm that avoids the expensive manual or semiautomated contour annotation to obtain accurate extraction of cardiac wall boundaries.

In this chapter, we first review related techniques for cardiac segmentation and modeling in medical images mostly from CMR. In Sect. 12.2, we present a novel deep learning method to handle segmentation of multiple structures in cine CMR data. Then, we describe the methodologies for shape refinement and 3D cardiac motion modeling in Sects. 12.3 and 12.4, respectively. Lastly, we discuss future research directions and use cases of cardiac analytics.

12.1.1 Deformable models for cardiac modeling

An important family of algorithms in cardiac segmentation are based on deformable models, which have been widely used in medical image analysis [9–11]. The name "deformable models" is derived from the mechanics of material deformation, which describes how elastic objects deform based on applied forces [12–16]. They are based on physics, geometry, and estimation theory, and provide powerful tools for image-based cardiac analytics.

Paragios utilized GVF-based level-sets to segment MR cardiac images [17]. Santarelli et al. [18] applied GVF snake for segmentation based on manual input of rough contour of the internal cavity. Gotardo et al. [19] presented a snake-like deformable model based on complex Fourier descriptors for tracking the LV endocardial and epicardial boundaries and detection of intra-ventricular dyssynchrony. Uzunbaş et al. [20] integrated deformable models with graphical models for myocardium segmentation. Besides, many other deformable model based methods were reviewed in [21].

Despite the different formulations and implementations, deformable models rely on primarily edge information from image gradient to derive external image forces to drive a shape-based model. Thus, they are sensitive to image noise and artifacts. For instance, a model may leak through small or large gaps on the object boundary, or it may get stuck in local minima due to spurious edges inside the object or clutter around the true boundary.

To address these limitations, Huang et al. [22] have developed a new class of deformable models, named "metamorphs". This method naturally integrates both shape and texture information, and unifies the boundary and region information into a variational framework. This type of method is suitable for medical image segmentation, where both boundary and texture information are necessary. The metamorphs have been applied to segment the left ventricle endocardium in MRI image and tagged MRI image [22,23].

Besides the image segmentation task, researchers have introduced deformable models to build the heart model by shape reconstruction [24,25]. To obtain reliable motion analysis, Park et al. [26,9] proposed a physics-based volumetric deformable model to characterize and quantify the 3D shape and motion of left ventricle (LV) wall from tagged MRI. The left ventricle is initially modeled geometrically using a 3D volumetric mesh. Then, the 3D motion is driven by Lagrangian dynamics using a finite element framework that takes into account tagging line constraints. Given the nonlinear movement of the heart, the parameter functions of the dynamic model are estimated and they correspond to the longitudinal and radial contraction, axial twisting, and long axial deformation. Haber et al. [27] utilized a similar physics-based model to study the volumetric motion of right ventricle (RV) over time from tagged MRI. Because the reconstruction of cardiac motion field can also quantify important clinical information, e.g., the myocardial strain, and detect regional heart functional loss. Chen et al. [28] presented a three-step method for this task in tagged MRI by using a Gabor filter bank, robust point matching, and a meshless deformable model. Recently, Yu et al. [29] designed a robust meshless deformable model by integrating seamlessly a hybrid norm (L_1 and L_2) regularization. This deformable model was applied to solve mouse left ventricle (LV) motion analysis using tagged MRI (tMRI).

12.1.2 Learning based cardiac segmentation

Several statistical geometric model-based segmentation methods have been developed for cardiac segmentation, such as methods based on Active Shape Models (ASM) [30] and Active Appearance Models (AAM) [31,32]. Kaus et al. [33] integrated various sources of prior knowledge learned from training data into a deformable model for myocardium segmentation in 3D MRI. Lekadir et al. [34] utilized ASM with outlier correction. Andreopoulos and Tsotsos [35] combined 3D AAM with hierarchical 2D ASM and temporal constraints. Zheng et al. [36] proposed an automatic four-chamber heart segmentation system for 3D cardiac CT images by using statistical shape model (SSM) and marginal space learning to detect boundary landmarks of the heart.

In recent years, researchers have been using increasingly machine learning for cardiac analytics due to their improved results. Afshin et al. [37] extracted image features and used linear discriminant analysis and linear SVM classifiers to detect and localize regional myocardial abnormalities in MRI. Bai et al. [38] used SVM classifier instead of KNN in their multiatlas framework for patch-based segmentation. Zhen et al. [39] proposed a method using multioutput regression with random forest in four-chamber volume estimation.

There have been several works that focus on using deep learning techniques for the analysis of cardiac MRI [40–42]. Kong et al. [43] first proposed a deep temporal regression network to recognize end-diastolic and end-systolic frames from the cardiac cycle, using a 2D CNN with a recurrent neural network. Subsequently, Ngo et al. [44] developed a new method that combines deep learning and level sets for the automated segmentation of the left ventricle of the heart from cine CMR data. Avendi et al. combined deep learning algorithms and deformable models to develop a fully automatic framework for segmentation of left ventricle [45] and right ventricle [46] in short-axis (SAX) cardiac MRI data. Yang et al. [47] also combined deep learning and deformable models to segment cardiac wall and blood. Isensee et al. [48] integrated segmentation and disease classification into a fully automatic processing pipeline using time–series segmentation and domain specific features. More recently, Khened et al. [49] proposed a ensemble system for cardiac disease classification. Xue et al. [50] proposed a deep multitask relationships-learning method for left ventricle quantification.

In addition to these deep learning based algorithms and methods, there have been several datasets and challenges released in recent years for the cardiac MRI segmentation. For example, the goal of 2015 Kaggle Data Science Bowl was to automatically measure ED and ES volumes from cardiac MRI. In 2017, the Automated Cardiac Diagnosis Challenge (ACDC) took place during the MICCAI conference, which focused on the segmentation of the left ventricular endocardium and epicardium and the right ventricular endocardium, as well as the classification of the data in five classes (normal case, heart failure with infarction, dilated cardiomyopathy, hypertrophic cardiomyopathy, abnormal right ventricle). Accordingly, Bernard et al. [51] summarized this challenge and discussed clinical implications. In 2018, Statistical Atlases and Computational Modeling of the Heart Workshop (STACOM) in MICCAI conference launched two challenges for atrial segmentation and LV full quantification. Both winners of the challenges employed deep learning based approaches [52,53].

12.2. Deep learning based segmentation of ventricles

Although the above methods have achieved some successes in cardiac MRI boundary segmentation, accurate and robust cardiac structures segmentation in cine CMR data is still an open and challenging task. Since cine CMR data usually have low resolution in the cardiac long axis, and short-axis slice misalignments often exist in the data [54], deep learning methods in 3D do not work as well as in 2D as discussed in [48]. In addition, the shapes and appearances of the cardiac structures vary significantly from ED phase to ES phase. Deformable model based approaches require good initialization and suffer from getting stuck in spurious local minima due to noise and often unclear boundaries.

To address these limitations, we have developed a novel end-to-end framework for the automated segmentation of multiple structures in cine CMR.

The U–Net [55] is one of the most widely employed deep neural networks for the segmentation of medical images, which can effectively segment objects in image by contracting path to capture context and a symmetric expanding path that enables precise localization. However, the skip connections (from contracting path to expanding path) in the U–Net are linear and shallow aggregation (aggregate the shallowest layers the least). For the interested structures (e.g., RVC, LVM, LVC) in cardiac MRI, the diverse shapes and low boundary contrast pose significant challenges when directly using U–Net for the cardiac MRI segmentation. Therefore, we propose a method based on a modified deep layer aggregation [56], which can effectively locate and segment cardiac structures in short-axis (SAX) or long-axis (LAX) cardiac MR scans. The aggregation architecture can better fuse semantic and spatial information from local to global, which is easy to recognize and represent image features related to cardiac structures. Additionally, in the path of upsampling features, we introduce two strategies, i.e., Refinement Residual Block (RRB) and Channel Attention Block (CAB) [57], to further boost the segmentation performance. The proposed framework is validated on the MICCAI ACDC 2017 public dataset [51], showing its excellent performance for the segmentation of cardiac structures such as RVC, LVM, and LVC.

Network architecture

The overview of the proposed framework is presented in Fig. 12.1. Unlike previous methods which directly tackle the segmentation using 3D data, we focus on improving the segmentation of 2D slices, due to the large slice distance and misalignment in the cine CMR data. As shown in Fig. 12.1, a deep layer aggregation (DLA) [58] based network is employed, which can effectively obtain features to discriminate and represent the cardiac MRI slices. In the training stage, we first perform data preprocessing and data augmentation to process images for the training of the deep neural network. Given the training images and the corresponding labels, a multilabel (i.e., RVC, LVM, LVC, and background) segmentation deep neural network is trained end-to-end. In the testing

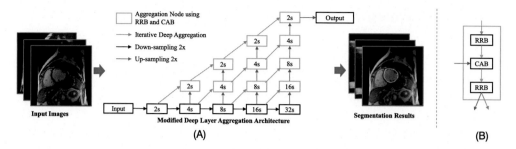

Figure 12.1 *Framework overview.* (A) The proposed framework for boundary segmentation in cardiac MRI. (B) Aggregation node using RRB and CAB [56].

stage, the unseen testing images undergo the preprocessing step before being processed by the trained network to obtain the segmentation results.

Preprocessing and data augmentation

Before the end-to-end training, we first prepare the training images to make them applicable for the training process. Specifically, in the data preprocessing step, images are first normalized so that the intensities follow standard normal distribution. The mean and standard deviation are calculated at the patient level. Then, the training images and corresponding ground truth are resampled to have the same spatial resolution. Such preprocessing is simple yet efficient. Therefore we ensure that the training and testing samples have the same distribution.

During the deep neural network training, we adopt multiple data augmentation strategies for the cardiac MRI data, such as random histogram matching, rotation, shifting, scaling, elastic deformation, and mirroring. Due to the large variance in the data (introduced by between-subject variance and different acquisition parameters) and limited size of training dataset, the data augmentation can avoid model overfitting by increasing the training data samples.

Modified deep layer aggregation network

As illustrated in Fig. 12.1, we design the segmentation framework by a modified DLA network. We choose DLA-34 2s as the backbone network [58] because of the good balance of the number of parameters and the performance compared with other variants with more layers. It can produce dense prediction for semantic segmentation and contour detection in 2-stride resolution. DLA extends neural networks by two types of layer aggregations: Iterative Deep Aggregation (IDA) and Hierarchical Deep Aggregation (HDA). As discussed in [58], IDA can refine features from shallowest, smallest scale and then iteratively merges deeper, larger scales. HDA aggregates representations within one scale. It can merge blocks and stages in a tree to preserve and combine feature channels.

Formally, in a network consisting of a series of layers $r_1, \ldots, r_n$ with increasingly deeper and semantic information, the IDA function I is defined as

$$I(r_1, \ldots, r_n) = \begin{cases} r_1 & \text{if } n = 1, \\ I(N(r_1, r_2), \ldots, r_n) & \text{otherwise,} \end{cases} \tag{12.1}$$

where N is some aggregation node. HDA function T_n for layer r with depth n is defined as

$$T_n(r) = N(R_{n-1}^n(r), R_{n-2}^n(r), \ldots, R_1^n(r), L_1^n(r), L_2^n(r)), \tag{12.2}$$

where functions R and L are defined as

$$L_2^n(r) = ConvBlock(L_1^n(r)), \quad L_1^n(r) = ConvBlock(R_1^n(r)), \tag{12.3}$$

$$R_m^n(r) = \begin{cases} T_m(r) & \text{if } m = n - 1, \\ T_m(R_{m+1}^n(r)) & \text{otherwise.} \end{cases} \tag{12.4}$$

The ConvBlock may represent different variants of convolutional blocks [58], while the aggregation function N used in this work is

$$N(r_1, \ldots, r_n) = ReLU(BatchNorm(\sum_i \omega_i r_i + b)), \tag{12.5}$$

where ReLU is the Rectified Linear Unit [59] and BatchNorm is Batch Normalization [60]; ω_i and b are the learnable parameters.

In order to match the original image resolution, DLA-34 2s is followed by two additional layers. The first one is a convolutional layer with 1×1 kernel size and 32 feature maps. The second one is a deconvolutional layer with 4×4 kernel, 2×2 stride, and padding size 1. Given a set of training datasets, the proposed network can learn to exploit the aggregation to fuse local and global information in cardiac MRI slices.

For the cardiac structures, one critical issue during segmentation is the intraclass inconsistency, where one structure may have different expressions and textures, especially for the cardiac MRI data ranging from ES to ED frame. Meanwhile, the interclass indistinction between structures and background context also needs to be considered in the cardiac data. In addition to the modified DLA, we also introduce techniques embedded in the neural network architectures to further improve the segmentation performance. In our framework, two improvements have been developed, i.e., CAB and RRB, in the path of upsampling features. As discussed in [57], the CAB is designed to change the weights of features on each layer. This design mimics feature selection to obtain discriminative features stagewise to enhance the intraclass consistency. RRB is basically a small residual block, which can refine the feature map and combine the information across all channels.

Loss function

In multilabel classification problems, one commonly used loss function is the cross entropy loss. However, in medical image segmentation tasks, usually the anatomy of interest occupies only a very small region in the image. Thus, the number of the background pixels are far more than those of the interested regions. In order to tackle such class imbalance, previous approaches resorted to weighted cross entropy based on sample reweighting, where foreground regions are given more importance during training. The weights can be set empirically or computed by the number of samples for each class. However, it is hard to find the optimal weights.

On the other hand, the Dice similarity coefficient (DSC), which measures the amount of agreement between two regions, is widely used as a metric to evaluate the segmentation performance compared with the given ground truth in medical images. The DSC metric of regions O_1 and O_2 is defined as

$$DSC(O_1, O_2) = -\frac{2|O_1 \cap O_2|}{|O_1| + |O_2|}. \tag{12.6}$$

In segmentation tasks, O_1 represents the segmentation result and O_2 is the ground truth mask; $|\cdot|$ operation indicates the number of pixels or voxels in that region. In order to make this function differentiable, Milletari et al. [61] proposed a continuous version, which can be directly used as loss in the optimization of deep neural network. In this work, we use a multilabel DSC loss to drive the optimization of the network model as follows:

$$Loss_{DSC} = -\frac{2}{C} \sum_{c=1}^{C} \frac{\sum_i \ell_{i,c} p_{i,c}}{\sum_i \ell_{i,c} + \sum_i p_{i,c}}, \tag{12.7}$$

where C is the number of classes; $p_{i,c}$ is the predicted probability (after softmax) of class c for sample i, and $\ell_{i,c}$ is the binary indicator if c is the correct label of sample i.

Dataset and evaluation metrics

To demonstrate the effectiveness, the proposed cardiac MRI segmentation method is validated on the MICCAI 2017 Automated Cardiac Diagnosis Challenge (ACDC) dataset [51] for performance comparison with the state-of-the-art. This dataset comprises SAX scans of cine CMR of 100 patients acquired at the University Hospital of Dijon using two MR scanners of different magnetic strengths (1.5 and 3.0 T). The

SAX data has in-plane resolution ranging from 0.49 to 3.69 mm^2 and 5 to 10 mm slice thickness in the direction of the long axis of the heart. The segmentation ground truth is provided for ED and ES phases. The structures of the LVC, LVM, and RVC are annotated manually by clinical experts.

We validate the proposed method in the segmentation tasks of multiple cardiac structures in cine CMR, and compare them with some state-of-the-art methods based on two error metrics. One is the Dice score as noted in Eq. (12.6), which ranges between [0, 1] (the higher the better). Since Dice score cannot reflect the accuracy of the boundaries, Hausdorff distance [62] is used as another metric, which is defined as:

$$dist_H(S_1, S_2) = \max\{dist(S_1, S_2), dist(S_2, S_1)\}, \tag{12.8}$$

where $dist(S_1, S_2)$ represents the maximum of the distances of all points in shape S_1 to their corresponding closest points in shape S_2. Note that $dist(S_1, S_2)$ is not symmetric: $dist(S_1, S_2) \neq dist(S_2, S_1)$. In our settings, the segmentation is conducted in 2D images, while the evaluation is conducted in 3D by considering the original voxel spacing.

Implementation details

In the preprocessing step, we resampled all data into 1.25 mm^2 in-plane resolution. We conducted 5-fold cross-validation. During the training, Adaptive Moment Estimation (Adam) [63] is used to optimize the neural network according to the Dice loss. The training process takes 500 epochs, with the initial learning rate as 0.001. The learning rate decreases by 99% in each epoch. The training image patches are cropped of size 256×256. For data augmentation, each training sample has 50% chance undergoing histogram matching with a random template picked from the rest of the training set. Similarly, it could be mirrored, rotated by any angle between 0 and 360 degrees, scaled by $0.7 \sim 1.3$, deformed and cropped around different locations, randomly with a two-thirds chance. All experiments are carried out on a Linux system with 1 Titan XP GPU by using Pytorch.

Results

Our method is compared with a U–Net based 2D segmentation method, which is specifically designed for the cine CMR segmentation [48] and won the first rank in the ACDC 2017. Table 12.1 records the average performances of 5-fold cross-validation results on ACDC 2017 data [51] in considering both the Dice metric and Hausdorff distance (in mm). In Table 12.1, the first row is quoted from [48]. After reproducing the results by using their source codes without statistical inference, the second row is obtained. According to the results in Table 12.1, the first row results are better than those in the second row in terms of Hausdorff distance, which may come from the strategy of the statistical inference by collecting 8 results from each testing case (2 predictions with

Table 12.1 5-fold cross-validation results on ACDC 2017 dataset [56].

Methods	Dice (%)			Hausdorff (mm)		
	RVC	LVM	LVC	RVC	LVM	LVC
Unet–2D [48]	90.2	90.5	94.5	14.294	8.899	7.055
Unet–2D w/o	90.0±7.4	**90.1±3**	**94.5±4.7**	16.227±10.66	9.368±7.29	7.655±6.76
DLA [58]	89.7±7.4	89.7±3.4	94.2±5.4	13.953±9.89	9.097±6.99	6.809±4.66
Proposed	**90.3±6.9**	89.2±3.4	94.2±5.5	**13.830±8.97**	**8.786±5.33**	**6.641±4**

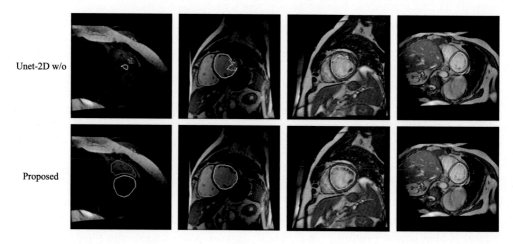

Figure 12.2 *Visual comparison.* Comparison of segmentation results between Unet-2D w/o and the proposed method. Yellow, blue, and green lines represent the boundaries of LVC, LVM, and RVC, respectively [56].

unfixed dropout layer on 4 mirrored inputs). Since the statistical inference significantly increases the testing time, we do not use it in our experiments (rows 2–4). Besides, the DLA indicates the results we trained with original DLA architecture [58] without CAB and RRB improvements, while the Proposed indicates the results we trained with all the proposed components.

According to Table 12.1, the proposed method produces comparable Dice scores and clearly better shape distances (even better than reported results in [48]). This excellent performance is the result of the modified DLA strategy, which can effectively explore the cardiac MRI structures from local to global to better fuse information across layers when training the deep neural networks. Moreover, the employed CAB and RRB [57] improve the DLA during the segmentation of related structures to obtain more accurate boundaries. Fig. 12.2 shows more examples of segmentation results where the Unet-2D w/o method has clear failures and the proposed method still works well.

Another example of segmented results is shown in Fig. 12.3. In this figure, all images are from one subject, but at different location and phases. Three rows represent the base

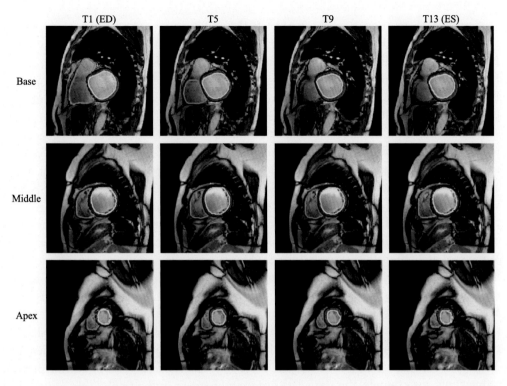

Figure 12.3 *One example of segmentation results in different slices along the cardiac cycle in ACDC dataset.* Only ED and ES phases have ground truth shown in dashed lines. Yellow, blue, and green lines represent the boundaries of LVC, LVM, and RVC, respectively.

(close to two atria), middle, and apex regions of the heart, respectively. Each column represents one phase in the cardiac cycle from ED to ES. Note that only ED and ES phases have ground truth in dashed lines. From these results, we can see that the proposed framework is robust and accurate in terms of different locations and phases. The same end-to-end framework can be easily applied to obtain LV segmentation in long-axis cardiac MRI.

12.3. Shape refinement by sparse shape composition

After the segmentation of cardiac structures in previous section, the left endocardium and epicardium contours can be extracted from the segmented regions as the boundaries shown in Fig. 12.3. We can see that the region boundaries are not very smooth. In order to extract smooth contours for the endocardium and epicardium, and ensure the correct topology, some sophisticate postprocessing of shapes is necessary.

Statistical shape models, such as ASM [64], have been proven an effective strategy to ensure the derived shape follows the shape patterns learned from a training database. However, these traditional methods cannot deal well with non-Gaussian distributions. In practice, these errors can be easily caused by erroneous detection or segmentation. Recently, sparsity based methods have been widely used in computer vision and image processing communities to deal with gross errors or outliers. The sparse shape representation is based on the observation that a small subset of the existing data is necessary to represent the statistical variation of shapes. Therefore, it is less sensitive to weak or misleading local appearance cues. One of its successful applications is medical image segmentation and modeling. Particularly, Zhang et al. [65] proposed Sparse Shape Composition model (SSC) to incorporate shape priors on-the-fly instead of using any parametric model of shape statistics. Zhang et al. [66] integrated the SSC and sparse dictionary learning in a deformable model for robust and efficient image segmentation. Wang et al. [67,68] further extended the SSC for fast and accurate shape prior modeling in liver surgical planning. Since SSC requires iterative sparse optimization, the run-time efficiency is limited when the shape repository is large. Besides, in medical imaging applications, training shapes seldom come in one batch. Thus, Zhang et al. [69] proposed an online learning method to dynamically update the dictionary to model shape priors from a large number of training shapes without sacrificing run-time efficiency. The sparse representation can not only be used in modeling priors, but also in shape refinements, for example, the fascia lata surface refinement in the thigh [70].

Formally, the shape repository can be represented as a data matrix $D = [d_1, \ldots, d_k] \in R^{m \times k}$, where k is the number of training shapes and d_i is the column vector containing the coordinates of all vertices in ith shape; m is the product of the number of vertices in each shape by the degree of freedom. All training shapes are prealigned [65]. Given an input shape u and the data matrix D, the sparse shape representation is formulated as an optimization problem

$$\underset{\phi, e, \beta}{\arg\min} \| T(u, \beta) - D\phi - e \|_2^2 + \lambda_1 \|\phi\|_1 + \lambda_2 \|e\|_1, \tag{12.9}$$

where $T(u, \beta)$ is a global transformation operator with parameter β. It aligns the input shape to the mean shape of the shape database; ϕ is the parameters for linear combination of D; e is an error vector. By optimizing the first term, the transformed input shape can be refined as $D\phi$. It can be transformed back by the inverse of T using parameter β. The second and third terms embed L_1 regularization to keep the ϕ and e sparse; λ_1 and λ_2 control the weights of two sparsity terms.

Note that the shapes of the LV wall vary significantly in different subjects, cardiac region (i.e., base, middle, apex) and cardiac cycle (from ED to ES). In order to better retrieve the similar shapes, we can cluster the shape repository into nonoverlapping subsets $\{G_1, \ldots, G_K\}$, and solve the shape refinement by using group sparsity [71]. Now the second term in Eq. (12.9) is replaced by a group-sparsity regularization ($L_{2,1}$ norm) as follows:

$$\arg\min_{\phi,e,\beta} \| T(u, \beta) - D\phi - e\|_2^2 + \lambda_1 \sum_{j=1}^{K} \|\phi_{G_j}\|_2 + \lambda_2\|e\|_1. \tag{12.10}$$

12.4. 3D modeling

Over the past two decades, advances in CMR data quality have significantly advanced the research on 3D cardiac modeling, which provides additional cues for the analysis of cardiovascular diseases. In this section, we describe our approach for 3D shape modeling and motion reconstruction in detail.

In CMR, it is not easy to build an accurate 3D heart model because of the motion artifacts caused by varying respiration during data acquisition. Although the cine MR sequences are captured at fixed spatial locations during breath-holding, the respiration phases at different slices of the cine MRI are hardly to remain the same. As a result, the MR scans at different locations are inevitably misaligned with spatial offsets and in-plane deformation. In order to build precise 3D models to analyze the function of the heart, we first correct the misalignment issue in the data based on 2D segmentation results.

According to a recent study [72], the cardiac motion under respiration is mainly a rigid-body translation in the craniocaudal direction, with minimum deformation. Therefore, we employ in-plane rigid translation to compensate the primary respiration effect for the MR slices. Particularly, to compute the rigid translation in a SAX slice for its misalignment correction, we utilize the previously extracted LV contours and the 3D spatial information (i.e., the origin, orientation and voxel spacing) of this SAX slice and the intersecting LAX slices. Let u_S denote the point set of LV contours in the SAX plane, and $u_{L,j}$ denote the contour of the jth intersecting LAX slice. We first collect point set u_p as the union of all intersection points of each $u_{L,j}$ and the SAX planes. Considering u_p as the target point set, we apply iterative closest point (ICP) algorithm to rigidly (translation only) register the u_S to u_p. Note that u_S contains much more points than u_p, we treat u_p as the source point cloud and u_S as the reference to compute the translation, and apply the inverse translation to u_S to obtain the corrected contour in SAX plane. The same algorithm can be applied for the correction of the LAX slices as well. The correction can be applied several times for all the slices to obtain better results. Fig. 12.4 shows an example of the misalignment correction.

After correcting misalignment, we first use point cloud registration method, e.g., coherent point drifting (CPD) [73], to register a template model to the aligned segmentation contour points at phase ED. The warped template model is the initialization. We use a meshless deformable model to fine-tune it to better fit the target model at ED, and generate the models for the following cardiac phases.

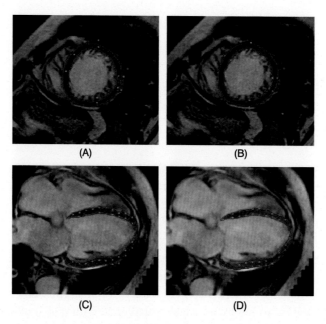

Figure 12.4 *Correction of misalignment.* Example of misalignment correction on SAX and LAX slices. The red lines are LV contours. The green points are intersection points u_p in each slice. Panels (A) and (C) show misaligned slices before correction; (B) and (D) show the corrected results.

Let v denote a set of discretized vertices. Each vertex has a neighborhood structure, which can be defined by the connectivity for the mesh model, or the distance for the meshless model. Here, we use a meshless model, which is directly represented by the positions of all vertices in v. A vertex $i \in v$ is represented by the homogeneous coordinate $v_i = (x_i, y_i, z_i, 1)^T$. After deformation, the vertex is represented by the cartesian coordinate $v_i' = (x_i', y_i', z_i')^T$. Thus, the deformed model is represented by $V' = [v_1'^T \ldots v_\eta'^T]^T$, where $\eta = |v|$. Let subset $v_o \subset v$ of size τ denote the selected control points based on the observations. The goal of the deformable model is to track the motion of the whole shape, given the position V_o' of the control points. The deformation is formulated as a minimization problem of the total energy:

$$E_{total} = E_{model}(V') + \alpha E_{ext}(V', V_o'),   (12.11)$$

where the model energy term E_{model} introduces an internal force to preserve the local shape structure in V' by regularizing the differences of the transformation matrices between neighboring vertices. The energy term E_{ext} introduces an external force by the observations to minimize the distance between the deformed model and the target positions; α is a parameter to balance between two energy terms.

The model energy term can be defined as

$$E_{model} = \sum_{i \in v} \sum_{j \in \aleph(i)} w_{ij} \| T_i v_i - T_j v_i \|_2^2,$$ (12.12)

where $\aleph(i) \subset v$ is the neighboring node set of vertex i. The weight w_{ij} is the strength of connection between vertex i and j, which could be defined as some kernel function (see detail discussions in [29]). The transformation matrix T_i is defined as

$$T_i = \begin{pmatrix} s_i & -h_i^1 & h_i^2 & t_i^x \\ h_i^1 & s_i & -h_i^3 & t_i^y \\ -h_i^2 & h_i^3 & s_i & t_i^z \end{pmatrix},$$ (12.13)

where the scalar s_i controls isotropic 3D scaling, (t_i^x, t_i^y, t_i^z) is the translation vector and parameters h_i^1, h_i^2, h_i^3 form a skew-symmetric matrix for linear approximation of rotations with small angles. On the other hand, the external energy is defined as

$$E_{ext} = \sum_{k \in v_o} \| T_k v_k - v_k' \|_2^2.$$ (12.14)

In order to solve the energy minimization problem with unknown arguments in T_i, we reformulate T_i into a vector $\mathbf{t}_i = (s_i, h_i^3, h_i^2, h_i^1, t_i^x, t_i^y, t_i^z)^T$, and vertex coordinates v_i into a matrix $A_i \in R^{3 \times 7}$:

$$A_i = \begin{pmatrix} x_i & 0 & z_i & -y_i & 1 & 0 & 0 \\ y_i & -z_i & 0 & x_i & 0 & 1 & 0 \\ z_i & y_i & -x_i & 0 & 0 & 0 & 1 \end{pmatrix}.$$ (12.15)

We further define a matrix $K_i = W_i \otimes A_i$, where $\otimes$ is Kronecker product, and w_{ij} is encoded in $W_i \in R^{|\aleph(i)| \times \eta}$ (for each neighbor j of i, there is one row in W_i, where the ith element is w_{ij} and the jth element is $-w_{ij}$, while the rest are all zeros). In this way, the model energy term (Eq. (12.12)) can be rewritten as

$$E_{model} = \| K\mathbf{t} \|_2^2,$$ (12.16)

where $K = [K_1^T \cdots K_n^T]^T$, and $\mathbf{t} = [\mathbf{t}_1^T \cdots \mathbf{t}_n^T]^T$. Similarly, Eq. (12.14) can be rewritten as

$$E_{ext} = \| U_o \mathbf{t} - V_o' \|_2^2,$$ (12.17)

where U_o is a sparse matrix with $\tau \times \eta$ blocks. Each $k \in v_o$ corresponds to one row in U_o with A_k placed in the kth column. Finally, the optimization problem is reformulated as

$$\arg \min_{\mathbf{t}} \{ \| K\mathbf{t} \|_2^2 + \alpha (\| U_o \mathbf{t} - V_o' - \epsilon \|_2^2 + \gamma \| \epsilon \|_1) \},$$ (12.18)

by utilizing both L_1 and L_2 norms, where ϵ represents the gross errors in the observations while γ controls the sparsity of ϵ. The above problem can be solved efficiently by a two-step optimization algorithm proposed in [29].

12.5. Conclusion and future directions

In this chapter, we first reviewed deformable model and machine learning based approaches for cardiac segmentation and wall motion analysis. Then, we presented a novel method for the automated segmentation of multiple cardiac structures in cine CMR, e.g., RVC, LVM, and LVC. The method is based on the recently proposed deep layer aggregation architecture (DLA), which can effectively fuse semantic and spatial information from local to global. This architecture is suitable for the segmentation of cardiac structures with low boundary contrast and diverse shapes. In addition, we further improve the segmentation performance by introducing two strategies in the deep network, i.e., channel attention block (CAB) and refinement residual block (RRB). The modified DLA network can better overcome the intraclass inconsistency and interclass indistinction that usually exist in cardiac MRI data. We also described the methodologies for 3D shape and motion reconstruction of the LV wall in detail including sparse methods. The whole framework is effective and efficient. It can automatically detect and segment important structures, and reconstruct heart model in different phases of cardiac cycle without any human interaction.

This framework could benefit clinical practices and researches by providing efficient and objective annotation and quantification of cardiac wall motion, such as the automatic detection of diseases such as hypertrophic cardiomyopathy, or assessment of cardiac dyssynchrony for improved cardiac resynchronization therapy (CRT). Currently, the quantitative assessment of cardiac function is limited due to lack of 3D cardiac shape and motion analytics. Computer-aided cardiac analytics can be used to obtain more detailed metrics than those currently used such as the quantification of the 17 segments of the left ventricle. The quantification of the heart's shape and motion promises to enable better understanding of cardiac function, early disease diagnosis and improved patient outcomes.

References

[1] Key facts of cardiovascular diseases (cvds), http://www.who.int/en/news-room/fact-sheets/detail/cardiovascular-diseases-(cvds). (Accessed 21 November 2018).

[2] D. Mozaffarian, E.J. Benjamin, A.S. Go, D.K. Arnett, M.J. Blaha, M. Cushman, et al., Heart disease and stroke statistics—2016 update: a report from the American Heart Association, Circulation (2015) e38–e360.

[3] A. Prakash, A.J. Powell, T. Geva, Multimodality noninvasive imaging for assessment of congenital heart disease, Circulation: Cardiovascular Imaging 3 (1) (2010) 112–125.

[4] A.K. Attili, A. Schuster, E. Nagel, J.H. Reiber, R.J. van der Geest, Quantification in cardiac MRI: advances in image acquisition and processing, The International Journal of Cardiovascular Imaging 26 (1) (2010) 27–40.

[5] X. Zhuang, K.S. Rhode, R.S. Razavi, D.J. Hawkes, S. Ourselin, A registration-based propagation framework for automatic whole heart segmentation of cardiac MRI, IEEE Transactions on Medical Imaging 29 (9) (2010) 1612–1625.

[6] M.P. Jolly, C. Guetter, X. Lu, H. Xue, J. Guehring, Automatic segmentation of the myocardium in cine MR images using deformable registration, in: International Workshop on Statistical Atlases and Computational Models of the Heart, Springer, 2011, pp. 98–108.

[7] X. Zhuang, J. Shen, Multi-scale patch and multi-modality atlases for whole heart segmentation of MRI, Medical Image Analysis 31 (2016) 77–87.

[8] R. Shahzad, Q. Tao, O. Dzyubachyk, M. Staring, B.P. Lelieveldt, R.J. van der Geest, Fully-automatic left ventricular segmentation from long-axis cardiac cine MR scans, Medical Image Analysis 39 (2017) 44–55.

[9] J. Park, D. Metaxas, A.A. Young, L. Axel, Deformable models with parameter functions for cardiac motion analysis from tagged MRI data, IEEE Transactions on Medical Imaging 15 (3) (1996) 278–289.

[10] T. McInerney, D. Terzopoulos, Deformable models in medical image analysis: a survey, Medical Image Analysis 1 (2) (1996) 91–108.

[11] D. Metaxas, X. Huang, T. Chen, Integrating shape and texture in deformable models: from hybrid methods to metamorphs, in: Handbook of Mathematical Models in Computer Vision, Springer, 2006, pp. 113–129.

[12] D. Terzopoulos, D. Metaxas, Dynamic 3D models with local and global deformations: deformable superquadrics, in: Third International Conference on Computer Vision, 1990, Proceedings, IEEE, 1990, pp. 606–615.

[13] C. Xu, J.L. Prince, Snakes, shapes, and gradient vector flow, TIP 7 (3) (1998) 359–369.

[14] T.F. Chan, L.A. Vese, Active contours without edges, IEEE Transactions on Image Processing 10 (2) (2001) 266–277.

[15] D.N. Metaxas, Physics-Based Deformable Models: Applications to Computer Vision, Graphics, and Medical Imaging, 1st ed., Kluwer Academic Publishers, Norwell, MA, USA, ISBN 0792398408, 1996.

[16] D.N. Metaxas, Physics-Based Deformable Models: Applications to Computer Vision, Graphics and Medical Imaging, vol. 389, Springer Science & Business Media, 2012.

[17] N. Paragios, A variational approach for the segmentation of the left ventricle in cardiac image analysis, International Journal of Computer Vision 50 (3) (2002) 345–362.

[18] M. Santarelli, V. Positano, C. Michelassi, M. Lombardi, L. Landini, Automated cardiac MR image segmentation: theory and measurement evaluation, Medical Engineering & Physics 25 (2) (2003) 149–159.

[19] P.F. Gotardo, K.L. Boyer, J. Saltz, S.V. Raman, A new deformable model for boundary tracking in cardiac MRI and its application to the detection of intra-ventricular dyssynchrony, in: 2006 IEEE Computer Society Conference on Computer Vision and Pattern Recognition, Vol. 1, IEEE, 2006, pp. 736–743.

[20] M.G. Uzunbaş, S. Zhang, K.M. Pohl, D. Metaxas, L. Axel, Segmentation of myocardium using deformable regions and graph cuts, in: 2012 9th IEEE International Symposium on Biomedical Imaging (ISBI), IEEE, 2012, pp. 254–257.

[21] P. Peng, K. Lekadir, A. Gooya, L. Shao, S.E. Petersen, A.F. Frangi, A review of heart chamber segmentation for structural and functional analysis using cardiac magnetic resonance imaging, Magnetic Resonance Materials in Physics, Biology and Medicine 29 (2) (2016) 155–195.

[22] X. Huang, D.N. Metaxas, Metamorphs: deformable shape and appearance models, IEEE Transactions on Pattern Analysis and Machine Intelligence 30 (8) (2008) 1444–1459.

[23] X. Cui, S. Zhang, J. Huang, X. Huang, D.N. Metaxas, L. Axel, Left endocardium segmentation using spatio-temporal metamorphs, in: 2012 9th IEEE International Symposium on Biomedical Imaging (ISBI), 2012, pp. 226–229.

[24] D. Terzopoulos, A. Witkin, M. Kass, Constraints on deformable models: recovering 3D shape and nonrigid motion, Artificial Intelligence 36 (1) (1988) 91–123.

[25] S. Zhang, X. Wang, D. Metaxas, T. Chen, L. Axel, LV surface reconstruction from sparse tMRI using Laplacian surface deformation and optimization, in: IEEE International Symposium on Biomedical Imaging: From Nano to Macro, ISBI'09, IEEE, 2009, pp. 698–701.

[26] J. Park, D. Metaxas, L. Axel, Analysis of left ventricular wall motion based on volumetric deformable models and MRI-SPAMM, Medical Image Analysis 1 (1) (1996) 53–71.

[27] I. Haber, D.N. Metaxas, L. Axel, Three-dimensional motion reconstruction and analysis of the right ventricle using tagged MRI, Medical Image Analysis 4 (4) (2000) 335–355.

[28] T. Chen, X. Wang, S. Chung, D. Metaxas, L. Axel, Automated 3D motion tracking using Gabor filter bank, robust point matching, and deformable models, IEEE Transactions on Medical Imaging 29 (1) (2010) 1–11.

[29] Y. Yu, S. Zhang, K. Li, D. Metaxas, L. Axel, Deformable models with sparsity constraints for cardiac motion analysis, Medical Image Analysis 18 (6) (2014) 927–937.

[30] H.C. Van Assen, M.G. Danilouchkine, A.F. Frangi, S. Ordás, J.J. Westenberg, J.H. Reiber, et al., SPASM: a 3D-ASM for segmentation of sparse and arbitrarily oriented cardiac MRI data, Medical Image Analysis 10 (2) (2006) 286–303.

[31] S.C. Mitchell, B.P. Lelieveldt, R.J. Van Der Geest, H.G. Bosch, J. Reiver, M. Sonka, Multistage hybrid active appearance model matching: segmentation of left and right ventricles in cardiac MR images, IEEE Transactions on Medical Imaging 20 (5) (2001) 415–423.

[32] R.J. van der Geest, B.P. Lelieveldt, E. Angelié, M. Danilouchkine, C. Swingen, M. Sonka, et al., Evaluation of a new method for automated detection of left ventricular boundaries in time series of magnetic resonance images using an active appearance motion model, Journal of Cardiovascular Magnetic Resonance 6 (3) (2004) 609–617.

[33] M.R. Kaus, J. Von Berg, J. Weese, W. Niessen, V. Pekar, Automated segmentation of the left ventricle in cardiac MRI, Medical Image Analysis 8 (3) (2004) 245–254.

[34] K. Lekadir, R. Merrifield, G.Z. Yang, Outlier detection and handling for robust 3-d active shape models search, IEEE Transactions on Medical Imaging 26 (2) (2007) 212–222.

[35] A. Andreopoulos, J.K. Tsotsos, Efficient and generalizable statistical models of shape and appearance for analysis of cardiac MRI, Medical Image Analysis 12 (3) (2008) 335–357.

[36] Y. Zheng, A. Barbu, B. Georgescu, M. Scheuering, D. Comaniciu, Four-chamber heart modeling and automatic segmentation for 3-d cardiac CT volumes using marginal space learning and steerable features, IEEE Transactions on Medical Imaging 27 (11) (2008) 1668–1681.

[37] M. Afshin, I.B. Ayed, K. Punithakumar, M.W. Law, A. Islam, A. Goela, et al., Regional assessment of cardiac left ventricular myocardial function via MRI statistical features, IEEE Transactions on Medical Imaging 33 (2) (2014) 481–494.

[38] W. Bai, W. Shi, C. Ledig, D. Rueckert, Multi-atlas segmentation with augmented features for cardiac MR images, Medical Image Analysis 19 (1) (2015) 98–109.

[39] X. Zhen, A. Islam, M. Bhaduri, I. Chan, S. Li, Direct and simultaneous four-chamber volume estimation by multi-output regression, in: International Conference on Medical Image Computing and Computer-Assisted Intervention, Springer, 2015, pp. 669–676.

[40] R.P. Poudel, P. Lamata, G. Montana, Recurrent fully convolutional neural networks for multi-slice MRI cardiac segmentation, in: Reconstruction, Segmentation, and Analysis of Medical Images, Springer, 2016, pp. 83–94.

[41] L.K. Tan, Y.M. Liew, E. Lim, R.A. McLaughlin, Convolutional neural network regression for short-axis left ventricle segmentation in cardiac cine MR sequences, Medical Image Analysis 39 (2017) 78–86.

[42] L.K. Tan, R.A. McLaughlin, E. Lim, Y.F. Abdul Aziz, Y.M. Liew, Fully automated segmentation of the left ventricle in cine cardiac MRI using neural network regression, Journal of Magnetic Resonance Imaging 48 (1) (2018) 140–152.

[43] B. Kong, Y. Zhan, M. Shin, T. Denny, S. Zhang, Recognizing end-diastole and end-systole frames via deep temporal regression network, in: International Conference on Medical Image Computing and Computer-Assisted Intervention, Springer, 2016, pp. 264–272.

[44] T.A. Ngo, Z. Lu, G. Carneiro, Combining deep learning and level set for the automated segmentation of the left ventricle of the heart from cardiac cine magnetic resonance, Medical Image Analysis 35 (2017) 159–171.

[45] M. Avendi, A. Kheradvar, H. Jafarkhani, A combined deep-learning and deformable-model approach to fully automatic segmentation of the left ventricle in cardiac MRI, Medical Image Analysis 30 (2016) 108–119.

[46] M.R. Avendi, A. Kheradvar, H. Jafarkhani, Automatic segmentation of the right ventricle from cardiac MRI using a learning-based approach, Magnetic Resonance in Medicine 78 (6) (2017) 2439–2448.

[47] D. Yang, Q. Huang, L. Axel, D. Metaxas, Multi-component deformable models coupled with 2D–3D U-Net for automated probabilistic segmentation of cardiac walls and blood, in: 2018 IEEE 15th International Symposium on Biomedical Imaging, ISBI 2018, IEEE, 2018, pp. 479–483.

[48] F. Isensee, P.F. Jaeger, P.M. Full, I. Wolf, S. Engelhardt, K.H. Maier-Hein, Automatic cardiac disease assessment on cine-MRI via time-series segmentation and domain specific features, in: International Workshop on Statistical Atlases and Computational Models of the Heart, STACOM, Springer, 2017, pp. 120–129.

[49] M. Khened, V.A. Kollerathu, G. Krishnamurthi, Fully convolutional multi-scale residual densenets for cardiac segmentation and automated cardiac diagnosis using ensemble of classifiers, preprint, arXiv: 1801.05173, 2018.

[50] W. Xue, G. Brahm, S. Pandey, S. Leung, S. Li, Full left ventricle quantification via deep multitask relationships learning, Medical Image Analysis 43 (2018) 54–65.

[51] O. Bernard, A. Lalande, C. Zotti, F. Cervenansky, X. Yang, P.A. Heng, et al., Deep learning techniques for automatic MRI cardiac multi-structures segmentation and diagnosis: is the problem solved? IEEE Transactions on Medical Imaging 37 (11) (2018) 2514–2525.

[52] Q. Xia, Y. Yao, Z. Hu, A. Hao, Automatic 3D atrial segmentation from GE-MRIs using volumetric fully convolutional networks, in: International Workshop on Statistical Atlases and Computational Modeling of the Heart, STACOM, Springer, 2018.

[53] J. Li, Z. Hu, Left ventricle full quantification using deep layer aggregation based multitask relationship learning, in: International Workshop on Statistical Atlases and Computational Modeling of the Heart, STACOM, Springer, 2018.

[54] S. Queirós, D. Barbosa, B. Heyde, P. Morais, J.L. Vilaça, D. Friboulet, et al., Fast automatic myocardial segmentation in 4D cine CMR datasets, Medical Image Analysis 18 (7) (2014) 1115–1131.

[55] O. Ronneberger, P. Fischer, T. Brox, U-Net: convolutional networks for biomedical image segmentation, in: International Conference on Medical Image Computing and Computer-Assisted Intervention, Springer, 2015, pp. 234–241.

[56] Z. Li, Y. Lou, Z. Yan, S. Al'Aref, J.K. Min, L. Axel, D.N. Metaxas, Fully automatic segmentation of short-axis cardiac MRI using modified deep layer aggregation, in: 2019 IEEE 16th International Symposium on Biomedical Imaging, ISBI, 2019, pp. 793–797.

[57] C. Yu, J. Wang, C. Peng, C. Gao, G. Yu, N. Sang, Learning a discriminative feature network for semantic segmentation, in: Proceedings of the IEEE Conference on Computer Vision and Pattern Recognition, 2018, pp. 1–8.

[58] F. Yu, D. Wang, E. Shelhamer, T. Darrell, Deep layer aggregation, in: Proceedings of the IEEE Conference on Computer Vision and Pattern Recognition, 2018, pp. 2403–2412.

[59] V. Nair, G.E. Hinton, Rectified linear units improve restricted Boltzmann machines, in: Proceedings of the 27th International Conference on Machine Learning, ICML-10, 2010, pp. 807–814.

[60] S. Ioffe, C. Szegedy, Batch normalization: accelerating deep network training by reducing internal covariate shift, preprint, arXiv:1502.03167, 2015.

[61] F. Milletari, N. Navab, S.A. Ahmadi, V-net: fully convolutional neural networks for volumetric medical image segmentation, in: 2016 Fourth International Conference on 3D Vision (3DV), IEEE, 2016, pp. 565–571.

[62] R.T. Rockafellar, R.J.B. Wets, Variational Analysis, vol. 317, Springer Science & Business Media, 2009.

[63] D.P. Kingma, J.L. Ba, Adam: a method for stochastic optimization, in: Proc. 3rd Int. Conf. Learn. Representations, 2014.

[64] T.F. Cootes, C.J. Taylor, D.H. Cooper, J. Graham, Active shape models – their training and application, Computer Vision and Image Understanding 61 (1) (1995) 38–59.

[65] S. Zhang, Y. Zhan, M. Dewan, J. Huang, D.N. Metaxas, X.S. Zhou, Towards robust and effective shape modeling: sparse shape composition, Medical Image Analysis 16 (1) (2012) 265–277.

[66] S. Zhang, Y. Zhan, D.N. Metaxas, Deformable segmentation via sparse representation and dictionary learning, Medical Image Analysis 16 (7) (2012) 1385–1396.

[67] G. Wang, S. Zhang, F. Li, L. Gu, A new segmentation framework based on sparse shape composition in liver surgery planning system, Medical Physics 40 (5) (2013).

[68] G. Wang, S. Zhang, H. Xie, D.N. Metaxas, L. Gu, A homotopy-based sparse representation for fast and accurate shape prior modeling in liver surgical planning, Medical Image Analysis 19 (1) (2015) 176–186.

[69] S. Zhang, Y. Zhan, Y. Zhou, M. Uzunbas, D.N. Metaxas, Shape prior modeling using sparse representation and online dictionary learning, in: International Conference on Medical Image Computing and Computer-Assisted Intervention, Springer, 2012, pp. 435–442.

[70] C. Tan, K. Li, Z. Yan, D. Yang, S. Zhang, H.J. Yu, et al., A detection-driven and sparsity-constrained deformable model for fascia lata labeling and thigh inter-muscular adipose quantification, Computer Vision and Image Understanding 151 (2016) 80–89.

[71] D. Yang, P. Wu, C. Tan, K.M. Pohl, L. Axel, D. Metaxas, 3D motion modeling and reconstruction of left ventricle wall in cardiac MRI, in: International Conference on Functional Imaging and Modeling of the Heart, Springer, 2017, pp. 481–492.

[72] K. McLeish, D.L. Hill, D. Atkinson, J.M. Blackall, R. Razavi, A study of the motion and deformation of the heart due to respiration, IEEE Transactions on Medical Imaging 21 (9) (2002) 1142–1150.

[73] A. Myronenko, X. Song, Point set registration: coherent point drift, IEEE Transactions on Pattern Analysis and Machine Intelligence 32 (12) (2010) 2262–2275.

CHAPTER 13

Image registration with sliding motion

Mattias P. Heinrich[a]**, Bartłomiej W. Papież**[b]

[a]Institute of Medical Informatics, University of Lübeck, Lübeck, Germany
[b]Big Data Institute, University of Oxford, Oxford, United Kingdom

Contents

13.1.	Challenges of motion discontinuities in medical imaging	293
13.2.	Sliding preserving regularization for Demons	296
	13.2.1 Direction-dependent and layerwise regularization	297
	13.2.2 Locally adaptive regularization	297
	Demons with bilateral filtering	*297*
	GIFTed Demons	*299*
	13.2.2.1 Graph-based regularization for demons	*301*
13.3.	Discrete optimization for displacements	303
	13.3.1 Energy terms for discrete registration	305
	13.3.2 Practical concerns and implementation details for 3D discrete registration	306
	13.3.3 Parameterization of nodes and displacements	307
	13.3.3.1 Efficient inference of regularization	*308*
13.4.	Image registration for cancer applications	311
13.5.	Conclusions	313
	References	314

13.1. Challenges of motion discontinuities in medical imaging

Medical image registration is one of the most important subareas of medical image analysis. There have been numerous methodological developments over the last decades, beginning from the adaptation of optical flow techniques [20] for medical scans, the use of fluid–like demons forces [65], over the development of free-form deformations [51] to the use of discrete combinatorial optimization [13], as well as the use of deep neural networks [18]. Image registration deals with the spatial or spatiotemporal alignment of two or more 3D images of parts of the human body. Initially, the rigid alignment of two images acquired with different scanners (from multiple modalities) was the main clinical driver for algorithm development in that field, which led to the adaptation of the information theoretic measure mutual information to be applied to joint intensity histograms [72]. Currently, the field has matured and provides important support to a wide range of subsequent applications in both research and clinical practice [15]. In particular, registration can now address a large number of relevant tasks: assisting medical

Handbook of Medical Image Computing and Computer Assisted Intervention
https://doi.org/10.1016/B978-0-12-816176-0.00018-1

image interpretation and provide guidance for interventions. A comprehensive overview of the state-of-the-art can be found in [53]. Most work focuses on the establishment of dense spatial correspondences of multiple images of the same patient for motion estimation or the analysis of temporal changes, e.g., due to successful cancer treatment response. However, establishing common anatomical atlases by registering scans across different subjects can also be of great importance to neuroscience and population studies. In addition, image registration can be used to automatically propagate information from one scan to another, e.g., anatomical labels. For all these mentioned applications the estimation of a nonlinear transformation is necessary, that means it is no longer possible to parameterize the motion or deformation with a simple 3×4 transformation matrix. Instead, a dense deformation field is thought that assigns a − possibly different − 3D displacement vector to every voxel in the image with respect to a reference frame.

The estimation of a plausible displacement field that helps align two images is a challenging, often ill-posed problem. Many suitable transformations exist, there is often ambiguity when considering homogeneous tissues or in the presence of missing data due to scanner limitations. Furthermore there is no complete ground truth known to evaluate different algorithms, and surrogate measures, such as regional labels [49] or sparsely distributed anatomical landmarks, [36] have to be used. Another way to evaluate image registration is to use realistic 3D and 4D phantom imaging data such as XCAT [63].

A typical registration algorithm consists of at least three components: a similarity metric that reflects the (local) alignment quality based on image intensities; a regularization and transformation model that aims to avoid implausible noisy deformations; and an optimization strategy, which is used to find the best solution for a new image pair. These methodological components are either explicitly stated in a cost function or implicitly combined within the algorithm (the Demons algorithm [65], for instance, couples an optimization strategy and similarity metric). Often the three different components can be chosen in a modular fashion and are interchangeable across different software frameworks. We will in particular discuss image registration using two approaches, first the Demons framework in Sect. 13.2, which is widely used, easy to implement, and flexible in its parameterization. Subsequently, we will explain the concept and use of discrete registration and its potential for sliding motion in Sect. 13.3. The focus of this chapter will be on the modeling of complex motion patterns that can be found for the registration of different anatomical regions and are not always reflected correctly in standard regularization and transformation models. In general, a widely used assumption in medical image registration is that of a smooth displacement field. Since, body organs usually consist of soft compressible tissues and joints can freely rotate the majority of the three-dimensional motion within the inside of our bodies is indeed without spatial discontinuities. When considering optical flow estimation in natural (camera) videos, there are many rapid changes in motion due to occlusions and contrary motions of

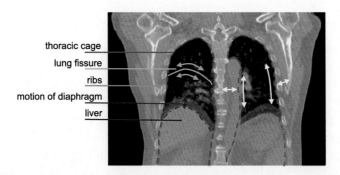

Figure 13.1 Overview of human anatomy that is mainly involved in respiratory sliding motion. The pleura acts as sliding interface between lungs and rib cage, while individual lung lobes can also slide against each other.

different objects against the background. But even in medical images, a fair amount of discontinuous motion can be found, which poses challenges for many commonly used algorithms.

In particular, when estimating motion within the thorax of lungs and liver, the occurrence of sliding motion along the individual lung lobes and even more pronounced along organ surfaces, in particular the lung pleura, becomes obvious. While the motion can be assumed to be smooth for the largest part of the image, severe errors would occur when this complex motion is not appropriately considered. Fig. 13.1 illustrates the anatomical implications of sliding motion, during respiration, on an example slice of a thoracic 4D CT scan. The inhale and exhale phases are overlaid to give a feeling of motion. Some key parts of the thoracic anatomy, as well as lung fissures and diaphragm motion, are outlined. The majority of lung motion is approximately in parallel to the lung boundary, as indicated by white arrows on right side; however, it has opposing directions for structures within and outside of the lung. This is the main reason for sliding and motion discontinuities at these interfaces. Due to respiratory, cardiac, or peristaltic motion, sliding can occur for the liver and many other anatomical regions including bowels, heart, kidneys, and others. Another situation where discontinuous deformations have to be addressed is present when aligning subjects with large anatomical variations, e.g., to build a population atlas. To construct a registration algorithm that handles sliding and discontinuous motion, a suitable adaptation of the regularization and transformation model is often essential, since the commonly employed global smoothness assumption is invalidated. In addition, it can be of advantage to intrinsically detect the locations, in particular surfaces, in a scan at which sliding might occur to use this information to obtain a better regularization model.

13.2. Sliding preserving regularization for Demons

The classic approaches to deformable image registration (DIR) rely on the estimation of smooth and continuous deformation fields, in particular, the Demons registration algorithm is decomposed into two alternating subproblems: minimizing the chosen similarity measure, followed by a general convolution-based regularization model [65,69]. In the original version of the Demons, the similarity measure $Sim(I_f, I_m(\vec{u}))$ between a fixed I_f and a moving image I_m is formulated as the sum of squared intensity differences (SSD) $\frac{1}{2}\|I_f - I_m(\vec{u})\|^2$, while a diffusion based regularization $Reg(\vec{u}) = \|\vec{u}\|^2$ of the deformation field $\vec{u}$ is performed by Gaussian smoothing. The final solution is approximated by an iterative Gaussian convolution $G_{\vec{x}}$ on the deformation field as follows:

$$\vec{u}_{i+1}(\vec{x}) = G_{\vec{x}} * \left(\vec{u}_i(\vec{x}) \circ \vec{du}_i(\vec{x}) \right) \tag{13.1}$$

where $\vec{u}_i$ is the deformation field estimated at iteration i, $\vec{du}$ is the force term that corresponds to the similarity measure Sim, and $\circ$ is the composition operator. However, such an isotropic and homogeneous regularization model is usually inadequate to enforce the plausibility of the estimated deformation field in many applications. Therefore, more advanced models are required to adequately mimic complex thoracic or abdominal motions, where locally discontinuous motion patterns (sliding) are typical, mostly due to respiratory motion. Estimation of local motion properties have been addressed by several deformable image registration algorithms including the use of an anisotropic, image-driven regularization [38,57,7], which smoothes the deformation field along edges but not across them. Considering that detection of edges in medical imaging could be challenging, e.g., due the low contrast of liver tissue in CT, later approaches also investigated flow-driven, and image-and-flow regularization models to reliably estimate the direction and magnitude of the deformation field [48,77]. Filtering of deformation fields within the predefined region to preserve rigidity of the ribs was introduced in [55], where the deformation field was repeatedly averaged within a mask. However, none of these approaches have explicitly addressed the discontinuities at sliding interfaces.

For most Demons-based DIR methods, the existing diffusion-based regularization models that accommodate sliding motion can be classified into two categories: direction-dependent regularization [60,39] and locally adaptive regularization [42,40, 46,26,41]. Some of these methods rely on estimating different domains or layers of motion first, often with help of segmentation approaches. We will give a brief overview of direction-dependent and layer-wise regularization and then explain locally adaptive regularization in more details.

Aside from Demons registration, other approaches have been proposed for DIR that use locally adaptive regularization to produce the sliding motion at the pleural cavity boundaries. These include spline-based registration methods, i.e., performing independent Free Form Deformation (FFD) of regions on either side of a discontinuity using masks [73], the decomposition of a B-Spline transformation into the tangential and normal directions at the control points [8], or eXtended FFD that adds an auxiliary structure describing the location of the discontinuity surface [19]. Similarly, the Large Deformation Diffeomorphic Metric Mapping (LDDMM) framework was extended towards a piecewise-diffeomorphic registration to model sliding motion [52].

13.2.1 Direction-dependent and layerwise regularization

Earlier work on estimating sliding motion in medical scans focused on the development of direction-dependent regularization (DDR) methods [60,39], where the modeling of discontinuities between the neighboring structures was explicitly incorporated into the regularization model. Direction-dependent regularization extends diffusion-like regularization by decomposing the estimated deformation field $\vec{u}$ into two components: normal $\vec{u}^{\perp}$ and tangential $\vec{u}^{\parallel}$ directions at the sliding interfaces as follows:

$$Reg(\vec{u}) = \int_{\Omega} \|\vec{u}^{\perp}\|^2 d\vec{x} + \int_{\Gamma} \|\vec{u}^{\parallel}\|^2 d\vec{x} + \int_{\Omega - \Gamma} \|\vec{u}^{\parallel}\|^2 d\vec{x}. \tag{13.2}$$

Smoothing in the normal direction is performed on the whole volume domain Ω, while smoothing between sliding surfaces is performed independently for each object Γ and $\Omega - \Gamma$, respectively. Encoding anatomical knowledge about organ motion properties is hence required to localize the interface where sliding motion occurs in order to reduce smoothing across these objects. This may be considered itself a challenging problem as a priori knowledge in the form of organ segmentation is required [39]; however, a method for an automated detection of sliding organ motion was presented in [60].

The idea of estimating multiple motion fields separately for different complementary regions in an image sequence has also been proposed in computer vision for a piecewise affine optical flow model [70] and later been extended to simultaneous motion layer segmentation and displacement estimation [62]. In [71] both motion layers and a learned PCA basis of statistically likely motion fields was employed. A first method that uses a thoracic segmentation as motion mask was presented for medical 4D CT images in [67] and later used in a similar way in [52]. Once, different subdomains are defined the motion in each part of the volume is treated independently. An important limitation of these methods is that at the interface implausible folding (crossing-over of motion vectors) across domains.

13.2.2 Locally adaptive regularization
Demons with bilateral filtering

To address both the sliding motion occurring at the pleural cavity boundary and the smooth motion within the lungs without the necessity for a prior segmentation, a modified Demons method was proposed in [42]. A pragmatic way to model sliding motion was to replace the Gaussian kernel (Eq. (13.1)) by a regularization kernel that can incorporate prior knowledge about the medical volumes to be registered. The standard Gaussian filtering of the deformation field was therefore replaced by a modified bilateral filtering technique [66] that prevents the deformation field to be filtered across sliding structure boundaries. The bilateral filtering is nonlinear filtering technique, widely used for image denoising, where an input image I_{input} at the spatial location $\vec{x}$ is filtered using a combination of two Gaussian kernels in the following way:

$$
I_{output}(\vec{x}) = \frac{1}{W(\vec{x})} \sum_{\vec{y} \in \mathcal{N}(\vec{x})} \underbrace{\exp\left(-\frac{(\vec{x}-\vec{y})^T(\vec{x}-\vec{y})}{2\sigma_{\vec{x}}^2}\right)}_{G_{\vec{x}}(\vec{x},\vec{y})}
$$
$$
\underbrace{\exp\left(-\frac{\|I_{input}(\vec{x}) - I_{input}(\vec{y})\|^2}{2\sigma_r^2}\right)}_{G_r(I(\vec{x}),I(\vec{y}))} I_{input}(\vec{y}), \tag{13.3}
$$

where $G_{\vec{x}}$ is a Gaussian kernel of variance $\sigma_{\vec{x}}^2$ defined on the spatial domain, and G_r is a Gaussian kernel of variance σ_r^2 defined on the intensity domain I_{input}, $\vec{y}$ is a spatial location within the local neighborhood $\mathcal{N}$ (centered on the position $\vec{x}$, e.g., a square window of size N), and $W(\vec{x})$ is a normalization factor for this image neighborhood. Using spatial proximity and intensity differences only in the regularization scheme, namely

$$
\vec{u}_{i+1}(\vec{x}) = G_x G_r * (\vec{u}_i(\vec{x}) \circ \vec{du}(\vec{x})), \tag{13.4}
$$

introduces *motion oversegmentation*, as each intensity change in the image (within a range of σ_r^2) imposes artificial deformation field discontinuities, resulting in nonphysically plausible deformation, which is typical for image-driven regularization [77]. Additionally, some organs have very similar intensity values, but slide along each other.

Therefore, to evade such a problem, a supplementary kernel to detect discontinuities in the motion field was added to the original bilateral filtering for deformation fields in the following way:

$$
\vec{u}_{i+1}(\vec{x}) = \frac{1}{W(\vec{x})} \sum_{\vec{y} \in \mathcal{N}(\vec{x})} G_{\vec{x}}(\vec{x},\vec{y}) G_r(I(\vec{x}), I(\vec{y}))
$$
$$
\underbrace{\exp\left(-\frac{(\vec{u}_{i-1}(\vec{x}) - \vec{u}_{i-1}(\vec{y}))^T (\vec{u}_{i-1}(\vec{x}) - \vec{u}_{i-1}(\vec{y}))}{2\sigma_{\vec{u}}^2}\right)}_{G_{\vec{u}}(\vec{u}(\vec{x}),\vec{u}(\vec{y}))} \vec{u}_i(\vec{y}), \tag{13.5}
$$

where $G_{\vec{u}}$ describes a Gaussian kernel based on the local deformation field dissimilarity and $\vec{u}_i(\vec{x}) = \vec{u}_{i-1}(\vec{x}) \circ \vec{du}(\vec{x})$. The filtering procedure with the new kernel $G_{\vec{u}}$ helps

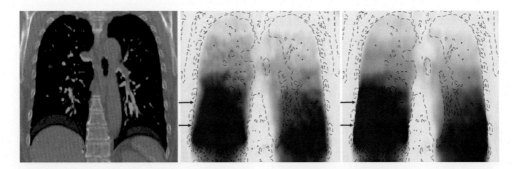

Figure 13.2 Example of Demons registration using isotropic Gaussian filtering and bilateral filtering for a CT lung data inhale/exhale pair. From left to right: coronal view of reference lung CT with the corresponding overlap of exhale image (red and green); and color-coded deformations for the standard Demons [69], and Demons with bilateral filtering [42]. The results demonstrate that Demons with bilateral filtering improves registration accuracy yielding a smooth deformation field inside the pleura cavity and simultaneously preserving sliding motion at the lung boundary.

reduce smoothing across the boundaries of structures having both different intensities and deformation field patterns, hence maintaining both continuous and discontinuous deformations in the whole image domain.

Visual analysis of registration results using the Demons with bilateral filtering is presented in Fig. 13.2. As can be seen, the Demons with bilateral filtering decreases the amount of smoothing between lungs and the mediastinum, thus remarkably enhances a level of sliding.

GIFTed Demons

Adding supplementary kernels to the bilateral filtering procedure appears to be a simple way to achieve a more accurate handling of sliding motion, however, due to spatially-varying filtering methodology, which is applied to the deformation fields at each iteration, a substantial amount of computational time is required. From a technical point of view, this limitation could be alleviated using more efficient algorithms, e.g., an approximated version of kernels (for a comprehensive review, see [44]) or a recursive bilateral filtering [75]. However, in order to easily increase the options of replacing a Gaussian kernel by a wide spectrum of available filtering techniques, a GIFTed Demons [40], based on the **G**uided **I**mage **F**itering **T**echnique [23], was proposed. Such a substitution offers the opportunity to design regularization kernels using additional (e.g., anatomical) information from so-called *guidance* images, providing accurate and fast locally adaptive regularization. To define the guided image filtering, the (output) filtered image I_{output} is considered as a locally linear model with respect to the guidance image I_g:

$$I_{output}(\vec{x}) = \gamma_{\mathcal{N}} I_g(\vec{x}) + \beta_{\mathcal{N}}, \tag{13.6}$$

where $\gamma_\mathcal{N}$ and $\beta_\mathcal{N}$ are coefficients estimated within the local neighborhood $\mathcal{N}$, by minimizing the difference between the input I_{input} and output image I_{output}, as follows:

$$\gamma_\mathcal{N} = \frac{\mu_{(I_g I_{input})} + \mu_{I_g}\mu_{I_{input}}}{\sigma^2_{I_g} + \varepsilon}, \qquad \beta_\mathcal{N} = \mu_{I_{input}} + \gamma_\mathcal{N}\mu_{I_g}, \qquad (13.7)$$

where μ_{I_g}, $\mu_{I_{input}}$, and $\mu_{(I_g I_{input})}$ are the intensity means of the guidance image I_g, input image I_{input}, and $I_g I_{input}$, respectively, and $\sigma^2_{I_g}$ is the intensity variance of the guidance image I_g estimated in the local neighborhood $\mathcal{N}$. The weighting parameter $\varepsilon > 0$ controls the degree of the edge-preserving properties for guided image filtering, while in the proposed regularization model can be considered as the degree of how much of the local structures are transferred from any guidance image I_g to the output displacement field.

For the GIFTed Demons, the guided image filter was used as a weighted averaging operator on the deformation field $\vec{u}$, replacing the convolution by a Gaussian kernel $G_{\vec{x}}$ (compare with Eq. (13.1)) in the following way:

$$\vec{u}_{i+1}(\vec{x}) = \sum_{\vec{y}\in\mathcal{N}} W_{GIF}(I_g, \vec{x}, \vec{y})\vec{u}_i(\vec{y}). \qquad (13.8)$$

The filtered deformation field $\vec{u}_{i+1}$ can be also considered as a weighted average of the guidance image I_g, and thus it can be expressed in the explicit form of kernel weights $W_{GIF}(I_g)$ operating at a spatial location $(\vec{x})$:

$$W_{GIF}(I_g, \vec{x}, \vec{y}) = 1 + \frac{(I_g(\vec{x}) - \mu_{I_g})(I_g(\vec{y}) - \mu_{I_g})}{\sigma^2_{I_g} + \varepsilon}. \qquad (13.9)$$

This regularization method requires the provision of the guidance image I_g that could propagate information about sliding interfaces to the estimated displacement field, while preserving smoothness inside organs of interest. In the simplest scenario, such information about sliding surfaces could come directly from the images to be registered (so-called *self-guidance*), however, such an approach suffers from the drawbacks of the aforementioned image-driven regularizers. An alternative approach would be to use motion mask (as described in Sect. 13.2.1) to detect sliding surfaces [47,73,67], then such a segmentation mask can be used as an auxiliary image to guide filtering of the displacement field. As discussed before, the automatic segmentation of lung motion can be considered as relatively straightforward task due primarily to the fact that there is a large difference in attenuation between normal lung parenchyma and the surrounding tissue, while generating motion masks of sliding surfaces in the abdomen may be challenging due low contrast of liver tissue in CT. Additionally, liver motion is also far more complex than that of the lungs, as the liver exhibits not only sliding motions against thoracic cage; but also moves against other surrounding organs in the abdomen and the abdominal wall [5].

For this reason, in [41] an alternative approach to generate an appropriate guidance image for a particular DIR application based on pseudo-segmentation using a clustering method was exploited. The Simple Linear Iterative Clustering (SLIC) algorithm [2] generates a regular and compact clustering, corresponding to spatial proximity and appearance similarity. Such clustering reduces redundant intensity information of voxels in essentially homogeneous areas, however, it also tends to give quite inconsistent results in large constant image regions, as noise estimates dominate the behavior of the algorithm. In the context of filtering the displacement field during registration, this is a major drawback, because filtering with respect to the inaccurately clustered image would introduce artificial discontinuities (similar to using self-guidance). In order to avoid such a problem, multiple channels of supervoxels (with randomly perturbed initial cluster centers) to obtain a piecewise smooth displacement model while preserving true motion discontinuities for image areas with sufficient structural content, cf. [21]. Then, each layer of supervoxels is used as a separate channel of guidance image I_g performing filtering of the displacement field with respect to such a multichannel guidance image.

More recently, spatially adaptive filtering of the displacement field using the guided image filtering technique was extended to its 4D regularization counterpart, where the estimated deformation field is additionally filtered by considering the temporal context of the guidance information encoded in the dynamic imaging [45]. The 4D regularization method is composed of two main steps: spatial adaptive filtering of the deformation field to enforce discontinuity preserving properties at lung interfaces; and an additional adaptive temporal filtering of the deformation fields to capture of temporal changes of the patient's irregular motion pattern.

13.2.2.1 Graph-based regularization for demons

For a number of medical applications, the direction-dependent [60,39], bilateral-like [42], and guided filter [40] regularization models provide very reasonable deformations to model complex motion patterns. Although the use of such regularizers considerably improves performance, it remains the case that such approaches perform regularization considering only the predefined local neighborhood around the point of interest, despite the fact that some organs can also deform in a manner that is not captured in such local neighborhood. However, extending the spatial range (e.g., a window of kernel size N) of the regularization of the deformations to become less local is usually computationally prohibitive. In such cases, neither global nor local regularization models are sufficiently versatile to handle the complexity of the organ motion, and thus graph-based regularization was introduced [46]. The graphical models have ability to represent complex connection between structures in a perceptually meaningful way, and thus graph-based

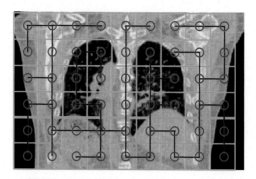

Figure 13.3 Visualization of graph derived from image and corresponding minimum spanning tree extracted from this graph as proposed in [16].

regularization provides a mathematical framework within which local, semilocal, and global constraints can be accommodated in a natural manner. The structures and connections between them can be represented, for example, by a Minimum Spanning Tree (MST), which has been shown to replicate well the underlying tissue properties and structure of anatomical connectivity [16]. In contrast to bilateral filter [42] and guided image filter [40] models, the proposed new regularization model implicitly extends local filter kernels to their nonlocal counterparts by simultaneous consideration of spatial and intensity proximity together with the connectivity of voxel-based nodes. First, a graph $G = (V, E)$ is defined comprising a set of nodes V (corresponding to voxels of the image volume) and a set of edges E (connecting all nearest neighbor nodes). For the constructed weighted graph G, an MST is found, connecting all nodes in the graph in the form of a tree, thus removing edges with large weights often marking edges crossing different organs. An example of MST is shown in Fig. 13.3, generated from the graph representing a 2D coronal slice of a lung CT. The remaining connections between nodes form the adaptive implicit support region composed by the voxels with large kernel weights in the entire image domain. Such kernels have a big advantage over the predefined local box window [39,42,41] in presenting the structure of an image for the reason that MST can efficiently present the structure of an image, and so the kernel weights of the filter defined on the MST avoid regularization across organ boundaries. To visualize the key differences between the local regularization models and the graph-based regularization model, example kernels for the bilateral model [42], and the graph-based regularization model [46] are shown in Fig. 13.4.

From a computational point of view, a major advantage of the guided filtering and graph-based regularization is a possibility to use a moving sum method [23] or an MST cost aggregation method [76] for efficient implementation. Guided image filtering has linear complexity with respect to the number of image voxels significantly improving performance compared to the bilateral filtering approach, which may be particularly

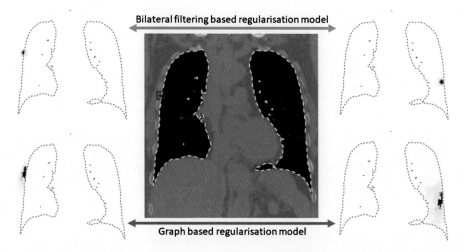

Figure 13.4 Visualization of two different kernels based on input image for the local model [42], and the graph-based regularization model for two distinctive areas selected inside (red cross) and outside the thoracic cage (magenta cross). The implicit support region provided by the graph-based regularization method can efficiently extend to the structure of an image contrary to the predefined local region support of [42,40].

important for long temporal acquisitions. From a biological point of view, all regularization methods show promising performance on publicly available lung data set, and the state-of-the-art accuracy on liver CT data set. DIR that use locally adaptive regularization may be, however, preferable as does not require organ segmentation, which may be challenging to obtain due to low contrast of liver tissue in CT.

To further extend the abilities of handling sliding motion in cases of large deformation, we will discuss the use of graphical models for discrete optimization in the next section.

13.3. Discrete optimization for displacements

Most image registration algorithms rely on iterative solutions, where the motion between scans is estimated in several small steps and usually also in a coarse-to-fine manner. This procedure will often lead to excellent solutions when the cost function is smooth and the similarity metric contains few local optima. When looking at the challenges of registration of scans with sliding organ motion, it becomes obvious that these two prerequisites are often not fulfilled. An alternative strategy to address this problem is to reformulate the registration into a discrete optimization framework based on the graphical representation introduced above. Early research in computer vision for the estimation of disparities between two images (left and right) of a stereo camera has explored this concept (see [61] for a review) and it was shown that discrete displacement

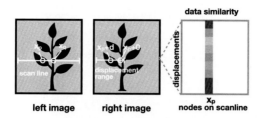

Figure 13.5 Concept of discrete optimization for finding stereo correspondences. Given a pixel (node) in the left camera image, one can calculate the unary data term with respect to each of the specified displacements of this pixel in the right image. For each scan-line (sequence of nodes in left image), we obtain a 2D array of displacement beliefs.

estimation works in particular well for discontinuous, piecewise smooth solutions. Estimating depth from stereo images, which can be seen as a 1D image registration task, has in itself several applications in medical imaging, cf. [35], but in this chapter it will be used to introduce the general principle of discrete optimization, which will later on be extended to 3D motion. In this section we begin by explaining the concept in detail on the example of finding discrete displacements in stereo optimization. Subsequently, we briefly discuss some advantages and challenges of graphical or combinatorial optimization strategies for the estimation of deformations in medical imaging, and sliding motion in particular. Finally, we present two well-known discrete registration algorithms, **drop** [13] and **deeds** [16], that are often used in practice in medical imaging research.

As mentioned before, the aim of stereo processing is to estimate the displacement between left and right camera frames. The notation in the section will follow [50]. First, we represent the reference image (left in our case) as a graph $G = (V, E)$, by subdividing the image domain into a set of nodes (or vertices) V and a set of pairwise edges E. The nodes could be either directly represent the pixels or another lower dimensional representation such as a supervoxel graph [17] or control points in a free-form deformation [51]. Consider a pixel at node p, which is located on the object in the left frame of a stereo pair as shown in Fig. 13.5. The same corresponding object pixel will be displaced by a certain distance in the right image depending on the depth. We can imagine a potential range of displacements $\mathcal{L}$, which will correspond to a discrete set of displacement labels $d_i, d_j, \ldots$ (which are inversely related to scene depth). In order to automatically find the best assignment $f : \{p, q, \ldots\} \to \{d_k, d_i, \ldots\}$, a data term (similarity metric) $\mathcal{D}(p, d_k)$ is first defined for each individual label assignment from a node to a displacement (see Fig. 13.6). Note that in contrast to previous registration approaches, where the (local) deformation was represented by a real-valued variable for each pixel (or control point), in a discrete registration approach we find a probability distribution over the range of potential displacements.

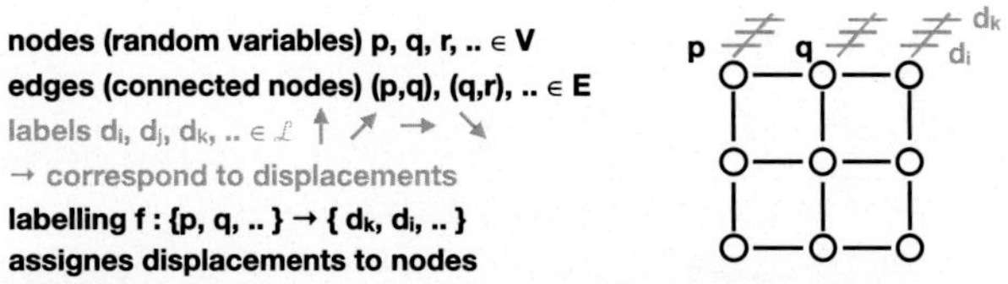

nodes (random variables) p, q, r, .. ∈ **V**

edges (connected nodes) (p,q), (q,r), .. ∈ **E**

labels d_i, d_j, d_k, .. ∈ $\mathcal{L}$ ↑ ↗ → ↘

→ correspond to displacements

labelling **f** : {p, q, .. } → { d_k, d_i, .. }

assignes displacements to nodes

Figure 13.6 Basics of graphical optimization for estimating discretized displacements. Local minima (globally poor solutions) can be avoided by sampling a dense and large enough range of motion vectors.

13.3.1 Energy terms for discrete registration

The **data term** $\mathcal{D}(k, d_q)$ is calculated in advance and could be as simple as absolute intensity differences (SAD), or a patch-based measure (such as local mutual information) and potentially be a learned metric. Subsequently, a displacement field could be obtained by selecting the optimal the displacement as the one with lowest data costs for each node individually. However, in practice the similarity metric does not entirely reflect the quality of a correspondence and in particular in areas of homogenous tissues it will be ambiguous. This brings us to the second part of graphical models, the definition of an edge system that can be employed to restrict the label assignment on two neighboring pairs of nodes jointly and serves as a **regularization term** $\mathcal{R}(d_p, d_q)$ that ensures piecewise smoothness.

Within a so called scan-line (sequence of horizontally connected nodes or chain) the optimization of both unary data costs and pairwise regularization terms can be solved using dynamic programming also known as Viterbi algorithm. The basic principle works as follows: instead of directly finding an optimal "hard assignment", we keep the probabilistic distribution of each potential solution for each node, which describes the accumulated belief of all previously visited nodes that a certain labeling is probable. We then continue to recursively optimize these displacement beliefs by computing an update formula. For a graph without loops, in general any tree, belief propagation can be used to find the exact marginal probabilities for each displacement at each node. Starting from the leaf nodes, messages m are passed along the edges $(p, q) \in E$ of the graph (from current node p to parent node q) and updated with the following computation of one element of m_{pq} [9]:

$$m_{kq}(d_q) = \min_{d_p} \mathcal{D}(p, d_q) + \mathcal{R}(d_p, d_q) + \sum_c m_{cp}(d_p), \qquad (13.10)$$

here c are the children of p. Since the last node (root) has no successor node, the forward path of the algorithm ends by simply selecting the displacement label with lowest cost and traversing back to select the best label for each node (given some additional stored information of label changes at each node). Alternatively, a second backward path

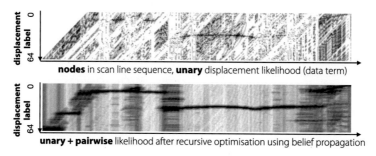

Figure 13.7 Visual example of displacement space for single line in image before (only unary term) and after spatial regularization. It becomes obvious that given the right choice of regularization penalty, a more confident choice for the right displacement label can be made and motion discontinuities can be preserved at the same time.

yields the probabilistic distribution for each node in the graph [21]. For arbitrary regularization terms $\mathcal{R}(d_p, d_q)$, every potential combination of two displacements d_p (from the current node p) and d_q (its parent q) would have to be calculated. A good choice for a very efficient regularization term that also enables the preservation of sliding motion will be discussed in Sect. 13.3.3.1. The effect of this sequential optimization and its regularizing effect of the displacement beliefs is visualized in Fig. 13.7. We can also note that given a suitably chosen pairwise term, the costs of neighboring pixel that are located at displacement discontinuities do not "bleed" into another and therefore a clear distinction of sliding motion becomes possible.

13.3.2 Practical concerns and implementation details for 3D discrete registration

Graph–based discrete optimization overcomes some aspects of continuous optimization: the restriction to sufficiently-differentiable similarity metrics and the avoidance of local minima and thereby the potential to correctly model large motion that may contain discontinuities, making it an attractive choice for deformable medical image registration involving complex motion. However, this comes at the cost of highly increased computational complexity, because the space of deformations needs to be discretized and therefore the number of degrees of freedom is drastically increased. This problem is naturally increased when moving from 1D displacement estimation (stereo processing) to full 3D motion. Consequently, suitable approximations have to be made so that the discrete optimization problem becomes computationally tractable, while retaining its superior robustness against local minima, and in order to make full use of the higher flexibility of the search space and similarity metric.

The complexity of the optimization problem is in the best case linearly dependent on the number of nodes n times all possible displacements of the label space $\mathcal{L}$. Considering a typical 3D registration problem with $n = 10^7$ voxels and a maximum motion of 15 voxels in each direction, so that $|\mathcal{L}| \approx 3 \times 10^4$, this problem will be intractable both in terms of computation time and memory requirements. In general, there are three approximations that can be made to find a suitable trade-off between the optimality of the solution and its tractability for practical application. These resolve around (1) the reduction of numbers or a hierarchical organization of nodes, (2) the restriction of the displacement space to fewer labels, and (3) the use of efficient optimization strategies.

13.3.3 Parameterization of nodes and displacements

A hierarchical subdivision of the image domain into groups of pixels has been proposed for discrete optimization for stereo by [10]. The solution is propagated from one to the next level in a coarse-to-fine manner. Still, the label-space is kept the same for all levels, resulting in very many degrees of freedom (for a 3D registration) at the finest scale. Another related approach to reduce the complexity is a parameterization of the transformation using a multilevel B-spline scheme [59], that was first proposed by [13] for discrete medical image registration. For a given level, the image is subdivided according to the control point grid into nonoverlapping cubic groups of voxels, which preserves the independence of the unary similarity term computation for all nodes. The data cost, which is incurred when moving a control point in the B-spline grid and thereby applying a discrete displacement to a cube is aggregated for all voxels within a cubic block. Subsequently, the regularization term is calculated only for each pair of control points.

Several hierarchical levels with decreasing grid-spacing g can be used, increasing the number of nodes for each finer level. The maximum number of displacement steps in the label space l_{max} can then be decreased correspondingly. The search space is defined as $\mathcal{L} = d \cdot \{0, \pm q, \pm 2q, \ldots, ql_{max}\}^3$ voxels, where q is a discretization step. Using this refinement approach, both high spatial accuracy and low computational complexity are achieved. By using same numbers for g and l_{max} for each level, the complexity is kept constant for all levels, because the number of similarity computations is $\sim K \cdot n/g^3 \cdot (2l_{max} + 1)^3 \approx 8Kn$, and thus linear with the number of voxels. For a finer level, the previous deformation field is obtained using the B-spline interpolation for voxels between control points and used as the prior deformation. In our experience, using a first order (linear) B-spline function provides best results for estimating lung motion, that contains sliding.

Another concept for reducing the number of free parameters is to employ only a sparse sampling of the deformation space in 3D, as done in the well-known discrete registration framework **drop** presented in [14] (see Fig. 13.8). This further reduces the complexity (especially the memory requirements of the employed FastPD optimization) of the registration, since instead of densely sampling the deformations in all three dimensions, only displacements along the three axes are considered. This may, however, lead to problems similar to the ones known for gradient-based optimization (local

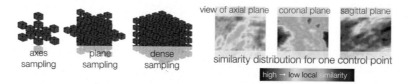

Figure 13.8 Overview of different approaches for sampling displacements in 3D space. Restricting the number of displacements to only axial directions can reduce the registration accuracy. While 2D or better 3D sampling enables high-quality alignment, it requires the use of efficient inference strategies to reduce computational demand.

minima, bias of initialization) and a nonoptimal registration with reduced accuracy, as shown in [64,16].

In the **deeds** framework (dense displacement sampling) [16] this approximation is therefore avoided, which led to improved results for intrapatient lung motion estimation (first place in EMPIRE10 challenge [50]) and abdominal intersubject registration (first place in independent comparison of six registration techniques on Beyond the Cranial Vault Dataset [74]). However, to limit the memory demand to few GBytes and the computation time to less than 5 minutes, two concepts originally proposed in computer vision in [68] and [10] have to be adapted. They are explained in the next section and form the basis for the **deeds** algorithm.

13.3.3.1 Efficient inference of regularization

First, the use of restricted graphical model relies on the minimum-spanning-tree, which has been introduced in Sect. 13.2.2.1. Second, the decomposition of the otherwise time-consuming optimization of the regularization term of 3D displacement spaces will be discussed using separable distance transforms and lower-envelope computations.

The aim is to avoid any potential local minima in the regularized cost function to fully exploit the potential of discrete registration for accurate sliding preserving alignment. For lung motion the search for potential matches could be over a range of finely quantized displacements as large as $d \in \mathcal{L} = \{0, \pm 2, \pm 4, \dots, \pm 32\}^3$ mm, resulting in a number of potential displacements of $|\mathcal{L}| = 35937$. First, for each of the $|\mathcal{L}|$ potential displacements, the matching likelihood is computed by summing over each element in the cubic block $|P_p|$ and its voxelwise dissimilarity costs. In practice, using a patch-size of 7^3 voxels with a stride of 2 is sufficient and yields $|P_p| = 64$ computations. Note that this step is directly related to traditional block-matching approaches [11], however, now instead of selecting an optimal displacement for each node p independently, we employ a diffusion–like regularizer $\mathcal{R}(d_p, d_q)$ that can also deal with sliding motion:

$$\mathcal{R}(d_p, d_q) := \frac{\alpha ||d_p - d_q||_2^2}{||x_p - x_q||_2 + |\mathcal{F}(p) - \mathcal{F}(q)|/\sigma_I}. \tag{13.11}$$

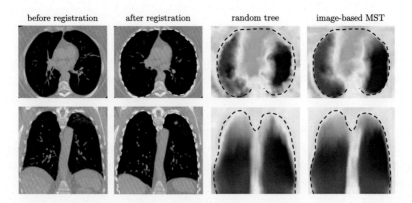

Figure 13.9 Example outcome of **deeds** registration for sliding motion estimation in lung CT. In contrast to an arbitrary randomly selected minimum-spanning-tree the image-adaptive regularization better preserves the discontinuity at the pleura. From Mattias P. Heinrich, Mark Jenkinson, Michael Brady, Julia A. Schnabel, MRF-based deformable registration and ventilation estimation of lung CT, IEEE Transactions on Medical Imaging, 32 (7) (July 2013), © 2013 IEEE.

Here, α is a user-determined weighting term that regularizes the degree of smoothness; the squared differences of displacements of two neighboring nodes p and q, which are connected by an edge (p, q), are penalized (normalized by their spatial and intensity distance of the fixed image F, with a modality-specific σ_I). Minimizing $\sum_{p \in V} \mathcal{D}(p, d_q) + \sum_{(p,q) \in E} \mathcal{R}(d_p, d_q)$ for a minimum-spanning-tree can be done exactly and efficiently using belief propagation as commonly done in part-based models [9,43]. It is important to note that the regularizer chosen in Eq. (13.11) for the computation of each message vector m_{pq} is particularly efficient when using fast distance transforms [9]. The so-called min-convolution technique reduces the complexity of regularization cost computations per pair of nodes from $|\mathcal{L}|^2$ to $|\mathcal{L}|$. It can be used for most common (pairwise) regularization terms, such as diffusion (squared difference of displacements) and total variation (absolute difference) regularization, by employing a lower envelope computation. When considering 2D or 3D displacement spaces a separable min-convolution is applicable similar to higher-dimensional Gaussian filtering. Each displacement label can be represented by an upward facing parabola rooted at $(d_p, D(d_p) + \sum_c m_{cp}(d_p))$. The minimization in Eq. (13.10) is defined by the lower envelope of these parabolas. There exists a simple graphical solution to find this lower envelope by calculating the intersection between the parabola of the current label and the right-most parabola of the lower envelope. This technique requires the definition of displacement labels $\mathcal{L}$ of both nodes to be equivalent. In [16], we made an extension to this method, which enables the use of an incremental regularization in a multilevel scheme.

In Fig. 13.9, we demonstrate the ability of the described discrete optimization framework with image-adaptive graphical regularization to handle sliding motion in lung CT. In terms of target registration errors, discrete optimization has set new state-of-the-art accuracies in two common registration tasks [50,74]. A combination with a subsequent continuous optimization was shown to improve the quality and smoothness of estimated transformations in [50]. When considering intersubject abdominal registration in [74] the use of discrete and partially discontinuous deformations proved essential to accurately resolve the very large displacements across subjects due to anatomical variability.

Nonlocal regularization. While the previously discussed approaches only consider the immediate neighbors (six in 3D) of a voxel to be part of $\mathcal{N}$ for the regularization energy, it may be beneficial to include a larger, nonlocal neighborhood to explicitly enforce smoothness across larger objects. In addition to the graph-regularized Demons approach in Sect. 13.2.2.1 [46], many state-of-the-art optical flow estimation methods use nonlocal filtering of the motion field (as a postprocessing) to ensure both discontinuity preservation across object boundaries and smoothness within an object [28,58].

Learning of regularization term. Within the context of discrete optimization, the work on fully-connected CRFs [27] provides the most comprehensive approach to model long-range pairwise interactions. Their work uses a fast high-dimensional filtering approach to obtain a very good approximation to nonlocal regularization, when restricting themselves to Gaussian pairwise potentials. A particularly interesting aspect of their work is that it can learn the optimal interlabel regularization priors directly from labeled data. Improved multiclass segmentation results have been demonstrated, however, for discrete image registration the large number of labels currently limits its practical implementation - yet recent work in this direction shows great promise [22]. In [12] nonlocal interactions are modeled by starting from a fully connected graph and learning the codependencies of control points with a clustering approach from training data. When applying these learned deformation priors for the registration of unseen images, promising improvements over the conventional local regularization was shown in particular for images with strong noise or artifacts. Another way of making use of supervised learning for discontinuity-preserving regularization was presented in [24]. Similar to [71] (in computer vision) a principal component basis of a statistical deformation model was learned from previous MRI sequences within a radiotherapy application context in a supervised manner (using the **deeds** framework). This low-dimensional motion basis contained the apparent sliding motion and could therefore be used to preserve these discontinuities in all subsequent frames.

The presented optimization strategies are, of course, not the only possible ones and several other suitable choices exist for different medical image registration problems. Apart from belief propagation on a tree, a number of other methods can be used to solve the MRF labeling, e.g., loopy belief propagation (LBP) [10] or sequential tree-reweighted message passing (TRW-S) [30]. Both of them are very similar to the described tree-based message passing and merely differ in the definition of graph edge systems and the schedule of message updates. When looking into combinatorial or linear programming approaches: α-expansion move graph cuts (α-GC) [3] are a popular choice, e.g., in image segmentation. Graph cuts can solve binary energy minimization problems exactly by finding the minimum cut, which separates a graph, in which each node is connected to its neighbors and two additional nodes (source and sink). To extend this approach to multilabel problems, such as image registration, α-expansion moves or QPBO [31] can be used. The fast primal–dual strategy (FastPD) [33] is another alternative for solving the graph cut problem that shows an improved performance compared to α-GC and relaxes the metric-requirement. However, this comes at the cost of substantially increased memory requirements. Another well-known combinatorial optimization technique is "Simulated annealing" [34] that has the advantage that it can theoretically find the global optimum for such problems by escaping out of local minima by accepting worse intermediate solutions that have a higher energy with a certain probability (determined by the annealing temperature). However, the high computational complexity limits its use in practical applications.

13.4. Image registration for cancer applications

Recently, modeling and analyzing lung and abdominal motion has been recognized as an important element of many biomedical image analysis applications [54], which could lead to improvements in diagnosis and treatment by formulating a personalized patient treatment plan. Dynamic imaging modalities such as Computed Tomography Perfusion (CTP) or Dynamic Contrast Enhanced Magnetic Resonance Imaging (DCE-MRI) have attracted significant interest in clinical cancer research providing a potential for the noninvasive, quantitative assessment of tumor microenvironment. These dynamic modalities have been widely used in clinical applications including neuroimaging, and head and neck radiotherapy, but their usability has been rather limited in lung and abdominal applications, not least because of the deformations caused by breathing.

Motion correction for intrasubject dynamic contrast-enhanced imaging of lungs and abdomen is challenging due to the complexity of motion to be estimated stemming from patient breathing during acquisition, and local intensity changes due to wash-in/out of tracer. In [4], the Demons framework was extended to accommodate localized intensity differences by a simultaneous pharmacokinetic model fitting and estimation of the deformation field. Such an approach, however, could be biased towards a chosen pharmacokinetic model, which, in turn, may limit its application in cancer imaging to assess the tumor heterogeneity as a single model is rarely appropriate for the whole tumor [32]. In order to avoid a potentially invalid pharmacokinetic model, Demons with contrast-invariant representation were used to contrast-enhanced abdominal imaging, further extended by spatially adaptive filtering of deformation field to model respiratory and hepatic motion [40]. This motion correction framework is well-suited to investigate how different compartment models describe kinetics of tumor uptake, and to determine how such model-derived parameters correlate with the gold-standard imaging

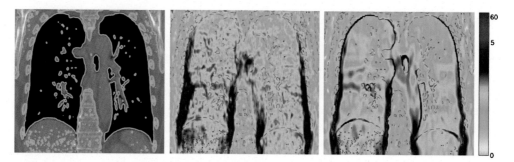

Figure 13.10 Example of quantification of sliding motion estimated by the Demons registration using isotropic Gaussian filtering and bilateral filtering for a CT lung data inhale/exhale pair. From left to right: coronal view of lung CT; and color-coded maximal shear stretch γ_{max} calculated for deformations estimated using the standard Demons [69], and Demons with bilateral filtering [42]. The results demonstrate that the framework with sliding motion model efficiently handles deformation discontinuities for estimation of complex motion, which is exhibited by high values of γ_{max}, while classic Demons smooths the deformation field across the lung boundaries.

methods (e.g., histopathology obtained from excised tumor slices). It has been shown to make the segmentation of the rectal tumor from DCE-MRI based on model-free tissue contrast enhancement characteristics more robust, particularly at the edges of the tumor [25]. Motion correction applied to various dynamic contrast-enhanced imaging techniques have been also used to derive the dynamic imaging-based parameters including tumor perfusion in preclinical and human tumors that can be considered as potential biomarkers in clinical trials to predict tumor response to adjuvant therapies [29].

Modeling of sliding motion has also potential to increase understanding of the level and nature of sliding especially in the context of lung lobe sliding. In order to analyze such discontinuous motion, the maximum shear stretch γ_{max} of the estimated deformation field as a sliding motion criterion was proposed in the literature [1]. The maximum shear stretch of the deformation field is defined as follows:

$$\gamma_{max} = \frac{\gamma_1 - \gamma_3}{2}, \tag{13.12}$$

where γ_1 and γ_3 are the maximal and minimal principal stretch components, respectively, obtained from eigenvalue decomposition of the deformation field gradients. As shown in Fig. 13.10, the sliding motion at the pleural cavity boundaries is more prominent when using the Demons registration with the appropriate regularization [42]. Furthermore, minor sliding motion patterns could be observed inside the lungs (around fissures) suggesting that lung lobes slides against each other, and such measurement may lead to better lung disease diagnosis, or better understanding of regional lung deformation with possible implications for image guided radiotherapy.

Deformable image registration is also a key component to produce ventilation volumes from 4D lung CT, which have shown a potential for a noninvasive local lung function assessment, and thus to deliver personalized functional avoidance in radiotherapy planning that could spare well-ventilated parts of the lungs. The most widely used methods estimating local lung ventilation are based on either quantification of breathing-induced lung density changes, or breathing-induced lung volume changes between inhale and exhale CT volumes [6]. To assess lung density changes, the inhale/exhale volumes from 4D CT are registered first, and the intensity differences (expressed in the Hounsfield units) between corresponding regions (in voxel-by-voxel manner) are calculated. The approach measuring lung volume changes requires also to perform deformable image registration between lung volumes, and subsequently the determinant of the Jacobian for the estimated deformation fields is calculated as a surrogate measure of local lung volume expansion/shrinkage. In both methods, accuracy of the performed deformable image registration is crucial, and, in particular, the chosen regularization model may highly influence the obtained results. The earliest work on ventilation estimation used the standard deformable image registration methods, however, more recently the use of dedicated frameworks, which incorporated sliding motion regularization, have been proposed [16,56] showing high correlation values for ventilated and nonventilated regions of lungs. Multimodal image registration has been also investigated for pulmonary applications. For example, a framework to register a standard 4D-CT used for radiotherapy planning to the experimental functional Xe-MRI measuring functional respiratory parameters was proposed in [56]. Fusion of structural information provided in CT, and functional information from Xe-MRI could be employed to optimize radiotherapy treatment planning to spare well-functioning regions of lung in patients (functional lung avoidance planning) [37].

13.5. Conclusions

In this chapter, we have presented an in-depth introduction and discussion of current approaches for medical image registration with sliding motion. Starting from early work in computer vision for the estimation of edges in optical flow fields, we have highlighted current work that enables locally-adaptive regularization firstly within the Demons framework and secondly within the discrete optimization approach **deeds**. In both cases, no specifically computed segmentation mask is necessary and substantial improvements over baseline approaches can be reached both in terms of visually plausible sliding in the obtained motion fields and in reducing the target registration error with respect to expert landmarks. A suitable handling of motion discontinuities has great clinical impact and future work is likely to further improve these strategies by incorporation of nonlocal adaptive regularization and providing more advanced graph-based edge priors through supervised learning.

References

[1] R.E. Amelon, K. Cao, J.M. Reinhardt, G.E. Christensen, M.L. Raghavan, A measure for characterizing sliding on lung boundaries, Annals of Biomedical Engineering (2013) 1–9.

[2] Radhakrishna Achanta, Appu Shaji, Kevin Smith, Aurélien Lucchi, Pascal Fua, Sabine Süsstrunk, SLIC Superpixels compared to state-of-the-art superpixel methods, IEEE Transactions on Pattern Analysis and Machine Intelligence 34 (11) (2012) 2274–2282.

[3] Y. Boykov, V. Kolmogorov, An experimental comparison of min-cut/max-flow algorithms for energy minimization in vision, IEEE Transactions on Pattern Analysis and Machine Intelligence 26 (9) (2004) 1124–1137.

[4] M. Bhushan, J.A. Schnabel, L. Risser, M.P. Heinrich, M. Brady, M. Jenkinson, Motion correction and parameter estimation in dceMRI sequences: application to colorectal cancer, in: MICCAI, Springer, 2011, pp. 476–483.

[5] M.A. Clifford, F. Banovac, E. Levy, K. Cleary, Assessment of hepatic motion secondary to respiration for computer assisted interventions, Computer Aided Surgery 7 (5) (2002) 291–299.

[6] Richard Castillo, Edward Castillo, Josue Martinez, Thomas Guerrero, Ventilation from four-dimensional computed tomography: density versus jacobian methods, Physics in Medicine and Biology 55 (16) (2010) 4661.

[7] Nathan D. Cahill, J. Alison Noble, David J. Hawkes, A Demons algorithm for image registration with locally adaptive regularization, in: Medical Image Computing and Computer-Assisted Intervention – MICCAI 2009, Springer, 2009, pp. 574–581.

[8] V. Delmon, S. Rit, R. Pinho, D. Sarrut, Registration of sliding objects using direction dependent B-splines decomposition, Physics in Medicine and Biology 58 (5) (2013) 1303–1314.

[9] Pedro F. Felzenszwalb, Daniel P. Huttenlocher, Pictorial structures for object recognition, International Journal of Computer Vision 61 (2005) 55–79.

[10] Pedro Felzenszwalb, Daniel Huttenlocher, Efficient belief propagation for early vision, International Journal of Computer Vision 70 (2006) 41–54.

[11] Vincent Garcia, Olivier Commowick, Grégoire Malandain, A robust and efficient block matching framework for nonlinear registration of thoracic CT images, in: Grand Challenges in Medical Image Analysis (MICCAI Workshop), 2010, pp. 1–10.

[12] Ben Glocker, Nikos Komodakis, Nassir Navab, Georgios Tziritas, Nikos Paragios, Dense registration with deformation priors, in: International Conference on Information Processing in Medical Imaging, Springer, 2009, pp. 540–551.

[13] Ben Glocker, Nikos Komodakis, Georgios Tziritas, Nassir Navab, Nikos Paragios, Dense image registration through MRFs and efficient linear programming, Medical Image Analysis 12 (6) (2008) 731–741.

[14] B. Glocker, A. Sotiras, N. Komodakis, N. Paragios, Deformable medical image registration: setting the state-of-the-art with discrete methods, Annual Review of Biomedical Engineering 13 (2011) 219–244.

[15] J.V. Hajnal, L.G.D. Hill, J.D. Hawkes, Medical Image Registration (Biomedical Engineering), CRC Press, Cambridge, June 2001.

[16] M.P. Heinrich, M. Jenkinson, M. Brady, J.A. Schnabel, MRF-based deformable registration and ventilation estimation of lung CT, IEEE Transactions on Medical Imaging 32 (7) (2013) 1239–1248.

[17] Mattias P. Heinrich, Mark Jenkinson, Bartlomiej W. Papiez, Fergus V. Glesson, Michael Brady, Julia A. Schnabel, Edge- and detail-preserving sparse image representations for deformable registration of chest MRI and CT volumes, in: Information Processing in Medical Imaging, in: LNCS, vol. 7917, Springer, Berlin Heidelberg, 2013, pp. 463–474.

[18] Yipeng Hu, Marc Modat, Eli Gibson, Wenqi Li, Nooshin Ghavami, Ester Bonmati, Guotai Wang, Steven Bandula, Caroline M. Moore, Mark Emberton, et al., Weakly-supervised convolutional neural networks for multimodal image registration, Medical Image Analysis 49 (2018) 1–13.

[19] Rui Hua, Jose M. Pozo, Zeike A. Taylor, Alejandro F. Frangi, Multiresolution eXtended Free-Form Deformations (XFFD) for non-rigid registration with discontinuous transforms, Medical Image Analysis 36 (2017) 113–122.

[20] Berthold K.P. Horn, Brian G. Schunck, Determining optical flow, Artificial Intelligence 17 (1–3) (1981) 185–203.

[21] Mattias P. Heinrich, Ivor J.A. Simpson, Bartłomiej W. Papież, Michael Brady, Julia A. Schnabel, Deformable image registration by combining uncertainty estimates, Medical Image Analysis 27 (2016) 57–71.

[22] Mattias P. Heinrich, Closing the gap between deep and conventional image registration using probabilistic dense displacement networks, in: Medical Image Computing and Computer-Assisted Intervention – MICCAI 2019, Springer, 2019, pp. 1–9.

[23] K. He, J. Sun, X. Tang, Guided image filtering, IEEE Transactions on Pattern Analysis and Machine Intelligence 35 (6) (2013) 1397–1409.

[24] In Young Ha, Matthias Wilms, Heinz Handels, Mattias Heinrich, Model-based sparse-to-dense image registration for realtime respiratory motion estimation in image-guided interventions, IEEE Transactions on Biomedical Engineering 66 (2) (2018) 302–310.

[25] Benjamin Irving, James M. Franklin, Bartłomiej W. Papież, Ewan M. Anderson, Ricky A. Sharma, Fergus V. Gleeson, Michael Brady, Julia A. Schnabel, Pieces-of-parts for supervoxel segmentation with global context: application to DCE-MRI tumour delineation, Medical Image Analysis 32 (2016) 69–83.

[26] Christoph Jud, Nadia Mori, Philippe C. Cattin, Sparse kernel machines for discontinuous registration and nonstationary regularization, in: Proceedings of the IEEE Conference on Computer Vision and Pattern Recognition Workshops, 2016, pp. 9–16.

[27] Krähenbühl Philipp, Vladlen Koltun, Efficient inference in fully connected CRFs with Gaussian edge potentials, in: Advances in Neural Information Processing Systems, 2011, pp. 109–117.

[28] Krähenbühl Philipp, Vladlen Koltun, Efficient nonlocal regularization for optical flow, in: European Conference on Computer Vision, Springer, 2012, pp. 356–369.

[29] Pavitra Kannan, Warren W. Kretzschmar, Helen Winter, Daniel R. Warren, Russell Bates, Philip D. Allen, Nigar Syed, Benjamin Irving, Bartłomiej W. Papież, Jakob Kaeppler, et al., Functional parameters derived from magnetic resonance imaging reflect vascular morphology in preclinical tumors and in human liver metastases, Clinical Cancer Research 24 (19) (2018) 4694–4704.

[30] V. Kolmogorov, Convergent tree-reweighted message passing for energy minimization, IEEE Transactions on Pattern Analysis and Machine Intelligence 28 (10) (2006) 1568–1583.

[31] Vladimir Kolmogorov, Carsten Rother, Minimizing nonsubmodular functions with graph cuts – a review, IEEE Transactions on Pattern Analysis and Machine Intelligence 29 (7) (2007).

[32] Jesper Folsted Kallehauge, Kari Tanderup, Chong Duan, Søren Haack, Erik Morre Pedersen, Jacob Christian Lindegaard, Lars Ulrik Fokdal, Sandy Mohamed Ismail Mohamed, Thomas Nielsen, Tracer kinetic model selection for dynamic contrast-enhanced magnetic resonance imaging of locally advanced cervical cancer, Acta Oncologica 53 (8) (2014) 1064–1072.

[33] Nikos Komodakis, Georgios Tziritas, Nikos Paragios, Performance vs computational efficiency for optimizing single and dynamic MRFs: setting the state-of-the-art with primal–dual strategies, Computer Vision and Image Understanding 112 (1) (2008) 14–29.

[34] S. Kirkpatrick, M.P. Vecchi, et al., Optimization by simulated annealing, Science 220 (4598) (1983) 671–680.

[35] Lena Maier-Hein, Peter Mountney, Adrien Bartoli, Haytham Elhawary, D. Elson, Anja Groch, Andreas Kolb, Marcos Rodrigues, J. Sorger, Stefanie Speidel, et al., Optical techniques for 3D surface reconstruction in computer-assisted laparoscopic surgery, Medical Image Analysis 17 (8) (2013) 974–996.

[36] Keelin Murphy, Bram Van Ginneken, Joseph M. Reinhardt, Sven Kabus, Kai Ding, Xiang Deng, Kunlin Cao, Kaifang Du, Gary E. Christensen, Vincent Garcia, et al., Evaluation of registration methods on thoracic CT: the EMPIRE10 challenge, IEEE Transactions on Medical Imaging 30 (11) (2011) 1901–1920.

[37] Martin J. Menten, Andreas Wetscherek, Martin F. Fast, Mri-guided lung SBRT: present and future developments, Physica Medica 44 (2017) 139–149.

[38] Hans-Hellmut Nagel, Wilfried Enkelmann, An investigation of smoothness constraints for the estimation of displacement vector fields from image sequences, IEEE Transactions on Pattern Analysis and Machine Intelligence 8 (5) (1986) 565–593.

[39] D.F. Pace, S.R. Aylward, M. Niethammer, A locally adaptive regularization based on anisotropic diffusion for deformable image registration of sliding organs, IEEE Transactions on Medical Imaging 32 (11) (2013) 2114–2126.

[40] Bartłomiej W. Papież, Jamie Franklin, Mattias P. Heinrich, Fergus V. Gleeson, Julia A. Schnabel, Liver motion estimation via locally adaptive over-segmentation regularization, in: Medical Image Computing and Computer-Assisted Intervention – MICCAI 2015, Springer, 2015, pp. 427–434.

[41] Bartłomiej W. Papież, James M. Franklin, Mattias P. Heinrich, Fergus V. Gleeson, Michael Brady, Julia A. Schnabel, Gifted demons: deformable image registration with local structure-preserving regularization using supervoxels for liver applications, Journal of Medical Imaging 5 (2) (2018) 024001.

[42] Bartłomiej W. Papież, Mattias P. Heinrich, Jérome Fehrenbach, Laurent Risser, Julia A. Schnabel, An implicit sliding-motion preserving regularisation via bilateral filtering for deformable image registration, Medical Image Analysis 18 (8) (2014) 1299–1311.

[43] Vaclav Potesil, Timor Kadir, Günther Platsch, Michael Brady, Personalized graphical models for anatomical landmark localization in whole-body medical images, International Journal of Computer Vision 111 (1) (2015) 29–49.

[44] Sylvain Paris, Pierre Kornprobst, Jack Tumblin, Frédo Durand, A gentle introduction to bilateral filtering and its applications, in: ACM SIGGRAPH 2007 Courses, ACM, 2007, p. 1.

[45] Bartłomiej W. Papież, Daniel R. McGowan, Michael Skwarski, Geoff S. Higgins, Julia A. Schnabel, Michael Brady, Fast groupwise 4D deformable image registration for irregular breathing motion estimation, in: International Workshop on Biomedical Image Registration, Springer, 2018, pp. 37–46.

[46] Bartłomiej W. Papież, Adam Szmul, Vicente Grau, J. Michael Brady, Julia A. Schnabel, Non-local graph-based regularization for deformable image registration, in: Medical Computer Vision and Bayesian and Graphical Models for Biomedical Imaging, Springer, 2016, pp. 199–207.

[47] Rietzel Eike, George T.Y. Chen, Deformable registration of 4D computed tomography data, Medical Physics 33 (11) (2006) 4423–4430.

[48] D. Ruan, S. Esedoglu, J.A. Fessler, Discriminative sliding preserving regularization in medical image registration, in: IEEE International Symposium on Biomedical Imaging: From Nano to Macro, 2009, ISBI '09, 2009, pp. 430–433.

[49] Torsten Rohlfing, Image similarity and tissue overlaps as surrogates for image registration accuracy: widely used but unreliable, IEEE Transactions on Medical Imaging 31 (2) (2012) 153–163.

[50] Jan Rühaak, Thomas Polzin, Stefan Heldmann, Ivor J.A. Simpson, Heinz Handels, Jan Modersitzki, Mattias P. Heinrich, Estimation of large motion in lung CT by integrating regularized keypoint correspondences into dense deformable registration, IEEE Transactions on Medical Imaging 36 (8) (2017) 1746–1757.

[51] Daniel Rueckert, L.I. Sonoda, Carmel Hayes, Derek L.G. Hill, Martin O. Leach, David J. Hawkes, Non-rigid registration using free-form deformations: application to breast MR images, IEEE Transactions on Medical Imaging 18 (8) (1999) 712–721.

[52] L. Risser, F.-X. Vialard, H.Y. Baluwala, J.A. Schnabel, Piecewise-diffeomorphic image registration: application to the motion estimation between 3D CT lung images with sliding conditions, Medical Image Analysis 17 (2) (2013) 182–193.

[53] Aristeidis Sotiras, Christos Davatzikos, Nikos Paragios, Deformable medical image registration: a survey, IEEE Transactions on Medical Imaging 32 (7) (2013) 1153–1190.

[54] Julia A. Schnabel, Mattias P. Heinrich, Bartłomiej W. Papież, J. Michael Brady, Advances and challenges in deformable image registration: from image fusion to complex motion modelling, Medical Image Analysis 33 (2016) 145–148.

[55] M. Staring, S. Klein, J.P.W. Pluim, Nonrigid registration with tissue-dependent filtering of the deformation field, Physics in Medicine and Biology 52 (2007) 6879–6892.

[56] Adam Szmul, Tahreema Matin, Fergus V. Gleeson, Julia A. Schnabel, Vicente Grau, B.W. Papiez, Patch-based lung ventilation estimation using multi-layer supervoxels, Computerized Medical Imaging and Graphics 74 (2019) 49–60.

[57] Radu Stefanescu, Xavier Pennec, Nicholas Ayache, Grid powered nonlinear image registration with locally adaptive regularization, Medical Image Analysis 8 (3) (Sept. 2004) 325–342.

[58] D. Sun, S. Roth, M.J. Black, Secrets of optical flow estimation and their principles, in: Computer Vision and Pattern Recognition, Proceedings of IEEE Int. Conference, 2010.

[59] Julia Schnabel, Daniel Rueckert, Marcel Quist, Jane Blackall, Andy Castellano-Smith, Thomas Hartkens, Graeme Penney, Walter Hall, Haiying Liu, Charles Truwit, Frans Gerritsen, Derek Hill, David Hawkes, A generic framework for non-rigid registration based on non-uniform multi-level free-form deformations, in: Wiro Niessen, Max Viergever (Eds.), Medical Image Computing and Computer-Assisted Intervention, MICCAI 2001, in: Lecture Notes in Computer Science, vol. 2208, Springer, Berlin/Heidelberg, 2001, pp. 573–581.

[60] A. Schmidt-Richberg, R. Werner, H. Handels, J. Ehrhardt, Estimation of slipping organ motion by registration with direction-dependent regularization, Medical Image Analysis 16 (2012) 150–159.

[61] Daniel Scharstein, Richard Szeliski, A taxonomy and evaluation of dense two-frame stereo correspondence algorithms, International Journal of Computer Vision 47 (1–3) (2002) 7–42.

[62] Deqing Sun, Erik B. Sudderth, Michael J. Black, Layered segmentation and optical flow estimation over time, in: 2012 IEEE Conference on Computer Vision and Pattern Recognition, CVPR, IEEE, 2012, pp. 1768–1775.

[63] W.P. Segars, G. Sturgeon, S. Mendonca, Jason Grimes, Benjamin M.W. Tsui, 4d xcat phantom for multimodality imaging research, Medical Physics 37 (9) (2010) 4902–4915.

[64] Ronald W.K. So, Tommy W.H. Tang, Albert C.S. Chung, Non-rigid image registration of brain magnetic resonance images using graph-cuts, Pattern Recognition 44 (10) (2011) 2450–2467.

[65] J.-P. Thirion, Image matching as a diffusion process: an analogy with Maxwell's demons, Medical Image Analysis 2 (3) (Sep. 1998) 243–260.

[66] C. Tomasi, R. Manduchi, Bilateral filtering for gray and color images, in: Proceedings of the Sixth International Conference on Computer Vision, ICCV-98, 1998, pp. 839–846.

[67] Jef Vandemeulebroucke, Olivier Bernard, Simon Rit, Jan Kybic, Patrick Clarysse, David Sarrut, Automated segmentation of a motion mask to preserve sliding motion in deformable registration of thoracic CT, Medical Physics 39 (2) (2012) 1006–1015.

[68] O. Veksler, Stereo correspondence by dynamic programming on a tree, in: Computer Vision and Pattern Recognition, CVPR 2005, vol. 2, 2005, pp. 384–390.

[69] T. Vercauteren, X. Pennec, A. Perchant, N. Ayache, Diffeomorphic Demons: efficient non-parametric image registration, NeuroImage 45 (2009) S61–S72.

[70] John Wang, Edward H. Adelson, Spatio-temporal segmentation of video data, in: Image and Video Processing II, vol. 2182, International Society for Optics and Photonics, 1994, pp. 120–132.

[71] Jonas Wulff, Michael J. Black, Efficient sparse-to-dense optical flow estimation using a learned basis and layers, in: Proceedings of the IEEE Conference on Computer Vision and Pattern Recognition, 2015, pp. 120–130.

[72] William M. Wells III, Paul Viola, Hideki Atsumi, Shin Nakajima, Ron Kikinis, Multi-modal volume registration by maximization of mutual information, Medical Image Analysis 1 (1) (1996) 35–51.

[73] Ziji Wu, Eike Rietzel, Vlad Boldea, David Sarrut, Gregory C. Sharp, Evaluation of deformable registration of patient lung 4D CT with subanatomical region segmentations, Medical Physics 35 (2) (Feb. 2008) 775–781.

[74] Zhoubing Xu, Christopher P. Lee, Mattias P. Heinrich, Marc Modat, Daniel Rueckert, Sebastien Ourselin, Richard G. Abramson, Bennett A. Landman, Evaluation of six registration methods for the

human abdomen on clinically acquired CT, IEEE Transactions on Biomedical Engineering 63 (8) (2016) 1563–1572.

[75] Qingxiong Yang, Recursive bilateral filtering, in: Computer Vision – ECCV 2012, Springer, 2012, pp. 399–413.

[76] Qingxiong Yang, Stereo matching using tree filtering, IEEE Transactions on Pattern Analysis and Machine Intelligence 37 (4) (2015) 834–846.

[77] H. Zimmer, A. Bruhn, J. Weickert, Optic flow in harmony, International Journal of Computer Vision 93 (2011) 368–388.

CHAPTER 14

Image registration using machine and deep learning

Xiaohuan Cao[a], **Jingfan Fan**[b], **Pei Dong**[a], **Sahar Ahmad**[b], **Pew-Thian Yap**[b], **Dinggang Shen**[b]

[a]Shanghai United Imaging Intelligence Co., Ltd., Shanghai, China
[b]Department of Radiology and BRIC, University of North Carolina, Chapel Hill, NC, United States

Contents

14.1. Introduction	319
14.2. Machine-learning-based registration	322
14.2.1 Learning initialized deformation field	322
14.2.2 Learning intermediate image	324
14.2.3 Learning image appearance	325
14.3. Machine-learning-based multimodal registration	326
14.3.1 Learning similarity metric	328
14.3.2 Learning common feature representation	330
14.3.3 Learning appearance mapping	331
14.4. Deep-learning-based registration	332
14.4.1 Learning similarity metric	332
14.4.2 Learning preliminary transformation parameters	334
14.4.3 End-to-end learning for deformable registration	335
References	338

14.1. Introduction

Image registration is a crucial and fundamental procedure in medical image analysis. The aim of registration algorithm is to obtain a spatial transformation that can align a floating image to a reference image. The resulting anatomical correspondences allow image comparison for applications such as population analyses, longitudinal studies, and image–guided interventions. Image registration involves determining the transformation ϕ^* that minimizes the image dissimilarity:

$$\phi^* = \underset{\phi}{\operatorname{argmin}}\ dissim\left(I_R, \phi\left(I_F\right)\right), \qquad (14.1)$$

where I_R and I_F denote the reference image and the floating image, respectively; $\phi\left(I_F\right)$ is the floating image warped using transformation ϕ. Image dissimilarity can be defined as the intensity sum of squared distance (SSD) [1], mean squared distance (MSD) [2],

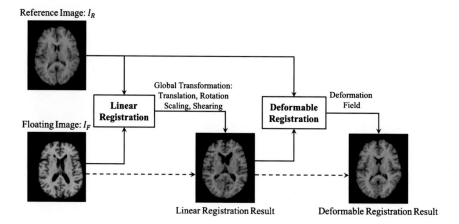

Figure 14.1 A typical image registration procedure.

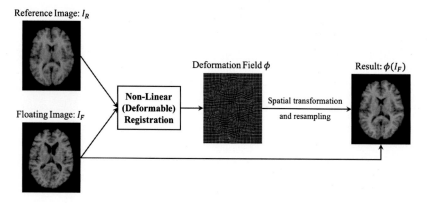

Figure 14.2 An illustration of deformable registration.

correlation ratio (CR) [3], (normalized) cross-correlation (CC/NCC) [4], (normalized) mutual information (MI/NMI) [5,6], etc. Based on the spatial transformation model, the registration method can be categorized as linear (including rigid and affine) and nonlinear (nonrigid and deformable). Fig. 14.1 shows a typical brain image registration procedure.

Linear registration accounts for translation, rotation, scaling, and shearing. Non-linear deformable registration determines voxel-to-voxel correspondences, as shown in Fig. 14.2. Determining the deformation field is a high-dimensional ill-posed optimization problem. Deformation smoothness is imposed to avoid implausible deformations and to preserve topology. The cost function of deformable registration can be reformulated as

$$\phi^* = \underset{\phi}{\operatorname{argmin}} \ dissim \left(I_R, \phi \left(I_F \right) \right) + \lambda reg \left(\phi \right), \tag{14.2}$$

where $reg\left(\phi\right)$ is a regularization term for ensuring smoothness of the estimated deformation field ϕ; λ is a regularization parameter that controls the degree of smoothness. Regularity of the deformation field can be achieved by Gaussian smoothing [6–8], by minimizing the bending energy, or by utilizing a spline [4,9,1] or diffeomorphic [10,11] deformation model.

Comprehensive reviews on deformable registration can be found in [12–15]. Performance comparison of some popular registration algorithms based on different databases and registration tasks are reported in [16,17]. According to [12], registration algorithms can be summarized in terms of (1) deformable models, i.e., physical models, interpolation models, etc., (2) matching criteria, i.e., volumetric-based, landmark-based, etc., and (3) numerical optimization techniques, i.e., continuous or discrete. The common underlying objective is to estimate an optimal transformation based on cost functions defined in the form of Eq. (14.2).

Machine learning [18] and deep learning [19] techniques have been widely applied to various medical image analysis tasks [20,21]. The increasing popularity of learning-based methods is mainly due to the following two reasons: First, it is generally difficult to optimize the large deformations between images with large anatomical differences. This is further complicated if images of two different imaging modalities with large appearance differences need to be registered. Second, with the advent of cutting-edge imaging technology, the scale and diversity of imaging data has increased significantly, posing significant challenges to registration. Modern registration methods need to be sufficiently versatile to deal with diverse imaging data with high efficiency, accuracy, and robustness.

Fortunately, machine learning techniques applied to image registration tasks can help address the aforementioned issues. Specifically, different machine learning techniques can be employed to learn from prior registration results to improve the registration performance in some challenging tasks. For instance, they can be employed for learning an appearance mapping model, learning an effective initialization for the optimization, etc. Recent studies [22–24] have also demonstrated the potential of deep learning methods in addressing challenging registration problems.

This chapter will be dedicated to summarize state-of-the-art learning-based registration algorithms, particularly methods for deformable registration. Methods for linear registration will also be discussed where necessary. In the following section, the methods will be divided into three categories: (1) machine-learning-based registration, (2) machine-learning-based multimodal registration, and (3) deep-learning-based registration.

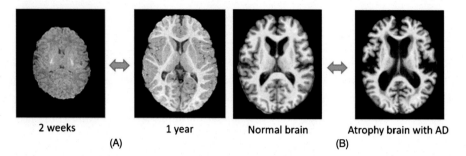

| 2 weeks | 1 year | Normal brain | Atrophy brain with AD |

(A)　(B)

Figure 14.3 Two challenging registration cases: (A) Image registration with large image appearance difference – registration of infant brain MRI at two different time points; (B) image registration with a large anatomical difference – registration between a normal brain MRI and an atrophied brain MRI suffered from Alzheimer's Disease (AD).

14.2. Machine-learning-based registration

In this section, we introduce the machine-learning-based image registration methods. Fig. 14.3 shows two registration cases that are challenging for traditional registration methods. As shown in Fig. 14.3(A), the infant brain MR images at different time points exhibit large appearance differences. Fig. 14.3(B) is a comparison between the normal brain MRI and the brain MRI with Alzheimer's Disease (AD), where the brain image with AD has significant atrophy. Conventional registration methods cannot solve these challenging tasks well. To solve them, machine learning can be applied to learn prior registration knowledge based on a training dataset, in order to simplify these challenging registration tasks. Basically, based on the learning objective, the learned model can be classified into the following three categories: (1) learning the initialized deformation field to simplify the complicated optimization, (2) learning intermediate image(s) that provides a bridge/link between the to-be-registered floating and reference images, and (3) learning the image appearance changes to eliminate the appearance difference. Table 14.1 summarizes the state-of-the-art machine-learning-based registration methods. In the following, we will elaborate the learning-based registration methods according to the three categories.

14.2.1 Learning initialized deformation field

One registration problem is to align images with large anatomical differences, as shown in Fig. 14.3(B). This is difficult to solve using traditional registration methods since the complex optimization process often falls into the local minima when the large deformations need to be estimated, which yields inaccurate registration result. Learning-based-registration method can elevate this problem by providing a good initialized deformation, which can transform the floating image close to the reference image. Then, the subsequent registration is simplified to estimate the remaining deformations,

Table 14.1 Representative studies for machine learning based registration methods.

Learning objective	Method	Data	Ref.
Initialized deformation field	Regression forest	Elderly brain MRI	[25]
	Support vector regression	Adult brain MRI	[26]
	Sparse learning	Adult brain MRI	[27]
Intermediate template	PCA	Adult brain MRI	[28]
	Sparse learning	Adult brain MRI Elderly brain MRI Infance brain MRI	[29,30]
Image appearance	Logistic intensity model	Monkey brain MRI	[31]
	Random forest	Infant brain MRI	[32,33]

which are usually small and can be effectively optimized. To date, many machine learning approaches, such as support vector regression [34], random forest [35], and sparse learning [36], have been proposed to learn a model from a training dataset for predicting an initialized deformation.

For example, Kim et al. [26] proposed to use support vector regression to learn the correlation between image appearance and their respective deformation field, which can efficiently warp the reference image to an intermediate image space that is close to the floating image. Then, the registration task can be easily achieved by aligning the similar-looking images between the floating image and the intermediate image. In the later work, Kim et al. [27] further proposed a sparse learning technique to estimate the initialized deformation field between the floating and the reference images in a patchwise fashion. In the training stage, a set of deformation fields is first acquired by registering all the training images to a preselected reference image used as a template. In the application stage, a small number of patches are first selected based on key points, and each patch can be sparsely represented by the image patches in the training dataset, which already have the associated deformations. Then the initialized deformation can be obtained by interpolation. With this fast initialization, the remaining deformations can be estimated more effectively.

Han et al. [25] proposed to train a regression forest model for detecting distinctive landmarks that can be used for registering the images with large anatomical variations. In this work, the regression forest is used for learning a set of features to well characterize each landmark and then establish the mapping between the local image patch and the image displacement towards each landmark. Specifically, in the training stage, a set of salient landmarks were annotated on each training MR image. Then, a regression forest was used to learn the mapping between the local image patch and the annotated landmarks. In the application stage, the trained regression forest can be used to predict the displacement of each point in the new image towards a corresponding landmark. From the predicted displacements, the location of the landmark on the new image can be detected, where these detected landmarks can be used as a good initialization for registering images efficiently and accurately.

Generally, for the learning-based registration in this category, machine learning technologies can be used to provide a good initialization model for the difficult registration tasks, which can accelerate the convergence in the registration optimization process, thus improving the registration performance in terms of efficiency, accuracy and also robustness.

14.2.2 Learning intermediate image

Another way to solve the registration of images with large anatomical variations is to introduce a bridge/link between the reference and the floating images by an intermediate image [29,28,30]. In this scenario, the intermediate image is located between the reference and floating images on the image manifold, and the registration can be decomposed into two separated pathways, i.e., (1) registering the floating image to its similar-looking intermediate image, and then (2) registering the intermediate image to the reference image. These methods are similar but different from learning an initialized deformation in last section. By learning an initialized deformation, the intermediate image is derived from the floating image. But in this category, machine learning techniques can help generate the intermediate image from following two ways: (1) simulating the intermediate image from an available training dataset, or (2) selecting the intermediate image from an available training dataset.

To simulate the intermediate image that is close to the floating image, Tang et al. [28] proposed to build an intermediate reference image space generated by a statistical deformation model, which is learned by using principal component analysis (PCA) on a set of training samples with deformation fields. The statistical deformation model can capture the statistical variation of brain deformation. When registering the new floating image to the predefined reference image, the statistical deformation model is used to generate a deformation field for estimating an intermediate image that is close to the floating image. The final registration result can be further refined by a conventional registration algorithm to register the floating image with the intermediate image. Despite the statistical model can achieve fast registration, the registration accuracy can be affected by the limited training samples and the biased assumption of data normality which does not follow the Gaussian distribution.

Instead of generating intermediate images, machine learning techniques can also be used for selecting intermediate images from an available training set. For example, instead of simply choosing only one intermediate image for bridging the floating image and the reference image, Wang et al. [29] proposed to utilize the patch-scale guidance from the intermediate images for improving the registration accuracy of brain MR images. They assumed that if points in the floating and the intermediate images share similar local appearance, they may share the common correspondence to the common reference image. Thus, instead of locating only one correspondence for each certain subject point in the intermediate image, the authors proposed a method to locate several candidate points in the intermediate images for each certain subject point by using sparse learning techniques. Then, the selected intermediate candidates can bridge the correspondence from the floating point to the template space, yielding the transformation associated with the floating point at the confidence level that relates to the learned sparse coefficients. After predicting the transformation fields on the key points, the dense transformation field that covers the entire image space can then be reconstructed immediately. In another study, Dong et al. [30] proposed a joint segmentation and registration method for iteratively refining the registration of infant brain images at different time points by using spatial–temporal trajectories learned from a large number of training subjects with complete longitudinal data. In this work, the preregistered atlas images at different time points act as intermediate images bridging the time gap between the two new images under registration. By using a multi-atlas-based label fusion method [37], which was incorporated with additional label fusion priors borrowed from the reference time domain, both segmentation and registration performance can be progressively improved.

The above-mentioned learning-based registration method is also suitable for registering images with large anatomical variations. By using the intermediate image(s), the floating and the reference image space, which are far away on the image manifold, can be effectively bridged to make the registration more efficient and accurate.

14.2.3 Learning image appearance

The similarity metric used in traditional registration methods are usually defined on image intensities, thus, these registration methods are less robust when the to-be-registered image pair have large appearance difference or intensity inhomogeneity. As an example shown in Fig. 14.4, registering infant brain images at different time points is a very challenging task due to the brain anatomical variation, and also the dynamic image appearance changes. Particularly, at the age around 3–6 months, due to the myelination of white matter (WM), the image contrast between the WM and the gray matter (GM) is very low, thus making the registration even more challenging. Recently, many studies attempted to address this issue by learning appearance mapping models to eliminate the image appearance change overtime, so that the conventional registration algorithms can more effectively solve this kind of registration problem.

The image appearance mapping model can be built via different machine learning methods. Csapo et al. [31] proposed a logistical model to adjust the image intensity change between two time points. Then, instead of registering the image pair with both image intensity and morphological changes, the authors eliminated the image intensity change by using the image adjustment model, and decoupled the problem into the traditional registration between the two intensity-adjusted images. Other studies [32,33]

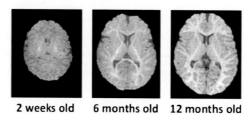

2 weeks old   6 months old   12 months old

Figure 14.4 An example of image appearance changes in infant brain longitudinal studies during the first year of life.

proposed to use random forest [38] for predicting both the image appearance change and anatomical variations. In the training stage, Hu et al. [32] used random forest to train two models for predicting both the initialized deformation and appearance changes, where one model was trained for learning the relationship between the image appearance and its displacement to a template image, and another model was trained for learning the appearance change between the two images at different time points. In a later work, Wei et al. [33] proposed to use a random forest regression coupled with an autocontext model to further improve the registration performance. In the application stage, the registration between the two infant images at different time points is composed of two phases: (1) the learned model is used to predict the initialized deformation field and image appearance changes; (2) a traditional image registration method is then applied to get the final registration result.

In summary, the learning-based registration methods are favorable to solve various image registration problems that pose different difficulties. By learning different kinds of prior knowledge based on the training dataset, the robustness, accuracy, and efficiency are significantly improved compared with traditional registration methods.

14.3. Machine-learning-based multimodal registration

Multimodal registration aims to relate clinically relevant and often complementary information from different imaging scans. It is a fundamental step to conduct the multimodal information fusion and facilitate the clinical diagnosis and treatment subsequently. It can compensate the deformations for the patient motion caused by different positioning or breathing level, and pathological changes between different imaging scans. Fig. 14.5 shows two typical multimodal images that need to be registered in clinical applications. The first one is the abdominal CT and MRI used for pancreas or other organs related diagnosis and treatment, and the second one is the brain T1w and T2w MRI used for brain related quantification and analysis.

As shown in Fig. 14.5, in addition to the geometric distortion caused by patient motion, multimodal registration also needs to deal with the large appearance difference

Abdominal CT and MRI   Brain T1w and T2w

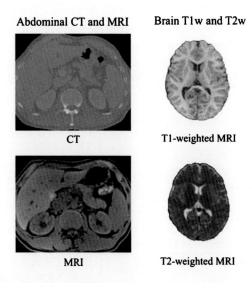

CT   T1-weighted MRI

MRI   T2-weighted MRI

Figure 14.5 Examples of multimodal images that need to be registered.

across modalities. Usually, the appearance relationship between different modalities is highly complex and nonlinear. In contrast to the monomodal registration, where many similarity metrics (e.g., NCC, SSD, etc.) can be leveraged, it is difficult to define an effective similarity metric to measure the anatomical correspondence across different modalities. Thus, deformable registration of multimodal images remains a challenging task in medical image analysis.

In conventional multimodal registration methods, mutual information (MI) is often used for multimodal registration. MI is an information theory-based metric, which aims to build a statistical intensity relationship by maximizing the shared information between the two images. It has been successfully used in linear registration of multimodal images, but it still has limitations when dealing with the deformable registration. MI is basically a global measure, which is less robust for conducting the local matching, since the insufficient number of voxels within a patch makes the intensity distribution less robust to compute MI. Besides MI-based multimodal registration, some feature-based registration methods can also be applied by using the high-order appearance information, e.g., Gabor attributes [39] and SIFT [40], however, these features are not invariant for large intensity differences, thus cannot be directly used for establishing the local correspondence across modalities.

Machine learning techniques applied in multimodal registration can help address the above issues and solve this challenging registration problem. It can be used to learn (1) an effective similarity metric, (2) a common feature representation, or (3) an appearance mapping model, in order to make the registration method more effective and feasible to deal with the large appearance difference. Under these three categories, the current

Table 14.2 A summary of learning-based multimodal image registration methods.

Learning objective	Learning method/manner	Data	Ref.
Similarity metric	Joint Intensity Distribution (Maximum Likelihood)	Brain CT and MRI Brain PET and MRI	[41]
	Joint Intensity Distribution (Kullback–Leibler Divergence)	Brain T1w and T2w DSA and MRA	[42–44]
		Brain T1w and T2w Thorax SPECT and CT Thorax PET and CT	[45,46]
		Brain CT and MRI	[47]
	Joint Intensity Distribution (Bhattacharyya Divergence)	Brain CT and MRI	[48]
	Joint Intensity Distribution (Jensen–Renyi Divergence)	Brain T1w, T2w and PD Brain PET and MRI	[49]
	Max-margin Structured Learning	Brain CT and MRI Brain PET and MRI	[50]
	Boosting	Brain CT and MRI Brain PET and MRI	[51]
	Neural Network	Brain CT and MRI	[52]
Common feature representation	Canonical Correlation Analysis (CCA)	Pelvic CT and MRI	[53]
	Manifold Learning	Brain T1w, T2w and PD	[54]
Appearance mapping	Polynomial Fitting	Brain MRI and ultrasound	[55]
	Fully Convolutional Network	Brain CT and MRI	[56]
	Random Forest	Pelvic CT and MRI	[57–59]

learning-based multimodal registration methods are summarized in Table 14.2. In the following, we will discuss the methods in these three categories.

14.3.1 Learning similarity metric

Since conventional similarity metric cannot be directly applied for measuring the similarity of multimodal images, one way to solve this problem is to learn an effective (dis)similarity metric that can well measure the anatomical correspondences across modalities. It can be implemented in two different ways: (1) learning an expected intensity distribution of multimodal images to make the existing metrics easy to distinguish the similarity between the new to-be-registered images, or (2) directly learning a metric that can measure the similarity across modalities.

In the first category, a prealigned multimodal image dataset is needed to learn an expected intensity distribution, which acts as a domain-specific model or a priori knowledge. Then, the registration method employs a metric with the expected intensity distribution to evaluate the similarity between the reference and floating images. Although it does not directly learn a new metric, it makes the existing metrics more effective and powerful to measure the anatomical difference of multimodal images. Leventon et al. [41] proposed to estimate the underlying joint intensity distribution from registered image pairs and then employed a maximum likelihood method to define the similarity metric for new to-be-registered image pairs. Chung et al. [42] minimized the Kullback–Leibler divergence (KLD) between the expected intensity distribution and the joint intensity distribution of the new images. By using KLD, the learning-based multimodal registration methods were extended in [43,44] and also used for deformable multimodal registration in [45–47]. Later on, as demonstrated in [60], Bhattacharyya divergence (BD) provided better performance than KLD, then, a new learning-based multimodal registration method using BD was proposed for both linear and deformable multimodal registration [48]. Similarly, Sabuncu et al. [49] used the entropic graph-based Jensen–Renyi divergence (JRD) for solving the same kind of problem. Compared with MI-based multimodal registration algorithms, the experimental results of these works demonstrated that, by incorporating the learned prior knowledge, e.g., the expected intensity distribution, the multimodal registration results can be improved in terms of accuracy and/or robustness.

The second category of learning-based multimodal registration methods can directly learn an effective similarity metric in a discriminative manner, and under the learned similarity metric, the reference image and correctly aligned floating image receive high similarity values. Intuitively, a training dataset is also needed with prealigned multimodal images, to train a distinctive similarity metric in a supervised manner. However, using supervised learning to learn a similarity metric is challenging. Unlike the traditional classification problem that can judge whether the images (or local patches) are similar or not, an effective similarity metric for registration task should provide a continuous similarity score, i.e., a similarity degree. Yet, the learning objective is not easy to clearly define in the training stage. Several approaches have been proposed to deal with this challenging task.

Lee et al. [50] proposed to learn a similarity function based on features extracted from the neighborhoods of both the reference and floating image positions in a patchwise manner. Specifically, they used joint kernels depending on structured input–output pairs, which provided an efficient way to model nonlinear dependencies between the reference and floating image patches for multimodal registration, and a maximum margin structured output learning method [61] was adopted to learn the similarity metric. The learned metric was then employed in a standard registration algorithm to realize the CT–MRI and PET–MRI registration. Compared with the methods in the first category, this algorithm can overcome the computational and data-scarcity problems. Another similar approach can be found in [51], in which a boosting algorithm was applied to learn a similarity metric to parameterize the anatomical similarity of multimodal images. Neural network is also employed to construct a similarity metric across modalities. In [52], the corresponding and noncorresponding CT and MRI patches were jointly used for metric learning. Then, during registration, the similarity degree of local patches can be obtained based on this learned similarity metric, to subsequently guide the local matching for deformable multimodal registration. According to the experimental results reported in this literature, the learned similarity metric is more productive compared with the traditional similarity metrics, e.g., mutual information (MI) or cross-correlation (CC), and the multimodal registration performance can be significantly boosted.

14.3.2 Learning common feature representation

Since the hand-engineered image features cannot directly work well for multimodal registration task due to the large appearance/intensity gap across modalities, some learning-based methods have been developed to learn a common feature representation for imaging data from different modalities.

In [53], the common feature representation was learned by projecting the two native feature spaces (derived from the two image modalities) to a common space. In this common space, the correlation between the corresponding anatomies or corresponding features are maximized. Since the appearance information of multimodal medical images can be completely different and statistically uncorrelated, the kernel canonical correlation analysis (KCCA) was applied in this work to reveal such nonlinear feature mappings. Then, the multimodal registration can take advantage of the learned common features to effectively establish the reliable correspondences for conducting the local matching. The experiments were performed on pelvic CT–MR images and the longitudinal infant brain MR images. The deformable multimodal registration results demonstrated the improved registration accuracy, compared with the conventional multimodal registration methods.

In [54], a manifold learning method was proposed for multimodal registration, to calculate dense features that represent the structural information of multimodal image patches. The Laplacian eigenmaps were used to learn the structural representation. The learned structural information of a patch only depend on the anatomy in the patch, not the intensity values. Then, the input multimodal images were replaced by the dense set of the learned descriptor, and a regular intensity-based registration algorithm can be performed.

Additionally, there are still some other methods that learn the common feature representations across multiple imaging modalities [62–64]. Although these methods are not designed for multimodal registration purpose, they have the potentials to further improve/investigate the multimodal registration problem.

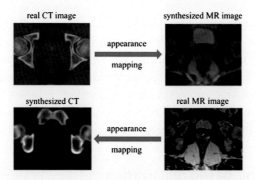

Figure 14.6 An example of bi-directional image synthesis results of pelvic CT and MRI.

14.3.3 Learning appearance mapping

The multimodal registration is more challenging compared with the mono-modal registration, since the large appearance difference across modalities makes it difficult to use the existing similarity metrics. To eliminate the appearance difference, some machine learning techniques have been applied to learn an image synthesis model between two modalities. Afterwards, the multimodal registration can be simplified as a monomodal registration problem, then, many effective similarity metrics can be applied. For example, Roche et al. [55] synthesized an ultrasound image and then estimated rigid registration between the ultrasound and MR images. Zhao et al. [56] simulated CT image from MRI to realize the brain CT and MRI registration. However, in these approaches, the image synthesis is often performed in single direction, and the synthetic direction is from the image modality with rich anatomical information to that with limited anatomical information, e.g., synthesizing ultrasound/CT from MRI.

To further improve the accuracy of multi-modal registration, a bi-directional image synthesis based multimodal registration algorithms were proposed [57,58] to nonlinearly register the pelvic CT and MR images. In these works, a structured random forest was applied to learn the image synthesis model in both directions, i.e., not only synthesizing CT from MRI, but also synthesizing MRI from CT. One novelty in this study is that the MR image is synthesized from a single CT modality, which is a "simple-to-complex" image synthesis problem, since the anatomical information of MRI is more complex than that in CT image. Fig. 14.6 shows an example of the bi-directional image synthesis results in this study. Afterwards, a dual-core steered multimodal registration method was proposed by using the complementary anatomical information from both modalities, to more accurately steer the deformable registration. Experimental results demonstrated that, the bi-directional image synthesis can help significantly improve the multimodal registration performance. Based on the learning-based bi-directional image synthesis framework, a region-adaptive multimodal registration method was further proposed to solve the pelvic CT and MRI registration problem [59].

In summary, machine learning algorithms can be applied in learning the prior knowledge in different aspects, to help solve or simplify the challenging multimodal registration problem. This includes learning the similarity metric, the common feature representation, and the appearance mapping model. By leveraging machine learning, many multimodal registration problems can be effectively resolved. Based on more precise multimodal information fusion achieved by accurate registration, various clinical applications can be facilitated accordingly.

14.4. Deep-learning-based registration

Recently, deep learning methods, such as convolutional neural network (CNN) has shown promising capability in achieving end-to-end learning in many medical image analysis tasks, such as image segmentation [65,66] and image classification [67]. However, unlike segmentation and classification tasks, it is not straightforward to directly solve the image registration problem by using deep learning, due to the following two reasons. First, the input image pair and the target dense deformation field belong to different physical spaces, thus the mapping from the intensity image pair and the target deformation field is highly complex and nonlinear. Second, under the commonly used supervised learning manner, the "ground-truth" deformation field is difficult to obtain in practice.

In order to circumvent the prediction of tremendous number of spatial parameters in the deformation fields, researchers first employed patch-based learning framework to improve the applicability of traditional registration method. As shown in Fig. 14.7(A), this includes learning (1) similarity metric for two images [52,68,69], (2) rigid transformation parameters [70,71], or (3) patch center displacement [22]. More recently, with the improvement of the voxel-to-voxel mapping capability achieved by deep learning, the end-to-end learning for the deformable registration task was gradually achieved [72–74,24]. As shown in Fig. 14.7(B), the dense deformation field can be directly predicted under different learning manners. By performing end-to-end learning, the network can be trained by using the "ground-truth" deformation field, which usually obtained by a traditional registration algorithm under the help of tissue segmentation map [22,23]. The network can also be trained in more advanced unsupervised learning manner [69,75–77]. In this case, we do not need carefully prepare the "ground-truth" deformation field.

Table 14.3 summarizes the deep-learning-based registration methods according to three categories, which will be elaborated separately in the following sections.

14.4.1 Learning similarity metric

As given by Eq. (14.1), the registration task can be mathematically formulated as finding an optimal transformation that minimizes the dissimilarity between the images defined

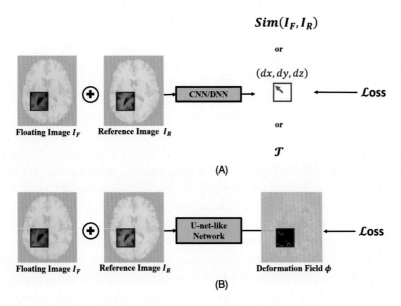

Figure 14.7 Two typical frameworks of the deep-learning-based registration methods: (A) patch-based model and (B) dense prediction model (voxel-to-voxel).

Table 14.3 Representative studies for deep learning based registration methods.

Learning objective	Supervision manner	Architecture	Data	Ref.
Similarity metric	Supervised	DNN	Brain CT/MRI	[52]
		CNN	Brain MRI	[68]
	Unsupervised	Conv ISA	Brain MRI	[69]
Transformation parameters	Supervised	CNN	X-Ray Image (Rigid registration)	[70]
		CNN	Brain MRI (Rigid registration)	[71]
		CNN	Brain MRI (Sparse matching)	[22]
		U–Net–like	Brain MRI (Initial momentum)	[23]
Deformation field	Supervised	U–Net–like	Brain/Cardiac MRI	[72–74,24]
	Unsupervised	U–Net–like	Brain MRI	[75–77]

by the degree of spatial alignment. An effective similarity metric is important in image registration. The intensity-based metrics, including SSD, NCC, and MI, have been successfully employed in many image registration methods to quantify the degree of similarity based on image intensities. However, these similarity metrics highly depend on the intensity distributions of images, which makes them ineffective in dealing with diverse data. In contrast to traditional image registration methods, deep-learning-based methods can directly learn an effective similarity metric from training data.

One such method was proposed by Cheng et al. in [52], where a binary classifier was trained to determine whether the two image patches were similar or not. A DNN, which consists of two stacked autoencoders (SAEs), was used as the classifier. It was trained and tested on sampled (non)corresponding image patches from same subject. Then, the predicted classification results were transformed into continuous probability values, which can be used as the similarity measurement. The proposed similarity metric was shown to correctly find the corresponding patches, which makes it effective in improving the registration accuracy. Inspired by this idea, Simonovsky et al. [68] used CNN to estimate a similarity metric between two patches from different images. Moreover, they also evaluated the proposed similarity metric on the actual 3D registration task by directly optimizing the transformation parameters via CNN. The similarity metric learned by CNN has shown better registration performance than DNN in capturing the complex-to-define image similarity between different medical images.

By using the supervised learning manner, a well-prepared training dataset with accurately aligned image pairs is required to conduct the training process, where the prealigned image pairs and their deformation fields are usually obtained by certain traditional registration methods. Thus, the precision of the employed registration methods may affect the training accuracy. Accordingly, Wu et al. [69] sought the correspondences directly from the image data in an unsupervised manner, by combining independent subspace analysis (ISA) and convolutional layers to extract features. The resultant feature vectors were used to incorporate into the HAMMER registration algorithm [78], instead of using the hand-engineered features. The learned feature is more distinctive, which can be used to effectively measure the image/patch similarity, and can consequently improve both accuracy and efficiency of registration results.

14.4.2 Learning preliminary transformation parameters

Image registration is a high dimensional optimization task as the deformation field consists of dense and smooth displacement vectors. To simplify the complicated optimization procedure, some studies focused on learning preliminary transformation parameters, such as rigid transformation parameters [70,71] and displacements of key points [22] by using patch-based CNN architecture.

In order to assess the pose and location of an implanted object during surgery, Miao et al. [70] used a CNN regression approach to achieve real-time 2D/3D registration. For this rigid registration task, the learning model aimed to predict 6 transformation parameters, including rotation and translation. To simplify the complex regression task in registration, the transformation parameter space was partitioned into different zones and the CNN model was trained in each zone separately. Then, the transformation parameters were decomposed in a hierarchical manner. The CNN model was trained using simulated data generated by manually adapting the transformation parameters. Salehi et al. [71] also proposed a deep CNN regression model for 3D rigid registration. They estimated rigid transformation based on 3D volumetric or sectional image representations. Specifically, the bi-invariant geodesic distance was used as the loss function. Moreover, the deep residual regression network was augmented with a correction network to estimate translation parameters, and then to initialize the optimization-based registration, in order to achieve robust and accurate registration at the widest plausible range of 3D rotations. Besides improving the registration accuracy, this method also significantly improved the computational speed.

Predicting the registration parameters for deformable registration is more challenging than rigid registration. Cao et al. [22] used an equalized active-points sampling strategy to build a similarity-steered CNN model, to predict the displacements associated with the active points, then the dense deformation field can be obtained by interpolation. This strategy significantly enhanced the accuracy when estimating the deformation field and did not require further refinement by traditional registration methods. Based on this framework, a cue-aware deep regression network was further proposed to more effectively train a registration network [79]. In these two methods, the "ground-truth" displacements were obtained with the help of tissue segmentations by using existing registration tools.

14.4.3 End-to-end learning for deformable registration

All the aforementioned methods aim to learn a prior knowledge to simplify or improve the registration task. Compared with these learning-based registration methods, conducting end-to-end learning in registration task can directly establish the mapping model from the input images to the final deformation field. This provides a more flexible way to solve the complicated registration problem. Unlike the traditional registration algorithms which often need iterative optimization along with careful parameter tuning, the end-to-end learning method can directly predict the dense deformation field without the need of parameter tuning. Recently, fully convolutional network [80] and U-Net [66] architectures have shown their efficacy in voxel-to-voxel prediction. Considering the success of these deep networks in image segmentation tasks, researchers show keen interest in using these networks for predicting the dense deformation field in image registration task. Basically, as shown in Fig. 14.8, the end-to-end deep-learning-based registration network can be trained in supervised, unsupervised, and semisupervised learning manner.

For *supervised learning manner*, the registration network is trained based on the ground-truth deformation fields. Uzunova et al. [72] focused on synthesizing huge amount of realistic ground-truth training data for deep-learning-based medical image registration. Basically, they learned a statistical appearance model from the available training images and applied this model to synthesize an arbitrary number of new images

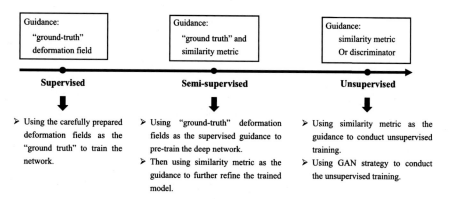

Figure 14.8 Deep-learning-based end-to-end registration methods using supervised, semisupervised, and unsupervised learning.

with varying shape and appearance. Rohe et al. [73] proposed a U–Net-like architecture, namely SVF-Net, to perform image registration. In order to obtain an accurate ground-truth mapping between the image pair, they built reference deformations for training by registering the segmented regions-of-interest (ROIs) instead of registering the intensity images. Sokooti et al. [74] proposed RegNet to estimate the displacement field from a pair of chest CT images. The training process was conducted on a variety of simulated deformations acting as the ground truth, while the testing stage used the trained model for aligning the baseline and follow-up CT images of a same patient. In another study, Yang et al. [23] predicted the momenta of the deformation in large deformation diffeomorphic metric mapping (LDDMM) setting [81]. LDDMM model takes an initial momentum value for each voxel (which is often computationally expensive) as input to calculate the final deformation field. The authors circumvented this by training a U–Net-like architecture to predict the dense momentum map from the input images. They trained the prediction network using training images and the ground-truth initial momentum obtained by numerical optimization of the LDDMM registration model. Visually comparable results were obtained but the computational time was significantly improved (i.e., 1500x speed-up for 2D and 66x speed-up for 3D registration). For the *supervised learning*, the ground-truth deformation is needed, but the real "ground-truth" deformations cannot be obtained in practice for the deformable registration task. Consequently, it is difficult to outperform the accuracy of conventional registration methods that are used for generating the ground truth.

Unlike *supervised learning*, the *unsupervised* learning strategies allow the registration network to learn the deformation field from the to-be-registered image pair automatically [75,82,77,83]. The unsupervised learning models estimate voxel-to-voxel displacements by maximizing the image similarity metric between the to-be-registered image pair, without the need of the ground-truth deformations. The target output is still the deformation field, but the loss is defined on the similarity between the reference image and the floating image warped by the output deformation field. That is, if the predicted deformation field is accurate, the warped floating image should be similar to the reference image. Some standard similarity metrics, which are derivable, such as SSD and NCC, can be employed to define the loss function during the training of the registration network. Since the similarity loss is defined on the images, not directly on the output deformation field, the loss gradient needs to backpropagate to the network to update the parameters during training. To achieve this goal, the spatial transformer network (STN) [84] is applied to perform the grid sampling on the image using the output deformation field. The STN can help propagate the gradient from the loss to the network without introducing additional training parameters. In addition, regularization loss [85] is also adopted to constrain the smoothness of the predicted deformation field. This unsupervised end-to-end learning procedure makes it realizable to train the registration network on large-scale unlabeled images.

Some additional properties are also applied to further improve the registration performance. Fan et al. [24] proposed a semisupervised U–Net–like network to deal with the lack of "ground-truth" deformations when training a deformable registration network. In this work, the deformation field achieved by a conventional registration method was used as the coarse guidance to pretrain the network, then the similarity between the reference image and the warped floating image was served as a fine guidance to further refine the trained model. Dalca et al. [86] added diffeomorphic property in this unsupervised learning framework. In this method, the output of the registration network is the velocity field and then uses several squaring and scaling layers to finally obtain the diffeomorphic field.

By using unsupervised learning strategy, the registration model can be trained without the need of ground-truth deformations, but a specific similarity metric, which is derivable, needs to be used, such as NCC or SSD. However, it is sometimes difficult to determine which metric is the most effective when dealing with different registration tasks. To avoid this issue, a generative adversarial network (GAN) was applied to train a registration network without using any specific similarity metric [87]. In this method, a generator is used to train a registration model and a discriminator is used to automatically judge whether the images are well-aligned or not. The generator plays the same role with the registration network, as the input is the to-be-registered image pair and the output is the deformation field. For the discriminator, the registration result generated by the generator was regarded as a "negative" case, and the well-aligned image pair was regarded as a "positive" case. The adversarial training strategy is applied to alternatively train the generator and discriminator until getting the final convergence. In the testing stage, only using the generator can predict the final deformation field. By applying GAN strategy, the registration network can be trained without using similarity metric, instead, the discriminator will evaluate the image similarity automatically.

In summary, deep learning techniques have been applied to simplify the deformable image registration problem from a complex spatial matching to a regression learning problem. Besides learning some prior knowledge as a good registration initialization, voxel-to-voxel learning framework helps in realizing end-to-end learning of the deformable image registration task. Under this framework, the registration can be implemented without iterative optimization and parameter tuning, which provides a more flexible and applicable way to solve the diverse registration problems. As a result, the efficient, accurate, and robust registration derived by deep-learning-based methods will become a core component of precise and intelligent medicine.

References

[1] D. Rueckert, L. Sonoda, C. Hayes, D. Hill, M. Leach, D. Hawkes, Nonrigid deformations using free form deformations: an application to breast MR images, IEEE Transactions on Medical Imaging 18 (8) (1999) 712–721.

[2] L.G. Brown, A survey of image registration techniques, ACM Computing Surveys 24 (4) (1992) 325–376.

[3] A. Roche, G. Malandain, X. Pennec, N. Ayache, The correlation ratio as a new similarity measure for multimodal image registration, in: International Conference on Medical Image Computing and Computer-Assisted Intervention, Springer, 1998, pp. 1115–1124.

[4] G. Wu, M. Kim, Q. Wang, D. Shen, Hierarchical attribute-guided symmetric diffeomorphic registration for MR brain images, in: International Conference on Medical Image Computing and Computer-Assisted Intervention, Springer, 2012, pp. 90–97.

[5] C. Studholme, D.L. Hill, D.J. Hawkes, An overlap invariant entropy measure of 3D medical image alignment, Pattern Recognition 32 (1) (1999) 71–86.

[6] P. Viola, W.M. Wells III, Alignment by maximization of mutual information, International Journal of Computer Vision 24 (2) (1997) 137–154.

[7] R.P. Woods, S.T. Grafton, C.J. Holmes, S.R. Cherry, J.C. Mazziotta, Automated image registration: I. General methods and intrasubject, intramodality validation, Journal of Computer Assisted Tomography 22 (1) (1998) 139–152.

[8] J. Thirion, Image matching as a diffusion process: an analogy with Maxwell's demons, Medical Image Analysis 2 (3) (1998) 243–260.

[9] P. Hellier, J. Ashburner, I. Corouge, C. Barillot, K.J. Friston, Inter-subject registration of functional and anatomical data using SPM, in: International Conference on Medical Image Computing and Computer-Assisted Intervention, Springer, 2002, pp. 590–597.

[10] T. Vercauteren, X. Pennec, A. Perchant, N. Ayache, Diffeomorphic demons: efficient non-parametric image registration, NeuroImage 45 (1, Supplement 1) (2009) S61–S72.

[11] B. Avants, C. Epstein, M. Grossman, J. Gee, Symmetric diffeomorphic image registration with cross-correlation: evaluating automated labeling of elderly and neurodegenerative brain, Medical Image Analysis 12 (2008) 26–41.

[12] A. Sotiras, C. Davatzikos, N. Paragios, Deformable medical image registration: a survey, IEEE Transactions on Medical Imaging 32 (7) (2013) 1153–1190.

[13] B. Zitova, J. Flusser, Image registration methods: a survey, Image and Vision Computing 21 (11) (2003) 977–1000.

[14] M. Holden, A review of geometric transformations for nonrigid body registration, IEEE Transactions on Medical Imaging 27 (2008) 111–128.

[15] M.A. Viergever, J.A. Maintz, S. Klein, K. Murphy, M. Staring, J.P. Pluim, A survey of medical image registration – under review, Medical Image Analysis 33 (2016) 140–144.

[16] Y. Ou, H. Akbari, M. Bilello, X. Da, C. Davatzikos, Comparative evaluation of registration algorithms in different brain databases with varying difficulty: results and insights, IEEE Transactions on Medical Imaging 33 (10) (2014) 2039–2065.

[17] A. Klein, J. Andersson, B.A. Ardekani, J. Ashburner, B. Avants, M.C. Chiang, et al., Evaluation of 14 nonlinear deformation algorithms applied to human brain MRI registration, NeuroImage 46 (3) (2009) 786–802.

[18] E. Alpaydin, Introduction to Machine Learning, MIT Press, 2014.

[19] Y. LeCun, Y. Bengio, G. Hinton, Deep learning, Nature 521 (7553) (2015) 436.

[20] G. Litjens, T. Kooi, B.E. Bejnordi, S. Aaa, F. Ciompi, M. Ghafoorian, et al., A survey on deep learning in medical image analysis, Medical Image Analysis 42 (9) (2017) 60–88.

[21] D. Shen, G. Wu, H.I. Suk, Deep learning in medical image analysis, Annual Review of Biomedical Engineering 19 (1) (2017) 221–248.

[22] X. Cao, J. Yang, J. Zhang, D. Nie, M. Kim, Q. Wang, et al., Deformable image registration based on similarity-steered CNN regression, in: International Conference on Medical Image Computing and Computer-Assisted Intervention, 2017.

[23] X. Yang, R. Kwitt, M. Styner, M. Niethammer, Quicksilver: fast predictive image registration – a deep learning approach, NeuroImage 158 (2017) 378–396.

[24] J. Fan, X. Cao, P.T. Yap, D. Shen, BIRNet: brain image registration using dual-supervised fully convolutional networks, preprint, arXiv:1802.04692, 2018.

[25] D. Han, Y. Gao, G. Wu, P.T. Yap, D. Shen, Robust anatomical landmark detection with application to MR brain image registration, Computerized Medical Imaging and Graphics 46 (2015) 277–290.

[26] M. Kim, G. Wu, P. Yap, D. Shen, A general fast registration framework by learning deformation-appearance correlation, IEEE Transactions on Image Processing 21 (2012) 1823–1833.

[27] M. Kim, G. Wu, Q. Wang, S.W. Lee, D. Shen, Improved image registration by sparse patch-based deformation estimation, NeuroImage 105 (2015) 257–268.

[28] S. Tang, Y. Fan, G. Wu, M. Kim, D. Shen, RABBIT: rapid alignment of brains by building intermediate templates, NeuroImage 47 (2009) 1277–1287.

[29] Q. Wang, M. Kim, Y. Shi, G. Wu, D. Shen, Predict brain MR image registration via sparse learning of appearance and transformation, Medical Image Analysis 20 (2015) 61–75.

[30] P. Dong, L. Wang, W. Lin, D. Shen, G. Wu, Scalable joint segmentation and registration framework for infant brain images, Neurocomputing 229 (2017) 54–62.

[31] I. Csapo, B. Davis, Y. Shi, M. Sanchez, M. Styner, M. Niethammer, Longitudinal image registration with temporally-dependent image similarity measure, IEEE Transactions on Medical Imaging 32 (2013) 1939–1951.

[32] S. Hu, L. Wei, Y. Gao, Y.W. Guo, G. Wu, D. Shen, Learning-based deformable image registration for infant MR images in the first year of life, Medical Physics 44 (2017) 158–170.

[33] L. Wei, X. Cao, Z. Wang, Y. Gao, S. Hu, L. Wang, et al., Learning-based deformable registration for infant MRI by integrating random forest with auto-context model, Medical Physics 44 (2017) 6289–6303.

[34] M.A. Hearst, S.T. Dumais, E. Osuna, J. Platt, B. Scholkopf, Support vector machines, IEEE Intelligent Systems & Their Applications 13 (4) (1998) 18–28.

[35] L. Breiman, Random forests, Machine Learning 45 (1) (2001) 5–32.

[36] Z. Zhang, Y. Xu, J. Yang, X. Li, D. Zhang, A survey of sparse representation: algorithms and applications, IEEE Access 3 (2015) 490–530.

[37] D. Zhang, Q. Guo, G. Wu, D. Shen, Sparse patch-based label fusion for multi-atlas segmentation, in: Advances in Neural Information Processing Systems, 2012, pp. 94–102.

[38] A. Criminisi, D. Robertson, E. Konukoglu, J. Shotton, S. Pathak, S. White, et al., Regression forests for efficient anatomy detection and localization in computed tomography scans, Medical Image Analysis 17 (8) (2013) 1293–1303.

[39] Y. Ou, C. Davatzikos, Dramms: deformable registration via attribute matching and mutual-saliency weighting, Medical Image Analysis 15 (4) (2011) 622.

[40] D.G. Lowe, Object recognition from local scale-invariant features, in: Iccv, 1999, p. 1150.

[41] M.E. Leventon, W.E.L. Grimson, Multi-modal volume registration using joint intensity distributions, in: International Conference on Medical Image Computing and Computer-Assisted Intervention, Springer, 1998, pp. 1057–1066.

[42] A.C. Chung, W.M. Wells, A. Norbash, W.E.L. Grimson, Multi-modal image registration by minimising Kullback–Leibler distance, in: International Conference on Medical Image Computing and Computer-Assisted Intervention, Springer, 2002, pp. 525–532.

[43] H.M. Chan, A.C. Chung, S.C. Yu, A. Norbash, W.M. Wells, Multi-modal image registration by minimizing Kullback–Leibler distance between expected and observed joint class histograms, in: 2003 IEEE Computer Society Conference on Computer Vision and Pattern Recognition, Proceedings, Vol. 2, IEEE, 2003, pp. II–570.

[44] R. Gan, J. Wu, A.C. Chung, C. Simon, W.M. Wells, Multiresolution image registration based on Kullback–Leibler distance, in: International Conference on Medical Image Computing and Computer-Assisted Intervention, Springer, 2004, pp. 599–606.

[45] C. Guetter, C. Xu, F. Sauer, J. Hornegger, Learning based non-rigid multi-modal image registration using Kullback–Leibler divergence, in: Medical Image Computing and Computer-Assisted Intervention, 2005, pp. 255–262.

[46] A. Gholipour, N. Kehtarnavaz, R.W. Briggs, K.S. Gopinath, Kullback–Leibler distance optimization for non-rigid registration of echo-planar to structural magnetic resonance brain images, in: IEEE International Conference on Image Processing, ICIP 2007, Vol. 6, IEEE, 2007, pp. VI–221.

[47] R.W. So, A.C. Chung, Multi-modal non-rigid image registration based on similarity and dissimilarity with the prior joint intensity distributions, in: 2010 IEEE International Symposium on Biomedical Imaging: From Nano to Macro, IEEE, 2010, pp. 368–371.

[48] R. So, A. Chung, A novel learning-based dissimilarity metric for rigid and non-rigid medical image registration by using Bhattacharyya distances, Pattern Recognition 62 (2017) 161–174.

[49] M.R. Sabuncu, P. Ramadge, Using spanning graphs for efficient image registration, IEEE Transactions on Image Processing 17 (5) (2008) 788–797.

[50] D. Lee, M. Hofmann, F. Steinke, Y. Altun, N.D. Cahill, B. Scholkopf, Learning similarity measure for multi-modal 3D image registration, in: IEEE Conference on Computer Vision and Pattern Recognition, 2017.

[51] M.M. Bronstein, A.M. Bronstein, F. Michel, N. Paragios, Data fusion through cross-modality metric learning using similarity-sensitive hashing, in: 2010 IEEE Conference on Computer Vision and Pattern Recognition (CVPR), IEEE, 2010, pp. 3594–3601.

[52] X. Cheng, L. Zhang, Y. Zheng, Deep similarity learning for multimodal medical images, Computer Methods in Biomechanics and Biomedical Engineering: Imaging & Visualization 6 (3) (2018) 248–252.

[53] H. Ge, G. Wu, L. Wang, Y. Gao, D. Shen, Hierarchical multi-modal image registration by learning common feature representations, in: International Workshop on Machine Learning in Medical Imaging, 2015.

[54] C. Wachinger, N. Navab, Manifold learning for multi-modal image registration, in: British Machine Vision Conference, 2010.

[55] A. Roche, X. Pennec, G. Malandain, N. Ayache, Rigid registration of 3-d ultrasound with mr images: a new approach combining intensity and gradient information, IEEE Transactions on Medical Imaging 20 (10) (2001) 1038–1049.

[56] C. Zhao, A. Carass, J. Lee, Y. He, J.L. Prince, Whole brain segmentation and labeling from ct using synthetic mr images, in: International Workshop on Machine Learning in Medical Imaging, Springer, 2017, pp. 291–298.

[57] X. Cao, Y. Gao, J. Yang, G. Wu, D. Shen, Learning-based multimodal image registration for prostate cancer radiation therapy, in: International Conference on Medical Image Computing and Computer-Assisted Intervention, Springer, 2016.

[58] X. Cao, J. Yang, Y. Gao, Y. Guo, G. Wu, D. Shen, Dual-core steered non-rigid registration for multi-modal images via bi-directional image synthesis, Medical Image Analysis 41 (2017) 18–31.

[59] X. Cao, Region-adaptive deformable registration of CT/MRI pelvic images via learning-based image synthesis, IEEE Transactions on Image Processing 27 (7) (2018) 3500–3512.

[60] T. Kailath, The divergence and Bhattacharyya distance measures in signal selection, IEEE Transactions on Communication Technology 15 (1) (1967) 52–60.

[61] I. Tsochantaridis, T. Joachims, T. Hofmann, Y. Altun, Large margin methods for structured and inter-dependent output variables, Journal of Machine Learning Research 6 (Sep.) (2005) 1453–1484.

[62] H.I. Suk, S.W. Lee, D. Shen, A.D.N. Initiative, et al., Hierarchical feature representation and multi-modal fusion with deep learning for AD/MCI diagnosis, NeuroImage 101 (2014) 569–582.

[63] P. Vincent, H. Larochelle, I. Lajoie, Y. Bengio, P.A. Manzagol, Stacked denoising autoencoders: learn-ing useful representations in a deep network with a local denoising criterion, Journal of Machine Learning Research 11 (Dec.) (2010) 3371–3408.

[64] N. Srivastava, R.R. Salakhutdinov, Multimodal learning with deep Boltzmann machines, in: Advances in Neural Information Processing Systems, 2012, pp. 2222–2230.

[65] D. Nie, L. Wang, E. Adeli, C. Lao, W. Lin, D. Shen, 3-D fully convolutional networks for multimodal isointense infant brain image segmentation, IEEE Transactions on Cybernetics 32 (2018) 1939–1951.

[66] O. Ronneberger, P. Fischer, T. Brox, U-Net: convolutional networks for biomedical image segmen-tation, in: International Conference on Medical Image Computing and Computer-Assisted Interven-tion, Springer, 2015, pp. 234–241.

[67] K. He, X. Zhang, S. Ren, J. Sun, Delving deep into rectifiers: surpassing human-level performance on ImageNet classification, in: Proceedings of the IEEE International Conference on Computer Vision, 2015, pp. 1026–1034.

[68] M. Simonovsky, B. Gutiérrez-Becker, D. Mateus, N. Navab, N. Komodakis, A deep metric for multimodal registration, in: International Conference on Medical Image Computing and Computer-Assisted Intervention, Springer, 2016, pp. 10–18.

[69] G. Wu, M. Kim, Q. Wang, Y. Gao, S. Liao, D. Shen, Unsupervised deep feature learning for de-formable registration of MR brain images, in: International Conference on Medical Image Computing and Computer-Assisted Intervention, 2013.

[70] S. Miao, Z.J. Wang, R. Liao, A CNN regression approach for real-time 2D/3D registration, IEEE Transactions on Medical Imaging 35 (5) (2016) 1352–1363.

[71] S. Salehi, S. Khan, D. Erdogmus, A. Gholipour, Real-time deep registration with geodesic loss 2018, preprint, arXiv:1803.05982.

[72] H. Uzunova, M. Wilms, H. Handels, J. Ehrhardt, Training CNNs for image registration from few samples with model-based data augmentation, in: International Conference on Medical Image Com-puting and Computer-Assisted Intervention, Springer, 2017, pp. 223–231.

[73] M.M. Rohé, M. Datar, T. Heimann, M. Sermesant, X. Pennec, SVF-Net: learning deformable image registration using shape matching, in: International Conference on Medical Image Computing and Computer-Assisted Intervention, 2017.

[74] H. Sokooti, B. de Vos, F. Berendsen, B.P.F. Lelieveldt, I. Išgum, M. Staring, Nonrigid image regis-tration using multi-scale 3D convolutional neural networks, in: International Conference on Medical Image Computing and Computer-Assisted Intervention, 2017.

[75] G. Balakrishnan, A. Zhao, M. Sabuncu, J. Guttag, A. Dalca, An unsupervised learning model for deformable medical image registration, preprint, arXiv:1802.02604, 2018.

[76] H. Li, Y. Fan, Non-rigid image registration using self-supervised fully convolutional networks without training data, preprint, arXiv:1801.04012, 2018.

[77] B. de Vos, F. Berendsen, M. Viergever, M. Staring, I. Išgum, End-to-end unsupervised deformable image registration with a convolutional neural network, in: Deep Learning in Medical Image Analysis and Multimodal Learning for Clinical Decision Support, Springer, 2017, pp. 204–212.

[78] D. Shen, C. Davatzikos, Hammer: hierarchical attribute matching mechanism for elastic registration, IEEE Transactions on Medical Imaging 21 (11) (2002) 1421–1439.

[79] X. Cao, J. Yang, J. Zhang, Q. Wang, P.T. Yap, D. Shen, Deformable image registration using cue-aware deep regression network, IEEE Transactions on Biomedical Engineering (2018).

[80] J. Long, E. Shelhamer, T. Darrell, Fully convolutional networks for semantic segmentation, in: Proceedings of the IEEE Conference on Computer Vision and Pattern Recognition, 2015, pp. 3431–3440.

[81] Y. Cao, M.I. Miller, R.L. Winslow, L. Younes, et al., Large deformation diffeomorphic metric mapping of vector fields, IEEE Transactions on Medical Imaging 24 (9) (2005) 1216–1230.

[82] H. Li, Y. Fan, Non-rigid image registration using self-supervised fully convolutional networks without training data, 2018, pp. 1075–1078.

[83] G. Balakrishnan, A. Zhao, M.R. Sabuncu, J. Guttag, A.V. Dalca, VoxelMorph: a learning framework for deformable medical image registration, IEEE Transactions on Medical Imaging 38 (8) (2019) 1788–1800.

[84] Jaderberg M. Simonyan, K. ZA, Spatial transformer networks, 2015, pp. 2017–2025.

[85] V. Vishnevskiy, T. Gass, G. Szekely, C. Tanner, O. Goksel, Isotropic total variation regularization of displacements in parametric image registration, IEEE Transactions on Medical Imaging 36 (2) (2016) 385–395.

[86] A.V. Dalca, G. Balakrishnan, J. Guttag, M.R. Sabuncu, Unsupervised learning for fast probabilistic diffeomorphic registration, 2019, pp. 729–738.

[87] J. Fan, X. Cao, Z. Xue, P.T. Yap, D. Shen, Adversarial similarity network for evaluating image alignment in deep learning based registration, 2018, pp. 739–746.

CHAPTER 15

Imaging biomarkers in Alzheimer's disease

Carole H. Sudre, M. Jorge Cardoso, Marc Modat, Sebastien Ourselin
School of Biomedical Engineering & Imaging Sciences, King's College London, London, United Kingdom

Contents

15.1. Introduction	344
15.2. Range of imaging modalities and associated biomarkers	345
15.2.1 Structural imaging	345
15.2.1.1 Grey matter assessment	*345*
15.2.1.2 White matter damage	*346*
15.2.1.3 Microstructural imaging	*347*
15.2.2 Functional and metabolite imaging	347
15.2.2.1 Functional imaging	*347*
15.2.2.2 Molecular imaging	*348*
15.3. Biomarker extraction evolution	349
15.3.1 Acquisition improvement	349
15.3.2 Biomarkers extraction: from visual scales to automated processes	349
15.3.3 Automated biomarker extraction: behind the scene	351
15.3.4 Automated methodological development validation	352
15.4. Biomarkers in practice	353
15.4.1 Practical use	353
15.4.2 Biomarkers' path to validation	354
15.4.3 Current challenges	355
15.5. Biomarkers' strategies: practical examples	356
15.5.1 Global vs local	356
15.5.1.1 Spatial patterns of abnormality – from global to local	*356*
15.5.1.2 The case of the hippocampus	*358*
15.5.2 Longitudinal vs cross-sectional	358
15.5.2.1 Challenges in longitudinal analyses	*359*
15.5.2.2 The case of the boundary shift integral (BSI)	*360*
15.6. Future avenues of image analysis for biomarkers in Alzheimer's disease	360
15.6.1 Community initiatives	360
15.6.1.1 Interfield collaboration	*360*
15.6.1.2 Standardization initiatives, challenges and open-source data	*360*
15.6.2 Technical perspectives	361
15.6.2.1 Combination of modalities and biomarkers – traditional approaches	*361*
15.6.2.2 Ever-increasing potential of AI technologies: reproduction, combination, discovery	*361*
15.6.3 Longitudinal prediction, simulation and ethical considerations	362
References	363

Handbook of Medical Image Computing and Computer Assisted Intervention
https://doi.org/10.1016/B978-0-12-816176-0.00020-X

15.1. Introduction

As per the definition of the Biomarkers Definition Working Group, a biomarker is a characteristic that is objectively measured and evaluated as an indicator of normal biological processes, pathogenic processes, or pharmacologic responses to a therapeutic intervention. In the context of Alzheimer's disease (AD) and neurodegenerative diseases, such characteristic can be used in different settings (research, pharmacological trials, clinical practice) and for different purposes (diagnostic, inclusion/exclusion criteria, stratification, end-point, safety assessment, statistical covariate). Compared to other biological markers of pathologies extracted from blood or cerebrospinal fluid (CSF) samples, imaging provides refined information on the regional pathological changes. The importance of imaging biomarkers of pathological change has largely blossomed since the acknowledgment of their use in preclinical phases of AD as per the diagnosis guidelines released by the NIA-AA in 2011 [1]. Since then, the recent update of the research framework guidelines classifying the different biomarkers according to their representation of amyloid pathology (A), tau injury (T) and neurodegeneration (N) has further contributed to an increased interest into this research field [2].

In the context of Alzheimer's Disease, clinical symptoms of cognitive degradation are preceded by pathophysiological changes that are initially silent such as accumulation of amyloid plaques, formation of tau tangles or neuronal loss. These changes occur over years or even decades before cognitive symptoms are noticed. The longitudinal evolution of these markers has been shown to associate closely to cognitive deterioration. Over the years, associations have been documented between histologically verified brain changes, cognitive decline and measures extracted from brain imaging. These measures include the observation of macrostructural neuronal loss either globally or regionally on computed tomography (CT) or magnetic resonance (MR) imaging, the aggregation of pathological proteins with amyloid or tau positron emission tomography (PET) imaging, the degradation of the functional pathway (lower metabolism through FDG-PET, changes in resting state in fMRI or lowering of cerebral blood flow with arterial spin labeling (ASL)). For the last 40 years, in vivo neuroimaging using CT, MRI, or PET has been used to provide insight over these pathological processes and find or assess potential therapeutic targets. As biomarkers, such imaging derived measurements are designed to provide indicators of the pathological stages, predict the risk of dementia onset, help in the process of a differential diagnosis, and become endpoints measures of disease-modifying treatment in the context of pharmacological trials in association with measures of cognitive decline.

With the accelerated development of more powerful neuroimaging acquisition techniques, providing more complex imaging data, the requirements over imaging analysis techniques have grown stronger. To ensure efficient use of imaging techniques, measurement extraction methods are required to be highly accurate, robust, and reproducible in variable settings and conditions.

After an overview of the range of possible imaging biomarkers in the context of Alzheimer's Disease obtained using different imaging modalities and acquisition sequences, the natural development towards automated extraction of imaging measurement and associated challenges will be presented. The practical use of biomarkers will be detailed before describing practical strategies adopted and their relevance in the context of the pathology (global vs local measures, cross-sectional vs longitudinal). The last part of the chapter will present samples of current trends, strategies, and methodologies adopted in the use of biomarkers for AD with the development of more holistic and robust methods arising thanks to recently acquired computational capacities.

15.2. Range of imaging modalities and associated biomarkers

15.2.1 Structural imaging

Structural imaging as per its name refers to the acquisition sequences and methods allowing to visualize the anatomical disposition of biological tissues with no information on their function. Structural imaging can be subdivided into macrostructural measures (volumes, shape, thickness) and microstructural information informing about tissue properties such as myelin or axonal damage.

15.2.1.1 Grey matter assessment

With a focus on measures of neurodegeneration and consequently grey matter loss, markers of the status of the grey matter either per its volume, shape, or thickness have been extensively developed using diverse imaging techniques. Since the early days of brain imaging, computer tomography (CT) has been used to successfully assess whole brain volumes [3,4] and is still commonly used in clinical practice [5] to assess whole brain atrophy notably in subjects for which an magnetic resonance imaging (MRI) exam is impossible due to the presence of MR incompatible implants, or patient claustrophobia. Due to stronger soft tissue contrast and the absence of radiation administration, MR imaging is, however, classically privileged in research settings on neurodegeneration. Since the mid-1980s, T1 weighted MR imaging has been extensively used due to its ability to provide images with a strong contrast between grey and white matter [6]. Due to the strong parallel found between local region of grey matter loss and cognitive performance [7], the assessment of neuronal loss and observation of cortical cerebral atrophy both globally and regionally has become central to the evaluation of neurodegeneration. Hippocampal volumetry, noted as an early region structurally impacted by the pathology has become over time one of the most used biomarkers of the disease. Other regions such as the entorhinal cortex as well as subcortical structures (thalamus, caudate, amygdala) have also been considered as potential markers for the investigation of Alzheimer's disease. The shape of relevant structures (hippocampus or amygdala) [8,9] as well as a measure of asymmetrical evolution in time [10] have been further reported in the investigation of AD.

15.2.1.2 White matter damage

Grey matter is not the only tissue impacted by the neurodegenerative diseases and white matter may also be damaged in Alzheimer's disease as well as other types of dementia. When damage affects the myelin, used around the axons as an insulator favoring the speed of the saltatory conduction, the tissue lipidic content is lowered and replaced by water which results in an altered fat/water ratio and ultimately a signal rise in T2-weighted images. This type of damage may be due to vascular function degradation leading to partial ischemia through cerebral small vessel disease or inflammatory processes. Alternatively, deposition of amyloid protein along the vessel wall as seen in cerebral amyloid angiopathy may also be at the origin of the development of such lesions [11]. In complement and synergy to the classical amyloid cascade of Alzheimer's pathology [12], the vascular pathway of pathological evolution has been receiving more attention in recent years. As an alternative to the vascular pathway, white matter degradation may be induced secondary to grey matter through Wallerian degeneration [13]. Hypotheses have also been proposed linking the presence of intracellular neurofibrillary tangles and an imbalance to the myelin susceptible to subsequent damage [14]. Although the observed lesions are not specific to a pathophysiological pathway, their increased presence has been associated with a higher risk of dementia onset and an acceleration of the cognitive decline [15]. Classically some of these white matter changes can be observed close to the ventricles (periventricular lesions) and are thus best assessed using Fluid Attenuated Inversion Recovery (FLAIR) MR acquisition that allows for a strong separation between CSF and tissue.

Lacunes, small infarcts in the white matter best observed on FLAIR and T2-weighted images, as per the recent guidelines on standardization over markers of cerebral small vessel disease are an additional marker that has been associated with Alzheimer's disease and vascular dementia [16,17].

Another impactful marker of vascular damage, microbleeds, that are hemosiderin deposits in the brain parenchyma appear to have a higher prevalence in AD while located mostly in the occipital region. Such markers are best observed using blood sensitive sequences such as Susceptibility Weighted Imaging or T2* in which iron-rich areas appear hypointense [18].

Beyond the spectrum of pathologically induced vascular damage, white matter changes have been observed as associated with the effect of amyloid drugs. Called amyloid-related imaging abnormalities (ARIA), cerebral microhemorrhages (ARIA-H) and transient vasogenic oedema changes in white matter signal (ARIA-E) have been observed after administration of high doses of amyloid immunotherapy treatments thus making the monitoring of these biomarkers crucial to ensure the safety of clinical trials [19].

15.2.1.3 Microstructural imaging

Diffusion-weighted imaging (DWI) and diffusion tensor imaging (DTI) image the movement of water within brain tissue and the constraints applied to it for instance along the axons. This has thus opened the door to the study of WM tracts and the investigation of associated microstructural properties. These techniques have the ability to indirectly inform about the damage of the underlying tissue such as demyelination, axonal loss or gliosis. Measures extracted from diffusion imaging such as fractional anisotropy or mean diffusivity have been shown to be altered in both Alzheimer's Disease subjects and mild cognitive impairment [20] compared to healthy controls and are thought to be potentially used as markers of prediction of conversion from MCI to AD [21–23]. Magnetic transfer ratio (MTR) measures the ratio between free protons and those attached to macromolecular structures, and thereby reflects the integrity of cell membranes. Widely used in the context of Multiple Sclerosis, a decreased MTR is thought to represent the damage sustained by the myelin. In AD, decreased MTR has notably been reported over the whole brain [24,25], the hippocampus [26], and the corpus callosum [27].

15.2.2 Functional and metabolite imaging

15.2.2.1 Functional imaging

Imaging the glucose consumption throughout the brain provides a means to assess brain metabolism and variations from normal expected observations. With radiotracers such as 18 fluorodeoxyglucose (FDG) binding to glucose, uptake (consumption) in the cortical areas can be imaged consequently presenting a visualization of the underlying metabolic dynamics. In the early stages of AD, decreased metabolism in the precuneus, entorhinal cortex and hippocampus have been observed mapping accurately with areas known to be early affected by neuronal loss [28,29]. The IWG-2 diagnosis workforce has highlighted the topographic contribution of FDG-PET in the consideration of disease evolution while patterns of decreased metabolism have been shown to provide strong discriminative properties between neurodegeneration subtypes especially FTD and dementia with Lewy bodies [29]. Thus, reduced glucose uptake observed on FDG-PET is considered as a sign of neurodegeneration [30].

As an alternative to the injection of a radiotracer, arterial spin labeling that uses water in the blood as an endogenous tracer allows for the quantification of blood flow throughout the brain. It has not only been shown to be able to accurately classify between normal and AD subjects but recent results have reported the ability of measures extracted from this imaging modality to relate closely to cognitive decline and different disease stages [31]. However, hypotheses of the early decrease of cerebral blood flow even prior to the presentation of amyloid deposition [32] are still in need for validation in order to evaluate the potential of such measurement in a preclinical presentation of AD. Compared to the use of FDG-PET, the sensitivity of such technique still appears to be slightly reduced [33]. Due to a large number of natural factors susceptible to impact cerebral blood flow and consequently ASL measurement, such as caffeine consumption, medication, blood composition, heart rate or mental state, a deeper understanding of each subject physiological status seems warranted to transform ASL in the path to validated biomarkers [34].

As a measure of brain activity, functional Magnetic Resonance Imaging (fMRI) through the blood oxygen level dependent (BOLD) signal uses the principle of oxygenation level variation as a measure of consumption and thus of indirect measure of neural activity [35]. Time course investigation of the signal in different brain region guides towards an interpretation of simultaneous activation and of the neural network of association between brain regions. The study of such networks either at rest (resting state fMRI) [36] or during specific tasks (task fMRI) has been reported to be different in AD subjects compared to controls and MCI subjects [19,37].

15.2.2.2 Molecular imaging

Proton magnetic resonance spectroscopy (1H-MRS) is used for the quantitation of biochemical compounds in biological tissue. A reduced level of N-acetyl aspartate (NAA) that reflects the status of neuronal mitochondria has been reported in Alzheimer's disease and such quantitation of tissue cellular function has been shown to be altered by pharmacological treatments [38].

Since the pathological process of AD appears to causally relate to the apparition of abnormal protein aggregation through extracellular amyloid plaques and intracellular neurofibrillary tangle tau to neuronal loss that parallel a downstream effect on cognitive ability, investigating and quantifying changes of the brain prior to neuronal loss has risen hopes for an earlier detection of pathological processes. Imaging of tau and amyloid pathology has become possible via the use of PET imaging and the development of radiotracers sensitive to the pathologically aggregated proteins.

Imaging of the binding of the radiotracers to these proteins enables the visualization of areas with an increased concentration of amyloid or tau pathology, that have been shown to preempt neuronal loss observed on macrostructural imaging and subsequent cognitive decline. The validation of the sensitivity of the C11 PiB tracer to amyloid plaques deposit and the association between binding and histopathological findings [39] of amyloid plaques has made amyloid PET one of the core acquisitions confirming the presence of amyloid pathology in suspected Alzheimer's disease cases. Since the development of the 11C-PIB tracer, other markers with longer half-life have been put on the market, easing the logistic burden of such examinations.

Development of radiotracers sensitive to tau pathology with postmortem histological validation [40] has recently become possible. Challenges related to the intracellular and multiform nature of the tau tangles requiring very sensitive tracers able to cross the cell membrane explain why appropriate solutions have been so long to be developed [14]. Although nonspecific binding to markers of astrogliosis was observed in first generation tracers, recently proposed improvements appear to present less off-target binding [41] and confirm the potential of imaging measures of tau pathology to become a useful biomarker in Alzheimer's disease [42].

15.3. Biomarker extraction evolution

15.3.1 Acquisition improvement

Through the years, neuroimaging has drastically improved thanks to a combination of advances in imaging hardware and the improvement and development of acquisition sequences. In the case of MR, hardware changes have seen the broad adoption of scanners with higher field strength from 1.5 T to 3 T, changes in head coils. As a consequence, images have become faster to acquire, with less distortion and higher resolution. As an example, while 16 T1-weighted 1 cm thick slices were acquired in about 20 min in 1983 on 1.5 T scanners, standard MPRAGE T1-weighted sequences 1 mm isotropic can now be acquired in less than 5 min on a 3 T scanner.

Investigation of the impact of increase in field strength from 1.5 T to 3 T on biomarkers measurements has shown a higher signal to noise ratio favoring more accurate delineation of the regions of interest such as the hippocampus, as well as a stronger sensitivity to vascular markers notably microbleeds [43] and WMH [44,45]. With shorter acquisition times, the risk for subject motion has been lowered and it has become possible to combine multiple acquisitions in a single MR session. For vascular markers, acquisition of 3D sequences instead of 2D has led to a reduction in the amount of observed artefact and of an increase in sensitivity to these pathological changes [46,47].

In the case of PET imaging, more sensitive detectors, improved reconstruction algorithms and optimized radiotracers have similarly contributed to drastic changes in the quality of the acquired images [48,49]. Lately, a combination of modalities in hybrid systems such as PET/CT and PET/MR scanners has allowed for the joint acquisition of metabolic/PET functional data and structural sequences. Advantages and limitations of such new technological development in the field of dementia have been largely documented since the first development of hybrid PET/MR [50] scanners and have led to the development of new methodological solutions to overcome inherent challenges such as the need for tissue attenuation coefficient maps [51,52].

15.3.2 Biomarkers extraction: from visual scales to automated processes

The development of new imaging biomarkers in Alzheimer's Disease follows a very standardized evolutionary paths. Starting from visual qualitative observations on a limited numbers of cases that are if possible validated through histological observation, methodological tools are then developed to provide relevant quantifiable measurements. These are then further enhanced and automated to precisely and robustly quantify at a larger scale, more complex data.

From all observations of pathological changes, the need to create normative frameworks to quantify the level of abnormality has led to the creation of assessment protocols and grading scales that reflect specific pathological patterns. Various protocols of grading the observed level of grey matter atrophy either in a specific region, known to be affected early by the pathology like the medial temporal lobe, or assessing ventricle enlargement have been developed and are currently broadly used [53,54]. Visual scales have also been validated for the assessment of white matter hyperintensities [55–58]. Such tools have been shown to relate well to cognitive functioning and to be highly predictive of the diagnosis [59]. Their popularity in the clinical research community has, however, not reached completely clinical practice. To that effect, recent initiatives have been started in order to facilitate their broader application [60].

However, their use is limited by the inherent need for categorization and the associated risk of ceiling and flooring effect. Furthermore, although their relevance has been proven for cross-sectional use, their ability to detect change over time is poor [61]. Longitudinal visual scales have been developed in the case of white matter hyperintensities but outcomes can further be biased by the way the longitudinal display is performed [62]. Despite the fact that most of them were originally developed for either other modalities (CT) or field strength (1.5 T), such scales have not been revalidated on recently developed acquisitions.

Quantification by categorization is limited and cannot reflect appropriately the continuum of the pathological evolution. In both the case of grey matter atrophy and white matter hyperintensity, volumetry measurements have been the natural development towards more quantifiable measurements. Volumetry requires the ability to appropriately and robustly delineate a region of interest. When these criteria are not met, no additional interest can be found in their use compared to visual scales as observed in early studies [63]. Such delineation can be performed totally freely by a rater according to a detailed protocol explaining, for instance, how to scale the windowing of the image, in which order/orientation to consider the slices to segment, how to define the borders of the region of interest. Validation of these manual protocols is often based on the relevance of the extracted measures in clinical classification as well as inter- and intrarater measures of agreement. Due to the time-consuming nature of such processes, semiautomated protocols have been introduced. Interactive segmentation tools allowing for region growing, morphological changes or automated thresholding are available in most medical imaging viewing platforms (MIDAS [64], ITKSnap, 3DSlicer) and contribute to reduce the operating time and increase the segmentation reproducibility. Nonetheless, these solutions are difficult to apply at scale and demands for fully automated solutions have grown accordingly. Manual segmentation despite its variability is still classically considered as providing a gold standard against which newly developed automated algorithms have to be validated. Automated processes of biomarkers extraction, in turn, are often developed and gathered in open source software suites (SPM, FSL, Freesurfer) [65–67] or packages (NiftySeg/Reg, MRTrix, AFNI) to be used by a large range of users in the community. Given the complexity and large choice of variants to be used at each step of a processing framework and in order to ensure consistency and reproducibility, efforts have been recently put into the creation of standardizing pipelines such as Nipype [68]. With a stronger demand in direct processing, web-based services have also emerged offering on-demand processing [69,70].

15.3.3 Automated biomarker extraction: behind the scene

Quantitative automatically extracted measurements used as biomarkers generally rely on the application of other methodological frameworks (registration, segmentation, partial volume correction) that have to be thoroughly validated as any error at early stages of the process will be propagated and impact the extracted value. Such effects can be for instance observed on PET imaging regarding the influence of MR segmentation errors [71]. The quality and validity of automated imaging biomarker extraction relies indeed heavily on other steps of data manipulation and correction due to the need for normalization, artifact correction or the extraction of additional measures to be used as nuisance covariates.

Head size measurement, while not reflective of the pathology, is, for instance, essential for any alignment to normative data and correction in statistical analysis. Accuracy of this measurement in volumetric studies has been shown to significantly affect resulting sample sizes [72,73] and has thus benefited from various methodological advances. In order to avoid the dependence on head size measurement present in volumetric studies, some have favored measures of cortical thickness that do not require this normalization step [74].

Moreover, additional steps may be required to correct for the presence of artifact induced by the imaging process. For instance, in the case of structural MRI, the presence of intensity inhomogeneities due to variation in magnetic field strength can affect greatly any quantitative output if not properly accounted for. Algorithms either correct for this beforehand using well-established methods, integrate the modeling of smooth varying intensities or ensure the proposed method is robust to such artifact [75–77].

In the case of PET imaging, quantitative analysis requires the creation of an attenuation correction map that accounts for the signal attenuation due to the cortical bone. While this measure is readily available when CT imaging is available, it is not the case when MR only is the additional acquired modality as is the case in hybrid PET/MR imaging. Associated methods have thus been developed to synthesize accurate attenuation correction maps even in the absence of CT imaging [51]. Additional processing includes partial volume correction and the choice of a reference region in order to calculate the standardized uptake value ratio that quantifies the specific binding to the targeted protein. The choice of the region of reference has fueled many discussions, the choice among the supratentorial white matter, cerebellar region, or pons being still debated [78]. In any case, such steps require generally the registration of the acquired T1 image. In light of the impact of the propagation of such processing errors on the final extracted value [79], these methodological fields of research have seen continuous development in recent years.

In the context of AD and neurodegenerative pathology, the concomitant presence of pathology has also been shown to affect biomarker measurements. For instance, the presence of white matter hyperintensities [80], hallmark of cerebral small vessel disease, is known to affect the accuracy of grey matter segmentation, cortical thickness measurement [81] as well as nonlinear registration due to its hypointense appearance on T1-weighted images. In order to account for such errors, processes of correction of the T1 images by replacing voxels in which lesions have been detected by healthy appearing tissue, also called inpainting [82], have successfully been adopted in other fields of research, notably multiple sclerosis, in which atrophy and white matter lesion coexist [83,84]. In a similar fashion effect of atrophy on PET signal in longitudinal assessment can be quantified and should be corrected for [85].

15.3.4 Automated methodological development validation

When it comes to the validation of newly developed automatic methods of biomarkers extraction, different methods have been employed according to the existence of a gold standard, a realization by other methods, or its performance in terms of predictive power or sample size estimates. Alternatively, when manual gold standard over a large amount of data is unavailable, correlation with cognitive tests has been used for validation. In the case of segmentation analysis, multiple evaluation metrics have been designed focusing on different assessment of error and bias may it be the distance between surfaces (average distance, Hausdorff distance) or measures of overlap (Jaccard coefficient, Dice coefficient). Their combined use allows for a more complete description of the performance and the study of their distribution can help to describe specific patterns of erroneous behavior. Performance in the classification of subjects (Controls vs MCI vs AD) or the ability to predict clinical conversion are additional measures of the relevance of such extracted metrics. In the development of methodological tools used as the backbone of the extracted imaging biomarkers, the choice of such evaluation metrics needs always to be driven by the context of the underlying application. In the situation where ground truth is impossible to access and/or normative data is available, the absence of difference in predictive accuracy yields to an equal consideration in the performance of compared automated tools [86], even if a large quantitative differences between extracted measurements is observed.

In the perspective of the use of such outcome measures in clinical practice and for clinical trials, evaluation of reproducibility, repeatability, and dependence on imaging acquisition, as well as the analysis potentially impacting results, accuracy is required. Investigation of the use of these quantification tools in multicenter studies is essential in order to assess the ratio between measurement variability across centers and expected signal difference.

15.4. Biomarkers in practice

15.4.1 Practical use

Imaging biomarkers are used at different levels of pathology course in the continuum of Alzheimer's disease.

In the context of clinical trials, their use may differ greatly ranging from their employ in selection criteria or enrichment or their incorporation as surrogate end-points. In order to minimize sample sizes, limit bias, and be applied to the appropriate population, selection criteria are of paramount importance in such trials. Due to site expertise variability, it appears that from 10% to 20% of the population taking part in clinical trials is wrongly included thus at risk of diluting measured effects [87]. Additionally, according to the expected drug effect, specific inclusion criteria may be required. For instance, when assessing a treatment targeting amyloid plaques, one may want to only consider participants presenting with amyloid deposition. In such a case, screening for amyloid-positive participants via either CSF measures or Amyloid PET positive result would be recommended [88].

It has been further shown that hippocampal volumetry was beneficial for the enrichment of clinical trials and has recently been accepted by the European Medicines Agency as potential biomarker to be used for such purpose [89,90]. In order to limit the inclusion of subjects with a mixed form of neurodegeneration, quantitative measures of the presence of vascular pathology can be used to exclude subjects in which the treatment process may be altered. Alternatively, imaging biomarkers may be of further use to ensure the safety of applied drugs as it has been observed that adverse dose-dependent effects could be observed with the occurrence of ARIA in treatments with bapineuzumab [91] or ganternerumab [92].

More recently appearing as surrogate end-points of clinical trials, imaging biomarkers have the advantage to account disease-modifying effects of the drugs and to require smaller sample sizes thanks to their relative more objective quantification and lower variability [93]. Furthermore, while cognitive assessments cannot be revisited, imaging data can be reanalyzed at a later stage and conclusions amended accordingly. For the most part, such imaging end-points currently report measures of structural grey matter atrophy (whole brain, medial temporal volume, or ventricular enlargement).

In addition to pathological imaging biomarkers, as mentioned above, other imaging derived measurements such as total intracranial volume may be required for appropriate analysis over a population or for the use of normative data.

15.4.2 Biomarkers' path to validation

Initial analytical validation of an observed difference between healthy and diseased subjects regarding a specific quantitative measure on a small and homogenous sample is only the first of many steps in the characterization and validation of imaging biomarkers. The ideal construction of a biomarker for Alzheimer's disease would detect a fundamental feature of the pathology, be validated in histologically confirmed cases, present high sensitivity and specificity, be reliable, reproducible, noninvasive, inexpensive, simple to perform [94].

There are many situations in which the imaging modality/sequence although it may reflect an underlying change is not specific to the biological pathway leading to it. Thus contradictory and compensatory changes may simultaneously occur. Alternatively, according to the impacted structure, different directions of changes may be observed. For instance, in the case of diffusion imaging, degradation of a single white matter tract at a region where the direction of present fibres is highly heterogeneous will lead to an increase in fractional anisotropy (FA) [95] while similar degradation in the region of concentrated similarly directed fibres will result in a reduction in fractional anisotropy. Therefore, a direct interpretation of a decreased FA as damage to the underlying white matter is a strong oversimplification of the actual biological situation [96]. Such interpretation oversimplification of extracted quantities may jeopardize the validity of extracted biomarkers and must be accounted for with caution. As another example, in fMRI, a reduction in the BOLD signal may not only be due to a change in activation networks but also reflect a disruption in the neurovascular unit, potentially caused by vascular-induced white matter damage [97]. In light of these examples, the nonspecific nature of imaging observations and the possibility of canceling effects must be kept in mind when assessing the histological validity of a proposed imaging derived biomarker.

Recently, a guideline on the steps to take for a new imaging biomarker to be accepted has been described [98], highlighting the gaps between initial analytical validation of a marker and the requirements to be met for its acceptance in clinical practice. As noted in this position paper, most of the imaging markers available for Alzheimer's disease have shown evidence of analytical validity but most of them lack evidence of clinical validity and utility. One of the key steps in that path to validation is the display of evidence that the power of the proposed biomarker is maintained in a multicenter setting. The difficulty arises with the complexity, variability, and duration of the sequence required for extraction of the biomarker of interest, and is currently a key limitation in the adoption of fMRI [99] and ASL [100] in practice.

In addition, in the perspective of regulatory agencies for the design clinical trials, one of the crucial points of debate relates to the very long development of the pathology before the observation of clinical symptoms. With the repeated failure of drug trials targeting subjects already diagnosed with the disease, some have hypothesized that an earlier treatment prior to any functional degradation was required. This situation makes even more complex the validation of disease-modifying treatments in terms of their functional assessment.

15.4.3 Current challenges

Atrophy, as observed on MR imaging, has been shown to strongly correlate with the neuronal loss on histological data but quantitative measurements extracted from images are only to be used as a surrogate of the histological ground truth and can never be entirely validated. This fact is further exemplified by the measurement variability observed across scanner and sequence acquisitions.

In the field of Alzheimer's disease and dementia, the democratization of neuroimaging worldwide in the last decades translates in the existence of many different scanners on which different sequence protocols are being implemented for similar assessments. The variability of the appearance of resulting images naturally puts a strain on the assumed correspondence between imaging and histological truth. Processes of harmonization among research centers and guidelines of imaging protocols have been felt necessary and various initiatives have been started in an attempt to reduce such source of measurement noise, known to hinder the transfer of imaging biomarker into clinical and pharmacological practice [101,102]. Comparative studies between established methods of processing attempt to provide objective guidelines based on an investigation of the validity of the findings on common standardized datasets. Such investigations have been widely performed in the field of structural MR for measurement of atrophy rates [103] more recently using normalized ground truth [104] but also to investigate the relevance of variation of processing in longitudinal PET amyloid imaging [105] where 1024 processing variants were assessed. Even in established structural volumetric measurement, more unexpected confounding factors such as acquisition time of day, have been shown to contribute to measurement variability [106].

Numerous studies have tried to document the changes in imaging quality resulting from sequence/hardware change over the years. For instance, the effect of field strength changes has been investigated on commonly employed automated solutions for TIV, grey and white matter segmentation [107]. Effect of change of field strength on cortical thickness measurement has resulted in the observation of a thicker cortical sheet at 3 T compared to 1.5 T [108] and the increased signal to noise ratio led to statistically more powerful extraction of hippocampus volumes [109]. Variations in acquisition protocols of T1-weighted images have shown to result in volumetric changes of the order of magnitude of expected pathological changes when using automated algorithms, thereby highlighting the need for corrective processes in data normalization [110]. In the consideration of longitudinal trials, where the stability of the scanner cannot be ensured, investigation of the impact of scanner change or upgrade needs to be documented [111]. While knowledge on the mean effect is of interest and allow for a linear correction, one must, however, be mindful of the potential nonlinear effect of such changes.

Image quality either impacted by scanning issues or by patient behavior is an additional hurdle that may significantly impact the automated extraction of imaging biomarkers. Changes in signal or contrast to noise ratio have also been shown to affect longitudinal measures of brain changes [112] and volumetric tissue measurement [113]. Head motion has been reported as contributing to a significant reduction of measurements of cortical volume and thickness [114]. This observation is of particular importance in dementia where more severely affected subjects are more likely to have difficulty staying still during the imaging session. Furthermore, such constraint may lead to the impossibility to acquire the last sequences if some of the early sequences had to be repeated. This situation may result in a bias in the exclusion or the analysis of the acquired data.

Motion correction algorithms have been applied to partially reduce the introduced bias [115]. Recently, models of motion correction have been developed for hybrid imaging in order to account for longer acquisition protocols using MRI data to retrieve a motion model to correct the PET acquisition [116].

The risk for artifacts in longer acquisitions sequences such as diffusion imaging and the known confounding effect of physiological noise in fMRI have been a major limitation to the translation of associated markers of pathological process into clinical practice. Recent development has pushed for the inclusion of measures of physiological data over the acquisition and model reducing noise in fMRI [117]. In parallel, specific motion model to correct diffusion data have been proposed.

The need to limit the bias introduced by image selection based on data quality, limit the appearance of outliers due to algorithmic failure and control quality of the processing in large scale data has led to an increase in methodological development in the field of quality control either on the images themselves [118,119] or on the output of a segmentation [120] or registration process [121].

15.5. Biomarkers' strategies: practical examples

15.5.1 Global vs local

15.5.1.1 Spatial patterns of abnormality – from global to local

As a global measure of atrophy, whole brain volume changes over time have been shown to be a good predictor of Alzheimer's disease. Global measures have been used early in the study of the disease with the availability of CT images.

However, the neurodegenerative process does not occur uniformly across the brain and patterns of progressive degeneration have been highlighted [122,123]. Overall spatial patterns of pathological changes may be particularly useful for differential diagnosis and to further refine the understanding of specific pathological processes. Beyond the single case of Alzheimer's Disease, information on the pattern of degeneration can also be employed to ensure a more accurate diagnosis, allowing, for instance, to differentiate between Alzheimer's Disease and other neurodegenerative diseases with other subtypes of atrophy patterns such as dementia with Lewy bodies or Fronto-Temporal Dementia. The topography of the pathological patterns is thus highlighted in the working document of the IWG 2 in the definition of useful biomarkers for AD [124]. Patterns of cortical thinning have, for instance, been observed to be relevant in distinguishing between AD and FTD [125].

Within the AD spectrum, apart from the typical amnestic presentation of AD, three main symptomatic variants (behavioral, logopenic, and visual variants) have been associated with different pattern of tau deposition, metabolic consumption, and structural atrophy. Noticeably, the regions implicated via neuroimaging were well aligned with their symptomatic correlates. These atypical symptomatic presentations are more frequent in the early presentation of the disease contributing further to the difficulty in formulating an accurate diagnosis in those cases [126].

More recently, three subtypes of AD pathology distribution as observed at autopsy by the regional count of neurofibrillary tangles tau (typical AD, hippocampal sparing, limbic predominant) have also been shown to present strong neuroimaging correlates [127]. Such information and study of volumetric patterns of atrophy can be used to refine group target and substratify AD population [128].

In order to better understand differences between pathology subtypes and their associations to clinical symptoms, methods have been developed to assess at the population level the pattern of changes namely voxelbased morphometry [129] and deformation based morphometry [130]. These methods, although relevant in the validation and formulation of new hypotheses, are, however, limited in the perspective of an individual diagnosis as they are grounded on group statistics.

The characterization of spatial pattern of evolution is essential to better understand the disease path and consequently improve the potential staging of individual subjects, refine trial targets and develop new biological hypotheses. In order to reduce intersubject variability and discordances between imaging and clinical evaluation, populations with known mutations leading to AD are the focus of many investigation [131]. The theory of the spatio-temporal pattern of pathological development in AD is being refined to better account for individual variability. Methodological developments inferring the ordering of observable changes such as event based modeling have shown to reflect well documented patterns of evolution [132].

15.5.1.2 The case of the hippocampus

Due to the noticeable structural changes observed in early phases of the disease and its association with early complaints of memory impairment, the medial temporal lobe and more specifically the entorhinal cortex and hippocampal region have received a large interest from the research community requiring methods to quantify its volumetric and morphologic properties. On CT scans, where the hippocampal fissure has long been considered as a potent marker of AD [3], visual ratings of the choroidal hippocampal fissure are used to assess the degree of atrophy. When a GM/WM contrast is observed as on T1-weighted images, the delineation of the individual structures such as the hippocampus becomes feasible. Although very sensitive to the existence of a neurodegenerative process, hippocampal volume loss is not specific to AD and has also been reported in other neurodegenerative diseases such as Parkinson's Disease [133], Vascular Dementia [134], and Fronto-Temporal Dementia [135]. Its involvement at the earliest stages of noticeable macrostructural neuronal loss has made the hippocampus the focus of numerous studies in Alzheimer's Disease. It has been further shown that volumetry of the hippocampus had a stronger predictive value than whole brain volume of later conversion to AD in MCI subjects [136].

The definition of this brain structure itself is however very varied and has led to more than 50 manual protocols of delineation [137,138]. Variations may relate to the definition of the borders of the structure or pertain to the processing of the image (reorientation of the scan, caudal or rostral direction of processing). Such variations in the definition of the hippocampal structure and in the protocol of delineation have been reported to provide up to 2.5-fold volume difference and have a direct impact on the design of any automated delineation tool. Recently, the HarP initiative has provided guidelines in order to harmonize hippocampus segmentation which has resulted in a standard validated protocol [139]. This initiative resulted also in the creation of validated examples of manual delineation that have since then been used for the validation and comparison of automated pipelines [140].

Going beyond the delineation of the whole hippocampus paralleling the emergence of hypotheses linking differential subfield involvement in neurodegenerative pathologies, automated methods linking histopathology and MR imaging have been developed to further parcellate the hippocampus into its subfields [141]. In this case again, many different manual protocols of parcellation have been defined and similar standardization as the HarP effort may be required [142]. Analysis of hippocampal subfields has further shown different patterns in terms of atrophy rates and shape across neurodegenerative diseases [143].

15.5.2 Longitudinal vs cross-sectional

Given the evolutionary process of neurodegenerative diseases, quantifying the worsening or stabilization of biomarkers is essential. Observation of changes (or absence of change) is of practical interest when imaging biomarkers are used as surrogate end-point of disease modifying drugs assessing treatment effect over time. Furthermore, atrophy rates have been shown to yield better predictive power compared to cross-sectional baseline measurement in the prediction of the conversion from MCI to AD [144]. Different approaches can be adopted to account for change over time. Naturally, one may adopt a cross-sectional method and apply it on multiple time points. Such approach is, however, subject to measurement noise issues that are further increased in case of change in acquisition protocol over time. Use of atrophy automated methods has been shown to relate to a decreased needed sample size compared to a cross-sectional repeated manual segmentation of the hippocampus [145]. Focusing on hippocampal structure, measures of atrophy over time have been shown to be more predictive of diagnosis than cross-sectional direct volumetric measures [146]. Longitudinal analyses are, however, methodologically more challenging due to the increased presence of source of bias.

15.5.2.1 Challenges in longitudinal analyses

For longitudinal follow-up, MR structural analysis has been the focus of many methodological developments. Sources of possible methodologically induced confounders have been documented over the years warranting for a good understanding of the tools employed to extract quantified measurements and associated limitations. One of the difficulty of applying validated cross-sectional volumetric methods in longitudinal settings pertains to the inherent measurement variability that may be related to scanner modifications, positioning with respect to the magnetic coils, or the use of even slightly different protocols. Recently reported unexpected growth in hippocampal volumes over time, inconsistent across tested segmentation tools shows the difficulty in reliably extrapolating validated cross-sectional methods for longitudinal findings [147].

When considering serial imaging, enforcing consistency in the way all images are processed is crucial. Interpolation asymmetries (for instance, when only one of the images undergo interpolation) and choice of reference image for the change has been shown to be the source of strong bias in the estimation of atrophy rate [148] in the hippocampus. Beyond interpolation asymmetries, other documented types of bias include the lack of inverse consistency in registration algorithms that have caused the reporting of peculiar atrophy trajectories [149] or a bias in the information transfer when for instance information from single time point only is transferred onto the other [150]. Methods have thus been developed to create unbiased template space [151] and ensure the absence of bias with respect to the ordering of the images in the extraction of specific pathological biomarkers [152]. Presence of artifacts such as magnetic field inhomogeneities at different time points may require a dedicated joined treatment in order to further improve reliability of later extracted measurement. To this end, the differential bias field correction [153] allows for a consistent correction for remaining bias field of serial scans.

15.5.2.2 The case of the boundary shift integral (BSI)

In order to study macrostructural brain changes over time and quantify atrophy, the boundary shift integral method and its local variants for ventricular enlargement investigation (VBSI) or focusing on the hippocampal structure (H-BSI) are currently widely used in the AD field. These measures have also been included as a core part of the processing from the Alzheimer's Disease Neuroimaging Initiative (REF). The boundary shift integral framework includes the registration of the two considered images to a common space and the integration over the boundary region of the object of interest of the variation in intensity between the two scans based on the assumption of a monotonic intensity change with tissue loss (from grey matter to CSF, for instance) so as to measure the actual volume loss.

In the perspective of multiple center and changes over time of protocol, improvement to the original method using tissue based intensity normalization for adjustment of window parameters has been shown to reduce the required sample size in a hypothetical trial [154]

More recently, the generalized version of the BSI further improved on those results by incorporating probabilistic segmentation in the definition of the segmented region of interest at the two time points [155].

15.6. Future avenues of image analysis for biomarkers in Alzheimer's disease

15.6.1 Community initiatives

15.6.1.1 Interfield collaboration

Methodological developments in the extraction of imaging biomarkers answer to needs expressed by the practising community in a specific clinical field. The solutions proposed are, however, rarely restricted to the given domain and may be successfully applied to other clinical challenges where similar problems and requirements are encountered. For instance, solutions developed to ensure robustness to ventriculomegaly in preterm infants can also be used to account for atrophy and associated ventricular enlargement at the other end of the age spectrum [156] while knowledge about PET challenges in oncology can be used to facilitate the development of PET biomarkers in AD [157]. Inspiration from other fields of clinical research is not limited to image analysis methodology but can be extended to broader strategies in the way such methods have to be validated to become translatable in clinical practice [98].

15.6.1.2 Standardization initiatives, challenges and open-source data

As noted repeatedly in previous sections, variability in extracted biomarkers rises from many different fields ranging from the variability in acquisition protocols to the diversity in automated processes through the variation in the biological definition of regions of interest. For each of the acquisitions of interest following the impulse given in that direction in the least challenged ones (T1-weighted imaging, hippocampal segmentation), collaborative workgroups and initiatives have started to determine standardized ways of acquiring and processing images in the perspective of AD research. With the observation of the rate at which innovative improvements are currently made, the main challenge of the outcome of such proposals is the possibility to further adapt and integrate new concepts and validated improvement in time and the subsequent difficulty to make these changes accepted in practice. In terms of automated processes, exhaustive combination search comparisons is only feasible when using dedicated software platforms [105]. In contrast, organization of methodological challenges offers the opportunity to consistently assess the validity of developed methodologies while producing key standardized test datasets [158,103,159]. With the rise in the number of acquired imaging data, technical solution for the curation, and standardized processing and access such as LORIS or XNat have been pushed forward [160,161]. These developments are notably required in the current context of worldwide effort towards the creation and open-source distribution of imaging data (ADNI, PREVENT-AD, OASIS) [162,163].

15.6.2 Technical perspectives

15.6.2.1 Combination of modalities and biomarkers – traditional approaches

Since different extracted biomarkers in Alzheimer's disease such as brain atrophy and measure of hypometabolism have been shown to be complementary but not interchangeable [164] the development of biomarkers in AD has also focused on ways to combine such outputs to improve the associated prediction. As such, the development of more powerful techniques able to combine multiple outputs with the purpose of either classification or prediction have widely shown that the combined use of multiple extracted biomarkers was more accurate and powerful in the separation between disease stages [165]. Combination of features extracted from different imaging modalities has also been shown to be more powerful than single modality features [166]. In addition to the creation of scores built from the aggregation of imaging biomarkers, a large body of research has focused on the development of machine learning methods destined to discover the most appropriate combinations of relevant biomarkers for diagnosis and/or risk of conversion [167] Random forest [168], Support Vector Machine [169], and Multiple Kernel Learning [170] have notably been shown to provide promising results.

15.6.2.2 Ever-increasing potential of AI technologies: reproduction, combination, discovery

Computational facilitation has brought new avenues of investigation in the field of medical imaging as a whole with notably the successful recent entry of deep learning techniques. In the context of Alzheimer's disease, one may imagine developing such tools not only to derive in a more reliable and accurate way historical biomarkers but reconsider the combination of modalities and acquisitions to derive new ways of understanding the underlying data, proposing new hypotheses that may push forward our understanding of the pathology. Such techniques have shown to provide state-of-the-art results in the domain of segmentation [171,172] but also diagnosis classification [173–176] and onset prediction [177,178], by combining multiple sources of input. In relation to the aforementioned challenges related to scanning inconsistency and quality, a new interest in ways to make such tools more robust to quality variations has risen, and new ways to increase the observed variability present in the data have been proposed [179]. Others have developed methods to account for missing acquisition sequences that may occur due to subject compliance issues [180,181]. With the possibility to include appropriate quantification over the uncertainty of extracted measurement, such techniques detain the ability to be used for safer and more consistent predictions while allowing for a reduction of sample size in clinical trials.

Furthermore, instead of reproducing biomarkers, traditionally created at the risk of reproducing human bias and potential error, these new data driven techniques also hold the potential to provide alternative biomarkers using a more holistic consideration of the data. Such approach may enable the uncovering of new pathological patterns and lead to the rise of new hypotheses in the perspective of an iterative process fully integrating machine learning development and clinical interpretation.

15.6.3 Longitudinal prediction, simulation and ethical considerations

It is known that the imaging biomarkers so far identified in association with Alzheimer's disease do not follow the same longitudinal path with some displaying changes before other [182]. Event based modeling methods have been developed to account for such temporal relationships, combining timelines of evolution of different imaging biomarkers to provide a better understanding of possible pathophysiological pathways, distinguish different pathology subtypes, and increase the performance of predictive methods [183]. Probabilistic models of disease evolution have further shown to be able to model diagnosis uncertainty and biomarkers variability [184]. Following biological hypotheses of the spread of misfolded amyloid protein at the core of Alzheimer's disease, mathematical models of prion-like spread have been developed to better model and understand patterns of longitudinal pathological evolution. Such models have been shown to appropriately reproduce expected biomarkers curves and provide ways to simulate drug effect according to the intended therapeutical target [185].

Combination of longitudinal information on the macrostructural changes observed in different structures have enabled the development of realistic simulation methods to predict grey matter atrophy patterns [186]. In parallel, building on biological hypothesis of functional network disruption, others have attempted to simulate networks progressive disruption [187]. Simulation works on the evolution of extracted biomarkers can then be used to infirm or validate new biological hypotheses [188] and may become essential to the design of clinical trials [189] and on a societal scale to better evaluate the impact of health policies [190,191]. The highly multifactorial expression of risk factors and pathological processes and the observation that generic therapeutic approaches are likely to fail have led to the development of new approaches under the paradigm of personalized medicine [192,193] with patient specific prediction [194] and the use of biomarkers in such a framework [195].

The specific context of discrepancy between biological markers and clinical expression of the pathology has contributed, along with the development of early new imaging biomarkers to the reflection on the ethical considerations associated with the disclosure of biomarkers results highlighting the need for appropriate education about the meaning of such markers and the understanding of their associated uncertainty [196–198]. To date, such considerations appear essential to address when observing the high potential of newly formulated data-driven paradigms and the high explanatory and predictor potential of artificial intelligence applied to the extraction, combination, and creation of new imaging biomarkers in Alzheimer's disease.

References

[1] Guy M. McKhann, David S. Knopman, Howard Chertkow, Bradley T. Hyman, Clifford R. Jack, Claudia H. Kawas, William E. Klunk, Walter J. Koroshetz, Jennifer J. Manly, Richard Mayeux, Richard C. Mohs, John C. Morris, Martin N. Rossor, Philip Scheltens, Maria C. Carrillo, Bill Thies, Sandra Weintraub, Creighton H. Phelps, The diagnosis of dementia due to Alzheimer's disease: recommendations from the National Institute on Aging-Alzheimer's Association workgroups on diagnostic guidelines for Alzheimer's disease, Alzheimer's & Dementia 7 (3) (May 2011) 263–269.

[2] Clifford R. Jack, David A. Bennett, Kaj Blennow, Maria C. Carrillo, Billy Dunn, Samantha Budd Haeberlein, David M. Holtzman, William Jagust, Frank Jessen, Jason Karlawish, Enchi Liu, Jose Luis Molinuevo, Thomas Montine, Creighton Phelps, Katherine P. Rankin, Christopher C. Rowe, Philip Scheltens, Eric Siemers, Heather M. Snyder, Reisa Sperling, Cerise Elliott, Eliezer Masliah, Laurie Ryan, Nina Silverberg, NIA-AA Research Framework: toward a biological definition of Alzheimer's disease, Alzheimer's & Dementia 14 (4) (Apr. 2018) 535–562.

[3] A.E. George, M.J. de Leon, L.A. Stylopoulos, J. Miller, A. Kluger, G. Smith, D.C. Miller, CT diagnostic features of Alzheimer disease: importance of the choroidal/hippocampal fissure complex, American Journal of Neuroradiology 11 (1) (Jan. 1990) 101–107.

[4] Abdullah Bin Zahid, Artem Mikheev, Neha Srivatsa, James Babb, Uzma Samadani, Henry Rusinek, Accelerated brain atrophy on serial computed tomography: potential marker of the progression of Alzheimer disease, Journal of Computer Assisted Tomography 40 (5) (2016) 827–832.

[5] Farshad Falahati, Seyed-Mohammad Fereshtehnejad, Dorota Religa, Lars-Olof Wahlund, Eric Westman, Maria Eriksdotter, The use of MRI, CT and lumbar puncture in dementia diagnostics: data from the SveDem registry, Dementia and Geriatric Cognitive Disorders 39 (1–2) (2015) 81–91.

[6] Henry Rusinek, Mony J. De Leon, Ajax E. George, Leonidas A. Stylopoulos, Ramesh Chandra, Gwenn Smith, Thomas Rand, Manuel Mourino, Henryk Kowalski, Alzheimer disease: measuring loss of cerebral gray matter with mr imaging, Radiology 178 (1) (1991) 109–114.

[7] J.M. Schott, J.W. Bartlett, J. Barnes, K.K. Leung, S. Ourselin, N.C. Fox, Reduced sample sizes for atrophy outcomes in Alzheimer's disease trials: baseline adjustment, Neurobiology of Aging 31 (8) (Aug. 2010) 1452–1462.e2.

[8] Dorothee Schoemaker, Claudia Buss, Kevin Head, Curt A. Sandman, Elysia P. Davis, M. Mallar Chakravarty, Serge Gauthier, Jens C. Pruessner, Hippocampus and amygdala volumes from magnetic resonance images in children: assessing accuracy of FreeSurfer and FSL against manual segmentation, NeuroImage 129 (Apr. 2016) 1–14.

[9] Xiaoying Tang, Yuanyuan Qin, Jiong Wu, Min Zhang, Wenzhen Zhu, Michael I. Miller, Shape and diffusion tensor imaging based integrative analysis of the hippocampus and the amygdala in Alzheimer's disease, Magnetic Resonance Imaging 34 (8) (Oct. 2016) 1087–1099.

[10] Christian Wachinger, David H. Salat, Michael Weiner, Martin Reuter, Whole-brain analysis reveals increased neuroanatomical asymmetries in dementia for hippocampus and amygdala, Brain 139 (12) (Dec. 2016) 3253–3266.

[11] Margaret Esiri, Steven Chance, Catharine Joachim, Donald Warden, Aidan Smallwood, Carolyn Sloan, Sharon Christie, Gordon Wilcock, A. David Smith, Cerebral amyloid angiopathy, subcortical white matter disease and dementia: literature review and study in OPTIMA, Brain Pathology 25 (1) (2015) 51–62.

[12] Kie Honjo, Sandra E. Black, Nicolaas P.L.G. Verhoeff, Alzheimer's disease, cerebrovascular disease, and the β-amyloid cascade, Canadian Journal of Neurological Sciences 39 (6) (Dec. 2014) 712–728.

[13] Francesca Caso, Federica Agosta, Massimo Filippi, Insights into white matter damage in Alzheimer's disease: from postmortem to in vivo diffusion tensor MRI studies, Neurodegenerative Diseases 16 (1–2) (Dec. 2015) 26–33.

[14] Benjamin Hall, Elijah Mak, Simon Cervenka, Franklin I. Aigbirhio, James B. Rowe, John T. O'Brien, In vivo tau PET imaging in dementia: pathophysiology, radiotracer quantification, and a systematic review of clinical findings, Ageing Research Reviews 36 (July 2017) 50–63.

[15] H. Jokinen, J. Lipsanen, R. Schmidt, F. Fazekas, A.A. Gouw, W.M. van der Flier, F. Barkhof, S. Madureira, A. Verdelho, J.M. Ferro, A. Wallin, L. Pantoni, D. Inzitari, T. Erkinjuntti, LADIS Study Group, Brain atrophy accelerates cognitive decline in cerebral small vessel disease: the LADIS study, Neurology 78 (22) (May 2012) 1785–1792.

[16] Joanna M. Wardlaw, Eric E. Smith, G.J. Biessels, Charlotte Cordonnier, Franz Fazekas, Richard Frayne, Richard I. Lindley, John T. O'Brien, Frederik Barkhof Oscar, R. Benavente, Sandra E. Black, Carol Brayne, Monique M.B. Breteler, Hugues Chabriat, Charles DeCarli, Frank-Erik de Leeuw, Fergus Doubal, Marco Duering, Nick C. Fox, Steven Greenberg, Vladimir Hachinski, Ingo Kilimann, Vincent Mok, Robert van Oostenbrugge, Leonardo Pantoni, Oliver Speck, Blossom C.M. Stephan, Stefan Teipel, Viswanathan Anand, David Werring, Christopher Chen, Colin Smith, Mark A. van Buchem, Bo Norrving, Philip B. Gorelick, Martin Dichgans, Neuroimaging standards for research into small vessel disease and its contribution to ageing and neurodegeneration, The Lancet Neurology 12 (2013) 822–838.

[17] Joanna M. Wardlaw, What is a lacune?, Stroke 39 (11) (Nov. 2008) 2921–2922.

[18] Bhavini Patel, Hugh S. Markus, Magnetic resonance imaging in cerebral small vessel disease and its use as a surrogate disease marker, International Journal of Stroke 6 (February) (2011) 47–59.

[19] Reisa A. Sperling, Paul S. Aisen, Laurel A. Beckett, David A. Bennett, Suzanne Craft, Anne M. Fagan, Takeshi Iwatsubo, Clifford R. Jack, Jeffrey Kaye, Thomas J. Montine, Denise C. Park, Eric M. Reiman, Christopher C. Rowe, Eric Siemers, Yaakov Stern, Kristine Yaffe, Maria C. Carrillo, Bill Thies, Marcelle Morrison-Bogorad, Molly V. Wagster, Creighton H. Phelps, Toward defining the preclinical stages of Alzheimer's disease: recommendations from the National Institute on Aging-Alzheimer's Association workgroups on diagnostic guidelines for Alzheimer's disease, Alzheimer's & Dementia 7 (3) (May 2011) 280–292.

[20] Satoshi Takahashi, Hisashi Yonezawa, Junko Takahashi, Masako Kudo, Takashi Inoue, Hideo Tohgi, Selective reduction of diffusion anisotropy in white matter of Alzheimer disease brains measured by 3.0 Tesla magnetic resonance imaging, Neuroscience Letters 332 (1) (Oct. 2002) 45–48.

[21] Olivier Naggara, Catherine Oppenheim, Dorothée Rieu, Nadine Raoux, Sebastian Rodrigo, Gianfranco Dalla Barba, Jean-François Meder, Diffusion tensor imaging in early Alzheimer's disease, Psychiatry Research. Neuroimaging 146 (3) (Apr. 2006) 243–249.

[22] Y. Zhang, N. Schuff, G-H. Jahng, W. Bayne, S. Mori, L. Schad, S. Mueller, A-T. Du, J.H. Kramer, K. Yaffe, H. Chui, W.J. Jagust, B.L. Miller, M.W. Weiner, Diffusion tensor imaging of cingulum fibers in mild cognitive impairment and Alzheimer disease, Neurology 68 (1) (Jan. 2007) 13–19.

[23] Stefan J. Teipel, Martin Wegrzyn, Thomas Meindl, Giovanni Frisoni, Arun L.W. Bokde, Andreas Fellgiebel, Massimo Filippi, Harald Hampel, Stefan Klöppel, Karlheinz Hauenstein, Michael Ewers, EDSD study group, Anatomical MRI and DTI in the diagnosis of Alzheimer's disease: a European multicenter study, Journal of Alzheimer's Disease 31 (s3) (Sept. 2012) S33–S47.

[24] Noor Jehan Kabani, John G. Sled, Howard Chertkow, Magnetization transfer ratio in mild cognitive impairment and dementia of Alzheimer's type, NeuroImage 15 (3) (Mar. 2002) 604–610.

[25] Wiesje M. Van Der Flier, Dominique M.J. Van Den Heuvel, Annelies W.E. Weverling-Rijnsburger, Eduard L.E.M. Bollen, Rudi G.J. Westendorp, Mark A. Van Buchem, Huub A.M. Middelkoop, Magnetization transfer imaging in normal aging, mild cognitive impairment, and Alzheimer's disease, Annals of Neurology 52 (1) (July 2002) 62–67.

[26] Haruo Hanyu, Tetsuichi Asano, Hirofumi Sakurai, Masaru Takasaki, Hiroaki Shindo, Kimihiko Abe, Magnetization transfer measurements of the hippocampus in the early diagnosis of Alzheimer's disease, Journal of the Neurological Sciences 188 (1–2) (July 2001) 79–84.

[27] Haruo Hanyu, Tetsuichi Asano, Hirofumi Sakurai, Yukari Imon, Toshihiko Iwamoto, Masaru Takasaki, Hiroaki Shindo, Kimihiko Abe, Diffusion-weighted and magnetization transfer imaging of the corpus callosum in Alzheimer's disease, Journal of the Neurological Sciences 167 (1) (Aug. 1999) 37–44.

[28] Lisa Mosconi, Susan De Santi, Yi Li, Juan Li, Jiong Zhan Wai Hon Tsui, Madhu Boppana, Alberto Pupi, Mony J. de Leon, Visual rating of medial temporal lobe metabolism in mild cognitive impairment and Alzheimer's disease using FDG-PET, European Journal of Nuclear Medicine and Molecular Imaging 33 (2) (Feb. 2006) 210–221.

[29] Takashi Kato, Yoshitaka Inui, Akinori Nakamura, Kengo Ito, Brain fluorodeoxyglucose (FDG) PET in dementia, Ageing Research Reviews 30 (Sept. 2016) 73–84.

[30] Clifford R. Jack, David S. Knopman, William J. Jagust, Leslie M. Shaw, Paul Aisen, Michael W. Weiner, Ronald C. Petersen, John Q. Trojanowsky, Hypothetical model of dynamic biomarkers of the Alzheimer's pathological cascade, The Lancet Neurology 9 (1) (Jan. 2010) 119–128.

[31] Maja A.A. Binnewijzend, Marije R. Benedictus, Joost P.A. Kuijer, Wiesje M. van der Flier, Charlotte E. Teunissen, Niels D. Prins, Mike P. Wattjes, Bart N.M. van Berckel, Philip Scheltens, Frederik Barkhof, Cerebral perfusion in the predementia stages of Alzheimer's disease, European Radiology 26 (2) (Feb. 2016) 506–514.

[32] Chelsea C. Hays, Zvinka Z. Zlatar, Christina E. Wierenga, The utility of cerebral blood flow as a biomarker of preclinical Alzheimer's disease, Cellular and Molecular Neurobiology 36 (2) (Mar. 2016) 167–179.

[33] Isabelle Riederer, Karl Peter Bohn, Christine Preibisch, Eva Wiedemann, Claus Zimmer, Panagiotis Alexopoulos, Stefan Förster, Alzheimer disease and mild cognitive impairment: integrated pulsed arterial spin-labeling MRI and [18]f-FDG PET, Radiology 288 (1) (July 2018) 198–206.

[34] Patricia Clement, Henk-Jan Mutsaerts, Lena Václav, Eidrees Ghariq, Francesca B. Pizzini, Marion Smits, Marjan Acou, Jorge Jovicich, Ritva Vanninen, Mervi Kononen, Roland Wiest, Egill Rostrup, Antó Nio, J. Bastos-Leite, Elna-Marie Larsson, Eric Achten, Variability of physiological brain perfusion in healthy subjects-a systematic review of modifiers. Considerations for multi-center ASL studies, Journal of Cerebral Blood Flow & Metabolism 38 (9) (2018) 1418–1437.

[35] Nikos K. Logothetis, Brian A. Wandell, Interpreting the BOLD signal, Annual Review of Physiology 66 (1) (Mar. 2004) 735–769.

[36] Frank de Vos, Marisa Koini, Tijn M. Schouten, Stephan Seiler, Jeroen van der Grond, Anita Lechner, Reinhold Schmidt, Mark de Rooij, Serge A.R.B. Rombouts, A comprehensive analysis of resting state fMRI measures to classify individual patients with Alzheimer's disease, NeuroImage 167 (Feb. 2018) 62–72.

[37] Peiying Liu, Andrew C. Hebrank, Karen M. Rodrigue, Kristen M. Kennedy, Jarren Section, Denise C. Park, Hanzhang Lu, Age-related differences in memory-encoding fMRI responses after accounting for decline in vascular reactivity, NeuroImage 78 (Sept. 2013) 415–425.

[38] Harald Hampel, Richard Frank, Karl Broich, Stefan J. Teipel, Russell G. Katz, John Hardy, Karl Herholz, Arun L.W. Bokde, Frank Jessen, Yvonne C. Hoessler, Wendy R. Sanhai, Henrik Zetterberg, Janet Woodcock, Kaj Blennow, Biomarkers for Alzheimer's disease: academic, industry and regulatory perspectives, Nature Reviews Drug Discovery 9 (7) (July 2010) 560–574.

[39] William E. Klunk, Henry Engler, Agneta Nordberg, Yanming Wang, Gunnar Blomqvist, Daniel P. Holt, Mats Bergström, Irina Savitcheva, Guo-Feng Huang, Sergio Estrada, Birgitta Ausén, Manik L. Debnath, Julien Barletta, Julie C. Price, Johan Sandell, Brian J. Lopresti, Anders Wall, Pernilla Koivisto, Gunnar Antoni, Chester A. Mathis, Bengt Långström, Imaging brain amyloid in Alzheimer's disease with Pittsburgh Compound-B, Annals of Neurology 55 (3) (Mar. 2004) 306–319.

[40] Marta Marquié, Marc D. Normandin, Charles R. Vanderburg, Isabel M. Costantino, Elizabeth A. Bien, Lisa G. Rycyna, William E. Klunk, Chester A. Mathis, Milos D. Ikonomovic, Manik L. Debnath, Neil Vasdev, Bradford C. Dickerson, Stephen N. Gomperts, John H. Growdon, Keith A. Johnson, Matthew P. Frosch, Bradley T. Hyman, Teresa Gómez-Isla, Validating novel tau positron emission tomography tracer [F-18]-AV-1451 (T807) on postmortem brain tissue, Annals of Neurology 78 (5) (Nov. 2015) 787–800.

[41] Nobuyuki Okamura, Ryuichi Harada, Aiko Ishiki, Akio Kikuchi, Tadaho Nakamura, Yukitsuka Kudo, The development and validation of tau PET tracers: current status and future directions, Clinical and Translational Imaging 6 (4) (Aug. 2018) 305–316.

[42] Anne Maass, Susan Landau, Suzanne L. Baker, Andy Horng, Samuel N. Lockhart, Renaud La Joie, Gil D. Rabinovici, William J. Jagust, Comparison of multiple tau-PET measures as biomarkers in aging and Alzheimer's disease, NeuroImage 157 (Aug. 2017) 448–463.

[43] Christoph Stehling, Heike Wersching, Stephan P. Kloska, Paulus Kirchhof, Janine Ring, Isabelle Nassenstein, Thomas Allkemper, Stefan Knecht, Rainald Bachmann, Walter Heindel, Detection of asymptomatic cerebral microbleeds: a comparative study at 1.5 and 3.0 T, Academic Radiology 15 (7) (July 2008) 895–900.

[44] James M. Stankiewicz, Bonnie I. Glanz, Brian C. Healy, Ashish Arora, Mohit Neema, Ralph H.B. Benedict, Zachary D. Guss, Shahamat Tauhid, Guy J. Buckle, Maria K. Houtchens, Samia Khoury, Howard L. Weiner, Charles R.G. Guttmann, Rohit Bakshi, 1.5T vs 3T, Journal of Neuroimaging 21 (2) (2011) 1–15.

[45] Carol Di Perri, Michael G. Dwyer, Niels Bergsland, Claudiu Schirda, Guy U. Poloni, David Wack, Jennifer L. Cox Turi, O. Dalaker, Laura Ranza, Erik Saluste, Sara Hussein, Stefano Bastianello, Robert Zivadinov, White matter hyperintensities on 1.5 and 3 Tesla brain MRI in healthy individuals, Journal of Biomedical Graphics and Computing 3 (3) (2013).

[46] Meike W. Vernooij, M. Arfan Ikram, Piotr A. Wielopolski, Gabriel P. Krestin, Monique M.B. Breteler, Aad van der Lugt, Cerebral microbleeds: accelerated 3D T2*-weighted GRE MR imaging versus conventional 2D T2*-weighted GRE MR imaging for detection, Radiology 248 (1) (July 2008) 272–277.

[47] Á. Paniagua Bravo, J.J. Sánchez Hernández, L. Ibáñez Sanz, I. Alba de Cáceres, J.L. Crespo San José, B. García-Castaño Gandariaga, A comparative MRI study for white matter hyperintensities detection: 2D-FLAIR, FSE PD 2D, 3D-FLAIR and FLAIR MIP, British Journal of Radiology 87 (1035) (Mar. 2014) 20130360.

[48] D.W. Townsend, Physical Principles and Technology of Clinical PET Imaging, Technical Report 2, 2004.

[49] Piotr J. Slomka, Tinsu Pan, Guido Germano, Recent advances and future progress in PET instrumentation, Seminars in Nuclear Medicine 46 (1) (Jan. 2016) 5–19.

[50] Henryk Barthel, Matthias L. Schroeter, Karl-Titus Hoffmann, Osama Sabri, PET/MR in dementia and other neurodegenerative diseases, Seminars in Nuclear Medicine 45 (3) (May 2015) 224–233.

[51] Ninon Burgos, M. Jorge Cardoso, Kris Thielemans, Marc Modat, Stefano Pedemonte, John Dickson, Anna Barnes, Rebekah Ahmed, Colin J. Mahoney, Jonathan M. Schott, John S. Duncan, David Atkinson, Simon R. Arridge, Brian F. Hutton, Sebastien Ourselin, Attenuation correction synthesis for hybrid PET-MR scanners: application to brain studies, IEEE Transactions on Medical Imaging 33 (12) (Dec. 2014) 2332–2341.

[52] Jorge Cabello, Mathias Lukas, Elena Rota Kops, André Ribeiro, N. Jon Shah, Igor Yakushev, Thomas Pyka, Stephan G. Nekolla, Sibylle I. Ziegler, Comparison between MRI-based attenuation correction methods for brain PET in dementia patients, European Journal of Nuclear Medicine and Molecular Imaging 43 (12) (Nov. 2016) 2190–2200.

[53] Philip Scheltens, Leonore J. Launer, Frederik Barkhof, Henri C. Weinstein, Willem A. van Gool, Visual assessment of medial temporal lobe atrophy on magnetic resonance imaging: interobserver reliability, Journal of Neurology 242 (9) (1995) 557–560.

[54] Maiken K. Brix, Eric Westman, Andrew Simmons, Geir Andre Ringstad, Per Kristian Eide, Kari Wagner-Larsen, Christian M. Page, Valeria Vitelli, Mona K. Beyer, The Evans' Index revisited: new cut-off levels for use in radiological assessment of ventricular enlargement in the elderly, European Journal of Radiology 95 (Oct. 2017) 28–32.

[55] Franz Fazekas, John B. Chawluk, Abass Alavi, Howard I. Hurtig, Robert A. Zimmerman, MR signal abnormalities on 1.5 T in Alzheimer's dementia and normal ageing, American Journal of Neuroradiology 8 (1987) 421–426.

[56] Philip Scheltens, Frederik Barkhof, D. Leys, J.P. Pruvo, J.J.P. Nauta, P. Vermersch, M. Steinling, Jacob Valk, P. Vermersch, M. Steinling, Jacob Valk, A semiquantitative rating scale for the assessment of signal hyperintensities on magnetic resonance imaging, Journal of the Neurological Sciences 114 (1) (1993) 7–12.

[57] W.T. Longstreth, T.A. Manolio, A. Arnold, G.L. Burke, N. Bryan, C.A. Jungreis, P.L. Enright, D. O'Leary, L. Fried, Cardiovascular Health Study Collaborative Research Group, Clinical correlates of white matter findings on cranial magnetic resonance imaging of 3301 elderly people: the cardiovascular health study, Stroke 27 (8) (Aug. 1996) 1274–1282.

[58] A.M. Tiehuis, K.L. Vincken, W.P.T.M. Mali, L.J. Kappelle, P. Anbeek, A. Algra, G.J. Biessels, Automated and visual scoring methods of cerebral white matter hyperintensities: relation with age and cognitive function, Cerebrovascular Diseases 25 (1–2) (Jan. 2008) 59–66.

[59] Lorna Harper, Frederik Barkhof, Nick C. Fox, Jonathan M. Schott, Using visual rating to diagnose dementia: a critical evaluation of MRI atrophy scales, Journal of Neurology, Neurosurgery and Psychiatry 86 (11) (Nov. 2015) 1225–1233.

[60] Lars-Olof Wahlund, Eric Westman, Danielle van Westen, Anders Wallin, Sara Shams, Lena Cavallin, Elna-Marie Larsson, Imaging Cognitive Impairment Network (ICINET), Imaging biomarkers of dementia: recommended visual rating scales with teaching cases, Insights into Imaging 8 (1) (Feb. 2017) 79–90.

[61] Basil H. Ridha, Josephine Barnes, Laura A. van de Pol, Jonathan M. Schott, Richard G. Boyes, Musib M. Siddique, Martin N. Rossor, Philip Scheltens, Nick C. Fox, Application of automated medial temporal lobe atrophy scale to Alzheimer disease, Archives of Neurology 64 (6) (June 2007) 849.

[62] N.D. Prins, E.C.W. van Straaten, E.J. van Dijk, M. Simoni, R.A. van Schijndel, H.A. Vrooman, P.J. Koudstaal, P. Scheltens, M.M.B. Breteler, F. Barkhof, Measuring progression of cerebral white matter lesions on MRI: visual rating and volumetrics, Neurology 62 (9) (May 2004) 1533–1539.

[63] A.A. Gouw, W.M. Van der Flier, E.C.W. van Straaten, F. Barkhof, J.M. Ferro, H. Baezner, L. Pantoni, D. Inzitari, T. Erkinjuntti, L.O. Wahlund, G. Waldemar, R. Schmidt, F. Fazekas, Ph. Scheltens, Simple versus complex assessment of white matter hyperintensities in relation to physical performance and cognition: the LADIS study, Journal of Neurology 253 (9) (Sept. 2006) 1189–1196.

[64] Peter A. Freeborough, Nick C. Fox, Richard I. Kitney, Interactive algorithms for the segmentation and quantitation of 3-D MRI brain scans, Computer Methods and Programs in Biomedicine 53 (1) (May 1997) 15–25.

[65] Stephen M. Smith, Mark Jenkinson, Mark W. Woolrich, Christian F. Beckmann, Timothy E.J. Behrens, Heidi Johansen-Berg, Peter R. Bannister, Marilena De Luca, Ivana Drobnjak, David E. Flitney, Rami K. Niazy, James Saunders, John Vickers, Yongyue Zhang, Nicola De Stefano, J. Michael Brady, Paul M. Matthews, Advances in functional and structural MR image analysis and implementation as FSL, NeuroImage 23 (Jan. 2004) S208–S219.

[66] John Ashburner, Computational anatomy with the SPM software, Magnetic Resonance Imaging 27 (8) (Oct. 2009) 1163–1174.

[67] Bruce Fischl, FreeSurfer, NeuroImage 62 (2) (Aug. 2012) 774–781.

[68] Krzysztof Gorgolewski, Christopher D. Burns, Cindee Madison, Dav Clark, Yaroslav O. Halchenko, Michael L. Waskom, Satrajit S. Ghosh, Nipype: a flexible, lightweight and extensible neuroimaging data processing framework in Python, Frontiers in Neuroinformatics 5 (13) (Aug. 2011).

[69] F. Prados Carrasco, M.J. Cardoso, Ninon Burgos, C.A.M. Wheeler-Kingshott, S. Ourselin, Nifty-Web: web based platform for image processing on the cloud, in: Scientific Meeting and Exhibition of the International Society for Magnetic Resonance in Medicine – ISMRM 2016, 2016.

[70] Yang Li, Peiying Liu, Yue Li, Hongli Fan, Pan Su, Shin-Lei Peng, Denise C. Park, Karen M. Rodrigue, Hangyi Jiang, Andreia V. Faria Can Ceritoglu, Michael Miller, Susumu Mori, Hanzhang Lu, ASL-MRICloud: an online tool for the processing of ASL MRI data, NMR in Biomedicine 32 (2) (Feb. 2019) e4051.

[71] Marcus Högenauer, Matthias Brendel, Andreas Delker, Sonja Därr, Mayo Weiss, Peter Bartenstein, Axel Rominger, Alzheimer's Disease Neuroimaging Initiative, Impact of MRI-based segmentation artifacts on amyloid- and FDG-PET quantitation, Current Alzheimer Research 13 (5) (2016) 597–607.

[72] T.I. Hansen, V. Brezova, L. Eikenes, A. Håberg, T.R. Vangberg, How does the accuracy of intracranial volume measurements affect normalized brain volumes? Sample size estimates based on 966 subjects from the HUNT MRI cohort, American Journal of Neuroradiology 36 (8) (Aug. 2015) 1450–1456.

[73] Ian B. Malone, Kelvin K. Leung, Shona Clegg, Josephine Barnes, Jennifer L. Whitwell, John Ashburner, Nick C. Fox, Gerard R. Ridgway, Accurate automatic estimation of total intracranial volume: a nuisance variable with less nuisance, NeuroImage 104 (Jan. 2015) 366–372.

[74] Adam J. Schwarz, Peng Yu, Bradley B. Miller, Sergey Shcherbinin, James Dickson, Michael Navitsky, Abhinay D. Joshi, Michael D. Devous, Mark S. Mintun, Regional profiles of the candidate tau PET ligand ^{18}F-AV-1451 recapitulate key features of Braak histopathological stages, Brain 139 (5) (May 2016) 1539–1550.

[75] J.G. Sled, A.P. Zijdenbos, A.C. Evans, A nonparametric method for automatic correction of intensity nonuniformity in MRI data, IEEE Transactions on Medical Imaging 17 (1) (1998) 87–97.

[76] Koen Van Leemput, Frederik Maes, Dirk Vandermeulen, Paul Suetens, Automated model-based bias field correction of MR images of the brain, IEEE Transactions on Medical Imaging 18 (10) (1999) 885–896.

[77] John Ashburner, Karl J. Friston, Unified segmentation, NeuroImage 26 (3) (July 2005) 839–851.

[78] Per Borghammer, Kristjana Yr Jonsdottir, Paul Cumming, Karen Ostergaard, Kim Vang, Mahmoud Ashkanian, Manoucher Vafaee, Peter Iversen, Albert Gjedde, Normalization in PET group comparison studies – the importance of a valid reference region, NeuroImage 40 (2) (Apr. 2008) 529–540.

[79] Christopher G. Schwarz, David T. Jones, Jeffrey L. Gunter, Val J. Lowe, Prashanthi Vemuri, Matthew L. Senjem, Ronald C. Petersen, David S. Knopman, Clifford R. Jack, Contributions of imprecision in PET-MRI rigid registration to imprecision in amyloid PETSUVR measurements, Human Brain Mapping 38 (7) (Apr. 2017) 3323–3336.

[80] Naama Levy-Cooperman, Joel Ramirez, Nancy J. Lobaugh, Sandra E. Black, Misclassified tissue volumes in Alzheimer disease patients with white matter hyperintensities: importance of lesion segmentation procedures for volumetric analysis, Stroke 39 (2008) 1134–1141.

[81] Mahanand Belathur Suresh, Bruce Fischl, David H. Salat, Factors influencing accuracy of cortical thickness in the diagnosis of Alzheimer's disease, Human Brain Mapping 39 (4) (Apr. 2018) 1500–1515.

[82] Ferran Prados, Manuel Jorge Cardoso, Baris Kanber, Olga Ciccarelli, Raju Kapoor, Claudia A.M. Gandini Wheeler-Kingshott, Sebastien Ourselin, A multi-time-point modality-agnostic patch-based method for lesion filling in multiple sclerosis, NeuroImage 139 (Oct. 2016) 376–384.

[83] Declan T. Chard, Jonathan S. Jackson, David H. Miller, Claudia A.M. Wheeler-Kingshott, Reducing the impact of white matter lesions on automated measures of brain gray and white matter volumes, Journal of Magnetic Resonance Imaging 32 (2010) 223–228.

[84] Marco Battaglini, Mark Jenkinson, Nicola De Stefano, Evaluating and reducing the impact of white matter lesions on brain volume measurements, Human Brain Mapping 33 (2012) 2062–2071.

[85] L.S. Jonasson, J. Axelsson, K. Riklund, C.J. Boraxbekk, Simulating effects of brain atrophy in longitudinal PET imaging with an anthropomorphic brain phantom, Physics in Medicine and Biology 62 (13) (July 2017) 5213–5227.

[86] Alberto Redolfi, David Manset, Frederik Barkhof, Lars-Olof Wahlund, Tristan Glatard, Jean-François Mangin, Giovanni B. Frisoni, neuGRID Consortium, for the Alzheimer's Disease Neuroimaging Initiative, Head-to-head comparison of two popular cortical thickness extraction algorithms: a cross-sectional and longitudinal study, PLoS ONE 10 (3) (Mar. 2015) e0117692.

[87] Paul S. Aisen, Clinical trial methodologies for disease-modifying therapeutic approaches, Neurobiology of Aging 32 (Dec. 2011) S64–S66.

[88] Mara ten Kate, Silvia Ingala, Adam J. Schwarz, Nick C. Fox, Gaël Chételat, Bart N.M. van Berckel, Michael Ewers, Christopher Foley, Juan Domingo Gispert, Derek Hill, Michael C. Irizarry, Adriaan A. Lammertsma, José Luis Molinuevo, Craig Ritchie, Philip Scheltens, Mark E. Schmidt, Pieter Jelle Visser, Adam Waldman, Joanna Wardlaw, Sven Haller, Frederik Barkhof, Secondary prevention of Alzheimer's dementia: neuroimaging contributions, Alzheimer's Research & Therapy 10 (1) (Dec. 2018) 112.

[89] M. Lorenzi, M. Donohue, D. Paternicò, C. Scarpazza, S. Ostrowitzki, O. Blin, E. Irving, G.B. Frisoni, Enrichment through biomarkers in clinical trials of Alzheimer's drugs in patients with mild cognitive impairment, Neurobiology of Aging 31 (8) (Aug. 2010) 1443–1451.e1.

[90] Derek L.G. Hill, Adam J. Schwarz, Maria Isaac, Luca Pani, Spiros Vamvakas, Robert Hemmings, Maria C. Carrillo, Peng Yu, Jia Sun, Laurel Beckett, Marina Boccardi, James Brewer, Martha Brumfield, Marc Cantillon, Patricia E. Cole, Nick Fox, Giovanni B. Frisoni, Clifford Jack, Thomas Kelleher, Feng Luo, Gerald Novak, Paul Maguire, Richard Meibach, Patricia Patterson, Lisa Bain, Cristina Sampaio, David Raunig, Holly Soares, Joyce Suhy, Huanli Wang, Robin Wolz, Diane Stephenson, Coalition Against Major Diseases/European Medicines Agency biomarker qualification of hippocampal volume for enrichment of clinical trials in predementia stages of Alzheimer's disease, Alzheimer's & Dementia 10 (4) (July 2014) 421–429.e3.

[91] Nzeera Ketter, H. Robert Brashear, Jennifer Bogert, Jianing Di, Yves Miaux, Achim Gass, Derk D. Purcell, Frederik Barkhof, H. Michael Arrighi, Central review of amyloid-related imaging abnormalities in two phase III clinical trials of bapineuzumab in mild-to-moderate Alzheimer's disease patients, Journal of Alzheimer's Disease 57 (2) (Mar. 2017) 557–573.

[92] Susanne Ostrowitzki, Dennis Deptula, Lennart Thurfjell, Frederik Barkhof, Bernd Bohrmann, David J. Brooks, William E. Klunk, Elizabeth Ashford, Kisook Yoo, Zhi-Xin Xu, Hansruedi Loetscher, Luca Santarelli, Mechanism of amyloid removal in patients with Alzheimer disease treated with gantenerumab, Archives of Neurology 69 (2) (Feb. 2012) 198.

[93] David M. Cash, Jonathan D. Rohrer, Natalie S. Ryan, Sebastien Ourselin, Nick C. Fox, Imaging endpoints for clinical trials in Alzheimer's disease, Alzheimer's Research & Therapy 6 (9) (Dec. 2014) 87.

[94] Richard A. Frank, Douglas Galasko, Harald Hampel, John Hardy, Mony J. de Leon, Pankaj D. Mehta, Joseph Rogers, Eric Siemers, John Q. Trojanowski, Biological markers for therapeutic trials in Alzheimer's disease: proceedings of the biological markers working group; NIA initiative on neuroimaging in Alzheimer's disease, Neurobiology of Aging 24 (4) (July 2003) 521–536.

[95] Gwenaëlle Douaud, Saâd Jbabdi, Timothy E.J. Behrens, Ricarda A. Menke, Achim Gass, Andreas U. Monsch, Anil Rao, Brandon Whitcher, Gordon Kindlmann, Paul M. Matthews, Stephen Smith, DTI measures in crossing-fibre areas: increased diffusion anisotropy reveals early white matter alteration in MCI and mild Alzheimer's disease, NeuroImage 55 (2011) 880–890.

[96] Derek K. Jones, Thomas R. Knösche, Robert Turner, White matter integrity, fiber count, and other fallacies: the do's and don'ts of diffusion MRI, NeuroImage 73 (June 2013) 239–254.

[97] Ute Lindauer, Ulrich Dirnagl, Martina Füchtemeier, Caroline Böttiger, Nikolas Offenhauser, Christoph Leithner, Georg Royl, Pathophysiological interference with neurovascular coupling – when imaging based on hemoglobin might go blind, Frontiers in Neuroenergetics 2 (Jan. 2010).

[98] Giovanni B. Frisoni, Marina Boccardi, Frederik Barkhof, Kaj Blennow, Stefano Cappa, Konstantinos Chiotis, Jean-Francois Démonet, Valentina Garibotto, Panteleimon Giannakopoulos, Anton Gietl, Oskar Hansson, Karl Herholz, Clifford R. Jack, Flavio Nobili, Agneta Nordberg, Heather M. Snyder, Mara Ten Kate, Andrea Varrone, Emiliano Albanese, Stefanie Becker, Patrick Bossuyt, Maria C. Carrillo, Chiara Cerami, Bruno Dubois, Valentina Gallo, Ezio Giacobini, Gabriel Gold, Samia Hurst, Anders Lönneborg, Karl-Olof Lovblad, Niklas Mattsson, José-Luis Molinuevo, Andreas U. Monsch, Urs Mosimann, Alessandro Padovani, Agnese Picco, Corinna Porteri Osman Ratib, Laure Saint-Aubert, Charles Scerri, Philip Scheltens, Jonathan M. Schott, Ida Sonni, Stefan Teipel, Paolo Vineis, Pieter Jelle Visser, Yutaka Yasui, Bengt Winblad, Strategic roadmap for an early diagnosis of Alzheimer's disease based on biomarkers, The Lancet Neurology 16 (8) (Aug. 2017) 661–676.

[99] Stefan J. Teipel, Coraline D. Metzger, Frederic Brosseron, Katharina Buerger, Katharina Brueggen, Cihan Catak, Dominik Diesing, Laura Dobisch, Klaus Fliebach, Christiana Franke, Michael T. Heneka, Ingo Kilimann, Barbara Kofler, Felix Menne, Oliver Peters, Alexandra Polcher, Josef Priller, Anja Schneider, Annika Spottke, Eike J. Spruth, Manuela Thelen, René J. Thyrian, Michael Wagner, Emrah Düzel, Frank Jessen, Martin Dyrba, DELCODE study group, Multicenter resting state functional connectivity in prodromal and dementia stages of Alzheimer's disease, Journal of Alzheimer's Disease 64 (3) (July 2018) 801–813.

[100] David C. Alsop, Weiying Dai, Murray Grossman, John A. Detre, Arterial spin labeling blood flow MRI: its role in the early characterization of Alzheimer's disease, Journal of Alzheimer's Disease 20 (3) (2010) 871–880.

[101] Eric E. Smith, Geert Jan Biessels, François De Guio, Frank Erik de Leeuw, Simon Duchesne, Marco Düring, Richard Frayne, M. Arfan Ikram, Eric Jouvent, Bradley J. MacIntosh, et al., Harmonizing brain magnetic resonance imaging methods for vascular contributions to neurodegeneration, Alzheimer's & Dementia: Diagnosis, Assessment & Disease Monitoring 11 (2019) 191–204.

[102] Simon Duchesne, Isabelle Chouinard, Olivier Potvin, Vladimir S. Fonov, April Khademi, Robert Bartha, Pierre Bellec, D. Louis Collins, Maxime Descoteaux, Rick Hoge, et al., The Canadian dementia imaging protocol: harmonizing national cohorts, Journal of Magnetic Resonance Imaging 49 (2) (2019) 456–465.

[103] David M. Cash, Chris Frost, Leonardo O. Iheme, Devrim Ünay, Melek Kandemir, Jurgen Fripp, Olivier Salvado, Pierrick Bourgeat, Martin Reuter, Bruce Fischl, Marco Lorenzi, Giovanni B. Frisoni, Xavier Pennec, Ronald K. Pierson, Jeffrey L. Gunter, Matthew L. Senjem, Clifford R. Jack, Nicolas Guizard, Vladimir S. Fonov, D. Louis Collins, Marc Modat, M. Jorge Cardoso, Kelvin K. Leung, Hongzhi Wang, Sandhitsu R. Das, Paul A. Yushkevich, Ian B. Malone, Nick C. Fox, Jonathan M. Schott, Sebastien Ourselin, Sebastien Ourselin, Assessing atrophy measurement techniques in dementia: results from the MIRIAD atrophy challenge, NeuroImage 123 (Dec. 2015) 149–164.

[104] Giovanni B. Frisoni, Clifford R. Jack, HarP: the EADC-ADNI Harmonized Protocol for manual hippocampal segmentation. A standard of reference from a global working group, Alzheimer's & Dementia 11 (2) (Feb. 2015) 107–110.

[105] Christopher G. Schwarz, Matthew L. Senjem, Jeffrey L. Gunter, Nirubol Tosakulwong, Stephen D. Weigand, Bradley J. Kemp, Anthony J. Spychalla, Prashanthi Vemuri, Ronald C. Petersen, Val J. Lowe, Clifford R. Jack, Optimizing PiB-PET SUVR change-over-time measurement by a large-scale analysis of longitudinal reliability, plausibility, separability, and correlation with MMSE, NeuroImage 144 (Jan. 2017) 113–127.

[106] Aaron Trefler, Neda Sadeghi, Adam G. Thomas, Carlo Pierpaoli, Chris I. Baker, Cibu Thomas, Impact of time-of-day on brain morphometric measures derived from T1-weighted magnetic resonance imaging, NeuroImage 133 (June 2016) 41–52.

[107] Rutger Heinen, Willem H. Bouvy, Adrienne M. Mendrik, Max A. Viergever, Geert Jan Biessels, Jeroen de Bresser, Robustness of automated methods for brain volume measurements across different MRI field strengths, PLoS ONE 11 (10) (Oct. 2016) e0165719.

[108] Xiao Han, Jorge Jovicich, David Salat, Andre van der Kouwe, Brian Quinn, Silvester Czanner, Evelina Busa, Jenni Pacheco, Marilyn Albert, Ronald Killiany, Paul Maguire, Diana Rosas, Nikos Makris, Anders Dale, Bradford Dickerson, Bruce Fischl, Reliability of MRI-derived measurements of human cerebral cortical thickness: the effects of field strength, scanner upgrade and manufacturer, NeuroImage 32 (1) (Aug. 2006) 180–194.

[109] N. Chow, K.S. Hwang, S. Hurtz, A.E. Green, J.H. Somme, P.M. Thompson, D.A. Elashoff, C.R. Jack, M. Weiner, L.G. Apostolova, Alzheimer's Disease Neuroimaging Initiative, Comparing 3T and 1.5T MRI for mapping hippocampal atrophy in the Alzheimer's Disease Neuroimaging Initiative, American Journal of Neuroradiology 36 (4) (Apr. 2015) 653–660.

[110] Sven Haller, Pavel Falkovskiy, Reto Meuli, Jean-Philippe Thiran, Gunnar Krueger, Karl-Olof Lovblad, Tobias Kober, Alexis Roche, Bénédicte Marechal, Basic MR sequence parameters systematically bias automated brain volume estimation, Neuroradiology 58 (11) (Nov. 2016) 1153–1160.

[111] Hyunwoo Lee, Kunio Nakamura, Sridar Narayanan, Robert A. Brown, Douglas L. Arnold, Estimating and accounting for the effect of MRI scanner changes on longitudinal whole-brain volume change measurements, NeuroImage 184 (Jan. 2019) 555–565.

[112] Gregory M. Preboske, Jeff L. Gunter, Chadwick P. Ward, Clifford R. Jack, Common MRI acquisition non-idealities significantly impact the output of the boundary shift integral method of measuring brain atrophy on serial MRI, NeuroImage 30 (4) (May 2006) 1196–1202.

[113] Borys Shuter, Ing Berne Yeh, Steven Graham, Chris Au, Shih-Chang Wang, Reproducibility of brain tissue volumes in longitudinal studies: effects of changes in signal-to-noise ratio and scanner software, NeuroImage 41 (2) (June 2008) 371–379.

[114] Martin Reuter, M. Dylan Tisdall, Abid Qureshi, Randy L. Buckner, André J.W. van der Kouwe, Bruce Fischl, Head motion during MRI acquisition reduces gray matter volume and thickness estimates, NeuroImage 107 (Feb. 2015) 107–115.

[115] Natsuki Igata, Shingo Kakeda, Keita Watanabe, Atsushi Nozaki, Dan Rettmann, Hidekuni Narimatsu, Satoru Ide, Osamu Abe, Yukunori Korogi, Utility of real-time prospective motion correction (PROMO) for segmentation of cerebral cortex on 3D T1-weighted imaging: voxel-based morphometry analysis for uncooperative patients, European Radiology 27 (8) (Aug. 2017) 3554–3562.

[116] Kevin T. Chen, Stephanie Salcedo, Daniel B. Chonde, David Izquierdo-Garcia, Michael A. Levine, Julie C. Price, Bradford C. Dickerson, Ciprian Catana, MR-assisted PET motion correction in simultaneous PET/MRI studies of dementia subjects, Journal of Magnetic Resonance Imaging 48 (5) (Nov. 2018) 1288–1296.

[117] Lars Kasper, Steffen Bollmann, Andreea O. Diaconescu, Chloe Hutton, Jakob Heinzle, Sandra Iglesias, Tobias U. Hauser, Miriam Sebold, Zina-Mary Manjaly, Klaas P. Pruessmann, Klaas E. Stephan, The PhysIO toolbox for modeling physiological noise in fMRI data, Journal of Neuroscience Methods 276 (Jan. 2017) 56–72.

[118] Bénédicte Mortamet, Matt A. Bernstein, Clifford R. Jack, Jeffrey L. Gunter, Chadwick Ward, Paula J. Britson, Reto Meuli, Jean-Philippe Thiran, Gunnar Krueger, Automatic quality assessment in structural brain magnetic resonance imaging, Magnetic Resonance in Medicine 62 (2) (Aug. 2009) 365–372.

[119] Ricardo A. Pizarro, Xi Cheng, Alan Barnett, Herve Lemaitre, Beth A. Verchinski, Aaron L. Goldman, Ena Xiao, Qian Luo, Karen F. Berman, Joseph H. Callicott, Daniel R. Weinberger, Venkata S. Mattay, Automated quality assessment of structural magnetic resonance brain images based on a supervised machine learning algorithm, Frontiers in Neuroinformatics 10 (Dec. 2016) 52.

[120] Anisha Keshavan, Esha Datta, Ian M. McDonough, Christopher R. Madan, Kesshi Jordan, Roland G. Henry Mindcontrol, A web application for brain segmentation quality control, NeuroImage 170 (Apr. 2018) 365–372.

[121] Vladimir Fonov, Mahsa Dadar, The PREVENT-AD Research Group, D. Louis Collins, Deep learning of quality control for stereotaxic registration of human brain MRI, bioRxiv, Apr. 2018, p. 303487.

[122] Heiko Braak, Eva Braak, Morphological criteria for the recognition of Alzheimer's disease and the distribution pattern of cortical changes related to this disorder, Neurobiology of Aging 15 (3) (May 1994) 355–356.

[123] Rik Ossenkoppele, Daniel R. Schonhaut, Michael Schöll, Samuel N. Lockhart, Nagehan Ayakta, Suzanne L. Baker, James P. O'Neil, Mustafa Janabi, Andreas Lazaris, Averill Cantwell, Jacob Vogel, Miguel Santos, Zachary A. Miller, Brianne M. Bettcher, Keith A. Vossel, Joel H. Kramer, Maria L. Gorno-Tempini, Bruce L. Miller, William J. Jagust, Gil D. Rabinovici, Tau PET patterns mirror clinical and neuroanatomical variability in Alzheimer's disease, Brain 139 (5) (May 2016) 1551–1567.

[124] Bruno Dubois, Howard H. Feldman, Claudia Jacova, Harald Hampel, Luis Molinuevo, Kaj Blennow, Steven T. Dekosky, Serge Gauthier, Dennis Selkoe, Randall Bateman, Stefano Cappa, Sebastian Crutch, Sebastiaan Engelborghs, Giovanni B. Frisoni, Nick C. Fox, Douglas Galasko, Marie-Odile Habert, Gregory A. Jicha, Agneta Nordberg, Florence Pasquier, Gil Rabinovici, Philippe Robert, Christopher Rowe, Stephen Salloway, Marie Sarazin, Stéphane Epelbaum, Leonardo C. De Souza, Bruno Vellas, Pieter J. Visser, Lon Schneider, Yaakov Stern, Philip Scheltens, Jeff Rey, L. Cummings, Position Paper Advancing Research Diagnostic Criteria for Alzheimer's Disease: the IWG-2 Criteria, Technical report, 2014.

[125] A.-T. Du, N. Schuff, J.H. Kramer, H.J. Rosen, M.L. Gorno-Tempini, K. Rankin, B.L. Miller, M.W. Weiner, Different regional patterns of cortical thinning in Alzheimer's disease and frontotemporal dementia, Brain 130 (4) (Nov. 2006) 1159–1166.

[126] Jason D. Warren, Phillip D. Fletcher, Hannah L. Golden, The paradox of syndromic diversity in Alzheimer disease, Nature Reviews Neurology 8 (8) (Aug. 2012) 451–464.

[127] Jennifer L. Whitwell, Dennis W. Dickson, Melissa E. Murray, Stephen D. Weigand, Nirubol Tosakulwong, Matthew L. Senjem, David S. Knopman, Bradley F. Boeve, Joseph E. Parisi, Ronald C. Petersen, Clifford R. Jack, Keith A. Josephs, Neuroimaging correlates of pathologically defined subtypes of Alzheimer's disease: a case-control study, The Lancet Neurology 11 (10) (Oct. 2012) 868–877.

[128] Min Soo Byun, Song E. Kim, Jinsick Park, Dahyun Yi, Young Min Choe, Bo Kyung Sohn, Hyo Jung Choi, Hyewon Baek, Ji Young Han, Jong Inn Woo, Dong Young Lee, Alzheimer's Disease Neuroimaging Initiative, Heterogeneity of regional brain atrophy patterns associated with distinct progression rates in Alzheimer's disease, PLoS ONE 10 (11) (Nov. 2015) e0142756.

[129] John Ashburner, Karl J. Friston, Voxel-based morphometry – the methods, NeuroImage 11 (6) (June 2000) 805–821.

[130] John Ashburner, Chloe Hutton, Richard Frackowiak, Ingrid Johnsrude, Cathy Price, Karl Friston, Identifying global anatomical differences: deformation-based morphometry, Human Brain Mapping 6 (5–6) (Jan. 1998) 348–357.

[131] Brian A. Gordon, Tyler M. Blazey, Yi Su, Amrita Hari-Raj, Aylin Dincer, Shaney Flores, Jon Christensen, Eric McDade, Guoqiao Wang, Chengjie Xiong, Nigel J. Cairns, Jason Hassenstab, Daniel S. Marcus, Anne M. Fagan, Clifford R. Jack, Russ C. Hornbeck, Katrina L. Paumier, Beau M. Ances, Sarah B. Berman, Adam M. Brickman, David M. Cash, Jasmeer P. Chhatwal, Stephen Correia, Stefan Förster, Nick C. Fox, Neill R. Graff-Radford, Christian la Fougère, Johannes Levin, Colin L. Masters, Martin N. Rossor, Stephen Salloway, Andrew J. Saykin, Peter R. Schofield, Paul M. Thompson, Michael M. Weiner, David M. Holtzman, Marcus E. Raichle, John C. Morris, Randall J. Bateman, Tammie L.S. Benzinger, Spatial patterns of neuroimaging biomarker change in individuals from families with autosomal dominant Alzheimer's disease: a longitudinal study, The Lancet Neurology 17 (3) (Mar. 2018) 241–250.

[132] Neil P. Oxtoby, Alexandra L. Young, David M. Cash, Tammie L.S. Benzinger, Anne M. Fagan, John C. Morris, Randall J. Bateman, Nick C. Fox, Jonathan M. Schott, Daniel C. Alexander, Data-driven models of dominantly-inherited Alzheimer's disease progression, Brain 141 (5) (May 2018) 1529–1544.

[133] Christine B. Schneider, Markus Donix, Katharina Linse, Annett Werner, Mareike Fauser, Lisa Klingelhoefer, Matthias Löhle, Rüdiger von Kummer, Heinz Reichmann, Alexander Storch, Alexander Storch, Accelerated age-dependent hippocampal volume loss in Parkinson disease with mild cognitive impairment, American Journal of Alzheimer's Disease & Other Dementias 32 (6) (Sept. 2017) 313–319.

[134] Geon Ha Kim, Jae Hong Lee, Sang Won Seo, Jeong Hun Kim, Joon-Kyung Seong, Byoung Seok Ye, Hanna Cho, Young Noh, Hee Jin Kim, Cindy W. Yoon, Seung Jun Oh, Jae Seung Kim, Yearn Seong Choe, Kyung Han Lee, Sung Tae Kim, Jung Won Hwang, Jee Hyang Jeong, Duk L. Na, Hippocampal volume and shape in pure subcortical vascular dementia, Neurobiology of Aging 36 (1) (Jan. 2015) 485–491.

[135] Marina Boccardi, Mikko P. Laakso, Lorena Bresciani, Samantha Galluzzi, Cristina Geroldi, Alberto Beltramello, Hilkka Soininen, Giovanni B. Frisoni, The MRI pattern of frontal and temporal brain atrophy in fronto-temporal dementia, Neurobiology of Aging 24 (1) (Jan. 2003) 95–103.

[136] W.J.P. Henneman, J.D. Sluimer, J. Barnes, W.M. van der Flier, I.C. Sluimer, N.C. Fox, P. Scheltens, H. Vrenken, F. Barkhof, Hippocampal atrophy rates in Alzheimer disease: added value over whole brain volume measures, Neurology 72 (11) (Mar. 2009) 999–1007.

[137] E. Geuze, E. Vermetten, J.D. Bremner, MR-based in vivo hippocampal volumetrics: 1. Review of methodologies currently employed, Molecular Psychiatry 10 (2) (Feb. 2005) 147–159.

[138] C. Konrad, T. Ukas, C. Nebel, V. Arolt, A.W. Toga, K.L. Narr, Defining the human hippocampus in cerebral magnetic resonance images – an overview of current segmentation protocols, NeuroImage 47 (4) (Oct. 2009) 1185–1195.

[139] Giovanni B. Frisoni, Clifford R. Jack, Martina Bocchetta, Corinna Bauer, Kristian S. Frederiksen, Yawu Liu, Gregory Preboske, Tim Swihart, Melanie Blair, Enrica Cavedo, Michel J. Grothe, Mariangela Lanfredi, Oliver Martinez, Masami Nishikawa, Marileen Portegies, Travis Stoub, Chadwich Ward, Liana G. Apostolova, Rossana Ganzola, Dominik Wolf, Frederik Barkhof, George Bartzokis, Charles DeCarli, John G. Csernansky, Leyla DeToledo-Morrell, Mirjam I. Geerlings, Jeffrey Kaye, Ronald J. Killiany, Stephane Lehéricy, Hiroshi Matsuda, John O'Brien, Lisa C. Silbert,

Philip Scheltens, Hilkka Soininen, Stefan Teipel, Gunhild Waldemar, Andreas Fellgiebel, Josephine Barnes, Michael Firbank, Lotte Gerritsen, Wouter Henneman, Nikolai Malykhin, Jens C. Pruessner Lei Wang, Craig Watson, Henrike Wolf, Mony DeLeon, Johannes Pantel, Clarissa Ferrari, Paolo Bosco, Patrizio Pasqualetti, Simon Duchesne, Henri Duvernoy, Marina Boccardi, Marilyn S. Albert, David Bennet, Richard Camicioli, D. Louis Collins, Bruno Dubois, Harald Hampel, Tom DenHeijer, Christofer Hock, William Jagust, Leonore Launer, Jerome J. Maller, Susan Mueller, Perminder Sachdev, Andy Simmons, Paul M. Thompson, Peter-Jelle Visser, Lars-Olof Wahlund, Michael W. Weiner, Bengt Winblad, The EADC-ADNI Harmonized Protocol for manual hippocampal segmentation on magnetic resonance: evidence of validity, Alzheimer's & Dementia 11 (2) (Feb. 2015) 111–125.

[140] Azar Zandifar, Vladimir Fonov, Pierrick Coupé, Jens Pruessner, D. Louis Collins, Alzheimer's Disease Neuroimaging Initiative, A comparison of accurate automatic hippocampal segmentation methods, NeuroImage 155 (2017) 383–393.

[141] Juan Eugenio Iglesias, Jean C. Augustinack, Khoa Nguyen, Christopher M. Player, Allison Player, Michelle Wright, Nicole Roy, Matthew P. Frosch, Ann C. McKee, Lawrence L. Wald, Bruce Fischl, Koen Van Leemput, A computational atlas of the hippocampal formation using ex vivo, ultra-high resolution MRI: application to adaptive segmentation of in vivo MRI, NeuroImage 115 (Jul. 2015) 117–137.

[142] Paul A. Yushkevich, Robert S.C. Amaral, Jean C. Augustinack, Andrew R. Bender, Jeffrey D. Bernstein, Marina Boccardi, Martina Bocchetta, Alison C. Burggren, Valerie A. Carr, M. Mallar Chakravarty, Gaël Chételat, Ana M. Daugherty, Lila Davachi, Song-Lin Ding, Arne Ekstrom, Mirjam I. Geerlings, Abdul Hassan, Yushan Huang, J. Eugenio Iglesias, Renaud La Joie, Geoffrey A. Kerchner, Karen F. LaRocque, Laura A. Libby, Nikolai Malykhin, Susanne G. Mueller, Rosanna K. Olsen, Daniela J. Palombo, Mansi B. Parekh, John B. Pluta, Alison R. Preston, Jens C. Pruessner, Charan Ranganath, Naftali Raz, Margaret L. Schlichting, Dorothee Schoemaker, Sachi Singh, Craig E.L. Stark, Nanthia Suthana, Alexa Tompary, Marta M. Turowski, Koen Van Leemput, Anthony D. Wagner, Lei Wang, Julie L. Winterburn, Laura E.M. Wisse, Michael A. Yassa, Michael M. Zeineh, Quantitative comparison of 21 protocols for labeling hippocampal subfields and parahippocampal subregions in in vivo MRI: towards a harmonized segmentation protocol, NeuroImage 111 (May 2015) 526–541.

[143] Martina Bocchetta, Juan Eugenio Iglesias, Marzia A. Scelsi, David M. Cash, M. Jorge Cardoso, Marc Modat, Andre Altmann, Sebastien Ourselin, Jason D. Warren, Jonathan D. Rohrer, Hippocampal subfield volumetry: differential pattern of atrophy in different forms of genetic frontotemporal dementia, Journal of Alzheimer's Disease 64 (2) (Jun. 2018) 497–504.

[144] T. Heinonen, I.P. Dastidar, P. Kauppinen, I.J. Malmivuo, H. Eskola, Semi-Automatic Tool for Segmentation and Volumetric Analysis of Medical Images, Technical report, 1998.

[145] Keith S. Cover, Ronald A. van Schijndel, Paolo Bosco, Soheil Damangir, Alberto Redolfi, Can measuring hippocampal atrophy with a fully automatic method be substantially less noisy than manual segmentation over both 1 and 3 years?, Psychiatry Research. Neuroimaging 280 (Oct. 2018) 39–47.

[146] Kelvin K. Leung, Matthew J. Clarkson, Jonathan W. Bartlett, Shona Clegg, Clifford R. Jack, Michael W. Weiner, Nick C. Fox, Sébastien Ourselin, Alzheimer's Disease Neuroimaging Initiative, Robust atrophy rate measurement in Alzheimer's disease using multi-site serial MRI: tissue-specific intensity normalization and parameter selection, NeuroImage 50 (2) (Apr. 2010) 516–523.

[147] Tejas Sankar, Min Tae, M. Park, Tasha Jawa, Raihaan Patel, Nikhil Bhagwat, Aristotle N. Voineskos, Andres M. Lozano, M. Mallar Chakravarty, Your algorithm might think the hippocampus grows in Alzheimer's disease: caveats of longitudinal automated hippocampal volumetry, Human Brain Mapping 38 (6) (June 2017) 2875–2896.

[148] Paul A. Yushkevich, Brian B. Avants, Sandhitsu R. Das, John Pluta, Murat Altinay, Caryne Craige, Bias in estimation of hippocampal atrophy using deformation-based morphometry arises from asym-

metric global normalization: an illustration in ADNI 3 T MRI data, NeuroImage 50 (2) (Apr. 2010) 434–445.

[149] Nick C. Fox, Gerard R. Ridgway, Jonathan M. Schott, Algorithms, atrophy and Alzheimer's disease: cautionary tales for clinical trials, NeuroImage 57 (1) (July 2011) 15–18.

[150] Martin Reuter, Bruce Fischl, Avoiding asymmetry-induced bias in longitudinal image processing, NeuroImage 57 (1) (July 2011) 19–21.

[151] Martin Reuter, Nicholas J. Schmansky, H. Diana Rosas, Bruce Fischl, Within-subject template estimation for unbiased longitudinal image analysis, NeuroImage 61 (4) (July 2012) 1402–1418.

[152] Carole H. Sudre, M. Jorge Cardoso, Sebastien Ourselin, Longitudinal segmentation of age-related white matter hyperintensities, Medical Image Analysis (Feb. 2017).

[153] Josephine Barnes, Rachael I. Scahill, Richard G. Boyes, Chris Frost, Emma B. Lewis, Charlotte L. Rossor, Martin N. Rossor, Nick C. Fox, Differentiating AD from aging using semiautomated measurement of hippocampal atrophy rates, NeuroImage 23 (2) (Oct. 2004) 574–581.

[154] Kelvin K. Leung, Josephine Barnes, Gerard R. Ridgway, Jonathan W. Bartlett, Matthew J. Clarkson, Kate Macdonald, Norbert Schuff, Nick C. Fox, Sebastien Ourselin, Automated cross-sectional and longitudinal hippocampal volume measurement in mild cognitive impairment and Alzheimer's disease, NeuroImage 51 (4) (July 2010) 1345–1359.

[155] Ferran Prados, Manuel Jorge Cardoso, Kelvin K. Leung, David M. Cash, Marc Modat, Nick C. Fox, Claudia A.M. Wheeler-Kingshott, Sebastien Ourselin, Alzheimer's Disease Neuroimaging Initiative, Measuring brain atrophy with a generalized formulation of the boundary shift integral, Neurobiology of Aging 36 (Suppl. 1) (Jan. 2015) S81–S90.

[156] M. Jorge Cardoso, Andrew Melbourne, Giles S. Kendall, Marc Modat, Nicola J. Robertson, Neil Marlow, S. Ourselin, AdaPT: an adaptive preterm segmentation algorithm for neonatal brain MRI, NeuroImage 65 (2013) 97–108.

[157] Ronald Boellaard, Standards for PET image acquisition and quantitative data analysis, Journal of Nuclear Medicine 50 (2009) 11–20.

[158] Esther E. Bron, Marion Smits, Wiesje M. van der Flier, Hugo Vrenken, Frederik Barkhof, Philip Scheltens, Janne M. Papma, Rebecca M.E. Steketee, Carolina Méndez Orellana, Rozanna Meijboom, Madalena Pinto, Joana R. Meireles, Carolina Garrett, António J. Bastos-Leite, Ahmed Abdulkadir, Olaf Ronneberger, Nicola Amoroso, Roberto Bellotti, David Cárdenas-Peña, Andrés M. Álvarez-Meza, Chester V. Dolph, Khan M. Iftekharuddin, Simon F. Eskildsen, Pierrick Coupé, Vladimir S. Fonov, Katja Franke, Christian Gaser, Christian Ledig, Ricardo Guerrero, Tong Tong, Katherine R. Gray, Elaheh Moradi, Jussi Tohka, Alexandre Routier, Stanley Durrleman, Alessia Sarica, Giuseppe Di Fatta, Francesco Sensi, Andrea Chincarini, Garry M. Smith, Zhivko V. Stoyanov, Lauge Sørensen, Mads Nielsen, Sabina Tangaro, Paolo Inglese, Christian Wachinger, Martin Reuter, John C. van Swieten, Wiro J. Niessen, Stefan Klein, Standardized evaluation of algorithms for computer-aided diagnosis of dementia based on structural MRI: the CADDementia challenge, NeuroImage 111 (May 2015) 562–579.

[159] Razvan V. Marinescu, Neil P. Oxtoby, Alexandra L. Young, Esther E. Bron, Arthur W. Toga, Michael W. Weiner, Frederik Barkhof, Nick C. Fox, Stefan Klein, Daniel C. Alexander, et al., Tadpole challenge: prediction of longitudinal evolution in Alzheimer's disease, preprint, arXiv:1805.03909, 2018.

[160] Robert L. Harrigan, Benjamin C. Yvernault, Brian D. Boyd, Stephen M. Damon, Kyla David Gibney, Benjamin N. Conrad, Nicholas S. Phillips, Baxter P. Rogers, Yurui Gao, Bennett A. Landman, Vanderbilt university institute of imaging science center for computational imaging xnat: a multimodal data archive and processing environment, NeuroImage 124 (2016) 1097–1101.

[161] Samir Das, Alex P. Zijdenbos, Dario Vins, Jonathan Harlap, Alan C. Evans, Loris: a web-based data management system for multi-center studies, Frontiers in Neuroinformatics 5 (2012) 37.

[162] Daniel S. Marcus, Tracy H. Wang, Jamie Parker, John G. Csernansky, John C. Morris, Randy L. Buckner, Open access series of imaging studies (oasis): cross-sectional mri data in young, middle aged, nondemented, and demented older adults, Journal of Cognitive Neuroscience 19 (9) (2007) 1498–1507.

[163] Susanne G. Mueller, Michael W. Weiner, Leon J. Thal, Ronald C. Petersen, Clifford R. Jack, William Jagust, John Q. Trojanowski, Arthur W. Toga, Laurel Beckett, Ways toward an early diagnosis in Alzheimer's disease: the Alzheimer's disease neuroimaging initiative (ADNI), Alzheimer's & Dementia 1 (1) (2005) 55–66.

[164] Agnès Benvenutto, Bernard Giusiano, Lejla Koric, Claude Gueriot, Mira Didic, Olivier Felician, Maxime Guye, Eric Guedj, Mathieu Ceccaldi, Imaging biomarkers of neurodegeneration in Alzheimer's disease: distinct contributions of cortical MRI atrophy and FDG-PET hypometabolism, Journal of Alzheimer's Disease 65 (4) (2018) 1147–1157.

[165] Lauge Sørensen, Christian Igel, Akshay Pai, Ioana Balas, Cecilie Anker, Martin Lillholm, Mads Nielsen, Alzheimer's Disease Neuroimaging Initiative, Differential diagnosis of mild cognitive impairment and Alzheimer's disease using structural MRI cortical thickness, hippocampal shape, hippocampal texture, and volumetry, NeuroImage: Clinical 13 (2017) 470–482.

[166] Kerstin Ritter, Julia Schumacher, Martin Weygandt, Ralph Buchert, Carsten Allefeld, John-Dylan Haynes, Multimodal prediction of conversion to Alzheimer's disease based on incomplete biomarkers, Alzheimer's & Dementia: Diagnosis, Assessment & Disease Monitoring 1 (2) (June 2015) 206–215.

[167] Jonathan Young, Marc Modat, Manuel J. Cardoso, Alex Mendelson, Dave Cash, Sebastien Ourselin, Accurate multimodal probabilistic prediction of conversion to Alzheimer's disease in patients with mild cognitive impairment, NeuroImage: Clinical 2 (Jan. 2013) 735–745.

[168] Alexander Kautzky, Rene Seiger, Andreas Hahn, Peter Fischer, Wolfgang Krampla, Siegfried Kasper, Gabor G. Kovacs, Rupert Lanzenberger, Prediction of autopsy verified neuropathological change of Alzheimer's disease using machine learning and MRI, Frontiers in Aging Neuroscience 10 (Dec. 2018) 406.

[169] Massimiliano Grassi, David A. Loewenstein, Daniela Caldirola, Koen Schruers, Ranjan Duara, Giampaolo Perna, A clinically-translatable machine learning algorithm for the prediction of Alzheimer's disease conversion: further evidence of its accuracy via a transfer learning approach, International Psychogeriatrics (Nov. 2018) 1–9.

[170] Jane Maryam Rondina Luiz Kobuti Ferreira, Fabio Luis de Souza Duran, Rodrigo Kubo, Carla Rachel Ono, Claudia Costa Leite, Jerusa Smid, Ricardo Nitrini, Carlos Alberto Buchpiguel, Geraldo F. Busatto, Selecting the most relevant brain regions to discriminate Alzheimer's disease patients from healthy controls using multiple kernel learning: a comparison across functional and structural imaging modalities and atlases, NeuroImage: Clinical 17 (Jan. 2018) 628–641.

[171] Siqi Bao, Albert C.S. Chung, Multi-scale structured CNN with label consistency for brain MR image segmentation, Computer Methods in Biomechanics and Biomedical Engineering: Imaging & Visualization 6 (1) (Jan. 2018) 113–117.

[172] Liang Cao, Long Li, Jifeng Zheng, Xin Fan, Feng Yin, Hui Shen, Jun Zhang, Multi-task neural networks for joint hippocampus segmentation and clinical score regression, Multimedia Tools and Applications 77 (22) (Nov. 2018) 29669–29686.

[173] Hongyoon Choi, Kyong Hwan Jin, Predicting cognitive decline with deep learning of brain metabolism and amyloid imaging, Behavioural Brain Research 344 (May 2018) 103–109.

[174] Xiaonan Liu, Kewei Chen, Teresa Wu, David Weidman, Fleming Lure, Jing Li, Use of multimodality imaging and artificial intelligence for diagnosis and prognosis of early stages of Alzheimer's disease, Translational Research 194 (Apr. 2018) 56–67.

[175] Jun Shi, Xiao Zheng, Yan Li, Qi Zhang, Shihui Ying, Multimodal neuroimaging feature learning with multimodal stacked deep polynomial networks for diagnosis of Alzheimer's disease, IEEE Journal of Biomedical and Health Informatics 22 (1) (Jan. 2018) 173–183.

[176] Simeon E. Spasov, Luca Passamonti, Andrea Duggento, Pietro Lio, Nicola Toschi, A multi-modal convolutional neural network framework for the prediction of Alzheimer's disease, in: 2018 40th Annual International Conference of the IEEE Engineering in Medicine and Biology Society, EMBC, IEEE, July 2018, pp. 1271–1274.

[177] Andrés Ortiz, Jorge Munilla, Juan M. Górriz, Javier Ramírez, Ensembles of deep learning architectures for the early diagnosis of the Alzheimer's disease, International Journal of Neural Systems 26 (07) (Nov. 2016) 1650025.

[178] Nicola Amoroso, Domenico Diacono, Annarita Fanizzi, Marianna La Rocca, Alfonso Monaco, Angela Lombardi, Cataldo Guaragnella, Roberto Bellotti, Sabina Tangaro, Deep learning reveals Alzheimer's disease onset in MCI subjects: results from an international challenge, Journal of Neuroscience Methods 302 (May 2018) 3–9.

[179] Richard Shaw, Carole Sudre, Sebastien Ourselin, M. Jorge Cardoso, MRI k-space motion artefact augmentation: model robustness and task-specific uncertainty, in: Proceedings of Machine Learning Research, vol. 102, 2019, pp. 427–436.

[180] Mohammad Havaei, Nicolas Guizard, Nicolas Chapados, Yoshua Bengio, HEMIS: hetero-modal image segmentation, in: International Conference on Medical Image Computing and Computer-Assisted Intervention, Springer, 2016, pp. 469–477.

[181] Thomas Varsavsky, Zach Eaton-Rosen, Carole H. Sudre, Parashkev Nachev, M. Jorge Cardoso Pimms, Permutation invariant multi-modal segmentation, in: Deep Learning in Medical Image Analysis and Multimodal Learning for Clinical Decision Support, Springer, 2018, pp. 201–209.

[182] Clifford R. Jack, David S. Knopman, William J. Jagust, Ronald C. Petersen, Michael W. Weiner, Paul S. Aisen, Leslie M. Shaw, Prashanthi Vemuri, Heather J. Wiste, Stephen D. Weigand, Timothy G. Lesnick, Vernon S. Pankratz, Michael C. Donohue, John Q. Trojanowski, Tracking pathophysiological processes in Alzheimer's disease: an updated hypothetical model of dynamic biomarkers, The Lancet Neurology 12 (2) (Feb. 2013) 207–216.

[183] Alexandra L. Young, Neil P. Oxtoby, Sebastien Ourselin, Jonathan M. Schott, Daniel C. Alexander, A simulation system for biomarker evolution in neurodegenerative disease, Medical Image Analysis 26 (1) (Dec. 2015) 47–56.

[184] Marco Lorenzi, Maurizio Filippone, Giovanni B. Frisoni, Daniel C. Alexander, Sebastien Ourselin, Probabilistic disease progression modeling to characterize diagnostic uncertainty: application to staging and prediction in Alzheimer's disease, NeuroImage 190 (Apr. 2019) 56–68.

[185] Sveva Fornari, Amelie Schafer, Mathias Jucker, Alain Goriely, Ellen Kuhl, Prion-like spreading of Alzheimer's disease within the brain's connectome, bioRxiv, Jan. 2019, p. 529438.

[186] Bishesh Khanal, Marco Lorenzi, Nicholas Ayache, Xavier Pennec, Simulating patient specific multiple time-point MRIs from a biophysical model of brain deformation in Alzheimer's disease, in: Computational Biomechanics for Medicine, Springer International Publishing, Cham, 2016, pp. 167–176.

[187] Xiangrui Li, Paul S. Morgan, John Ashburner, Jolinda Smith, Christopher Rorden, The first step for neuroimaging data analysis: DICOM to NIfTI conversion, Journal of Neuroscience Methods 264 (May 2016) 47–56.

[188] Jeffrey R. Petrella, Wenrui Hao, Adithi Rao, P. Murali Doraiswamy, Computational causal modeling of the dynamic biomarker cascade in Alzheimer's disease, Computational & Mathematical Methods in Medicine 2019 (Feb. 2019) 1–8.

[189] Magali Haas, Diane Stephenson, Klaus Romero, Mark Forrest Gordon, Neta Zach, Hugo Geerts, Big data to smart data in Alzheimer's disease: real-world examples of advanced modeling and simulation, Alzheimer's & Dementia 12 (9) (Sept. 2016) 1022–1030.

[190] Igor Koval, J.-B. Schiratti, Alexandre Routier, Michael Bacci, Olivier Colliot, Stéphanie Allassonnière, Stanley Durrleman, Statistical learning of spatiotemporal patterns from longitudinal manifold-valued networks, in: Medical Image Computing and Computer Assisted Intervention – MICCAI 2017, Sept. 2017, pp. 451–459.

[191] Anuraag R. Kansal, Ali Tafazzoli, K. Jack Ishak, Stanmira Krotneva, Alzheimer's disease Archimedes condition-event simulator: development and validation, Alzheimer's & Dementia: Translational Research & Clinical Interventions 4 (Jan. 2018) 76–88.

[192] Christiane Reitz, Richard Mayeux, Alzheimer disease: epidemiology, diagnostic criteria, risk factors and biomarkers, Biochemical Pharmacology 88 (4) (Apr. 2014) 640–651.

[193] Yasser Iturria-Medina, Félix M. Carbonell, Alan C. Evans, Multimodal imaging-based therapeutic fingerprints for optimizing personalized interventions: application to neurodegeneration, NeuroImage 179 (Oct. 2018) 40–50.

[194] R. Guerrero, A. Schmidt-Richberg, C. Ledig, T. Tong, R. Wolz, D. Rueckert, Instantiated mixed effects modeling of Alzheimer's disease markers, NeuroImage 142 (Nov. 2016) 113–125.

[195] H. Hampel, S.E. O'Bryant, S. Durrleman, E. Younesi, K. Rojkova, V. Escott-Price, J-C. Corvol, K. Broich, B. Dubois, S. Lista, Alzheimer Precision Medicine Initiative, A precision medicine initiative for Alzheimer's disease: the road ahead to biomarker-guided integrative disease modeling, Climacteric 20 (2) (Mar. 2017) 107–118.

[196] José L. Molinuevo, Jordi Cami, Xavier Carné, Maria C. Carrillo, Jean Georges, Maria B. Isaac, Zaven Khachaturian, Scott Y.H. Kim, John C. Morris, Florence Pasquier, Craig Ritchie, Reisa Sperling, Jason Karlawish, Ethical challenges in preclinical Alzheimer's disease observational studies and trials: results of the Barcelona summit, Alzheimer's & Dementia 12 (5) (May 2016) 614–622.

[197] Eline M. Bunnik, Edo Richard, Richard Milne, Maartje H.N. Schermer, On the personal utility of Alzheimer's disease-related biomarker testing in the research context, Journal of Medical Ethics 44 (2018) 830–834.

[198] Winston Chiong, Challenges in communicating and understanding predictive biomarker imaging for Alzheimer disease, JAMA Neurology 75 (1) (Jan. 2018) 18.

CHAPTER 16

Machine learning based imaging biomarkers in large scale population studies: A neuroimaging perspective

Guray Erus, Mohamad Habes, Christos Davatzikos

Artificial Intelligence in Biomedical Imaging Lab (AIBIL), Center for Biomedical Image Computing and Analytics (CBICA), Perelman School of Medicine, University of Pennsylvania, Philadelphia, PA, United States

Contents

16.1.	Introduction	379
16.2.	Large scale population studies in neuroimage analysis: steps towards dimensional neuroimaging; harmonization challenges	382
	16.2.1 The ENIGMA project	382
	16.2.2 The iSTAGING project	383
	16.2.3 Harmonization of multisite neuroimaging data	383
16.3.	Unsupervised pattern learning for dimensionality reduction of neuroimaging data	385
	16.3.1 Finding imaging patterns of covariation	386
16.4.	Supervised classification based imaging biomarkers for disease diagnosis	387
	16.4.1 Automated classification of Alzheimer's disease patients	388
	16.4.2 Classification of schizophrenia patients in multisite large cohorts	388
16.5.	Multivariate pattern regression for brain age prediction	389
	16.5.1 Brain development index	389
	16.5.2 Imaging patterns of brain aging	390
16.6.	Deep learning in neuroimaging analysis	392
16.7.	Revealing heterogeneity of imaging patterns of brain diseases	393
16.8.	Conclusions	394
References		395

16.1. Introduction

In vivo brain magnetic resonance imaging (MRI) methods play an increasingly important role in the research for diagnosis and treatment of neuro-degenerative diseases and mental illnesses, as well as in understanding brain changes occurring during development and aging [5,38,46,27]. Modern imaging methods offer the opportunity to quantify and study multifaceted aspects of brain changes in ways that were previously impossible. Neuroimaging data is both very large and very complex, as it encompasses many dimensions related to structure, function, and pathology. Multivariate patterns of disease related brain changes are subtle and confounded to a great extent by significant anatomical and functional variations due to differences in patient populations. Understanding the interrelationship among multimodal imaging measurements and relating them to cognitive and clinical measures, as well as to demographic and genetic risk factors, is challenging and requires informed data summarization. Moreover, for these complex imaging measures to eventually become routine assays in the clinic, they need to be condensed down to a relatively small and manageable, yet maximally informative set of imaging biomarkers.

A growing interest towards this direction has been focused on the use of machine learning methods for the analysis of large and complex brain imaging data [5,33,65,67]. Machine learning models extract patterns from the raw data in order to predict an output, without being explicitly programmed to do so. In supervised learning, the most common type of machine learning approaches, the algorithms use training data with known outcome values, or labels, in order to discover an optimal mapping between the provided input data and the output values. The trained model is subsequently applied to new, previously unseen data to predict the output values. Yet, in unsupervised learning, only unlabeled input data is available, and the goal is to model the underlying structure of the data, for example, to identify inherent subtypes within the sample population, or clusters/groups within the input features. Machine learning methods are increasingly popular in neuroimaging studies due to their ability to model high-dimensional datasets. In contrast to mass-univariate analyses [3], in which a statistical model is applied on each individual measurement, e.g., voxel intensity values on image maps, volumes of anatomical regions, or brain activity in a region or network, machine learning can learn a model that operates on the high-dimensional multivariate data in order to find the optimal mapping between the complex input data and the desired output. Importantly, the machine learning framework fits well into the concept of a biomarker, defined as "a characteristic that is objectively measured and evaluated as an indicator of normal biological processes, pathogenic processes, or pharmacologic responses to a therapeutic intervention" [56], which contains within it the idea of associating a pattern of structural or functional brain change with a particular clinical outcome [5].

There are major challenges in developing accurate and reproducible imaging biomarkers that can correctly predict relevant clinical endpoints in neurologic and neuropsychiatric diseases. Indisputably, the best way to address these challenges is by increasing the sample size, i.e., the number of scanned subjects [64]. In fact, the success of machine learning approaches in neuroimaging depends greatly on the existence of large-scale studies that are complemented with a broad and deep phenotyping. Most neuroimaging studies have traditionally relied on modest sample sizes (e.g., $n < 100$), which may contribute to low reproducibility of the findings [59]. However, with the increased accessibility of medical imaging technology we have witnessed a growing interest towards larger scale population studies (e.g., $n > 300$) that acquire multimodal scans and associated clinical data. In recent years, a small number of "big data" neuroimaging studies started to collect imaging data with even larger samples (e.g., $n > 1000$) [61,42]. Finally, "mega-analyses" start to emerge by pooling thousands of samples together, as in [4]. While large sample sizes present opportunities for neuroimaging research, they also introduce important new challenges, such as harmonization of datasets from different scanners and imaging protocols, a task that may benefit from statistical learning techniques. The increasing availability of such studies also renders data-driven machine learning analyses increasingly pertinent. The large samples allow machine learning methods to identify and quantify subtle and spatially complex patterns of disease-induced changes in the brain in a more accurate and generalizable way, providing more interpretable representations of the complex data, as well as powerful predictive biomarkers on an individual basis for early diagnosis [46,40]. They also enable the application of techniques that typically require very large sample sizes for model training, such as deep neural networks, as well as advanced and exploratory analytic techniques that go beyond classical machine learning methods, such as the semisupervised methods for disease heterogeneity detection, which we describe below.

In the remainder of this chapter, we present multifaceted sample of methods and studies involving machine learning principles applied to large scale population studies. We by no means intend to provide an exhaustive overview of this rapidly growing field, but we largely draw from our laboratory work examples of different analyses that can be performed using machine learning. We first discuss some current efforts towards large scale neuroimaging analyses in Sect. 16.2. We give as example large, consortium-based imaging studies of brain aging and mental diseases, with a specific focus on data harmonization across studies for analysis of pooled multi-site data. In Sect. 16.3, we touch upon dimensionality reduction techniques for effective summarization of the high-dimensional imaging data. We describe an unsupervised learning methodology that decomposes brain images into patterns of covariation across subjects. Section 16.4 presents the supervised multivariate learning framework for disease classification, with examples of learning algorithms and their use in large scale studies. In Sect. 16.5 we explain the application of multivariate pattern regression methods for brain age prediction on developmental and aging datasets. Deep learning methods, which are gaining increasing popularity for addressing various major problems in neuroimaging analysis, are briefly described in Sect. 16.6. Section 16.7 addresses the issue of disease heterogeneity in the context of machine learning, and presents as a potential solution a semisupervised learning approach for detecting interpretable imaging subtypes of disease, while Sect. 16.8 concludes this chapter.

16.2. Large scale population studies in neuroimage analysis: steps towards dimensional neuroimaging; harmonization challenges

In recent years, there has been a significant interest toward neuroimaging "big data" analyses [62,60,11]. Many studies have acquired multimodal scans of hundreds or low-thousands of participants to study different aspects of structural and functional brain changes, such as the Alzheimer's Disease Neuroimaging Initiative (ADNI) [69], Baltimore Longitudinal Study of Aging (BLSA) [22], Philadelphia Neurodevelopmental cohort (PNC) [50], SHIP [68], UK-BIOBANK [57], and Human Connectome Project [25]. This has opened the way for pooling together large and diverse datasets for joint analysis, aiming to link neuroimaging phenotypes with neurocognitive phenotypes. Such pooling will significantly mitigate the challenge of undertraining and undertesting machine learning algorithms. Importantly, it will also allow us to investigate heterogeneity of brain imaging phenotypes, which calls for very large sample sizes. The following two subsections offer two examples of large-scale imaging data integration for meta-analysis purposes.

16.2.1 The ENIGMA project

One of these initiatives, the ENIGMA project, conducted by a collaborative network of research groups worldwide involved in neuroimaging and genetics, combines data from 70 institutions for the genetic analysis of brain imaging [58,4]. The initial aim of the study was to perform genome-wide association study (GWAS) analyses on measures derived from brain images to identify associations between variations in the genome and changes in the brain structure and function. Standard GWAS studies, such as the univariate analysis of SNP effects, require very large sample sizes to identify genetic markers of imaging phenotypes and to replicate them across independent datasets. The ENIGMA project was initiated to address this challenge by pooling data from many existing neuroimaging studies and for the metaanalysis of the data. The primary imaging measures that were used in ENIGMA GWAS analyses have been the volumes of major subcortical structures that were derived through automatic segmentation of anatomical regions of interest (ROIs). Importantly, image processing for these analyses was performed by each participating center using their own algorithm, as it would not be feasible to request these centers to use a single specific algorithm.

At a later phase of the project, "disease working groups" were formed to investigate the effects of various mental disorders on the brain using pooled imaging data from patients with psychiatric illnesses. From these, the Schizophrenia and Bipolar Disorder working group collected MRI data of 2028 patients and 2540 controls from 15 centers. High-resolution T1-weighted structural scans of these subjects were segmented into subcortical ROIs using the Freesurfer package [23]. The data analysis involved univariate analysis of group differences for each ROI within each subsample and univariate linear regression for the metaanalysis of these group differences. The results have indicated a robust pattern of subcortical brain differences between healthy controls and patients with schizophrenia [17]. Importantly, these results were consistent with previous retrospective metaanalyses of published work, evidencing the validity of prospective data pooling approaches and their potential for further more advanced analyses on these pooled datasets with very large sample sizes. Despite its impressive sample size and richness of data, ENIGMA is currently somewhat limited by the lack of pooling of the raw datasets, and reliance on independently derived measures via Freesurfer, which limits the ability to more broadly test richer feature sets and machine learning methods like convolutional neural networks.

16.2.2 The iSTAGING project

The iSTAGING project (Imaging-based coordinate system for aging and neurodegenerative diseases) is another collaborative effort that pools together multiparametric imaging datasets of over 20,000 participants from more than 10 studies spanning ages 45 to 89, forming one of the largest existing MRI imaging databases of aging [9]. iSTAGING has a particular focus on leveraging advances in current machine learning methods to study diverse brain changes present in aging, cerebrovascular disease (CeVD) and Alzheimer disease (AD). Application of machine learning methods to such large studies has started to highlight a second very important strength of machine learning methods, beyond their ability to form individualized biomarkers. In particular, using semisupervised learning methods [14,63,16], we can now distill complex multiparametric imaging data down to perhaps a few dozens of dimensions, thereby allowing us to establish concise and clinically informative brain reference systems. Each of these dimensions reflects a different pattern of brain alterations, for instance age related brain atrophy, AD-like patterns of brain change, functional connectivity and local coherence loss, spatial pattern of amyloid deposition or white matter abnormalities, hence capturing the underlying neuroanatomical, neurofunctional, and neuropathological heterogeneity in quantifiable and replicable metrics (Fig. 16.1).

16.2.3 Harmonization of multisite neuroimaging data

While data pooling enables building unprecedented sample sizes, it also raises novel methodological and statistical challenges. The most important challenge of multisite, multistudy analyses is "data harmonization". In individual studies, defining a standardized scan protocol is the first step for minimizing the scanner-related variability [53]. However, even in multicenter studies with consistent standardized protocols and field strengths, systematic differences in imaging measurements of the normal and abnormal brain tissues were found [52]. On the other hand, data pooled from multiple studies are subject to more significant scanner-related variations, due to differences in scan protocols, scanner manufacturers, models and field strengths. Various analyses have

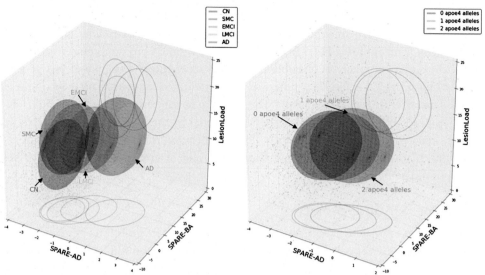

APOE4 and clinical diagnosis correlate with development of AD-like patterns of atrophy (SPARE-AD) more than with patterns of advanced brain aging (SPARE-BA). Limited correlations with lesion load.

Figure 16.1 Preliminary results from six cohorts (ADNI1, ADNI2, SHIP, BLSA1, BLSA2, Penn ADC; $n = 3,179$) covering a heterogeneous spectrum of cognitively normal brain aging, MCI and AD were harmonized and used to prototype a dimensional system. For clarity, three dimensions are visualized herein, using machine-learning: (1) SPARE-BA, a subject-specific index of age-related brain atrophy patterns; (2) SPARE-AD, an index previously developed to capture AD-like atrophy patterns; (3) white matter hyperintensities (WMH) burden. (From [9].)

demonstrated that scanner and protocol differences cause systematic bias in final imaging measurements [6,31,34,24]. These scanner effects should be taken into consideration in all studies that combine data across platforms and across field-strengths.

One approach to harmonization focuses on the image processing stage, and aims to derive interstudy compatible measures by standardizing image characteristics and image processing steps that derive these measures. For example, in [19] a method for calculating longitudinally and intersite consistent regional anatomy volumes in the BLSA study was proposed for longitudinal scans with scanner changes from a 1.5 T SPGR to a 3 T MPRAGE scanner. The method extended the multiatlas ROI segmentation framework using harmonized scanner-specific atlases. Consecutive SPGR and MPRAGE scans of a subset of the participants were pairwise registered to each other to create scanner specific atlas image sets. The reference labels of these atlases were calculated by applying multiatlas segmentation with external atlases, but only for one type of scan, so that atlas pairs preserve original scan characteristics while sharing a single set of common anatomical labels. Each scan in the complete sample was segmented using the harmonized atlas set for the specific scanner type. The segmentation using the proposed harmonization method resulted in reduced scanner-related differences in cross-sectional age trends of

ROI volumes, and improved longitudinal consistency between SPGR and MPRAGE scans. A major requirement of this method, however, is the availability of a small set of subjects that were scanned in both sites. While this requirement is satisfied in longitudinal studies, data that is pooled retrospectively does generally not include subjects scanned in multiple sites to be used for creating the scanner specific atlases.

An alternative approach is to perform postprocessing data harmonization, i.e., correcting final imaging measurements derived from processed images for site differences using statistical techniques. An "adjusted residuals harmonization" method was described in [24]. This technique fits a linear regression model separately for each imaging measurement as a dependent variable to estimate coefficients associated with both biological covariates of interest, such as age and sex, and the scanner indicator. The parameters of the model are estimated using regular ordinary least squares (OLS). Scanner effects are removed by subtracting the estimated scanner effects only. The Combat model, a popular correction method that was initially proposed for genomics data, extended this model by defining prior distribution hyperparameters on the estimated site effect parameters. The main assumption of Combat is that input features (e.g., voxel values or regional measurements) share a common distribution. Thus, instead of estimating site effects independently for each input feature, information pooled across features was used to improve the statistical estimation of the site effects [24]. In comparative evaluations on functional anisotropy (FA) and mean diffusivity (MD) maps extracted from multisite diffusion tensor imaging (DTI) scans Combat successfully removed unwanted sources of scan variability and effectively mitigated scanner effects.

16.3. Unsupervised pattern learning for dimensionality reduction of neuroimaging data

A major challenge for the multivariate analysis of neuroimaging data is the curse of dimensionality, as input scans contain a large number of variables (voxel values; derived features), possibly from multiple image modalities, while relatively much lower number of samples are often available, even in large scale studies. Some form of data reduction is typically performed to eliminate redundant variables or to map the data into a lower-dimensional representation of it. A straightforward approach for dimensionality reduction has been to partition the brain into a set of a priori defined anatomical or functional regions of interest (ROIs) and to use summary measurements within ROIs (e.g., regional volumes or average signal from the input image maps) for subsequent analysis steps. While the ROI segmentation approach is simple and provides interpretable measurements for further data analyses, it is based on regional hypotheses reflected in the definitions of the reference segmentations. In recent years, the use of unsupervised learning techniques has shown promising results for automatically identifying reproducible and interpretable imaging patterns from a collection of scans without need for

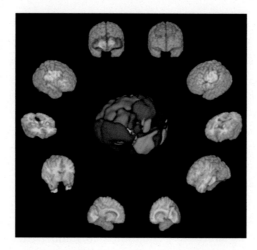

Figure 16.2 Nonnegative parts of the brain estimated using GM tissue density maps from a healthy elder population.

a priori region definitions. A major advantage of these data–driven approaches that de-compose the brain into a set of components is that they generalize well to new datasets. They can be applied on any type of image maps (tissue densities, cortical thickness val-ues, diffusion or functional activation maps) and on diverse subject groups in order to identify imaging patterns that characterize the specific dataset.

16.3.1 Finding imaging patterns of covariation

In [54], an unsupervised pattern analysis method was proposed for finding imaging pat-terns of structural covariance via Nonnegative Matrix Factorization (NNMF), which has previously been used with great success in computer vision for parts-based decom-positions [37]. The method derives components that correspond to brain regions that covary across individuals in a consistent way (Fig. 16.2). NNMF uses image maps in a common atlas space from a group of subjects as input, and computes a decomposition of the data matrix (of voxel values from all subjects) into two matrices: a predefined number of basis vectors, i.e., components, and their loadings for each subject. The for-mulation includes a nonnegativity constraint that leads to a parts-based representation of the data, and an orthogonality constraint that favors nonoverlapping components, which together combine to form the whole brain. The NNMF methodology allows deriving decompositions at different resolutions by varying the number of estimated components. While this is a desirable property of the methodology, it's also important to determine the "optimal number of components" for a specific dataset. For this pur-pose, two metrics were used jointly: the reconstruction error of the initial data using the derived components and the reproducibility of the components from split-half data. The optimal decomposition would have low reconstruction error and high reproducibility.

Application of the NNMF method on gray matter tissue density maps in a common atlas space from a healthy elder population produced sparse and well localized structural covariance components [54]. These components also aligned well with known anatomical parcellations. On a pediatric dataset (ages 9–21) NNMF decomposed the developing brain into components that were not only consistent with previous manual decompositions based on anatomy, but also consistent with major functional parcellations. Furthermore, the maturation of these components with age followed trends that were consistent with the evolutionary development of different brain regions [55]. Application on white matter lesion segmentations on MRI scans of 1836 subjects from the cross-sectional Study of Health in Pomerania resulted in spatially heterogeneous lesion patterns encoded by four components [28]. The decomposition was consistent with known categorizations into periventricular vs deep white matter lesions. However, the data-driven approach further divided periventricular lesions into frontal, dorsal, and posterior components. The results on these diverse datasets demonstrate the potential of unsupervised machine learning techniques to uncover coordinated patterns of brain changes, providing interpretable and quantifiable representations of the high dimensional data and efficiently reducing the data dimensionality for further analyses.

16.4. Supervised classification based imaging biomarkers for disease diagnosis

In the last few decades, there has been a growing interest in the use of supervised machine learning methods to derive neuroimaging biomarkers for early diagnosis and for individual patient management. The objective of supervised classification is to use imaging data and known outcome labels from a set of subjects, such as healthy controls and patients, to learn a model that automatically classifies individuals into one of the target classes. In the model training phase, a training set with known labels is used to "learn" the mapping between the complex multivariate input data and the labels. The training model is then applied on new samples to make predictions.

A supervised learning algorithm that was relatively widely used in neuroimaging analysis has been the support vector machines (SVM) [7]. In SVM classification, a separating hyperplane between data samples from two different classes is found by maximizing the margin between these two classes. The decision function, that is, the classification hyperplane, is fully specified by only the data samples on the margin boundaries, which are called the support vectors. SVMs have many advantages that make them suitable for high-dimensional pattern recognition problem, such as high generalization performance, as well as easy computation that allows dealing with the curse of dimensionality. Ensemble-based methods, where a collection of individual classifiers are cooperatively trained on the same task, have also been very effective ways to derive reliable and reproducible classifiers, while reducing confounding noise effects [21,48]

16.4.1 Automated classification of Alzheimer's disease patients

Machine learning methods have been applied for single subject classification of various mental diseases, such as schizophrenia, autism spectrum disorder, bipolar disease, attention deficit hyperactivity disorder, and major depression [10,2]. However, the most widespread application of them in neuroimaging was for classification of AD, the most common neurodegenerative disorder. A recent review paper has identified 409 studies for machine learning based classification of AD in PubMed and Google Scholar, from January 1985 to June 2016 [43]. The ADNI multisite longitudinal study [69], which was conducted by researchers at 63 sites in the US and Canada, was a major driving force for this intense research activity, evidencing the importance of large scale studies in neuroimaging research. ADNI has been one of the earliest examples of large scale neuroimaging initiatives, collecting, from 2004 until now, multimodal longitudinal scans of more than 1000 patients with AD and mild cognitive impairment (MCI), as well as of healthy controls. The number of machine learning papers on AD classification using ADNI data has dramatically increased in recent years [20,43], with converging results for cross-validated classification accuracy values. For an objective comparison of different approaches [47] proposed a framework for reproducible classification experiments using 1519 baseline T1 MR images and 1102 baseline FDG PET images from ADNI. The framework included data extraction, image processing and machine learning components for benchmarking different feature extraction and classification tools in a reproducible manner. A voxel-based linear SVM and a spatially and anatomically regularized SVM were used separately for T1 and FDG PET scans for classification. Overall, the use of FDG PET with a linear SVM obtained the highest accuracy for AD vs CN classification with 91% accuracy and 94.2% AUC.

16.4.2 Classification of schizophrenia patients in multisite large cohorts

These results on AD and a very large number of other studies evidence the great potential of machine learning methods for single subject prediction of various mental diseases. However, a major limitation of the majority of existing neuroimaging studies is the small sample size, which significantly impacts the generalizability of the findings and replications on independent sets. For example, previous results from small sample size, single-site imaging studies for schizophrenia, a major mental disorder and a serious public health problem characterized by deficits in cognition, provided evidence of patterns of gray matter deficits in schizophrenia [12]. ROI-based machine learning approaches were found to be potentially helpful in automatic classification of patients with schizophrenia [66]. However, these results have often been heterogeneous, leading investigators to retrospective metaanalyses of published data [30]. However, the increasing number of studies examining structural brain abnormalities in schizophrenia in recent years provides an opportunity to machine learning methods for computing more robust and generalizable imaging biomarkers of the disease by pooling the available data. In [45] a neuroanatomical signature of patients with schizophrenia was found via multivariate pattern classification using pooled data from 5 sites (941 adult participants, including 440 patients with schizophrenia). A linear SVM was used for classification. Input features included a combination of voxelwise tissue density values, regional volumes, and regional shape, intensity and texture features, which were harmonized across sites by intracranial volume (ICV), site, age, and sex effects using a pooled sample of control subjects. Cross-validated classification using pooled data achieved a prediction accuracy of 76% (AUC = 0.84). Importantly, leave-site-out validation of the model obtained accuracy/AUC range of 72–77%/0.73–0.91, showing that the model generalized well to data from previously unseen sites. These results emphasize the potential for machine learning methods to provide robust and reproducible imaging signatures of schizophrenia using pooled datasets with large sample sizes.

16.5. Multivariate pattern regression for brain age prediction

In addition to binary disease classification, the supervised learning framework can also be applied to compute a predictive model that maps the high dimensional imaging data into a continuous outcome variable. A popular application of multivariate pattern regression methods in neuroimaging in recent years has been the "brain age" models. These models aim to predict the chronological age of subjects from their MRI images. Importantly, as a subject's age is a ground truth that is easily ascertained, the putative clinical utility of the approach is in the quantification of how much a subject deviates from normative age trajectories, particularly in stages of life when the most significant brain changes occur, such as childhood, adolescence, and aging. Even further, the pattern of deviation from normative brain age trajectories might provide more precise/specific indications of the underlying neuropathology.

16.5.1 Brain development index

Human brain maturation during childhood and adolescence is very complex and involves dynamic processes of progressive and regressive brain changes that occur simultaneously. The brain development index (BDI) model [18] was proposed for summarizing complex imaging patterns of structural brain maturation along a single dimension using a machine learning methodology. The model was trained using the multimodal MRI data of 621 subjects of ages 8–22. Input image features included a combination of tissue density (RAVENS) map values for gray matter (GM), white matter (WM), and lateral ventricles (VN) derived from T1-weighted scans, and functional anisotropy (FA) and apparent diffusion coefficient (ADC) maps derived from DTI scans and aligned to a common template image. A support vector regression (SVR) method was used for the BDI model. SVR is a supervised learning technique based on the concept of support vector machines (SVM), but generalizes the categorical classification of SVM to predict continuous variables, such as the age. The regression model found a consistent developmental trajectory with predictions achieving a cross-validated correlation coefficient of $r = 0.89$ between chronological age and the BDI, and a mean absolute error of 1.22 years. Importantly, deviations from the age trajectory was related to cognitive performance. Subjects that had a BDI higher than their chronological age displayed significantly superior cognitive processing speed compared with subjects whose BDI was lower than their actual age. These results indicate the potential of machine learning-based indices to provide early biomarkers of pathologic deviations from the trajectory of typical brain development.

16.5.2 Imaging patterns of brain aging

The application of predictive machine learning methods has also provided new insights in studying the course of brain aging. Previous studies have found specific patterns of cortical gray matter loss due to older age in individuals without concurrent pathology [41,8]. However, characterizing and quantifying "advanced" brain aging and associating it with risk factors and clinical and cognitive outcomes has been a challenge. Detection of subjects with brains appearing older than their chronological age may provide further explanations on factors leading to "acceleration" or "resilience" in brain aging. For example, it is well-established in the literature that age is the strongest risk factor for AD. An important question, however, is how aging related patterns of brain atrophy overlap with (or differ from) those found in Alzheimer disease (AD).

In [27] machine learning based multivariate pattern analysis was applied on a large sample from the population-based Study of Health in Pomerania (SHIP) (20–90 years, $n = 2705$) to derive multiple imaging indexes that independently capture and quantify atrophy patterns associated with Alzheimer's disease (SPARE-AD) and brain aging (SPARE-BA) (Fig. 16.3). The SPARE-BA index was used to identify subjects with advanced brain aging (ABA), defined as significant deviation from typical BA trajectories. Multivariate regression models revealed risk factor associations with SPARE-AD that were different from those associated with SPARE-BA. Also, ABA individuals displayed atrophy patterns that were partially overlapping with, but notably deviating from those typically found in AD, supporting the hypothesis that distinct mechanisms might underlie lifetime brain aging and late-life neurodegeneration.

Notably, summarizing the high dimensional imaging data with a relatively small set of quantitative imaging signatures can help studying other comorbidities prevalent in elderly. Vascular brain injury in the white matter (or white matter hyperintensities,

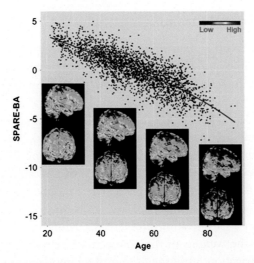

Figure 16.3 SPARE-BA values for SHIP participants ($n = 2705$) plotted against age. Red line represents local polynomial fitted curve. Higher/lower values indicate less/more aging-specific brain atrophy patterns, captured by the SPARE-BA index. Brain rendering shows the gray matter RAVENS (regional volumetric) maps for age groups 20–80. (From [27].)

WMHs) is part of the spectrum of small vessel disease (SVD) and is characterized pathologically by demyelination and axonal loss often attributed to ischemia. The ischemic damage has been hypothesized to "accelerate" brain aging and dementia. Using structural equation modeling with SPARE-BA and SPARE-AD scores of $n = 2367$ subjects from the SHIP study, and their WMH load automatically calculated from MRI images, [26] investigated causal relationships between WMHs, accelerated brain aging and AD. The study demonstrated a high proportion of WMH contribution to accelerated brain aging (10.4%) and to AD–like atrophy (32.8%). In similar fashion, computation of machine learning based indexes enables more effective integration of imaging and non-imaging data, such as genetic data. Apolipoprotein E (APOE) $\epsilon4$ allele is the strongest sporadic genetic risk factor in Alzheimer disease. In [29] SPARE-AD and SPARE-BA indexes of $n = 1472$ subjects from the SHIP study (ages 30 to 90) were used to quantify differences in imaging patterns between APOE $\epsilon4$ carriers and noncarriers, for investigating early brain changes prior to AD diagnosis. The study did not find any significant association between the APOE genotype and the imaging signatures of AD, accelerated aging or with regional gray matter volumes (lateral frontal, lateral temporal, medial frontal, and hippocampus), suggesting that measurable APOE related brain atrophy does not occur in early adulthood and midlife, but more proximal to the onset of clinical symptoms of dementia.

16.6. Deep learning in neuroimaging analysis

In recent years, deep learning algorithms have witnessed growing popularity, due to their top performance in many major machine learning problems, in computer vision, natural language processing and other fields [51,36]. The term "deep" in deep learning refers to the depth of the hidden layers of an artificial neural network. A deep neural network has an input layer, two or more hidden layers and an output layer. The input layer of a deep neural network consists of the input data, while the hidden layers encode linear or nonlinear transformations of the data, using densely interconnected simple processing nodes called neurons. The cascade of multiple layers allow representations of the data with higher complexity with increasingly higher levels. The output layer encodes possible outcomes of the specific problem, for instance, the class labels of the input samples in a classification problem. Learning in a deep network consists of iteratively adjusting the weights of the connections between the neurons through a process called backpropagation, until the output of the model gets as close as possible to the desired output for the given input data.

In comparison to other machine learning algorithms, deep neural networks have a much higher number of parameters to estimate. Thus, a large amount of labeled input data is required to train them for obtaining accurate results. For this reason, early applications of deep learning focused on tasks for which it was relatively easier to collect training data, such as object recognition on natural images. In recent years, however, deep learning emerged as a powerful framework in neuroimaging analysis, achieving state-of-the-art accuracies in various tasks such as brain extraction, tissue segmentation, anatomy segmentation, disease classification, and detection of brain lesions and tumors [32,13,1,35,39,49]. Two main factors that enabled the more widespread use of deep learning in neuroimaging were recent technological advances in computer hardware (e.g., increased power of graphics processing units) that allowed time efficient processing of medical imaging datasets with very high dimensionality, and the availability of imaging datasets with larger sample sizes.

A majority of neuroimaging applications of deep learning use a technique called "convolutional neural networks" (CNNs) [36]. Unlike standard neural networks that input the data in the form of a one dimensional vector, the general architecture of CNNs is specifically designed considering that the input data consists of images, either two- or three-dimensional. CNNs include one or more convolutional layers, which compute local convolutions of the input data, thus extracting representative regional features from the images. Convolutional layers are often followed by pooling layers, which combine the outputs of the local convolutions and reduce the spatial dimensions of the data. In recent years, specialized architectures were designed to address specific challenges of working with neuroimaging data, such as high image dimensionality and lack of large numbers of annotated data. From these, the U-Net architecture [44] combined a contracting path of convolution and pooling layers to capture the context and

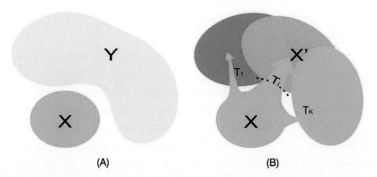

Figure 16.4 CHIMERA method overview: X is the reference distribution and Y is the patient distribution. (B) Model assumption: X is transformed into a distribution X' covering the distribution Y, by a set of K different transformations. (From Aoyan Dong, Nicolas Honnorat, Bilwaj Gaonkar, Christos Davatzikos, CHIMERA: clustering of heterogeneous disease effects via distribution matching of imaging patterns, IEEE Transactions on Medical Imaging 35 (2) (Feb. 2016) 612–621, © 2016 IEEE.)

a symmetric expanding path that enables precise localization. The U–Net architecture has been adapted to different segmentation problems and obtained very accurate results that outperform other machine learning methods.

16.7. Revealing heterogeneity of imaging patterns of brain diseases

Many neurodegenerative diseases and conditions exhibit heterogeneous symptoms and imaging characteristics. However, commonly used methods for group comparisons, such as the general linear model or linear multivariate pattern analysis/classification methods, search for a single direction of group difference between patients and control subjects, or between two subgroups of patients. Although nonlinear classifiers (e.g., via kernels) produce complex hypersurfaces that capture this heterogeneity, they do so in a way that is impractical from the perspective of clinical and biological interpretation. To address this limitation, [14] proposed a semisupervised learning method that uses a novel, regularized, clustering method based on mapping of statistical distributions. The method, based on a generative probabilistic framework, models the heterogeneous disease effects as a set of transformations from a reference set of healthy controls to the patients, with a different transformation for each patient subgroup (Fig. 16.4). An expectation-maximization method is used to find the transformations and cluster membership assignment of patients that maximizes the similarity between the transformed control subjects and the patients.

CHIMERA was applied on ADNI2 to characterize the heterogeneity of the MCI and AD cohort. The 4 subgroups that were identified in this cohort, and that were replicated using ADNI1 cohort, reflected a different type of anatomic difference relative to matched cognitive normal subjects in ADNI2. Also, these 4 subgroups displayed significant differences in their progression from MCI to AD, as well as in their rate of cognitive decline [14]. A complementary approach, using supervised clustering and multi-plane SVM, was proposed in [63].

The application of these semisupervised learning methods to brain aging has begun to provide insights into the heterogeneity of brain aging, which is a first step toward precision diagnosis and prognosis. Brain aging involves diverse pathologic processes that lead to complex neurodegenerative changes in brain structure and function. Characterizing the heterogeneity of brain aging in cognitively normal older adults is critical to better understand these underlying processes. A recent analysis addressed this problem by applying an advanced multivariate pattern analysis method on the structural and resting state functional MRI scans of 400 participants (ages 50 to 96) from the Baltimore Longitudinal Study of Aging [15]. Cross-validated brain age models have been first constructed independently for structural and functional image features. Predicted structural and functional brain age values have been jointly used for identifying "resilient" agers as the reference group and the "advanced" agers as the target group for the subsequent heterogeneity analysis. A mixture of experts (MOE) method, which combines unsupervised modeling of mixtures of distributions with supervised learning of classifiers, was applied using a combination of structural and functional image features to identify subgroups in the advanced aging group. The method discovered five distinct phenotypes of advanced brain aging. The subgroups have shown differences in their structural and functional brain change patterns with respect to the reference group and their total white matter lesion burden, suggesting that various pathological processes are likely to generate these phenotypes.

16.8. Conclusions

The increasing availability of large scale population studies brings both new opportunities and challenges for clinical and basic neuroscience analyses. Machine learning plays, and will most likely continue to play, an increasingly important role for addressing the challenges of the new big data analysis efforts towards development of imaging biomarkers with high accuracy and high diagnostic and prognostic value. Machine learning techniques are critical for building individualized imaging biomarkers via sufficiently discriminative imaging patterns, for reducing the dimensionality of the complex imaging data, and for automatically identifying disease subgroups within a patient group. Although the most widely use of machine learning methods has been in discriminating between groups (e.g., patients and controls), large-scale imaging databases have opened the way for perhaps a more important use of machine learning methods: the reduction of very complex multiparametric imaging signals down to a small, yet comprehensive and informative set of imaging patterns. This approach will eventually lead to dimensional neuroimaging paradigms that will allow for highly interpretable and predictive reduction of such complex data to a small panel of measures that are easy to interpret and adopt in the clinic.

References

[1] Z. Akkus, A. Galimzianova, A. Hoogi, D.L. Rubin, B.J. Erickson, Deep learning for brain MRI segmentation: state-of-the-art and future directions, Journal of Digital Imaging 30 (4) (Aug. 2017) 449–459, URL https://www.ncbi.nlm.nih.gov/pmc/articles/PMC5537095/.

[2] M.R. Arbabshirani, S. Plis, J. Sui, V.D. Calhoun, Single subject prediction of brain disorders in neuroimaging: promises and pitfalls, NeuroImage 145 (Pt B) (2017) 137–165.

[3] J. Ashburner, K.J. Friston, Voxel-based morphometry – the methods, NeuroImage 11 (6 Pt 1) (Jun. 2000) 805–821.

[4] C.E. Bearden, P.M. Thompson, Emerging global initiatives in neurogenetics: the Enhancing Neuroimaging Genetics through Meta-analysis (ENIGMA) Consortium, Neuron 94 (2) (Apr. 2017) 232–236.

[5] M. Brammer, The role of neuroimaging in diagnosis and personalized medicine – current position and likely future directions, Dialogues in Clinical Neuroscience 11 (4) (2009) 389–396.

[6] K.A. Clark, R.P. Woods, D.A. Rottenberg, A.W. Toga, J.C. Mazziotta, Impact of acquisition protocols and processing streams on tissue segmentation of T1 weighted MR images, NeuroImage 29 (1) (Jan. 2006) 185–202.

[7] C. Cortes, V. Vapnik, Support-vector networks, Machine Learning 20 (3) (Sep. 1995) 273–297, https://doi.org/10.1007/BF00994018.

[8] F. Crivello, N. Tzourio-Mazoyer, C. Tzourio, B. Mazoyer, Longitudinal assessment of global and regional rate of grey matter atrophy in 1,172 healthy older adults: modulation by sex and age, PLoS ONE 9 (12) (Dec. 2014) e114478, URL https://journals.plos.org/plosone/article?id=10.1371/journal.pone.0114478.

[9] C. Davatzikos, Brain aging heterogeneity elucidated via machine learning: the multi-site ISTAGING dimensional neuroimaging reference system, Alzheimer's & Dementia 14 (7) (2018) P1476–P1477.

[10] M. de Bruijne, Machine learning approaches in medical image analysis: from detection to diagnosis, Medical Image Analysis 33 (2016) 94–97.

[11] S.J. de Wit, P. Alonso, et al., Multicenter voxel-based morphometry mega-analysis of structural brain scans in obsessive-compulsive disorder, The American Journal of Psychiatry 171 (3) (Mar. 2014) 340–349.

[12] L.E. DeLisi, K.U. Szulc, H.C. Bertisch, M. Majcher, K. Brown, Understanding structural brain changes in schizophrenia, Dialogues in Clinical Neuroscience 8 (1) (Mar. 2006) 71–78, URL https://www.ncbi.nlm.nih.gov/pmc/articles/PMC3181763/.

[13] J. Dolz, C. Desrosiers, I. Ben Ayed, 3D fully convolutional networks for subcortical segmentation in MRI: a large-scale study, NeuroImage 170 (Apr. 2018) 456–470, URL http://www.sciencedirect.com/science/article/pii/S1053811917303324.

[14] A. Dong, N. Honnorat, B. Gaonkar, C. Davatzikos, CHIMERA: clustering of heterogeneous disease effects via distribution matching of imaging patterns, IEEE Transactions on Medical Imaging 35 (2) (Feb. 2016) 612–621.

[15] H. Eavani, M. Habes, T.D. Satterthwaite, Y. An, M.-K. Hsieh, N. Honnorat, G. Erus, J. Doshi, L. Ferrucci, L.L. Beason-Held, S.M. Resnick, C. Davatzikos, Heterogeneity of structural and functional imaging patterns of advanced brain aging revealed via machine learning methods, Neurobiology of Aging 71 (Nov. 2018) 41–50, URL http://www.sciencedirect.com/science/article/pii/S0197458018302173.

[16] H. Eavani, M.K. Hsieh, Y. An, G. Erus, L. Beason-Held, S. Resnick, C. Davatzikos, Capturing heterogeneous group differences using mixture-of-experts: application to a study of aging, NeuroImage 125 (Jan. 2016) 498–514, URL https://www.ncbi.nlm.nih.gov/pmc/articles/PMC5460911/.

[17] T.G.M.v. Erp, D.P. Hibar, et al., Subcortical brain volume abnormalities in 2028 individuals with schizophrenia and 2540 healthy controls via the ENIGMA consortium, Molecular Psychiatry 21 (4) (Apr. 2016) 547–553, URL https://www.nature.com/articles/mp201563.

[18] G. Erus, H. Battapady, T.D. Satterthwaite, H. Hakonarson, R.E. Gur, C. Davatzikos, R.C. Gur, Imaging patterns of brain development and their relationship to cognition, Cerebral Cortex (New York, N.Y.: 1991) 25 (6) (Jun. 2015) 1676–1684.

[19] G. Erus, J. Doshi, Y. An, D. Verganelakis, S.M. Resnick, C. Davatzikos, Longitudinally and inter-site consistent multi-atlas based parcellation of brain anatomy using harmonized atlases, NeuroImage 166 (2018) 71–78.

[20] F. Falahati, E. Westman, A. Simmons, Multivariate data analysis and machine learning in Alzheimer's disease with a focus on structural magnetic resonance imaging, Journal of Alzheimer's Disease 41 (3) (2014) 685–708.

[21] S. Farhan, M.A. Fahiem, H. Tauseef, An ensemble-of-classifiers based approach for early diagnosis of Alzheimer's disease: classification using structural features of brain images, Computational & Mathematical Methods in Medicine 2014 (2014), URL https://www.ncbi.nlm.nih.gov/pmc/articles/PMC4172935/.

[22] L. Ferrucci, The Baltimore longitudinal study of aging (BLSA): a 50-year-long journey and plans for the future, The Journals of Gerontology. Series A, Biological Sciences and Medical Sciences 63 (12) (Dec. 2008) 1416–1419, URL https://www.ncbi.nlm.nih.gov/pmc/articles/PMC5004590/.

[23] B. Fischl, FreeSurfer, NeuroImage 62 (2) (Aug. 2012) 774–781.

[24] J.-P. Fortin, N. Cullen, et al., Harmonization of cortical thickness measurements across scanners and sites, NeuroImage 167 (2018) 104–120.

[25] M.F. Glasser, S.M. Smith, D.S. Marcus, J.L.R. Andersson, E.J. Auerbach, T.E.J. Behrens, T.S. Coalson, M.P. Harms, M. Jenkinson, S. Moeller, E.C. Robinson, S.N. Sotiropoulos, J. Xu, E. Yacoub, K. Ugurbil, D.C. Van Essen, The Human Connectome Project's neuroimaging approach, Nature Neuroscience 19 (9) (2016) 1175–1187.

[26] M. Habes, G. Erus, et al., White matter hyperintensities and imaging patterns of brain ageing in the general population, Brain: A Journal of Neurology 139 (Pt 4) (Apr. 2016) 1164–1179.

[27] M. Habes, D. Janowitz, G. Erus, J.B. Toledo, S.M. Resnick, J. Doshi, S. Van der Auwera, K. Wittfeld, K. Hegenscheid, N. Hosten, R. Biffar, G. Homuth, H. Völzke, H.J. Grabe, W. Hoffmann, C. Davatzikos, Advanced brain aging: relationship with epidemiologic and genetic risk factors, and overlap with Alzheimer disease atrophy patterns, Translational Psychiatry 6 (Apr. 2016) e775.

[28] M. Habes, A. Sotiras, G. Erus, J.B. Toledo, D. Janowitz, D.A. Wolk, H. Shou, N.R. Bryan, J. Doshi, H. Völzke, U. Schminke, W. Hoffmann, S.M. Resnick, H.J. Grabe, C. Davatzikos, White matter lesions: spatial heterogeneity, links to risk factors, cognition, genetics, and atrophy, Neurology 91 (10) (Sep. 2018) e964–e975.

[29] M. Habes, J.B. Toledo, S.M. Resnick, J. Doshi, S.V.d. Auwera, G. Erus, D. Janowitz, K. Hegenscheid, G. Homuth, H. Völzke, W. Hoffmann, H.J. Grabe, C. Davatzikos, Relationship between APOE genotype and structural MRI measures throughout adulthood in the study of health in Pomerania population-based cohort, American Journal of Neuroradiology (May 2016), URL http://www.ajnr.org/content/early/2016/05/12/ajnr.A4805.

[30] S.V. Haijma, N. Van Haren, W. Cahn, P.C.M.P. Koolschijn, H.E. Hulshoff Pol, R.S. Kahn, Brain volumes in schizophrenia: a meta-analysis in over 18 000 subjects, Schizophrenia Bulletin 39 (5) (Sep. 2013) 1129–1138, URL https://www.ncbi.nlm.nih.gov/pmc/articles/PMC3756785/.

[31] X. Han, J. Jovicich, D. Salat, A. van der Kouwe, B. Quinn, S. Czanner, E. Busa, J. Pacheco, M. Albert, R. Killiany, P. Maguire, D. Rosas, N. Makris, A. Dale, B. Dickerson, B. Fischl, Reliability of MRI-derived measurements of human cerebral cortical thickness: the effects of field strength, scanner upgrade and manufacturer, NeuroImage 32 (1) (Aug. 2006) 180–194.

[32] M. Havaei, A. Davy, D. Warde-Farley, A. Biard, A. Courville, Y. Bengio, C. Pal, P.-M. Jodoin, H. Larochelle, Brain tumor segmentation with Deep Neural Networks, Medical Image Analysis 35 (Jan. 2017) 18–31, URL http://www.sciencedirect.com/science/article/pii/S1361841516300330.

[33] G.E. Hinton, Machine learning for neuroscience, Neural Systems & Circuits 1 (1) (Aug. 2011) 12, https://doi.org/10.1186/2042-1001-1-12.

[34] J. Jovich, S. Czanner, X. Han, D. Salat, A. van der Kouwe, B. Quinn, J. Pacheco, M. Albert, R. Killiany, D. Blacker, P. Maguire, D. Rosas, N. Makris, R. Gollub, A. Dale, B.C. Dickerson, B. Fischl, MRI-derived measurements of human subcortical, ventricular and intracranial brain volumes: reliability effects of scan sessions, acquisition sequences, data analyses, scanner upgrade, scanner vendors and field strengths, NeuroImage 46 (1) (May 2009) 177–192.

[35] J. Kleesiek, G. Urban, A. Hubert, D. Schwarz, K. Maier-Hein, M. Bendszus, A. Biller, Deep MRI brain extraction: a 3D convolutional neural network for skull stripping, NeuroImage 129 (Apr. 2016) 460–469.

[36] Y. Lecun, Y. Bengio, G. Hinton, Deep learning, Nature 521 (7553) (2015) 436–444.

[37] D.D. Lee, H.S. Seung, Learning the parts of objects by non-negative matrix factorization, Nature 401 (6755) (Oct. 1999) 788–791.

[38] S.N. Lockhart, C. DeCarli, Structural imaging measures of brain aging, Neuropsychology Review 24 (3) (Sep. 2014) 271–289.

[39] F.J. Martinez-Murcia, J.M. Górriz, J. Ramírez, A. Ortiz, Convolutional neural networks for neuroimaging in Parkinson's disease: is preprocessing needed? International Journal of Neural Systems (Jul. 2018) 1850035, URL https://www.worldscientific.com/doi/abs/10.1142/S0129065718500351.

[40] J.M. Mateos-Pérez, M. Dadar, M. Lacalle-Aurioles, Y. Iturria-Medina, Y. Zeighami, A.C. Evans, Structural neuroimaging as clinical predictor: a review of machine learning applications, NeuroImage: Clinical 20 (Jan. 2018) 506–522, URL http://www.sciencedirect.com/science/article/pii/S2213158218302602.

[41] H. Matsuda, Voxel-based morphometry of brain MRI in normal aging and Alzheimer's disease, Aging and Disease 4 (1) (Feb. 2013) 29–37.

[42] K.L. Miller, F. Alfaro-Almagro, et al., Multimodal population brain imaging in the UK Biobank prospective epidemiological study, Nature Neuroscience 19 (11) (2016) 1523–1536.

[43] S. Rathore, M. Habes, M.A. Iftikhar, A. Shacklett, C. Davatzikos, A review on neuroimaging-based classification studies and associated feature extraction methods for Alzheimer's disease and its prodromal stages, NeuroImage 155 (2017) 530–548.

[44] O. Ronneberger, P. Fischer, T. Brox, U-Net: convolutional networks for biomedical image segmentation, in: N. Navab, J. Hornegger, W.M. Wells, A.F. Frangi (Eds.), Medical Image Computing and Computer-Assisted Intervention – MICCAI 2015, in: Lecture Notes in Computer Science, Springer International Publishing, 2015, pp. 234–241.

[45] M. Rozycki, T.D. Satterthwaite, et al., Multisite machine learning analysis provides a robust structural imaging signature of schizophrenia detectable across diverse patient populations and within individuals, Schizophrenia Bulletin 44 (5) (Aug. 2018) 1035–1044.

[46] M.R. Sabuncu, E. Konukoglu, Alzheimer's Disease Neuroimaging Initiative, Clinical prediction from structural brain MRI scans: a large-scale empirical study, Neuroinformatics 13 (1) (Jan. 2015) 31–46.

[47] J. Samper-González, N. Burgos, S. Fontanella, H. Bertin, M.-O. Habert, S. Durrleman, T. Evgeniou, O. Colliot, Yet another ADNI machine learning paper? Paving the way towards fully-reproducible research on classification of Alzheimer's disease, in: Q. Wang, Y. Shi, H.-I. Suk, K. Suzuki (Eds.), Machine Learning in Medical Imaging, in: Lecture Notes in Computer Science, Springer International Publishing, 2017, pp. 53–60.

[48] A. Sarica, A. Cerasa, A. Quattrone, Random forest algorithm for the classification of neuroimaging data in Alzheimer's disease: a systematic review, Frontiers in Aging Neuroscience 9 (2017), URL https://www.frontiersin.org/articles/10.3389/fnagi.2017.00329/full.

[49] S. Sarraf, D.D. DeSouza, J. Anderson, G. Tofighi, Alzheimer's Disease Neuroimaging Initiative, DeepAD: Alzheimer's disease classification via deep convolutional neural networks using MRI and fMRI, bioRxiv, 070441. URL https://www.biorxiv.org/content/early/2017/01/14/070441, Jan. 2017.

[50] T.D. Satterthwaite, J.J. Connolly, K. Ruparel, M.E. Calkins, C. Jackson, M.A. Elliott, D.R. Roalf, K.P. Ryan Hopsona, M. Behr, H. Qiu, F.D. Mentch, R. Chiavacci, P.M.A. Sleiman, R.C. Gur, H. Hakonarson, R.E. Gur, The Philadelphia neurodevelopmental cohort: a publicly available resource for the study of normal and abnormal brain development in youth, NeuroImage 124 (Pt B) (Jan. 2016) 1115–1119.

[51] J. Schmidhuber, Deep learning in neural networks: an overview, Neural Networks 61 (Jan. 2015) 85–117, URL http://www.sciencedirect.com/science/article/pii/S0893608014002135.

[52] R.T. Shinohara, J. Oh, et al., Volumetric analysis from a harmonized multi-site brain MRI study of a single-subject with multiple sclerosis, American Journal of Neuroradiology 38 (8) (Aug. 2017) 1501–1509, URL https://www.ncbi.nlm.nih.gov/pmc/articles/PMC5557658/.

[53] J.H. Simon, D. Li, A. Traboulsee, P.K. Coyle, D.L. Arnold, F. Barkhof, J.A. Frank, R. Grossman, D.W. Paty, E.W. Radue, J.S. Wolinsky, Standardized MR imaging protocol for multiple sclerosis: consortium of MS centers consensus guidelines, American Journal of Neuroradiology 27 (2) (Feb. 2006) 455–461, URL http://www.ajnr.org/content/27/2/455.

[54] A. Sotiras, S.M. Resnick, C. Davatzikos, Finding imaging patterns of structural covariance via non-negative matrix factorization, NeuroImage 108 (Mar. 2015) 1–16.

[55] A. Sotiras, J.B. Toledo, R.E. Gur, R.C. Gur, T.D. Satterthwaite, C. Davatzikos, Patterns of coordinated cortical remodeling during adolescence and their associations with functional specialization and evolutionary expansion, Proceedings of the National Academy of Sciences of the United States of America 114 (13) (2017) 3527–3532.

[56] K. Strimbu, J.A. Tavel, What are biomarkers? Current opinion in HIV and, AIDS 5 (6) (Nov. 2010) 463–466, URL https://www.ncbi.nlm.nih.gov/pmc/articles/PMC3078627/.

[57] C. Sudlow, J. Gallacher, N. Allen, V. Beral, P. Burton, J. Danesh, P. Downey, P. Elliott, J. Green, M. Landray, B. Liu, P. Matthews, G. Ong, J. Pell, A. Silman, A. Young, T. Sprosen, T. Peakman, R. Collins, UK Biobank: an open access resource for identifying the causes of a wide range of complex diseases of middle and old age, PLoS Medicine 12 (3) (Mar. 2015), URL https://www.ncbi.nlm.nih.gov/pmc/articles/PMC4380465/.

[58] P.M. Thompson, J.L. Stein, et al., The ENIGMA Consortium: large-scale collaborative analyses of neuroimaging and genetic data, Brain Imaging and Behavior 8 (2) (Jun. 2014) 153–182.

[59] B.O. Turner, E.J. Paul, M.B. Miller, A.K. Barbey, Small sample sizes reduce the replicability of task-based fMRI studies, Communications Biology 1 (1) (Jun. 2018) 62, URL https://www.nature.com/articles/s42003-018-0073-z.

[60] J.A. Turner, The rise of large-scale imaging studies in psychiatry, GigaScience 3 (2014) 29.

[61] D.C. Van Essen, S.M. Smith, D.M. Barch, T.E.J. Behrens, E. Yacoub, K. Ugurbil, WU-Minn HCP Consortium, The WU-Minn Human Connectome Project: an overview, NeuroImage 80 (Oct. 2013) 62–79.

[62] J.D. Van Horn, A.W. Toga, Human neuroimaging as a "Big Data" science, Brain Imaging and Behavior 8 (2) (Jun. 2014) 323–331, URL https://www.ncbi.nlm.nih.gov/pmc/articles/PMC3983169/.

[63] E. Varol, A. Sotiras, C. Davatzikos, Alzheimer's Disease Neuroimaging Initiative, HYDRA: revealing heterogeneity of imaging and genetic patterns through a multiple max-margin discriminative analysis framework, NeuroImage 145 (Pt B) (2017) 346–364.

[64] G. Varoquaux, Cross-validation failure: small sample sizes lead to large error bars, arXiv:1706.07581 [q-bio.QM], Jun. 2017.

[65] G. Varoquaux, B. Thirion, How machine learning is shaping cognitive neuroimaging, GigaScience 3 (2014) 28.

[66] E. Veronese, U. Castellani, D. Peruzzo, M. Bellani, P. Brambilla, Machine learning approaches: from theory to application in schizophrenia, Computational & Mathematical Methods in Medicine 2013 (2013) 867924.

[67] N. Vogt, Machine learning in neuroscience, Nature Methods 15 (Jan. 2018) 33, https://doi.org/10.1038/nmeth.4549.

[68] H. Völzke, D. Alte, et al., Cohort profile: the study of health in Pomerania, International Journal of Epidemiology 40 (2) (Apr. 2011) 294–307.

[69] M.W. Weiner, D.P. Veitch, et al., The Alzheimer's Disease Neuroimaging Initiative: a review of papers published since its inception, Alzheimer's & Dementia 9 (5) (Sep. 2013) e111–e194, URL https://www.ncbi.nlm.nih.gov/pmc/articles/PMC4108198/.

CHAPTER 17

Imaging biomarkers for cardiovascular diseases

Avan Suinesiaputra, Kathleen Gilbert, Beau Pontre, Alistair A. Young
Department of Anatomy and Medical Imaging, University of Auckland, Auckland, New Zealand

Contents

17.1. Introduction   401
17.2. Cardiac imaging   402
17.3. Cardiac shape and function   404
    17.3.1 Left ventricular mass   405
    17.3.2 Ejection fraction   407
    17.3.3 Remodeling   407
17.4. Cardiac motion   409
    17.4.1 Wall motion analysis   409
    17.4.2 Myocardial strain   410
    17.4.3 Dyssynchrony   411
17.5. Coronary and vascular function   412
    17.5.1 Coronary artery disease   412
    17.5.2 Myocardial perfusion   413
    17.5.3 Blood flow   414
    17.5.4 Vascular compliance   416
17.6. Myocardial structure   416
    17.6.1 Tissue characterization   416
    17.6.2 Fiber architecture   418
17.7. Population-based cardiac image biomarkers   419
References   420

17.1. Introduction

In the 1940s, the Framingham Study established four major risk factors for cardio-vascular disease (CVD): smoking, raised blood pressure, raised serum cholesterol, and diabetes mellitus [1]. Subsequent studies have found other risk factors, including body mass index, alcohol consumption, diet, physical inactivity, and several environmental factors (ambient air pollution, household air pollution, and lead exposure). Risk factors are diagnostic tools to identify individuals at risk for developing CVD, who may require treatment or a change in lifestyle, and therefore finding new risk factors is always an active area of research. However, none of the above risk factors were derived from imaging data.

Handbook of Medical Image Computing and Computer Assisted Intervention
https://doi.org/10.1016/B978-0-12-816176-0.00022-3

Recent epidemiological studies have been collecting medical images as part of their study protocol to identify novel risk factors for CVD [2], including the Multi-Ethnic Study of Atherosclerosis [3], the Canadian Alliance for Healthy Hearts and Minds [4], and the UK Biobank [5]. Imaging biomarkers have therefore started to emerge as new risk factors or mechanistic indicators for CVD. As medical image acquisition becomes part of routine clinical examination, imaging biomarkers will be inevitably included for risk assessment alongside with other physiological assessments.

This chapter describes image-derived biomarkers that show promising results in the evaluation and prediction of CVD outcomes. The following sections are organized as follows. First, we begin with an overview of the nomenclature and acquisition protocols in cardiac imaging. Next, we describe how CVD biomarkers can be derived from cardiac shape and function, cardiac motion, blood flow, and myocardial structure. We close this chapter by showing how imaging informatics methods can be used to analyze large amounts of clinical imaging data for patient and population evaluation.

17.2. Cardiac imaging

Echocardiographic two-dimensional imaging is the most widely used clinical technique, although 1D (M-mode) and 3D acquisitions are common. Standard 2D image planes are usually oriented based on the geometry of the heart (see Fig. 17.1). The left ventricle (LV) is used as the reference for two perpendicular imaging axes: short and long-axis views. A long-axis image slice typically runs from the apex to the base and creates either a view with two chambers (the LV and left atrium) or all four chambers. The two-chamber view is also called the vertical long-axis and the four-chamber view is also called the horizontal long-axis (see Fig. 17.1(A)). Sometimes nonstandard long-axis views are acquired to show structures of interest in a particular region of the heart, such as in patients with congenital heart diseases or right ventricular pathologies. The short-axis view shows both the LV and the right ventricle (RV) in cross-section perpendicular to the long-axis. Multiple short-axis views are usually acquired with a fixed slice gap for volumetric analysis.

Many morphometric biomarkers can be derived from anatomical images by means of a 3D geometric model. Multislice CT, 3D echocardiography and 3D MRI can provide volumetric data, allowing 3D segmentation of the heart anatomy. For 2D acquisitions, either a mathematical model or a mesh structure can be fitted to multislice image data. This approach requires an accurate registration method to align the images with the model, since in many cases each 2D slice is acquired in a separate breath-hold [6]. There are three common geometric models of the heart: LV, biventricular (left and right ventricles), and whole heart (both ventricles and atria). The LV model is the most commonly used, because the LV is the high pressure chamber and is most at risk of disease. LV volumes, mass, and ejection fraction are common parameters that

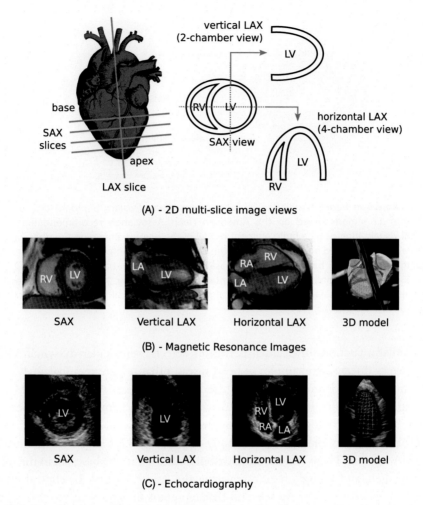

Figure 17.1 *Two-dimensional cardiac image acquisition.* Standard acquisition plan to acquire images of the heart: (A) acquisition diagram, (B) examples from cardiac MRI slices, and (C) examples from echocardiography. Abbreviations: SAX = short-axis, LAX = long-axis, LV = left ventricle, RV = right ventricle, LA = left atrium, RA = right atrium. *(Source: (A) Wikimedia (CC BY-SA 3.0), (B)–(C) acquired by the authors.)*

determine the physiological status of the heart (see Table 17.1 for the definition of these parameters). A biventricular model can be defined by registering a cubic Hermite mesh [7] or by interactive guide–point modeling [8]. RV function is a useful biomarker in congenital heart disease or pulmonary disease, while the combination of LV and RV function is useful for the assessment of interventricular dyssynchrony. The whole heart model enables the quantification of electrical activation and mechanics of all four chambers [9].

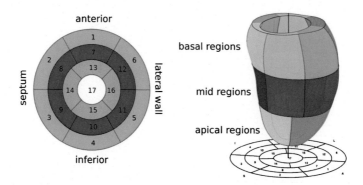

Figure 17.2 *American Heart Association regional myocardium division.* Standard division of myocardium into 17 regions based on the American Heart Association recommendations. Three-dimensional visualization using a finite element model of the heart is shown on the right figure. The 17 regions are labeled based on the anatomy of the heart: 1 = basal anterior, 2 = basal anteroseptal, 3 = basal inferoseptal, 4 = basal inferior, 5 = basal inferolateral, 6 = basal anterolateral, 7 = mid-anterior, 8 = mid-anteroseptal, 9 = mid-inferoseptal, 10 = mid-inferior, 11 = mid-inferolateral, 12 = mid-anterlateral, 13 = apical anterior, 14 = apical septum, 15 = apical inferior, 16 = apical lateral, 17 = apex.

Myocardial infarction, myocardial perfusion defects, ventricular dyssynchrony, and coronary artery disease are examples of heart diseases that require regional analysis. The 17-segments regional definition based on the American Heart Association (AHA) recommendation [10] applies to images from magnetic resonance imaging (MRI), echocardiography, computed tomography (CT), single photon emission computed tomography (SPECT), and positron emission tomography (PET). Fig. 17.2 shows the definition of the 17 AHA regions. These regions are distributed into six in the base, six in the middle, four in the apex, and a single region covering the apical tip area. In clinical practice, three short-axis view images are selected that represent the apical, midventricular and basal levels. The apical slice is chosen at the bottom part of the LV where the LV cavity is still visible at end-systole, the basal slice is the slice below the LV outflow tract, and the middle slice is the short-axis image slice between the apical and basal slices. For the apical tip region (region number 17), the area is defined on the two-chamber view image as a region below the apical slice comprising apical myocardium only [11]. A more accurate regional division can be defined from a 3D model of the LV (see Fig. 17.2), where regional volumes can be maintained throughout the whole cardiac cycle.

17.3. Cardiac shape and function

Measurements derived from geometry of the heart (e.g., volume, mass, and wall thickness) as well as cardiac function (e.g., stroke volume, ejection fraction, and cardiac output) have been used in many studies for CVD risk assessment. As listed in Ta-

Table 17.1 List of global cardiac volume, mass, and function.

Name		Unit	Calculation
LVEDV	LV End-Diastolic[†] Volume	ml	Summation of endocardium volumes for all slices (2D MRI), or cavity volume calculation based on prolate ellipsoidal assumption (2D echo), or direct volume calculation (3D MRI/echo). All measurements are at end-diastole.
LVESV	LV End-Systolic[‡] Volume	ml	Similar to LVEDV but at end-systole.
LVM	LV mass	g	Total volume enclosed by the epicardium at end-diastole subtracted by LVEDV and then multiplied by the myocardial density (1.05 g/ml).
RVEDV	RV End-Diastolic Volume	ml	Similar to LVEDV but for the RV.
RVESV	RV End-Systolic Volume	ml	Similar to LVESV but for the RV.
RVM	RV mass	g	Similar to LVM but for the RV.
SV*	Stroke Volume	ml	LVEDV − LVESV
EF*	Ejection Fraction	%	$\dfrac{SV}{LVEDV} \times 100$
CO*	Cardiac Output	ml/min	SV × HeartRate

[†] End-diastole (ED) is a cardiac frame just before the semilunar valves open, which shows the largest amount of blood in the LV.
[‡] End-systole (ES) is a cardiac frame where the LV holds the smallest amount of blood.
* These measurements by default are calculated for the LV, but it is also possible to measure the RV function similarly.

ble 17.1, cardiac volume, mass, and function measurements require segmentation of LV and RV endocardial and epicardial borders. There has been a large body of research into automated segmentation in the last two decades (see reviews in [12–14]). Several grand challenges have also been held to compare and evaluate segmentation algorithms using benchmark datasets for validation. These include consensus ground truth for the LV [15,16], the RV [17], and the left atrium [18].

17.3.1 Left ventricular mass

Several clinical studies have found that LV mass (LVM) is an independent predictor for cardiovascular events [19]. An abnormally increased LVM, known as LV hypertrophy (LVH), increases the risk of heart failure and coronary heart disease. The heart wall in LVH typically thickens due to a chronically increased workload of the myocardium.

LVM assessment is not a trivial task [20], since 3D information is often not available and body size variation must be taken into account [21]. The American Society of Echocardiography (ASE) has recommended several formulae for LVM assessment from 2D echocardiography based on geometric assumptions and empirical regression data

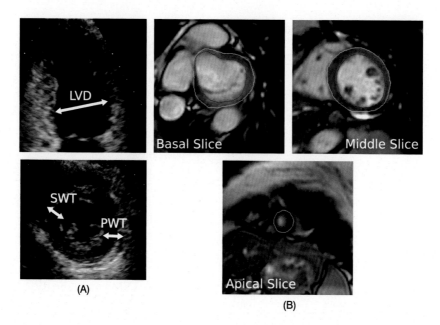

Figure 17.3 *Volume calculation.* Ventricular volume calculation from (A) 2D echocardiography, and (B) 2D MRI slices. LVD is the LV minor axis diameter, PWT is the posterior wall thickness, and SWT is the septal wall thickness. Only three MRI slices are visualized (base, middle, and apex), but usually there are more slices acquired between base and apex. Endocardium and epicardium are shown as red and cyan lines, respectively. *(Source: (A) acquired by the authors, (B) from the collection of consensus contour study at the Cardiac Atlas Project [22].)*

to estimate mass from diameter and wall thickness measurements in standard locations (Fig. 17.3(A)) [21]. However, these geometric assumptions are not valid in patients with irregular shape of the heart, such as patients with chronic myocardial infarction and congenital heart diseases.

LVM calculation from 2D MRI requires delineation of myocardium to calculate the ventricular volume (see Fig. 17.3(B)). Myocardial volume is the area between the epicardium and endocardium, multiplied by interslice distance. LVM is usually defined at end-diastole and it is the product of myocardial volume with myocardial density (1.05 g/ml). There is an ongoing debate of including or excluding papillary muscle and trabeculae, but based on the lack of reproducibility [23], these structures are usually excluded from the LVM calculation. However, trabeculated mass above 20% of the global LVM is highly sensitive and specific for the diagnosis of patients with LV non-compaction [24], which needs a specialized automated segmentation and evaluation of trabeculated mass, e.g., by fractal analysis [25].

Echocardiography is widely available and less expensive, which makes it practical to measure LVM. However, LVM assessment by MRI is more accurate and precise [26]. Three-dimensional echocardiography has been introduced recently with improved accuracy and reproducibility, but can still suffer from interoperator variability [27]. Nevertheless, LVM measurements from both imaging modalities are highly correlated, but their absolute values can differ markedly [28]. Hence, the two methods cannot be used interchangeably without correction for bias due to imaging modality or different parameters within the same modality [29].

In clinical studies, LVM is usually adjusted by height, weight or body surface area to eliminate the size factor, where taller people tend to have bigger hearts. There is no established protocol to normalize LVM. In [30], LVM was normalized with an allometric technique, which adjusted LV mass, volume and wall thickness based on fat-free mass. In an asymptomatic population study [31], LVM was divided by LVEDV (LV mass-to-volume ratio) to predict coronary heart disease and stroke. However, statistical arguments indicate that this normalization can lead to spurious results. A better approach is to include height and weight parameters in a multivariate regression [32].

17.3.2 Ejection fraction

Ejection fraction (EF) is another widely used biomarker for assessing the heart performance. EF is quantified by the percentage of blood being ejected out from the LV per heart beat, which is calculated from the cavity volumes at end-diastole and at end-systole (see Table 17.1). The normal range of EF is between 50% and 70%. Reduced EF under 40% is an indicator of heart failure or cardiomyopathy, and also as one of the criteria to select patients with LV dyssynchrony for cardiac resynchronization therapy. Too high EF (more than 70%), which is called a hyperdynamic LVEF, is commonly found in patients with trauma in the intensive care unit [33].

Reduced EF in heart failure is caused by muscle damage that remodels the cells and reduces contractility. The most common causes of heart failure are ischemic heart disease and myocardial infarction. This leads to a reduction in systolic contraction (heart failure with reduced ejection fraction or HFrEF). However, there are heart failure patients with apparently normal EF, known as heart failure with preserved EF or HFpEF. In these patients, systolic function appears normal, but the heart cannot relax properly (diastolic dysfunction) [34].

17.3.3 Remodeling

Cardiac remodeling is a process in which the shape of the heart changes to maintain normal physiology. Remodeling can be maladaptive (due to the onset of injury or disease [35]) or adaptive (ageing [36] or physical exercise [37]). There are three pathophysiological pathways of maladaptive remodeling: (1) an increase of a pressure load that leads to the thickening of myocardium (concentric hypertrophy), (2) an increase of volume load that enlarges the ventricular size (eccentric hypertrophy), and (3) remodeling due to myocardial infarction, where infarcted tissue causes both volume and pressure

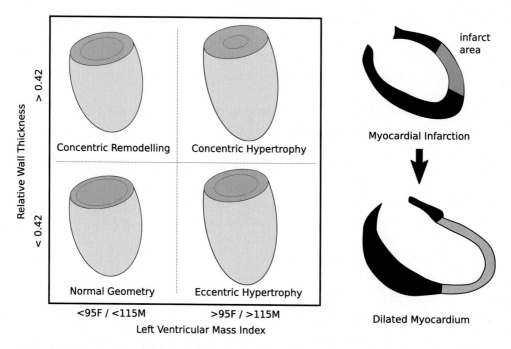

Figure 17.4 *Cardiac remodeling patterns.* (Left) A map to classify cardiac remodeling patterns by using relative wall thickness (RWT) and LV mass index. The cutoff values are based on [38]. (Right) Remodeling pattern due to myocardial infarction. *(Source: redrawn from [38].)*

overload to the noninfarcted regions. Fig. 17.4 illustrates these three remodeling patterns. Fibrosis contributes to all of these patterns.

A combination of two indices has been investigated to classify cardiac remodeling patterns into 4-tiers: normal geometry, concentric remodeling, concentric hypertrophy, and eccentric hypertrophy [38]. These are LVM adjusted for body surface area with the cutoff value of 95 g/m^2 for female and 115 g/m^2 for male, and the relative wall thickness (RWT) of 0.42 for both male and female. RWT is derived from echocardiography, calculated by

$$RWT = 2 \frac{PWT}{LVD}, \qquad (17.1)$$

where PWT is the posterior wall thickness and LVD is the LV internal diameter (see Fig. 17.3(A)). Fig. 17.4 shows the classification map for remodeling patterns. In MRI, LV mass-to-volume ratio can be used to replace RWT in the classification of remodeling patterns [31]. Recently, statistical shape analysis techniques, such as principal component analysis [39] and partial least squares [40], have been investigated to define new remodeling indices.

Cardiac remodeling is highly associated with heart failure [41]. During the progression of heart failure, a series of structural and functional changes of the heart occur. The LV becomes stiff and thick, and there is a reduction in EF (HFrEF). Around 50% of the heart failure patient population exhibit normal ejection fraction at rest (HFpEF), but does not increase appropriately during stress [42]. LV volumes, mass, and ejection fraction less than 50% can be used to identify HFrEF patients. However, identifying HFpEF patients based on volumes and mass is still problematic because symptoms are nonspecific. Instead of systolic function, some studies have been looking into the mechanics of diastolic function to discover a new biomarker for HFpEF patients [43,44].

17.4. Cardiac motion

Cardiac motion is an important biomarker for several cardiovascular diseases, as cardiac function is critically dependent on the motion of the heart. CVD biomarkers based on motion can be extracted from the whole cardiac frames in terms of motion patterns, velocity vector fields or strain. Motion can be assessed regionally to indicate the degree of synchronization across the myocardium.

17.4.1 Wall motion analysis

Disruption in the supply of blood to the myocardium triggers a cascade of regional adaptations of the myocardium to match the demand and supply of the blood. Prior to infarction, some the affected regions may still viable after a revascularization procedure (stenting or bypass surgery). Identifying viable regions is therefore a subject of great interest, which can be performed by comparing wall motion from a rest condition to a dobutamine-induced stress condition [45].

Visual wall motion analysis is the current clinical standard that visually categorizes each myocardial region into either normokinetic (normal motion), hypokinetic (reduced motion), akinetic (no motion), or dyskinetic (paradoxical motion) from cine image sequences. A viable region can be defined as a hypokinetic region at rest, but normokinetic at stress. Several automated classification methods of regional wall motion have been proposed in the last decade, e.g., [46–48]. Wall motion analyses are also used in the assessment of LV dyssynchrony, as discussed below. Recent methods have fused wall motion with other data, including temporal patterns of valvular dynamics, to analyze the effects of heart failure [49].

Automated tracking of individual pixels inside the myocardium is another approach to analyze wall motion. Planar motion tracking based on optic flow algorithms can estimate myocardial wall motion from a sequence of 2D images. In echocardiography, this is known as *speckle tracking* [50], while in MRI it is called *feature tracking* [51]. Typically motion estimation must be combined with additional features, such as features from low dimensional spaces [52], to avoid the aperture problem. Two-dimensional speckle tracking echocardiography has been standardized by the European Association of Cardiovascular Imaging (EACVI) and the American Society of Echocardiography (ASE) [53], while MR feature tracking is still being developed and validated against the current gold standard which is MR tagging [54].

In practice, not all image pixels are tracked, but rather small regions-of-interests are defined at end-diastole. These regions are usually positioned equally spaced along myocardial borders: endocardial, epicardial, and mid-wall borders. Three velocity directions are calculated: radial, circumferential, and longitudinal. Radial velocity with the positive direction towards the center can be estimated from either short or long-axis views. Circumferential velocity can only be estimated from the short-axis view, while longitudinal velocities with positive values in the direction from base to apex can only be estimated from the long-axis view.

17.4.2 Myocardial strain

Physiologically, cardiac myocytes shorten uniaxially by approximately 15% during systole. Myocardial strain varies across the heart wall following the helical fiber architecture of the heart. At end-systole, circumferential strain varies from 10% at the epicardium to 25% at the endocardium. Due to the geometry of the heart and the incompressibility of heart muscle, myocardial strain can be reduced in thick-walled ventricles which is commonly observed in cardiomyopathy [55]. Strain and flow imaging, in particular Doppler echocardiography, has been used to derive several indices to assess elevated filling pressure [56,57].

In MRI, strain is usually derived from nonselective tagging pulses [58]. The MRI tagging protocol artificially creates stripe or grid markers on the acquired images by spatially modulating the degree of magnetization prior to imaging. These markers follow the deformation of the heart, albeit decaying over time, giving the myocardium a trackable image texture. A method called HARP (harmonic phase) analysis [59] is widely used to measure strains from tagged MRI. HARP computes local myocardial motion by analyzing the phase associated with the complex images, which correspond to the isolated spectral peaks of the Fourier transformed tagged images. Another MRI technique called DENSE (displacement encoded with stimulated echoes) was developed to generate a map of myocardial displacement [60]. DENSE is able to create a vector valued image that shows pixel displacement, which can be directly used to compute strains.

Feature tracking or speckle tracking can also be used to estimate myocardial strain. However, there are differences in regional circumferential strain between feature/speckle tracking and MR tagging [61]. Since tagged MRI artificially creates tag patterns that follow the deformation of the heart, tagged MR images contain more features for the circumferential motion than cine MRI. Different approaches have also been proposed to

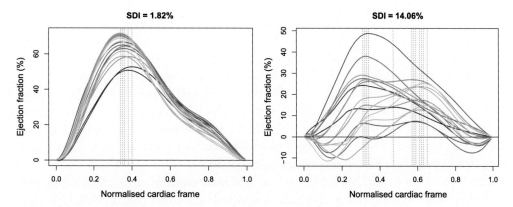

Figure 17.5 *Regional ejection fraction.* A comparison of regional ejection fraction curves between (A) healthy subject and (B) LV dyssynchrony. Systolic dyssynchrony index (SDI) measures how synchronized the motion between regions is. Smaller SDI defines more synchronized motion. Vertical bars denote the time to reach the peak contraction for each region. SDI is calculated by the standard deviation of these peaks.

compute strain, such as a graph theoretic approach to compute 3D biventricular cardiac strain from tagged MRI [62]. For recent reviews on MR tagging, see [63,64].

17.4.3 Dyssynchrony

Blood flow circulation inside the heart chambers and the great vessels is a product of synchronous and coordinated electrical and mechanical activation. Electromechanical delays lead to dyssynchronous movements of the LV (intraventricular dyssynchrony) or inefficient motion between the LV and the RV (interventricular dyssynchrony). Regional scars also contribute to intraventricular dyssynchrony. One clinical intervention for dyssynchrony is cardiac resynchronization therapy (CRT), where a cardiac pacemaker with pacing leads is implanted into the heart to help synchronize the contraction pattern. However, 30% of patients who underwent CRT did not respond to the treatment [65]. Hence, accurate selection and prediction of patients who will respond to the treatment is a subject of great interest.

Due to this high percentage of non CRT responders, there have been several dyssynchrony indices proposed for patient selection. All of them involve regional analysis, where the 17 AHA regions are commonly used (see Fig. 17.2). LV assessment is categorized into indices calculated either from wall motion, velocity or strain. For wall motion, a dyssynchrony index can be defined based on the time to reach minimum volume from each region. Fig. 17.5 shows two examples of regional ejection fraction profiles from a healthy subject (left), where the peaks are clustered closely around end-systole, and a patient with dyssynchrony (right), where the peaks are widely distributed. Based on the standard deviation of the peak distribution, the systolic dyssynchrony index [66] was proposed to quantify dyssynchrony. Another way to quantify dyssynchrony from regional wall motion is to look into opposing segments, such as the septal and posterior wall, known as the septal-to-posterior wall motion delay [67].

Dyssynchrony indices based on velocity are usually measured from tissue Doppler echocardiography imaging. Let T_s be the time from QRS[1] onset in the electrocardiogram to the maximal velocity during systole. The distribution of T_s across regions indicates the degree of dyssynchrony [68]. The maximum delay, such as the delay from four basal segments [69] or the delay between frontal and posterior walls from apical long-axis view [70], has been used to assess dyssynchrony.

Strain-based dyssynchrony indices are defined from radial or circumferential strains. A method called CURE (Circumferential Uniform Ratio Estimate), or RURE (Radial Uniform Ratio Estimate), was proposed by [71] to measure the uniformity of local circumferential or radial strains. It is defined as

$$\text{CURE/RURE} = \sqrt{\sum_{s=\text{base}}^{\text{apex}} \sum_{t=0}^{RR} \frac{A_0^s(t)}{A_0^s(t) + 2A_1^s(t)}}, \qquad (17.2)$$

where A_0 and A_1 are the zeroth and first order terms from the Fourier analysis of the strain curve. The more oscillatory the plot, the more dyssychronous the motion of the heart. CURE/RURE values range from 0 (dyssynchronous contraction) to 1 (all segments contracting synchronously).

More advanced cardiac motion modeling methods, such as a combination of motion and nonmotion information using a machine learning algorithm [72] and a manifold learning algorithm to measure the distance between dyssynchronous motion and normal wall motion [73], have been proposed to predict CRT responders.

17.5. Coronary and vascular function

Blood flow patterns, in the great arteries, the chambers of the heart, or the coronary arteries, are indicative of healthy and diseased cardiovascular function [74]. In the great vessels, altered patterns of flow are thought to be related to inefficiencies in the pump function leading to adverse remodeling of the left and right ventricles. In the coronary arteries, blocking or narrowing of the arteries alters the blood supply to the myocardium, which can trigger ischemic heart disease leading to myocardial infarction.

17.5.1 Coronary artery disease

The percentage of coronary artery diameter reduction (degree of stenosis) is an indicator of developing coronary artery disease (CAD). CT angiography, echocardiography, and

---

[1] QRS is a pattern in echocardiogram indicating the pulse of the heart beat and their duration.

MRI are able to visualize coronary vessels, allowing quantification of the degree of stenosis. Vessel wall MRI can provide more information about the characteristics of deposits inside a coronary artery, known as the plaque burden. Automated segmentation of lumen and vessel wall boundaries are needed to assess plaque burden before plaque classification into lumen, outer wall, calcified plaque, and haemorrhage [75].

Quantification of calcified plaques, in the form of a coronary artery calcium score, has been used as a primary diagnostic tool to calculate CAD risk among asymptomatic individuals. The Agatson score, derived from CT images, is the reference standard and the most widely used coronary artery calcium score in clinical practice. A threshold of 130 Hounsfield units is used to identify lesions when the area is ≥ 1 mm. The Agatson score is therefore calculated as the sum of all lesions in all coronary arteries. Alternatively, coronary artery calcium can also be scored based on volume [76]. Coronary artery calcium score has been shown by the population of asymptomatic subjects to have independent predictive value for future adverse events [77].

Another useful biomarker derived from CT coronary imaging is the fractional flow reserve estimate (CT-FFR) [78,79], which is an estimate of the haemodynamic severity of the stenosis in terms of pressure drop across the lesion. CT-FFR is used to guide the decision to implant a stent to widen the coronary artery. The combination of computational modeling and medical imaging to provide important information needed to guide treatment illustrates the power of these methods in benefiting patient outcomes.

17.5.2 Myocardial perfusion

Myocardial perfusion imaging is used to assess how much blood is being perfused into the myocardial tissue per unit time. Decreases in perfusion can be indicative of CAD, or narrowing or blockage of the myocardial microvasculature, which puts patients at increased risk of adverse cardiac events [80]. Of particular importance is the capacity for the heart and coronary arteries to provide increased blood flow to the myocardium when the heart is under stress. Scans are typically done both under stress and at rest to get an indication of myocardial perfusion reserve (MPR), which measures the capacity for increased myocardial blood flow from rest to stress. The stress condition is achieved by elevating heart rate either induced pharmacologically with substances such as adenosine or dobutamine, or by exercise [81].

Myocardial perfusion imaging is most commonly performed with either single photon emission computed tomography (SPECT) or positron emission tomography (PET) following administration of an exogenous radioactive tracer, such as thallium-201 or technetium-99m in SPECT, or rubidium-86 in PET [82,83]. The standardized uptake value determined from these techniques provides a direct measure of the presence of radiotracer in the myocardium. MRI is also being increasingly used to assess myocardial perfusion. In cardiac MR perfusion, gadolinium-based contrast agents are used as a tracer, producing signal increase as it perfuses through the myocardium as a result of T1^2 shortening in the vicinity of gadolinium.

In SPECT and PET, perfusion is assessed on a regional basis with the standardized uptake value ratio between stress and rest. The results are displayed as a polar map based on the 17 AHA regions with a score assigned to each of the regions according to the degree of tissue perfusion. The score is a 5-point scale ranging from 0 for normal perfusion to 4, which representing a complete absence of blood flow in the region [84]. Diverse image processing methods have been proposed to automatically score myocardial perfusion (see a survey in [85]).

Owing to its higher temporal resolution and soft tissue contrast, MRI-based methods allow for more precise quantification of perfusion reserve. Images are acquired using a cardiac gated saturation recovery protocol during a breath-hold. Although the scans are breath-held, motion correction is often required to ensure that images from all time-points are coregistered so that a pixelwise analysis can be performed [86]. The exchange of the tracer from the blood into the extracellular volume is represented by the volume transfer constant (K^{trans}). Using Toft's two-compartment model the concentration of the tracer in the myocardial tissue (C_{myo}) is given by

$$C_{\text{myo}}(t) = C_{\text{blood}}(t) \circledast K^{\text{trans}} \, e^{-k_{\text{ep}}t}, \tag{17.3}$$

where $\circledast$ is a convolution operator, k_{ep} is the rate constant of tracer flow from the extracellular space to the vasculature, and C_{blood} is the concentration of the tracer in the blood, which can be determined from signal measurements on the LV blood pool [87]. The concentration of the tracer is related to the signal in the respective tissues and depends on the native T1 of the tissue, the relaxivity of the contrast agent, as well as sequence-specific parameters. Other models with additional tissue compartments as well as model independent methods can also be used to measure K^{trans} [87].

The myocardial perfusion reserve is the ratio of the K^{trans} under stress to the K^{trans} measured at rest

$$\text{MPR} = \frac{K^{\text{trans}}_{\text{rest}}}{K^{\text{trans}}_{\text{stress}}}. \tag{17.4}$$

Myocardial perfusion is considered to be clinically impaired when MPR < 2 [88].

17.5.3 Blood flow

Blood flow patterns are particularly important in congenital heart disease. Over 80% of patients with repaired tetralogy of Fallot develop moderate to severe pulmonary blood

---

^{2} T1 is the longitudinal relaxation time, which determines the rate at which excited protons return to equilibrium during MRI.

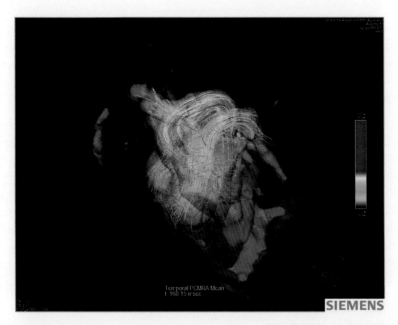

Figure 17.6 *4D Flow MRI.* A screenshot of 4D Flow MRI analysis software developed by Siemens Healthineers, showing streamlines of blood flow inside the great arteries. The 3D volume is rendered by the maximum intensity projection technique. Colors of the streamlines indicate the velocity magnitude. *(Source: acquired by the authors.)*

regurgitation in adulthood, which is associated with adverse right ventricular remodeling leading to eventually heart failure. Blood velocity and flow can be quantified using Doppler echocardiography and phase contrast velocity sensitive MRI. Recent advances in MRI have enabled accurate noninvasive evaluation of time-resolved velocity measurements along all three flow directions with three-dimensional anatomic coverage, known as 4D Flow MRI [89]. Fig. 17.6 shows a screenshot example of 4D Flow MRI analysis that visualizes the blood flow streamlines inside the great arteries, color coded by the velocity magnitude.

Flow vortices have been characterized as a fundamental feature of normal blood flow in the heart, and may aid the efficiency of flow through the chambers. For example, vortices around the mitral valve leaflets may aid valve closure. However, pathology may disrupt natural vortices and may introduce new flow features which reduces flow efficiency [90–92]. Vortical features may also be useful in characterizing myocardial rotational patterns [93].

Turbulence and kinetic energy are flow features that have been investigated for a biomarker in congenital heart disease and valvular diseases [94,95]. These features alter the mechanics of the blood vessels, affecting the vessel wall. Regions of lower and higher wall shear stress have been linked with adverse remodeling of vascular tissue. Automated methods to quantify shear stress are therefore required to examine these effects [96]. In the left and right atrium, blood flow is commonly affected by atrial fibrillation with the risk of thrombus formation in the right atrium leading to pulmonary embolism [97].

17.5.4 Vascular compliance

The stiffness or compliance of the main arteries is a useful biomarker for CVD. Increased stiffness is related to increased likelihood of adverse events [98]. Aortic compliance can be measured using a variety of techniques including distensibility, pulse wave velocity, and elastography. Distensibility requires measurement of the aortic diameter change in response to central pressure changes during the heart beat [99]. Central aortic pressure can be measured using cuff recordings transformed to the central aorta using transmission line theory [100]. Diameter can be recorded using MRI or ultrasound. Pulse wave velocity measures the propagation of the blood velocity or pressure waveform [101]. Elastography exploits an external driver providing shear waves, the propagation of which along the aorta give information on wall stiffness [102].

17.6. Myocardial structure

Cardiomyopathies are a result of changes to the cellular structure of the myocardial tissue [103], which can be assessed through images that show the structure of myocytes. Changes in myocardial fiber architecture is also observed in patients with myocardial infarction. MRI can now be used to probe the microstructural structure of myocardium in many ways. A contrast agent can be administered prior to image acquisition to enhance the visibility of myocytes of diseased tissue. Alternatively, a specialized noncontrast MR imaging has been developed to detect changes in the tissue structure by combining different protocols during acquisition. MRI can also be used to derive the architecture of myocardial tissue by exploiting the anisotropic nature of water diffusion in myocytes.

17.6.1 Tissue characterization

MRI is well suited to evaluate the cellular changes in the myocardium, owing to the fact that soft tissue structure influences both longitudinal and transverse relaxation times (T1 and T2, respectively). However, the resulting MR signal is not dependent on T1 and T2 alone, and is influenced by other factors. As a consequence, specialized imaging protocols and automated analysis are required to accurately quantify the tissue characteristics of the myocardium.

Sensitivity to changes in tissue structure can be improved through the use of an exogenous contrast agents such as those based on gadolinium. These contrast agents are often used in delayed contrast enhanced MRI to identify fibrotic tissue in the heart [104]. Fig. 17.7 (left) shows an example of a delayed contrast enhanced MRI showing hyperenhanced intensity of an infarction in the subendocardium of the anterio-septal area

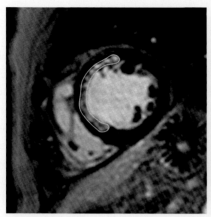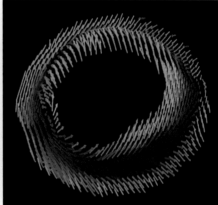

Figure 17.7 *Extracting myocardial structure from MRI.* (Left) An example of late-gadolinium enhanced MRI showing hyperintensity scarred tissue (cyan contour). (Right) Fiber architecture of the myocardium derived from diffusion tensor MR imaging. *(Source: left image was taken from the DE-TERMINE cohort shared by the Cardiac Atlas Project [22], right image was acquired and analyzed by the authors.)*

(contoured). The imaging protocol is based on an inversion recovery protocol which eliminates the signal from normal myocardium. The introduction of gadolinium-based contrast agents into the myocardium following intravascular administration produces an increase in signal related to the shortening of T1. In normal myocardium, the gadolinium washes out over the course of a few cardiac cycles and the apparent signal remains low. In fibrotic tissue, the gadolinium accumulates in the extracellular space resulting in prolonged hyperintensity.

Without contrast agents, standard MRI techniques are not sufficiently sensitive to detect the changes in the inherent (or "native") relaxation times. These issues can be overcome by parametric mapping, which provides complete quantification of the relaxation times on a pixelwise basis. Unlike standard imaging methods, parametric mapping requires multiple image acquisitions of the same tissue with varying parameters, followed by postprocessing of the resulting images to quantify the relaxation times. Since the heart is in constant motion, conventional techniques are too slow to obtain sufficient image data in a suitable time. Recent MR techniques are now able to show different map of images, weighted on T1, T2 and T2★ relaxation times[3] to characterize myocardial tissues for each pixel [105–107]. To distinguish the images from standard T1 or T2-weighted imaging, a color lookup table is typically applied to the image data. The decay model assumes that the relaxation properties of the tissues are monoexponential in nature. However, the actual decay is influenced by multiple compartments and more

---

[3] T2 is the true transverse relaxation time, while T2★ is the observed transverse relaxation time.

complex models have been used to account for the multiexponential nature of the signal decay [108].

T1, T2, and T2★ mapping have been used in a wide variety of cardiomyopathies with many showing promising results for clinical use. Studies on myocarditis show increases in native T1 and T2 [109]. T2★ mapping has been used to evaluate the presence of iron in the myocardium in patients with iron-overload diseases, where the presence of iron shortens T2★ [107]. In addition to these applications with native relaxation times, parametric mapping is also being used in delayed contrast enhanced scans to further improve sensitivity in the uptake of contrast agents [110]. Further, the use of T1 mapping before and after the injection of a gadolinium based contrast agent allows for quantification of the extracellular volume, which is linked to myocarditis and diffuse fibrosis [111].

17.6.2 Fiber architecture

Finding the correct description of the architecture of the heart is still an active area of research. Seven models of cardiac structures have been proposed so far [112]. Recently, the application of diffusion-based MRI technique, called diffusion tensor imaging (DTI), has enabled the examination of the whole fiber structure of the heart. DTI exploits the random motion of water and lipid molecules to estimate anisotropic cellular structures [113]. When applied to the heart, DTI provides information about the myocardial fiber architecture without the need for exogenous contrast agents.

Anisotropic diffusion with a single fiber family can be represented mathematically by a symmetric second-order tensor in 3D space. In cardiac DTI, the three orthogonal eigenvectors of this tensor (ordered based on their eigenvalues) are related to the laminar and fibrous structure of the myocardium (sheetlets). The primary eigenvector (the largest) will be along the fiber long axis, the second eigenvector will lie on the sheetlet plane orthogonal to the long axis, and the last eigenvector will be normal to the sheetlet plane.

With this model of diffusion and other prior information [114], fiber architecture of the myocardium can be inferred. Fig. 17.7 (right) shows a typical fiber architecture from a cardiac DTI image. Fiber tracking or tractography is a method to analyze fiber architecture by creating connections based on the primary eigenvector [115]. However, fiber tractography for the heart is problematic since cardiac myocytes form a 3D branching syncytium rather than discrete bundles, with each myocyte connected up to 10 neighbors in a complex pattern. The nonrigid deformation of the heart during its cardiac cycle further complicates DTI analysis.

Myocyte longitudinal axis alignment is a characteristic feature of mammalian hearts, with a myocyte orientation ("fiber angle") that varies from $-60°$ at the epicardium to $+70°$ or higher at endocardium. In addition, myocardial sheetlets enable transmural shearing to facilitate wall thickening [116]. Recently imaging fiber architecture has been possible from X-ray phase contrast microtomography [117]. Shape features can be combined with a computational model of fiber architecture to achieve a personalized modeling of atrial electrophysiology [118]. Although limited in spatial resolution, it is becoming possible to quantify fiber architecture in vivo, which could give valuable biomarkers of fiber disarray or remodeling [119].

17.7. Population-based cardiac image biomarkers

Advancements in imaging technology have enabled detailed examination of cardiac function using noninvasive methods. These are now being applied in large scale research studies and are being translated to clinical practice. Studies such as MESA and UK Biobank have enabled the development of novel imaging biomarkers for risk prediction and quantitative evaluation of patient heart health status. The Cardiac Atlas Project[4] has been contributing to accelerating population-based cardiac image analysis research by sharing thousands of cardiac MRI studies [22] and providing benchmark data for the development of automated analysis [2].

Large scale epidemiological and imaging studies have the potential to provide new information on the progression of heart disease. Mechanistic insights into new treatment targets may be found using either hypothesis-driven biophysical analysis or data-driven pattern analysis [120]. In the UK Biobank, 500,000 participants have been studied using physical examination, blood tests, and questionnaires [121]. The cardiac MRI extension will result in approximately 100,000 of these participants undergoing a 20 minute MRI exam, including right and left ventricular function, aortic distensibility, native T1 mapping, and myocardial tagging [122].

Automated processing of the population-based cardiac image analysis is becoming available [123,124]. Relationships between imaging biomarkers and clinical information will provide new insights into disease progression [125]. In MESA, cardiac MRI derived mass and volume provides independent information on the likelihood of future adverse events [126]. Shape indices such as sphericity also add predictive value [127]. Atlas-based analysis of left ventricular shape and shape changes are more powerful than traditional indices of remodeling, giving stronger relationships with known risk factors [40].

Machine learning methods have recently begun to be applied to predict outcomes from imaging and clinical biomarkers, trained with large scale imaging data [128]. In the future, new informatics and machine learning methods will enable advanced automated processing and fusion of information from different sources, which will assist clinical decision making and treatment planning.

---

[4] www.cardiacatlas.org.

References

[1] T.R. Dawber, G.F. Meadors, F.E. Moore Jr, Epidemiological approaches to heart disease: the Framingham Study, Am. J. Public Health Nation's Health 41 (3) (1951) 279–281.

[2] A. Suinesiaputra, P. Medrano-Gracia, B.R. Cowan, A.A. Young, Big heart data: advancing health informatics through data sharing in cardiovascular imaging, IEEE J. Biomed. Health Inform. 19 (4) (2015) 1283–1290, https://doi.org/10.1109/JBHI.2014.2370952.

[3] D.E. Bild, D.A. Bluemke, G.L. Burke, R. Detrano, A.V. Diez Roux, A.R. Folsom, et al., Multi-Ethnic Study of Atherosclerosis: objectives and design, Am. J. Epidemiol. 156 (9) (2002) 871–881.

[4] S.S. Anand, J.V. Tu, P. Awadalla, S. Black, C. Boileau, D. Busseuil, et al., Rationale, design, and methods for Canadian alliance for healthy hearts and minds cohort study (CAHHM) – a Pan Canadian cohort study, BMC Public Health 16 (2016) 650, https://doi.org/10.1186/s12889-016-3310-8.

[5] S.E. Petersen, P.M. Matthews, J.M. Francis, M.D. Robson, F. Zemrak, R. Boubertakh, et al., UK Biobank's cardiovascular magnetic resonance protocol, J. Cardiovasc. Magn. Reson. 18 (2016) 8, https://doi.org/10.1186/s12968-016-0227-4.

[6] M. Sinclair, W. Bai, E. Puyol-Antón, O. Oktay, D. Rueckert, A.P. King, Fully automated segmentation-based respiratory motion correction of multiplanar cardiac magnetic resonance images for large-scale datasets, in: M. Descoteaux, L. Maier-Hein, A. Franz, P. Jannin, D.L. Collins, S. Duchesne (Eds.), Medical Image Computing and Computer-Assisted Intervention – MICCAI 2017, Springer International Publishing, Cham, ISBN 978-3-319-66185-8, 2017, pp. 332–340.

[7] P. Lamata, S. Niederer, D. Nordsletten, D.C. Barber, I. Roy, D.R. Hose, et al., An accurate, fast and robust method to generate patient-specific cubic Hermite meshes, Med. Image Anal. 15 (6) (2011) 801–813, https://doi.org/10.1016/j.media.2011.06.010.

[8] K. Gilbert, B. Pontre, C.J. Occleshaw, B.R. Cowan, A. Suinesiaputra, A.A. Young, 4D modelling for rapid assessment of biventricular function in congenital heart disease, Int. J. Cardiovasc. Imaging 34 (3) (2018) 407–417, https://doi.org/10.1007/s10554-017-1236-6.

[9] N.A. Trayanova, Whole-heart modeling: applications to cardiac electrophysiology and electromechanics, Circ. Res. 108 (1) (2011) 113–128, https://doi.org/10.1161/CIRCRESAHA.110.223610.

[10] M.D. Cerqueira, N.J. Weissman, V. Dilsizian, A.K. Jacobs, S. Kaul, W.K. Laskey, et al., Standardized myocardial segmentation and nomenclature for tomographic imaging of the heart. A statement for healthcare professionals from the Cardiac Imaging Committee of the Council on Clinical Cardiology of the American Heart Association, Circulation 105 (4) (2002) 539–542.

[11] B.S.N. Selvadurai, V.O. Puntmann, D.A. Bluemke, V.A. Ferrari, M.G. Friedrich, C.M. Kramer, et al., Definition of left ventricular segments for cardiac magnetic resonance imaging, JACC Cardiovasc. Imaging 11 (6) (2018) 926–928, https://doi.org/10.1016/j.jcmg.2017.09.010.

[12] P. Peng, K. Lekadir, A. Gooya, L. Shao, S.E. Petersen, A.F. Frangi, A review of heart chamber segmentation for structural and functional analysis using cardiac magnetic resonance imaging, MAGMA 29 (2) (2016) 155–195, https://doi.org/10.1007/s10334-015-0521-4.

[13] A.F. Frangi, W.J. Niessen, M.A. Viergever, Three-dimensional modeling for functional analysis of cardiac images: a review, IEEE Trans. Med. Imaging 20 (1) (2001) 2–25, https://doi.org/10.1109/42.906421.

[14] C. Petitjean, J.N. Dacher, A review of segmentation methods in short axis cardiac MR images, Med. Image Anal. 15 (2) (2011) 169–184, https://doi.org/10.1016/j.media.2010.12.004.

[15] A. Suinesiaputra, B.R. Cowan, A.O. Al-Agamy, M.A. Elattar, N. Ayache, A.S. Fahmy, et al., A collaborative resource to build consensus for automated left ventricular segmentation of cardiac MR images, Med. Image Anal. 18 (1) (2014) 50–62, https://doi.org/10.1016/j.media.2013.09.001.

[16] A. Suinesiaputra, D.A. Bluemke, B.R. Cowan, M.G. Friedrich, C.M. Kramer, R. Kwong, et al., Quantification of LV function and mass by cardiovascular magnetic resonance: multi-center variability and consensus contours, J. Cardiovasc. Magn. Reson. 17 (2015) 63, https://doi.org/10.1186/s12968-015-0170-9.

[17] C. Petitjean, M.A. Zuluaga, W. Bai, J.N. Dacher, D. Grosgeorge, J. Caudron, et al., Right ventricle segmentation from cardiac MRI: a collation study, Med. Image Anal. 19 (1) (2015) 187–202, https://doi.org/10.1016/j.media.2014.10.004.

[18] C. Tobon-Gomez, A. Geers, J. Peters, J. Weese, K. Pinto, R. Karim, et al., Benchmark for algorithms segmenting the left atrium from 3D CT and MRI datasets, IEEE Trans. Med. Imaging (2015), https://doi.org/10.1109/TMI.2015.2398818.

[19] D. Levy, R.J. Garrison, D.D. Savage, W.B. Kannel, W.P. Castelli, Prognostic implications of echocardiographically determined left ventricular mass in the Framingham Heart Study, N. Engl. J. Med. 322 (22) (1990) 1561–1566, https://doi.org/10.1056/NEJM199005313222203.

[20] S.S. Gidding, Controversies in the assessment of left ventricular mass, Hypertension 56 (1) (2010) 26–28, https://doi.org/10.1161/HYPERTENSIONAHA.110.153346.

[21] A.C. Armstrong, S. Gidding, O. Gjesdal, C. Wu, D.A. Bluemke, J.A.C. Lima, LV mass assessed by echocardiography and CMR, cardiovascular outcomes, and medical practice, JACC Cardiovasc. Imaging 5 (8) (2012) 837–848, https://doi.org/10.1016/j.jcmg.2012.06.003.

[22] C.G. Fonseca, M. Backhaus, D.A. Bluemke, R.D. Britten, J.D. Chung, B.R. Cowan, et al., The Cardiac Atlas Project – an imaging database for computational modeling and statistical atlases of the heart, Bioinformatics 27 (16) (2011) 2288–2295, https://doi.org/10.1093/bioinformatics/btr360.

[23] T. Papavassiliu, H.P. Kühl, M. Schröder, T. Süselbeck, O. Bondarenko, C.K. Böhm, et al., Effect of endocardial trabeculae on left ventricular measurements and measurement reproducibility at cardiovascular MR imaging, Radiology 236 (1) (2005) 57–64, https://doi.org/10.1148/radiol.2353040601.

[24] A. Jacquier, F. Thuny, B. Jop, R. Giorgi, F. Cohen, J.Y. Gaubert, et al., Measurement of trabeculated left ventricular mass using cardiac magnetic resonance imaging in the diagnosis of left ventricular noncompaction, Eur. Heart J. 31 (9) (2010) 1098–1104, https://doi.org/10.1093/eurheartj/ehp595.

[25] G. Captur, V. Muthurangu, C. Cook, A.S. Flett, R. Wilson, A. Barison, et al., Quantification of left ventricular trabeculae using fractal analysis, J. Cardiovasc. Magn. Reson. 15 (2013) 36, https://doi.org/10.1186/1532-429X-15-36.

[26] P.B. Bottini, A.A. Carr, L.M. Prisant, F.W. Flickinger, J.D. Allison, J.S. Gottdiener, Magnetic resonance imaging compared to echocardiography to assess left ventricular mass in the hypertensive patient, Am. J. Hypertens. 8 (3) (1995) 221–228, https://doi.org/10.1016/0895-7061(94)00178-E.

[27] R. Hoffmann, G. Barletta, S. von Bardeleben, J.L. Vanoverschelde, J. Kasprzak, C. Greis, et al., Analysis of left ventricular volumes and function: a multicenter comparison of cardiac magnetic resonance imaging, cine ventriculography, and unenhanced and contrast-enhanced two-dimensional and three-dimensional echocardiography, J. Am. Soc. Echocardiogr. 27 (3) (2014) 292–301, https://doi.org/10.1016/j.echo.2013.12.005.

[28] K. Alfakih, T. Bloomer, S. Bainbridge, G. Bainbridge, J. Ridgway, G. Williams, et al., A comparison of left ventricular mass between two-dimensional echocardiography, using fundamental and tissue harmonic imaging, and cardiac MRI in patients with hypertension, Eur. J. Radiol. 52 (2) (2004) 103–109, https://doi.org/10.1016/j.ejrad.2003.09.015.

[29] P. Medrano-Gracia, B.R. Cowan, D.A. Bluemke, J.P. Finn, A.H. Kadish, D.C. Lee, et al., Atlas-based analysis of cardiac shape and function: correction of regional shape bias due to imaging protocol for population studies, J. Cardiovasc. Magn. Reson. 15 (2013) 80, https://doi.org/10.1186/1532-429X-15-80.

[30] F.E. Dewey, D. Rosenthal, D.J. Murphy Jr, V.F. Froelicher, E.A. Ashley, Does size matter? Clinical applications of scaling cardiac size and function for body size, Circulation 117 (17) (2008) 2279–2287, https://doi.org/10.1161/CIRCULATIONAHA.107.736785.

[31] D.A. Bluemke, R.A. Kronmal, J.A.C. Lima, K. Liu, J. Olson, G.L. Burke, et al., The relationship of left ventricular mass and geometry to incident cardiovascular events: the MESA (Multi-Ethnic Study of Atherosclerosis) study, J. Am. Coll. Cardiol. 52 (25) (2008) 2148–2155, https://doi.org/10.1016/j.jacc.2008.09.014.

[32] R.A. Kronmal, Spurious correlation and the fallacy of the ratio standard revisited, J. R. Stat. Soc., Ser. A, Stat. Soc. 156 (3) (1993) 379–392, URL http://www.jstor.org/stable/2983064.

[33] J.R. Paonessa, T. Brennan, M. Pimentel, D. Steinhaus, M. Feng, L.A. Celi, Hyperdynamic left ventricular ejection fraction in the intensive care unit, Crit. Care 19 (2015) 288, https://doi.org/10.1186/s13054-015-1012-8.

[34] C.G. Fonseca, A.M. Dissanayake, R.N. Doughty, Three-dimensional assessment of left ventricular systolic strain in patients with type 2 diabetes mellitus, diastolic dysfunction, and normal ejection fraction, Am. J. Cardiol. 94 (11) (2004) 1391–1395, https://doi.org/10.1016/j.amjcard.2004.07.143.

[35] L.H. Opie, P.J. Commerford, B.J. Gersh, M.A. Pfeffer, Controversies in ventricular remodelling, Lancet 367 (9507) (2006) 356–367, https://doi.org/10.1016/S0140-6736(06)68074-4.

[36] B.A. Carabello, Is cardiac hypertrophy good or bad? The answer, of course, is yes, JACC Cardiovasc. Imaging 7 (11) (2014) 1081–1083, https://doi.org/10.1016/j.jcmg.2014.07.013.

[37] A.L. Spence, L.H. Naylor, H.H. Carter, C.L. Buck, L. Dembo, C.P. Murray, et al., A prospective randomised longitudinal MRI study of left ventricular adaptation to endurance and resistance exercise training in humans, J. Physiol. 589 (Pt 22) (2011) 5443–5452, https://doi.org/10.1113/jphysiol.2011.217125.

[38] M.A. Konstam, D.G. Kramer, A.R. Patel, M.S. Maron, J.E. Udelson, Left ventricular remodeling in heart failure: current concepts in clinical significance and assessment, JACC Cardiovasc. Imaging 4 (1) (2011) 98–108, https://doi.org/10.1016/j.jcmg.2010.10.008.

[39] X. Zhang, B.R. Cowan, D.A. Bluemke, J.P. Finn, C.G. Fonseca, A.H. Kadish, et al., Atlas-based quantification of cardiac remodeling due to myocardial infarction, PLoS ONE 9 (10) (2014) e110243, https://doi.org/10.1371/journal.pone.0110243.

[40] X. Zhang, P. Medrano-Gracia, B. Ambale-Venkatesh, D.A. Bluemke, B.R. Cowan, J.P. Finn, et al., Orthogonal decomposition of left ventricular remodeling in myocardial infarction, Gigascience 6 (3) (2017) 1–15, https://doi.org/10.1093/gigascience/gix005.

[41] X. Zhang, B.L. Schulz, C. Punyadeera, The current status of heart failure diagnostic biomarkers, Expert Rev. Mol. Diagn. 16 (4) (2016) 487–500, https://doi.org/10.1586/14737159.2016.1144474.

[42] M.M. Redfield, Heart failure with preserved ejection fraction, N. Engl. J. Med. 376 (9) (2017) 897, https://doi.org/10.1056/NEJMc1615918.

[43] V.Y. Wang, H.I. Lam, D.B. Ennis, B.R. Cowan, A.A. Young, M.P. Nash, Modelling passive diastolic mechanics with quantitative MRI of cardiac structure and function, Med. Image Anal. 13 (5) (2009) 773–784, https://doi.org/10.1016/j.media.2009.07.006.

[44] T. Ohara, C.L. Niebel, K.C. Stewart, J.J. Charonko, M. Pu, P.P. Vlachos, et al., Loss of adrenergic augmentation of diastolic intra-LV pressure difference in patients with diastolic dysfunction: evaluation by color M-mode echocardiography, JACC Cardiovasc. Imaging 5 (9) (2012) 861–870, https://doi.org/10.1016/j.jcmg.2012.05.013.

[45] A. Suinesiaputra, A.F. Frangi, T.A.M. Kaandorp, H.J. Lamb, J.J. Bax, J.H.C. Reiber, et al., Automated regional wall motion abnormality detection by combining rest and stress cardiac MRI: correlation with contrast-enhanced MRI, J. Magn. Reson. Imaging 34 (2) (2011) 270–278, https://doi.org/10.1002/jmri.22601.

[46] A. Suinesiaputra, A.F. Frangi, T.A.M. Kaandorp, H.J. Lamb, J.J. Bax, J.H.C. Reiber, et al., Automated detection of regional wall motion abnormalities based on a statistical model applied to multislice short-axis cardiac MR images, IEEE Trans. Med. Imaging 28 (4) (2009) 595–607, https://doi.org/10.1109/TMI.2008.2008966.

[47] M. Afshin, I. Ben Ayed, K. Punithakumar, M. Law, A. Islam, A. Goela, et al., Regional assessment of cardiac left ventricular myocardial function via MRI statistical features, IEEE Trans. Med. Imaging 33 (2) (2014) 481–494, https://doi.org/10.1109/TMI.2013.2287793.

[48] K. Punithakumar, I. Ben Ayed, A. Islam, A. Goela, I.G. Ross, J. Chong, et al., Regional heart motion abnormality detection: an information theoretic approach, Med. Image Anal. 17 (3) (2013) 311–324, https://doi.org/10.1016/j.media.2012.11.007.

[49] S. Sanchez-Martinez, N. Duchateau, T. Erdei, A.G. Fraser, B.H. Bijnens, G. Piella, Characterization of myocardial motion patterns by unsupervised multiple kernel learning, Med. Image Anal. 35 (2017) 70–82, https://doi.org/10.1016/j.media.2016.06.007.

[50] Y. Notomi, P. Lysyansky, R.M. Setser, T. Shiota, Z.B. Popović, M.G. Martin-Miklovic, et al., Measurement of ventricular torsion by two-dimensional ultrasound speckle tracking imaging, J. Am. Coll. Cardiol. 45 (12) (2005) 2034–2041, https://doi.org/10.1016/j.jacc.2005.02.082.

[51] K.N. Hor, W.M. Gottliebson, C. Carson, E. Wash, J. Cnota, R. Fleck, et al., Comparison of magnetic resonance feature tracking for strain calculation with harmonic phase imaging analysis, JACC Cardiovasc. Imaging 3 (2) (2010) 144–151, https://doi.org/10.1016/j.jcmg.2009.11.006.

[52] M.M. Rohé, M. Sermesant, X. Pennec, Low-dimensional representation of cardiac motion using Barycentric Subspaces: a new group-wise paradigm for estimation, analysis, and reconstruction, Med. Image Anal. 45 (2018) 1–12, https://doi.org/10.1016/j.media.2017.12.008.

[53] J.U. Voigt, G. Pedrizzetti, P. Lysyansky, T.H. Marwick, H. Houle, R. Baumann, et al., Definitions for a common standard for 2D speckle tracking echocardiography: consensus document of the EACVI/ASE/Industry Task Force to standardize deformation imaging, J. Am. Soc. Echocardiogr. 28 (2) (2015) 183–193, https://doi.org/10.1016/j.echo.2014.11.003.

[54] J.J. Cao, N. Ngai, L. Duncanson, J. Cheng, K. Gliganic, Q. Chen, A comparison of both DENSE and feature tracking techniques with tagging for the cardiovascular magnetic resonance assessment of myocardial strain, J. Cardiovasc. Magn. Reson. 20 (1) (2018) 26, https://doi.org/10.1186/s12968-018-0448-9.

[55] M.H. Vandsburger, B.A. French, P.A. Helm, R.J. Roy, C.M. Kramer, A.A. Young, et al., Multiparameter in vivo cardiac magnetic resonance imaging demonstrates normal perfusion reserve despite severely attenuated beta-adrenergic functional response in neuronal nitric oxide synthase knockout mice, Eur. Heart J. 28 (22) (2007) 2792–2798, https://doi.org/10.1093/eurheartj/ehm241.

[56] J.J. Cao, Y. Wang, J. McLaughlin, E. Haag, P. Rhee, M. Passick, et al., Left ventricular filling pressure assessment using left atrial transit time by cardiac magnetic resonance imaging, Circ. Cardiovasc. Imaging 4 (2) (2011) 130–138, https://doi.org/10.1161/CIRCIMAGING.110.959569.

[57] S.F. Nagueh, Non-invasive assessment of left ventricular filling pressure, Eur. J. Heart Fail. 20 (1) (2018) 38–48, https://doi.org/10.1002/ejhf.971.

[58] L. Axel, L. Dougherty, Heart wall motion: improved method of spatial modulation of magnetization for MR imaging, Radiology 172 (2) (1989) 349–350, https://doi.org/10.1148/radiology.172.2.2748813.

[59] N.F. Osman, E.R. McVeigh, J.L. Prince, Imaging heart motion using harmonic phase MRI, IEEE Trans. Med. Imaging 19 (3) (2000) 186–202, https://doi.org/10.1109/42.845177.

[60] A.H. Aletras, S. Ding, R.S. Balaban, H. Wen, DENSE: displacement encoding with stimulated echoes in cardiac functional MRI, J. Magn. Res. 137 (1) (1999) 247–252, https://doi.org/10.1006/jmre.1998.1676.

[61] B.R. Cowan, S.M. Peereboom, A. Greiser, J. Guehring, A.A. Young, Image feature determinants of global and segmental circumferential ventricular strain from cine CMR, JACC Cardiovasc. Imaging 8 (12) (2015) 1465–1466, https://doi.org/10.1016/j.jcmg.2014.10.005.

[62] M. Li, H. Gupta, S.G. Lloyd, L.J. Dell'Italia, T.S. Denney Jr, A graph theoretic approach for computing 3D+time biventricular cardiac strain from tagged MRI data, Med. Image Anal. 35 (2017) 46–57, https://doi.org/10.1016/j.media.2016.06.006.

[63] E.S.H. Ibrahim, Myocardial tagging by cardiovascular magnetic resonance: evolution of techniques–pulse sequences, analysis algorithms, and applications, J. Cardiovasc. Magn. Reson. 13 (2011) 36, https://doi.org/10.1186/1532-429X-13-36.

[64] H. Wang, A.A. Amini, Cardiac motion and deformation recovery from MRI: a review, IEEE Trans. Med. Imaging 31 (2) (2012) 487–503, https://doi.org/10.1109/TMI.2011.2171706.

[65] C. Ypenburg, R.J. van Bommel, C.J.W. Borleffs, G.B. Bleeker, E. Boersma, M.J. Schalij, et al., Long-term prognosis after cardiac resynchronization therapy is related to the extent of left ventricular reverse remodeling at midterm follow-up, J. Am. Coll. Cardiol. 53 (6) (2009) 483–490, https://doi.org/10.1016/j.jacc.2008.10.032.

[66] S. Kapetanakis, M.T. Kearney, A. Siva, N. Gall, M. Cooklin, M.J. Monaghan, Real-time three-dimensional echocardiography: a novel technique to quantify global left ventricular mechanical dyssynchrony, Circulation 112 (7) (2005) 992–1000, https://doi.org/10.1161/CIRCULATIONAHA.104.474445.

[67] M.V. Pitzalis, M. Iacoviello, R. Romito, F. Massari, B. Rizzon, G. Luzzi, et al., Cardiac resynchronization therapy tailored by echocardiographic evaluation of ventricular asynchrony, J. Am. Coll. Cardiol. 40 (9) (2002) 1615–1622.

[68] C.M. Yu, W.H. Fung, H. Lin, Q. Zhang, J.E. Sanderson, C.P. Lau, Predictors of left ventricular reverse remodeling after cardiac resynchronization therapy for heart failure secondary to idiopathic dilated or ischemic cardiomyopathy, Am. J. Cardiol. 91 (6) (2003) 684–688.

[69] J.J. Bax, G.B. Bleeker, T.H. Marwick, S.G. Molhoek, E. Boersma, P. Steendijk, et al., Left ventricular dyssynchrony predicts response and prognosis after cardiac resynchronization therapy, J. Am. Coll. Cardiol. 44 (9) (2004) 1834–1840, https://doi.org/10.1016/j.jacc.2004.08.016.

[70] J. Gorcsan 3rd, H. Kanzaki, R. Bazaz, K. Dohi, D. Schwartzman, Usefulness of echocardiographic tissue synchronization imaging to predict acute response to cardiac resynchronization therapy, Am. J. Cardiol. 93 (9) (2004) 1178–1181, https://doi.org/10.1016/j.amjcard.2004.01.054.

[71] R.J. Taylor, F. Umar, W.E. Moody, C. Meyyappan, B. Stegemann, J.N. Townend, et al., Feature-tracking cardiovascular magnetic resonance as a novel technique for the assessment of mechanical dyssynchrony, Int. J. Cardiol. 175 (1) (2014) 120–125, https://doi.org/10.1016/j.ijcard.2014.04.268.

[72] D. Peressutti, M. Sinclair, W. Bai, T. Jackson, J. Ruijsink, D. Nordsletten, et al., A framework for combining a motion atlas with non-motion information to learn clinically useful biomarkers: application to cardiac resynchronisation therapy response prediction, Med. Image Anal. 35 (2017) 669–684, https://doi.org/10.1016/j.media.2016.10.002.

[73] N. Duchateau, M. De Craene, G. Piella, A.F. Frangi, Constrained manifold learning for the characterization of pathological deviations from normality, Med. Image Anal. 16 (8) (2012) 1532–1549, https://doi.org/10.1016/j.media.2012.07.003.

[74] P.J. Kilner, G.Z. Yang, A.J. Wilkes, R.H. Mohiaddin, D.N. Firmin, M.H. Yacoub, Asymmetric redirection of flow through the heart, Nature 404 (6779) (2000) 759–761, https://doi.org/10.1038/35008075.

[75] J. Wang, N. Balu, G. Canton, C. Yuan, Imaging biomarkers of cardiovascular disease, J. Magn. Reson. Imaging 32 (3) (2010) 502–515, https://doi.org/10.1002/jmri.22266.

[76] M.J. Blaha, M.B. Mortensen, S. Kianoush, R. Tota-Maharaj, M. Cainzos-Achirica, Coronary Artery Calcium Scoring: is it time for a change in methodology?, JACC Cardiovasc. Imaging 10 (8) (2017) 923–937, https://doi.org/10.1016/j.jcmg.2017.05.007.

[77] R. Detrano, A.D. Guerci, J.J. Carr, D.E. Bild, G. Burke, A.R. Folsom, et al., Coronary calcium as a predictor of coronary events in four racial or ethnic groups, N. Engl. J. Med. 358 (13) (2008) 1336–1345, https://doi.org/10.1056/NEJMoa072100.

[78] C.A. Taylor, T.A. Fonte, J.K. Min, Computational fluid dynamics applied to cardiac computed tomography for noninvasive quantification of fractional flow reserve: scientific basis, J. Am. Coll. Cardiol. 61 (22) (2013) 2233–2241, https://doi.org/10.1016/j.jacc.2012.11.083.

[79] L. Itu, P. Sharma, V. Mihalef, A. Kamen, C. Suciu, D. Lomaniciu, A patient-specific reduced-order model for coronary circulation, in: 2012 9th IEEE International Symposium on Biomedical Imaging, ISBI, 2012, pp. 832–835.

[80] R. Hachamovitch, S.W. Hayes, J.D. Friedman, I. Cohen, D.S. Berman, Stress myocardial perfusion single-photon emission computed tomography is clinically effective and cost effective in risk strati-

fication of patients with a high likelihood of coronary artery disease (CAD) but no known CAD, J. Am. Coll. Cardiol. 43 (2) (2004) 200–208.

[81] M.G. Levine, A.W. Ahlberg, A. Mann, M.P. White, C.C. McGill, et al., C. Mendes de Leon, et al., Comparison of exercise, dipyridamole, adenosine, and dobutamine stress with the use of Tc-99m tetrofosmin tomographic imaging, J. Nucl. Cardiol. 6 (4) (1999) 389–396.

[82] G.A. Beller, S.R. Bergmann, Myocardial perfusion imaging agents: SPECT and PET, J. Nucl. Cardiol. 11 (1) (2004) 71–86, https://doi.org/10.1016/j.nuclcard.2003.12.002.

[83] R. Nakazato, D.S. Berman, E. Alexanderson, P. Slomka, Myocardial perfusion imaging with PET, Imaging Med. 5 (1) (2013) 35–46, https://doi.org/10.2217/iim.13.1.

[84] P.L. Tilkemeier, C.D. Cooke, E.P. Ficaro, D.K. Glover, C.L. Hansen, B.D. McCallister Jr, et al., American Society of Nuclear Cardiology information statement: standardized reporting matrix for radionuclide myocardial perfusion imaging, J. Nucl. Cardiol. 13 (6) (2006) e157–e171, https://doi.org/10.1016/j.nuclcard.2006.08.014.

[85] V. Gupta, H.A. Kirişli, Cardiac MR perfusion image processing techniques: a survey, Med. Image Anal. 16 (4) (2012) 767–785, https://doi.org/10.1016/j.media.2011.12.005.

[86] B. Pontre, B.R. Cowan, E. DiBella, S. Kulaseharan, D. Likhite, N. Noorman, et al., An open benchmark challenge for motion correction of myocardial perfusion MRI, IEEE J. Biomed. Health Inform. 21 (5) (2017) 1315–1326, https://doi.org/10.1109/JBHI.2016.2597145.

[87] N.A. Pack, E.V.R. DiBella, Comparison of myocardial perfusion estimates from dynamic contrast-enhanced magnetic resonance imaging with four quantitative analysis methods, Magn. Reson. Med. 64 (1) (2010) 125–137, https://doi.org/10.1002/mrm.22282.

[88] V.K. Dandekar, M.A. Bauml, A.W. Ertel, C. Dickens, R.C. Gonzalez, A. Farzaneh-Far, Assessment of global myocardial perfusion reserve using cardiovascular magnetic resonance of coronary sinus flow at 3 Tesla, J. Cardiovasc. Magn. Reson. 16 (2014) 24, https://doi.org/10.1186/1532-429X-16-24.

[89] P.D. Gatehouse, J. Keegan, L.A. Crowe, S. Masood, R.H. Mohiaddin, K.F. Kreitner, et al., Applications of phase-contrast flow and velocity imaging in cardiovascular MRI, Eur. Radiol. 15 (10) (2005) 2172–2184, https://doi.org/10.1007/s00330-005-2829-3.

[90] G. Pedrizzetti, G. La Canna, O. Alfieri, G. Tonti, The vortex – an early predictor of cardiovascular outcome?, Nat. Rev. Cardiol. 11 (9) (2014) 545–553, https://doi.org/10.1038/nrcardio.2014.75.

[91] W.Y. Kim, P.G. Walker, E.M. Pedersen, J.K. Poulsen, S. Oyre, K. Houlind, et al., Left ventricular blood flow patterns in normal subjects: a quantitative analysis by three-dimensional magnetic resonance velocity mapping, J. Am. Coll. Cardiol. 26 (1) (1995) 224–238.

[92] G.Z. Yang, R.H. Mohiaddin, P.J. Kilner, D.N. Firmin, Vortical flow feature recognition: a topological study of in vivo flow patterns using MR velocity mapping, J. Comput. Assist. Tomogr. 22 (4) (1998) 577–586.

[93] S. Sanz-Estébanez, L. Cordero-Grande, T. Sevilla, A. Revilla-Orodea, R. de Luis-García, M. Martín-Fernández, et al., Vortical features for myocardial rotation assessment in hypertrophic cardiomyopathy using cardiac tagged magnetic resonance, Med. Image Anal. 47 (2018) 191–202, https://doi.org/10.1016/j.media.2018.03.005.

[94] S.F. Hussaini, D.R. Rutkowski, A. Roldán-Alzate, C.J. François, Left and right ventricular kinetic energy using time-resolved versus time-average ventricular volumes, J. Magn. Reson. Imaging 45 (3) (2017) 821–828, https://doi.org/10.1002/jmri.25416.

[95] M.D. Hope, T.A. Hope, S.E.S. Crook, K.G. Ordovas, T.H. Urbania, M.T. Alley, et al., 4D flow CMR in assessment of valve-related ascending aortic disease, JACC Cardiovasc. Imaging 4 (7) (2011) 781–787, https://doi.org/10.1016/j.jcmg.2011.05.004.

[96] J. Eriksson, C.J. Carlhäll, P. Dyverfeldt, J. Engvall, A.F. Bolger, T. Ebbers, Semi-automatic quantification of 4D left ventricular blood flow, J. Cardiovasc. Magn. Reson. 12 (2010) 9, https://doi.org/10.1186/1532-429X-12-9.

[97] V.P. Kamphuis, J.J.M. Westenberg, R.L.F. van der Palen , N.A. Blom, A. de Roos, R. van der Geest, et al., Unravelling cardiovascular disease using four dimensional flow cardiovascular magnetic resonance, Int. J. Cardiovasc. Imaging 33 (7) (2017) 1069–1081, https://doi.org/10.1007/s10554-016-1031-9.

[98] P. Boutouyrie, A.I. Tropeano, R. Asmar, I. Gautier, A. Benetos, P. Lacolley, et al., Aortic stiffness is an independent predictor of primary coronary events in hypertensive patients: a longitudinal study, Hypertension 39 (1) (2002) 10–15.

[99] M.C. Whitlock, W.G. Hundley, Noninvasive imaging of flow and vascular function in disease of the aorta, JACC Cardiovasc. Imaging 8 (9) (2015) 1094–1106, https://doi.org/10.1016/j.jcmg.2015.08.001.

[100] A.C.W. Lin, A. Lowe, K. Sidhu, W. Harrison, P. Ruygrok, R. Stewart, Evaluation of a novel sphygmomanometer, which estimates central aortic blood pressure from analysis of brachial artery suprasystolic pressure waves, J. Hypertens. 30 (9) (2012) 1743–1750, https://doi.org/10.1097/HJH.0b013e3283567b94.

[101] P.A. Roberts, B.R. Cowan, Y. Liu, A.C.W. Lin, P.M.F. Nielsen, A.J. Taberner, et al., Real-time aortic pulse wave velocity measurement during exercise stress testing, J. Cardiovasc. Magn. Reson. 17 (2015) 86, https://doi.org/10.1186/s12968-015-0191-4.

[102] H. Dong, R. Mazumder, V.S.P. Illapani, X. Mo, R.D. White, A. Kolipaka, In vivo quantification of aortic stiffness using MR elastography in hypertensive porcine model, Magn. Reson. Med. 78 (6) (2017) 2315–2321, https://doi.org/10.1002/mrm.26601.

[103] P.A. Harvey, L.A. Leinwand, The cell biology of disease: cellular mechanisms of cardiomyopathy, J. Cell Biol. 194 (3) (2011) 355–365, https://doi.org/10.1083/jcb.201101100.

[104] B.L. Gerber, J. Garot, D.A. Bluemke, K.C. Wu, J.A.C. Lima, Accuracy of contrast-enhanced magnetic resonance imaging in predicting improvement of regional myocardial function in patients after acute myocardial infarction, Circulation 106 (9) (2002) 1083–1089.

[105] S.K. Piechnik, V.M. Ferreira, E. Dall'Armellina, L.E. Cochlin, A. Greiser, S. Neubauer, et al., Shortened Modified Look-Locker Inversion recovery (ShMOLLI) for clinical myocardial T1-mapping at 1.5 and 3 T within a 9 heartbeat breathhold, J. Cardiovasc. Magn. Reson. 12 (2010) 69, https://doi.org/10.1186/1532-429X-12-69.

[106] T.Y. Huang, Y.J. Liu, A. Stemmer, B.P. Poncelet, T2 measurement of the human myocardium using a T2-prepared transient-state TrueFISP sequence, Magn. Reson. Med. 57 (5) (2007) 960–966, https://doi.org/10.1002/mrm.21208.

[107] M. Westwood, L.J. Anderson, D.N. Firmin, P.D. Gatehouse, C.C. Charrier, B. Wonke, et al., A single breath-hold multiecho T2* cardiovascular magnetic resonance technique for diagnosis of myocardial iron overload, J. Magn. Reson. Imaging 18 (1) (2003) 33–39, https://doi.org/10.1002/jmri.10332.

[108] T. He, P.D. Gatehouse, G.C. Smith, R.H. Mohiaddin, D.J. Pennell, D.N. Firmin, Myocardial T2* measurements in iron-overloaded thalassemia: an in vivo study to investigate optimal methods of quantification, Magn. Reson. Med. 60 (5) (2008) 1082–1089, https://doi.org/10.1002/mrm.21744.

[109] P. Lurz, C. Luecke, I. Eitel, F. Föhrenbach, C. Frank, M. Grothoff, et al., Comprehensive cardiac magnetic resonance imaging in patients with suspected myocarditis: the MyoRacer-trial, J. Am. Coll. Cardiol. 67 (15) (2016) 1800–1811, https://doi.org/10.1016/j.jacc.2016.02.013.

[110] D.R. Messroghli, K. Walters, S. Plein, P. Sparrow, M.G. Friedrich, J.P. Ridgway, et al., Myocardial T1 mapping: application to patients with acute and chronic myocardial infarction, Magn. Reson. Med. 58 (1) (2007) 34–40, https://doi.org/10.1002/mrm.21272.

[111] J.C. Moon, D.R. Messroghli, P. Kellman, S.K. Piechnik, M.D. Robson, M. Ugander, et al., Myocardial T1 mapping and extracellular volume quantification: a Society for Cardiovascular Magnetic Resonance (SCMR) and CMR Working Group of the European Society of Cardiology consensus statement, J. Cardiovasc. Magn. Reson. 15 (2013) 92, https://doi.org/10.1186/1532-429X-15-92.

[112] S.H. Gilbert, A.P. Benson, P. Li, A.V. Holden, Regional localisation of left ventricular sheet structure: integration with current models of cardiac fibre, sheet and band structure, Eur. J. Cardiothorac. Surg. 32 (2) (2007) 231–249, https://doi.org/10.1016/j.ejcts.2007.03.032.

[113] P.J. Basser, J. Mattiello, D. LeBihan, MR diffusion tensor spectroscopy and imaging, Biophys. J. 66 (1) (1994) 259–267, https://doi.org/10.1016/S0006-3495(94)80775-1.

[114] A. Nagler, C. Bertoglio, C.T. Stoeck, S. Kozerke, W.A. Wall, Maximum likelihood estimation of cardiac fiber bundle orientation from arbitrarily spaced diffusion weighted images, Med. Image Anal. 39 (2017) 56–77, https://doi.org/10.1016/j.media.2017.03.005.

[115] D.E. Sosnovik, R. Wang, G. Dai, T.G. Reese, V.J. Wedeen, Diffusion MR tractography of the heart, J. Cardiovasc. Magn. Reson. 11 (2009) 47, https://doi.org/10.1186/1532-429X-11-47.

[116] I.J. LeGrice, Y. Takayama, J.W. Covell, Transverse shear along myocardial cleavage planes provides a mechanism for normal systolic wall thickening, Circ. Res. 77 (1) (1995) 182–193.

[117] F. Varray, I. Mirea, M. Langer, F. Peyrin, L. Fanton, I.E. Magnin, Extraction of the 3D local orientation of myocytes in human cardiac tissue using X-ray phase-contrast micro-tomography and multi-scale analysis, Med. Image Anal. 38 (2017) 117–132, https://doi.org/10.1016/j.media.2017.02.006.

[118] T.E. Fastl, C. Tobon-Gomez, A. Crozier, J. Whitaker, R. Rajani, K.P. McCarthy, et al., Personalized computational modeling of left atrial geometry and transmural myofiber architecture, Med. Image Anal. 47 (2018) 180–190, https://doi.org/10.1016/j.media.2018.04.001.

[119] S. Nielles-Vallespin, Z. Khalique, P.F. Ferreira, R. de Silva, A.D. Scott, P. Kilner, et al., Assessment of myocardial microstructural dynamics by in vivo diffusion tensor cardiac magnetic resonance, J. Am. Coll. Cardiol. 69 (6) (2017) 661–676, https://doi.org/10.1016/j.jacc.2016.11.051.

[120] P. Lamata, Teaching cardiovascular medicine to machines, Cardiovasc. Res. 114 (8) (2018) e62–e64, https://doi.org/10.1093/cvr/cvy127.

[121] C. Sudlow, J. Gallacher, N. Allen, V. Beral, P. Burton, J. Danesh, et al., UK biobank: an open access resource for identifying the causes of a wide range of complex diseases of middle and old age, PLoS Med. 12 (3) (2015) e1001779, https://doi.org/10.1371/journal.pmed.1001779.

[122] S.E. Petersen, P.M. Matthews, F. Bamberg, D.A. Bluemke, J.M. Francis, M.G. Friedrich, et al., Imaging in population science: cardiovascular magnetic resonance in 100,000 participants of UK Biobank – rationale, challenges and approaches, J. Cardiovasc. Magn. Reson. 15 (2013) 46, https://doi.org/10.1186/1532-429X-15-46.

[123] A. Suinesiaputra, M.M. Sanghvi, N. Aung, J.M. Paiva, F. Zemrak, K. Fung, et al., Fully-automated left ventricular mass and volume MRI analysis in the UK Biobank population cohort: evaluation of initial results, Int. J. Cardiovasc. Imaging 34 (2) (2018) 281–291, https://doi.org/10.1007/s10554-017-1225-9.

[124] Q. Zheng, H. Delingette, N. Duchateau, N. Ayache, 3D consistent & robust segmentation of cardiac images by deep learning with spatial propagation, IEEE Trans. Med. Imaging 37 (9) (2018) 2137–2148, https://doi.org/10.1109/TMI.2018.2820742.

[125] M.M. Sanghvi, N. Aung, J.A. Cooper, J.M. Paiva, A.M. Lee, F. Zemrak, et al., The impact of menopausal hormone therapy (MHT) on cardiac structure and function: insights from the UK Biobank imaging enhancement study, PLoS ONE 13 (3) (2018) e0194015, https://doi.org/10.1371/journal.pone.0194015.

[126] K. Yoneyama, B.A. Venkatesh, D.A. Bluemke, R.L. McClelland, J.A.C. Lima, Cardiovascular magnetic resonance in an adult human population: serial observations from the multi-ethnic study of atherosclerosis, J. Cardiovasc. Magn. Reson. 19 (1) (2017) 52, https://doi.org/10.1186/s12968-017-0367-1.

[127] B. Ambale-Venkatesh, K. Yoneyama, R.K. Sharma, Y. Ohyama, C.O. Wu, G.L. Burke, et al., Left ventricular shape predicts different types of cardiovascular events in the general population, Heart 103 (7) (2017) 499–507, https://doi.org/10.1136/heartjnl-2016-310052.

[128] B. Ambale-Venkatesh, X. Yang, C.O. Wu, K. Liu, W.G. Hundley, R. McClelland, et al., Cardiovascular event prediction by machine learning: the Multi-Ethnic Study of Atherosclerosis, Circ. Res. 121 (9) (2017) 1092–1101, https://doi.org/10.1161/CIRCRESAHA.117.311312.

CHAPTER 18

Radiomics
Data mining using quantitative medical image features

Martijn P.A. Starmans[a,b,c]**, Sebastian R. van der Voort**[a,b,c]**,**
Jose M. Castillo Tovar[a,b]**, Jifke F. Veenland**[a,b]**, Stefan Klein**[a,b]**, Wiro J. Niessen**[a,b,d]

[a]Erasmus MC, Department of Radiology and Nuclear Medicine, Rotterdam, the Netherlands
[b]Erasmus MC, Department of Medical Informatics, Rotterdam, the Netherlands
[d]Delft University of Technology, Faculty of Applied Sciences, Delft, the Netherlands

Contents

18.1.	Introduction	430
18.2.	Data acquisition & preparation	431
	18.2.1 Introduction	431
	18.2.2 Patient selection	432
	18.2.3 Imaging data collection	432
	18.2.4 Label data collection	433
	18.2.5 Conclusion	433
18.3.	Segmentation	434
	18.3.1 Introduction	434
	18.3.2 Segmentation methods	434
	18.3.3 Influence of segmentation on radiomics pipeline	436
	18.3.4 Conclusion	436
18.4.	Features	437
	18.4.1 Introduction	437
	18.4.2 Common features	437
	18.4.2.1 Morphological features	437
	18.4.2.2 First order features	438
	18.4.2.3 Higher order features	438
	18.4.3 Uncommon features	440
	18.4.4 Feature extraction	440
	18.4.5 Feature selection and dimensionality reduction	441
	18.4.6 Conclusion	441
18.5.	Data mining	441
	18.5.1 Introduction	441
	18.5.2 Correlation	442
	18.5.3 Machine learning	442
	18.5.4 Deep learning	443
	18.5.5 Conclusion	444
18.6.	Study design	444

[c] The first two authors are shared first authors.

Handbook of Medical Image Computing and Computer Assisted Intervention
https://doi.org/10.1016/B978-0-12-816176-0.00023-5
429

18.6.1 Introduction   444
18.6.2 Training, validation and evaluation set   444
18.6.3 Generating sets   445
    18.6.3.1 Cross-validation   *445*
    18.6.3.2 Separate evaluation set   *446*
18.6.4 Evaluation metrics   446
    18.6.4.1 Confidence intervals   *447*
    18.6.4.2 Conclusion   *447*
18.7. Infrastructure   447
18.7.1 Introduction   447
18.7.2 Data storage and sharing   448
18.7.3 Feature toolboxes   449
18.7.4 Learning toolboxes   450
18.7.5 Pipeline standardization   450
18.7.6 Conclusion   451
18.8. Conclusion   451
Acknowledgment   452
References   452

18.1. Introduction

Analysis of quantitative medical image features has been performed for several decades. Early studies showed relationships between features and clinical variables through the use of, e.g., correlation coefficients [1] and Receiver Operating Characteristic (ROC) analysis [2]. In 2012, the area which considers multiple features simultaneously was coined "radiomics" [3] and gained more attention. Currently, a typical radiomics study makes use of large numbers of quantitative features combined with machine learning methods to determine relationships between the image and relevant clinical outcomes. Deep learning, which in recent years has gained more attention, shows many similarities to radiomics. Especially convolutional neural networks could be a tool employed in radiomics as an alternative or complementary to the hand–crafted features used in radiomics.

Many studies have shown the potential of radiomics in various areas such as the lung [4], liver [5], brain [6], kidney [7], throat [8], and sarcomas [9]. Studies also vary in the use of imaging modality, e.g., Magnetic Resonance Imaging (MRI), Computed Tomography (CT), Positron Emission Tomography (PET), mammography, and X-ray. Several clinical outcomes can be predicted, such as survival [4], therapy response liver [5], and genetic mutations [7] (a field which is often coined "radiogenomics"). Lastly, applications are not only limited to diseased sites such as tumors, but can also be applied to, e.g., the musculoskeletal system, (healthy) organs [10], and other tissue structures.

Although papers use similar approaches, the field of radiomics lacks standardization. Several initiatives have tried to address this issue by providing roadmaps [11], schematic

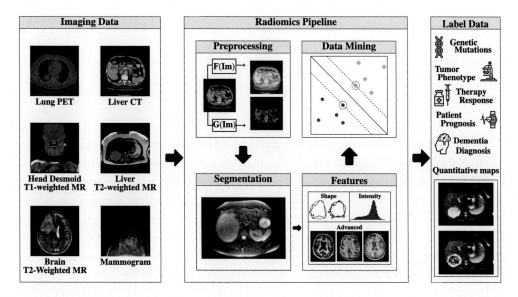

Figure 18.1 Overview of the radiomics pipeline.

reviews [12], standardization [13], and guidelines [14] for creating a radiomics signature. Despite these efforts, a wide variety of approaches still exist.

This chapter provides a guide through the several aspects of designing a radiomics study. An overview of popular approaches is provided, while focusing on the impact of each step on the final result. The structure follows that of a typical radiomics pipeline [14] as illustrated in Fig. 18.1. The first step is the gathering of data, as described in Sect. 18.2. Next, the process of segmentation of the Region Of Interest (ROI) will be discussed in Sect. 18.3. Possible preprocessing approaches will shortly be discussed in Sect. 18.4. The ROI can be used to extract several quantitative radiomics features, as shown in Sect. 18.4. Using these features, several data mining approaches can be employed that are discussed in Sect. 18.5. An overview of proper design of a radiomics study combining these steps will be detailed in Sect. 18.6. Several different software toolkits and their influence will be discussed in Sect. 18.7, after which the chapter will be concluded in Sect. 18.8.

18.2. Data acquisition & preparation

18.2.1 Introduction

Every radiomics study starts with either prospectively or retrospectively collecting data. At least two types of data have to be collected: imaging data and label data. Apart from this, additional clinical data is usually collected, which are relevant for the problem at hand.

This section will address the inclusion of patients and collection of clinical data in Sect. 18.2.2, the collection of the imaging data in Sect. 18.2.3 and the collection of label data in Sect. 18.2.4.

18.2.2 Patient selection

The first step in data collection is the decision which patients to include in the study. When prospectively collecting data, the inclusion criteria are stated in the study protocol. In the case of a retrospective study, the inclusion criteria will be based on data that is available for a group of patients. In the vast majority of the cases the study will only comprise a single disease or organ of interest, for example, the liver, prostate, or brain. Therefore, the first approach would be to include all patients for which there is imaging and label data available of a specific disease or organ. However, this might not always result in a clinically relevant dataset, depending on the clinical use case that should be addressed by the radiomics pipeline.

In clinical practice, it is possible that a preselection of patients is made based on some imaging or clinical characteristics. For example, in the neuro-oncology field a treatment decision is made based on the contrast enhancement of the tumor in the MR image. Although one could include all patients with a tumor, without considering whether they are enhancing or not, this would not lead to a clinically relevant dataset since clinicians will primarily look at the enhancement regardless of what other outcomes the radiomics pipeline might predict (e.g., survival or genetics). Therefore, if the clinical aspect is not taken into account when constructing the dataset, this could ultimately lead to solving a clinically irrelevant question. Furthermore, the problem that is then solved could be either harder or easier than the clinical question, misrepresenting the actual performance of the pipeline.

18.2.3 Imaging data collection

Once the patients to be included in the study have been selected, the imaging data to be used in the radiomics pipeline are collected. Radiomics is based on the hypothesis that a relation exists between the imaging data and the label data. It is important to keep this hypothesis in mind when the imaging data is collected, to ensure imaging data is collected which may contain predictive features. It is also important to keep in mind that there should not be a bias in the selection of the imaging data. For example, some of the patients in the dataset might have undergone a clinical procedure such as a biopsy, which will influence the imaging data. Instead of predicting the task at hand, the radiomics pipeline might then predict whether a clinical procedure was performed. Therefore, it is important to select imaging data that have been acquired before such a clinical procedure has taken place.

The diversity of the collected imaging data also plays a role. When collecting imaging data from a single scanner or single institute, this might make it easier to solve the task at hand as the data is likely more consistent. However, by collecting data from multiple scanners and institutes a more realistic expectation of the performance of the radiomics pipeline in routine clinical practice can be given, and the pipeline might become more generally applicable.

18.2.4 Label data collection

In order to train and evaluate the radiomics pipeline, it is important to have label data. The type of label data depends on the question that is addressed.

Label data can consist of manual labels provided by a clinician, or the result of a clinical analysis, e.g., a genetic subtype derived from tissue analysis, or derived from clinical follow-up such as survival time. In all cases the obtained labels might not be perfectly accurate and might still be different from the ground truth. Especially manual labels are not objective and can be observer dependent. Even when a clinical analysis is used, which might seem to give an objective label, different methods can lead to different labels [15,16]. In the case where the labels are obtained from a clinical procedure, one should therefore keep in mind the accuracy of this procedure. As these labels are taken as the ground truth, flaws in their accuracy will influence the performance and evaluation of the pipeline.

When collecting label data for patients, it is important to record when the label data was collected. In the case of a tissue analysis it is best to use imaging data that is as close as possible to the date of the tissue analysis, but before the actual analysis. This is important since the tissue characteristics could change between the imaging and analysis. If the labels are observed labels, the imaging data that is used should correspond with the imaging data that was used to determine the label.

18.2.5 Conclusion

The acquisition of high quality data to be used in the radiomics pipeline is a very important first step for a radiomics analysis. Without the foundation of a proper dataset, the pipeline will most likely not achieve a good performance, nor will it be possible to properly evaluate the pipeline, regardless of whether or not a model that can achieve good performance has actually been constructed. It is therefore important to do quality assurance, both during the data acquisition and once the dataset has been completely collected. If a method does not seem to work, it is also important to keep in mind that this could be due to the data, either because of quality or because the data that is being used might not have a relationship with what the pipeline is trying to predict.

18.3. Segmentation

18.3.1 Introduction

Segmentation is an important part of most medical imaging processing pipelines, which is also true for radiomics as it determines the region of interest (ROI) in the radiomics pipeline. In general, two types of segmentation can be distinguished. Firstly, an ROI that indicates a general region of interest for example the brain or the liver. Secondly, an ROI that indicates a specific part like a tumor or other disease within an organ. The first type can be used to perform image normalization or to determine the location of a disease with respect to the organ in which it is located. The second type is often used to determine the ROI from which features are extracted.

Since segmentation is used in a lot of different medical imaging processing pipelines, and many literature on the topic can be found, it will not be discussed in depth here. However, it is important to note some particular aspects of segmentation which are important in the radiomics pipeline. Therefore, we first provide a broad overview of segmentation methods in Sect. 18.3.2, after which the impact of the segmentation on the radiomics pipeline will be discussed in Sect. 18.3.3.

Note that while the majority of radiomics studies use segmentation, it is not a strict requirement. Features can also be extracted on the full image. Alternatively, approaches such as deep learning (see Sect. 18.5.4) may be able to determine the most salient regions without an explicit segmentation.

18.3.2 Segmentation methods

Segmentation methods can be split into three categories: manual, semiautomatic, and automatic. Each method has its own advantages and disadvantages.

Manual segmentation is usually performed by an expert: often a radiologist or a specialized clinician. This is usually done in a slice-by-slice manner, but is also possible in 3D, with the expert either encircling the ROI or annotating the voxels of interest. While an advantage of this segmentation method is that we can utilize expert knowledge, drawbacks of this method are that it is very time consuming and prone to intra and interobserver variability, as can be seen in Fig. 18.2. Thus, although manual segmentation is usually regarded as the golden standard, it often has a large variability, which can result in a large difference in the extracted radiomics values [17,18].

Semiautomatic segmentation tries to solve some of the problems related to manual segmentation. By assisting the segmentation with algorithms, for example, by growing the segmentation over a region or expanding the segmentation to other slices to eliminate the need for a slice-by-slice segmentation, the effort and time required from the user can be reduced. There are a lot of variations in semiautomatic methods, where some algorithms assist during (or even before) the segmentation, whereas others help with finalizing the segmentation. Furthermore, by providing an initial "objective"

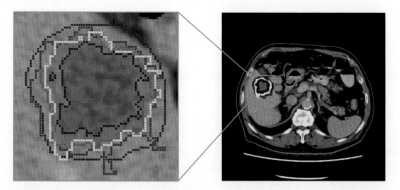

Figure 18.2 Manual segmentations of multiple observers of a colorectal liver metastasis on an axial slice of a CT scan.

segmentation, semi-automatic algorithms aim to reduce the inter- and intraobserver variability [17,19]. However, interobserver variability will still be present, as the manual part of the segmentation and the settings of the algorithm influence the result.

Automatic segmentation methods do not rely on user interaction, and can be split into two categories: learning and nonlearning based. Deep learning recently has become very popular as a learning-based method, where the segmentation is performed by a neural network that is trained with labeled examples. A popular deep learning approach is the U–Net architecture [20]. The advantage of this approach is that once the method has been constructed, the segmentations can be performed relatively quickly. Depending on the image, this can range from seconds to minutes, but it is usually much faster than when user interaction is required. The disadvantage of deep learning is that it usually requires a lot of labeled data to train an accurate model, as well as a long training time and specialized hardware (GPU) to construct the model. These methods are often trained on the segmentations from a single observer, meaning that the constructed model will have the same bias as the observer. Learning based approaches might not generalize well since an algorithm that has been trained on a specific dataset might perform very poorly on a different dataset. Furthermore, the segmentations that are used for the training data also still have to be done using a manual or semiautomatic method.

Nonlearning-based methods are usually application specific, where properties of the image and disease are used to perform the segmentation task [21]. Since these nonlearning-based methods are application specific, a completely different method has to be constructed when performing a different segmentation task.

An advantage of automatic segmentation methods is that they produce segmentations that are consistent and reproducible. This does not mean that the segmentation is accurate, but merely that if the same image is supplied to the algorithm multiple times it will always yield the same segmentation. As such, the errors that the method makes in the segmentation are systematic errors instead of incidental errors as in the case of manual or semiautomatic methods.

18.3.3 Influence of segmentation on radiomics pipeline

In a radiomics pipeline the segmentations themselves are usually not the end goal, but merely a means to the goal of classification. Therefore segmentations do not have to be perfect in terms of accuracy. It is more important that they capture the essential information that could be relevant for the subsequent radiomics analysis.

The effect of the segmentation on the radiomics pipeline depends on what the segmentation is used for: either for normalization of the image or for the extraction of features. If the segmentation is used for normalization, e.g., using a brain mask to normalize a brain MRI, an inaccuracy in the segmentation will have an effect on the features based on image intensity; see Sect. 18.4.2. A segmentation of an ROI can also be used to calculate, for example, a relative location, which will then also be impacted. Whether the influence of an inaccurate segmentation is large will depend on the magnitude of the inaccuracy, as well as whether this is a consistent inaccuracy or if it only occurs in a subset of the data.

On the other hand, there can be inaccuracies in the segmentation of the actual ROI of the organ from which the radiomics features are extracted [18]. If such a segmentation has an inaccuracy this will affect all features, instead of only the intensity based features. The segmentation that is used for feature extraction usually has a larger effect on the radiomics prediction than the segmentation that is used for normalization.

Segmentations can introduce both an over- and underestimation bias on the results of the pipeline. There is an overestimation bias if there is a bias in the segmentation towards one of the classes which is being predicted. It will then be easier to predict this class; however, if a different segmentation is given the results will not be as good. There is an underestimation bias if inaccuracies in the segmentation lead to variation of the features due to the segmentation and not just due to a difference in label. As a result, the radiomics pipeline will have difficulty differentiating the relevant from the irrelevant feature leading to a reduced performance.

18.3.4 Conclusion

Although segmentation is usually not the main goal of the radiomics pipeline, it is an important aspect to take into account in the pipeline. As has been discussed in this section, segmentation can influence the radiomics pipeline in different ways, resulting in a misrepresentation of the performance. Therefore it is important to be aware of these effects in the radiomics pipeline and measure the sensitivity of the pipeline to small changes in the segmentation. The robustness to these differences could be improved by, e.g., either creating a robust segmentation method or removing the need for segmentation altogether.

18.4. Features

18.4.1 Introduction

Originating from computer vision, a feature is any piece of information which can be relevant for solving the task at hand. In radiomics, features can be divided into two groups. The first group consists of computational or imaging features, which are extracted from the medical images in an automated way. The second group consists of semantic features, which are not computed, but manually annotated. Semantic features contain clinical factors which may be relevant for a radiomics signature. Examples include tumor statistics, genetic profiles, and the age of the patient. A specific combination of features, often selected for a certain application, is often referred to as a radiomics *signature*.

Due to the wide variety of image processing methods available, many computational features can be found in literature. This section will address the most commonly used radiomics features in Sect. 18.4.2, some of the more recently developed and therefore uncommon features in Sect. 18.4.3, common methods used for feature selection and dimensionality reduction in Sect. 18.4.5 and the process of extracting computational features in Sect. 18.4.4.

18.4.2 Common features

Several imaging features frequently occur in radiomics and are regarded as the basis of radiomics features [22]. Different divisions can be made. Many studies use the group of *morphological* features, which are used to describe the shape of an object. Another set of features can be computed on the intensity data, either using the image or a histogram of the image. These will be referred to as *first order* features, as they are based on first order representation of the image, i.e., the intensity.

Most of the remaining features are computed using filtering operations or higher order representations. Although these are often split in separate classes, these features are all used to detect specific patterns or *textures* in the image. We therefore group these features in a single class. These will be referred to as texture or *higher order* features, since the statistics used in these features are based on higher order representations of the image. This roughly follows the division as used in Zwanenburg et al. [13].

18.4.2.1 Morphological features

Morphological or shape features are used to describe the shape of an object. They are based solely on the ROI and do not require the underlying image intensity data. See Fig. 18.3 for some examples.

Many features compare the ROI with a template, e.g., a sphere in 3D or a circle in 2D. These comparisons are used to define, for example, the compactness, roughness, and convexity of an object [23].

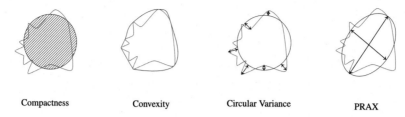

| Compactness | Convexity | Circular Variance | PRAX |

Figure 18.3 Four examples of morphological features.

18.4.2.2 First order features

First order features describe the distribution of gray levels or intensities in an image using statistical measures [24]. Most first order features resemble observations clinicians take into account as well, e.g., the mean and maximum intensity. Other statistics are more difficult to directly estimate from the image as an observer, such as the intensity skewness and kurtosis. These statistics potentially detect texture patterns, thus overlapping with the texture feature class.

First order features can either be computed directly from the image, or derived from the intensity histogram, i.e., after discretization of the gray levels in a number of bins. Through discretization, some information is lost. Some features may, however, be more robust to noise when derived from the histogram. For example, when the maximum intensity on the image is caused by noise, discretization may remove such an outlier. This trade-off between information loss and robustness is application dependent and may not be trivial.

18.4.2.3 Higher order features

Higher order features are used to detect specific patterns in images, such as stripes or blobs. A majority of the features require a transformation to another representation of the image, e.g., through filtering, after which statistics are extracted from the results. Although subgroups are originally aimed to detect specific patterns, the majority of texture feature classes are highly correlated.

Filter based

Filter-based features are constructed by computing statistical measures on a filtered version of the image. Most filters are defined in both 2D and 3D. Two filtering techniques commonly used for texture analysis in radiomics studies are the Gabor filter and the Laplacian of Gaussian (LoG) filter [24]. After the filtering operation, first order features can be extracted from the resulting image representation. The Gabor filter consists of a Gaussian convolved with a plane wave and is used to detect line patterns; see Fig. 18.4 for examples. The LoG filter is created by convolving the Laplacian operator with a Gaussian kernel and is used to detect blob patterns.

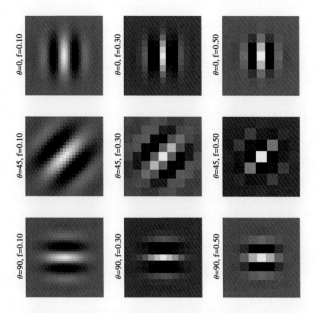

Figure 18.4 Gabor filters for various frequencies (*f*) and angles (*θ*).

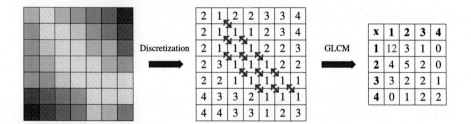

Figure 18.5 Examples of discretization of an image and GLCM construction.

Gray level matrix features

A gray level matrix is constructed from the intensity image by discretizing the image in a fixed number of levels; see Fig. 18.5. This is similar to the binning of the image when creating a histogram. Based on this matrix, different texture matrices can be constructed which describe the distribution of gray levels, of which the three most popular ones are discussed.

The Grey Level Cooccurrence Matrix (GLCM) expresses how frequent combinations of pixel intensities cooccur within a set distance in a specific direction; see Fig. 18.5. The Grey Level Run Length Matrix (GLRLM) describes the run length distribution in an image. A run length is defined as the length of a consecutive sequence of pixels or voxels with the same gray level along a specific direction. The GLRLM thereby closely correlates to the Gabor filter features in detecting stripe patterns. Lastly, the Grey Level Size Zone Matrix (GLSZM) expresses the distribution of connected components or zones of the same gray level in the image. Each gray level matrix has its own set of features that can be extracted from the matrix.

18.4.3 Uncommon features

The texture features mentioned above require relatively few computation steps and detect relatively simple patterns. These low level features have therefore successfully been used in many different radiomics approaches. However, new features are still being developed. These often target patterns specific to an application and consist of more advanced methods. Examples include the Co-occurrence of Local Anisotropic Gradient Orientations (CoLlAGe) feature, which is used to detect a form of heterogeneity in brain images [25], the RADIomic Spatial TexturAl descripTor (RADISTAT) feature, which is also used to describe heterogeneity but for multiple applications [26]. Additionally, image processing methods from other fields can be adopted to the radiomics field, such as Local Binary Patterns (LBPs) [27]. Hence the set of radiomics features keeps growing steadily.

18.4.4 Feature extraction

Although the mathematics of the mentioned features is widely agreed upon, extracting features is nontrivial. Most features require parameters to be set, for example, for scale and orientation. These parameters have to be tuned per application.

Additionally, several preprocessing steps are often involved before extracting the features; see Fig. 18.1. These can include a.o. discretization (e.g., for creating a histogram or gray level matrix), resampling and interpolation, normalization, and histogram matching. These operations are applied to reduce the influence of unwanted variations in the data due to for example scan protocol variations, as many features are not robust to these types of variation [28].

Lastly, the alterations in the ROI can heavily influence feature extraction as detailed in Sect. 18.3.3.

As stated earlier, all these (hyper)parameters have to be tuned per application either manually or by using optimization methods. An alternative specifically for features is to extract the features within a range of hyperparameter settings. Combining these features with some of the feature selection methods from Sect. 18.4.5 could be used to automatically identify relevant hyperparameter settings. Various machine learning methods from Sect. 18.5 are also able to identify which features and thereby hyperparameter settings are optimal. However, this procedure can become computationally expensive when a large search space for the hyperparameters is used.

18.4.5 Feature selection and dimensionality reduction

Due to the large amount of features used in a typical radiomics study, a form of selection or dimensionality reduction is often required in order to build reliable models [4]. Feature selection can be performed using simple ranking with statistical measures such as a t-test. Other methods perform a step-by-step approach of either including or excluding features, i.e., forward- or backward-selection, respectively, to estimate the added value of features. Lastly, correlation measures can be employed; see Sect. 18.5.2.

Contrary to selecting features, dimensionality reduction methods reduce the number of features by combining multiple features in new, more informative features. One of the most popular approaches for this is Principal Component Analysis (PCA), which transforms the feature space to components ranked based on the amount of variance they express in the dataset [29]. These components can be linear combinations of the original features, or nonlinear combinations by using a kernel method.

Note that several selection and dimensionality reduction approaches use the actual object labels. Hence these methods are *supervised* and should be trained and tested on independent datasets; see Sect. 18.6.

18.4.6 Conclusion

Radiomics studies show a large overlap in the computational features used, which have been described in this section. These features aim to describe various aspects of the ROI, such as the shape, intensity distribution, and texture patterns. However, variations in the feature computation between studies occur in feature extraction and selection methods, but also due to the preceding steps such as segmentation and preprocessing. Additionally, variations occur due to the choice of software as described in Sect. 18.7.3. Selecting the appropriate features extraction methods for a particular radiomics study therefore has to be done with care.

18.5. Data mining

18.5.1 Introduction

Several methods can be used to discover associations between the aforementioned quantitative image features and the clinical factors of interest. Earlier work tried to identify possible high-potential features by looking at the correlation matrix as described in Sect. 18.5.2. More recent radiomics work makes use of machine learning techniques as described in Sect. 18.5.3, which are often more advanced and are able to use a combination of features. Lastly, deep learning has shown a lot of potential in recent years in tasks similar to radiomics. Hence Sect. 18.5.4 will discuss how these fields relate to each other.

18.5.2 Correlation

A correlation matrix can be created by computing a correlation coefficient for each radiomics feature and the clinical factor of interest. Features with high potential are identified by thresholding the coefficient. A statistical test can be used to investigate the significance of the association between these single high potential features or a combination of them.

Methods vary in the statistical methods used for both calculating the correlation matrix as well as testing the significance of association. Examples of correlation co-efficients used include the inter- or intraclass correlation [8], Pearson and Spearman coefficients. Associations can be found with these coefficients, but also measures like the concordance index or a t-test [7] might be used. For example, Aerts et al. [4] make use of the χ^2-test to construct a correlation matrix, after which the concordance index is used to estimate the performance of several signatures comprising features with a high correlation index.

Correlation coefficients and statistical tests are well standardized, have relatively few parameters, and are relatively fast to compute. Finding the proper settings therefore often can be achieved by an exhaustive search. Note, however, that correlation measures are often restricted to univariate feature testing and lack the complexity to create higher order signatures.

18.5.3 Machine learning

An alternative to correlation measure is the use of machine learning. Several machine learning methods can provide multivariate testing and can fit more complex models, but suffer from their own drawbacks such as potential over-fitting and the need of parameter tuning. A wide variety of methods exist for both classification and regression problems. The optimal choice depends on the complexity of the problem at hand.

Less complex *estimators* (i.e., classification and regression methods) often model the outcome as linear combinations of features. Simple features, e.g., first order intensity features, generally provide too little information to determine significant relationships in a linear manner. These estimators are therefore more suited for complex features, e.g., higher order texture features. Examples include linear and logistic regression [5], linear determinant analysis [9], nearest neighbors, decision trees, naive Bayes estimators, and Gaussian processes.

Alternatively, Cox regression is a popular approach in regression problems, probably due to its wide use in clinical survival studies. These methods model the impact of each feature as a basis function, e.g., an exponential, modulated by a so-called *hazard* ratio. The hazard ratio is used to identify the impact of the feature on the outcome of interest. Cox regression is also a linear model.

More complex methods generally perform better in high-dimensional level feature spaces (i.e., more features than patients). Due to the often large number of radiomics features (see Sect. 18.4) and often relatively small datasets, methods generally will have to cope with high-dimensional features spaces. Popular choices therefore include Support Vector Machines (SVMs) [30] and Random Forests (RFs) [6]. Both SVMs and RFs fare relatively well in high-dimensional features spaces, are often less prone to over-fitting than the previously mentioned estimators, and can be both used for classification and regression. Additionally, the complexity of both classifiers can be tuned to the application.

Alternatively, the radiomics feature space can be mapped to a higher or lower dimensional feature space prior to employing machine learning; see Sect. 18.4.5. When mapping to a low-dimensional feature space, simple classifiers may work equally well as or even better than more complex ones.

18.5.4 Deep learning

One of the most recent approaches in the analysis of medical imaging is deep learning [31,32]. In contrast to traditional machine learning methods, deep learning does not require features as an input, but can directly learn features from the images and will optimize these for the task at hand. In the field of medical imaging, and radiomics specifically, deep learning has gained a lot of popularity in a short time as it eliminates the need for handcrafted features. Deep learning might also increase performance of the radiomics pipeline compared to traditional machine learning methods [33].

The most popular approach in deep learning for imaging is to use a Convolutional Neural Network (CNN). CNNs use convolutional filters that are trained to extract the features, while the last layer of this network is a fully connected layer to predict the final label. The popularity of CNNs started with AlexNet [34], but nowadays a lot more CNN architectures have become popular like Inception [35], VGGNet [36], and ResNet [37]. Although these architectures can often serve as a basis, performance improves when tailoring a network for a specific task.

Although CNNs have multiple advantages, there are also disadvantages. It takes a large amount of labeled data to train a CNN, especially to make it generalizable. Although CNNs should generalize well in theory when enough data is provided (and if there is enough heterogeneity in this data), in practice CNNs are still required to focus on a specific, small task. Training a CNN takes a lot of time, even when using specialized hardware. Whereas, for example, an SVM can be trained in a couple of minutes, training a CNN usually takes at least a couple of hours up to a few days even on specialized hardware. Furthermore, a huge restriction on CNNs, and in particular the hardware, is the limited memory capability, which still restricts the widespread use of 3D CNNs.

To try and alleviate the problem of the need for a large dataset, transfer learning has gained increasing popularity [32,38]. The idea behind transfer learning is to train a neural network with a dataset that is not (directly) related to the problem, and fine-tuning the network using the data that is related to the problem. In this way, a large dataset can be used to actually train the network, whereas only a small dataset is required for fine-tuning. The results of CNNs are more difficult to interpret, since it is not known which specific features are used by the CNN to make the prediction. However, recent advances like attention maps try to solve this issue [39].

The field of deep learning in general and also in radiomics is rapidly developing. The latest research focuses on combining deep learning with more traditional machine learning approaches [40], but new architectures and other approaches of doing deep learning are developed as well, for example, generative adversarial networks [41] and siamese networks [42].

18.5.5 Conclusion

Correlation, machine learning and deep learning can all be used to determine relationships between features and label data. The choice of method depends on the complexity of the task at hand, but is also a matter of user preference and the amount of available labeled data. The areas can also be combined and can potentially complement each other. As for each area a wide variety of methods exist, selecting the best approach for an application is not always trivial.

18.6. Study design

18.6.1 Introduction

Perhaps the most important part of a radiomics pipeline is a correct study design to test the performance of the pipeline.

In Sect. 18.6.2 the difference between the training, validation and evaluation set will be discussed, while Sect. 18.6.3 discusses how the different sets are obtained. This section concludes with an overview of different evaluation metrics in Sect. 18.6.4.

18.6.2 Training, validation and evaluation set

In this section a distinction between a training, validation, and evaluation (often also called a test) set will be made.

- A training set is a (sub)set of data that is used to train the pipeline.
- A validation set is a (sub)set of data that is used to optimize the parameters of the pipeline.
- An evaluation set is a (sub)set of data that is used to evaluate the performance of the pipeline.

The most important aspect here is that the three different sets are independent of each other, aside from the label distribution. Especially keeping the training/validation and evaluation sets independent is important, as a correlation in these sets could have a large impact on the performance evaluation. For example, if a pipeline is based on a slice-based approach, one cannot include slices from the same patient in the training, validation, and evaluation sets. The pipeline could then learn the features of the individual patients instead of learning a generalized representation of the dataset.

Often the training and validation set together are referred to as the training set, where no clear distinction is being made between which data is used for training and which data is used for parameter optimization. This is especially common in traditional machine learning approaches where the validation of hyperparameters is usually performed using a cross-validation.

18.6.3 Generating sets

There are two ways of generating the different (sub)sets of data to use as the training, validation, and evaluation sets. First of all, one can generate the sets by getting random subsets of the data from a larger data set – this process is known as cross-validation. Otherwise, a predefined separate set can be used as the evaluation set.

18.6.3.1 Cross-validation

Often in a radiomics pipeline, there is a single dataset with no clear distinction between different subsets. Cross-validation can then be used to generate random subsets from the data to be used as the different sets. Several methods of cross-validation exist [43].

One of the methods that is often used is K-fold cross-validation. In a K-fold cross-validation, the data is split in K parts, called folds, each of them containing N/K samples of the dataset, where N being the total size of the dataset. One can then iterate over the folds, usually taking 1-fold as the evaluation set. The remainder of the folds can then be used as the training and validation sets, where usually $(K - 2)$-fold are used for training and 1-fold for validation. However, the exact number of folds for each group can be freely selected, as long as samples from different folds are not mixed.

Another common method is leave-one-out, where one sample of the dataset is left out as the evaluation set. This is a specific instance of K-fold cross-validation with K being equal to N.

Another method frequently used is random sampling, where a certain number P of samples are randomly selected from the complete dataset to be used as the evaluation set and the remainder as the train/validation set. This process is then repeated a number of times to get different samples for the training, validation, and evaluation sets.

The main difference between the random sampling and K-fold sampling method is that with K-fold it is guaranteed that every sample will be in the different sets at least once (if iterated over all folds). On the contrary, due to the stochastic nature, in case of random sampling this is not guaranteed, however, when the number of iterations is large enough, a sample will on average occur an equal number of times in the different sets.

Both methods can be performed in a stratified way, meaning that the distribution of the samples from different classes will be the same in the different folds or in the training, validation, and evaluation sets. The advantage of using a stratified approach is that otherwise the results might be skewed because the training or evaluation of the method might then be biased towards a certain class.

18.6.3.2 Separate evaluation set

Besides generating training, validation, and evaluation sets from a single dataset, it is also possible to have a separate dataset that is used solely as an evaluation set, while using cross-validation to generate the training and validation sets. This approach is most suitable when there is a clear distinction between the datasets that would create a logical separation of the data. For example, if an open source data set is available or if data have been obtained from a different institute, this would make a logical evaluation set. Of course, the evaluation set that is being used needs to be representative for the dataset that is used for training and validation. In this case, it is very important to keep the evaluation set purely as an evaluation set and not to use it as a validation set as well. This means that the separate evaluation set can only be used once the whole radiomics pipeline has been constructed and trained, and nothing will be changed with the introduction of the evaluation set. This also includes, for example, normalization, which cannot be done on a group basis if the evaluation is already included in the group, and the optimization of hyperparameters. The advantage of using a separate evaluation set over cross-validation methods is that in this way a typical performance in a new setting can be evaluated.

18.6.4 Evaluation metrics

A correct study design also involves the choice of appropriate metrics to evaluate the pipeline. Often, the first choice for an evaluation metric is accuracy, which is reported in almost every study. However, accuracy is in most of the cases an inappropriate measure. Whenever there is a class imbalance in the evaluation data, accuracy will always give a skewed view of the performance. For example, imagine a dataset where there are 90 samples of class 1 and 10 samples of class 2. When the algorithm then predicts class 1 for all samples, it has an accuracy of 90%, while the performance is clearly of no value.

Some metrics that alleviate this problem are the sensitivity and specificity, which report the accuracy within a single class. However, often the total performance of the pipeline over all classes is important. In that case two metrics that can be used are the area under the receiver operating characteristic curve and the F1-score.

The receiver operating characteristic (ROC) curve shows the True Positive Rate (TPR) (the sensitivity) vs the False Positive Rate (FPR) (1 − the specificity) for various thresholds of the classifier [44]. The Area Under Curve (AUC) is the area under the ROC curve, which can vary between 0 and 1, with 0.5 being equal to random guessing.

When reporting the AUC it is helpful to show the corresponding ROC as well, since although two curves can have the same AUC they can have a very different shape. Finally, the F1-score, the harmonic mean of precision and recall (sensitivity), and average precision are other metrics which are robust against imbalanced datasets. An overview of all these measures and their exact definitions can be found in [45].

18.6.4.1 Confidence intervals

Reporting metrics on a single evaluation set can be very misleading, especially when a cross-validation approach is used. If cross-validation is used and performance on only one evaluation set is shown, this still gives no clear indication of the performance of the pipeline. The current split of training and evaluation set might be ideal or nonideal and result in a high or low score. Furthermore, there is no clear reason as to why a specific train/evaluation split would be chosen to be presented in the results. The results will also not be easily reproducible, as a different split will lead to different results. In the case of metrics like the accuracy and AUC a better option is to use a confidence interval. Often the 95% confidence interval is chosen to be reported. When plotting the ROC it is also helpful to plot the confidence "bands" along with the curve [46].

When reporting the confidence interval it is important to keep in mind that the confidence intervals need to be adjusted because of the cross-validation that is being applied. More details about this confidence interval correction can be found in [47].

18.6.4.2 Conclusion

Measuring the performance of a radiomics pipeline is the last step in the construction of the pipeline, and is often the result that one is interested in. Depending on the performance, changes to the pipeline may be made to achieve better results. As discussed in this section, it is important to use a proper study design and select the appropriate measure to analyze the performance of the pipeline. Especially when presenting the results of a pipeline this is important as otherwise a fair comparison between methods cannot be made. When evaluating a published pipeline it is also important be aware of these pitfalls, and to be aware that the presented and the actual performance of the pipeline might differ.

18.7. Infrastructure

18.7.1 Introduction

In the previous chapters, a theoretical basis for radiomics pipelines has been presented. Implementation and execution of such a pipeline requires appropriate hardware for storage of the data and results and software for the execution. Due to the rise of popularity of radiomics in recent years, several research groups have created their own toolkits.

Therefore, a wide variety of feature toolboxes, storage solutions, segmentation and classification software packages have been created. Although all packages do use the same theoretical basis, variations in outcomes occur due to implementation differences.

The standardization of infrastructures is not studied much. A majority of the radiomics related papers do not mention the toolboxes used and do not release the used code publicly. Additionally, the settings of a toolbox such as initialization, approximation, and discretization methods are hardly mentioned. Hence, replication of the results, comparison with other methods, and applying existing methods to new areas is complicated. Recently, there has been some attention to standardization of biomarkers [13], providing a solid theoretical basis for many radiomics features. Similar initiatives for radiomics infrastructures could provide a valuable asset for the research field.

The impact of software variations and the current status of software will be discussed in this chapter. It covers data storage and sharing solutions in Sect. 18.7.2, feature toolboxes in Sect. 18.7.3, learning toolboxes in Sect. 18.7.4, and standardization of radiomics pipelines in Sect. 18.7.5. Segmentation software will not be discussed, as this area is already widely covered in (nonradiomics) related works.

18.7.2 Data storage and sharing

A lot of data and data types are involved in radiomics. Usually data is stored on a local hard drive, and experiments are run using the data from there. However, in this way it is easy to mix up data for different subjects, to lose data, or to lose overview of the data. Furthermore, there is no easy way of sharing the data and restricting access to the data.

XNAT is a (medical) imaging platform that can store imaging data in a standardized way [48]. On XNAT, imaging and clinical data can be stored together, and are easily accessible through either the web interface or the API. If during the analysis of the data something goes wrong, it is then easy to go back to the original data on XNAT, and data cannot be easily mixed up. Furthermore, because the data is stored on XNAT in a standardized way, it is easy to run experiments, also for others.

Apart from imaging data, there is usually a lot of clinical data collected as well. Although XNAT is able to store nonimaging data, this is not its strong point, and often other tools are used in combination with XNAT, for example, OpenClinica, which is a tool for clinical data management [49]. It allows for the tracking of a patient, and association of clinical data with different visit moments.

Another platform that can store images and clinical data is ePad [50]. Not only does it allow for the storage of medical images, it intends to collect quantitative imaging features, which are often extracted in radiomics.

Although no single solution might be the best, it is clear that using a data platform has advantages over using data stored locally on a hard disk. Having a more standardized approach to collect and store data, on whatever specific platform, will most likely prevent a lot of problems in the development of the radiomics pipeline. Furthermore, by making data access easier, radiomics research is also able to expand faster.

18.7.3 Feature toolboxes

Features can be seen as the core part of radiomics, which could explain the wide variety of toolboxes available. These toolboxes differ among others in software language, the features they implement, the preprocessing applied, and the routines to compute features. As these variations influence the final result, it is important to select the correct toolbox for each application.

Court et al. [51] mention five different toolboxes for radiomics, each having their own specific advantages and drawbacks. One of these is IBEX [52], a MATLAB[1] and C/C++ based platform. Although mainly a feature toolbox, it also has capabilities for displaying images and their corresponding features, as well as several preprocessing and feature selection methods. One of the more recently developed and popular toolboxes is PyRadiomics [53], a Python based platform. PyRadiomics includes most of the features mentioned in Sect. 18.4.2, including several filters that can be applied to the image. However, PyRadiomics is solely a feature extraction toolbox, thus it does not provide any segmentation or learning solutions. Another major player is CaPTk [54], which was originally developed for the quantitative analysis of brain tumors. CaPTk is based on the Insight ToolKit (ITK), Visualization ToolKit (VTK), and OpenCV. It includes feature extraction, feature selection, but also segmentation and preprocessing, including visualization options. Lastly, PREDICT [55] is a feature toolbox that additionally provides preprocessing, feature selection, and several machine learning capabilities through scikit-learn; see also Sect. 18.7.4.

Although these platforms all use the same basis of radiomics, there are many differences. There is a large overlap in features, but each platform has a different set of features that can be extracted. Each platform additionally is combined with different segmentation and preprocessing methods. Moreover, the different back-ends (e.g., MATLAB, Python, and OpenCV) may cause further variations in outcome. As there is not yet a computational standard in radiomics, it is difficult to assess which feature toolbox would therefore be most suitable for a specific application.

The platforms also share some similar drawbacks. There are a lot of possibilities provided in terms of configurations, but there is often no best setting or optimization process. Users will have to tune the parameters and settings themselves for each application. Radiomics often involves high throughput batch-processing of numerous images. Some of these toolboxes can be wrapped in command line executables, which has to be done by the user. Others only provide graphical user interfaces through which each image has to be processed manually.

---

[1] MATLAB® is a trademark of The MathWorks.

18.7.4 Learning toolboxes

As the area of machine learning is much older than radiomics, the software solutions are better organized. In `Python`, the main machine learning toolbox is `scikit-learn`, which incorporates many classification and regressions methods, along with useful methods such as dimensionality reduction and model selection. `MATLAB` has the native Statistics and Machine Learning Toolbox. Both are mainly based on `C/C++` implementations such as `libsvm` [56].

For deep learning, the community is more scattered. Most toolboxes are based on `NVIDIA's` `CUDA` and are `Python` based, although `MATLAB` has the native Neural Network Toolbox. One of the first widely used toolboxes is `Theano` [57]. However, as `Theano` will not be supported in the future, a popular alternative is `Google's` `Tensorflow` [58], which is used in the `Keras` [59] (which can also use `Theano`) and `NiftyNet` [60] toolboxes. `NiftyNet` is especially designed to incorporate networks targeted for the use in medical imaging. `Facebook` has launched an alternative to `Tensorflow` in the form of `PyTorch` [61]. Lastly, `Caffe` [62] is another alternative, which is not `Python` or `MATLAB` based, but rather a toolbox on its own.

At the moment, there is no single toolbox that stands out. As most frameworks are under active development, specifications change frequently.

18.7.5 Pipeline standardization

As discussed in this chapter and illustrated in Fig. 18.1, a radiomics pipeline consists of four major steps: preprocessing, segmentation, feature extraction, and data mining. In the previous sections, several theoretical and methodological issues have been addressed. When executing a radiomics study, these steps have to be combined in a single pipeline. As stated earlier, the choice of software used, e.g., the feature toolbox, can have a major influence on the outcome. Additionally, the ordering of all required processing steps has an influence on the results. Thus, standardization of software pipelines in radiomics is important for correct reporting and comparison of results.

The problem is twofold. On the one hand, there is a lack of complete radiomics pipeline solution. On the other hand, there is a lack of standardization. As seen in the previous subsections, toolboxes typically only implement a single step of the radiomics pipeline instead of the full process. Exceptions are `CaPTk`, which does provide all steps except the learning part, and `PREDICT`, which provides all parts but not a standardized pipeline. Hence, it is difficult to interpret and compare results. For example, all feature toolboxes mentioned might call a feature "entropy" and assign it a certain value. This label does not actually tell how this value was computed, e.g., which preprocessing was used or which routine to compute an histogram.

Hence, it is difficult to assess which methods are most suitable for an application. `WORC` [63] is an initiative that standardizes the radiomics pipeline based on `fastr` [64] using mainly the `PREDICT` toolbox. Such initiatives could help in the comparison of results and the search for the optimal radiomics solution.

18.7.6 Conclusion

For each step in the radiomics pipeline, a wide variety of software solutions exist. Each toolkit has its own advantages and drawbacks, some of these hidden in internal operations of the language the package is based on. Hence, comparison of results and methods, as well as the use of existing methods on new applications is difficult. Initiatives for standardization of the radiomics pipeline do exist, but in most applications, the construction of the pipeline and tuning of the settings still has to be manually done by the user.

18.8. Conclusion

Recent advances in the machine learning field, as well as the wider and easier availability of medical imaging data and associated clinical labels, have accelerated the popularity of the radiomics field. A lot of promising studies have already been carried out, and the research field is rapidly expanding.

In this chapter the components of a radiomics pipeline and their impact on the performance of the pipeline have been discussed. Different elements from medical image analysis come together in the pipeline, and as such bring together a lot of the complexities from the different elements. Although there are many pitfalls, most of them can easily be avoided and radiomics could be a powerful tool for the clinic.

The next steps of radiomics will lie in the translation from research to clinical application. Even though studies have shown promising results, the conversion to clinical usage has still been limited. The field of radiomics faces various challenges, such as the standardization of both the theoretical components and their implementations. Moreover, while many methods show promising results on a specific application, generalization of these methods is rarely studied. Lastly, robustness to changes in the imaging and segmentation protocol appear mandatory for successful conversion to the clinic.

Radiomics still holds a lot of promises for the future. Currently, most studies focus on a single aspect of a bigger clinical process, however, ultimately radiomics can also focus on the complete process. In this case, the pipeline will not focus on predicting a specific subclass or genetics of a disease, but can, for example, predict survival or suggest which treatment option might work best for a patient. This will probably require additional clinical data, but can ultimately have a bigger impact.

Another point of future interest is the continuous inclusion of data. When constructing a radiomics pipeline usually a fixed dataset is used, but in practice during or after the construction of the pipeline new patients will come in which could also be included. Instead of then constructing the pipeline from scratch again, which takes time and resources, updating the pipeline with the new information would be a better approach. This requires a different approach, both on the machine learning side to select the appropriate algorithms and the study design side to ensure that the performance does not decrease when including new data.

All in all, the field of radiomics is a quickly expanding and promising field, with multiple opportunities to be clinically impactful.

Acknowledgment

Martijn Starmans and Jose Tovar acknowledge the research program STRaTeGy with project numbers 14929, 14930 and 14931, which is (partly) financed by the Netherlands Organisation for Scientific Research (NWO). Sebastian van der Voort acknowledges funding from the Dutch Cancer Society (KWF project number EMCR 2015-7859). We want to thank Karin van Garderen and Maria Garcia Sanz for proofreading the chapter.

References

[1] Eran Segal, Claude B. Sirlin, Clara Ooi, Adam S. Adler, Jeremy Gollub, Xin Chen, Bryan K. Chan, George R. Matcuk, Christopher T. Barry, Howard Y. Chang, Michael D. Kuo, Decoding global gene expression programs in liver cancer by noninvasive imaging, Nature Biotechnology (ISSN 1087-0156) 25 (6) (June 2007) 675–680, https://doi.org/10.1038/nbt1306.

[2] Kenneth A. Miles, Balaji Ganeshan, Matthew R. Griffiths, Rupert C.D. Young, Christopher R. Chatwin, Colorectal cancer: texture analysis of portal phase hepatic CT images as a potential marker of survival, Radiology 250 (2) (2009) 444–452.

[3] Philippe Lambin, Emmanuel Rios-Velazquez, Ralph Leijenaar, Sara Carvalho Ruud, G.P.M. van Stiphout, Patrick Granton, Catharina M.L. Zegers, Robert Gillies, Ronald Boellard, André Dekker, Hugo J.W.L. Aerts, Radiomics: extracting more information from medical images using advanced feature analysis, European Journal of Cancer (ISSN 0959-8049) 48 (4) (March 2012) 441–446, https://doi.org/10.1016/j.ejca.2011.11.036.

[4] Hugo J.W.L. Aerts, Emmanuel Rios Velazquez, Ralph T.H. Leijenaar, Chintan Parmar, Patrick Grossmann, Sara Cavalho, Johan Bussink, René Monshouwer, Benjamin Haibe-Kains, Derek Rietveld, Frank Hoebers, Michelle M. Rietbergen, C. René Leemans, Andre Dekker, John Quackenbush, Robert J. Gillies, Philippe Lambin, Decoding tumour phenotype by noninvasive imaging using a quantitative radiomics approach, Nature Communications (ISSN 2041-1723) 5 (June 2014), https://doi.org/10.1038/ncomms5006.

[5] Sheng-Xiang Rao, Doenja M.J. Lambregts, Roald S. Schnerr, Rianne C.J. Beckers, Monique Maas, Fabrizio Albarello, Robert G. Riedl, Cornelis H.C. Dejong, Milou H. Martens, Luc A. Heijnen, Walter H. Backes, Geerard L. Beets, Meng-Su Zeng, Regina G.H. Beets-Tan, CT texture analysis in colorectal liver metastases: a better way than size and volume measurements to assess response to chemotherapy? United European Gastroenterology Journal (ISSN 2050-6406) 4 (2) (Apr. 2016) 257–263, https://doi.org/10.1177/2050640615601603, ISSN 2050-6414.

[6] Hao Zhou, Martin Vallières, Harrison X. Bai, Chang Su, Haiyun Tang, Derek Oldridge, Zishu Zhang, Bo Xiao, Weihua Liao, Yongguang Tao, Jianhua Zhou, Paul Zhang, Li Yang, MRI features predict survival and molecular markers in diffuse lower-grade gliomas, Neuro-Oncology (ISSN 1522-8517) 19 (6) (June 2017) 862–870, https://doi.org/10.1093/neuonc/now256, ISSN 1523-5866.

[7] Christoph A. Karlo, Pier Luigi Di Paolo, Joshua Chaim, A. Ari Hakimi, Irina Ostrovnaya, Paul Russo, Hedvig Hricak, Robert Motzer, James J. Hsieh, Oguz Akin, Radiogenomics of clear cell renal cell carcinoma: associations between CT imaging features and mutations, Radiology 270 (2) (2014) 464–471.

[8] Lijun Lu, Wenbing Lv, Jun Jiang, Jianhua Ma, Qianjin Feng, Arman Rahmim, Wufan Chen, Robustness of radiomic features in [^{11}c]Choline and [^{18}f]FDG PET/CT imaging of nasopharyngeal carcinoma: impact of segmentation and discretization, Molecular Imaging and Biology (ISSN 1536-1632) 18 (6) (Dec. 2016) 935–945, https://doi.org/10.1007/s11307-016-0973-6, ISSN 1860-2002.

[9] Rebecca E. Thornhill, Mohammad Golfam, Adnan Sheikh, Greg O. Cron, Eric A. White, Joel Werier, Mark E. Schweitzer, Gina Di Primio, Differentiation of lipoma from liposarcoma on MRI using texture and shape analysis, Academic Radiology (ISSN 1076-6332) 21 (9) (Sept. 2014) 1185–1194, https://doi.org/10.1016/j.acra.2014.04.005.

[10] Sheng-Xiang Rao, Doenja M.J. Lambregts, Roald S. Schnerr, Wenzel van Ommen, Thiemo J.A. van Nijnatten, Milou H. Martens, Luc A. Heijnen, Walter H. Backes, Cornelis Verhoef, Meng-Su Zeng, Geerard L. Beets, Regina G.H. Beets-Tan, Whole-liver CT texture analysis in colorectal cancer: does the presence of liver metastases affect the texture of the remaining liver? United European Gastroenterology Journal (ISSN 2050-6406) 2 (6) (Dec. 2014) 530–538, https://doi.org/10.1177/2050640614552463, ISSN 2050-6414.

[11] James P.B. O'Connor, Eric O. Aboagye, Judith E. Adams, Hugo J.W.L. Aerts, Sally F. Barrington, Ambros J. Beer, Ronald Boellaard, Sarah E. Bohndiek, Michael Brady, Gina Brown, David L. Buckley, Thomas L. Chenevert, Laurence P. Clarke, Sandra Collette, Gary J. Cook, Nandita M. deSouza, John C. Dickson, Caroline Dive, Jeffrey L. Evelhoch, Corinne Faivre-Finn, Ferdia A. Gallagher, Fiona J. Gilbert, Robert J. Gillies, Vicky Goh, John R. Griffiths, Ashley M. Groves, Steve Halligan, Adrian L. Harris, David J. Hawkes, Otto S. Hoekstra, Erich P. Huang, Brian F. Hutton, Edward F. Jackson, Gordon C. Jayson, Andrew Jones, Dow-Mu Koh, Denis Lacombe, Philippe Lambin, Nathalie Lassau, Martin O. Leach, Ting-Yim Lee, Edward L. Leen, Jason S. Lewis, Yan Liu, Mark F. Lythgoe, Prakash Manoharan, Ross J. Maxwell, Kenneth A. Miles, Bruno Morgan, Steve Morris, Tony Ng, Anwar R. Padhani, Geoff J.M. Parker, Mike Partridge, Arvind P. Pathak, Andrew C. Peet, Shonit Punwani, Andrew R. Reynolds, Simon P. Robinson, Lalitha K. Shankar, Ricky A. Sharma, Dmitry Soloviev, Sigrid Stroobants, Daniel C. Sullivan, Stuart A. Taylor, Paul S. Tofts, Gillian M. Tozer, Marcel van Herk, Simon Walker-Samuel, James Wason, Kaye J. Williams, Paul Workman, Thomas E. Yankeelov, Kevin M. Brindle, Lisa M. McShane, Alan Jackson, John C. Waterton, Imaging biomarker roadmap for cancer studies, Nature Reviews Clinical Oncology (ISSN 1759-4774) 14 (3) (Oct. 2016) 169–186, https://doi.org/10.1038/nrclinonc.2016.162, ISSN 1759-4782.

[12] Stephen S.F. Yip, Hugo J.W.L. Aerts, Applications and limitations of radiomics, Physics in Medicine and Biology (ISSN 0031-9155) 61 (13) (July 2016) R150–R166, https://doi.org/10.1088/0031-9155/61/13/R150, ISSN 1361-6560.

[13] Alex Zwanenburg, Stefan Leger, Martin Vallières, Steffen Löck, Image Biomarker Standardisation Initiative, Image biomarker standardisation initiative, arXiv:1612.07003 [cs], Dec. 2016.

[14] Robert J. Gillies, Paul E. Kinahan, Hedvig Hricak, Radiomics: images are more than pictures, they are data, Radiology (ISSN 0033-8419) 278 (2) (Feb. 2016) 563–577, https://doi.org/10.1148/radiol.2015151169, ISSN 1527-1315.

[15] H. Broholm, P.W. Born, D. Guterbaum, H. Dyrbye, H. Laursen, Detecting chromosomal alterations at 1p and 19q by fish and DNA fragment analysis – a comparative study in human gliomas, Clinical Neuropathology 27 (6) (2008) 378–387.

[16] Carmen Franco-Hernández, Victor Martínez-Glez, Jose M. de Campos, Alberto Isla, Jesús Vaquero, Manuel Gutiérrez, Cacilda Casartelli, Juan A. Rey, Allelic status of 1p and 19q in oligodendrogliomas and glioblastomas: multiplex ligation-dependent probe amplification versus loss of heterozygosity, Cancer Genetics and Cytogenetics 190 (2) (2009) 93–96.

[17] Tobias Heye, Elmar M. Merkle, Caecilia S. Reiner, Matthew S. Davenport, Jeffrey J. Horvath, Sebastian Feuerlein, Steven R. Breault, Peter Gall, Mustafa R. Bashir, Brian M. Dale, et al., Reproducibility of dynamic contrast-enhanced MR imaging. Part II. Comparison of intra- and interobserver variability with manual region of interest placement versus semiautomatic lesion segmentation and histogram analysis, Radiology 266 (3) (2013) 812–821.

[18] Chintan Parmar, Emmanuel Rios Velazquez, Ralph Leijenaar, Mohammed Jermoumi, Sara Carvalho, Raymond H. Mak, Sushmita Mitra, B. Uma Shankar, Ron Kikinis, Benjamin Haibe-Kains, et al., Robust radiomics feature quantification using semiautomatic volumetric segmentation, PLoS ONE 9 (7) (2014) e102107.

[19] Paul A. Yushkevich, Joseph Piven, Heather Cody Hazlett, Rachel Gimpel Smith, Sean Ho, James C. Gee, Guido Gerig, User-guided 3D active contour segmentation of anatomical structures: significantly improved efficiency and reliability, NeuroImage 31 (3) (2006) 1116–1128.

[20] Olaf Ronneberger, Philipp Fischer, Thomas Brox, U-net: convolutional networks for biomedical image segmentation, in: International Conference on Medical Image Computing and Computer-Assisted Intervention, Springer, 2015, pp. 234–241.

[21] D. Louis Collins, Colin J. Holmes, Terrence M. Peters, Alan C. Evans, Automatic 3D model-based neuroanatomical segmentation, Human Brain Mapping 3 (3) (1995) 190–208.

[22] Vishwa Parekh, Michael A. Jacobs, Radiomics: a new application from established techniques, Expert Review of Precision Medicine and Drug Development (ISSN 2380-8993) 1 (2) (2016) 207–226, https://doi.org/10.1080/23808993.2016.1164013.

[23] Markus Peura, Jukka Iivarinen, Efficiency of simple shape descriptors, in: Proceedings of the Third International Workshop on Visual Form, 1997, pp. 443–451.

[24] Rafael C. Gonzalez, Richard E. Woods, Digital Image Processing, 3rd edition, Prentice-Hall, Inc., Upper Saddle River, NJ, USA, ISBN 013168728X, 2006.

[25] Prateek Prasanna, Pallavi Tiwari, Anant Madabhushi, Co-occurrence of Local Anisotropic Gradient Orientations (CoLlAGe): a new radiomics descriptor, Scientific Reports (ISSN 2045-2322) 6 (2016), https://doi.org/10.1038/srep37241.

[26] Maxime Descoteaux, Lena Maier-Hein, Alfred Franz, Pierre Jannin, D. Louis Collins, Simon Duchesne (Eds.), Medical Image Computing and Computer-Assisted Intervention – MICCAI 2017, Lecture Notes in Computer Science, vol. 10434, Springer International Publishing, Cham, ISBN 978-3-319-66184-1, 2017, ISBN 978-3-319-66185-8.

[27] Timo Ojala, Matti Pietikainen, Topi Maenpaa, Multiresolution gray-scale and rotation invariant texture classification with local binary patterns, IEEE Transactions on Pattern Analysis and Machine Intelligence 24 (7) (2002) 971–987.

[28] Binsheng Zhao, Yongqiang Tan, Wei-Yann Tsai, Jing Qi, Chuanmiao Xie, Lin Lu, Lawrence H. Schwartz, Reproducibility of radiomics for deciphering tumor phenotype with imaging, Scientific Reports (ISSN 2045-2322) 6 (Mar. 2016), https://doi.org/10.1038/srep23428.

[29] Ian Jolliffe, Principal Component Analysis, Springer, 2011.

[30] Corinna Cortes, Vladimir Vapnik, Support-vector networks, Machine Learning 20 (3) (1995) 273–297.

[31] Hayit Greenspan, Bram van Ginneken, Ronald M. Summers, Guest editorial deep learning in medical imaging: overview and future promise of an exciting new technique, IEEE Transactions on Medical Imaging 35 (5) (2016) 1153–1159.

[32] Hoo-Chang Shin, Holger R. Roth, Mingchen Gao Le Lu, Ziyue Xu, Isabella Nogues, Jianhua Yao, Daniel Mollura, Ronald M. Summers, Deep convolutional neural networks for computer-aided detection: CNN architectures, dataset characteristics and transfer learning, IEEE Transactions on Medical Imaging 35 (5) (2016) 1285–1298.

[33] June-Goo Lee, Sanghoon Jun, Young-Won Cho, Hyunna Lee, Guk Bae Kim, Joon Beom Seo, Namkug Kim, Deep learning in medical imaging: general overview, Korean Journal of Radiology 18 (4) (2017) 570–584.

[34] Alex Krizhevsky, Ilya Sutskever, Geoffrey E. Hinton, ImageNet classification with deep convolutional neural networks, in: Advances in Neural Information Processing Systems, 2012, pp. 1097–1105.

[35] Christian Szegedy, Sergey Ioffe, Vincent Vanhoucke, Alexander A. Alemi, Inception-v4, Inception-ResNet and the impact of residual connections on learning, in: AAAI, vol. 4, 2017, p. 12.

[36] Karen Simonyan, Andrew Zisserman, Very deep convolutional networks for large-scale image recognition, preprint, arXiv:1409.1556, 2014.

[37] Kaiming He, Xiangyu Zhang, Shaoqing Ren, Jian Sun, Deep residual learning for image recognition, in: Proceedings of the IEEE Conference on Computer Vision and Pattern Recognition, 2016, pp. 770–778.

[38] Annegreet Van Opbroek, M. Arfan Ikram, Meike W. Vernooij, Marleen De Bruijne, Transfer learning improves supervised image segmentation across imaging protocols, IEEE Transactions on Medical Imaging 34 (5) (2015) 1018–1030.

[39] Bolei Zhou, Aditya Khosla, Agata Lapedriza, Aude Oliva, Antonio Torralba, Learning deep features for discriminative localization, in: 2016 IEEE Conference on Computer Vision and Pattern Recognition, CVPR, IEEE, 2016, pp. 2921–2929.

[40] Yi Sun, Xiaogang Wang, Xiaoou Tang, Hybrid deep learning for face verification, in: 2013 IEEE International Conference on Computer Vision, ICCV, IEEE, 2013, pp. 1489–1496.

[41] Ian Goodfellow, Jean Pouget-Abadie Mehdi Mirza, Bing Xu, David Warde-Farley, Sherjil Ozair, Aaron Courville, Yoshua Bengio, Generative adversarial nets, in: Advances in Neural Information Processing Systems, 2014, pp. 2672–2680.

[42] Luca Bertinetto, Jack Valmadre, Joao F. Henriques, Andrea Vedaldi, H.S. Philip Torr, Fully-convolutional siamese networks for object tracking, in: European Conference on Computer Vision, Springer, 2016, pp. 850–865.

[43] Ron Kohavi, et al., A study of cross-validation and bootstrap for accuracy estimation and model selection, in: IJCAI, vol. 14, Montreal, Canada, 1995, pp. 1137–1145.

[44] Tom Fawcett, An introduction to ROC analysis, Pattern Recognition Letters 27 (8) (2006) 861–874.

[45] Marina Sokolova, Nathalie Japkowicz, Stan Szpakowicz, Beyond accuracy, F-score and ROC: a family of discriminant measures for performance evaluation, in: Australasian Joint Conference on Artificial Intelligence, Springer, 2006, pp. 1015–1021.

[46] Sofus A. Macskassy, Foster Provost, Saharon Rosset, ROC confidence bands: an empirical evaluation, in: Proceedings of the 22nd International Conference on Machine Learning, ACM, 2005, pp. 537–544.

[47] Claude Nadeau, Yoshua Bengio, Inference for the generalization error, Machine Learning 3 (52) (2003) 239–281.

[48] Daniel S. Marcus, Timothy R. Olsen, Mohana Ramaratnam, Randy L. Buckner, The extensible neuroimaging archive toolkit, Neuroinformatics 5 (1) (2007) 11–33.

[49] Marinel Cavelaars, Jacob Rousseau, Cuneyt Parlayan, Sander de Ridder, Annemarie Verburg, Ruud Ross, Gerben Rienk Visser, Annelies Rotte, Rita Azevedo, Jan-Willem Boiten, et al., Openclinica, Journal of Clinical Bioinformatics 5 (2015) S2.

[50] Dilvan A. Moreira, Cleber Hage, Edson F. Luque, Debra Willrett, Daniel L. Rubin, 3D markup of radiological images in ePAD, a web-based image annotation tool, in: 2015 IEEE 28th International Symposium on Computer-Based Medical Systems, CBMS, IEEE, 2015, pp. 97–102.

[51] Laurence E. Court, Xenia Fave, Dennis Mackin, Joonsang Lee, Jinzhong Yang, Lifei Zhang, Computational resources for radiomics, Translational Cancer Research (ISSN 2218-676X) 5 (4) (August 2016) 340–348, https://doi.org/10.21037/tcr.2016.06.17, ISSN 2219-6803.

[52] Lifei Zhang, David V. Fried, Xenia J. Fave, Luke A. Hunter, Jinzhong Yang, Laurence E. Court, IBEX: an open infrastructure software platform to facilitate collaborative work in radiomics, Medical Physics 42 (3) (2015) 1341–1353.

[53] Joost J.M. van Griethuysen, Andriy Fedorov, Chintan Parmar, Ahmed Hosny, Nicole Aucoin, Vivek Narayan, Regina G.H. Beets-Tan, Jean-Christophe Fillion-Robin, Steve Pieper, Hugo J.W.L. Aerts, Computational radiomics system to decode the radiographic phenotype, Cancer Research (ISSN 0008-5472) 77 (21) (Nov. 2017) e104–e107, https://doi.org/10.1158/0008-5472.CAN-17-0339, ISSN 1538-7445.

[54] Saima Rathore, Spyridon Bakas, Sarthak Pati, Hamed Akbari, Ratheesh Kalarot, Patmaa Sridharan, Martin Rozycki, Mark Bergman, Birkan Tunc, Ragini Verma, Michel Bilello, Christos Davatzikos, Brain cancer imaging phenomics toolkit (brain-CaPTk): an interactive platform for quantitative analysis of glioblastoma, Brainlesion (2017) 10670 (2018) 133–145, https://doi.org/10.1007/978-3-319-75238-9_12.

[55] Sebastian R. van der Voort, Martijn P.A. Starmans, PREDICT: a radiomics extensive differentiable interchangeable classification toolkit, URL https://github.com/Svdvoort/PREDICTFastr, Feb. 2018, original-date: 2017-05-24 T14:03:08Z.

[56] LIBSVM – a library for support vector machines, URL https://www.csie.ntu.edu.tw/~cjlin/libsvm/.

[57] James Bergstra, Olivier Breuleux, Pascal Lamblin, Razvan Pascanu, Olivier Delalleau, Guillaume Desjardins, Ian Goodfellow, Arnaud Bergeron, Yoshua Bengio, Pack Kaelbling, Theano: Deep Learning on GPUs with Python.

[58] Martín Abadi, Ashish Agarwal, Paul Barham, Eugene Brevdo, Zhifeng Chen, Craig Citro, Greg S. Corrado, Andy Davis, Jeffrey Dean, Matthieu Devin, Sanjay Ghemawat, Ian Goodfellow, Andrew Harp, Geoffrey Irving, Michael Isard, Yangqing Jia, Rafal Jozefowicz, Lukasz Kaiser, Manjunath Kudlur, Josh Levenberg, Dandelion Mané, Rajat Monga, Sherry Moore, Derek Murray, Chris Olah, Mike Schuster, Jonathon Shlens, Benoit Steiner, Ilya Sutskever, Kunal Talwar, Paul Tucker, Vincent Vanhoucke, Vijay Vasudevan, Fernanda Viégas, Oriol Vinyals, Pete Warden, Martin Wattenberg, Martin Wicke, Yuan Yu, Xiaoqiang Zheng, TensorFlow: large-scale machine learning on heterogeneous systems, URL https://www.tensorflow.org/, 2015, software available from tensorflow.org.

[59] François Chollet, et al., Keras, https://keras.io, 2015.

[60] Eli Gibson, Wenqi Li, Carole Sudre, Lucas Fidon, Dzoshkun Shakir, Guotai Wang, Zach Eaton-Rosen, Robert Gray, Tom Doel, Yipeng Hu, Tom Whyntie, Parashkev Nachev, Dean C. Barratt, Sebastien Ourselin, M. Jorge Cardoso, Tom Vercauteren, NiftyNet: a deep-learning platform for medical imaging, Computer Methods and Programs in Biomedicine 158 (2018) 113–122.

[61] Adam Paszke, Sam Gross, Soumith Chintala, Gregory Chanan, Edward Yang, Zachary DeVito, Zeming Lin, Alban Desmaison, Luca Antiga, Adam Lerer, Automatic differentiation in PyTorch, in: NIPS-W, 2017.

[62] Yangqing Jia, Evan Shelhamer, Jeff Donahue, Sergey Karayev, Jonathan Long, Ross Girshick, Sergio Guadarrama, Trevor Darrell, Caffe: convolutional architecture for fast feature embedding, preprint, arXiv:1408.5093, 2014.

[63] Martijn P.A. Starmans, Workflow for Optimal Radiomics Classification (WORC), URL https://github.com/MStarmans91/WORC, Feb. 2018, original-date: 2017-05-24 T13:31:31Z.

[64] Hakim C. Achterberg, Marcel Koek, Wiro J. Niessen, Fastr: a workflow engine for advanced data flows in medical image analysis, Frontiers in ICT (2016) 15, https://doi.org/10.3389/fict.2016.00015.

CHAPTER 19

Random forests in medical image computing

Ender Konukoglu[a], **Ben Glocker**[b]

[a]Computer Vision Laboratory, ETH Zürich, Zürich, Switzerland
[b]Department of Computing, Imperial College London, London, United Kingdom

Contents

19.1. A different way to use context	457
19.2. Feature selection and ensembling	459
19.3. Algorithm basics	460
19.3.1 Inference	460
19.3.2 Training	462
19.3.3 Integrating context	466
19.4. Applications	467
19.4.1 Detection and localization	468
19.4.2 Segmentation	469
19.4.3 Image-based prediction	471
19.4.4 Image synthesis	473
19.4.5 Feature interpretation	474
19.4.6 Algorithmic variations	475
19.5. Conclusions	476
References	476

19.1. A different way to use context

Machine learning (ML) algorithms have served as essential tools in medical image computing since the early days of the field. Supervised methods were used for localization and detection of objects and pathological structures [72,40], unsupervised learning was the corner stone of statistical shape modeling [36], and both were extensively used in neuroimaging studies [46,10]. In the earlier days, roughly before 2009, despite the interest, ML algorithms were not able to compete with atlas-based methods when it comes to segmentation of anatomical structures and defining regions of interest, two of the most critical tasks in medical image computing. ML approaches were still useful but it was common to use an atlas-based approach to first restrict the field-of-view and then initialize a subsequent ML-based method for further analysis, such as [62,4].

The main missing piece in the ML-based approaches of those days was the integration of *contextual information*. Context is an extremely important cue in medical images.

Handbook of Medical Image Computing and Computer Assisted Intervention
https://doi.org/10.1016/B978-0-12-816176-0.00024-7

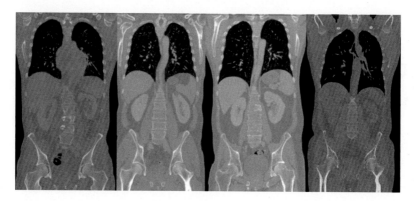

Figure 19.1 Example CT scans showing intersubject variation in shapes and intensities of objects as well as similarity in context and spatial constellation.

Despite possible variations, anatomy is largely very similar across different individuals. Fig. 19.1 shows images of CT scans from different individuals. It is clear that images show variations in the shape and intensity of corresponding anatomical structures. However, the positioning of the organs in the different scans are the same. To segment a liver in this large field-of-view (FOV) image, one can use the surrounding structures both for rough initialization and then detailed, voxelwise semantic segmentation. Similar applies for detecting/segmenting specific pathological structures. Specific lesions, e.g., traumatic brain injuries, occur more frequently at particular locations, which again can be identified using contextual information.

Atlas-based approaches leverage the anatomical similarity across individuals explicitly by using image registration. A group of *atlas* images, either population averages or a selected set of images, are manually labeled for the structures of interest. When analyzing a new image, the atlas(es) are aligned with the image to identify point correspondences between the images, as best as possible. Labels are then propagated from the atlases to the new image based on the correspondences, and aggregated into the final segmentation using various label fusion strategies, as illustrated in Fig. 19.2. Atlas-based approaches are still used in many of the well known research-oriented software suites. However, reliance on the image registration was problematic for two main reasons. First, the registration accuracy was not always satisfactory, especially when the new image differed from the atlases, for instance in the case of images bearing lesions. Second, image registration can be computationally expensive limiting its use in large-scale studies.

Random Forests (RFs), also known as random decision forests, were among the first algorithms that introduced a substantial change in terms of integrating context within an ML-based approach. The important development was to use internal feature selection and voting. Leveraging both of these techniques, RFs became an important tool for detection, localization, segmentation, and image-based prediction. In order to

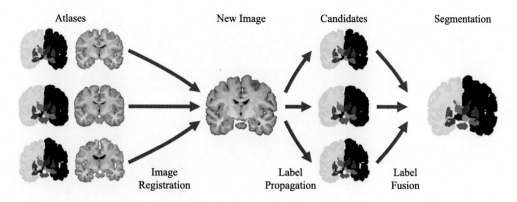

Figure 19.2 Illustration of multiatlas segmentation with label fusion.

understand the value of implicit feature selection and voting, let us compare RFs with previous algorithms.

19.2. Feature selection and ensembling

ML-based methods in image analysis that preceded Random Forests were mostly using well-defined features that were carefully extracted from images. One of the best examples is morphological measurements that are widely used in neuroimaging, such as hippocampal volume or thickness of the cortex. These features have proven to be useful for developing automatic methods for diagnosis, e.g., [60]; however, hand-crafted features are not easy to construct for integrating context in an ML-based method. This difficulty can be easily explained on an example.

In Fig. 19.3, we show a CT image and highlight a patch as a green square in the liver. Let us assume the task at hand is to identify the organ this patch belongs to, also known as semantic segmentation. For humans, the context around this patch, i.e., the image content, makes it easy to identify the organ. It is, however, unclear how to numerically represent this content. Which well-defined measurement or feature should one extract? Can the same type of feature be used for other organs? Note that for atlas-based methods we the context is explicitly integrated in the alignment procedure (i.e., image registration).

RFs overcame this difficulty by removing the need for carefully extracting well-defined features from the images. First, RFs replaced this task with extracting a large pool of simple features, which are fast and easy to extract, and employing an internal feature selection mechanism to identify the most useful (i.e., most discriminative features) for the potentially very large pool. Second, RFs used a voting mechanism that aggregated information from multiple weak classifiers. It is also important to note that RFs is not the only algorithm that follow this approach. Boosting methods are based

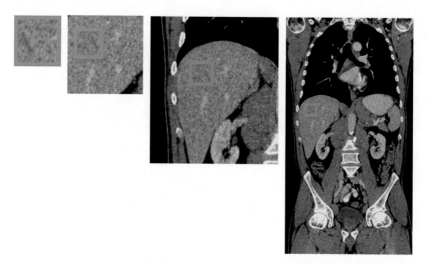

Figure 19.3 Context helps us decide what organ a region in the image belongs to. In the figure, green box is shown from left to right with increasing image content around it. While it is difficult to understand it is a liver region on the left patch, content as we go right makes it clear.

on very similar ideas and have also been used both in medical image computing [11,68] and computer vision [65].

In the next sections we briefly explain the basics of the algorithm and then present some applications where RFs proved to be very successful. Our presentation is brief and we focus on supervised learning. We refer the reader to resources solely focusing on RFs, such as [17,8], for a more detailed discussion of the subject.

19.3. Algorithm basics

The Random Forests algorithm was first proposed by Amit and Geman in [5] and later made popular by Brieman [8]. It is based on an ensemble of decision trees, which are sets of hierarchically nested binary tests evaluated on the features. The sets can be graphically represented as trees as shown in Fig. 19.4. It is simpler to start the description by the inference stage. We will first describe the algorithm as general as possible then provide the link to image analysis.

19.3.1 Inference

Let us represent a sample $\mathbf{x}$ with a set of features $\mathbf{f}(\mathbf{x}) = \{f_j(\mathbf{x})\}_{j=1}^{D}$ and its label $l(\mathbf{x})$, categorical or continuous; for simplicity of notation, we drop the dependence of both $\mathbf{f}$ and l on $\mathbf{x}$. At inference, the goal of a decision tree is to predict a label for $\mathbf{x}$. A tree is composed of three types of nodes: (i) root, (ii) internal, and (iii) leaf nodes, and at each

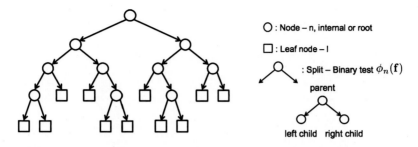

Figure 19.4 Illustration of a decision tree on the left and different components on the right.

root and internal node there is a binary test, simplest example being the binary stump:

$$\phi_n(\mathbf{f}) = \begin{cases} 0, & f_{j(n)} < \tau_n, \\ 1, & f_{j(n)} \geq \tau_n, \end{cases} \tag{19.1}$$

where the subscript n denotes the node, $f_{j(n)}$ is the $j(n)$th element of $\mathbf{f}$ and τ_n is the threshold at the node n. Both the feature index and threshold depend on n, and we will describe how they are determined in Sect. 19.3.2. Other alternative tests have also been proposed in the literature, and we discuss some of them in Sect. 19.4.6.

The decision tree is a directed graph with each node connected to a single parent and two child nodes. The direction of the connection is from parents to children. The sample $\mathbf{x}$ starts its journey at the root node $n = 0$ with the binary question ϕ_n (i.e., a feature test). Depending on the answer, it is sent either to the right ($\phi_n(\mathbf{f}) = 0$) or the left child ($\phi_n(\mathbf{f}) = 1$) of the root node. The process is repeated at the new node and $\mathbf{x}$ travels further down the tree until it reaches a leaf node, which does not have any further children or a binary test. At the leaf node, a prediction is made for the sample $\hat{l}(\mathbf{x})$ (based on empirical distributions over labels determined at training time).

As mentioned, a forest is an ensemble of many decision trees where each tree differs, i.e., feature tests and the structure of the tree are different. Each tree makes an independent prediction for a given test sample and the predictions are aggregated to get the final prediction. The aggregation method depends on the type of the label. For categorical variables it is common to aggregate the predictions in a histogram

$$p(\hat{l}_F = l_i) = \frac{1}{T} \sum_{t=1}^{T} \delta(\hat{l}_t = l_i), \tag{19.2}$$

where subscript F denotes the forest prediction while t denotes individual tree predictions, l_i is the ith possible label category, T is the total number of trees in the forest and $\delta(\cdot)$ is the Dirac's delta function. Once the histogram is computed, a single prediction can be defined as the most likely category, in other words, by doing majority voting

$$\hat{l}_F = \arg\max_{l_i} p(\hat{l}_F = l_i). \tag{19.3}$$

For continuous labels, one can compute the mean of tree predictions as the final prediction:

$$\hat{l}_F = \frac{1}{T} \sum_{t=1}^{T} \hat{l}_t. \tag{19.4}$$

Median is also a good choice for robustness to outliers, or if the predictions form multimodal distributions over the continuous label space, a mode seeking procedure might be considered.

Being an ensemble method, RFs directly provide probabilistic predictions, as in the histogram for categorical label prediction, which can be used to estimate uncertainties. To this end, different tree predictions are seen as independent samples, and various statistics, such as sample standard deviation or confidence intervals, can be computed.

19.3.2 Training

The parameters of the RF algorithm, the binary tests and tree structure, are determined in a training phase using a training set composed of samples with ground truth labels. Let us denote a training set of M samples with $\mathcal{D} = \{(\mathbf{f}(\mathbf{x}_m), l(\mathbf{x}_m))\}_{m=1}^{M} = \{(\mathbf{f}_m, l_m)\}_{m=1}^{M}$ and use the latter notation for simplicity. During training each decision tree is independently constructed starting from the root node and growing the following nodes sequentially in an identical manner based on a greedy strategy to optimize prediction accuracy on the training set. Let us focus on a specific node n and denote the set of training samples at this node by $\mathcal{D}_n$. To determine the test at this node, we optimize a cost that is defined by the potential split of training data into two subsets

$$\tau_n, j(n) = \arg\max_{\tau, j} \mathcal{L}(\mathcal{D}, \mathcal{D}_R, \mathcal{D}_L), \tag{19.5}$$

where $\mathcal{D}_R$ and $\mathcal{D}_L$ are the training samples that follow to the right and left child depending on the feature test at the current node. In abstract terms, this optimization determines the test that best partitions the training dataset $\mathcal{D}$ in two subsets according to the cost function. Once such a test is determined, two child nodes of n are created, n_R and n_L, and $\mathcal{D}_R$ and $\mathcal{D}_L$ are sent to the respective children. The optimization and the partitioning procedure are repeated in the new nodes with the corresponding set of samples.

Cost

Exact definition of the cost $\mathcal{L}$ depends on the application. When labels are categorical and the task is classification, a common definition is the information gain:

$$\mathcal{L}(\mathcal{D}, \mathcal{D}_R, \mathcal{D}_L) = I_G(\mathcal{D}, \mathcal{D}_R, \mathcal{D}_L) = H(\mathcal{D}) - \frac{|\mathcal{D}_R|}{|\mathcal{D}|} H(\mathcal{D}_R) - \frac{|\mathcal{D}_L|}{|\mathcal{D}|} H(\mathcal{D}_L), \qquad (19.6)$$

$$H(\mathcal{A}) = - \sum_{i=1}^{K} p(l = l_i | \mathcal{A}) \ln p(l = l_i | \mathcal{A}), \qquad (19.7)$$

$$p(l = l_i | \mathcal{A}) = \frac{|\{\mathbf{x} : \mathbf{x} \in \mathcal{A} \text{ and } l(\mathbf{x}) = l_i\}|}{|\mathcal{A}|}, \qquad (19.8)$$

where $H(\cdot)$ is the entropy computed from sample histograms in the set $\mathcal{A}$ and $|\cdot|$ denotes set size. The information gain quantifies the reduction in entropy which achieves its lowest value when all the samples in the dataset have the same label. Therefore, the highest information gain would be achieved when dataset $\mathcal{D}$ is divided into two partitions each with homogeneous labels.

For regression problems with continuous labels, reduction in variance is widely used as the cost function:

$$\mathcal{L}(\mathcal{D}, \mathcal{D}_R, \mathcal{D}_L) = \sigma_{\mathcal{D}}^2 - \frac{|\mathcal{D}_R|}{|\mathcal{D}|} \sigma_{\mathcal{D}_R}^2 - \frac{|\mathcal{D}_L|}{|\mathcal{D}|} \sigma_{\mathcal{D}_L}^2, \qquad (19.9)$$

$$\sigma_{\mathcal{A}}^2 = \frac{1}{|\mathcal{A}| - 1} \sum_{\mathbf{x} \in \mathcal{A}} \left(l(\mathbf{x}) - \mu_{\mathcal{A}} \right)^2, \qquad (19.10)$$

$$\mu_{\mathcal{A}} = \frac{1}{|\mathcal{A}|} \sum_{\mathbf{x} \in \mathcal{A}} l(\mathbf{x}), \qquad (19.11)$$

where $\sigma_{\mathcal{A}}^2$ and $\mu_{\mathcal{A}}$ are respectively the sample variance and mean of l in the set $\mathcal{A}$. As in the case of categorical labels, the cost $\mathcal{L}$ is also maximized when the partitions have the lowest variance, in other words, become homogeneous.

Optimization

In general, the optimization of the cost function $\mathcal{L}$ can be a difficult problem since it is optimizing over the feature index. However, at each time only one index is considered while evaluating the cost. This 1D nature of the problem makes a brute force approach feasible. In practice, the most commonly used approach is to perform grid search or a golden section search to determine the best threshold for each feature independently and choose the feature index and the threshold that yields the maximum. We should note that for tests other than binary stumps, this approach might not be feasible.

Stopping criteria

The growth of the tree is a sequential process that implements a greedy optimization strategy. As the tree grows deeper, two things happen. First, the number of training samples that can be used to optimize a node decreases due to successive partitioning. Second, assuming the optimization works, the homogeneity of the samples in each node increases. The criteria for stopping the growth of a tree are based on two conditions that check these points:

1. If $|\mathcal{D}| < \tau_{\mathcal{D}}$ then stop. A node is not partitioned any further if the number of samples is less than a certain threshold.
2. If $H(\mathcal{D}) < \tau_H$ for classification and $\sigma_{\mathcal{D}}^2 < \tau_{\sigma^2}$ for regression then stop. A node is not partitioned if it is homogeneous.

When a node reaches either of these conditions, the tree growth is stopped in that branch and the node is set as a leaf node. The thresholds for the stopping criteria are typically user defined. The lower the thresholds, the deeper the trees will grow while higher threshold will lead to shallow trees.

Leaf predictions

Tree predictions are made based on the training samples that arrive at each leaf node. In theory, when the optimization works, samples at the leaf nodes will be homogeneous in terms of their labels. Any unseen sample that reaches the same leaf node is assumed to have a label similar to the training samples that arrived in the same node during training. As the decision tree, at least in its original form, is composed of binary tests, a sample will follow a unique path in the tree and will reach a single leaf node, therefore, will have only one prediction from each tree.

At the end of training, a number of training samples may be residing at each leaf node. To get a single prediction, labels of these samples are summarized in a single statistic. For a regression problem, a common statistic is the mean label value

$$\hat{l}_{t,n} = \frac{1}{|\mathcal{D}_n|} \sum_{\mathbf{x} \in \mathcal{D}_n} l(\mathbf{x}), \qquad (19.12)$$

where the subscript (t, n) denotes the nth leaf node in the tree t and $\mathcal{D}_n$ is the set of training samples in the leaf node. For a test sample, $\hat{l}_t = \hat{l}_{t,n(\mathbf{x})}$, where $n(\mathbf{x})$ is the leaf node $\mathbf{x}$ ends up in, due to the uniqueness of the path.

Similar to regression, for a classification task a common summary statistic is the mode of the sample histogram of labels in the leaf node:

$$\hat{l}_{t,n} = \arg \max_{l_i} |\{\mathbf{x} : \mathbf{x} \in \mathcal{D}_n \text{ and } l(\mathbf{x}) = l_i\}|. \qquad (19.13)$$

From trees to random forest

As mentioned earlier, a Random Forest is an ensemble of many decision trees. It has been empirically shown that having each tree being different than the others leads to better generalization accuracy [8,17] and gives the RF algorithm its advantage over nonensemble methods. Difference between trees is ensured by decorrelation using two randomization strategies. First, each tree is trained using only a subset of the pool of features $\mathbf{f}_t \subset \mathbf{f}$, where $\mathbf{f}_t$ only consists of $d < D$ dimensions randomly selected from the entire set. As a result of this randomization, each decision tree in the forest, performs prediction based on a different subspace of the entire feature space, effectively helping against overfitting [5,8,17]. Another variant of feature randomization is to randomly select a different feature set at each node while optimizing for the binary feature tests. This alternative is particularly interesting for applications where the number of features per sample can be very large, hence extracting the features beforehand and holding them in a matrix has a large memory footprint, but where extracting individual features is computationally efficient, they can be extracted on-the-fly during training. Most of the medical image computing tasks fit well to this scenario.

The second randomization strategy is implemented by randomly subsampling the training set for each tree (also known as bagging). Instead of using $\mathcal{D}_F^{tr}$ for training every tree, $\mathcal{D}_t^{tr} \subset \mathcal{D}_F^{tr}$ is sampled and used for constructing the tree t. As before, this helps avoid overfitting and ensures variability across different trees. This randomization can also be implemented at the node level instead of the tree level. For medical image computing tasks, where reading different volumetric images from memory can be slow, sampling the samples at the tree level can be a more practical option.

Effect of model parameters

The RF algorithm has various parameters that need to be set by the user when training a model. Criminisi et al. in [17] and Brieman in [8] analyzed the effect of different parameters in depth. Through empirical evaluations, these works provide some guidelines for the effect of these parameters:

1. Larger number of trees is beneficial for generalization, however, the effect saturates at some point.
2. Deeper trees have the risk of overfitting. In order to build deeper trees, more samples are required. From our own experience, however, overfitting with RFs on tasks such as image segmentation seems less of a problem and deeper trees typically improve performance.
3. In the randomization of features d/D depends on the problem. For a large set of problems, it has been demonstrated that generalization accuracy may not be very sensitive to this parameter for a large range. A typical heuristic is setting $d = \sqrt{(D)}$.
4. $|\mathcal{D}_t^{tr}|/|\mathcal{D}_F^{tr}|$ also depends on the problem, and the generalization accuracy is not very sensitive to this parameter for a large range as well.

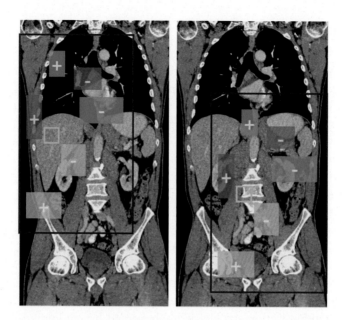

Figure 19.5 Image illustrates example of contextual features, Haar-like mean intensity differences, often used in applications of RF in medical image computing. Regions indicated with green squares are characterized with features extracted from larger regions shown in red squares. Haar-like features simply compute differences between mean intensities of two different regions computed at a certain offset from the central green square. Three such features are shown in the image on the right. For a different point, as shown in the right image, same features are computed at the same offsets. Note that these features are not necessarily discriminative. It is common to extract large number of such weak features and internal feature selection of RF selects the ones that are discriminative for the task.

5. Good performance has been observed even when only one randomization strategy was utilized.

19.3.3 Integrating context

Having described the inference and the training phases, we now provide the details on how RFs make use of contextual information. Let us focus on the example shown in Fig. 19.3 once again. The task is semantic segmentation and, in order to decide on the organ to which the green patch belongs to, one has to take into account the contextual information, e.g., image information in the red rectangle. The approach to this problem with RFs is to represent the green patch with features extracted from all around the image, as illustrated in Fig. 19.5. However, it is unclear what feature to extract in this large image region. This is where the internal feature selection becomes critical.

The node optimization that is used during training of decision trees is actually performing feature selection. It sifts through all the features in $\mathbf{f}_t$ (or a random subset of it) and selects the optimal one for partitioning the training data according to the task at hand (defined by the cost function). Using this mechanism, context can be easily integrated. In RFs, we extract a very large number of simple to compute features from a large spatial area around the green patch and which forms **f**. The training procedure then selects the contextual features that are the most helpful at different nodes in the decision trees for optimizing the splitting cost.

One can think of various alternatives for simple to compute features. The important aspect of such features is that they can be computed in large quantities very efficiently, so on-the-fly feature evaluation can be performed at node level. Arguably the most commonly used type is Haar-like features computed using integral images [64]. These features are defined as differences of mean intensities in two rectangular regions in the image, as illustrated in Fig. 19.5. To represent a local patch with contextual features, Haar-like features are computed using regions at different random offsets from the patch [15]. A large number of such features (i.e., the feature pool) are extracted and considered during training.

The difference in intensities assume that intensities are comparable across different images. This may not be the case for a variety of imaging modalities in medical imaging. For images where intensities are not calibrated, such as in Magnetic Resonance Imaging (MRI), Pauly et al. proposed to extract local binary patterns similar to integral features [57].

The second critical part in integrating context is the ensemble of multiple trees and their aggregation. Although the feature selection can sift through large number of features, at every node, only a finite number of features can be explored. Therefore, it is likely that individual tree predictions may not be very accurate. Aggregation of predictions from many different trees has been empirically shown to lead to accurate predictions as, for example, shown in [29].

19.4. Applications

In this section, we will describe several applications of RFs in medical image computing, where integrating contextual features allowed RFs to outperform previous approaches. This section is not intended to be a complete literature review of all related articles in medical image computing. We only provide some examples and the interested reader may find more works in the literature.

We will analyze applications in five coarse categories. Naturally, this categorization is artificial and there are several works that can fit in several categories. For each part, we also provide a brief description of the basic principle of how RFs, as explained in the previous section, are applied.

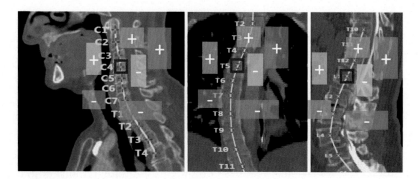

Figure 19.6 Illustration of how the contextual features change for the problem of detecting and identifying individual vertebral bodies in spinal CT.

19.4.1 Detection and localization

The first application where RFs made a substantial contribution to the field is detection and localization, where the goal is to identify the location of a point of interest, e.g., a landmark or a boundary point of an object, in the images. For instance, in Fig. 19.6 we show an example application where the goal is to identify the center of vertebrae in the volumetric CT images. Examining the problem in Fig. 19.6, it is clear that having a good representation for the context in the image and integrating it in the prediction seems useful for accurate localization.

Cootes et al. in [14] (later extended in [50]), Criminisi et al. in [15,18,16], Glocker et al. in [29] were among the early works that tackled the localization challenge using RFs. The main idea behind these works was to cast the localization as a regression problem and use RFs to solve it. More specifically, $l \in \mathbb{R}^3$, assuming volumetric images, represented the coordinates of the point of interest. During inference, each point in the image, $p \in \Omega \subset R^3$, predicted independently its offset to the point of interest, $l - p$, using local and contextual image information. As feature values, all the three works used Haar-like features extracted at different offsets from p to represent the point. Aggregating the independent predictions yielded the final prediction for the point of interest as well as an associated uncertainty. A very similar idea was also used in computer vision during the same time for various tasks [25].

To train these localization approaches random points in each volume are extracted as independent samples and offsets to the respective points of interests are associated as labels. The training procedure for regression explained in Sect. 19.3.2 can then be directly applied. These approaches also allow to predict locations of multiple landmarks simultaneously by simply increasing the dimensionality of $l \in \mathbb{R}^{3 \times \text{number of points of interest}}$. For instance, in [15] the authors predicted multiple bounding boxes with six values per bounding box in CT volumes.

An interesting design in the mentioned methods was that samples were pixels extracted from images rather than samples being entire images. This led to having multiple independent samples, and therefore predictions, from the same image. This choice was important for improving robustness to varying field-of-views as well as artifacts in the images. For example, if a part of the anatomy was missing in one image, predictions from that part were missing but predictions from the other parts were sufficient to localize the points of interest. Similarly, if there were artifacts, predictions from points affected by the artifacts were misleading but points that were not affected were sufficient for accurate localization.

Another approach for localization was to use classification instead of regression. In [32] authors classified each point as being the point of interest or not. In this case, once again each point was seen as a sample. During training, the authors considered points close to the point of interest as positive samples and points that are far as negative samples. A similar strategy was combined with regression forests for improved accuracy in [22] for localizing multiple repeating structures. Authors in [31] used localization with RFs for further registration of pathological CT spine images and a regression approach was also used in [9] for identifying individual vertebrae in X-ray absorptiometry (DXA) images. Lastly, Liu et al. [52] used classification RFs to locate mediastinal lymph nodes in CT images with multiatlas label fusion providing prior information.

19.4.2 Segmentation

Semantic segmentation was arguably the most popular application area for RFs and where the approach made the biggest impact. In one of the earliest works [49], Lempitsky et al. demonstrated the accuracy of RF based segmentation on the notoriously difficult echocardiography images, where they segmented the myocardium. Segmentation was cast as a classification problem, $l \in \{0, 1\}$ was a voxelwise binary variable, and each voxel's contextual information was represented by calculating mean intensities over varying sized boxes around each voxel while adding location information as additional features. Each voxel was considered as an independent sample, the training and inference of RFs followed the descriptions in Sect. 19.3.

Following Lempitsky et al.'s work, numerous extensions of the initial segmentation framework were proposed. Geremia et al. in [27] proposed an extended set of different features for segmenting Multiple Sclerosis lesions. They used Haar-like features, as used in regression RFs, symmetry features, which compare intensities between corresponding points at two halves of the brain assuming a lesion would only affect one side of the brain, and coarse initial segmentation of the brain MRI into gray matter, white matter and CSF. All these features focused on integrating different aspects of spatial context for the segmentation. That system achieved state-of-the-art performance at the time and their analysis on feature importance showed that context features were selected most often during training and used in testing. A very similar system was later applied to segmenting brain tumors in MRI by Zikic et al. in [74].

Both [49] and [27] considered images with limited field-of-view. Extending the classification forests to larger field-of-view images, where structure of interest may be smaller compared to the entire image, was challenging. To address this challenge, three approaches that integrated regression with RF in segmentation were proposed in [30,19, 51]. Glocker et al. [30] used a joint cost function where for each voxel, not only its label but also its distance to certain landmarks were predicted. Predicting multiple outputs, in the spirit of multitask learning, improved accuracy compared to using only classification. Cuingnet et al. in [19] a cascaded localization step, where they estimated a bounding box around kidneys in CT images in two successive applications of RF regression, as a preprocessing step to voxelwise classification and deformable template matching. In an approach similar in principle, Lindner et al. in [51] used localization with RF-based regression, similar to [14], to initialize and constrain a shape model. Authors were able to segment the femur bone in 2D pelvic radiographs with complicated artifacts, such as implants.

In the same spirit as [27], several other works explored adding different set of features to represent voxels for segmentation. Mitra et al. and Khalifa et al. in [56,42] investigated using tissue probability masks, extracted by a Bayesian model with Markov random field (MRF) prior, and shape features, respectively. Yaqub et al., on the other hand, questioned the random feature selection used during node optimization and showed in [69] that improved segmentation accuracy was possible with some prior information on what feature is more useful. Authors in the same work also proposed to use a weighted strategy while aggregating predictions of individual trees to form the final prediction.

While Yaqup et al. was questioning the feature selection, Lombaert et al. questioned randomly sampling the images during training of individual trees in Laplacian Forests [53]. Given the possibly high anatomical variations, they proposed to use images that show similar anatomy while training individual trees. In this case, each tree would not try to capture the entire anatomical variation in the population, as seen in the training dataset, but focus on a smaller set with limited variation. As different trees would focus on different sets, the entire forest would still capture the overall population variation. During inference, the appropriate trees would be identified automatically. In their experiments, the authors showed that this approach made it easier to learn powerful trees with higher forest prediction accuracy. Context was integrated using the same type of features as previous works.

Lombaert et al.'s idea was partly motivated by an earlier work by Zikic et al. in [73], which took a very different view on the RF algorithm. Instead of capturing any variability, Zikic et al. trained each tree with only one image but relatively deep, effectively overfitting to a single image, with number of trees equal to the number of training examples. This approach, maybe surprisingly, showed good segmentation performance on brain MRI. This algorithm is important in the sense that it suggested explicit links between the RF algorithm and approaches that implement database retrieval ideas for segmentation, such as [59].

One other interesting direction to explore was the scale of prediction. All the works mentioned so far performed predictions at the voxel level while solving the classification problem with RFs. Geremia et al. in [28] took an alternative approach and used supervoxels as samples in prediction. They partitioned the images into mutually exclusive and exhaustive regions at different scales using the SLIC algorithm [1]. During training the trees see the supervoxels at all scales, training starts at the coarsest scale and proceeds to finer scale supervoxels.

The idea of using supervoxels in RFs was later also used by Gu et al. in [34] but this time to perform semisupervised learning, where a large number of unlabeled images are used along with a small number of labeled images to improve segmentation accuracy over only using the labeled set. Authors here modified the SLIC algorithm to use forest predictions and used unlabeled images to create an auxiliary tool that predicts where a segmentation method will have low confidence predictions. This auxiliary prediction is later integrated for the final prediction of the segmentation method and shown to improve performance.

19.4.3 Image-based prediction

Image-based prediction was another area where RFs influenced medical image computing. The problem here is to summarize the entire content in an image to predict a label, which might correspond to demographic information, such as age, phenotypical variables, clinical diagnosis, or outcome prediction. This is, in principle, similar to segmentation, where the problem is often cast as a classification task, but features extracted here represent the entire image rather than individual voxels.

The aspect that made RFs an important tool for image-based prediction is the feature selection. In most such problems in medical image computing, the dimensions of images, i.e., number of voxels, are much higher than the number of samples. This situation makes training prone to overfitting. ML approaches that were popular in medical image computing prior to RF, addressed this issue in two ways, as exemplified in [60]. First, instead of using the entire image, carefully extracted features, such as morphological measurements, were used. Such features were low in number and therefore, overfitting was less of a problem with smaller sample sizes. The second approach was to use regularized ML models, where the model parameters were constrained with a regularization or a prior term, for example, as in [70,67]. Regularization prevented overfitting by limiting the number on nonzero parameters, and thus avoided fitting the noise in the training dataset.

RFs took a different approach. As we have seen in Sect. 19.3.2, the internal feature selection mechanism is able to sift through a large number of features and choose those that yield the best partitionings during the node optimization. This internal selection mechanism was how RFs were able to integrate contextual information for localization and segmentation. The same mechanism, for the image-based prediction problem, helps with the dimensionality of the problem and allows RF-based methods to generalize to unseen data and achieve high classification accuracy, as shown, for instance, in [60].

The basic RF classification algorithm has been applied to classify various conditions based on imaging data. Some recent examples are that of Lebedev et al. [48], where authors studied Alzheimer's disease and Mild Cognitive Impairment using morphological measurements with RFs. Venkataraman et al. [63] focused on classifying patients with chronic schizophrenia from healthy volunteers with functional connectivity. Wade et al. [66] studied depression with shape features of subcortical structures in the brain. Eshagi et al. [23] showed classification results for distinguishing Neuromyelitis optica from Multiple Sclerosis using brain MRI. Chincarini et al. [12] proposed to diagnose prodromal Alzheimer's disease with brain imaging data. These are just some examples of works successfully applying RFs; we selected these to provide a range of applications both in terms of data and clinical problems.

Besides the direct applications, several works proposed algorithmic modifications that extended the RF classification model. In one of the earliest works [54], Menze et al. focused on the feature selection mechanism and used RF as a tool to select features in high-dimensional spectral datasets through recursive feature elimination [35]. Langs et al. [47] applied a similar strategy to analyze functional MRI images to detect stable brain activity using RFs as a feature selection tool.

Gray et al. in [33] built a system using RF classification as the building block that integrates multimodal imaging data in an innovative manner. Using RFs, they convert imaging data into similarity metrics between different samples, which can be combined despite differences in the data. Using their model, the authors showed improved classification between AD as well as MCI and healthy controls. Dmirtiev et al., on the other hand, combined RFs and convolutional neural networks (CNNs) to classify among four different types of pancreatic cyst in [21]. The RF was using patient demographic information and shape features while the CNN was integrating texture information for the classification.

All the works mentioned above focused on classification among two or more groups. Désir et al. in [20], used RFs for unsupervised outlier detection. The problem here is to learn a classifier using only data from one group, for example, healthy looking tissue, and at inference time identify samples that are not from this group. They solved this problem by generating synthetic out-of-group samples and train classification RFs that can distinguish abnormal samples.

One recent interesting application, which somehow deviates from the prediction works described above, was proposed by Kanavati et al. [41] and further developed by Conze et al. in [13]. These works propose to use RF classification as a basis for pairwise

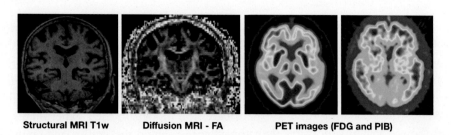

Structural MRI T1w   **Diffusion MRI - FA**   **PET images (FDG and PIB)**

Figure 19.7 Different modalities characterizing different aspects of the brain. The first two are structural T1-weighted MRI and diffusion MRI derived Fractional Anisotropy image while the last two are PET images acquired with FDG and PIB compounds.

image registration, i.e., determining point correspondences between two volumes often referred to as source and target. They divide the source image into superpixels and, in a similar spirit as in [73], learned a classification RF where labels are superpixel indices. Classifying superpixel representation of the target image provides correspondences between the two volumes, which were then used for registering the images.

19.4.4 Image synthesis

Image synthesis is a relatively recent application of RFs in medical image computing. Multimodality is a critical aspect in medical imaging. Different images show different physical characteristics of the underlying tissue. For instance, in Fig. 19.7 we show different modalities that show different characteristics of a subject's brain. The first two are MRI images, showing structural information, while the last is a Positron Emission Tomography (PET) image showing metabolic activity, specifically glucose consumption levels. Visualizing the tissue in multiple modalities provides a richer characterization of the tissue.

In certain cases not all modalities are available for the required level of characterization. This might be due to missing acquisitions in population imaging or lack of time in clinical practice. One specific example is CT and MRI for PET imaging. Tissue density is important for acquiring and interpreting PET images, specifically for attenuation correction in the imaging signal. CT images are useful for this purpose as they provide noninvasive measurements of tissue density; they are often acquired alongside PET. However, MRI also provides crucial information due to its superior soft-tissue contrast and is sometimes the preferred modality for interpreting the PET information. Despite both being useful, CT and MRI are rarely acquired together.

If there is a statistical relationship between the modalities, it might be possible to *synthesize* one image that's missing from existing modalities. Naturally, the relationship between the existing and missing modalities should be either one-to-one or many-to-one, which is much more often the case. When such a relationship exists, accurate synthesis might be possible.

In one of the early works, Huynh et al. in [37] proposed to use RFs for synthesizing CT from MRI for the purpose of attenuation correction in PET. They show the possibility of synthesizing realistic CT images using the regression framework of RFs. In [39,38], Jog et al. proposed a similar algorithm, the first version appearing earlier than [37], for synthesizing T2-weighted and FLAIR images from T1-weighted MPRAGE sequences using the RF-based regression model. In their experiments, the authors showed that an automatic algorithm that segmented the synthesized compared to ground truth images yielded similar results.

Another problem that is comparable to image synthesis is "superresolution". We use quotes as superresolution may not only relate to increasing the spatial resolution of an image but also angular resolution in diffusion weighted imaging (DWI). Alexander et al. in [3,2] proposed to use RF-based regression to improve spatial resolution of diffusion tensor imaging (DTI) as well as parameter mapping for images that would normally require high angular resolution DWI. Bahrami et al. in [6] and Zhang et al. in [71], on the other hand, used RF-based regression to improve resolution of structural MRI. The first work showed that slice thickness can be improved using the synthesis approach good enough for high-resolution atlas construction by groupwise registration. The second work, on the other hand, improved resolution of 3T images using a database of 7T MRI.

19.4.5 Feature interpretation

One aspect of RFs that we have not yet discussed is the feature selection property. We already mentioned that feature selection is essential for integrating contextual information for prediction and, related, managing high-dimensional feature spaces. However, the feature selection mechanism in RFs also provides a way to identify features related to conditions of interest, e.g., regions in the brain affected by a disease, forming an alternative to other well known univariate (e.g., regression analysis), and multivariate techniques such as Elastic Nets and Lasso [75,61].

The most commonly used methods that use RFs for identifying feature relevance rely on statistics obtained during the node optimization in the training stage. During node optimization, the algorithm sifts through a set of features to determine the one that yields the best partitioning for the task at hand. The number of times a feature is selected, the *selection frequency*, or the related information gain, *Gini index* or *feature importance*, can be used to assess the value or importance of a feature for the task. For example, if we are considering classification of AD patients versus healthy controls, a selected feature holds predictive information for this classification. It is important to note that a feature that is affected by the disease will not necessarily be selected during the node optimization if there is another feature that yields a better training partitioning.

Menze et al. [54] performed one of the first analyses of the feature selection mechanism in RFs for medical image computing. The authors were interested in identifying features in high-dimensional spectral images useful for prediction. They showed that the RF-based mechanism, specifically the Gini importance measure, when used in a recursive feature elimination algorithm, can identify a small set of features that capture most of the predictive power. Langs et al. [47] used the same idea to identify task-related stable activation patterns in fMRI data. They showed that the essentially multivariate feature selection mechanism was able to identify areas that were not detected by univariate methods.

In [26], Ganz et al. observed that when using RFs directly or through recursive feature elimination it was not possible to identify *all* the features related to the condition. In the presence of redundant information, not all features were chosen during the node optimization or the number of times they were chosen were divided among similar features. As a result, features identified via direct application of RFs may only cover a small portion of the set of features relevant to the condition of interest. In the same article, the authors proposed to employ a knock-out strategy, where a set of features is identified using RFs, then removed from the entire set of features, and the procedure is repeated on the remaining features. This approach substantially improved the detection accuracy of relevant features and showed that areas which might be missed with other alternative methods can be detected.

Lastly, methods for assigning relevance to features with RFs do not necessarily have statistical measures, such as false-positive rates, associated with them. Thresholds for distinguishing between relevant and irrelevant features are often set using heuristics. In [44], Konukoglu and Ganz proposed a method for identifying thresholds in feature selection frequency measure to approximately limit the false-positive rate associated with the threshold.

19.4.6 Algorithmic variations

In addition to the works we described above, there were also algorithmic developments that can be applied to any application using RFs. We would like to point out two of such works. In [55], Menze et al. questioned the node optimization using binary stumps and analyzed the *oblique* alternative. Instead of using binary tests, as given in Eq. (19.1), they used the linear model

$$\beta_n^T \mathbf{f} \geq \tau_n, \tag{19.14}$$

where β_n and τ_n are the model parameters at the node n. Using this model, they showed improvement in classification accuracy for a variety of tasks. The oblique node optimization model can naturally be integrated into any type of RF model, whether classification or regression.

Konukoglu et al. [45], on the other hand, questioned whether it was necessary to define different cost functions for different tasks. Observing that all RF models effectively perform partitioning of the training dataset, they introduced Neighborhood

Approximation Forests (NAFs) that used one cost function for all, evaluating the quality of a clustering based on a user defined similarity metric. They showed in [45] that numerous tasks can be solved with this model, in particular, tasks that are difficult to solve with conventional RFs, such as patch-based segmentation improving results over conventional voxelwise classification RFs. They also presented results for age regression from MRI.

19.5. Conclusions

A decade after Random Forests have been introduced to medical imaging computing, one might ask the question whether they still deserve a place in a researcher's image analysis toolbox. Given the recent trend towards deep learning models which seem to surpass performance on almost all applications where RFs had been the state-of-the-art, maybe it's time to conclude that RFs are of limited importance these days. We would argue that RFs are still one of the most powerful ML methods to consider in real-world applications and should not be abandoned easily. They are easy to implement and extremely efficient both at training and testing. They don't require particular hardware such as graphical processing units, and work well in memory and computed limited environments (e.g., mobile computers, hospital infrastructure).

Interestingly, in the context of deep learning, decision trees seem to recently gain new attention with a few works considering how to combine both worlds [58,43,7]. There is another aspect of interpretability which we haven't discussed at all as it is not the focus of the article. Interpretability in ML, whatever the term implies, is a hot topic and of particular importance in healthcare application such as medical imaging. Arguably, decision trees have been always on the more interpretable side of "black box" algorithms, as decisions that lead to predictions are relatively easy to distill. It is therefore not surprising to find works that try to leverage this aspect, for example, by mapping neural networks to decision trees [24]. A direction that shows great promise for future work.

References

[1] R. Achanta, A. Shaji, K. Smith, A. Lucchi, P. Fua, S. Süsstrunk, et al., SLIC superpixels compared to state-of-the-art superpixel methods, IEEE Transactions on Pattern Analysis and Machine Intelligence 34 (11) (2012) 2274–2282.

[2] D.C. Alexander, D. Zikic, A. Ghosh, R. Tanno, V. Wottschel, J. Zhang, E. Kaden, T.B. Dyrby, S.N. Sotiropoulos, H. Zhang, et al., Image quality transfer and applications in diffusion MRI, NeuroImage 152 (2017) 283–298.

[3] D.C. Alexander, D. Zikic, J. Zhang, H. Zhang, A. Criminisi, Image quality transfer via random forest regression: applications in diffusion MRI, Springer, Cham, 2014, pp. 225–232.

[4] P. Aljabar, R.A. Heckemann, A. Hammers, J.V. Hajnal, D. Rueckert, Multi-atlas based segmentation of brain images: atlas selection and its effect on accuracy, NeuroImage 46 (3) (2009) 726–738.

[5] Y. Amit, D. Geman, Shape quantization and recognition with randomized trees, Neural Computation 9 (7) (1997) 1545–1588.

[6] K. Bahrami, F. Shi, I. Rekik, Y. Gao, D. Shen, 7T-guided super-resolution of 3T MRI, Medical Physics 44 (5) (2017) 1661–1677.

[7] R. Balestriero, Neural decision trees, preprint, arXiv:1702.07360, 2017.

[8] L. Breiman, Random forests, Machine Learning 45 (1) (2001) 5–32.

[9] P.A. Bromiley, J.E. Adams, T.F. Cootes, Localisation of vertebrae on DXA images using constrained local models with random forest regression voting, Springer, Cham, 2015, pp. 159–171.

[10] V.D. Calhoun, T. Adali, G.D. Pearlson, J. Pekar, A method for making group inferences from functional mri data using independent component analysis, Human Brain Mapping 14 (3) (2001) 140–151.

[11] G. Carneiro, B. Georgescu, S. Good, D. Comaniciu, Detection of fetal anatomies from ultrasound images using a constrained probabilistic boosting tree, IEEE Transactions on Medical Imaging 27 (9) (2008) 1342–1355.

[12] A. Chincarini, P. Bosco, P. Calvini, G. Gemme, M. Esposito, C. Olivieri, L. Rei, S. Squarcia, G. Rodriguez, R. Bellotti, et al., Local MRI analysis approach in the diagnosis of early and prodromal Alzheimer's disease, NeuroImage 58 (2) (2011) 469–480.

[13] P.-H. Conze, F. Tilquin, V. Noblet, F. Rousseau, F. Heitz, P. Pessaux, Hierarchical multi-scale supervoxel matching using random forests for automatic semi-dense abdominal image registration, in: 2017 IEEE 14th International Symposium on Biomedical Imaging, ISBI 2017, IEEE, Apr. 2017, pp. 490–493.

[14] T.F. Cootes, M.C. Ionita, C. Lindner, P. Sauer, Robust and accurate shape model fitting using random forest regression voting, Springer, Berlin, Heidelberg, 2012, pp. 278–291.

[15] A. Criminisi, D. Robertson, E. Konukoglu, J. Shotton, S. Pathak, S. White, K. Siddiqui, Regression forests for efficient anatomy detection and localization in computed tomography scans, Medical Image Analysis 17 (8) (Dec. 2013) 1293–1303.

[16] A. Criminisi, J. Shotton, S. Bucciarelli, Decision forests with long-range spatial context for organ localization in CT volumes, in: Medical Image Computing and Computer-Assisted Intervention, MICCAI, 2009, pp. 69–80.

[17] A. Criminisi, J. Shotton, E. Konukoglu, et al., Decision forests: a unified framework for classification, regression, density estimation, manifold learning and semi-supervised learning, Foundations and Trends in Computer Graphics and Vision 7 (2–3) (2012) 81–227.

[18] A. Criminisi, J. Shotton, D. Robertson, E. Konukoglu, Regression forests for efficient anatomy detection and localization in CT studies, in: International MICCAI Workshop on Medical Computer Vision, Springer, 2010, pp. 106–117.

[19] R. Cuingnet, R. Prevost, D. Lesage, L.D. Cohen, B. Mory, R. Ardon, Automatic detection and segmentation of kidneys in 3D CT images using random forests, Springer, Berlin, Heidelberg, 2012, pp. 66–74.

[20] C. Désir, S. Bernard, C. Petitjean, L. Heutte, A random forest based approach for one class classification in medical imaging, Springer, Berlin, Heidelberg, 2012, pp. 250–257.

[21] K. Dmitriev, A.E. Kaufman, A.A. Javed, R.H. Hruban, E.K. Fishman, A.M. Lennon, J.H. Saltz, Classification of pancreatic cysts in computed tomography images using a random forest and convolutional neural network ensemble, Springer, Cham, 2017, pp. 150–158.

[22] R. Donner, B.H. Menze, H. Bischof, G. Langs, Global localization of 3D anatomical structures by pre-filtered Hough Forests and discrete optimization, Medical Image Analysis 17 (8) (Dec. 2013) 1304–1314.

[23] A. Eshaghi, V. Wottschel, R. Cortese, M. Calabrese, M.A. Sahraian, A.J. Thompson, D.C. Alexander, O. Ciccarelli, Gray matter MRI differentiates neuromyelitis optica from multiple sclerosis using random forest, Neurology 87 (23) (Dec. 2016) 2463–2470.

[24] N. Frosst, G. Hinton, Distilling a neural network into a soft decision tree, preprint, arXiv:1711.09784, 2017.

[25] J. Gall, A. Yao, N. Razavi, L. Van Gool, V. Lempitsky, Hough forests for object detection, tracking, and action recognition, IEEE Transactions on Pattern Analysis and Machine Intelligence 33 (11) (2011) 2188–2202.

[26] M. Ganz, D.N. Greve, B. Fischl, E. Konukoglu, A.D.N. Initiative, et al., Relevant feature set estimation with a knock-out strategy and random forests, NeuroImage 122 (2015) 131–148.

[27] E. Geremia, O. Clatz, B.H. Menze, E. Konukoglu, A. Criminisi, N. Ayache, Spatial decision forests for MS lesion segmentation in multi-channel magnetic resonance images, NeuroImage 57 (2) (Jul. 2011) 378–390.

[28] E. Geremia, B.H. Menze, N. Ayache, Spatially adaptive random forests, in: 2013 IEEE 10th International Symposium on Biomedical Imaging, IEEE, Apr. 2013, pp. 1344–1347.

[29] B. Glocker, J. Feulner, A. Criminisi, D.R. Haynor, E. Konukoglu, Automatic localization and identification of vertebrae in arbitrary field-of-view ct scans, in: International Conference on Medical Image Computing and Computer-Assisted Intervention, Springer, 2012, pp. 590–598.

[30] B. Glocker, O. Pauly, E. Konukoglu, A. Criminisi, Joint classification-regression forests for spatially structured multi-object segmentation, in: European Conference on Computer Vision, Springer, 2012, pp. 870–881.

[31] B. Glocker, D. Zikic, D.R. Haynor, Robust registration of longitudinal spine ct, in: International Conference on Medical Image Computing and Computer-Assisted Intervention, Springer, 2014, pp. 251–258.

[32] B. Glocker, D. Zikic, E. Konukoglu, D.R. Haynor, A. Criminisi, Vertebrae localization in pathological spine CT via dense classification from sparse annotations, in: International Conference on Medical Image Computing and Computer-Assisted Intervention, Springer, 2013, pp. 262–270.

[33] K.R. Gray, P. Aljabar, R.A. Heckemann, A. Hammers, D. Rueckert, Random forest-based similarity measures for multi-modal classification of Alzheimer's disease, NeuroImage 65 (Jan. 2013) 167–175.

[34] L. Gu, Y. Zheng, R. Bise, I. Sato, N. Imanishi, S. Aiso, Semi-supervised learning for biomedical image segmentation via forest oriented super pixels (voxels), Springer, Cham, 2017, pp. 702–710.

[35] I. Guyon, J. Weston, S. Barnhill, V. Vapnik, Gene selection for cancer classification using support vector machines, Machine Learning 46 (1–3) (2002) 389–422.

[36] T. Heimann, H.-P. Meinzer, Statistical shape models for 3D medical image segmentation: a review, Medical Image Analysis 13 (4) (2009) 543–563.

[37] T. Huynh, Y. Gao, J. Kang, L. Wang, P. Zhang, J. Lian, D. Shen, Alzheimer's Disease Neuroimaging Initiative, Estimating CT image from MRI data using structured random forest and auto-context model, IEEE Transactions on Medical Imaging 35 (1) (Jan. 2016) 174–183.

[38] A. Jog, A. Carass, D.L. Pham, J.L. Prince, Random forest flair reconstruction from T1, T2, and PD-weighted MRI, in: 2014 IEEE 11th International Symposium on Biomedical Imaging, ISBI, IEEE, 2014, pp. 1079–1082.

[39] A. Jog, A. Carass, S. Roy, D.L. Pham, J.L. Prince, Random forest regression for magnetic resonance image synthesis, Medical Image Analysis 35 (Jan. 2017) 475–488.

[40] T.R. Jones, A.E. Carpenter, M.R. Lamprecht, J. Moffat, S.J. Silver, J.K. Grenier, A.B. Castoreno, U.S. Eggert, D.E. Root, P. Golland, et al., Scoring diverse cellular morphologies in image-based screens with iterative feedback and machine learning, Proceedings of the National Academy of Sciences 106 (6) (2009) 1826–1831.

[41] F. Kanavati, T. Tong, K. Misawa, M. Fujiwara, K. Mori, D. Rueckert, B. Glocker, Supervoxel classification forests for estimating pairwise image correspondences, Pattern Recognition 63 (2017) 561–569.

[42] F. Khalifa, A. Soliman, A.C. Dwyer, G. Gimel'farb, A. El-Baz, A random forest-based framework for 3D kidney segmentation from dynamic contrast-enhanced CT images, in: 2016 IEEE International Conference on Image Processing, ICIP, IEEE, Sept. 2016, pp. 3399–3403.

[43] P. Kontschieder, M. Fiterau, A. Criminisi, S. Rota Bulo, Deep neural decision forests, in: Proceedings of the IEEE International Conference on Computer Vision, 2015, pp. 1467–1475.

[44] E. Konukoglu, M. Ganz, Approximate false positive rate control in selection frequency for random forest, Oct. 2014.

[45] E. Konukoglu, B. Glocker, D. Zikic, A. Criminisi, Neighbourhood approximation using randomized forests, Medical Image Analysis 17 (7) (2013) 790–804.

[46] N. Kriegeskorte, R. Goebel, P. Bandettini, Information-based functional brain mapping, Proceedings of the National Academy of Sciences 103 (10) (2006) 3863–3868.

[47] G. Langs, B.H. Menze, D. Lashkari, P. Golland, Detecting stable distributed patterns of brain activation using Gini contrast, NeuroImage (2011).

[48] A. Lebedev, E. Westman, G. Van Westen, M. Kramberger, A. Lundervold, D. Aarsland, H. Soininen, I. Kłoszewska, P. Mecocci, M. Tsolaki, B. Vellas, S. Lovestone, A. Simmons, Random Forest ensembles for detection and prediction of Alzheimer's disease with a good between-cohort robustness, NeuroImage: Clinical 6 (Jan. 2014) 115–125.

[49] V. Lempitsky, M. Verhoek, J.A. Noble, A. Blake, Random forest classification for automatic delineation of myocardium in real-time 3D, in: Echocardiography, Springer, Berlin, Heidelberg, 2009, pp. 447–456.

[50] C. Lindner, P.A. Bromiley, M.C. Ionita, T.F. Cootes, Robust and accurate shape model matching using random forest regression-voting, IEEE Transactions on Pattern Analysis and Machine Intelligence 37 (9) (Sept. 2015) 1862–1874.

[51] C. Lindner, S. Thiagarajah, J. Wilkinson, T. Consortium, G. Wallis, T. Cootes, Fully automatic segmentation of the proximal femur using random forest regression voting, IEEE Transactions on Medical Imaging 32 (8) (Aug. 2013) 1462–1472.

[52] J. Liu, J. Hoffman, J. Zhao, J. Yao, L. Lu, L. Kim, E.B. Turkbey, R.M. Summers, Mediastinal lymph node detection and station mapping on chest CT using spatial priors and random forest, Medical Physics 43 (7) (June 2016) 4362–4374.

[53] H. Lombaert, D. Zikic, A. Criminisi, N. Ayache, Laplacian forests: semantic image segmentation by guided bagging, Springer, Cham, 2014, pp. 496–504.

[54] B.H. Menze, B.M. Kelm, R. Masuch, U. Himmelreich, P. Bachert, W. Petrich, F.A. Hamprecht, A comparison of random forest and its Gini importance with standard chemometric methods for the feature selection and classification of spectral data, BMC Bioinformatics 10 (1) (July 2009) 213.

[55] B.H. Menze, B.M. Kelm, D.N. Splitthoff, U. Koethe, F.A. Hamprecht, On oblique random forests, Springer, Berlin, Heidelberg, 2011, pp. 453–469.

[56] J. Mitra, P. Bourgeat, J. Fripp, S. Ghose, S. Rose, O. Salvado, A. Connelly, B. Campbell, S. Palmer, G. Sharma, S. Christensen, L. Carey, Lesion segmentation from multimodal MRI using random forest following ischemic stroke, NeuroImage 98 (Sept. 2014) 324–335.

[57] O. Pauly, B. Glocker, A. Criminisi, D. Mateus, A.M. Möller, S. Nekolla, N. Navab, Fast multiple organ detection and localization in whole-body mr Dixon sequences, in: International Conference on Medical Image Computing and Computer-Assisted Intervention, Springer, 2011, pp. 239–247.

[58] S. Rota Bulo, P. Kontschieder, Neural decision forests for semantic image labelling, in: Proceedings of the IEEE Conference on Computer Vision and Pattern Recognition, 2014, pp. 81–88.

[59] F. Rousseau, P.A. Habas, C. Studholme, A supervised patch-based approach for human brain labeling, IEEE Transactions on Medical Imaging 30 (10) (2011) 1852–1862.

[60] M.R. Sabuncu, E. Konukoglu, A.D.N. Initiative, et al., Clinical prediction from structural brain mri scans: a large-scale empirical study, Neuroinformatics 13 (1) (2015) 31–46.

[61] R. Tibshirani, Regression shrinkage and selection via the lasso, Journal of the Royal Statistical Society, Series B, Methodological (1996) 267–288.

[62] K. Van Leemput, F. Maes, D. Vandermeulen, P. Suetens, Automated model-based tissue classification of mr images of the brain, IEEE Transactions on Medical Imaging 18 (10) (1999) 897–908.

[63] A. Venkataraman, T.J. Whitford, C.-F. Westin, P. Golland, M. Kubicki, Whole brain resting state functional connectivity abnormalities in schizophrenia, Schizophrenia Research 139 (1–3) (Aug. 2012) 7–12.

[64] P. Viola, M. Jones, Rapid object detection using a boosted cascade of simple features, in: Proceedings of the 2001 IEEE Computer Society Conference on Computer Vision and Pattern Recognition, Vol. 1, CVPR 2001, IEEE, 2001, pp. I–I.

[65] P. Viola, M.J. Jones, Robust real-time face detection, International Journal of Computer Vision 57 (2) (2004) 137–154.

[66] B.S.C. Wade, S.H. Joshi, T. Pirnia, A.M. Leaver, R.P. Woods, P.M. Thompson, R. Espinoza, K.L. Narr, Random forest classification of depression status based on subcortical brain morphometry following electroconvulsive therapy, in: 2015 IEEE 12th International Symposium on Biomedical Imaging, ISBI, IEEE, Apr. 2015, pp. 92–96.

[67] Y. Wang, Y. Fan, P. Bhatt, C. Davatzikos, High-dimensional pattern regression using machine learning: from medical images to continuous clinical variables, NeuroImage 50 (4) (2010) 1519–1535.

[68] M. Wels, G. Carneiro, A. Aplas, M. Huber, J. Hornegger, D. Comaniciu, A discriminative model-constrained graph cuts approach to fully automated pediatric brain tumor segmentation in 3D MRI, in: International Conference on Medical Image Computing and Computer-Assisted Intervention, Springer, 2008, pp. 67–75.

[69] M. Yaqub, M.K. Javaid, C. Cooper, J.A. Noble, Investigation of the role of feature selection and weighted voting in random forests for 3D volumetric segmentation, IEEE Transactions on Medical Imaging 33 (2) (Feb. 2014) 258–271.

[70] J. Ye, M. Farnum, E. Yang, R. Verbeeck, V. Lobanov, N. Raghavan, G. Novak, A. DiBernardo, V.A. Narayan, Sparse learning and stability selection for predicting MCI to ad conversion using baseline ADNI data, BMC Neurology 12 (1) (2012) 46.

[71] J. Zhang, L. Zhang, L. Xiang, Y. Shao, G. Wu, X. Zhou, D. Shen, Q. Wang, Brain atlas fusion from high-thickness diagnostic magnetic resonance images by learning-based super-resolution, Pattern Recognition 63 (2017) 531–541.

[72] Y. Zheng, A. Barbu, B. Georgescu, M. Scheuering, D. Comaniciu, Four-chamber heart modeling and automatic segmentation for 3D cardiac CT volumes using marginal space learning and steerable features, IEEE Transactions on Medical Imaging 27 (11) (2008) 1668–1681.

[73] D. Zikic, B. Glocker, A. Criminisi, Atlas encoding by randomized forests for efficient label propagation, Springer, Berlin, Heidelberg, 2013, pp. 66–73.

[74] D. Zikic, B. Glocker, E. Konukoglu, A. Criminisi, C. Demiralp, J. Shotton, O.M. Thomas, T. Das, R. Jena, S.J. Price, Decision forests for tissue-specific segmentation of high-grade gliomas in multi-channel MR, in: International Conference on Medical Image Computing and Computer-Assisted Intervention, Springer, 2012, pp. 369–376.

[75] H. Zou, T. Hastie, Regularization and variable selection via the elastic net, Journal of the Royal Statistical Society, Series B, Statistical Methodology 67 (2) (2005) 301–320.

CHAPTER 20

Convolutional neural networks

Jonas Teuwen[a,b], Nikita Moriakov[a]

[a]Radboud University Medical Center, Department of Radiology and Nuclear Medicine, Nijmegen, the Netherlands
[b]Netherlands Cancer Institute, Department of Radiation Oncology, Amsterdam, the Netherlands

Contents

20.1.	Introduction	481
20.2.	Neural networks	482
	20.2.1 Loss function	483
	20.2.2 Backpropagation	484
20.3.	Convolutional neural networks	487
	20.3.1 Convolutions	488
	20.3.2 Nonlinearities	490
	20.3.3 Pooling layers	491
	20.3.4 Fully connected layers	492
20.4.	CNN architectures for classification	492
20.5.	Practical methodology	495
	20.5.1 Data standardization and augmentation	495
	20.5.2 Optimizers and learning rate	496
	20.5.3 Weight initialization and pretrained networks	497
	20.5.4 Regularization	498
20.6.	Future challenges	499
References		500

20.1. Introduction

Convolutional neural networks (CNNs) – or *convnets*, for short – have in recent years achieved results which were previously considered to be purely within the human realm. In this chapter we introduce CNNs, and for this we first consider regular neural networks, and how these methods are trained. After introducing the convolution, we introduce CNNs. They are very similar to the regular neural networks as they are also made up of neurons with learnable weights. But, in contrast to MLPs, CNNs make the explicit assumption that inputs have specific structure like images. This allows encoding this property into the architecture by sharing the weights for each location in the image and having neurons respond only locally.

Handbook of Medical Image Computing and Computer Assisted Intervention
https://doi.org/10.1016/B978-0-12-816176-0.00025-9
481

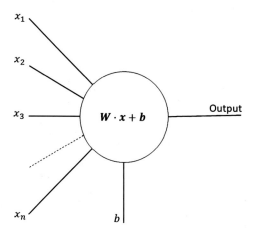

Figure 20.1 Schematic version of neuron.

20.2. Neural networks

To understand convolutional neural networks, we need to take one step back and first look into regular neural networks. Most concepts can readily be explained by using these simpler networks. The initial development of these networks originates in the work of Frank Rosenblatt on perceptrons and starts with the definition of a neuron. Mathematically, a neuron is a nonlinearity applied to an affine function. The input features $x = (x_1, x_2, \ldots, x_n)$ are passed through an affine function composed with a nonlinearity φ:

$$T(x) = \varphi\left(\sum_i W_i x_i + b\right) = \varphi(W \cdot x + b) \tag{20.1}$$

with given *weights* W and *bias* b. Schematically this is represented in Fig. 20.1. A typical nonlinearity, or *activation function* is the *sigmoid* defined by

$$\sigma(x) = \frac{1}{1 + e^{-x}}. \tag{20.2}$$

There are many choices for such nonlinearities, and different choices will be given when we discuss CNNs in Sect. 20.3.2.

Such a neural network can be modeled as a collection of neurons which are connected in an acyclic graph. That is, the output of some of the neurons become inputs to other neurons, and cycles where the output of a neuron maps back to an earlier intermediate input are forbidden. Commonly such neurons are organized in layers of neurons. Such a network consists of an input layer, one or more *hidden layers,* and an output layer. In contrast to the hidden layers, the output layer usually does not have

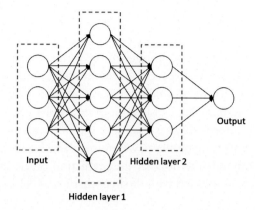

Figure 20.2 A 3-layer neural network with three inputs, two hidden layers of respectively 5 and 3 neurons, and one output layer. Notice that in both cases there are connections between neurons across layers, but not within a layer.

an activation function. Such networks are usually referred to as Multilinear Perceptron (MLP) or less commonly as Artificial Neural Network (ANN). If we want to be more explicit about the number of layers, we could refer to such a network as an N-layer network where N counts the number of layers, excluding the input layer. An example of this is given in Fig. 20.2. To use a neural network for prediction, we need to find the proper values for the parameters (W, b) and define a function to map the output of the neural network to a prediction; this could, for instance, be a class (i.e., malignant or benign) or a real value in the case of a regression problem. These parameters are the so-called *trainable parameters,* and the number of these parameters serves as a metric for the size (or capacity) of the neural network. In the example of Fig. 20.2, there are in total 8 neurons, where the hidden layers have $3 \cdot 5$ and $5 \cdot 3$ weights, and 5 and 3 biases, respectively. The output layer has 3 weights and 1 bias. In total this network has 27 learnable parameters. In modern neural network architectures, these numbers can run into the millions.

As mentioned, the output layer most commonly does not have an activation function because the output layer is often used to represent, for instance, class scores through a softmax function, which we will discuss in more detail below or some other real-valued target in the case of regression.

20.2.1 Loss function

Depending on a task, neural networks can be trained in a supervised or unsupervised way. For the type of tasks most frequently encountered in medical imaging, we are typically working with discriminative models, meaning that we have two spaces of objects X ("the inputs") and Y ("the labels") and we would like to learn a neural network f_θ

with parameters θ, the hypothesis, which outputs an object in Y given an object in X, or $f_\theta : X \rightarrow Y$. To do this, we have a training set of size m at our disposal $(X_i, y_i)_{i=1}^m$ where X_i is the input, for instance, an image, and y_i is the corresponding label. To put it differently, y_i is the response we expect from the model g_θ with X_i as input.

Putting this more formally, we assume there is a joint probability distribution $P(x, y)$ over $X \times Y$ and that the training set consists out of m samples $(X_i, y_i)_{i=1}^m$ independently drawn from $\mathbb{P}(x, y)$. In this formality, y is a random variable with conditional probability $\mathbb{P}(y \mid x)$. To formulate the training problem, we assume there is a nonnegative real–valued loss function L which can measure how far the prediction of the hypothesis y_{pred} from the real value y is. The risk associated with the hypothesis g_θ is defined as the expectation of the loss function

$$R(g_\theta) = \mathbb{E}_{(X,y)\sim\mathbb{P}(x,y)} [L(g_\theta(X), y)]. \tag{20.3}$$

The goal of learning is to find parameters θ such that R is minimal, that is, we want to find θ^* such that $\theta^* = \arg\min_{\theta\in\mathbf{R}^m} R(g_\theta)$, where m is the number of parameters of the neural network.

In general, the risk $R(g_\theta)$ cannot be computed because the distribution $\mathbb{P}(x, y)$ is unknown. In this case we replace the expectation with the average over the training set to obtain the *empirical risk* as an approximation to the expectation:

$$R_{\text{emp}}(g_\theta) = \frac{1}{m} \sum_{i=1}^m L(g_\theta(X_i), y_i). \tag{20.4}$$

The process of minimizing the empirical risk is called *empirical risk minimization*.

20.2.2 Backpropagation

Nearly all neural networks encountered in practice are almost-everywhere differentiable with respect to parameters θ and are optimized with gradient-based optimization:

$$\nabla_\theta R_{\text{emp}}(g_\theta) = [\frac{\partial}{\partial\theta_1}, \frac{\partial}{\partial\theta_2}, \ldots, \frac{\partial}{\partial\theta_M}]R_{\text{emp}}(g_\theta). \tag{20.5}$$

Backpropagation is an algorithm that allows us to compute the gradients and apply gradient-based optimization schemes such as gradient descent, which is explained in more detail in Sect. 20.5.2.

The structure of a neural network allows for a very efficient computation of the gradient by a process called *backpropagation*, which can be readily understood by applying the chain rule.

For a bit more detail, consider a feedforward neural network, which accepts an input x which is propagated through the network to produce an output y. This process is the *forward propagation* step and results in a scalar loss R_{emp}. Computing the derivative for such a network is straightforward, but numerically evaluating such an expression is not only computationally expensive, it is also sensitive to numerical rounding errors, especially for deeper networks. Using the backpropagation algorithm, we can evaluate this derivative in a computationally efficient way with the additional advantage that the computations can be reused in subsequent steps. Once we have the gradient, we can apply an algorithm such as stochastic gradient descent (SGD) to compute updates to the network weights.

To be able to understand backpropagation properly, we introduce the *computation graph* language. A computation graph is a directed graph where on each node we have an *operation*, and an operation is a function of one or more variables and returns either a number, multiple numbers, or a tensor. The chain rule can now be used to compute the derivatives of functions formed by composing other functions with known derivatives. The backpropagation algorithms allows us to do this in a highly efficient manner.

Before we continue, let us recall the chain rule. For this let f and g be real-valued functions. Suppose additionally that $y = g(x)$ and $z = f(g(x)) = f(y)$ (i.e., two operations on the computation graph). The chain rule is now given by

$$\frac{dz}{dx} = \frac{dz}{dy}\frac{dy}{dx}.$$

The generalization to higher dimensions is trivial. Suppose now that $x \in \mathbf{R}^n$ and $y \in \mathbf{R}^m$, $g : \mathbf{R}^n \to \mathbf{R}^m$, and $f : \mathbf{R}^m \to \mathbf{R}$. Then if $y = g(x)$ and $z = f(y)$, we have

$$\frac{\partial z}{\partial x_i} = \sum_j \frac{\partial z}{\partial y_j}\frac{\partial y_j}{\partial x_i}. \tag{20.6}$$

Using the chain rule (20.6), the back propagation algorithm is readily explained. Before we proceed, we fix some notation. Consider an MLP where the jth neuron in the ℓth layer has weighted output (i.e., before the activation function φ) z_j^ℓ and activation $a_j^\ell := \varphi(z_j^\ell)$. Similarly, the jth neuron in the layer ℓ weights output of the kth neuron in the $(\ell-1)$th by w_{kj}^ℓ with corresponding bias b_j^ℓ.

As we intend to minimize the empirical risk function R_{emp} through gradient optimization, we are interested in the derivatives

$$\frac{\partial R_{\text{emp}}}{\partial w_{kj}^\ell} \quad \text{and} \quad \frac{\partial R_{\text{emp}}}{\partial b_j^\ell}.$$

These derivatives can readily be computed using the chain rule (20.6):

$$\frac{\partial R_{\text{emp}}}{\partial w_{kj}^\ell} = \sum_k \frac{R_{\text{emp}}}{\partial z_k^\ell}\frac{\partial z_k^\ell}{\partial w_{kj}^\ell}.$$

As

$$z_k^\ell := \sum_j w_{kj}^\ell a_j^{\ell-1} + b_k^\ell, \tag{20.7}$$

the last derivative is equal to $a_j^{\ell-1}$ when $j = k$ and 0 otherwise, so,

$$\frac{\partial R_{\text{emp}}}{\partial w_{kj}^\ell} = \frac{\partial R_{\text{emp}}}{\partial z_k^\ell} a_j^{\ell-1}.$$

Using the chain rule again, we can see that

$$\frac{\partial R_{\text{emp}}}{\partial b_j^\ell} = \frac{\partial R_{\text{emp}}}{\partial z_j^\ell}.$$

Using these, we can see how the backpropagation rule works by efficiently computing $\varepsilon_j^\ell := \partial R_{\text{emp}}/\partial z_j^\ell$ where we will refer to ε_j^ℓ as the *error* of the jth node in the ℓth layer.

The backpropagation algorithm is an efficient way to compute the error ε^ℓ iteratively using error $\varepsilon^{\ell+1}$, so we proceed by computing the error from the last layer L, again, using the chain rule:

$$\varepsilon_j^L = \sum_k \frac{\partial R_{\text{emp}}}{\partial a_k^L} \frac{\partial a_k^L}{\partial z_j^L}, \tag{20.8}$$

and, when $k \neq L$, the terms vanish and we obtain:

$$\varepsilon_j^L = \frac{\partial R_{\text{emp}}}{\partial a_j^L} \frac{\partial a_j^L}{\partial z_j^L} = \frac{\partial R_{\text{emp}}}{\partial a_j^L} \varphi'(z_j^L).$$

If we can derive a rule to compute ε_j^ℓ from $\varepsilon_j^{\ell+1}$ efficiently, we are done. This rule can be found, again, through the chain rule:

$$\varepsilon_j^\ell = \frac{\partial R_{\text{emp}}}{\partial z_j^\ell} = \sum_k \frac{\partial R_{\text{emp}}}{\partial z_k^{\ell+1}} \frac{\partial z_k^{\ell+1}}{\partial z_j^\ell}$$

$$= \sum_k \varepsilon_k^{\ell+1} \frac{\partial z_k^{\ell+1}}{\partial z_j^\ell}.$$

Using (20.7) we can compute the last derivative as

$$\frac{\partial z_k^{\ell+1}}{\partial z_j^\ell} = w_{kj}^{\ell+1} \varphi'(z_j^\ell),$$

so, the backpropagation rule becomes

$$\varepsilon_j^\ell = \sum_k \varepsilon_j^{\ell+1} w_{kj}^{\ell+1} \varphi'(z_j^\ell). \tag{20.9}$$

In summary, to compute the derivatives of the empirical risk R_{emp} with respect to the weights and biases, it is sufficient to compute the error ε^ℓ. This can be done iteratively, by first computing the error for the final layer by (20.8) and then proceeding to the input by applying (20.9) for each layer consecutively.

20.3. Convolutional neural networks

Convolutional neural networks (CNNs), or *convnets* for short, are a special case of *feed-forward* neural networks. They are very similar to the neural networks presented above in the sense that they are made up of neurons with learnable weights and biases. The essential difference is that the CNN architecture makes the implicit assumption that the input are image-like, which allows us to encode certain properties in the architecture. In particular, convolutions capture *translation invariance* (i.e., filters are independent of the location).

This in turns makes the forward function more efficient, vastly reduces the number of parameters, and therefore makes the network easier to optimize and less dependent on the size of the data.

In contrast to regular neural networks, the layers of CNNs have neurons arranged in a few dimensions: channels, width, height, and number of filters in the simplest 2D case. A convolution neural network consists, just as an MLP, of a sequence of layers, where every layer transforms the activations or outputs of the previous layer through another differentiable function. There are several such layers employed in CNNs, and these will be explained in subsequent sections, however, the most common building blocks which you will encounter in most CNN architectures are: the convolution layer, pooling layer, and fully connected layers. In essence, these layers are like feature extractors, dimensionality reduction and classification layers, respectively. These layers of a CNN are stacked to form a full convolutional layer.

Before we proceed with an overview of the different layers, we pause a bit at the convolution layer. Essentially, a convolution layer uses a convolutional kernel as a filter for the input. Usually, there are many of such *filters*.

During a forward pass, a filter slides across the input volume and computes the *activation map* of the filter at that point by computing the pointwise product of each value and adding these to obtain the activation at the point. Such a sliding filter is naturally implemented by a *convolution* and, as this is a linear operator, it can be written as a dot-product for efficient implementation.

Intuitively, this means that when training such a CNN, the network will learn filters that capture some kind of visual information such as an edge, orientation, and eventually, in a higher layer of the network, entire patterns. In each such convolution layer, we have an entire set of such filters, each of which will produce a separate activation map. These activation maps are stacked to obtain the output map or *activation volume* of this layer.

20.3.1 Convolutions

Mathematically, the convolution $(x * w)(a)$ of functions x and w is defined in all dimensions as

$$(x * w)(a) = \int x(t)w(a - t)\, da, \tag{20.10}$$

where a is in $\mathbf{R}^n$ for any $n \geqslant 1$, and the integral is replaced by its higher-dimensional variant. To understand the idea behind convolutions, it is interesting to pick the Gaussian function $w(a) = \exp(-x^2)$ as an example. If we were taking a photo with a camera and shaking the camera a bit, the blurry picture would be the real picture x convolved with a Gaussian function w.

In the terminology of convolutional neural networks, x is called the *input*, w is called the *filter* or *kernel*, and the output is often referred to as *activation, or feature map*.

Note that we modeled the input and kernel in (20.10) as a continuous function. Due to the discrete nature of image sensors, this will not be the case in practice and it is more realistic to assume that parameter t is *discrete*. If we assume that this is the case, then we can define the discrete convolution

$$(x * w)(a) = \sum_a x(t)w(t - a), \tag{20.11}$$

where a runs over all values in the space, and can be in any dimension. In deep learning, usually x is a multidimensional array of data and the kernel w involves learnable parameters and usually has finite support, that is, there are only finitely many values a for which $w(a)$ is nonzero. This means that we can implement (20.11) as a finite summation. The definition of (20.11) is independent of dimension, but in medical imaging we will mainly be working with 2- or 3-dimensional convolutions:

$$(I * K)(i, j) = \sum_m \sum_n I(m, n)K(i - m, j - n), \tag{20.12}$$

or

$$(I * K)(i, j, k) = \sum_m \sum_n \sum_\ell I(m, n, \ell)K(i - m, j - n, k - \ell). \tag{20.13}$$

The convolutions (20.10) and (20.11) are commutative, which means that $I * K = K * I$, so that we can also write (20.12) as

$$(I * K)(i, j) = \sum_m \sum_n I(i - m, j - n) K(m, n). \tag{20.14}$$

As K has finite support, this a priori infinite sum becomes finite. Some neural network libraries also implement an operation called the *cross-correlation*, but from a deep learning perspective these operations are equivalent, as one weight set can be directly translated into the other.

Convolutions as an infinitely strong priors

As a convolution is a linear transformation, it can be written in the form of $w \cdot x + b$ and therefore as a fully connected layer. However, as the kernels are often much smaller than the input, only a small number of inputs will interact with the output (the so-called *receptive field*), and the weight tensor w will be very *sparse*. Additionally, the weight tensor will contain many similar elements, caused by the fact that the kernel is applied to every location in the input. This effect is referred to as *weight sharing*, and, together with the sparsity, this not only means that we need to store fewer parameters, which improves both the memory requirements and statistical efficiency, but additionally puts a prior on the weights: we implicitly assume that a filter, such as an edge filter, can be relevant to every part of the image and that most interactions between pixels are local. For most images, this is definitely a reasonable assumption, but this can break down in the case of other type of image data such a CT sinograms or MRI k-space where local information in the imaging domain can translate to global information in the acquisition space. Sometimes, we refer to this by saying that a convolution is an *infinitely strong prior* in contrast to weaker priors such as ℓ^p-regularization discussed below.

Much research has gone into adapting convolutions and imposing new strong priors, for instance, the *group convolution* [1] additionally enforces a certain symmetry group to hold for the image. Further discussion of this topic is beyond the scope of this chapter.

Equivariance

Next to sparsity and weight sharing, convolutions put another prior on the kernel weights in the form of translation equivariance, which to a translation (for instance, shifting) of the convolution means that if we apply a translation to the image, and then apply convolutions, we obtain the same result as first applying the convolution and then translating the feature map. More specifically, an operator T is said to be equivariant with respect to f if for each x we have $T(f(x)) = f(T(x))$. Translation equivariance is a sensible assumption for images, as the features to detect an object in the image should only depend on the object itself and not on its precise location.

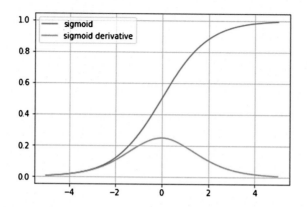

20.3.2 Nonlinearities

Nonlinearities are essential for neural network design: without nonlinearities a neural network would compute a linear function of its input, which is too restrictive. The choice of a nonlinearity can have a large impact on the training speed of a neural network.

sigmoid   This nonlinearity is defined as

$$\sigma(x) = \frac{1}{1+e^{-x}}, \quad x \in \mathbb{R}. \tag{20.15}$$

It is easy to show that $\sigma(x) \in (0, 1)$ for all $x \in \mathbb{R}$. Furthermore, σ is monotone increasing, $\lim_{x \to \infty} \sigma(x) = 1$ and $\lim_{x \to -\infty} \sigma(x) = 0$.

This makes the sigmoid nonlinearity suitable when the goal is to produce outputs contained in the $[0, 1]$ range, such as probabilities or normalized images. One can also show that $\lim_{x \to \infty} \sigma'(x) = \lim_{x \to -\infty} \sigma'(x) = 0$. This fact implies that the sigmoid nonlinearity may lead to *vanishing gradients*: when the input x to the sigmoid is far from zero, the neuron will saturate and the gradient of $\sigma(x)$ with respect to x will be close to zero, which will make successive optimization hard. This is the reason why sigmoid nonlinearities are rarely used in the intermediate layers of CNNs.

tanh   The *tanh* nonlinearity is defined as

$$\tanh(x) = \frac{e^x - e^{-x}}{e^x + e^{-x}}, \quad x \in \mathbb{R}. \tag{20.16}$$

It is easy to show that $\tanh(x) \in (-1, 1)$ for all $x \in \mathbb{R}$. Furthermore, tanh is monotone increasing, $\lim_{x \to \infty} \tanh(x) = 1$ and $\lim_{x \to -\infty} \tanh(x) = -1$. Similar to the sigmoid nonlinearity, tanh can lead to vanishing gradients and is rarely used in intermediate layers of CNNs.

ReLU   This nonlinearity is defined as

$$\mathrm{ReLU}(x) = \max(0, x), \quad x \in \mathbb{R}. \tag{20.17}$$

It is easy to see that $\mathrm{ReLU}'(x) = 1$ for $x > 0$ and that $\mathrm{ReLU}'(x) = 0$ for $x < 0$. ReLU nonlinearity generally leads to faster convergence compared to sigmoid or tanh nonlinearities, and it typically works well in CNNs with properly chosen weight initialization strategy and learning rate. Several modifications of ReLU activation function such as Exponential Linear Units (ELUs) [2] have been proposed.

softmax   Softmax nonlinearity is more specialized compared to the general nonlinearities listed above. It is defined as

$$\mathrm{softmax}(x)_i := \frac{\exp(x_i)}{\sum\limits_{j=1}^{n} \exp(x_j)}, \quad x \in \mathbb{R}^n,$$

and maps a vector $x \in \mathbb{R}^n$ to a probability vector of length n. The intuition behind softmax is as follows: map $x \mapsto \exp(x)$ gives an order-preserving bijection between the set of real numbers $\mathbb{R}$ and the set of strictly positive real numbers $\mathbb{R}_{>0}$, so that for any indexes i, j we have $x_i < x_j$ if and only if $\exp(x_i) < \exp(x_j)$. Subsequent division by $\sum\limits_{j=1}^{n} \exp(x_j)$ normalizes the result, giving probability vector as the output. This nonlinearity is used, e.g., in classification tasks, after the final fully connected layer with n outputs in a n-class classification problem. It should be noted, however, that softmax outputs do not truly model prediction uncertainty in the scenario of noisy labels (such as noisy organ segmentations in medical imaging).

20.3.3 Pooling layers

The goal of a pooling layer is to produce a summary statistic of its input and to reduce the spatial dimensions of the feature map (hopefully without losing essential information). For this the *max pooling* layer reports the maximal values in each rectangular neighborhood of each point (i, j) (or (i, j, k) for 3D data) of each input feature while the *average pooling* layer reports the average values. Most common form of maxpooling uses stride 2 together with kernel size 2, which corresponds to partitioning the feature map spatially into a regular grid of square or cubic blocks with side 2 and taking max or average over such blocks for each input feature.

While pooling operations are common building blocks of CNNs when the aim is to reduce the feature map spatial dimension, it should be noted that one can achieve similar goal by using, e.g., 3×3 convolutions with stride 2 if working with 2D data. In this case one can also simultaneously double the number of filters to reduce information loss while at the same time aggregating higher level features. This downsampling strategy is used, e.g., in ResNet [3] architecture.

20.3.4 Fully connected layers

Fully connected layer with n input dimensions and m output dimensions is defined as follows. The layer output is determined by the following parameters: the weight matrix $W \in M_{m,n}(\mathbb{R})$ having m rows and n columns, and the bias vector $b \in \mathbb{R}^m$. Given input vector $x \in \mathbb{R}^n$, the output of a fully-connected layer FC with activation function f is defined as

$$FC(x) := f(Wx + b) \in \mathbb{R}^m. \tag{20.18}$$

In the formula above, Wx is the matrix product and the function f is applied componentwise.

Fully connected layers are used as final layers in classification problems, where a few (most often one or two) fully-connected layers are attached on top of a CNN. For this, the CNN output is flattened and viewed as a single vector. Another example would be various autoencoder architectures, where FC layers are often attached to the latent code in both encoder and decoder paths of the network. When working with convolutional neural network it is helpful to realize that for a feature map with n channels one can apply a convolution filter with kernel size 1 and m output channels, which would be equivalent to applying a same fully-connected layer with m outputs to each point in the feature map.

20.4. CNN architectures for classification

Convolutional neural networks were originally introduced more than 20 years ago with the development of the LeNet CNN architecture [4,5]. Originally, the applications of CNNs were limited to relatively simple problems like handwritten digit recognition, but in the recent years CNN-based approaches have become dominant in image classification, object localization, and image segmentation tasks. This popularity can be attributed to two major factors: availability of computational resources (mostly GPUs) and data, on the one hand, and improvements in CNN architectures, on the other. Today CNN architectures have been developed that are quite successful in the tasks of image classification, object localization and image/instance segmentation. Below we will discuss a few noteworthy CNN architectures for image classification problems.

A neural network needs to have enough expressive power, depending on the task, to perform well. A naive approach towards increasing the capacity is increasing the number of filters in convolutional layers and the depth of the network. This approach was taken in the *AlexNet* [6] architecture, which was the first architecture that popularized CNNs in computer vision by winning the ImageNet ILSVRC challenge [7] in 2012. It featured 5 convolutional layers and only feed-forward connections with the total of 60M trainable parameters. Shortly after it was outperformed by

- *ZF Net* [8] in 2013;
- *GoogLeNet* [9], the winning solution for the 2014 version of the challenge;
- *VGG16/VGG19* [10], which scored the second-best in this challenge but showed better single-net performance and was conceptually simpler.

VGG19 features 19 trainable layers connected in a feed-forward fashion, of which 16 layers are convolutional and relies on 3×3 convolutions with stride 1 and ReLU activations. Convolutional layers are gathered in 2 blocks of 2 layers for the first convolutional blocks and in 3 blocks of 4 layers for the last convolutional blocks. Maxpooling is performed in between the convolutional blocks, and the number of features in convolutional blocks doubles after each maxpooling operation. An important difference between AlexNet and VGG (as well as more modern architectures) is how large effective receptive field size is created: AlexNet used 11×11 filters in its initial layer while VGG uses stacks of 3×3 filters, and it can be easily shown that this is more parameter-efficient way of increasing receptive field size. Compared to VGG19, GoogLeNet has much less trainable parameters (4M for 22 layers vs. 140M for 19 layers of VGG19) which is due to the introduction of the so-called *inception module*, which is a deviation from the standard feedforward pattern, and helps to improve parameter efficiency.

However, all the architectures above still largely rely on feedforward information flow similar to the original LeNet-5 [4,5], while the benefits of these architectures mostly stem from their depth. Making the feedforward architectures even deeper leads to a number of challenges in addition to increased number of parameters. The first obstacle is the problem of vanishing/exploding gradients [11,23,12]. This can be largely addressed by normalized weight initialization and intermediate normalization layers, such as Batch Normalization [13]. Yet another obstacle is the performance degradation problem [3]: as the depth of a feedforward neural network increases, both testing and training accuracies get saturated and degrade afterwards. Such performance degradation is not explained by overfitting, and indicates that such networks are generally harder to optimize. Alternative CNN architectures have been suggested to deal with these shortcomings. A common feature of such architectures is the use of skip connections, which carry over information directly from earlier layers into the later layers without passing through intermediate convolutional layers. This, supposedly, helps in general to prevent information from "washing out". This general idea has been implemented in a number of ways.

ResNet [3] architecture, which was the basis for the winning solution in ILSVRC 2015 challenge [7], deals with the aforementioned issues by introducing *residual blocks*. Suppose that we are considering a residual block with two convolutional layers. In such a block the original input x goes through the first convolutional layer (typically a 3×3 convolution), after that Batch Normalization is applied and then the ReLU nonlinearity follows. The result is fed into the next convolutional layer, after which Batch Normalization is performed. This gives the output $F(x)$, to which x is added pointwise and then ReLU nonlinearity is applied. The output of the block hence equals $\text{ReLU}(F(x) + x)$. In general, ResNets are

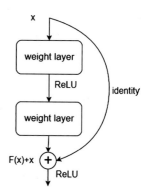

build out of a varying number of such residual blocks with 2–3 convolutional layers in each block. In particular, it is interesting to note that, according to [3], using only a single convolutional layer in a residual block did not give any advantages compared to the plain feedforward architecture without residual connections. For feature map downsampling, convolutions with stride 2 are used, while the number of feature maps is doubled at the same time. This architecture choice allows training networks with more than a 100 layers and no performance degradation, as is shown in [3]. ResNet-based architectures are often used up to this day, and several extensions were proposed as well [14]. Furthermore, ResNet is often used as a CNN feature extractor for object detection and instance segmentation, e.g., in Mask R–CNN [15].

A more recent development is the DenseNet architecture [16], which is build from a collection of *dense blocks*, with "transition layers" (1×1 convolutions and 2×2 average pooling) to reduce the size of the feature maps in between. The main insight is that each such dense block consist of a few "convolutional layers", which, depending on a DenseNet variant, are either a stack of a 3×3 convolutional layer, Batch Normalization layer, and ReLU nonlinearity, or, alternatively, contain an initial 1×1 convolutional layer with Batch Normalization and ReLU nonlinearity to reduce the number of input features. Each such "convolutional layer" provides its output features to *all* successive convolutional layers in the block, leading to a "dense" connectivity pattern. The output of a dense block is the stack of all resulting feature maps and the input features, and as a result the successive dense blocks have access to these features and don't need to relearn them. This architecture achieves comparable or better performance on ILSVRC as compared to a ResNet architecture while also using significantly less parameters. For more details, we refer to [16].

20.5. Practical methodology

20.5.1 Data standardization and augmentation

Prior to feeding the data to the neural network for training, some preprocessing is usually done. Many beginners fail to obtain reasonable results not because of the architectures or methods or lack of regularization, but instead because they simply did not normalize and visually inspect their data. Two most important forms of pre-processing are *data standardization* and *dataset augmentation*. There are a few data standardization techniques common in imaging.

- **Mean subtraction.** During mean subtraction, the mean of every channel is computed over the training dataset, and these means are subtracted channelwise from both the training and the testing data.
- **Scaling.** Scaling amounts to computing channelwise standard deviations across the training dataset, and dividing the input data channelwise by these values so as to obtain a distribution with standard deviation equal to 1 in each channel. In place of division by standard deviation one can divide, e.g., by 95-percentile of the absolute value of a channel.
- **Specialized methods.** In addition to these generic methods, there are also some specialized standardization methods for medical imaging tasks, e.g., in chest X-ray one has to work with images coming from different vendors, furthermore, X-ray tubes might be deteriorating. In [17] local energy-based normalization was investigated for chest X-ray images, and it was shown that this normalization technique improves model performance on supervised computer-aided detection tasks. For another example, when working with hematoxylin and eosin (H&E) stained histological slides, one can observe variations in color and intensity in samples coming from different laboratories and performed on different days of the week. These variations can potentially reduce the effectiveness of quantitative image analysis. A normalization algorithm specifically designed to tackle this problem was suggested in [18], where it was also shown that it improves the performance for a few computer-aided detection tasks on these slide images. Finally, in certain scenarios (e.g., working directly with raw sinogram data for CT or Digital Breast Tomosynthesis [19]) it is reasonable to take log-transform of the input data as an extra preprocessing step.

Neural networks are known to benefit from large amounts of training data, and it is a common practice to artificially enlarge an existing dataset by adding data to it in a process called "*augmentation*". We distinguish between train-time augmentation and test-time augmentation, and concentrate on the first for now (which is also more common). In case of train-time augmentation, the goal is to provide a larger training dataset to the algorithm. In a supervised learning scenario, we are given a dataset $\mathcal{D}$ consisting of pairs (x_j, y_j) of a training sample $x_j \in \mathbb{R}^d$ and the corresponding label y_j. Given the dataset $\mathcal{D}$, one should design transformations $T_1, T_2, \ldots, T_n : \mathbb{R}^d \to \mathbb{R}^d$ which are label-preserving in a sense that for every sample $(x_j, y_j) \in \mathcal{D}$ and every transformation T_i the resulting vector $T_i x_j$ still looks like a sample from $\mathcal{D}$ with label y_j. Multiple transformations can be additionally stacked, resulting in greater number of new samples. The resulting new samples with labels assigned to them in this way are added to the training dataset and optimization as usual is performed. In case of the test-time augmentation the goal is to improve test-time performance of the model as follows. For a predictive model f, given a test sample $x \in \mathbb{R}^d$, one computes the model predictions $f(x), f(T_1 x), \ldots, f(T_n x)$ for different augmenting transformations and aggregates these predictions in a certain way (e.g., by averaging softmax-output from classification layer [6]). In general, choice of the augmenting transformation depends on the dataset, but there are a few common strategies for data augmentation in imaging tasks:

- **Flipping.** Image x is mirrored in one or two dimensions, yielding one or two additional samples. Flipping in horizontal dimension is commonly done, e.g., on the ImageNet dataset [6], while on medical imaging datasets flipping in both dimensions is sometimes used.
- **Random cropping and scaling.** Image x of dimensions $W \times H$ is cropped to a random region $[x_1, x_2] \times [y_1, y_2] \subseteq [0, W] \times [0, H]$, and the result is interpolated to obtain original pixel dimensions if necessary. The size of the cropped region should still be large enough to preserve enough global context for correct label assignment.
- **Random rotation.** An image x is rotated by some random angle φ (often limited to the set $\varphi \in [\pi/2, \pi, 3\pi/2]$). This transformation is useful, e.g., in pathology, where rotation invariance of samples is observed; however, it is not widely used on datasets like ImageNet.
- **Gamma transform.** A grayscale image x is mapped to image x^γ for $\gamma > 0$, where $\gamma = 1$ corresponds to identity mapping. This transformation in effect adjusts the contrast of an image.
- **Color augmentations.** Individual color channels of the image are altered in order to capture certain invariance of classification with respect to variation in factors such as intensity of illumination or its color. This can be done, e.g., by adding small random offsets to individual channel values; an alternative scheme based on PCA can be found in [6].

20.5.2 Optimizers and learning rate

As discussed above, the optimization goal when training neural networks is minimization of the empirical risk R_{emp}. This is done by, firstly, computing the gradient $\nabla_\theta R_{\mathrm{emp}}$ of the risk on a minibatch of training data with respect to the neural network parameters θ using backpropagation, and, secondly, updating the neural network weights θ accordingly. This update in its most basic form of *stochastic gradient descent* is given by the formula

$$\theta := \theta - \eta \cdot \nabla_\theta R_{\text{emp}},$$

where $\eta > 0$ is the hyperparameter called the *learning rate*. A common extension of this algorithm is the addition of *momentum*, which in theory should accelerate the convergence of the algorithm on flat parts of the loss surface. In this case, the algorithm remembers the previous update direction and combines it with the newly computed gradient to determine the new update direction:

$$\delta\theta := \alpha \cdot \delta\theta - \eta \cdot \nabla_\theta R_{\text{emp}},$$
$$\theta := \theta + \delta\theta.$$

More recent variations to stochastic gradient descent are adaptive methods such as RMSProp and Adam [20], which extends RMSProp by adding momentum for the gradient updates. All these methods (SGD, RMSProp, Adam) are implemented in deep learning frameworks such as Tensorflow and PyTorch. Adam, in particular, is a popular choice once a good starting learning rate is picked. However, one should note that there is some recent research (see, e.g., [21]) suggesting that adaptive methods such as Adam and RMSProp may lead to poorer generalization and that properly tuned SGD with momentum is a safer option.

Choice of a proper learning rate is still driven largely by trial and error up to this date, including learning rate for adaptive optimizers such as Adam. This choice depends heavily on the neural network architecture, with architectures such as ResNet and DenseNet including Batch Normalization known to work well with relatively large learning rates in the order of 10^{-1}, and the batch size, with larger batches allowing for higher learning rate and faster convergence. In general, it makes sense to pick the batch size as large as possible given the network architecture and image size, and then to choose the largest possible learning rate which allows for stable learning. If the error keeps oscillating (instead of steadily decreasing), it is advised to reduce the initial learning rate. Furthermore, it is common to use *learning rate schedule*, i.e., to change the learning rate during training depending on the current number of epochs and/or validation error. For instance, one can reduce the learning rate by a factor of 10 two times when the epoch count exceeds 50% and 75% of the total epoch budget; or one can choose to decrease the learning rate once the mean error on validation dataset stops decreasing in the process of training.

20.5.3 Weight initialization and pretrained networks

It is easy to see that if two neurons (or convolutional filters) in the same place of a computational graph have exactly the same bias and weights, then they will always get exactly the same gradients, and hence will never be able to learn distinct features, and this would result in losing some expressive power of the network. The connection between random initialization and expressive power of the network was explicitly examined in [22].

To "break the symmetry" when cold-starting the neural network training it is a common practice to initialize the weights randomly with zero mean and variance depending on the "input size" of the neuron [23,24], while biases are still initialized by zeros. The initialization strategy [24], which is more recent and was particularly derived for ReLU activations, suggests to initialize the weights by a zero–mean Gaussian distribution whose standard deviation equals $\sqrt{\frac{2}{n}}$, where n is determined as follows:

- When initializing a fully-connected layer, n equals the number of input features of a layer;
- When initializing, e.g., a two–dimensional convolutional layer of dimension $k \times k$ with m input feature maps, n equals the product $k^2 \cdot m$.

Most practical initialization strategies such as He initialization are already implemented in deep learning frameworks such as PyTorch and Tensorflow.

A second option to training from cold start is to use a pretrained convolutional network, stack fully connected layers with randomly initialized weights atop for a particular classification task, and then fine-tune the resulting network on a particular dataset. This strategy is motivated by the heuristic that the ImageNet dataset is fairly generic, hence convolutional features learned on ImageNet should be useful for other imaging datasets as well. Pretrained networks such as VGG, ResNet, and DenseNet variants are easy to find online. When fine-tuning a pretrained CNN for a particular classification task, it often makes sense to choose a lower learning rate for updates of the convolutional feature extraction layers and a higher learning rate for the final classification layers.

20.5.4 Regularization

Regularization, generally speaking, is a wide range of ML techniques aimed at reducing overfitting of the models while maintaining theoretical expressive power.

- **L^1/L^2 regularization.** These regularization methods are one of the most well-known regularization methods originating in classical machine learning theory in connection with maximum a posteriori (MAP) estimates for Laplace and Gaussian priors, respectively [25]. So suppose now that we have a neural network with parameters θ and loss function $L(\theta)$. In case of L^2 regularization, the term $\frac{\lambda_2}{2} \cdot \|\theta\|_2^2$ is added to the loss function; in case of L^1 regularization, the term $\lambda_1 \cdot \|\theta\|_1$ is added instead; λ_1, λ_2 are hyperparameters. Intuitively speaking, L^2 regularization encourages the network to use all of its inputs a little, rather than some of the inputs a lot, while L^1 regularization encourages the network to learn sparse weight vectors (which can be used, e.g., for feature selection tasks). Also L^1/L^2 regularization is often already implemented in deep learning frameworks and is easy to use (e.g., in

PyTorch L^2 regularization is added by passing a nonzero parameter λ_2 to an optimizer), however, one should note that there are regularization methods specifically designed for neural networks which can be more effective.

- **Max norm constraints.** Another form of regularization is enforcing an absolute upper bound $\|\theta\|_2 \leqslant c$ on the norm of the weight. In practice, this corresponds to performing the parameter update as usual, and then scaling the resulting θ back to the ball $\{x : \|x\|_2 \leqslant c\}$ of radius c. As a consequence, this form of regularization prevents weights from exploding.

- **Dropout.** Introduced in [26], dropout is a very powerful and simple regularization method for neural networks. While training, dropout is implemented by keeping a neuron active with some probability $p \in (0, 1)$ (which is a hyperparameter that can be different for different layers) while also dividing the output activation by p, and setting it to zero otherwise. During inference, all neurons are kept active and no scaling is applied. Very often probabilities p are chosen in a way that early convolutional layers are kept intact with probabilities close or equal to 1, while the probability of keeping neuron active goes down for deeper layers. Activation scaling during training time in this procedure is introduced in order to keep mean activations the same as during inference time, while saving computation cost at inference time. Dropout is implemented as a layer in frameworks such as PyTorch and Tensorflow and it is straightforward to add it to a model. Dropout is included in many classical NN architectures for classification and segmentation, see, e.g., [16] and [27]. An interesting recent development is the work [28], where it was shown that dropout training in deep neural networks can be viewed as a form of approximate Bayesian inference.

20.6. Future challenges

Despite the enormous success of CNNs in computer vision, in general, and in medical imaging, in particular, in recent years, there remain important challenges as well. Firstly, there is a well-known problem of the lack of interpretability of predictions. For example, in an image classification problem a neural network can produce accurate predictions, but the internal CNN features remain a black box and do not reveal much information. In medical imaging, however, we would like to know what image features are responsible for the prediction. Some work is done in this direction, e.g., there are a few approaches to the visualization of saliency maps [29]. Furthermore, we would be interested in image features that have clear clinical interpretation, but extracting those in an unsupervised manner is challenging.

Secondly, there is often a problem of domain shift, which emerges when a neural network is trained on a dataset from one domain and then it is applied to a related, but different domain. Some examples would be when

- We make a model for object detection in urban scenes and train it on scenes generated in a computer game, then try to apply it on real-life scenes [30];
- We have multiple vendors for, e.g., mammography scanners, which apply some amount of vendor-specific processing so that resulting images look different [31].

In general, developing models that are robust to variations in acquisition equipment remains challenging.

Thirdly, the neural networks remain data-hungry, and there is ongoing work on improving the parameter efficiency [1].

References

[1] T.S. Cohen, M. Welling, Group equivariant convolutional networks, preprint, arXiv:1602.07576, 2016.

[2] D.A. Clevert, T. Unterthiner, S. Hochreiter, Fast and accurate deep network learning by exponential linear units (ELUs), preprint, arXiv:1511.07289, 2015.

[3] K. He, X. Zhang, S. Ren, J. Sun, Deep residual learning for image recognition, in: CVPR, IEEE Computer Society, 2016, pp. 770–778.

[4] Y. LeCun, B. Boser, J.S. Denker, D. Henderson, R.E. Howard, W. Hubbard, et al., Backpropagation applied to handwritten zip code recognition, Neural Computation 1 (4) (1989) 541–551, https://doi.org/10.1162/neco.1989.1.4.541.

[5] Y. LeCun, L. Bottou, Y. Bengio, P. Haffner, Gradient-based learning applied to document recognition, Proceedings of the IEEE 86 (11) (1998) 2278–2324.

[6] A. Krizhevsky, I. Sutskever, G.E. Hinton, Imagenet classification with deep convolutional neural networks, in: F. Pereira, C.J.C. Burges, L. Bottou, K.Q. Weinberger (Eds.), Advances in Neural Information Processing Systems, vol. 25, Curran Associates, Inc., 2012, pp. 1097–1105, http://papers.nips.cc/paper/4824-imagenet-classification-with-deep-convolutional-neural-networks.pdf.

[7] O. Russakovsky, J. Deng, H. Su, J. Krause, S. Satheesh, S. Ma, et al., ImageNet large scale visual recognition challenge, International Journal of Computer Vision 115 (3) (2015) 211–252, https://doi.org/10.1007/s11263-015-0816-y.

[8] M.D. Zeiler, R. Fergus, Visualizing and understanding convolutional networks, CoRR, abs/1311.2901, 2013, URL http://dblp.uni-trier.de/db/journals/corr/corr1311.html#ZeilerF13.

[9] C. Szegedy, W. Liu, Y. Jia, P. Sermanet, S. Reed, D. Anguelov, et al., Going deeper with convolutions, in: Computer Vision and Pattern, Recognition, CVPR, 2015, preprint, arXiv:1409.4842.

[10] K. Simonyan, A. Zisserman, Very deep convolutional networks for large-scale image recognition, CoRR, abs/1409.1556, 2014.

[11] Y. Bengio, P. Simard, P. Frasconi, Learning long-term dependencies with gradient descent is difficult, IEEE Transactions on Neural Networks 5 (2) (1994) 157–166, https://doi.org/10.1109/72.279181.

[12] J. Hochreiter, Untersuchungen zu dynamischen neuronalen Netzen, Diploma thesis, Institut für Informatik, Lehrstuhl Prof. Brauer, Technische Universität München, 1991.

[13] S. Ioffe, C. Szegedy, Batch normalization: accelerating deep network training by reducing internal covariate shift, in: Proceedings of the 32Nd International Conference on International Conference on Machine Learning, ICML'15, vol. 37, JMLR.org, 2015, pp. 448–456, URL http://dl.acm.org/citation.cfm?id=3045118.3045167.

[14] S. Xie, R.B. Girshick, P. Dollár, Z. Tu, K. He, Aggregated residual transformations for deep neural networks, in: CVPR, IEEE Computer Society, 2017, pp. 5987–5995.

[15] K. He, G. Gkioxari, P. Dollár, R.B. Girshick, Mask R-CNN, in: IEEE International Conference on Computer Vision, ICCV 2017, Venice, Italy, October 22–29, 2017, 2017, pp. 22–29.

[16] G. Huang, Z. Liu, L. van der Maaten, K.Q. Weinberger, Densely connected convolutional networks, in: 2017 IEEE Conference on Computer Vision and Pattern Recognition, CVPR 2017, Honolulu, HI, USA, July 21–26, 2017, 2017, pp. 21–26.

[17] R.H.H.M. Philipsen, P. Maduskar, L. Hogeweg, J. Melendez, C.I. Sánchez, B. van Ginneken, Localized energy-based normalization of medical images: application to chest radiography, IEEE Transactions on Medical Imaging 34 (9) (2015) 1965–1975, https://doi.org/10.1109/TMI.2015.2418031.

[18] B.E. Bejnordi, G. Litjens, N. Timofeeva, I. Otte-Höller, A. Homeyer, N. Karssemeijer, et al., Stain specific standardization of whole-slide histopathological images, IEEE Transactions on Medical Imaging 35 (2) (2016) 404–415, https://doi.org/10.1109/TMI.2015.2476509.

[19] N. Moriakov, K. Michielsen, J. Adler, R. Mann, I. Sechopoulos, J. Teuwen, Deep learning framework for digital breast tomosynthesis reconstruction, preprint, arXiv:1808.04640, 2018.

[20] D.P. Kingma, J. Ba, Adam: a method for stochastic optimization, preprint, arXiv:1412.6980, 2014.

[21] A.C. Wilson, R. Roelofs, M. Stern, N. Srebro, B. Recht, The marginal value of adaptive gradient methods in machine learning, preprint, arXiv:1705.08292.

[22] A. Daniely, R. Frostig, Y. Singer, Toward deeper understanding of neural networks: the power of initialization and a dual view on expressivity, in: D.D. Lee, M. Sugiyama, U.V. Luxburg, I. Guyon, R. Garnett (Eds.), Advances in Neural Information Processing Systems, vol. 29, Curran Associates, Inc., 2016, pp. 2253–2261, http://papers.nips.cc/paper/6427-toward-deeper-understanding-of-neural-networks-the-power-of-initialization-and-a-dual-view-on-expressivity.pdf.

[23] X. Glorot, Y. Bengio, Understanding the difficulty of training deep feedforward neural networks, in: Proceedings of the Thirteenth International Conference on Artificial Intelligence and Statistics, AISTATS 2010, Chia Laguna Resort, Sardinia, Italy, May 13–15, 2010, 2010, pp. 249–256, URL http://www.jmlr.org/proceedings/papers/v9/glorot10a.html.

[24] K. He, X. Zhang, S. Ren, J. Sun, Delving deep into rectifiers: surpassing human-level performance on ImageNet classification, in: Proceedings of the 2015 IEEE International Conference on Computer Vision, ICCV'15, IEEE Computer Society, Washington, DC, USA, ISBN 978-1-4673-8391-2, 2015, pp. 1026–1034.

[25] C.M. Bishop, Pattern Recognition and Machine Learning, Information Science and Statistics, Springer-Verlag, Berlin, Heidelberg, ISBN 0387310738, 2006.

[26] N. Srivastava, G. Hinton, A. Krizhevsky, I. Sutskever, R. Salakhutdinov, Dropout: a simple way to prevent neural networks from overfitting, Journal of Machine Learning Research 15 (2014) 1929–1958, URL http://jmlr.org/papers/v15/srivastava14a.html.

[27] S. Jégou, M. Drozdzal, D. Vázquez, A. Romero, Y. Bengio, The one hundred layers Tiramisu: fully convolutional DenseNets for semantic segmentation, CoRR, abs/1611.09326, 2016.

[28] Y. Gal, Z. Ghahramani, Dropout as a Bayesian approximation: representing model uncertainty in deep learning, preprint, arXiv:1506.02142, 2015.

[29] K. Simonyan, A. Vedaldi, A. Zisserman, Deep inside convolutional networks: visualising image classification models and saliency maps, in: 2nd International Conference on Learning Representations, ICLR 2014, Banff, AB, Canada, April 14–16, 2014, Workshop Track Proceedings, 2014, pp. 14–16, arXiv:1312.6034.

[30] Y. Chen, W. Li, C. Sakaridis, D. Dai, L.V. Gool, Domain adaptive faster R-CNN for object detection in the wild, CoRR, abs/1803.03243, 2018.

[31] J. van Vugt, E. Marchiori, R. Mann, A. Gubern-Mérida, N. Moriakov, J. Teuwen, Vendor-independent soft tissue lesion detection using weakly supervised and unsupervised adversarial domain adaptation, CoRR 2018, abs/1808.04909.

CHAPTER 21

Deep learning: RNNs and LSTM

Robert DiPietro, Gregory D. Hager
Johns Hopkins University, Department of Computer Science, Baltimore, MD, United States

Contents

21.1.	From feedforward to recurrent	503
	21.1.1 Simple motivating example	504
	21.1.2 Naive solution	505
	21.1.3 Simple RNNs	505
	21.1.4 Representation power of simple RNNs	506
	21.1.5 More general recurrent neural networks	507
21.2.	Modeling with RNNs	507
	21.2.1 Discriminative sequence models	508
	21.2.2 Generative sequence models	509
	21.2.3 RNN-based encoder–decoder models	509
21.3.	Training RNNs (and why simple RNNs aren't enough)	510
	21.3.1 The chain rule for ordered derivatives	510
	21.3.2 The vanishing gradient problem	511
	21.3.3 Truncated backpropagation through time	513
	21.3.4 Teacher forcing	513
21.4.	Long short-term memory and gated recurrent units	514
21.5.	Example applications of RNNs at MICCAI	517
	References	518

Recurrent neural networks (RNNs) are a class of neural networks that are naturally suited to processing time-series data and other sequential data. Here we introduce recurrent neural networks as an extension to feedforward networks, in order to allow the processing of variable-length (or even infinite-length) sequences, and some of the most popular recurrent architectures in use, including long short-term memory (LSTM) and gated recurrent units (GRUs). In addition, various aspects surrounding RNNs are discussed in detail, including various probabilistic models that are often realized using RNNs and various applications of RNNs that have appeared within the MICCAI community.

21.1. From feedforward to recurrent

The transition from feedforward neural networks to recurrent neural networks is conceptually simple. Feedforward networks traditionally map from fixed-size inputs to fixed-size outputs, for example, to map from an image of fixed spatial extent to its class,

Handbook of Medical Image Computing and Computer Assisted Intervention
https://doi.org/10.1016/B978-0-12-816176-0.00026-0

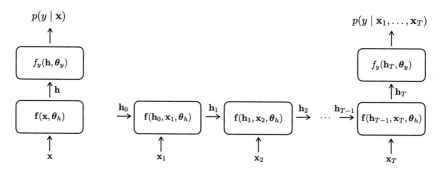

Figure 21.1 An example feedforward network (left) and an example recurrent neural network (right). In the recurrent example, the function **f** and its parameters θ_h are shared over time.

or to a segmentation map of the same spatial extent. In contrast, recurrent neural networks naturally operate on variable-length input sequences and map to variable-length output sequences, for example, to map from an image to various sentences that describe that image. This capability is achieved by sharing parameters and transformations over time.

21.1.1 Simple motivating example

We begin with a straightforward example. Consider a scenario in which we wish to map from a set of measurements describing a tumor, **x**, to probability of malignancy, $p(y \mid \mathbf{x})$. Suppose we wish to use feedforward neural networks to solve this problem, and that we begin with the simple network

$$\mathbf{h} = \tanh(\mathbf{W}_{xh}\mathbf{x} + \mathbf{b}_h), \tag{21.1}$$

$$p(y \mid \mathbf{x}) = \sigma(\mathbf{W}_{hy}\mathbf{h} + b_y), \tag{21.2}$$

where all weights **W** and all biases **b** are parameters to be learned, tanh is the hyperbolic tangent function, and σ is the sigmoid function, the output of which is between 0 and 1. Given this network and a training set of ground-truth $(\mathbf{x}_i, y_i)$ pairs, say, one per patient, we typically proceed by maximizing the conditional log-likelihood $\sum_i \log p(y_i \mid \mathbf{x}_i)$. (This is equivalent to minimizing the overall cross-entropy between our predicted distributions, given by the network, and the ground-truth distributions, given by our training data, as usually done in practice.) Optimization is typically carried out using a variant of stochastic gradient descent, and this is usually carried out in practice by (1) forming a computation graph that corresponds to this network (and loss function) and (2) computing gradients via backpropagation [1].

We now ask the following question: what if each patient is not associated with a single measurement vector, but rather with a *sequence* of measurement vectors, each associated with a single examination? How can we modify the network above to map from a sequence of measurement vectors to a single probability of malignancy, corresponding to the latest examination date?

21.1.2 Naive solution

Perhaps the most straightforward approach is to stack each patient's measurement vectors into one, forming a new input of increased dimensionality. However, this approach is unsatisfactory for a number of reasons. First, we note that such a model makes no attempt to capture the inductive biases we might hope for in our model: it would treat all elements across all time steps in exactly the same way, rather than incorporating any explicit mechanism to capture local dynamics. Second, we expect the number of examinations per patient to vary, and as a reminder, the input to our network, $\mathbf{x}$, has fixed dimensionality. Thus if we proceed in this way, we will be forced to proceed with heuristics, either by throwing away past information for some patients (those with many examinations) or by padding the inputs of other patients (those with fewer examinations).

21.1.3 Simple RNNs

Instead, let's proceed by modifying the simple network above to carry over latent information from time step to time step (after training, these latent states can be interpreted as learned representations that are specific to our task). First, let's modify our notation so that the single-examination case more explicitly corresponds to a sequence of length 1:

$$\mathbf{h}_1 = \tanh(\mathbf{W}_{xh}\mathbf{x}_1 + \mathbf{b}_h), \tag{21.3}$$

$$p(y_1 \mid \mathbf{x}_1) = \sigma(\mathbf{W}_{hy}\mathbf{h}_1 + b_y). \tag{21.4}$$

Next, let's modify the linear transformation used in the hidden-state computation to depend not only our input $\mathbf{x}$ but also on information from the past, which is carried through the hidden state. We will set our previous hidden state to $\mathbf{0}$, which can be interpreted as carrying over no information from the past:

$$\mathbf{h}_0 = \mathbf{0}, \tag{21.5}$$

$$\mathbf{h}_1 = \tanh(\mathbf{W}_{hh}\mathbf{h}_0 + \mathbf{W}_{xh}\mathbf{x}_1 + \mathbf{b}_h), \tag{21.6}$$

$$p(y_1 \mid \mathbf{x}_1) = \sigma(\mathbf{W}_{hy}\mathbf{h}_1 + b_y). \tag{21.7}$$

Notice that, from a modeling perspective, this network is precisely equivalent to our original network; it differs only in notation and operation counts (introduced by the unnecessary matrix-vector multiply involving $\mathbf{h}_0 = \mathbf{0}$). However, our network now naturally extends to patients with any number of examinations:

$$\mathbf{h}_0 = \mathbf{0}, \tag{21.8}$$

$$\mathbf{h}_1 = \tanh(\mathbf{W}_{hh}\mathbf{h}_0 + \mathbf{W}_{xh}\mathbf{x}_1 + \mathbf{b}_h), \tag{21.9}$$

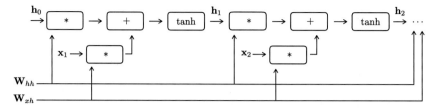

Figure 21.2 A computation graph corresponding to a simple RNN. The bias ($\mathbf{b}_h$) is omitted for simplicity. Note that all parameters, here $\mathbf{W}_{hh}$ and $\mathbf{W}_{xh}$, are shared over time. Two time steps are shown, but the computation graph can be unrolled indefinitely. The symbol $*$ denotes matrix multiplication (with implicit ordering assumed, e.g., $\mathbf{W}_{hh}\mathbf{h}_0$, not $\mathbf{h}_0\mathbf{W}_{hh}$).

$$\mathbf{h}_2 = \tanh(\mathbf{W}_{hh}\mathbf{h}_1 + \mathbf{W}_{xh}\mathbf{x}_2 + \mathbf{b}_h), \qquad (21.10)$$

$$\cdots \qquad (21.11)$$

$$\mathbf{h}_T = \tanh(\mathbf{W}_{hh}\mathbf{h}_{T-1} + \mathbf{W}_{xh}\mathbf{x}_T + \mathbf{b}_h), \qquad (21.12)$$

$$p(y_T \mid \mathbf{x}_1, \ldots, \mathbf{x}_T) = \sigma(\mathbf{W}_{hy}\mathbf{h}_T + b_y). \qquad (21.13)$$

This RNN is capable of processing sequences of any length, for example, one with a length of $T = 1$ and another with a length of $T = 7$, because *the transition function and its parameters are shared over time.*

Once defined, training the network is carried out in a way that is nearly identical to the process described above for feedforward networks. Each patient now corresponds to a *sequence* of exams, $\mathbf{x}_1, \ldots, \mathbf{x}_T$, along with a label y_T. We form our computation graph by unrolling the RNN over these time steps, and by adding operations to compute the probability of malignancy and the loss. Then we obtain gradients via backpropagation, and optimize via stochastic gradient descent.

Equations (21.9)–(21.12) represent one of the first RNN variants that can be found in the literature – that of *simple* RNNs or *Elman* RNNs [2]. In the literature, we typically see the more compact representation

$$\mathbf{h}_t = \tanh(\mathbf{W}_{hh}\mathbf{h}_{t-1} + \mathbf{W}_{xh}\mathbf{x}_t + \mathbf{b}_h), \qquad (21.14)$$

in which the initial hidden state is omitted, and, unless otherwise specified, is often assumed to be $\mathbf{h}_0 = 0$. A simplified computation graph corresponding to Eq. (21.14) is shown in Fig. 21.2.

21.1.4 Representation power of simple RNNs

A well known result is that a feedforward network with only one hidden layer, under fairly unrestrictive assumptions and given enough hidden units, can approximate continuous functions to arbitrary accuracy [3]. The analogous result for simple RNNs is that they can approximate sequence-to-sequence mappings to arbitrary accuracy [4,5].

(In fact, again under fairly unrestrictive assumptions, one can even show that simple RNNs are capable of simulating a Turing machine with only a small, fixed number of units (886), under which binary streams are provided as the inputs and outputs of the RNN [6,7].)

Thus even this extremely simple architecture is very powerful from the perspective of *representation*. However, in practice representational power is not our only concern, and it is important to note that these powerful results on representation in no way indicate that we can *learn* such representations from data in any reasonable amount of time. Indeed, we will later see that a major drawback of simple RNNs is their inability to learn long-term dependencies from data, and that long short-term memory (LSTM) was introduced explicitly to alleviate this issue.

21.1.5 More general recurrent neural networks

Simple RNNs map from hidden state to hidden state through Eq. (21.14). More generally, RNNs typically map a sequence of inputs $\mathbf{x}_1, \ldots, \mathbf{x}_T$ to a sequence of hidden states $\mathbf{h}_1, \ldots, \mathbf{h}_T$ through a set of parameters $\boldsymbol{\theta}$ via

$$\mathbf{h}_t = f(\mathbf{h}_{t-1}, \mathbf{x}_t, \boldsymbol{\theta}), \tag{21.15}$$

where we emphasize that here f should *not* be interpreted as a simple activation function, e.g., tanh or σ. For example, below we will discuss long short-term memory, for which f is a composition involving various gates and nonlinearities.

In addition, the inputs $\mathbf{x}_t$ are not restricted to be our observed (input) data, and similarly, $\mathbf{h}_t$ does not need to be related to our observed (output) data through a simple transformation, as seen in the motivating example above. From this perspective, RNNs are another building block that we can use to build rich models that can be trained in an end-to-end fashion. For example, we can compose what is often referred to as a *deep* RNN by applying Eq. (21.15) multiple times: first, an RNN is applied to our observed inputs, yielding a sequence of hidden states; and these hidden states are fed as inputs into another RNN; and so on.

21.2. Modeling with RNNs

RNNs were motivated above through a simple example: mapping from a sequence of measurement vectors describing a tumor, $\mathbf{x}_1$ through $\mathbf{x}_T$, to the probability of malignancy as of the last measurement, $p(y_T \mid \mathbf{x}_1, \ldots, \mathbf{x}_T)$. This was an example of a *discriminative* model, and in particular a discriminative model which maps from *a sequence of inputs* to *a single output*. However, RNNs are also applicable to many other modeling scenarios, and this section aims to introduce some of the most common types of models found in the literature.

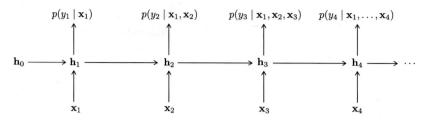

Figure 21.3 Example RNN-based discriminative model. Here, each time step is associated with exactly one input, $\mathbf{x}_t$, and one output label, y_t. Notice that each distribution over y_t is conditioned not only on the current input $\mathbf{x}_t$ but also on all previous inputs.

21.2.1 Discriminative sequence models

We have already seen one simple discriminative model above, where we modeled the probability of malignancy given a sequence of patient measurements, $p(y_T \mid \mathbf{x}_1, \ldots, \mathbf{x}_T)$. Another common application of RNNs is to discriminatively model the distribution over a sequence of outputs, $y_1, \ldots, y_T$, given a sequence of inputs, $\mathbf{x}_1, \ldots, \mathbf{x}_T$, under the assumption that the outputs are conditionally independent *given the input sequence*. As an example, one can consider surgical activity recognition from hand-movement data during robot-assisted surgery, where for each time step we aim to predict the current activity (e.g., suturing or knot tying), conditioned on either past motion data (in the online setting) or past and future motion data (in the offline setting) [8].

In the online setting, we are restricted to leveraging only past and current inputs. Here, we model $p(y_t \mid \mathbf{x}_1, \ldots, \mathbf{x}_t)$ for all t. This model can be realized with RNNs (again assuming binary classification for simplicity) via

$$\mathbf{h}_t = f(\mathbf{h}_{t-1}, \mathbf{x}_t, \boldsymbol{\theta}_h), \tag{21.16}$$

$$p(y_t \mid \mathbf{x}_1, \ldots, \mathbf{x}_t) = \text{softmax}(\mathbf{W}_{hy}\mathbf{h}_t + \mathbf{b}_y), \tag{21.17}$$

which is illustrated in Fig. 21.3. This is also useful as a simple baseline even when online inference is not mandatory.

In the offline setting, we can also make use of *future* inputs, and this is done using *bidirectional RNNs*. The idea is simple: in order to leverage both past and future inputs, one RNN is run in the forward direction, and another is run in the reverse direction, after which hidden states are concatenated and finally used together for prediction:

$$\mathbf{h}_t^{(\rightarrow)} = \mathbf{f}(\mathbf{h}_{t-1}, \mathbf{x}_t, \boldsymbol{\theta}_h^{(\rightarrow)}) \quad \text{for} \quad t = 1, 2, \ldots, T, \tag{21.18}$$

$$\mathbf{h}_t^{(\leftarrow)} = \mathbf{f}(\mathbf{h}_{t+1}, \mathbf{x}_t, \boldsymbol{\theta}_h^{(\leftarrow)}) \quad \text{for} \quad t = T, T-1, \ldots, 1, \tag{21.19}$$

$$\mathbf{h}_t = [\mathbf{h}_t^{(\rightarrow)}; \mathbf{h}_t^{(\leftarrow)}], \tag{21.20}$$

$$p(y_t \mid \mathbf{x}_1, \ldots, \mathbf{x}_T) = \text{softmax}(\mathbf{W}_{hy}\mathbf{h}_t + \mathbf{b}_y). \tag{21.21}$$

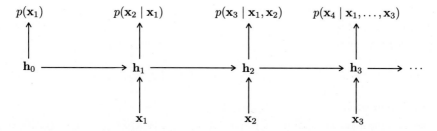

Figure 21.4 Example RNN-based generative model. At training time, each $\mathbf{x}_t$ fed into the model is taken directly from the observed sequence; this is known as *teacher forcing*. In contrast, at inference time, each input is *sampled* from the distribution governed by the previous time step.

21.2.2 Generative sequence models

Another common use of RNNs is autoregressive density estimation, in which we model a full joint distribution by making use of the factorized form

$$p(\mathbf{x}_1, \mathbf{x}_2, \ldots, \mathbf{x}_T) = p(\mathbf{x}_1)p(\mathbf{x}_2 \mid \mathbf{x}_1) \cdots p(\mathbf{x}_T \mid \mathbf{x}_1, \mathbf{x}_2, \ldots, \mathbf{x}_{T-1}). \tag{21.22}$$

Again we can consider hand-motion data in the context of robot-assisted surgery, this time for representation learning (e.g., for data exploration or down-stream tasks such as motion-based search, as considered in [9]). Notice that the factorization above does *not* make any independence assumptions over time; this model has the potential to generate full trajectories of surgical motion through intermediate (learned) representations. For simplicity, assume the motion data at each time step has been discretized, so that at each time step we have a categorical distribution. (It is not difficult to instead associate each time step with, e.g., a mixture of multimodal continuous distributions, but this is beyond the scope of this chapter; see, e.g., [9].) Each RNN step is then associated with one factor in the joint distribution:

$$\mathbf{h}_t = f(\mathbf{h}_{t-1}, \mathbf{x}_{t-1}, \boldsymbol{\theta}_h), \tag{21.23}$$

$$p(\mathbf{x}_t \mid \mathbf{x}_1, \ldots, \mathbf{x}_{t-1}) = \mathrm{softmax}(\mathbf{W}_{hy}\mathbf{h}_t + \mathbf{b}_y). \tag{21.24}$$

This is illustrated in Fig. 21.4.

21.2.3 RNN-based encoder–decoder models

Above we have seen some of the versatility of RNN-based modeling. In this section we consider one more discriminative model which essentially combines the ideas from the simple discriminative and generative models that we have already discussed.

In Sect. 21.2.1, we saw an example of surgical activity recognition from hand-motion data through the discriminative model $p(y_1, \ldots, y_T \mid \mathbf{x}_1, \ldots, \mathbf{x}_T)$. However, recall that we made the assumption that our outputs $y_1, \ldots, y_T$ are conditionally independent when conditioned on the input sequence $\mathbf{x}_1, \ldots, \mathbf{x}_T$. How can we relax this assumption? We can proceed with a discriminative model $p(y_1, \ldots, y_T \mid \mathbf{x}_1, \ldots, \mathbf{x}_T)$ that *without any independence assumptions over the outputs* using the factorization

$$p(y_1, \ldots, y_T \mid \mathbf{x}_1, \ldots, \mathbf{x}_T) = p(y_1 \mid \mathbf{x}_1, \ldots, \mathbf{x}_T) p(y_2 \mid y_1, \mathbf{x}_1, \ldots, \mathbf{x}_T) \cdots. \tag{21.25}$$

The simplest approach to realizing this model with RNNs is to (a) run one RNN over $\mathbf{x}_1, \ldots, \mathbf{x}_T$ and (b) feed the final hidden state of this first RNN to a second RNN which captures the joint distribution over the labels, as in Sect. 21.2.2:

$$\mathbf{h}_t^{(\text{enc})} = f(\mathbf{h}_{t-1}^{(\text{enc})}, \mathbf{x}_t, \boldsymbol{\theta}_h), \tag{21.26}$$

$$\mathbf{h}_0^{(\text{dec})} \equiv \mathbf{h}_T^{(\text{enc})}, \tag{21.27}$$

$$\mathbf{h}_t^{(\text{dec})} = f(\mathbf{h}_{t-1}^{(\text{dec})}, \mathbf{x}_t, \boldsymbol{\theta}_h), \tag{21.28}$$

$$p(y_t \mid y_1, \ldots, y_{t-1}, \mathbf{x}_1, \ldots, \mathbf{x}_T) = \text{softmax}(\mathbf{W}_{hy} \mathbf{h}_t^{(\text{dec})} + \mathbf{b}_y). \tag{21.29}$$

This is an example of an RNN-based encoder–decoder model, which was first introduced for machine translation to model p(sentence in target language | sentence in source language) [10]. Similar ideas can also be applied even if we do not desire structure over our outputs. For example, this approach was taken in [9] to model future motion as a function of past motion through an embedding (for the purpose of representation learning).

21.3. Training RNNs (and why simple RNNs aren't enough)

As with feedforward networks, recurrent neural networks are typically trained using gradient-based optimization, where gradients are obtained using backpropagation [11,1]. (In the literature, a habit has formed of referring to *backpropagation through time* when backpropagation is discussed in the context of RNNs; but this just leads to confusion, since the difference is only one of terminology: in [1], the application of error backpropagation to RNNs was discussed; and in [12], *backpropagation through time* does not refer to an RNN-specific algorithm, but rather to an algorithm that applies to a set of computations with well-defined order.) In this section, we introduce the *chain rule for ordered derivatives* [12], highlight the *vanishing gradient problem* [13], and discuss various tricks that are often used to train RNNs in practice.

21.3.1 The chain rule for ordered derivatives

First let's disambiguate notation, since the symbol $\frac{\partial \mathbf{f}}{\partial \mathbf{x}}$ is routinely overloaded in the literature. Consider the Jacobian of $\mathbf{f}(\mathbf{x}, \mathbf{u}(\mathbf{x}))$ with respect to $\mathbf{x}$. We let $\frac{\partial^+ \mathbf{f}}{\partial \mathbf{x}}$ denote $\frac{\partial \mathbf{f}(\mathbf{x})}{\partial \mathbf{x}}$, a collection of full derivatives, and we let $\frac{\partial \mathbf{f}}{\partial \mathbf{x}}$ denote $\frac{\partial \mathbf{f}(\mathbf{x}, \mathbf{u})}{\partial \mathbf{x}}$, a collection of partial derivatives. For example, using this notation, the *ordinary* chain rule can be expressed as

$\frac{\partial^+ \mathbf{f}}{\partial \mathbf{x}} = \frac{\partial \mathbf{f}}{\partial \mathbf{x}} \frac{\partial^+ \mathbf{x}}{\partial \mathbf{x}} + \frac{\partial \mathbf{f}}{\partial \mathbf{u}} \frac{\partial^+ \mathbf{u}}{\partial \mathbf{x}}$. (This notation is consistent with [14,12], and is the exact opposite of the convention used in [13].)

Now consider an ordered system of n vectors $\mathbf{v}_1, \mathbf{v}_2, \ldots, \mathbf{v}_n$, where each is a function of all previous:

$$\mathbf{v}_i \equiv \mathbf{v}_i(\mathbf{v}_{i-1}, \mathbf{v}_{i-2}, \ldots, \mathbf{v}_1), \quad 1 \le i \le n. \tag{21.30}$$

The chain rule for ordered derivatives, which can be derived from the ordinary chain rule [14], expresses the full derivatives $\frac{\partial^+ \mathbf{v}_i}{\partial \mathbf{v}_j}$ for any $j < i$ in terms of the full derivatives that relate $\mathbf{v}_i$ to all previous $\mathbf{v}_k$:

$$\frac{\partial^+ \mathbf{v}_i}{\partial \mathbf{v}_j} = \sum_{i \ge k > j} \frac{\partial^+ \mathbf{v}_i}{\partial \mathbf{v}_k} \frac{\partial \mathbf{v}_k}{\partial \mathbf{v}_j}, \quad j < i. \tag{21.31}$$

Before moving on, it will be useful to relate the gradient components associated with any $\mathbf{v}_i$ and $\mathbf{v}_i$ to the paths between them (see Figs. 21.1 and 21.2 for specific examples). We will now apply Eq. (21.31) recursively, first to expand $\frac{\partial^+ \mathbf{v}_i}{\partial \mathbf{v}_j}$, then to expand each term in the sum, and so on.

For each intermediate $\mathbf{v}_k$, we see that Eq. (21.31) has exactly one component in the sum involving the partial $\frac{\partial \mathbf{v}_k}{\partial \mathbf{v}_j}$. This implies that if $\mathbf{v}_k$ is not computed directly in terms of $\mathbf{v}_j$, then the corresponding partial is $\mathbf{0}$, and so the component itself is also $\mathbf{0}$. In other words, upon a first application of Eq. (21.31), we obtain exactly one component for each $\mathbf{v}'$ that is computed directly from $\mathbf{v}_j$. For each such $\mathbf{v}'$, the component is the product $\frac{\partial^+ \mathbf{v}_i}{\partial \mathbf{v}'} \frac{\partial \mathbf{v}'}{\partial \mathbf{v}_j}$. Each $\mathbf{v}'$ then yields one component for each $\mathbf{v}''$ that is computed directly from $\mathbf{v}'$. Taken together, this yields exactly one component for each path $\mathbf{v}_j \to \mathbf{v}' \to \mathbf{v}''$. For each $\mathbf{v}', \mathbf{v}''$ pair, the component is the product $\frac{\partial^+ \mathbf{v}_i}{\partial \mathbf{v}''} \frac{\partial \mathbf{v}''}{\partial \mathbf{v}'} \frac{\partial \mathbf{v}'}{\partial \mathbf{v}_j}$. Recursively applying Eq. (21.31) until only partials remain, we finally obtain a sum with exactly one additive gradient component for each path from $\mathbf{v}_j$ to $\mathbf{v}_i$; and each component itself consists of a product of partials, with one partial for each edge along the path.

21.3.2 The vanishing gradient problem

Consider Fig. 21.1 (right), along with a loss $f_l(\mathbf{h}_T, \boldsymbol{\theta}_y)$ which is computed directly from $\mathbf{h}_T$ (under which $f_y(\mathbf{h}_T, \boldsymbol{\theta}_y)$ and $p(y \mid \mathbf{x}_1, \ldots, \mathbf{x}_T)$ are computed implicitly). Suppose we are interested in obtaining the gradients with respect to $\boldsymbol{\theta}$, the parameters belonging to the RNN itself (as in the figure). Using the ordinary chain rule, we can write the Jacobian (or transposed gradient) as

$$\frac{\partial^+ f_l}{\partial \boldsymbol{\theta}} = \frac{\partial f_l}{\partial \mathbf{h}_T} \frac{\partial^+ \mathbf{h}_T}{\partial \boldsymbol{\theta}} \tag{21.32}$$

because $\frac{\partial^+ \theta_y}{\partial \theta} = \mathbf{0}$. Now, applying the chain rule for ordered derivatives to $\frac{\partial^+ \mathbf{h}_T}{\partial \theta}$ with $\mathbf{v}_1 = \theta$, $\mathbf{v}_2 = \mathbf{h}_0$, $\mathbf{v}_3 = \mathbf{x}_1$, $\mathbf{v}_4 = \mathbf{h}_1$, ... immediately gives

$$\frac{\partial^+ \mathbf{h}_T}{\partial \theta} = \frac{\partial^+ \mathbf{h}_T}{\partial \mathbf{h}_T}\frac{\partial \mathbf{h}_T}{\partial \theta} + \frac{\partial^+ \mathbf{h}_T}{\partial \mathbf{h}_{T-1}}\frac{\partial \mathbf{h}_{T-1}}{\partial \theta} + \frac{\partial^+ \mathbf{h}_T}{\partial \mathbf{x}_{T-1}}\frac{\partial \mathbf{x}_{T-1}}{\partial \theta} + \frac{\partial^+ \mathbf{h}_T}{\partial \mathbf{h}_{T-2}}\frac{\partial \mathbf{h}_{T-2}}{\partial \theta} + \cdots . \quad (21.33)$$

Finally, noticing that $\frac{\partial \mathbf{x}_t}{\partial \theta} = \mathbf{0}$ for all t and that $\frac{\partial \mathbf{h}_0}{\partial \theta} = \mathbf{0}$, we have

$$\frac{\partial^+ \mathbf{h}_T}{\partial \theta} = \sum_{\tau=0}^{T-1} \frac{\partial^+ \mathbf{h}_T}{\partial \mathbf{h}_{T-\tau}}\frac{\partial \mathbf{h}_{T-\tau}}{\partial \theta}. \quad (21.34)$$

This decomposition breaks $\frac{\partial^+ \mathbf{h}_T}{\partial \theta}$ into its temporal components, making it clear that the spectral norm of $\frac{\partial^+ \mathbf{h}_T}{\partial \mathbf{h}_{T-\tau}}$ plays a major role in how $\mathbf{h}_{T-\tau}$ affects the final gradient $\frac{\partial^+ f_l}{\partial \theta}^T$. In particular, if the spectral norm of $\frac{\partial^+ \mathbf{h}_T}{\partial \mathbf{h}_{T-\tau}}$ is extremely small, then $\mathbf{h}_{T-\tau}$ has a negligible effect on the final gradient, which in turn makes it extremely difficult to learn from events that occurred at time $T - \tau$. We also emphasize that this discussion applies unchanged for a loss computed at any time step t (e.g., when losses are computed at every time step rather than only at the end of the sequence).

The final step is to consider $\frac{\partial^+ \mathbf{h}_T}{\partial \mathbf{h}_{T-\tau}}$ in more detail. Notice that, for simple RNNs, there is exactly one path from $\mathbf{h}_{T-\tau}$ to $\mathbf{h}_T$ (see Fig. 21.2), and this corresponds to only one gradient component,

$$\frac{\partial^+ \mathbf{h}_T}{\partial \mathbf{h}_{T-\tau}} = \frac{\partial \mathbf{h}_T}{\partial \mathbf{h}_{T-1}}\frac{\partial \mathbf{h}_{T-1}}{\partial \mathbf{h}_{T-2}} \cdots \frac{\partial \mathbf{h}_{T-\tau+1}}{\partial \mathbf{h}_{T-\tau}}, \quad (21.35)$$

and so, in terms of the spectral norm, we have

$$\left\| \frac{\partial^+ \mathbf{h}_T}{\partial \mathbf{h}_{T-\tau}} \right\| \leq \left\| \frac{\partial \mathbf{h}_T}{\partial \mathbf{h}_{T-1}} \right\| \left\| \frac{\partial \mathbf{h}_{T-1}}{\partial \mathbf{h}_{T-2}} \right\| \cdots \left\| \frac{\partial \mathbf{h}_{T-\tau+1}}{\partial \mathbf{h}_{T-\tau}} \right\|. \quad (21.36)$$

In the case of simple RNNs, each partial is the product of two Jacobians, one corresponding to tanh (which is diagonal) and the other corresponding to the matrix multiplication (which is $\mathbf{W}_{hh}$); and this in turn means that the spectral norms associated with these partials can vary dramatically during training. In particular, we can see that if largest spectral norm of any partial is $\lambda < 1$, then we have $\|\frac{\partial^+ \mathbf{h}_T}{\partial \mathbf{h}_{T-\tau}}\| \leq \lambda^\tau$, and so the contribution to gradients from events at time $T - \tau$ fall off exponentially fast with τ. Many attempts have been made at alleviating this issue, for example, by regularizing the norms directly [13], initializing or restricting weight matrices to be orthogonal [15,16], or including direct connections between nonadjacent hidden states [17,9]. However, the architecture that gained widespread success is long short-term memory [18,19], which introduces additional paths between $\mathbf{h}_{T-\tau}$ and $\mathbf{h}_T$ that are associated with more stable spectral norms (long short-term memory is the subject of Sect. 21.4). We also remark that exploding gradients can also be an issue (for example, if the minimum singular value across partials is $\lambda > 1$); however, gradient clipping is routinely used in practice to mitigate this issue, with the simplest solution being to clip the derivative with respect to each θ_i, so that each lies in a specified range.

21.3.3 Truncated backpropagation through time

Notice that the computational complexity of RNNs, during both the forward and backward passes, grows linearly with sequence length; and recall that backpropagation requires us to cache outputs during the forward pass (so that they can be reused during the backward pass). This means that, during training, the amount of memory we need grows linearly with sequence length; and the amount of compute *per gradient update* also grows linearly with sequence length. This can be prohibitive when sequences are long, and *truncated backpropagation through time* (TBTT) [20] is a heuristic that alleviates this issue. TBTT is applicable when we form predictions at the subsequence level, and is most commonly used when we have predictions (and associated losses during training) at *every* time step.

This is perhaps easiest explained through an example. Consider a single training sequence with length $T = 10000$. Using backpropagation through time, we would compute a complete forward pass, caching all intermediate results in memory, and then a complete backward pass, in the end visiting each time step twice. To instead proceed with truncated backpropagation, we first choose a maximum number of time steps $\tilde{T} \leq T$ to visit before performing a gradient update; moving forward with the example, let's choose $\tilde{T} = 100$. Proceeding with TBTT, we perform a forward, backward pass using only the first 100 time steps, after which we perform a gradient update and discard all cached outputs except $\mathbf{h}_{100}$ from memory. Next, we proceed to time step 101, *carrying over the stale hidden state* $\mathbf{h}_{100}$ (which was computed with our *old* parameters, before the gradient update). We now complete a forward, backward pass using time steps 101 through 200, take an optimization step, and discard cached outputs from memory. In repeating this process until our sequence is exhausted, we require only 1% of the memory as for full backpropagation; we perform 100x as many gradient updates; and in doing so we end up performing the same amount of overall computation as one full forward, backward pass. This is illustrated in Fig. 21.5 (with $T = 10$ and $\tilde{T} = 2$).

21.3.4 Teacher forcing

When training RNN-based generative models using the factorized representation $p(\mathbf{x}_1, \mathbf{x}_2, \ldots, \mathbf{x}_T) = p(\mathbf{x}_1)p(\mathbf{x}_2 \mid \mathbf{x}_1) \cdots p(\mathbf{x}_T \mid \mathbf{x}_1, \mathbf{x}_2, \ldots, \mathbf{x}_{T-1})$, we usually have access to only a limited training dataset which consists of a fixed number of training sequences. For example, in the case of modeling surgical hand motion, imagine that the beginning

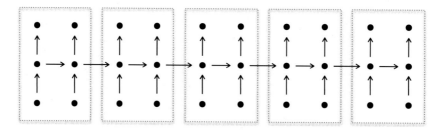

Figure 21.5 Depiction of truncated backpropagation with a sequence of $T = 10$ time steps, performing updates every $\tilde{T} = 2$ time steps. As in Figs. 21.3 and 21.4, inputs are fed to an RNN to form hidden states, and these hidden states are used to compute per-time-step outputs; and during training, each output is associated with a loss (e.g., cross-entropy). We first compute a forward and backward pass using the first group alone (time steps 1 and 2), and we use the obtained gradients to update model parameters. Next, we pass the *stale* hidden state to the next group (this hidden state is not recomputed using the updated parameters). Next, we compute a forward and backward pass using the second group alone (time steps 3 and 4), and again update the model parameters. And so on. This heuristic demands 1/5 the working memory as typical backpropagation (since we only need to cache states on a per-group basis during backpropagation), and it yields 5x as many gradient updates per computation.

of a sequence consists of a surgeon beginning to suture. The true underlying distribution captures many possible ways to complete the sequence (as there are many possible ways that the suture will be completed); however, we often have access to only one such future – the specific future that was observed in the sequence that we collected. Because of this, there is a disconnect between *training* an RNN-based generative model and *sampling* from an RNN-based generative model at inference time. At training time, we resort to *teacher forcing*: at time t, when computing $f(\mathbf{h}_{t-1}, \mathbf{x}_{t-1}, \boldsymbol{\theta})$, we do not sample $\mathbf{x}_{t-1}$ from our model, but rather use the observed $\mathbf{x}_{t-1}$ that comes directly from our training data.

21.4. Long short-term memory and gated recurrent units

Long short–term memory (LSTM) was introduced to alleviate the vanishing gradient problem [18], and has become one of the most popular RNN architectures to date. Gated recurrent units (GRUs) [10] were later introduced as a simpler alternative to LSTM, and have also become quite popular. Here we will introduce both architectures in the context of the vanishing gradient problem, and we will see that LSTM and GRUs alleviate this problem in very similar ways. For an intuitive view of the primary difference between simple RNNs and LSTM / GRUs, see Fig. 21.6.

We first remark that many different variants of LSTM and GRUs exist in literature, and that even the default implementations in various major deep learning frameworks often differ. (Performance is often similar – see, e.g., [21] – but this can nevertheless lead to confusion when reproducing results.) The most common variant of LSTM is

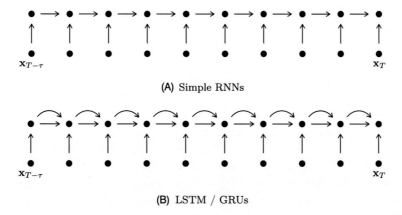

(A) Simple RNNs

(B) LSTM / GRUs

Figure 21.6 Illustration of paths for simple RNNs, LSTM, and GRUs. Simple RNNs yield exactly one path between times T and $T - \tau$, with each step inhibited by linear transformations and nonlinearities. LSTM and GRUs give exponentially many paths between times T and $T - \tau$, with one path inhibited by neither linear transformations nor nonlinearities.

described by

$$\mathbf{f}_t = \sigma(\mathbf{W}_{fh}\mathbf{h}_{t-1} + \mathbf{W}_{fx}\mathbf{x}_t + \mathbf{b}_f), \tag{21.37}$$

$$\mathbf{i}_t = \sigma(\mathbf{W}_{ih}\mathbf{h}_{t-1} + \mathbf{W}_{ix}\mathbf{x}_t + \mathbf{b}_i), \tag{21.38}$$

$$\mathbf{o}_t = \sigma(\mathbf{W}_{oh}\mathbf{h}_{t-1} + \mathbf{W}_{ox}\mathbf{x}_t + \mathbf{b}_o), \tag{21.39}$$

$$\tilde{\mathbf{c}}_t = \tanh(\mathbf{W}_{ch}\mathbf{h}_{t-1} + \mathbf{W}_{cx}\mathbf{x}_t + \mathbf{b}_c), \tag{21.40}$$

$$\mathbf{c}_t = \mathbf{f}_t \odot \mathbf{c}_{t-1} + \mathbf{i}_t \odot \tilde{\mathbf{c}}_t, \tag{21.41}$$

$$\mathbf{h}_t = \mathbf{o}_t \odot \tanh(\mathbf{c}_t). \tag{21.42}$$

At a high level, LSTM is often interpreted as maintaining a memory cell, $\mathbf{c}_t$, which is reset, written to, and read from according to the forget gate $\mathbf{f}_t$, the input gate $\mathbf{i}_t$, and the output gate $\mathbf{o}_t$ [5], which all vary over time. We can see the clear similarity between the updates for these different gates; they differ only in that they have distinct weight matrices and biases (to be learned). In particular, all three gates very much resemble simple RNNs, but with the key difference being the sigmoid activation function (restricting outputs to lie between 0 and 1), rather than the tanh activation function. These gates therefore have elements that can be interpreted as lying between fully off (0), shutting down information flow; and fully on (1), allowing full information flow. Next, we see the formation of the *candidate* update to our memory cell, $\tilde{\mathbf{c}}_t$. Notice that this transformation is identical to that of a simple RNN. Next, in Eq. (21.41), the elements of the previous cell $\mathbf{c}_{t-1}$ are combined with the candidate update $\tilde{\mathbf{c}}_t$, according to the forget gate $\mathbf{f}_t$ and the input gate $\mathbf{i}_t$. And finally the new hidden state $\mathbf{h}_t$ is formed by applying

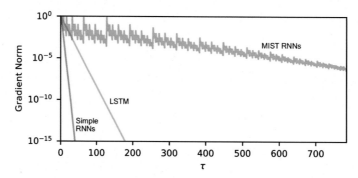

Figure 21.7 Empirical gradient magnitudes $\| \frac{\partial^+ f_T}{\partial \mathbf{h}_{T-\tau}} \|$ while training on the flattened-MNIST task (images of digits are flattened and scanned sequentially, pixel by pixel, and the goal is to output the digit upon completion).

a final activation function to the memory cell and then weighting elements according to the output gate.

Eq. (21.41), the formation of the new memory cell, is at the core of alleviating the vanishing gradient problem. Notice here that there is one path between $\mathbf{c}_{t-1}$ and $\mathbf{c}_t$ that is modulated *only* by the forget gate. In the context of Sect. 21.3, we have exponentially many paths from $\mathbf{c}_{T-\tau}$ to $\mathbf{c}_T$, but one of these paths corresponds simply to elementwise multiplications by forget gates. This in turn means that we have an additive gradient component which itself is the product of diagonal Jacobians with diagonal elements corresponding to the forget gates. Hence gradient contributions can still decay exponentially with τ, but *if the forget gates have elements that are close to 1, then the base of the exponential decay is also close to 1.* This is precisely why it is common in practice to initialize the bias $\mathbf{b}_f$ of the forget gate to be positive (e.g., 1 or 2) at the start of training. Fig. 21.6 illustrates this idea.

Before moving on to GRUs, we make a few closing remarks about LSTM in hope of avoiding confusion. First, our notation was chosen to be consistent with literature. However, note that the true hidden state – the collection of all information passed from one time step to the next – is actually a concatenation of $\mathbf{h}_t$ and $\mathbf{c}_t$. Second, it is worth noting that some sources state that LSTM "solves" the vanishing gradient problem and/or that LSTM alleviates the exploding-gradient problem. Both of these statements are incorrect. As we have seen, gradient norms still decay exponentially fast with delay. This is also illustrated in Fig. 21.7, which shows gradient magnitude vs. delay during training. And with regard to the second statement, we know of no theoretical argument or empirical result that suggests that LSTM alleviates the exploding-gradient problem, and indeed many practitioners still find it necessary to clip gradients when training LSTM networks.

After encountering LSTM, one may wonder what parts of LSTM are most necessary, and whether it is possible to simplify the architecture while retaining its key benefits.

One recently proposed architecture that was inspired by LSTM is that of gated recurrent units (GRUs) [10]. GRUs are simpler than LSTM, as they use one less gate and eliminate the need for distinguishing between hidden states and memory cells. The most common variant is described by

$$\mathbf{u}_t = \sigma(\mathbf{W}_{uh}\mathbf{h}_{t-1} + \mathbf{W}_{ux}\mathbf{x}_t + \mathbf{b}_u), \tag{21.43}$$

$$\mathbf{r}_t = \sigma(\mathbf{W}_{rh}\mathbf{h}_{t-1} + \mathbf{W}_{rx}\mathbf{x}_t + \mathbf{b}_r), \tag{21.44}$$

$$\tilde{\mathbf{h}}_t = \tanh(\mathbf{W}_{hh}(\mathbf{r}_t \odot \mathbf{h}_{t-1}) + \mathbf{W}_{hx}\mathbf{x}_t + \mathbf{b}_h), \tag{21.45}$$

$$\mathbf{h}_t = \mathbf{u}_t \odot \mathbf{h}_{t-1} + (1 - \mathbf{u}_t) \odot \tilde{\mathbf{h}}_t. \tag{21.46}$$

Notice that GRUs mitigate the vanishing gradient problem using a mechanism very similar to that of LSTM; from Eq. (21.46), we can see that if $u_{t,i}$ is nearly 1, then the corresponding partial $\frac{\partial h_{t,i}}{\partial h_{t-1,i}}$ is also nearly 1; $\mathbf{r}_t$ and $\mathbf{u}_t$ are referred to as the reset and update gates, respectively.

21.5. Example applications of RNNs at MICCAI

Here we explain some example applications of RNNs that have appeared at MICCAI. We do not intend to provide an exhaustive list, but rather intend to provide the reader with some concrete and in-depth examples of the material discussed above.

Recognizing surgical activities from motion in robot-assisted surgery. In [8], surgical activities are recognized from motion using long short-term memory, specifically in the benchtop training setting for robot-assisted surgery. Here two types of activities are considered: short, low-level activities, or *gestures*, and longer, mid-level activities, or *maneuvers*. Results match state-of-the-art performance in the case of gesture recognition and surpass previous state-of-the-art performance in the case of maneuver recognition. In the latter case, each time step was classified as one of 4 activities: suture throw, knot tying, grasp pull run suture, and intermaneuver segment. The error rate in this setting was reduced to $10.5 \pm 4.0\%$ (from $18.3 \pm 6.2\%$), and the segmentwise edit distance was reduced to $19.5 \pm 5.2\%$ (from $29.7 \pm 6.8\%$).

Perimysium segmentation from HE stained microscopy images. In [22], clockwork RNNs (which at their core operate at multiple time scales) are extended from 1D to 2D for perimysium segmentation. Their approach is shown to perform favorably to multiple baselines, for example, achieving an intersection over union of 0.84, in comparison to 0.77 with the common U-Net segmentation architecture [23].

Mitosis event detection and stage localization from phase-contrast microscopy images. In [24], CNNs and bidirectional LSTM are combined for detecting mitosis events in phase-contrast microscopy image sequences, and, when present, for localizing various stages (interphase, start of mitosis, formation of daughter cells, separation of daughter cells) in the sequence. Here, CNNs are trained to detect the start-of-mitosis phase from image and motion images, and the features extracted from these CNNs are fed to bidirectional LSTM (and processed further) to predict whether a mitosis event has occurred (at the sequence level) and to regress the frames at which the various stages occur. For event detection, they achieve an F1 score of $97.7 \pm 1.2\%$, outperforming the previous state-of-the-art result of $95.8 \pm 0.8\%$, based on CNNs alone. For stage localization, *given that a mitosis event is known to have occurred*, they achieve a stage-3 localization error of 0.62 ± 0.62 frames, which is comparable to prior methods for this task.

Assessing the quality of image sequences in echocardiography. In [25], CNNs are combined with LSTM to assess quality in echocardiographic cines. Five standard imaging planes are assessed, with lower-level CNN layers shared among planes and high-level layers being plane specific. Here, LSTM is used to aggregate features over time, such that a single quality score is obtained for each sequence of 20 images for any given plane. With assessment scores normalized to the [0, 1] range, they achieve $15 \pm 12\%$ error (as measured by L1 distance to ground-truth scores provided by clinicians).

Unsupervised learning for surgical motion in robot-assisted surgery. In [26], representations of surgical motion are learned using an LSTM-based encoder–decoder architecture, where past motion is encoded and subsequently decoded to predict future actions. The resulting encodings end up clustering into high-level activities, and these encodings are used in an information-retrieval setting to search a database of surgical motion using motion-based queries. In this application, they increase state-of-the-art performance for suturing queries from an F1 score of 0.60 ± 0.14 to 0.77 ± 0.05.

References

[1] D.E. Rumelhart, G.E. Hinton, R.J. Williams, Learning representations by back-propagating errors, Nature 323 (6088) (1986) 533.

[2] J.L. Elman, Finding structure in time, Cognitive Science 14 (2) (1990) 179–211.

[3] K. Hornik, M. Stinchcombe, H. White, Multilayer feedforward networks are universal approximators, Neural Networks 2 (5) (1989) 359–366.

[4] B. Hammer, On the approximation capability of recurrent neural networks, Neurocomputing 31 (1–4) (2000) 107–123.

[5] A. Graves, Supervised sequence labelling, in: Supervised Sequence Labelling with Recurrent Neural Networks, Springer, 2012.

[6] H. Siegelmann, E. Sontag, On the computational power of neural nets, Journal of Computer and System Sciences 50 (1) (1995) 132–150.

[7] I. Goodfellow, Y. Bengio, A. Courville, Deep Learning, MIT Press, Cambridge, 2016.

[8] R. DiPietro, C. Lea, A. Malpani, N. Ahmidi, S.S. Vedula, G.I. Lee, et al., Recognizing surgical activities with recurrent neural networks, in: International Conference on Medical Image Computing and Computer-Assisted Intervention, 2016, pp. 551–558.

[9] R. DiPietro, C. Rupprecht, N. Navab, G.D. Hager, Analyzing and exploiting NARX recurrent neural networks for long-term dependencies, arXiv preprint, arXiv:1702.07805, 2017.

[10] K. Cho, B. van Merriënboer, Ç. Gülçehre, D. Bahdanau, F. Bougares, H. Schwenk, et al., Learning phrase representations using RNN encoder–decoder for statistical machine translation, in: EMNLP, 2014.

[11] P.J. Werbos, Applications of advances in nonlinear sensitivity analysis, in: System Modeling and Optimization, Springer, 1982, pp. 762–770.

[12] P.J. Werbos, Backpropagation through time: what it does and how to do it, Proceedings of the IEEE 78 (10) (1990) 1550–1560.

[13] R. Pascanu, T. Mikolov, Y. Bengio, On the difficulty of training recurrent neural networks, in: International Conference on Machine Learning (ICML), vol. 28, 2013, pp. 1310–1318.

[14] P.J. Werbos, Maximizing long-term gas industry profits in two minutes in lotus using neural network methods, IEEE Transactions on Systems, Man, and Cybernetics 19 (2) (1989) 315–333.

[15] M. Arjovsky, S. Amar, Y. Bengio, Unitary evolution recurrent neural networks, in: International Conference on Machine Learning (ICML), 2016.

[16] M. Henaff, A. Szlam, Y. LeCun, Orthogonal RNNs and long-memory tasks, in: International Conference on Machine Learning (ICML), 2016.

[17] T. Lin, B.G. Horne, P. Tino, Learning long-term dependencies in NARX recurrent neural networks, IEEE Transactions on Neural Networks 7 (6) (1996) 1329–1338.

[18] S. Hochreiter, J. Schmidhuber, Long short-term memory, Neural Computation 9 (8) (1997) 1735–1780.

[19] F.A. Gers, J. Schmidhuber, F. Cummins, Learning to forget: continual prediction with LSTM, Neural Computation 12 (10) (2000) 2451–2471.

[20] I. Sutskever, Training Recurrent Neural Networks, University of Toronto, Toronto, Ontario, Canada, 2013.

[21] K. Greff, R.K. Srivastava, J. Koutník, B.R. Steunebrink, J. Schmidhuber, LSTM: a search space odyssey, IEEE Transactions on Neural Networks and Learning Systems 28 (10) (2017) 2222–2232.

[22] Y. Xie, Z. Zhang, M. Sapkota, L. Yang, Spatial clockwork recurrent neural network for muscle perimysium segmentation, in: International Conference on Medical Image Computing and Computer-Assisted Intervention, Springer, 2016, pp. 185–193.

[23] O. Ronneberger, P. Fischer, T. Brox, U-Net: convolutional networks for biomedical image segmentation, in: International Conference on Medical Image Computing and Computer-Assisted Intervention, Springer, 2015, pp. 234–241.

[24] Y. Mao, Z. Yin, A hierarchical convolutional neural network for mitosis detection in phase-contrast microscopy images, in: International Conference on Medical Image Computing and Computer-Assisted Intervention, Springer, 2016, pp. 685–692.

[25] A.H. Abdi, C. Luong, T. Tsang, G. Allan, S. Nouranian, J. Jue, et al., Automatic quality assessment of echocardiograms using convolutional neural networks: feasibility on the apical four-chamber view, IEEE Transactions on Medical Imaging 36 (6) (2017) 1221–1230.

[26] R. DiPietro, G.D. Hager, Unsupervised learning for surgical motion by learning to predict the future, arXiv preprint, arXiv:1806.03318, 2018.

CHAPTER 22

Deep multiple instance learning for digital histopathology

Maximilian Ilse, Jakub M. Tomczak, Max Welling
University of Amsterdam, Amsterdam Machine Learning Lab, Amsterdam, the Netherlands

Contents

22.1.	Multiple instance learning	522
22.2.	Deep multiple instance learning	524
22.3.	Methodology	525
22.4.	MIL approaches	526
	22.4.1 Instance-based approach	526
	22.4.2 Embedding-based approach	527
	22.4.3 Bag-based approach	528
22.5.	MIL pooling functions	528
	22.5.1 Max	530
	22.5.2 Mean	530
	22.5.3 LSE	530
	22.5.4 (Leaky) Noisy-OR	531
	22.5.5 Attention mechanism	531
	22.5.6 Interpretability	532
	22.5.7 Flexibility	532
22.6.	Application to histopathology	533
	22.6.1 Data augmentation	534
	22.6.1.1 Cropping	*534*
	22.6.1.2 Rotating and flipping	*535*
	22.6.1.3 Blur	*535*
	22.6.1.4 Color	*535*
	22.6.1.5 Elastic deformations	*537*
	22.6.1.6 Generative models	*537*
	22.6.2 Performance metrics	537
	22.6.2.1 Accuracy	*538*
	22.6.2.2 Precision, recall and F1-score	*538*
	22.6.2.3 Receiver Operating Characteristic Area Under Curve	*539*
	22.6.3 Evaluation of MIL models	540
	22.6.3.1 Experimental setup	*540*
	22.6.3.2 Colon cancer	*542*
	22.6.3.3 Breast cancer	*543*
References		545

Handbook of Medical Image Computing and Computer Assisted Intervention
https://doi.org/10.1016/B978-0-12-816176-0.00027-2
521

Nowadays, a typical benchmark image data sets contain thousands of images of size up to 256×256 pixels. Current hardware and software allow us to easily parallelize computations and efficiently train a machine learning model. However, in medical imaging only a small number of images is available for training (10^1–10^2 of medical scans) and an image consists of billions of pixels (roughly $10,000 \times 10,000$ pixels). Moreover, very often only a single label for one image is available. Therefore, a naturally arising question is how to process such large images and learn from weakly-labeled training data. A possible solution is to look for local patterns and combine them into a global decision. Opposite to the classical supervised learning, where one label corresponds to one image, we consider now a situation with one label for a collection (a *bag*) of multiple images (*instances*). We can handle a large image by processing all smaller images in parallel, in a similar manner how a minibatch is processed.

In machine learning the problem of inferring a label for a bag of i.i.d. instances is called the *multiple instance learning* (MIL). The main goal of MIL is to learn a model that predicts a bag label (e.g., a medical diagnosis). An additional task is to find the instances that trigger the bag label a.k.a. *key instances* [17]. Discovering key instances is of special interest due to legal issues. According to the European Union General Data Protection Regulation (taking effect 2018), a user should have the right to obtain an explanation of the decision reached. In order to solve the primary task of a bag classification, different methods are proposed, such as utilizing similarities among bags [4], embedding instances to a compact low-dimensional representation that is further fed to a bag-level classifier [1,2], and combining responses of an instance-level classifier [19,20,30]. From these three approaches only the last one could provide interpretable results. However, it was shown that the instance level accuracy of such methods is low [11], and in general there is a disagreement among MIL methods at the instance level [3]. All these issues force us to rethink the usability of current MIL models for interpreting the final decision.

In this chapter, we aim at explaining the idea of the multiple instance learning and show its natural fit in medical imaging illustrated by the example of the computational pathology. We formally define the MIL problem and outline a theoretical prescription of formulating MIL methods in Sect. 22.3. Next, we present different MIL approaches in Sect. 22.4 and then discuss components of MIL models in Sect. 22.5. Eventually, we present the application of MIL to histopathology data in Sect. 22.6.

22.1. Multiple instance learning

The multiple instance learning framework was originally introduced by [7]. That paper deals with the problem of predicting the drug activity of molecules. Most drugs are small molecules that work by binding to much larger molecules such as enzymes and cell surface receptors. Each drug molecule can adopt different shapes by rotating its bonds, which are called conformations. A drug molecule is labeled "active" if at least one of its conformations can bind to a binding site. In case of an "inactive" molecule none of its possible conformations can bind to a binding site. Here, a single conformation of a molecule is referred to as an instance and all conformations of a certain molecule are referred to as a bag. The only available observation is if a molecule is "active" or "inactive". In the paper, each conformation was represented by 166 shape features and a bag could contain up to hundreds of conformations. The task was to infer drug activity of unseen molecules. This seminal paper formulated a new problem of classifying sets of objects, called multiple instance learning (MIL).

Andrews et al. [1] proposed a support vector machine based MIL model for the automatic annotation of images and text. Here an image consists of a set of patches and a text consists of a set of words. Each patch or word is referred to as an instance and the image or text is referred to as a bag, respectively. Considering image and text data sets from the MIL perspective pointed out its major advantage, namely, the ability of working with *weakly annotated* data. Annotating whole images is far less time consuming than providing pixel–level annotations. The same kind of reasoning applies to text data as well. In general, documents that contain a relevant passage are considered to be relevant with respect to a specific topic, however, most of the time class labels are not available on the passage level. They are rather associated with the document as a whole. As in [7] the models are optimized using precomputed features, such as, color, texture, and shape features in case of the image data sets and features related to word frequency in case of the text data sets. Furthermore, they were among the first to investigate two different approaches of predicting bag labels. The first approach tries to first predict a label for each instance in a bag. Afterwards these instance labels are used to infer the corresponding bag label. The second approach does not predict instance labels but aims at predicting the bag label directly. In Sect. 22.4, we will discuss these two approaches in greater detail.

In the following years, a variety of extensions of these methods were proposed with a steadily improving performance on a variety of MIL data sets. Ranging from methods based on graphs, where each bag is represented by a graph in which instances correspond to nodes [12], to methods which convert the multiple instance learning problem to a standard supervised learning problem by embedded instance selection [2].

In addition to the classical MIL assumption described above that is discussed in detail in Sect. 22.3, various new MIL assumptions were proposed. For example, instead of single instances that trigger the bag label, there could be a setting where most, if not all, instances contribute to the bag label. In such a scenario, utilizing (dis)similarities among bags instead of instance features is favorable [4]. Even though this approach has certain advantages, it is not necessarily well suited for the field of medical imaging, as we will discuss in Sect. 22.4.

Before we move on to discuss the use of deep neural networks in MIL, we have to highlight another key aspect of MIL. In many real life application we are not only interested in inferring the labels of before unseen bags, we are also concerned with finding the instances that are responsible for the bag label. These instances are called *key instances*. Being able to point out key instances adds a great deal of interpretability to an MIL model. Moreover, it has been shown that a model that is successfully detecting key instances is more likely to achieve better bag label predictions [17].

22.2. Deep multiple instance learning

Before the advent of deep neural networks, the majority of machine learning systems consisted of two separated entities: a feature extractor and a classifier. A crucial step in the design of such systems was the extraction of discriminant features from the given data. This process was done manually by human researchers, therefore we speak of *handcrafted features*. After the extraction of those features, they were subsequently fed into statistical classifiers, e.g., support vector machines, random forests, and Gaussian processes. The classifier was then trained in a fully supervised manner using a labeled training set.

The clear advantage of deep neural network is that they can be trained from end-to-end. In other words, deep neural networks are able to learn the features that optimally represent the given training data. This concept lies at the basis of many deep learning algorithms: networks composed of many layers that find a mapping from the input space (e.g., images) to the output space (e.g., class label) while learning increasingly higher level features.

Convolutional neural networks (CNNs) are a class of deep neural networks which have been widely applied to image data. CNNs are using (small) convolutional filters to extract local features of an image. Hereby, CNNs are exploiting a key property of images, which is that nearby pixels are more strongly correlated than more distant pixels. As a result, CNNs are more robust to transformations such as translating, rotating, scaling, and elastic deformations than fully connected networks (FCNs). Currently, there is a fast developing research of making CNNs invariant to rotations and other group-theoretic properties [5], with successful applications to medical imaging [25].

As with computer vision, CNNs have become the standard technique for feature extractions in MIL. In contrast to a fully supervised setting, the challenge is to design a system that can be trained end-to-end without instance labels. In other words, the information represented by the bag label has to be backpropagated through the entire network. Deep neural network architectures that are applicable for MIL can be found in [27]. Standard CNNs consist of 3 types of layers: convolutional layers, fully connected layers, and pooling layers. In classical supervised learning, pooling layers are used to reduce the dimensions of the latent space after every layer of neurons. In MIL problem, the pooling layers are also used to pool instance representations to obtain bag representations (i.e., pooling over instances). As we will see in Sects. 22.4 and 22.5, there is a wide variety of architectures and MIL pooling layers that we can choose from to design a deep MIL model.

22.3. Methodology

In (binary) fully supervised learning, one tries to find a mapping from an instance $\mathbf{x} \in \mathbb{R}^D$ to a label $y \in \{0, 1\}$, whereas in MIL one tries to find a mapping from a bag of instances $X = \{\mathbf{x_1}, \ldots, \mathbf{x_K}\}$ to a label $Y \in \{0, 1\}$. It is important to notice that the number of instances K in a bag is not necessarily constant for all bags in X. In MIL we assume that instances in a bag are unordered and independent of each other. Furthermore, we assume that there is a binary label for each instance in a bag, i.e., $y_1, \ldots, y_K$, $y_k \in \{0, 1\}$ for all $k = 1, \ldots, K$, though during training we have no access to these instance labels.

We now can define the main assumption of MIL as follows:

$$Y = \begin{cases} 0, & \text{if and only if } \sum_{k=1}^{K} y_k = 0, \\ 1, & \text{otherwise.} \end{cases} \tag{22.1}$$

Since our label Y is a binary random variable, we use Bernoulli distribution to model the probability of Y given the bag of instances X:

$$p(Y|X) = S(X)^Y (1 - S(X))^{(1-Y)}, \tag{22.2}$$

where $S(X) = p(Y = 1|X)$ is a scoring function of a bag X.

In order to train the scoring function, we utilize the negative log-likelihood of Bernoulli distribution in (22.2), which yields

$$\frac{1}{K} \sum_{k=1}^{K} -\log p(Y_k|X_k) = \frac{1}{k} \sum_{k=1}^{K} -Y_k \log(S(X_k)) - (1 - Y_k) \log(1 - S(X_k)), \tag{22.3}$$

where X_k and Y_k denote the training pair of a bag and a label, respectively.

In the following, we will introduce a framework to construct scoring functions $S(X)$ that successfully map a bag of instances $X = \{\mathbf{x_1}, \ldots, \mathbf{x_K}\}$ to a label $Y \in \{0, 1\}$. Since the instances in a bag are unordered and independent of each other, a valid scoring function has to be permutation invariant by design. In general, a scoring function $S(X)$ is considered permutation invariant (a.k.a. a symmetric function) if and only if

$$S(\{\mathbf{x_1}, \ldots, \mathbf{x_K}\}) = S(\{\mathbf{x}_{\sigma(1)}, \ldots, \mathbf{x}_{\sigma(K)}\}), \tag{22.4}$$

for any permutation σ.

The following two theorems provide sufficient and necessary conditions of defining a permutation invariant scoring function. The difference between Theorems 22.1

and 22.2 is that the former is a universal decomposition while the latter provides an arbitrary approximation.

Theorem 22.1. ([29]) *A scoring function for a set of instances X, $S(X) \in \mathbb{R}$, is a symmetric function (i.e., permutation invariant to the elements in X) if and only if it can be decomposed in the following form:*

$$S(X) = g\left(\sum_{x \in X} f(\mathbf{x})\right), \tag{22.5}$$

where f and g are suitable transformations.

Theorem 22.2. ([18]) *For any $\epsilon > 0$, a Hausdorff continuous symmetric function $S(X) \in \mathbb{R}$ can be arbitrarily approximated by a function in the form $g(\max_{x \in X} f(x))$, where max is the elementwise vector maximum pooling function and f and g are continuous functions, that is,*

$$|S(X) - g(\max_{x \in X} f(x))| < \epsilon. \tag{22.6}$$

From Theorems 22.1 and 22.2 we can see how one can design an algorithm to approximate any permutation-invariant scoring function $S(X)$:
1. Embedding all instances into a low-dimensional space using the function f.
2. Combining the embedded instances using a permutation-invariant (symmetric) function, e.g., the sum and max of embedded instances as shown in Eqs. (22.5) and (22.6).
3. Mapping of the combination of embedded instances to a single scalar (the score) using the function g.

Here, the choices of g and f are of crucial importance for the performance of a MIL model. Therefore, in the following, we presume that the functions f and g are parameterized by deep neural networks. Since, in theory, deep neural networks can approximate any nonlinear function.

22.4. MIL approaches

In MIL literature, three approaches prevail, namely: instance-based approach, embedding-based approach, and bag-based approach. In the following, we will explain each of them in detail. Later we will show that there are models that are not necessarily restricted to one of the three approaches. In all cases we will refer to the functions $S(\cdot)$, $f(\cdot)$, and $g(\cdot)$ as introduced in Sect. 22.3.

22.4.1 Instance-based approach

When using the instance-based approach, we try to directly infer instance scores. Consequently, we train a deep neural network, that is shared among instances, to compute

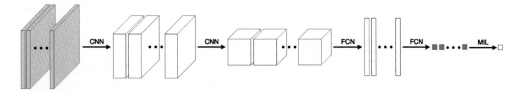

Figure 22.1 Instance-level approach: For each instance in a bag an instance score is obtained using a combination convolutional and fully connected layers. At last, an MIL pooling layer is used to infer the bag label.

a score (a scalar value between 0 and 1) for every instance. In a second step, an MIL pooling layer combines the score for every instance and computes a label for the entire bag of instances. Fig. 22.1 shows a possible architecture for an end-to-end trainable deep neural network that is using the instance-based approach.

The advantage of the instance-based approach is its ability to highlight key instances. This makes the approach highly interpretable, since a practitioner can investigate the highlighted instances, i.e., instances with a high instance score. When compared to the embedding-based approach (Sect. 22.4.2) and the bag-based approach (Sect. 22.4.3), multiple studies showed that the instance-based approach results generally in worse classification performance [27]. Since the instance labels are unknown during training, the deep neural network predicting instance scores might be trained insufficiently and introduces an additional error to the bag label prediction. In case of the instance-based approach, f is parameterized by a deep neural network and g is the identity function (see Eq. (22.5)). In Sect. 22.5 an overview of MIL pooling functions is given. The majority of the presented MIL pooling functions are suitable when an instance-based approach is used.

22.4.2 Embedding-based approach

The embedding-based approach has the same building blocks as the instance-based approach. The main difference of the two approaches lies in the ordering of fully connected layers, used for classification, and the MIL pooling layer. In case of the embedding-based approach, our main goal is finding a compact embedding (latent representation) of a bag. In a second step, we combine the instance embeddings to a single embedding that represents the entire bag. Similar to the instance-based approach, an MIL pooling layer is used to combine the instance embeddings. Though, in this case the MIL pooling layer must be able to handle a vector input in contrast to a scalar value. By sharing the same deep neural network we are guaranteed that all bag embeddings share the same latent space. Fig. 22.2 shows a possible architecture for an end-to-end trainable deep neural network that is using the embedding-based approach. When compared to the instance-based approach, MIL models using the embedding-based approach are known to have a better bag classification performance [27]. However, there is no

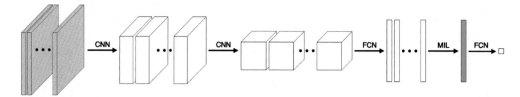

Figure 22.2 Embedded-level approach: First, convolutional and fully connected layers are used to embed each instance in a bag into a low dimensional space. Second, an MIL pooling layer is used to combine the instance embeddings to a single bag embedding. Last, a series of fully connected layers are used to infer the bag label.

way to infer instance scores when using the embedding-based approach. This makes this approach infeasible in a wide variety of settings where interpretability plays a crucial role. In case of the embedded-based approach, f and g are both parameterized by deep neural networks.

22.4.3 Bag-based approach

Bag-based approaches aim at looking for (dis)similarities among bags. They use different metrics like bag distances, bag kernels, or dissimilarities between bags to rephrase an MIL task as a regular supervised problem. Here, the bag is treated as a whole and the implicit assumption is made that bag labels can be related to distances between bags. The biggest challenge of this approach is to find a suitable definition of distance or similarity. Most of the time, a distance or similarity measure is only suited for one task and has to be chosen a priori, i.e., the measure is fixed during training. According to our knowledge, there is no research combining the bag-based approach with deep learning. Additionally, since bags are treated as a whole, there is substantial difficulty to infer instance scores. In the remaining part of this chapter, we will focus on the instance-based approach and embedding-based approach.

22.5. MIL pooling functions

In Sect. 22.4 we emphasized the advantages and disadvantages of the instance-based approach and embedding-based approach. One of the challenges in both approaches, and the MIL problem in general, is the choice of an appropriate MIL pooling functions. In the context of deep neural networks a pooling function is used inside of a pooling layer. Depending on the approach, the pooling layer is responsible for either combing instance scores (instance-based approach) or instance embeddings (embedded-based approach). We turn now to an exploration of the most widely-used MIL pooling functions. The pooling functions introduced in this section will also serve another important purpose, namely, to provide us with opportunity to discuss some key concepts, such as

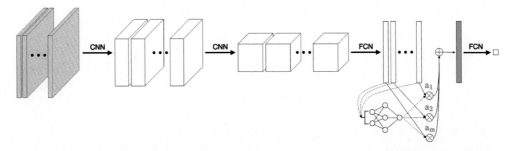

Figure 22.3 Attention-based approach: First, convolutional and fully connected layers are used to embed each instance in a bag into a low dimensional space. Afterwards, the attention mechanism is used to combine the instance embeddings into a single bag embedding. The attention mechanism consists of two fully connected layers that are used to compute an attention weight for each instance. Therefore, instances with a higher attention weight are contributing more to the bag embedding. Last, a series of fully connected layers are used to infer the bag label.

interpretability and *flexibility*, at the end of the section. We shall also show that different pooling functions have different purposes. Understanding those purposes enables us to choose the right pooling function.

Let us consider a bag of instances,

$$X = \{\mathbf{x}_1, \ldots, \mathbf{x}_K\}, \tag{22.7}$$

where instance $\mathbf{x}_k \in \mathbb{R}^D$ is, e.g., an image represented by its raw pixel values. Using the function f_θ, parameterized by a deep neural network shared among instances, we obtain a bag of embeddings,

$$H = \{\mathbf{h}_1, \ldots, \mathbf{h}_K\}, \tag{22.8}$$

where $\mathbf{h}_k = f_\theta(\mathbf{x}_k)$. Depending on the approach we choose, the embedding of an instance is either a scalar in case of the instance-based approach, $h_k \in [0, 1]$, or a vector in case of the embedding-based approach, $\mathbf{h}_k \in \mathbb{R}^M$, where $M < D$.

After having obtained the embeddings for all instances in a bag, we use a pooling function to combine the instance embedding to a bag embedding $\mathbf{z}$. We note that $\mathbf{z}$ has the same dimensionality as each of the instance embeddings, i.e., dimension 1 in case of the instance-based approach, or dimension M in case of the embedding-based approach. The aim of the bag embedding is to capture the most important information of a bag using a low dimensional representation. In contrast to a bag of instance embeddings, a bag embedding can be straightforwardly mapped to the corresponding bag label.

In the following section, we focus on most prominent MIL pooling functions. Our list is not exhaustive and there are many other, more specialized MIL pooling functions, e.g., ISR and Noisy-AND [14].

22.5.1 Max

The most commonly used MIL function is the max function. It can be used in two settings, namely, for a single vector $\mathbf{h} \in \mathbb{R}^K$:

$$z = \max_{k=1,\dots,K} \{h_k\}, \tag{22.9}$$

or as an elementwise operation over K vectors:

$$\text{for all } m = 1, \dots, M, \quad z_m = \max_{k=1,\dots,K} \{h_{km}\}. \tag{22.10}$$

22.5.2 Mean

Another widely used MIL pooling function is the mean function, which, in case of the instance-based approach, averages individual scores:

$$z = \frac{1}{K} \sum_{k=1}^{K} h_k, \tag{22.11}$$

or calculates an average embedding in the embedding-based approach:

$$\mathbf{z} = \frac{1}{K} \sum_{k=1}^{K} \mathbf{h_k}. \tag{22.12}$$

22.5.3 LSE

A continuous relaxation of the max function is the log–sum–exp (LSE) MIL pooling. The LSE function has an additional hyperparameter $r > 0$. In the instance-based approach it is defined as follows:

$$z = r \log \left[\frac{1}{K} \sum_{k=1}^{K} \exp(rh_k) \right], \tag{22.13}$$

while in the embedding-based approach it is given by

$$\text{for all } m = 1, \dots, M, \quad z_m = r \log \left[\frac{1}{K} \sum_{k=1}^{K} \exp(rh_{km}) \right]. \tag{22.14}$$

Interestingly, for $r \to \infty$, this function is equivalent to the maximum, and, for $r \to 0$, it results in the mean. In practice the choice of r might be quite problematic, however, it introduces some degree of flexibility of this MIL pooling.

22.5.4 (Leaky) Noisy-OR

Another continuous version of the max function is the Noisy-OR that acts similarly to the logic OR gate. The Noisy-OR is only used with the instance-based approach, where it is defined as

$$z = 1 - \prod_{k=1}^{K}(1 - h_k),$$

(22.15)

where $h_k \in [0, 1]$ corresponds to the *success* probability. This function could be further generalized by introducing a *leaky* parameter $h_0 \in [0, 1]$, that is,

$$z = 1 - (1 - h_0) \prod_{k=1}^{K}(1 - h_k).$$

(22.16)

22.5.5 Attention mechanism

All pooling functions mentioned in previous subsections have the clear disadvantage that they are predefined and nontrainable, and thus they reduce the flexibility of a MIL model drastically. Therefore, it would be beneficiary to have a fully flexible MIL pooling that can be trained alongside other components of a model. A solution that fulfills this goal is the attention-based MIL pooling [10] that is defined as a weighted sum,

$$\mathbf{z} = \sum_{k=1^K} a_k \mathbf{h}_k,$$

(22.17)

with

$$a_k = \frac{\exp\{\mathbf{w}^\mathsf{T} \ \tanh(V)\mathbf{h}_k^\mathsf{T}\}}{\sum_{j=1}^{K} \exp\{\mathbf{w}^\mathsf{T} \ \tanh(V)\mathbf{h}_j^\mathsf{T}\}},$$

(22.18)

where $\mathbf{w} \in \mathbb{R}^{L \times 1}$ and $\mathbf{V} \in \mathbb{R}^{L \times M}$.

The attention-based MIL pooling layer utilizes an auxiliary network that consists of two fully connected layers. In the first hidden layer, the hyperbolic tangent activation $\tanh(\cdot)$ is used since it is symmetric in its outputs, in contrast to the commonly used activation functions, such as sigmoid or ReLU. The second layer uses the softmax nonlinearity, so that the attention weights sum to 1. The resulting MIL pooling is fully trainable and highly flexible. In addition, the attention weights can be easily interpreted. The higher the attention weight, the higher the relative importance of the object. In case of the positive class, we can use the attention weights to determine the key instances. The attention-based MIL pooling layer can be seen in Fig. 22.3.

Moreover, we can get an extra insight into the attention-based MIL pooling by inspecting its gradient. Calculating the gradient with respect to the parameters of the f transformation, one gets

$$\frac{\partial a_k \mathbf{h}_k}{\partial \theta} = \frac{\partial a_k f_\theta(\mathbf{x}_k)}{\partial \theta} = a_k \frac{\partial f_\theta(\mathbf{x}_k)}{\partial \theta}. \tag{22.19}$$

The attention mechanism can be seen a gradient filter that determines the amount of gradient flow for individual instances [26].

One possible short coming of the attention-based MIL pooling layer is the use of the tanh($\cdot$) nonlinearity. The expressiveness of tanh($\cdot$) is limited since it is approximately linear for $x \in [-1, 1]$. It was proposed in [10] to additionally use the *gating mechanism* [6] together with tanh($\cdot$) nonlinearity, yielding

$$a_k = \frac{\exp\left\{\mathbf{w}^\top\left(\tanh\left(\mathbf{V}\mathbf{h}_k^\top\right) \odot \mathrm{sigm}\left(\mathbf{U}\mathbf{h}_k^\top\right)\right)\right\}}{\sum\limits_{j=1}^{K} \exp\left\{\mathbf{w}^\top\left(\tanh\left(\mathbf{V}\mathbf{h}_j^\top\right) \odot \mathrm{sigm}\left(\mathbf{U}\mathbf{h}_j^\top\right)\right)\right\}}, \tag{22.20}$$

where $\mathbf{U} \in \mathbb{R}^{L \times M}$ are parameters, $\odot$ is an elementwise multiplication and sigm($\cdot$) is the sigmoid nonlinearity. The gating mechanism introduces a learnable nonlinearity.

22.5.6 Interpretability

As mentioned before, only the instance-based approach and the attention-based pooling provide interpretability by highlighting the key instances. In case of the MIL, for a positive bag a high instance score or attention weight should ideally correspond with a positive instance label. Nevertheless, the interpretability of the instance-based approach comes with a loss in classification performance.

In the medical imaging domain interpretability is a key attribute of any machine learning method. Gaining insight in the inner workings of a machine learning model is of special interest for human doctors to properly analyze the diagnosis and prescribe appropriate treatment. For example, in digital pathology such a model can be used to highlight Regions Of Interest (ROI) that can be examined by a pathologist. ROIs could serve as indicators for "where-to-look" parts of an image and can drastically decrease the time a pathologist needs per image. Another scenario is the classification of lung CT screenings, where the malignancy of each nodule has to be assessed to derive a final diagnosis for the whole scan [15]. Again, an MIL approach could assist a human doctor in her daily routines.

22.5.7 Flexibility

Classical MIL methods utilized a feature extraction method and one of MIL pooling functions that is nontrainable like max or mean. An MIL pooling that has a hyperparameter that could be tuned is the LSE. In case of the LSE, if r is chosen to be small, it will approximate the mean and if r is sufficiently large, it will approximate the maximum. However, there are two limitations. First, the LSE can only provide instance scores in the instance-based approach. Second, the hyperparameter r is global, thus, it is not adaptive to new instances. The only MIL pooling that is learnable and adaptive is the attention-based pooling. The attention-based pooling layer can approximate the argmax function over instance if a single a_k equals 1 and the others are 0, and the mean if all attention weights have the same value $1/K$. Furthermore, since the attention weights are functions of the instance embeddings, the attention pooling layer can work as the maximum for positive bags and at the same time as the mean for negative bags.

22.6. Application to histopathology

The examination of a biopsy or surgical specimen can give insights into the state of a disease that other modalities, like CT, MRI, or US, cannot provide. After the specimen has been processed and the tissue have been placed onto glass slides, a pathologist can examine the tissue using a microscope. Unfortunately, the majority of cellular structures are colorless and transparent. Therefore, a wide array of chemicals is used to stain different structures so that they become visible. Staining usually works by using a dye that stains some of the cells components a bright color, together with a counterstain that stains the remaining of the cell in a different color. The most common staining system is Hematoxylin and Eosin (H&E). On the one hand, Hematoxylin stains nuclei blue since it binds to nucleic acids in the cell nucleus. On the other hand, Eosin stains the cytoplasm pink. Fig. 22.4 shows an example of H&E stained tissue.

In recent years, with the advent of digital microscopy, it has become possible to convert glass slides into digital slides. This results in large scale whole–slide images (WSI) of tissue specimen, containing billions of pixels and tens of thousands of cells. The reading of a WSI is a laborious task. Even a highly trained pathologist needs several hours in order to read a single slide thoroughly. Therefore, deep learning, with its capabilities of processing huge amounts of data, holds a great promise to support pathologists in their daily routines.

Already, deep learning methods have shown human-like performance on a set of (restricted) tasks. Common tasks for deep learning systems are: cell segmentation and cell type classification, segmentation and grading of organs, detecting and classifying the disease at the lesion- or WSI-level [16]. Because of the variability of the staining of WSI, deep learning methods have also been applied for normalization of histopathology images.

22.6.1 Data augmentation

Deep neural networks have millions of parameters that need to be tuned in order to learn a mapping from an input to an output, e.g., from an image to a label. To obtain a good final performance, the amount of examples in the training set needs to be proportional to the number of parameters in the network. Also, the number of parameters needed is proportional to the complexity of the task the model has to perform.

However, in the medical domain, where labeling is very time consuming and requires special training, data sets usually consists only of a few hundred or thousand of examples. Furthermore, the tasks, when compared to classical computer vision tasks, are typically significantly more challenging. For example, a histopathology data set might contain only a few dozen WSI. However, a single WSI will usually contain a billion pixels. To increase the number of training examples, data augmentation techniques are used. In the following section, we will look into methods to artificially enlarge data sets. With the help of data augmentation we can reduce overfitting of machine learning models, due to the increased amount of training data.

Another way of looking at the data augmentation is from the perspective of equivariance or invariance. By providing a network with all possible variations of the input data, the network can learn to disregard certain changes in the input. For instance, a translation in the input space should not change the predicted class label (invariance), furthermore it should only result in a translation of the segmentation by the same amount of pixels (equivariance).

Next, we will describe the most common data augmentation techniques utilized in deep learning methods applied to histopathology images. In contrast to other domains like computer vision, medical imaging is a field where safety plays a crucial role. Therefore, all the described data augmentation methods should be carefully considered and used only if they reflect possible real-life variants of the data. If the presented methods are used too extensively the model will become too confident when encountering abnormal changes. We might still see a performance gain but severe side effects may occur when these models are used in practice.

22.6.1.1 Cropping

In many practical scenarios one relies on existing neural network architectures, e.g., inception networks [24], that are proven to have a good performance. In order to use those models, we have to adjust the size of the images to match the input dimensions of the network. In medical imaging it is quite likely that the images are larger than the input dimensions of the model. Here, multiple smaller patches are extracted from the original images by randomly shifting the center of the cropped area by a few pixels left and right, and up and down. By shifting the input patch the network becomes robust to translations in the input space. As mentioned above, a translation in the input space should not lead to unforeseen changes of the output of a network.

22.6.1.2 Rotating and flipping

For a human observer a rotated or flipped image still contains the same content. Unfortunately, (convolutional) neural networks are very sensitive to such transformations [5]. In other words, the rotation of the input can lead to very different class predictions. To prevent such a behavior rotations and flips to the input images are applied. In case of rotation by an arbitrary angle the problem of interpolation arises, since the two images (original and rotated) are no longer sharing the same grid. In addition, one has to fill the corners in case where these are empty for the rotated image. Therefore, the simplest way of data augmentation is a rotation by 90, 180 and 270 degrees, as seen in Fig. 22.4. In addition, it is a common practice to flip images around the vertical and horizontal axis.

22.6.1.3 Blur

In the majority of cases, blurriness of digital histopathology images is introduced during the digitalization of the WSI. Since sections of the tissue slice are unevenly aligned, due to the different thickness of tissue sections, with the microscope focal plane the degree of blurriness varies across the WSI. By training with blurred images the model should become invariant to blurriness. In practice a Gaussian filter is used to artificially blur images:

$$G(x, y) = \frac{1}{2\pi\sigma^2} \exp\left\{\frac{x^2 + y^2}{2\sigma^2}\right\}. \tag{22.21}$$

The degree of blurriness can be tuned by changing the value of σ. Fig. 22.4 shows an example of an artificially blurred histopathology image.

22.6.1.4 Color

As described before, different dyes are applied to WSI in order to make certain cellular structures visible. Since staining is a nondigital process, it has a high variability, it is a common practice to slightly modify the colors of a histopathology image. There are two mainly used methods to deal with staining variability. The bottom row of Fig. 22.4 shows one example image for each method.

Color decomposition

Here, the RGB channels of a WSI are decomposed into the Hematoxylin, Eosin, and DAB channels. It is assumed that the obtained channels are uncorrelated. Afterwards the magnitude of H&E for a pixel is multiplied by two i.i.d. Gaussian random variables with expectation equal to one. The third, DAB channel remains constant. Finally, we map the channels back into the RGB color space.

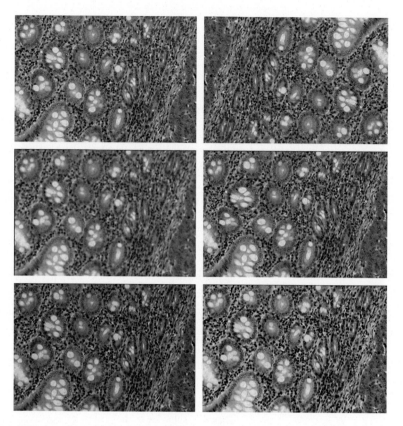

Figure 22.4 Different data augmentation methods applied to a histopathology image. Clockwise, starting at the upper left corner: No augmentation. Rotation: Rotation by 180°. Elastic Deformation: Deformation using a 3 × 3 grid and a displacement of 30 pixels. Color normalization: $l\alpha\beta$ channels are normalized using a target image. Color Augmentation: multiplying the magnitude of H&E for a pixel by two i.i.d. Gaussian random variables with expectation equal to one and $\sigma = 0.02$. Blur: Gaussian blur with σ set to 1.3.

Color normalization

The main idea of the color normalization technique is that the characteristics of all images in the data set are changed towards the characteristics of a predefined target image [21]. First, we map the RGB channels of the original image to a new color space, called $l\alpha\beta$. This new color space has two main advantages: **(i)** the three channels in the new color space have minimal correlation, in contrast to RGB where channels show a high amount of correlation, **(ii)** the $l\alpha\beta$ color space is logarithmic, thus, uniform changes lead to equally detectable changes in intensity. Second, we whiten the image in $l\alpha\beta$ space by subtracting the mean and dividing by the standard deviation, **(iii)** we multiply the channels by the standard deviation of the target image and add the mean of the target image. The resulting image now features the image characteristics of the target image. Last, we map the image bag to RGB space.

22.6.1.5 Elastic deformations

Elastic deformations have been proven to be useful especially for segmentation tasks of cellular structures [22]. First, we subdivide the image in patches. Second, we make use of random displacement field to deform images. A displacement field is a matrix that causes pixel values in each patch to be moved to new locations. A 2D matrix with uniformly distributed random numbers will lead to random displacements of the pixels of the original image. In order to guarantee a smooth displacement, we have to convolve the displacement matrix with a Gaussian blur in (22.21). Applying elastic deformation to the images in our training set the network learns to be invariant such deformations. This is particularly since deformation is one of the most common variation in tissue and realistic deformations can be simulated accurately, see Fig. 22.4 for an example image.

22.6.1.6 Generative models

One of the most promising new approaches for data augmentation is the use of generative models. Recent publications were able to show that generative models for data augmentation are also applicable in the field of medical imaging [28]. There are two major classes of deep generative model: Generative Adversarial Networks [9] and Variational Autoencoders [13]. Both classes of models have shown their effectiveness to learn from unlabeled data to generate photo realistic images. After training, generative models are able to synthesize images with particular characteristics. In this paper we do not use this approach for data augmentation, however, we want to highlight its huge potential.

22.6.2 Performance metrics

In Sect. 22.6.3, we are going to compare the performance of different settings and models on two histopathology data sets. As we defined in Sect. 22.3, in the MIL problem the distribution of the bag labels is a Bernoulli distribution. Therefore, we can make use of a wide array of performance metrics that assume binary class labels. In the following, we consider the illustrative example of classifying WSI using the labels malignant (1) or benign (0). Furthermore, we assume that only 10% of the WSI contain malignant changes. On the one hand, such a ratio is not an unrealistic one in practice; on the other hand, it will help us to highlight the shortcomings of some of the metrics when dealing with unbalanced data sets. In this section we will make use of the following notation: True positive (TP), label is 1 prediction is 1; False positive (FP), label is 0 prediction is 1; True negative (TN), label is 0 prediction is 0; False negative (FN), label is 1 prediction is 0.

22.6.2.1 Accuracy

The most widely-used measure is the classification accuracy. The accuracy is defined by the fraction of correctly classified data points:

$$\text{accuracy} = \frac{TP + TN}{TP + TN + FP + FN}. \tag{22.22}$$

Considering our example of classifying WSIs, we can easily see that accuracy will fail to assess the performance of a model that is always predicting 0. In this case the model would achieve an accuracy of 0.9. The second drawback of the classification accuracy is the necessity of choosing a classification threshold for the output values of the model to provide either 0 or 1. The output of the model is a real number between 0 and 1, $\hat{Y} \in [0, 1]$, while the labels of the WSI are binary, $Y \in \{0, 1\}$. To be able to compute TP, FP, TN, and FN, we need to threshold the model's output. A commonly used threshold is 0.5, i.e., if $\hat{Y} \geq 0.5$, the final prediction will be equal to 1, otherwise it will be 0. Since the threshold is not represented by the loss function, there is no guarantee that, e.g., 0.5 will lead to the best possible classification performance of the model.

22.6.2.2 Precision, recall and F1-score

After noticing possible limitations of the classification accuracy as a performance metric, we now look at precision and recall, and one particular combination of the two, namely, the F1-score. Precision is the ratio of WSI that were correctly classified as malignant and all WSI that were classified as malignant,

$$\text{precision} = \frac{TP}{TP + FP}. \tag{22.23}$$

Precision is the ratio of WSI that were correctly classified as malignant and the all correctly classified WSI as either malignant or benign,

$$\text{recall} = \frac{TP}{TP + FN}. \tag{22.24}$$

In case of the unbalanced WSI image and a classifier always predicting benign for all WSIs, we can see that the precision equals 0 as well as the recall. It is easy to see that for an imbalanced data set precision and recall are better suited than accuracy. Often, there is an inverse relationship between precision and recall, where it is possible to increase one at the cost of reducing the other. The F1-score is one particular and commonly used way of combining precession and recall into one performance measure,

$$\text{F1-score} = 2\frac{\text{precision} \times \text{recall}}{\text{precision} + \text{recall}}. \tag{22.25}$$

One common criticism of the measures mentioned earlier is that the true negative, TN, is not taken into account. This results in zero precision and recall for our WSI example. Again, precision, recall and F1-score suffer from the same problem of having only one single classification threshold. In the next section we introduce a performance measure that does not suffer from this issue.

22.6.2.3 Receiver Operating Characteristic Area Under Curve

In contrast to the performance metrics described above, the Receiver Operating Characteristic Area Under Curve (ROC AUC, commonly denoted as AUC) is not restricted to a single classification threshold. The ROC curve allows us to compare multiple pairs of sensitivity and specificity values, where the sensitivity, or the true positive rate, is given by

$$\text{sensitivity} = \frac{TP}{TP + FN}, \tag{22.26}$$

and the specificity, or the true negative rate, is given by

$$\text{specificity} = \frac{TN}{TP + FN}. \tag{22.27}$$

The ROC curve can be drawn using the sensitivities as the y-coordinates and the specificities as the x-coordinates. As the classification threshold decreases, the specificity decreases as well, while the sensitivity increases, and vice versa. Each point on the graph is called an operating point. Each operating point is generated using a different classification threshold. Since the ROC curve displays the sensitivity and the specificity at all possible classification thresholds, it can be used to evaluate the performance of a machine learning model independently of the classification threshold. As in case of the F1-score, we are interested in finding one metric that combines all the information represented by the ROC curve. This is most commonly done by measuring the area under the receiver operating characteristic curve. It is a measure of the overall classification performance of a machine learning model interpreted as the mean value of sensitivity for all possible values of specificity. The AUC can have any value between 0 and 1, since both the x and y axes are strictly positive. The closer the value of AUC is to 1, the better the overall classification performance of a machine learning model.

If we were to rely on pure chance to classify data samples, the ROC curve would fall along the diagonal line segment from $(0, 0)$ to $(1, 1)$. The resulting ROC curve has an area of 0.5. At last, we want to note that having machine learning models with the same classification performance result in ROCs and the same AUC value does not mean that the machine learning models are identical.

22.6.3 Evaluation of MIL models

In this section we evaluate MIL methods in a quantitative manner, using the performance metrics introduced in Sect. 22.6.2. We investigate the performance of the two deep MIL approaches with different pooling layers on two histopathology data sets, called Breast Cancer and Colon Cancer. In both cases we frame the learning task as a MIL task where we try to infer the binary labels of a bag of patches. The two data sets comprise images extracted from WSI, where the size of the extracted images range from 500×500 pixels to 896×768 pixels. In order to process such large images, we will make use of MIL methods. Here, each image is represented as a collection of smaller patches containing a nuclei and adjacent tissue, where each image is treated as a bag while each patch is an instance. During training we only use information about the label of the original image. By focusing on single cells and their nuclei, the MIL models are able to learn various cell attributes such as shape, size, and smoothness of the boundary. These morphological properties of cells are crucial for classifying dysplastic changes. The diagnosis of dysplastic changes in surveillance biopsies is one of the strongest independent risk factors for progression.

One crucial part of the presented MIL experiments is extracting patches from histopathology images. There are two common classes of methods to generate an MIL data set. The first class makes use of a preceding detector. The detector can be either a human or a computer program, e.g., another machine learning model, that finds regions of interest and discards parts of the image that are considered irrelevant for the task. The Colon Cancer data set is an example of this class, here the cells were presegmented by a pathologist. The second class of methods is subdividing the image into patches using a rigid grid. Depending on the number of resulting patches and computational resources, sampling methods can be used to reduce the number of patches. Here, it is common practice to discard patches that are not containing any cells. The Breast Cancer data set is an example of this generation method. In this case the model not only has to differentiate between benign and malignant tissue but also find important cellular structures. The presented results show that, in general, MIL works better the higher the quality of the provided instances.

For both data sets we use the same experimental setup. We will see how the two MIL approaches shape the architecture of the MIL models. By carefully studying the experimental setup we are able to make connections between the mathematical framework introduced in Sect. 22.3 and a real-world application.

22.6.3.1 Experimental setup

Tables 22.1 and 22.2 show the architecture of different MIL models for the embedded-based approach and the instance-based approach. This particular architecture, including the size and number of filters and layers, is proven to have good classification performance on patches containing single cells [23]. For both approaches the network has

Table 22.1 Model architecture for embedding-based approach. The neural network consists of convolutional layers (conv(kernel size, stride, padding)-number of filters + activation function), fully connected layers (fc-output dimensions + activation function) and MIL pooling layers. Here, ReLU represents the Rectified Linear Unit activation function and sigm the sigmoid activation function.

Layer	Type
1	conv(4,1,0)-36 + ReLU
2	maxpool(2,2)
3	conv(3,1,0)-48 + ReLU
4	maxpool(2,2)
5	fc-512 + ReLU
6	dropout
7	fc-512 + ReLU
8	dropout
9	mil-pooling
10	fc-1 + sigm

the same number of layers. Therefore we can have a fair comparison of the different approaches. An important difference, as discussed in Sect. 22.4, is the order of layers. In case of the embedded-based approach, the patches are embedded using two convolutional layers and two fully connected layers. All layers are shared among the instances. An MIL pooling layer is used to combine the embeddings to a single embedding representing the entire bag. Lastly, a single fully connected layer is used for classifying the bag.

In contrast, using the instance-based approach, each instance is processed using two convolutional layers and three fully connected layers. The output of the last layer is a single score, a real number between 0 and 1, for each instance. In a final step all scores are combined by a MIL pooling layer. The combination of the instance scores results in the final bag score.

All models are trained using the same hyperparameters. For training we use the Adam optimizer with the default settings $\beta_1 = 0.9$, $\beta_2 = 0.999$, and a learning rate equal to 0.0001. Since the number of samples in both data sets is very limited, weight decay and the early stopping were used to prevent overfitting. As mentioned frequently in this chapter, one of the biggest challenges in medical imaging is the difficulty of obtaining high quality labels. This results in comparably small data sets. In order to compensate for the small number of training examples data augmentation methods are used. First, the center of a patch is randomly shifted by a small number of pixels. Second, each

Table 22.2 Model architecture for instance-based approach. The neural network consists of convolutional layers (conv(kernel size, stride, padding)-number of filters + activation function), fully connected layers (fc-output dimensions + activation function) and MIL pooling layers. Here, ReLU represents the Rectified Linear Unit activation function and sigm the sigmoid activation function.

Layer	Type
1	conv(4,1,0)-36 + ReLU
2	maxpool(2,2)
3	conv(3,1,0)-48 + ReLU
4	maxpool(2,2)
5	fc-512 + ReLU
6	dropout
7	fc-512 + ReLU
8	dropout
9	fc-1 + sigm
10	mil-pooling

patch was randomly rotated and flipped. Third, the patches are randomly blurred using a Gaussian kernel. Fourth, the H&E staining of each patch are randomly adjusted.

22.6.3.2 Colon cancer

Colorectal cancer (colon cancer) is known to originate from epithelial cells lining the colon and rectum. Therefore, tagging epithelial cells is highly relevant from a clinical point of view. One way to explore these cell types is to use special biomarkers which can highlight certain cells in the cancer tissue. However, such an approach is time consuming and requires the selection of the appropriate markers a priori. Furthermore, a single histopathology image can contain thousands of epithelial cells, where malignant epithelial cells often appear highly cluttered together with irregular shaped nuclei. For the former reason a fully supervised approach that relies on class labels for every single cell is not well suited. Using MIL we make use of the ability of MIL models to find cells of a certain type while only using image labels during training. The weak image labels can be obtained, e.g., by knowing the area where the tissue was extracted from. The Colon Cancer data set has been made publicly available by the University of Warwick and comprises 100 H&E images of colorectal adenocarcinomas [23]. The images come from a variety of tissue appearance from both benign and malignant regions. In each image the nuclei of all cells are marked. In total there are 22,444 nuclei with 4 associated class labels: epithelial, inflammatory, fibroblast, and miscellaneous. For every cell a patch

Table 22.3 Results on Colon Cancer data set. Experiments were run 5 times and an average ($\pm$ one standard error of the mean) is reported.

METHOD	ACCURACY	PRECISION	RECALL	F-SCORE	AUC
Instance+max	0.842 ± 0.021	0.866 ± 0.017	0.816 ± 0.031	0.839 ± 0.023	0.914 ± 0.010
Instance+mean	0.772 ± 0.012	0.821 ± 0.011	0.710 ± 0.031	0.759 ± 0.017	0.866 ± 0.008
Embedding+max	0.824 ± 0.015	0.884 ± 0.014	0.753 ± 0.020	0.813 ± 0.017	0.918 ± 0.010
Embedding+mean	0.860 ± 0.014	0.911 ± 0.011	0.804 ± 0.027	0.853 ± 0.016	0.940 ± 0.010
Attention	$\mathbf{0.904 \pm 0.011}$	$\mathbf{0.953 \pm 0.014}$	$\mathbf{0.855 \pm 0.017}$	$\mathbf{0.901 \pm 0.011}$	$\mathbf{0.968 \pm 0.009}$
Gated-Attention	$\mathbf{0.898 \pm 0.020}$	$\mathbf{0.944 \pm 0.016}$	$\mathbf{0.851 \pm 0.035}$	$\mathbf{0.893 \pm 0.022}$	$\mathbf{0.968 \pm 0.010}$

of 27×27 pixel was extracted. Furthermore, a bag of patches is given a positive label if it contains one or more nuclei from the epithelial class. While the primary task is to predict the bag label of an unseen image, assuming presegmented cells, we are even more interested in highlighting all epithelial cells. A task that only the attention-based MIL pooling layers and MIL pooling layers used with an instance-level approach can solve.

The results of experiments on the Colon Cancer data set are presented in Table 22.3. First, we notice that models of the instance-level approach are performing worse than all other models, disregard of the used MIL pooling layer. Furthermore, attention-based MIL pooling layers perform the best across all metrics. It is most likely that they benefit from the properties described in Sect. 22.5.5. In case of the embedding-level approach the mean pooling layer is performing significantly better than the max pooling layer. This finding indicates that the mean pooling layer is better suited if a bag contains a high number of positive instances, as it is the case for the Colon Cancer data set.

In Fig. 22.5, we compare the ability of the best performing instance-level approach model and the best performing attention-based model with respect to their ability to discover key instances. We can easily see that the attention-based pooling layer is able to highlight more epithelial cells than the max-instance pooling layer. By using an auxiliary network, the MIL pooling layer is not restricted to either have interpretable instance scores or discriminative instance embeddings. As a result the attention-based MIL pooling layers show the best classification performance together with having highly interpretable attention weights a_k.

22.6.3.3 Breast cancer

After abnormal findings during a mammography, a biopsy is used to gain further insight into the conditions of a patient. A biopsy removes tissue from the suspicious area of the breast. After the extraction, the tissue is stained and fixed to a glass slide. At last, the obtained histopathology slide is digitalized. The Breast Cancer data set is part of a bigger corpus of medical data, the UCSB Bio-Segmentation Benchmark [8]. It consists of 58 weakly labeled 896×768 H&E images. Unlike the Colon Cancer data set, the image label is 1 if an image contains malignant changes. An image is labeled as benign

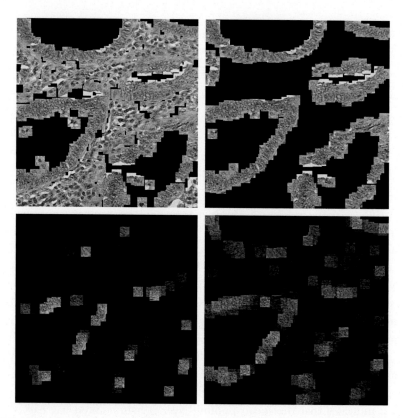

Figure 22.5 Clockwise, starting in the upper left corner: Instances: 27×27 patches centered around all marked nuclei. Ground truth: Patches that belong to the class epithelial. Attention heatmap: Every patch multiplied by its attention weight. Instance+max heatmap: Every patch multiplied by its instance score. We rescaled the attention weights and instance scores using $a'_k = (a_k - \min(\mathbf{a}))/(\max(\mathbf{a}) - \min(\mathbf{a}))$.

(0) if no abnormal changes are present. In case of the Breast Cancer data set the images were not presegmented. We divide every image into 32×32 patches. This results in 672 patches per bag. A patch is discarded if it contains 75% or more of white pixels. Compared to the Colon Cancer data set this is considerably more challenging task since not all patches will contain a centered cell. The lower performance values in Table 22.4 reflect the challenging nature of the task. In addition, the data set contains fewer images than the Colon Cancer data set.

Once more the attention-based pooling layers are among the best performing models. Even though the embedded-mean model leads to similar classification results on the bag level, it does not provide any interpretable results on the instance level. In addition, it is important to notice that one of the most common MIL pooling layers, the max pooling layer, is having low values across all metrics.

Table 22.4 Results on Breast Cancer data set. Experiments were run 5 times and an average ($\pm$ one standard error of the mean) is reported.

METHOD	ACCURACY	PRECISION	RECALL	F-SCORE	AUC
Instance+max	0.614 ± 0.020	0.585 ± 0.03	0.477 ± 0.087	0.506 ± 0.054	0.612 ± 0.026
Instance+mean	0.672 ± 0.026	0.672 ± 0.034	0.515 ± 0.056	0.577 ± 0.049	0.719 ± 0.019
Embedding+max	0.607 ± 0.015	0.558 ± 0.013	0.546 ± 0.070	0.543 ± 0.042	0.650 ± 0.013
Embedding+mean	$\mathbf{0.741 \pm 0.023}$	$\mathbf{0.741 \pm 0.023}$	0.654 ± 0.054	0.689 ± 0.034	$\mathbf{0.796 \pm 0.012}$
Attention	$\mathbf{0.745 \pm 0.018}$	0.718 ± 0.021	$\mathbf{0.715 \pm 0.046}$	$\mathbf{0.712 \pm 0.025}$	0.775 ± 0.016
Gated-Attention	$\mathbf{0.755 \pm 0.016}$	$\mathbf{0.728 \pm 0.016}$	$\mathbf{0.731 \pm 0.042}$	$\mathbf{0.725 \pm 0.023}$	$\mathbf{0.799 \pm 0.020}$

References

[1] Stuart Andrews, Ioannis Tsochantaridis, Thomas Hofmann, Support vector machines for multiple-instance learning, in: NIPS, 2003, pp. 577–584.

[2] Yixin Chen, Jinbo Bi, James Ze Wang, MILES: multiple-instance learning via embedded instance selection, IEEE Transactions on Pattern Analysis and Machine Intelligence 28 (12) (2006) 1931–1947.

[3] Veronika Cheplygina, Lauge Sørensen, David Tax, Marleen de Bruijne, Marco Loog, Label stability in multiple instance learning, in: MICCAI, 2015, pp. 539–546.

[4] Veronika Cheplygina, David M.J. Tax, Marco Loog, Multiple instance learning with bag dissimilarities, Pattern Recognition 48 (1) (2015) 264–275.

[5] Taco S. Cohen, Max Welling, Group equivariant convolutional networks, in: ICML, 2016.

[6] Yann N. Dauphin, Angela Fan, Michael Auli, David Grangier, Language modeling with gated convolutional networks, arXiv preprint arXiv:1612.08083, 2016.

[7] Thomas G. Dietterich, Richard H. Lathrop, Tomás Lozano-Pérez, Solving the multiple instance problem with axis-parallel rectangles, Artificial Intelligence 89 (1–2) (1997) 31–71.

[8] Elisa Drelie Gelasca, Jiyun Byun, Boguslaw Obara, B.S. Manjunath, Evaluation and benchmark for biological image segmentation, in: IEEE International Conference on Image Processing, 2008, pp. 1816–1819.

[9] Ian J. Goodfellow, Jean Pouget-Abadie, Mehdi Mirza, Bing Xu, David Warde-Farley, Sherjil Ozair, Aaron Courville, Yoshua Bengio, Generative adversarial networks, in: NIPS, 2014.

[10] Maximilian Ilse, Jakub M. Tomczak, Max Welling, Attention-based deep multiple instance learning, in: ICML, 2018.

[11] Melih Kandemir, Fred A. Hamprecht, Computer-aided diagnosis from weak supervision: a benchmarking study, Computerized Medical Imaging and Graphics 42 (2015) 44–50.

[12] Melih Kandemir, Chong Zhang, Fred A. Hamprecht, Empowering multiple instance histopathology cancer diagnosis by cell graphs, in: MICCAI, 2014, pp. 228–235.

[13] Diederik P. Kingma, Max Welling, Auto-encoding variational Bayes, in: ICLR, 2013.

[14] Oren Z. Kraus, Jimmy Lei Ba, Brendan J. Frey, Classifying and segmenting microscopy images with deep multiple instance learning, Bioinformatics 32 (12) (2016) i52–i59.

[15] Fangzhou Liao, Ming Liang, Zhe Li, Xiaolin Hu, Sen Song, Evaluate the malignancy of pulmonary nodules using the 3D deep leaky noisy-or network, URL http://arxiv.org/abs/1711.08324.

[16] Geert Litjens, Thijs Kooi, Babak Ehteshami Bejnordi, Arnaud Arindra Adiyoso Setio, Francesco Ciompi, Mohsen Ghafoorian, Jeroen A.W.M. van der Laak, Bram van Ginneken, Clara I. Sánchez, A survey on deep learning in medical image analysis, Medical Image Analysis 42 (2017) 60–88.

[17] Guoqing Liu, Jianxin Wu, Zhi-Hua Zhou, Key instance detection in multi-instance learning, in: JMLR, vol. 25, 2012, pp. 253–268.

[18] Charles R. Qi, Hao Su, Kaichun Mo, Leonidas J. Guibas, PointNet: deep learning on point sets for 3D classification and segmentation, in: CVPR, 2017.

[19] Jan Ramon, Luc De Raedt, Multi instance neural networks, in: ICML Workshop on Attribute-value and Relational Learning, 2000, pp. 53–60.

[20] Vikas C. Raykar, Balaji Krishnapuram, Jinbo Bi, Murat Dundar, R. Bharat Rao, Bayesian multiple instance learning: automatic feature selection and inductive transfer, in: ICML, 2008, pp. 808–815.

[21] Erik Reinhard, Michael Ashikhmin, Bruce Gooch, Peter Shirley, Color transfer between images, IEEE Computer Graphics and Applications (2001).

[22] Olaf Ronneberger, Philipp Fischer, Thomas Brox, U-Net: convolutional networks for biomedical image segmentation, in: MICCAI, 2015.

[23] Korsuk Sirinukunwattana, Shan E. Ahmed Raza, Yee-Wah Tsang, David R.J. Snead, Ian A. Cree, Nasir M. Rajpoot, Locality sensitive deep learning for detection and classification of nuclei in routine colon cancer histology images, IEEE Transactions on Medical Imaging 35 (5) (2016) 1196–1206.

[24] Christian Szegedy, Wei Liu, Yangqing Jia, Pierre Sermanet, Scott Reed, Dragomir Anguelov, Dumitru Erhan, Vincent Vanhoucke, Andrew Rabinovich, Going deeper with convolutions, in: CVPR, 2015.

[25] Bastiaan S. Veeling, Jasper Linmans, Jim Winkens, Taco Cohen, Max Welling, Rotation equivariant CNNs for digital pathology, in: MICCAI, 2018.

[26] Fei Wang, Mengqing Jiang, Chen Qian, Shuo Yang, Cheng Li, Honggang Zhang, Xiaogang Wang, Xiaoou Tang, Residual attention network for image classification, in: CVPR, 2017.

[27] Xinggang Wang, Yongluan Yan, Peng Tang, Xiang Bai, Wenyu Liu, Revisiting multiple instance neural networks, Pattern Recognition 74 (2016) 15–24.

[28] Jelmer M. Wolterink, Tim Leiner, Ivana Isgum, Blood vessel geometry synthesis using generative adversarial networks, URL http://arxiv.org/abs/1804.04381.

[29] Manzil Zaheer, Satwik Kottur, Siamak Ravanbakhsh, Barnabas Poczos, Ruslan Salakhutdinov, Alexander Smola, Deep sets, in: NIPS, 2017.

[30] Cha Zhang, John C. Platt, Paul A. Viola, Multiple instance boosting for object detection, in: NIPS, 2006, pp. 1417–1424.

CHAPTER 23

Deep learning: Generative adversarial networks and adversarial methods

Jelmer M. Wolterink[a], **Konstantinos Kamnitsas**[b], **Christian Ledig**[c], **Ivana Išgum**[a]

[a]Image Sciences Institute, University Medical Center Utrecht, Utrecht, the Netherlands
[b]Imperial College London, London, United Kingdom
[c]Imagen Technologies, New York, NY, United States

Contents

23.1. Introduction		547
23.2. Generative adversarial networks		549
	23.2.1 Objective functions	549
	23.2.2 The latent space	552
	23.2.3 Conditional GANs	553
	23.2.4 GAN architectures	553
23.3. Adversarial methods for image domain translation		554
	23.3.1 Training with paired images	555
	23.3.2 Training without paired images	556
23.4. Domain adaptation via adversarial training		558
23.5. Applications in biomedical image analysis		559
	23.5.1 Sample generation	560
	23.5.2 Image synthesis	561
	23.5.3 Image quality enhancement	562
	23.5.4 Image segmentation	564
	23.5.5 Domain adaptation	565
	23.5.6 Semisupervised learning	567
23.6. Discussion and conclusion		568
References		570

23.1. Introduction

Recent years have seen a strong increase in deep learning applications to medical image analysis [1]. Many of these applications are supervised, consisting of a convolutional neural network (CNN) that is optimized to provide a desired prediction given an input image. For example, given a medical image, we may require the CNN to obtain a segmentation of a number of anatomical structures. These are *discriminative* models, in which the CNN tries to discriminate between images or image voxels that correspond to different classes. Optimization of this CNN is *supervised* by a loss function that quantifies the agreement between model predictions and reference labels. Convolutional layers and downsampling layers are used to discard redundant information from the input, obtain invariance to, e.g., translations, and transform a high-dimensional input into a low-dimensional prediction.

In contrast to discriminative models, *generative models* aim to learn the underlying distribution of the data and the generative process that creates them. By learning the factors that govern this process, the natural features of a dataset (e.g., object categories, illumination, pose, etc.), they enable analysis of the data and can potentially provide novel intuitions about the world. Furthermore, they also allow generation of new data by sampling from the model. As an example, a low-dimensional input, such as a noise vector or a vector that encodes the required characteristics of the output, can be transformed into a high-dimensional output, such as an image. Generative adversarial networks (GANs) have recently emerged as a powerful class of generative models [2]. Central to the idea of GANs is the joint optimization of two neural networks with opposing goals, i.e., *adversarial* training. The first network is a generator network that maps input from a source domain, which is often low-dimensional, to a target domain such as the high-dimensional space of natural images. This network is jointly optimized with a second, adversarial network, called the discriminator network. The generator tries to generate outputs that the discriminator network cannot distinguish from a dataset of real examples. Both the generator and discriminator are optimized based on the output of the discriminator: if the discriminator can easily distinguish the generator's outputs from samples in the real dataset, the weights of the generator need to be adjusted accordingly.

It has been shown that the training of discriminative or regression models such as segmentation CNNs can also benefit from the signal of an adversarial network. For example, an adversarial network with a large receptive field that processes full predicted and real segmentations can provide an additional cost term to a segmentation CNN that quantifies how well the global arrangement of predicted segmentations agrees with that of real segmentations. It has been shown empirically that such an approach can reduce mistakes such as segmentation maps with holes or fragments [3]. This is a task for which it is challenging to hand-craft an appropriate loss function. This type of adversarial training has found its way to many applications in biomedical image analysis.

This chapter provides an introduction to GANs and adversarial methods with a focus on applications in biomedical image analysis. In Sect. 23.2 we describe GANs and methods to optimize GANs. In Sect. 23.3 we describe the use of adversarial networks to map images from one domain to another, which could benefit many medical image analysis techniques such as segmentation, modality synthesis, and artifact reduction. Section 23.4 provides an introduction to domain adaptation with adversarial methods. Section 23.5 describes a number of applications of GANs and adversarial methods in biomedical image analysis. Section 23.6 provides a discussion of some of the current strengths and limitations of GANs and adversarial methods in biomedical image analysis, as well as a discussion of potential future research directions.

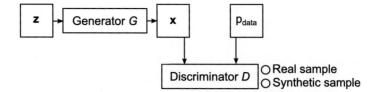

Figure 23.1 Generative adversarial network. The generator G takes a noise vector $\mathbf{z}$ sampled from a distribution p_z as input and uses fully connected or convolutional layers to transform this vector into a sample $\mathbf{x}$. The discriminator D tries to distinguish these samples from samples drawn from the real data distribution p_{data}.

23.2. Generative adversarial networks

Generative adversarial networks consist of two neural networks [2]. The first network, the *generator*, tries to generate synthetic but perceptually convincing samples $\mathbf{x} \in p_{\text{fake}}$ that appear to have been drawn from a real data distribution p_{data}. It transforms noise vectors $\mathbf{z}$ drawn from a distribution p_z into new samples, i.e., $\mathbf{x} = G(\mathbf{z})$ (Fig. 23.1). The second network, the *discriminator*, has access to real samples from p_{data} and to the samples generated by G, and tries to discriminate between these two. GANs are trained by solving the following optimization problem that the discriminator is trying to maximize and the generator is trying to minimize:

$$\min_G \max_D V(D, G) = \mathop{\mathbb{E}}_{\mathbf{x} \sim p_{\text{data}}} [\log D(\mathbf{x})] + \mathop{\mathbb{E}}_{\mathbf{z} \sim p_z} [\log (1 - D(G(\mathbf{z})))], \qquad (23.1)$$

where G is the generator, D is the discriminator, $V(D, G)$ is the objective function, p_{data} is the distribution of real samples, and p_z is a distribution from which noise vectors are drawn, e.g., a uniform distribution or spherical Gaussian. The final layer of the discriminator network contains a sigmoid activation function, so that $D(\mathbf{x}), D(G(\mathbf{z})) \in [0, 1]$. By maximizing the value function, the discriminator minimizes the error of its predictions with respect to target values 1 and 0 for real and fake samples, respectively. Conversely, the generator tries to minimize the chance that the discriminator will predict a 0 for fake samples. Hence, the loss of the generator depends directly on the performance of the discriminator.

23.2.1 Objective functions

The iterative approach when training GANs, i.e., finding a saddle point in Eq. (23.1), tends to be unstable. This makes the optimization process challenging in practice. Optimization of the generator depends directly on gradients provided by the discriminator for synthetic samples. A problem arises when the discriminator can easily distinguish samples in p_{fake} from those in p_{data}, as is common at the beginning of GAN training. In that case, the gradient for $\log (1 - D(G(\mathbf{z})))$ is close to zero (Fig. 23.2). Consequently,

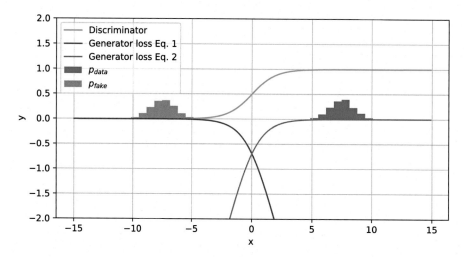

Figure 23.2 Objective function on real and fake data. When using the generator loss in Eq. (23.1), gradients for fake samples saturate when real and fake data are easily separated. When using the alternative loss in Eq. (23.2), gradients for fake samples do not saturate.

the generator will fail to update its parameters and minimize its loss. Therefore, an alternative loss function for the generator is used in practice [2]:

$$\min_{G} V(D, G) = - \mathop{\mathbb{E}}_{\mathbf{z} \sim p_z} [\log D(G(\mathbf{z}))]. \tag{23.2}$$

While in Eq. (23.1) the objective for the generator is to minimize the probability that the discriminator identifies generated samples as fake, in Eq. (23.2) the objective is to maximize the probability that the discriminator identifies generated samples as real. Fig. 23.2 shows how this objective has a strong gradient for fake samples that are far from the discriminator's decision boundary, and how this is not the case when using the objective in Eq. (23.1).

Nevertheless, GANs can still suffer from unstable training. This is partly due to the way in which the discriminator computes the difference between p_{data} and p_{fake}. In the original GAN definition (Eq. (23.1)), this difference is computed as the Jensen–Shannon divergence. This is a symmetric divergence measure, which unfortunately is poorly defined when two distributions are disjoint. To address this, alternative objective functions have been proposed that use the Pearson chi-square divergence [4] or the Earth Mover's or Wasserstein distance [5]. Table 23.1 lists several alternative objective functions for the discriminator and generator that could be used to optimize a GAN.

One attractive way to optimize GANs is to use the Wasserstein distance for the divergence between the real and fake distributions. An analogy for this distance is that of two piles that are different but both contain the same amount of earth: the Wasserstein distance is the minimum amount of work required to transform one pile into the other,

Table 23.1 Discriminator and generator objectives in different GAN variants: original GAN (GAN, Eq. (23.1)), an alternative in which the generator maximizes the probability that its samples are identified as real (GAN-MA, Eq. (23.2)), least-squares GAN (LSGAN), Wasserstein GAN (WGAN, Eq. (23.3)), and Wasserstein GAN with gradient penalty (WGAN-GP, Eq. (23.4)). In all cases, the discriminator or generator is trying to minimize the listed loss.

	Discriminator loss	Generator loss
GAN [2]	$-\displaystyle\mathop{\mathbb{E}}_{\mathbf{x}\sim p_{data}} [\log D(\mathbf{x})] - \mathop{\mathbb{E}}_{\mathbf{z}\sim p_z} [\log(1-D(G(\mathbf{z})))]$	$\displaystyle\mathop{\mathbb{E}}_{\mathbf{z}\sim p_z} [\log(1-D(G(\mathbf{z})))]$
GAN-MA [2]	$-\displaystyle\mathop{\mathbb{E}}_{\mathbf{x}\sim p_{data}} [\log D(\mathbf{x})] - \mathop{\mathbb{E}}_{\mathbf{z}\sim p_z} [\log(1-D(G(\mathbf{z})))]$	$-\displaystyle\mathop{\mathbb{E}}_{\mathbf{z}\sim p_z} [\log D(G(\mathbf{z}))]$
LSGAN [4]	$\displaystyle\mathop{\mathbb{E}}_{\mathbf{x}\sim p_{data}} [(D(\mathbf{x})-1)^2] + \mathop{\mathbb{E}}_{\mathbf{z}\sim p_z} [D(G(\mathbf{z}))^2]$	$\displaystyle\mathop{\mathbb{E}}_{\mathbf{z}\sim p_z} [(D(G(\mathbf{z}))-1)^2]$
WGAN [5]	$-\displaystyle\mathop{\mathbb{E}}_{\mathbf{x}\sim p_{data}} [D(\mathbf{x})] + \mathop{\mathbb{E}}_{\mathbf{z}\sim p_z} [D(G(\mathbf{z}))]$	$-\displaystyle\mathop{\mathbb{E}}_{\mathbf{z}\sim p_z} [D(G(\mathbf{z}))]$
WGAN-GP [6]	$-\displaystyle\mathop{\mathbb{E}}_{\mathbf{x}\sim p_{data}} [D(\mathbf{x})] + \mathop{\mathbb{E}}_{\mathbf{z}\sim p_z} [D(G(\mathbf{z}))] +$ $\lambda \displaystyle\mathop{\mathbb{E}}_{\hat{\mathbf{x}}\sim p_{\hat{\mathbf{x}}}} [(\|\nabla_{\hat{\mathbf{x}}} D(\hat{\mathbf{x}})\|_2 - 1)^2]$	$-\displaystyle\mathop{\mathbb{E}}_{\mathbf{z}\sim p_z} [D(G(\mathbf{z}))]$

in which work is defined as the amount of earth moved multiplied with the distance it is moved. In GANs, the discriminator could use this metric to compute the divergence between p_{data} and p_{fake}. Computing the Wasserstein distance is intractable, but through the Kantorovich–Rubinstein duality a Wasserstein GAN objective can be formulated [5] as

$$\min_{G} \max_{D \in \mathcal{D}} V(D, G) = \mathop{\mathbb{E}}_{\mathbf{x}\sim p_{data}} [D(\mathbf{x})] - \mathop{\mathbb{E}}_{\mathbf{z}\sim p_z} [D(G(\mathbf{z}))], \qquad (23.3)$$

where D is in $\mathcal{D}$, the set of 1-Lipschitz continuous functions for which the norm of the gradient should not exceed 1 [5]. While standard GANs are driven by a classifier separating real from fake samples, Wasserstein GANs are driven by a distance measure that quantifies the similarity of two distributions. Hence, discriminators in Wasserstein GANs do not return a probability but a scalar value, and are also referred to as *critics*. While the value of Eq. (23.1) does not necessarily correspond with image quality, the distance in Eq. (23.3) has been empirically shown to correlate with image quality [5].

There are several ways to obtain 1-Lipschitz continuity in the discriminator, among which weight clipping [5] and the use of a gradient penalty [6] are most commonly used. With weight clipping, the weights of the discriminator network are clipped to, e.g., $[-0.01, 0.01]$ at the end of each iteration. With gradient penalty, linearly interpolated samples are obtained between random real and synthesized samples. For each of these samples, the discriminator gradient should be less than 1. The objective function then becomes

$$\min_{G} \max_{D \in \mathcal{D}} V(D, G) = \mathop{\mathbb{E}}_{\mathbf{x}\sim p_{data}} [D(\mathbf{x})] - \mathop{\mathbb{E}}_{\mathbf{z}\sim p_z} [D(G(\mathbf{z}))] - \lambda \mathop{\mathbb{E}}_{\hat{\mathbf{x}}\sim p_{\hat{\mathbf{x}}}} [(\|\nabla_{\hat{\mathbf{x}}} D(\hat{\mathbf{x}})\|_2 - 1)^2], \quad (23.4)$$

where $p_{\hat{\mathbf{x}}}$ is the distribution of points along straight lines between randomly selected pairs of samples in p_{data} and p_{fake}. The gradient penalty is weighted by a factor λ.

Another commonly encountered phenomenon is that of *mode collapse*, in which the generator consistently synthesizes similar samples with little diversity. While such samples may be able to fool the discriminator, for obvious reasons it would be preferable if the generator provides more diverse samples. Mode collapse is addressed in Salimans et al. [7] by letting the discriminator not only look at individual samples, but also at the variation within a minibatch. Another solution is to unroll the GAN [8] by computing generator updates through multiple versions of the discriminator. Furthermore, Wasserstein GANs have been shown to generate more diverse samples, potentially reducing the problem of mode collapse [5].

23.2.2 The latent space

During training of a GAN, the generator G learns to map points in the low–dimensional latent space to points in the high-dimensional sample space. The latent space p_z consists of a distribution with dimensionality m, such as a spherical Gaussian. It has been shown empirically that points that are close to each other in p_z tend to result in samples that are also close in sample space [9]. Therefore, a walk through the latent space of a GAN may result in smooth interpolations between samples. This could also allow arithmetic in the latent space. Radford et al. [9] found that for a GAN trained to synthesize face images, subtracting the latent space point for "man without glasses" from that of "man with glasses" and adding that to "woman without glasses" could result in an image of a "woman with glasses".

Although neighboring points in the latent space may correspond to samples with similar characteristics, there is no guarantee that the individual dimensions in the latent space correspond to interpretable and meaningful features. In fact, dimensions in the latent space may be highly entangled. One way to disentangle these dimensions is to use an InfoGAN [10]. InfoGANs include a latent code $\mathbf{c}$ in addition to the noise vector $\mathbf{z}$, so that $\mathbf{x} = G(\mathbf{z}, \mathbf{c})$. The GAN is trained so that the latent code represents disentangled features, such as the angle or thickness of a handwritten digit. To prevent the generator from simply ignoring the latent codes, the mutual information $I(\mathbf{c}; G(\mathbf{z}, \mathbf{c}))$ between $\mathbf{c}$ and $G(\mathbf{z}, \mathbf{c})$ is added to the objective in Eq. (23.1). This is implemented using a separate neural network that tries to retrieve the latent code $\mathbf{x}$ from generated samples $G(\mathbf{z}, \mathbf{c})$.

It may also be useful to not only obtain a mapping from the latent space to the sample space, but also the reverse mapping from the sample space to the latent space. This will lead to m–dimensional feature descriptors that have been learned in an unsupervised manner. Such feature descriptors can characterize real data samples and may be used in subsequent analysis. One way to obtain a mapping to latent space is to consider finding the location $\mathbf{z} \in p_z$ of a sample as a separate optimization problem. Given a sample $\mathbf{x} \in p_{\text{data}}$, the point in $\mathbf{z} \in p_z$ should be retrieved that minimizes the difference between $G(\mathbf{z})$ and $\mathbf{x}$, with fixed G [11]. Alternatively, GANs can be extended with an

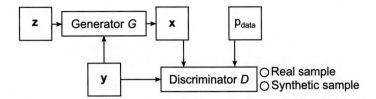

Figure 23.3 In a conditional GAN, the generator and discriminator both take an additional conditioning vector **y** as input.

additional encoder neural network that maps real and synthesized samples to a latent space representation [12].

23.2.3 Conditional GANs

GAN training results in a generator model that can synthesize samples, but generally does not allow control over the characteristics of samples that are being generated. In practice, it may be beneficial to have more control over what is represented in the generated samples. In conditional GANs (cGANs), both the generator and the discriminator can take additional side-information into account [13] (Fig. 23.3). This side-information is represented by an input vector **y** so that the objective function becomes

$$\min_{G} \max_{D} V(D, G) = \underset{\mathbf{x} \sim p_{\text{data}}}{\mathbb{E}} [\log D(\mathbf{x}|\mathbf{y})] + \underset{\mathbf{z} \sim p_z}{\mathbb{E}} [\log (1 - D(G(\mathbf{z}|\mathbf{y})|\mathbf{y}))]. \tag{23.5}$$

The generator uses the information in **y** in addition to the noise vector **z** to synthesize plausible samples. The discriminator assesses whether these samples resemble real samples in p_{data}, given the information provided in **y**. An example application is the synthesis of specific handwritten MNIST digits [13]. The conditioning vector **y** in that cases contains a one-hot encoding of the ten digit classes, i.e., a vector in which one element is set to 1 and all other elements are set to 0. However, the conditioning vector is not restricted to such encodings. Mirza et al. [13] also show how a text tag generator can be conditioned on a feature vector describing a natural image. Conversely, Zhang et al. [14] used cGANs to synthesize images from text descriptions.

23.2.4 GAN architectures

Most GAN research has focused on the synthesis of 2D natural images using neural networks. Early applications of GANs used multilayer perceptrons (MLPs) for the discriminator and generator. While this may be sufficient for the synthesis of smaller images, the number of network parameters may rapidly increase when MLPs are used for larger images. Therefore, a CNN is typically used for the generator as well as for the discriminator. To allow the generator to gradually increase the size of its representations, it is common to use fractionally strided or transposed convolutions for upsampling. Denton et al. [15] proposed a Laplacian GAN to gradually increase the size of synthesized images using a sequence of conditional GANs, in which each image is conditioned on the upsampled version of a previous lower-resolution image. This allows synthesis of 64×64 pixel RGB images, but requires training and evaluation of several GANs. Alternatively, Radford et al. [9] proposed three architectural choices to allow direct training of deep convolutional GANs (DCGANs). First, downsampling and upsampling should be performed with strided convolutions instead of pooling operations. Second, the use of fully connected layers should be prevented. Third, batch normalization should be used to normalize the inputs to activation functions. This allowed direct synthesis of 64×64 pixel RGB images.

Due to the advent of alternative loss functions such as those based on the Wasserstein distance, GAN training stability has much improved in recent years. Nevertheless, synthesis of large images is still challenging. The current state-of-the-art allows synthesis of 1024×1024 pixel RGB images, by progressively blending in additional upsampling layers (generator) and downsampling layers (discriminator) [16]. By carefully increasing the image resolution, collapse of the training process can be prevented.

23.3. Adversarial methods for image domain translation

In a conditional GAN, the generator is trained to synthesize plausible samples given a noise vector **z** and additional information provided in **y**. Depending on the information encoded in the conditioning vector **y**, the outputs of the generator could become heavily constrained: for a given input **y** the generator will always predict the same output, regardless of **z**. For example, Isola et al. [17] found that when training a conditional GAN to translate an image from one domain to another domain, the generator mostly ignored the noise vector. Nevertheless, the discriminator network can provide valuable feedback to networks performing image domain translation: adversarial feedback can replace hand-crafted loss functions to quantify to what extent an image belongs to a particular target domain.

Two scenarios for training of an image domain translation model can be distinguished. In the first situation, a reference image in domain B may be available for each image in domain A. For example, when domain A contains grayscale photos and domain B contains color photos. Hence, these problems can be approached by training *with* paired images. In the second class of problems, one wishes to translate images from domain A to a semantically related domain B, but domain B does not necessarily contain a reference image for each image in domain A. This may be the case when translating between photos of horses and photos of zebras. In this scenario, training is performed *without* paired training images.

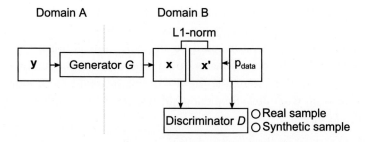

Figure 23.4 In image domain translation *with* paired training images in domains A and B, the generator G minimizes the voxelwise loss between its output **x** and a reference image **x′**, and the discriminator D provides an adversarial loss that reflects how well **x** corresponds to real images in domain B.

23.3.1 Training with paired images

Isola et al. [17] trained a generator to translate images from one domain to another domain. For each input image **y** in domain A, a reference image **x′** in domain B was available (Fig. 23.4). The generator was trained to minimize the pixelwise difference between its prediction and this reference image. In addition, an adversarial network was used to assess whether the output images looked perceptually convincing compared to other images in domain B. The objective function used was

$$
\min_{G} \max_{D} V(D, G) = \lambda_1 \left(\mathop{\mathbb{E}}_{\mathbf{x} \sim p_{\text{data}}} [\log D(\mathbf{x}|\mathbf{y})] + \mathop{\mathbb{E}}_{\mathbf{y} \sim p_y} [\log (1 - D(G(\mathbf{y})|\mathbf{y}))] \right)
$$
$$
+ \lambda_2 \mathop{\mathbb{E}}_{\mathbf{x}' \sim p_{\text{data}}, \mathbf{y} \sim p_y} [\|\mathbf{x}' - G(\mathbf{y})\|_1], \tag{23.6}
$$

where **x′** and **y** are assumed to be spatially aligned (Fig. 23.4). When $\lambda_1 = 0$ and $\lambda_2 > 0$, the system is effectively reduced to only the generator, which tries to minimize the pixelwise unstructured loss between its output $G(\mathbf{y})$ and a reference image. When $\lambda_1 > 0$ and $\lambda_2 = 0$, network G is trained to transform the input into an image that looks similar to other images in domain B. However, because this output image is not directly linked to a reference image in domain B, it does not necessarily correspond to the generator's input. The combination of $\lambda_1 > 0$ and $\lambda_2 > 0$ ties the output image $G(\mathbf{y})$ to the reference image **x** and the target domain through both the L_1-norm and the adversarial loss.

Similar ideas were proposed for image segmentation [3] and image colorization. Ledig et al. [18] proposed to use adversarial training for super-resolution and thus to translate low-resolution images into high-resolution images. The discriminator tries to distinguish the reconstructed high-resolution images from natural images in a reference database. Correspondence between the reconstructed image and the original high-resolution image is enforced using an L_2 content loss term calculated in feature space (e.g., of a VGG-network) while the adversarial loss component encourages perceptually convincing samples.

Adversarial networks performing image domain translation tend to be more stable than regular GANs, as the feature maps are heavily conditioned on an existing image. Architectures used for the generator could be any fully convolutional network architecture, such as [19–21]. The discriminator could look either at the full image, or only at subimages [17,22]. In the latter case, the discriminator could focus more on high-frequency information, while low-frequency information is captured in a different loss term such as the L_1-norm.

23.3.2 Training without paired images

The objective function in Eq. (23.6) assumes that for each input image $\mathbf{y}$ there is an aligned corresponding reference image $\mathbf{x}'$ in domain B. However, corresponding pairs of images in two different domains may often be unavailable in practice, e.g., when translating between different imaging modalities. Even if the same patient is scanned with two modalities, it may be impossible to correctly align the resulting images in order to use a voxelwise loss term. If the assumption of aligned pairs of training images were to be removed from Eq. (23.6), the objective function would be

$$\min_G \max_D V(D, G) = \mathop{\mathbb{E}}_{\mathbf{x} \sim p_{\text{data}}} [\log D(\mathbf{x})] + \mathop{\mathbb{E}}_{\mathbf{y} \sim p_y} [\log (1 - D(G(\mathbf{y})))]. \qquad (23.7)$$

This objective resembles that of a GAN (Eq. (23.1)) with deterministic inputs from input images $\mathbf{y}$. In this formulation the generator will learn to generate samples that mimic the target domain, but there is no guarantee that these samples match the actual content of the input image in the source domain. This problem can be mitigated by adding additional loss terms through either self-regularization or cyclic consistency.

Self-regularization introduces an additional loss term that minimizes the difference between the input and the output image to encourage that they maintain the same content [23] (Fig. 23.5). In that case, the objective becomes

$$\min_G \max_D V(D, G) = \mathop{\mathbb{E}}_{\mathbf{x} \sim p_{\text{data}}} [\log D(\mathbf{x})] + \mathop{\mathbb{E}}_{\mathbf{y} \sim p_y} [\log (1 - D(G(\mathbf{y})))]$$
$$+ \lambda \mathop{\mathbb{E}}_{\mathbf{y} \sim p_y} [\|\mathbf{y} - G(\mathbf{y})\|_1]. \qquad (23.8)$$

However, this is only feasible when some similarity between the input and output image can be expected. For example, Shrivastava et al. [23] use self-regularization to refine simulated images of the eye. In that case, the low-frequency information in the final image is expected to be similar to that in the input image. However, when $G(\mathbf{y})$ and $\mathbf{y}$ are in two very different domains, self-regularization may lead to undesirable results.

Cycle consistency assumes that an image $\mathbf{y}_A$ in domain A that is translated into an image $\mathbf{x}_B$ in domain B can also be mapped back to an image $\mathbf{y}'_A$ in domain A.

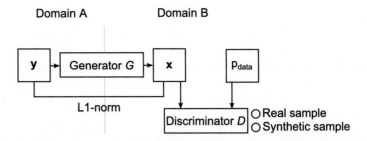

Figure 23.5 In the image domain translation *without* paired training images in domains A and B, self-supervision could be used. The generator *G* minimizes the voxelwise loss between its output **x** and the input image **y**. In addition, the discriminator *D* provides an adversarial loss that reflects how well **x** corresponds to real images in domain *B*.

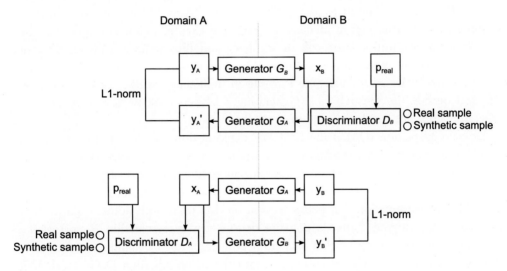

Figure 23.6 A CycleGAN consists of two generator networks and two discriminator networks. The generators translate images from domain *A* to domain *B* and vice versa. The discriminators differentiate between real and synthetic samples in each domain. A pixel-wise *L*1-loss in each domain determines whether images are consistently recovered after cyclic translation.

The reconstructed image $\mathbf{y}'_A$ should be similar to the original image $\mathbf{y}_A$. In addition, as before, images that are mapped to a target domain should be indistinguishable from other images in the target domain (Fig. 23.6). Models trained with cycle consistency therefore contain a generator G_B that transforms images from domain A to domain B, a generator G_A that transforms images from domain B to domain A, a discriminator D_B in domain B and a discriminator D_A in domain A. Two cycles are trained simultaneously, one from domain A to domain B and back, and one from domain B to domain A and back. This idea was proposed in [22,24,25] and is commonly referred to as a CycleGAN.

To train a CycleGAN, the generator networks try to minimize the discrepancy between input images as well as their reconstruction in the original domain. In addition, the generators try to maximize the loss of the discriminators, which in turn try to distinguish synthetic samples from real samples in their respective domains. Zhu et al. [22] showed how a CycleGAN can be used to transform, e.g., photographs into paintings with different styles.

23.4. Domain adaptation via adversarial training

A common underlying assumption in machine learning is that training and test data are drawn from the same distribution. A predictive model trained on data from a *source* domain S and distribution p_S may under-perform when applied to data from a *target* domain T and a distribution p_T that differs from p_S. Many factors can contribute to this problem of *domain shift* in medical imaging. For example, clinical centers may be using different acquisition protocols or scanners, and thus acquire scans of different modalities, quality, resolution, or contrast. These variations are a significant practical obstacle towards the use of machine learning in multicenter studies or its large-scale adoption outside the research labs. Generating a labeled database for every possible target domain is not a realistic solution.

Domain adaptation (DA) is the field that explores how to learn a predictor using labeled data in domain S and adapt it to generalize on domain T without any or with limited additional labels [26]. Of great interest is *unsupervised* domain adaptation (UDA), which assumes no labeled data from domain T. The basic assumption of DA is that there exists a predictive function that performs well on data from both domains [26]. UDA methods learn mappings between domains or to a new representation $\mathcal{H}$, so that the predictor C learned using labeled data from domain S can be applied on data from domain T when appropriately combined with the mappings. Ben-David et al. [26] showed that to learn how to map samples to a representation $\mathcal{H}$ that allows predictor C trained on embedded labeled samples from S to generalize on embedded samples from T, the learning algorithm has to minimize a *trade-off* between the source error and the divergence of the two distributions of the embedded samples. They pointed out that a strategy to minimize this divergence is to find a representation where samples from the two domains are indistinguishable by a domain classifier. This idea formed the basis for domain adaptation via adversarial training [27], which treats the domain classifier as an adversarial network.

The basic framework for domain adaptation with adversarial networks [27] is shown in Fig. 23.7. The primary network F (e.g., a classifier) is decomposed into the feature extractor H (e.g., all hidden layers), which maps the input to a latent-representation $\mathcal{H}$, and the label predictor C (e.g., the last linear classifier). An auxiliary network, the domain classifier D, tries to distinguish the domain of the input based on the extracted

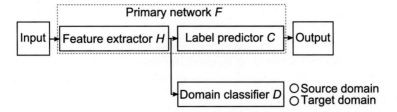

Figure 23.7 Domain adaptation with adversarial methods. The primary network *F* is split into a feature extractor *H* and a label predictor *C*. The feature extractor tries to embed samples in a space that expresses only the domain-independent information that is necessary for *C* to perform the primary task. An auxiliary domain classifier network *D* tries to classify the domain of the input based on the latent representation. The feature extractor and domain classifier are trained as adversaries.

features. To train H to extract a domain invariant representation that simultaneously enables the primary task on both domains, two cost functions are considered. The first cost, $\mathcal{L}_c$, is for learning the primary task, such as cross–entropy between predictions of classifier $F(\mathbf{x}) = C(H(\mathbf{x}))$ and the training labels. The second cost is the negative log–likelihood of the domain discriminator:

$$\mathcal{L}_d = - \underset{\mathbf{x} \sim p_S}{\mathbb{E}} \left[\log D(H(\mathbf{x})) \right] - \underset{\mathbf{x} \sim p_T}{\mathbb{E}} \left[\log \left(1 - D(H(\mathbf{x})) \right) \right]. \tag{23.9}$$

Note this is related to the objective of standard GANs (Table 23.1), where instead of real and synthetic data, it involves representations of samples from the two domains. During training, D is trained to classify the domain of input samples, hence to minimize $\mathcal{L}_d$. The primary network simultaneously learns the primary task on the source labeled data and minimizes $\mathcal{L}_c$, while learning a feature extractor H such that the domain discriminator's loss $\mathcal{L}_d$ is maximized. Such a training objective results in a mapping $H(\mathbf{x})$ that does not preserve domain-specific features, rather only the information necessary to perform the primary task. Assuming that both the domains contain the information necessary for the primary task, the network $F(\mathbf{x}) = C(H(\mathbf{x}))$ is able to make predictions for unseen input regardless its domain. Otherwise a *trade-off* between domain invariance and performance is necessary.

23.5. Applications in biomedical image analysis

Recent years have seen applications of GANs and adversarial methods to a wide range of problems in biomedical image analysis. This section discusses a number of these applications. Section 23.5.1 describes studies focused on *de novo* generation of data through sampling from a latent distribution using GANs, and the use of GANs to detect novelties or abnormalities in medical images. In Sect. 23.5.2, adversarial methods that convert images from one modality to another are described. Furthermore, adversarial methods can be used to improve the quality of biomedical images, e.g., by reducing image acquisition artifacts or improving image resolution (Sect. 23.5.3). Section 23.5.4 describes the use of adversarial methods for biomedical image segmentation. Section 23.5.5 describes adversarial domain adaptation methods for transfer learning between different kinds of images. Section 23.5.6 describes how GANs can be integrated in methods for semisupervised learning.

A common factor in many applications is that the discriminator is only used during training. The generator performs the main task, and is used during training as well as during testing. One exception to this is semisupervised learning (Sect. 23.5.6), in which the generator is discarded and the discriminator is kept.

23.5.1 Sample generation

GANs have been used for *de novo* generation of samples of medical images or anatomical structures from a latent distribution p_z. Generated samples could potentially be used to enlarge training sets for discriminative models, or synthesize data for training of human experts. This is a challenging task: whereas there may be a certain tolerance for errors in synthesized samples in some domains such as natural images, such errors can have strong negative effects in medical imaging.

An example of de novo synthesis of images is the work by Chuquicusma et al. [28], who used a DCGAN to synthesize 56×56 pixel 2D CT image patches showing lung nodules. The appearance of synthesized lung nodules was assessed in an observer study, which showed that in many cases the synthesized patches were able to fool the radiologist. Nevertheless, the small size of these images may be a limiting factor for some applications. To allow synthesis of larger images, Beers et al. [29] used the progressive GAN method by Karras et al. [16] to generate 256×256 pixel slices of multimodal MRI images and 512×512 pixel retinal fundus images. The method jointly synthesized the medical image and a corresponding segmentation mask for brain tumors in MRI, and for retinal vessels in fundus images. The results showed that joint synthesis of the image and the segmentation mask led to higher quality synthesized images. Korkinof et al. [30] showed that progressive GANs without the use of any prior information such as manual segmentations are capable of generating realistic mammograms of high resolution, up to 1280×1024 pixels.

Synthesis of 3D anatomical structures using GANs is challenging, as de novo generation of voxelized 3D volumes can lead to holes and fragments in synthesized structures. This issue may be addressed by using specific data representations. Wolterink et al. [31] used a Wasserstein GAN with gradient penalty to obtain 1D representations of contiguous 3D coronary artery geometries. Using a training set of semiautomatically extracted coronary centerlines from coronary CT angiography (CCTA) scans, a GAN was trained to synthesize vessels. An analysis of the latent space showed that latent feature representations can distinguish between left and right coronary arteries and short and long arteries.

The property that GANs learn to only generate samples that resemble those coming from the distribution of data shown during training can be used to identify cases deviating from it, i.e., identify abnormalities or novelties. This is a highly relevant topic in medical image analysis, where a common goal is the detection of deviations from the normal. Schlegl et al. [32] used GANs for the analysis of retinal OCT images. A GAN was trained to generate images of healthy patients based on noise vectors sampled from a uniform distribution. To identify anomalies in new and unseen images, an iterative process was used to find the noise vector in the latent space corresponding to the image with the lowest reconstruction error with respect to the input sample. Each image sample was assigned an anomaly score, which was based on the reconstruction error, as well as on the output of the discriminator for the sample. Hence, both the generator and discriminator were used to identify anomalies.

23.5.2 Image synthesis

In clinical practice, information from multiple medical imaging modalities is often combined. However, depending on the application, the information contained in a particular image modality may already be present in other modalities. Accurate conversion of images from one imaging domain to another imaging domain could help lower the number of acquisitions required, thereby reducing patient discomfort and costs.

One example of a clinical problem in which accurate conversion from one modality to another may be desirable is radiotherapy treatment planning. In conventional treatment planning, tumors and organs-at-risk are delineated in MR, and electron-density values for radiation dose calculation are measured using CT. These two are then combined in radiation treatment planning. Research on MR-only radiotherapy treatment planning attempts to synthesize a CT image based on the MR scan. This approach avoids the requirement for a CT image during treatment planning, thereby reducing imaging burden for the patient. Several methods have used regression CNNs to learn a direct mapping between MR images and CT images [33,34] by minimizing a voxelwise loss between synthesized and corresponding paired target images. However, a potential side-effect of voxelwise loss minimization is blurring: The MR and CT image are two separate acquisitions and there is no perfect spatial overlap between the images, even after image registration. Consequently, similar MR inputs may correspond to different CT outputs in the training set, and during testing the CNN will predict a blurred image.

To improve how well synthesized CT images resemble real CT images, Nie et al. [36] combined the voxelwise loss of a regression CNN with adversarial feedback from a discriminator, similarly to the method described in Sect. 23.3.1. However, this method – and similar approaches like [37] – still require aligned images in the MR and the CT domains. As mentioned above, accurate alignment of these two modalities is challeng-

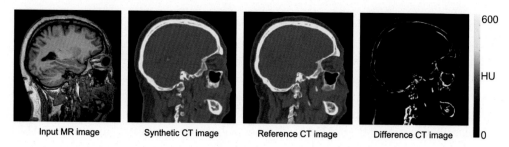

Input MR image   Synthetic CT image   Reference CT image   Difference CT image

Figure 23.8 Result from Wolterink et al. [35], showing how a GAN with cycle consistency can be used to convert T1-weighted MR images into CT images. This example shows the input MR image, the synthetic CT image, the reference CT image and the difference between the synthetic and reference CT image.

ing. Furthermore, aligned training images may not always be available. To overcome this, Wolterink et al. [35] used a CycleGAN as described in Sect. 23.3.2 to allow MR to CT synthesis without paired MR and CT training images. A forward CycleGAN was trained to transform MR into CT and back to MR, and a backward CycleGAN was trained to transform CT images into MR and back to CT. Fig. 23.8 shows an example of results obtained in [35].

Similarly, Chartsias et al. [38] trained a CycleGAN to synthesize a cardiac MR image and corresponding segmentation from a real cardiac CT scan and manual segmentation made on it. Such conversion allowed transferring information from the CT to the MR domain. The synthetic MR images and segmentations were used along with real MR images and manual segmentations, to enlarge the amount of available training data for learning better segmentation model of the myocardium in MR. Likewise, Huo et al. [39] showed that a CycleGAN that synthesizes CT from MR can be potentially useful for training a network to segment splenomegaly in CT using only manual annotations performed on MR. GANs have also been used to synthesize, e.g., structural MR images based on amyloid PET images [40] for analysis in patients with Alzheimer's disease, and brain MR angiography images based on T1-weighted and T2-weighted MR images [41]. Moreover, it has been shown that conditional GANs can be used to synthesize 2D X-ray images of the lumbar spine based on a simple sketch of the vertebrae [42].

23.5.3 Image quality enhancement

Medical image acquisition often includes a trade-off between image quality and factors such as time, costs and patient discomfort. For example, lower ionizing radiation dose levels in CT could prevent radiation-induced cancer, but will typically lead to increased image noise levels, and undersampled MR image reconstruction could reduce scan time but may lead to image artifacts. Adversarial methods have been used to avert such effects in the acquisition domain or the image domain.

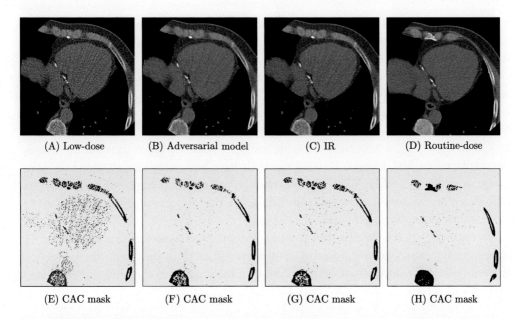

Figure 23.9 Result from Wolterink et al. [43]. Example CT slice of (A) 20% low-dose FBP reconstruction and (E) corresponding coronary artery calcification (CAC) scoring mask, (B) 20% dose GAN-based noise reduction and (F) corresponding CAC scoring mask, (C) 20% dose iterative reconstruction (IR) and (G) corresponding CAC scoring mask, and (D) routine-dose FBP reconstruction and (H) corresponding CAC scoring mask. All images have window level/width 90/750 HU. CAC scoring masks show all voxels $\geq$ 130 HU in black, and voxels selected by CAC scoring with connected component labeling in red.

To allow CT scanning at low radiation dose, regression CNNs have been proposed to convert low-dose CT images to routine-dose CT images [44]. One problem is that even routine-dose CTs contain low amounts of image noise, and training a regression model can lead to blurred predictions. Wolterink et al. [43] proposed a 3D model to translate low-dose CT images into routine-dose CT images. The method was evaluated on phantom CT data as well as in-vivo CT images. In phantom CT images, where the low-dose CT and routine-dose CT image were perfectly aligned, the adversarial loss was combined with an L_1-loss term between the generated image and a reference routine-dose CT image. In real cardiac CT studies, low-dose and routine-dose images were not aligned and self-regularization was used (Eq. (23.8)). Fig. 23.9 shows a low-dose CT image and the same image denoised using the proposed method or by commercially available iterative reconstruction (IR) software. Both denoising methods compare well with the reference routine-dose CT. However, IR requires CT projection data to be available, while the adversarial method operates on already reconstructed CT images.

Yang et al. [45] proposed an alternative adversarial training approach for artifact reduction in low-dose CT. Instead of using the original GAN objective (Eq. (23.1)) as in [43], Yang et al. proposed to use a Wasserstein distance objective (Eq. (23.3)) to train the GAN. In addition, a perceptual loss term based on a pre-trained CNN was added to the loss term. Similarly, Wang et al. [46] proposed to use adversarial methods to synthesize full-dose PET images from low-dose PET images.

In addition to CT artifact reduction, adversarial methods have been found to be useful to speed up MR image acquisition. In compressed sensing MR imaging, the k-space is undersampled. The undersampled acquisition can be reconstructed to an MR image, but this image will likely contain aliasing artifacts. In the method proposed by Quan et al. [47], a generator network tries to transform the reconstructed images into artifact-free MR images. Related methods have been proposed to speed up MR image acquisition with GANs [48,49], with variations using high-resolution images with different contrasts as additional input alongside the low-resolution image to provide more information to the generator.

Because the source domain and the target domain are typically strongly related in image quality enhancement problems, it is often sufficient to only train the generator to predict the difference image between the original image and the artifact-free image. This was used by, e.g., Wolterink et al. [43] and Quan et al. [47].

23.5.4 Image segmentation

Accurate segmentation of anatomical structures is an important topic in medical image analysis and in recent years CNNs have led to many advances in medical image segmentation. One problem when using CNNs is that they are typically trained using a voxelwise unstructured loss, such as the cross-entropy loss. This may lead to holes and fragments in automatically obtained segmentations. To overcome this, postprocessing schemes have been used, such as morphological operations and conditional random fields [50]. Alternatively, structurally correct segmentations can be imposed by an adversarial network that assesses whether a segmentation, or a combination of segmentation and input image, is plausible. This approach was successfully employed in medical image segmentation problems.

Moeskops et al. [51] used an adversarial approach to segment brain tissues in $T1$-weighted MR brain images. A voxelwise categorical cross-entropy loss was combined with adversarial feedback from a discriminator network that assessed combinations of images and segmentations. Experiments showed that adversarial training helped prevent segmentation errors and substantially improved Dice similarity indices between automatically obtained and reference segmentations. Moreover, for tumor segmentation in prostate MR Kohl et al. [52] completely omitted the voxelwise loss term from the loss function. Hence, in this case optimization was fully driven by the adversarial loss. This resulted in higher Dice similarity indices than training with only a voxelwise loss, or training with a combination of voxelwise and adversarial losses.

One problem of adversarial segmentation methods is that reference segmentations contain discrete label masks, while the generator produces a continuous probability value for each class in each voxel. An adversarial network working directly on reference segmentations and generator outputs could thus learn to distinguish these two by learning to discriminate between discrete and continuous values. One way to overcome this is to let the discriminator look at the product of the input image and the segmentation [3]. Xue et al. [53] proposed to let an adversarial encoder network look at the product of the input image and the predicted segmentation, as well as at the product of the input image and the reference segmentation. Features were extracted at multiple scales for both inputs and the L_1-loss between the two sets of features served as a scalar adversarial loss for the segmentation CNN, showing to be beneficial for brain tumor segmentation in MR.

Adversarial training could also be used for weakly supervised segmentation of anomalies, in which a label is known for the images but not for individual voxels. Baumgartner et al. [54] employed adversarial training with a Wasserstein objective to transform MR images of patients with Alzheimer's disease (AD) into images that show what the patient's brain might look like without AD. In this case, the real data distribution contained patients without known AD. The generator was trained to generate a visual attribution map which, when added to the input image, showed a brain without AD. To make sure that the synthesized image matches the anatomical structure in the original image, self-regularization was used (Sect. 23.3.2). Results showed that obtained attribution maps are more specific than commonly used methods such as class activation mapping.

23.5.5 Domain adaptation

The theory and framework for domain adaptation via adversarial training presented in Sect. 23.4 has formed the basis for several works in biomedical image analysis. Kamnitsas et al. [55] proposed employing domain adversarial networks for alleviating problematic segmentation due to domain shift between MR acquisition protocols. Extending the basic framework, they proposed multiconnected adversarial nets, which enable the domain discriminator to process information from several layers of the feature extractor (Fig. 23.10). Empirical analysis showed that this leads to a higher quality domain classifier, hence flow of better gradients to the primary network and improved adaptation. By applying the technique to adapt between two databases of multimodal MR brain scans with traumatic brain lesions, where one of the modalities differed (Fig. 23.11), they showed that domain adversarial training is applicable to 3D CNNs for volumetric image processing. This was previously questioned in the literature [56] due to memory constraints.

Recently adversarial networks were employed for adaptation of more segmentation systems. Adaptation with this technique in the case of larger domain shift was recently attempted by Dou et al. [57]. Starting with a segmentation network of the cardiac structures, trained only with labeled MR data, promising results were shown by adapting

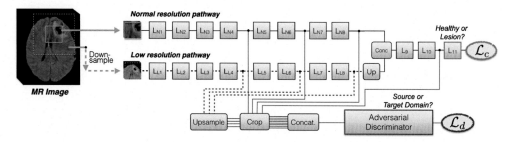

Figure 23.10 Multiconnected adversarial nets for domain adaptation. The domain discriminator processes activations from several depths and scales, which leads to better domain classifier and improved flow of adversarial gradients for better adaptation. Figure adapted from [55].

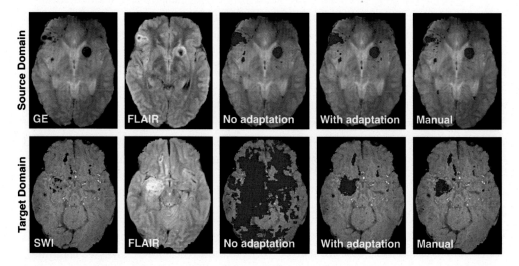

Figure 23.11 Result from Kamnitsas et al. [55]. A CNN for segmentation of brain lesions is trained on a database of multimodal MR scans, which include gradient echo (GE) sequence. The CNN fails when it is applied on another study, where susceptibility weighted imaging was acquired instead of GE. Domain adaptation alleviates the issue.

it to segment CT data, without any labels in CT. In [58] the authors investigated the potential of this method for alleviating domain shift in 3D ultrasound between devices of different manufacturers and settings. Adversarial UDA offered significant improvements for the segmentation of the left atrium, which were also complementary to benefits obtained from shape priors [59].

Besides segmentation tasks, Lafarge et al. [60] investigated the approach in the context of mitosis detection in breast cancer histopathology images. As different pathology labs may have slightly different methods for image staining, a model trained on data from one lab may underperform on data from another. The authors showed that adversarial domain adaptation can offer significant benefits and complement well the more traditional method of color augmentation.

The above works [60,57,58] adopted domain discriminators that process information from different depths and scales of the main network. This type of domain discriminators was originally proposed by [55] and is appropriate for approaches that learn a domain-invariant *latent space*.

In contrast to the aforementioned approaches, recent works learn mappings between the two domains in *image space*. In Bousmalis et al. [61], simulated images (domain *S*) for which labels are available were mapped to the target domain of real natural images via conditional GANs. A classifier was then trained on the synthetic, labeled, real-looking images, and was afterwards applied on real images. The reverse approach has been shown promising on medical data [62]. A self-regularized conditional GAN mapped real endoscopy images to the domain of simulated images, which were then processed by a predictor trained on simulated data. The mapping of domains in image space has also been attempted via CycleGANs [39,63]. In these works, mapping between the domains was also regularized by encouraging semantics to be preserved, so that a segmentor trained with source labels can segment the synthesized images. The approach was found promising in mapping between abdominal MR and CT [39] and between X-ray scans from different clinical centers [63].

Learning to map samples between domains in image space offers interpretability in comparison to mapping them in latent space. However, the former assumes no information is exclusive to one domain, otherwise it is an ill-posed problem. In many applications this may not hold. Adaptation in a latent space that only encodes information specific for the primary task (e.g., segmentation) avoids this issue. A more detailed discussion follows in Sect. 23.6.

23.5.6 Semisupervised learning

Supervised learning methods assume that labels are available for all training samples. In semisupervised learning (SSL), besides the labeled data, it is assumed that there are also unlabeled data available at training time. The goal of SSL methods is to extract information from the unlabeled data that could facilitate learning a discriminative model with higher performance.

Salimans et al. [7] described a method to use GANs for SSL (Fig. 23.12). The discriminator network receives three kinds of samples: samples that have been synthesized by the generator G, labeled samples from the data distribution p_{data} that belong to one of a number of classes, and unlabeled samples from the same data distribution. The cost function combines a standard cross-entropy term for the labeled samples with a binary cross-entropy term for the unlabeled and synthetic samples. In other words, the discriminator uses the synthetic and unlabeled samples to learn better feature representations. After training, the discriminator is kept, while the generator is discarded. This method

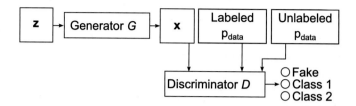

Figure 23.12 Semisupervised learning with a GAN, as proposed in [7]. The discriminator D receives samples synthesized by G, labeled samples from p_{data} that belong to any of a finite number of classes, and samples from the same distribution that belong to a class, but for which the label is not known.

has been applied in Madani et al. [64] for the classification of normal chest X-ray scans versus scans that show cardiac disease. Although the study was performed on limited test data with comparably small networks on downsampled 32×32 scans, it presented preliminary indications that the technique can offer beneficial regularization.

Another approach for SSL with GANs was investigated in Zhang et al. [65]. The method was inspired by the supervised segmentation method of Luc et al. [3] and is also related to Isola et al. [17]. In the latter works, a segmentor is interpreted as the generator of a conditional GAN, producing segmentation maps given an input image, while the discriminator tries to differentiate between predicted and manual segmentations. In Zhang et al. [65] this framework was adapted for SSL. The segmentor is applied on both labeled and unlabeled data. The discriminator of the GAN then tries to distinguish whether a prediction is made on data from the labeled or unlabeled database. Adversarial training regularizes the segmentor so that predictions on unlabeled data have similar quality as those on labeled data. This regularization was found beneficial when applied to segmentation of glands in histology images and fungus in electron microscopy [65].

23.6. Discussion and conclusion

Adversarial training is a powerful technique that has helped to further advance deep learning in biomedical image analysis for a large number of tasks. When used for data synthesis, GANs allow the generation of perceptually convincing samples of images or anatomical geometries. The majority of applications of adversarial methods in biomedical image analysis have focused on image synthesis, quality enhancement, or segmentation. This has many interesting applications, as shown in the previous section. Despite these benefits, applications of adversarial methods in biomedical image analysis should be critically considered.

Like all automatic image analysis in medical applications, errors caused by such methods could have grave clinical consequences. For one, a potential hazard is that generators start "hallucinating" content in order to convince the discriminator that their data belongs to the target distribution. This was illustrated in an experiment by Cohen et al.

[66], who used a set of FLAIR MR brain images *with* tumors and a set of T1-weighted MR brain images *without* tumors to train a CycleGAN. Application of the trained model to a new and unseen FLAIR MR brain image with a tumor led to a perceptually convincing T1-weighted image that nevertheless did not show the tumor. Conversely, a CycleGAN could be trained to synthesize tumors in images of patients that actually did not have tumors. Such side-effects could have dangerous implications, and hence applications should be carefully selected. A second problem with CycleGANs arises in the fact that the intermediate representation obtained after application of the first generator network may contain high-frequency information that the second generator network uses to translate the image back to the original domain [67]. It is important to consider that differences exist between real images and synthesized images in the target domain which may not be directly visible. This hidden high-frequency information may affect follow-up analysis with automated methods. For example, a segmentation method that has been trained on real images in the target domain, may have problems dealing with information that the CycleGAN encodes in synthesized images in the target domain.

An important issue for consideration arises when comparing the two approaches presented in Sect. 23.5.5 for adapting a network to perform a task in two domains. Mapping samples between domains in *image space* instead of *latent space* offers the advantage of interpretability. For example, visual inspection of the synthesized images may reveal failure of the domain transfer and inform that predictions are not trustworthy. On the other hand, learning to map samples between domains in image-space requires translating all information present in the images, a broader problem than preserving and translating only the information relevant for the primary task. For instance, reconstruction by CycleGANs demands all patterns in the images to be preserved during the transfer from one domain to the other and back. This not only requires more complex models [63,39], but it may also be an ill-posed problem in some applications. This is the case when some information is exclusively present in images from one domain. For instance, certain structures may only be visible in MR but not in CT, and vice versa. Enforcing a translation could make the mapping function, such as the generator of a CycleGAN, to "hallucinate" patterns in order to make the synthetic images look realistic, a behavior particularly perilous in medical imaging. These issues are mitigated by matching the two distributions in a task-specific *latent space*. This is because the latent space encodes only the information that is relevant for the primary task, which is present in both domains provided that the domains are appropriate for it.

One problem for GANs and adversarial methods is that it is challenging to find an appropriate measure for the quality of generated samples. Many works using adversarial techniques aim to generate samples that look "realistic", but it is not trivial how this should be measured. In natural image analysis, the quality of samples generated by GANs is often assessed using the Inception Score [7] or the Fréchet Inception Distance [68]. Both depend on an *inception* image classification CNN trained on the ImageNet dataset of natural images [69]. The Inception Score is high if the CNN can clearly assign individual generated samples to a class and generated samples are classified into many different classes. The Fréchet Inception Distance compares feature vectors of real and generated samples, extracted from the inception CNN. The distance between the distribution of both kinds of feature vectors should be low. However, these metrics are typically not used to evaluate generated samples in biomedical image analysis. Further, it has been shown that low distortion and high perceptual quality are competing goals in image restoration algorithms [70].

Future applications of adversarial methods are likely to be found in the same subfields as those described in Sect. 23.5. First, de novo generation of new samples with GANs could help enlarge datasets for training of discriminative models. However, this may not directly lead to improved performance of discriminative models trained using this data. It is possible that there is no additional information in the synthesized samples beyond that which is already present in the training dataset. Furthermore, despite recent advances in the training of GANs (Sect. 23.2.1), successfully training a GAN to generate perceptually convincing samples can be challenging and further advances are needed in this respect. Second, we expect that there will be many applications for conversion of images from one modality to another, for removal of artifacts, or for image segmentation. This may lead to a decrease in the number of medical images that are being acquired, which could benefit patients directly. Additionally, acquisition of images with lower radiation dose or sparse sampling of k-space could directly affect patients. Finally, future applications of adversarial methods may focus on the identification of abnormalities. Given that a large numbers of images are available for healthy patients, models could be trained to learn the distribution of healthy patients and to identify patients with disease as deviating from this distribution.

We conclude that – when used with caution – adversarial techniques have many potential applications in medical imaging. Adding adversarial feedback to a model performing tasks such as segmentation or image synthesis, for which it is hard to hand-craft a loss function, will in many cases yield images that more closely match real images in the target domain and are more likely to be valuable in clinical practice.

References

[1] G. Litjens, T. Kooi, B.E. Bejnordi, A.A.A. Setio, F. Ciompi, M. Ghafoorian, J.A. van der Laak, B. Van Ginneken, C.I. Sánchez, A survey on deep learning in medical image analysis, Medical Image Analysis 42 (2017) 60–88.

[2] I. Goodfellow, J. Pouget-Abadie, M. Mirza, B. Xu, D. Warde-Farley, S. Ozair, A. Courville, Y. Bengio, Generative adversarial nets, in: Advances in Neural Information Processing Systems, 2014, pp. 2672–2680.

[3] P. Luc, C. Couprie, S. Chintala, J. Verbeek, Semantic segmentation using adversarial networks, in: NIPS Workshop on Adversarial Training, 2016.

[4] X. Mao, Q. Li, H. Xie, R.Y. Lau, Z. Wang, S.P. Smolley, Least squares generative adversarial networks, in: IEEE International Conference on Computer Vision (ICCV), 2017, pp. 2813–2821.

[5] M. Arjovsky, S. Chintala, L. Bottou, Wasserstein generative adversarial networks, in: Proceedings of the 34th International Conference on Machine Learning, vol. 70, 2017, pp. 214–223.

[6] I. Gulrajani, F. Ahmed, M. Arjovsky, V. Dumoulin, A.C. Courville, Improved training of Wasserstein GANs, in: Advances in Neural Information Processing Systems, 2017, pp. 5769–5779.

[7] T. Salimans, I. Goodfellow, W. Zaremba, V. Cheung, A. Radford, X. Chen, Improved techniques for training GANs, in: Advances in Neural Information Processing Systems, 2016, pp. 2234–2242.

[8] L. Metz, B. Poole, D. Pfau, J. Sohl-Dickstein, Unrolled generative adversarial networks, in: International Conference on Learning Representations, 2016.

[9] A. Radford, L. Metz, S. Chintala, Unsupervised representation learning with deep convolutional generative adversarial networks, in: International Conference on Learning Representations, 2016.

[10] X. Chen, Y. Duan, R. Houthooft, J. Schulman, I. Sutskever, P. Abbeel, InfoGAN: interpretable representation learning by information maximizing generative adversarial nets, in: Advances in Neural Information Processing Systems, 2016, pp. 2172–2180.

[11] Z.C. Lipton, S. Tripathi, Precise recovery of latent vectors from generative adversarial networks, in: International Conference on Learning Representations, 2017.

[12] J. Donahue, P. Krähenbühl, T. Darrell, Adversarial feature learning, in: International Conference on Learning Representations, 2016.

[13] M. Mirza, S. Osindero, Conditional generative adversarial nets, arXiv preprint arXiv:1411.1784, 2014.

[14] H. Zhang, T. Xu, H. Li, S. Zhang, X. Huang, X. Wang, D. Metaxas, StackGAN: text to photo-realistic image synthesis with stacked generative adversarial networks, in: IEEE International Conference on Computer Vision (ICCV), 2017, pp. 5907–5915.

[15] E.L. Denton, S. Chintala, A. Szlam, R. Fergus, Deep generative image models using a Laplacian pyramid of adversarial networks, in: Advances in Neural Information Processing Systems, 2015, pp. 1486–1494.

[16] T. Karras, T. Aila, S. Laine, J. Lehtinen, Progressive growing of GANs for improved quality, stability, and variation, in: International Conference on Learning Representations, 2018.

[17] P. Isola, J.-Y. Zhu, T. Zhou, A.A. Efros, Image-to-image translation with conditional adversarial networks, in: The IEEE Conference on Computer Vision and Pattern Recognition (CVPR), 2017, pp. 5967–5976.

[18] C. Ledig, L. Theis, F. Huszár, J. Caballero, A. Cunningham, A. Acosta, A. Aitken, A. Tejani, J. Totz, Z. Wang, et al., Photo-realistic single image super-resolution using a generative adversarial network, in: The IEEE Conference on Computer Vision and Pattern Recognition (CVPR), 2016, pp. 4681–4690.

[19] J. Long, E. Shelhamer, T. Darrell, Fully convolutional networks for semantic segmentation, in: The IEEE Conference on Computer Vision and Pattern Recognition (CVPR), 2015, pp. 3431–3440.

[20] O. Ronneberger, P. Fischer, T. Brox, U-Net: convolutional networks for biomedical image segmentation, in: International Conference on Medical Image Computing and Computer-Assisted Intervention, 2015, pp. 234–241.

[21] F. Yu, V. Koltun, Multi-scale context aggregation by dilated convolutions, in: International Conference on Learning Representations, 2016.

[22] J.-Y. Zhu, T. Park, P. Isola, A.A. Efros, Unpaired image-to-image translation using cycle-consistent adversarial networks, in: IEEE International Conference on Computer Vision (ICCV), 2017, pp. 2223–2232.

[23] A. Shrivastava, T. Pfister, O. Tuzel, J. Susskind, W. Wang, R. Webb, Learning from simulated and unsupervised images through adversarial training, in: The IEEE Conference on Computer Vision and Pattern Recognition (CVPR), vol. 2, 2017, pp. 2107–2116.

[24] Z. Yi, H.R. Zhang, P. Tan, M. Gong, DualGAN: unsupervised dual learning for image-to-image translation, in: IEEE International Conference on Computer Vision (ICCV), 2017, pp. 2868–2876.

[25] T. Kim, M. Cha, H. Kim, J.K. Lee, J. Kim, Learning to discover cross-domain relations with generative adversarial networks, in: International Conference on Machine Learning, 2017, pp. 1857–1865.

[26] S. Ben-David, J. Blitzer, K. Crammer, A. Kulesza, F. Pereira, J.W. Vaughan, A theory of learning from different domains, Machine Learning 79 (2010) 151–175.

[27] Y. Ganin, E. Ustinova, H. Ajakan, P. Germain, H. Larochelle, F. Laviolette, M. Marchand, V. Lempitsky, Domain-adversarial training of neural networks, Journal of Machine Learning Research 17 (59) (2016) 1–35.

[28] M.J. Chuquicusma, S. Hussein, J. Burt, U. Bagci, How to fool radiologists with generative adversarial networks? A visual Turing test for lung cancer diagnosis, in: IEEE International Symposium on Biomedical Imaging (ISBI), 2018, pp. 240–244.

[29] A. Beers, J. Brown, K. Chang, J.P. Campbell, S. Ostmo, M.F. Chiang, J. Kalpathy-Cramer, High-resolution medical image synthesis using progressively grown generative adversarial networks, arXiv preprint arXiv:1805.03144, 2018.

[30] D. Korkinof, T. Rijken, M. O'Neill, J. Yearsley, H. Harvey, B. Glocker, High-resolution mammogram synthesis using progressive generative adversarial networks, arXiv preprint arXiv:1807.03401, 2018.

[31] J.M. Wolterink, T. Leiner, I. Isgum, Blood vessel geometry synthesis using generative adversarial networks, arXiv preprint arXiv:1804.04381, 2018.

[32] T. Schlegl, P. Seeböck, S.M. Waldstein, U. Schmidt-Erfurth, G. Langs, Unsupervised anomaly detection with generative adversarial networks to guide marker discovery, in: International Conference on Information Processing in Medical Imaging, Springer, 2017, pp. 146–157.

[33] X. Han, MR-based synthetic CT generation using a deep convolutional neural network method, Medical Physics 44 (4) (2017) 1408–1419.

[34] A.M. Dinkla, J.M. Wolterink, M. Maspero, M.H. Savenije, J.J. Verhoeff, E. Seravalli, I. Isgum, P.R. Seevinck, C.A. van den Berg, MR-only brain radiotherapy: dosimetric evaluation of synthetic CTs generated by a dilated convolutional neural network, International Journal of Radiation Oncology, Biology, Physics 102 (4) (2018) 801–812.

[35] J.M. Wolterink, A.M. Dinkla, M.H.F. Savenije, P.R. Seevinck, C.A.T. van den Berg, I. Išgum, Deep MR to CT synthesis using unpaired data, in: Simulation and Synthesis in Medical Imaging, 2017, pp. 14–23.

[36] D. Nie, R. Trullo, J. Lian, C. Petitjean, S. Ruan, Q. Wang, D. Shen, Medical image synthesis with context-aware generative adversarial networks, in: International Conference on Medical Image Computing and Computer-Assisted Intervention, 2017, pp. 417–425.

[37] M. Maspero, M.H. Savenije, A.M. Dinkla, P.R. Seevinck, M.P. Intven, I.M. Jurgenliemk-Schulz, L.G. Kerkmeijer, C.A. van den Berg, Dose evaluation of fast synthetic-CT generation using a generative adversarial network for general pelvis MR-only radiotherapy, Physics in Medicine & Biology 63 (18) (2018) 185001.

[38] A. Chartsias, T. Joyce, R. Dharmakumar, S.A. Tsaftaris, Adversarial image synthesis for unpaired multi-modal cardiac data, in: Simulation and Synthesis in Medical Imaging, 2017, pp. 3–13.

[39] Y. Huo, Z. Xu, S. Bao, A. Assad, R.G. Abramson, B.A. Landman, Adversarial synthesis learning enables segmentation without target modality ground truth, in: IEEE International Symposium on Biomedical Imaging (ISBI), IEEE, 2018, pp. 1217–1220.

[40] H. Choi, D.S. Lee, Generation of structural MR images from amyloid pet: application to MR-less quantification, Journal of Nuclear Medicine 59 (7) (2018) 1111–1117.

[41] S. Olut, Y.H. Sahin, U. Demir, G. Unal, Generative adversarial training for MRA image synthesis using multi-contrast MRI, in: International Workshop on PRedictive Intelligence in MEdicine, Springer, 2018, pp. 147–154.

[42] F. Galbusera, F. Niemeyer, M. Seyfried, T. Bassani, G. Casaroli, A. Kienle, H.-J. Wilke, Exploring the potential of generative adversarial networks for synthesizing radiological images of the spine to be used in *in silico* trials, Frontiers in Bioengineering and Biotechnology 6 (2018) 53.

[43] J.M. Wolterink, T. Leiner, M.A. Viergever, I. Išgum, Generative adversarial networks for noise reduction in low-dose CT, IEEE Transactions on Medical Imaging 36 (12) (2017) 2536–2545.

[44] E. Kang, J. Min, J.C. Ye, A deep convolutional neural network using directional wavelets for low-dose X-ray CT reconstruction, Medical Physics 44 (10) (2017).

[45] Q. Yang, P. Yan, Y. Zhang, H. Yu, Y. Shi, X. Mou, M.K. Kalra, Y. Zhang, L. Sun, G. Wang, Low dose CT image denoising using a generative adversarial network with Wasserstein distance and perceptual loss, IEEE Transactions on Medical Imaging 37 (2018) 1348–1357.

[46] Y. Wang, B. Yu, L. Wang, C. Zu, D.S. Lalush, W. Lin, X. Wu, J. Zhou, D. Shen, L. Zhou, 3D conditional generative adversarial networks for high-quality PET image estimation at low dose, NeuroImage 174 (2018) 550–562.

[47] T.M. Quan, T. Nguyen-Duc, W.-K. Jeong, Compressed sensing MRI reconstruction using a generative adversarial network with a cyclic loss, IEEE Transactions on Medical Imaging 37 (2018) 1488–1497.

[48] M. Mardani, E. Gong, J.Y. Cheng, S. Vasanawala, G. Zaharchuk, M. Alley, N. Thakur, S. Han, W. Dally, J.M. Pauly, et al., Deep generative adversarial networks for compressed sensing automates MRI, in: Medical Imaging Meets NIPS Workshop, 2017.

[49] K.H. Kim, W.-J. Do, S.-H. Park, Improving resolution of MR images with an adversarial network incorporating images with different contrast, Medical Physics 45 (2018) 3120–3131.

[50] K. Kamnitsas, C. Ledig, V.F. Newcombe, J.P. Simpson, A.D. Kane, D.K. Menon, D. Rueckert, B. Glocker, Efficient multi-scale 3D CNN with fully connected CRF for accurate brain lesion segmentation, Medical Image Analysis 36 (2017) 61–78.

[51] P. Moeskops, M. Veta, M.W. Lafarge, K.A.J. Eppenhof, J.P.W. Pluim, Adversarial training and dilated convolutions for brain MRI segmentation, in: Deep Learning in Medical Image Analysis and Multimodal Learning for Clinical Decision Support, 2017, pp. 56–64.

[52] S. Kohl, D. Bonekamp, H.-P. Schlemmer, K. Yaqubi, M. Hohenfellner, B. Hadaschik, J.-P. Radtke, K. Maier-Hein, Adversarial networks for the detection of aggressive prostate cancer, arXiv preprint arXiv:1702.08014, 2017.

[53] Y. Xue, T. Xu, H. Zhang, L.R. Long, X. Huang, SegAN: adversarial network with multi-scale L_1 loss for medical image segmentation, Neuroinformatics 16 (3–4) (2018) 383–392.

[54] C.F. Baumgartner, L.M. Koch, K.C. Tezcan, J.X. Ang, E. Konukoglu, Visual feature attribution using Wasserstein GANs, in: The IEEE Conference on Computer Vision and Pattern Recognition (CVPR), 2018, pp. 8309–8319.

[55] K. Kamnitsas, C. Baumgartner, C. Ledig, V. Newcombe, J. Simpson, A. Kane, D. Menon, A. Nori, A. Criminisi, D. Rueckert, et al., Unsupervised domain adaptation in brain lesion segmentation with adversarial networks, in: International Conference on Information Processing in Medical Imaging, Springer, 2017, pp. 597–609.

[56] R. Bermúdez-Chacón, C. Becker, M. Salzmann, P. Fua, Scalable unsupervised domain adaptation for electron microscopy, in: International Conference on Medical Image Computing and Computer-Assisted Intervention, 2016, pp. 326–334.

[57] Q. Dou, C. Ouyang, C. Chen, H. Chen, P.-A. Heng, Unsupervised cross-modality domain adaptation of convnets for biomedical image segmentations with adversarial loss, in: Proceedings of the 27th International Joint Conference on Artificial Intelligence, IJCAI'18, AAAI Press, 2018, pp. 691–697.

[58] M.A. Degel, N. Navab, S. Albarqouni, Domain and geometry agnostic CNNs for left atrium segmentation in 3D ultrasound, in: International Conference on Medical Image Computing and Computer-Assisted Intervention, 2018.

[59] O. Oktay, E. Ferrante, K. Kamnitsas, M. Heinrich, W. Bai, J. Caballero, S.A. Cook, A. de Marvao, T. Dawes, D.P. O'Regan, et al., Anatomically constrained neural networks (ACNNs): application to cardiac image enhancement and segmentation, IEEE Transactions on Medical Imaging 37 (2) (2018) 384–395.

[60] M.W. Lafarge, J.P. Pluim, K.A. Eppenhof, P. Moeskops, M. Veta, Domain-adversarial neural networks to address the appearance variability of histopathology images, in: Deep Learning in Medical Image Analysis and Multimodal Learning for Clinical Decision Support, Springer, 2017, pp. 83–91.

[61] K. Bousmalis, N. Silberman, D. Dohan, D. Erhan, D. Krishnan, Unsupervised pixel-level domain adaptation with generative adversarial networks, in: The IEEE Conference on Computer Vision and Pattern Recognition (CVPR), 2017, p. 7.

[62] F. Mahmood, R. Chen, N.J. Durr, Unsupervised reverse domain adaption for synthetic medical images via adversarial training, IEEE Transactions on Medical Imaging 37 (12) (2018) 2572–2581.

[63] C. Chen, Q. Dou, H. Chen, P.-A. Heng, Semantic-aware generative adversarial nets for unsupervised domain adaptation in chest X-ray segmentation, arXiv preprint arXiv:1806.00600, 2018.

[64] A. Madani, M. Moradi, A. Karargyris, T. Syeda-Mahmood, Semi-supervised learning with generative adversarial networks for chest X-ray classification with ability of data domain adaptation, in: IEEE International Symposium on Biomedical Imaging (ISBI), IEEE, 2018, pp. 1038–1042.

[65] Y. Zhang, L. Yang, J. Chen, M. Fredericksen, D.P. Hughes, D.Z. Chen, Deep adversarial networks for biomedical image segmentation utilizing unannotated images, in: International Conference on Medical Image Computing and Computer-Assisted Intervention, 2017, pp. 408–416.

[66] J.P. Cohen, M. Luck, S. Honari, Distribution matching losses can hallucinate features in medical image translation, in: International Conference on Medical Image Computing and Computer-Assisted Intervention, 2018.

[67] C. Chu, A. Zhmoginov, M. Sandler, CycleGAN: a master of steganography, in: NIPS 2017 Workshop on Machine Deception, 2017.

[68] M. Heusel, H. Ramsauer, T. Unterthiner, B. Nessler, S. Hochreiter, GANs trained by a two time-scale update rule converge to a local Nash equilibrium, in: Advances in Neural Information Processing Systems, 2017, pp. 6626–6637.

[69] C. Szegedy, W. Liu, Y. Jia, P. Sermanet, S. Reed, D. Anguelov, D. Erhan, V. Vanhoucke, A. Rabinovich, Going deeper with convolutions, in: Proceedings of the IEEE Conference on Computer Vision and Pattern Recognition, 2015, pp. 1–9.

[70] Y. Blau, T. Michaeli, The perception-distortion tradeoff, in: The IEEE Conference on Computer Vision and Pattern Recognition (CVPR), 2018, pp. 6228–6237.

CHAPTER 24

Linear statistical shape models and landmark location

T.F. Cootes

The University of Manchester, Manchester, United Kingdom

Contents

24.1.	Introduction	576
24.2.	Shape models	576
24.2.1	Representing structures with points	576
24.2.2	Comparing two shapes	577
24.2.3	Aligning two shapes	578
24.2.4	Aligning a set of shapes	578
24.2.5	Building linear shape models	579
	24.2.5.1 Choosing the number of modes	*580*
	24.2.5.2 Examples of shape models	*581*
	24.2.5.3 Matching a model to known points	*581*
24.2.6	Analyzing shapes	582
24.2.7	Constraining parameters	583
24.2.8	Limitations of linear models	583
24.2.9	Dealing with uncertain data	584
24.2.10	Alternative shape models	584
	24.2.10.1 Level set representations	*584*
	24.2.10.2 Medial representations	*585*
	24.2.10.3 Models of deformations	*585*
24.2.11	3D models	585
24.3.	Automated landmark location strategies	586
24.3.1	Exhaustive methods: searching for individual points	586
	24.3.1.1 Template matching	*587*
	24.3.1.2 Generative approaches	*587*
	24.3.1.3 Discriminative approaches	*587*
	24.3.1.4 Regression-based approaches	*588*
	24.3.1.5 Estimating score maps with CNNs	*590*
24.3.2	Alternating approaches	590
	24.3.2.1 Constrained local models	*591*
24.3.3	Iterative update approaches	592
	24.3.3.1 Updating parameters	*593*
	24.3.3.2 Regression-based updates	*594*
	24.3.3.3 Locating landmarks with agents	*595*
24.4.	Discussion	595
	Appendix 24.A	595
24.A.1	Computing modes when fewer samples than ordinates	595

Handbook of Medical Image Computing and Computer Assisted Intervention
https://doi.org/10.1016/B978-0-12-816176-0.00029-6

24.A.2   Closest point on a plane   596
24.A.3   Closest point on an ellipsoid   596
References   597

24.1. Introduction

Information about the shape and size of anatomical structures is of great importance when studying, diagnosing, or treating disease. For instance, there are clear changes in the shapes of the ventricles in the brain as various diseases progress, and bones are changed by osteoarthritis. To quantify shapes and shape changes, it is necessary to represent them in a flexible way that is amenable to analysis. A very effective approach is to describe the shape as a set of points (for instance, spaced around the boundary of the object). Shapes can then be compared by studying the relative positions of equivalent points on different examples.

In the following we will focus on 2D shape models initially, but there is a natural extension to 3D shape models.

24.2. Shape models

24.2.1 Representing structures with points

A structure (or set of structures) can be represented using a set of *landmark* points. These define the location of interesting parts of the structure (such as boundaries or clinically important points).

The positions of such points should be well defined so that each can be consistently located on a new image. Choosing the points to be used to represent an example is an important part of defining a model. Each landmark has a unique definition and effectively defines a *correspondence* between structures in one image and those in another; see Fig. 24.1.

In 2D there are three types of such landmarks:

1. Points which are well defined in 2D (such as corners, centers of small structures, etc.);
2. Points which are well defined in 1D (such as points on boundaries);
3. Points which are weakly defined (such as points at the intersections of occluding boundaries).

Most shapes consist of types 1 and 2 only. A shape is usually defined by some well defined corners, together with points along boundaries between them. The latter are only present to define the curve of the boundary, so their exact position along the curve can vary; see Fig. 24.1.

An important advantage of the point-based representation is that it can be use for structures containing multiple parts – for instance, in Fig. 24.1 we could represent ad-

Figure 24.1 Points used to represent the outline of a structure. Each point is numbered and defines a particular position on the object. The same number of points are used on each example. Those in red are well defined in 2D (Type 1). Other points are used to define the boundary (Type 2).

ditional bones just by adding more points on to them. The curves are just used for visualization of the shape model.

24.2.2 Comparing two shapes

In 2D an individual shape is represented by the set of n points, $\{(x_i, y_i)\}$, which can be encoded in a single vector

$$\mathbf{x} = (x_1, y_1, \ldots, x_n, y_n)^T. \tag{24.1}$$

A mathematical definition of shape (a generalization of that due to Kendall [16]) as "*that geometric information which is invariant to some class of transformations*".

Usually one works with similarity transformations (translation, rotation, scale), but in some cases one may use translations, rigid transformations (translation+rotations), dilations (translation+scale), or affine transformations.

For instance, when the absolute size of an object is important (for instance, when studying growth), then one would use information invariant to rigid transformations (sometimes called *shape-and-size* [14]).

Suppose $T(\mathbf{x}; \mathbf{t})$ applies a transformation to the points defined in $\mathbf{x}$ with parameters $\mathbf{t}$. Common linear transformations can be defined as follows (when applied to a single point):

Transformation	Form
Translation	$T(\mathbf{x}; \mathbf{t}) = \mathbf{x} + (t_x, t_y)^T$
Dilation	$T(\mathbf{x}; \mathbf{t}) = s\mathbf{x} + (t_x, t_y)^T$
Euclidean (rigid)	$T(\mathbf{x}; \mathbf{t}) = \begin{pmatrix} \cos\theta & -\sin\theta \\ -\sin\theta & \cos\theta \end{pmatrix}\mathbf{x} + (t_x, t_y)^T$
Similarity	$T(\mathbf{x}; \mathbf{t}) = s\mathbf{R}_\theta\mathbf{x} + (t_x, t_y)^T = \begin{pmatrix} a & -b \\ b & a \end{pmatrix}\mathbf{x} + (t_x, t_y)^T$
Affine	$T(\mathbf{x}; \mathbf{t}) = \begin{pmatrix} a & b \\ c & d \end{pmatrix}\mathbf{x} + (t_x, t_y)^T$

The simplest way of comparing two shapes is to compute the sum of square distances between corresponding points. If $\mathbf{x}_i$ is point i from shape $\mathbf{x}$, then this is given by

$$D = \sum_{i=1}^{n} |\mathbf{x}_i - \mathbf{z}_i|^2 = |\mathbf{x} - \mathbf{z}|^2. \tag{24.2}$$

Two shapes $\mathbf{x}$ and $\mathbf{z}$ can be considered to be the same under a particular class of transformations if one can transform one to exactly match the other, so that

$$\min_{\mathbf{t}} |\mathbf{z} - T(\mathbf{x}; \mathbf{t})|^2 = 0. \tag{24.3}$$

24.2.3 Aligning two shapes

To align shape $\mathbf{x}$ to $\mathbf{z}$, we find the transformation parameters $\mathbf{t}$ to minimize

$$Q(\mathbf{t}) = |\mathbf{z} - T(\mathbf{x}; \mathbf{t})|^2. \tag{24.4}$$

For the linear classes of transformation, there are simple linear solutions to this. For notational convenience, let the vector $\mathbf{x}_x = (x_1, \dots, x_n)^T$ be the x values from $\mathbf{x}$, $\mathbf{x}_y = (y_1, \dots, y_n)^T$ the y values from $\mathbf{x}$. Similarly, let $\mathbf{z}_x$ and $\mathbf{z}_y$ be the x and y values from shape $\mathbf{z}$.

Let us also assume that $\mathbf{x}$ has been translated so that its center of gravity is at the origin. This can be achieved by applying a translation by $(-\mathbf{x}_x.\mathbf{1}, -\mathbf{x}_y.\mathbf{1})^T/n$.

In all cases the optimal choice of translation parameters is given by $t_x = \mathbf{z}_x.\mathbf{1}/n$, $t_y = \mathbf{z}_y.\mathbf{1}/n$. Other parameters are as follows:

Translation	$t_x = \mathbf{z}_x.\mathbf{1}/n$
	$t_y = \mathbf{z}_y.\mathbf{1}/n$
Dilation	$s = \mathbf{x}.\mathbf{z}/|\mathbf{x}|$
Similarity	$a = \mathbf{x}.\mathbf{z}/|\mathbf{x}|,$
	$b = (\mathbf{x}_x.\mathbf{z}_y - \mathbf{x}_y.\mathbf{z}_x)/|\mathbf{x}|$
Affine	$\begin{pmatrix} a & b \\ c & d \end{pmatrix} = \begin{pmatrix} |\mathbf{x}_x|^2 & \mathbf{x}_x.\mathbf{x}_y \\ \mathbf{x}_x.\mathbf{x}_y & |\mathbf{x}_y|^2 \end{pmatrix}^{-1} \begin{pmatrix} \mathbf{x}_x.\mathbf{z}_x & \mathbf{x}_x.\mathbf{z}_y \\ \mathbf{x}_y.\mathbf{z}_x & \mathbf{x}_y.\mathbf{z}_y \end{pmatrix}$

These assume equal, isotropic weights for every point; see below for cases in which this assumption is relaxed, for instance, to deal with missing or noisy point position estimates.

24.2.4 Aligning a set of shapes

If we wish to analyze a set of N shapes, $\{\mathbf{x}_j\}$, we need to first align them into a common reference frame – a process known as Generalized Procrustes Analysis [12]. A common approach is to estimate the mean shape $\bar{\mathbf{x}}$ and a set of transformations $\{T_j\}$ such that $|\bar{\mathbf{x}}| = 1$ and the following is minimized

$$\sum_{j=1}^{N} |T_j(\mathbf{x}_j) - \bar{\mathbf{x}}|^2 \quad \text{where} \quad \bar{\mathbf{x}} = \tfrac{1}{N} \sum_{j=1}^{N} T_j(\mathbf{x}_j). \tag{24.5}$$

In morphometry it is common to normalize all shapes so that their center of gravity is at the origin, and their scale is unity [14]. The normalized shapes then live on the unit hypersphere, which is a curved space. The only free parameter in the alignment is rotation, which is selected so as to minimize (24.5).

However, if one wishes to build a linear model of the data, it is better to project the shapes into the tangent plane to the unit hypersphere at the mean, otherwise the model will be forced to deal with the nonlinearities caused by the curvature of the sphere.

Thus when building a linear shape model, it is better to choose the transformations which minimize

$$\sum_{j=1}^{N} |\mathbf{x}_j - T_j(\bar{\mathbf{x}})|^2 \quad \text{where} \quad \bar{\mathbf{x}} = \tfrac{1}{N} \sum_{j=1}^{N} T_j^{-1}(\mathbf{x}_j). \tag{24.6}$$

The (inverse) transformed shapes will all be in the tangent plane by construction. This has the added appeal that (24.6) is selecting a mean which minimizes the errors measured in the original frame of the shapes.

There have been a range of algorithms proposed for aligning sets of shapes [17,14, 12,4]. A simple iterative approach is as follows:

Choose one shape to define the orientation, say $\mathbf{x}_r = \mathbf{x}_0$
Center $\mathbf{x}_r$ so its CoG is at the origin
Scale $\mathbf{x}_r$ to have unit size ($|\mathbf{x}_r| = 1$)
Set initial estimate of mean $\bar{\mathbf{x}} = \mathbf{x}_r$
repeat
    For each shape compute T_j to minimize $|T_j(\bar{\mathbf{x}}) - \mathbf{x}_j|^2$
    Update estimate of mean: $\bar{\mathbf{x}} = \tfrac{1}{N} \sum_{j=1}^{N} T_j^{-1}(\mathbf{x}_j)$
    Align $\bar{\mathbf{x}}$ to $\mathbf{x}_r$ to fix rotation, then scale so that $|\bar{\mathbf{x}}| = 1$
until convergence

This usually converges in a few iterations, so is very quick to run.

24.2.5 Building linear shape models

Given a set of aligned shapes $\{\mathbf{x}_i\}$, a linear statistical shape model can be built by using principal component analysis (PCA) to identify the main modes of shape variation.

This involves the following steps:

1) Compute the mean of the set $\bar{\mathbf{x}} = \frac{1}{N}\sum_i \mathbf{x}_i$
2) Compute the covariance about the mean, $\mathbf{S} = \frac{1}{N-1}\sum_i (\mathbf{x}_i - \bar{\mathbf{x}})(\mathbf{x}_i - \bar{\mathbf{x}})^T$
3) Compute the eigenvectors, $\{\mathbf{p}_j\}$, and associated eigenvalues λ_j of $\mathbf{S}$
4) Choosing the number of modes t to retain

The final model has the form

$$\mathbf{x} = \bar{\mathbf{x}} + \mathbf{P}\mathbf{b} \qquad (24.7)$$

where $\mathbf{P} = (\mathbf{p}_1|\dots|\mathbf{p}_t)$ is a matrix whose columns are the t eigenvectors associated with the largest eigenvalues.

Note that when there are many points, and few examples, there are more efficient methods of computing the eigenvectors and eigenvalues than creating the whole covariance matrix (see Appendix 24.A.1).

24.2.5.1 Choosing the number of modes

The number of modes retained, t, defines the amount of flexibility in the model and will affect the performance of any system which uses the resulting model. If too few modes are retained, the model will not be able to represent the full variation seen in class of shapes.

The eigenvalues, λ_i, describe the variance of the training data projected onto the associated eigenvector, $\mathbf{p}_i$. The total variance about the mean in the training set is given by the sum of all eigenvalues, $V_T = \sum_i \lambda_i$. A widely used approach is to choose t to represent a particular proportion of the total variance, p_t, such as 0.95 or 0.98;

$$\sum_{i=1}^{t} \lambda_i > p_t V_T, \qquad (24.8)$$

where the eigenvalues are sorted, $\lambda_i \geq \lambda_{i+1}$.

This ensures that most of the main modes of variation are encoded in the model, which is usually sufficient for most applications. The optimal number of modes retained will depend on the application, and is best found by experiment.

An extended version of the shape model explicitly models the residuals at each point:

$$\mathbf{x} = \bar{\mathbf{x}} + \mathbf{P}\mathbf{b} + \mathbf{r}, \qquad (24.9)$$

where $\mathbf{b}$ is distributed as $p(\mathbf{b})$ (such as a multivariate Gaussian) and each element of $\mathbf{r}$ is independent and normally distributed, so $\mathbf{r}$ has distribution $p(\mathbf{r}) = N(\mathbf{r}; \mathbf{0}, \sigma_r^2 \mathbf{I})$. This

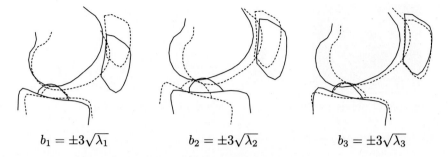

$$b_1 = \pm 3\sqrt{\lambda_1} \qquad b_2 = \pm 3\sqrt{\lambda_2} \qquad b_3 = \pm 3\sqrt{\lambda_3}$$

Figure 24.2 First three modes of a shape model of the lateral knee.

is the model underlying Probabilistic PCA [33]. Given enough examples, the optimal number of modes to retain can be estimated.

24.2.5.2 Examples of shape models

Fig. 24.2 shows the first three modes of a shape model of the bones of the knee as seen in a lateral X-ray.[1]

24.2.5.3 Matching a model to known points

Given a set of points $\mathbf{z}$, one often wishes to find the best approximation with the shape model, enabling one to estimate the shape parameters representing $\mathbf{z}$. In the simplest case one finds the shape and pose parameters to minimize

$$Q_2(\mathbf{b}, \mathbf{t}) = |T(\bar{\mathbf{x}} + \mathbf{P}\mathbf{b}; \mathbf{t}) - \mathbf{z}|^2. \tag{24.10}$$

A fast alternating algorithm for this is as follows:

Initialize $\mathbf{b}$, for instance, $\mathbf{b} = 0$
repeat
    Find the optimal pose, $\mathbf{t}$ to minimize $Q_2(\mathbf{b}, \mathbf{t})$;
    Project $\mathbf{z}$ into the model space: $\mathbf{z}' = T^{-1}(\mathbf{z}; \mathbf{t})$;
    Estimate the shape using $\mathbf{b} = \mathbf{P}^T(\mathbf{z}' - \bar{\mathbf{x}})$;
until converged

This will usually converge in a small number of iterations.

[1] Thanks to L. Minciullo.

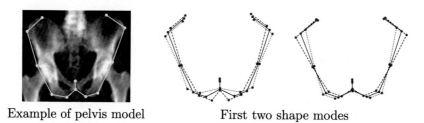

Example of pelvis model   First two shape modes

Figure 24.3 Simple model of pelvis shape using 12 points.

Minimizing (24.10) is equivalent to finding the most likely parameters if (a) the uncertainties on all the points in $\mathbf{z}$ are equal isotropic Gaussians, and (b) that the prior distribution of shape and pose parameters is flat.

A more general case is to assume that each point in $\mathbf{z}$, $\mathbf{z}_i$, has a Gaussian uncertainty with an inverse covariance matrix, $\mathbf{W}_i$. Missing points can be represented using $\mathbf{W}_i = 0$.

In this case the optimal parameters are found by minimizing

$$Q_w(\mathbf{b}, \mathbf{t}) = 0.5 \sum_{i=1}^{n} (\mathbf{x}_i(\mathbf{b}, \mathbf{t}) - \mathbf{z}_i)^T \mathbf{W}_i (\mathbf{x}_i(\mathbf{b}, \mathbf{t}) - \mathbf{z}_i) - \log p_b(\mathbf{b}), \qquad (24.11)$$

where $\mathbf{x}_i(\mathbf{b}, \mathbf{t})$ is the position of model point i after transformation, and $p_b(\mathbf{b})$ is the prior distribution of the shape parameters.

24.2.6 Analyzing shapes

Once images are annotated with points, each can be represented by the shape parameters which best fit the model to the landmarks. This gives a compact feature vector enabling further analysis. One can, for instance, classify the shape using the parameter vector, or perform regression to study the links between shape changes and disease.

For example, Fig. 24.3 shows the first two modes of a simple 12 point shape model describing the outline of the pelvis as viewed in whole body DXA images. There is a significant difference between the shape in males and females, which can be observed in the scatter plot shown in Fig. 24.4(A).

Note that since PCA extracts the linear modes which explain the largest variance in the data, they do not necessarily always correspond to particular differences. In this case one could apply linear discriminant analysis to the parameter vectors to learn the single linear direction which best separates males from females – useful for visualizing the differences; see, for instance, Fig. 24.4(B)–(C).

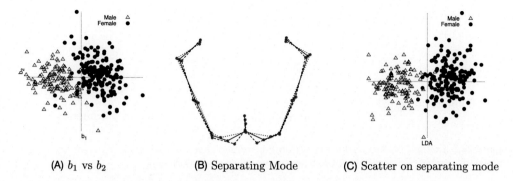

(A) b_1 vs b_2 (B) Separating Mode   (C) Scatter on separating mode

Figure 24.4 (A) Scatter of parameters for males and females, (B) the best linear mode separating the two classes, and (C) the scatter along that direction.

24.2.7 Constraining parameters

Suppose we wish to apply hard constraints on the parameters, to ensure they remain in the ranges found in the training set. The effect of the PCA used in training is to ensure that each shape parameter b_i is linearly independent and has a variance λ_i.

If we assume that the original data is normally distributed (which appears to be a good model in a wide variety of cases), then the shape parameters $\{b_i\}$ are each univariate Gaussian, and $p(\mathbf{b}) = N(\mathbf{b} : \mathbf{0}, \Lambda)$ where $\Lambda = diag(\lambda_1, \ldots, \lambda_t)$.

A natural constraint on $\mathbf{b}$ is then the isocontour ellipsoid, $M(\mathbf{b}) \leq M_t$ where M_t is a threshold on the Mahalanobis distance, $M(\mathbf{b})$,

$$M(\mathbf{b}) = \mathbf{b}^T \Lambda^{-1} \mathbf{b} = \sum_{i=1}^{t} \frac{b_i^2}{\lambda_i}. \tag{24.12}$$

Since $M(\mathbf{b})$ has a χ^2 distribution, we can use the inverse of the cumulative χ^2 distribution to estimate M_t so that a desired proportion of the training data is within the threshold.

Appendix 24.A.3 gives an algorithm for finding the closest point on the ellipsoid to an external point, which can be used to constrain the shape parameters.

24.2.8 Limitations of linear models

The linear form of the model is simple and effective for many classes of object. However, it is not always the best parameterization of shape variation. A particular example is when an object contains joints about which one part can rotate. A natural parameterization would include the angle at such a joint. However, a linear model will approximate a pure rotation with two modes, potentially leading to more modes of variation than are strictly necessary (see Fig. 24.5).

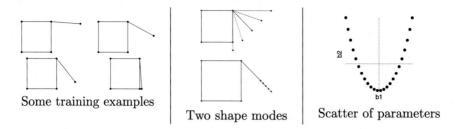

| Some training examples | Two shape modes | Scatter of parameters |

Figure 24.5 Example of linearization of rotation. Pure rotation about an axis leads to parameter values following a curved path, which is not well represented by a single Gaussian.

24.2.9 Dealing with uncertain data

The algorithms for building models described above assume that the point coordinates are all known accurately, and that any uncertainty is small and isotropic for every point. In many cases there will be some uncertainty on each training point, particularly when points are placed along a boundary (and so could slide along it). In such cases one could estimate the covariance of the error for each point. Well defined (Type 1) points would have near isotropic uncertainties, but points on boundaries (Type 2) may have nonisotropic covariance matrices, with more uncertainty parallel to the boundary compared to normal to it.

It is possible to build statistical shape models which take this uncertainty in the training data into account [28].

24.2.10 Alternative shape models

The landmark based approach to shape modeling described above is perhaps the most widely used. However, there are many alternatives which are suitable for different situations.

24.2.10.1 Level set representations

A closed shape in 2D can be represented as the region which satisfies $F(x, y) < 0$ for some level set function F. The points which satisfy $F(x, y) = 0$ are on the boundary of the shape. For a particular shape one can construct F using a signed distance function from the shape (negative distances inside, positive distances to the boundary outside). Such a distance function image can be represented as a single vector, $\mathbf{d}$, by concatenating the rows.

Given multiple example shapes, aligned to minimize the sum of square distances between $F(x, y)$ for each, the mean and covariance of the resulting vectors, $\{\mathbf{d}_i\}$, can be calculated and PCA can be applied to create a linear model [19]. Since the linear interpolation of two distance transforms is not necessarily a distance transform itself, such models are not good for synthesizing shapes. However, they are useful for applying constraints to geodesic active contours.

24.2.10.2 Medial representations

Medial representations describe a shape in terms of a set of elements making up a skeleton, together with a description of the distance of the surface of the shape to each skeleton node [31]. Statistical analysis of the parameters can lead to generative statistical models. For certain objects this is a natural representation, and can encode variation in a set with fewer parameters than the linear approaches described above. However, reconstructing the surface from the medial representation is a nonlinear optimization problem.

24.2.10.3 Models of deformations

Given a set of images, one can apply nonrigid registration to learn the deformation field from a reference image to each other image. PCA can be applied to the parameters of the deformation field to learn a statistical model of deformation that doesn't require any explicit landmarks [10].

An important class of deformations are diffeomorphisms (smooth, invertible mappings). There is now an extensive literature on building statistical models from sets of diffeomorphisms, building on [1].

24.2.11 3D models

Although much of the above described 2D shape models, the modeling and matching techniques are equally valid for 3D models. One of the main challenges is the initial annotation of the training images. In 2D it is practical to have human experts place all the points (often with semiautomatic support). However, to represent 3D surfaces requires hundreds, or even thousands of landmarks, which cannot be placed by hand.

Usually the 3D volumetric image is segmented (often with slice-by-slice manual editing) to create binary masks for the structures of interest. The challenge then is to place landmarks on the surfaces of each such structure so as to define useful correspondences. There are two broad approaches to this:

1. Convert each mask to a surface. Place points on each surface then slide them around to optimize some measure of correspondence [7].
2. Use volumetric nonlinear registration to deform each image (and mask) into a reference frame, place landmarks on the mean in this frame then propagate them back to the training images [9,10,2].

24.3. Automated landmark location strategies

In order to analyze the shape of an object in a new image, it is first necessary to locate the landmarks representing the shape in the image. Many strategies for this use shape models to ensure that the resulting points satisfy the constraints imposed by the model.

Fitting such a shape model to an image (finding the parameters which lead to points which best match to image structures) is a challenging optimization task, which is usually performed with an iterative approach.

There are three broad classes of approach used:

1. **Exhaustive search**, in which each point is searched for independently in an image region.
2. **Alternating approaches**, in which candidates for each point are found with independent local searches, then a shape model is used to constrain the set of points to a valid shape (such as the Active Shape Model [4]).
3. **Iterative approaches**, in which the model parameters are modified using estimates of the optimal update vector estimated using gradient descent or regression techniques (such as the Active Appearance Model [3] or Supervised Descent Method [35]).

Note that many practical approaches use a combination of such methods, for instance, using regression to estimate each point or part then regularizing results with a shape model.

Most practical applications use a global search to estimate the approximate pose (position, orientation, scale) of the target object before refining the points. Global search is typically done with an object detector, either by looking for key points or by an exhaustive search over scales/orientations with a detector such as that in [27].

In addition, it is usually both quicker and more robust to use a multistage technique, in which initial models are trained and run on low resolution versions of the image to get initial approximations to point positions, which are then improved by using models and information from higher resolution images.

24.3.1 Exhaustive methods: searching for individual points

Given an input image, I, several methods exist for computing score maps, $S(\mathbf{x}|I)$, indicating how likely a landmark point is to be at any given pixel. With no other information, the pixel with the highest value of $S(\mathbf{x}, I)$ is the best estimate of the location of the point.

There are two widely used approaches, (i) those that use features around each pixel to compute a score at the pixel and (ii) those that use regression techniques to vote for point positions.

Both approaches involve computing image features from a region around each pixel, $\mathbf{v} = f_v(I, \mathbf{x})$, which is then used to estimate match scores or relative positions.

Examples of features that have been used include
- Raw pixel values in a region around the point
- The response of filter banks, such as Gabor filters
- Haar-like filters [27,20]
- SIFT [23] or SURF [13] features
- Features learnt using Convolutional Neural Networks (CNNs)

24.3.1.1 Template matching

The simplest approach to finding matches is to find the feature vectors which are closest to a template vector. The template is the mean of vectors extracted at representative points in the training set, $\bar{\mathbf{v}}$. The score is given by normalized correlation between the template and the image features at each point, $\mathbf{v}.\bar{\mathbf{v}}/(|\mathbf{v}||\bar{\mathbf{v}}|)$.

24.3.1.2 Generative approaches

Given a training set one can estimate the distribution of the feature vectors sampled at a point, $p(\mathbf{v}|L)$. This can be used to assess the probability that any point in a new image is the true landmark position.

Strictly one is interested in estimating the probability that the vector at a particular point is associated with a landmark position, $p(L|\mathbf{v})$, which is given by

$$p(L|\mathbf{v}) = \frac{p(\mathbf{v}|L)p(L)}{p(\mathbf{v})}. \tag{24.13}$$

Since usually one cannot easily estimate either $p(L)$ or $p(\mathbf{v})$, it is common to score each point using $p(\mathbf{v}|L)$ directly.

For instance, a simple assumption is that the feature vectors have a multivariate Gaussian distribution, described by the mean, $\bar{\mathbf{v}}$, and covariance matrix, $\mathbf{S}_v$, which can be estimated from the training examples.

Then

$$S(\mathbf{x}) = \log(p(L|\mathbf{v})) = C - 0.5(\mathbf{v} - \bar{\mathbf{v}})^T \mathbf{S}_v^{-1}(\mathbf{v} - \bar{\mathbf{v}}) = C - M_v, \tag{24.14}$$

so one seeks the point which minimizes the Mahalanobis distance, M_v [4].

24.3.1.3 Discriminative approaches

One can train a classifier to discriminate between positions which are likely to be landmark locations and those which are not. A classifier function, $C(\mathbf{v})$, is learned which gives a larger value when at the true landmark location. A response image can be computed by evaluating $C(\mathbf{v})$ at each pixel, and local peaks in this give candidates for the true position.

A key challenge when training the classifier is to identify suitable negative examples. If the true landmark position on a training image is given by $\mathbf{x}$, then positive samples can be collected by sampling feature vectors centered at points $\mathbf{x} + \mathbf{d}$ where $|\mathbf{d}| < r_1$ for some small radius r_1. Negative samples can be taken from elsewhere in the image, but are often taken nearby, at $\mathbf{x} + \mathbf{d}$ where $r_2 < |\mathbf{d}| < r_3$. This avoids including ambiguous examples in the annulus r_2 to r_3.

If the landmark is on a boundary, then nearby points on the same boundary are likely to have very similar feature vectors, so would confuse a classifier if treated as negative samples. In this case one may treat points on the boundary as positives, and those away from it as negatives. More specifically, if $\mathbf{u}$ is the unit normal to the boundary then points sampled at $\mathbf{x} + a\mathbf{u}$ will be positive examples if $|a| < r_1$ and negative if $r_2 < |a| < r_3$.

A wide range of classifiers have been used for this task including linear discriminators, support vector machines, random forests, and neural networks.

24.3.1.4 Regression-based approaches

Rather than attempting to classify each pixel, a more powerful approach is to use the features to vote for where the target point is likely to be. The idea is that one trains a regressor to predict the offset $(\delta_x, \delta_y) = R(\mathbf{v})$. During search one scans the region of interest. If the feature vector sampled at point (x, y), is $\mathbf{v}$, one computes $(\delta_x, \delta_y) = R(\mathbf{v})$, then uses this to vote into an accumulator array at $(x + \delta_x, y + \delta_y)$.

To create a training set for such a system for a particular point, we do the following (see Fig. 24.6(A)):

---

for all Images I_i with associated points $\mathbf{x}_i$ **do**
    Generate a set of m random displacements $\mathbf{d}_{ij}$ with $|\mathbf{d}_{ij}| < r$
    Generate small random scale, orientation displacement poses T_{ij}
    Sample the feature vectors $\mathbf{v}_{ij}$ from image I_i at pose T_{ij} (Fig. 24.6(A))
end for

The pairs $\{(T_{ij}^{-1}(\mathbf{d}_{ij}), \mathbf{v}_{ij})\}$ are used to train a regressor, $\mathbf{d} = R(\mathbf{v})$. The transformation of the displacement by T_{ij}^{-1} calculates the displacement in the transformed frame (the landmark position as seen from the sampling reference frame).

Random Forests [18,5] are widely used for this regression task because of their efficiency and flexibility. A forest contains a set of decision trees. Each decision node in each tree applies a threshold to a particular feature measured from the image patch. One of the simplest features to use is the difference between intensities at two chosen positions within the patch [29]. More robust features can be computed from the means of intensities over rectangular patches, which can be efficiently computed from integral images [27]. Common examples are the difference between two random rectangles [5], and the use of Haar features [27,20].

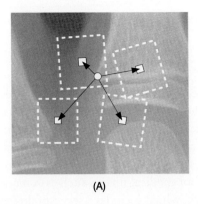
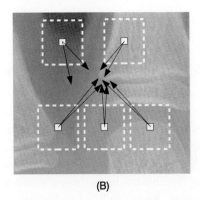

(A)   (B)

Figure 24.6 Regression voting. During training random displacements in position, scale, and orientation are used to improve generalization. During search samples are taken at a fixed scale and orientation at regular grid positions. (A) Training: sample at displaced positions; (B) Search: one vote per tree.

Training a tree. To train a tree in a Random Forest, one selects a feature and a threshold at each node so as to best split the data arriving at that node from its parent. When the tree is to be used to predict a location, one seeks to encourage the set of displacement vectors $\{\mathbf{d}_k\}$ which reach a node to be as compact as possible. Let the samples arriving at the node be pairs $\{(\mathbf{d}_k, \mathbf{v}_k)\}$. Let $g(\mathbf{v})$ compute a scalar feature from the vector. Then during training one tries a random selection of possible features g and thresholds t, choosing the one which minimizes

$$G_T(t) = G(\{\mathbf{d}_k : g(\mathbf{v}_k) < t\}) + G(\{\mathbf{d}_k : g(\mathbf{v}_k) \geq t\}), \tag{24.15}$$

where $G()$ is an entropy measure $G(\{\mathbf{d}_k\}) = N \log|\Sigma|$ where Σ is the covariance matrix of the N samples.

During training one recursively selects features and thresholds to add new nodes to a tree until either a maximum depth is reached or the number of samples reaching a node falls below a threshold. The resulting leaf nodes then record (a) the mean of the displacement vectors reaching them, $\bar{\mathbf{d}}$, and (b) a weight $w = \min(0.5, |\Sigma|^{-0.5})$. The latter is used to reduce the importance of ambiguous cases (where the samples reaching the node are widely spread, with a large covariance, Σ).

A common way to combine the results of multiple trees is to compute the mean of the output of each. However, it has been found [20] to be better to allow each tree to vote independently (with a weight given by the value in the leaf, w), combining the results in the accumulator array (see Fig. 24.6(B)).

This has two key advantages over scanning with a classifier:

1. There is no need for an arbitrary threshold to define positive/negative regions in training;
2. During search one can sample sparsely, significantly speeding up the process.

This regression voting approach has also been shown to lead to more accurate and robust results [20].

24.3.1.5 Estimating score maps with CNNs

An approach that has been found to be very effective in many unconstrained landmark location tasks (such as finding body joints in photographs of people [26]) is to train a CNN to compute the score maps indicating likely point positions. Fully convolutional networks are trained to output score maps (the same size as the original image) which should have a Gaussian blob centered on the true position (sometimes known as a "heatmap"). This has been shown to work well for medical images such as X-ray [25].

A U-Net [30] is a fully convolutional network, which includes a series of downsampling and upsampling layers together with skip connections. Given an input image, it can be trained to produce an output image, and effectively transforms one image into another. If each input training image is paired with a target output image which has a Gaussian blob centered on the position of the landmark, a U-Net can be trained to predict point positions. The accuracy of the prediction increases as the number of training examples increases. This approach can easily be adapted to predict multiple landmark points, by adding extra planes to the output image (one per point) [25,8].

Summary. Of the above methods, the two most effective are those that use CNNs to estimate score maps, and the random forest regression voting approach. Current experience on X-ray images [8] suggests that where small numbers of training examples are available (fewer than a few hundred) the Random Forest methods work better, but that with larger training sets the CNN methods are more robust (have smaller numbers of large errors).

24.3.2 Alternating approaches

Alternating approaches are variants of the Active Shape Model algorithm [4], which involves iterating through three steps (Fig. 24.7);

Initialize shape and pose parameters, $\mathbf{b}, \mathbf{t}$
repeat
    1) Estimate point positions $\mathbf{x} = T(\bar{\mathbf{x}} + \mathbf{Pb}; \mathbf{t})$
    2) Search the image around each point $\mathbf{x}_i$ for a better position $\mathbf{x}'_i$
    3) Update the shape and pose parameters to fit to the new points $\mathbf{x}'$
until converged

The key is to have a model for each individual landmark point which can search the image in a region to find the most likely position for the point. The simplest approach is to search for a strong edge nearby. However, most systems use variants of the exhaustive

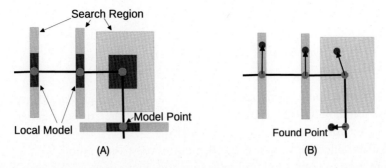

Figure 24.7 Active Shape Model steps. (A) Search for each point nearby; (B) Move towards best local matches.

search techniques described in Sect. 24.3.1, applied to regions sampled around each of the current points as follows:

> **for** $j \leftarrow 1$ to n **do**
>   Compute normal, $\mathbf{u}_j$ and tangent $\mathbf{v}_j$ at point $\mathbf{x}_j$
>   Sample image patch around point, $P(a, b) = I(\mathbf{x}_j + a\mathbf{u}_j + b\mathbf{v}_j)$
>   Search patch $P(a, b)$ to get response $S(a, b)$
>   Find a, b with largest score $S(a, b)$
>   Set $\mathbf{x}'_j = \mathbf{x}_j + a\mathbf{u}_j + b\mathbf{v}_j$
> **end for**

The Active Shape Model involves selecting a candidate for each point independently, which loses information if it chooses the wrong point (due to noise or inherent ambiguity in the image).

A more effective alternative (the "Constrained Local Model" approach) is to retain all the information in the score images for each point and to search them all together [6,20].

24.3.2.1 Constrained local models

The individual shape model points can be computed using

$$\mathbf{x}_j = T(\bar{\mathbf{x}}_j + \mathbf{P}_j\mathbf{b}; \mathbf{t}), \qquad (24.16)$$

where $\bar{\mathbf{x}}_j$ is the mean position of the point in the model frame and $\mathbf{P}_j$ defines the effect of each shape mode on the point.

One iteration of the CLM algorithm involves searching around each point $\mathbf{x}_j$ to compute a score image $S_j(\mathbf{x}_j)$, then finding the pose and shape parameters, $\mathbf{t}, \mathbf{b}$ to maximize

$$Q(\mathbf{t}, \mathbf{b}) = \sum_{j=1}^{n} S_j(T(\bar{\mathbf{x}}_j + \mathbf{P}_i\mathbf{b}; \mathbf{t})) - R(\mathbf{b}), \qquad (24.17)$$

where $R(\mathbf{b})$ is an optional regularization term used to encourage plausible shapes.

The cost function $Q(\mathbf{t}, \mathbf{b})$ can then be optimized either using a general purpose optimizer [6], or using a mean–shift approach [15].

A particularly effective variant is the Random Forest Regression Voting CLM [20] which uses regression voting and multiple stages to achieve state-of-the-art performance on a variety of bone shape detection tasks in radiographs.

24.3.3 Iterative update approaches

Many techniques aim to move toward the best point positions using a sequence of update steps. If $\mathbf{p}$ is a vector combining all the parameters (for instance, the shape and pose vectors), one iteration on an image I has the following steps:

---

1) Sample features from image based on current points, $\mathbf{v} = f(I, \mathbf{x})$

2) Estimate updates to parameters, $\delta\mathbf{p} = h(\mathbf{v})$

3) Modify current parameters, $\mathbf{p} \rightarrow \mathbf{p} + \delta\mathbf{p}$

Two widely used ways of collecting features from the image are:

1. Sample across the region defined by a triangulation of the points;
2. Sample features around each point and concatenate to form $\mathbf{v}$.

The first is the equivalent of using the points and a triangular mesh to warp the image into a standard reference frame (usually defined by the mean points of the model).

Sampling with a mesh. If the region is covered by a triangular mesh (Fig. 24.8(A)) then the position of each sample point can be defined relative to the nodes of its containing triangle using barycentric coordinates, $\mathbf{x}_s = \alpha\mathbf{x}_1 + \beta\mathbf{x}_2 + \gamma\mathbf{x}_3$. This defines a correspondence between sampling points within the mesh and those in a standard reference frame. The values of α, β, γ, and the corner point indices for each sampling point can be precomputed, enabling rapid image sampling given a new set of points [3]. If necessary, the samples can be used to reconstruct an image in the reference frame (with the mean shape), which can then be processed to obtain feature vectors. For instance, to reduce variance caused by illumination effects, it is usually better to work with gradient information than raw pixel values.

Sampling around points. In order to take account of the pose, $\mathbf{t}$, of the object, we calculate the effect of scale and orientation encoded in basis vectors, $\mathbf{u} = T((w, 0); \mathbf{t}) - T((0, 0); \mathbf{t})$ and $\mathbf{v} = T((0, w); \mathbf{t}) - T((0, 0); \mathbf{t})$, where w defines the sampling step size in the reference frame. Around each point we resample the image over a

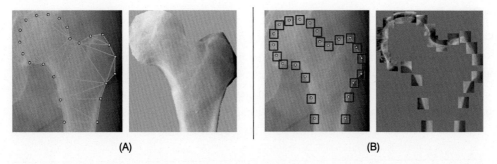

Figure 24.8 Sampling from images. (A) Sampling using a triangular mesh; (B) Sampling around points.

grid $P_j(a, b) = I(\mathbf{x}_j + a\mathbf{u} + b\mathbf{v})$, where a, b are integers. We then sample features from the image patch $P_j(a, b)$ and concatenate them to form $\mathbf{v}$. The feature values may simply be the pixel values (Fig. 24.8(B)), or they may be the elements of SIFT features or other transformations.

24.3.3.1 Updating parameters

Given the features sampled from the image, $\mathbf{v}$, an update is calculated using some function $\delta\mathbf{p} = h(\mathbf{v})$. The function can either be computed as a gradient descent step (where an explicit cost function is being optimized), or can be trained as a regressor.

Explicit cost functions. Suppose that for a particular structure we have a generative model, which computes the feature vector given a set of parameters, $\mathbf{q}$, $\hat{\mathbf{v}} = V(\mathbf{q})$. An example are statistical appearance models which apply PCA to feature vectors sampled from a training set, modeled as $\hat{\mathbf{v}} = \bar{\mathbf{v}} + \mathbf{P}_v\mathbf{q}$ [3].

The quality of fit of a model with parameters $\mathbf{p} = (\mathbf{b}^T, \mathbf{t}^T, \mathbf{q}^T)^T$ could be given by a sum of square error term, such as $Q(\mathbf{p}) = |D(\mathbf{p})|^2$, where D is the vector of differences between sampled and reconstructed features,

$$D(\mathbf{p}) = \mathbf{v}(\mathbf{b}, \mathbf{t}) - V(\mathbf{q}). \tag{24.18}$$

The quadratic form of Q means that near the minimum, a step towards the minimum is given by

$$\delta\mathbf{p} = -(\mathbf{J}_D)^{-1}D(\mathbf{p}), \tag{24.19}$$

where $\mathbf{J}_D$ is the Jacobian of $D(\mathbf{p})$ w.r.t. $\mathbf{p}$.

This general approach can be improved by careful choice of reference frame and the use of compositional updates, leading to the Inverse Compositional algorithm and its variants [24,34], which enable efficient and accurate model fitting.

24.3.3.2 Regression-based updates

Rather than fitting an explicit appearance (or feature) model to the target image, regression techniques aim to estimate good parameter updates directly from the current feature values, in a manner similar to the regression voting approach described in Sect. 24.3.1.4.

Suppose we have a training set of N images, I_i, and the best shape and pose parameters to match to the labeled points in the image are $\mathbf{p}_i$.

We can construct a set of training pairs $\{(\mathbf{v}_{ij}, \delta\mathbf{p}_{ij})\}$ as follows:

---

for all images I_i with associated points $\mathbf{x}_i$ **do**
    Generate a set of m random displacements $\delta\mathbf{p}_{ij}$
    Sample the feature vectors $\mathbf{v}_{ij} = f(I_i, \mathbf{p}_i + \delta\mathbf{p}_{ij})$
end for

This set is then used to train a regression function, $\delta\mathbf{p} = h(\mathbf{v})$.

This regression function estimates the parameter displacements required to get to the target position from any current position, and thus forms the basis of an iterative update scheme. The accuracy of the prediction depends on (i) how similar the current offset is to that used in training, (ii) how broad the training set was, and (iii) the form of the regression function.

In general, models trained on small displacements will give good predictions when applied to cases where the current position is near the true answer, but will break down when the current position is far from the right one. Models trained on large displacements are less accurate, but may give a useful step toward the right position.

Thus a useful strategy is to train a series of models, the first trained on large displacements, with later models trained on increasingly small ranges. For instance, the Supervised Descent Method [35] uses a sequence of linear predictors, each leading to a more accurate estimate of the target position.

An example of a very fast technique is to use ensembles of trees to generate sparse binary vectors from input features, followed by sparse linear regression on these vectors to predict the parameter updates [29]. During training, a set of trees is trained to predict the offset of each point. However, rather than using the outputs stored in the leaves, each tree returns a binary vector which indicates which leaf was reached. The resulting binary vectors from all trees and all points are concatenated together and a linear regressor is trained to predict the actual parameter updates. The use of the trees builds nonlinearity into the system, enabling it to deal with a wide range of variation in appearance.

Sequences of deep convolutional networks have also been used to estimate parameter updates in a similar way [32].

24.3.3.3 Locating landmarks with agents

A very effective approach to detecting landmarks is to train artificial agents to move toward the true landmark position [11]. Given an arbitrary starting point, the agent samples the image features and computes a move in a direction which should be closer to the target landmark. This can be implemented as a classifier which chooses which neighboring pixel or voxel to move to. The agent then crawls through the image until it converges on the true landmark position. Such agents can be trained with deep reinforcement learning, aiming to learn the optimal path towards the landmark from any starting point. This technique has been shown to be very effective for locating landmarks in 3D CT images, and for identifying when a landmark is outside the image [11]. It is also very efficient – rather than scanning the whole image (as exhaustive techniques do), it needs only sample image features from around the path from an initial point to the landmark.

24.4. Discussion

There have been many approaches proposed for locating landmarks in images – the above summary picks out some of the major themes. For 2D tasks (such as locating the outlines of bones in radiographs) the best techniques are approaching the accuracy and robustness of experienced human annotators [21,22]. The best technique for a particular problem will depend on the data itself. The random forest regression methods (both the voting techniques RFRV-CLM [20]) and the iterative update methods [29] seem to be applicable to a range of problems and can deal with significant variation in training sets. Where sufficient training examples are available, the more recent fully convolutional CNN methods [25,8] are achieving slightly better results, and seem to reduce the number of large errors. Where points are well localized the agent-based search [11] has been shown to perform very well.

Research challenges include dealing with missing or occluded data and dealing with large outliers in shape robustly.

Appendix 24.A

24.A.1 Computing modes when fewer samples than ordinates

Suppose we wish to apply a PCA to N n-D vectors, $\{\mathbf{x}_j\}$, where $N < n$. The covariance matrix is $n \times n$, which may be very large. However, we can calculate its eigenvectors and eigenvalues from a smaller $N \times N$ matrix derived from the data. Because the time taken for an eigenvector decomposition goes as the cube of the size of the matrix, this can give considerable savings.

Subtract the mean from each data vector and put them into the matrix $\mathbf{D}$

$$\mathbf{D} = ((\mathbf{x}_1 - \bar{\mathbf{x}})|\ldots|(\mathbf{x}_N - \bar{\mathbf{x}})) \tag{24.20}$$

Consider the two matrices

$$\mathbf{S} = \mathbf{D}\mathbf{D}^T/N \qquad \mathbf{T} = \mathbf{D}^T\mathbf{D}/N \tag{24.21}$$

$\mathbf{S}$ is the $n \times n$ covariance matrix of the data. $\mathbf{T}$ is a $N \times N$ matrix.

Let $\mathbf{e}_i$ be the s eigenvectors of $\mathbf{T}$ with corresponding eigenvalues λ_i, sorted into descending order. It can be shown that the $N-1$ vectors $\mathbf{D}\mathbf{e}_i$ are all eigenvectors of $\mathbf{S}$ with corresponding eigenvalues λ_i, and that all remaining eigenvectors of $\mathbf{S}$ have zero eigenvalues. Note that $\mathbf{D}\mathbf{e}_i$ is not necessarily of unit length so may require normalizing.

24.A.2 Closest point on a plane

Consider the plane $\mathbf{w}.\mathbf{x} = t$ and the point $\mathbf{y}$. Let $\hat{\mathbf{y}}$ be the closest point on the plane to $\mathbf{y}$. Then

$$\hat{\mathbf{y}} = \mathbf{y} - \beta\mathbf{w} \quad \text{where} \quad \beta = \frac{\mathbf{w}.\mathbf{y} - t}{|\mathbf{w}|^2} \tag{24.22}$$

Proof: Since $\mathbf{w}$ is normal to the plane, $\hat{\mathbf{y}}$ must lie on the line $\mathbf{x} = \mathbf{y} - \beta\mathbf{w}$ for some β. Substituting into $\mathbf{w}.\mathbf{x} = t$ to find the intersection with the plane yields $\mathbf{w}.\mathbf{y} - \beta\mathbf{w}.\mathbf{w} = t$, from which we obtain β.

24.A.3 Closest point on an ellipsoid

We seek the closest point on an ellipsoid to the external point $\mathbf{y}$. Assuming the ellipsoid is centered on the origin, it has the equation $\mathbf{x}^T\mathbf{A}\mathbf{x} = k$ where $\mathbf{A}$ is symmetric. If $\mathbf{z}$ is a point on the ellipsoid, the tangent plane at that point has equation $\mathbf{x}.(\mathbf{A}\mathbf{z}) = k$. By (24.22) the closest point on this plane to $\mathbf{y}$ is given by

$$\hat{\mathbf{y}} = \mathbf{y} - \beta\mathbf{A}\mathbf{z} \quad \text{where} \quad \beta = \frac{(\mathbf{A}\mathbf{z}).\mathbf{y} - k}{|\mathbf{A}\mathbf{z}|^2} \tag{24.23}$$

An algorithm for finding the closest point on an ellipsoid to an external point $\mathbf{y}$ is thus to start at one point on the ellipsoid, move to the closest point on the tangent plane, then project onto the ellipsoid. Repeating will converge to the correct position, effectively sliding around the ellipsoid. More precisely:

$$\hat{\mathbf{y}}_0 = \mathbf{y}/\sqrt{\mathbf{y}^T \mathbf{A}\mathbf{y}/k}, \; i = 0$$
repeat
$$\hat{\mathbf{y}}_{i+1} = \mathbf{y} - \beta_i \mathbf{A}\hat{\mathbf{y}}_i \text{ where } \beta_i = \frac{(\mathbf{A}\hat{\mathbf{y}}_i).\mathbf{y} - k}{|\mathbf{A}\hat{\mathbf{y}}_i|^2}$$
$$\hat{\mathbf{y}}_{i+1} \rightarrow \hat{\mathbf{y}}_{i+1}/\sqrt{\hat{\mathbf{y}}_{i+1}^T \mathbf{A}\hat{\mathbf{y}}_{i+1}/k}$$
until $|\hat{\mathbf{y}}_{i+1} - \hat{\mathbf{y}}_i| < \epsilon$

References

[1] M.F. Beg, M. Miller, A. Trouvé, L. Younes, Computing large deformation metric mappings via geodesic flows of diffeomorphisms, International Journal of Computer Vision 61 (2) (2005) 139–157.

[2] T.F. Cootes, C.J. Twining, V.S. Petrović, K.O. Babalola, C.J. Taylor, Computing accurate correspondences across groups of images, IEEE Transactions on Pattern Analysis and Machine Intelligence 32 (11) (2010) 1994–2005.

[3] T.F. Cootes, G.J. Edwards, C.J. Taylor, Active appearance models, IEEE Transactions on Pattern Analysis and Machine Intelligence 23 (6) (2001) 681–685.

[4] T.F. Cootes, C.J. Taylor, D. Cooper, J. Graham, Active Shape Models – their training and application, Computer Vision and Image Understanding 61 (1) (Jan. 1995) 38–59.

[5] A. Criminisi, J. Shotton (Eds.), Decision Forests for Computer Vision and Medical Image Analysis, Springer, 2013.

[6] D. Cristinacce, T.F. Cootes, Automatic feature localisation with constrained local models, Pattern Recognition 41 (10) (2008) 3054–3067.

[7] R. Davies, C. Twining, T. Cootes, C. Taylor, A minimum description length approach to statistical shape modelling, IEEE Transactions on Medical Imaging 21 (2002) 525–537.

[8] A. Davison, C. Lindner, D. Perry, W. Luo, T.F. Cootes, Landmark localisation in radiographs using weighted heatmap displacement voting, in: Proc. Int. Workshop on Computational Methods and Clinical Applications in Musculoskeletal Imaging, 2018.

[9] S. Duchesne, D. Collins, Analysis of 3D deformation fields for appearance-based segmentation, in: Proc. MICCAI, 2001, pp. 1189–1190.

[10] A. Frangi, D. Rueckert, J. Schnabel, W. Niessen, Automatic construction of multiple-object three-dimensional statistical shape models: application to cardiac modeling, IEEE Transactions on Medical Imaging 21 (2002) 1151–1166.

[11] F.C. Ghesu, B. Georgescu, S. Grbic, A. Maier, J. Hornegger, D. Comaniciu, Towards intelligent robust detection of anatomical structures in incomplete volumetric data, Medical Image Analysis 48 (2018) 203–213.

[12] C. Goodall, Procrustes methods in the statistical analysis of shape, Journal of the Royal Statistical Society B 53 (2) (1991) 285–339.

[13] T.T.H. Bay, A. Ess, L.V. Gool, Surf: speeded up robust features, Computer Vision and Image Understanding 10 (3) (2008) 346–359.

[14] I.L. Dryden, K.V. Mardia, Statistical Shape Analysis, Wiley, 1998.

[15] J.M. Saragih, S. Lucey, J.F. Cohn, Deformable model fitting by regularized mean-shifts, International Journal of Computer Vision (2011) 200–215.

[16] D. Kendall, The diffusion of shape, Advances in Applied Probability 9 (1977) 428–430.

[17] J. Kent, The complex Bingham distribution and shape analysis, Journal of the Royal Statistical Society B 56 (1994) 285–299.

[18] L. Breiman, Random forests, Machine Learning 45 (2001) 5–32.

[19] M. Leventon, E. Grimson, O. Faugeras, Statistical shape influence in geodesic active contours, in: IEEE Proc. Computer Vision and Pattern Recognition, vol. 1, 2000, pp. 316–323.

[20] C. Lindner, P. Bromiley, M. Ionita, T. Cootes, Robust and accurate shape model matching using random forest regression-voting, IEEE Transactions on Pattern Analysis and Machine Intelligence 37 (9) (Sept. 2015) 1862–1874.

[21] C. Lindner, S. Thiagarajah, J.M. Wilkinson, arcOGEN, G. Wallis, T.F. Cootes, Fully automatic segmentation of the proximal femur using random forest regression voting, IEEE Transactions on Medical Imaging 32 (8) (2013) 1462–1472.

[22] C. Lindner, C.-W. Wang, C.-T. Huang, J.-H. Lee, C.-H. Li, S.-W. Chang, T. Cootes, Fully automatic system for accurate localisation and analysis of cephalometric landmarks in lateral cephalograms, Scientific Reports 6 (Sept. 2016).

[23] D. Lowe, Distinctive image features from scale-invariant keypoints, International Journal of Computer Vision 60 (2) (2004) 91–110.

[24] I. Matthews, S. Baker, Active appearance models revisited, International Journal of Computer Vision 60 (2) (Nov. 2004) 135–164.

[25] C. Payer, D. Stern, H. Bischof, M. Urschler, Regressing heatmaps for multiple landmark localization using CNNs, in: MICCAI, vol. 9901, 2016, pp. 230–238.

[26] T. Pfister, J. Charles, A. Zisserman, Flowing convnets for human pose estimation in videos, in: IEEE International Conference on Computer Vision, ICCV, 2015, pp. 1913–1921.

[27] P. Viola, M. Jones, Rapid object detection using a boosted cascade of simple features, in: CVPR, Vol. 1, 2001, pp. 511–518.

[28] H. Ragheb, N. Thacker, P. Bromiley, D. Tautz, A. Schunke, Quantitative shape analysis with weighted covariance estimates for increased statistical efficiency, Frontiers in Zoology 10 (16) (2013).

[29] S. Ren, X. Cao, Y. Wei, J. Sun, Face alignment via regressing local binary features, IEEE Transactions on Image Processing 25 (3) (Mar. 2016) 1233–1245.

[30] O. Ronneberger, P. Fischer, T. Brox, U-Net: convolutional networks for biomedical image segmentation, in: N. Navab, J. Hornegger, W.M. Wells, A.F. Frangi (Eds.), Medical Image Computing and Computer-Assisted Intervention – MICCAI 2015, Springer International Publishing, Cham, 2015, pp. 234–241.

[31] S.M. Pizer, P. Fletcher, S. Joshi, et al., Deformable M-Reps for 3D medical image segmentation, International Journal of Computer Vision 2–3 (55) (2003) 85–106.

[32] Y. Sun, X. Wang, X. Tang, Deep convolutional network cascade for facial point detection, in: IEEE Conference on Computer Vision and Pattern Recognition, 2013, pp. 3476–3483.

[33] M.E. Tipping, C. Bishop, Probabilistic principal component analysis, Journal of the Royal Statistical Society, Series B 21 (3) (Jan. 1999) 611–622.

[34] G. Tzimiropoulos, M. Pantic, Fast algorithms for fitting active appearance models to unconstrained images, International Journal of Computer Vision 122 (1) (Mar. 2017) 17–33.

[35] Xuehan Xiong, F. De la Torre, Supervised descent method and its application to face alignment, in: IEEE CVPR, 2013.

CHAPTER 25

Computer-integrated interventional medicine: A 30 year perspective

Russell H. Taylor[a]

Department of Computer Science, Johns Hopkins University, Baltimore, MD, United States

Contents

25.1. Introduction: a three-way partnership between humans, technology, and information to improve patient care 599
25.2. The information flow in computer-integrated interventional medicine 603
    25.2.1 Patient-specific information 604
    25.2.2 Patient-specific models 604
    25.2.3 Diagnosis 605
    25.2.4 Treatment planning 605
    25.2.5 Intervention 606
    25.2.6 Assessment and follow-up 607
    25.2.7 Multipatient information and statistical analysis 607
    25.2.8 Intensive care, rehabilitation, and other treatment venues 608
25.3. Intraoperative systems for CIIM 608
    25.3.1 Intraoperative imaging systems 609
    25.3.2 Navigational trackers 611
    25.3.3 Robotic devices 612
    25.3.4 Human–machine interfaces 614
25.4. Emerging research themes 615
References 616

25.1. Introduction: a three-way partnership between humans, technology, and information to improve patient care

The potential of computer-assisted processes to fundamentally change the practice of medicine has long been recognized. Over the past 30 years, we have seen the emergence of systems that incorporate imaging, robots, and other technology to enhance patient care. A three-way partnership between physicians, technology, and information

---

[a] **Disclosures:** Some of the work reported in this chapter incorporates intellectual property that is owned by Johns Hopkins University and that has been or may be licensed to outside entities, including Intuitive Surgical, Varian Medical Systems, Philips Nuclear Medicine, Galen Robotics, and other corporate entities. The author has received or may receive some portion of the license fees. In addition, the author is a paid consultant to Galen Robotics and has an equity interest in that company. These arrangements have been reviewed and approved by JHU in accordance with its conflict of interest policy.

Handbook of Medical Image Computing and Computer Assisted Intervention
https://doi.org/10.1016/B978-0-12-816176-0.00030-2

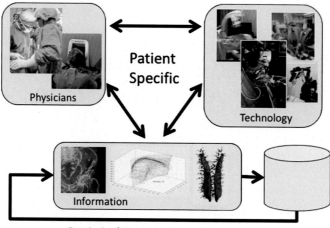

Statistical Process Improvement

Figure: Copyright © Russell Taylor, 2019, Used by permission

Figure 25.1 *This three-way partnership* between physicians, technology, and information can transcend human limitations in treating individual patients. Further, the information from each individual intervention can be used to help determine the best way to treat future patients.

is beginning to have the same impact on patient care that a comparable partnership has had on industrial production and other sectors of our society. (See Fig. 25.1.)

Humans are tool makers, and surgical instruments (first made of stone and later of metal) have been used in surgery since prehistoric times. As technology and manufacturing processes improved, these tools became more sophisticated. The introduction of X-ray (and later other) imaging devices further enhanced treatment capabilities by giving physicians the ability to visualize anatomy beneath the surface of tissues. Combined with advances in medical knowledge, sterile processes, and anesthesia, these technological advances enabled dramatic improvements in the ability of physicians to treat a wide range of conditions.

Traditionally, physicians have relied overwhelmingly on their own direct senses, memory, and judgment to guide them in planning, guiding, and carrying out interventional procedures. As elsewhere in our society, computers have begun to have a profound effect on interventional medicine by exploiting the complementary capabilities of humans, technology, and computer-based information processing (see Table 25.1). Medical imaging is heavily dependent on computation. Interventional devices are increasingly incorporating sophisticated computer control. Computer-based methods provide unprecedented ability to combine multiple forms of information and to use the results to help control surgical devices or to provide intraoperative guidance during procedures.

In addition to enabling increased precision, lower invasiveness, and improved safety for individual patients, computer-integrated interventional systems can enable improve-

Table 25.1 Complementary strengths and limitations of humans, technology, and computers.

	Strengths	Limitations
Humans	Astonishingly versatile Able to synthesize information from multiple sources & relate it to task at hand Excellent judgment & ability to modify plans in response to new circumstances Excellent vision, visual processing, and pattern recognition Reasonable short- and long-term memory Excellent eye–hand coordination Reasonable strength Excellent dexterity and good manipulation precision within fairly broad range Excellent tactile and force sensing within fairly broad range	Occasionally forgetful and may omit critical steps in procedures Limited ability to recall massive amounts of information Vision limited to specific spectrum Limited visual acuity for tiny structures Unable to see through tissue Hands are big and require large openings to access internal structures Affected by ionizing radiation, chemical, and biological contaminants Very limited geometric accuracy Hand tremor limits ability to perform very precise manipulation tasks Susceptible to fatigue Not naturally sterile – can spread infections
Technology	Capable of extremely precise motions Capable of providing very high degrees of geometric accuracy Devices can be made very small (much smaller than human hands) Can be made much stronger than humans Not necessarily affected by ionizing radiation Multiple imaging devices can sense anatomy beneath tissue surfaces Can sense wavelengths and forces beyond human perceptual thresholds Can sense biological processes Can be sterilized	Fabrication processes and materials still limit device capabilities, especially at small sizes Some materials create biocompatibility problems Device and system reliability can be difficult to guarantee Advanced imaging and robotic systems are complex, and system verification can be challenging Systems can present safety challenges both for patients and medical personnel

(continued on next page)

Table 25.1 (*continued*)

	Strengths	Limitations
Computers and information technology	Can store and retrieve vast quantities of information indefinitely Can transform complex sensor information into images that are understandable by humans and are also useful in further computations Can control complex machinery such as robots or other therapy devices Can enable sophisticated visualization and "augmented reality" methods for displaying information Increasingly able to perform sophisticated image segmentation and interpretation tasks Capable of developing statistical models of anatomy & using these in clinical applications Increasingly powerful machine learning and optimization capabilities Computational power still increasing exponentially	Ability to understand human intention is still limited Programming is complicated and often contains errors System security and system integrity are difficult to ensure Machine learning methods still developing Image segmentation and interpretation capabilities still inferior to humans in most cases (though progress is being made) Less ability to cope with unexpected or unfamiliar input

ment in treatment processes, in many of the same ways that computer-integrated manufacturing systems have enabled advanced electronics manufacturing or flight data recorders have enabled aviation safety. Computer-assisted processes tend to be more consistent than traditional "freehand" processes. The information used in each individual procedure can be saved, along with outcome and other follow-up data. Statistical methods can then be used to help assess effectiveness of different treatment options and to assist patient-specific diagnosis and planning for future patients. Similarly, an information-aware operating room or interventional suite can provide information for improving clinical workflow and physician training.

A 30-year evolution from "CAS" to "CAI" to "CIIM": Computers and computer-controlled systems have played a role in medicine since at least the 1950s [1,2]. Radiation therapy [3] has been heavily dependent on computing for dosimetry planning, and the radiation beam systems are computer-controlled. The emergence of adequately powerful and relatively inexpensive computer workstations in the 1980s and

1990s facilitated the introduction of computers into operating room settings for neurosurgery [4–11], ENT [12,13], orthopaedics [14–19], and other clinical applications [20–23]. These systems were often referred to as "computer assisted surgery (CAS)" systems, and this phrase is still commonly used for surgical navigation systems. Since not all interventional procedures are strictly surgery, others introduced phrases like "computer assisted medical interventions (CAMI)" [24] or "computer assisted Interventions (CAI)" for much the same concepts.[1] My personal preference for a number of years has been "computer-integrated surgery (CIS)" [25] or "computer-integrated interventional medicine (CIIM)", emphasizing the importance of computing throughout the entire treatment cycle and the increasingly strong parallels with computer-integrated manufacturing. This nomenclature seems to me to be even more apropos today, as statistical process control and machine learning methods are becoming more and more prevalent in interventional medicine and at the MICCAI conference.

The balance of this chapter is intended to provide an introduction to the "CAI" portion of this book. In it, I will first discuss the information flow associated with CIIM processes, and I will briefly mention some of the emerging research issues associated with each component subprocess. Next, I will outline the basic architectural components of intraoperative CIIM systems and will provide brief forward links to the remaining chapters in this section of the book. Finally, I will offer some thoughts about future research opportunities and system evolution.

25.2. The information flow in computer-integrated interventional medicine

The information and work flow in computer-integrated interventional medicine is illustrated in Fig. 25.2. The brief discussion below will discuss each of the components in this picture and will identify a few of the key research issues involved. It is also important to remember that the actual workflow occurs at many different time scales and is often a much more iterative process than this simple figure indicates. Very broadly, the blue arrows within the figure emphasize the use of information to treat each patient in an optimal way, and the red arrows emphasize the use of statistical methods to improve treatment for future patients.

---

[1] **One historical note.** When the MICCAI conference was formed in 1998 from the merger of three separate meetings – "Visualization in Biomedical Computing (VBC)", "Medical Robotics and Computer Assisted Surgery", and "Computer Vision, Virtual Reality, and Robotics in Medicine (CVRMED)" – there was considerable discussion about what to call the combined meeting. The "Medical Image Computing (MIC)" part was fairly clear, but how to recognize the other aspects of the meeting was more difficult. One candidate was "Medical Image Computing and Robotics (MICR)", which I thought was too restrictive. Another was "MICCAS", which again seemed too restrictive. In the end, we settled on "Computer Assisted Interventions (CAI)".

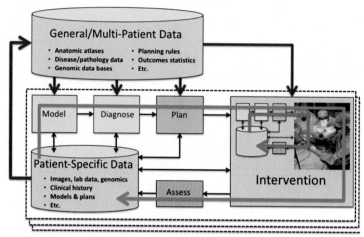

Figure: Copyright © Russell Taylor, 2019, Used by permission

Figure 25.2 *The information flow in computer-integrated interventional medicine.* The blue arrows illustrate the use of information for treating individual patients. The red arrows illustrate the ability of statistical methods to combine the experience gained from treating many patients to improve treatment processes for future patients.

25.2.1 Patient-specific information

Essentially, we are dealing with a unified electronic health record (EHR) for each individual patient, containing all available data about that patient that may be useful in diagnosis, treatment planning, plan execution, assessment, and follow-up. In the case of surgical interventions, much of this information may be in the form of medical images taken before, during, or after the intervention. It may also include other clinical data such as lab results, past history, genomic data, etc., as well information derived from this data, such as models derived from images, diagnoses, treatment plans, and other information that may be used during the intervention itself.

Research issues. In addition to research issues associated with individual steps in the interventional workflow (discussed below), there are challenges relating to extending traditional EHRs to fully support computer-integrated interventions. These include issues associated with the acquiring, storing and retrieving the individual images and other sensor data. Many of the details depend on the individual sensing modality, but common themes include extending the support provided by conventional PACS systems to support real-time access, together with means for dynamically adjusting or controlling intraoperative imaging devices or sensors.

25.2.2 Patient-specific models

Generally, the unprocessed medical images and other data associated with an individual must be processed into a form that is useful for the various steps of the treatment process. The goal here is to produce data structures that support the various computational and visualization processes associated with diagnosis, planning, intervention, and assessment. Further, the resulting models and the algorithms to produce them need to be computationally efficient, especially if they are to be used to update intraoperative models of for decision support or control of intraoperative treatment processes.

Research issues. There are many research issues (segmentation, registration, etc.) associated with the analysis of medical images in order to construct models of the patient's anatomy. Many of these are discussed in the first ("MIC") section of this book. Of particular importance for interventional systems is the requirement that these models often need to be constructed or updated in real time in response to deforming anatomy or intraoperative sensing. There is also increasing use of prior statistical information about patient anatomy to assist in image segmentation and in "labeling" of anatomic structures and to infer information that may not be present in patient-specific data. Another emerging challenge is finding ways to correlate nonanatomic data in the medical record into a usable and comprehensive model.

25.2.3 Diagnosis

The goal of diagnosis is to determine what is wrong with the patient. Generally, this process relies heavily on human judgment and experience, although computers are playing an increasingly important role, both in synthesizing and presenting all relevant information about the patient and in relating this data to diagnostic data bases and rule sets derived from statistical analysis of many prior cases.

Research issues. Better machine learning methods are needed to develop effective decision support rules synthesizing multiple sources of information. For example, cancer diagnosis and staging may require information from medical images, genomics, histology, and other information in the patient's clinical history. Within image analysis, better methods to recognize abnormal anatomy are needed. In addition, better methods for visualizing and interacting with patient models and other data are needed.

25.2.4 Treatment planning

Once a diagnosis is made, a decision must be made about how best to treat the patient. These decisions may be made by an individual physician, but they are increasingly made by multispecialty teams of physicians who can help choose the best treatment modality, based on the patient's specific characteristics and clinical experience and outcomes for previous similar patients. Once an overall treatment approach has been selected, additional planning is usually required to produce more detailed information needed to carry out the planned intervention. For example, a radiation therapy plan needs to include the planned dose distribution, the machine settings required to produce the desired dose, and information needed to align the patient to the radiation therapy machine. The likelihood of complications from the treatment may be predicted and steps to ameliorate these effects may also be planned. A surgical intervention might similarly include models of the targeted anatomy, details of the planned surgical approach, and information needed for plan-to-patient registration. Although a complete "rehearsal" of a planned surgical intervention is seldom done, some "key frame" animations or visualizations may sometimes be prepared. Treatment planning is discussed further in Chapter 32 of this book.

Research issues. Treatment planning involves many of the same research issues as diagnosis, especially in the earlier stages of providing decision support for selecting the most appropriate treatment strategy for a specific patient, based on experience with previous similar patients. Again, this phase involves many issues of machine learning and combining many sources of (often incomplete) information from many patients. Issues involved in formulating specific plans, once a basic strategy is chosen may include significant geometric planning for things like surgical approach, planning for intraoperative imaging and other sensing needed for registration and feedback, estimation of predicted accuracy of treatment delivery, etc. Surgical simulations for the purpose of planning or to provide reference predictions for intraoperative control also pose significant research opportunities. One key aspect of any treatment plan is that it must be executable in order to be useful. Consequently, there are important research issues in finding plan representations that permit very efficient intraoperative execution.

25.2.5 Intervention

Essentially all the processes in the interventional workflow (sensing, modeling, diagnosis, planning, executing, and assessment) may be found at multiple time scales within the actual intervention. Here, we focus on what happens within the operating room or interventional suite. Intraoperative imaging devices, navigational trackers, or other sensors are used to register the preoperative models and interventional plan to the physical patient. Once this step is accomplished, a wide variety of technology may be used to assist the physician in carrying out the planned procedure. Typical examples include robotic systems, "augmented reality" displays, surgical navigation systems, and other devices. Intraoperative imaging is often incorporated for guidance and control feedback and for assessing the results of the procedure as work proceeds. Also, we are beginning to see the use of room cameras and other sensors to monitor surgical workflow and teamwork within the room. Before, during, and after the procedure, there are also computer-integrated processes accessing hospital databases to monitor supplies uses, assist in room and personnel scheduling, etc.

Research issues. Virtually all research issues concerning medical imaging (acquisition, segmentation, registration) and modeling are highly relevant during the intervention phase. Modalities such as video images from microscopes and endoscopes and intraoperative ultrasound are especially natural for intraoperative use. One distinguishing feature within the interventional environment is the requirement for real time performance, with acceptable latencies ranging from 30 milliseconds up to 1–2 minutes, depending on application. In cancer cases, it is not uncommon to perform histology to verify resection margins, and there is increasing interest in intraoperative imaging using modalities such as confocal microscopy to speed up this process. There are also significant research issues involving human–machine interfaces, including latency, ergonomics, visualization, and haptics. Other issues include real time sensing and control for robotic devices and integration and communication for multiple devices and subsystems within the operating room.

As operating rooms become increasingly computer-intensive, a huge amount of data may be generated. With the explosion of inexpensive data storage capacity, it is (in principle) possible to capture and retain all of this data to provide a comprehensive record of what actually was done in each procedure for each patient. This "flight data recorder" capability can be used both for per-patient assessments and for statistical studies designed to improve care for future patients (§25.2.7). One important area for research is development of efficient online methods for compressing or segmenting this data stream to retain the most relevant data. In addition to use in postoperative analysis, such online processes may potentially be used to provide "near miss" safety warnings or to adapt the forms of assistance provided, depending on the particular subtasks being performed.

25.2.6 Assessment and follow-up

Postoperative images and other tests are routinely done to assess the technical and clinical results of the procedure. This stage involves many of the same technologies and computational methods used in preoperative modeling, diagnosis, and interventional stages. Based on the results, further interventional or postoperative care steps may be planned and carried out.

Research issues. Many of the research issues involved in assessment are the same as those in earlier stages of the process. Several issues of particular salience include the challenge of comparing predicted versus achieved technical results from the intervention, developing more sensitive and effective clinical outcomes measures, and detecting incipient complications resulting from the intervention.

25.2.7 Multipatient information and statistical analysis

At least since the time of Imhotep, medicine has been fundamentally an empirical, experience-driven undertaking. Modern computer and information technology has the potential to significantly enhance the ability of physicians to diagnose and treat disease and deformity. Every step of the patient-specific treatment cycle discussed in §25.2.2–§25.2.6 relies on prior knowledge obtained from experience with prior patients. This information includes labeled "atlases" and statistical models of patient anatomy, physiology, and pathology, genomic data bases, algorithms for helping develop and optimize interventional plans, statistical data bases and methods for predicting the results that may be expected from different interventional options, etc.

Research issues. The creation of a truly integrated information system to assist in interventional medicine presents enormous challenges at every level. These include the ability to retrieve, index, and search data from thousands of individual patients for the purposes of statistical analysis and machine learning while also preserving patient privacy. Once the data are obtained, the machine learning, information fusion, and statistical model representations themselves present significant research challenges. One of the great research challenges and great opportunities for "surgical data science" is developing effective models linking outcomes to patient data in a way that will allow prediction of outcomes for different treatment plans for specific patients. Other research needs include development of robust methods for analyzing surgical workflow and surgical task performance. These may be used both in skill assessment for surgical training and (potentially) in correlating variations in specific surgical task execution with outcomes.

25.2.8 Intensive care, rehabilitation, and other treatment venues

Although the discussion in this section has focused on active treatment modalities such as surgery, interventional radiology, or radiation oncology, the overall concepts are more broadly applicable. For example, many of the data gathering, work flow analysis, and machine-learning based decision support methods discussed above are applicable in intensive care units (ICUs). Similarly, rehabilitation after surgery or stroke includes all the steps of data gathering, modeling, diagnosis, treatment planning, and assessment. Both ICU and rehabilitation are properly subjects of this expanded notion of "Surgical Data Science" [26,27], which is explored further in Chapter 38. More generally, "Surgical Data Science" should naturally be considered within the broader context of "Medical Data Science", including drug therapies and home health care.

25.3. Intraoperative systems for CIIM

Fig. 25.3 illustrates the emerging architecture of a computer-integrated interventional room. At the heart is a powerful **computational infrastructure**, which acts as an information and control hub for activities within the room. Key functions for this system include:

- **Information fusion**, combining information from preoperative patient models and other data, intraoperative imaging systems, video cameras, robots, surgeon interfaces, patient monitors, and other sensors within the room;

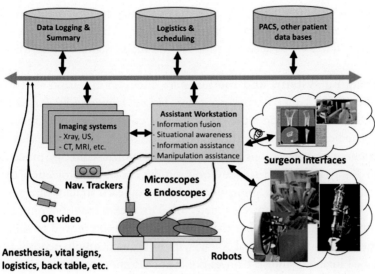

Figure: Copyright © Russell Taylor, 2019, Used by permission

Figure 25.3 The information-intensive interventional suite.

- **Situational awareness**, i.e., relating the fused information to the current interventional plan, in order to provide appropriate assistance at each step in the procedure;
- **Information assistance** that can be used by the surgeon and other personnel within the interventional room to carry out the procedure; and
- **Manipulation assistance** using robotic devices to manipulate the patient or surgical tools.

The intraoperative system also includes interfaces to the broader hospital information infrastructure, including the PACS system, other patient data bases, operating room scheduling & supplies logistics systems, and data logging capabilities.

As mentioned, this is an *emerging* architecture that has yet to be fully implemented, although the basic elements can be seen in current practice and there have been a number of efforts to develop interoperability and communication standards for perioperative use (e.g., [28,29]).

25.3.1 Intraoperative imaging systems

Although diagnostic imaging systems designed for use in diagnosis and treatment planning are often used intraoperatively, the requirements for intraoperative imaging are rather different. Whereas the main requirement for most diagnostic systems is *image quality*, the overriding requirement for intraoperative imaging is *timeliness*. Although quality is still important, a perfect image obtained some hours (or even several minutes) after it is taken is not so useful in an operating room setting. Generally, one needs the images to provide sufficient information for positioning an instrument relative to target anatomy or monitoring an interventional process within acceptable latencies that may range from fractions of seconds to a few minutes, depending on the particular task.

X-ray imaging systems and methods are discussed in Chapter 26. Mobile fluoroscopic c-arms and larger fixed c-arms are designed specifically for interventional applications. Since X-ray images provide excellent contrast for bone, they are widely used in orthopaedics. Combined with suitable contrast material, they are also commonly used for angiographic applications and other interventional radiology procedures. One limitation of X-ray images is that they only produce a single projection through the patient, essentially showing the absorption of X-rays on each straight line path from the X-ray source to each pixel on an X-ray detector. This means that obtaining accurate 3D information typically requires either that the X-ray c-arm be moved to different poses relative to the patient or that several X-ray systems be used simultaneously (e.g., in so-called "biplane" imaging suites). Conventional CT scanners produce very high quality 3D X-ray volume images. Although these systems are expensive and can be difficult to deploy in operating rooms, they are becoming more common in specialized surgical suites, where they are used periodically to perform 3D assessments on the progress of an intervention. They are also used more commonly for guidance of needle placement procedures such as biopsies. Large motorized c-arm systems typically provide "cone beam CT" volume images. Although these systems generally do not produce quite as good images as those from high quality CT scanners, they are extremely versatile and well suited to interventional applications. One advantage is that the CT volumes produced are inherently coregistered with individual X-ray projections taken with the same system.

Ultrasound (US) is, in many ways, an ideal modality for interventional use. Ultrasound is fast, inexpensive, and nonionizing. Systems for producing both 2D cross-sectional and 3D volumetric images are readily available, and sophisticated techniques such as ultrasound elastography (e.g., [30–33]), ultrasound thermography [34], and photoacoustic imaging (e.g., [35–40]) provide many options for guiding and monitoring interventional processes. Although ultrasound probes are typically manipulated freehand, there is increasing interest in the use of robots for this purpose (e.g., [32,41–51]). The state-of-the-art is discussed in Chapter 28.

Magnetic resonance imaging (MRI) systems produce superb soft tissue contrast and also are capable of imaging many biological processes. Their potential for use in interventional applications has long been recognized [52,53], as have many of the practical difficulties with using them in interventional applications. The fundamental challenges involve preserving MR compatibility within a surgical environment and working in a confined space. Although "open" MRI systems (e.g., [54–56]) have been developed for intraoperative use, the field strength (and image resolution) for these systems has typically been less than that for more conventional "closed tunnel" systems. However, the development of high field "short" and "wide" bore closed systems and the use of robotics (e.g., [57–61]) within the MR system bore has led to increasing use of interventional MRI. The state-of-the-art is discussed in Chapter 27.

Video cameras are becoming more and more prevalent in the operating room. The most common are simple monoscopic or stereoscopic video cameras/display systems used with video endoscopes or surgical microscopes. However, there is increasing emphasis on processing the video data streams for purposes such as anatomic modeling & registration, tracking of surgical instruments, or support of augmented reality information supports for the surgeon. There has also been recent work on use of collections of in-room cameras to track intraoperative workflow. The state-of-the-art is discussed in Chapter 29.

25.3.2 Navigational trackers

Surgical navigation systems were introduced in the 1980s to provide intraoperative information support to surgeons. Essentially, these systems track surgical tools and other objects within the operating room and display the positions of tools relative to registered images of the patient's anatomy. The initial applications were for neurosurgery [62], but these systems were soon applied to orthopaedics [63,64], craniofacial surgery [65–67], ENT [12], and other medical applications for which precise location of tools relative to anatomic targets is important. The first tracking devices were encoded mechanical linkages (e.g., [4,68]), but ultrasound [6,69], electromagnetic (e.g., [70,71]), and optical trackers (e.g., [66,72–74]) have all been used. Currently, most commercial systems use electromagnetic (e.g., [75,76]) or optical (e.g., [77–79]) tracking devices. The optical trackers can be very accurate, but have some drawbacks. Since the optical targets being tracked must be outside the patient's body, any angular uncertainty in determining tracking target orientation can increase the positional uncertainty of a tool tip locate some distance away. Similarly, the requirement to maintain a clear line of sight between the tracking camera and the target can significantly complicate surgical workflow. Electromagnetic (EM) tracking systems do not have line of sight restrictions, and the tracking targets are commonly embedded in surgical tools or catheters. The tracking targets can also be made to be quite small. On the other hand, EM systems can suffer from signal strength and field distortions caused by nearby metal or magnetic objects or from sources of EM interference, which can constrain the choice of surgical tools and other equipment. The choice of which system is most appropriate for a given application requires careful analysis of specific requirements and of how various measurement errors interact. A more extensive discussion of the state of the art may be found in Chapter 31.

25.3.3 Robotic devices

Robotic devices can transcend human limitations in many ways, including geometric accuracy, precision, ability to manipulate tools in very confined spaces, physical strength, etc. And there has been a steady evolution of systems that exploit their capabilities to improve patient care.

Initial applications focused on geometric accuracy. Generally, these applications require that the robot be accurately registered to images used either in pre-treatment planning or for intraoperative control of the system. Although the fact is sometimes overlooked, the first "medical robots" arguably were radiation beam therapy systems [3, 80], and these systems continue to be widely deployed. Within "surgical" applications, robotic systems positioning a needle guide for stereotactic neurosurgery were introduced in the late 1980s and early 1990s [9,11,81–83]. Since then, many robotic systems for image-guided needle placement have been developed (e.g., [60,61,84–89]), often exploiting the ability of the robot to work in X-ray, MRI, or other imaging environments. Other applications exploiting the geometric accuracy of robotic devices include systems for joint reconstruction surgery (e.g., [19,90–92]), spine surgery (e.g., [93,94]), craniofacial surgery (e.g., [95,96]), and ENT surgery (e.g., [97–100]).

By far the most successful use of robotic devices for interventional applications has been in the area of minimally-invasive surgery (MIS). Here, the first systems (e.g., [101, 102]) manipulated laparoscopic cameras, typically with some form of joystick, foot pedal, or voice interface to command motion of the camera. Several early research groups also explored the possibility of video tracking of surgical instruments or anatomic landmarks for controlling endoscope motion (e.g., [102,103]). Subsequent systems (e.g., [104,105]) provided high dexterity telemanipulation of surgical instruments with stereo visualization. Of commercial systems, the Intuitive Surgical da Vinci systems (Intuitive Surgical, Sunnyvale, Ca. [106]) has been very widely deployed, although several competitor systems are also available commercially, and other manufacturers are expected to enter the market soon. The primary value proposition (to the surgeon) for these systems is "telepresence" [107] – i.e., giving the surgeon the feeling that he or she is operating inside the patient's body, with surgical tool motions following the motion of high dexterity hand controllers. Within this paradigm, the basic robotic system functions as a platform that can be customized for particular application by the use of a variety of custom tools manipulated by the robot. In recent years, these systems have begun to evolve to exploit the ability of a computer to augment the information available to the surgeon through integrated imaging or "augmented reality" overlays or to assist in controlling the surgical tools by means of "virtual fixtures" (e.g., [108–114]).

As robotic devices are developed to operate in progressively confined spaces, they necessarily become smaller. This need for miniaturization poses significant design and manufacturability challenges. One response has been to replace traditional mechanisms with continuum mechanisms [115]. These systems – which are usually teleoperated –

pose their own design, control, and sensing challenges. The use of highly flexible robotic systems for endoluminal, transluminal, and intravascular applications is a growing focus area for research, and we are beginning to see a number of clinically deployed systems for these applications (e.g., [116–120]).

Systems exploiting the precision of robotic devices for microsurgery and similar applications were also introduced in the late 1980s (e.g., [121–123]), and this area has been an active focus for research ever since. Here, the value proposition for surgeons is the ability to make very small, controlled motions without the effects of hand tremor. In addition to MIS, other common application domains include ophthalmology [124], neurosurgery, "open" microsurgery.

Although teleoperation is often used as the primary means for surgeons to control motion of the robot, other methods are also possible. Perhaps the most common alternative is what I call "steady hand" cooperative control [125], in which the surgeon and the robot hold the surgical tool. A force sensor detects forces exerted by the surgeon, and the robot moves to comply. Since the robot makes the actual motion, the motion can be very stable and precise, and virtual fixtures or other methods can be used to assist the surgeon. This control method has been used in many applications, including orthopaedics [19,92,126], endoscopic surgery [102], ophthalmology [125,127,128], otology [128–130], and other head-and-neck procedures [100,131,132]. One advantage for microsurgery applications is that it is highly intuitive for most surgeons and can be introduced with minimum disruption to clinical workflow.

Research issues. A more extensive discussion of robotic systems may be found in Chapter 34. Broadly, the research issues associated with robotic interventional devices are similar to those in other subfields of robotics. These include basic technology, materials, "scaling" for very small sizes with high dexterity, integration of sensing & control, etc. Although not unique to interventional robots, several topics seem especially pertinent for this area. Examples include safety, sterility, and autonomy. This last topic has received considerable discussion, within the popular press, regulatory bodies, and the research community. One recent *Science Robotics* editorial [133] discusses six levels of autonomy in medical robots and lays out some of the considerations involved. Much of the popular discussion has centered on the distinction between systems in which the robot motions directly correspond to motions of a "master" hand controller or forces exerted by the surgeon on a tool and those in which the computer uses information about the surgical task in some more complex way.

In considering autonomy, research issues fall into two broad categories: (1) how can a human tell the computer unambiguously what the system is to do; and (2) how can the system reliably execute what it is instructed to do? The answers to these questions for currently deployed have so far been rather simple. In the case of teleoperation or "steady hand" control, the computer must map motions of the hand controller or forces exerted by the surgeon directly into corresponding robot motions. Decisions on what motions to command are still made by the surgeon. Similarly, tool paths in bone machining robots are computed from medical images, and the computed determines the corresponding robot motions after the planning images and robot coordinates are registered to the patient in the operating room. The challenge comes in cases where more complex decisions must be made (often interactively) based on a shared situational awareness between the human and the computer, as discussed in Sect. 25.2, above.

25.3.4 Human–machine interfaces

Effective two-way human–machine communication is essential for computer-integrated interventional systems, in which physicians and other medical personnel are cooperating with computer-based technology to treat patients. Human–machine interfaces are discussed in Chapter 33.

The earliest widely deployed systems primarily used computer terminals and display monitors for this purpose. For example, surgical navigation systems typically use a cross-hair or circular cursor to indicate the position of a tracked surgical tool relative to medical images which have been registered to the patient's anatomy. Similarly, radiation therapy treatments are planned using conventional interactive computer display terminals, as are many orthopaedic, craniofacial, and other image-based procedures. Comparable displays are frequently used within the operating room to provide information feedback during the procedure and for interactive replanning. Conventional keyboards and mice are sometimes used intraoperatively, but sterility constraints have led researchers to explore alternative technologies, including sterile touch screens, video gesture recognition, and voice recognition.

Within telerobotic systems, the dominant interface is some combination of joystick-like hand controllers and video display. With proper attention to ergonomic factors, systems like the da Vinci surgical robots can provide a strong sense for the physician that he or she is inside the patient's body [107,134–136]. One significant limitation with commercially deployed systems has been that they provide only limited haptic feedback through the hand controllers of tool-to-tissue interaction forces, although this area has been a subject of considerable research [137–139]. There has also been considerable interest in developing non-haptic "sensory substitution" methods for displaying tool-tissue forces [140] and other sensory data. Commonly used methods include video overlays (e.g., [141,142]) or auditory cues (e.g., [143]). Auditory feedback is often preferred by physicians in situations where video displays may prove distracting from close visual attention to the anatomy being manipulated.

More generally, there is increasing interest in augmented reality methods in surgery and other medical applications [144–147]. Voice interfaces for medical applications have been explored since at least the 1980s (e.g., [23,104,148,149]). As technology has improved, voice interfaces are becoming more and more sophisticated and are increasingly integrated with augmented reality applications.

25.4. Emerging research themes

Many of the important research issues associated with CIIM systems have already been mentioned earlier in this chapter and are expanded upon further in subsequent chapters in this volume. Here is a brief mention of a few points that I see as particularly salient in coming years in further enhancing the fundamental three-way partnership of computer-integrated interventional medicine.

- **Physician interactions with CIIM systems.** Key research areas include sophisticated systems for real-time intraoperative decision support, immersive environments for displaying pertinent information to the physician, methods for physicians to unambiguously express what the system is to do, and ergonomic optimization of human–machine interfaces to support meaningful interaction without getting in the physician's way or slowing down the procedure. Similarly, further advances are needed for computers to track and interpret human activity in interventional rooms, and to use this capability both to provide context-appropriate assistance during procedures and to develop skill metrics for surgical training.

- **Technology and devices.** Broadly, we can expect continued advances in device technology across the board. Novel devices permitting useful work on progressively smaller scale (down to microns) will enable less invasive and better targeted interventions. Together with this, we may expect to see robotic systems with higher dexterity and precision at fine scales. Similarly, both hand-held and robotically manipulated tools will increasingly incorporate devices for sensing tool-to-tissue interactions and local tissue properties. Continued development of novel imaging methods and "medical image computing methods" will play a crucial role in enhancing the information available within interventional rooms. We may expect imaging capabilities to be more fully integrated with interventional systems, and the ability of robotic systems to manipulate image sensors will be exploited in novel ways.

- **Information.** Although the information associated with the preoperative and intraoperative aspects of interventional medicine is crucial for improving patient care, it will become more and more important to focus on all aspects of the treatment cycle, and to integrate all this information to provide optimal care. One crucial need is to develop better methods for comprehensive modeling of all relevant aspects of the patient state for each stage of the intervention and to make this information available in a form and in a timely enough manner so that it can be used effectively at all stages of the treatment cycle. Another need is development of better metrics and methods for relating surgical technical endpoints to clinical results, together with methods for using these methods to improve treatment planning.

Finally, we should again emphasize that we are concerned with *systems* that integrate these three broad areas.

References

[1] M. Lipkin, Historical background on the origin of computer medicine, in: Proc Annu Symp Appl Med Care, Nov 7, 1984, pp. 987–990, PMC2578563.

[2] L.P. Sewell, L.Q. Thede, Computer development and health care information systems 1950 to present, in: Informatics and Nursing: Opportunities and Challenges, 4th edition, Lippincott Williams & Wilkins, Philadelphia, 2013, online supplemental material, http://dlthede.net/informatics/chap01introni/healthcare_computers.html.

[3] J.M. Slater, From X-rays to ion beams: a short history of radiation therapy, in: U. Linz (Ed.), Ion Beam Therapy, Springer-Verlag, Berlin, 2012, pp. 3–15.

[4] Y. Kosugi, E. Watanabe, J. Goto, T. Watanabe, S. Yoshimoto, K. Takakura, J. Ikebe, An articulated neurosurgical navigation system using MRI and CT images, IEEE Transactions on Biomedical Engineering (February 1988) 147–152.

[5] E. Watanabe, The neuronavigator: a computer-controlled navigation system in neurosurgery, in: R.H. Taylor, S. Lavallee, G. Burdea, R. Mosges (Eds.), Computer-Integrated Surgery, MIT Press, Cambridge, Mass., 1996, pp. 319–327.

[6] H.F. Reinhardt, Neuronavigation: a ten years review, in: R. Taylor, S. Lavallee, G. Burdea, R. Moegses (Eds.), Computer-Integrated Surgery, MIT Press, Cambridge, 1996, pp. 329–342.

[7] R.L. Galloway, C.A. Edwards, J.G. Thomas, S. Schreiner, R.J. Maciunas, A new device for interactive, image guided surgery, in: Proc. SPIE Medical Imaging V, 1991.

[8] J.M. Drake, M. Joy, A. Goldenberg, D. Kreindler, Robotic and computer assisted resection of brain tumors, in: Fifth Int. Conf. on Advanced Robotics, Pisa, 1991, pp. 888–892.

[9] P. Cinquin, J. Troccaz, J. Demongeot, S. Lavallee, G. Champleboux, L. Brunie, F. Leitner, P. Sautot, B. Mazier, A. Perez, M. Djaid, T. Fortin, M. Chenic, A. Chapel, IGOR: image guided operating robot, Innovation et Technologie en Biologie et Medicine 13 (4) (1992) 374–394.

[10] Y.S. Kwoh, J. Hou, E.A. Jonckheere, S. Hayati, A robot with improved absolute positioning accuracy for CT guided stereotactic brain surgery, IEEE Transactions on Biomedical Engineering 35 (1988) 153–160.

[11] A.L. Benabid, S. Lavallee, D. Hoffmann, P. Cinquin, J. Demongeot, F. Danel, Potential use of robots in endoscopic neurosurgery, Acta Neurochirurgica. Supplementum 54 (1992) 93–97.

[12] L. Adams, J.M. Gilsbach, W. Krybus, D. Meyer-Ebrecht, R. Mosges, G. Schlondorff, CAS – a navigation support for surgery, in: 3D Imaging in Medicine, Springer-Verlag, Berlin, Heidelberg, 1990, pp. 411–423.

[13] G. Schlöndorff, Computer-assisted surgery: historical remarks, Computer Aided Surgery 3–4 (1998) 150–152, https://doi.org/10.3109/10929089809148137.

[14] R. Haaker, History of computer-assisted surgery, in: R. Haaker, W. Konermann (Eds.), Computer and Template Assisted Orthopedic Surgery, Springer Berlin Heidelberg, Berlin, Heidelberg, 2013, pp. 3–9.

[15] G. Brandt, K. Radermacher, S. Lavallee, H.-W. Staudte, G. Rau, A compact robot for image-guided orthopaedic surgery: concept and preliminary results, in: Proc. First Joint Conference of CVRMed and MRCAS, Grenoble, France, 1997, p. 767.

[16] S. Lavallee, R. Orti, R. Julliard, S. Martelli, V. Dessenne, P. Cinquin, Computer-assisted knee anterior cruciate ligament reconstruction: first clinical trials, in: First Int. Symp. on Medical Robotics and Computer Assisted Surgery (MRCAS 94), Pittsburgh, 1994, pp. 11–16.

[17] R. Taylor, H.A. Paul, B. Mittelstadt, et al., Robotic hip replacement surgery in dogs, in: Eleventh Annual Conference on Engineering in Medicine and Biology, Seattle, Nov. 9–12, 1989, pp. 887–889.

[18] H. Paul, B. Mittelstadt, W. Bargar, B. Musits, R. Taylor, P. Kazanzides, J. Zuhars, B. Williamson, W. Hanson, A surgical robot for total hip replacement surgery, in: Int. Conference on Robotics and Automation, Nice, France, May 1992.

[19] R.H. Taylor, H.A. Paul, P. Kazanzides, B.D. Mittelstadt, W. Hanson, J.F. Zuhars, B. Williamson, B.L. Musits, E. Glassman, W.L. Bargar, An image-directed robotic system for precise orthopaedic surgery, IEEE Transactions on Robotics and Automation 10 (3) (1994) 261–275.

[20] C. Cutting, R. Taylor, R. Bookstein, D. Khorramabadi, B. Haddad, A. Kalvin, H. Kim, M. Nox, Computer aided planning and execution of craniofacial surgical procedures, in: Proc. IEEE Engineering in Medicine and Biology Conference, Paris, France, 1992, pp. 1069–1070.

[21] R.H. Taylor, G.B. Bekey, J. Funda, in: Proc. of NSF Workshop on Computer Assisted Surgery, Washington, D.C., 1993.

[22] J. Troccaz, Y. Menguy, M. Bolla, P. Cinquin, P. Vassal, N. Laieb, L. Desbat, A. Dussere, S. Dal Soglio, Conformal external radiotherapy of prostatic carcinoma: requirements and experimental results, Radiotherapy and Oncology 29 (1993) 176–183.

[23] R.H. Taylor, J. Funda, L. Joskowicz, A. Kalvin, S. Gomory, A. Gueziec, L. Brown, An overview of computer-integrated surgery research at the IBM T.J. Watson Research Center, IBM Journal of Research and Development (March 1996).

[24] S. Lavallée, P. Cinquin, Computer assisted medical interventions, in: 3D Imaging in Medicine, Springer, Berlin, Heidelberg, 1990, pp. 301–312.

[25] R.H. Taylor, S. Lavallee, G.C. Burdea, R. Mosges (Eds.), Computer-Integrated Surgery, Technology and Clinical Applications, The MIT Press, 1995.

[26] L. Maier-Hein, S.S. Vedula, et al., Surgical data science for next-generation interventions, Nature Biomedical Engineering 1 (September 2017) 691–696.

[27] L. Maier-Hein, M. Eisenmann, et al., Surgical data science: a consensus perspective, https://arxiv.org/pdf/1806.03184.pdf, 2018.

[28] M. Kasparick, B. Andersen, H. Ulrich, S. Franke, E. Schreiber, M. Rockstroh, F. Golatowski, D. Timmermann, J. Ingenerf, T. Neumuth, IEEE 11073 SDC and HL7 FHIR: emerging standards for interoperability of medical systems, International Journal of Computer Assisted Radiology and Surgery 13 (Suppl 1) (2018), pp. S135–6.

[29] H. Lemke, M. Vannier, The operating room and the need for an IT infrastructure and standards, International Journal of Computer Assisted Radiology and Surgery 1 (2006) 117–121.

[30] J. Ophir, I. Cespedes, H. Ponnekanti, Y. Yazdi, X. Li, Elastography: a quantitative method for imaging the elasticity of biological tissues, Ultrasonic Imaging 13 (1991) 111–134.

[31] H. Rivaz, E. Boctor, M.A. Choti, G.D. Hager, Real-time regularized ultrasound elastography, IEEE Transactions on Medical Imaging 30 (4) (2011) 928–945.

[32] S. Billings, N. Deshmukh, H.J. Kang, R. Taylor, E. Boctor, System for robot-assisted real-time laparoscopic ultrasound elastography, in: SPIE Medical Imaging: Image-Guided Procedures, Robotic Interventions and Modeling, San Diego, Feb 5–7, 2012, pp. 8316–8367.

[33] S. Salcudean, X.u. Wen, S. Mahdavi, M. Moradi, J.W. Morris, I. Spadinger, Ultrasound elastography – an image guidance tool for prostate brachytherapy, Brachytherapy 8 (2) (April–June 2009) 125–126.

[34] E.S. Ebbini, C. Simon, D. Liu, Real-time ultrasound thermography and thermometry [Life Sciences], IEEE Signal Processing Magazine 35 (2) (2018) 166–174, https://doi.org/10.1109/MSP.2017.2773338.

[35] G. Ku, B.D. Fornage, X. Jin, M. Xu, K.K. Hunt, L.V. Wang, Thermoacoustic and photoacoustic tomography of thick biological tissues toward breast imaging, Technology in Cancer Research & Treatment 4 (5) (2005) 559–565.

[36] J. Su, A. Karpiouk, B. Wang, S. Emelianov, Photoacoustic imaging of clinical metal needles in tissue, Journal of Biomedical Optics 15 (2) (2010) 021309, pp. 1–6.

[37] S. Vyas, S. Su, R. Kim, N. Kuo, R. Taylor, J. Kang, E. Boctor, Intraoperative ultrasound to stereocamera registration using interventional photoacoustic imaging, in: SPIE Medical Imaging, San Diego, February 2012, p. 83160S.

[38] A. Cheng, J.U. Kang, R.H. Taylor, E.M. Boctor, Direct 3D ultrasound to video registration using photoacoustic markers, Journal of Biomedical Optics 18 (6) (June 2013) 066013.

[39] A. Cheng, X. Guo, H.J. Kang, M.A. Choti, J.U. Kang, R.H. Taylor, E.M. Boctor, Direct ultrasound to video registration using photoacoustic markers from a single image pose, in: Proc. SPIE 9313, Advanced Biomedical and Clinical Diagnostic and Surgical Guidance Systems, San Francisco, 8–10 Feb, 2015, p. 93130X.

[40] A. Cheng, Y. Kim, Y. Itsarachaiyot, H.K. Zhang, C.R. Weiss, R.H. Taylor, Emad M. Boctor, Photoacoustic-based catheter tracking: simulation, phantom, and in vivo studies, Journal of Medical Imaging 5 (2) (2018) 021223, https://doi.org/10.1117/1.JMI.5.2.021223.

[41] E. Boctor, M. de Oliviera, M. Awad, R. Taylor, G. Fichtinger, M.A. Choti, Robot-assisted 3D strain imaging for monitoring thermal ablation of liver, in: Annual Congress of the Society of American Gastrointestinal Endoscopic Surgeons (SAGES), 2005, pp. 240–241.

[42] B. Meng, L. Chen, A. Cheng, S. Billings, F. Aalamifar, R.H. Taylor, E. Boctor, Robot-assisted mirror ultrasound scanning for deep venous thrombosis using depth image: a preliminary tracking study, in: Computer Assisted Radiology and Surgery (CARS 2015), Barcelona, June 24–27, 2015, pp. 13–16.

[43] T.-Y. Fang, H.K. Zhang, R. Finocchi, R.H. Taylor, E.M. Boctor, Force-assisted ultrasound imaging system through dual force sensing and admittance robot control, International Journal of Computer Assisted Radiology and Surgery 12 (6) (June 2017) 983–991.

[44] R. Finocchi, F. Aalamifar, T.Y. Fang, R.H. Taylor, E.M. Boctor, Co-robotic ultrasound imaging: a cooperative force control approach, in: Medical Imaging 2017: Image-Guided Procedures, Robotic Interventions, and Modeling, Feb 11–16, 2017, p. 10135ff.

[45] J. Leven, D. Burschka, R. Kumar, G. Zhang, S. Blumenkranz, X. Dai, M. Awad, G. Hager, M. Marohn, M. Choti, C. Hasser, R.H. Taylor, DaVinci canvas: a telerobotic surgical system with integrated, robot-assisted, laparoscopic ultrasound capability, in: Medical Image Computing and Computer-Assisted Interventions, Palm Springs, CA, 2005, pp. 811–818, PMID: 16685945.

[46] R.P. Goldberg, M. Dumitru, R.H. Taylor, D. Stoianovici, A modular robotic system for ultrasound image acquisition, in: Medical Image Computing and Computer-Assisted Intervention – MICCAI 2001, Utrecht, October 2001, pp. 1430–1434.

[47] R. Kojcev, A. Khakzar, B. Fuerst, O. Zettinig, C. Fahkry, R. DeJong, J. Richmon, R. Taylor, E. Sinibaldi, N. Navab, On the reproducibility of expert-operated and robotic ultrasound acquisitions, International Journal of Computer Assisted Radiology and Surgery 12 (6) (June 2017).

[48] O. Mohareri, J. Ischia, P.C. Black, C. Schneider, J. Lobo, L. Goldenberg, S.E. Salcudean, Intraoperative registered transrectal ultrasound guidance for robot-assisted laparoscopic radical prostatectomy, The Journal of Urology 193 (1) (2015) 302–312, https://doi.org/10.1016/j.juro.2014.05.124, http://www.sciencedirect.com/science/article/pii/S0022534714042621.

[49] C. Schneider, C. Nguan, R. Rohling, S. Salcudean, Tracked "pick-up" ultrasound for robot-assisted minimally invasive surgery, IEEE Transactions on Biomedical Engineering 63 (2) (2016) 260–268, https://doi.org/10.1109/TBME.2015.2453173.

[50] R. Monfaredi, E. Wilson, B. Azizi Koutenaei, B. Labrecque, K. Leroy, J. Goldie, E. Louis, D. Swerdlow, K. Cleary, Robot-assisted ultrasound imaging: overview and development of a parallel telerobotic system, Minimally Invasive Therapy & Allied Technologies 24 (1) (2015) 54–62, https://doi.org/10.3109/13645706.2014.992908.

[51] C. Schneider, P. Peng, R. Taylor, G. Dachs, C. Hasser, S. DiMaio, M. Choti, Robot-assisted laparoscopic ultrasonography for hepatic surgery, Surgery 151 (5) (May 2012) 756–762, https://doi.org/10.1016/j.surg.2011.07.040, PMID: 21982071.

[52] F.A. Jolesz, S.M. Blumenfeld, Interventional use of magnetic resonance imaging and spectroscopic analysis and associated apparatus, Magnetic Resonance Quarterly 10 (2) (1994) 85–96.

[53] T. Kahn, H. Busse (Eds.), Interventional Magnetic Resonance Imaging, Springer, Heidelberg, 2012.

[54] J. Schenck, F. Jolesz, P. Roemer, H. Cline, W. Lorensen, R. Kikinis, S. Silverman, C. Hardy, W. Barber, E. Laskaris, Superconducting open-configuration MR imaging system for image-guided therapy, Radiology 195 (3) (1995) 805–814.

[55] R.J. Bohinski, R.E. Warnick, M.F. Gaskill-Shipley, M. Zuccarello, H.R. van Loveren, D.W. Kormos, J.M. Tew Jr., Intraoperative magnetic resonance imaging to determine the extent of resection of pituitary macroadenomas during transsphenoidal microsurgery, Neurosurgery 49 (5) (1 November 2001) 1133–1144.

[56] F. Fischbach, J. Bunke, M. Thormann, G. Gaffke, K. Jungnickel, J. Smink, J. Ricke, MR-guided freehand biopsy of liver lesions with fast continuous imaging using a 1.0-T open MRI scanner: experience in 50 patients, Cardiovascular and Interventional Radiology 34 (1) (2011) 188–192, https://doi.org/10.1007/s00270-010-9836-8.

[57] K. Chinzei, N. Hata, F.A. Jolesz, K. Kikinis, MRI compatible surgical assist robot: system integration and preliminary feasibility study, in: Medical Image Computing and Computer-Assisted Intervention (MICCAI), 2000, pp. 921–930.

[58] S.P. DiMaio, G.S. Fischer, S.J. Haker, N. Hata, I. Iordachita, C.M. Tempany, R. Kikinis, G. Fichtinger, A system for MRI-guided prostate interventions, in: BioRob, Pisa, 2006.

[59] A. Krieger, G. Fichtinger, G. Metzger, E. Atalar, L.L. Whitcomb, A hybrid method for 6-DOF tracking of MRI-compatible robotic interventional devices, in: IEEE International Conference on Robotics and Automation, Orlando, Florida, 2006.

[60] R. Monfaredi, R. Seifabadi, I. Iordachita, R. Sze, N.M. Safdar, K. Sharma, S. Fricke, A. Krieger, K. Cleary, A prototype body-mounted MRI-compatible robot for needle guidance in shoulder arthrography, in: 5th IEEE RAS/EMBS International Conference on Biomedical Robotics and Biomechatronics, 2014, pp. 40–45.

[61] G. Tilak, K. Tuncali, S.-E. Song, J. Tokuda, O. Olubiyi, F. Fennessy, A. Fedorov, T. Penzkofer, C. Tempany, N. Hata, 3T MR-guided in-bore transperineal prostate biopsy: a comparison of robotic and manual needle-guidance templates, Journal of Magnetic Resonance Imaging 42 (1) (2014) 63–71, https://doi.org/10.1002/jmri.24770.

[62] R.J. Maciunas, Interactive Image-Guided Neurosurgery, American Association of Neurological Surgeons, 1993.

[63] L.P. Nolte, H. Visarius, et al., Computer Assisted Orthopaedic Surgery, Hofgrefe & Huber, 1996.

[64] G. Zheng, L.P. Nolte, Computer-assisted orthopedic surgery: current state and future perspective, Frontiers in Surgery (online journal), 23 December, 2015. https://doi.org/10.3389/fsurg.2015.00066.

[65] R.H. Taylor, C.B. Cutting, Y. Kim, A.D. Kalvin, D.L. Larose, B. Haddad, D. Khoramabadi, M. Noz, R. Olyha, N. Bruun, D. Grimm, A model-based optimal planning and execution system with active sensing and passive manipulation for augmentation of human precision in computer-integrated surgery, in: Second Int. Symposium on Experimental Robotics, Toulouse, France, June 25–27, 1991.

[66] C. Cutting, R. Taylor, D. Khorramabadi, B. Haddad, Optical tracking of bone fragments during craniofacial surgery, in: Proc. 2nd Int. Symp. on Medical Robotics and Computer Assisted Surgery, Baltimore, Md., Nov 4–7, 1995, 1995, pp. 221–225.

[67] G. Enislidis, A. Wagner, O. Ploder, R. Ewers, Computed intraoperative navigation guidance; a preliminary report on a new technique, British Journal of Oral and Maxillofacial Surgery 35 (4) (1997) 271–274, https://doi.org/10.1016/S0266-4356(97)90046-2.

[68] H. Reinhardt, H. Meyer, A. Amrein, A computer-assisted device for intraoperative CT-correlated localization of brain tumors, European Surgical Research 20 (1988) 51–58.

[69] R. Bucholz, K. Smith, A comparison of sonic digitizers versus light emitting diode-based localization, in: Robert J. Maciunas (Ed.), Interactive Image-Guided Neurosurgery, American Association of Neurological Surgeons, 1993, pp. 179–200.

[70] M.P. Fried, J. Kleefield, H. Gopal, E. Reardon, B.T. Ho, F.A. Kuhn, Image-guided endoscopic surgery: results of accuracy and performance in a multicenter clinical study using an electromagnetic tracking system, The Laryngoscope 107 (5) (2009) 594–601, https://doi.org/10.1097/00005537-199705000-00008.

[71] F. Attivissimo, A.D. Nisio, A.M.L. Lanzolla, S. Selicato, P. Larizza, Evaluation of noise performance of an electromagnetic image-guided surgery system, in: 2018 IEEE International Instrumentation and Measurement Technology Conference (I2MTC), 2018, pp. 1–6.

[72] K.R. Smith, K.J. Frank, R.D. Bucholz, The Neurostation – a highly accurate minimally invasive solution to frameless stereotactic neurosurgery, Computerized Medical Imaging and Graphics 18 (1994) 247–256.

[73] M.P. Heilbrun, S. Koehler, P. McDonald, W. Peters, V. Sieminov, C. Wiker, Implementation of a machine vision method for stereotactic localization and guidance, in: R. Maciunas (Ed.), Interactive Image-Guided Neurosurgery, AANS, 1993, pp. 169–177.

[74] A.M. Franz, T. Haidegger, W. Birkfellner, K. Cleary, T.M. Peters, L. Maier-Hein, Electromagnetic tracking in medicine—a review of technology, validation, and applications, IEEE Transactions on Medical Imaging 33 (8) (2014) 1702–1725.

[75] A.M. Franz, T. Haidegger, W. Birkfellner, K. Cleary, T.M. Peters, L. Maier-Hein, Polhemus electronic tracking systems, https://polhemus.com/applications/electromagnetics/, 2018.

[76] A.M. Franz, T. Haidegger, W. Birkfellner, K. Cleary, T.M. Peters, L. Maier-Hein, Northern digital electromagnetic tracking systems, https://www.ndigital.com/products/electromagnetic-tracking-systems/, 2018.

[77] A.M. Franz, T. Haidegger, W. Birkfellner, K. Cleary, T.M. Peters, L. Maier-Hein, Northern digital optical measurement systems, https://www.ndigital.com/products/optical-measurement-systems/, 2018.

[78] A.M. Franz, T. Haidegger, W. Birkfellner, K. Cleary, T.M. Peters, L. Maier-Hein, Atracsys optical measurement systems, https://www.atracsys-measurement.com/products/, 2018.

[79] A.M. Franz, T. Haidegger, W. Birkfellner, K. Cleary, T.M. Peters, L. Maier-Hein, Claron Micron-Tracker system, https://www.claronav.com/microntracker/, 2018.

[80] J. Adler, A. Schweikard, R. Tombropoulos, J.-C. Latombe, Image-guided robotic radiosurgery, in: Proceedings of the First International Symposium on Medical Robotics and Computer-Assisted Surgery, Pittsburgh, 1994, pp. 291–297.

[81] Y.S. Kwoh, J. Hou, E.A. Jonckheere, et al., A robot with improved absolute positioning accuracy for CT guided stereotactic brain surgery, IEEE Transactions on Biomedical Engineering 35 (2) (1988) 153–161.

[82] S. Lavallee, P. Cinquin, J. Demongeot, A. Benabid, I. Marque, M. Djaïd, Computer assisted interventionist imaging: the instance of stereotactic brain surgery, in: MEDINFO 89: The Sixth Conference on Medical Informatics, Beijing, China and Singapore, 1989, pp. 613–617.

[83] J.M. Drake, M. Joy, A. Goldenberg, D. Kreindler, Computer- and robot-assisted resection of thalamic astrocytomas in children, Neurosurgery 29 (1) (1991) 27–31.

[84] K. Masamune, E. Kobayashi, Y. Masutani, M. Suzuki, T. Dohi, H. Iseki, K. Takakura, Development of an MRI-compatible needle insertion manipulator for stereotactic neurosurgery, Journal of Image Guided Surgery 1 (1995) 242–248.

[85] J.T. Bishoff, D. Stoianovici, B.R. Lee, J. Bauer, R.H. Taylor, L.L. Whitcomb, J.A. Cadeddu, D. Chan, L.R. Kavoussi, RCM-PAKY: clinical application of a new robotics system for precise needle placement, Journal of Endourology 12 (1998) S82.

[86] K. Masamune, A. Patriciu, D. Stoianovici, R. Susil, G. Fichtinger, L. Kavoussi, J. Anderson, R. Taylor, I. Sakuma, T. Dohi, Development of CT-PAKY frame system – CT image guided needle puncturing manipulator and a single slice registration for urological surgery, in: Proc. 8th Annual Meeting of JSCAS, Kyoto, 1999, pp. 89–90.

[87] S.P. DiMaio, S. Pieper, K. Chinzei, N. Hata, S.J. Haker, G. Fichtinger, C.M. Tempany, R. Kikinis, Robot-assisted needle placement in open-MRI: system architecture, integration and validation, Journal of Computer Aided Surgery 12 (1) (2007) 15–24.

[88] S.E. Salcudean, T.D. Prananta, W.J. Morris, I. Spadinger, A robotic needle guide for prostate brachytherapy, in: IEEE International Conference on Robotics and Automation, Pasadena, California, May 19–23, 2008, pp. 2975–2981.

[89] N. Cowan, K. Goldberg, G. Chirikjian, G. Fichtinger, R. Alterovitz, K. Reed, V. Kallem, W. Park, S. Misra, A.M. Okamura, Robotic needle steering: design, modeling, planning, and image guidance, in: J. Rosen, B. Hannaford, R.M. Satava (Eds.), Surgical Robotics – Systems Applications and Visions, Springer, New York, 2011.

[90] W. Bargar, A. DiGioia, R. Turner, J. Taylor, J. McCarthy, D. Mears, Robodoc multi-center trial: an interim report, in: Proc. 2nd Int. Symp. on Medical Robotics and Computer Assisted Surgery, Baltimore, Md., Nov 4–7, 1995, pp. 208–214.

[91] B. Davies, S. Harris, M. Jakopec, J. Cobb, A novel hands-on robot for knee replacement surgery, in: Computer Assisted Orthopaedic Surgery USA (CAOS USA), Pittsburgh, 1999, pp. 70–74.

[92] A.D. Pearle, P.F. O'Loughlin, D.O. Kendoff, Robot-assisted unicompartmental knee arthroplasty, The Journal of Arthroplasty 25 (2) (2010) 230–237.

[93] D.P. Devito, L. Kaplan, et al., Clinical acceptance and accuracy assessment of spinal implants guided with SpineAssist surgical robot – retrospective study, Spine 35 (24) (2010) 2109–2115.

[94] C.C. Zygourakis, A.K. Ahmed, S. Kalb, A.M. Zhu, A. Bydon, N.R. Crawford, N. Theodore, Technique: open lumbar decompression and fusion with the Excelsius GPS robot, Neurosurgical Focus 45-VideoSuppl1 (2018) V6, https://doi.org/10.3171/2018.7.FocusVid.18123.

[95] R.H. Taylor, H.A. Paul, C.B. Cutting, B. Mittelstadt, W. Hanson, P. Kazandides, B. Musits, Y.-Y. Kim, A. Kalvin, B. Haddad, D. Khoramabadi, D. Larose, Augmentation of human precision in computer-integrated surgery, Innovation et Technologie en Biologie et Medicine 13 (4) (1992) 450–459 (special issue on computer assisted surgery).

[96] C.B. Cutting, F.L. Bookstein, R.H. Taylor, Applications of simulation, morphometrics and robotics in craniofacial surgery, in: R.H. Taylor, S. Lavallee, G. Burdea, R. Mosges (Eds.), Computer-Integrated Surgery, MIT Press, Cambridge, Mass., 1996, pp. 641–662.

[97] S. Weber, N. Gerber, K.A. Gavaghan, T. Williamson, W. Wimmer, J. Ansó, L. Brogna-Salas, D. Chen, C. Weisstanner, M. Caversaccio, B. Bell, Image guided and robotic assisted minimally invasive cochlear implantation, in: The Hamlyn Symposium on Medical Robotics, London, June 22–25, 2013, pp. 22–25.

[98] K.C. Olds, P. Chalasani, P. Pacheco-Lopez, I. Iordachita, L.M. Akst, R.H. Taylor, Preliminary evaluation of a new microsurgical robotic system for head and neck surgery, in: IEEE Int. Conf on Intelligent Robots and Systems (IROS), Chicago, Sept 14–18, 2014, pp. 1276–1281.

[99] K. Olds, Robotic Assistant Systems for Otolaryngology-Head and Neck Surgery, PhD Thesis in Biomedical Engineering, Johns Hopkins University, Baltimore, March 2015.

[100] L. Akst, K. Olds, M. Balicki, P. Chalasani, R. Taylor, Robotic microlaryngeal phonosurgery: testing of a "steady-hand platform", Laryngoscope 128 (Jan. 2018) 126–132, https://doi.org/10.1002/lary.26621, PMID: 28498632.

[101] J.M. Sackier, Y. Wang, Robotically assisted laparoscopic surgery. From concept to development, Surgical Endoscopy 8 (1) (Jan 1994) 63–66, http://www.ncbi.nlm.nih.gov/entrez/query.fcgi?cmd=Retrieve&db=PubMed&dopt=Citation&list_uids=8153867.

[102] R.H. Taylor, J. Funda, B. Eldgridge, S. Gomory, K. Gruben, D. LaRose, M. Talamini, L. Kavoussi, J. Anderson, Telerobotic assistant for laparoscopic surgery, IEEE Engineering in Medicine and Biology Magazine 14 (3) (April–May 1995) 279–288.

[103] A. Casals, J. Amat, E. Laporte, Automatic guidance of an assistant robot in laparoscopic surgery, in: Proceedings of IEEE International Conference on Robotics and Automation, vol. 1, 1996, pp. 895–900.

[104] H. Reichenspurner, R. Demaino, M. Mack, D. Boehm, H. Gulbins, C. Detter, B. Meiser, R. Ellgass, B. Reichart, Use of the voice controlled and computer-assisted surgical system Zeus for endoscopic

coronary artery surgery bypass grafting, Journal of Thoracic and Cardiovascular Surgery 118 (1) (1999).

[105] G.S. Guthart, J.K. Salisbury, The intuitive telesurgery system: overview and application, in: Proc. of the IEEE International Conference on Robotics and Automation (*ICRA*2000), San Francisco, 2000, pp. 618–621.

[106] G.S. Guthart, J.K. Salisbury, Intuitive surgical, https://www.intuitive.com, 2018.

[107] P. Green, R. Satava, J. Hill, I. Simon, Telepresence: advanced teleoperator technology for minimally invasive surgery (abstract), Surgical Endoscopy 6 (91) (1992).

[108] L.B. Rosenberg, Virtual fixtures: perceptual tools for telerobotic manipulation, in: Proceedings of IEEE Virtual Reality International Symposium, 1993, pp. 76–82.

[109] M. Li, A.M. Okamura, Recognition of operator motions for real-time assistance using virtual fixtures, in: 11th International Symposium on Haptic Interfaces for Virtual Environment and Teleoperator Systems, 2003, pp. 125–131.

[110] J.J. Abbott, A.M. Okamura, Stable forbidden-region virtual fixtures for bilateral telemanipulation, ASME Journal of Dynamic Systems, Measurement, and Control 53 (64) (2006).

[111] M. Li, M. Ishii, R.H. Taylor, Spatial motion constraints in medical robot using virtual fixtures generated by anatomy, IEEE Transactions on Robotics 23 (1) (2007) 4–19.

[112] A. Kapoor, R. Taylor, A constrained optimization approach to virtual fixtures for multi-handed tasks, in: IEEE International Conference on Robotics and Automation (ICRA), Pasadena, May 19–23, 2008, pp. 3401–3406.

[113] B. Becker, R. MacLachlan, L. Lobes, G. Hager, C. Riviere, Vision-based control of a handheld surgical micromanipulator with virtual fixtures, IEEE Transactions on Robotics 29 (3) (2013) 674–683, NIHMSID: 429749.

[114] L. Wang, Z. Chen, P. Chalasani, J. Pile, P. Kazanzides, R.H. Taylor, N. Simaan, Updating virtual fixtures from exploration data in force-controlled model-based telemanipulation, in: ASME 2016 International Design Engineering Technical Conferences & Computers and Information in Engineering Conference, Charlotte, Aug. 21–24, 2016, p. V05AT07A031.

[115] J. Burgner-Kahrs, D.C. Rucker, H. Choset, Continuum robots for medical applications: a survey, IEEE Transactions on Robotics 31 (6) (2015) 1261–1280, https://doi.org/10.1109/TRO.2015.2489500.

[116] H. Rafii-Tari, C.J. Payne, G.-Z. Yang, Current and emerging robot-assisted endovascular catheterization technologies: a review, Annals of Biomedical Engineering 42 (4) (2014) 697–715, https://doi.org/10.1007/s10439-013-0946-8.

[117] H. Rafii-Tari, C.J. Payne, G.-Z. Yang, Auris Monarch Platform, https://www.aurishealth.com/monarch-platform.html, 2018.

[118] B. Azizi Koutenaei, E. Wilson, R. Monfaredi, C. Peters, G. Kronreif, K. Cleary, Robotic natural orifice transluminal endoscopic surgery (R-NOTES): literature review and prototype system, Minimally Invasive Therapy & Allied Technologies 24 (1) (2015) 18–23, https://doi.org/10.3109/13645706.2014.992907.

[119] B. Po, M. Yeung, P.W.Y. Chiu, Application of robotics in gastrointestinal endoscopy: a review, World Journal of Gastroenterology 22 (5) (2016) 1811–1825.

[120] K. Kume, Flexible robotic endoscopy: current and original devices, Computer Assisted Surgery 21 (1) (2016) 150–159, https://doi.org/10.1080/24699322.2016.1242654.

[121] S. Charles, R.E. Williams, B. Hamel, Design of a surgeon–machine interface for teleoperated microsurgery, in: Proceedings of the Annual International Conference of the IEEE Engineering in Medicine and Biology Society, 1989, pp. 11:883–884.

[122] S.J.E. Yang, G.C. Mathie, C.I. Phillips, R.S. Bartholomew, Feasibility of using micromachines for cataract surgery, in: IEEE Proceedings on Micro Electro Mechanical Systems, An Investigation of Micro Structures, Sensors, Actuators, Machines and Robots, 1990, pp. 136–141.

[123] A. Guerrouad, P. Vidal, SMOS: stereotaxical microtelemanipulator for ocular surgery, in: Images of the Twenty-First Century. Proceedings of the Annual International Engineering in Medicine and Biology Society, vol. 3, 1989, pp. 879–880.

[124] M. Roizenblatt, T.L. Edwards, P.L. Gehlbach, Robot-assisted vitreoretinal surgery: current perspectives, Robotic Surgery 5 (2018) 1–11, https://doi.org/10.2147/RSRR.S122301, PMC5842029.

[125] R. Taylor, P. Jensen, L. Whitcomb, A. Barnes, R. Kumar, D. Stoianovici, P. Gupta, Z.X. Wang, E. deJuan, L. Kavoussi, Steady-hand robotic system for microsurgical augmentation, International Journal of Robotics Research 18 (12) (1999) 1201–1210.

[126] S.C. Ho, R.D. Hibberd, B.L. Davies, Robot assisted knee surgery, IEEE EMBS Magazine Sp. Issue on Robotics in Surgery (April–May 1995) 292–300.

[127] X. He, D. Roppenecker, D. Gierlach, M. Balicki, Kevin Olds, James Handa, P. Gehlbach, R.H. Taylor, I. Iordachita, Toward a clinically applicable Steady-Hand Eye Robot for vitreoretinal surgery, in: ASME 2012 International Mechanical Engineering Congress & Exposition, Houston, Texas, Nov 9–15, 2012, p. 88384.

[128] A. Gijbels, J. Smits, L. Schoevaerdts, K. Willekens, E.B. Vander Poorten, P. Stalmans, D. Reynaerts, In-human robot-assisted retinal vein cannulation, a world first, Annals of Biomedical Engineering 46 (10) (2018) 1676–1685, https://doi.org/10.1007/s10439-018-2053-3.

[129] D.L. Rothbaum, J. Roy, P. Berkelman, G. Hager, D. Stoianovici, R.H. Taylor, L.L. Whitcomb, M. Howard Francis, J.K. Niparko, Robot-assisted stapedotomy: micropick fenestration of the stapes footplate, Otolaryngology – Head and Neck Surgery 127 (5) (November 2002) 417–426.

[130] S. Gurbani, P. Wilkening, M. Zhao, B. Gonenc, G.W. Cheon, I. Iordachita, W. Chien, R. Taylor, J. Niparko, J.U. Kang, Robot-assisted three-dimensional registration for cochlear implant surgery using a common-path swept-source optical coherence tomography probe, Journal of Biomedical Optics 19 (5) (2014) 057004.

[131] K.C. Olds, P. Chalasani, P. Pacheco-Lopez, I. Iordachita, L.M. Akst, R.H. Taylor, Preliminary evaluation of a new microsurgical robotic system for head and neck surgery, in: 2014 IEEE/RSJ International Conference on Intelligent Robots and Systems, 2014, pp. 1276–1281.

[132] A.L. Feng, C.R. Razavi, P. Lakshminarayanan, Z. Ashai, K. Olds, M. Balicki, Z. Gooi, A.T. Day, R.H. Taylor, J.D. Richmon, The robotic ENT microsurgery system: a novel robotic platform for microvascular surgery, The Laryngoscope 127 (November 2017) 2495–2500.

[133] G.-Z. Yang, J. Cambias, K. Cleary, E. Daimler, J. Drake, P.E. Dupont, N. Hata, P. Kazandides, S. Martel, R.V. Patel, V.J. Santos, R.H. Taylor, Medical robotics—regulatory, ethical, and legal considerations for increasing levels of autonomy [Editorial], Science Robotics 2 (4) (15 March 2017) eaam8638, https://doi.org/10.1126/scirobotics.aam8638.

[134] R.L. Cornum, J.C. Bowersox, Telepresence: a 21st century interface for urologic surgery, Journal of Urology 155 (1996) 489.

[135] P. Green, J. Jensen, J. Hill, A. Shah, Mobile telepresence surgery, in: Proc. 2nd Int. Symp. on Medical Robotics and Computer Assisted Surgery, Baltimore, Md., 1995, pp. 97–103.

[136] J.W. Hill, J.F. Jensen, Telepresence technology in medicine: principles and applications, Proceedings of the IEEE 86 (3) (1998) 569–580.

[137] B.T. Bethea, A.M. Okamura, M. Kitagawa, T.P. Fitton, S.M. Cattaneo, V.L. Gott, W.A. Baumgartner, D.D. Yuh, Application of haptic feedback to robotic surgery, Journal of Laparoendoscopic and Advanced Surgical Techniques 14 (3) (2004) 191–195.

[138] A.M. Okamura, Methods for haptic feedback in teleoperated robot-assisted surgery, Industrial Robot 31 (6) (2004) 499–508.

[139] E.P. Westebring - van der Putten, R.H.M. Goossens, J.J. Jakimowicz, J. Dankelman, Haptics in minimally invasive surgery – a review, Minimally Invasive Therapy & Allied Technologies 17 (1) (2008) 3–16, https://doi.org/10.1080/13645700701820242.

[140] M.J. Massimino, T.B. Sheridan, Sensory substitution for force feedback in teleoperation, IFAC Symposia Series 5 (1993) 109–114.

[141] M. Kitagawa, D. Dokko, A.M. Okamura, B.T. Bethea, D.D. Yuh, Effect of sensory substitution on suture manipulation forces for surgical teleoperation, in: Medicine Meets Virtual Reality, vol. 12, 2004, pp. 157–163.

[142] T. Akinbiyi, C.E. Reiley, S. Saha, D. Burschka, C.J. Hasser, D.D. Yuh, A.M. Okamura, Dynamic Augmented reality for sensory substitution in robot-assisted surgical systems, in: 28th Annual International Conference of the IEEE Engineering in Medicine and Biology Society, 2006, pp. 567–570.

[143] N. Cutler, M. Balicki, M. Finkelstein, J. Wang, P. Gehlbach, J. McGready, I. Iordachita, R. Taylor, J. Handa, Auditory force feedback substitution improves surgical precision during simulated ophthalmic surgery, Investigative Ophthalmology & Visual Science 54 (2) (2013) 1316–1324, https://doi.org/10.1167/iovs.12-11136, PMC3597188.

[144] H. Fuchs, M.A. Livingston, R. Raskar, D. Colucci, K. Keller, A. State, J.R. Crawford, P. Rademacher, S.H. Drake, A.A. Meyer, Augmented reality visualization for laparoscopic surgery, in: MICCAI '98, Boston, 1998.

[145] M. Rosenthal, A. State, J. Lee, G. Hirota, J. Ackerman, K. Keller, E.D. Pisano, M. Jiroutek, K. Muller, H. Fuchs, Augmented reality guidance for needle biopsies: a randomized, controlled trial in phantoms, in: Fourth International Conference on Medical Image Computing and Computer-Assisted Intervention, 2001, pp. 240–248.

[146] S. Bernhardt, S.A. Nicolau, L. Soler, C. Doignon, The status of augmented reality in laparoscopic surgery as of 2016, Medical Image Analysis 37 (2017) 66–90, https://doi.org/10.1016/j.media.2017.01.007, http://www.sciencedirect.com/science/article/pii/S1361841517300178.

[147] D.K. Baker, C.T. Fryberger, B.A. Ponce, The emergence of augmented reality in orthopaedic surgery and education, The Orthopaedic Journal at Harvard Medical School 16 (June 2015).

[148] R.G. Confer, R.C. Bainbridge, Voice control in the microsurgical suite, in: Proc. of the Voice I/O Systems Applications Conference '84, Arlington, VA, 1984.

[149] R. Sturges, S. Laowattana, A voice-actuated, tendon-controlled device for endoscopy, in: R.H. Taylor, S. Lavallee, G. Burdea, R. Mosges (Eds.), Computer-Integrated Surgery, MIT Press, Cambridge, Mass., 1996.

CHAPTER 26

Technology and applications in interventional imaging: 2D X-ray radiography/fluoroscopy and 3D cone-beam CT

Sebastian Schafer[a], Jeffrey H. Siewerdsen[b]
[a]Advanced Therapies, Siemens Healthineers, Forchheim, Germany
[b]Department of Biomedical Engineering, Johns Hopkins University, Baltimore, MD, United States

Contents

26.1.	The 2D imaging chain	626
26.1.1	Production of X-rays for fluoroscopy and CBCT	626
26.1.2	Large-area X-ray detectors for fluoroscopy and cone-beam CT	628
26.1.3	Automatic exposure control (AEC) and automatic brightness control (ABC)	631
26.1.4	2D image processing	631
	26.1.4.1 Detector corrections / image preprocessing	*631*
	26.1.4.2 Postprocessing	*632*
26.1.5	Radiation dose (fluoroscopy)	633
	26.1.5.1 Measurement of fluoroscopic dose	*633*
	26.1.5.2 Reference dose levels	*634*
26.2.	The 3D imaging chain	635
26.2.1	3D imaging prerequisites	635
	26.2.1.1 Geometrical calibration	*635*
	26.2.1.2 I_0 calibration	*637*
	26.2.1.3 Other correction factors	*638*
26.2.2	3D image reconstruction	640
	26.2.2.1 Filtered backprojection	*640*
	26.2.2.2 Emerging methods: optimization-based (iterative) image reconstruction (OBIR)	*644*
	26.2.2.3 Emerging methods: machine learning methods for cone-beam CT	*646*
26.2.3	Radiation dose (CBCT)	647
	26.2.3.1 Measurement of dose in CBCT	*647*
	26.2.3.2 Reference dose levels	*648*
26.3.	System embodiments	649
26.3.1	Mobile systems: C-arms, U-arms, and O-arms	649
26.3.2	Fixed-room C-arm systems	651
26.3.3	Interventional multi-detector CT (MDCT)	654
26.4.	Applications	654
26.4.1	Interventional radiology	655
	26.4.1.1 Neurological interventions	*655*

Handbook of Medical Image Computing and Computer Assisted Intervention
https://doi.org/10.1016/B978-0-12-816176-0.00031-4

        26.4.1.2 Body interventions (oncology and embolization)   657
    26.4.2 Interventional cardiology   659
    26.4.3 Surgery   661
References   664

26.1. The 2D imaging chain

26.1.1 Production of X-rays for fluoroscopy and CBCT

The physical principles and basic technology for X-ray production for medical imaging applications are discussed in detail in a variety of texts on the physics of medical imaging [1]. The most prevalent technology uses an X-ray vacuum tube containing a hot cathode (X-ray tube filament) through which a current is delivered to produce electrons by thermionic emission. The electrons accelerate across the vacuum under a high voltage (~50–150 kV) applied across the X-ray tube and impinge on an anode typically composed of a material with high atomic number to produce a continuous spectrum of bremsstrahlung radiation, as well as a discrete spectrum corresponding to direct interaction with innershell electrons of the anode material. Example X-ray spectra computed using the *spektr* toolkit [2] implementation of the TASMICS algorithm [3] are shown in Fig. 26.1. Noteworthy features include the continuous bremsstrahlung spectrum with maximum energy (E_{max}) determined by the tube voltage (kV, referred to sometimes as "peak kilovoltage," kVp) and the characteristic "spikes" at X-ray energies corresponding to the K-shell binding energy of the anode material (tungsten).

Emerging technologies for X-ray production include carbon nanotube (CNT) systems [4], which could offer a number of possible advantages over the hot cathode approach, including compact form factor, enabling systems with distributed arrays of multiple X-ray sources. Although CNT systems have faced some challenges in their early development with respect to X-ray output (i.e., generating a sufficiently high X-ray flux) and reliability, CNT systems are emerging for applications in dental imaging [5] and tomosynthesis [6]. Ongoing research to address the technical, material, and manufacturing challenges associated with such technologies could offer a new base technology for X-ray production.

Interventional X-ray imaging typically involves an X-ray tube operated at ~60–120 kV with a rotating tungsten anode and hot cathode in pulsed mode, with X-ray pulse width ranging ~10–50 ms and pulse rate ranging up to ~60 pulses/s. A tungsten anode provides a high heat capacity to allow high X-ray tube current (up to ~500 mA) and/or extended run-times associated with fluoroscopic or cone-beam CT (CBCT) image acquisition series.

The image acquisition technique for fluoroscopic imaging is characterized by selection of the kV (typically ~60–100 kV), tube current (mA), and focal spot size (FS). The selection of technique factors depends on considerations such as patient size, anatomical site, orientation (e.g., posterior–anterior (PA) or lateral (LAT) views), and the imaging

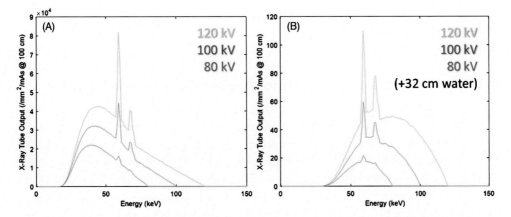

Figure 26.1 Example X-ray spectra in fluoroscopy or cone-beam CT: (A) example spectra incident on the patient; (B) the same spectra attenuated by 32 cm water (approximating the spectra incident on the detector), amounting to ~800× reduction in fluence.

task. As illustrated in Fig. 26.1, the selection of tube potential determines the maximum energy of the X-ray beam, with higher kV typically required for thicker body sites. The FS affects spatial resolution due to focal spot magnification (finer FS for higher resolution imaging) and affects anode heat loading (higher instantaneous heat load for a finer FS), with focal spot size typically ~0.3–0.6 mm. Note that FS specification (e.g., 0.6 FS) and focal spot width (mm) are not the same – related instead by categorization specified in [7] and [8]. For pulsed fluoroscopy systems, the X-ray tube current may be characterized in terms of the effective mA, i.e., the equivalent constant current corresponding to the amount of charge for the X-ray pulse. For example, a fluoroscopic sequence with width 10 ms, pulse rate of 30 /s, and (actual, instantaneous) current of 300 mA may be stated to have an effective tube current of 3 mA. The current-time product (mA × pulse width) is referred to as mAs.

The image acquisition technique for CBCT imaging is characterized by numerous factors, including the kV and mAs as described above, as well as the number of projection views (typically ~100–500 views) and the orbit of the X-ray source and detector about the patient (e.g., an isocentric circular orbit). Selection of technique factors depends on considerations of, e.g., patient size, imaging task, and workflow requirements while delivering as low a dose as reasonably achievable.

A simple calculation illustrates the fairly steep requirements in quantum efficiency required of X-ray imaging systems in fluoroscopy and CBCT. For example, a particular combination of technique factors delivering ~3×10^5 X-rays/mm^2/mR at 100 cm in-air from the source and attenuated by 32 cm of water amounts to ~200 X-rays/mm^2/mR at the detector (assumed 150 cm from the source). For a detector with 0.2 mm pixel aperture, this amounts to fewer than 10 X-rays/pixel for an exposure of 1 mR. The incident fluence is often assumed to be Poisson–distributed (although such low count rates suggest using more sophisticated compound statistical models).

26.1.2 Large-area X-ray detectors for fluoroscopy and cone-beam CT

A major advance in interventional X-ray imaging was accomplished in the development of modern, large-area, active matrix flat-panel detectors (FPDs) over the course of the 1990s [9,10]. The enabling technology underlying these systems is a thin-film transistor (TFT) based on hydrogenated amorphous silicon (a–Si:H), which acts as a switching element on each detector pixel for active matrix readout. Two broad categories of FPD had emerged by 2001, "direct-detection" FPDs in which detection of incident X-rays is achieved by a photoconductive layer (typically amorphous selenium, a–Se) coupled to a storage capacitor on each pixel, and "indirect-detection" FPDs in which the sensitive element is an a–Si:H photodiode coupled to an overlying scintillator. Each technology has come to play a role in various applications of digital X-ray imaging, but the latter (indirect-detection FPDs) are more common in interventional imaging and are the focus of discussion below, unless otherwise noted.

The physical principles of the indirect-detection FPD imaging chain are well described by a cascade of the following physical processes [11]. Incident X-rays are detected by interaction (photoelectric absorption or Compton scatter) in a scintillator at the input to the FPD. The most common scintillator in current use is CsI:Tl, forming a crystalline layer (typically $\sim$0.5–0.6 mm thick) over the active matrix array. The probability of X-ray interaction in the scintillator is described by Beers Law, with quantum detection efficiency (QDE) of $\sim$0.6–0.8 at X-ray energies ($\sim$80–120 kV) typical of interventional procedures.

X-ray interactions in the scintillator deposit energy that is converted to optical photons by scintillation or phosphorescence. (Alternatively, X-rays above the K-edge of the scintillator material can produce a fluorescent X-ray, which in turn may be absorbed in the scintillator or escape.) The optical conversion efficiency typically yields $\sim$800–1500 optical photons per X-ray interaction, providing a fairly high input signal analogous to the input phosphor of X-ray image intensifiers (XRIIs). The statistical distribution in the number of optical photons generated per interaction is typically broader than a Poisson distribution (described by the absorbed energy distribution (AED), Poisson excess, or Swank factor) and presents an important additional source of noise in the imaging chain. For example, the upper limit in detective quantum efficiency (DQE) for a scintillator is given by the product of the QDE and Swank factor.

Optical photons produced by X-ray interactions in the scintillator are emitted isotropically from the point of interaction and thus spread some distance within the scintillator before interacting with the detector matrix. This presents a significant source of blur in indirect-detection FPDs. CsI:Tl scintillators have a needle-like crystalline struc-

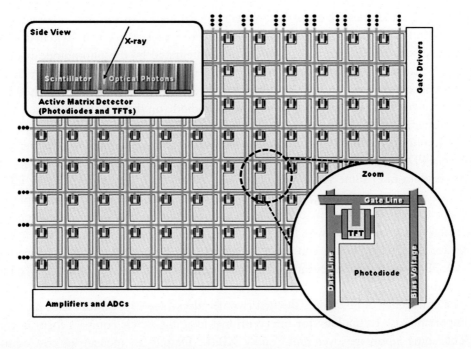

Figure 26.2 Detection and readout architecture for a flat-panel X-ray detector. Active matrix readout involves sequential activation of each row (switching each TFT on that row via gate drivers) and transfer of signal from each pixel on that row to amplifiers and ADCs. The side view (top left) illustrates the basic physical principle of X-ray interaction in the overlying scintillator, conversion to optical photons that in turn propagate and spread to the detector array, which is addressed via active matrix readout to charge-integrating amplifiers and ADCs. The zoom view (lower right) shows a single pixel of the detector array, featuring an a-Si:H photodiode and TFT.

ture oriented orthogonal to the plane of the detector, providing a degree of internal reflection at crystal interfaces and helping to limit the extent of lateral spread. Many scintillators incorporate a reflective layer at the input surface to return photons emitted in directions away from the detector back toward the sensitive detector matrix. For indirect-detection FPDs based on a-Si:H photodiodes and TFTs, the CsI:Tl is usually deposited through a special process directly on the detector matrix, providing a fairly high degree of optical coupling between the scintillator and photodiodes.

Underlying the scintillator is an active matrix array of a-Si:H photodiodes and TFTs as illustrated in Fig. 26.2. A wide variety of FPD designs are now commercially available, with key characteristics that include sensitive area (typically $\sim$20–40 cm on a side), pixel pitch (typically 0.1–0.3 mm), and readout rate (typically 15–30 fps). The photodiode element on each pixel is optically sensitive (typical quantum efficiency $\sim$0.8 over the emission spectrum of CsI:Tl) and convert interacting photons to electron–hole (e–h) pairs. A bias voltage (typically $\sim$4–6 V) applied across the ($\sim$0.001 mm thick) intrinsic layer of the photodiodes separates the e–h pairs, generating a current that is integrated within the capacitance of the photodiode. When the TFT element is switched to a conducting state via its gate voltage, the charge integrated by the photodiode is read out via a "data line" connected the source (or drain) of the TFT. The active matrix readout concept is shown in Fig. 26.2, where individual rows of TFTs are switched on and off sequentially, and the signal from each photodiode on that row is transferred to a charge-integrating amplifier.

Each column of the FPD is thus connected to a charge-integrating amplifier. In practice, FPDs may feature dual-sided readout, giving a factor of 2 increase in active matrix readout rate. Some systems incorporate a variety of "gain modes" on the integrating amplifier, e.g., "dual gain" or "dynamic gain" readout in which the amplifier feedback features capacitors in parallel that may be switched to increase or decrease the charge capacitance (i.e., switch to low or high gain, respectively) [12]. The charge integrated by the amplifier is subsequently digitized by an analog-to-digital converter (ADC). FPDs in current interventional imaging systems typically incorporate 14–16 bit digitization.

The emergence of FPDs over the first two decades of the 21st century thus presents an important base technology for interventional imaging. Their compact form factor presents some advantage over more bulky XRIIs. Despite an increase in cost compared to XRIIs, these detectors have become fairly ubiquitous in fluoroscopy – on both mobile and fixed-room imaging platforms – and they enabled the emergence of high-quality CBCT. They are now prevalent in mammography, radiography, and fluoroscopy, and as described below, their application to CBCT presents the state-of-the-art X-ray imaging technology in image-guided radiotherapy [13], interventional radiology and cardiology [14], and image-guided surgery [15].

A rapidly emerging technology – in many areas, now fully emerged – includes FPDs with a different underlying semiconductor technology based on complementary metal oxide semiconductor (CMOS) sensor elements. CMOS detectors also employ a scintillator (commonly CsI:Tl, similar to that described above) and therefore have similar characteristics with respect to input QDE and blur. However, CMOS detectors have a number of potentially advantageous technical performance characteristics, including higher frame rate, lower image lag, and reduced electronic noise. Potential tradeoffs compared to FPDs based on a-Si:H sensors (at the time of writing) include somewhat smaller active area (recognizing the ability to tile larger arrays by tiling) and reduced optical coupling associated with the fiber optic face plate between the scintillator and optoelectronic sensor array (and also shields the CMOS components from X-ray irradiation not absorbed in the scintillator).

X-ray detector technologies continue to present an area of active research and development. Areas of active research include novel materials [16–20] such as PbI_2, HgI_2, and CdTe or CdZnTe, as well as novel pixel readout architectures [21,22] giving on-pixel amplification. The potential for single photon counting by way of highly efficient materials and/or avalanche-mode operation, for example, using direct or indirect detector arrays operated at higher voltage with novel pixel architectures [23,24].

26.1.3 Automatic exposure control (AEC) and automatic brightness control (ABC)

Automatic exposure control (AEC) in 2D and 3D imaging on C-arm X-ray systems aims at keeping the dose at the detector entrance constant (e.g. 100 nGy/frame). In 3D imaging, this is in contrast to conventional MDCT scanners that employ a constant kV/mAs setting for a given image acquisition protocol (recognizing that MDCT scanners can also employ kV/mA modulation to improve noise and dose performance). The AEC draws as input the X-ray exposure to the detector in a certain region of the projection image. Using this input, the AEC varies first mAs, followed by kV to achieve the desired dose using prescribed exposure curves [25]. In some instances, dependent on object thickness, copper filtration is added or removed at the tube side or the focal spot size is changed during the adjustment phase (2–3 images) to increase X-ray tube output [26]. Voltage is varied lastly and may be predetermined for a specific detection task in 2D imaging, such as iodine or certain metal/metal compounds (e.g., nitinol or platinum, the main components of stents).

The use of AEC in 2D/3D imaging is aimed at reducing over- and underexposure, minimizing detector saturation and photon starvation and the corresponding information loss and object visualization challenges in 2D and reconstruction artifacts in 3D. When working with C-arm X-ray systems, it is important to keep this functionality in mind when performing 3D/2D registration as well as when attempting 3D image reconstruction from fluoroscopic images. (See Sect. 26.1.4.2 on fluoroscopic image postprocessing.) The exposure variation with angulation requires intensity calibration across a variety of energies and mAs (Sect. 26.2.1.2). Image postprocessing and incorrect intensity correction can produce image reconstruction errors ranging from incorrect Hounsfield Unit (HU) values in the reconstructed image to streak artifacts and distortion.

26.1.4 2D image processing
26.1.4.1 Detector corrections / image preprocessing

Each pixel of a FPD presents signal contributions from dark current and X-ray exposure. Prior to clinical use of a detector, both sources of pixel signal have to be calibrated across the detector to achieve a homogeneous image. To generate the dark current offset map, repeat image acquisition without X-ray exposure is performed. The array of images is then averaged and a unique offset correction factor is determined for each pixel [12,27]. It is common for clinical systems to update this map in the background when the system is idle. Gain maps require a valid offset map and can be determined for either a single, high-dose map at approximately three-fourths of saturation of the detector assuming a linear response over the exposures of interest, or a multipoint calibration that accounts for nonlinearities, particularly at dose close to the saturation level [27]. Using both the offset and gain map, defective pixels can be determined as pixels with high deviation from their surrounding neighbors (indicating unresponsive or always saturated pixel) or a high standard deviation from their average value (indicating an unstable pixel). While defects can be hard to perceive visually in 2D, the impact on 3D imaging in form or ring artifacts is a substantial detriment to low-contrast resolution. Further detector correction modes include lag or ghosting correction from prior acquired images, temperature-dependent gain for nonactively cooled detectors and delta correction for wandering heel effect for 3D imaging [28–30]. In addition, deviations from pixel-binning used for calibration, such as for specialized 3D imaging modes, require repeat of the offset and gain maps.

26.1.4.2 Postprocessing

CT or CBCT image reconstruction uses different filtration kernels in the Fourier domain to preprocess projection image data to achieve a certain image impression, trading of spatial and contrast resolution. Analogous methods exist in 2D image processing but are less explicit. To reduce patient and occupational dose, linear and nonlinear filters are commonly applied to the 2D raw image (after detector correction) to minimize the detrimental effects of quantum and electronic noise on image quality. While each vendor uses proprietary approaches, the filters can be split generally into temporal and image domain filtration. Temporal filtration incorporates prior images to reduce noise, using temporal weights and body site dependent motion models to reduce temporal blur [31,32]. Image domain filtration uses edge enhancement, frequency- and wavelet-domain filters, as well as custom designed filters focused on iodinated contrast enhanced vessels. In addition, image impression filters are applied, such as dynamic brightness rescaling (creating a flatter image with lower contrast) and intensity clustering (e.g., 2D roadmap), creating a custom image impression that varies from user to user. It is not uncommon that each user at a hospital uses a custom designed processing parameter set. It is important to note that each of these filtration steps introduces a temporal delay accumulating to ~100–200 ms in some instances. Fig. 26.3 illustrates the different image impressions obtained on a clinical angiography system. Images were acquired using the NEMA SCA&I cardiovascular fluoroscopic benchmark phantom (CIRS, Norfolk, VA). The phantom employs a rotary stage using a straight wire (simulating guidewire movement) as well as larger objects (numbers) and a stationary bar pattern.

It is also important to note that the image data output from the 2D image processing chain is typically not suitable to direct (linear or log) processing for 3D image reconstruction. Potential problems arise from log-transformation of image data, bit-depth

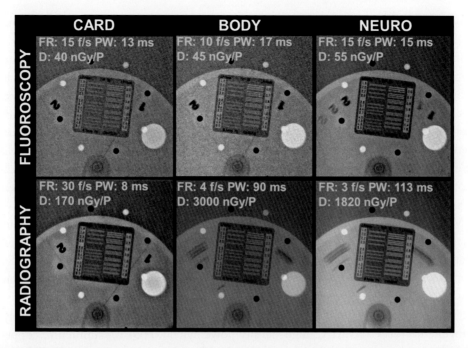

Figure 26.3 (Top row) Image impression after postprocessing of fluoroscopic images for various interventional specialties. Cardiology requires high frame rate imaging due to multiple motion sources and can only use limited temporal integration, resulting in higher quantum noise. Interventional radiology employs lower frame rates and limited temporal filtration and increased dose to account for increased object density. Neurovascular imaging can employ high temporal filtration due to limited motion of both object and devices. (Bottom row) Image impression in digital radiography. While no temporal filtration is used in these three modes, dose and pulse width length result in vastly different noise characteristics, temporal correlation, and blur. Similar to fluoroscopy, cardiac imaging uses a short pulse width due to strong object motion, with a gradual increase over body acquisition to neuro acquisitions. Note that cardiac imaging uses high frame rate at low dose, while body and neuro imaging uses low frame rates and higher dose according to the imaging requirements posed by each specialty.

conversion, nonlinear and temporal filtration, as well as redistribution and rescaling of intensity values. This processing may also need to be taken into account as well for 3D–2D image registration.

26.1.5 Radiation dose (fluoroscopy)

26.1.5.1 Measurement of fluoroscopic dose

As part of continuous quality control, annual tests on X-ray emitting equipment are performed. These include measurement of the X-ray output in terms of half value layer (HVL – thickness of attenuating material to reduce dose or exposure by a factor of 2) as well as the performance of the AEC. Dosimetry tools used in this context include ionization chambers, silicon diodes, and an array of slab or cylindrical phantoms simulating a variety of pertinent exposure conditions.

In an ionization chamber, X-ray photons interact with the electrons in the gas to create ion pairs. The ions migrate to either the anode or cathode, with electrons arriving at the anode providing a measure of radiation exposure. Solid state diodes based on silicon make use of *n-* and *p-type silicon*, impure silicon mixed with small amounts of phosphorus/boron and lithium. Incident X-rays interact with the silicon to create electron–hole pairs in the conduction/valence bands. Through an applied electric field, the electrons migrate to the anode on the *n-type* side and the holes will migrate to the negative voltage on the *p-side*. Again, the charge collected gives a measure of incident exposure.

Measurements performed using reference standards [33] can be used to estimate incident air kerma (K) and kerma area product (P). Air kerma, the estimated patient entrance dose at a reference level based on reference measurements, is currently used in prospective dose monitoring of patients. To test the reference air kerma, specific phantoms (depending on local regulatory requirements) or various thicknesses of attenuating material are used. For instance, a phantom can comprise various thicknesses of polymethylmethacrylate (PMMA), high-density polyethylene (HDPE), aluminum, copper, or a combination thereof. The phantom is placed on a stand on the patient table and positioned at image center in the anterior–posterior direction and at isocenter in the lateral position. The dosimeter is placed at a prescribed distance from the X-ray source at image center, and exposure is tested in either integration or rate modes [34]. Kerma-area product (or dose-area product) is conventionally measured at the tube exit windows using an ionization chamber and is reported by the manufacturer. This direct measure of X-ray radiation incorporates various factors influencing the amount of radiation impinging on the patient and is a potentially good control measure to assess problems with the system; however, dose reporting can be somewhat variable among vendors.

26.1.5.2 Reference dose levels

Due to the broad range in anatomical sites, body habitus, image quality preference, complexity, and type of intervention, as well as the variety of systems in the field, reference dose levels can be difficult to interpret generally. A survey of reference dose levels in endovascular procedures was reported in 2009 [35]. Societies focusing on various endovascular applications have established national registries aimed at providing members insight into average dose levels in their respective fields [36]. Ongoing work aims to minimize radiation dose to both patients and staff (occupational dose) through improved hardware in the imaging chain as well as software postprocessing methods [26,37–39]. Table 26.1 gives an overview of dose-area product (DAP) and exposure values reported in the literature. Regulatory bodies and medical physicists usually establish alert levels

Table 26.1 Reference dose characteristics for five common interventional procedures.

Intervention type	DAP (μGy m^2)	Air kerma (mGy)	Reference
Diagnostic Cerebral Angiography	10,620	697	[40]
Cerebral Aneurysm Embolization	21,880	3365	[40]
Percutaneous Coronary Interventions	5560	551	[43]
Electrophysiology	91	16	[41]
Transcatheter Arterial Chemoembolization	16,401	972	[42]

at particular dose levels, such as 2 Gy and 5 Gy of single case exposure to follow up for potentially deterministic effects of X-ray radiation on the patient.

Table 26.1 presents a summary of 2D imaging dose levels for different interventional specialties [40–43]. The dose levels cited for 2D interventional procedures are representative of currently reported values and can vary highly from site to site.

26.2. The 3D imaging chain

26.2.1 3D imaging prerequisites

To achieve artifact-free 3D image reconstructions, a variety of calibration and correction steps must be performed. Missing or incorrect corrections can result in image artifacts, noise, and inaccuracy in 3D image reconstruction. Due to manufacturing tolerances, resolution requirements, physical variability, and variations in system positioning in the interventional suite, these calibrations are unique for every system. In addition, system use and aging necessitates repeated calibration to be performed over time.

26.2.1.1 Geometrical calibration

Geometric calibration is performed for every 3D acquisition sequence available on the interventional X-ray system. Geometric calibration may vary due to the variations in acquisition sequences, speed, angulation step between images, frame rate, detector binning, C-arm start position, and C-arm trajectory. Additionally, mechanical factors such as C-arm gantry sag and trajectory inhomogeneity due to mechanical tolerances need to be accounted for. A C-arm pose at a given position during an acquisition arc consists of the angular position (α, β, γ) and possible translation (T) of the system, factors commonly referred to as extrinsic parameters. Intrinsic parameters completing the pose description are the source to axis and (SAD) the source to image distance (SID), the source position (X_s, Y_s, Z_s), detector position (X_d, Y_d, Z_d) (Fig. 26.4), and detector tilt and rotation (Roll (φ), Pitch (θ), Yaw (η)), as well as piercing point (u_0, v_0), pixel pitch (du, dv).

The procedure of geometric calibration involves a physical phantom, commonly a combination of a low attenuation encasing material and high attenuation metallic markers. Spherical markers of varying size are embedded in the casing material to create a

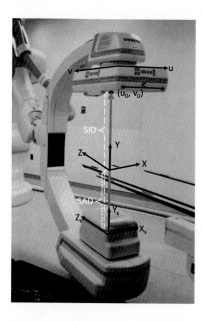

Figure 26.4 Illustration of C-arm system geometry.

distinct, stable geometric pattern satisfying the following criteria: minimal overlap of markers in 2D projection images, nonambiguity of projected pattern and easy detection in image and projection space. Different shapes have been described in literature, such as helix, single-, dual-, and multiplane ellipsoids, cubical setups, and circular arranged shapes [44–48]. In addition to the physical phantom, an exact numerical replica is available for the calibration procedure. For each 3D acquisition sequence, and each C-arm pose contained therein, projection images with the geometric calibration phantom positioned at isocenter are acquired.

Two basic approaches are commonly used to arrive at the system geometry description – pose determination and analytical calibration. Pose determination is based on the pin-hole camera model for the formation of 2D X-ray images on the FPD as a conic projection [47,49–54]. In this approach, the relationship between image domain 3D coordinates (x, y, z) and the 2D coordinates (u, v) can be modeled as a linear transformation of homogenous coordinates

$$m(u, v) = PM(x, y, z). \tag{26.1}$$

The 3×4 projection matrix P can be decomposed as a product of three matrices

$$P(\xi) = A(u_0, v_0, SID) R(\alpha, \beta, \gamma) T(x_s, y_s, z_s) \tag{26.2}$$

where $\xi = (u_0, v_0, SID, \alpha, \beta, \gamma, x_s, y_s, z_s)$ describes the acquisition geometry. The matrix A contains the intrinsic information on the acquisition system, the source-to-image distance (SID), the piercing point (u_0, v_0) and the pixel pitch (du, dv),

$$A(u_0, v_0, SID) = \begin{bmatrix} u_0/SID & du & 0 \\ v_0/SID & 0 & dv \\ 1/SID & 0 & 0 \end{bmatrix}, \tag{26.3}$$

$R(\alpha, \beta, \gamma)$ is an Euler-angle based rotation matrix, and $T(x_s, y_s, z_s)$ frame-to-frame translation matrix. Pose determination is generally the model chosen by industrial vendors due to its simplicity.

Analytical calibration approaches seek to define the imaging system geometry in exact terms, resulting in numerical values for all the system parameters defined. This approach allows deeper evaluation of the impact on parameter perturbation and image quality, theoretically allowing better hardware design to mitigate long-term effects of system mechanical degradation. A variety of approaches have been presented in literature, each using a specific approach in relating the 3D position of the physical phantom to the measured projection image information. Two approaches can be generalized: nonlinear optimization based [55,56] and direct analytical solution [44,45,57–59]. While pose estimation can be used with a variety of phantom shapes, analytical approaches tend to use phantoms with a specific design complementary to the derived approach.

26.2.1.2 I_0 calibration

A basic underlying principle of image reconstruction in transmission-based computed tomography is the Beer–Lambert Law, relating the incident X-ray fluence, tissue thickness, composition, and transmitted X-ray fluence:

$$I = I_0 e^{-\int \mu x dx}. \tag{26.4}$$

Different approaches to estimate I_0 exist in varying complexity. A good approximation for I_0 can be achieved by measuring a region in the projection image in which the beam was not attenuated. This must be performed for each image if the system is governed by an AEC. Challenges with this method are the potential absence of an unattenuated region, detector saturation, and image bit-depth conversion before evaluation. A more refined approach is to calibrate across a dose-area product (DAP) spectrum for a given kV. In such an approach, the kV is held constant and increased tube load is added through copper filtration, while keeping an area of the beam unattenuated. A lookup table (LUT) is created for a given kV as a function of DAP and can later be correlated with object acquisition DAP. Most commercial units do not follow these two methods due to the AEC and the varying imaging targets. These systems determine I_0 for a given system using a prior calibration to create a LUT of I_0 values as a function of tube setting (kV, mAs). In practice, only a limited number of measurements are taken at common dose points for a system with multiple kV settings. An attenuator (e.g., copper sheets) is placed in the X-ray beam and the AEC is allowed to select the mAs to achieve the requested dose at a given kV setting. The applied voltage determines the X-ray spectrum and the resulting effective energy of the X-ray beam and the mAs product. After all images (kV/dose pairs) have been acquired, an LUT is derived. During I_0 normalization, the recorded exposure parameters of a scan are correlated to the determined LUT, and the I_0 values are interpolated.

26.2.1.3 Other correction factors

In addition to detector gain, offset, and defect correction, as well as exposure normalization mentioned above, 2D projection data requires a number of additional corrections to yield high-quality CBCT reconstructions. Chief among these is correction of X-ray scatter. Within the typical diagnostic energy range of X-rays typical in CBCT imaging (~50–150 keV), X-ray scatter is a strong component of X-ray interaction in the body, and depending on the system geometry (e.g., distance of the detector from the patient) and body site, scattered photons can constitute the majority of X-rays incident on the detector. For example, at 50 keV, the likelihood of Compton scatter in water is more than 7 times that of photoelectric absorption.

X-ray scatter therefore presents a large (and spatially varying) bias in projection data that leads to shading and streaks in CBCT reconstructions, as illustrated in Fig. 26.5. The first defense against X-ray scatter is system geometry, with a larger distance between the patient and detector ("air gap") providing a strong degree of selectivity [60], recognizing competing effects of reduced exposure to the detector and increased focal spot blur [61]. Second is the possibility to incorporate an antiscatter grid on the detector array, absorbing X-rays that are incident on the detector at angles other than that in line with the focal spot. The use of antiscatter grids is somewhat variable in interventional imaging – fairly common in fluoroscopy but somewhat less so for CBCT image acquisition, since a grid may introduce subtle gridline artifacts in the projection data (rings in CBCT reconstructions) and may carry a dose penalty due to partial absorption of the primary (unscattered X-ray beam). Numerous other considerations, e.g., body site, pediatric or adult, etc., weigh in the consideration of whether to use a grid in CBCT imaging, and at the time of writing, systems in commercial use vary in this regard. Finally, correction of X-ray scatter from the 2D projections is a common – and in many instances, essential – data correction for high-quality CBCT. Methods for X-ray scatter correction vary widely, each aiming to estimate the X-ray scatter fluence in the projection image. A broad variety of methods have been reported [62,63], and fast Monte Carlo models [64] have shown good performance in correcting the high levels of X-ray scatter in CBCT. For example, Fig. 26.5 shows a CBCT image of a head phantom with and without scatter correction using the fast Monte Carlo method reported in

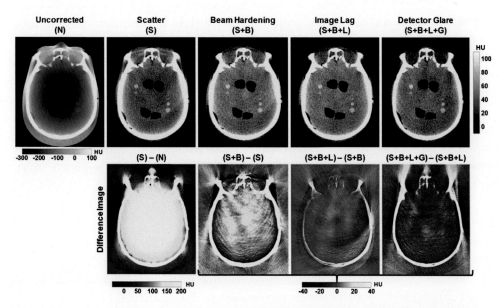

Figure 26.5 Artifacts and corrections. Scatter, beam-hardening, lag, and glare. The top row shows axial CBCT images of a head phantom with no corrections (N) as well as incremental application of corrections for X-ray scatter (S), beam hardening (B), image lag (L), and detector glare (G). The bottom row shows difference images as noted, illustrating the magnitude of each artifact individually. For example, (S)–(N) illustrates the magnitude and distribution of scatter artifacts. Similarly (S+B)–(S) shows beam-hardening, (S+B+L)–(S+B) shows lag artifacts, and (S+B+L+G)–(S+B+L) shows artifacts primarily associated with detector glare. *Images courtesy of Dr. Alejandro Sisniega (Department of Biomedical Engineering, Johns Hopkins University, Baltimore MD).*

[65]. More recently, deep learning methods demonstrate a potentially useful means of estimating scatter fluence in projection data as well [66].

Other artifacts can also be a detriment to CBCT image quality, depending on the imaging task. For example, beam–hardening effects are comparable to those in diagnostic CT and can be mitigated at least in part by similar means, e.g., correction based on iterative approximation of the object according to water and bone components [67,68, 65]. Artifacts somewhat more prevalent for CBCT systems with FPDs include effects arising from image lag and glare, as illustrated in Fig. 26.5: the former corrected in part by temporal deconvolution (i.e., correction of signal carried over from previous projection views) and the latter by low–frequency spatial deconvolution (i.e., correction of long–range signal correlation not associated simply with system blur). And, of course, metal instrumentation can present a major source of image degradation in CBCT in interventional imaging, including metallic implants and instrumentation. A variety of metal artifact reduction (MAR) techniques have been reported [69–71], most aiming to identify (segment) the region associated with metallic components in the 2D and/or

3D image domains and correct the projection data therein by "in-painting" from surrounding regions or using more sophisticated model-based, polyenergetic approaches.

Finally, patient motion during the CBCT scan can present a significant detriment to image quality, including involuntary motion from bowel gas, cardiac motion, and/or respiration. Such motion presents an inconsistency in the projection data that is evident as distortion and/or streaks in CBCT reconstructions. A variety of methods have been developed to manage or compensate for patient motion, including retrospective selection of projection data that is consistent in phase with periodic motion and image-domain motion compensation that solves an iterative optimization with respect to some characteristic of image sharpness in the CBCT image [72–78].

26.2.2 3D image reconstruction

Methods for CBCT image reconstruction are numerous and varied, constituting a vibrant area of ongoing research. A detailed description of the mathematics, algorithms, and computer implementations of such reconstruction methods is beyond the scope of a single chapter, and a basic overview of the most pertinent established and emerging methodologies is provided below.

26.2.2.1 Filtered backprojection

Filtered backprojection (FBP) has represented the primary means of CT image reconstruction throughout most of its history in clinical use, including FBP variations suitable to axial CT, helical/spiral CT, multidetector CT (MDCT), and CBCT, as described well in a variety of textbooks [79–81]. The essence and simplicity of FBP can be appreciated from the Fourier slice-projection theorem, which relates an object $\mu(x, y)$, its (parallel-beam) projections over angles θ, and the Fourier transform of the object $M(f_x, f_y)$. Consider a 2D axial slice of the object $\mu(x, y)$. A parallel-beam projection of the object at angle θ is

$$p(x', \theta) = \int_{-\infty}^{+\infty} dy' \mu(x', y'), \tag{26.5}$$

where (x', y') is a coordinate system rotated by θ with respect to (x, y). The Fourier transform of the projection, denoted $P(f_x, \theta)$, gives a 1D "spoke" in the Fourier domain,

$$P(f_x, \theta) = \int_{-\infty}^{+\infty} \int_{-\infty}^{+\infty} dx dy \, \mu(x, y) e^{-i2\pi f_x(x \cos \theta + y \sin \theta)}, \tag{26.6}$$

which is a 1D "spoke" of the 2D Fourier transform of $\mu(x, y)$ at angle θ:

$$M(f_x, f_y) = \Im [\mu(x, y)] = \int_{-\infty}^{+\infty} \int_{-\infty}^{+\infty} dx dy \, \mu(x, y) e^{-i2\pi (f_x x + f_y y)}. \tag{26.7}$$

Therefore, by acquiring projections over all angles θ from 0 to π, the 2D Fourier transform of the object can be built up spoke-by-spoke – and the object itself obtained (in principle) by inverse Fourier transform. The Fourier slice-projection theorem gives an important – if basic – connection between (the Fourier transform of) an object and (the Fourier transform of) its projections, though it is limited with respect to how tomographic projection is actually performed – for reasons of polar/Cartesian sampling and extension to divergent beams.

We can maintain a degree of mathematical intuition beyond that of the Fourier slice-projection theorem by considering further the progression from (a) 2D axial FBP for a parallel beam; (b) 2D axial FBP for a divergent fan beam; and (c) 3D volumetric FBP for a divergent "cone" beam as follows. The discussion below follows that of J. Hsieh [80] with minor changes in notation and an emphasis on the weighting terms appearing in the (a)–(b)–(c) variations of FBP.

Closed-form representation of tomographic reconstruction for (a) 2D axial FBP for a parallel beam can be obtained by considering again the domain (x', y') rotated by θ with respect to (x, y) and writing $dx'dy' = f_r df_r d\theta$. The object obtained by inverse Fourier transform is

$$
\begin{aligned}
\mu(x, y) &= \int_0^{2\pi} d\theta \int_{-\infty}^{+\infty} f_r df_r M(f_r \cos\theta, f_r \sin\theta) e^{+i2\pi f_r(x\cos\theta + y\sin\theta)} \\
&= \int_0^{\pi} d\theta \int_{-\infty}^{+\infty} df_r P(f_r, \theta) |f_r| e^{+i2\pi f_r(x\cos\theta + y\sin\theta)} \\
&= \int_0^{\pi} d\theta\, p(x\cos\theta + y\sin\theta) h'(x).
\end{aligned}
\tag{26.8}
$$

The second integral represents the inverse Fourier transform of $P(f_r, \theta)|f_r|$, which in the spatial domain is $p(x', \theta)$ filtered by the spatial-domain kernel $h'(x)$ corresponding to the "ramp" $|f_r|$. The solution to $\mu(x, y)$ can therefore be seen as a sum of ramp-filtered projection data backprojected over angles θ from 0 to π.

Extension to 2D axial fan-beam reconstruction introduces two important weighting factors to account for divergence in the axial plane. We again assume equiangular sampling and a curved detector centered on the source. Writing in a similar form as above, we have

$$
\mu(x, y) = \int_0^{2\pi} d\theta \frac{1}{L^2} \int_{-\gamma_{max}}^{+\gamma_{max}} d\gamma\, D\cos\gamma\, p(\gamma, \theta) h'(\gamma),
\tag{26.9}
$$

where γ is the angle between the source and a particular pixel on the detector ("detector angle"), and the filter $h'(\gamma)$ carries weighting that is dependent on detector angle. The two weighting terms of note in fan-beam FBP are: (1) the $w = D\cos\gamma$ term, where D is the source-to-isocenter distance, representing divergent-beam cosine weights applied to each pixel measurement; and (2) the angle-dependent ($\frac{1}{L^2}$) term, where L is the distance from the X-ray source to a particular voxel in the reconstruction.

Before continuing the progression to CBCT, we consider a variation of 2D fan-beam reconstruction in which the detector is flat. We represent the object function in the voxel domain described by (r, ϕ) instead of (x, y), where r is the distance from isocenter to the ray containing a given pixel, and ϕ is the angle between a line from the voxel to isocenter and a line through isocenter and parallel to the detector. The weighted filtered backprojection becomes

$$\mu(r, \phi) = \int_0^{2\pi} d\theta \frac{D^2}{[D + r\sin(\theta - \phi)]^2} \int_{-\infty}^{+\infty} dx' \frac{D}{\sqrt{D^2 + x'^2}} p(x', \theta) h(x' - x), \quad (26.10)$$

where the divergent-beam weights applied to each pixel measurement are now $\frac{D}{\sqrt{D^2 + x'^2}}$, and the angle-dependent term becomes $\frac{D^2}{[D + r\sin(\theta - \phi)]^2}$.

Extension to 3D cone-beam reconstruction with a flat detector introduces additional weighting factors to account for the fully 3D divergent volumetric beam. A broadly used practical implementation of cone-beam FBP is the Feldkamp–Davis–Kress (FDK) algorithm [82], which introduced the "Feldkamp" weights (alternatively, cosine weights) w_{FDK} that vary in inverse proportion to ray density in the 2D projection domain and are analogous to the ($\frac{1}{L^2}$) term in 2D fan-beam projection. Analytical forms and practical algorithms for FDK cone-beam reconstruction are detailed in textbooks by Hsieh [80] and Buzug [81].

The key elements of weighting, filtering, and backprojection are explicit in the formulations above. An additional term deserves mention, namely the "smoothing" or "apodization" filter. The ramp filter $|f_r|$ represents a high-pass filter arising from the radial density in the Fourier domain (for parallel or divergent beams). It is not intended as a "sharpening" filter per se; rather, it accounts exactly for the $(1/r)$ blur that would otherwise be imparted in backprojection. As a high-pass filter, however, it tends to amplify high-frequency noise; therefore, a low-pass "smoothing" filter is often applied to modulate such high-frequency noise. A broad variety of linear filters are suitable, e.g., the raised cosine Hann filter,

$$T_{win}(f) = \frac{1}{2}\left[1 - \cos\left(2\pi\frac{f}{F}\right)\right] \quad \text{for } 0 \le f \le F, \quad (26.11)$$

and the "smoothing" filter can be tuned in its cutoff frequency according to the imaging task, noting that whatever choice is made for T_{win}, it affects the resulting reconstruction in the manner of a linear filter (e.g., blur and noise correlation). For example, a filter with higher cutoff frequency can be selected for a sharper image at the cost of increased noise (perhaps suitable for visualization of high-contrast details), or a filter with lower cutoff frequency can be selected to smooth the image and reduce noise (perhaps suitable for visualization of large, low-contrast lesions). Of course, a dataset obtained from a given scan can be reconstructed with numerous filters appropriate to the task, e.g., a sharp "bone reconstruction" and a smooth "soft-tissue reconstruction," yielding separate volumes for distinct imaging tasks. Note also that application of the smoothing filter in the process of 3D filtered backprojection (e.g., FDK reconstruction) could certainly be implemented as a 2D filter – in the "row" direction of the projection data to counter high-frequency noise amplification as usual, and in the "column" direction to provide isotropic smoothing and better maintain isotropic spatial resolution characteristics in the 3D image reconstruction.

While an intuition for FBP can be appreciated in simple terms from the Fourier projection-slice theorem and the progression of analytical expressions described above, such is not – in practice – how 3D image reconstruction is usually performed in practical implementation. Instead, 3D image reconstruction is usually based on an algorithmic implementation of "voxel-driven" reconstruction. Generic pseudocode is as follows:

(1) Apply data corrections (gain, offset, defect, X-ray scatter, etc.) to projection data $p[x'; \theta]$;

(2) Apply ramp filter $h[u]$, apodization filter $T_{win}[f_u]$, and cosine weights $w_{FDK}[u, v]$;

(3) Define 3D voxel grid $\mu[i, j, k]$, including voxel size $[a_{xy}, a_z]$ and FOV;

(4) for all projection views $N_i = 1:N_{views}$

(5)   for all voxels i = 1:FOV_x, j = 1:FOV_y, and k = FOV_z

(6)   Compute intersection (u, v) of ray $(x_{source}, y_{source}, k_{source}) \rightarrow (i, j, k) \rightarrow$ Detector plane

(7)   Determine detector signal at intersection (6) by interpolation of detector data (2)

(8)   Scale detector signal (7) by angle-dependent weights

(9)   Add (average) the weighted signal (8) to voxel value at position (i, j, k)

(10)   end k; end j; end i; end N_i

Following data preprocessing (steps 1–2), including gain-offset and projection-domain artifact corrections, the 3D reconstruction matrix for $\mu(i, j, k)$ is defined. Then, for each projection view (at angle θ) and for each voxel (i, j, k), the intersection point (u, v) on the detector is computed for a ray containing the source and voxel. Note that geometric calibration (i.e., complete pose determination of the source and detector for angles θ) is implicit at this stage (6) in order to determine the position of the source and detector. The weighted and filtered detector signal at the (u, v) intersection point is computed by interpolation of neighboring measurements, scaled according to the angle-dependent weights described above, and added to the value at voxel (i, j, k). The process is repeated for all voxels and all views. Note that the process is fully parallelizable in the projection, weighting / filtering, and backprojection operations for each voxel.

Alternative analytical reconstruction methods present an additional important area of ongoing development [83–91]. Such methods are suitable to a broad variety of noncircular orbits, including orbits that may be executed on the interventional C-arm systems described below, offering potential improvements in image noise, artifacts, and field of view.

26.2.2.2 Emerging methods: optimization-based (iterative) image reconstruction (OBIR)

While FBP has represented the mainstay of 3D image reconstruction in clinical CT, it is not without its limitations. Chief among these is sensitivity to noise and/or bias in the detector measurements (e.g., Poisson noise due to the discrete nature of incident photons, as well as other sources of noise or blur arising from the detector itself) which translate to noise, artifacts, and resolution losses in the 3D image reconstruction. Broad families of iterative optimization-based image reconstruction (OBIR) – alternatively, model-based image reconstruction (MBIR) – methods have been developed in recent decades, motivated in part to overcome such limitations, improve CT image quality, and reduce radiation dose. By 2011, such methods became commonly available on clinical diagnostic MDCT systems and are now routinely employed as an alternative to FBP – especially in relation to low-dose imaging protocols.

Such methods involve iterative approximation of $\mu(x, y, z)$ – or more specifically, the discrete volumetric parameterization $\mu[i, j, k]$ – beginning with some initialization (e.g., a zero image or the FBP image) and refining the estimate according to a particular objective function and optimization/update scheme. The objective function typically invokes a forward model of the imaging system to compare the current image estimate to the projection data measurements, and the optimization seeks to minimize some form of difference between the measurements and the forward projection of the image estimate

$$\mu = \arg \min \|y, F(\mu)\| \qquad (26.12)$$

Such forward models may be as simple as a forward projection of the image volume (e.g., Siddon's method) for the particular system geometry, and they can be made increasingly sophisticated to better account for the discrete parameterization of system geometry (e.g., the "footprint" of the 3D voxel in forward projection to the 2D detector domain) as well as the physics of the imaging system (e.g., a polyenergetic beam, energy-dependent attenuation in the object, blur in the detector, electronic noise, etc.). Note also that such methods typically do not require a particular source–detector orbit (e.g., a circular orbit as described above for FBP); rather, the forward model is applicable to essentially any known geometry, and such methods are therefore well suited to cases in which the source–detector trajectory is arbitrarily complex.

Broad categorization of OBIR methods can be considered as "algebraic" or "statistical." Algebraic reconstruction techniques (ART) seek an iterative estimation of μ by applying a correction to the current estimate determined by the residual error between the projection (represented by the system matrix projection geometry A) and backprojection (represented by A^T) and the measured line integrals

$$\hat{\mu}^{(m+1)} = \hat{\mu}^{(m+1)} + A^T[l - A\mu], \tag{26.13}$$

where normalization of the projection/backprojection operators has been omitted for simplicity. A broad variety of ART approaches have been reported, usually involving this basic linearization of the forward model (Beers' law forward projection in arbitrary system geometry) and under some conditions is equivalent to a least-squares objective function $\arg\min \|y - A\mu\|^2$.

Statistical approaches extend the forward model described above to include a model for stochastic variations (noise) in the measurements. For example, likelihood-based approaches consider the joint probability that measurements y result from the image estimate μ, denoted $p(y \mid \mu)$. The maximum-likelihood (ML) method, as its name implies, maximizes the objective function

$$\hat{\mu} = \arg\max L(y, \mu), \tag{26.14}$$

where L represents the joint probability – alternatively the log-likelihood $L(y \mid \mu) = \ln p(y \mid \mu)$. A variety of statistical models can be envisioned, including a basic Poisson distribution in incident X-rays, a Gaussian approximation to the image statistics, and higher-fidelity models that seek to describe other physical factors of noise and blur in the imaging chain [92,93].

The maximum likelihood estimate can be regularized to enforce particular qualities ("priors") in the resulting image. Such regularization is imparted by way of a penalty function

$$\hat{\mu} = \arg\max L(g \mid \mu) - \beta R(\mu), \tag{26.15}$$

where R is the regularization term, which penalizes particular undesirable image characteristics, and β is the regularization strength. For example, image smoothness (e.g., homogeneous, piecewise constancy) can be enforced via a regularizer than penalizes differences in neighboring voxels, $R(\mu) = \sum_j \sum_k \psi(\mu_j, \mu_k)$. Many forms of the penalty function ψ can be invoked, including the sum of squared differences $\psi = (\mu_j - \mu_k)^2$ (which tends toward simple smoothing) and forms that more strongly preserve edges, such as linear total variation based on the 1-norm and others. Such penalized likelihood (PL) approaches have demonstrated strong improvements in imaging performance compared to FBP in a variety of applications.

OBIR approaches are also amenable to incorporation of prior information (e.g., a previously acquired image of the patient or knowledge of a particular structure known to be within the patient) via additional regularization. Prior image-based reconstruction has demonstrated promising advances in image quality by incorporation of such prior information – especially under conditions of undersampled data (e.g., sparse projection views), data inconsistency (e.g., patient motion during the scan), and/or a high degree of image noise (low-dose projection data). Among the more prominent approaches is the PICCS method (prior image constrained compressed sensing), which mixes prior image information with the current data in a controlled manner [94]. Extension of the PL methods described above have been described to combine deformably registered prior information with the current data and a noise model, e.g., prior-image-registered PL estimate (PIRPLE) [95,96]. The PIRPLE approach combines the advantages of a noise model with prior image information and can be similarly controlled in the strengths of prior image regularization.

OBIR approaches remain an active area of ongoing research and clinical translation in applications ranging from diagnostic CT to interventional CBCT [97]. Topics include modeling of image quality characteristics for nonlinear OBIR methods [98], spatially varying regularization to improve quality and uniformity throughout the FOV [99,100], and novel optimization schemes aimed at maximizing imaging performance with respect to an imaging task – termed "task-driven" imaging [101,102].

26.2.2.3 Emerging methods: machine learning methods for cone-beam CT

Deep learning approaches hold tremendous promise for 3D image reconstruction as well, burgeoning since ~2015 thanks in part to advances in parallel computing capacity and the availability of large datasets for training neural networks of various architectures. Such learning-based approaches applied to medical image analysis, classification, registration, and reconstruction represent a large area of current research, as evidenced by a recent IEEE-TMI special issue [103] and MICCAI workshops on the topic [104]. Deep learning methods are covered in greater detail in the section of this book entitled *Machine Learning for Medical Image Analysis* herein. Below, a brief overview is provided with a focus on applications of machine learning methods in interventional imaging and X-ray cone-beam CT.

Among the "low-hanging fruit" [105] of deep learning approaches in 3D imaging is application to image denoising (whereby a neural network learns the relationship between "noisy" low-dose images and low-noise (higher dose) images) and X-ray scatter correction (in which the network learns the relationship between projection data measurements and the scatter fluence therein). These amount to image processing methods that can work in concert with 3D FBP or OBIR described above [106–109].

In another sense, a deep neural network can be trained to solve the inverse problem associated with tomographic reconstruction itself, i.e., learning the relationship between projection data measurements and 3D image reconstructions [110–113]. For example, a neural network trained on large sets of noisy projection data and their corresponding FBP reconstructions (alternatively, ART or ML or PL reconstructions) learn the transfer characteristics associated with such correspondence and can form image reconstructions of comparable quality as the underlying algorithm by which it was trained. Somewhat distinct from the image processing methods described above, the projection data measurements correspond to the features, and the image reconstruction itself is the output. Such methods often present the advantage of computational speed (once trained) in comparison to computationally intense OBIR. A number of challenges persist and are the subject of ongoing research, for example, the availability of suitable training sets in a broad spectrum of 3D imaging applications, the susceptibility of a neural net to statistical discrepancies between the training and test data, the sensitivity to rare semantic features not present in the training data, and the means by which deep learning based 3D imaging performance can be assessed relative to conventional metrics of spatial resolution, noise, dose dependence, and task performance.

In summary, the broad and burgeoning scope of 3D image reconstruction methods surveyed above – ranging from analytical forms to iterative optimization and deep learning networks – present opportunities for innovation within the algorithms themselves, in the rigorous, quantitative, and meaningful evaluation of imaging performance, and in the translation to clinical applications that will benefit from such advances. Analytical, physics- and model-based methods are well suited to high-fidelity, well sampled, "clean" data, especially in scenarios in which very few, if any, priors are available and the imaging task may not be well defined. Lower-fidelity data, e.g., noisy data associated with reduction of radiation dose and/or sparse data associated with few-view acquisition, may often be better handled by iterative optimization-based and/or example-based learning methods, especially when one has access to strong priors and/or reliable definition of the imaging task.

26.2.3 Radiation dose (CBCT)

26.2.3.1 Measurement of dose in CBCT

The radiation dose distribution in an axial plane for a CBCT acquisition is neither radially nor rotationally symmetric. A full appreciation of dose deposition in the object therefore requires – at a minimum – measurements at central and peripheral positions in a cylindrical or anthropomorphic phantom. Dose values, analogous to $CTDI_W$ defined for axial MDCT, can be computed as $D_w = (1/3) D_{center} + (2/3) \overline{D_{periph}}$. Measurements of D_{center} and $\overline{D_{periph}}$ can be obtained from a 16-cm CTDI phantom positioned at isocenter [14,114–116]. CTDI phantoms typically contain five bore holes for dosimetry purposes, one at the center and four at cardinal points at the periphery. To perform the measurements, a small ion chamber or solid-state detector is positioned at the center of a given bore hole, and a scan is acquired for a selected CBCT protocol. The measurement is repeated for each bore hole (and repeated three times) to yield the average value at each location. The center bore average yields D_{center} and the average across all peripheral measurements yields $\overline{D_{periph}}$. A 16 cm diameter CTDI phantom is typically used in relation

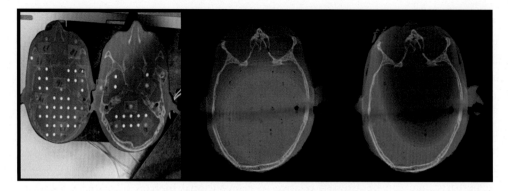

Figure 26.6 (Left) TLD setup for dose measurement in an anthropomorphic head phantom. (Middle) Dose distribution measured for a diagnostic MDCT scan. (Right) Dose distribution for a CBCT scan. Note that the color scale dose images were scaled independently. MDCT exhibits a more symmetric, homogeneous dose distribution, whereas the C-arm CBCT dose distribution can vary strongly, depending on acquisition protocol, e.g., a tube-under-table short-scan acquisition in the case shown here. *[Image courtesy of T. Szczytukowicz, University of Wisconsin–Madison.]*

to head imaging, and a 32 cm diameter phantom is typically used to measure dose for body sites [116].

Thermoluminescence detectors (TLDs) can be used for measurements of effective organ dose, calculations of which are somewhat more involved and usually only performed if thorough assessment of a particular image acquisition protocol is required, e.g., in regulatory approval. TLD are disks with minimal thickness and diameter of ~2.5 mm. Anthropomorphic phantoms are commercially available with small bore holes that can hold the disks at discrete locations. During image acquisition, radiation dose accumulates in the disks, and the absorbed dose can be read by heating the TLD and measuring the light emitted by it. Fig. 26.6 gives an illustration of TLD setup in anthropomorphic head phantom.

Measurements should be performed for each CBCT acquisition protocol and body site due to the uniqueness of both. CBCT protocols can vary by application in the starting position, extent of the source–detector orbit, angular rotation per frame, dose per frame, kV, field of view, and other factors, illustrating the need to characterize the dosimetry for each such protocol. For example, Fig. 26.6 shows the difference in dose distribution for a cranial MDCT scan (left) and a typical C-arm CBCT scan. Both measurements were performed using a TLD based approach as in Fig. 26.6(left). Note the strongly asymmetric dose distribution associated with the CBCT scan protocol.

26.2.3.2 Reference dose levels

Considerable insight into the radiation dose characteristics for a given CBCT acquisition protocol on a clinical system can be gained by examining the dose report generated

Table 26.2 Radiation dose (effective dose, mSv) reported for different 3D acquisition protocols.

Acquisition site – Single scan dose CBCT	mSv	Reference
3D DR – Head	0.5	[118]
3D DSA – Head	0.9	[118]
High-Quality Cranial Imaging	2.9–5.4	[118,124]
Lung	0.98	[120]
Abdomen	15–37	[124]
Cardiac	6.6	[122,123]

at the end of the case. The dose-area product (DAP, or Air-Kerma product KAP) and Air Kerma approximation of skin exposure are commonly reported with respect to a system reference point (e.g., 15 cm toward the tube from isocenter). The reported dose will vary due to acquisition protocol as well as patient anatomy (e.g., BMI, implants). An overview of reference values published for select body sites and acquisition protocols is shown in Table 26.2 [117–123], each determined by TLD measurements. Fig. 26.7 shows an example of a dose report available at the end of a procedure, giving an abbreviated overview of the case. Deeper insight can be gained from DICOM structured dose reports (DICOM SR) available on newer angiography systems. These reports record system parameters at each press of the foot pedal. While this data may be difficult to parse manually, they are important in quality assurance dose monitoring programs.

26.3. System embodiments

26.3.1 Mobile systems: C-arms, U-arms, and O-arms

A variety of mobile intraoperative imaging systems emerged in the first two decades of the 20th century with capability for 2D fluoroscopy and 3D CBCT. The shape of the gantry and source–detector orbit about the patient can be categorized as C-arms, U-arms, and O-arms as described below and illustrated in Fig. 26.8.

A C-arm is characterized by an X-ray source and detector on a C-shaped gantry that typically approaches the patient and operating table from the lateral (left or right) side. Alternative setups can be found for imaging of the extremities, e.g., in orthopaedic trauma surgery involving an arm board or leg board attachment to the operating table. The source–detector orbit is in the azimuthal direction along the curvature of the C, typically following a "half-scan" semicircular orbit of 180° + fan angle. Among the first such systems was the Iso-C^{3D} (later versions including the Arcadis Orbic 3D, Siemens Healthcare), featuring an X-ray image intensifier (XRII) as the detector. More recent C-arm embodiments for higher quality CBCT are based on a FPD, including the Vario 3D (Ziehm, Nuremberg Germany) and Cios Spin (Siemens Healthineers, Forchheim Germany) shown in Fig. 26.8. One of the differentiating features among such C-arms

```
                               Exam Protocol
-------------------------------------------------------------------------------
Patient Info:
Name:    ████  ██████          Sex: █  ID:  ██████
-------------------------------------------------------------------------------
Patient Position:  HFS                                     03-Mar-14 07:19:11

1    3D          FIXED    5sDCT 70kV Card              5s  60F/s  03-Mar-14 10:10:03
A   70kV   316mA  3.6ms   0.0CL large 0.0Cu 39cm  624.43µGym² 33.2mGy  98RAO  0CRA 248F

2    CARD        FIXED    Card15  <6kg              6s  30F/s  03-Mar-14 10:38:15
A   60kV   330mA  3.4ms   0.0CL small 0.3Cu 32cm   24.18µGym²  3.0mGy   5RAO  41CRA 175F

2    CARD        FIXED    Card15  <6kg              6s  30F/s  03-Mar-14 10:38:15
B   60kV   334mA  3.4ms   0.0CL small 0.3Cu 20cm   17.49µGym²  3.6mGy  90LAO   0CRA 175F

3    CARD        FIXED    Card15  <6kg              3s  30F/s  03-Mar-14 10:56:15
A   60kV   181mA  3.4ms   0.0CL small 0.3Cu 32cm    6.76µGym²  0.9mGy   3LAO   3CAU  88F

4    CARD        FIXED    Card15  <6kg              3s  30F/s  03-Mar-14 11:01:49
A   60kV   183mA  3.4ms   0.0CL small 0.3Cu 32cm    7.47µGym²  0.9mGy   3LAO   3CAU  96F

5    CARD        FIXED    Card15  <6kg              2s  30F/s  03-Mar-14 11:05:00
A   60kV   214mA  3.4ms   0.0CL small 0.3Cu 32cm    6.18µGym²  0.8mGy   3LAO   3CAU  69F

6    CARD        FIXED    Card15  <6kg              5s  30F/s  03-Mar-14 11:11:45
A   60kV   131mA  3.4ms   0.0CL small 0.3Cu 39cm   14.97µGym²  1.0mGy   3LAO   3CAU 156F


***Accumulated exposure data***                           03-Mar-14 11:39:47
-------------------------------------------------------------------------------
Performing Physician:  ████ ██████           Exposures: 7
Total Fluoro:  18.6min Max.Skin Entrance Dose: 27mGy   Total: 806.37µGym²    57.1mGy
A    Fluoro:  17.6min  98.33µGym²        12.4mGy   Total: 782.32µGym²    52.3mGy
B    Fluoro:   1.0min   6.56µGym²         1.3mGy   Total:  24.05µGym²     4.8mGy
===============================================================================
-------------------------------------------------------------------------------
```

Figure 26.7 Example dose report for an interventional procedure involving treatment of a pediatric congenital heart defect. The exam protocol gives an overview of the DAP and exposure for each radiographic acquisition (2D and 3D) as well as the type, the tube exposure parameters and tube angulations (Artis Q.zen, Siemens Healthineers, Forchheim, Germany). *Example provided courtesy of L. Lamers (American Family Children's Hospital, Madison WI).*

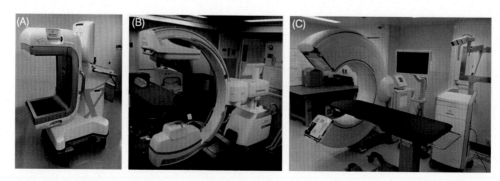

Figure 26.8 Mobile intraoperative imaging systems with 3D imaging capability: (A) the xCAT XL mobile U-arm (Xoran, Ann Arbor MI); (B) the Cios Spin mobile C-arm (Siemens Healthineers, Forcheim Germany); (C) the O-arm and Stealth Station (Medtronic, Minneapolis MN). *Image (A) is courtesy of Dr. Robert Labadie and Antonio "Drew" Scheffano (Department of Otolaryngology and Vanderbilt Institute of Surgery and Engineering, Vanderbilt University, Nashville TN).*

is whether the gantry is isocentric: an isocentric gantry maintains the center of the FOV as it rotates through the source-detector orbit; as a result, the orbital arc is approximately circular, and system geometry for 3D image reconstruction is essentially that in Sect. 26.2, similar to a diagnostic CT scanner, recognizing of course the need for geometric calibration (Sect. 26.2.1.1) to account for gantry flex. In fluoroscopy, an isocentric C-arm also maintains the center of the FOV as the C-arm is rotated from PA to LAT views. A nonisocentric C-arm (e.g., the Ziehm Vario 3D) can still perform 3D image reconstruction, of course, but the source–detector orbit is modified by way of additional translational motion of the gantry during rotation, and 3D image reconstruction methods are accordingly modified. State-of-the-art mobile C-arms regularly feature such additional motorization of the gantry, easing positioning at tableside and enabling noncircular orbits that can improve expand the 3D image FOV and improve image quality.

A U-arm is characterized by an X-ray source and detector on a U-shaped gantry that typically approaches the patient and operating table from the superior aspect (i.e., on the longitudinal axis of the patient). The source–detector orbit is in the axial plane, of course, just as for the C-arm systems mentioned above, but perpendicular to the U-shaped gantry itself. This allows a complete 360° orbit about the patient, although the range of body sites that may be imaged is limited by the "throat" of the U-arm, i.e., sufficient to reach the head, neck, and upper thorax (alternatively, the distal lower extremities), but usually not the abdomen or pelvis. An example system is the X-Cat (Xoran, Ann Arbor MI) shown in Fig. 26.8(A), used for CBCT guidance of head-and-neck / otolaryngology and cranio-maxillofacial surgery.

An O-arm is characterized by an X-ray source and detector within an O-shaped ring gantry as with a typical diagnostic CT scanner, allowing a complete 360° orbit about the patient. A key innovation in such embodiments involves a "breakable" gantry as evident in the O-arm system by Medtronic (Minneapolis MN). In such a system, the O-arm gantry "breaks" as shown in Fig. 26.8(C) to allow the system to approach the patient and operating table from the lateral (left or right) side as with a C-arm (allowing the system to reach a full range of body sites, including the thorax and pelvis) and then "closes" to a ring allowing a 360° orbit of the source and detector. The closed O-arm gantry also means that the orbit is executed without exposed moving parts and thereby reduces risk of collision during the scan.

26.3.2 Fixed-room C-arm systems

Like the mobile systems described above, fixed-room C-arm systems consist of an X-ray tube and detector, a C-arm capable of angular and/or azimuthal rotation, and a base. Fixed-room C-arms, however, typically employ a larger SDD, flexible detector positioning, various detector sizes depending on clinical specialty, a more powerful X-ray tube, and increased 2D and 3D imaging acquisition capabilities. Additionally, fixed C-arm systems are usually integrated with other aspects of the interventional suite, e.g., the patient support table, in order to avoid collision during fast rotation. The systems are conventionally designed with an accompanying angiographic table, patient collision detection, as well as position sensors in the C-arm base. Image display systems have been developed allowing flexible display of multiple inputs and satisfying the need to incorporate the imaging system into the complex data stream during advanced angiographic procedures. Finally, fixed-room C-arm systems are available in different base configurations – affixed to the floor or ceiling – geared toward the different requirements of various specialties in interventional/angiographic fields.

The arm supporting the X-ray tube and detector pair can support fast rotation in lateral as well as cranial/caudal positions with smaller deformation due to flex than described above for mobile systems. This stiffness also allows the support of actively cooled X-ray tubes (conventional power of 25 to 90 kW depending on focal spot size) and large flat-panel detectors (up to 40×40 cm^2) with wide focus antiscatter grids. X-ray tubes may feature multiple focal spot sizes, allowing more tailored 2D and 3D image acquisition sequences according to both power requirements and the imaging task. Active cooling of the X-ray tube is necessary due to the potentially long procedure duration (>2 hours) and power/X-ray dose requirement due to large patient habitus. Motion systems on the detector allow change in SID for 2D procedures for dose efficiency, while the imaging chain commonly enables different zoom modes to visualize endovascular devices of sub-mm size with individual strands of <50 nm.

The C-arm and base incorporate position sensors with the patient support table. The table is usually designed to support patients weighing up to 450 pounds while maintaining free-floating capability in lateral and longitudinal directions. Depending on manufacturer, all axes may be motorized to facilitate positioning and recall, as well as tracking of patient position to minimize dose during interventional procedures. Tables may additionally tilt, swivel, and cradle, providing flexibility that can improve vascular access and patient loading. Recent years have seen the incorporation of surgical tables with fixed-room C-arms to enable complex surgical procedures that would benefit from advanced intraoperative 2D and 3D imaging.

Information density in the angiographic suite is continuously increasing with multiple data streams (e.g., hematology, neural monitoring) as well as additional imaging equipment (e.g., Ultrasound, IVUS, OCT) needed to be displayed at the interventionalists finger tips. Current solutions include large ceiling-mount displays (>50 inch) with multiple input streams and layout capabilities. Requirements for these displays differ from conventional TV screens, requiring medical grade X-ray image display (monochromatic) as well as color display, and a nonmirroring protective screen imbedded due to hits and scrapes from other in-room equipment. Finally, the hanging of the equipment needs to support easy positioning alongside the patient table.

Embedded sensors on some systems help to make the imaging system more semi-aware of the positioning of its respective parts and better enable advanced imaging

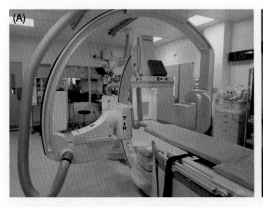 

Figure 26.9 Example fixed-room C-arm systems for fluoroscopy and CBCT: (A) bi-plane C-arm system (Artis Zee, Siemens Healthineers, Forcheim Germany). In this configuration, the floor-mounted C-arm is capable of fluoroscopy and CBCT, while the ceiling-mounted system provides fluoroscopy; (B) robotic C-arm for interventional imaging in interventional radiology (Artis Zeego, Siemens Healthineers, Forcheim Germany). *Images (A)–(B) courtesy of Dr. Clifford Weiss (Department of Radiology, Johns Hopkins University, Baltimore MD) and Ms. Sarah Capostagno (Department of Biomedical Engineering, Johns Hopkins University, Baltimore MD).*

procedures with fusion and overlay of preoperative volumetric data. Advanced 3D applications and workflows using this information are conventionally performed on a connected workstation and are focused on improving procedure guidance and shortening time. Workflows focus on automatic extraction of vessel path and targets for embolization procedures (e.g., liver, prostate), extraction of data from preoperative data (e.g., CTO guidance), or needle guidance for percutaneous procedures (e.g., biopsy, drainage, ablation) combined with live overlay of 3D structures on 2D image stream.

Depending on the clinical specialty, systems can be manufactured in a variety of configurations. Among the most common designs is a single C-arm mounted on the floor as prevalent in cardiac catheterization labs, due to the comparably lower cost and installation requirements. In recent years, both interventional radiology and cardiology suites have tended toward ceiling–mounted units to allow increased patient long–axis coverage, left and right side access as well as multiple 3D acquisition positions. The ceiling mount requires somewhat increased installation cost due to high–strength ceiling rigging to support the suspended C–arm. A combined approach is the bi–planar system commonly found in neurovascular interventional labs (Fig. 26.9(A)). Complex cranial vascular anatomy often requires two planes to improve mental visualization of pathways during diagnosis and intervention.

Some systems have emerged with more specialized configurations geared toward surgery. Examples are the Discovery IGS 740 (GE Healthcare, Waukesha, WI) and the Zeego and Pheno systems (Siemens Healthineers, Forchheim, Germany). The Discovery system uses a movable base to allow flexible positioning of the system while the

Zeego and Pheno systems are mounted on a robotic arm to achieve a large variety of approaches and table positions (Fig. 26.9(B)). Due to this flexibility, the Zeego and Pheno systems have become common in conventional angiography procedures and mixed-use/"hybrid" interventional theaters as well. With imaging requirements increasing in ever more complex interventional procedures, many hospitals have installed multimodality systems in such "hybrid" rooms. A combination of CT or MR with an angiographic C-arm with streamlined patient transfer between the systems represents the current state-of-the-art in multimodality image-guided therapies.

26.3.3 Interventional multi-detector CT (MDCT)

A variety of other interventional 3D X-ray imaging systems are worth mentioning, though they are beyond the scope of this chapter, which focuses on systems for CBCT. Most notable are systems for intraoperative multidetector CT (MDCT) that are similar in principle to diagnostic CT but are embodied in a form suitable to application in image-guided interventions – the main differences being portability, lower power requirements, integration with a diversity of operating table setups, and a larger central bore (inner diameter of the CT gantry) to accommodate a variety of patient setups and provide better access to the surgical field. Example systems include the BodyTom (Samsung/Neurologica, Boston MA) and the Airo (Brainlab, Munich Germany).

Alternatively, direct translation of a diagnostic-quality CT scanner into the operating theater has been a subject of interest for decades [125]. Challenges include integration/transfer between the operating table and the patient support for helical scanning. Emerging systems include CT scanners "on rails" such that the CT scanner moves along the patient's longitudinal axis to effect helical motion and volumetric acquisition.

The CBCT systems summarized in Sects. 26.3.1 and 26.3.2 provide combined capability for 3D imaging and fluoroscopy – the former for purposes of navigation and 3D visualization of the surgical product, for example, and the latter for real-time imaging during device placement, e.g., placement of a catheter or K-wire under fluoroscopic guidance. The CT systems mentioned above typically do not provide fluoroscopic imaging, motivating the addition of a fluoroscopic C-arm in combination with the CT scanner. An early example of CT mated to C-arm fluoroscopy in the 1990s was seen in a Picker CT scanner (Picker, Cleveland OH). A more recent example is the Angio CT (Siemens Healthineers, Forcheim Germany) featuring a CT on rails optionally integrated with a fixed-room angiographic C-arm.

26.4. Applications

The field of interventional radiology has changed substantially within the last decade. This has not only been enabled by improved imaging equipment, but also by new disruptive devices entering the marketplace and pivotal clinical studies showing the benefit of minimally invasive treatments. These factors have worked in combination to transform the state-of-the-art in medical interventions from highly invasive procedures (such as aneurysm clipping with craniotomy or open-heart surgery) to minimally invasive procedures offering reduced morbidity, mortality and recovery time.

Another major area of application for 2D radiographic/fluoroscopic imaging and CBCT is image-guided radiation therapy (IGRT). In fact, such areas were among the first areas for CBCT to emerge in medicine (apart from dental imaging), motivated by the need to reduce margins and escalate dose in increasingly conformal radiotherapy procedures in the late 1990s [13,126]. Such technology has become a prevalent standard of care in radiation therapy, though beyond the scope of this chapter, which focuses on interventional procedures in radiology (Sect. 26.4.1), cardiology (Sect. 26.4.2), and surgery (Sect. 26.4.3).

26.4.1 Interventional radiology

26.4.1.1 Neurological interventions

Neurovascular interventions generally employ biplane angiography systems with large detectors (40×30 cm^2) allowing full coverage of the adult head for 2D and 3D imaging. Current state-of-the-art treatments in minimally invasive neurological interventions have three main targets: the treatment of ruptured and unruptured aneurysm, the embolization of arterial–venous malformations (AVM), and the treatment of acute hemorrhagic and ischemic stroke. Enabling imaging technologies required for these treatments is 2D fluoroscopy, digital subtraction angiography (2D DSA), and 3D vascular and soft tissue imaging. Nonacute patients generally undergo diagnostic imaging first, involving 2D DSA and 3D imaging to evaluate existing disease state (Fig. 26.10). The use of 3D DSA enables the physician to evaluate vessel topology with high-spatial resolution (~0.5 mm isotropic voxel size) and plan the approach to the procedure with respect to factors such as aneurysm dimensions, vessel bifurcations, and AVM architecture with a focus on supplying arterial vessels, venous drainage, and intranidal aneurysm.

Treatment of aneurysms involves an array of devices, depending on aneurysm locations and dimensions, such as stent and endovascular coil constructs [127], flow diverting stents [128], or intrasaccular flow diverters [129]. A procedure typically involves a 3D DSA image once access has been gained to manually define the C-arm working angles using the intrinsic connection between C-arm, angiographic table, and patient. Endovascular tools are advanced to the site of disease under 2D roadmap fluoroscopic guidance (Sect. 26.1.4) or using 3D/2D overlay of the acquired 3D DSA image. Deployment of devices is then performed using general fluoroscopy or short sequences of digital radiography scenes (see Sect. 26.1.5). After deployment, 3D imaging of the construct is performed, using either 3D DSA or high-quality CBCT with a concurrent contrast injection [130,131].

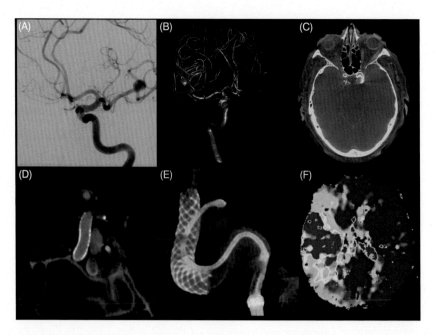

Figure 26.10 Example of imaging modes in neuroendovascular applications: (A) 2D DSA acquisition showing an aneurysm on the top right ACA; (B) 3D DSA of same patient; (C) high-quality C-Arm CBCT acquisition after flow diverting stent placement; (D) zoom-in view of a flow diverter; (E) volumetric rendering of flow diverting stent and catheter placed inside an aneurysm; (D) time-to-peak (TTP) map from a research study involving CBCT for perfusion imaging. *[Image courtesy of C. Strother, University of Wisconsin–Madison.]*

Postprocessing of 3D DSA enables visualization of the construct with respect to the vessel topology, while the high-quality CBCT, with potential combination of metal artifact reduction, allows the understanding of the construct with respect to the full cranial anatomy (Fig. 26.10). A similar approach is taken for the treatment of AVMs, with the main difference being the potential to acquire 4D DSA images, enabling the physician to evaluate the fill sequence of the nidus feeding arteries, as well as deeper insight into the AVM structure [132]. During the procedure, the physician advances a guidewire/catheter combination into the feeding arteries to inject an embolization agent, aiming at reducing the inflow of blood into the aneurysm nidus to enable either continued medical treatment, or as preparation for surgical resection and follow-up to radiation therapy [133]. Follow-up imaging is conventionally similar to aneurysm treatments, and recent years have seen an increased interest in using high-quality CBCT with low-concentration contrast injection as a planning tool for radiation therapy [134].

Recent years have also seen a pivotal shift in the treatment of ischemic stroke. While endovascular stenting and coiling of acute hemorrhagic stroke has been a long-standing treatment option, recent clinical studies have shown the benefit of endovascular treatment in acute ischemic stroke patients [135–137]. Treatment of acute ischemic stroke involving a large vessel occlusion (internal carotid artery up to the Circle of Willis) appears to be shifting from medical treatment alone to active removal of the clot under interventional guidance. For patients undergoing an ischemic event, the time to recanalization is crucial, therefore bypassing the emergency suite (involving CT and MR imaging) and transferring directly to angiography is an ongoing topic of research. Currently, several efforts have been made to show the feasibility of the concept [138–140]. Besides the clinical challenges involved, interventional 3D imaging requirements are the highest for this setting. Three imaging modes need to be generated depending on the patient time of presentation: a high-quality CBCT to exclude hemorrhage [138], a multiphase CTA image to assess the site of occlusion [139,141], and cranial perfusion imaging to evaluate the affected tissue and the remaining viable sections of brain (Fig. 26.10) [142–144]. Following a decision to treat, a guidewire/catheter combination is advanced to the site of occlusion, and either a mechanical thrombectomy stent is deployed and retracted to remove the clot or the clot is aspirated and removed through suction catheters.

Outside the three main treatment areas, other neurovascular treatment areas include percutaneous ablation and sklerosing of lesions, spinal interventions, and tumor vessel embolization.

26.4.1.2 Body interventions (oncology and embolization)

Interventional radiology procedures focusing on the torso and pelvis include a multitude of applications. Two main treatment areas are intravascular/intraarterial embolization and percutaneous tissue ablation. Imaging systems commonly employed in such procedures are fixed-room C-arm systems allowing the flexibility to cover a large range of the patient extent. Ceiling-mounted systems as described in Sect. 26.3 can traverse most of the room, offering 2D and 3D imaging from left-, head-, or right-side. Robotic systems can offer even greater flexibility, allowing access of the patient from varying angulations for 2D and allowing table-rotation to left or right side for 3D imaging.

Embolization procedures are typically performed to occlude a vascular bed and/or deliver a cancer treatment drug. Common applications include the liver, kidney, and prostate. While treatment indications and agents vary, the imaging requirements for the applications are similar. Without loss in generality, the treatment of liver cancer will be focused upon here. Treatment of metastatic liver cancer involves staging via MDCT with intravenous contrast injection and 2D DSA using intraarterial contrast injection to assess the extent of the disease and determine the dosage of drug to be delivered. In addition, CBCT imaging with concurrent contrast injection (either whole organ or vessel selective) is performed at time of treatment to assess distribution of the agent through the organ. In the case of chemo- or radio-embolization, the site of injection (systemic, selective, superselective) is very important. Supporting tools in current use are

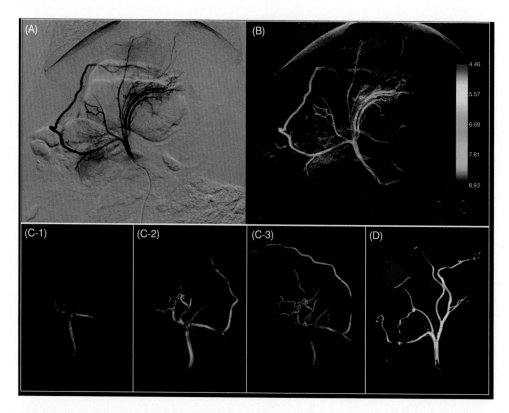

Figure 26.11 Applications of C-arm imaging in central body interventions – in this case, liver embolization: (A) 2D DSA image of liver vasculature; (B) time of arrival map of 2D DSA image; (c 1–3) time-resolved images from 4D-DSA to enhance understanding of vascular filling prior to embolization treatment; (D) segmented target volume and feeding artery delineated by semiautomatic algorithm. The data can be overlaid on live fluoroscopic imaging for guidance. *[Images courtesy of Paul Laeseke, University of Wisconsin, Madison WI.]*

focused on automatically segmenting the path from the catheter tip, situated commonly in the hepatic artery, to the tumor [145] as shown in Fig. 26.11. Following planning, the 3D path is overlaid on live fluoroscopy. While not accounting for breathing motion, such an overlay aids in accessing higher order branches in the liver anatomy [145]. For overlay of data derived from a CBCT scan, no additional registration is required, since fixed-room C-arm angiography systems are calibrated with respect to gantry rotation, detector zoom, and table motion without loss of 3D to 2D correspondence.

Percutaneous procedures commonly involve placement of needles (or needle-like structures) to achieve biopsy samples, fluid drainage, tissue ablation, or bone augmentation [146,147]. Such procedures commonly use the C-arm capability for both 3D and 2D imaging with coregistration. Procedural workflow often begins with the acquisition of a CBCT image of the patient and may be registered with volumetric imaging from CT or MR and preinterventional planning (structures, paths). The interventional-ist then designs needle paths on a planning workstation and transfers the information to the interventional tableside. Commonly, the system offers three preset viewing angles, a bulls-eye for site of entrance and centering, a perpendicular view for needle ad-vancement, and an oblique view for depth orientation and confirmation. During tool placement, the physician alternates between the viewing angles to gain understanding of the 3D object trajectory. In some circumstances the tool placement is followed by 3D image acquisition to gain full understanding of targeting. Since many such tools include dense metallic components, recent years have seen the introduction of metal artifact reduction algorithms [148] for C-arm CBCT. These algorithms often follow the approach of a user-defined segmentation of the metallic object, forward projection of the segmented object into the projection domain, removal of the metallic object, and in-painting of surrounding values. The 3D reconstruction is repeated and merged with the user-segmented 3D object.

Other clinical procedures in body interventions include placement of central lines and other catheters for various drug therapies, treatment of lower limb ischemia, and placement or removal of inferior vena cava filters. These treatments are commonly short in time and may not require advanced imaging support, often performed using standard 2D imaging modes.

An additional area presenting particular imaging challenges is TIPS (Transjugular Intrahepatic Portosystemic Shunt) procedures, in which an artificial shunt is created from the pulmonary vein to hepatic artery to increase liver blood circulation and relieve potential occlusions. The placement of the shunt is performed with a needle catheter in highly deformable tissue, and solutions such as 3D/2D overlay of structures and needle guidance have shown some success in targeting, while not resolving the need of repeat needle placement completely [149,150].

26.4.2 Interventional cardiology

The largest field of interventional procedures is focused on minimally invasive treatment of cardiovascular disease. Procedures covering diagnostics of the heart, including image and pressure–based assessments and interventions to alleviate vascular stenosis, are the bulk of the procedures performed; however, the last decade saw a considerable increase in more complex interventions. These more complex interventions include implanta-tion of valves [151,152], closure of appendages [153], electro-physiology (to treat atrial fibrillation), as well as opening of chronically occluded coronary arteries (CTO) [154]. A small subset of interventions focus on the pulmonary artery, especially in pediatric congenital disease and treatment of pulmonary stenosis. Finally, acute cardiac infarc-tion has primarily moved to the angiographic suite and minimally invasive treatment with angioplasty and stenting. Angiographic systems in most common use are single-plane, small detector (22×22 cm^2) systems. Ceiling-mounted systems have become increasingly popular, while floor-mounted systems are still commonly found. Electrophysiology interventions employ biplane systems as well as electromagnetic navigational guidance.

Cardiac interventions may be performed under fluoroscopic guidance and 2D digital radiography sequences (cine) to assess the extent of coronary artery disease. Further assessments can be done using endovascular ultrasound (IVUS), optical coherence tomography (OCT), and via pressure and flow reserve measurements. While procedural guidance relies on visualization of guidewires and catheters in standard fluoroscopic images, and the vasculature can be visualized via iodine injections during X-ray image acquisition, advanced image processing has been developed to mitigate motion effects and improve stent and balloon visibility. A recent focus includes deriving fractional flow reserve measurements through angiographic evaluation from biplane views [155]. Approaches commonly use the geometry from epipolar reconstruction of two cine acquisitions followed by CFD calculation for flow behavior [155]. This approach has been verified and commercialized for coronary MDCTA (Heartflow, Redwood City, CA) and will likely enter the angiography suite in the near future [156].

Both valve implant and appendage closure procedures rely on a combination of X-ray and ultrasound guidance (Transesophageal ultrasound – TEE): the former to visualize devices and the latter for visualizing the target itself and functional analysis of valve placement and performance. Ultrasound guidance is mainly performed using transesophageal transducers, achieving good visualization of most cardiac structure. The current generation angiographic equipment allows coregistration of X-ray and ultrasound images by detection of the TEE probe in fluoroscopic images [157,158]. The information from the ultrasound image (B-mode data, geometric shapes) is translated into the C-arm viewing direction and overlaid onto the live fluoroscopic images (Fig. 26.12).

Electrophysiology procedures are aimed at reducing arrhythmia of the heart. Dependent on guidance, these procedures can rely heavily on fluoroscopic imaging or use only minimal to no fluoroscopy. The main difference is if the case allows use of an electromagnetic (EM) guidance/navigation system, with adult cases in larger patients mainly relying on fluoroscopy alone due to the limitations of EM field size. When EM is used, as in pediatric cases, fluoroscopy time tends to be minimized. EM systems are incorporated with the angiographic equipment and are in most cases connected to the system to allow simultaneous fluoroscopic and EM guidance without electromagnetic interference with the imaging chain. During the case, an ablation catheter is navigated to areas of the heart mapped from a preprocedural MR scan. Once in position, an ablation is performed aimed at stopping the conductivity of the underlying tissue to prevent erratic conduction of electric impulses.

Complex coronary interventions and chronic total occlusions (CTO) are currently performed under conventional X-ray guidance. Workflows have been introduced that

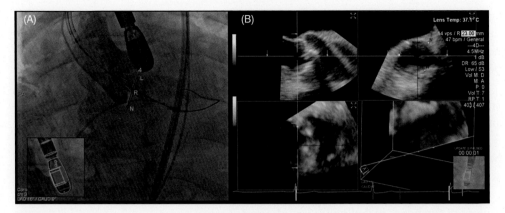

Figure 26.12 (A) Overlay of objects created using echo/X-ray fusion. The noncoronary (N), right (R), and left (L) hinge points of the aortic valve are labeled. This fluoroscopic frame was acquired immediately prior to valve deployment. (B) Markers in 3D ultrasound. The hinge points of the aortic valve have been marked on the upper-right multiplanar reformation from 3D TEE. The indicator in the bottom right shows the status of the probe identification by EXF software at the time of freezing of this image. Points N, R, and L correspond to fluoroscopic image in (A). *[Image Courtesy of Ignacio Inglessis, MGH, Boston MS.]*

include a preintervention CTA aimed at supporting the reduction in procedure time and amount of contrast agent. In these workflows, the CTA is segmented to remove bone anatomy and segment the coronary arteries. After registering the CTA and the angiography system coordinates, the user can adjust C-arm angulation based on the CTA aiming to minimize vessel shortening due to coplanar direction of vessel and X-ray beam. Following that, the vessel centerline is overlaid on live fluoroscopic images to aid in orientation [159].

26.4.3 Surgery

CBCT guidance has become a common foundation for surgical navigation in image-guided surgery, providing an up-to-date 3D view of the patient at the time of surgery. By comparison, surgical navigation within the context of preoperative CT or MRI is subject to errors introduced by anatomical deformation between the preoperative scan and the procedure, and intraoperative CBCT not only provides a more up-to-date view at the beginning of the case, the image can in principle be updated during the case to provide visualization of anatomical change. In some scenarios, the CBCT image serves as a basis for accurate (potentially deformable) registration of the preoperative CT or MRI, and navigation is still within the context of the preoperative image. In others, navigation may be within the CBCT image directly.

Intraoperative CBCT also presents an opportunity to acquire a 3D image at the conclusion of the case to evaluate/validate the surgical product and/or provide a check against complications (e.g., hemorrhage) – with opportunity to revise immediately if necessary. By comparison, suboptimal surgical constructs or complications detected in postoperative CT outside the OR introduce costly factors of time, morbidity, and a possible repeat/revision surgery.

In scenarios wherein CBCT serves simply as a basis for rigid registration of bone anatomy, image quality requirements are fairly low; however, work in recent years has aimed to elevate CBCT image quality on mobile intraoperative systems to a near-diagnostic level of image quality sufficient to visualize soft-tissue anatomy, provide a basis for deformable registration, and allow a reliable check against complications, such as intracranial hemorrhage [160].

Perhaps the most widespread area of clinical application in this context is neuro-surgery of the brain, including biopsy, electrode/stimulator placement, tumor resection and other procedures for which neuro-navigation is a fairly common standard of care. Systems such as the Medtronic O-arm are commonly used to enable high-precision neuro-intervention, where the primary imaging tasks are registration to preoperative MRI, visualization of the ventricles, and detection of hemorrhage. As a key element of a complex arsenal of imaging, navigation, and advanced neurosurgical instrumentation, CBCT has helped advance the field of high-precision neurosurgery. Remaining challenges include the physical form of the CBCT system (e.g., bulky gantry at tableside), minimization of radiation dose (especially in pediatric cases), image quality supporting soft-tissue visualization and reliable detection of hemorrhage, and streamlined integration with emerging systems for high-precision navigation, neuro-endoscopy, and robotics.

CBCT guidance has become fairly prevalent as well in spine surgery, including neurological and orthopaedic spine surgery. In this context, 3D intraoperative imaging provides similar utility to that mentioned above for intracranial neurosurgery with respect to improved surgical navigation. For example, Fig. 26.13 shows a CBCT image obtained in spinal neurosurgery as a basis for 3D navigation and robot-assisted pedicle screw placement. The utility is further increased with respect to 2D fluoroscopic imaging, where spine surgery regularly employs fluoroscopic/radiographic imaging for vertebral level localization, visualization of K-wires/Jamshidi needles, and pedicle screws. For example, placement of a screw may be checked within the pedicle (avoiding medial breach of the spinal canal) can be visualized in a PA fluoroscopic image, and its depth visualized in a LAT fluoroscopic image. In this context, both fluoroscopy and CBCT can be acquired from a single device. Remaining challenges include the need to minimize radiation dose, improve image quality, image in the presence of dense surgical instrumentation (i.e., reduce metal artifacts in CBCT), and provide streamlined integration with spinal navigation and robotics.

In orthopaedic trauma surgery, navigation is less prevalent, and CBCT is accordingly less common in routine, mainstream utilization. Such procedures commonly rely on

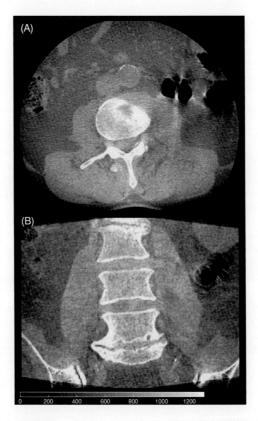

Figure 26.13 Intraoperative CBCT in spine surgery. Images were acquired using the O2 O-arm (Medtronic, Minneapolis MN) under research protocol and reconstructed with a custom 3D filtered backprojection algorithm. (A) Axial; (B) coronal. *Images courtesy of Ms. Xiaoxuan Zhao (Department of Biomedical Engineering, Johns Hopkins University, Baltimore MD).*

direct fluoroscopic visualization throughout the case, and mobile C-arms are a very common component of the surgical arsenal. Such mobile systems with 3D imaging capability could provide a basis for navigation in scenarios where navigation is consistent with workflow. Even without navigation, there are circumstances in which the ability to obtain a 3D image in the OR is of value, e.g., to evaluate the quality of the surgical construct and/or visualize the completeness of reduction that may not be conspicuous in fluoroscopic views.

As mobile systems with 3D imaging capability become more prevalent and stream-lined in their deployment, a variety of other surgical procedures present emerging areas of potential application. These include: thoracic surgery (e.g., ability to obtain a 3D image of the deflated lung in wedge resection); abdominal surgery (e.g., ability to visualize hepatic vessels during biopsy or tumor resection); pelvic surgery (e.g., ability to visualize normal soft-tissue anatomy adjacent to the surgical target); and vascular surgeries targeting aneurysms (as mentioned above in the context of neurovascular intervention) and arteriovenous malformations (AVMs).

References

[1] J.T. Bushberg, J.M. Boone, The Essential Physics of Medical Imaging, Lippincott Williams & Wilkins, 2011.

[2] J. Punnoose, J. Xu, A. Sisniega, W. Zbijewski, J.H. Siewerdsen, Technical Note: spektr 3.0 – a computational tool for X-ray spectrum modeling and analysis, Med. Phys. 43 (8) (Aug. 2016) 4711.

[3] A.M. Hernandez, J.M. Boone, Tungsten anode spectral model using interpolating cubic splines: unfiltered X-ray spectra from 20 kV to 640 kV, Med. Phys. 41 (4) (Apr. 2014) 042101.

[4] C. Puett, et al., An update on carbon nanotube-enabled X-ray sources for biomedical imaging, Wiley Interdiscip. Rev. Nanomed. Nanobiotechnol. 10 (1) (2018).

[5] J. Shan, et al., Stationary intraoral digital tomosynthesis using a carbon nanotube X-ray source array, Dentomaxillofacial Radiol. 44 (9) (2015) 20150098.

[6] J. Shan, et al., Stationary chest tomosynthesis using a carbon nanotube X-ray source array: a feasibility study, Phys. Med. Biol. 60 (1) (Jan. 2015) 81–100.

[7] I.E. Commission, X-Ray Tube Assemblies for Medical Diagnosis – Characteristics of Focal Spots, Bureau Central de la Commission Electrotechnique Internationale, 1993.

[8] K. Bavendiek, U. Ewert, A. Riedo, U. Heike, U. Zscherpel, New measurement methods of focal spot size and shape of X-ray tubes in digital radiological applications in comparison to current standards, in: Proceedings 18th World Conference on Nondestructive Testing, Apr. 16–20, 2012, Durban, South Africa, South African Institute for Non-Destructive Testing (SAINT), Pretoria, South Africa, 2012.

[9] L.E. Antonuk, et al., A real-time, flat-panel, amorphous silicon, digital X-ray imager, Radiographics 15 (4) (Jul. 1995) 993–1000.

[10] W. Zhao, J.A. Rowlands, X-ray imaging using amorphous selenium: feasibility of a flat panel self-scanned detector for digital radiology, Med. Phys. 22 (10) (Oct. 1995) 1595–1604.

[11] J.H. Siewerdsen, L.E. Antonuk, Y. El-Mohri, J. Yorkston, W. Huang, I.A. Cunningham, Signal, noise power spectrum, and detective quantum efficiency of indirect-detection flat-panel imagers for diagnostic radiology, Med. Phys. 25 (5) (May 1998) 614–628.

[12] P.G. Roos, et al., Multiple-gain-ranging readout method to extend the dynamic range of amorphous silicon flat-panel imagers, in: Medical Imaging 2004, 2004, pp. 139–149.

[13] D.A. Jaffray, J.H. Siewerdsen, J.W. Wong, A.A. Martinez, Flat-panel cone-beam computed tomography for image-guided radiation therapy, Int. J. Radiat. Oncol. Biol. Phys. 53 (5) (Aug. 2002) 1337–1349.

[14] R. Fahrig, R. Dixon, T. Payne, R.L. Morin, A. Ganguly, N. Strobel, Dose and image quality for a cone-beam C-arm CT system, Med. Phys. 33 (12) (Dec. 2006) 4541–4550.

[15] J.H. Siewerdsen, et al., Volume CT with a flat-panel detector on a mobile, isocentric C-arm: pre-clinical investigation in guidance of minimally invasive surgery, Med. Phys. 32 (1) (Jan. 2005) 241–254.

[16] Z. Su, et al., Systematic investigation of the signal properties of polycrystalline HgI2 detectors under mammographic, radiographic, fluoroscopic and radiotherapy irradiation conditions, Phys. Med. Biol. 50 (12) (June 2005) 2907–2928.

[17] K.S. Shah, et al., X-ray imaging with PbI2-based a-Si:H flat panel detectors, Nucl. Instrum. Methods Phys. Res., Sect. A, Accel. Spectrom. Detect. Assoc. Equip. 458 (1–2) (2001) 140–147.

[18] H. Jiang, Q. Zhao, L.E. Antonuk, Y. El-Mohri, T. Gupta, Development of active matrix flat panel imagers incorporating thin layers of polycrystalline HgI2 for mammographic X-ray imaging, Phys. Med. Biol. 58 (3) (Feb. 2013) 703–714.

[19] A.M.D. Ede, E.J. Morton, P. DeAntonis, Thin-film CdTe for imaging detector applications, Nucl. Instrum. Methods Phys. Res., Sect. A, Accel. Spectrom. Detect. Assoc. Equip. 458 (1–2) (2001) 7–11.

[20] Y. El-Mohri, et al., Active pixel imagers incorporating pixel-level amplifiers based on polycrystalline-silicon thin-film transistors, Med. Phys. 36 (7) (2009) 3340–3355.

[21] S. Kasap, et al., Amorphous and polycrystalline photoconductors for direct conversion flat panel X-ray image sensors, Sensors (Basel) 11 (5) (2011) 5112–5157.

[22] L.E. Antonuk, et al., Strategies to improve the signal and noise performance of active matrix, flat-panel imagers for diagnostic X-ray applications, Med. Phys. 27 (2) (Feb. 2000) 289–306.

[23] M.M. Wronski, J.A. Rowlands, Direct-conversion flat-panel imager with avalanche gain: feasibility investigation for HARP-AMFPI, Med. Phys. 35 (12) (Dec. 2008) 5207–5218.

[24] W. Zhao, et al., Indirect flat-panel detector with avalanche gain: fundamental feasibility investigation for SHARP-AMFPI (scintillator HARP active matrix flat panel imager), Med. Phys. 32 (9) (Sept. 2005) 2954–2966.

[25] K.A. Wunderle, J.T. Rakowski, F.F. Dong, Approaches to interventional fluoroscopic dose curves, J. Appl. Clin. Med. Phys. 17 (1) (2016) 342–352.

[26] M. Dehairs, H. Bosmans, W. Desmet, N.W. Marshall, Evaluation of automatic dose rate control for flat panel imaging using a spatial frequency domain figure of merit, Phys. Med. Biol. 62 (16) (2017) 6610.

[27] C. Schmidgunst, D. Ritter, E. Lang, Calibration model of a dual gain flat panel detector for 2D and 3D X-ray imaging, Med. Phys. 34 (9) (2007) 3649.

[28] A.L.C. Kwan, J.A. Seibert, J.M. Boone, An improved method for flat-field correction of flat panel X-ray detector, Med. Phys. 33 (2) (2006) 391.

[29] N. Mail, D.J. Moseley, J.H. Siewerdsen, D.A. Jaffray, An empirical method for lag correction in cone-beam CT, Med. Phys. 35 (11) (2008) 5187.

[30] J.H. Siewerdsen, D.A. Jaffray, A ghost story: spatio-temporal response characteristics of an indirect-detection flat-panel imager, Med. Phys. 26 (8) (Aug. 1999) 1624–1641.

[31] M. Tomic, S. Loncaric, D. Sersic, Adaptive spatio-temporal denoising of fluoroscopic X-ray sequences, Biomed. Signal Process. Control 7 (2) (2012) 173–179.

[32] C. Amiot, C. Girard, J. Chanussot, J. Pescatore, M. Desvignes, Spatio-temporal multiscale denoising of fluoroscopic sequence, IEEE Trans. Med. Imaging 35 (6) (2016) 1565–1574.

[33] A.K. Jones, et al., Ongoing quality control in digital radiography: report of AAPM Imaging Physics Committee Task Group 151, Med. Phys. 42 (11) (2015) 6658–6670.

[34] AAPM Task Group No. 150, C. Willis, N. Ranger, D. Gauntt, A.K. Jones, A. Walz-Flannigan, B. Schueler, D. Peck, E. Gingold, F. Ranallo, J. Yorkston, I. Rutel, I. Bercha, L. Goldman, R. Layman, Y. Fang, AAPM task group report no. 150: acceptance testing and quality control of digital radiographic imaging systems, Med. Phys. (2019), in process.

[35] D.L. Miller, D. Kwon, G.H. Bonavia, Reference levels for patient radiation doses in interventional radiology: proposed initial values for U.S. practice, Radiology (2009).

[36] D.F. Vener, M. Gaies, J.P. Jacobs, S.K. Pasquali, Clinical databases and registries in congenital and pediatric cardiac surgery, cardiology, critical care, and anesthesiology worldwide, World J. Pediatr. Congenit. Hear. Surg. 8 (1) (2017) 77–87.

[37] L.R.C. Dekker, et al., New image processing and noise reduction technology allows reduction of radiation exposure in complex electrophysiologic interventions while maintaining optimal image quality: a randomized clinical trial, Heart Rhythm 10 (11) (2013) 1678–1682.

[38] L. Eloot, et al., Novel X-ray imaging technology enables significant patient dose reduction in interventional cardiology while maintaining diagnostic image quality, Catheter. Cardiovasc. Interv. 86 (5) (2015) E205–E212.

[39] E.N. Kahn, et al., Radiation dose reduction during neurointerventional procedures by modification of default settings on biplane angiography equipment, J. Neurointerv. Surg. 8 (8) (2016).

[40] Y.K. Ihn, et al., Patient radiation exposure during diagnostic and therapeutic procedures for intracranial aneurysms: a multicenter study, Neurointervention 11 (2) (2016) 78–85.

[41] F. Bourier, et al., Evaluation of a new very low dose imaging protocol: feasibility and impact on X-ray dose levels in electrophysiology procedures, Europace (2016).

[42] R. Kohlbrenner, et al., Patient radiation dose reduction during transarterial chemoembolization using a novel X-ray imaging platform, J. Vasc. Interv. Radiol. 26 (9) (2015) 1331–1338.

[43] J.E. Boland, L.W. Wang, B.J. Love, M. Christofi, D.W.M. Muller, Impact of new-generation hybrid imaging technology on radiation dose during percutaneous coronary interventions and trans-femoral aortic valve implantations: a comparison with conventional flat-plate angiography, Hear. Lung Circ. 25 (7) (2016) 668–675.

[44] Y. Cho, D.J. Moseley, J.H. Siewerdsen, D.A. Jaffray, Accurate technique for complete geometric calibration of cone-beam computed tomography systems, Med. Phys. 32 (4) (2005) 968.

[45] F. Noo, R. Clackdoyle, C. Mennessier, T.A. White, T.J. Roney, Analytic method based on identification of ellipse parameters for scanner calibration in cone-beam tomography, Phys. Med. Biol. 45 (11) (Nov. 2000) 3489–3508.

[46] A.J. Fox, R. Graumann, Dynamic geometrical calibration for 3-D cerebral angiography, in: Med. Imaging 1996, 11–13 Febr. 1996, Newport Beach, California, in: Phys. Med. Imaging, vol. 1, 1996, p. 361.

[47] A. Rougée, C. Picard, C. Ponchut, Y. Trousset, Geometrical calibration of X-ray imaging chains for three-dimensional reconstruction, Comput. Med. Imaging Graph. 17 (4) (1993) 295–300.

[48] A. Rougee, C.L. Picard, Y.L. Trousset, C. Ponchut, Geometrical calibration for 3D X-ray imaging, in: Medical Imaging 1993, 1993, pp. 161–169.

[49] R.R. Galigekere, K. Wiesent, D.W. Holdsworth, Cone-beam reprojection using projection-matrices, IEEE Trans. Med. Imaging 22 (10) (2003) 1202–1214.

[50] J. Labuz, M. Thaker, B. Venkateswaran, S. Carolina, Decomposition of the Camera Calibration Matrix, 1991, pp. 89–93.

[51] M. Mitschke, N. Navab, Recovering the X-ray projection geometry for three-dimensional tomographic reconstruction with additional sensors: attached camera versus external navigation system, Med. Image Anal. 7 (1) (Mar. 2003) 65–78.

[52] N. Navab, A. Bani-Hashemi, 3D reconstruction from projection matrices in a C-arm based 3D-angiography system, in: Medical Image Computing and Computer-Assisted Intervention – MICCAI'98, 1998.

[53] M.D. Silver, A. Sen, S. Oishi, Determination and correction of the wobble of a C-arm gantry, in: Medical Imaging 2000, 2000, pp. 1459–1468.

[54] K. Wiesent, et al., Enhanced 3-D-reconstruction algorithm for C-arm systems suitable for interventional procedures, IEEE Trans. Med. Imaging 19 (5) (May 2000) 391–403.

[55] G.T. Gullberg, B.M.W. Tsui, C.R. Crawford, J.G. Ballard, J.T. Hagius, Estimation of geometrical parameters and collimator evaluation for cone beam tomography, Med. Phys. 17 (2) (1990) 264–272.

[56] P. Rizo, P. Grangeat, R. Guillemaud, Geometric calibration method for multiple-head cone-beam SPECT system, IEEE Trans. Nucl. Sci. 41 (6) (1994) 2748–2757.

[57] J.C. Ford, D. Zheng, J.F. Williamson, Estimation of CT cone-beam geometry using a novel method insensitive to phantom fabrication inaccuracy: implications for isocenter localization accuracy, Med. Phys. 38 (6) (2011) 2829–2840.

[58] C. Mennessier, R. Clackdoyle, F. Noo, Direct determination of geometric alignment parameters for cone-beam scanners, Phys. Med. Biol. 54 (6) (Mar. 2009) 1633–1660.

[59] N. Robert, K.N. Watt, X. Wang, J.G. Mainprize, The geometric calibration of cone-beam systems with arbitrary geometry, Phys. Med. Biol. 54 (24) (Dec. 2009) 7239–7261.

[60] U. Neitzel, Grids or air gaps for scatter reduction in digital radiography: a model calculation, Med. Phys. 19 (2) (1992) 475–481.

[61] J.H. Siewerdsen, D.A. Jaffray, Optimization of X-ray imaging geometry (with specific application to flat-panel cone-beam computed tomography), Med. Phys. 27 (8) (Aug. 2000) 1903–1914.

[62] E.-P. Rührnschopf, K. Klingenbeck, A general framework and review of scatter correction methods in X-ray cone-beam computerized tomography. Part 1: scatter compensation approaches, Med. Phys. 38 (7) (July 2011) 4296–4311.

[63] E.-P. Ruhrnschopf And, K. Klingenbeck, A general framework and review of scatter correction methods in cone beam CT. Part 2: scatter estimation approaches, Med. Phys. 38 (9) (Sept. 2011) 5186–5199.

[64] A. Sisniega, et al., Monte Carlo study of the effects of system geometry and antiscatter grids on cone-beam CT scatter distributions, Med. Phys. 40 (5) (May 2013) 051915.

[65] A. Sisniega, et al., High-fidelity artifact correction for cone-beam CT imaging of the brain, Phys. Med. Biol. 60 (4) (Feb. 2015) 1415–1439.

[66] S. Xu, P. Prinsen, J. Wiegert, R. Manjeshwar, Deep residual learning in CT physics: scatter correction for spectral CT, preprint, arXiv:1708.04151, 2017.

[67] J. Hsieh, R.C. Molthen, C.A. Dawson, R.H. Johnson, An iterative approach to the beam hardening correction in cone beam CT, Med. Phys. 27 (1) (Jan. 2000) 23–29.

[68] R.A. Brooks, G. Di Chiro, Beam hardening in X-ray reconstructive tomography, Phys. Med. Biol. 21 (3) (1976) 390.

[69] A. Hahn, M. Knaup, M. Brehm, S. Sauppe, M. Kachelrieß, Two methods for reducing moving metal artifacts in cone-beam CT, Med. Phys. (Jun. 2018).

[70] B. Kratz, I. Weyers, T.M. Buzug, A fully 3D approach for metal artifact reduction in computed tomography, Med. Phys. 39 (11) (Nov. 2012) 7042–7054.

[71] M. Meilinger, C. Schmidgunst, O. Schütz, E.W. Lang, Metal artifact reduction in cone beam computed tomography using forward projected reconstruction information, Z. Med. Phys. 21 (3) (Sept. 2011) 174–182.

[72] S. Rit, J. Nijkamp, M. van Herk, J.-J. Sonke, Comparative study of respiratory motion correction techniques in cone-beam computed tomography, Radiother. Oncol. 100 (3) (Sept. 2011) 356–359.

[73] R.E. Kincaid, E.D. Yorke, K.A. Goodman, A. Rimner, A.J. Wu, G.S. Mageras, Investigation of gated cone-beam CT to reduce respiratory motion blurring, Med. Phys. 40 (4) (Apr. 2013) 041717.

[74] M. Berger, et al., Marker-free motion correction in weight-bearing cone-beam CT of the knee joint, Med. Phys. 43 (3) (Mar. 2016) 1235–1248.

[75] A. Sisniega, J.W. Stayman, J. Yorkston, J.H. Siewerdsen, W. Zbijewski, Motion compensation in extremity cone-beam CT using a penalized image sharpness criterion, Phys. Med. Biol. 62 (9) (May 2017) 3712–3734.

[76] M. Berger, et al., Motion compensation for cone-beam CT using Fourier consistency conditions, Phys. Med. Biol. 62 (17) (Aug. 2017) 7181–7215.

[77] S. Ouadah, M. Jacobson, J.W. Stayman, T. Ehtiati, C. Weiss, J.H. Siewerdsen, Correction of patient motion in cone-beam CT using 3D–2D registration, Phys. Med. Biol. 62 (23) (Nov. 2017) 8813–8831.

[78] S. Sauppe, J. Kuhm, M. Brehm, P. Paysan, D. Seghers, M. Kachelrieß, Motion vector field phase-to-amplitude resampling for 4D motion-compensated cone-beam CT, Phys. Med. Biol. 63 (3) (Feb. 2018) 035032.

[79] A.C. Kak, M. Slaney, Principles of Computerized Tomographic Imaging, IEEE Press, New York, 1988.

[80] J. Hsieh, Computed Tomography: Principles, Design, Artifacts, and Recent Advances, SPIE, 2009.

[81] T.M. Buzug, Computed Tomography: From Photon Statistics to Modern Cone-Beam CT, Springer Science & Business Media, 2008.

[82] L.A. Feldkamp, L.C. Davis, J.W. Kress, Practical cone-beam algorithm, J. Opt. Soc. Am. A 1 (6) (1984) 612–619.

[83] F. Noo, R. Clack, M. Défrise, Cone-beam reconstruction from general discrete vertex sets using Radon rebinning algorithms, IEEE Trans. Nucl. Sci. 44 (3) (1997) 1309–1316.

[84] H. Kudo, T. Saito, Fast and stable cone-beam filtered backprojection method for non-planar orbits, Phys. Med. Biol. 43 (4) (1998) 747.

[85] G.L. Zeng, G.T. Gullberg, A cone-beam tomography algorithm for orthogonal circle-and-line orbit, Phys. Med. Biol. 37 (3) (1992) 563.

[86] F. Noo, M. Defrise, R. Clack, Direct reconstruction of cone-beam data acquired with a vertex path containing a circle, IEEE Trans. Image Process. 7 (6) (1998) 854–867.

[87] A. Katsevich, Image reconstruction for the circle-and-arc trajectory, Phys. Med. Biol. 50 (10) (2005) 2249.

[88] X. Wang, R. Ning, A cone-beam reconstruction algorithm for circle-plus-arc data-acquisition geometry, IEEE Trans. Med. Imaging 18 (9) (1999) 815–824.

[89] A. Katsevich, An improved exact filtered backprojection algorithm for spiral computed tomography, Adv. Appl. Math. 32 (4) (2004) 681–697.

[90] J.D. Pack, F. Noo, H. Kudo, Investigation of saddle trajectories for cardiac CT imaging in cone-beam geometry, Phys. Med. Biol. 49 (11) (2004) 2317.

[91] H. Yang, M. Li, K. Koizumi, H. Kudo, View-independent reconstruction algorithms for cone beam CT with general saddle trajectory, Phys. Med. Biol. 51 (15) (2006) 3865.

[92] S. Tilley, J.H. Siewerdsen, J.W. Stayman, Model-based iterative reconstruction for flat-panel cone-beam CT with focal spot blur, detector blur, and correlated noise, Phys. Med. Biol. 61 (1) (Jan. 2016) 296–319.

[93] S. Tilley, et al., Penalized-likelihood reconstruction with high-fidelity measurement models for high-resolution cone-beam imaging, IEEE Trans. Med. Imaging 37 (4) (Apr. 2018) 988–999.

[94] G.-H. Chen, J. Tang, S. Leng, Prior image constrained compressed sensing (PICCS), Proc. SPIE Int. Soc. Opt. Eng. 6856 (Mar. 2008) 685618.

[95] J.W. Stayman, H. Dang, Y. Ding, J.H. Siewerdsen, PIRPLE: a penalized-likelihood framework for incorporation of prior images in CT reconstruction, Phys. Med. Biol. 58 (21) (Nov. 2013) 7563–7582.

[96] H. Dang, A.S. Wang, M.S. Sussman, J.H. Siewerdsen, J.W. Stayman, dPIRPLE: a joint estimation framework for deformable registration and penalized-likelihood CT image reconstruction using prior images, Phys. Med. Biol. 59 (17) (Sep. 2014) 4799–4826.

[97] L.L. Geyer, et al., State of the art: iterative CT reconstruction techniques, Radiology 276 (2) (2015) 339–357.

[98] W. Wang, G.J. Gang, J.H. Siewerdsen, J.W. Stayman, Spatial resolution and noise prediction in flat-panel cone-beam CT penalized-likelihood reconstruction, Proc. SPIE Int. Soc. Opt. Eng. 10573 (Feb. 2018).

[99] J.H. Cho, J.A. Fessler, Regularization designs for uniform spatial resolution and noise properties in statistical image reconstruction for 3-D X-ray CT, IEEE Trans. Med. Imaging 34 (2) (Feb. 2015) 678–689.

[100] H. Dang, et al., Task-based statistical image reconstruction for high-quality cone-beam CT, Phys. Med. Biol. 62 (22) (Nov. 2017) 8693–8719.

[101] G.J. Gang, J.W. Stayman, T. Ehtiati, J.H. Siewerdsen, Task-driven image acquisition and reconstruction in cone-beam CT, Phys. Med. Biol. 60 (8) (Apr. 2015) 3129–3150.

[102] G.J. Gang, J.H. Siewerdsen, J.W. Stayman, Task-driven optimization of fluence field and regularization for model-based iterative reconstruction in computed tomography, IEEE Trans. Med. Imaging 36 (12) (2017) 2424–2435.

[103] H. Greenspan, B. Van Ginneken, R.M. Summers, Guest editorial deep learning in medical imaging: overview and future promise of an exciting new technique, IEEE Trans. Med. Imaging 35 (5) (2016) 1153–1159.

[104] S.K. Zhou, Deep learning guide to MICCAI 2015, in: 18th Int. Conf. Med. Image Comput. Comput. Assisted Intervent., 2015.

[105] G. Wang, A perspective on deep imaging, preprint, arXiv:1609.04375, 2016.

[106] H. Chen, et al., Low-dose CT via convolutional neural network, Biomed. Opt. Express 8 (2) (Feb. 2017) 679–694.

[107] E. Kang, W. Chang, J. Yoo, J.C. Ye, Deep convolutional framelet denosing for low-dose CT via wavelet residual network, IEEE Trans. Med. Imaging 37 (6) (June 2018) 1358–1369.

[108] H. Shan, et al., 3-D convolutional encoder-decoder network for low-dose CT via transfer learning from a 2-D trained network, IEEE Trans. Med. Imaging 37 (6) (June 2018) 1522–1534.

[109] Q. Yang, et al., Low-dose CT image denoising using a generative adversarial network with Wasserstein distance and perceptual loss, IEEE Trans. Med. Imaging 37 (6) (Jun. 2018) 1348–1357.

[110] E. Kang, J. Min, J.C. Ye, A deep convolutional neural network using directional wavelets for low-dose X-ray CT reconstruction, Med. Phys. 44 (10) (Oct. 2017) e360–e375.

[111] H. Gupta, K.H. Jin, H.Q. Nguyen, M.T. McCann, M. Unser, CNN-based projected gradient descent for consistent CT image reconstruction, IEEE Trans. Med. Imaging 37 (6) (June 2018) 1440–1453.

[112] Z. Zhang, X. Liang, X. Dong, Y. Xie, G. Cao, A sparse-view CT reconstruction method based on combination of DenseNet and deconvolution, IEEE Trans. Med. Imaging 37 (6) (June 2018) 1407–1417.

[113] J.C. Montoya, Y. Li, C. Strother, G.-H. Chen, 3D deep learning angiography (3D-DLA) from C-arm conebeam CT, Am. J. Neuroradiol. 39 (5) (May 2018) 916–922.

[114] M.A. Rafferty, et al., Intraoperative cone-beam CT for guidance of temporal bone surgery, Otolaryngol. Head Neck Surg. 134 (5) (2006) 801–808.

[115] M.J. Daly, J.H. Siewerdsen, D.J. Moseley, D.A. Jaffray, J.C. Irish, Intraoperative cone-beam CT for guidance of head and neck surgery: assessment of dose and image quality using a C-arm prototype, Med. Phys. 33 (10) (2006) 3767.

[116] S. Schafer, et al., Mobile C-arm cone-beam CT for guidance of spine surgery: image quality, radiation dose, and integration with interventional guidance, Med. Phys. 38 (2011) 4563.

[117] T. Berris, R. Gupta, M.M. Rehani, Radiation dose from cone-beam CT in neuroradiology applications, Am. J. Roentgenol. 200 (4) (2013) 755–761.

[118] T. Struffert, M. Hauer, R. Banckwitz, C. Köhler, K. Royalty, A. Doerfler, Effective dose to patient measurements in flat-detector and multislice computed tomography: a comparison of applications in neuroradiology, Eur. Radiol. 24 (6) (2014) 1257–1265.

[119] G. Reinke, et al., Three-dimensional rotational angiography in congenital heart disease: estimation of radiation exposure, Open J. Radiol. 3 (03) (2013) 124.

[120] W. Hohenforst-Schmidt, et al., Radiation exposure of patients by cone beam CT during endobronchial navigation-a phantom study, J. Cancer 5 (3) (2014) 192.

[121] A.A. Schegerer, U. Lechel, M. Ritter, G. Weisser, C. Fink, G. Brix, Dose and image quality of cone-beam computed tomography as compared with conventional multislice computed tomography in abdominal imaging, Invest. Radiol. 49 (10) (2014) 675–684.

[122] J.-Y. Wielandts, K. Smans, J. Ector, S. De Buck, H. Heidbüchel, H. Bosmans, Effective dose analysis of three-dimensional rotational angiography during catheter ablation procedures, Phys. Med. Biol. 55 (3) (Feb. 2010) 563–579.

[123] J.-Y. Wielandts, et al., Three-dimensional cardiac rotational angiography: effective radiation dose and image quality implications, Europace 12 (2) (2009) 194–201.

[124] Y.M. Kwok, F.G. Irani, K.H. Tay, C.C. Yang, C.G. Padre, B.S. Tan, Effective dose estimates for cone beam computed tomography in interventional radiology, Eur. Radiol. 23 (11) (2013) 3197–3204.

[125] L.D. Lunsford, R. Parrish, L. Albright, Intraoperative imaging with a therapeutic computed tomographic scanner, Neurosurgery 15 (4) (Oct. 1984) 559–561.

[126] D.A. Jaffray, J.H. Siewerdsen, Cone-beam computed tomography with a flat-panel imager: initial performance characterization, Med. Phys. 27 (6) (June 2000) 1311–1323.

[127] A. Biondi, V. Janardhan, J.M. Katz, K. Salvaggio, H.A. Riina, Y.P. Gobin, Neuroform stent-assisted coil embolization of wide-neck intracranial aneurysms: strategies in stent deployment and midterm follow-up, Neurosurgery 61 (3) (2007) 460–469.

[128] P.K. Nelson, P. Lylyk, I. Szikora, S.G. Wetzel, I. Wanke, D. Fiorella, The pipeline embolization device for the intracranial treatment of aneurysms trial, Am. J. Neuroradiol. 32 (1) (2011) 34–40.

[129] J. Klisch, V. Sychra, C. Strasilla, T. Liebig, D. Fiorella, The Woven EndoBridge cerebral aneurysm embolization device (WEB II): initial clinical experience, Neuroradiology 53 (8) (2011) 599–607.

[130] N.S. Heran, J.K. Song, K. Namba, W. Smith, Y. Niimi, A. Berenstein, The utility of DynaCT in neuroendovascular procedures, Am. J. Neuroradiol. 27 (2) (2006) 330–332.

[131] S.C. Wong, O. Nawawi, N. Ramli, K.A.A. Kadir, Benefits of 3D rotational DSA compared with 2D DSA in the evaluation of intracranial aneurysm, Acad. Radiol. 19 (6) (2012) 701–707.

[132] C. Sandoval-Garcia, et al., Comparison of the diagnostic utility of 4D-DSA with conventional 2D- and 3D-DSA in the diagnosis of cerebrovascular abnormalities, Am. J. Neuroradiol. (2017).

[133] I. Saatci, S. Geyik, K. Yavuz, H.S. Cekirge, Endovascular treatment of brain arteriovenous malformations with prolonged intranidal Onyx injection technique: long-term results in 350 consecutive patients with completed endovascular treatment course, J. Neurosurg. 115 (1) (2011) 78–88.

[134] M.G. Safain, et al., Use of cone-beam computed tomography angiography in planning for gamma knife radiosurgery for arteriovenous malformations: a case series and early report, Neurosurgery (2014).

[135] M. Goyal, et al., Randomized assessment of rapid endovascular treatment of ischemic stroke, N. Engl. J. Med. 372 (11) (2015) 1019–1030.

[136] M. Goyal, et al., Endovascular thrombectomy after large-vessel ischaemic stroke: a meta-analysis of individual patient data from five randomised trials, Lancet 387 (10029) (2016) 1723–1731.

[137] G.W. Albers, et al., Thrombectomy for stroke at 6 to 16 hours with selection by perfusion imaging, N. Engl. J. Med. 378 (8) (2018) 708–718.

[138] J.R. Leyhe, et al., Latest generation of flat detector CT as a peri-interventional diagnostic tool: a comparative study with multidetector CT, J. Neurointerv. Surg. (2017).

[139] M.-N. Psychogios, et al., One-stop management of acute stroke patients: minimizing door-to-reperfusion times, Stroke 48 (11) (2017) 3152–3155.

[140] I.L. Maier, et al., Diagnosing early ischemic changes with the latest-generation flat detector CT: a comparative study with multidetector CT, Am. J. Neuroradiol. (2018).

[141] M.N. Psychogios, J.H. Buhk, P. Schramm, A. Xyda, A. Mohr, M. Knauth, Feasibility of angiographic CT in peri-interventional diagnostic imaging: a comparative study with multidetector CT, Am. J. Neuroradiol. (2010).

[142] T. Struffert, et al., Flat detector CT in the evaluation of brain parenchyma, intracranial vasculature, and cerebral blood volume: a pilot study in patients with acute symptoms of cerebral ischemia, Am. J. Neuroradiol. 31 (8) (Sept. 2010) 1462–1469.

[143] A. Ganguly, et al., Cerebral CT perfusion using an interventional c-arm imaging system: cerebral blood flow measurements, Am. J. Neuroradiol. 32 (8) (2011) 1525–1531.

[144] K. Niu, et al., C-arm conebeam CT perfusion imaging in the angiographic suite: a comparison with multidetector CT perfusion imaging, Am. J. Neuroradiol. 37 (7) (2016) 1303–1309.

[145] V. Tacher, A. Radaelli, M. Lin, J.-F. Geschwind, How I do it: cone-beam CT during transarterial chemoembolization for liver cancer, Radiology 274 (2) (2015) 320–334.

[146] C. Floridi, et al., Percutaneous needle biopsy of mediastinal masses under C-arm conebeam CT guidance: diagnostic performance and safety, Med. Oncol. 34 (4) (2017) 67.

[147] D.-C. Jiao, et al., Clinical applications of the C-arm cone-beam CT-based 3D needle guidance system in performing percutaneous transthoracic needle biopsy of pulmonary lesions, Diagnostic Interv. Radiol. 20 (6) (2014) 470.

[148] G. Chintalapani, et al., Evaluation of C-arm CT metal artifact reduction algorithm during intra-aneurysmal coil embolization: assessment of brain parenchyma, stents and flow-diverters, Eur. J. Radiol. 85 (7) (2016) 1312–1321.

[149] M.J. Wallace, M.D. Kuo, C. Glaiberman, C.A. Binkert, R.C. Orth, G. Soulez, Three-dimensional C-arm cone-beam CT: applications in the interventional suite, J. Vasc. Interv. Radiol. 19 (6) (2008) 799–813.

[150] D. Ketelsen, et al., Three-dimensional C-arm CT-guided transjugular intrahepatic portosystemic shunt placement: feasibility, technical success and procedural time, Eur. Radiol. 26 (12) (2016) 4277–4283.

[151] M.B. Leon, et al., Transcatheter or surgical aortic-valve replacement in intermediate-risk patients, N. Engl. J. Med. 374 (17) (2016) 1609–1620.

[152] M. Puls, et al., One-year outcomes and predictors of mortality after MitraClip therapy in contemporary clinical practice: results from the German transcatheter mitral valve interventions registry, Eur. Heart J. 37 (8) (2015) 703–712.

[153] D.R. Holmes, et al., Prospective randomized evaluation of the Watchman Left Atrial Appendage Closure device in patients with atrial fibrillation versus long-term warfarin therapy: the PREVAIL trial, J. Am. Coll. Cardiol. 64 (1) (2014) 1–12.

[154] E.S. Brilakis, et al., Procedural outcomes of chronic total occlusion percutaneous coronary intervention: a report from the NCDR (National Cardiovascular Data Registry), JACC Cardiovasc. Interv. 8 (2) (2015) 245–253.

[155] M. Pellicano, et al., Validation study of image-based fractional flow reserve during coronary angiography, Circ. Cardiovasc. Interv. 10 (9) (2017) e005259.

[156] B.L. Nørgaard, et al., Diagnostic performance of noninvasive fractional flow reserve derived from coronary computed tomography angiography in suspected coronary artery disease: the NXT trial (Analysis of Coronary Blood Flow Using CT Angiography: Next Steps), J. Am. Coll. Cardiol. 63 (12) (2014) 1145–1155.

[157] S. Gafoor, et al., Use of EchoNavigator, a novel echocardiography-fluoroscopy overlay system, for transseptal puncture and left atrial appendage occlusion, J. Interv. Cardiol. 28 (2) (2015) 215–217.

[158] K. Sinclair, et al., TCT-505 feasibility of a novel echo/X-ray fusion software to determine implant angulation during transcatheter aortic valve replacement, J. Am. Coll. Cardiol. 68 (18 Supplement) (2016) B203.

[159] B.B. Ghoshhajra, et al., Real-time fusion of coronary CT angiography with X-ray fluoroscopy during chronic total occlusion PCI, Eur. Radiol. 27 (6) (2017) 2464–2473.

[160] J. Xu, et al., Technical assessment of a prototype cone-beam CT system for imaging of acute intracranial hemorrhage, Med. Phys. 43 (10) (Oct. 2016) 5745.

CHAPTER 27

Interventional imaging: MR

Eva Rothgang[a], **William S. Anderson**[b], **Elodie Breton**[c], **Afshin Gangi**[d,c],
Julien Garnon[d,c], **Bennet Hensen**[e], **Brendan F. Judy**[b], **Urte Kägebein**[e],
Frank K. Wacker[e]

[a]Department of Medical Engineering, Technical University of Applied Sciences Amberg-Weiden, Weiden, Germany
[b]Department of Neurosurgery, Johns Hopkins Hospital, Baltimore, MD, United States
[c]ICube UMR7357, University of Strasbourg, CNRS, Strasbourg, France
[d]Department of Interventional Imaging, Strasbourg University Hospital (HUS), Strasbourg, France
[e]Department of Diagnostical and Interventional Radiology, Hannover Medical School, Hannover, Germany

Contents

27.1. Motivation	674
27.2. Technical background	675
27.2.1 Design, operation, and safety of an interventional MRI suite	675
27.2.2 MR conditional devices	677
27.2.2.1 *Needles and biopsy guns*	677
27.2.2.2 *Ablation systems*	678
27.2.3 Visualization requirements	678
27.2.4 Intraprocedural guidance	679
27.2.4.1 *Passive tracking*	680
27.2.4.2 *Active tracking – radiofrequency coils*	681
27.2.4.3 *Semiactive tracking – gradient-based tracking*	682
27.2.4.4 *Gradient-based tracking*	682
27.2.4.5 *Optical tracking*	682
27.2.5 MR thermometry	683
27.2.6 MR elastography	683
27.3. Clinical applications	684
27.3.1 Applications in oncology	684
27.3.1.1 *Clinical setup*	685
27.3.1.2 *Clinical workflow*	685
27.3.1.3 *MR-guided biopsies*	686
27.3.1.4 *MR-guided thermal ablations*	687
27.3.2 MR-guided functional neurosurgery	689
27.3.2.1 *Intraoperative MRI and deep brain stimulation*	689
27.3.2.2 *Intraoperative MRI and laser interstitial thermal therapy*	689
27.3.2.3 *Safety considerations*	690
References	692

Handbook of Medical Image Computing and Computer Assisted Intervention
https://doi.org/10.1016/B978-0-12-816176-0.00032-6

27.1. Motivation

Minimally invasive image-guided interventions are gaining increased interest in medicine, ranging from radiology and cardiology to urology and neuroradiology. Compared to open surgery, they tend to be less invasive, less painful and produce smaller wounds, thus reducing the patient's burden and shortening the recovery. Additionally, the healthcare system benefits from more precise treatments with less complications and reduced costs due to shortened hospital stays.

In this context, Ultrasound (US) and Computer Tomography (CT) have emerged as primary means for accurate, safe, and reliable image-guided interventions [30,114].

Interventional MRI (iMRI) refers to the use of magnetic resonance (MR) imaging for performing and monitoring a minimally invasive diagnostic or therapeutic intervention in a manner analogous to conventional fluoroscopy, ultrasound (US), or computed tomography (CT).

US imaging has the advantage of being compact and mobile, and thus widely available [13,89,98]. Its disadvantages include a low penetration depth of the ultrasonic waves, making it difficult to access lower-lying structures, in particular in obese patients. Bone and air further reflect ultrasound which adds to the complexity when US is used for image guidance. This is important for tumor ablation where thermal energy is used to heat cancerous tissues to cytotoxic levels. During heating, the generated gas bubbles adversely affect the ultrasound images, making it impossible to see the lesion [48,70,114].

CT is less prone to artifacts. It usually provides adequate images of the entire area of interest during an intervention. However, it requires ionizing radiation which can be harmful for both the patient and the medical staff. Since this is especially true for real-time guidance (CT-fluoroscopy) under continuous imaging [49,75], CT interventions are primarily carried out as an in–out procedure. This means that only control scans are acquired, to limit the exposure to ionizing radiation. However, imaging of the target area is usually restricted to a transversal image plane. This not only restricts the access route but can also lead to a time-consuming workflow with the increased risk of involuntarily damaging structures such as the pleural cavity during liver interventions [9, 114]. Another disadvantage of CT is the low soft-tissue contrast. This can be improved by using contrast agents that facilitate vessel and tissue differentiation. Contrast media, however, wash out, which usually makes it difficult to visualize lesions on repeated scans.

The advantages of using MR imaging to guide minimally invasive procedures are manifold. MRI has an excellent soft-tissue contrast, with most lesions visible without contrast agent [72,114]. In comparison to CT, MRI uses no ionizing radiation. Especially the capability of selecting arbitrary slice orientation makes it an ideal tool for image guidance as it enables complex trajectories often necessary to reach difficult areas such as the liver dome or lesions close to the heart or diaphragm without causing damage to the pleural cavity [3,92]. In addition, MRI has the unique ability to measure physical parameters such as temperature (MR-thermometry), ventilation, diffusion, and perfusion in-vivo [2,6,92].

The following paragraphs will provide background on why interventional MRI is a unique tool to guide and monitor tumor ablations, biopsies, endovascular or neurosurgical interventions, and what is needed to make it a clinical reality beyond specialized centers. Interventional MRI has clearly grown from primarily a preclinical field, into an image guidance modality for safe, effective, and personalized patient care [113]. Having explained the technical background of iMRI, example clinical applications are illustrated in this chapter.

27.2. Technical background

So far, iMRI is mainly limited to specialized hospitals, most of them with a biomedical engineering backbone. This is required because all commercially available MRI are designed for diagnostic imaging. Using such scanners for interventions beyond simple biopsies requires serious tweaking, best performed by a team of physicians, physicists, and engineers. There are different challenges that need to be addressed in order to make iMRI a clinical reality.

27.2.1 Design, operation, and safety of an interventional MRI suite

In prior years, more open systems (e.g., horizontal magnet poles, double donut design) with sufficient patient access have been on the market [48,70,114]. However, these open systems could not compete in the diagnostic realm. The main reason was their low field strength and low gradient strength that resulted in lower image quality, lower spatial and lower temporal resolution in comparison to standard closed-bore MRI scanners. This was especially true for the only dedicated interventional MRI scanner, the Signa double donut, which at the time was an engineering masterpiece [98]. Most of these open MRI scanners are taken off the market.

Thus, the strategy evolved to using conventional diagnostic scanners with "add-on" interventional MRI packages [45]. The currently predominant design of MRI scanners is tube-like. Conventional high-field (≥ 1 T) MRI scanners have a narrow (≤ 60 cm) and long (≥ 150 cm) bore to achieve a homogeneous main magnetic field crucial for image quality. Patient access inside the magnet bore is thus severely limited [13,89,98]. Up to date, simple procedures such as biopsies are primarily performed as in–out procedures. Here, the patient is moved into the MRI for imaging and pulled out to insert the needle. Although feasible, this is time consuming, making interventions on moving organs difficult [48,70,114] and neglecting important advantages of MRI. Recent development of wide-bore (70 cm) scanners with shorter bore length has improved patient access [114]. In addition to improved scanner design, dedicated interventional sequences were developed [15] with focus on improved image quality and reduced im-

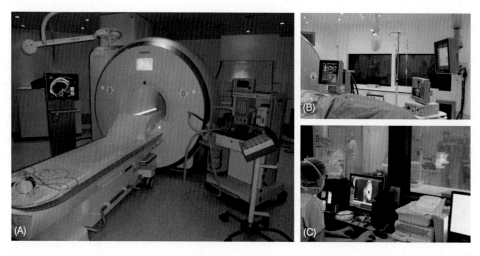

Figure 27.1 MRI suite room layout (Interventional Imaging Department, Hôpitaux Universitaires de Strasbourg, France): (A) wide bore 1.5 T MRI scanner equipped with dockable patient table, in-room monitor (left) for image display, MR conditional anesthesia, patient monitoring and cryoablation systems (right), operating light (ceiling); (B) a second in-room monitor (right, ceiling) allows monitoring the ablation time course. Wide windows offer good visual contact between in-room and control desk staff; (C) MR technician controlling image planes and in-room display.

age acquisition time. This shift of MR-guided interventions to conventional wide-bore systems has greatly pushed the field of interventional MRI. Especially patients with oncologic diseases could tremendously benefit from guidance and monitoring under real-time MRI as thermometry can assure complete destruction of the tumor while simultaneously protecting the surrounding tissue. According to Barkhausen et al., an accurate MRI-guided intervention reduces mortality, achieves a lower recurrence rate, and shortens the hospital stay. This, in turn, lowers the total cost, while creating more capacity for a higher number of minimal invasive interventions [3,92].

For diagnostic imaging, MR scans are planned and conducted from the control room. However, during interventional procedures, there is a need for visualization of the MR images and control of the scanner at the table in the MRI scanner room. To follow catheter manipulation in the heart or advancement of a needle, real-time changes to the scanning plane and sequence parameters are required. In addition to MR compatible monitors, appropriate MR-compatible anesthetic and patient monitoring equipment is essential (Fig. 27.1). Another challenge for performing MR-guided interventions is the acoustic noise generated during scanning [41,63,73]. This makes it challenging for the team to communicate (Fig. 27.2). Special noise canceling headsets exist but are not widespread, yet.

iMRI has demonstrated a low risk profile for the patient being treated [5,38,74]; however, the strong magnetic field requires special safety measures [80,106,116]. An

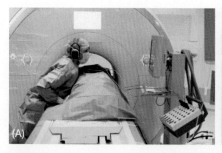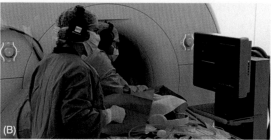

Figure 27.2 (A) The massive noise of switching gradients requires continuous ear protection during the intervention strongly hampering the communication. (B) Interventional Radiology Department, Hannover Medical School: The wide bore layout and the need to scan at the isocenter requires the physician to lean into the magnet bore while adjusting the interventional device under real-time imaging with the freehand-technique. A second physician assists the practitioner during the procedure.

MRI scanner produces static and gradient magnetic forces in addition to radiofrequency pulses. The static magnetic force (e.g., 1.5 T or 3 T) exerts a powerful effect on ferromagnetic objects, causing objects to take flight and potentially harm persons or medical equipment [102]. Care must be taken to remove all ferromagnetic objects from the vicinity of the scanner. Thus, also no conventional needles or guidewires made with ferromagnetic material can be used within an MRI scanner as they are subject to translational and rotational movement. The gradient force (20 to 100 mT/m) occurs rapidly throughout scanning and is sufficiently powerful to disrupt electrophysiological monitoring. Finally, in order to generate an MR signal from the net magnetization, the radiofrequency pulses are needed to excite the spin system, i.e. tilt the proton spins away from their original orientation. These radiofrequency pulses release thermal energy into the environment, which have the potential to harm medical equipment, personnel, and patients. In particular for interventional MRI, the potential heating of wires, needles, implants, and other instruments needs to be considered. Specially designed devices have to be used and a comprehensive safety protocol must be established to minimize possible hazards.

27.2.2 MR conditional devices

27.2.2.1 Needles and biopsy guns

MR conditional needles and biopsy guns are made of nonferromagnetic materials (titanium and nickel alloys, carbon fibers), chosen in order to obtain an appropriate balance between appearance in MR images and material strength. In practice, nonmagnetic MR conditional cannula and stylets are more flexible than regular instruments. The size of the artifact depends on the material of the device, but also on its orientation with regards to the B0 main magnetic field, sequence ponderation, and readout direction [57,59]. The size and contrast of the artifact should be sufficient to allow for clear visibility of the shaft in MR images, while remaining small enough so that the surrounding anatomy is not masked.

Current commercially available MR conditional needles and biopsy guns include: Chiba needles 20 to 22 G, coaxial puncture needles 12 to 18 G, and automatic and semiautomatic biopsy guns 14 to 18 G. These devices are MR conditional for magnetic fields up to 1.5 T, some of them being MR conditional for magnetic fields up to 3 T, allowing for MR guided procedure in the vast majority of MRI suites.

27.2.2.2 Ablation systems

Most ablation systems require specific MR conditional probes (radio-frequency probe, microwave antenna, cryoprobe with similar constraints as needles) and dedicated MR hardware, including signal filters and waveguides on the Faraday shield. However, most clinical laser ablation systems may be directly used in the MR environment (MR conditional) as long as the ablation optical fiber includes no conducting, metallic or magnetic part on the patient side (inside the MR room). This can be achieved with long optical fibers and/or fiber extensions ($\sim$5 to 10 m) that allow for all electronic items and the metallic optical fiber connector to remain outside of the MR room, the optical fiber crossing the Faraday cage in a waveguide. Care must be taken for all ferromagnetic devices to remain outside of the MR room at all time, for instance, the optical fiber should be passed from the control room to the MR room, the metallic connector remaining outside.

27.2.3 Visualization requirements

One of the most important requirements for an accurate MR-guided intervention besides patient access is rapid and reliable visualization and tracking of both the instrument as well as the target lesion. This is best realized by advancing the interventional tool to the target under continuous real-time imaging [15,101]. Thus, imaging sequences for iMRI have several key differences from their diagnostic counterparts. Visualization requirements include real-time acquisition and near real-time reconstruction, rapid sequence changes, and interactive control. The images need to be displayed immediately after acquisition and be acquired at a frame rate high enough to ensure continuous display of the instrument, the target lesion, and the surrounding sensitive structures. One often works with either up to three parallel or orthogonal slices (Fig. 27.3), which are planned along the desired trajectory [30,114]. However, the clinical realization is still challenging as important contrasts like T2 weighted images are by nature too slow for interventional MR. New developments in the field of rapid contrast imaging, however, constantly improve the sequences to meet the imaging needs of interventions [15]. With new parallel imaging techniques, frame rates of as high as 20 images can be achieved while maintaining suitable spatial resolution for interventional applications

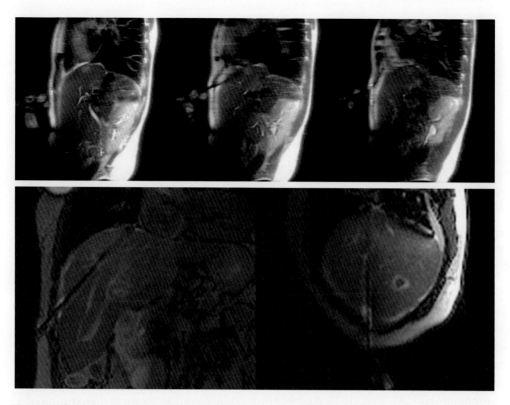

Figure 27.3 Real-time image guidance in the liver can be performed with the aid of either three parallel slices using a T2 weighted sequence (top) or two orthogonal slices using a T1 weighted sequence (bottom). Due to the slow acquisition rate of the T2 weighted sequence, the breathing induced liver motion leads to a blurred representation of the used instrument whereas the tumor is still clearly visible.

[84]. Although real-time MRI still has lower frame rate than X-ray, real-time MRI is comparably information-rich [91].

The acquired near real-time images are displayed on MR-compatible in-room monitors [114]. In addition to conventional MRI scanner, user interfaces, dedicated interactive environments are needed, which provide features like graphical slice control, multislice display, and real-time modification of scan parameters. There are various interventional MR platforms of the different manufacturers [66,92,120] and other methods to enhance the workflow like augmented reality [65].

27.2.4 Intraprocedural guidance

The insertion of the interventional instrument under real-time imaging guidance is often conducted with the freehand-technique, meaning the manual insertion of the needle by the radiologist comparable to CT or US guided interventions. The technique

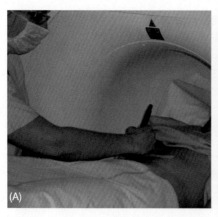 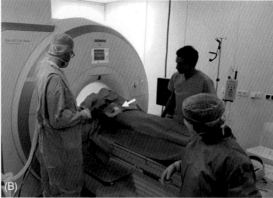

Figure 27.4 (A) Marking the skin entry point under the laser light crosshair. (B) Sterilization process of the patient, performing physician, MRI scanner user interface, and used surface coils (white arrow).

is simple and does not require additional devices [31,114]. In comparison to CT or US, however, the workflow is hampered by the massive noise of switching gradients. For an efficient, safe, and effective procedure, it is important to continuously know where the interventional device is. This requires significant input from a skilled MR technician being in the control room to manipulate the imaging plane to keep the device within slice. In particular for complex trajectories this process can be cumbersome and time consuming [6,27,30,70,92,101]. Another important workflow factor is the creation of a sterile field (Fig. 27.4). Especially the receiver coils represent a challenge as their opening, further limited by additional drapes, leads to a restricted operation area. However, surface coils are strongly needed for both image quality and the ability to use imaging acceleration techniques like parallel imaging.

In addition, the localization of the interventional instrument – especially the tip – within the MR image is prone to errors. Interventional instruments like needles cause image distortions (artifacts). Both the size and position of the artifact is affected by a variety of factors: needle material, pulse sequence, field strength of the main magnetic field, orientation of the needle relative to the main magnetic field, receiver bandwidth, and frequency coding direction [57,59,114]. This in turn can make it difficult to accurately position the interventional instrument, in particular, if the needle artifact is very large or small [104].

Due to these challenges, a variety of instrument tracking methods have been developed to support and simplify the procedure.

27.2.4.1 Passive tracking

Passive tracking is an image-based technique, in which the instruments are automatically detected in the image slice. For this purpose, the instrument itself or additional attached markers either produce MR signal amplifications or signal voids [25,47,53,76,78,83,92, 94].

The latter can be, for instance, produced with the aid of small paramagnetic rings locally distorting the magnetic field and causing a negative contrast. Local field distortions can be further produced by applying direct currents through an integrated wire. The distortion size can be directly controlled through the current amplitude. However, as this technique utilizes long electrically conducting wires, radiofrequency (RF) induced heating can lead to local tissue burns.

A positive contrast instead can be created by filling the instrument or coating its surface with a paramagnetic T1-shortening contrast agent [25,47,53,76,78,83,92,94]. Oliveira et al., for instance, used a cylinder filled with a gel as a positive contrast marker for MR-guided prostate biopsies [25,47,53,76,78,83,92,94]. The position of these markers within an MR image can be automatically determined using dedicated image postprocessing techniques.

The main advantage of passive tracking is simplicity. No additional hardware is needed, and the absence of a wire connection from the device to the scanner eliminates the risk radiofrequency heating posed by long conductive wires.

However, the tracking precision strongly depends on the marker artifact, and thus on parameters like field strength, the used pulse sequence type, as well as partial volume effects. Furthermore, the temporal resolution can be a limiting factor. If the instrument is advanced too fast, it will no longer be visible within the acquired images, causing a time-consuming manual readjustment of imaging planes [25,47,53,76,78,83,92,94]. Acceleration techniques like parallel imaging or projection imaging [93] can help overcome this limitation of image based tracking. The passive tracking approach also does not allow tracking more than one device at a time [94].

27.2.4.2 Active tracking – radiofrequency coils

An alternative to passive instrument tracking utilizes small RF coils. Those coils are locally attached to the instrument tip and connected to the MR receiver system. Once a special RF pulse is transmitted during the MR-imaging process, the coil position can be determined in 3-dimensional space within 10 to 20 ms [32,115]. On the one hand, the detected instrument tip can be overlaid on a previously acquired roadmap. On the other hand, the coil position can be used to automatically realign the imaging slice in real-time. Certain image acquisition parameters, like field of view or resolution, can be influenced by the instrument behavior, too [110]. The RF coils at the tip can be furthermore used for high resolution imaging in endovascular interventions [26]. So far, RF coils were mainly used in conjunction with catheters. Furthermore, they are prone to RF heating.

27.2.4.3 Semiactive tracking – gradient-based tracking

Instead of being directly connected to the MR receiver system, resonant circuits are inductively coupled to the imaging coils [40,54,86]. They are locally attached to the instrument and amplify the local magnet field during RF excitation, causing a significant higher signal in the proximity of the resonant circuit. The position of the resonant circuit can be detected with special image postprocessing techniques. Although they are relatively simple and cost effective, resonant circuits can be only used for the certain field strength they are tuned for.

27.2.4.4 Gradient-based tracking

The gradient-based tracking utilizes small sensors to measure the spatially varying gradient fields. The EndoScout tracking system (Robin Medical, Baltimore, USA), for instance, detects local voltages, being induced during the gradient ramping, to calculate the local sensor position [85]. This in turn is used to automatically reposition the imaging slice. The sensor can be integrated into small devices like an electrophysiology catheter or up to instruments like endoscopes or needle holders [6,27,30,70,92,101]. Compared to the above-mentioned tracking techniques, the gradient-based tracking has the advantage of being able to be simultaneously applied with the image acquisition process. However, the sensors have to be positioned within the homogeneous volume of the gradient coil. Thus, in clinical practice, the device can be only used in the center of the bore being difficult for strongly angulated trajectories.

27.2.4.5 Optical tracking

Another common method is the tracking of optical sensors attached to the distal end of the instrument. Optical tracking combines the accuracy of a stereotactic approach with the simplicity of the freehand-technique, thus allowing interactive manipulation of image planes in a variety of trajectories [77,114]. For this purpose, either several light-emitting diodes or retroreflective markers are attached to the end of the interventional instrument with the aid of a corresponding holding device. A stereo camera, located outside the MRI, detects the positions and sends them to an interventional platform or the MRI computer for real-time control [71]. Line-of-sights problems, however, strongly restrict the available tracking space within the MRI scanner. Busse et al. therefore developed an approach, in which the performing physicians navigate the instrument within a previously recorded 3D dataset outside the magnet using optically tracked markers for an in–out approach [13,14]. This sacrifices the real-time capability of MRI. Thus, moving organs such as the liver can only be targeted when breathing and motion correction or general anesthesia are used [13]. Another approach uses an MR compatible camera mounted inside the bore close to the magnets isocenter to track markers attached at the end of the rigid instrument in real-time (Fig. 27.5) [47].

Figure 27.5 An MR-compatible tracking camera detects the position and orientation of a planar Moiré Phase Tracking marker (left) being attached at the end of a rigid instrument (right, white arrow) to automatically align two perpendicular imaging planes along the instrument and centered at its tip [47].

27.2.5 MR thermometry

Several temperature-dependent MR parameters such as the longitudinal relaxation time [81], the molecular diffusion coefficient [56], or the proton resonance frequency shift (PRFS) [46] can be exploited for the purpose of temperature mapping.

As of today, the PRFS based phase mapping method is the most popular MR thermal imaging method [121]. It shows a linear correlation with temperature over a wide range of temperatures from −15°C to 100°C [42,121], covering the temperature range of interest for high-temperature thermal ablation and also low-temperature hyperthermia. In addition, its temperature sensitivity coefficient is almost constant and nearly independent of tissue type, except for tissue with high content of fat. However, the PRFS method is sensitive to magnet susceptibility associated with tissue anatomy and interventional devices [8], motion artifacts, magnetic field drift, and requires special correction methods in tissue with high fat content [119]. It only provides relative temperature changes (Fig. 27.6) and although several methods have been proposed to correct for motion [108], it is still not ideal for abdominal MR thermometry in patients with irregular breath or when tumor tissue deforms during the intervention.

27.2.6 MR elastography

MR Elastography (MRE) has been proposed for the monitoring of thermal ablations as a complementary biomarker to thermometry [55,118]. Shortly, MRE is a virtual palpation means, providing elasticity maps of tissues, through MR phase contrast imaging of mechanical waves propagated in tissues, and inverse problem solving. Thermal ablations alter the mechanical properties of tissues, either when heated or frozen. MRE has been shown to be able to monitor such changes in mechanical properties [18,19,55,118], and can provide both elasticity and PRFS thermometry maps from the same dataset [55].

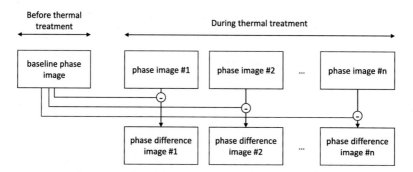

Figure 27.6 Principle of PRFS based MR thermometry which provides relative temperature measurements; thus, it is highly sensitive to tissue motion. For each voxel the phase at time *t* is subtracted from the corresponding voxel in the baseline phase image. The temperature change can then be directly calculated from the phase difference image.

27.3. Clinical applications

MR-guided procedures can be performed in almost every MRI suite with main magnetic fields up to 3 T. There are two main manners for performing MR guided procedures, depending on whether instruments and imaging are performed sequentially or simultaneously.

Most clinical centers practice interventional MRI in conventional diagnostic scanners, equipped with in-room monitor(s). Performing the procedure under real-time continuous MR acquisition may not be feasible given geometrical constraints from the bore (length, inner diameter, access). For such "in–out" procedures, MR images are acquired, and the needle is sequentially advanced towards its target once the patient is back outside of the bore, with alternating phases of imaging and instrument advancement.

Alternatively, with so-called "wide bore" scanners, the practitioner may advance the instrument during MR image acquisitions, hence benefiting of real-time MR-guidance. Obviously, "real-time" in the context of MR-guidance is different from US real-time guidance: image acquisition and reconstruction with state-of-the-art MRI induce a delay on the order of 1 s between image acquisition and display. Hence, practitioners may take some learning time in the beginning of the procedure in order to observe organ displacement with physiological motions such as breathing and cardiac motion.

27.3.1 Applications in oncology

The use of image-guided interventions in the field of oncology has gained wide acceptance over the past years. Percutaneous biopsies allow obtaining histological diagnostic in the vast majority of the cases; and thermal ablation has been proven to be an effective alternative to surgery in selected situations, notably for small liver and renal tumors in the abdominal area. Most of the authors advocate the use of ultrasound and/or CT to guide an abdominal procedure, as they represent cost-effective guidance modalities and are accessible in almost all centers dealing with cancer patients. However, both techniques have their inner limitations which can lead to mistargeting of a lesion and/or damages of vulnerable surrounding structure(s). In this perspective, MR-guidance offers new perspective for both diagnostic and therapeutic interventions.

27.3.1.1 Clinical setup

MR-guided interventions in the abdomen encompass both diagnostic (biopsy) and therapeutic (ablations) procedures. Typically, the practitioner collaborates with two MR technologists, one for in-room support (Fig. 27.2) and one at the MR-scanner desk, driving sequence acquisition and image display on the in-room monitor.

The MR scanner room is equipped with at least one in-room monitor, displaying MR acquisitions. One additional in-room monitor is a plus during thermal ablations, so that the practitioner can control the time-course of the ongoing therapy. Additional specific hardware includes MR compatible anesthesia and patient monitoring, and operating light (Fig. 27.1).

27.3.1.2 Clinical workflow

The typical clinical workflow is shown as a flowchart for in-bore-procedures in Fig. 27.7. The workflow is identical for in–out procedures, except for the needle guidance that does not use real-time acquisitions (see details below). Comfortable patient positioning is crucial in order to avoid pain and related motion in sedated patient, or joint injury for longer procedures under general anesthesia. Patient dockable tables can be rolled outside of the MRI suite, and simplify patient positioning.

After scout imaging, a stack of high resolution images is acquired in order to define the needle trajectory, from the skin entry point to the target lesion. Position of the entry point on the patient skin is determined in both its head–foot distance to the zero patient laser light and its left–right position with regards to the laser light cross-hairs. The plane of the entry point is moved out below the laser light, so that the entry point can be marked according to its left–right position from the laser light cross-hairs as determined with a ruler (Fig. 27.4(A)).

Similar to CT guided procedures, skin prepping at the entry point is followed by sterile draping of both patient and MR bore (Fig. 27.4(B)).

The instrument is first inserted by a couple centimeters before the patient is moved back into the MRI bore for imaging and needle advancement. The practitioner can watch the MR images on the in-room monitor (Fig. 27.2), which display is typically controlled by the MR technician sitting at the MR control room (Fig. 27.1(C)). During needle positioning, "in–out" procedures alternate image acquisition and out-of-bore needle advancement. Alternatively, "in-bore" procedures really take advantage of the real-time imaging capability of MR. Real-time MR fluoroscopic sequences allow for

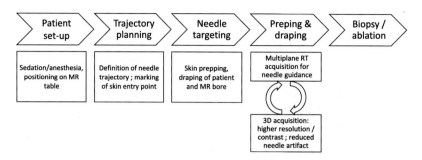

Figure 27.7 Flowchart of the clinical workflow during a percutaneous in-bore MR guided procedure in the abdomen.

continuous imaging of multiple image planes, typically aligned to the needle shaft main axis, and eventually orthogonal to this axis. Such guidance allows for 3D visualization of the needle trajectory, with tissue contrast for the surrounding anatomy. Real-time acquisitions are interlaced with 3D control acquisitions, typically allowing for better spatial depiction of the needle and organs, with improved resolution and/or contrasts and/or reduced needle artifact.

27.3.1.3 MR-guided biopsies

MRI offers several advantages when targeting a lesion located in the abdominal cavity. The high intrinsic contrast resolution of MR allows identifying most lesions without contrast media, including those poorly/not visible in ultrasound and CT-scan. During needle progression, the real-time imaging capabilities of MR enables the operator to identify all surrounding vulnerable structures, including those moving with respiration (liver, kidney, spleen) and bowels. Moreover, vessels are visible without contrast enhancement, which greatly limits the risk of incidental vascular injury [33]. Hence, MRI allows navigating safely between the different organs while identifying precisely the target lesion. An additional benefit of MRI is the possibility to perform real-time imaging in multiplanar acquisition planes. With such guidance, there is no limitation for steep sagittal or even double oblique approaches [111]. This is particularly interesting to avoid the posterior pleural recess for lesions located in the upper part of the abdomen [50].

MRI can potentially be used for any abdominal biopsies. Of note, because of all the listed advantages, MRI has mostly been reported to guide:

• Liver biopsies, with a special interest for lesions which are not visible in ultrasound and CT-scan [99].
• Kidney biopsies, particularly for lesions completely embedded in the renal parenchyma (because of the high contrast resolution of MRI) and lesions of the upper pole (because the pleural recess can easily be avoided) [34].

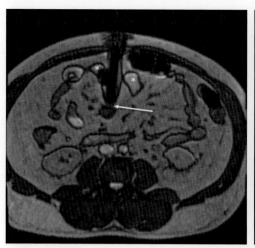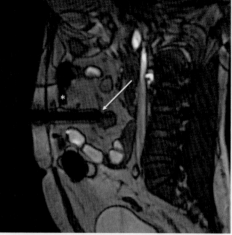

Figure 27.8 Biopsy of a mesenteric lymph node. Axial (left) and sagittal (right) multiplanar real-time sequences show the coaxial needle close to the lymph node (arrows). The needle was safely advanced in-between the bowel loops (asterisks) using real-time imaging.

- Adrenal biopsies, as these biopsies typically require a double oblique approach. The clear visualization of the inferior vena cava is also very helpful to sample a tumor located on the right adrenal [50].
- Retroperitoneal masses, as vessels and ureter are clearly depicted during the whole procedure without contrast injection.

An example of an MR-guided biopsy of a lymph node in the mesentery is shown in Fig. 27.8. The needle was safely advanced between the bowel loops (asterisks) using multiplanar real-time MRI.

27.3.1.4 MR-guided thermal ablations

MR-guidance has the same advantages for biopsy and ablation during needle insertion. An additional advantage of MRI for thermal ablation procedures requiring multiple needles (mostly cryoablation) is the possibility to assess precisely in all planes the correct repartition and distance in between each probe, in order to optimize treatment's efficacy. However, the major advantage of MRI is the possibility to continuously monitor the necrotic zone throughout the ablation process. With MRI it is possible to depict in all planes the extent of the ablation without contrast injection, which allows immediately assessing if the lesion has been completely covered with safety margins, or if additional treatment is required.

This special feature of MR compared to CT and ultrasound is useful both during heat-based and cold-based ablations. MR-guided radiofrequency and microwave ablations have mostly been studied in the liver, where the ablation is visible as a spontaneous

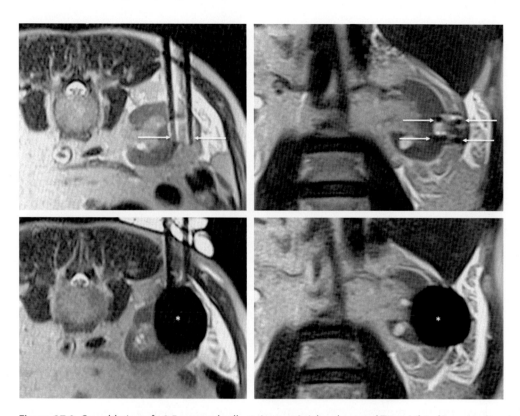

Figure 27.9 Cryoablation of a 3.5 cm renal cell carcinoma. Axial and coronal T2 weighted imaging (top images) demonstrate 4 cryoprobes (arrows) positioned inside the tumor with 1.5 cm gaps between probes. Same planes after completion of the whole double freeze cycle (bottom images) show the iceball (asterisk) which covers completely the tumor with safety margins.

hyperdensity on T1 sequences. The visualization of the ablation zone with cryoablation is even more impressive, as the iceball appears as a signal void on all sequences, thus is clearly distinguishable from the surrounding anatomy (Fig. 27.9). This offers maximal precision and safety as the boundaries of the ablation zone are visible during the whole procedure. Complete coverage of tumor without unintended freezing of peripheral organs can therefore be assessed in real-time and multiplanar [17].

Similarly to biopsies, almost all abdominal lesions can be ablated under MR-guidance. Radiofrequency and microwave ablations are well suited for liver ablations, and can therefore be used to ablate lesions measuring less than 3 cm, especially those not visible with other imaging modalities and/or located in areas difficult to access (liver dome especially) [43]. MR-guided cryoablation has mainly been reported to treat renal tumors less than 4 cm in diameter, and is particularly interesting to target intraparenchymatous lesions and lesions close to the ureter and/or digestive structures [17]. The field of indications is likely to enlarge in the near future, as other locations (adrenal, mesentery) can benefit from MR-guidance, both for targeting and monitoring of the ablation zone. A review of the various ablation techniques can be found in [37].

27.3.2 MR-guided functional neurosurgery

Intraoperative MRI (iMRI) is a powerful tool that delivers precise neurological intervention in functional neurosurgery. Since its inception in the field of neuro-oncology [51], iMRI has expanded to deep brain stimulation (DBS) and laser-induced thermal therapy (LITT) [103]. iMRI offers similar accuracy in DBS lead placement in comparison to electrophysiological targeting methods [20,79,97,100] and provides effective ablation of epileptogenic foci while offering precision with thermography [21]. iMRI allows for "brain-shift," [39] intraoperative edema, intraoperative hemorrhage, and surgical manipulation of tissue to be addressed in "real-time" [20,28,69]. In this section we describe the utility and safety of iMRI in functional neurosurgery.

27.3.2.1 Intraoperative MRI and deep brain stimulation

DBS offers patients an effective treatment for movement disorders including Parkinson's Disease (PD) [4,24], essential tremor [52], dystonia [109], and shows promise for a plethora of other disease, including depression [62], chronic pain [90], and obsessive compulsive disorder [36]. DBS alters pathological neural circuitry through precise lead placement.

Traditionally, DBS leads have been placed intraoperatively using electrophysiologic monitoring in an awake patient due to the neuromodulatory effects of general anesthesia [1,60,61,107]. This requires preoperative brain imaging in addition to intraoperative or postoperative confirmation of lead placement [44]. iMRI allows for the patient to be under general anesthesia and includes intraoperative lead confirmation [79,97]. Importantly, general anesthesia allows for patients that would not tolerate an awake surgery to receive care. This includes patients with severe high amplitude movements, claustrophobia, and anxiety disorders [7]. iMRI is also useful for pediatric cases and for dystonia patients who would be uncomfortable on the operating room table during long awake procedures. Intraoperative lead placement with MRI has been shown to have excellent accuracy [79,97,100] and similar clinical outcomes in comparison with awake surgery with stereotaxy and electrophysiology [79,97]. Intraoperative CT has also been used for DBS lead placement utilizing preoperative merging of CT and MRI [12,51,67,95]; however, CT does not have the excellent soft-tissue discrimination available with modern MR-imaging. Additionally, the bony anatomy surrounding the midbrain makes tissue discrimination and target delineation difficult on CT [68].

27.3.2.2 Intraoperative MRI and laser interstitial thermal therapy

Within the neurosurgeon's armament, the ability to resect and ablate pathological neural tissue is essential for the treatment of medically refractory epilepsy [21,58,82,105]. Laser interstitial thermal therapy (LITT) offers a minimally invasive treatment of tumor, both in brain and spine [16,103], in addition to ablation of epileptogenic neural tissue. Similar to DBS placement, precision is key with LITT. This technique has been shown to safely ablate neural tissue with heat reaching up to 1 cm away from the applicator [11, 64]. Magnetic resonance thermal imaging (MRTI) allows for real-time monitoring of ablation. Fig. 27.10 shows an example MR-guided LITT for intractable complex partial seizures.

The FDA has approved iMRI-compatible LITT systems which allow for visual software provided feedback of the ablation, ability to contour the tissue destruction, and offer multiple passes of the applicator if needed [21,105]. Furthermore, these systems have been associated with a reduced operating time and decreased inpatient hospitalization [112].

27.3.2.3 Safety considerations

Neurophysiological monitoring, such as electroencephalography (EEG) and electromyography (EMG), concurrently with iMRI may be associated with complications. EEG and EMG use metal leads or subdermal needles to record the central and peripheral nervous system. The radiofrequency energy produced by iMRI may generate heat at the end of the leads or needles which has been reported in the literature to cause thermal injury and image artifact [10,23]. The safety of subdermal needles with MRI has been explored in two separate studies [22,23]. These studies demonstrated that needle length and higher energy MRI sequencing correlate with increased heat production at the needle tip. One study demonstrated favorable safety profile of stainless steel and platinum–iridium needles with painless heat production. Platinum–iridium needles were shown to cause minimal imaging artifact, are low cost, and overall may be the most viable option for a Federal Drug Administration (FDA)-approved MRI-compatible subdermal needle, which currently does not exist.

Compatibility of preexisting medical devices, such as pacemakers and implanted cardioverter defibrillators (ICDs), with MRI-guided functional neurosurgery is also a growing area of interest. Roughly 50% to 75% of patients with implanted cardiac devices will need an MRI within one decade of implantation [29,35]. However, static magnetic fields in most scanners are powerful enough to dislodge implanted metal objects and potentially cause tremendous harm to the patient. The "magnetohydrodynamic effect" is also produced by the static magnetic field and produces currents in blood, which may alter ECG reading during scanning. The resulting ECG may resemble S–T elevation [29,96,117].

The FDA's Center for Devices and Radiological Health (CDRH) plays an active role in regulation of iMRI and the surgical instrumentation and software used for DBS and laser ablation. The FDA, in conjunction with the medical device companies, has issued warnings to instruct medical personnel on safest practice [87,88].

(A) Preoperative

(B) Intraoperative

(C) Postoperative

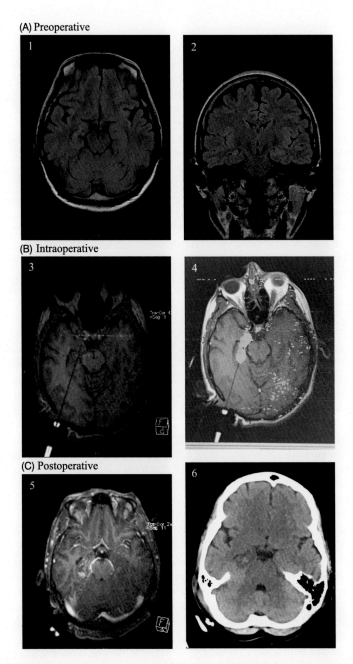

Figure 27.10 MR-guided laser-induced thermal therapy (MRgLITT) for intractable complex partial seizures. (A) Preoperative axial (1) and coronal (2) T2-weighted FLAIR post gadolinium MRI demonstrating right mesial temporal sclerosis. (B) Intraoperative T1-weighted magnetic resonance thermal imaging (MRTI) for MRgLITT (3) and the damage estimate demonstrated by the MRgLITT software (4). (C) Postoperative axial T1-weighted MRI post gadolinium (5) and noncontrast CT scan (6) with right temporal lobe lesion.

References

[1] A. Abosch, A. Lozano, Stereotactic neurosurgery for movement disorders, The Canadian Journal of Neurological Sciences (Le journal canadien des sciences neurologiques) 30 (S1) (2003) S72–S82, https://doi.org/10.1017/S0317167100003279.

[2] V. Auboiroux, L. Petrusca, M. Viallon, A. Muller, S. Terraz, R. Breguet, et al., Respiratory-gated MRgHIFU in upper abdomen using an MR-compatible in-bore digital camera, BioMed Research International 2014 (2014) 421726, https://doi.org/10.1155/2014/421726.

[3] J. Barkhausen, T. Kahn, G.A. Krombach, C.K. Kuhl, J. Lotz, D. Maintz, et al., White Paper: Interventionelle MRT: Status Quo und Entwicklungspotenzial unter ökonomischen Perspektiven, Teil 1: Generelle Anwendungen, RoFo: Fortschritte auf dem Gebiete der Rontgenstrahlen und der Nuklearmedizin 189 (7) (2017) 611–623, https://doi.org/10.1055/s-0043-110011.

[4] A.L. Benabid, P. Pollak, A. Louveau, S. Henry, J. de Rougemont, Combined (thalamotomy and stimulation) stereotactic surgery of the VIM thalamic nucleus for bilateral Parkinson disease, Stereotactic and Functional Neurosurgery 50 (1–6) (2004) 344–346, https://doi.org/10.1159/000100803.

[5] S. Bisdas, C. Roder, U. Ernemann, M.S. Tatagiba, Intraoperative MR imaging in neurosurgery, Clinical Neuroradiology 25 (Suppl 2) (2015) 237–244, https://doi.org/10.1007/s00062-015-0443-6.

[6] M. Bock, F.K. Wacker, MR-guided intravascular interventions: techniques and applications, Journal of Magnetic Resonance Imaging: JMRI 27 (2) (2008) 326–338, https://doi.org/10.1002/jmri.21271.

[7] C.E. Boone, T. Wojtasiewicz, E. Moukheiber, A. Butala, L. Jordao, K.A. Mills, et al., MR-guided functional neurosurgery: laser ablation and deep brain stimulation, Topics in Magnetic Resonance Imaging: TMRI 27 (3) (2018) 171–177, https://doi.org/10.1097/RMR.0000000000000152.

[8] A. Boss, H. Graf, B. Müller-Bierl, S. Clasen, D. Schmidt, P.L. Pereira, et al., Magnetic susceptibility effects on the accuracy of MR temperature monitoring by the proton resonance frequency method, Journal of Magnetic Resonance Imaging: JMRI 22 (6) (2005) 813–820, https://doi.org/10.1002/jmri.20438.

[9] A. Boss, H. Rempp, P. Martirosian, S. Clasen, C. Schraml, A. Stenzl, et al., Wide-bore 1.5 Tesla MR imagers for guidance and monitoring of radiofrequency ablation of renal cell carcinoma: initial experience on feasibility, European Radiology 18 (7) (2008) 1449–1455, https://doi.org/10.1007/s00330-008-0894-0.

[10] P.A. Bottomley, Turning up the heat on MRI, Journal of the American College of Radiology: JACR 5 (7) (2008) 853–855, https://doi.org/10.1016/j.jacr.2008.04.003.

[11] C. Brace, Thermal tumor ablation in clinical use, IEEE Pulse 2 (5) (2011) 28–38, https://doi.org/10.1109/MPUL.2011.942603.

[12] K.J. Burchiel, S. McCartney, A. Lee, A.M. Raslan, Accuracy of deep brain stimulation electrode placement using intraoperative computed tomography without microelectrode recording, Journal of Neurosurgery 119 (2) (2013) 301–306, https://doi.org/10.3171/2013.4.JNS122324.

[13] H. Busse, N. Garnov, G. Thörmer, D. Zajonz, W. Gründer, T. Kahn, et al., Flexible add-on solution for MR image-guided interventions in a closed-bore scanner environment, Magnetic Resonance in Medicine 64 (3) (2010) 922–928, https://doi.org/10.1002/mrm.22464.

[14] H. Busse, T. Riedel, N. Garnov, G. Thörmer, T. Kahn, M. Moche, Targeting accuracy, procedure times and user experience of 240 experimental MRI biopsies guided by a clinical add-on navigation system, PLoS ONE 10 (7) (2015) e0134370, https://doi.org/10.1371/journal.pone.0134370.

[15] A.E. Campbell-Washburn, A.Z. Faranesh, R.J. Lederman, M.S. Hansen, Magnetic resonance sequences and rapid acquisition for MR-guided interventions, Magnetic Resonance Imaging Clinics of North America 23 (4) (2015) 669–679, https://doi.org/10.1016/j.mric.2015.05.006.

[16] A. Carpentier, R.J. McNichols, R.J. Stafford, J. Itzcovitz, J.-P. Guichard, D. Reizine, et al., Real-time magnetic resonance-guided laser thermal therapy for focal metastatic brain tumors, Neurosurgery 63 (1 Suppl 1) (2008), ONS21-8; discussion ONS28-9. https://doi.org/10.1227/01.neu.0000335007.07381.df.

[17] R.L. Cazzato, J. Garnon, B. Shaygi, G. Tsoumakidou, J. Caudrelier, G. Koch, et al., How to perform a routine cryoablation under MRI guidance, Topics in Magnetic Resonance Imaging: TMRI 27 (1) (2018) 33–38, https://doi.org/10.1097/RMR.0000000000000158.

[18] J. Chen, D.A. Woodrum, K.J. Glaser, M.C. Murphy, K. Gorny, R. Ehman, Assessment of in vivo laser ablation using MR elastography with an inertial driver, Magnetic Resonance in Medicine 72 (1) (2014) 59–67, https://doi.org/10.1002/mrm.24891.

[19] N. Corbin, J. Vappou, E. Breton, Q. Boehler, L. Barbé, P. Renaud, et al., Interventional MR elastography for MRI-guided percutaneous procedures, Magnetic Resonance in Medicine 75 (3) (2016) 1110–1118, https://doi.org/10.1002/mrm.25694.

[20] Z. Cui, L. Pan, H. Song, X. Xu, B. Xu, X. Yu, et al., Intraoperative MRI for optimizing electrode placement for deep brain stimulation of the subthalamic nucleus in Parkinson disease, Journal of Neurosurgery 124 (1) (2016) 62–69, https://doi.org/10.3171/2015.1.JNS141534.

[21] D.J. Curry, A. Gowda, R.J. McNichols, A.A. Wilfong, MR-guided stereotactic laser ablation of epileptogenic foci in children, Epilepsy & Behavior: E&B 24 (4) (2012) 408–414, https://doi.org/10.1016/j.yebeh.2012.04.135.

[22] G. D'Andrea, A. Angelini, C. Foresti, P. Familiari, E. Caroli, A. Frati, Platinum–iridium subdermal magnetic resonance imaging-compatible needle electrodes are suitable for intraoperative neurophysiological monitoring during image-guided surgery with high-field intraoperative magnetic resonance imaging: an experimental study, Neurosurgery 10 (Suppl 3) (2014) 387–392, discussion 392. https://doi.org/10.1227/NEU.0000000000000432.

[23] T.M. Darcey, E.J. Kobylarz, M.A. Pearl, P.J. Krauss, S.A. Ferri, D.W. Roberts, et al., Safe use of subdermal needles for intraoperative monitoring with MRI, Neurosurgical Focus 40 (3) (2016) E19, https://doi.org/10.3171/2015.12.FOCUS15555.

[24] G. Deuschl, C. Schade-Brittinger, P. Krack, J. Volkmann, H. Schäfer, K. Bötzel, et al., A randomized trial of deep-brain stimulation for Parkinson's disease, The New England Journal of Medicine 355 (9) (2006) 896–908, https://doi.org/10.1056/NEJMoa060281.

[25] W. Dominguez-Viqueira, H. Karimi, W.W. Lam, C.H. Cunningham, A controllable susceptibility marker for passive device tracking, Magnetic Resonance in Medicine 72 (1) (2014) 269–275, https://doi.org/10.1002/mrm.24899.

[26] D.R. Elgort, C.M. Hillenbrand, S. Zhang, E.Y. Wong, S. Rafie, J.S. Lewin, et al., Image-guided and -monitored renal artery stenting using only MRI, Journal of Magnetic Resonance Imaging: JMRI 23 (5) (2006) 619–627, https://doi.org/10.1002/jmri.20554.

[27] D.R. Elgort, E.Y. Wong, C.M. Hillenbrand, F.K. Wacker, J.S. Lewin, J.L. Duerk, Real-time catheter tracking and adaptive imaging, Journal of Magnetic Resonance Imaging: JMRI 18 (5) (2003) 621–626, https://doi.org/10.1002/jmri.10402.

[28] W.J. Elias, Editorial: deep brain stimulation and intraoperative MRI, Journal of Neurosurgery 126 (1) (2016) 59–61, https://doi.org/10.3171/2015.2.JNS1556.

[29] A.M. Ferreira, F. Costa, A. Tralhão, H. Marques, N. Cardim, P. Adragão, MRI-conditional pacemakers: current perspectives, Medical Devices (Auckland, N.Z.) 7 (2014) 115–124, https://doi.org/10.2147/MDER.S44063.

[30] F. Fischbach, J. Bunke, M. Thormann, G. Gaffke, K. Jungnickel, J. Smink, et al., MR-guided freehand biopsy of liver lesions with fast continuous imaging using a 1.0-T open MRI scanner: experience in 50 patients, Cardiovascular and Interventional Radiology 34 (1) (2011) 188–192, https://doi.org/10.1007/s00270-010-9836-8.

[31] G.S. Fischer, A. Deguet, C. Csoma, R.H. Taylor, L. Fayad, J.A. Carrino, et al., MRI image overlay: application to arthrography needle insertion, Computer Aided Surgery: Official Journal of the International Society for Computer Aided Surgery 12 (1) (2007) 2–14, https://doi.org/10.3109/10929080601169930.

[32] C. Flask, D. Elgort, E. Wong, A. Shankaranarayanan, J. Lewin, M. Wendt, et al., A method for fast 3D tracking using tuned fiducial markers and a limited projection reconstruction FISP (LPR-FISP) sequence, Journal of Magnetic Resonance Imaging: JMRI 14 (5) (2001) 617–627.

[33] J. Garnon, N. Ramamurthy, J. Caudrelier, G. Erceg, E. Breton, G. Tsoumakidou, et al., MRI-guided percutaneous biopsy of mediastinal masses using a large bore magnet: technical feasibility, Cardiovascular and Interventional Radiology 39 (5) (2016) 761–767, https://doi.org/10.1007/s00270-015-1246-5.

[34] J. Garnon, A. Schlier, X. Buy, G. Tsoumakidou, M. de Mathelin, E. Breton, et al., Evaluation of percutaneous biopsies of renal masses under MRI-guidance: a retrospective study about 26 cases, European Radiology 25 (3) (2015) 617–623, https://doi.org/10.1007/s00330-014-3449-6.

[35] M.R. Gold, T. Sommer, J. Schwitter, A. Al Fagih, T. Albert, B. Merkely, et al., Full-body MRI in patients with an implantable cardioverter-defibrillator: primary results of a randomized study, Journal of the American College of Cardiology 65 (24) (2015) 2581–2588, https://doi.org/10.1016/j.jacc.2015.04.047.

[36] B.D. Greenberg, D.A. Malone, G.M. Friehs, A.R. Rezai, C.S. Kubu, P.F. Malloy, et al., Three-year outcomes in deep brain stimulation for highly resistant obsessive-compulsive disorder, Neuropsychopharmacology: Official Publication of the American College of Neuropsychopharmacology 31 (11) (2006) 2384–2393, https://doi.org/10.1038/sj.npp.1301165.

[37] R.W.Y. Habash, R. Bansal, D. Krewski, H.T. Alhafid, Thermal therapy, part III: ablation techniques, Critical Reviews in Biomedical Engineering 35 (1–2) (2007) 37–121, https://doi.org/10.1615/CritRevBiomedEng.v35.i1-2.20.

[38] W.A. Hall, H. Liu, A.J. Martin, C.H. Pozza, R.E. Maxwell, C.L. Truwit, Safety, efficacy, and functionality of high-field strength interventional magnetic resonance imaging for neurosurgery, Neurosurgery 46 (3) (2000) 632–641, discussion 641-642.

[39] C.H. Halpern, S.F. Danish, G.H. Baltuch, J.L. Jaggi, Brain shift during deep brain stimulation surgery for Parkinson's disease, Stereotactic and Functional Neurosurgery 86 (1) (2008) 37–43, https://doi.org/10.1159/000108587.

[40] S. Hegde, M.E. Miquel, R. Boubertakh, D. Gilderdale, V. Muthurangu, S.F. Keevil, et al., Interactive MR imaging and tracking of catheters with multiple tuned fiducial markers, Journal of Vascular and Interventional Radiology: JVIR 17 (7) (2006) 1175–1179, https://doi.org/10.1097/01.RVI.0000228466.09982.8B.

[41] B. Heismann, M. Ott, D. Grodzki, Sequence-based acoustic noise reduction of clinical MRI scans, Magnetic Resonance in Medicine 73 (3) (2015) 1104–1109, https://doi.org/10.1002/mrm.25229.

[42] J.C. Hindman, Proton resonance shift of water in the gas and liquid states, The Journal of Chemical Physics 44 (12) (1966) 4582–4592, https://doi.org/10.1063/1.1726676.

[43] R. Hoffmann, H. Rempp, D.-E. Keßler, J. Weiß, P.L. Pereira, K. Nikolaou, et al., MR-guided microwave ablation in hepatic tumours: initial results in clinical routine, European Radiology 27 (4) (2017) 1467–1476, https://doi.org/10.1007/s00330-016-4517-x.

[44] K.L. Holloway, S.E. Gaede, P.A. Starr, J.M. Rosenow, V. Ramakrishnan, J.M. Henderson, Frameless stereotaxy using bone fiducial markers for deep brain stimulation, Journal of Neurosurgery 103 (3) (2005) 404–413, https://doi.org/10.3171/jns.2005.103.3.0404.

[45] S.G. Hushek, A.J. Martin, M. Steckner, E. Bosak, J. Debbins, W. Kucharzyk, MR systems for MRI-guided interventions, Journal of Magnetic Resonance Imaging: JMRI 27 (2) (2008) 253–266, https://doi.org/10.1002/jmri.21269.

[46] Y. Ishihara, A. Calderon, H. Watanabe, K. Okamoto, Y. Suzuki, K. Kuroda, A precise and fast temperature mapping using water proton chemical shift, Magnetic Resonance in Medicine 34 (6) (1995) 814–823.

[47] U. Kägebein, F. Godenschweger, B.S.R. Armstrong, G. Rose, F.K. Wacker, O. Speck, et al., Percutaneous MR-guided interventions using an optical Moiré Phase tracking system: initial results, PLoS ONE 13 (10) (2018) e0205394, https://doi.org/10.1371/journal.pone.0205394.

[48] J. Kariniemi, R. Blanco Sequeiros, R. Ojala, O. Tervonen, MRI-guided abdominal biopsy in a 0.23-T open-configuration MRI system, European Radiology 15 (6) (2005) 1256–1262, https://doi.org/10.1007/s00330-004-2566-z.

[49] R. Kloeckner, D.P. dos Santos, J. Schneider, L. Kara, C. Dueber, M.B. Pitton, Radiation exposure in CT-guided interventions, European Journal of Radiology 82 (12) (2013) 2253–2257, https://doi.org/10.1016/j.ejrad.2013.08.035.

[50] G. Koch, J. Garnon, G. Tsoumakidou, F. Edalat, J. Caudrelier, R.L. Cazzato, et al., Adrenal biopsy under wide-bore MR imaging guidance, Journal of Vascular and Interventional Radiology: JVIR 29 (2) (2018) 285–290, https://doi.org/10.1016/j.jvir.2017.04.023.

[51] R.B. Kochanski, M.G. Kerolus, G. Pal, L.V. Metman, S. Sani, Use of intraoperative CT to predict the accuracy of microelectrode recording during deep brain stimulation surgery. A proof of concept study, Clinical Neurology and Neurosurgery 150 (2016) 164–168, https://doi.org/10.1016/j.clineuro.2016.09.014.

[52] W.C. Koller, K.E. Lyons, S.B. Wilkinson, A.I. Troster, R. Pahwa, Long-term safety and efficacy of unilateral deep brain stimulation of the thalamus in essential tremor, Movement Disorders: Official Journal of the Movement Disorder Society 16 (3) (2001) 464–468.

[53] A.J. Krafft, P. Zamecnik, F. Maier, A. de Oliveira, P. Hallscheidt, H.-P. Schlemmer, et al., Passive marker tracking via phase-only cross correlation (POCC) for MR-guided needle interventions: initial in vivo experience, Physica Medica: PM: An International Journal Devoted to the Applications of Physics to Medicine and Biology: Official Journal of the Italian Association of Biomedical Physics (AIFB) 29 (6) (2013) 607–614, https://doi.org/10.1016/j.ejmp.2012.09.002.

[54] T. Kuehne, S. Weiss, F. Brinkert, J. Weil, S. Yilmaz, B. Schmitt, et al., Catheter visualization with resonant markers at MR imaging-guided deployment of endovascular stents in swine, Radiology 233 (3) (2004) 774–780, https://doi.org/10.1148/radiol.2333031710.

[55] Y. Le, K. Glaser, O. Rouviere, R. Ehman, J.P. Felmlee, Feasibility of simultaneous temperature and tissue stiffness detection by MRE, Magnetic Resonance in Medicine 55 (3) (2006) 700–705, https://doi.org/10.1002/mrm.20801.

[56] D. Le Bihan, J. Delannoy, R.L. Levin, Temperature mapping with MR imaging of molecular diffusion: application to hyperthermia, Radiology 171 (3) (1989) 853–857, https://doi.org/10.1148/radiology.171.3.2717764.

[57] J.S. Lewin, J.L. Duerk, V.R. Jain, C.A. Petersilge, C.P. Chao, J.R. Haaga, Needle localization in MR-guided biopsy and aspiration: effects of field strength, sequence design, and magnetic field orientation, AJR. American Journal of Roentgenology 166 (6) (1996) 1337–1345, https://doi.org/10.2214/ajr.166.6.8633445.

[58] R. Liscak, H. Malikova, M. Kalina, Z. Vojtech, T. Prochazka, P. Marusic, et al., Stereotactic radiofrequency amygdalohippocampectomy in the treatment of mesial temporal lobe epilepsy, Acta Neurochirurgica 152 (8) (2010) 1291–1298, https://doi.org/10.1007/s00701-010-0637-2.

[59] H. Liu, W.A. Hall, A.J. Martin, C.L. Truwit, Biopsy needle tip artifact in MR-guided neurosurgery, Journal of Magnetic Resonance Imaging: JMRI 13 (1) (2001) 16–22.

[60] M.B. Maciver, H.M. Bronte-Stewart, J.M. Henderson, R.A. Jaffe, J.G. Brock-Utne, Human subthalamic neuron spiking exhibits subtle responses to sedatives, Anesthesiology 115 (2) (2011) 254–264, https://doi.org/10.1097/ALN.0ch27b013e3182217126.

[61] D. Maltête, S. Navarro, M.-L. Welter, S. Roche, A.-M. Bonnet, J.-L. Houeto, et al., Subthalamic stimulation in Parkinson disease: with or without anesthesia?, Archives of Neurology 61 (3) (2004) 390–392, https://doi.org/10.1001/archneur.61.3.390.

[62] H.S. Mayberg, A.M. Lozano, V. Voon, H.E. McNeely, D. Seminowicz, C. Hamani, et al., Deep brain stimulation for treatment-resistant depression, Neuron 45 (5) (2005) 651–660, https://doi.org/10.1016/j.neuron.2005.02.014.

[63] M. McJury, F.G. Shellock, Auditory noise associated with MR procedures: a review, Journal of Magnetic Resonance Imaging: JMRI 12 (1) (2000) 37–45.

[64] R.J. McNichols, A. Gowda, M. Kangasniemi, J.A. Bankson, R.E. Price, J.D. Hazle, MR thermometry-based feedback control of laser interstitial thermal therapy at 980 nm, Lasers in Surgery and Medicine 34 (1) (2004) 48–55, https://doi.org/10.1002/lsm.10243.

[65] A. Mewes, F. Heinrich, U. Kägebein, B. Hensen, F. Wacker, C. Hansen, Projector-based augmented reality system for interventional visualization inside MRI scanners, The International Journal of Medical Robotics + Computer Assisted Surgery: MRCAS (2018) e1950, https://doi.org/10.1002/rcs.1950.

[66] B.C. Meyer, A. Brost, D.L. Kraitchman, W.D. Gilson, N. Strobel, J. Hornegger, et al., Percutaneous punctures with MR imaging guidance: comparison between MR imaging-enhanced fluoroscopic guidance and real-time MR Imaging guidance, Radiology 266 (3) (2013) 912–919, https://doi.org/10.1148/radiol.12120117.

[67] Z. Mirzadeh, K. Chapple, M. Lambert, R. Dhall, F.A. Ponce, Validation of CT-MRI fusion for intra-operative assessment of stereotactic accuracy in DBS surgery, Movement Disorders: Official Journal of the Movement Disorder Society 29 (14) (2014) 1788–1795, https://doi.org/10.1002/mds.26056.

[68] Z. Mirzadeh, K. Chapple, M. Lambert, V.G. Evidente, P. Mahant, M.C. Ospina, et al., Parkinson's disease outcomes after intraoperative CT-guided "asleep" deep brain stimulation in the globus pallidus internus, Journal of Neurosurgery 124 (4) (2016) 902–907, https://doi.org/10.3171/2015.4.JNS1550.

[69] J.M.K. Mislow, A.J. Golby, P.M. Black, Origins of intraoperative MRI, Neurosurgery Clinics of North America 20 (2) (2009) 137–146, https://doi.org/10.1016/j.nec.2009.04.002.

[70] M. Moche, S. Heinig, N. Garnov, J. Fuchs, T.-O. Petersen, D. Seider, et al., Navigated MRI-guided liver biopsies in a closed-bore scanner: experience in 52 patients, European Radiology 26 (8) (2016) 2462–2470, https://doi.org/10.1007/s00330-015-4097-1.

[71] M. Moche, R. Trampel, T. Kahn, H. Busse, Navigation concepts for MR image-guided interventions, Journal of Magnetic Resonance Imaging: JMRI 27 (2) (2008) 276–291, https://doi.org/10.1002/jmri.21262.

[72] M. Moche, D. Zajonz, T. Kahn, H. Busse, MRI-guided procedures in various regions of the body using a robotic assistance system in a closed-bore scanner: preliminary clinical experience and limitations, Journal of Magnetic Resonance Imaging: JMRI 31 (4) (2010) 964–974, https://doi.org/10.1002/jmri.21990.

[73] A. Moelker, R.A.J.J. Maas, F. Lethimonnier, P.M.T. Pattynama, Interventional MR imaging at 1.5 T: quantification of sound exposure, Radiology 224 (3) (2002) 889–895, https://doi.org/10.1148/radiol.2243010978.

[74] I. Mutchnick, T.M. Moriarty, Intraoperative MRI in pediatric neurosurgery – an update, Translational Pediatrics 3 (3) (2014) 236–246, https://doi.org/10.3978/j.issn.2224-4336.2014.07.09.

[75] R.D. Nawfel, P.F. Judy, S.G. Silverman, S. Hooton, K. Tuncali, D.F. Adams, Patient and personnel exposure during CT fluoroscopy-guided interventional procedures, Radiology 216 (1) (2000) 180–184, https://doi.org/10.1148/radiology.216.1.r00jl39180.

[76] P. Nordbeck, H.H. Quick, M.E. Ladd, O. Ritter, Real-time magnetic resonance guidance of interventional electrophysiology procedures with passive catheter visualization and tracking, Heart Rhythm 10 (6) (2013) 938–939, https://doi.org/10.1016/j.hrthm.2011.12.017.

[77] R. Ojala, R.B. Sequeiros, R. Klemola, E. Vahala, L. Jyrkinen, O. Tervonen, MR-guided bone biopsy: preliminary report of a new guiding method, Journal of Magnetic Resonance Imaging: JMRI 15 (1) (2002) 82–86.

[78] A. de Oliveira, J. Rauschenberg, D. Beyersdorff, W. Semmler, M. Bock, Automatic passive tracking of an endorectal prostate biopsy device using phase-only cross-correlation, Magnetic Resonance in Medicine 59 (5) (2008) 1043–1050, https://doi.org/10.1002/mrm.21430.

[79] J.L. Ostrem, N. Ziman, N.B. Galifianakis, P.A. Starr, M.S. Luciano, M. Katz, et al., Clinical outcomes using ClearPoint interventional MRI for deep brain stimulation lead placement in Parkinson's disease, Journal of Neurosurgery 124 (4) (2016) 908–916, https://doi.org/10.3171/2015.4.JNS15173.

[80] L.P. Panych, B. Madore, The physics of MRI safety, Journal of Magnetic Resonance Imaging: JMRI 47 (1) (2018) 28–43, https://doi.org/10.1002/jmri.25761.

[81] D.L. Parker, Applications of NMR imaging in hyperthermia: an evaluation of the potential for localized tissue heating and noninvasive temperature monitoring, IEEE Transactions on Bio-Medical Engineering 31 (1) (1984) 161–167, https://doi.org/10.1109/TBME.1984.325382.

[82] A.G. Parrent, W.T. Blume, Stereotactic amygdalohippocampotomy for the treatment of medial temporal lobe epilepsy, Epilepsia 40 (10) (1999) 1408–1416.

[83] J.M. Peeters, J.-H. Seppenwoolde, L.W. Bartels, C.J.G. Bakker, Development and testing of passive tracking markers for different field strengths and tracking speeds, Physics in Medicine and Biology 51 (6) (2006) N127–N137, https://doi.org/10.1088/0031-9155/51/6/N04.

[84] K. Pushparajah, H. Chubb, R. Razavi, MR-guided cardiac interventions, Topics in Magnetic Resonance Imaging: TMRI 27 (3) (2018) 115–128, https://doi.org/10.1097/RMR.0000000000000156.

[85] K. Qing, L. Pan, B. Fetics, F.K. Wacker, S. Valdeig, M. Philip, et al. (Eds.), Proceedings of the Joint Annual Meeting ISMRM-ESMRMB, Stockholm, Sweden, 2018.

[86] H.H. Quick, M.O. Zenge, H. Kuehl, G. Kaiser, S. Aker, S. Massing, et al., Interventional magnetic resonance angiography with no strings attached: wireless active catheter visualization, Magnetic Resonance in Medicine 53 (2) (2005) 446–455, https://doi.org/10.1002/mrm.20347.

[87] T. Reimann, Suggested Techniques for Sterotactic Laser Amygdalohippocampotomy, Medtronic, June 29, 2018.

[88] T. Reimann, Urgent: Medical Device Correction. Visualase Thermal Therapy System, Medtronic, June 1, 2018.

[89] H. Rempp, H. Loh, R. Hoffmann, E. Rothgang, L. Pan, C.D. Claussen, et al., Liver lesion conspicuity during real-time MR-guided radiofrequency applicator placement using spoiled gradient echo and balanced steady-state free precession imaging, Journal of Magnetic Resonance Imaging: JMRI 40 (2) (2014) 432–439, https://doi.org/10.1002/jmri.24371.

[90] D.E. Richardson, H. Akil, Pain reduction by electrical brain stimulation in man. Part 2: chronic self-administration in the periventricular gray matter, Journal of Neurosurgery 47 (2) (1977) 184–194, https://doi.org/10.3171/jns.1977.47.2.0184.

[91] T. Rogers, R.J. Lederman, Interventional CMR: clinical applications and future directions, Current Cardiology Reports 17 (5) (2015) 31, https://doi.org/10.1007/s11886-015-0580-1.

[92] E. Rothgang, W.D. Gilson, F. Wacker, J. Hornegger, C.H. Lorenz, C.R. Weiss, Rapid freehand MR-guided percutaneous needle interventions: an image-based approach to improve workflow and feasibility, Journal of Magnetic Resonance Imaging: JMRI 37 (5) (2013) 1202–1212, https://doi.org/10.1002/jmri.23894.

[93] J.-H. Seppenwoolde, M.A. Viergever, C.J.G. Bakker, Passive tracking exploiting local signal conservation: the white marker phenomenon, Magnetic Resonance in Medicine 50 (4) (2003) 784–790, https://doi.org/10.1002/mrm.10574.

[94] F. Settecase, A.J. Martin, P. Lillaney, A. Losey, S.W. Hetts, Magnetic resonance-guided passive catheter tracking for endovascular therapy, Magnetic Resonance Imaging Clinics of North America 23 (4) (2015) 591–605, https://doi.org/10.1016/j.mric.2015.05.003.

[95] M. Sharma, M. Deogaonkar, Accuracy and safety of targeting using intraoperative "O-arm" during placement of deep brain stimulation electrodes without electrophysiological recordings, Journal of Clinical Neuroscience: Official Journal of the Neurosurgical Society of Australasia 27 (2016) 80–86, https://doi.org/10.1016/j.jocn.2015.06.036.

[96] J.S. Shinbane, P.M. Colletti, F.G. Shellock, Magnetic resonance imaging in patients with cardiac pacemakers: era of "MR Conditional" designs, Journal of Cardiovascular Magnetic Resonance: Official Journal of the Society for Cardiovascular Magnetic Resonance 13 (2011) 63, https://doi.org/10.1186/1532-429X-13-63.

[97] C. Sidiropoulos, R. Rammo, B. Merker, A. Mahajan, P. LeWitt, P. Kaminski, et al., Intra-operative MRI for deep brain stimulation lead placement in Parkinson's disease: 1 year motor and neuropsychological outcomes, Journal of Neurology 263 (6) (2016) 1226–1231, https://doi.org/10.1007/s00415-016-8125-0.

[98] S.G. Silverman, B.D. Collick, M.R. Figueira, R. Khorasani, D.F. Adams, R.W. Newman, et al., Interactive MR-guided biopsy in an open-configuration MR imaging system, Radiology 197 (1) (1995) 175–181, https://doi.org/10.1148/radiology.197.1.7568819.

[99] E.A. Smith, J.J. Grove, A.F.L. van der Spek, M.D. Jarboe, Magnetic-resonance-guided biopsy of focal liver lesions, Pediatric Radiology 47 (6) (2017) 750–754, https://doi.org/10.1007/s00247-017-3788-y.

[100] P.A. Starr, A.J. Martin, J.L. Ostrem, P. Talke, N. Levesque, P.S. Larson, Subthalamic nucleus deep brain stimulator placement using high-field interventional magnetic resonance imaging and a skull-mounted aiming device: technique and application accuracy, Journal of Neurosurgery 112 (3) (2010) 479–490, https://doi.org/10.3171/2009.6.JNS081161.

[101] J. Stattaus, S. Maderwald, H.A. Baba, G. Gerken, J. Barkhausen, M. Forsting, et al., MR-guided liver biopsy within a short, wide-bore 1.5 Tesla MR system, European Radiology 18 (12) (2008) 2865–2873, https://doi.org/10.1007/s00330-008-1088-5.

[102] K. Strach, C.P. Naehle, A. Mühlsteffen, M. Hinz, A. Bernstein, D. Thomas, et al., Low-field magnetic resonance imaging: increased safety for pacemaker patients?, Europace: European Pacing, Arrhythmias, and Cardiac Electrophysiology: Journal of the Working Groups on Cardiac Pacing, Arrhythmias, and Cardiac Cellular Electrophysiology of the European Society of Cardiology 12 (7) (2010) 952–960, https://doi.org/10.1093/europace/euq081.

[103] C.E. Tatsui, R.J. Stafford, J. Li, J.N. Sellin, B. Amini, G. Rao, et al., Utilization of laser interstitial thermotherapy guided by real-time thermal MRI as an alternative to separation surgery in the management of spinal metastasis, Journal of Neurosurgery. Spine 23 (4) (2015) 400–411, https://doi.org/10.3171/2015.2.SPINE141185.

[104] C. Thomas, H. Wojtczyk, H. Rempp, S. Clasen, M. Horger, C. von Lassberg, et al., Carbon fibre and nitinol needles for MRI-guided interventions: first in vitro and in vivo application, European Journal of Radiology 79 (3) (2011) 353–358, https://doi.org/10.1016/j.ejrad.2010.07.007.

[105] Z. Tovar-Spinoza, D. Carter, D. Ferrone, Y. Eksioglu, S. Huckins, The use of MRI-guided laser-induced thermal ablation for epilepsy, Child's Nervous System: ChNS: Official Journal of the International Society for Pediatric Neurosurgery 29 (11) (2013) 2089–2094, https://doi.org/10.1007/s00381-013-2169-6.

[106] L.L. Tsai, A.K. Grant, K.J. Mortele, J.W. Kung, M.P. Smith, A practical guide to MR imaging safety: what radiologists need to know, Radiographics: A Review Publication of the Radiological Society of North America, Inc 35 (6) (2015) 1722–1737, https://doi.org/10.1148/rg.2015150108.

[107] L. Venkatraghavan, E. Rakhman, V. Krishna, F. Sammartino, P. Manninen, W. Hutchison, The effect of general anesthesia on the microelectrode recordings from pallidal neurons in patients with dystonia, Journal of Neurosurgical Anesthesiology 28 (3) (2016) 256–261, https://doi.org/10.1097/ANA.0000000000000200.

[108] K.K. Vigen, B.L. Daniel, J.M. Pauly, K. Butts, Triggered, navigated, multi-baseline method for proton resonance frequency temperature mapping with respiratory motion, Magnetic Resonance in Medicine 50 (5) (2003) 1003–1010, https://doi.org/10.1002/mrm.10608.

[109] J. Volkmann, A. Wolters, A. Kupsch, J. Müller, A.A. Kühn, G.-H. Schneider, et al., Pallidal deep brain stimulation in patients with primary generalised or segmental dystonia: 5-year follow-up of a randomised trial, The Lancet Neurology 11 (12) (2012) 1029–1038, https://doi.org/10.1016/S1474-4422(12)70257-0.

[110] F.K. Wacker, D. Elgort, C.M. Hillenbrand, J.L. Duerk, J.S. Lewin, The catheter-driven MRI scanner: a new approach to intravascular catheter tracking and imaging-parameter adjustment for interventional MRI, AJR. American Journal of Roentgenology 183 (2) (2004) 391–395, https://doi.org/10.2214/ajr.183.2.1830391.

[111] L. Wang, M. Liu, L. Liu, Y. Zheng, Y. Xu, X. He, et al., MR-guided percutaneous biopsy of focal hepatic dome lesions with free-hand combined with MR fluoroscopy using 1.0-T open high-field scanner, Anticancer Research 37 (8) (2017) 4635–4641, https://doi.org/10.21873/anticanres.11865.

[112] H. Waseem, A.C. Vivas, F.L. Vale, MRI-guided laser interstitial thermal therapy for treatment of medically refractory non-lesional mesial temporal lobe epilepsy: outcomes, complications, and current limitations: a review, Journal of Clinical Neuroscience: Official Journal of the Neurosurgical Society of Australasia 38 (2017) 1–7, https://doi.org/10.1016/j.jocn.2016.12.002.

[113] C.R. Weiss, J. Fritz, The state-of-the-art of interventional magnetic resonance imaging: part 2, Topics in Magnetic Resonance Imaging: TMRI 27 (3) (2018) 113–114, https://doi.org/10.1097/RMR.0000000000000171.

[114] C.R. Weiss, S.G. Nour, J.S. Lewin, MR-guided biopsy: a review of current techniques and applications, Journal of Magnetic Resonance Imaging: JMRI 27 (2) (2008) 311–325, https://doi.org/10.1002/jmri.21270.

[115] M. Wendt, M. Busch, R. Wetzler, Q. Zhang, A. Melzer, F. Wacker, et al., Shifted rotated keyhole imaging and active tip-tracking for interventional procedure guidance, Journal of Magnetic Resonance Imaging: JMRI 8 (1) (1998) 258–261.

[116] M.J. White, J.S. Thornton, D.J. Hawkes, D.L.G. Hill, N. Kitchen, L. Mancini, et al., Design, operation, and safety of single-room interventional MRI suites: practical experience from two centers, Journal of Magnetic Resonance Imaging: JMRI 41 (1) (2015) 34–43, https://doi.org/10.1002/jmri.24577.

[117] B.L. Wilkoff, D. Bello, M. Taborsky, J. Vymazal, E. Kanal, H. Heuer, et al., Magnetic resonance imaging in patients with a pacemaker system designed for the magnetic resonance environment, Heart Rhythm 8 (1) (2011) 65–73, https://doi.org/10.1016/j.hrthm.2010.10.002.

[118] T. Wu, J.P. Felmlee, J.F. Greenleaf, S.J. Riederer, R.L. Ehman, Assessment of thermal tissue ablation with MR elastography, Magnetic Resonance in Medicine 45 (1) (2001) 80–87.

[119] J. Yuan, C.-S. Mei, L.P. Panych, N.J. McDannold, B. Madore, Towards fast and accurate temperature mapping with proton resonance frequency-based MR thermometry, Quantitative Imaging in Medicine and Surgery 2 (1) (2012) 21–32, https://doi.org/10.3978/j.issn.2223-4292.2012.01.06.

[120] S.R. Yutzy, J.L. Duerk, Pulse sequences and system interfaces for interventional and real-time MRI, Journal of Magnetic Resonance Imaging: JMRI 27 (2) (2008) 267–275, https://doi.org/10.1002/jmri.21268.

[121] M. Zhu, Z. Sun, C.K. Ng, Image-guided thermal ablation with MR-based thermometry, Quantitative Imaging in Medicine and Surgery 7 (3) (2017) 356–368, https://doi.org/10.21037/qims.2017.06.06.

CHAPTER 28

Interventional imaging: Ultrasound

Ilker Hacihaliloglu[a], Elvis C.S. Chen[b], Parvin Mousavi[c], Purang Abolmaesumi[d], Emad Boctor[e], Cristian A. Linte[f]

[a]Rutgers University, Piscataway, NJ, United States
[b]Western University, London, ON, Canada
[c]Queen's University, Kingston, ON, Canada
[d]University of British Columbia, Vancouver, BC, Canada
[e]Johns Hopkins University, Baltimore, MD, United States
[f]Rochester Institute of Technology, Rochester, NY, United States

Contents

28.1. Introduction: ultrasound imaging		702
28.2. Ultrasound-guided cardiac interventions		702
	28.2.1 Cardiac ultrasound imaging technology	703
	28.2.1.1 Transthoracic echocardiography – TTE	*704*
	28.2.1.2 Transesophageal echocardiography – TEE	*704*
	28.2.1.3 Intracardiac echocardiography – ICE	*704*
	28.2.2 3D cardiac ultrasound imaging	704
	28.2.2.1 Reconstructed 3D imaging	*704*
	28.2.2.2 Real-time 3D imaging	*705*
28.3. Ultrasound data manipulation and image fusion for cardiac applications		705
	28.3.1 Multimodal image registration and fusion	706
	28.3.2 Integration of ultrasound imaging with surgical tracking	706
	28.3.3 Fusion of ultrasound imaging via volume rendering	707
28.4. Ultrasound imaging in orthopedics		708
	28.4.1 Bone segmentation from ultrasound images	709
	28.4.1.1 Segmentation methods using image intensity and phase information	*709*
	28.4.1.2 Machine learning-based segmentation	*710*
	28.4.1.3 Incorporation of bone shadow region information to improve segmentation	*710*
	28.4.2 Registration of orthopedic ultrasound images	711
28.5. Image-guided therapeutic applications		711
	28.5.1 Fluoroscopy & TEE-guided aortic valve implantation	711
	28.5.2 US-guided robot-assisted mitral valve repair	712
	28.5.3 Model-enhanced US-guided intracardiac interventions	712
	28.5.4 ICE-guided ablation therapy	713
	28.5.5 Image-guided spine interventions	714
28.6. Summary and future perspectives		715
Acknowledgments		715
References		716

Handbook of Medical Image Computing and Computer Assisted Intervention
https://doi.org/10.1016/B978-0-12-816176-0.00033-8

28.1. Introduction: ultrasound imaging

The first use of ultrasound (US) imaging in medicine was in 1956 for fetal imaging in Glasgow [1]; however, it was not until the 1990s when it was employed for interventional guidance [2], starting with neurosurgical procedures. US can acquire real-time images at various user-controlled positions and orientations, with a spatial resolution ranging from 0.2 to 2 mm. In concert with recent technological advancements, US has become one of the most widely employed imaging modality in medicine. The collection of real time data, coupled with the ability to provide quantitative blood flow information, and its ability to acquire both 2D and 3D images are some of the critical properties that render US imaging as a suitable intraoperative guidance and monitoring tool. Furthermore, US imaging is portable, cost-effective, and versatile. Thanks to these characteristics, US has been employed in various interventional procedures such as: (1) cardiac and vascular applications for imaging blood flow, ventricular wall motion, and valve opening/closing; (2) orthopedic applications for intraoperative imaging of bone or real-time needle guidance; (3) neurosurgery applications for intraoperative tumor imaging; and (4) cancer management and monitoring for guiding biopsy applications.

It is generally agreed that the quality of US images is inferior to that of the CT or MR images [3]. The presence of multiple speckle reflections, shadowing, and variable contrast are some of the disadvantages that have contributed to the slow progress of employing US imaging intraoperatively. Several approaches to enhance anatomical visualization have included the acquisition of 2D US image series to generate volumetric datasets [4], optical or magnetic tracking of the 2D US transducer to reconstruct 3D images [5], and fusion of US and preoperative CT or MRI images [6,7].

28.2. Ultrasound-guided cardiac interventions

Cardiac therapy involved a wide variety of procedures, including the replacement or repair of a malfunctioning valve, restoration of myocardial perfusion by stenting or grafting, or treatment of arrhythmic conditions by electrically isolating tissue regions via thermal or cryoablation. Cardiac interventions are unique in several perspectives, namely, restricted access and surgical instrument manipulation, limited visualization, as well as the challenge to operate on the beating heart. Procedure invasiveness extends beyond the typical measurement of the incision size, and in fact, arises from two equally important sources: access to the surgical target via a median sternotomy and rib-spreading, and the use of cardiopulmonary bypass after the heart is stopped. Supplying circulatory support via cardiopulmonary bypass (i.e., heart–lung machine) represents a significant source of invasiveness that may lead to severe inflammatory response and neurological damage [8]. Moreover, despite various approaches employed to stabilize the motion of the heart at the site of interest during surgery [9], the delivery of therapy to a soft tissue organ enclosing a blood-filled environment in continuous motion is still a significant challenge. Successful therapy requires versatile instrumentation, robust visualization, and superior surgical skills.

Due to the challenges associated with visualization and access, cardiac interventions have been among the last surgical applications to embrace the use of less invasive therapeutic methods [10] that originated in the mid-1990s following the introduction of laparoscopic techniques and their use in video-assisted thoracic surgery. The adoption of less invasive techniques posed significant problems in terms of their workflow integration and yield of clinically acceptable outcomes. However, the morbidity associated with the surgery rather than the therapy, together with the successful experience with the less invasive approaches in other surgical specialties, have fueled their emergence into cardiac therapy.

Over the past couple of decades, medical imaging has provided a means for visualization and guidance during interventions where direct visual feedback could not be achieved without significant trauma. Initial image-guided techniques, including robot-assisted procedures, relied on thorascopic video or fluoroscopic imaging for surgical guidance [11,12]. The advent of "CT fluoroscopy" has opened the door for promoting CT as a high-quality intraprocedure image-guidance technique. Lauritsch et al. [13] have investigated the feasibility of C-arm guidance both *in vitro*, using phantom experiments, as well as in *in vivo* preclinical studies. McVeigh et al. [14] have shown that interventional MRI systems can provide the surgeon with detailed and comprehensive dynamic cardiac images for intraprocedure guidance.

As an alternative to CT or MRI, US imaging is an attractive modality for intraoperative cardiac guidance, especially due to its safety, low cost, wide availability, and lack of ionizing radiation. The main drawback of US is that standard 2D images cannot appropriately portray a 3D surgical scene, which often includes delivery instruments and anatomical targets [15]. This visualization impediment can be improved by complementing the 2D images with appropriate anatomical context provided by high-quality preoperative information. In fact, recently developed image-guided therapy systems for cardiac surgery have fused data from pre- and intraoperative imaging and tracking technologies to form sophisticated visualizations for surgical guidance [16–18].

28.2.1 Cardiac ultrasound imaging technology

US transducers of varying size and invasiveness, some of which image natively in 3D, have been employed for cardiac interventions. Furthermore, integration of US imaging with surgical tracking technologies has enabled visualization of the acquired images relative to the tracked surgical instruments, as described in the following sections.

28.2.1.1 Transthoracic echocardiography – TTE

These probes are held against the patient's chest and are simple to use and completely noninvasive. However, acoustic windows where the ribs and lungs do not impede imaging are limited, and depth penetration is problematic in obese patients or those with chronic lung disease. Because the probe must remain in contact with the patient's chest, the surgeon needs to manipulate the US transducer at the same time as the instruments, leading to a cumbersome workflow.

28.2.1.2 Transesophageal echocardiography – TEE

TEE transducers are inserted into the patient's esophagus or upper stomach to image from directly behind the heart. Most are multiplanar, meaning that the imaging plane can be electronically rotated through 180°. The viewing direction can also be manipulated by translating, flexing, and tilting the probe. The proximity of the probe to the heart allows for higher frequency transducers, which increases spatial resolution and overall image quality compared to TTE. During interventions, the transducer is conveniently out of the way inside the patient, but this necessitates general anesthesia and makes imaging more technically challenging.

28.2.1.3 Intracardiac echocardiography – ICE

Fixed to a steerable catheter, these transducers are navigated directly into the heart via the femoral or jugular vein. In particular, ICE is often used to visualize interventional catheters during percutaneous procedures. A very high imaging frequency provides excellent image quality and general anesthesia is not required. However, the single-use nature of ICE makes it expensive. In addition, ICE probes are difficult for the clinician to manipulate inside the heart, and given the proximity of the transducer to the imaged tissue, ICE images have a limited field of view and are difficult to interpret without additional anatomical context.

28.2.2 3D cardiac ultrasound imaging

28.2.2.1 Reconstructed 3D imaging

A single volume or a time series of 3D US images can be built from multiple 2D images that cover 3D space, and are acquired by moving the US probe manually or mechanically [19]. Cardiac gating is required when imaging the beating heart with this approach. Each 2D US image must be accurately localized in 3D space by tracking the US probe, or, for mechanical probe manipulation, using actuator feedback or sensor-less approaches. US reconstruction is flexible and can generate 3D images with good spatial resolution and a large field of view (Fig. 28.1), but it can be a lengthy procedure and is subject to artifacts caused by tracking error, cardiac gating error, or respiratory or patient motion.

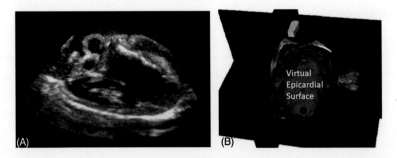

Figure 28.1 (A) Example 3D US reconstruction of an excised porcine heart in a water bath, acquired using a TEE probe with rotational acquisition; (B) Example visualization of a reconstructed 4D US dataset registered to a dynamic cardiac surface model (single frame showed here) using a beating heart phantom (The Chamberlain Group, Great Barrington, MA, USA).

28.2.2.2 Real-time 3D imaging

A 2D matrix array transducer with electronic beam steering natively acquires pyramidal 3D images at 20–30 frames per second with real-time volume rendering [20]. Both TTE and TEE transducers are currently available and real-time 3D ICE is on the horizon. Trade-offs between spatial resolution, frame rate, and field of view are caused by the finite speed of sound in tissue, so only a small section of the heart can be imaged at any point in time. It is therefore common to stitch together several electrocardiography (ECG)-gated images acquired over multiple cardiac cycles from different viewing directions with electronic beam steering. Such "wide-angle" scans are generated without probe tracking while assuming a stationary transducer and patient. The resulting composite scans are subject to stitching artifacts at the interfaces between the original real-time 3D images.

28.3. Ultrasound data manipulation and image fusion for cardiac applications

Image processing and analysis algorithms designed specifically for US images are required when integrating US imaging within image-guided therapy systems. Strategies for fusing US imagery with other datasets are particularly important. Intraoperative US images are often used to bring preoperative images into the coordinate system of the intraoperative patient (patient-to-image registration). Tracking technologies used to align data spatially must be integrated into the operating room while not impeding US imaging or standard workflows. Finally, US imagery must be integrated within three-dimensional scenes alongside additional image, geometric and/or functional data.

28.3.1 Multimodal image registration and fusion

Image registration is critical for image-guided therapy and multimodal data fusion. Monomodal and multimodal registration of cardiac US images remains challenging because they show few distinctive features and because of the relatively poor image quality of US imaging. Approaches for image-to-patient registration via intraoperative US have been based on matching anatomical landmarks such as the valve annuli [21], aortic centerline [22], and endocardial surface coordinates [23].

Intensity-based image registration is often ideal for intraoperative use since it does not rely on potentially inaccurate feature localization, requires no user interaction, and may be implemented in real-time. Example algorithms registering intra-operative US to high-quality CT or MRI cardiac images include those of Sun et al. [6], who maximized the normalized cross-correlation between 2D ICE images and the gradient magnitude of intraoperative CT images, Huang et al. [7], who enabled fast intra-operative registration between tracked 2D US and preoperative CT images by computing a very close registration initialization, and King et al. [24], who optimized the statistical likelihood that 3D US images arose from a preoperative surface model using a simple model of US physics.

28.3.2 Integration of ultrasound imaging with surgical tracking

Real-time tracking of moving surgical tools and imaging devices is required for data to be properly displayed relative to each other. Although optical tracking systems can be used to track intraoperative transthoracic probes, their line-of-sight constraints make electromagnetic tracking more suitable when using transesophageal or intracardiac echocardiography (Fig. 28.2). Image-based tracking of surgical tools within US images using physical markers [25] and voxel classification [26] has also been investigated, but is not in widespread use at present.

Relatively simple surgical guidance systems visualizing tracked real-time 2D US imaging alongside virtual representations of tracked surgical tools, such as needles or anastomosis (fastening) devices, have been proposed for beating-heart intracardiac interventions and even for prenatal cardiac interventions to guide needles through the maternal abdomen and into the fetal heart.

Perhaps one of the most efficient and complete platforms for image guidance and navigation that facilitate the integration of tracked US imaging is the PLUS framework [27]. PLUS is an open-source software toolkit for data acquisition, pre-processing, and calibration for image-guided navigation and visualization. PLUS was originally developed for US-guided interventions (hence the name, PLUS – Public software Library for UltraSound imaging research) and it contains all essential functions for implementing tracked US systems. However, over the past few years, the PLUS platform has been widely used to build image-guided navigation frameworks for orthopedic, neuro and

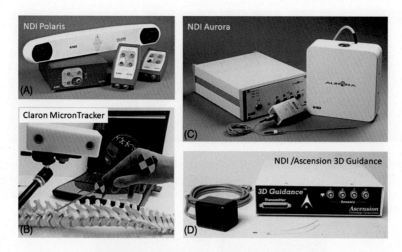

Figure 28.2 Commonly employed optical tracking systems: (A) Polaris Spectra from NDI, and (B) Micron Tracker from Claron Technologies; and electromagnetic tracking systems: (C) Aurora from NDI, and (D) 3D Guidance from Ascension.

cardiac applications, with and without US imaging. The PLUS toolkit, its development, applications and additional details are disseminated in detail in another chapter of this collection by Lasso et al. [27].

28.3.3 Fusion of ultrasound imaging via volume rendering

Although overlaying virtual representations of tracked surgical tools onto echocardiography should enhance image interpretability during surgical tasks, greater improvements can be provided by fusing echocardiography with information from other imaging modalities.

Volume rendering is the most common technique for visualizing real-time 3D US within image guidance systems designed for cardiac therapy, as it utilizes all the original 3D imaging data, rather than discarding most of it when surfaces are extracted using segmentation. "Viewing rays" are cast through the intact volumes and individual voxels in the dataset are mapped onto the viewing plane, maintaining their 3D relationship while making the display appearance meaningful to the observer.

The interventional system described by Wein et al. [28], which registers real-time 3D ICE images with intraoperative C-arm CT imagery, uses volume rendering to visualize the US data within its augmented reality display. Ma et al. [22] have developed a guidance system fusing complementary X-ray and transthoracic 3D echocardiography data, using a master–slave robotic system to manipulate the US probe in the presence of X-ray radiation and overlaying volume rendered 3D US onto the 2D X-ray images (Fig. 28.3).

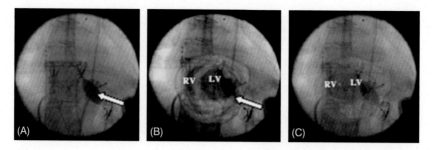

Figure 28.3 (A) Traditional 2D X-ray image used for catheter navigation; (B) Manual segmentations of the left (green) and right ventricle (blue) and electrical measurement catheter (red) overlaid onto 2D X-ray image; (C) Volume rendering of the masked 3D echo image was also used and overlaid onto the 2D X-ray images.

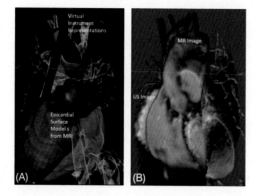

Figure 28.4 (A) Procedure simulation showing volume rendered cardiac MR dataset augmented with surgical instruments, displayed using different translucency levels for feature enhancement; (B) Fused cardiac MR and 3D US datasets, showing enhancement of the preoperative MR data. Images courtesy of Qi Zhang, PhD, Robarts Research Institute.

Using GPUs, artifact-free interactive volume rendering of medical datasets was achieved [29] without compromising image fidelity, as also demonstrated by Zhang et al. (Fig. 28.4) [30].

28.4. Ultrasound imaging in orthopedics

In order to provide a radiation-free, cost-effective alternative to standard 2D fluoroscopy, US imaging has been investigated as an alternative imaging modality in orthopedics [31–39]. Despite several clear advantages of US imaging over standard fluoroscopy – real-time 2D and 3D imaging capabilities – widespread adoption of US imaging in orthopedic procedures has been limited. Low signal-to-noise ratio (SNR), bone surfaces appearing several millimeters in thickness, reverberation artifacts, and operator-dependent, manual data collection are the main problems associated with US [40]. Another disadvantage of US is related to the fact that collected images only display the outer layer of periosteum bone (subsurface) and a complete tomographic imaging is not possible. This causes further difficulties during the interpretation of collected data. In order to provide solutions to these problems and increase the applicability of US, research has focused on automatic bone segmentation and registration approaches [40, 41].

28.4.1 Bone segmentation from ultrasound images

Segmentation approaches can be divided into four main categories: (1) segmentation methods using image intensity information; (2) segmentation methods using image phase information; (3) segmentation methods using joint (intensity and phase) information; and (4) machine learning-based segmentation.

28.4.1.1 Segmentation methods using image intensity and phase information

Early work on automatic segmentation of bone surfaces from US data focused on the use of image intensity and gradient information [31,37,42,43]. Intensity-based approaches have low sensitivity and specificity if the collected scans have low contrast bone surfaces and high intensity soft tissue interfaces. Fig. 28.5 shows two different scans obtained *in vivo* from the distal radius without changing the transducer position; however, a slight tilt was introduced to collect the image shown on the right. The image shown on the left exhibits typical bone surface response characteristics: high intensity interface followed by an intensity dropout. These characteristics are not visible in the image shown on the right due to a different transducer orientation with respect to the imaged bone surface. Processing these two images using intensity-based approaches would result in two different segmentation outputs.

In order to overcome the difficulties of intensity-based approaches and provide a more robust solution, the use of image phase information has been investigated by various groups [44–47]. Image phase information is obtained by filtering the Fourier transformed B-mode US image with band-pass quadrature filters [48]. Most widely used filters for processing US data include Log-Gabor filters, monogenic signal filter, and Gabor filters. The image phase-based methods usually result in the enhancement of bone features, followed by a postprocessing method [49] to obtain a final segmented surface.

Lastly, joint methods combine the strengths of both intensity and phase-based methods and have shown to provide segmentation results with higher sensitivity and specificity [50,51].

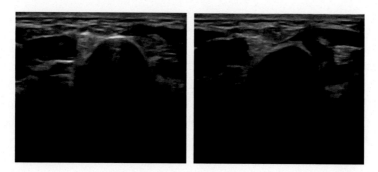

Figure 28.5 Both images show *in vivo* distal radius US scans. The scans were obtained from the same anatomical region (distal radius) without changing the transducer position. However, a slight tilt of the transducer was introduced to obtain the image show on the right.

28.4.1.2 Machine learning-based segmentation

The use of machine learning in the context of US bone segmentation has been most recently investigated. In [52], an approach using random forests was investigated. In [53], a graphical modeling approach based on image intensity and phase features, was proposed. Due to the very successful results obtained for segmenting medical image data, deep learning based bone segmentation has also been investigated [54,55]. In [55], the proposed convolutional neural network (CNN)-based methods achieved significantly improved results over phase-based approaches.

28.4.1.3 Incorporation of bone shadow region information to improve segmentation

The high acoustic impedance mismatch between the soft tissue and bone interface causes most of the propagating US signal to reflect back to the transducer surface at the bone boundary. This results in the formation of a low intensity region after the high intensity bone surface response. This low intensity region is denoted as the bone shadow region. Some of the methods mentioned previously, have improved the accuracy of the segmentation by incorporating bone shadow image feature into their framework [50, 51,53,56].

Most of the bone segmentation and/or enhancement methods developed so far have only been validated on individual bone anatomy for specific orthopedic procedures. Development of a method for segmenting any bone surface, independent of the clinical application, is still an open research question. In order to make US a dominant imaging modality in orthopedics, extensive validation in clinical trials is necessary. Recently, several groups have also investigated new beamforming methods specifically designed for imaging specular bone surfaces [57], and methods based on the use of elastography [58].

28.4.2 Registration of orthopedic ultrasound images

Image registration is one of the main components of computer-assisted orthopedic intervention platforms. For US-guided orthopedic procedures, registration is performed to (1) align a pre-operative (CT-derived) plan to intra-operative patient data obtained using US, (2) overcome the limited field of view of US by providing context from CT or MRI images, and (3) augment the US data with 3D anatomical models generated from tomographic images. In orthopedic procedures, point-based registration methods have dominated the field due to their computational advantage over intensity-based registration methods [41].

Automatic, real-time and accurate registration is critical for effective image guidance and anatomical restoration for various orthopedic procedures. Most of the registration methods developed have not been extensively validated in clinical trials and the clinical accuracy requirements for certain surgical procedures still exceed the reported registration accuracies. Finally, most of the proposed registration approaches require a manual initialization to begin the registration process.

28.5. Image-guided therapeutic applications

Although US imaging technology has been around for quite some time, it was mainly employed as a diagnostic imaging tool. During the past decade or less, the use of US has expanded toward interventional imaging, leading to several pre-clinical and clinical successes in surgical guidance, while others are still under development.

28.5.1 Fluoroscopy & TEE-guided aortic valve implantation

Transapical aortic valve implantations have received significant attention over the past few years. Such procedures have been successful under real-time MR imaging, as well as real-time cone-beam CT and US imaging. Walther et al. [59] have reported the use of real-time fluoroscopy guidance combined with echocardiography to guide the implantation of aortic valves via the left ventricular apex during rapid ventricular pacing. The guidance environment integrates both a planning and a guidance module. The pre-operative planning is conducted based on DynaCT Axiom Artis images (Siemens Inc., Erlangen, Germany) and interactive anatomical landmark selection to determine the size and optimal position of the prosthesis. The intraoperative fluoroscopy guidance allows tracking of the prosthesis and coronary ostia, while TEE enables real-time assessment of valve positioning [60]. The main benefit of these contemporary CBCT imaging systems is their ability to provide 3D organ reconstructions during the procedure. Because the fluoroscopy and CT images are intrinsically registered, no further registration is required to overlay the model of the aortic root reconstructed intraoperatively with the real-time fluoroscopy images [61]. Moreover, since this therapy approach makes use of imaging modalities already employed in the OR, it has the potential to be adopted as a clinical standard of care for such interventions.

28.5.2 US-guided robot-assisted mitral valve repair

Real-time 3D (4D) US imaging of the heart has been employed extensively in clinical practice, enabling the performance of new surgical procedures [62,63], and making possible real-time therapy evaluation on the beating heart. However, the rapid cardiac motion introduces serious challenges to the surgeons, especially for procedures which require the manipulation of moving intracardiac structures. Howe et al. [64] have proposed the use of a 3D US-based robotic motion compensation system to synchronize instruments with the motion of the heart. The system consists of a real-time 3D US tissue tracker that is integrated with a 1 degree-of-freedom actuated surgical instrument and a real-time 3D US instrument tracker. The device first identifies the position of the instrument and target tissue, then drives the robot such that the instrument matches the target motion.

For mitral valve repair procedures, two instruments were introduced through the wall of the left atrium: one instrument deployed an annuloplasty ring with a shape-memory-alloy frame, and the other instrument applied anchors to attach the ring to the valve annulus. This approach allows the surgeon to operate on a "virtually motionless" heart when placing the annuloplasty ring and anchors. Initial studies have demonstrated the potential of such motion-compensation techniques to increase the success rate of surgical anchor implantation. Moreover, in a recent study [65], this group also reported submillimeter accuracy in tracking the mitral valve using a similar motion-compensation approach for catheter servoing.

28.5.3 Model-enhanced US-guided intracardiac interventions

The development of model-enhanced US assisted guidance draws its origins from the principle that therapeutic interventions consist of two processes: navigation, during which the surgical instrument is brought close to the target, and positioning, when the actual therapy is delivered by accurately placing the tool on target. The integration of pre- and intraoperative imaging and surgical tracking enables the implementation of the navigation-positioning paradigm formulated in this work. The preoperative anatomical models act as guides to facilitate tool-to-target navigation, while the US images provide real-time guidance for on-target tool positioning.

This platform has been employed pre-clinically to guide several *in vivo* intracardiac beating heart interventions in swine models, including mitral valve implantation and septal defect repair [21]. As described in the work by Guiraudon et al. [66,21], access to the chambers of the beating heart was achieved using the Universal Cardiac Introducer (UCI) [66] attached to the left atrial appendage of the swine heart exposed via a left minithoracotomy. The guidance environment employed magnetically tracked real-time

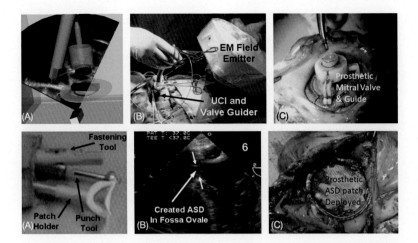

Figure 28.6 Mitral valve implantation – upper panel: (A) Guidance environment showing virtual models of the US probe and surgical tools; (B) OR setup during model-enhanced US guided interventions; (C) Postprocedure assessment image. Septal defect repair – lower panel: (A) Tools employed during the ASD creation and repair; (B) 2D US image showing the septal defect; (C) Postoperative image showing successful ASD repair.

2D TEE augmented with preoperative models of the porcine heart and virtual representations of the valve-guiding tool and valve-fastening tool. The procedure involved the navigation of the tools to the target under guidance provided by the virtual models, followed by the positioning of the valve and application of the surgical clips under real-time US imaging (Fig. 28.6).

The ASD repair procedure was similar to the mitral valve implantation; however, the surgical target was not readily defined. The septal defect was created in the swine models by removing a circular disc of tissue from the fossa ovale under US guidance, using a custom-made hole-punch tool (15 mm diameter) introduced via the UCI. The created septal defect was confirmed using color Doppler US for blood flow imaging. The repair patch was guided to the target under virtual model guidance. Once on target, the surgeon correctly positioned the patch on the created ASD and anchored it to the underlying tissue under real-time US image guidance (Fig. 28.6).

28.5.4 ICE-guided ablation therapy

Recently, intraoperative 2D ICE has been proposed as an alternative to preoperative MR/CT for the generation of endocardial surface models. ICE-derived surface models have been used within surgical guidance systems used in patients to perform pulmonary vein and linear ablations [67] and left ventricular tachycardia ablations [68]. A set of spatially-localized 2D ICE images can be acquired by sweeping a magnetically-tracked 2D ICE probe to view the left atrium, left ventricle, pulmonary veins or any other structures of interest, typically under ECG and respiratory gating. Although ICE-derived surface models have a lower spatial resolution than those segmented from preoperative MR or CT, they can be generated in the operating room and may be argued to provide the intraoperative heart with higher fidelity.

Intraoperative endocardial surface data derived from 2D ICE have been used to integrate preoperative MR/CT surface models with the intraoperative patient. This approach takes advantage of ICE's ability to collect endocardial surface points without deforming the cardiac wall, which leads to improved registration accuracy while still integrating a high-quality surface model, as demonstrated by Zhong et al. [23]. Real-time 2D ICE imaging can also be integrated into the surgical guidance system along with a cardiac model and representation of the ablation catheter, as demonstrated by den Uijl et al. [69].

28.5.5 Image-guided spine interventions

Due to visualization of the bone anatomy and soft tissue structures, easy portability, and lack of radiation exposure, various US-guided systems have been developed for spinal pain management [70] and surgical procedures. Pain management of the spine is one of the most common medical procedures, affecting up to 90% of people at some point in their lifetime [71]. For patients not responsive to conservative treatment options (such as physical therapy, oral analgesics, or chiropractic treatment), minimally invasive spine injections have been employed as a more cost-effective and less harmful treatment option than surgery. Epidural, facet joint, and sacroiliac joint injections are the most commonly performed interventional spine procedures. Epidural injections are also very common in obstetrics, with 50–80% of women in labor electing to receive an epidural injection [72]. In order to reduce neurovascular complications and provide a safe procedure, image guidance has been used in most of these procedures. Two-dimensional (2D) fluoroscopy has been the most dominant imaging modality used in these procedures.

To provide a safer and more accurate guidance alternative, US imaging began to emerge as an imaging technique in spine pain management procedures [73]. The added advantage of US in these procedures includes: (1) visualization of soft tissues interfaces such as muscles, tendons, and ligaments together with bony anatomical landmarks, (2) portability, allowing the procedures performed within clinic, (3) real-time imaging resulting in cost savings and decreased time for the procedure, and (4) zero radiation exposure, which is a very important advantage in obstetrics. The primary disadvantage of US-guided spine injections, aside from the other challenges mentioned previously, is the need for simultaneous operation of the transducer and insertion of needles, difficulty in localizing needle from US data (specifically for steep insertion angles), and correct interpretation of the collected scans. In order to overcome solutions to these problems, various groups have focused on developing segmentation and registration tools in order to provide enhanced guidance [74–80]. Recently, robotic-guided solutions have also been proposed [80]. Main advantage for these systems is low variability of the collected scans since the transducer is controlled by a robotic arm.

Compared to pain management procedures, application of US in spine surgery has not been investigated extensively. Early work focused on the enhancement and registration steps [32,81]. Using tracked 2D US snapshots was investigated in [82] for pedicle screw insertion. In [83], 2D US was used for identification of pedicle scan plane. In [55], segmented US bone surfaces were registered to intraoperative fluoroscopy scans in the context of lumbar hernia surgery, however, surgical accuracy was not investigated. Feasibility of using A-mode and/or intravascular US for guiding pedicle drill hole generation and pedicle screw insertion was also explored [84–87]. US was also investigated in the context of scoliosis diagnosis and monitoring [88,89]. Commercial platforms based on US for scoliosis imaging are also available (Scolioscan, Talefield Medical Imaging, Hong Kong, China).

28.6. Summary and future perspectives

In this chapter we have presented a condensed view of recent work in US-based interventions. Specific focus was given on cardiac, orthopedic, and intra-vascular applications.

Even though US has been widely investigated as an imaging modality in orthopedic interventions, its clinical adaptability in this field is far behind compared to cardiology, neurosurgery, or computer aided diagnosis. In orthopedics there is an urgent need for increased effort on segmentation validation. Such an effort will provide a better understanding of the strengths and limitations of the developed methods compared to each other and on larger database. This requires the establishment of a publicly available database ideally with multiexpert segmentations. Although robotic systems, such as Mazor Robotics or Srtyker Mako, are widely employed in orthopedic surgery (with successful clinical outcomes) the incorporation US into these systems has not been investigated extensively. Recently, some research groups are investigating the combination of robotics and US in orthopedic surgery [90,80]. Finally, efforts on combining augmented reality (AR) and US imaging in orthopedic interventions is also attracting a lot of attention [91].

Acknowledgments

Work presented in this chapter has been supported by several sources of funding: National Sciences and Engineering research Council of Canada (Abolmaesumi, Chen, Linte and Mousavi), Heart and Stroke Foundation of Canada (Linte), Canadian Institutes of Health Research (Abolmaesumi, Chen, Linte and Mousavi), North American Spine Society (NASS) 2017 Young Investigator Basic Research Grant Award (Hacihaliloglu), National Institutes of Health – National Institute of General Medical Sciences Grant No. R35GM128877 (Linte), and National Science Foundation – Advanced Cyber-infrastructure Award No. 1808530 (Linte).

References

[1] M. Nicolson, J.E. Fleming, Imaging and Imagining the Fetus: The Development of Obstetric Ultrasound, JHU Press, 2013.

[2] V. van Velthoven, L.M. Auer, Practical application of intraoperative ultrasound imaging, Acta Neurochirurgica (Wien) 105 (1990) 5–13.

[3] R. Steinmeier, R. Fahlbusch, O. Ganslandt, C. Nimsky, W. Huk, M. Buchfelder, et al., Intraoperative magnetic resonance imaging with the magnetom open scanner: concepts, neurosurgical indications, and procedures: a preliminary report, Neurosurgery 43 (1998) 739–747.

[4] R.N. Rohling, A.H. Gee, L. Berman, Automatic registration of 3-D ultrasound images, Ultrasound in Medicine & Biology 24 (1998) 841–854.

[5] D.F. Pace, A.D. Wiles, J. Moore, C. Wedlake, D.G. Gobbi, T.M. Peters, Validation of four-dimensional ultrasound for targeting in minimally-invasive beating-heart surgery, in: Proc. SPIE Medical Imaging 2009: Visualization, Image-Guided Procedures and Modeling, vol. 7261, 2009, p. 726115–1–12.

[6] Y. Sun, S. Kadoury, Y. Li, M. John, F. Sauer, J. Resnick, et al., Image guidance of intracardiac ultrasound with fusion of pre-operative images, in: Proc. Med. Image Comput. Comput. Assist. Interv., in: Lect. Notes Comput. Sci., vol. 10, 2007, pp. 60–67.

[7] X. Huang, J. Moore, G.M. Guiraudon, D.L. Jones, D. Bainbridge, J. Ren, et al., Dynamic 2D ultrasound and 3D CT image registration of the beating heart, IEEE Transactions on Medical Imaging 28 (2009) 1179–1189.

[8] L.H. Edmunds, Why cardiopulmonary bypass makes patients sick: strategies to control the blood-synthetic surface interface, Advances in Cardiac Surgery 6 (1995) 131–167.

[9] V.A. Subramanian, J.C. McCabe, C.M. Geller, Minimally invasive direct coronary artery bypass grafting: two-year clinical experience, The Annals of Thoracic Surgery 64 (1997) 1648–1653.

[10] M.J. Mack, Minimally invasive cardiac surgery, Surgical Endoscopy 20 (2006) S488–S492.

[11] A. Cribier, H. Eltchaninoff, A. Bash, N. Borenstein, C. Tron, F. Bauer, et al., Percutaneous transcatheter implantation of an aortic valve prosthesis for calcific aortic stenosis, Circulation 106 (2002) 3006–3008.

[12] A. Carpentier, D. Loulmet, B. Aupecle, J.P. Kieffer, D. Tournay, P. Guibourt, et al., First computer assisted open heart surgery: first case operated on with success, Comptes Rendus de l'Academie des Sciences – Series III 321 (1998) 437–442.

[13] G. Lauritsch, J. Boese, L. Wigström, H. Kemeth, R. Fahrig, Towards cardiac C-arm computed tomography, IEEE Transactions on Medical Imaging 25 (2006) 922–934.

[14] E.R. McVeigh, M.A. Guttman, P. Kellman, A.A. Raval, R.J. Lederman, Real-time, interactive MRI for cardiovascular interventions, Academic Radiology 12 (2005) 1221–1227.

[15] T.M. Peters, Image-guidance for surgical procedures, Physics in Medicine and Biology 51 (2006) R505–R540.

[16] C.A. Linte, J. White, R. Eagleson, G.M. Guiraudon, T.M. Peters, Virtual and augmented medical imaging environments: enabling technology for minimally invasive cardiac interventional guidance, IEEE Reviews in Biomedical Engineering 3 (2010) 25–47.

[17] C.A. Linte, J. Moore, C. Wedlake, T.M. Peters, Evaluation of model-enhanced ultrasound-assisted interventional guidance in a cardiac phantom, IEEE Transactions on Biomedical Engineering 57 (2010) 2209–2218.

[18] C.A. Linte, J. Moore, A. Wiles, C. Wedlake, T. Peters, Virtual reality-enhanced ultrasound guidance: a novel technique for intracardiac interventions, Computer Aided Surgery 13 (2008) 82–94.

[19] A. Fenster, D.B. Downey, Three dimensional ultrasound imaging, Annual Review of Biomedical Engineering 2 (2000) 457–475.

[20] I.S. Salgo, 3D echocardiographic visualization for intracardiac beating heart surgery and intervention, Journal of Thoracic and Cardiovascular Surgery 19 (2007) 325–329.

[21] C.A. Linte, J. Moore, C. Wedlake, D. Bainbridge, G.M. Guitaudon, D.L. Jones, et al., Inside the beating heart: an *in vivo* feasibility study on fusing pre- and intra-operative imaging for minimally invasive therapy, International Journal of Computer Assisted Radiology and Surgery 4 (2009) 113–122.

[22] Y.L. Ma, G.P. Penney, C.A. Rinaldi, M. Cooklin, R. Razavi, K.S. Rhode, Echocardiography to magnetic resonance image registration for use in image-guided cardiac catheterization procedures, Physics in Medicine and Biology 54 (2009) 5039–5055.

[23] H. Zhong, T. Kanade, D. Schwartzman, "Virtual touch": an efficient registration method for catheter navigation in left atrium, in: Proc. Med. Image Comput. Comput. Assist. Interv., in: Lect. Notes Comput. Sci., vol. 4190, 2006, pp. 437–444.

[24] A.P. King, Y.L. Ma, C. Yao, C. Jansen, R. Razavi, K.S. Rhode, et al., Image-to-physical registration for image-guided interventions using 3-D ultrasound and an ultrasound imaging model, in: Information Processing in Medical Imaging, in: Lect. Notes Comput. Sci., vol. 5636, 2009, pp. 188–201.

[25] J. Stoll, P. Dupont, Passive markers for ultrasound tracking of surgical instruments, in: Proc. Med. Image Comput. Comput. Assist. Interv., in: Lect. Notes Comput. Sci., vol. 3750, 2005, pp. 41–48.

[26] M.G. Linguraru, N.V. Vasilyev, P.J. del Nido, R.D. Howe, Statistical segmentation of surgical instruments in 3-D ultrasound images, Ultrasound in Medicine & Biology 33 (2007) 1428–1437.

[27] A. Lasso, T. Heffter, A. Rankin, C. Pinter, T. Ungi, G. Fichtinger, PLUS: open-source toolkit for ultrasound-guided intervention systems, IEEE Transactions on Biomedical Engineering 61 (2014) 2527–2537.

[28] W. Wein, E. Camus, M. John, M. Diallo, C. Duong, A. Al-Ahmad, et al., Towards guidance of electrophysiological procedures with real-time 3D intracardiac echocardiography fusion to C-arm CT, in: Proc. Med. Image Comput. Comput. Assist. Interv., in: Lect. Notes Comput. Sci., vol. 5761, 2000, pp. 9–16.

[29] O. Kutter, R. Shams, N. Navab, Visualization and GPU-accelerated simulation of medical ultrasound from CT images, Computer Methods and Programs in Biomedicine 94 (2009) 250–266.

[30] Q. Zhang, R. Eagleson, T.M. Peters, Dynamic real-time 4D cardiac MDCT image display using GPU-accelerated volume rendering, Computerized Medical Imaging and Graphics 33 (2009) 461–476.

[31] D.V. Amin, T. Kanade, A.M. Digioia, B. Jaramaz, Ultrasound registration of the bone surface for surgical navigation, Computer Aided Surgery 8 (1) (2003) 1–16.

[32] B. Brendel, S. Winter, A. Rick, M. Stockheim, H. Ermert, Registration of 3D CT and ultrasound datasets of the spine using bone structures, Computer Aided Surgery 7 (3) (2002) 146–155.

[33] T.K. Chen, P. Abolmaesumi, D.R. Pichora, R.E. Ellis, A system for ultrasound-guided computer-assisted orthopaedic surgery, Computer Aided Surgery 10 (5–6) (2005) 281–292.

[34] T. Grau, R.W. Leipold, R. Conradi, E. Martin, J. Motsch, Efficacy of ultrasound imaging in obstetric epidural anesthesia, Journal of Clinical Anesthesia 14 (3) (2002) 169–175.

[35] J. Tonetti, L. Carrat, S. Blendea, P. Merloz, J. Troccaz, S. Lavallée, et al., Clinical results of percutaneous pelvic surgery. Computer assisted surgery using ultrasound compared to standard fluoroscopy, Computer Aided Surgery 6 (4) (2001) 204–211.

[36] M. Beek, P. Abolmaesumi, S. Luenam, R.E. Ellis, R.W. Sellens, D.R. Pichora, Validation of a new surgical procedure for percutaneous scaphoid fixation using intra-operative ultrasound, Medical Image Analysis 12 (2) (2008) 152–162.

[37] J. Kowal, C. Amstutz, F. Langlotz, H. Talib, M.G. Ballester, Automated bone contour detection in ultrasound B-mode images for minimally invasive registration in computer-assisted surgery—an in vitro evaluation, The International Journal of Medical Robotics and Computer Assisted Surgery 3 (4) (2007) 341–348.

[38] G. Ionescu, S. Lavallée, J. Demongeot, Automated registration of ultrasound with CT images: application to computer assisted prostate radiotherapy and orthopedics, in: International Conference on Medical Image Computing and Computer-Assisted Intervention, Springer, 1999, pp. 768–777.

[39] D.M. Muratore, Towards an Image-Guided Spinal Surgical System Using Three-Dimensional Ultrasound: From Concept to Clinic, PhD thesis, 2003.

[40] I. Hacihaliloglu, Ultrasound imaging and segmentation of bone surfaces: a review, Technology 5 (02) (2017) 74–80.

[41] S. Schumann, State of the art of ultrasound-based registration in computer assisted orthopedic interventions, in: Computational Radiology for Orthopaedic Interventions, Springer, 2016, pp. 271–297.

[42] V. Daanen, J. Tonetti, J. Troccaz, A fully automated method for the delineation of osseous interface in ultrasound images, in: International Conference on Medical Image Computing and Computer-Assisted Intervention, Springer, 2004, pp. 549–557.

[43] P. Foroughi, E. Boctor, M.J. Swartz, R.H. Taylor, G. Fichtinger, P6D-2 ultrasound bone segmentation using dynamic programming, in: Ultrasonics Symposium, 2007. IEEE, IEEE, 2007, pp. 2523–2526.

[44] E.M.A. Anas, A. Seitel, A. Rasoulian, P.S. John, T. Ungi, A. Lasso, et al., Bone enhancement in ultrasound based on 3D local spectrum variation for percutaneous scaphoid fracture fixation, in: MICCAI, 2016, pp. 465–473.

[45] I. Hacihaliloglu, R. Abugharbieh, A. Hodgson, R.N. Rohling, Bone surface localization in ultrasound using image phase-based features, Ultrasound in Medicine & Biology 35 (9) (2009) 1475–1487.

[46] I. Hacihaliloglu, P. Guy, A.J. Hodgson, R. Abugharbieh, Volume-specific parameter optimization of 3D local phase features for improved extraction of bone surfaces in ultrasound, The International Journal of Medical Robotics and Computer Assisted Surgery 10 (4) (2014) 461–473.

[47] I. Hacihaliloglu, P. Guy, A.J. Hodgson, R. Abugharbieh, Automatic extraction of bone surfaces from 3D ultrasound images in orthopaedic trauma cases, International Journal of Computer Assisted Radiology and Surgery 10 (8) (2015) 1279–1287.

[48] S.A. Jantzi, K.W. Martin, A.S. Sedra, Quadrature bandpass $\Delta\Sigma$ modulation for digital radio, IEEE Journal of Solid-State Circuits 32 (12) (1997) 1935–1950.

[49] I. Hacihaliloglu, Localization of bone surfaces from ultrasound data using local phase information and signal transmission maps, in: International Workshop and Challenge on Computational Methods and Clinical Applications in Musculoskeletal Imaging, Springer, 2017, pp. 1–11.

[50] N. Quader, A. Hodgson, R. Abugharbieh, Confidence weighted local phase features for robust bone surface segmentation in ultrasound, in: Workshop on Clinical Image-Based Procedures, Springer, 2014, pp. 76–83.

[51] R. Jia, S.J. Mellon, S. Hansjee, A. Monk, D. Murray, J.A. Noble, Automatic bone segmentation in ultrasound images using local phase features and dynamic programming, in: Biomedical Imaging (ISBI), 2016 IEEE 13th International Symposium on, IEEE, 2016, pp. 1005–1008.

[52] N. Baka, S. Leenstra, T. van Walsum, Random forest-based bone segmentation in ultrasound, Ultrasound in Medicine & Biology 43 (10) (2017) 2426–2437.

[53] F. Ozdemir, E. Ozkan, O. Goksel, Graphical modeling of ultrasound propagation in tissue for automatic bone segmentation, in: International Conference on Medical Image Computing and Computer-Assisted Intervention, Springer, 2016, pp. 256–264.

[54] M. Salehi, R. Prevost, J.L. Moctezuma, N. Navab, W. Wein, Precise ultrasound bone registration with learning-based segmentation and speed of sound calibration, in: International Conference on Medical Image Computing and Computer-Assisted Intervention, Springer, 2017, pp. 682–690.

[55] N. Baka, S. Leenstra, T. van Walsum, Ultrasound aided vertebral level localization for lumbar surgery, IEEE Transactions on Medical Imaging 36 (10) (2017) 2138–2147.

[56] I. Hacihaliloglu, Enhancement of bone shadow region using local phase-based ultrasound transmission maps, International Journal of Computer Assisted Radiology and Surgery 12 (6) (2017) 951–960.

[57] B. Zhuang, R. Rohling, P. Abolmaesumi, Accumulated angle factor-based beamforming to improve the visualization of spinal structures in ultrasound images, IEEE Transactions on Ultrasonics, Ferroelectrics, and Frequency Control 65 (2) (2018) 210–222.

[58] M.A. Hussain, A.J. Hodgson, R. Abugharbieh, Strain-initialized robust bone surface detection in 3-D ultrasound, Ultrasound in Medicine & Biology 43 (3) (2017) 648–661.

[59] T. Walther, G. Schuler, M.A. Borger, J. Kempfert, V. Falk, F.W. Mohr, et al., Transapical aortic valve implantation in 100 consecutive patients: comparison to propensity-matched conventional aortic valve replacement, European Heart Journal 31 (2010) 1398–1403.

[60] M.E. Karar, M. Gessat, T. Walther, V. Falk, O. Burgert, Towards a new image guidance system for assisting transapical minimally invasive aortic valve implantation, in: Proc. IEEE Eng. Med. Biol., 2009, pp. 3645–3648.

[61] J. Kempfert, V. Falk, G. Schuler, A. Linke, D. Merk, F.W. Mohr, et al., Dyna-CT during minimally invasive off-pump transapical aortic valve implantation, The Annals of Thoracic Surgery 88 (2009) 2041–2042.

[62] Y. Suematsu, G.R. Marx, J.A. Stoll, P.E. DuPont, R.D. Howe, R.O. Cleveland, et al., Three-dimensional echocardiography-guided beating-heart surgery without cardiopulmonary bypass: a feasibility study, Journal of Thoracic and Cardiovascular Surgery 128 (2004) 579–587.

[63] K. Liang, A.J. Rogers, E.D. Light, D. von Allmen, S.W. Smith, Three-dimensional ultrasound guidance of autonomous robotic breast biopsy: feasibility study, Ultrasound in Medicine & Biology 36 (2010) 173–177.

[64] R.D. Howe, Fixing the beating heart: ultrasound guidance for robotic intracardiac surgery, in: Proc. FIMH, in: Lect. Notes Comput. Sci., vol. 5528, 2009, pp. 97–103.

[65] S.B. Kesner, S.G. Yuen, R.D. Howe, Ultrasound servoing of catheters for beating heart valve repair, in: Proc. IPCAI, in: Lect. Notes Comput. Sci., vol. 6135, 2010, pp. 168–178.

[66] G. Guiraudon, D. Jones, D. Bainbridge, T. Peters, Mitral valve implantation using off-pump closed beating intracardiac surgery: a feasibility study, Interactive Cardiovascular and Thoracic Surgery 6 (2007) 603–607.

[67] Y. Okumura, B.D. Henz, S.B. Johnson, C.J. O'Brien, A. Altman, A. Govari, et al., Three-dimensional ultrasound for image-guided mapping and intervention: methods, quantitative validation, and clinical feasibility of a novel multimodality image mapping system, Circulation: Arrhythmia and Electrophysiology 1 (2008) 110–119.

[68] Y. Khaykin, A. Skanes, B. Whaley, C. Hill, L. Gula, A. Verma, Real-time integration of 2D intracardiac echocardiography and 3D electroanatomical mapping to guide ventricular tachycardia ablation, Heart Rhythm 5 (2008) 1396–1402.

[69] D.W. den Uijl, L.F. Tops, J.L. Tolosana, J.D. Schuijf, S.A.I.P. Trines, K. Zeppenfeld, et al., Real-time integration of intracardiac echocardiography and multislice computed tomography to guide radiofrequency catheter ablation for atrial fibrillation, Heart Rhythm 5 (2008) 1403–1410.

[70] U. Eichenberger, M. Greher, M. Curatolo, Ultrasound in interventional pain management, Techniques in Regional Anesthesia & Pain Management 8 (4) (2004) 171–178.

[71] J.W. Frymoyer, Back pain and sciatica, The New England Journal of Medicine 318 (5) (1988) 291–300.

[72] M.J. Osterman, J.A. Martin, Epidural and spinal anesthesia use during labor: 27-state reporting area, 2008, National Vital Statistics Reports: From the Centers for Disease Control and Prevention, National Center for Health Statistics, National Vital Statistics System 59 (5) (2011) 1–13.

[73] H. Jee, J.H. Lee, J. Kim, K.D. Park, W.Y. Lee, Y. Park, Ultrasound-guided selective nerve root block versus fluoroscopy-guided transforaminal block for the treatment of radicular pain in the lower cervical spine: a randomized, blinded, controlled study, Skeletal Radiology 42 (1) (2013) 69–78.

[74] J. Hetherington, V. Lessoway, V. Gunka, P. Abolmaesumi, R. Rohling, SLIDE: automatic spine level identification system using a deep convolutional neural network, International Journal of Computer Assisted Radiology and Surgery 12 (7) (2017) 1189–1198.

[75] D. Behnami, A. Sedghi, E.M.A. Anas, A. Rasoulian, A. Seitel, V. Lessoway, et al., Model-based registration of preprocedure MR and intraprocedure US of the lumbar spine, International Journal of Computer Assisted Radiology and Surgery 12 (6) (2017) 973–982.

[76] A. Seitel, S. Sojoudi, J. Osborn, A. Rasoulian, S. Nouranian, V.A. Lessoway, et al., Ultrasound-guided spine anesthesia: feasibility study of a guidance system, Ultrasound in Medicine & Biology 42 (12) (2016) 3043–3049.

[77] D. Behnami, A. Seitel, A. Rasoulian, E.M.A. Anas, V. Lessoway, J. Osborn, et al., Joint registration of ultrasound, CT and a shape+pose statistical model of the lumbar spine for guiding anesthesia, International Journal of Computer Assisted Radiology and Surgery 11 (6) (2016) 937–945.

[78] S. Nagpal, P. Abolmaesumi, A. Rasoulian, I. Hacihaliloglu, T. Ungi, J. Osborn, et al., A multi-vertebrae CT to US registration of the lumbar spine in clinical data, International Journal of Computer Assisted Radiology and Surgery 10 (9) (2015) 1371–1381.

[79] A. Rasoulian, A. Seitel, J. Osborn, S. Sojoudi, S. Nouranian, V.A. Lessoway, et al., Ultrasound-guided spinal injections: a feasibility study of a guidance system, International Journal of Computer Assisted Radiology and Surgery 10 (9) (2015) 1417–1425.

[80] J. Esteban, W. Simson, S.R. Witzig, A. Rienmüller, S. Virga, B. Frisch, et al., Robotic ultrasound-guided facet joint insertion, International Journal of Computer Assisted Radiology and Surgery (2018) 1–10.

[81] S. Winter, B. Brendel, I. Pechlivanis, K. Schmieder, C. Igel, Registration of CT and intraoperative 3-D ultrasound images of the spine using evolutionary and gradient-based methods, IEEE Transactions on Evolutionary Computation 12 (3) (2008) 284–296.

[82] T. Ungi, E. Moult, J.H. Schwab, G. Fichtinger, Tracked ultrasound snapshots in percutaneous pedicle screw placement navigation: a feasibility study, Clinical Orthopaedics and Related Research 471 (12) (2013) 4047–4055.

[83] X. Qi, L. Riera, A. Sarangi, G. Youssef, M. Vives, I. Hacihaliloglu, Automatic scan plane identification from 2D ultrasound for pedicle screw guidance, in: Annual Meeting of the International Society for Computer Assisted Orthopaedic Surgery (CAOS), 2018, pp. 6–9.

[84] A. Manbachi, R.S. Cobbold, H.J. Ginsberg, Guided pedicle screw insertion: techniques and training, The Spine Journal 14 (1) (2014) 165–179.

[85] A.H. Aly, H.J. Ginsberg, R.S. Cobbold, On ultrasound imaging for guided screw insertion in spinal fusion surgery, Ultrasound in Medicine & Biology 37 (4) (2011) 651–664.

[86] D.T. Raphael, J.H. Chang, Y.P. Zhang, D. Kudija, T.C. Chen, K.K. Shung, A-Mode ultrasound guidance for pedicle screw advancement in ovine vertebral bodies, The Spine Journal 10 (5) (2010) 422–432.

[87] S.R. Kantelhardt, H.C. Bock, L. Siam, J. Larsen, R. Burger, W. Schillinger, et al., Intra-osseous ultrasound for pedicle screw positioning in the subaxial cervical spine: an experimental study, Acta Neurochirurgica 152 (4) (2010) 655–661.

[88] T. Ungi, F. King, M. Kempston, Z. Keri, A. Lasso, P. Mousavi, et al., Spinal curvature measurement by tracked ultrasound snapshots, Ultrasound in Medicine & Biology 40 (2) (2014) 447–454.

[89] F. Berton, F. Cheriet, M.C. Miron, C. Laporte, Segmentation of the spinous process and its acoustic shadow in vertebral ultrasound images, Computers in Biology and Medicine 72 (2016) 201–211.

[90] P.J.S. Gonçalves, P.M. Torres, F. Santos, R. António, N. Catarino, J. Martins, A vision system for robotic ultrasound guided orthopaedic surgery, Journal of Intelligent & Robotic Systems 77 (2) (2015) 327–339.

[91] L. Ma, Z. Zhao, F. Chen, B. Zhang, L. Fu, H. Liao, Augmented reality surgical navigation with ultrasound-assisted registration for pedicle screw placement: a pilot study, International Journal of Computer Assisted Radiology and Surgery 12 (12) (2017) 2205–2215.

CHAPTER 29

Interventional imaging: Vision

Stefanie Speidel[a], Sebastian Bodenstedt[a], Francisco Vasconcelos[b], Danail Stoyanov[b]

[a]National Center for Tumor Diseases (NCT), Partner Site Dresden, Division of Translational Surgical Oncology (TSO), Dresden, Germany
[b]Wellcome/EPSRC Centre for Interventional and Surgical Sciences (WEISS), UCL Computer Sciences, London, United Kingdom

Contents

29.1.	Vision-based interventional imaging modalities	722
	29.1.1 Endoscopy	722
	29.1.1.1 Endoscope types	722
	29.1.1.2 Advances in endoscopic imaging	723
	29.1.2 Microscopy	724
29.2.	Geometric scene analysis	725
	29.2.1 Calibration and preprocessing	725
	29.2.1.1 Preprocessing	726
	29.2.2 Reconstruction	727
	29.2.2.1 Stereo reconstruction	727
	29.2.2.2 Simultaneous Localization and Mapping	728
	29.2.2.3 Shape-from-X	729
	29.2.2.4 Active reconstruction	730
	29.2.3 Registration	730
	29.2.3.1 Point-based registration	731
	29.2.3.2 Surface-based registration	731
29.3.	Visual scene interpretation	732
	29.3.1 Detection	732
	29.3.1.1 Surgical tools	733
	29.3.1.2 Phase detection	733
	29.3.2 Tracking	734
29.4.	Clinical applications	734
	29.4.1 Intraoperative navigation	734
	29.4.2 Tissue characterization	734
	29.4.3 Skill assessment	736
	29.4.4 Surgical workflow analysis	736
29.5.	Discussion	736
	Acknowledgments	738
	References	738

Handbook of Medical Image Computing and Computer Assisted Intervention
https://doi.org/10.1016/B978-0-12-816176-0.00034-X

721

29.1. Vision-based interventional imaging modalities

The most common interventional use of white light cameras is for diagnostic and therapeutic endoscopy and laparoscopy where the camera enables less invasive procedures by accessing the anatomy through natural orifices or through small ports. Another common usage is in procedures that require significant zoom into the surgical area and in which a microscope is used to perform microsurgical tasks. In both cases, the information provided by the camera is the primary sensory channel used by the clinician to carry out the procedure.

29.1.1 Endoscopy

An endoscope is an optical system used for both diagnostic and therapeutic purposes. It is inserted through natural or artificial orifices into the human body. The word originates from the greek and means "Endo=within" and "scopein=to observe". Nowadays, endoscopic procedures are the preferred approach for many interventions due to numerous patient benefits, e.g., less pain, reduced morbidity and mortality, as well as shorter hospital stays, and the applicability to at-risk groups enabled by reduced comorbidity. Interventional applications range from surgery within most anatomical regions to ablation therapy, laser therapy, photodynamic therapy, and cryotherapy [74].

29.1.1.1 Endoscope types

There exists two types of endoscope, rigid and flexible (see Fig. 29.1). Flexible endoscopes transmit light and an image feed through ordered fiber optic bundles and are controlled by cables or linkages. They can adapt to natural coils due to their flexibility and therefore are common for diagnostic and therapeutic purposes, e.g., in the gastrointestinal tract or bronchial tree. Rigid endoscopes are applied in minimally invasive surgery (MIS) and are usually based on rod lens technology. The endoscope is normally inserted via a trocar through small cuts.

A prerequisite for the use of endoscopic techniques and their rapid adoption at the end of the 20th century were technical inventions, namely the rod lens system and the advent of charge-coupled device (CCD) chips that paved the way for modern video endoscopy. A modern video endoscopic system consists of the endoscope itself (optical system), a cold light source, a camera system including a CCD or CMOS chip, and, optionally, channels through the device for the introduction of instruments, irrigation, or other support systems [8].

In both rigid and flexible systems, recently "chip-on-tip" systems were established due to the ongoing miniaturization of the imaging sensors. In this case, the imaging sensor chip is mounted directly on the tip of the endoscope and transmits a digital signal.

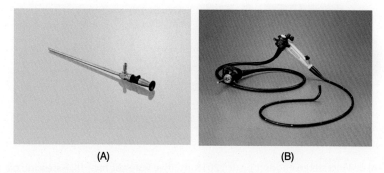

(A)   (B)

Figure 29.1 (A) Rigid endoscope (Laparoscope, © KARL STORZ SE & Co. KG.); (B) Flexible endoscope (Gastroscope, © KARL STORZ SE & Co. KG.).

Table 29.1 Examples of different endoscopes.

Endoscope	Treatment area
Arthroscope	Joints
Bronchoscope	Respiratory tract
Colonoscope	Colon
Cystoscope	Bladder
Gastroscope	Gastrointestinal tract
Laparoscope	Abdominal organs

There are different endoscopes depending on the application. Examples are shown in Table 29.1.

29.1.1.2 Advances in endoscopic imaging

Although endoscopic imaging has many benefits, it also carries drawbacks. In the special case of using a monocular system, the most significant drawback is the loss of 3D vision. To compensate for such a drawback, stereo endoscopes are employed. They enable a stereoscopic view by incorporating two optical channels and stereoscopic displays, either with lenticular arrays or with polarization glasses. Although stereoscopic based systems are necessary, they have yet to gain widespread clinical adoption. The da Vinci surgical system is a prominent example that integrates a stereo endoscope (see Fig. 29.2) to offer a comfortable and effective 3D view of the surgical site. Furthermore, different approaches have been proposed in research to examine the integration of structured light or time-of-flight technology into endoscopes to enable the recovery of 3D information [69].

More recently, wireless capsule endoscopy has evolved as an alternative to observe the gastrointestinal tract [46]. The capsule is swallowed and includes a miniaturized camera, LED light source, small battery, and transmitter that sends the image data to a recording device outside the patient's body. The capsule can be moved naturally through

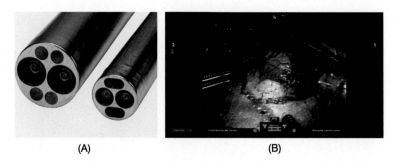

(A)   (B)

Figure 29.2 (A) da Vinci stereo endoscope (© 2018 Intuitive Surgical, Inc.); (B) Assessing parenchymal perfusion during tumor excision in Fluorescence Imaging mode during da Vinci Partial Nephrectomy (© 2018 Intuitive Surgical, Inc.).

the gastrointestinal system by physiological motion or it can be directed using external forces, for example, magnets.

To overcome the limitations of classic white light endoscopic imaging, biophotonic imaging techniques are a promising way to enable real-time feedback regarding subsurface structures or functional tissue characteristics [22,108]. Examples of such imaging techniques include autofluorescence imaging (see Fig. 29.2), multispectral as well as narrow-band imaging, optical coherence tomography, diffuse reflection spectroscopy, fluorescence imaging, photoacoustics imaging, and endomicroscopy.

29.1.2 Microscopy

In the 20th century, operating microscopes have been introduced to various surgical disciplines such as otologic, ophthalmologic, vascular, plastic, and neurological surgery [57]. The use of microscopic imaging in combination with special high-precision surgical tools made it possible to operate on delicate structures such as blood vessels and nerves. This led to the emergence of microsurgery, which became a surgical discipline in its own right [116].

An interventional microscope usually consists of a binocular head, objective lens, magnification changer, and illuminator. It achieves an optical magnification of up to 40x of the operation field. Recently, digital CCD microscopy has become more common, where a CCD is used for high definition image acquisition. These systems can be directly linked to the surgical display or be routed through prisms [79].

Similar to endoscopes, there have been different advances in microscopic imaging, e.g., microscopes with coaxial illumination, confocal microscopy [98], optical coherence tomography (OCT) [30], fluorescence imaging [68] (see Fig. 29.3), or even thermal imaging [51].

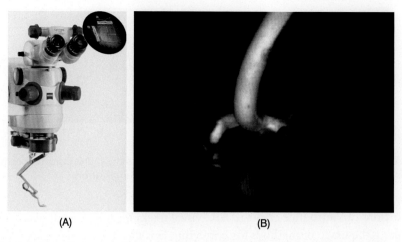

(A)   (B)

Figure 29.3 (A) OCT Microscope (Photo: Courtesy of ZEISS); (B) Fluorescence angiography in microscope (from [68]).

29.2. Geometric scene analysis

One of the most important metrics or information that can be extracted from white light images concerns the geometry of the surgical environment. This is performed by solving the inverse problem of how images are generated by modeling the geometric interaction between light emitted by the illumination source, reflected within the scene and detected at the image sensor. This model makes it possible to recover, or rather reconstruct, the original geometry from given images. These reconstructions can then be used to register information from other imaging modalities, such as preoperative data. In this section, the methods for geometric scene analysis are presented starting with camera calibration and image preprocessing, reconstruction, and registration.

29.2.1 Calibration and preprocessing

Modeling the geometry of the camera is a requirement for many applications, such as removing lens distortion, pose estimation, 3D reconstruction, and providing navigation information via Augmented Reality (AR). Commonly the extended pinhole model is used to describe how points from a 3D scene are projected onto a 2D image [119,42].

Camera calibration is the process of determining the parameters of the model, intrinsic (principal point, focal length, lens distortion) and extrinsic parameters (offset to world coordinate system or another camera, e.g., in a stereo rig). Given an object with a known geometry (e.g., a chessboard; see Fig. 29.4), there are multiple methods for recovering the camera parameters [44,119,133].

Wide angle optics, which are especially common in endoscopes, introduce a noticeable amount of lens distortion, especially radial distortions (see Fig. 29.4). If ignored,

Figure 29.4 (A) Chessboard calibration object. The image exhibits the radial distortion common to endoscopic images; (B) Specular highlights during thoracoscopic surgery (from [97]).

these distortions can introduce errors in AR, visual tracking, and other applications [31], hence making the usage of methods for correcting lens distortion a necessity [102,104].

Often endoscopes and microscopes incorporate a zoom function, which, when used, invalidates certain parameters of the camera calibration such as the focal length. Recalibrating the camera during surgery every time the zoom factor is changed is impractical. Given a camera with discrete zoom levels, such as a surgical microscope, permits to calibrate separately each zoom level [29]. A method for automatically adapting the focal length of an endoscopic stereo camera during surgery has been introduced in [109]. Here, the fundamental matrix is estimated during surgery, from which the focal length is then derived. A more general approach for calibrating the zoom level of a camera has been previously proposed in [125]. In this case, it is required to have the zoom motor information, which is not readily available, and correlated this with different values for the focal length.

If the camera is being tracked via an external tracking system, e.g., via an optical marker or a robot arm, a hand–eye calibration can be performed to determine the offset between the coordinate system of the camera and the tracking system [45].

29.2.1.1 Preprocessing

Prior to further analysis and interpretation of images acquired during an intervention, certain preprocessing steps are undertaken to improve image quality and suitability for tasks such as 3D reconstruction and registration. As mentioned earlier, given a calibrated camera, it is possible to correct certain effects of lens distortion in real-time [58,102, 104]. To facilitate solving the correspondence problem during stereo reconstruction, a given stereo image pair is rectified. For this, the images are projected onto a common image plane, thereby reducing the search for the correspondence of a given point to a horizontal line [35].

Interventional images generally contain artifacts specific to surgery, such as specular highlights due to the reflective properties of tissue, movement artifacts from instruments, and discolouration of tissue due to blood [33,58]. Especially artifacts due to specular highlights can be disruptive to segmentation and tracking tasks (see Fig. 29.4). Multiple methods for correcting specular highlights in surgical images have been proposed, ranging from approaches based on detection and inpainting [7,97] to temporal registration [111] and machine learning based approaches [33].

29.2.2 Reconstruction

3D reconstruction of human anatomy is an essential condition to register vision and other intra- and preoperative imaging modalities. Due to the nonrigid nature of soft-tissue and due to patient motion, reconstruction of the intraoperative environment is a dynamic task that requires real-time imaging feedback. This can be achieved by using single-shot reconstruction techniques [70] or by explicitly formulating nonrigid 3D models [78,24].

Reconstruction techniques vary in nature and can be achieved with different device configurations [69,70]. Passive methods infer shape by analyzing image cues alone and thus require no other equipment than conventional monocular or stereo cameras. On the other hand, active methods interact with the environment using controlled light sources. In the following paragraphs, we give an overview of three passive methods (Stereo, SLAM, Shape-from-X) and two active methods (Structured light, Time of Flight).

29.2.2.1 Stereo reconstruction

Stereo cameras provide single shot 3D reconstructions of the imaged scene by using perspective changes in two camera views (see Fig. 29.5). Such systems are most commonly found in laparoscopy, but there are also applications in microscopy [73]. The reconstruction process involves estimating point correspondences between the two camera views that represent the same point in the scene. Semidense methods establish a sparse set of reliable correspondences from which the rest of the scene is interpolated [110], while dense methods estimate a pairwise matching for every image pixel [19,95]. The difference in pixel position for each correspondence forms a disparity map that represents the scene depth from a camera's point of view. A metric for the 3D reconstruction is obtained from the pixel disparity map using a precalibrated geometric model of the stereo cameras to triangulate each of the point correspondences. Given that intraoperative scenes are typically continuous tissue surfaces, improved results can be achieved by including a regularizer to enforce surface smoothness and continuity.

Stereo reconstruction requires a preoperative calibration procedure to determine the intrinsic and extrinsic geometric properties of the stereo camera, so that each image pixel position can be mapped to a light ray trajectory reflected by the scene (as detailed in Sect. 29.2.1).

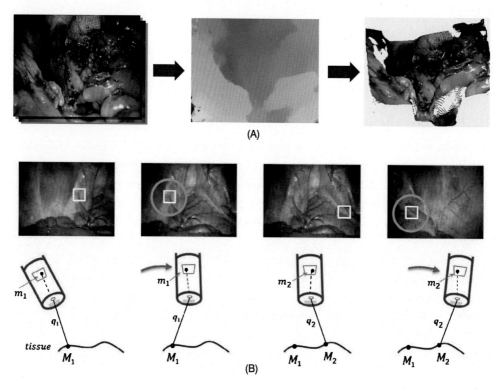

Figure 29.5 (A) Stereo reconstruction: from a given stereo image pair, a dense disparity map is created and used for triangulation of a 3D point cloud (from [95]); (B) Simultaneous Localization and Mapping (SLAM): A point m_1 (white square) is located in the image and added to the map. In the next frame, the predicted camera motion is used to project the points on the map onto the image, allowing for a local search (green circle) for matches, which are used to update the camera pose and map. New points are added to the map. The same steps are repeated on the new frame (from [71]).

29.2.2.2 Simultaneous Localization and Mapping

Simultaneous Localization and Mapping (SLAM) reconstructs scenes from video captures of a moving camera (see Fig. 29.5). While tracking image features across consecutive frames, SLAM methods solve the inverse problem of estimating both the camera trajectory and the 3D structure of the scene. SLAM methods can be broadly grouped into two approaches, filtering and bundle adjustment. In filtering approaches, a uniform motion model is typically used to predict the position of tracked features in the next video frame. The discrepancy between predictions and new observations is used to update a sparse 3D map of the imaged scene using a Kalman filter. Bundle adjustment approaches are usually formulated as a graph optimization problem, with camera poses as nodes and image correspondences as edges. The goal is to minimize the reprojection error of reconstructed 3D points in each of the camera views. Bundle adjustment performance depends on the succession of closed-form initializations of new camera poses and new scene features using multiple-view geometry [42].

The majority of SLAM pipelines only computes a sparse set of points from the scene for localization, while detailed dense 3D reconstructions being computed in a postprocessing step [117]. In some recent works, however, a dense reconstruction is part of the motion estimation pipeline. SLAM is applicable to both monocular and stereo cameras. In the monocular case, the metric scale of the reconstruction is unknown, while the scale of the scene can be recovered with stereo. Standard SLAM approaches work under the assumption that the imaged scene is static while the camera is moving, however, this assumption is often not applicable to the reconstruction of live soft-tissue. Therefore, accurate and robust SLAM in laparoscopy interventions requires incorporating deformable 3D models [78,24].

As SLAM is also a camera localization method, it has applications that go beyond generating a 3D model of the scene. These include AR applications to overlay organs, lesions, or other regions of interest on the laparoscopic view in real-time (see Sect. 29.4.1). In this context, SLAM is an alternative to frame-by-frame registration of preoperative models when this is not feasible due to deformations and occlusions. Additionally, mosaicing techniques can work on top of a SLAM pipeline to generate wide views of the scene that stitch multiple image frames together [10,77]. Although mosaicing can simply be an add-on to conventional SLAM, in some applications the reconstruction formulations can be simplified to increase computational efficiency and ease of implementation. For example, assuming that the reconstructed scene is a single plane has applications in creating mosaics in microscopy [38,93] and endoscopy [77].

29.2.2.3 Shape-from-X

Shape-from-X methods infer 3D object shapes from indirect cues such as lighting, focus, textures, or motion. In laparoscopic imaging, the lighting conditions have a very particular set-up that can be exploited with Shape-from-Shading methods. Shape-from-Motion largely overlaps with the SLAM literature (see Sect. 29.2.2.2), but also includes 3D reconstruction from sets of images with no particular temporal order using bundle adjustment approaches.

Shape-from-Shading models show how a light source interacts with an object, establishing the relationship between surface normals and intensity of reflected light. This requires a complete characterization of light propagation in the environment, object reflectance, and the radiometric response of the camera. While most methods assume a light source at a large distance from the object, this is not the case in laparoscopy, as the light source attached to the camera is only a few millimeters away from the scene. Near-lighting models have been specifically developed for this scenario [80]. Additionally, Shape-from-Shading and Shape-from-Motion can be combined together to build more detailed 3D reconstructions [126].

29.2.2.4 Active reconstruction

3D reconstructions can be obtained by directly interfering with the environment using light projectors. Active reconstruction systems that include an integrated RGB camera are called RGB-D sensors as both a color and a depth value can be associated with each image pixel. Since these methods require custom designed hardware, the main challenge in translation to an interventional setting, such as laparoscopy, is the miniaturization of light projectors to allow insertion into the surgical scene. There are two different approaches to active reconstruction, structured light and time of flight.

Structured light reconstructions are obtained by projecting a visible light pattern onto a scene and modeling the relationship between the appearance of those patterns on an image and the shape of an object. The principle is similar to Shape-from-Shading (see Sect. 29.2.2.3), however, in this case the light source is purposefully designed to project specific color and shape patterns. There are structured light methods based on both a static light pattern and sequences of light patterns. Although both approaches have been tested on laparoscopy settings, the former is more suitable for reconstructing deformable environments. Several designs for endoscopic and laparoscopic structured light systems have been proposed, including protruding arms with light projectors [54], a light source that fits into the working channel of a conventional endoscope [21], and an axially aligned light projector [100].

Time of flight (ToF) systems estimate depth by measuring the time it takes for projected light to reach an object and be reflected back to a sensor. Generally, these systems provide no color information, this would require a separate RGB sensor. This is a relatively recent addition to interventional reconstruction, with only a few ToF endoscope prototypes having been developed [41,83]. Although the working principle has been demonstrated experimentally, endoscopic ToF still has significantly lower accuracy than stereo or structured light techniques, which is mainly due to the low resolution of the currently available systems [70].

29.2.3 Registration

Registration is a prerequisite for many computer-assisted interventions (CAI) applications, especially for intraoperative navigation. The term intraoperative registration refers to aligning preoperative with intraoperative patient data. The preoperative data is generally acquired by tomographic imaging such as CT or MRI. In this chapter, intraoperative data refers to endoscopic or microscopic data, e.g., raw images, reconstructed surfaces or features in the images. Following the categorization in [86], registration methods are grouped in manual, point-, surface-, calibration-, or volume-based methods.

Manual registration refers to methods where both datasets are aligned by hand [72], whilst point-based means that either artificial or natural landmarks are used and surface-based methods register the intraoperatively reconstructed scene with preoperative data.

Calibration-based methods align two intraoperative imaging modalities (e.g., endoscope and ultrasound) to a common coordinate system by means of fiducials mounted on the modalities which are tracked [32,47] or by using the kinematic parameters of a robot in robotic-assisted surgeries [65]. Volume-based methods use an intraoperative imaging device that provides subsurface data (e.g., ultrasound) that is registered with preoperative data; no camera imaging device is involved, yet.

In general, we distinguish between rigid and nonrigid registration methods. Rigid registration refers to methods where the transformation between both data sources consists only of rotation and translation. Nonrigid registration methods also incorporate an elastic component to account for deformations. An example is soft-tissue registration, where the initial registration is continuously updated to account for deformations. A common strategy for continuous registration is the tracking of features in the intraoperative images. More details are given in Sect. 29.3.2.

In the following paragraphs we focus on point- and surface-based registration methods since these are the most common methods used for registering intraoperative images from cameras with preoperative data.

29.2.3.1 Point-based registration

In point-based registration, landmarks are used that can be detected in the camera image as well as in the preoperative data set. Landmarks are naturally occurring or artificial features that are distinct and can be easily identified. For registration, point correspondences between the two data sets have to be established. In case of deformation or camera movement, the correspondences also have to be updated, e.g., by tracking the landmarks (see Sect. 29.3.2) and/or the imaging modality. One can either use natural or artificial landmarks where the correspondences are either manually or (semi)automatically calculated. Manual registration with natural landmarks is usually rigid and involves a tracked pointer or instrument which is used for choosing the landmarks in the intraoperative and preoperative data set (see, e.g., [118,43]). These landmarks are usually not tracked. In the case of artificial landmarks, in general the correspondences are calculated (semi)automatically using an additional intraoperative imaging modality that provides volume information, e.g., an intraoperative ultrasound or C-arm. Examples for artificial landmarks include needle-shaped [103] or fluorescent markers [124] inserted in the tissue that can be tracked in the camera image to keep the registration valid. An extension to nonrigid registration approaches can be achieved by combining markers with biomechanical models that incorporate an elasticity model and use the marker displacements as boundary conditions [55] to account for deformations.

29.2.3.2 Surface-based registration

A prerequisite for surface-based registration is the 3D reconstruction of the intraoperative surface (Sect. 29.2.2) which is then matched with the preoperative shape of the target organ. In contrast to point-based approaches, this requires no additional hardware. Surface registration is a common problem in many domains [115], but special challenges arise in an intraoperative setting due to real-time requirements, tissue deformation and sparse sensor data resulting in only partially visible surfaces and ambiguous shape descriptors [76]. The most common methods use the iterative closest point (ICP) algorithm to match surfaces [13,90]. Biomechanical models combined with reconstructed surfaces are also a promising way of nonrigid registration, e.g., in open visceral surgery [96], neurosurgery [76], as well as laparoscopic surgery [112,92,88,85]. Shape matching can also be done with features derived from the images, e.g., the organ contour [56].

29.3. Visual scene interpretation

Extracting information from the visual scene, such as the type of a surgical instrument and its position, what organs are currently visible, or the current phase of the operation, is a requirement for many applications in CAI (see Sect. 29.4). The focus of this section lies in describing different methods for interpreting the contents of the surgical scene, mainly for detecting objects, scenes, and regions, and for tracking these over a temporal dimension.

29.3.1 Detection

Object detection plays an important role in visual scene interpretation for interventional vision. In this context, we define detection as a combination of classification ("Is the object located in the current scene?") and localization ("Where in the scene is the object located?"). In the context of CAI, detection generally focuses on surgical tools, e.g., surgical instruments or suture materials (see Fig. 29.6 for examples), and tissue as well as organs. Common tasks are locating a certain organ, e.g., for registration [91], differentiating tissues types [132], or detecting abnormal tissue and tissue changes such as polyps [11], ulcers/bleeding [66], tumors [50], or tissue atrophy [20,36].

Detecting objects in a scene generally requires the use of image features that make distinguishing objects from other objects and the background possible. For this, many approaches utilize handcrafted combinations of existing feature types, such as information from color, gradient (histogram of gradients), texture, shape, motion, and depth [11,17], which describe the contents of certain regions of an image, e.g., pixels, windows, or superpixels [16]. Recently, a trend in the direction of automatically selected features, namely through using convolutional neural networks (CNNs), has become apparent [11,28,37,60,61,99]. Often, to decide whether the selected features belong to a relevant object, heuristics such as thresholds on certain values of features are used [1, 105]. However, the majority of approaches rely on machine learning based discriminators, such as support vector machines [18,59], random forests [5,94,114], or neural networks [11,28,37,60,61,99], to classify features.

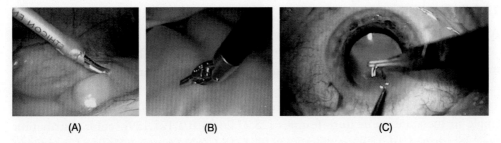

(A)   (B)   (C)

Figure 29.6 Examples of surgical instruments: (A) Conventional laparoscopic instrument (from [17]); (B) Robotic laparoscopic instrument with wrist joint (from [26]); (C) Instrument during microscopic retinal surgery (from [89]).

29.3.1.1 Surgical tools

The majority of approaches for surgical tool detection in interventional vision focus on surgical instruments, though approaches for detecting other tools, such as surgical thread [82] and suture needles [106], do exist. Many challenging factors are common to detecting surgical instruments in interventional vision, for example, parts of surgical instruments can be occluded by tissue, blood or specular highlights, which decreases detection accuracy [17,61]. Furthermore, the appearance of surgical instruments is variable as instruments in both endoscopic and microscopic surgery possess grasper joints whose angles frequently vary [61,113]. During robotic surgery, a further joint (wrist joint) is introduced, increasing the appearance variability of the instruments [4,3,28]. To account for these challenges, approaches for pose estimation are employed [3,17]. These approaches can be divided into discriminative approaches and generative approaches. Discriminative methods rely on initial data-driven models whose pose parameters are determined online. Generative approaches, which generally determine pose parameters via regression and ad hoc approaches, utilize low-level image processing techniques [17].

29.3.1.2 Phase detection

Apart from the detection of physical spatial objects, the detection of surgical phases in the temporal domain is also a relevant problem in visual scene interpretation. Estimating the progress of surgery is the cornerstone for workflow analysis and context-aware assistance during interventions (see Sect. 29.4.4). Up until recently, many methods for surgical phase detection relied on semantic features such as tool usage [14,25] and surgical activities [52], which are not always unique and can therefore result in ambiguities. More recent methods for phase detection utilize handcrafted image features such as low-level visual features [14,25,63] and spatio-temporal features [131]. Current state-of-the-art methods rely on CNNs and recurrent neural network architectures [34,49, 64,120,135].

29.3.2 Tracking

An important addition to detection methods are approaches that make it possible to connect detections in different frames temporally via tracking. This allows for smoother trajectories of features, such as instrument tips or natural landmarks, and for continuous registration (see Sect. 29.2.3).

Generally, landmarks are used as features for tracking [17]. The most prevalent example in literature are texture features [23,27,26,84,101,127,129], color distribution [94,128], shape [101,129], gradient [6,39,94,134], CNN features [28,60,61], and CAD models [130].

To propagate information, e.g., features, onto a future image frame, different approaches exist. Examples are stochastic filters like the Kalman filter [17,39,101,127] and the particle filter [17,107]. Other, nonstochastic, methods are also common, for example, block and template matching [23,26,94,122,130], graph matching [28], mean shift [128], optical flow [3,27,48,84], neural networks [60,61,134], and tracking by detection [6,123,129,134].

29.4. Clinical applications

The methods described above are the basis to realize different clinical applications. Some of them are briefly described in the following paragraphs.

29.4.1 Intraoperative navigation

Intraoperative navigation is a key clinical application in different kinds of surgeries and addresses the question of where subsurface structures are located and how they can be reached, e.g., the hidden tumor position or risk structures that should not be injured [67]. The image guidance is based on preoperative patient planning data which is registered with intraoperative imaging data. Especially in endoscopic and microscopic applications, the camera image can be used to do an intraoperative registration (Sect. 29.2.3) without additional hardware and to provide an AR visualization of the navigation information directly on the image [12,75] (see Fig. 29.7). Challenges arise due to soft-tissue deformation, real-time requirements, and integration into the surgical workflow.

29.4.2 Tissue characterization

Tissue characterization is one of the most important capabilities that an imaging modality can provide in real time during surgery. The ability to distinguish different structural and functional tissue properties is crucial for surgical decision making, for example, for determining tumor margins to ensure complete resection. Currently this is left almost entirely to the surgeon's interpretation and can vary in both difficulty, depending on the

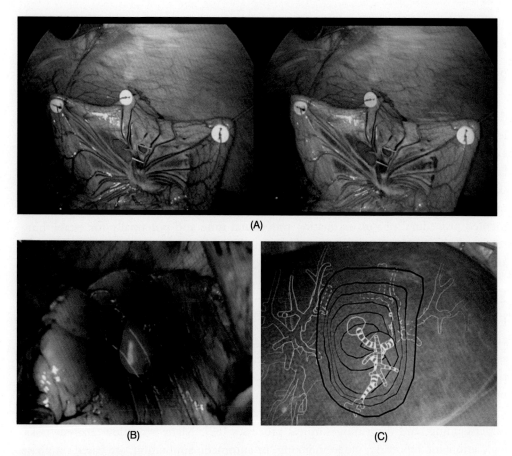

Figure 29.7 Examples of AR in interventional vision (from [12]): (A) AR visualization of blood perfusion from fluorescence; (B) AR using inverse realism; (C) AR using vascular contours.

condition of the tissue or the organ under investigation, and on the subjective cognitive decision of the operating surgeon.

The most common tissue characterization requirement is to differentiate between healthy and malignant tissue. This is important in many specializations and in particular in surgeries that aim to remove cancerous or abnormal tissue. Characterization can rely on imaging modalities, e.g., endomicroscopy, that can see structural patterns at a microscale and use such readings as means for intraoperative histopathology [53]. Multispectral modalities have also been successfully used to characterize different types of tissue [132].

Characterization can also be based purely on white light signals. This has been most widely explored in gastroenterology where artificial intelligence (AI) can be used as a computer-aided diagnostic tool to support detection and characterization of lesions

[11]. Experimental work in colonoscopy, small bowel investigations, oesophaegeal and gastric diagnostic or therapeutic interventions have been explored [11].

29.4.3 Skill assessment

Competency and skill assessment are important aspects of surgery that mostly rely on direct supervision by an experienced surgeon. In this context, one of the largest challenges is to establish objective skills metrics that are not affected by subjective expert evaluation [9]. Performance evaluation of standardized tasks on virtual reality simulators is becoming an increasingly more accepted surgical training tool. Partial automation of skills assessment can be achieved with motion analysis of tracked instruments [81]. Most recently, automated analysis of surgical or training video has become possible for segmented procedural phases, estimating procedural time and potentially for establishing relationships to risk or competence, for example, by linking to standard expert driven assessment systems [121].

29.4.4 Surgical workflow analysis

For many applications in CAI, such as providing the position of a tumor, predicting complications, or determining the remaining duration of surgery, a context–aware assistance would be desirable. Context-aware assistance refers to systems that provide the right information at the right time while automatically and continuously predicting the progress of an ongoing intervention. Analyzing the surgical workflow is a prerequisite for providing context-aware assistance and covers the challenging topic of perceiving, understanding, and describing surgical processes [62]. Many workflow analysis tasks, e.g., automatic reporting, video indexing, or automatic annotation, are based on phase detection (Sect. 29.3.1.2) using endoscopic or microscopic image data. Another example is the prediction of the remaining surgery time with purely image-based methods [2, 15]. Since integrated operating rooms are becoming more common, workflow analysis will not rely only on image data but also on additional device data [15].

29.5. Discussion

This chapter covered the most common optical imaging modalities and setups used for surgery and interventions, describing the basic techniques and the computational algorithms that can be used to provide additional computer-assisted enhanced systems. Vision can be used to infer additional information from the scene, such as geometry, which is useful for AR or for real-time measurements, or it can be used to provide automation in tissue classification or for example in assessing surgical skill.

Challenges to the clinical translation of vision capabilities are multiple from both technical and translational perspectives. Traditionally, vision algorithms typically suffer from limited robustness. While the newly dominant deep learning paradigm has dramatically enhanced robustness by avoiding hand crafted optimizational cost functions, it also requires sufficient data to train the model to regularize all fringe cases. In general computer vision, this capability has been partially driven by the availability of large datasets both for algorithm training and for evaluation. But such availability is still lacking in surgical vision. While datasets of surgical video are now emerging and more prevalent, the ground truth to such data is still very limited despite efforts such as EndoVis.[1] There are multiple reasons for this scarcity of ground truth. Often labels are difficult to generate due to the complexity and ambiguity of the labeling task and hence require expert time and effort, which is not only costly but also difficult to implement at scale. Initiative such as LABELS[2] have started addressing some of these problems in medical imaging as a whole but much work remains to be done. Additionally, surgical vision algorithms trained on certain datasets are not readily applicable to new data and the domain transferability of models is currently insufficiently understood. This holds true for both inter- and intraprocedural transfer problems. While more labeled data is likely to emerge, comprehensive coverage will take time. Additionally, data is likely to be heavily skewed towards commonly occurring procedures and events, thus remaining problematic for less frequent circumstances. An emerging field is to create large datasets of artificial training data with generative adversarial networks [40]. These datasets can be used to augment existing, realistic datasets, e.g. for training segmentation models [87].

Despite the promise of deep learning, additional challenges to research and development of vision systems remain. The diversity of different optical hardware and designs mean that geometric or radiometric calibration is not always easy in practice. With chip-on-tip systems, calibration can be fixed and predetermined. However, in other setups it may be very different and in fact unreliable due to, for example, frequent rotation between the sensor and the optical system or swapping of different scopes. Similarly for radiometric calibration, the wide range of illumination arrangement and the temporal change in illumination power or color can be problematic for accurate radiometry. Without either geometric or radiometric calibration accuracy, algorithms and systems for estimating camera ego motion and/or the geometry of the surgical site are all adversely affected.

Practical challenges also exist. While endoscopic data is normally anonymous (e.g., it is difficult to identify people from the appearance of their inner anatomy), this is not always the case (identifying information can be stored in the filename or on the metadata displayed on screen). For microscopic images, there may be additional concerns depending on the anatomical region, like the eye, where identification may be possible. Identifying information means that data handling is more complex and is under regula-

---

[1] https://endovis.grand-challenge.org/.
[2] https://www.miccailabels.org/.

tion, which is sometimes not sufficiently known or understood by either researchers or the clinical teams and can differ geographically.

Acknowledgments

The authors would like to thank Isabel Funke (TSO, NCT) for assisting in reviewing the literature.

References

[1] A. Agustinos, S. Voros, 2D/3D real-time tracking of surgical instruments based on endoscopic image processing, in: International Workshop on Computer-Assisted and Robotic Endoscopy, Springer, 2015, pp. 90–100.

[2] I. Aksamentov, A.P. Twinanda, D. Mutter, J. Marescaux, N. Padoy, Deep neural networks predict remaining surgery duration from cholecystectomy videos, in: International Conference on Medical Image Computing and Computer-Assisted Intervention (MICCAI), Springer, 2017, pp. 586–593.

[3] M. Allan, S. Ourselin, D. Hawkes, J. Kelly, D. Stoyanov, 3-D pose estimation of articulated instruments in robotic minimally invasive surgery, IEEE Transactions on Medical Imaging 37 (5) (2018) 1204–1213.

[4] M. Allan, P.-L. Chang, S. Ourselin, D.J. Hawkes, A. Sridhar, J. Kelly, D. Stoyanov, Image based surgical instrument pose estimation with multi-class labelling and optical flow, in: International Conference on Medical Image Computing and Computer-Assisted Intervention (MICCAI), Springer, 2015, pp. 331–338.

[5] M. Allan, S. Ourselin, S. Thompson, D.J. Hawkes, J. Kelly, D. Stoyanov, Toward detection and localization of instruments in minimally invasive surgery, IEEE Transactions on Biomedical Engineering 60 (4) (2013) 1050–1058.

[6] M. Alsheakhali, A. Eslami, H. Roodaki, N. Navab, CRF-based model for instrument detection and pose estimation in retinal microsurgery, Computational and Mathematical Methods in Medicine 2016 (2016) 1067509.

[7] M. Arnold, A. Ghosh, S. Ameling, G. Lacey, Automatic segmentation and inpainting of specular highlights for endoscopic imaging, Journal on Image and Video Processing 2010 (2010) 814319.

[8] M.E. Arregui, Robert J. Fitzgibbons Jr., N. Katkhouda, J.B. McKernan, H. Reich, et al., Principles of Laparoscopic Surgery: Basic and Advanced Techniques, Springer Science & Business Media, 2012.

[9] J. Beard, Objective assessment of technical surgical skills, British Journal of Surgery 97 (7) (2010) 987–988.

[10] T. Bergen, T. Wittenberg, Stitching and surface reconstruction from endoscopic image sequences: a review of applications and methods, IEEE Journal of Biomedical and Health Informatics 20 (1) (2016) 304–321.

[11] J. Bernal, N. Tajkbaksh, F.J. Sánchez, B.J. Matuszewski, H. Chen, L. Yu, Q. Angermann, O. Romain, B. Rustad, I. Balasingham, et al., Comparative validation of polyp detection methods in video colonoscopy: results from the MICCAI 2015 Endoscopic Vision Challenge, IEEE Transactions on Medical Imaging 36 (6) (2017) 1231–1249.

[12] S. Bernhardt, S.A. Nicolau, L. Soler, C. Doignon, The status of augmented reality in laparoscopic surgery as of 2016, Medical Image Analysis 37 (2017) 66–90.

[13] P.J. Besl, N.D. McKay, A method for registration of 3-D shapes, IEEE Transactions on Pattern Analysis and Machine Intelligence 14 (2) (1992) 239–256.

[14] T. Blum, H. Feußner, N. Navab, Modeling and segmentation of surgical workflow from laparoscopic video, in: International Conference on Medical Image Computing and Computer-Assisted Intervention (MICCAI), Springer, 2010, pp. 400–407.

[15] S. Bodenstedt, M. Wagner, L. Mündermann, H. Kenngott, B.P. Müller-Stich, M. Breucha, S.T. Mees, J. Weitz, S. Speidel, Prediction of laparoscopic procedure duration using unlabeled, multi-modal sensor data, International Journal of Computer Assisted Radiology and Surgery 14 (6) (2019) 1089–1095.

[16] S. Bodenstedt, J. Görtler, M. Wagner, H. Kenngott, B.P. Müller-Stich, R. Dillmann, S. Speidel, Superpixel-based structure classification for laparoscopic surgery, in: Medical Imaging 2016: Image-Guided Procedures, Robotic Interventions, and Modeling, Bd. 9786, International Society for Optics and Photonics, 2016, p. 978618.

[17] D. Bouget, M. Allan, D. Stoyanov, P. Jannin, Vision-based and marker-less surgical tool detection and tracking: a review of the literature, Medical Image Analysis 35 (2017) 633–654.

[18] D. Bouget, R. Benenson, M. Omran, L. Riffaud, B. Schiele, P. Jannin, Detecting surgical tools by modelling local appearance and global shape, IEEE Transactions on Medical Imaging 34 (12) (2015) 2603–2617.

[19] P.-L. Chang, D. Stoyanov, A.J. Davison, et al., Real-time dense stereo reconstruction using convex optimisation with a cost-volume for image-guided robotic surgery, in: International Conference on Medical Image Computing and Computer-Assisted Intervention (MICCAI), Springer, 2013, pp. 42–49.

[20] E.J. Ciaccio, G. Bhagat, S.K. Lewis, P.H. Green, Quantitative image analysis of celiac disease, World Journal of Gastroenterology 21 (9) (2015) 2577.

[21] N.T. Clancy, D. Stoyanov, L. Maier-Hein, A. Groch, G.-Z. Yang, D.S. Elson, Spectrally encoded fiber-based structured lighting probe for intraoperative 3D imaging, Biomedical Optics Express 2 (11) (2011) 3119–3128.

[22] S. Coda, P.D. Siersema, G.W. Stamp, A.V. Thillainayagam, Biophotonic endoscopy: a review of clinical research techniques for optical imaging and sensing of early gastrointestinal cancer, Endoscopy International Open 3 (5) (2015) E380.

[23] T. Collins, A. Bartoli, N. Bourdel, M. Canis, Robust, real-time, dense and deformable 3D organ tracking in laparoscopic videos, in: International Conference on Medical Image Computing and Computer-Assisted Intervention (MICCAI), Springer, 2016, pp. 404–412.

[24] T. Collins, B. Compte, A. Bartoli, Deformable shape-from-motion in laparoscopy using a rigid sliding window, in: MIUA, 2011, pp. 173–178.

[25] O. Dergachyova, D. Bouget, A. Huaulmé, X. Morandi, P. Jannin, Automatic data-driven real-time segmentation and recognition of surgical workflow, International Journal of Computer Assisted Radiology and Surgery 11 (6) (2016) 1081–1089.

[26] X. Du, M. Allan, A. Dore, S. Ourselin, D. Hawkes, J.D. Kelly, D. Stoyanov, Combined 2D and 3D tracking of surgical instruments for minimally invasive and robotic-assisted surgery, International Journal of Computer Assisted Radiology and Surgery 11 (6) (2016) 1109–1119.

[27] X. Du, N. Clancy, S. Arya, G.B. Hanna, J. Kelly, D.S. Elson, D. Stoyanov, Robust surface tracking combining features, intensity and illumination compensation, International Journal of Computer Assisted Radiology and Surgery 10 (12) (2015) 1915–1926.

[28] X. Du, T. Kurmann, P.-L. Chang, M. Allan, S. Ourselin, R. Sznitman, J.D. Kelly, D. Stoyanov, Artic-ulated multi-instrument 2D pose estimation using fully convolutional networks, IEEE Transactions on Medical Imaging 37 (5) (2018) 1276–1287.

[29] P.J. Edwards, A.P. King, C.R. Maurer, D.A. de Cunha, D.J. Hawkes, D.L. Hill, R.P. Gaston, M.R. Fenlon, A. Jusczyck, A.J. Strong, et al., Design and evaluation of a system for microscope-assisted guided interventions (MAGI), IEEE Transactions on Medical Imaging 19 (11) (2000) 1082–1093.

[30] J.P. Ehlers, J. Goshe, W.J. Dupps, P.K. Kaiser, R.P. Singh, R. Gans, J. Eisengart, S.K. Srivastava, Determination of feasibility and utility of microscope-integrated optical coherence tomography dur-ing ophthalmic surgery: the DISCOVER Study RESCAN Results, JAMA Ophthalmology 133 (10) (2015) 1124–1132.

[31] M. Feuerstein, T. Mussack, S.M. Heining, N. Navab, Intraoperative laparoscope augmentation for port placement and resection planning in minimally invasive liver resection, IEEE Transactions on Medical Imaging 27 (3) (2008) 355–369.

[32] M. Feuerstein, T. Reichl, J. Vogel, A. Schneider, H. Feussner, N. Navab, Magneto-optic tracking of a flexible laparoscopic ultrasound transducer for laparoscope augmentation, in: International Conference on Medical Image Computing and Computer-Assisted Intervention, Springer, 2007, pp. 458–466.

[33] I. Funke, S. Bodenstedt, C. Riediger, J. Weitz, S. Speidel, Generative adversarial networks for specular highlight removal in endoscopic images, in: Medical Imaging 2018: Image-Guided Procedures, Robotic Interventions, and Modeling, Bd. 10576, International Society for Optics and Photonics, 2018, p. 1057604.

[34] I. Funke, A. Jenke, S.T. Mees, J. Weitz, S. Speidel, S. Bodenstedt, Temporal coherence-based self-supervised learning for laparoscopic workflow analysis, in: OR 2.0 Context-Aware Operating Theaters, First International Workshop, Held in Conjunction with International Conference on Medical Image Computing and Computer-Assisted Intervention (MICCAI), Springer, 2018, p. 85.

[35] A. Fusiello, E. Trucco, A. Verri, A compact algorithm for rectification of stereo pairs, Machine Vision and Applications 12 (1) (2000) 16–22.

[36] M. Gadermayr, H. Kogler, M. Karla, D. Merhof, A. Uhl, A. Vécsei, Computer-aided texture analysis combined with experts' knowledge: improving endoscopic celiac disease diagnosis, World Journal of Gastroenterology 22 (31) (2016) 7124.

[37] L.C. García-Peraza-Herrera, W. Li, C. Gruijthuijsen, A. Devreker, G. Attilakos, J. Deprest, E. Vander Poorten, D. Stoyanov, T. Vercauteren, S. Ourselin, Real-time segmentation of non-rigid surgical tools based on deep learning and tracking, in: International Workshop on Computer-Assisted and Robotic Endoscopy, Springer, 2016, pp. 84–95.

[38] D.S. Gareau, Y. Li, B. Huang, Z. Eastman, K.S. Nehal, M. Rajadhyaksha, Confocal mosaicing microscopy in Mohs skin excisions: feasibility of rapid surgical pathology, Journal of Biomedical Optics 13 (5) (2008) 054001.

[39] S. Giannarou, M. Visentini-Scarzanella, G.-Z. Yang, Probabilistic tracking of affine-invariant anisotropic regions, IEEE Transactions on Pattern Analysis and Machine Intelligence 35 (1) (2013) 130–143.

[40] I. Goodfellow, J. Pouget-Abadie, M. Mirza, B. Xu, D. Warde-Farley, S. Ozair, A. Courville, Y. Bengio, Generative adversarial nets, in: Advances in Neural Information Processing Systems, Curran Associates, Inc., 2014, pp. 2672–2680.

[41] S. Haase, C. Forman, T. Kilgus, R. Bammer, L. Maier-Hein, J. Hornegger, ToF/RGB sensor fusion for 3-D endoscopy, Current Medical Imaging Reviews 9 (2) (2013) 113–119.

[42] R. Hartley, A. Zisserman, Multiple View Geometry in Computer Vision, Cambridge University Press, 2003.

[43] Y. Hayashi, K. Misawa, D.J. Hawkes, K. Mori, Progressive internal landmark registration for surgical navigation in laparoscopic gastrectomy for gastric cancer, International Journal of Computer Assisted Radiology and Surgery 11 (5) (2016) 837–845.

[44] J. Heikkila, O. Silven, A four-step camera calibration procedure with implicit image correction, in: IEEE Computer Society Conference on Computer Vision and Pattern Recognition, IEEE, 1997, pp. 1106–1112.

[45] R. Horaud, F. Dornaika, Hand-eye calibration, The International Journal of Robotics Research 14 (3) (1995) 195–210.

[46] G. Iddan, G. Meron, A. Glukhovsky, P. Swain, Wireless capsule endoscopy, Nature 405 (6785) (2000) 417.

[47] U.L. Jayarathne, J. Moore, E.C. Chen, S.E. Pautler, T.M. Peters, Real-time 3D ultrasound reconstruction and visualization in the context of laparoscopy, in: International Conference on Medical Image Computing and Computer-Assisted Intervention (MICCAI), Springer, 2017, pp. 602–609.

[48] S. Ji, X. Fan, D.W. Roberts, A. Hartov, K.D. Paulsen, Cortical surface shift estimation using stereovision and optical flow motion tracking via projection image registration, Medical Image Analysis 18 (7) (2014) 1169–1183.

[49] Y. Jin, Q. Dou, H. Chen, L. Yu, P.-A. Heng, EndoRCN: recurrent convolutional networks for recognition of surgical workflow in cholecystectomy procedure video, in: IEEE Transactions on Medical Imaging, 2016.

[50] S.A. Karkanis, D.K. Iakovidis, D.E. Maroulis, D.A. Karras, M. Tzivras, Computer-aided tumor detection in endoscopic video using color wavelet features, IEEE Transactions on Information Technology in Biomedicine 7 (3) (2003) 141–152.

[51] B. Kateb, V. Yamamoto, C. Yu, W. Grundfest, J.P. Gruen, Infrared thermal imaging: a review of the literature and case report, NeuroImage 47 (2009) T154–T162.

[52] D. Katić, A.-L. Wekerle, F. Gärtner, H. Kenngott, B.P. Müller-Stich, R. Dillmann, S. Speidel, Knowledge-driven formalization of laparoscopic surgeries for rule-based intraoperative context-aware assistance, in: International Conference on Information Processing in Computer-Assisted Interventions, Springer, 2014, pp. 158–167.

[53] R. Kiesslich, L. Gossner, M. Goetz, A. Dahlmann, M. Vieth, M. Stolte, A. Hoffman, M. Jung, B. Nafe, P.R. Galle, et al., In vivo histology of Barrett's esophagus and associated neoplasia by confocal laser endomicroscopy, Clinical Gastroenterology and Hepatology 4 (8) (2006) 979–987.

[54] E. Kolenovic, W. Osten, R. Klattenhoff, S. Lai, C. von Kopylow, W. Jüptner, Miniaturized digital holography sensor for distal three-dimensional endoscopy, Applied Optics 42 (25) (2003) 5167–5172.

[55] S.-H. Kong, N. Haouchine, R. Soares, A. Klymchenko, B. Andreiuk, B. Marques, G. Shabat, T. Piéchaud, M. Diana, S. Cotin, et al., Robust augmented reality registration method for localization of solid organs' tumors using CT-derived virtual biomechanical model and fluorescent fiducials, Surgical Endoscopy 31 (7) (2017) 2863–2871.

[56] B. Koo, E. Özgür, B.L. Roy, E. Buc, A. Bartoli, Deformable registration of a preoperative 3D liver volume to a laparoscopy image using contour and shading cues, in: International Conference on Medical Image Computing and Computer-Assisted Intervention (MICCAI), 2017.

[57] T.C. Kriss, V.M. Kriss, History of the operating microscope: from magnifying glass to microneurosurgery, Neurosurgery 42 (4) (1998) 899–907.

[58] S. Krüger, F. Vogt, W. Hohenberger, D. Paulus, H. Niemann, C. Schick, Evaluation of computer-assisted image enhancement in minimal invasive endoscopic surgery, Methods of Information in Medicine 43 (04) (2004) 362–366.

[59] S. Kumar, M.S. Narayanan, P. Singhal, J.J. Corso, V. Krovi, Product of tracking experts for visual tracking of surgical tools, in: IEEE International Conference on Automation Science and Engineering (CASE), IEEE, 2013, pp. 480–485.

[60] T. Kurmann, P.M. Neila, X. Du, P. Fua, D. Stoyanov, S. Wolf, R. Sznitman, Simultaneous recognition and pose estimation of instruments in minimally invasive surgery, in: International Conference on Medical Image Computing and Computer-Assisted Intervention (MICCAI), Springer, 2017, pp. 505–513.

[61] I. Laina, N. Rieke, C. Rupprecht, J.P. Vizcaíno, A. Eslami, F. Tombari, N. Navab, Concurrent segmentation and localization for tracking of surgical instruments, in: International Conference on Medical Image Computing and Computer-Assisted Intervention (MICCAI), Springer, 2017, pp. 664–672.

[62] F. Lalys, P. Jannin, Surgical process modelling: a review, International Journal of Computer Assisted Radiology and Surgery 9 (3) (2014) 495–511.

[63] F. Lalys, L. Riffaud, D. Bouget, P. Jannin, A framework for the recognition of high-level surgical tasks from video images for cataract surgeries, IEEE Transactions on Biomedical Engineering 59 (4) (2012) 966–976.

[64] C. Lea, J.H. Choi, A. Reiter, G.D. Hager, Surgical phase recognition: from instrumented ORs to hospitals around the world, in: M2CAI, International Workshop, Held in Conjunction with International Conference on Medical Image Computing and Computer-Assisted Intervention (MICCAI), 2016, pp. 45–54.

[65] J. Leven, D. Burschka, R. Kumar, G. Zhang, S. Blumenkranz, X.D. Dai, M. Awad, G.D. Hager, M. Marohn, M. Choti, C. Hasser, R.H. Taylor, DaVinci canvas: a telerobotic surgical system with integrated, robot-assisted, laparoscopic ultrasound capability, in: International Conference on Medical Image Computing and Computer-Assisted Intervention (MICCAI), 2005, pp. 811–818.

[66] B. Li, M.Q.-H. Meng, Computer-based detection of bleeding and ulcer in wireless capsule endoscopy images by chromaticity moments, Computers in Biology and Medicine 39 (2) (2009) 141–147.

[67] X. Luo, K. Mori, T.M. Peters, Advanced endoscopic navigation: surgical big data, methodology, and applications, Annual Review of Biomedical Engineering 20 (1) (2018).

[68] C.-Y. Ma, J.-X. Shi, H.-D. Wang, C.-H. Hang, H.-L. Cheng, W. Wu, Intraoperative indocyanine green angiography in intracranial aneurysm surgery: microsurgical clipping and revascularization, Clinical Neurology and Neurosurgery 111 (10) (2009) 840–846.

[69] L. Maier-Hein, P. Mountney, A. Bartoli, H. Elhawary, D. Elson, A. Groch, A. Kolb, M. Rodrigues, J. Sorger, S. Speidel, D. Stoyanov, Optical techniques for 3D surface reconstruction in computer-assisted laparoscopic surgery, Medical Image Analysis 17 (8) (2013) 974–996.

[70] L. Maier-Hein, A. Groch, A. Bartoli, S. Bodenstedt, G. Boissonnat, P.-L. Chang, N. Clancy, D.S. Elson, S. Haase, E. Heim, et al., Comparative validation of single-shot optical techniques for laparoscopic 3-D surface reconstruction, IEEE Transactions on Medical Imaging 33 (10) (2014) 1913–1930.

[71] L. Maier-Hein, P. Mountney, A. Bartoli, H. Elhawary, D. Elson, A. Groch, A. Kolb, M. Rodrigues, J. Sorger, S. Speidel, et al., Optical techniques for 3D surface reconstruction in computer-assisted laparoscopic surgery, Medical Image Analysis 17 (8) (2013) 974–996.

[72] J. Marescaux, F. Rubino, M. Arenas, D. Mutter, L. Soler, Augmented-reality–assisted laparoscopic adrenalectomy, JAMA 292 (18) (2004) 2211–2215.

[73] F. Marinello, P. Bariani, E. Savio, A. Horsewell, L. De Chiffre, Critical factors in SEM 3D stereo microscopy, Measurement Science and Technology 19 (6) (2008) 065705.

[74] J.M. Marks, B.J. Dunkin, Principles of Flexible Endoscopy for Surgeons, Springer, 2013.

[75] A. Meola, F. Cutolo, M. Carbone, F. Cagnazzo, M. Ferrari, V. Ferrari, Augmented reality in neurosurgery: a systematic review, Neurosurgical Review 40 (4) (2017) 537–548.

[76] M.I. Miga, Computational modeling for enhancing soft tissue image guided surgery: an application in neurosurgery, Annals of Biomedical Engineering 44 (1) (2016) 128–138.

[77] R. Miranda-Luna, C. Daul, W. Blondel, Y. Hernandez-Mier, D. Wolf, F. Guillemin, Mosaicing of bladder endoscopic image sequences: distortion calibration and registration algorithm, IEEE Transactions on Biomedical Engineering 55 (2) (2008) 541–553.

[78] P. Mountney, G.-Z. Yang, Motion compensated SLAM for image guided surgery, in: International Conference on Medical Image Computing and Computer-Assisted Intervention (MICCAI), Springer, 2010, pp. 496–504.

[79] D.B. Murphy, Fundamentals of Light Microscopy and Electronic Imaging, John Wiley & Sons, 2002.

[80] T. Okatani, K. Deguchi, Shape reconstruction from an endoscope image by shape from shading technique for a point light source at the projection center, Computer Vision and Image Understanding 66 (2) (1997) 119–131.

[81] I. Oropesa, P. Sánchez-González, P. Lamata, M.K. Chmarra, J.B. Pagador, J.A. Sánchez-Margallo, F.M. Sánchez-Margallo, E.J. Gómez, Methods and tools for objective assessment of psychomotor skills in laparoscopic surgery, Journal of Surgical Research 171 (1) (2011) e81–e95.

[82] N. Padoy, G.D. Hager, 3D thread tracking for robotic assistance in tele-surgery, in: IEEE/RSJ International Conference on Intelligent Robots and Systems (IROS), IEEE, 2011, pp. 2102–2107.

[83] J. Penne, K. Höller, M. Stürmer, T. Schrauder, A. Schneider, R. Engelbrecht, H. Feußner, B. Schmauss, J. Hornegger, Time-of-flight 3-D endoscopy, in: International Conference on Medical Image Computing and Computer-Assisted Intervention (MICCAI), Springer, 2009, pp. 467–474.

[84] V. Penza, X. Du, D. Stoyanov, A. Forgione, L.S. Mattos, E. De Momi, Long Term Safety Area Tracking (LT-SAT) with online failure detection and recovery for robotic minimally invasive surgery, Medical Image Analysis 45 (2018) 13–23.

[85] I. Peterlík, H. Courtecuisse, R. Rohling, P. Abolmaesumi, C. Nguan, S. Cotin, S. Salcudean, Fast elastic registration of soft tissues under large deformations, Medical Image Analysis 45 (2018) 24–40.

[86] T.M. Peters, C.A. Linte, Z. Yaniv, J. Williams, Mixed and Augmented Reality in Medicine, CRC Press, 2018.

[87] M. Pfeiffer, I. Funke, M.R. Robu, S. Bodenstedt, L. Strenger, S. Engelhardt, et al., Generating large labeled data sets for laparoscopic image processing tasks using unpaired image-to-image translation, in: International Conference on Medical Image Computing and Computer-Assisted Intervention (MICCAI), Springer, 2019.

[88] R. Plantefeve, I. Peterlik, N. Haouchine, S. Cotin, Patient-specific biomechanical modeling for guidance during minimally-invasive hepatic surgery, Annals of Biomedical Engineering 44 (1) (2016) 139–153.

[89] G. Quellec, K. Charrière, M. Lamard, Z. Droueche, C. Roux, B. Cochener, G. Cazuguel, Real-time recognition of surgical tasks in eye surgery videos, Medical Image Analysis 18 (3) (2014) 579–590.

[90] T.P. Rauth, P.Q. Bao, R.L. Galloway, J. Bieszczad, E.M. Friets, D.A. Knaus, D.B. Kynor, A.J. Herline, Laparoscopic surface scanning and subsurface targeting: implications for image-guided laparoscopic liver surgery, Surgery 142 (2) (2007) 207–214.

[91] D. Reichard, S. Bodenstedt, S. Suwelack, B. Mayer, A. Preukschas, M. Wagner, H. Kenngott, B. Müller-Stich, R. Dillmann, S. Speidel, Intraoperative on-the-fly organ-mosaicking for laparoscopic surgery, Journal of Medical Imaging 2 (4) (2015) 045001.

[92] D. Reichard, D. Häntsch, S. Bodenstedt, S. Suwelack, M. Wagner, H. Kenngott, B. Müller-Stich, L. Maier-Hein, R. Dillmann, S. Speidel, Projective biomechanical depth matching for soft tissue registration in laparoscopic surgery, International Journal of Computer Assisted Radiology and Surgery 12 (7) (2017) 1101–1110.

[93] R. Richa, B. Vágvölgyi, M. Balicki, G. Hager, R.H. Taylor, Hybrid tracking and mosaicking for information augmentation in retinal surgery, in: International Conference on Medical Image Computing and Computer-Assisted Intervention (MICCAI), Springer, 2012, pp. 397–404.

[94] N. Rieke, D.J. Tan, C.A. San Filippo, F. Tombari, M. Alsheakhali, V. Belagiannis, A. Eslami, N. Navab, Real-time localization of articulated surgical instruments in retinal microsurgery, Medical Image Analysis 34 (2016) 82–100.

[95] S. Röhl, S. Bodenstedt, S. Suwelack, H. Kenngott, B.P. Müller-Stich, R. Dillmann, S. Speidel, Dense GPU-enhanced surface reconstruction from stereo endoscopic images for intraoperative registration, Medical Physics 39 (3) (2012) 1632–1645.

[96] D.C. Rucker, Y. Wu, L.W. Clements, J.E. Ondrake, T.S. Pheiffer, A.L. Simpson, W.R. Jarnagin, M.I. Miga, A mechanics-based nonrigid registration method for liver surgery using sparse intraoperative data, IEEE Transactions on Medical Imaging 33 (1) (2014) 147–158.

[97] C.-A. Saint-Pierre, J. Boisvert, G. Grimard, F. Cheriet, Detection and correction of specular reflections for automatic surgical tool segmentation in thoracoscopic images, Machine Vision and Applications 22 (1) (2011) 171–180.

[98] N. Sanai, J. Eschbacher, G. Hattendorf, S.W. Coons, M.C. Preul, K.A. Smith, P. Nakaji, R.F. Spetzler, Intraoperative confocal microscopy for brain tumors: a feasibility analysis in humans, Operative Neurosurgery 68 (suppl_2) (2011) ons282–ons290.

[99] D. Sarikaya, J. Corso, K. Guru, Detection and localization of robotic tools in robot-assisted surgery videos using deep neural networks for region proposal and detection, IEEE Transactions on Medical Imaging 36 (7) (2017) 1542–1549.

[100] C. Schmalz, F. Forster, A. Schick, E. Angelopoulou, An endoscopic 3D scanner based on structured light, Medical Image Analysis 16 (5) (2012) 1063–1072.

[101] A. Schoob, D. Kundrat, L.A. Kahrs, T. Ortmaier, Stereo vision-based tracking of soft tissue motion with application to online ablation control in laser microsurgery, Medical Image Analysis 40 (2017) 80–95.

[102] R. Shahidi, M.R. Bax, C.R. Maurer, J.A. Johnson, E.P. Wilkinson, B. Wang, J.B. West, M.J. Citardi, K.H. Manwaring, R. Khadem, Implementation, calibration and accuracy testing of an image-enhanced endoscopy system, IEEE Transactions on Medical Imaging 21 (12) (2002) 1524–1535.

[103] T. Simpfendörfer, M. Baumhauer, M. Müller, C.N. Gutt, H.-P. Meinzer, J.J. Rassweiler, S. Guven, D. Teber, Augmented reality visualization during laparoscopic radical prostatectomy, Journal of Endourology 25 (12) (2011) 1841–1845.

[104] W.E. Smith, N. Vakil, S.A. Maislin, Correction of distortion in endoscope images, IEEE Transactions on Medical Imaging 11 (1) (1992) 117–122.

[105] S. Speidel, J. Benzko, S. Krappe, G. Sudra, P. Azad, B.P. Müller-Stich, C. Gutt, R. Dillmann, Automatic classification of minimally invasive instruments based on endoscopic image sequences, in: Medical Imaging 2009: Visualization, Image-Guided Procedures, and Modeling, Bd. 7261, International Society for Optics and Photonics, 2009, p. 72610A.

[106] S. Speidel, A. Kroehnert, S. Bodenstedt, H. Kenngott, B. Mueller-Stich, R. Dillmann, Image-based tracking of the suturing needle during laparoscopic interventions, in: Medical Imaging 2015: Image-Guided Procedures, Robotic Interventions, and Modeling, Bd. 9415, International Society for Optics and Photonics, 2015, p. 94150B.

[107] S. Speidel, E. Kuhn, S. Bodenstedt, S. Röhl, H. Kenngott, B. Müller-Stich, R. Dillmann, Visual tracking of da vinci instruments for laparoscopic surgery, in: Medical Imaging 2014: Image-Guided Procedures, Robotic Interventions, and Modeling, Bd. 9036, International Society for Optics and Photonics, 2014, p. 903608.

[108] D. Stoyanov, Surgical vision, Annals of Biomedical Engineering 40 (2) (2012) 332–345.

[109] D. Stoyanov, A. Darzi, G.-Z. Yang, Laparoscope self-calibration for robotic assisted minimally invasive surgery, in: International Conference on Medical Image Computing and Computer-Assisted Intervention (MICCAI), Springer, 2005, pp. 114–121.

[110] D. Stoyanov, M.V. Scarzanella, P. Pratt, G.-Z. Yang, Real-time stereo reconstruction in robotically assisted minimally invasive surgery, in: T. Jiang, N. Navab, J.P.W. Pluim, M.A. Viergever (Eds.), International Conference on Medical Image Computing and Computer-Assisted Intervention (MICCAI), Springer, 2010.

[111] D. Stoyanov, G.Z. Yang, Removing specular reflection components for robotic assisted laparoscopic surgery, in: IEEE International Conference on Image Processing (ICIP), Bd. 3, IEEE, 2005, S. III–632.

[112] S. Suwelack, S. Röhl, S. Bodenstedt, D. Reichard, R. Dillmann, T.dos Santos, L. Maier-Hein, M. Wagner, J. Wünscher, H. Kenngott, B.P. Müller, S. Speidel, Physics-based shape matching for intra-operative image guidance, Medical Physics 41 (11) (2014) 111901.

[113] R. Sznitman, K. Ali, R. Richa, R.H. Taylor, G.D. Hager, P. Fua, Data-driven visual tracking in retinal microsurgery, in: International Conference on Medical Image Computing and Computer-Assisted Intervention (MICCAI), Springer, 2012, pp. 568–575.

[114] R. Sznitman, C. Becker, P. Fua, Fast part-based classification for instrument detection in minimally invasive surgery, in: International Conference on Medical Image Computing and Computer-Assisted Intervention (MICCAI), Springer, 2014, pp. 692–699.

[115] G.K. Tam, Z.-Q. Cheng, Y.-K. Lai, F.C. Langbein, Y. Liu, D. Marshall, R.R. Martin, X.-F. Sun, P.L. Rosin, Registration of 3D point clouds and meshes: a survey from rigid to nonrigid, IEEE Transactions on Visualization and Computer Graphics 19 (7) (2013) 1199–1217.

[116] S. Tamai, History of microsurgery, Plastic and Reconstructive Surgery 124 (6S) (2009) e282–e294.

[117] T. Thormahlen, H. Broszio, P.N. Meier, Three-dimensional endoscopy, in: Falk Symposium, Kluwer Academic Publishers, 2002, pp. 199–214.

[118] P. Tinguely, M. Fusaglia, J. Freedman, V. Banz, S. Weber, D. Candinas, H. Nilsson, Laparoscopic image-based navigation for microwave ablation of liver tumors—a multi-center study, Surgical Endoscopy 31 (10) (2017) 4315–4324.

[119] R. Tsai, A versatile camera calibration technique for high-accuracy 3D machine vision metrology using off-the-shelf TV cameras and lenses, IEEE Journal on Robotics and Automation 3 (4) (1987) 323–344.

[120] A.P. Twinanda, S. Shehata, D. Mutter, J. Marescaux, M. De Mathelin, N. Padoy, EndoNet: a deep architecture for recognition tasks on laparoscopic videos, IEEE Transactions on Medical Imaging 36 (1) (2017) 86–97.

[121] S.S. Vedula, M. Ishii, G.D. Hager, Objective assessment of surgical technical skill and competency in the operating room, Annual Review of Biomedical Engineering 19 (2017) 301–325.

[122] D. Wesierski, A. Jezierska, Surgical tool tracking by on-line selection of structural correlation filters, in: Signal Processing Conference (EUSIPCO), IEEE, 2017, pp. 2334–2338.

[123] D. Wesierski, A. Jezierska, Instrument detection and pose estimation with rigid part mixtures model in video-assisted surgeries, Medical Image Analysis 46 (2018) 244–265.

[124] E. Wild, D. Teber, D. Schmid, T. Simpfendörfer, M. Müller, A.-C. Baranski, H. Kenngott, K. Kopka, L. Maier-Hein, Robust augmented reality guidance with fluorescent markers in laparoscopic surgery, International Journal of Computer Assisted Radiology and Surgery 11 (6) (2016) 899–907.

[125] R.G. Willson, Modeling and calibration of automated zoom lenses, in: Videometrics III, Bd. 2350, International Society for Optics and Photonics, 1994, pp. 170–187.

[126] C. Wu, S.G. Narasimhan, B. Jaramaz, A multi-image shape-from-shading framework for near-lighting perspective endoscopes, International Journal of Computer Vision 86 (2–3) (2010) 211–228.

[127] B. Yang, C. Liu, W. Zheng, S. Liu, Motion prediction via online instantaneous frequency estimation for vision-based beating heart tracking, Information Fusion 35 (2017) 58–67.

[128] B. Yang, W.-K. Wong, C. Liu, P. Poignet, 3D soft-tissue tracking using spatial-color joint probability distribution and thin-plate spline model, Pattern Recognition 47 (9) (2014) 2962–2973.

[129] M. Ye, S. Giannarou, A. Meining, G.-Z. Yang, Online tracking and retargeting with applications to optical biopsy in gastrointestinal endoscopic examinations, Medical Image Analysis 30 (2016) 144–157.

[130] M. Ye, L. Zhang, S. Giannarou, G.-Z. Yang, Real-time 3D tracking of articulated tools for robotic surgery, in: International Conference on Medical Image Computing and Computer-Assisted Intervention (MICCAI), Springer, 2016, pp. 386–394.

[131] L. Zappella, B. Béjar, G. Hager, R. Vidal, Surgical gesture classification from video and kinematic data, Medical Image Analysis 17 (7) (2013) 732–745.

[132] Y. Zhang, S. Wirkert, J. Iszatt, H. Kenngott, M. Wagner, B. Mayer, C. Stock, N.T. Clancy, D.S. Elson, L. Maier-Hein, Tissue classification for laparoscopic image understanding based on multispectral texture analysis, Journal of Medical Imaging 4 (1) (2017) 015001.

[133] Z. Zhang, A flexible new technique for camera calibration, IEEE Transactions on Pattern Analysis and Machine Intelligence 22 (2000) 1330–1334.

[134] Z. Zhao, S. Voros, Y. Weng, F. Chang, R. Li, Tracking-by-detection of surgical instruments in minimally invasive surgery via the convolutional neural network deep learning-based method, Computer Assisted Surgery 22 (sup1) (2017) 26–35.

[135] O. Zisimopoulos, E. Flouty, I. Luengo, P. Giataganas, J. Nehme, A. Chow, D. Stoyanov, DeepPhase: surgical phase recognition in cataracts videos, in: International Conference on Medical Image Computing and Computer-Assisted Intervention (MICCAI), Springer, 2018, pp. 265–272.

CHAPTER 30

Interventional imaging: Biophotonics

Daniel S. Elson
Hamlyn Centre for Robotic Surgery, Institute of Global Health Innovation and Department of Surgery and Cancer, Imperial College London, London, United Kingdom

Contents

30.1.	A brief introduction to light–tissue interactions and white light imaging	748
30.2.	Summary of chapter structure	749
30.3.	Fluorescence imaging	750
30.4.	Multispectral imaging	753
30.5.	Microscopy techniques	756
30.6.	Optical coherence tomography	760
30.7.	Photoacoustic methods	761
30.8.	Optical perfusion imaging	764
30.9.	Macroscopic scanning of optical systems and visualization	765
30.10.	Summary	767
References		767

Since the beginning of medicine, optical imaging has formed a central pillar for the diagnosis and treatment of disease. The 20th century saw the development of many other types of diagnostic imaging methods – CT, MRI, nuclear methods, etc. – but optical imaging remains of paramount importance. Within the last few decades optical imaging has started to become more widely used outside of simple detection with the naked eye. These developments, some of which will be introduced in this chapter, are primarily as a result of the minimally invasive surgery revolution. This was enabled by the detection of the surgical field with a color camera system that is either mounted on the proximal end of an endoscope or in more recent times miniaturized and placed at the tip. The color responses of the red–green–blue image data are well matched to the human eye and can be presented on a color display to the surgeon in the operating theater for direct visual guidance of the intervention. Imaging the reflected white light properties of the tissue is an approach that is purely based on providing a visually recognizable picture of the tissue to the surgeon and misses the potential of light to reveal otherwise invisible tissue information (although the digital format of this data and contemporary developments in computer vision methods can be used to improve the understanding of the surgical field – see, for instance, Chapter 29). It is the potential of biophotonics techniques to guide interventions that will be explored in this chapter, together with descriptions of how these additional signals may be collected and understood in detail.

Handbook of Medical Image Computing and Computer Assisted Intervention
https://doi.org/10.1016/B978-0-12-816176-0.00035-1

This content of this chapter is reproduced in a contemporaneous chapter on "Optical Imaging" submitted to a book on Bioengineering Innovative Solutions for Cancer [54].

30.1. A brief introduction to light–tissue interactions and white light imaging

It is well known that light interacts strongly with tissue, with the two principal mechanisms being absorption and scattering (see Fig. 30.1(A)). The absorption will depend on the concentration and extinction coefficient of optically active molecules within the tissue, but is dominated by oxy- and deoxy-haemoglobin, which have distinct absorption spectra in the visible and near infrared spectral regions [12]. Other significant absorbers within this spectral range include melanin and lipids, while water also absorbs strongly at longer wavelengths in the near-infrared. Since many diseases involve changes in vasculature or haemodynamics, it is to be anticipated that these could be detected by imaging the absorption properties of the tissue. For instance, optical imaging and near infrared spectroscopy (NIRS) was proposed to detect tissue changes resulting from breast cancer (see Fig. 30.1(B)) [40], or for minimally invasive real-time monitoring of brain cortical activation (see Fig. 30.1(C)) [84]. However, although optical wavelengths in the red and near-infrared can be selected to allow a good optical transmission through centimeter path lengths, the practical application of these methods is impacted by the very strong tissue optical scattering [12].

Tissue optical scattering arises from the molecular tissue content, and at microscopic and macroscopic scales it manifests itself whenever there is a change in refractive index. Tissues comprise numerous such inhomogeneities, from macromolecules at submicron length scales, through to fibrous collagen structures, cell membranes and layered tissue structures at microscopic to macroscopic scales. The compound result is that the scattering coefficient of tissue is high, meaning that light has a very short (~100 micron) mean free path between scattering events, although it does vary with wavelength, being reduced in the near infrared [12]. The large length scale of many scattering inclusions compared to the wavelength of light produces mainly "Mie" type scattering, which is preferentially in the forwards direction, mitigating the full effect of the high scattering coefficient. Although the tendency for forward scattering has enabled the tomographic approaches mentioned in the last paragraph, it does limit the spatial resolution that can be achieved at depths of greater than a few mean free paths, i.e., a few hundred microns. Therefore, with the exception of a couple of techniques, namely Optical Coherence Tomography (OCT) and Photoacoustic Tomography (PAT), this interventional imaging chapter will focus on imaging the surface or superficial properties of the tissue.

Returning to the standard clinical tissue imaging that uses reflected white light viewed by naked-eye or digital detection, what is generally observed is a combination of the absorption and scattering information. The primary source of coloration is

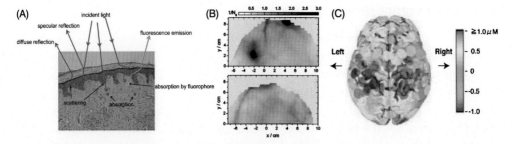

Figure 30.1 (A) Summary of common light tissue interaction processes. (B) "Optical mammogram" showing normalized photon counts (related to optical absorption) in a craniocaudal projection view of the left breast (top) and right breast (bottom). Superficial blood vessels are observed in both images as well as a tumor at (-2 cm, 2.5 cm) in the left breast. Adapted with permission from [40], The Optical Society. (C) Top down view of a sequential whole-head examination by NIRS with the activation (change in oxyhaemoglobin concentration) indicated for an apple peeling task. From [84].

the haemoglobin optical absorbers, whose color is revealed by the light that is scattered superficially in the tissue before being backscattered for detection, giving the tissue its turbid appearance. It is also a common feature of white light imaging that specular highlights appear as bright white regions or spots, which are enhanced in regions of the tissue that have a smooth surface or a mucus layer. These arise from the direct surface reflections which carry color information about the white light source only. They indicate that at these points the tissue surface normal is oriented in a direction that bisects the illumination and detection ray paths and this information has been used to imply geometrical information about tissues with computer vision techniques.

30.2. Summary of chapter structure

This chapter will explore how more complex information besides that mentioned above can be obtained from tissue during interventional imaging. This will begin with a description of fluorescence, initially considering autofluorescence followed by the use of contrast agents in the near infrared spectral range that can improve the ability to detect deeper tissue as well as improve targeting accuracy. The next section details how spectral information can be increased by modifying the light source or the camera to achieve a narrower spectral response, namely multi/hyperspectral imaging. Both fluorescence and reflectance imaging can be used in a microscopic format to achieve high resolution surface information about tissue and cellular structures, providing a further image-based mechanism for tissue diagnostics. The potential of OCT for interventional imaging of subsurface tissue will then be explored and this will be compared to photoacoustic methods. Methods that evaluate motion of tissue scatterers such as laser Doppler imaging and LASCA will be briefly introduced as well as methods for scanning optical devices to acquire data from large regions of tissue and organs.

30.3. Fluorescence imaging

Fluorescence offers the potential to detect and image the location of endogenous molecules with a good level of specificity, or to use extrinsic contrast agents that are able to target a specific process or biomarker within the tissue. There are some parallels with interventional nuclear/radio approaches with the benefits of not requiring ionizing radiation and potentially higher spatial resolution, but the disadvantage of worse imaging depth. Fluorescence is the process whereby molecules are excited by absorbing an incident photon, followed by a radiative decay involving the emission of a longer wavelength photon (with the energy difference accounted for as heat, see Fig. 30.2(A)) [55]. The efficiency of this process depends on the (wavelength-specific) absorption cross-section of a molecule – which in turn is determined by the molecule's electronic energy structure, which also determines the emission spectrum (see Fig. 30.2(A)). Many biomolecules tend to be naturally fluorescent, particularly when illuminated by blue and ultraviolet light where the individual photons carry more energy. The environment within which the molecule is situated also plays a role and can affect the quantum efficiency, i.e., the probability that the molecule emits a fluorescent photon rather than decaying through a competitive nonradiative path [55].

It is known that tissue contains a number of naturally occurring fluorophores such as collagen, elastin, porphyrins, and molecules involved in metabolism, meaning that tissue exhibits the property of *autofluorescence*, particularly when illuminated in the ultraviolet or blue spectral ranges. Since some of these molecules are implicated in the progression of various pathologies and diseases, effort has been made to develop and translate interventional molecular detection and imaging devices that can inform clinical decisions [112,105]. The main considerations when constructing clinical devices to image fluorescence are to (1) ensure that appropriate excitation and emission filters are selected to ensure a low nonfluorescence background (i.e., block nonfrequency-shifted directly reflected photons) and maximal photon efficiency, (2) to use sufficiently sensitive detectors due to the low yield of fluorescence photons, and (3) to allow the light source and camera system to operate in both fluorescence and white light modes to enable standard navigation.

One commercially available example is the Olympus Lucera flexible endoscope which has a violet excitation mode that can be selected at the flick of a switch to reveal information or contrast that is invisible to the naked eye. It is typically noted when observing epithelial tissues that the neoplastic and dysplastic thickening of this uppermost layer leads to a reduction in the green (collagen) fluorescence from the underlying stroma, and that there is potentially an increase in red fluorescence from porphyrins in lesions such as ulcerated squamous cell carcinomas [34]. Clinical studies have shown that various pathologies can be detected including cancers of the brain [108], lung [56], oesophagus [14], and colon [41] (see Fig. 30.2(B)–(C)).

Although autofluorescence imaging is a conceptually attractive method – requiring relatively simple device modifications and regulatory approval, provided that the wavelength is longer than potentially harmful ultraviolet range – it does not achieve the level of specificity that is required for many diagnostic applications. This may be due to the many confounding factors that can affect the image appearance, including variations in the illumination field, imaging distance, cross-talk with other fluorophores and nonspecific fluorescence background, etc. Fiber probe-based fluorescence spectroscopy devices can overcome some of these issues by recording the full fluorescence emission spectrum in a controlled measurement geometry, sometimes at multiple excitation wavelengths, providing a richer and more complete dataset with more potential for internal controls and normalization. Multiwavelength detection benefits from the hardware developments described in the section on MSI, although methods that rely on sequential images may be impractical due to the generally longer camera exposures that are required to detect the weaker fluorescence signals.

An alternative method is to record the fluorescence lifetime, where the nanosecond scale decay of the fluorescence is imaged using ultrafast lasers or megahertz frequency-modulated sources, which can improve the specificity to certain fluorophores, or remove nonspecific fluorescence background [73] (see Fig. 30.2(A), lower section). A further class of technologies combines reflectance and fluorescence multispectral imaging where a more detailed fluorescence spectrum is recorded, which has been used to detect cervical [9] and ovarian [95] cancers as well as guiding surgical procedures such as cholecystectomy [76]. Devices that use these technologies are mainly restricted to early clinical trials at present and have generally not been fully validated and commercialized.

The use of extrinsic fluorophore agents is also being actively pursued, where it is hoped that the high specificity and low background images obtained in microscopes for cell biology can be brought to human-scale applications. There many types of extrinsic labels ranging from organic fluorescent compounds through to synthetic nanoconstructs such as quantum dots, or even genetic labels such as green fluorescent protein (GFP) that render expressed proteins fluorescent. It is a natural step to ask whether these molecules could be used in a clinical context to improve the detection accuracy. However, there are safety and toxicity concerns with extrinsic markers and the targeting methods, and expensive time-consuming regulatory processes are required to pursue the commercialization of chemical probes or the associated hardware. Furthermore, when designing a fluorescent molecule for clinical application it is desirable to use infrared fluorophores so that there is less cross-talk with the spectra of the endogenous fluorophores, and so that the achievable sensing depth of the fluorescence is increased to 5–10 mm due to reduced scattering and absorption.

For these reasons many investigators and industry have focused on using an infrared fluorophore called indocyanine green (ICG), which received regulatory approval for systemic administration to measure perfusion in the eye and other organs [99]. ICB binds

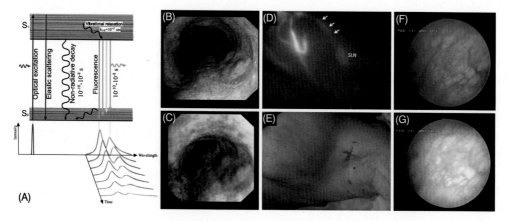

Figure 30.2 Illustration of fluorescence approaches and interventional examples. (A) "Jablonski diagram" showing a set of ground states S_0 and excited states S_1 for a molecule, as well as the possible transitions that can occur after absorbing an excitation photon. (B) White light and (C) autofluorescence image of a neoplastic lesion in Barrett's oesophagus showing a violet decoloration caused by a loss of fluorescence signal from the underlying tissue. From [14]. (D) Near infrared fluorescence image during breast surgery following local injection of ICG used to detect the lymphatic vessel (arrows) sentinel lymph node (SLN), and (E) matched white light image showing the position of the SLN marked on the tissue surface for excision. Reprinted/adapted by permission from Springer Nature [42]. (F) Urothelial carcinoma *in situ* exhibiting red/pink protoporphyrins IX fluorescence which is not visible in (G) standard white light cystoscopy. From [100].

to blood proteins such as serum albumen, resulting in an excitation peak at 805 nm with emission at 830 nm [77]. Although it is frequently used without further functionalization and is rapidly excreted, it has been observed to accumulate in certain tumors thanks to the enhanced permeability and retention (EPR) effect, where the increased number and leaky angiogenic blood vessels pass the protein-bound ICG, while at the same time the compromised lymphatics result in its accumulation. The EPR effect has been used to image breast cancer [99] and others. Direct intravascular ICG injection can also allow the perfusion of downstream blood vessels to be imaged, allowing organ perfusion to be assessed including in the GI tract [121] or in skin flaps [60]. ICG may be applied topically to tissue with the intent of imaging the time course of the fluorescence as the ICG drains into the lymphatic system. This can allow the identification of lymph nodes provided that they are within a few millimeters of the tissue surface (see Fig. 30.2(D)–(E)) [42]. The sentinel nodes can then be excised under image guidance for subsequent histopathological examination for the signs of the spread of cancer, an important prognostic indicator.

Various approved commercial imaging systems are available with 510(k) clearance for near infrared fluorescence imaging, including Novadaq Technologies SPY imaging system, the Quest Medical Spectrum and the Hamamatsu Photonics PDE Photodynamic Eye [26]. Endoscopic devices are manufactured by the major endoscope manufacturers

Karl Storz, Richard Wolf, Stryker, Olympus, etc. Clinical trials and preclinical imaging studies have investigated improvements to the targeting of ICG by binding it to antibodies or peptides [16]. There are also promising results reported from other near infrared fluorophores such as IRDye 800CW [20], which is brighter than ICG and may be targeted for use in margin assessment during breast cancer surgery [57].

Although increasingly popular, not all fluorescence studies use near-infrared contrast agents. For example, some visible fluorescence molecules are approved for clinical use including fluorescein, which is excited in the green spectral region and is used particularly with intraocular imaging and endoconfocal microscopy (described in a later section of this chapter). It has been used for large-area surgical guidance, investigated together with folate targeting for ovarian cancer staging and debulking using a multiplexed camera multispectral imaging device [114]. Another visible fluorophore, protoporphyrins IX, arises after a precursor molecule 5-aminolevulinic acid is delivered to tissue. This is metabolized to the fluorophore as part of haem biosynthesis pathway, but the process is altered in tumors compared with healthy tissues, resulting in increased protoporphyrins IX and a visible fluorescence signal. This mechanism has been applied to the image-guided surgery of bladder cancer using this agent under the marketing name Hexvix (see Fig. 30.2(F)–(G)), where the papillary or sessile carcinomas can be visualized when the surgeon switches to an endoscopic "blue light" mode [64,100]. A related agent under the marketing name Gliolan has also been approved for imaging of glioma and uses a fluorescence enabled operating microscope for image-guided intervention [129]. The applications of protoporphyrins IX continue to develop, including the use of its second excitation band in the red which can reduce the interference from autofluorescence and increase the sensing depth.

Finally, it is worth noting that a second near infrared region can be used to image fluorophores with wavelengths in the range 1.3–1.4 µm, where absorption remains relatively low but scattering is also reduced [44]. Imaging depths of 2 mm have been shown *in vivo*, including through mouse skull [44], and a range of new fluorophores are in development including single-walled carbon nanotubes and quantum dots [45]. Further information on the fluorophores and imaging systems can be found in an article by DSouza [26].

30.4. Multispectral imaging

Multispectral imaging is the extension of white light imaging to incorporate better spectral resolution resulting in improved ability to distinguish different chromophores in the tissue. As with other applications of multi/hyperspectral imaging (MSI), such as remote sensing or production line inspection, the use of this technology requires a compromise to be struck between the spatial, spectral, and temporal resolutions with the ideal interventional acquisition consisting of a detailed spectral signature for each pixel in the image at video rate.

A simple example of how these resolutions may be selected is in a commercially available endoscopic technique called narrow band imaging (NBI), which achieves video rate imaging by retaining a camera but modifying the light source for limited multiwavelength illumination. During NBI a filter wheel controls the light spectrum that is incident on the tissue, restricting it to three narrow (20–30 nm) bands of light in the red, green, and blue spectral regions (Fig. 30.3(C)) [37]. The principle is that the short wavelength bands, being more strongly absorbed by the haemoglobins, are absorbed by the superficial blood vessels, improving their visibility and contrast through the removal of other wavelengths that would result in blurring. Clinical examples of the use of NBI are numerous due to the general availability of the technique on Olympus endoscopes, including, for instance, in flexible endoscopy to improve the detection of adenomas or hyperplasia through better imaging of the pit pattern or microvascular tortuosity (Fig. 30.3(B)) [71], as well as in the oesophagus for supporting identification of Barrett's tissue (Fig. 30.3(A)) [37]. To overcome the variable accuracy and efficacy of NBI techniques for different users, as well as the effect of the learning curve, there have recently been attempts to standardize classification systems. For instance, methods have been proposed to predict the presence or absence of dysplasia in Barrett's oesophagus [102] or to stage colorectal cancer [98].

While NBI compromises potential spectral resolution in favor of high resolution imaging at video rate, the technique of diffuse reflection spectroscopy (DRS) takes a different approach, recording high spectral resolution data at video rate, but usually from only a single point, by placing a fiber based probe directly in contact with the tissue surface [113]. This is relevant to this chapter on interventional *imaging* because (1) this type of data can serve to guide the design of multispectral imaging instruments, particularly in the selection of the spectral bands that optimize the diagnostic sensitivity, and (2) because endoscopic scanning methods can be used to build up an image point by point. DRS has been shown to achieve high accuracy in identifying tissue pathology in a variety of different tissues [91] and the average depth of photon penetration into the tissue can be controlled by adjusting the source–detector fiber separation.

NBI and DRS are optimized for high spatial and high spectral resolution, respectively, and can acquire data at video rate or higher. Other multi- and hyperspectral instruments attempt to acquire a spectral hypercube (Fig. 30.3(D)) and may either acquire over longer time periods to maintain high spectral/spatial resolution, or may compromise spatial/spectral resolution to allow imaging in a single snapshot. One example is the use of tunable optical filters or arrays of filters placed in front of the light source or camera (Fig. 30.3(G)) [1,22]. In this case the spectral resolution and the acquisition time simply scales with the number of filter bands that are to be used, which in surgical applications may require registration of images to account for tissue motion and deformation [23]. Another popular MSI approach that is used in production line quality control and aerial surveillance applications is to acquire spatial information about

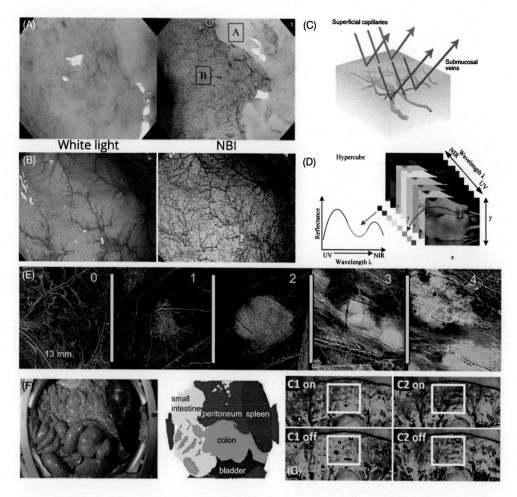

Figure 30.3 Illustration of different MSI approaches and interventional examples. (A) Conventional (left) and NBI (right) images of normal ("A") and Barrett's ("B") oesophagus showing enhanced pit pattern visualization for NBI. Adapted with permission from [37]. (B) Conventional (left) and NBI (right) images of sigmoid colon showing improved superficial vessel visualization. © Georg Thieme Verlag KG [71]. (C) Depiction of NBI blue and green light interacting with superficial vessels. From Maximilian J. Waldner, Stefan Wirtz, Clemens Neufert, Christoph Becker, Markus F. Neurath, Confocal laser endomicroscopy and narrow-band imaging-aided endoscopy for in vivo imaging of colitis and colon cancer in mice, Nature Protocols, volume 6, pages 1471–1481 (2011). Originally adapted from Olympus. (D) The principle of MSI, showing a stack of images acquired at different reflection wavelengths (hypercube) and an illustrative spectrum extracted from one pixel. Adapted with permission from [69]. (E) Pseudocolor processed HSI examples for normal tissue (0), benign tumor (1), intraductal carcinoma (2), papillary and cribriform carcinoma (3), and carcinoma with invasion (4). Reprinted by permission of the publisher (Taylor & Francis Ltd) [85]. (F) RGB (left) and HSI segmented (right) images of porcine abdomen classified using an artificial neural network. Reprinted/adapted by permission from Springer Nature [3]. (G) Oxygen saturation variation showing ischaemia (blue) during vessel occlusion in a section of porcine bowel. Reprinted with permission from [22].

a single line, using the other dimension of the imaging detector to record spectral data, usually by dispersing the light using a prism or grating [3]. However, the slow acquisition speed limits this method for interventional applications because the line must be scanned across the tissue to build the image content in the second spatial dimension, which is then limited by the frame rate of the camera.

Another class of MSI device is snapshot imagers which record all data simultaneously. For instance, the spatial detector may be divided by a spatially varying "Bayer" pattern of different filters to acquire more spectral bands over a larger range of wavelengths, usually at the expense of reduced spectral resolution [70]. Other methods include image mapping spectrometry that spreads the two spatial and one spectral dimensions across a single two-dimensional camera in such a way that a spectral data cube can still be reconstructed [32]. Alternatively, high spatial resolution white light imaging and low spatial resolution spectroscopy may be combined together using information processing approaches to recover higher resolution spectroscopic images [67].

When analyzing MSI data, it is possible to construct an analytical model since the majority of the tissue absorption spectra are known (Fig. 30.3(G)), allowing techniques such as spectral unmixing algorithms to recover the individual components [69]. Complexities that must be built into the model (or ignored/assumed insignificant for practical purposes) include (1) that different wavelengths of light penetrate to different depths and effectively sample a different volume, (2) that optical scattering is wavelength–dependent and will affect light penetration, and (3) that the flood illumination and wide-field detection means that the paths through which the photons travel within the tissue are less well defined compared to DRS. Therefore, as an alternative to modeling, feature extraction and classification holds promise using parallel processing hardware and machine/deep learning pathological diagnosis (Fig. 30.3(E)–(F)). In common with other biophotonics techniques, progress has been limited due to the requirement to test against ground truth (histology) data, which is impractical or time-consuming to achieve.

There are many applications of MSI, including: monitoring of diabetic feet [39]; emphysema [62]; imaging tissue ischaemia during transplant surgeries [10] or during tissue monitoring prior to anastomosis (Fig. 30.3(G)) [22]; detection of Hirschsprung's Disease [27]; characterizing skin bruises [93] detecting cancerous changes in the prostate [2], stomach [4], breast [93], etc. A broader range of MSI applications is presented in a review article by Lu and Fei [69], where the different acquisition strategies are also described in more detail.

30.5. Microscopy techniques

Most of the techniques and examples introduced so far have focused on large area surveillance with wide-field imaging, since this is well-matched to the scale of many surgical interventions. However, while many diseases will present gross changes visible at this scale, it is also the case that early stage disease involves microscopic changes to the biochemistry and tissue architecture that may be lost for lower resolution imaging. Also, many surgical procedures require precise small-scale tissue manipulation. When imaging an exposed tissue surface conventional image magnification optics can be used, for instance, skin lesions may be evaluated by directly placing a high magnification clinical microscope system in contact with the patient. Properties such as coloration, texture, lesion borders, and size may then be used to form an indicative score that may prompt biopsy, treatment, or watch-and-wait paths [53]. In the case of open surgery, operating microscopes use a large stand-off distance to allow microsurgical procedures such as small blood vessel anastomoses or precise tissue removal or brain dissection.

In endoscopic screening and surveillance of the gastrointestinal tract, neoplasia, and dysplasia will result in the abnormal growth and organization of the epithelial cells as well as molecular changes, and detection or diagnosis uses biopsy and standard histology as the gold standard. Under white light imaging these changes may appear similar to other conditions or inflammation, and it is also difficult to accurately survey a large area since multiple physical biopsies are either not possible or practical. Similar arguments apply for other epithelial tissues, as well as for the detection of microscopic metastatic deposits, for instance, in the peritoneal cavity, or for the detection of residual microscopic disease after a tumor has been excised in breast surgery. Therefore, various microscopic imaging devices have been proposed or are in standard clinical practice.

One way in which microscopic changes may be highlighted is through the use of chromoendoscopy, where methylene blue, toluidine blue, or other absorbing contrast agents are sprayed or applied to the tissue. Although not always applied as a microscopic technique, the microscopic cellular architectures manifest themselves as gross intensity variations in the visibility of the absorbing dye. More accurate diagnosis of ulcerative colitis has been achieved, as well as detection of intraepithelial neoplasia and cancer of the colon [50]. As with some of the autofluorescence endoscopy methods described in the section on fluorescence, there are varying results reported on the overall accuracy of the method, including for the diagnosis of Barrett's oesophagus [104].

Magnified endoscopy or zoom endoscopy uses a tip attachment or modified optics to achieve a short endoscopic working distance and high magnification compared to standard imaging. Suspicious regions can then be investigated in higher resolution and using color enhancement processing techniques to show cellular architecture [126]. High magnification can also be combined with narrow band imaging so that the microvasculature can be observed in higher detail so that clinicians can look for features such as branching vessels, dark spots or disorganized capillary patterns. This can improve performance over narrow band endoscopy alone, particularly for distinguishing sessile serrated adenomas from hyperplastic polyps (Fig. 30.4(A)–(B)) [125]. A low cost endoscopic accessory has also been developed, named high resolution microendoscopy (HRME), based on a millimeter diameter fiber-optic imaging bundle that can be placed

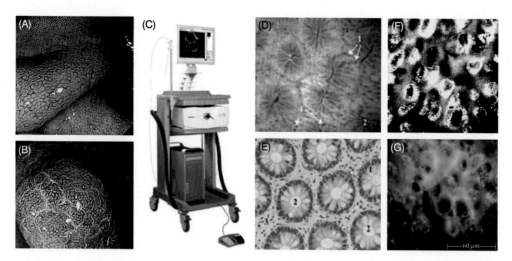

Figure 30.4 Illustration of microscopic approaches and interventional examples. (A)–(B) Magnifying narrow-band imaging of sessile serrated adenomas/polyps (SSA/Ps) illustrating (A) regular and (B) disorganized meshed capillary pattern. From [125]. (C) The Mauna Kea confocal endomicroscope system. Courtesy Mauna Kea Technologies. (D) Confocal endomicroscopy images following fluorescein injection, resulted in strong staining of the cecum epithelium and (E) a closely matched histological section: 1 indicates goblet cells, 2 indicates crypt lumen. From [89]. (F) A fluorescence intensity image of a malignant melanoma examined *ex vivo* at 40 μm depth showing an irregular distribution of pleomorphic cells. (G) A fluorescence lifetime image showing variation of lifetime between melanoma cells (short lifetime values, yellow). © 2012 Stefania Seidenari [101].

in gentle contact with the tissue [79]. This has been evaluated in a range of gastrointestinal applications, showing high accuracy for distinguishing neoplastic polyps [86] and oral neoplasia [80], and with potential to be deployed in resource-limited settings.

The magnification methods mentioned above can record high resolution images, but are affected by out-of-focus background scattered light, which results in cross-talk between the resolution elements and contributes to blurring of the images and loss of contrast. Confocal microscopy overcomes this issue by allowing out-of-focus light to be physically rejected by a pinhole in front of the detector to produce high contrast optically sectioned images, usually at the expense of requiring an image to be acquired point-by-point by beam scanning [103]. Clinical confocal microscopes have been used to record skin cancer architecture at high resolution across the different epithelial layers [17,92]. This can be extended to endoscopic application by miniaturizing the optics, which is usually achieved using optical fibers to simultaneously transport the light and to act as a pinhole. In the commercial Mauna Kea confocal endomicroscope a fiber image guide is used (Fig. 30.4(C)), with distal-mounted miniature microscope optics and a proximal raster beam scanning base station [59]. The probe is inserted though the biopsy/working channel of an endoscope and is usually used to detect tissue fluorescence for blue excitation, allowing either endogenous elastin or, more frequently, a topically or systemically applied fluorescein contrast agent to be imaged. This endoscope has been investigated preclinically and clinically and has shown promise for detecting microscopic blood vessels and angiogenesis [75], Barrett's-associated metaplasia [88], colonic pit patterns (Fig. 30.4(D)–(E)) [89], and parenchymal lung disease [82]. The small imaged field means that the probe must be scanned across the tissue surface for larger area surveillance or contextualization. Image mosaicing features are a standard part of the commercial system [116], and mechanical probe scanning methods are introduced later in this chapter. Image interpretation and histological validation remains a challenge, but there is a growing database of representative images across a range of specialties available in published research papers as well as on the Mauna Kea online archive.

Since the imaging depth for confocal endoscopy reaches only around 100 μm, there is interest in extending the working depth of confocal endomicroscopy by using *nonlinear* methods such as two photon excited fluorescence. This technique uses an illumination wavelength at approximately twice that typically used for single photon excitation, having the benefit of reduced scattering and absorption, leading to increased working depths. However, it does require more expensive and complex pulsed lasers to be used since the absorption cross-section is much smaller and scales nonlinearly with the photon flux [130]. These pulsed near infrared laser sources can also be used to record at the second harmonic, i.e., half the wavelength, and certain structures including collagen have a nonlinear response to intense driving electromagnetic fields. These two techniques (two photon excited fluorescence and second harmonic generation) have been used extensively in the laboratory to image tissue and produce detailed images of unstained tissue at up to 1 mm imaging depth [101,25]. Such systems have also been adapted for the inspection of skin lesions, including using the fluorescence lifetime (Fig. 30.4(F)–(G)). To be able to use these more complex techniques endoscopically at depth, the short intense pulses of infrared light must be passed through a significant length of optical fiber. To overcome the issues of fiber nonlinearity and dispersion which would destroy the short laser pulses, special fiber types such as photonic crystal or hollow core fibers are typically used [28]. Double-clad structures can also keep the excitation light tightly contained for focusing to a small spot while the emitted fluorescence can be collected with a larger detection target [29]. Since the optical fiber is effectively a single pixel detector, distal scanning of the beam is required for imaging, which often uses an MEMS device. Imaging of NADH and FAD together with collagen has been recorded from tissue *in vivo* as well as redox imaging in a perfusion animal model [66].

30.6. Optical coherence tomography

Optical Coherence Tomography (OCT) provides cross-sectional images of the optical scattering structures within a biological tissue. In early systems the time-of-flight of short pulses of light was recorded as they scattered from layers or structures within the tissue, a process which is often referred to as the optical equivalent to an ultrasound pulse-echo A-scan [47]. Due to the very fast ~10 picosecond ($\times 10^{-12}$ s) transit round-trip time of light over the mm length scales involved, (Michelson) interferometric detection is required that uses the detection of optical phase while a reference mirror is translated to change the interferometer arm length [30]. The maximum imaging depth is determined by the tissue scattering and absorption properties, as typically after a ~mm propagation distance the number of directly reflected photons reaching the surface becomes minimal compared to the number of diffusely scattered photons. The use of pulsed light sources has been superseded by Fourier or frequency domain methods that use broadband sources with spectrally-resolved detection, offering improved sensitivity through parallel detection of an entire A-scan in a single measurement with no requirement to scan the reference mirror [63]. In more recent systems the acquisition speed has been further improved by using frequency-swept laser sources and fast detectors to allow A-scans to be recorded at many 100s MHz frequencies [19]. Following signal extraction and processing, some form of spatial beam scanning is required to build up two- or three-dimensional images.

Due to the mm maximum depth scale, the availability of ophthalmoscopes and the layered structure of the retina, diagnostic ocular imaging has become the main application of OCT, with commercial devices found in specialist centers or even in high street opticians (see Fig. 30.4(A)–(E)). This has allowed retinal defects such as detachment, macular degeneration, and macular holes to be diagnosed. OCT has also been incorporated into ophthalmic image-guided therapy devices, for instance, it has allowed the guidance of microsurgical robotic devices to perform retinal surgery [7] and to allow precise manipulation of surgical forceps for membrane peeling [128]. In these studies OCT was used for its depth ranging capabilities to locate the precise position of the tissue surface, and this idea could be used as a surgical assistive technique beyond the retina.

A second major application area of OCT has been in detecting the layered structures within blood vessel walls, such as characterization of the thickness and vulnerability of the fibrous cap in atherosclerotic plaque or imaging of stent placement and complications [11,48]. Since OCT systems are generally implemented using optical fiber, they can be readily incorporated into a catheter device, provided that radial and axial scanning can be achieved and the blood briefly flushed from the imaging area [107]. Fast radial scanning can be achieved proximally by rotating a component the entire length of the catheter, or by distally rotating a small mirror/prism using a micromotor. The latter approach has achieved more than 4000 rotational frames per second with a 100 millimeters per second pullback speed, producing complete three-dimensional datasets in a single heartbeat (see Fig. 30.4(F)–(L)) [119]. OCT is also being combined with autofluorescence information since the functional fluorescence signal can complement the structural OCT data, for instance, distinguishing necrotic lipid pools from collagen [109]. With a standard reference guide produced by the Journal of the American College of Cardiology [107] and thousands of scans being performed every year, there is the potential for scaling to millions of scans per year for comprehensive longitudinal plaque characterization or OCT-based stent selection [15].

The uses of OCT for detection and diagnosis of cancer have been more modest to date, although there is much promising current research in this area. Reports suggest that morphological changes such as epithelial thickening can be detected *in vivo*, although the available axial and lateral resolutions are not sufficient to clearly see the cellular architecture when working at depth. There have been relatively few *in vivo* diagnostic studies with statistics reported and it has been suggested that new techniques that improve the spatial resolution and allow adoption into surgical formats will improve uptake [115]. Performance can also be improved by using automated image analysis approaches [90] such as texture analysis [38,33]. Other applications and findings in the gastrointestinal tract are summarized in a review article [52], while OCT has also been used during robotic prostatectomy to identify the neurovascular bundles [5] and detection of bladder lesions and tumor penetration [72] amongst many other cancer interventions [115]. The minimally invasive use of OCT has been enhanced through the use of needle-based probes that can obtain circumferential scans along the insertion path, as shown for prostate cancer detection [81], breast cancer diagnosis [117], guidance of transbronchial needle aspiration [65], and needle insertion guidance systems [49]. The depth ranging abilities of OCT have also been used as a method of precise surgical guidance.

30.7. Photoacoustic methods

The interventional imaging techniques in the above sections can record data in real-time for detection, diagnosis, and guidance, although they are primarily only able to sense the very superficial tissue properties, extending to around 1 mm for OCT or a few millimeters for near infrared fluorescence. There are also optical tomographic techniques using absorption or fluorescence contrast [24,12], which have low spatial resolution and are mainly used either in a small animal investigational setting or for diagnostic/preoperative imaging (not discussed further in this chapter). As an alternative approach, the combination of optical absorption contrast with ultrasound detection has potential to bridge this gap, allowing optical contrast but with a resolution determined by ultrasound. In a typical tomographic setup short (nanosecond) pulses of light are applied to a tissue in flood illumination, resulting in a rapid thermoelastic expansion and the creation of an acoustic wave. The temporal evolution of this wave can be detected by multiple ultrasound transducer elements at the tissue surface and reconstruction algorithms used for identifying the three-dimensional absorption (Fig. 30.6(A)–(D)) [118]. As with MSI, there

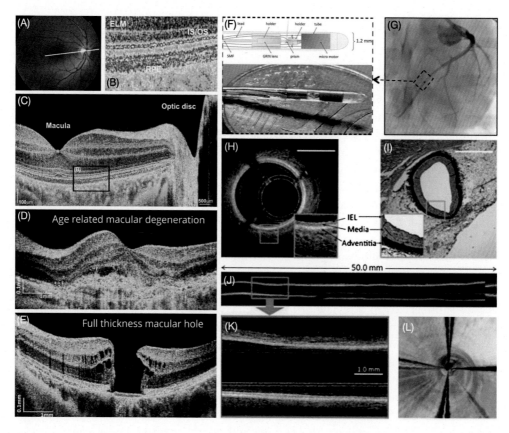

Figure 30.5 Illustration of OCT images of the (A)–(E) retina and (F)–(L) blood vessel. (A) White light ophthalmoscopic image showing the location of the OCT B-scan shown in (C), with the zoomed in region of the External Limiting Membrane (ELM), Inner Segment/Outer Segment junction (IS/OS) and Retinal Pigment Epithelium (RPE) shown in (B). Figures (D) and (E) show two conditions of the eye that involve a disruption of the retinal structures and may be detected from OCT images. Reprinted with permission from [122], The Optical Society. (F) An intravascular OCT catheter with distal scanning mechanism, which is visible under fluoroscopy (G). Figures (H) and (I) show a comparison of OCT and histology with arterial structures labeled including the Internal Elastic Lamina (IEL). (J) Longitudinal rendering with a zoomed in region (K) and reconstructed fly-through (L). Reprinted with permission from [119], The Optical Society.

is intrinsic absorption contrast from blood, although many other absorbing contrast agents can be used, including clinically approved agents such as ICG and fluorescein, as well as other dyes and emerging optical contrast agents or nanoconstructs [94,43,120]. Multispectral absorption contrast uses multiple illumination wavelengths to distinguish multiple chromophores within the tissue [94]. As with conventional ultrasound the image resolution scales inversely with the depth, with higher resolution achievable for more superficial sensing (see Fig. 30.5). At greater depths, the resolution is reduced and

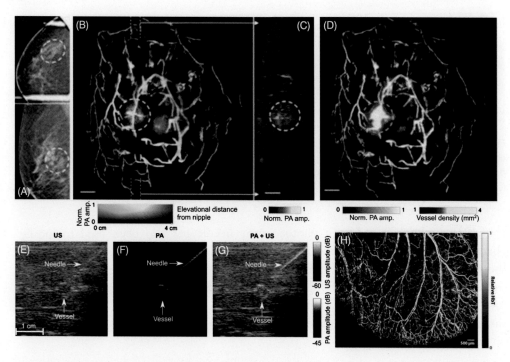

Figure 30.6 Illustration of photoacoustic approaches and interventional examples. (A)–(D) Images of breast tissue and a tumor showing (A) X-ray mammograms of right cranial-caudal (RCC) and right medio-lateral (RML) projections, (B) depth-encoded angiograms where the tumor is indicated by a white circle, (C) maximum amplitude sagittal projection within the volume indicated by the two dashed lines in (B), and (D) automatic tumor detection (red) displayed with the vasculature (grayscale). Adapted from [68] under a Creative Commons Attribution 4.0 International License http://creativecommons.org/licenses/by/4.0/. (E)–(G) Ultrasound, photoacoustic and combined images during needle insertion towards a vessel in a tissue phantom. Adapted from [123] under a Creative Commons Attribution 4.0 International License http://creativecommons.org/licenses/by/4.0/. (H) Photoacoustic microscopy image of relative total haemoglobin concentration in a mouse ear showing vascular and capillary anatomy. Reprinted with permission from [46], The Optical Society.

photon flux is also reduced by the absorption in shallower layers, and direct fiber deliver to deeper layers has been proposed using needles [87]. At more superficial depths, optical focusing can allow much higher resolutions, similar to microscopy but with acoustic detection of the signal (Fig. 30.6(H)) [118].

As a diagnostic tool, photoacoustic tomography is being applied for imaging of human breast vasculature and tissue oxygenation (Fig. 30.6(A)–(D)) as a harmless alternative to X-ray mammography for identifying breast cancer. Photoacoustic imaging has also been proposed as an interventional device guidance tool, for instance, for needle guidance in sentinel lymph node biopsy enabled by ICG contrast [51] or during the detection or avoidance of blood vessels for needle insertion (Fig. 30.6(E)–(G))

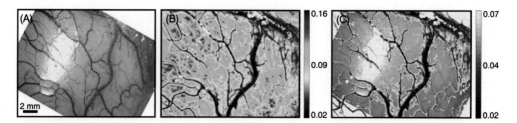

Figure 30.7 (A) Standard white light image of brain tissue under operating microscope. (B) LSCI image and (C) overlay of (A) and (B) illustrating high (red) and low (blue) blood flows intraoperatively. Reproduced under a Creative Commons Attribution 3.0 Unported License, DOI:10.1117/1.NPh.1.1.015006 © The authors [96].

[124,123]. Light delivered by a photoacoustic needle has also been used to locally characterize cancerous lesions and improve the guidance of biopsy needles [87]. Furthermore, brachytherapy seeds have been imaged during an animal model of prostate therapy [8]. The field is developing rapidly with new applications emerging regularly, such as multispectral discrimination between nerves and tendon [74], robotic–assisted surgical guidance [31] or for catheter tracking [18].

30.8. Optical perfusion imaging

It is not just the absorption from haemoglobin that can provide an optical signature for blood, but it is also possible to detect the signal scattered from moving red blood cells. This is used to sense flow within vessels or perfusion in bulk tissue, and hence may be used to record or monitor tissue conditions such as erythema, psoriasis, burn recovery, and skin patch viability. Light that is scattered by the moving blood cells is shifted in optical frequency due to the Doppler effect, which results in interference at detector between the frequency-shifted light and the light backscattered from stationary structures. When illuminated by a coherent laser, scattering from motionless structures and tissues forms a high contrast speckle pattern on an imaging detector due to randomly spatially varying constructive or destructive interference [13]. However, in regions of the image where there is tissue motion or blood flow then the local speckle contrast is reduced. The contrast information it typically converted into a false color image representing the blood flow rate (Fig. 30.7(A)–(C)) and this technique is termed laser speckle contrast imaging (LSCI). Similar information may also be found by recording a stack of images with time and analyzing the temporal variation in the signal intensity on a per–pixel basis [13]. In a closely related technique, the temporal evolution between the light scattered from stationary and moving structures can be recorded at a single point with a fast detector, called laser Doppler flowmetry. If this point is scanned across the tissue surface then the technique is referred to as laser Doppler imaging.

30.9. Macroscopic scanning of optical systems and visualization

This section will consider the bridge between what surgeons see by naked eye or standard endoscopy, and the information that may be acquired using optical techniques. There are four scenarios to consider: (1) For many implementations of MSI or fluorescence imaging the imaged field is identical to the white light image and may be directly registered or used to augment it; (2) For some OCT, confocal and photoacoustic devices, mechanical scanning or reconstruction is inherent to the design of the instrument, and produces stand-alone visualizations that the operator must learn to interpret and use as a complement to vision and endoscopy; (3) In microscopic methods and some OCT probes the imaged field must be tracked and understood with respect to the position on the bulk tissue surface, potentially including image mosaicking if the device is scanned across the surface; (4) Where single point (spectroscopic) sensing is performed, tracking and scanning across the tissue surface is essential to produce image data. For the first two cases, there are a range of image tracking and registration tools that may be applied that are covered elsewhere in the literature, including the use of augmented reality headgear and immersive displays. This section will mainly consider cases 3 and 4, including how they may be practically implemented into interventional devices.

For single point spectroscopy, where the data contains no image information, the scanning may be performed manually provided the position of the probe can be tracked in real-time. As described elsewhere, this could be achieved by visual instrument tracking, magnetic tracking or by using optical markers (see Chapter 31). Visual tracking is suited to the application of probe-based techniques when using the instrument channel of a flexible endoscope, since the on-board camera can be used to locate the instrument position or even reconstruct the tissue surface shape using SLAM [35,78]. Where multiple examinations are performed at different times the visual tracking can also help with retargeting the probe location for serial examination [127]. A similar concept can also be applied to bench-top devices, to allow a clinician to scan a spectroscopic probe across the tissue surface and have this diagnostic information displayed on a white light video that is recorded from a stationary camera. A similar concept has been used for *ex vivo* breast cancer specimen scanning using fluorescence lifetime spectroscopy [110]. Besides the potential benefit of such approaches for surgical decision making, they can also act as an important link between the excised specimen and the histology, which can allow optical spectroscopic methods to be validated more easily and accurately (see Fig. 30.8(A)–(C)) [111]. Where the optical probe is acquiring microscopic images, it is possible to use the stack of image fields acquired during probe motion to create a mosaic (Fig. 30.8(A)–(C)). In this case, any independently acquired positional data can be used to support the mosaic process or to help with the path closure problem [97].

Whilst manual scanning has the advantage of giving the clinician the ability to self-select the probed points on the tissue surface, mechanized or robotic scanning can play

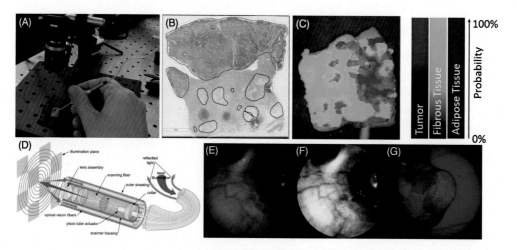

Figure 30.8 Illustration of point scanning approaches. (A)–(C) Acquisition and display of single-point time- and spectrally-resolved fluorescence data after a probe is scanned over a tissue surface (A). Image data records the position of the probe to create a registered overlay of the classified data (C). This can then be compared with histology with a classification made by the histologist (B). Adapted with permission from [110], The Optical Society. (D) Schematic of a distal fiber scanning method using a piezoelectric actuator and cantilevered fiber to trace a spiral scan pattern. (E)–(G) Three different imaging modes of bronchoscopic images ((E) white light, (F) a form of narrow band imaging and (G) fluorescence) acquired at 30 Hz. Blood vessels and inflamed tissue are better visualized in (F), and the red fluorescence in (G) shows hypericin localization within a renal cell carcinoma. Creative Commons. [61].

a role to either assist the targeting where manual probe control is cumbersome or to permit systematic scanning over a larger tissue surface area. For example, scanning a curved tissue surface while maintaining a specified probe-surface contact pressure can be difficult during endoscopy, and this may be supported by closed-loop force control [58,83]. More autonomous mechanisms can be used to comprehensively scan over extended tissues, with potential for surveying whole residual tumor beds [36] or for screening tubular organs such as the colon [6].

Scanning methods can also help to reduce the size of the imaging optics for ultra-minimal access surgery. Whilst there has been a drive towards smaller tip-mounted camera systems, their dimensions are ultimately limited by the desired resolution and a minimum pixel size. For very narrow endoscopes it is still common to find coherent fiber-optic bundles in use, although the resolution of these is also limited to the number of fibers in the bundle. An alternative is to use a single optical fiber and miniaturize a distil-mounted scanning mechanism for rapid pointwise reflectance data, and it is possible to use similar hardware to OCT. For instance, piezoelectric activation of the tip of an optical fiber can scan patterns on the tissue surface, using three lasers for white light imaging and with the possibility of acquiring other modalities such as confocal or fluorescence [61]. Spectral-encoding of the image field has also been proposed for single fiber imaging [106] and it is also possible to reconstruct images by imaging through multimode fiber although the calibration required has so far prevented the technique from being used in realistic scenarios [21].

30.10. Summary

A selection of optical imaging methods have been described in this chapter, many of which are applied during cancer diagnosis and intervention. The direct white light optical imaging of tissue is the primary interventional guidance method and relies on the scattering and absorption properties of the tissue to provide visible contrast to the clinician. It is the scattering that limits the imaging depth of most of the techniques that were presented, with the majority able to sense within the top 100 micron superficial layer. In this superficial regime, high resolution microscopic images can be acquired and contrast can exploit absorption from haemoglobin, or fluorescence and Raman processes to create molecular-sensitive contrasts. Optical coherence tomography pushes the imaging depth limit up to a depth of a few mm, where the number of directly backscattered photons reduces beneath detectable levels. Beyond this, diffuse optical tomography and photoacoustic tomography are able to image absorption or scattering contrast for ~5 cm tissue depths.

It remains a challenge to validate optical methods, which usually have to be compared against histology as the gold standard, but this involves a preparation method that can be difficult and time-consuming to orient and interpret with respect to the optical data. It is even harder to validate against clinical outcomes during larger trials due to the number of patients required and a lack of standardization between different studies. Other promising technologies such as near infrared fluorescence require new contrast agents to reach their full potential, although the high investment to prove safety and efficacy combined with the small established market is not driving this process. Overall, and despite these limitations, there is great promise for optical imaging and biophotonics methods to be used for interventional diagnosis and guidance thanks to the potential for harmless, real-time and highly detailed information to be acquired.

References

[1] M.A. Afromowitz, J.B. Callis, D.M. Heimbach, L.A. Desoto, M.K. Norton, Multispectral imaging of burn wounds: a new clinical instrument for evaluating burn depth, IEEE Transactions on Biomedical Engineering 35 (1988) 842–850.

[2] H. Akbari, L. Halig, D.M. Schuster, B. Fei, A. Osunkoya, V. Master, P. Nieh, G. Chen, Hyperspectral imaging and quantitative analysis for prostate cancer detection, Journal of Biomedical Optics 17 (1) (2012) 076005.

[3] H. Akbari, Y. Kosugi, K. Kojima, N. Tanaka, Wavelet-based compression and segmentation of hyperspectral images in surgery, in: International Workshop on Medical Imaging and Virtual Reality, Springer, 2008, pp. 142–149.

[4] H. Akbari, K. Uto, Y. Kosugi, K. Kojima, N. Tanaka, Cancer detection using infrared hyperspectral imaging, Cancer Science 102 (2011) 852–857.

[5] M. Aron, J.H. Kaouk, N.J. Hegarty, J.R. Colombo Jr., G.-P. Haber, B.I. Chung, M. Zhou, I.S. Gill, Second prize: preliminary experience with the Niris optical coherence tomography system during laparoscopic and robotic prostatectomy, Journal of Endourology 21 (2007) 814–818.

[6] F.B. Avila-Rencoret, G.P. Mylonas, D.S. Elson, Robotic wide-field optical biopsy endoscopy, in: Clinical and Translational Biophotonics, Optical Society of America, 2018, CF1B.5.

[7] M. Balicki, J.-H. Han, I. Iordachita, P. Gehlbach, J. Handa, R. Taylor, J. Kang, Single fiber optical coherence tomography microsurgical instruments for computer and robot-assisted retinal surgery, in: International Conference on Medical Image Computing and Computer-Assisted Intervention, Springer, 2009, pp. 108–115.

[8] M.A.L. Bell, N.P. Kuo, D.Y. Song, J.U. Kang, E.M. Boctor, In vivo visualization of prostate brachytherapy seeds with photoacoustic imaging, Journal of Biomedical Optics 19 (2014) 126011.

[9] J.M. Benavides, S. Chang, S.Y. Park, R. Richards-Kortum, N. Mackinnon, C. Macaulay, A. Milbourne, A. Malpica, M. Follen, Multispectral digital colposcopy for in vivo detection of cervical cancer, Optics Express 11 (2003) 1223–1236.

[10] S.L. Best, A. Thapa, M.J. Holzer, N. Jackson, S.A. Mir, J.A. Cadeddu, K.J. Zuzak, Minimal arterial in-flow protects renal oxygenation and function during porcine partial nephrectomy: confirmation by hyperspectral imaging, Urology 78 (2011) 961–966.

[11] H.G. Bezerra, M.A. Costa, G. Guagliumi, A.M. Rollins, D.I. Simon, Intracoronary optical coherence tomography: a comprehensive review: clinical and research applications, JACC: Cardiovascular Interventions 2 (2009) 1035–1046.

[12] D.A. Boas, D.H. Brooks, E.L. Miller, C.A. Dimarzio, M. Kilmer, R.J. Gaudette, Q. Zhang, Imaging the body with diffuse optical tomography, IEEE Signal Processing Magazine 18 (2001) 57–75.

[13] D.A. Boas, A.K. Dunn, Laser speckle contrast imaging in biomedical optics, Journal of Biomedical Optics 15 (2010) 011109.

[14] D.F. Boerwinkel, J.A. Holz, M.A. Kara, S.L. Meijer, M.B. Wallace, L.M.W.K. Song, K. Ragunath, H.C. Wolfsen, P.G. Iyer, K.K. Wang, Effects of autofluorescence imaging on detection and treatment of early neoplasia in patients with Barrett's esophagus, Clinical Gastroenterology and Hepatology 12 (5) (2014) 774–781.

[15] B.E. Bouma, M. Villiger, K. Otsuka, W.-Y. Oh, Intravascular optical coherence tomography, Biomedical Optics Express 8 (2017) 2660–2686.

[16] J.E. Bugaj, S.I. Achilefu, R.B. Dorshow, R. Rajagopalan, Novel fluorescent contrast agents for optical imaging of in vivo tumors based on a receptor-targeted dye-peptide conjugate platform, Journal of Biomedical Optics 6 (2001) 122–134.

[17] P. Calzavara-Pinton, C. Longo, M. Venturini, R. Sala, G. Pellacani, Reflectance confocal microscopy for in vivo skin imaging, Photochemistry and Photobiology 84 (2008) 1421–1430.

[18] A. Cheng, Y. Itsarachaiyot, Y. Kim, H.K. Zhang, R.H. Taylor, E.M. Boctor, Catheter tracking in an interventional photoacoustic surgical system, in: Medical Imaging 2017: Image-Guided Procedures, Robotic Interventions, and Modeling, International Society for Optics and Photonics, 2017, p. 1013527.

[19] S. Chinn, E. Swanson, J. Fujimoto, Optical coherence tomography using a frequency-tunable optical source, Optics Letters 22 (1997) 340–342.

[20] H.S. Choi, S.L. Gibbs, J.H. Lee, S.H. Kim, Y. Ashitate, F. Liu, H. Hyun, G. Park, Y. Xie, S. Bae, Targeted zwitterionic near-infrared fluorophores for improved optical imaging, Nature Biotechnology 31 (2013) 148.

[21] Y. Choi, C. Yoon, M. Kim, T.D. Yang, C. Fang-Yen, R.R. Dasari, K.J. Lee, W. Choi, Scanner-free and wide-field endoscopic imaging by using a single multimode optical fiber, Physical Review Letters 109 (2012) 203901.

[22] N.T. Clancy, S. Arya, D. Stoyanov, M. Singh, G.B. Hanna, D.S. Elson, Intraoperative measurement of bowel oxygen saturation using a multispectral imaging laparoscope, Biomedical Optics Express 6 (2015) 4179–4190.

[23] N.T. Clancy, D. Stoyanov, D.R.C. James, A.D. Marco, V. Sauvage, J. Clark, G.-Z. Yang, D.S. Elson, Multispectral image alignment using a three channel endoscope in vivo during minimally invasive surgery, Biomedical Optics Express 3 (2012) 2567–2578.

[24] A. Corlu, R. Choe, T. Durduran, M.A. Rosen, M. Schweiger, S.R. Arridge, M.D. Schnall, A.G. Yodh, Three-dimensional in vivo fluorescence diffuse optical tomography of breast cancer in humans, Optics Express 15 (2007) 6696–6716.

[25] W. Denk, J.H. Strickler, W.W. Webb, Two-photon laser scanning fluorescence microscopy, Science 248 (1990) 73–76.

[26] A.V. DSouza, H. Lin, E.R. Henderson, K.S. Samkoe, B.W. Pogue, Review of fluorescence guided surgery systems: identification of key performance capabilities beyond indocyanine green imaging, Journal of Biomedical Optics 21 (2016) 080901.

[27] P.K. Frykman, E.H. Lindsley, M. Gaon, D.L. Farkas, Spectral imaging for precise surgical intervention in Hirschsprung's disease, Journal of Biophotonics 1 (2) (2008) 97–103.

[28] L. Fu, M. Gu, Fibre-optic nonlinear optical microscopy and endoscopy, Journal of Microscopy 226 (2007) 195–206.

[29] L. Fu, A. Jain, H. Xie, C. Cranfield, M. Gu, Nonlinear optical endoscopy based on a double-clad photonic crystal fiber and a MEMS mirror, Optics Express 14 (2006) 1027–1032.

[30] J.G. Fujimoto, Optical coherence tomography for ultrahigh resolution in vivo imaging, Nature Biotechnology 21 (2003) 1361.

[31] N. Gandhi, M. Allard, S. Kim, P. Kazanzides, M.A.L. Bell, Photoacoustic-based approach to surgical guidance performed with and without a da Vinci robot, Journal of Biomedical Optics 22 (2017) 121606.

[32] L. Gao, R.T. Kester, N. Hagen, T.S. Tkaczyk, Snapshot Image Mapping Spectrometer (IMS) with high sampling density for hyperspectral microscopy, Optics Express 18 (2010) 14330–14344.

[33] P.B. Garcia-Allende, I. Amygdalos, H. Dhanapala, R.D. Goldin, G.B. Hanna, D.S. Elson, Morphological analysis of optical coherence tomography images for automated classification of gastrointestinal tissues, Biomedical Optics Express 2 (2011) 2821–2836.

[34] F.N. Ghadially, Red fluorescence of experimentally induced and human tumours, The Journal of Pathology and Bacteriology 80 (1960) 345–351.

[35] M. Giannarou, D.S. Elson, G.Z. Yang, Tracking of spectroscopic and microscopic optical probes in endoscopy using the endoscope image field, in: Optical Tissue Image Analysis in Microscopy, Histopathology and Endoscopy (OPTIMHisE), A Satellite Workshop at MICCAI, MICCAI, London, 2009.

[36] P. Giataganas, M. Hughes, C. Payne, P. Wisanuvej, B. Temelkuran, G.-Z. Yang, Intraoperative robotic-assisted large-area high-speed microscopic imaging and intervention, IEEE Transactions on Biomedical Engineering 66 (2018) 208–216.

[37] K. Gono, T. Obi, M. Yamaguchi, N. Oyama, H. Machida, Y. Sano, S. Yoshida, Y. Hamamoto, T. Endo, Appearance of enhanced tissue features in narrow-band endoscopic imaging, Journal of Biomedical Optics 9 (2004) 568–578.

[38] K.W. Gossage, T.S. Tkaczyk, J.J. Rodriguez, J.K. Barton, Texture analysis of optical coherence tomography images: feasibility for tissue classification, Journal of Biomedical Optics 8 (2003) 570–576.

[39] R.L. Greenman, S. Panasyuk, X. Wang, T.E. Lyons, T. Dinh, L. Longoria, J.M. Giurini, J. Freeman, L. Khaodhiar, A. Veves, Early changes in the skin microcirculation and muscle metabolism of the diabetic foot, The Lancet 366 (2005) 1711–1717.

[40] D. Grosenick, K.T. Moesta, H. Wabnitz, J. Mucke, C. Stroszczynski, R. Macdonald, P.M. Schlag, H. Rinneberg, Time-domain optical mammography: initial clinical results on detection and characterization of breast tumors, Applied Optics 42 (2003) 3170–3186.

[41] J. Haringsma, G.N. Tytgat, H. Yano, H. Iishi, M. Tatsuta, T. Ogihara, H. Watanabe, N. Sato, N. Marcon, B.C. Wilson, Autofluorescence endoscopy: feasibility of detection of GI neoplasms unapparent to white light endoscopy with an evolving technology, Gastrointestinal Endoscopy 53 (2001) 642–650.

[42] C. Hirche, D. Murawa, Z. Mohr, S. Kneif, M. Hünerbein, ICG fluorescence-guided sentinel node biopsy for axillary nodal staging in breast cancer, Breast Cancer Research and Treatment 121 (2010) 373–378.

[43] C.J.H. Ho, G. Balasundaram, W. Driessen, R. McLaren, C.L. Wong, U. Dinish, A.B.E. Attia, V. Ntziachristos, M. Olivo, Multifunctional photosensitizer-based contrast agents for photoacoustic imaging, Scientific Reports 4 (2014) 5342.

[44] G. Hong, S. Diao, J. Chang, A.L. Antaris, C. Chen, B. Zhang, S. Zhao, D.N. Atochin, P.L. Huang, K.I. Andreasson, Through-skull fluorescence imaging of the brain in a new near-infrared window, Nature Photonics 8 (2014) 723.

[45] G. Hong, J.T. Robinson, Y. Zhang, S. Diao, A.L. Antaris, Q. Wang, H. Dai, In vivo fluorescence imaging with Ag_2S quantum dots in the second near-infrared region, Angewandte Chemie International Edition 51 (2012) 9818–9821.

[46] S. Hu, K. Maslov, L.V. Wang, Second-generation optical-resolution photoacoustic microscopy with improved sensitivity and speed, Optics Letters 36 (2011) 1134–1136.

[47] D. Huang, E.A. Swanson, C.P. Lin, J.S. Schuman, W.G. Stinson, W. Chang, M.R. Hee, T. Flotte, K. Gregory, C.A. Puliafito, Optical coherence tomography, Science 254 (1991) 1178–1181.

[48] I.-K. Jang, B.E. Bouma, D.-H. Kang, S.-J. Park, S.-W. Park, K.-B. Seung, K.-B. Choi, M. Shishkov, K. Schlendorf, E. Pomerantsev, Visualization of coronary atherosclerotic plaques in patients using optical coherence tomography: comparison with intravascular ultrasound, Journal of the American College of Cardiology 39 (2002) 604–609.

[49] M.-C. Kao, Y.-T. Wu, M.-Y. Tsou, W.-C. Kuo, C.-K. Ting, Intelligent epidural needle placement using fiber-probe optical coherence tomography in a piglet model, Biomedical Optics Express 9 (2018) 3711–3724.

[50] R. Kiesslich, J. Fritsch, M. Holtmann, H.H. Koehler, M. Stolte, S. Kanzler, B. Nafe, M. Jung, P.R. Galle, M.F. Neurath, Methylene blue-aided chromoendoscopy for the detection of intraepithelial neoplasia and colon cancer in ulcerative colitis, Gastroenterology 124 (2003) 880–888.

[51] C. Kim, T.N. Erpelding, K.I. Maslov, L. Jankovic, W.J. Akers, L. Song, S. Achilefu, J.A. Margenthaler, M.D. Pashley, L.V. Wang, Handheld array-based photoacoustic probe for guiding needle biopsy of sentinel lymph nodes, Journal of Biomedical Optics 15 (2010) 046010.

[52] T.S. Kirtane, M.S. Wagh, Endoscopic Optical Coherence Tomography (OCT): advances in gastrointestinal imaging, Gastroenterology Research and Practice 2014 (2014).

[53] H. Kittler, H. Pehamberger, K. Wolff, M. Binder, Diagnostic accuracy of dermoscopy, The Lancet Oncology 3 (2002) 159–165.

[54] S. Ladame, Bioengineering Innovative Solutions for Cancer, Elsevier/Academic Press, 2019.

[55] J.R. Lakowicz, Principles of Fluorescence Spectroscopy, 2nd edition, Kluwer Academic/Plenum Publishers, New York, 1999.

[56] S. Lam, C. MacAulay, J.C. Leriche, B. Palcic, Detection and localization of early lung cancer by fluorescence bronchoscopy, Cancer 89 (2000) 2468–2473.

[57] L.E. Lamberts, M. Koch, J.S. de Jong, A.L. Adams, J. Glatz, M.E. Kranendonk, A.G.T. Van Scheltinga, L. Jansen, J. de Vries, M.N. Lub-de Hooge, Tumor-specific uptake of fluorescent bevacizumab–IRDye800CW microdosing in patients with primary breast cancer: a phase I feasibility study, Clinical Cancer Research 23 (2017) 2730–2741.

[58] W.T. Latt, R.C. Newton, M. Visentini-Scarzanella, C.J. Payne, D.P. Noonan, J. Shang, G.-Z. Yang, A hand-held instrument to maintain steady tissue contact during probe-based confocal laser endomicroscopy, IEEE Transactions on Biomedical Engineering 58 (2011) 2694–2703.

[59] G. Le Goualher, A. Perchant, M. Genet, C. Cavé, B. Viellerobe, F. Berier, B. Abrat, N. Ayache, Towards optical biopsies with an integrated fibered confocal fluorescence microscope, in: International Conference on Medical Image Computing and Computer-Assisted Intervention, Springer, 2004, pp. 761–768.

[60] B.T. Lee, M. Hutteman, S. Gioux, A. Stockdale, S.J. Lin, L.H. Ngo, J.V. Frangioni, The FLARE intraoperative near-infrared fluorescence imaging system: a first-in-human clinical trial in perforator flap breast reconstruction, Plastic and Reconstructive Surgery 126 (2010) 1472.

[61] C.M. Lee, C.J. Engelbrecht, T.D. Soper, F. Helmchen, E.J. Seibel, Scanning fiber endoscopy with highly flexible, 1 mm catheterscopes for wide-field, full-color imaging, Journal of Biophotonics 3 (2010) 385–407.

[62] J.-H. Lee, C.-H. Won, Characterization of lung tissues using liquid-crystal tunable filter and hyperspectral imaging system, in: 2009 Annual International Conference of the IEEE Engineering in Medicine and Biology Society, IEEE, 2009, pp. 1416–1419.

[63] R. Leitgeb, C. Hitzenberger, A.F. Fercher, Performance of fourier domain vs. time domain optical coherence tomography, Optics Express 11 (2003) 889–894.

[64] S.P. Lerner, A. Goh, Novel endoscopic diagnosis for bladder cancer, Cancer 121 (2015) 169–178.

[65] J. Li, B.C. Quirk, P.B. Noble, R.W. Kirk, D.D. Sampson, R.A. McLaughlin, Flexible needle with integrated optical coherence tomography probe for imaging during transbronchial tissue aspiration, Journal of Biomedical Optics 22 (2017) 106002.

[66] W. Liang, G. Hall, B. Messerschmidt, M.-J. Li, X. Li, Nonlinear optical endomicroscopy for label-free functional histology in vivo, Light: Science & Applications 6 (2017) e17082.

[67] J. Lin, N.T. Clancy, J. Qi, Y. Hu, T. Tatla, D. Stoyanov, L.M. Hein, D.S. Elson, Dual-modality endoscopic probe for tissue surface shape reconstruction and hyperspectral imaging enabled by deep neural networks, Medical Image Analysis 48 (2018) 162–176.

[68] L. Lin, P. Hu, J. Shi, C.M. Appleton, K. Maslov, L. Li, R. Zhang, L.V. Wang, Single-breath-hold photoacoustic computed tomography of the breast, Nature Communications 9 (2018) 2352.

[69] G. Lu, B. Fei, Medical hyperspectral imaging: a review, Journal of Biomedical Optics 19 (2014) 010901.

[70] A.S. Luthman, S. Dumitru, I. Quiros-Gonzalez, J. Joseph, S.E. Bohndiek, Fluorescence hyperspectral imaging (fHSI) using a spectrally resolved detector array, Journal of Biophotonics 10 (2017) 840–853.

[71] H. Machida, Y. Sano, Y. Hamamoto, M. Muto, T. Kozu, H. Tajiri, S. Yoshida, Narrow-band imaging in the diagnosis of colorectal mucosal lesions: a pilot study, Endoscopy 36 (2004) 1094–1098.

[72] M.J. Manyak, N.D. Gladkova, J.H. Makari, A.M. Schwartz, E.V. Zagaynova, L. Zolfaghari, J.M. Zara, R. Iksanov, F.I. Feldchtein, Evaluation of superficial bladder transitional-cell carcinoma by optical coherence tomography, Journal of Endourology 19 (2005) 570–574.

[73] L. Marcu, P.M. French, D.S. Elson, Fluorescence Lifetime Spectroscopy and Imaging: Principles and Applications in Biomedical Diagnostics, CRC Press, 2014.

[74] J.M. Mari, W. Xia, S.J. West, A.E. Desjardins, Interventional multispectral photoacoustic imaging with a clinical ultrasound probe for discriminating nerves and tendons: an *ex vivo* pilot study, Journal of Biomedical Optics 20 (2015) 110503.

[75] A. Meining, M.B. Wallace, Endoscopic imaging of angiogenesis in vivo, Gastroenterology 134 (2008) 915–918.

[76] K. Mitra, J. Melvin, S. Chang, R. Xu, K. Park, A. Yilmaz, S. Melvin, Indocyanine-green-loaded microballoons for biliary imaging in cholecystectomy, Journal of Biomedical Optics 17 (2012) 116025.

[77] S. Mordon, J.M. Devoisselle, S. Soulie-Begu, T. Desmettre, Indocyanine green: physicochemical factors affecting its fluorescence in vivo, Microvascular Research 55 (1998) 146–152.

[78] P. Mountney, S. Giannarou, D. Elson, G.Z. Yang, Optical biopsy mapping for minimally invasive cancer screening, in: G.Z. Yang, D. Hawkes, D. Rueckert, A. Nobel, C. Taylor (Eds.), Medical Image Computing and Computer-Assisted Intervention, 20–24 September, London, Springer, 2009, pp. 483–490.

[79] T.J. Muldoon, S. Anandasabapathy, D. Maru, R. Richards-Kortum, High-resolution imaging in Barrett's esophagus: a novel, low-cost endoscopic microscope, Gastrointestinal Endoscopy 68 (2008) 737–744.

[80] T.J. Muldoon, D. Roblyer, M.D. Williams, V.M. Stepanek, R. Richards-Kortum, A.M. Gillenwater, Noninvasive imaging of oral neoplasia with a high-resolution fiber-optic microendoscope, Head & Neck 34 (2012) 305–312.

[81] B.G. Muller, D.M. De Bruin, M.J. Brandt, W. Van Den Bos, S. Van Huystee, D. Faber, D. Savci, P.J. Zondervan, T.M. De Reijke, M.P. Laguna-Pes, Prostate cancer diagnosis by optical coherence tomography: first results from a needle based optical platform for tissue sampling, Journal of Biophotonics 9 (2016) 490–498.

[82] R.C. Newton, S.V. Kemp, G.-Z. Yang, D.S. Elson, A. Darzi, P.L. Shah, Imaging parenchymal lung diseases with confocal endomicroscopy, Respiratory Medicine 106 (2012) 127–137.

[83] D.P. Noonan, C.J. Payne, J. Shang, V. Sauvage, R. Newton, D. Elson, A. Darzi, G.-Z. Yang, Force adaptive multi-spectral imaging with an articulated robotic endoscope, in: International Conference on Medical Image Computing and Computer-Assisted Intervention, Springer, 2010, pp. 245–252.

[84] M. Okamoto, H. Dan, K. Shimizu, K. Takeo, T. Amita, I. Oda, I. Konishi, K. Sakamoto, S. Isobe, T. Suzuki, K. Kohyama, I. Dan, Multimodal assessment of cortical activation during apple peeling by NIRS and fMRI, NeuroImage 21 (4) (2004) 1275–1288.

[85] S.V. Panasyuk, S. Yang, D.V. Faller, D. Ngo, R.A. Lew, J.E. Freeman, A.E. Rogers, Medical hyperspectral imaging to facilitate residual tumor identification during surgery, Cancer Biology & Therapy 6 (2007) 439–446.

[86] N.D. Parikh, D. Perl, M.H. Lee, B. Shah, Y. Young, S.S. Chang, R. Shukla, A.D. Polydorides, E. Moshier, J. Godbold, In vivo diagnostic accuracy of high-resolution microendoscopy in differentiating neoplastic from non-neoplastic colorectal polyps: a prospective study, The American Journal of Gastroenterology 109 (2014) 68.

[87] D. Piras, C. Grijsen, P. Schutte, W. Steenbergen, S. Manohar, Photoacoustic needle: minimally invasive guidance to biopsy, Journal of Biomedical Optics 18 (2013) 070502.

[88] H. Pohl, T. Roesch, M. Vieth, M. Koch, V. Becker, M. Anders, A.C. Khalifa, A. Meining, Miniprobe confocal laser microscopy for the detection of invisible neoplasia in patients with Barrett's oesophagus, Gut 57 (2008) 1648–1653.

[89] A.L. Polglase, W.J. McLaren, S.A. Skinner, R. Kiesslich, M.F. Neurath, P.M. Delaney, A fluorescence confocal endomicroscope for in vivo microscopy of the upper- and the lower-GI tract, Gastrointestinal Endoscopy 62 (5) (2005) 686–695.

[90] X. Qi, Y. Pan, M.V. Sivak, J.E. Willis, G. Isenberg, A.M. Rollins, Image analysis for classification of dysplasia in Barrett's esophagus using endoscopic optical coherence tomography, Biomedical Optics Express 1 (2010) 825–847.

[91] A.J. Radosevich, N.N. Mutyal, J. Yi, Y. Stypula-Cyrus, J.D. Rogers, M.J. Goldberg, L. Bianchi, S. Bajaj, H.K. Roy, Ultrastructural alterations in field carcinogenesis measured by enhanced backscattering spectroscopy, Journal of Biomedical Optics 18 (2013) 097002.

[92] M. Rajadhyaksha, A. Marghoob, A. Rossi, A.C. Halpern, K.S. Nehal, Reflectance confocal microscopy of skin in vivo: from bench to bedside, Lasers in Surgery and Medicine 49 (2017) 7–19.

[93] L.L. Randeberg, I. Baarstad, T. Løke, P. Kaspersen, L.O. Svaasand, Hyperspectral imaging of bruised skin, in: Photonic Therapeutics and Diagnostics II, International Society for Optics and Photonics, 2006, 60780O.

[94] D. Razansky, C. Vinegoni, V. Ntziachristos, Multispectral photoacoustic imaging of fluorochromes in small animals, Optics Letters 32 (2007) 2891–2893.

[95] T.E. Renkoski, U. Utzinger, K.D. Hatch, Wide-field spectral imaging of human ovary autofluorescence and oncologic diagnosis via previously collected probe data, Journal of Biomedical Optics 17 (2012) 036003.

[96] L.M. Richards, E.L. Towle, D.J. Fox, A.K. Dunn, Intraoperative laser speckle contrast imaging with retrospective motion correction for quantitative assessment of cerebral blood flow, Neurophotonics 1 (1) (2014) 015006.

[97] B. Rosa, M.S. Erden, T. Vercauteren, B. Herman, J. Szewczyk, G. Morel, Building large mosaics of confocal endomicroscopic images using visual servoing, IEEE Transactions on Biomedical Engineering 60 (2012) 1041–1049.

[98] Y. Sano, S. Tanaka, S.E. Kudo, S. Saito, T. Matsuda, Y. Wada, T. Fujii, H. Ikematsu, T. Uraoka, N. Kobayashi, Narrow-band imaging (NBI) magnifying endoscopic classification of colorectal tumors proposed by the Japan NBI Expert Team, Digestive Endoscopy 28 (2016) 526–533.

[99] B.E. Schaafsma, J.S.D. Mieog, M. Hutteman, J.R. Van Der Vorst, P.J. Kuppen, C.W. Löwik, J.V. Frangioni, C.J. Van De Velde, A.L. Vahrmeijer, The clinical use of indocyanine green as a near-infrared fluorescent contrast agent for image-guided oncologic surgery, Journal of Surgical Oncology 104 (2011) 323–332.

[100] J. Schmidbauer, F. Witjes, N. Schmeller, R. Donat, M. Susani, M. Marberger, Hexvix PCB301/01 Study Group, Improved detection of urothelial carcinoma in situ with hexaminolevulinate fluorescence cystoscopy, The Journal of Urology 171 (1) (2004) 135–138.

[101] S. Seidenari, F. Arginelli, S. Bassoli, J. Cautela, P.M.W. French, M. Guanti, D. Guardoli, K. König, C. Talbot, C. Dunsby, Multiphoton laser microscopy and fluorescence lifetime imaging for the evaluation of the skin, Dermatology Research and Practice 2012 (2012) 810749.

[102] P. Sharma, J.J. Bergman, K. Goda, M. Kato, H. Messmann, B.R. Alsop, N. Gupta, P. Vennalaganti, M. Hall, V. Konda, Development and validation of a classification system to identify high-grade dysplasia and esophageal adenocarcinoma in Barrett's esophagus using narrow-band imaging, Gastroenterology 150 (2016) 591–598.

[103] C. Sheppard, D. Shotton, C. Sheppard, Confocal Laser Scanning Microscopy, BIOS Scientific Publishers, Oxford, 1997.

[104] M.B. Sturm, T.D. Wang, Emerging optical methods for surveillance of Barrett's oesophagus, Gut 64 (2015) 1816–1823.

[105] E. Te Velde, T. Veerman, V. Subramaniam, T. Ruers, The use of fluorescent dyes and probes in surgical oncology, European Journal of Surgical Oncology (EJSO) 36 (2010) 6–15.

[106] G. Tearney, M. Shishkov, B. Bouma, Spectrally encoded miniature endoscopy, Optics Letters 27 (2002) 412–414.

[107] G.J. Tearney, E. Regar, T. Akasaka, T. Adriaenssens, P. Barlis, H.G. Bezerra, B. Bouma, N. Bruining, J.-M. Cho, S. Chowdhary, Consensus standards for acquisition, measurement, and reporting of intravascular optical coherence tomography studies: a report from the International Working Group for Intravascular Optical Coherence Tomography Standardization and Validation, Journal of the American College of Cardiology 59 (2012) 1058–1072.

[108] S.A. Toms, W.-C. Lin, R.J. Weil, M.D. Johnson, E.D. Jansen, A. Mahadevan-Jansen, Intraoperative optical spectroscopy identifies infiltrating glioma margins with high sensitivity, Operative Neurosurgery 57 (2005), ONS-382–ONS-391.

[109] G.J. Ughi, H. Wang, E. Gerbaud, J.A. Gardecki, A.M. Fard, E. Hamidi, P. Vacas-Jacques, M. Rosenberg, F.A. Jaffer, G.J. Tearney, Clinical characterization of coronary atherosclerosis with dual-modality OCT and near-infrared autofluorescence imaging, JACC: Cardiovascular Imaging 9 (2016) 1304–1314.

[110] J. Unger, C. Hebisch, J.E. Phipps, M.A. Darrow, R.J. Bold, L. Marcu, Real-time visualization of tumor margins in breast specimen using fluorescence lifetime imaging, in: Biophotonics Congress: Biomedical Optics Congress 2018 (Microscopy/Translational/Brain/OTS), OSA Technical Digest (Optical Society of America), 2018, paper CTu4B.4.

[111] J. Unger, T. Sun, Y.-L. Chen, J.E. Phipps, R.J. Bold, M.A. Darrow, K.-L. Ma, L. Marcu, Method for accurate registration of tissue autofluorescence imaging data with corresponding histology: a means for enhanced tumor margin assessment, Journal of Biomedical Optics 23 (2018) 015001.

[112] P. Urayama, M.A. Mycek, Fluorescence lifetime imaging microscopy of endogenous biological fluorescence, in: M.A. Mycek, B.W. Pogue (Eds.), Handbook of Biomedical Fluorescence, Marcel Dekker, New York, 2003.

[113] U. Utzinger, R.R. Richards-Kortum, Fiber optic probes for biomedical optical spectroscopy, Journal of Biomedical Optics 8 (2003) 121–148.

[114] G.M. Van Dam, G. Themelis, L.M. Crane, N.J. Harlaar, R.G. Pleijhuis, W. Kelder, A. Sarantopoulos, J.S. de Jong, H.J. Arts, A.G. Van Der Zee, Intraoperative tumor-specific fluorescence imaging in ovarian cancer by folate receptor-α targeting: first in-human results, Nature Medicine 17 (2011) 1315.

[115] L. van Manen, J. Dijkstra, C. Boccara, E. Benoit, A.L. Vahrmeijer, M.J. Gora, J.S.D. Mieog, The clinical usefulness of optical coherence tomography during cancer interventions, Journal of Cancer Research and Clinical Oncology (2018) 1–24.

[116] T. Vercauteren, A. Perchant, G. Malandain, X. Pennec, N. Ayache, Robust mosaicing with correction of motion distortions and tissue deformations for in vivo fibered microscopy, Medical Image Analysis 10 (2006) 673–692.

[117] M. Villiger, D. Lorenser, R.A. McLaughlin, B.C. Quirk, R.W. Kirk, B.E. Bouma, D.D. Sampson, Deep tissue volume imaging of birefringence through fibre-optic needle probes for the delineation of breast tumour, Scientific Reports 6 (2016) 28771.

[118] L.V. Wang, L. Gao, Photoacoustic microscopy and computed tomography: from bench to bedside, Annual Review of Biomedical Engineering 16 (2014) 155–185.

[119] T. Wang, T. Pfeiffer, E. Regar, W. Wieser, H. Van Beusekom, C.T. Lancee, G. Springeling, I. Krabbendam, A.F. Van Der Steen, R. Huber, Heartbeat OCT: in vivo intravascular megahertz-optical coherence tomography, Biomedical Optics Express 6 (2015) 5021–5032.

[120] Y. Wang, X. Xie, X. Wang, G. Ku, K.L. Gill, D.P. O'Neal, G. Stoica, L.V. Wang, Photoacoustic tomography of a nanoshell contrast agent in the in vivo rat brain, Nano Letters 4 (2004) 1689–1692.

[121] J. Watanabe, M. Ota, Y. Suwa, S. Suzuki, H. Suwa, M. Momiyama, A. Ishibe, K. Watanabe, H. Masui, K. Nagahori, Evaluation of the intestinal blood flow near the rectosigmoid junction using the indocyanine green fluorescence method in a colorectal cancer surgery, International Journal of Colorectal Disease 30 (2015) 329–335.

[122] M. Wojtkowski, High-speed optical coherence tomography: basics and applications, Applied Optics 49 (2010) D30–D61.

[123] W. Xia, M. Kuniyil Ajith Singh, E. Maneas, N. Sato, Y. Shigeta, T. Agano, S. Ourselin, S.J. West, A.E. Desjardins, Handheld real-time LED-based photoacoustic and ultrasound imaging system for accurate visualization of clinical metal needles and superficial vasculature to guide minimally invasive procedures, Sensors 18 (2018) 1394.

[124] W. Xia, E. Maneas, D.I. Nikitichev, C.A. Mosse, G.S. Dos Santos, T. Vercauteren, A.L. David, J. Deprest, S. Ourselin, P.C. Beard, Interventional photoacoustic imaging of the human placenta with ultrasonic tracking for minimally invasive fetal surgeries, in: International Conference on Medical Image Computing and Computer-Assisted Intervention, Springer, 2015, pp. 371–378.

[125] M. Yamada, T. Sakamoto, Y. Otake, T. Nakajima, A. Kuchiba, H. Taniguchi, S. Sekine, R. Kushima, H. Ramberan, A. Parra-Blanco, T. Fuji, T. Matsuda, Y. Saito, Investigating endoscopic features of sessile serrated adenomas/polyps by using narrow-band imaging with optical magnification, Gastrointestinal Endoscopy 82 (1) (2015) 108–117.

[126] K. Yao, A. Iwashita, T. Yao, Early gastric cancer: proposal for a new diagnostic system based on microvascular architecture as visualized by magnified endoscopy, Digestive Endoscopy 16 (2004) S110–S117.

[127] M. Ye, S. Giannarou, A. Meining, G.-Z. Yang, Online tracking and retargeting with applications to optical biopsy in gastrointestinal endoscopic examinations, Medical Image Analysis 30 (2016) 144–157.

[128] H. Yu, J.-H. Shen, R.J. Shah, N. Simaan, K.M. Joos, Evaluation of microsurgical tasks with OCT-guided and/or robot-assisted ophthalmic forceps, Biomedical Optics Express 6 (2015) 457–472.

[129] S. Zhao, J. Wu, C. Wang, H. Liu, X. Dong, C. Shi, C. Shi, Y. Liu, L. Teng, D. Han, Intraoperative fluorescence-guided resection of high-grade malignant gliomas using 5-aminolevulinic acid-induced porphyrins: a systematic review and meta-analysis of prospective studies, PLoS ONE 8 (2013) e63682.

[130] W.R. Zipfel, R.M. Williams, W.W. Webb, Nonlinear magic: multiphoton microscopy in the biosciences, Nature Biotechnology 21 (2003) 1369.

CHAPTER 31

External tracking devices and tracked tool calibration

Elvis C.S. Chen[a]**, Andras Lasso**[b]**, Gabor Fichtinger**[b]
[a]Robarts Research Institute, Western University, London, ON, Canada
[b]Queen's University, Kingston, ON, Canada

Contents

31.1. Introduction	777
31.2. Target registration error estimation for paired measurements	778
31.3. External spatial measurement devices	780
31.3.1 Electromagnetic tracking system	780
31.3.2 Optical tracking system	781
31.3.3 Deployment consideration	782
31.4. Stylus calibration	782
31.5. Template-based calibration	784
31.6. Ultrasound probe calibration	785
31.7. Camera hand–eye calibration	787
31.8. Conclusion and resources	790
References	791

31.1. Introduction

Spatial measurement device, or tracking system, is the enabling technology for surgical navigation. Perhaps the first spatial measurement device used for surgery was the stereotactic frame by Horsley and Clarke [26], which enabled accurate electrolytic lesioning to be made in the animal brain. The first stereotaxis apparatus for human was designed by the Canadian neurologist Aubrey Mussen [41] and the utilization of the stereotactic frame is still the dominant approach for many types of neuronavigation. Many other types of tracking system have been applied to surgery, including mechanical linkage [15,1] and ultrasonic [43]. Optical and electromagnetic tracking devices remain the most widely used systems commercially and will be the focus for the remainder of this chapter. For a brief historic and technological overview of tracking devices used in surgery, readers may refer to [4].

Both the optical and electromagnetic tracking devices are capable of tracking their own pose sensors with submillimeter and subdegree accuracy under an ideal setting. To track the pose of surgical instruments, these sensors must be rigidly attached to surgical instruments. Spatial calibration must be performed to relate the geometry of a surgical instrument to the coordinate system of its pose sensor. Many issues in sensor design,

Handbook of Medical Image Computing and Computer Assisted Intervention
https://doi.org/10.1016/B978-0-12-816176-0.00036-3

integration, and spatial calibration can be formulated as a registration problem between homologous dataset. Framing tracking and calibration problems as registration problems admits the use of the wide range of techniques described in the registration literature, allowing one to understand tracking and calibration error, optimize the design of pose sensor, and optimize collection of calibration measurements.

31.2. Target registration error estimation for paired measurements

Optical tracking and several tool calibrations can be formulated as a registration problem between homologous measurements, more appropriately known as the Orthogonal Procrustes Analysis [21] (OPA). This admits the use of rich literature of target registration error (TRE) estimation models [16,33,12,8] to improve tracking accuracy of a calibrated instrument.

The simplest form of OPA is the registration between homologous point sets. Tracking of an optical pose sensor (Sect. 31.3.2), as an example, is achieved by the point-to-point registration between the known fiducial marker geometry to those measured by the optical tracking system. The solution to the rigid point-based registration problem is the rotation $\mathbf{R}$ and translation $\mathbf{t}$ that best aligns a set of points $\{\mathbf{x}_i\}$ to a set of corresponding points $\{\mathbf{y}_i\}$. The distance between a measured point $\mathbf{x}_i$ and the unknown true location of the point before the registration transformation is computed is called the fiducial localization error (FLE). If FLE is not zero, then the $\{\mathbf{x}_i\}$ will not coincide exactly with the $\{\mathbf{y}_i\}$ after the registration transformation is applied to $\{\mathbf{x}_i\}$; the root-mean-squared (RMS) distance between $\{\mathbf{x}_i\}$ and $\{\mathbf{y}_i\}$ after registration is called the fiducial registration error (FRE). For N points, FRE is given by

$$\mathrm{FRE}^2 = \frac{1}{N} \sum_{i=1}^{N} \left\| \mathbf{R}\mathbf{x}_i + \mathbf{t} - \mathbf{y}_i \right\|^2 \tag{31.1}$$

where the vector $\mathbf{FRE}_i = \mathbf{R}\mathbf{x}_i + \mathbf{t} - \mathbf{y}_i$ is the residual displacement error between the registered point $\mathbf{x}_i$ and its corresponding point $\mathbf{y}_i$.

In most surgical applications, the target of interest does not coincide with a fiducial marker. When the registration is applied to a point $\mathbf{r}$ not used in computing the registration, then the distance between $\mathbf{r}$ and its corresponding point $\mathbf{r}$ is called the target registration error (TRE).

The expected value of the squared magnitude of TRE as a function of zero-mean, independent, identical, isotropic, normally distributed FLE is given by [16]:

$$\langle \mathrm{TRE}^2(\mathbf{r}) \rangle = \frac{1}{N} \left(1 + \frac{1}{3} \sum_{k=1}^{3} \frac{d_k^2}{f_k^2} \right) \langle \mathrm{FLE}^2 \rangle \tag{31.2}$$

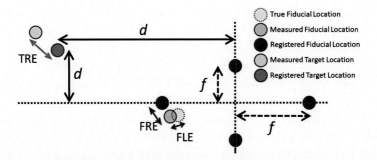

Figure 31.1 After registration, the expected value of the target registration error (displacement between blue circles) is a function of the number of fiducial makers (red circles) and their configurations. Refer to Eq. (31.2), *f* is the RMS distance of the fiducials, and *d* is the distance of the target from principal axis of the fiducial configuration.

where N is the number of fiducial markers, d_k is the distance of $\mathbf{r}$ from the principal axis k of the noise-free fiducial markers defined in $\{Y\}$, f_k^2 is the mean of the squared distances of the markers from axis k, and $\langle \text{FLE}^2 \rangle$ is the expected value of the squared magnitude of FLE (Fig. 31.1). In this scenario, closed-form and optimal solutions to Eq. (31.1) exist [25,2]. Eq. (31.2) concisely describes the behavior of the magnitude of TRE: TRE magnitude is proportional to the standard deviation of FLE, inversely proportional to the square root of the number of markers, minimized at the centroid of the markers, and the isocontours of TRE are ellipsoidal. Based on Eq. (31.2), West et al. proposed four guidelines [56] for fiducial configuration: (1) avoid collinear fiducial marker configuration, (2) the center of mass of fiducial configuration should be as close to the target as possible, (3) keep the markers as far from each other as possible, and (4) use as many fiducial markers as possible (although there is a diminishing returning after 5 or 6 markers are used).

Patient registration is often facilitated through the use of artificial (radioopaque) landmarks. Several authors examined practical consideration of incorporating these principles for fiducial placement in the context of neurosurgery [56,48]. We further argue that minimizing FLE throughout tracking, tool calibration, and fiducial digitizing process is equally important to achieve system accuracy of surgical navigation.

Eq. (31.2) applies directly to the design of optically-tracked instrument where the retroreflective markers are the registration fiducials, and the end-effector of the surgical instrument is the target. West and Maurer focused their studies on planar target configuration, although they briefly discussed some of the expected effect of using nonplanar targets [55]. Wiles and Peters studies the problem of predicting TRE of an optically tracked target when a reference target was used [57] and Wiles and Peters described a method to estimate FLE of a tracked optical pose sensor in real-time [58]. Seginer described a method to predict TRE directly from the vector fiducial registration error [45]. Sielhorst et al. described a covariance propagation technique to predict the covariance of TRE for an optically tracked target [49].

TRE estimation models for paired fiducial registration under anisotropic FLE (a common problem for optical tracking) was introduced in [60] and was later generalized to the case of heteroscedastic FLE in [35,12]. TRE estimation model for paired fiducial-surface registration under heteroscedastic FLE (a common problem for patient registration) was introduced in [33], and for paired fiducial-line registration (a common for tool calibration) under heteroscedastic FLE introduced in [34,8]. Theoretical optimal solution for the OPA under heteroscedastic FLE was introduced in [36]. Empirically, i.e. with no theoretical guarantees, a globally optimal solution for point-to-point, point-to-line, and point-to-plane registration under heteroscedastic FLE was introduced in [5].

31.3. External spatial measurement devices

External tracking devices conceptually comprise of two components: the tracker and the pose sensor. The tracking system defines a global reference frame, for which the pose of the sensor are measured with 5 or 6 degrees of freedom (DoF). Commercial optical and electromagnetic tracking devices are capable of tracking their pose sensors with submillimeter and subdegree accuracy [17,59,28] but environmental factors such as lighting and the presence of ferromagnetic materials may influence tracking accuracy.

31.3.1 Electromagnetic tracking system

Electromagnetic tracking systems operate on the principle of generating an artificial magnetic field where the strength and orientation of the magnetic field can be detected using either a search coil (for alternating current driven field), or a fluxgate coil (for direct current driven field) [18]. These coils tend to be tubular in shape, with a typical dimension of less than 1 mm in diameter and less than 10 mm in length. The pose of each coil can be determined up to 5 DoF, comprising translation (3-DoF) plus pitch and yaw angles. 6-DoF sensor comprises of two 5-DoF sensors arranged in an oblique (i.e. nonparallel) orientation, thus the diameter of a 6-DoF sensor tend to be slightly larger than that of a 5-DoF sensor. Measured poses are communicated to the tracker via a flexible wire. Due to its small dimension, electromagnetic tracking systems are particular suitable for tracking small (e.g. needle) or flexible (e.g. endoscopic ultrasound) instruments and does not suffer from line-of-sight problem. Overviews of the application of electromagnetic tracking system in medicine can be found [63,18].

The need for a tethered connection between the pose sensor and the tracker has practical implication in the surgical workflow. Sensor cables must be managed carefully to minimize impacts on existing surgical workflow. Embedding a coil which either sense, or induce, electrical current within surgical instrument has significant implication in the regulatory approval of the modified device. Electromagnetic tracking system are sensitive to the presence of ferromagnetic object and any object that can induce Eddy current within the surgical field. Newer model of the magnetic tracking systems (e.g. NDI Aurora) has a magnetic field generator with embedded shielding which minimizes tracking distortions caused by conductive or ferromagnetic materials located on the other side of the shield. Readers may refer to [28] for a discussion on the impact of metal presence and magnetic tracking in surgical field.

31.3.2 Optical tracking system

Optical tracking system can be further categorized as either infrared- (IR) or video-metric-based systems. In IR-based optical tracking systems, multiple cameras imaging in the infrared spectrum are arranged in a known configuration. The principal of tracking is based on triangulation and paired-point registration (Sect. 31.2). The optical pose sensor comprises of a set of fiducial markers arranged in a rigid and known configuration. During tracking, the 3D locations of individual fiducial marker are determined via triangulation and the pose of the pose sensor determined via registration to the known configuration. Fiducial markers can be either passive (i.e. retroreflective) or active (i.e. IR emitting). Both the number and spatial distribution of the fiducial marker influences the tracking accuracy of the optical pose sensor [55]. At least three fiducial markers must be arranged in a noncollinear configuration in order to resolve the pose in 6 DoF. Passive tracking system, such as MicronTracker (ClaroNav, Toronto, Ontario Canada) and Polaris (Northern Digital Inc., Waterloo, Ontario Canada), are wireless. In active tracking system, power supplied to the IRED emitter can be wired (as in Certus (Northern Digital Inc., Waterloo, Ontario, Canada)), or wireless and battery-powered (as in FusionTrack (Atracsys, Switzerland)). Hybrid systems are capable of tracking both passive and active fiducial markers.

In videometric tracking system the pose of planar marker patterns are determined on video image sequences using one or more cameras. Using only a monoscopic camera, the pose of a planar marker can be determined through homography. A dictionary of unique markers can be built, such as those freely available in ArUco [19], allowing robust tracking of multiple patterns simultaneously. Modern videometric tracking systems such as the Vuforia library[1] have the ability to track nonplanar pattern, relying on feature detection and image registration as the basis for tracking. The size of these image patterns must be optimized with respect to the size of the viewing frustum to ensure visibility and tracking accuracy.

The design of optical pose sensor must follow vendor-specific criteria, both with respect to intra- (i.e. location of individual fiducial marker within the pose sensor) and intercompatibility of multiple pose sensors. Intrasensor criteria assure that each

[1] https://www.vuforia.com/.

fiducial marker can be localized accurately, whereas intersensor criteria assure each pose sensor can be identified uniquely. Due to these constraints, the optical pose sensor is physically larger than a magnetic pose sensor. Integration of optical pose sensor into surgical instruments is limited by the finite sensor size, its inability to track flexible surgical tools, and line-of-sight issue.

31.3.3 Deployment consideration

As tracking accuracy is influenced by its environment, accuracy of the tracking system must be validated in the specific surgical setting [50,61,63]. Portable validation phantoms have been developed [30,18] to assess tracking accuracy in situ. When deciding which type of tracking system to be used, practical considerations must include [63]:

- Refresh rate: optical tracking system has a typical refresh rate higher than that of a magnetic tracking system,
- Concurrency: how many sensors can be tracked concurrently,
- Working Volume: tracker must provide a working volume sufficiently large to cover the anatomy of interest,
- Obtrusiveness: size and the weight (for optical), cable management (for magnetic), and positioning of the tracking sensor must not interfere with surgical workflow and has minimal impact on other surgical instrument,
- Accuracy: In a clean environment, both optical and magnetic tracking systems provides submillimeter and subdegree accuracy. Magnetic tracker may provide a better orientation tracking [32], and
- Robustness: Tracking may be interfered by environmental factors such as light, sound, ferromagnetic objects, etc.

31.4. Stylus calibration

The surgical stylus, a pen-shaped and spatially tracked instrument, is ubiquitous in any surgical navigation system. The primary utility of the stylus is *digitization*, used to infer the 3D location of a fiducial in some reference coordinate system (e.g. CT or MRI compatible skin markers). The secondary utility is *registration*: once a set of fiducial markers are digitized, their locations serve as the mathematical basis for several types of registration including paired-fiducial [25,2] and point-to-surface methods [3].

The act of digitization involves placing the calibrated stylus tip to be in physical contact with the fiducial. Assuming the stylus tip coincides with the fiducial exactly, the fiducial location is inferred as the instantaneous location of the tracked stylus tip. The fiducial localization error (FLE) during digitization is influenced by, among others: tracking and calibration error of the surgical stylus, the inability to coincide the calibrated tip with the fiducial exactly, and tissue deformation due to physical contact. As

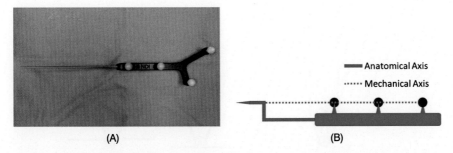

Figure 31.2 (A) Commercial optical-tracked surgical stylus with a blunt tip, and (B) in a typical pivot calibration approach, the tip location and the mechanical axis of the stylus is determined.

the magnitude of TRE is proportional to the magnitude of FLE (Eq. (31.2)), minimizing FLE throughout the digitization process is necessary to achieve accurate registration.

One way to perform stylus tip calibration is by pivoting the stylus tip about a stationary point. The motion of the pose sensor follows the surface of a sphere of which the stylus tip is at the center. Several algebraic and geometric solutions for pivot calibration are described in [62]. All stylus used in the clinical setting are equipped with a blunt tip (Fig. 31.2(A)). A sharp tip, i.e. needle like, has the potential for causing tissue damage during contact-based digitization and is rarely used even in the laboratory setting. Note that pivot calibration can only determine the tip location and the *mechanical axis* of the stylus (Fig. 31.2(B)). If the *anatomical axis* of the stylus does not align with its mechanical axis, the orientation of the anatomical axis can be calibrated using the template-based calibration (Sect. 31.5).

Relating to Eq. (31.2), tracking markers constitute registration fiducials and the stylus tip is the target. Hence there is a theoretical advantage to embed the sensor as close to the stylus tip (in the case of electromagnetic tracking) or designing a pose sensor configuration (in the case of optical tracking) that comprises of more than 3 retroreflective fiducial markers arranged noncollinearly. The use of blunt tip, however, introduces possible FLE during pivot calibration and digitization. The idealized tip location determined via pivot calibration often does not lie on the surface of the stylus tip, but rather is inside the physical construct of the stylus tip (Fig. 31.3). There is no guarantee that the ideal calibrated tip will be identical to the point of contact used for digitization. If the surgical scenario allows, one should employ a digitizing stylus with a spherical tip, with hemispherical divots of matching radius used as the contact fiducial. Pivot calibration of the spherical-tip stylus should also be performed about a stationary hemispherical divot.

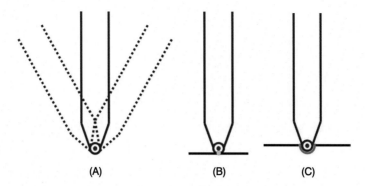

Figure 31.3 (A) Tip calibration using pivoting determines a calibration point that is inside the physical construct of the stylus tip (shown in red), (B) during digitization this produces fiducial localization error (FLE), (C) when situation allows, using a hemispherical divot with matching diameter minimizes FLE during digitization.

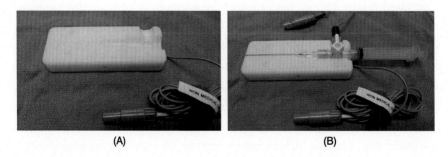

Figure 31.4 Spatial calibration of a hypodermic needle using a template: (A) a template is a tracked calibration jib with the negative imprint. The template itself is calibrated using the hemisphere divots, and (B) once mated, the spatial relation between the pose sensors of the needle and the template provides the needle calibration. Both the needle tip and the needle orientation can be calibrated using template calibration.

31.5. Template-based calibration

Spatial calibration of a surgical instrument with complex geometry can be achieved via a calibration jig, or template. A template is another tracked device with the negative imprint of the surgical instrument engraved. The geometrical relationship between the negative imprint to its own pose sensor is known by design or by another calibration step, and the manner of which the template is calibrated is a possible contributor to FLE.

Fig. 31.4 depicts an example of a calibration template for a hypodermic needle, where calibration of the needle tip location is not feasible due to its sharpness and the need for sterilization. By placing the tracked needle to mate with the tracked negative imprint, the geometrical relationship between these two tracked pose sensor provides the calibration matrix one seeks.

The calibration of the template to its pose sensor is often achieved using paired-point registration. In Fig. 31.4, a set of hemispherical divots were engraved throughout the needle calibration template and used as calibration fiducials. The number of divots and their spatial configuration should be optimized according to Eq. (31.2) as to (1) use as many divots as possible, (2) their spatial extent should be maximized, and (3) the negative imprint (i.e. the target) should be placed close to the geometrical centroid of the divots.

31.6. Ultrasound probe calibration

Ultrasound (US) is ubiquitous in modern health care environment, providing information support by visualizing anatomy beneath the organ surface. It enables noninvasive real-time visualization without using ionizing radiation and is relatively inexpensive. One way to extend the utility of US into interventional medicine is to augment the US transducer with a tracking system. Once tracked and calibrated, as an example, freehand 2D US image can be reconstructed to form a 3D US volume to provide better visualization and to serve as basis for volume-based registration with other imaging modalities.

Ultrasound calibration refers to the process to determine the geometrical relationship between the US image to its pose sensor (i.e. the transform denoted as $^{sensor}T_{image}$ in Fig. 31.5), and it remains as an area of active research. In two review papers [37,27], every aspect of US calibration was thoroughly discussed, including the design of calibration phantom, their advantages and disadvantages, effect of the speed-of-sound (SoS) of the ultrasound coupling medium, and method for accuracy validation. To achieve the desired US calibration, consideration must be given to the costs (materials and construction) and the computation efforts (data collection and image processing) required.

One difficulty in achieving accurate US calibration is FLE introduced by US physics, tracking uncertainty, inaccurate calibration tool calibration, and fiducial segmentation error. For example, the accuracy of point-based US calibration [13,39] depends on how well the point fiducial can be placed in the idealized US mid-plane, and how well the fiducial can be localized in the calibration tool and segmented from the US image [42,27]. These problems can be somewhat mitigated by the use of a *line fiducial* instead of point fiducial [10,29]. To obtain accurate calibration, it is necessary to scan the calibration phantom from a sufficiently diverse range of position and orientation, and its location spread throughout the B-mode image [42,37,27]. These recommendations are consistent with Eq. (31.2).

Clinical ultrasound scanners assume the average SoS in human tissue to be 1540 m/s. During probe calibration, if the ultrasound coupling medium does not exhibit appropriate SoS, image distortion will be produced [37]. For example, if a room-temperature

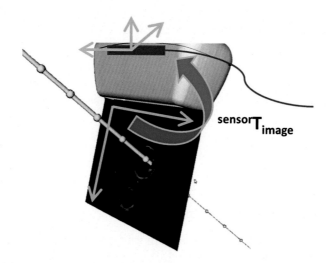

Figure 31.5 Ultrasound calibration determines the similarity transform, denoted as $^{sensor}T_{image}$, between the coordinate systems of the ultrasound image to its pose sensor. The similarity comprises of anisotropic scaling followed by rotation and translation.

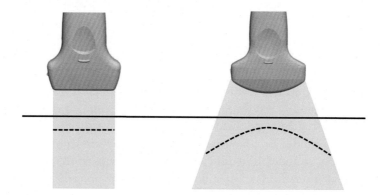

Figure 31.6 Image distortion (dotted lines) of imaging a plane in a pure water bath at room temperature. Because the speed-of-sound of the ultrasound medium is lower than what ultrasound machine expects, the line reflection will appear further away from the transducer. In the case of curvilinear transducer, the line reflection will also be curved.

pure water bath is used as the coupling medium (SoS $\approx$ 1485 m/s), then a straight line will appear either deeper (for linear probe), or deeper and curved (for curvilinear probe) in the ultrasound image (Fig. 31.6). These image distortions introduces calibration FLE. Additives such as glycerol [22] or alcohol [46,52] can be incorporated to room temperature water to increase SoS. Alternatively, the pure water bath can be heated up to approximately 50°C [53]. To prevent accidental damage to tissue *in situ*, however, mod-

(A)   (B)

Figure 31.7 Modern matrix-array based transducer are capable of acquiring single-plane, bi-plane, and real-time 3D ultrasound. Because these two mode of image acquisition shares a common coordinate system, calibration form bi-plane and real-time 3D ultrasound can be inferred from the calibration of the single-plane ultrasound.

ern ultrasound transducers have an electronic switch to prevent it from operating at high temperature.

Modern ultrasound transducers with 2D matrix array are capable of acquiring single-plane, bi-plane, and real-time 3D ultrasound (Fig. 31.7). Both plane- and point-fiducial techniques can be directly applied to the calibration of real-time 3D ultrasound. Segmenting calibration fiducial directly from the low-resolution 3D voxel introduces significant FLE. The neutral orientation of the single- and bi-plane ultrasound are aligned with the 3D coordinate system of the real-time ultrasound volume and share the same origin. Thus, one may achieve high-precision ultrasound calibration using high-resolution 2D ultrasound and to infer the calibration transform for real-time 3D, as shown in Fig. 31.7.

TRE estimation models can also be used to performed *guided* calibration. In calibration technique that employs paired-points or paired point–line registration, sequential imaging of calibration fiducial can be guided by TRE model by treating US pixel locations as targets. TRE estimation models can then be applied to suggest the location of subsequent fiducial placement such at estimated TRE can be decreased by the most amount throughout successive fiducial measurement. In this manner, accurate US calibration can be achieved by using minimal number of measurements [8].

31.7. Camera hand–eye calibration

Surgical cameras such as laparoscopes, endoscopes and pass-through head-mounted displays are prevalent in modern operating theater, used as a surrogate for direct vision. One way to extend the utility of these cameras is to augment them with a pose sensor, allowing advanced visualization techniques such as augmented or virtual reality environment to be implemented. Akin to ultrasound calibration (Sect. 31.6), the geometrical relationship between the optical axis of the camera lens must be related to its pose sensor via a calibration step.

Camera calibration refers to both the *intrinsic* and *extrinsic* calibrations. The intrinsic calibration determines the optical properties of the camera lens, including the focal point $((f_x, f_y))$, principal point $((c_x, c_y))$, and distortion coefficients [7]. Most of the techniques described in the medical imaging literature assumes the ideal pinhole camera geometry [23], with the intrinsic parameters of a camera represented as:

$$M = \begin{bmatrix} f_x & 0 & c_x \\ 0 & f_y & c_y \\ 0 & 0 & 1 \end{bmatrix}. \tag{31.3}$$

A point $Q = (X, Y, Z)^T$ in 3D space can be projected onto the image by:

$$q = MQ \tag{31.4}$$

where $q = (w, y, w)^T$. Given a pixel location, however, only the corresponding ray can be reconstructed by:

$$r = M^{-1}q \tag{31.5}$$

where $q = (x, y, 1)^T$ is the pixel location represented in the homogeneous coordinate system. Eqs. (31.3)–(31.5) together define a 3D optical axis, centered at the principal point, looking toward the focal point. The use of the pinhole camera with radial distortion model assumes the camera lens is radially symmetrical about its principal point. Among the camera intrinsic calibration techniques, the method proposed by Zhang remains most popular [64] due to its open-source implementation in popular software packages such as the OpenCV library[2] and Matlab.[3]

Hand–eye calibration thus determines the rigid geometrical relationship between the optical axis of the camera lens to its pose sensor (Fig. 31.8). Most of the techniques described in the medical imaging literature have roots from the robotic literature [47], where the camera view (i.e. the eye) must be linked with the kinematics of the robotic systems (i.e. the hand). These approaches rely on imaging salient features of a stationary object from different poses and then solving for rotation and translation either separately [54], jointly [11], or iteratively [14,24]. The quality of the hand–eye calibration result is highly dependent upon the data used for computing the unknown transformation; readers are referred to Schmidt and Niemann for a mathematical overview of hand–eye calibration and data selection approaches [44].

---

[2] https://opencv.org.
[3] MATLAB® is a trademark of The MathWorks. https://www.mathworks.com/products/matlab.html.

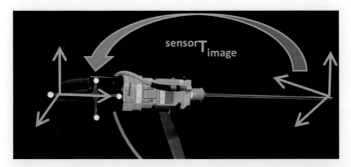

Figure 31.8 Hand–eye calibration determines the rigid-body (rotation followed by translation) transform, denoted as $^{sensor}T_{image}$, between the optical axis of the camera lens to its pose sensor.

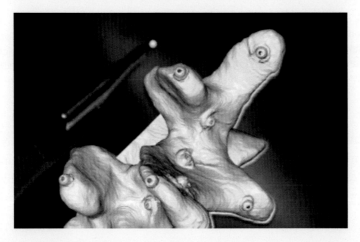

Figure 31.9 An Augmented Reality environment depicting the virtual representation of the spine and stylus tip projected onto an endoscopic video. Surface of a vertebra phantom was segmented from CT and projected onto the endoscopic video. The location of a calibrated and tracked stylus tip was also depicted by a virtual sphere.

Once calibrated, surgical guidance is performed by projecting preoperative imagery data or virtual representation of tracked surgical instruments to the surgical video via Eq. (31.4) (Fig. 31.9). The accurate image overlay depends on camera calibrations (both intrinsic and hand–eye) and tracking. Hand–eye calibration for rigid laparoscope is particular challenging [51] as the pose sensor are typically placed on the distal end of the scope and with the camera on the proximal end, thus any error tracking is amplified through the lever effect. Performing camera calibration in the surgical environment is limited by factors such as the need to maintain sterility without disrupting the surgical workflow.

In robotic-assisted minimally invasive surgery, the end effector of the robot may be used as a calibration fiducial, thus eliminating the need for an additional calibration ap-

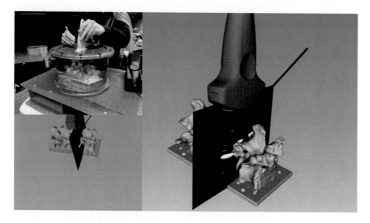

Figure 31.10 A mixed reality environment for ultrasound-guided needle intervention. (top) A user performing needle insertion into a spine phantom using HTC VIVE head-mounted display, (left) the mixed realty view as seen by the user through HMD, and (right) Alternative view depicting tracked needle, ultrasound image, and patient anatomy. The hyperechoic reflection of the needle and spine in ultrasound serve as visual indication to the accuracy of the ultrasound-guided needle navigation system.

paratus [40]. Accuracy of this type of approach is limited by the accurate measurement of the kinematics of the robot. Using Procrustean point–line registration, hand–eye calibration [38] can be formulated in the exact same manner as ultrasound calibration [8], and guided by a TRE estimation model to minimize the number of measurement required to achieve accurate calibration [9].

31.8. Conclusion and resources

Surgical navigation system operates on the principle of tracking surgical instruments and patient anatomy in a common coordinate system. This is accomplished through tool tracking and calibration, and patient registration. Once properly tracked, calibrated, and registered, advanced mixed reality environment can be implemented for the safe guidance of surgical instruments within patient anatomy (Fig. 31.10).

Commercial optical and electromagnetic spatial measurement devices provide highly accurate tracking of their own pose sensors. The manner of how these pose sensors are integrated and calibrated into the surgical instruments influences the tracking accuracy. In general, optical tracking system work on the principal of triangulation and can be formulated as point-based Orthogonal Procrustes Analysis [21]. This admits the use of the target registration error estimation models [35,12] to optimize optical pose sensor geometry and its placement within the surgical instrument. Issues such as line-of-sight, pose sensor size and weight must be considered for clinical deployment. The design of optical pose sensor must also follow vendor-specific criteria; an open-source library for optical pose sensor is publicly available [6].

Electromagnetic based tracking works on the principle of sensing the strength and orientation of an artificially generated magnetic field. It, too, offers submillimeter accuracy but such an accuracy may be compromised by the presence of ferromagnetic materials inside the surgical field. Due to the size of electromagnetic pose sensors, they are suitable for tracking of small (e.g. needle) or flexible (e.g. endoscopic ultrasound) surgical instruments. Electromagnetic pose sensors are also tethered; issues including sterilization and cable management must be considered.

Because these tracking systems can only track their pose sensors directly, a spatial calibration must be performed to align the geometry of the tracked surgical instrument to its pose sensor. Registration and calibration of many surgical instruments can be formulated as Orthogonal Procrustes Analysis, admitting the use of TRE estimation models to optimize calibration measurements [8,9]. TRE estimation models are available for paired points [35,12], paired point–line [8], and paired point–plane registration problems [33].

Vendor specific application programming interface (API) are needed to obtain pose information from a specific tracker. Open-source libraries such as the Image-Guided Surgery Toolkit [20] and the Plus Toolkit [31] provide a cross-platform and cross-vendor API to communicate with tracking systems.

References

[1] Essam Alshail, James T. Rutka, James M. Drake, Harold J. Hoffman, Robin Humphreys, John Phillips, Michael Cusimano, Vito Forte, Blake Papsin, Stephanie Holowka, Utility of frameless stereotaxy in the resection of skull base and basal cerebral lesions in children, Skull Base Surgery 8 (1) (1998) 29–38.

[2] K.S. Arun, T.S. Huang, S.D. Blostein, Least-squares fitting of two 3-D point sets, IEEE Transactions on Pattern Analysis and Machine Intelligence PAMI-9 (5) (1987) 698–700.

[3] Paul J. Besl, Neil D. McKay, A method for registration of 3-D shapes, IEEE Transactions on Pattern Analysis and Machine Intelligence 14 (2) (1992) 239–256.

[4] Wolfgang Birkfellner, Johann Hummel, Emmanuel Wilson, Kevin Cleary, Tracking devices, in: Terry M. Peters, Kevin Cleary (Eds.), Image-Guided Interventions, 2008, pp. 23–44, Chap. 2.

[5] Jesus Briales, Javier Gonzalez-Jimenez, Convex global 3D registration with lagrangian duality, in: The IEEE Conference on Computer Vision and Pattern Recognition (CVPR), 2017.

[6] Alisa Brown, Ali Uneri, Tharindu De Silva, Amir Manbachi, Jeffery H. Siewerdsen, Design and validation of an open-source library of dynamic reference frames for research and education in optical tracking, Journal of Medical Imaging 5 (2) (2018) 021215.

[7] Duane C. Brown, Decentering distortion of lenses, Photogrammetric Engineering 32 (3) (1966) 444–462.

[8] Elvis C.S. Chen, Terry M. Peters, Burton Ma, Guided ultrasound calibration: where, how, and how many calibration fiducials, International Journal of Computer Assisted Radiology and Surgery 11 (6) (2016) 889–898.

[9] Elvis C.S. Chen, Isabella Morgan, Uditha L. Jayarathne, Burton Ma, Terry M. Peters, Hand–eye calibration using a target registration error model, Healthcare Technology Letters 4 (5) (2017) 157–162.

[10] Roch M. Comeau, Aaron Fenster, Terence M. Peters, Integrated MR and ultrasound imaging for improved image guidance in neurosurgery, in: Kenneth M. Hanson (Ed.), Medical Imaging 1998: Image Processing, in: Proc. SPIE, vol. 3338, 1998, pp. 747–754.

[11] Konstantinos Daniilidis, Hand–eye calibration using dual quaternions, The International Journal of Robotics Research 18 (3) (1999) 286–298.

[12] Andrei Danilchenko, J. Michael Fitzpatrick, General approach to first-order error prediction in rigid point registration, IEEE Transactions on Medical Imaging 30 (3) (2011) 679–693.

[13] Paul R. Detmer, Gerard Bashein, Timothy Hodges, Kirk W. Beach, Eric P. Filer, David H. Burns, D. Eugene Strandness, 3D ultrasonic image feature localization based on magnetic scanhead tracking: in vitro calibration and validation, Ultrasound in Medicine & Biology 20 (9) (1994) 923–936.

[14] F. Dornaika, R. Horaud, Simultaneous robot–world and hand–eye calibration, IEEE Transactions on Robotics and Automation 14 (4) (1998) 617–622.

[15] P.V. Dyer, N. Patel, G.M. Pell, B. Cummins, D.R. Sandeman, The ISG viewing wand: an application to atlanto-axial cervical surgery using the le fort I maxillary osteotomy, British Journal of Oral and Maxillofacial Surgery 33 (6) (1995) 370–374.

[16] J. MichaelFitzpatrick, Jay B. West, Calvin R. Maurer, Predicting error in rigid-body point-based registration, IEEE Transactions on Medical Imaging 17 (5) (1998) 694–702.

[17] Donald D. Frantz, Andrew D. Wiles, S.E. Leis, S.R. Kirsch, Accuracy assessment protocols for electromagnetic tracking systems, Physics in Medicine and Biology 48 (14) (2003) 2241–2251.

[18] Alfred M. Franz, Tamas Haidegger, Wolfgang Birkfellner, Kevin Cleary, Terry M. Peters, Lena Maier-Hein, Electromagnetic tracking in medicine – a review of technology, validation, and applications, IEEE Transactions on Medical Imaging 33 (8) (2014) 1702–1725.

[19] S. Garrido-Jurado, R. Munoz-Salinas, F.J. Madrid-Cuevas, M.J. Marín-Jiménez, Automatic generation and detection of highly reliable fiducial markers under occlusion, Pattern Recognition 47 (6) (2014) 2280–2292.

[20] Kevin Gary, Luis Ibanez, Stephen Aylward, David Gobbi, M. Brian Blake, Kevin Cleary, IGSTK: an open source software toolkit for image-guided surgery, Computer 39 (4) (2006) 46–53.

[21] John C. Gower, Garmt B. Dijksterhuis, Procrustes Problems, Oxford Statistical Science Series, vol. 30, Oxford University Press, 2004.

[22] H. Samavat, J.A. Evans, An ideal blood mimicking fluid for Doppler ultrasound phantoms, Journal of Medical Physics 31 (4) (2006) 275–278.

[23] Richard Hartley, Andrew Zisserman, Multiple View Geometry in Computer Vision, 2nd ed., Cambridge University Press, Cambridge, 2004.

[24] J. Heller, M. Havlena, T. Pajdla, A branch-and-bound algorithm for globally optimal hand–eye calibration, in: 2012 IEEE Conference on Computer Vision and Pattern Recognition, 2012, pp. 1608–1615.

[25] Berthold K.P. Horn, Closed-form solution of absolute orientation using unit quaternions, Journal of the Optical Society of America A 4 (4) (1987) 629–642.

[26] Victor Horsley, R.H. Clarke, The structure and functions of the cerebellum examined by a new method, Brain 31 (1) (1908) 45–124.

[27] Po-Wei Hsu, Richard W. Prager, Andrew H. Gee, Graham M. Treece, Freehand 3D ultrasound calibration: a review, in: Christoph W. Sensen, Benedikt Hallgrímsson (Eds.), Advanced Imaging in Biology and Medicine: Technology, Software Environments, Applications, Springer Berlin Heidelberg, 2009, pp. 47–84.

[28] Johann B. Hummel, Michael R. Bax, Michael L. Figl, Yan Kang, Calvin R. Maurer Jr., Wolfgang W. Birkfellner, Helmar Bergmann, Ramin Shahidi, Design and application of an assessment protocol for electromagnetic tracking systems, Medical Physics 32 (7) (2005) 2371–2379.

[29] Ali Khamene, Frank Sauer, A novel phantom-less spatial and temporal ultrasound calibration method, in: James S. Duncan, Guido Gerig (Eds.), Medical Image Computing and Computer-Assisted Intervention – MICCAI 2005, Springer Berlin Heidelberg, 2005, pp. 65–72.

[30] Tapani Koivukangas, Jani P.A. Katisko, John P. Koivukangas, Technical accuracy of optical and the electromagnetic tracking systems, SpringerPlus 2 (1) (2013) 1–7.

[31] Andras Lasso, Tamas Heffter, Adam Rankin, Csaba Pinter, Tamas Ungi, Gabor Fichtinger, PLUS: open-source toolkit for ultrasound-guided intervention systems, IEEE Transactions on Biomedical Engineering 61 (10) (2014) 2527–2537.

[32] Elodie Lugez, Hossein Sadjadi, David R. Pichora, Randy E. Ellis, Selim G. Akl, Gabor Fichtinger, Electromagnetic tracking in surgical and interventional environments: usability study, International Journal of Computer Assisted Radiology and Surgery 10 (3) (2015) 253–362.

[33] Burton Ma, Randy E. Ellis, Analytic expressions for fiducial and surface target registration error, in: Rasmus Larsen, Mads Nielsen, Jon Sporring (Eds.), Medical Image Computing and Computer-Assisted Intervention – MICCAI 2006, Springer Berlin Heidelberg, 2006, pp. 637–644.

[34] Burton Ma, Terry M. Peters, Elvis C.S. Chen, Estimation of line-based target registration error, in: Robert J. Webster, Ziv R. Yaniv (Eds.), Medical Imaging 2016: Image-Guided Procedures, Robotic Interventions, and Modeling, in: Proc. SPIE, vol. 9786, 2016.

[35] Burton Ma, Mehdi H. Moghari, Randy E. Ellis, Purang Abolmaesumi, Estimation of optimal fiducial target registration error in the presence of heteroscedastic noise, IEEE Transactions on Medical Imaging 29 (3) (2010) 708–723.

[36] Bogdan C. Matei, Peter Meer, A general method for errors-in-variables problems in computer vision, in: Proceedings IEEE Conference on Computer Vision and Pattern Recognition. CVPR 2000 (Cat. No. PR00662), vol. 2, 2000, pp. 18–25.

[37] Laurence Mercier, Thomas Langø, Frank Lindseth, D. Louis Collins, A review of calibration techniques for freehand 3-D ultrasound systems, Ultrasound in Medicine & Biology 31 (4) (2005) 449–471.

[38] Isabella Morgan, Uditha L. Jayarathne, Adam Rankin, Terry M. Peters, Elvis C.S. Chen, Hand–eye calibration for surgical cameras: a procrustean perspective-n-point solution, International Journal of Computer Assisted Radiology and Surgery 12 (7) (2017) 1141–1149.

[39] Diane M. Muratore, Robert L. Galloway Jr., Beam calibration without a phantom for creating a 3-D freehand ultrasound system, Ultrasound in Medicine & Biology 27 (11) (2001) 1557–1566.

[40] K. Pachtrachai, M. Allan, V. Pawar, S. Hailes, D. Stoyanov, Hand–eye calibration for robotic assisted minimally invasive surgery without a calibration object, in: 2016 IEEE/RSJ International Conference on Intelligent Robots and Systems (IROS), 2016, pp. 2485–2491.

[41] Claude Picard, Andre Olivier, Gilles Bertrand, The first human stereotaxic apparatus. The contribution of Aubrey Mussen to the field of stereotaxis, Journal of Neurosurgery 59 (4) (1983) 673–676.

[42] R.W. Prager, R.N. Rohling, A.H. Gee, L. Berman, Rapid calibration for 3-D freehand ultrasound, Ultrasound in Medicine & Biology 24 (6) (1998) 855–869.

[43] Hans F. Reinhardt, Gerhard A. Horstmann, Otmar Gratzl, Sonic stereometry in microsurgical procedures for deep-seated brain tumors and vascular malformations, Neurosurgery 32 (1) (1993) 51–57.

[44] Jochen Schmidt, Heinrich Niemann, Data selection for hand–eye calibration: a vector quantization approach, The International Journal of Robotics Research 27 (9) (2008) 1027–1053.

[45] A. Seginer, Rigid-body point-based registration: the distribution of the target registration error when the fiducial registration errors are given, Medical Image Analysis 15 (4) (2011) 397–413.

[46] Chandra M. Sehgal, Burdett R. Porter, James F. Greenleaf, Ultrasonic nonlinear parameters and sound speed of alcohol–water mixtures, The Journal of the Acoustical Society of America 79 (2) (1986) 566–570.

[47] Mili Shah, Roger D. Eastman, Tsai Hong, An overview of robot–sensor calibration methods for evaluation of perception systems, in: Proceedings of the Workshop on Performance Metrics for Intelligent Systems (PerMIS '12), ACM, 2012, pp. 15–20.

[48] Reuben R. Shamir, Leo Joskowicz, Yigal Shoshan, Fiducial optimization for minimal target registration error in image-guided neurosurgery, IEEE Transactions on Medical Imaging 31 (3) (2012) 725–737.

[49] Tobias Sielhorst, Martin Bauer, Oliver Wenisch, Gudrun Klinker, Nassir Navab, Online estimation of the target registration error for n-ocular optical tracking systems, in: Nicholas Ayache, Sébastien Ourselin, Anthony Maeder (Eds.), Medical Image Computing and Computer-Assisted Intervention – MICCAI 2007, Springer Berlin Heidelberg, 2007, pp. 652–659.

[50] J.B. Stiehl, J. Bach, D.A. Heck, Validation and metrology in CAOS, in: James B. Stiehl, Werner H. Konermann, Rolf G. Haaker, Anthony M. DiGioia (Eds.), Navigation and MIS in Orthopedic Surgery, Springer Berlin Heidelberg, 2007, pp. 68–78, Chap. 9.

[51] Stephen Thompson, Danail Stoyanov, Crispin Schneider, Kurinchi Gurusamy, Sébastien Ourselin, Brian Davidson, David Hawkes, Matthew J. Clarkson, Hand–eye calibration for rigid laparoscopes using an invariant point, International Journal of Computer Assisted Radiology and Surgery 11 (6) (2016) 1071–1080.

[52] Audrey Thouvenot, Tamie Poepping, Terry M. Peters, Elvis C.S. Chen, Characterization of various tissue mimicking materials for medical ultrasound imaging, in: Medical Imaging 2016: Physics of Medical Imaging, in: Proc. SPIE, vol. 9783, 2016.

[53] Graham M. Treece, Andrew H. Gee, Richard W. Prager, Charlotte J.C. Cash, Laurence H. Berman, High-definition freehand 3-D ultrasound, Ultrasound in Medicine & Biology 29 (4) (2003) 529–546.

[54] R.Y. Tsai, R.K. Lenz, A new technique for fully autonomous and efficient 3D robotics hand/eye calibration, IEEE Transactions on Robotics and Automation 5 (3) (1989) 345–358.

[55] Jay B. West, Calvin R. Maurer Jr., Designing optically tracked instruments for image-guided surgery, IEEE Transactions on Medical Imaging 23 (5) (2004) 533–545.

[56] Jay B. West, J. Michael Fitzpatrick, Steven A. Toms, Calvin R. Maurer Jr., Robert J. Maciunas, Fiducial point placement and the accuracy of point-based, rigid body registration, Neurosurgery 48 (4) (2001) 810–6; discussion 816-7.

[57] Andrew D. Wiles, Terry M. Peters, Improved statistical TRE model when using a reference frame, in: Nicholas Ayache, Sébastien Ourselin, Anthony Maeder (Eds.), Medical Image Computing and Computer-Assisted Intervention – MICCAI 2007, Springer Berlin Heidelberg, 2007, pp. 442–449.

[58] Andrew D. Wiles, Terry M. Peters, Real-time estimation of FLE statistics for 3-D tracking with point-based registration, IEEE Transactions on Medical Imaging 28 (9) (2009) 1384–1398.

[59] Andrew D. Wiles, David G. Thompson, Donald D. Frantz, Accuracy assessment and interpretation for optical tracking systems, in: Robert L. Galloway Jr. (Ed.), Medical Imaging 2004: Visualization, Image-Guided Procedures, and Display, in: Proc. SPIE, vol. 5367, 2004, p. 421.

[60] Andrew D. Wiles, Alexander Likholyot, Donald D. Frantz, Terry M. Peters, A statistical model for point-based target registration error with anisotropic fiducial localizer error, IEEE Transactions on Medical Imaging 27 (3) (2008) 378–390.

[61] Emmanuel Wilson, Ziv Yaniv, Hui Zhang, Christopher Nafis, Eric Shen, Guy Shechter, Andrew D. Wiles, Terry M. Peters, David Lindisch, Kevin Cleary, A hardware and software protocol for the evaluation of electromagnetic tracker accuracy in the clinical environment: a multi-center study, in: Proc. SPIE, vol. 6509, 2007.

[62] Ziv Yaniv, Which pivot calibration?, in: Robert J. Webster, Ziv R. Yaniv (Eds.), Medical Imaging 2015: Image-Guided Procedures, Robotic Interventions, and Modeling, in: Proc. SPIE, vol. 9415, 2015, p. 941527.

[63] Ziv Yaniv, Emmanuel Wilson, David Lindisch, Kevin Cleary, Electromagnetic tracking in the clinical environment, Medical Physics 36 (3) (2009) 876–892.

[64] Z. Zhang, A flexible new technique for camera calibration, IEEE Transactions on Pattern Analysis and Machine Intelligence 22 (11) (2000) 1330–1334.

CHAPTER 32

Image-based surgery planning

Caroline Essert[a], Leo Joskowicz[b]
[a]ICube / Université de Strasbourg, Illkirch, France
[b]The Hebrew University of Jerusalem, Jerusalem, Israel

Contents

32.1. Background and motivation	795
32.2. General concepts	796
32.3. Treatment planning for bone fracture in orthopaedic surgery	798
32.3.1 Background	798
32.3.2 System overview	799
32.3.3 Planning workflow	799
32.3.4 Planning system	800
32.3.5 Evaluation and validation	803
32.3.6 Perspectives	804
32.4. Treatment planning for keyhole neurosurgery and percutaneous ablation	804
32.4.1 Background	804
32.4.2 Placement constraints	806
32.4.3 Constraint solving	807
32.4.4 Evaluation and validation	808
32.4.5 Perspectives	811
32.5. Future challenges	811
References	813

32.1. Background and motivation

The planning of surgeries based on preoperative images has a long history, starting with the first film X-ray images at the beginning of the 20th century. With the proliferation of clinical imaging modalities in the recent past, including X-rays, ultrasound (US), computed tomography (CT), and magnetic resonance imaging (MRI), it is now possible to assess the patient condition, make a diagnosis, explore the treatment options, and plan the surgery ahead of time. Image-based surgery planning allows the surgeon to consider a variety of approaches, evaluate their feasibility, foresee possible complications, and optimize the treatment, so as to reduce the risk of injury and improve the surgical outcome. The preoperative images allow the surgeon to visualize and locate the surgical access area, to plan the position of surgical instruments and implants with respect to the patient anatomical structures, and to assess the safety of their location and of the surgery execution. Preoperative images allow building patient-specific anatomy and pathology models which can then be used for advanced planning based on optimization and simulation. Preoperative planning based on these models allows the customization of the surgery to the specific characteristics of the patient. The rise of minimally invasive surgery, and more recently of image-based intraoperative navigation and medical robotics, has further increased the need for image-based surgery planning.

The types of surgeries for which image-based planning is used spans a very wide range across surgical procedures and specialties, e.g.,orthopaedic surgery, neurosurgery, abdominal surgery, and urology, to name only a few. By their very nature, each type of surgical procedure has its own characteristics, constraints, and requirements. For example, in orthopaedic surgery, preoperative planning systems are used for the selection and sizing of joint replacement implants and fracture fixation hardware and for their optimal positioning based on the patient bone geometry and bone quality derived from the patient preoperative CT scan. Advanced biomechanical analysis includes patient-specific kinematic and dynamic simulations of knee and hip joints, bone loading analysis, and fracture risk analysis. In stereotactic neurosurgery, the planning consists of determining an appropriate access location on the patient skull and defining a safe insertion trajectory to reach a brain tumor, perform a biopsy, and deliver therapy as needed.

Over the past 30 years, many preoperative planning systems have been developed, and some of them are in routine clinical use. In fact, some surgeries, e.g., radiation surgery and stereotactic neurosurgery, cannot be performed without accurate image-based preoperative planning. More broadly, the availability of Computer Assisted Surgery (CAS) technology, of which image-based preoperative planning is a key component, allows clinicians to explore more treatment options and surgical scenarios and execute them more precisely and reliably.

A detailed survey of image-based surgery planning is outside the scope of this chapter. In the following, we will briefly outline the general concept of image-guided surgical planning and present two applications: (1) reduction and fixation planning for orthopaedic bone fracture surgery, and (2) trajectory planning for keyhole neurosurgery and percutaneous ablations. We chose to include these case studies because they cover a variety of anatomies, organs, and planning. In particular, they include three types of surgery planning (neurosurgery, orthopaedic surgery and abdominal surgery) of three anatomies (brain, liver and kidneys, bones) with both hard and soft tissue, and involve both linear trajectories of simple and complex surgical instruments (needles) and implants (fracture fixation plate). We will then conclude with a brief discussion on trends and perspectives in image-guided surgery planning.

32.2. General concepts

The main components of preoperative planning systems are visualization, modeling, analysis, and plan generation. Visualization consists of showing the original images, structures of interest, implants and/or surgical tools in a way that is intuitive and useful for the clinician. Modeling consists of creating mathematical representations of the structures of interest, the surgical tasks and their constraints, and the physiological phenomena that are taken into account for the planning. Analysis consists of exploring the solution space of the planning problem by manual exploration, simulation, and/or optimization. Plan generation consists of selecting the solution that is most appropriate for the intervention based on the results of the visualization and the analysis.

The major types of surgical planning tasks are:

- **Surgical target identification** – determining the surgical target and its location in the preoperative patient images and identifying the relevant surrounding structures.
- **Surgical access planning** – planning the surgical access point/location and path to the predefined target structure that causes minimal or no damage to the relevant surrounding structures.
- **Surgical tools and implant positioning** – determining the position of surgical tools and probes for the delivery of treatment and/or the location of implants.
- **Assessment of the selected plan** – predicting and evaluating the expected effect of a treatment, e.g., radiotherapy, cryoablation, brachytherapy, the placement of a stent, a brain stimulation electrode, or an orthopaedic implant.

Advanced image-based planning also includes: (1) the design of patient-specific surgical aids and implants, such as 3D printed custom surgical guides and jigs, (2) positioning and plan design for intraoperative navigation and surgical robots, and (3) surgical workflow planning and optimization. We will not discuss these further in this chapter.

The main technical elements of image-based preoperative planning are:

- **Pre-treatment image processing** – image enhancement, region of interest selection, registration between multiple scans (when available), volumetric visualization of images.
- **Segmentation and model construction** – segmentation of the structures of interest, geometric modeling of these structures, biomechanical modeling, physiological modeling, and/or treatment delivery modeling for simulation.
- **Definition of task-specific goals and constraints** – when applicable, mathematical formulation of the task goals and constraints as a multiobjective constrained optimization problem.
- **Visual exploration of the anatomy** – interactive visualization of the anatomy of the patient in the context of the preoperative images.
- **Plan elaboration** – manual plan elaboration based on visualization of the anatomy and analysis of the constraints using a trial and error process, or automatic plan computation by simulation or by optimization of the defined multiobjective constrained optimization problem.

The advantages of image-based preoperative planning include the ability to explore treatment alternatives, e.g., various access points, surgical tools access points, paths, locations, and the selection of implants. It also allows increasing the precision of the surgery and its robustness, as well as reducing its risks. In difficult cases, image-based preoperative planning helps to find a feasible strategy, and allows the access to surgery for the patient.

In the operating theater, the preoperative plan is imported and implemented. The implementation can be qualitative, i.e., by serving as a visual guide to the surgeon, or quantitative, following the registration of the preoperative plan to the intraoperative situation. The plan can then be used for visual guidance, for image-based navigation, or for robotics-based assistance. In some cases, the plan may be modified intraoperatively based on new images acquired in the operating room, minimally invasive surgery, laparoscopic and endoscopic surgery for the purpose of observation, biopsy, brachytherapy, treatment delivery.

32.3. Treatment planning for bone fracture in orthopaedic surgery[1]

32.3.1 Background

Computer-based treatment planning for orthopaedic surgery, also termed Computer Aided Orthopaedic Surgery (CAOS) dates back to the early 1990s [1]. It is, together with neurosurgery, the first clinical specialty for which treatment planning, image guided navigation, and robotic systems were developed. CAOS planning methods and systems have been developed for most of the main surgery procedures, e.g., knee and hip joint replacement, cruciate ligament surgery, spine surgery, osteotomy, bone tumor surgery, and trauma surgery, among others. Commercial systems for some of these procedures have been in clinical use for over a decade. FRACAS, the first system for computer integrated orthopedic surgery system for closed femoral medullary nailing fixation, dates back to the 1990s [2].

The treatment for bone fractures is a routine procedure in orthopedic trauma surgery. Bone fractures can be intra/extraarticular, on load-bearing bones, and range from a simple, nondisplaced fissure of a single bone to complex, multifragment, comminuted, dislocated fractures across several bones. The main goal of orthopedic trauma surgery is to restore the anatomy of the bone fragments and their function in support of the bone healing process. The two main steps of the surgery are fracture reduction, to bring the bone fragments to their original anatomical locations, and fracture fixation to keep the bone fragments in place with fixation hardware including screws, nails, and plates. Surgery planning consists of determining the surgical approach, the bone fracture reduction, and the type, number, and locations of the fixation hardware [3].

For simple fractures, the planning is performed on X-ray images of the fracture site with software packages that support the overlay of translucent 2D digital templates of

---

[1] This section is based on the paper "Haptic computer-assisted patient specific preoperative planning for orthopaedic fracture surgery", I. Kovler, L. Joskowicz, A. Kronman, Y. Weill, J. Salavarrieta, International Journal of Computer-Aided Radiology and Surgery 10 (10) (2015) 1535–1546.

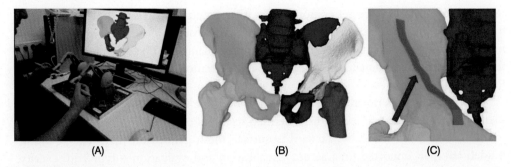

Figure 32.1 (A) Two-hand haptic system and screen view of (B) a 3D model of a pelvic fracture, (C) a custom fixation plate.

the fixation hardware on the digital X-ray images. For more complex cases, e.g., pelvic bone fractures and multifragment femoral neck/distal radius fractures, planning is performed on CT scans with 3D bone fragment models [3]. These fracture cases have a higher incidence of complications, including bone and/or fixation hardware misplacement and inaccurate fracture reduction resulting from bones fragment misalignment. Complications result in reduced functionality, higher risk of recurrent fractures, fracture reduction failure, and fracture osteosynthesis failure, and require revision surgery in 10–15% of all cases [4]. Various preoperative planning systems for fracture surgery based on 3D bone and implant models from CT scans are reported in the literature [5–10]. They include systems for maxillofacial surgery, hip fracture surgery simulation, proximal humerus fractures, and pelvic and acetabular fractures surgery.

The main drawbacks of these systems are that they do not support two-hand manipulation, that they do not account for ligaments, and that the custom hardware creation is not automated. Since bone fracture reduction is a time-consuming and challenging aspect of the planning, various methods have been proposed for this task [11–19].

32.3.2 System overview

We have developed a 3D two-hand haptic-based system that provides the surgeon with an interactive, intuitive, and comprehensive planning tool that includes 3D stereoscopic visualization and supports bone fragments model creation, manipulation, fracture reduction and fixation, and interactive custom fixation plate creation to fit the bone morphology (Fig. 32.1). We describe next the planning workflow, system architecture, and the fracture reduction method based on [20,21].

32.3.3 Planning workflow

The inputs to the planning system are a CT scan of the fracture site and geometric models of the standard fixation hardware, e.g., screws and plates. The planning proceeds in four steps: (1) automatic generation of the 3D geometric models of the relevant bone fragments selected on the CT scan slices, (2) fracture visualization and exploration, (3) fracture reduction planning, and (4) fracture fixation planning. The outputs are the bone fracture models, the standard and custom fracture fixation hardware models, and their locations.

The first step is performed by segmenting the bone fragments using the graph–cut method whose inputs are several user-defined scribbles on the fragments of interest on several CT slices followed by standard isosurface mesh generation [22]. The resulting models are then imported for fracture visualization and evaluation – type and severity of the fracture based on established classification schemes. The surgeon then manipulates the bone fragments to align them to their estimated original locations to restore their function. The fracture reduction can be manual, semiautomatic, or automatic (see below). Having obtained a virtual reduction of the fracture, the surgeon proceeds to plan its fixation with screws, nails, and/or reduction of the plates. The plan includes the screws – their lengths, diameters, locations, and number – and the custom plates. The surgeon can produce more than one fixation plan, and perform further analysis and comparison with finite-element methods [23]. The preoperative plan is then exported for use during the surgery.

32.3.4 Planning system

Fig. 32.2 shows the system architecture. It consists of six user interaction devices – a computer screen, a pair of glasses for stereoscopic viewing, a keyboard, a computer mouse, and two PHANTOM Omni haptic devices (SensAble Technologies Inc., USA), each with a hand-held 5 degree of freedom stylus that allow the user to touch and manipulate virtual objects. The haptic device has translational force feedback of 0.8–3.3 N and a spatial resolution of 0.05 mm. These values are the translational forces that can be generated by the PHANTOM Omni device according to the manufacturer's specifications. We use the entire range to stiffen the resistance as the interpenetration between surfaces increases.

The software modules of the system are as follows:

1. *Objects Manager* manages five types of objects from the database: (1) bone/bone fragments – surface meshes, centers of mass, locations, CT voxels; (2) screws – cylinders defined by their radius, length, axis origin, and axis orientation; (3) fixation plates – surface meshes; (4) ligaments – 1D springs defined by their start/end points; and (5) virtual pivot points – spheres defined by their origin and radius. The module manages individual objects and groups of objects.

2. *Physics Engine* performs real-time dynamic rigid and flexible body simulation. It simulates physical behavior and interaction between objects, prevents objects interpenetration, and provides the data for a realistic tactile experience of object grasping and objects contacts. The module uses the Bullet Physics Library physics engine [24].

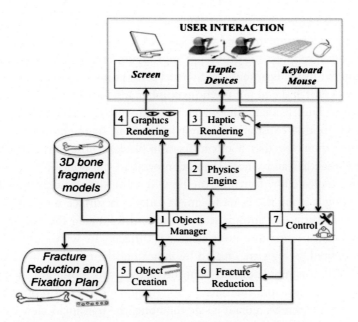

Figure 32.2 Block diagram of the planning system (reproduced with permission).

3. *Haptic Rendering* controls the manipulation of grasped objects and produces the forces that are acted upon by the haptic device for tactile perception. It ensures real-time and stable user interaction with the virtual environment and generates the coupling forces and torques for the Physics Engine and for the haptic devices. The interaction between the haptic device and an object is modeled with a proxy [25], which is a point that follows the position of the stylus. In free space, the locations of the proxy and of the stylus pointer are identical. When a contact with an object occurs, the proxy remains outside the object, but the stylus pointer penetrates slightly the object, exerting a reaction force akin to a virtual spring damper coupling. To facilitate grasping, a gravity well attracts the stylus pointer to the object surface with force whose strength is proportional to the stylus point distance to the object surface. The module is implemented with The Haptic Library and Haptic Device Application Program Interfaces [26].

4. *Graphics Rendering* generates the views of the virtual environment. The camera viewpoint is interactively changed by the user with a virtual trackball that is also used for the interactive spatial rotation of the models. Four viewing modes – monoscopic solid, monoscopic translucid, stereoscopic, and X-ray view – are available. The monoscopic solid mode is used for general scene viewing and for fracture exploration. The monoscopic translucid mode is a see through of the bones used for screws insertion and positioning inside the bone. The stereoscopic mode provides depth perception for accurate positioning during fracture reduction. The X-ray mode shows simulated X-ray

images of the bone fragments and their contours as they may appear in the X-ray fluoroscope. The module is implemented with the GLUT and OpenGL libraries [27].

5. *Object Creation* supports the grouping/ungrouping of bone fragments and the creation of fixation hardware, ligaments, and virtual pivot points. Ligaments are modeled as 1D springs with a start and end point whose number and locations are determined from anatomical atlases. They facilitate the interactive virtual fracture reduction by providing realistic anatomic motion constraints that restrict the bone fragments motions during reduction and hold them together. Custom fixation plates, whose purpose is to hold the bone fragments together and whose shape conforms to the bone surface morphology (Fig. 32.1(C)), are created by touching the bone fracture surface with the virtual stylus pointer and sliding it along the bone fragment surface. A surface mesh in contact with the bone fragment surface is automatically generated following the pointer trajectory. The plate can span one or more bone fragment surfaces. Its width and thickness can be adjusted as desired. Screws are created by indicating their start and end points with the virtual tip of the manipulator and then interactively positioning it in their desired location. During the insertion, the outside bone fragment surfaces resistance is turned off. To ensure that the screws remain inside the bone, the translucid view mode and/or turns on/off the internal resistance of the bone fragment surfaces to prevent the screws from protruding outside the bone.

6. *Fracture Reduction* computes the transformation between two bone fragments to reduce the fracture. It also supports the interactive annotation of fracture surface points for semiautomatic reduction. There are three fracture reduction modes:

(a) Manual fracture reduction. In this mode, the surgeon grasps a bone fragment or a bone fragments group with one of the haptic devices and moves it until the fracture is reduced. The main difficulty is to simultaneously align several contact surfaces. To allow the sequential alignment of the matching surfaces, the system provides the temporary reduction of the bone fragments freedom with virtual pivot points. A virtual pivot point constraints the translation of the bone fragment (or group) to the center of the pivot. By placing a virtual pivot point at the intersection of two bone fragment surfaces, a connection that allows one object/group with respect to the other is enabled. The virtual pivot point constraints the manipulation of the object/group and facilitates the alignment of the bone fragment surfaces in another location. The virtual pivot points can be added and removed at any time as necessary.

(b) Semiautomatic fracture reduction. When the bone fracture surface interface area is large, the precise alignment of the bone fracture surfaces requires many small and delicate manipulations. We automate this fine-tuning alignment by providing the surgeon with the ability to interactively mark the two bone fragments surfaces that are to be matched. The surgeon starts by interactively selecting the points on the surface of each bone fragment with the virtual tip of the haptic manipulator. The surgeon then brings two bone fragments into coarse alignment and instructs the computer to perform the fine alignment by Iterative Closest Point (ICP) rigid registration method with outlier point pairs' removal.

(c) Automatic pairwise fracture reduction. Automatic fracture reduction between two bone fragments is performed by computing the rigid motion transformation that best aligns one bone fragment with the other. This is a rigid registration problem that is solved by identifying the fracture surfaces to be matched in each bone fragment and then performing ICP registration in-between. The fracture surfaces are identified by finding the points on the surface model for which a neighborhood relation, defined on the intensity profile of the CT scan and on the curvature of the fragments surface, holds. The bone cortex voxels are identified by intensity thresholding since the density of the bone cortex is much higher than the densities of the interior spongy bone and the medullary cavity. Points on the outer bone surface whose corresponding voxel intensities are low are classified as fracture contact surface points. We also add points whose maximum principal curvature is high, as these correspond to sharp fracture edges.

7. *Control* handles the user commands and determines the actions of the system based on state machine automation. The mouse controls the camera viewpoint and allows the selection of menu options. The keyboard provides access to the modules' options, e.g., object type selection, viewing mode, motion scaling, and enabling/disabling the haptic rendering. The haptic device enables the user to manipulate virtual objects and to select fracture surface points for semiautomatic reduction.

32.3.5 Evaluation and validation

We evaluated our fracture planning system with two studies. In the first study, we evaluated the use of the system for manual fracture reduction and quantified the accuracy of the manual bone fracture reduction. First, we generated the ground-truth reference of the bone fracture reduction by simulating fractures on healthy bone models on four CT scans of patients whose pelvic bone was intact. We then virtually created on the 3D model of the pelvis six realistic perfect-fit two-fragment fractures with no comminution. The position of the resulting bone fragments is the ground-truth final position of the fracture reduction. For each model, we displaced one of the bone fragments, created six scenarios, and asked five surgeons from the Dept. of Orthopaedic Surgery, Hadassah Medical Center, to manually reduce the fracture with our system. We then compared the bone fragment positions to the ground truth. The anatomical alignment error is the Hausdorff distance between each of the bone fragments with respect to their ground-truth configuration. The user interaction times were 10–30 minutes depending on the surgeon's familiarity with the system. The surgeons expressed satisfaction with the system in an informal qualitative usability study. They achieved a mean and RMS surface match error of 1 mm or less. For some cases and for some surgeons, the maximum surface error in specific areas of the fracture surface was > 2 mm. These errors were considered by all surgeons to be very accurate and clinically adequate in all cases.

The second study quantifies the accuracy of the virtual bone fracture reduction algorithm. We created virtual fractures on four healthy femoral bone models as in the first study. We developed a new method for realistic fracture simulation which consists of computing a realistic fracture surface by segmenting a bone fracture surface in a CT scan of a fractured bone and then using it as a cutting surface template on a healthy bone model. For each model, we simulated three types of bone fractures: femoral neck fracture, proximal femoral shaft fracture, and distal femoral shaft fracture. We then applied our method and compared the configuration of the resulting reduced fracture to the original healthy bone. The mean final Target Registration Error is 1.79 mm (std = 1.09 mm). The algorithm running time was 3 minutes (std = 0.2 minutes). The surgeons examined each one of the cases and determined that the reduction was clinically acceptable in all cases.

32.3.6 Perspectives

Treatment planning for orthopaedic trauma surgery has the potential to improve patient outcomes, improve functionality, and reduce revision surgery rates. An effective user interface, coupled with automatic features and advanced analysis will go a long way towards providing an effective computer-based tools for treatment planning.

32.4. Treatment planning for keyhole neurosurgery and percutaneous ablation

Image-based surgical planning is also commonly used to help find an appropriate access to a pathology in minimally invasive interventions. In this type of interventions, the surgeon does not have a direct visualization of the surgical site. Therefore, image-based planning approaches are essential to select the most appropriate placement for the surgical tool before the start of the surgery. This is a very important aspect, as sometimes candidates to surgery cannot be treated because no feasible access can be found before surgery. Image-based preoperative planning consists in helping the surgeon in this decision-making process by solving automatically tool placement rules to propose feasible – or better, optimal – solutions. These are often called *trajectories* or *tool placements*.

Access planning has two different and complementary objectives: computing the entire set of feasible access sites, and computing the optimal one. In this section, we will discuss both problems, and illustrate them with two different interventions, keyhole neurosurgery and percutaneous thermal ablations in the abdomen.

32.4.1 Background

For both surgical applications, the general clinical objective is similar: insert one or several straight surgical tools in a specific part of the body, through the skin or the skull, towards a chosen target, and while maximizing the positive effects of the treatment and minimizing its risks or side effects.

Deep Brain Stimulation (DBS) for the treatment of Parkinson's disease, and Stereoelectroencephalography (SEEG) recording to detect the origin of seizures in epilepsy, are two representative examples of keyhole neurosurgery. DBS consists in implanting a permanent electrode in a deep and small nucleus of the brain, and stimulating it with a current sent by a pacemaker to reduce the tremors. It was first proposed in 1987 by Benabid et al. [28], and was successfully applied in 1994 to treat Parkinson's disease [29]. The treatment of choice consists of implanting one electrode per hemisphere to achieve a good laterality in the treatment. Because of the very small size of the targeted structures, i.e., the subthalamic nucleus (STN) and the globus pallidus interna (GPI), the insertion of the electrode must be performed with a millimeter accuracy. The choice of an optimal electrode placement is mostly a geometry problem, based on the anatomy of the patient's brain. In SEEG interventions [30], a higher number of electrodes have to be implanted – around 15 on one side of the skull. The electrodes are placed in such a way that all anatomical structures to be monitored are covered by the region that the contacts along the electrodes can record [31]. An optimal placement combines safety and good coverage and ensures that the electrodes do not interfere with each other, which adds a new complexity. Commercial solutions exist, such as BrainLab Element [32] or Medtronic StealthStation [33]. They are often used in clinical routine, and mostly provide assistance to interactive planning, thanks to image processing and fusion functionalities, and an interactive choice of the target and entry points.

Percutaneous thermal ablations [34] consist in the localized destruction of malignant cells by hyperthermia using either extreme cold or extreme heat delivered at the tip of custom-designed needles inserted through the skin inside the tumor. While treating pathologies with heat or cold has been studied from centuries, modern percutaneous techniques have made them very popular in the 1990s due to their minimal invasiveness and good efficacy. Examples of percutaneous thermal ablations include radiofrequency ablation, often used for liver tumors, or cryoablation, often used for renal tumors. Radiofrequency [35] consists in heating the tumor above 60°C for about 10–15 minutes to allow for the complete destruction of the malignant cells. A variety of devices and needle models are commercially available, including straight rigid, umbrella-shaped, and multiarray needles. Advanced needle designs allow the treatment of large volumes. Their advantage is that they require a single application in most cases to treat the entire tumor. However, in other situations, i.e., cryoablation [36], several needles are usually required to form an iceball large enough to cover the tumor. The tumor ablation process is also longer, as it requires two freezing cycles of 10 minutes, with a thawing cycle of 5 minutes in-between to achieve the complete tumor obliteration. For this type of abdominal percutaneous thermal ablation, no planning tool is currently commercially available. The surgeons usually plan the entry and target points based on preoperative images in their minds. This is a difficult task, especially for cryoablation, where several needles and a complex resulting iceball shape are involved.

In all these procedures, the placement of the surgical tool needs to be very accurate to guarantee full coverage of the tumor and include a safety margin, while avoiding damages to surrounding healthy structures and other side effects. To define accurately the insertion plan, the surgeons usually rely on preoperative images and on a set of placement rules gathered from the professional literature and learned from their mentors and from their own experience.

32.4.2 Placement constraints

One of the challenges of preoperative image-based surgery planning is to realistically model the placement rules before they are used to solve the placement problem. In fact, most of the placement rules can be expressed as geometric constraints between the anatomy of the patient and the tools to be inserted (electrodes or needles), or the shape of their resulting effect. To simplify, the tools can be at first modeled as straight line segments whose endpoints are their tip and the entry points. The effect shapes can also be approximated by simplified shapes, as described in earlier papers [37,38] to reduce computation times, or be simulated with realistic mathematical formulas for a better accuracy of the prediction [39,40] (See Fig. 32.3).

Surgical rules are most often expressed by the surgeon in natural language, so it is necessary to convert them to a formal, computer-enabled representation so they can be processed by a solver. The formal representation of these rules, called *surgical constraints*, can be expressions in a formal language [41], trees, or mathematical cost functions. While all these representations are conceptually equivalent, we found that the cost-functions' representation is the most convenient to implement.

The compilation and formalization of the surgical rules is a time-consuming and convoluted task, as some of these rules are implicit, may differ from one surgeon to another, and may change over time. To accommodate this, we chose to develop a generic and adaptable surgical constraint solver [42].

We distinguish between two types of surgical constraints, namely hard and soft surgical constraints. *Hard constraints*, also called *strict*, are mandatory, e.g., "*do not cross any vessel with the needle*". Their evaluation is a Boolean value, indicating if they are satisfied or not. All candidate trajectories that do not satisfy any of the hard constraints must be discarded. *Soft constraints* express preferences, e.g., "*keep the needle as far as possible from the vessels*". Their evaluation is a numerical value, indicating their degree of compliance. Note that this preference can be expressed as a rule describing the distance between the needle line and the vessels shape. When solving such constraints, the objective is to minimize or maximize their value.

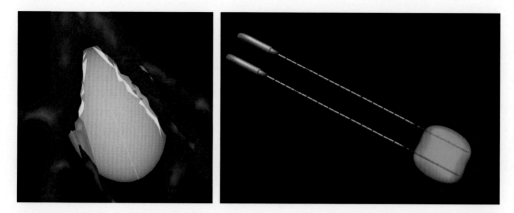

Figure 32.3 Volume of necrosis of an RFA intervention represented by a simplified deformed ellipsoid (left), and ice balls of a cryoablation with two interacting cryoprobes simulated using mathematical modeling (right).

32.4.3 Constraint solving

Once the surgical rules have been established and the patient-specific 3D model has been created from the preoperative images, the next step is constraint solving.

The hard and soft constraints can be solved separately or together. When solving them separately, a good approach is to first solve the hard constraints so as to restrict the solution space to the set of feasible solutions. This can be achieved by examining all possible solutions and eliminating those that do not satisfy all the strict constraints. Since the initial solution space is infinite, it is necessary to discretize it beforehand. One common way to do this is to set the target point (for instance, to the centroid of the targeted structure), and then examine the resulting entry points either by browsing the vertices of the skin's surface mesh, or the centers of its triangular cells, or to use an angular discretization of the space around the target point. The second step is to further explore the set of feasible solutions to find the solutions that best satisfy the soft constraints. This actually consists in the resolution of a multicriteria optimization problem. Depending on the clinical application, the target point can still be set in advance (either by using its centroid, or by asking the surgeon to select it) to examine only possible entry points, or it can be included in the search for an optimal solution, which is an optimal pair entry/target points. The latter approach increases the number of degrees of freedom and the search space but might be useful in some applications, in particular when multiple surgical tools – electrodes, needles – are involved.

The first and most commonly used technique to solve the soft constraints is the weighted sum method. It consists of representing the soft constraints as cost functions f_i to minimize, and then combining them using individual weighting factors w_i that can be predefined or adjusted by the surgeon. In this way, a unique global cost function f is defined as described in converting the multicriteria problem into a single-criterion problem that can be solved using a minimization algorithm. Formally, the function is

$$f = \frac{w_1 \cdot f_1 + w_2 \cdot f_2 + \cdots + w_n \cdot f_n}{\cdot w_1 + w_2 + \cdots + w_n}.$$

In this approach, the choice of the minimization function is key, as the results and the computation times will depend on it. When using a local minimization function, e.g., the Nelder–Mead downhill simplex method [43,44], an initialization is required to ensure convergence. Global approaches can also be considered, provided that adequate parameter values can be found that do not require readjusting for each patient [45].

Another very interesting approach is to find the best compromise between soft constraints based on a real multicriteria optimization method, such as Pareto front computation. The general idea is that since it is in general impossible to find a solution that simultaneously optimizes all of the soft constraints $f_i, \ldots, f_n$, the best is to find compromises between them. Each solution with a specific evaluation of functions $f_i, \ldots, f_n$ constitutes compromise. The compromises will always satisfy some of the constraints better than the others. The best among the compromises are called the Pareto-optimal solutions. The set of all Pareto-optimal solutions constitutes the Pareto front. Note that choosing a Pareto-optimal solution requires ranking the soft constraints by their importance, as all such solutions optimize equally the soft constraints, each one in its own way. In the end, the choice of which of the Pareto-optimal solutions are the most suitable for a specific case depends on which constraint(s) we want to satisfy most. This requires the quantification of optimality.

In [46], we defined an optimality quantification based on dominance and described how to compute the corresponding Pareto front for the specific case of trajectory planning for surgery. In this work, the weighted sum and the Pareto front approaches were compared. We showed that the weighted front approach, although more intuitive for the user in terms of presentation and visualization of the solutions, was missing many possible solutions. We also showed that the missed solutions found by the Pareto front method were those most often chosen by surgeons, suggesting the superiority of this approach.

Finally, note that it is also possible to simultaneously solve hard and soft constraints by representing hard constraints as cost functions with a maximum penalty outside the feasible area. This approach has the drawback of being computationally more expensive when parameters, such as weighting factors, are changed.

32.4.4 Evaluation and validation

The evaluation and validation of the planning solutions is performed in two ways. The first is to display the results for visual assessment and to provide the surgeon with the necessary information to decide which solution to adopt. The visualization consists of displaying color maps over the skin mesh as illustrated in Fig. 32.4. This is particularly

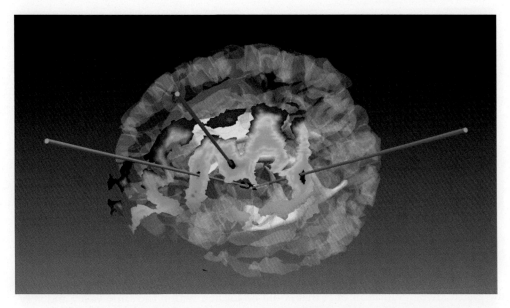

Figure 32.4 Color map representing the quality of each feasible insertion point on the skull (red – poor quality; green – high quality) for a Deep Brain Stimulation intervention, with the three most optimal electrodes positions located in three separate valleys (purple).

useful for visualizing the results of the weighted sum approach. Usually, the least appropriate zones are displayed in red, while the most appropriate ones in green or blue. The color map shows results from the two phases. Its border shows the limit of the feasible entry points, computed by solving the hard constraints, and the colors represent the quality of each feasible entry point, computed by solving the soft constraints. When hard and soft constraints are solved together, the zone outside the border is displayed in red.

It is important to note that this kind of display is partial and has bias. Indeed, color-coding an entry point to represent the quality of its associated trajectory presupposes that this trajectory is unique. However, an entry point may represent an entire family of trajectories, aiming at various target points when the target point was not set in advance. In this case, the color of the entry point should be determined by the value of the most optimal trajectory using this entry point. Note that, although color-coding is a good way to get a rough idea of the possible good locations for insertion points, this kind of visualization is not very accurate.

The second approach is to show the first few most optimal solutions. Indeed, when visualizing the color maps, it is very common to see that there is usually not a unique good location. Most often, there are a few good candidate areas, also called "valleys" that represent connected zones with the lowest values of f. A good way to indicate the most suitable entry points to the surgeon is therefore not to display the trajectories with

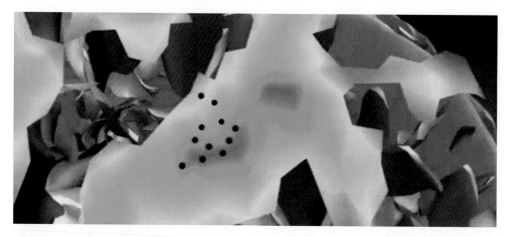

Figure 32.5 Pareto-optimal solutions (red spheres) displayed over a weighted-sum color map for a Deep Brain Stimulation intervention.

the global lowest evaluation of f, that could be located within the same valley and very close to each other, but rather to display the most optimal trajectory within each valley, as shown on Fig. 32.4.

When using the Pareto front method, the display can be somewhat different. All the entry points retained as equally optimal can be displayed with an equal visualization. However, this might be confusing when trying to select one of them, especially when the front is large and the solutions numerous. Some help to shrink the selection of the points can prove very useful, for instance, by setting minimal evaluations for all cost functions $f_i, \ldots, f_n$. It is also possible to ask the surgeon to rank the importance of soft constraints, which will allow a coloring to be done, or to display the Pareto-optimal solutions over a weighted-sum dynamic color map with adjustable weights as a hint, as illustrated in Fig. 32.5.

With both approaches, we see that ranking the importance given to each soft constraint helps in the resolution of the problem. An interaction from the user allows setting respective weights and updating the visualization in real time. Interactive repositioning of the surgical tool, real-time 2D/3D and tool-axis ("probe-eye") visualization, and numerical information displayed dynamically, such as the distance to major organs to avoid, are among the useful features that trajectory planning software should provide.

The evaluation of the result can also be seen in terms of clinical validation. Either to assess the robustness and accuracy of a method in general, or to evaluate the clinical relevance of a patient-specific solution, numerical validation is useful. In many other fields, this is usually done by comparing the results with some ground truth. However, in our case, defining ground truth is a delicate issue.

An option can be to study retrospective cases, in which the position of the tool chosen by the surgeon is retrieved from either automatic or interactive segmentation based on postoperative images. However, without assessing the quality of the surgeon planning in those cases, it is not possible to consider that the very best location was always selected. In many cases, the surgeon might have chosen purposely a suboptimal position for a variety of reasons, or might have lacked some information to find the most optimal one, or even the tool simply deviated from the planned trajectory when inserting it. Therefore, retrospective cases cannot be considered directly as ground truth. The best way to proceed is to gather candidate positions from different sources, manually planned from retrospective cases and automatically planned with the proposed methods, and have them blindly ranked by experts.

32.4.5 Perspectives

Image-based preoperative planning can also benefit from other features to improve their accuracy, especially when mechanical or physiological phenomena can influence the procedure. Simulating those phenomena help to anticipate them and provide a more optimal planning.

Deformations in general are the first cause of inaccuracies. Image-based planning means using still preoperative images to choose a strategy. However, even if the patient is in the exact same position during the intervention, many phenomena can cause motions of the anatomical structures surrounding the target. For abdominal interventions, breathing is, of course, the first cause of deformations. Movements due to friction and pressure forces also occur during insertion of needles into the soft tissues of the abdomen. In neurosurgery, the well-known phenomenon of brain shift is due to leaks of cerebrospinal fluid, gravity, and various other factors. Attempts have been made to take those phenomena into account to improve the predictability and the accuracy of the planning.

Another kind of phenomenon interesting to model is the effect that will be produced by the treatment. In the case of thermal ablations, such as radiofrequency or cryoablation, simulating the propagation of heat around the tip of the probe allows anticipating the coverage of the tumor by isotherm surfaces representing the zone of full necrosis, confirming that the treatment will be a success, or identifying potential surrounding structures that could be affected. In the case of DBS, simulating the electrical field around the tip of the electrode allows visualizing what structures will be included inside the stimulated volume.

32.5. Future challenges

Image-based preoperative planning is a key component of the trend towards precision and personalized medicine. Its role in an ever-growing number of procedures is increasing, and it is an enabler for new surgical systems and procedures for more structures and pathologies. This creates technical demands that need to be addressed with existing and new technologies.

We foresee several technical trends that will play an important role in the near future. For segmentation and model construction, we foresee an increase in the use of atlas-based segmentation and deep learning segmentation. A main challenge for these methods is the acquisition and/or generation of ground-truth organ and structures segmentation for atlas construction and for network training. For simulation, we foresee challenges in the development of multiphysics models and their simulation with high computational demands.

Another topic of interest is the integration of preoperative planning and intraoperative execution, hereby allowing plan modification and adaptation in the operating room. For some procedures, the progress of a surgical step, e.g., the insertion of a needle, is monitored with intraoperative images. For example, during cryoablation surgery of liver tumors, surgeons usually monitor the insertion of the needle to see if it matches the planned trajectory, and then follow the growth of the ice ball with 2D ultrasound or fluoroscopy X-ray images. Based on these intraoperative images, they may adjust the plan to correct possible inaccuracies of the needles placements or complement the ice ball formation. The original plan can then be automatically adjusted to adapt and preserve the optimality, safety and accuracy of the needles placements according to the observed structures deformations.

A third topic to explore is to link posttreatment imaging and evaluation to the preoperative plan. The goal is to establish a correlation between the preoperative plan and the postoperative outcome and to determine if the treatment was effective and if an alternative plan could have yielded better results. For example, for orthopaedic bone fracture surgery, a postoperative CT scan can help to determine if bone union was completed successfully and if the fixation plate and screws did not undergo displacement. Based on this assessment, it could be determined that thicker and/or longer screws should have been used. This conclusion can then be taken into account when planning the next surgery.

Finally, we note that image-based preoperative planning also have an important role in clinician training, education, and evaluation. Indeed, image-based surgical planning systems such as the bone fracture surgery system in orthopaedic surgery described in this chapter can serve as a component in simulation systems to provide a hands-on, realistic virtual environment in which the users can perform a variety of procedures, such as suturing and knot tying, with simulated instruments on virtual models of tissues and organs. Indeed, surgical simulators are gaining acceptance as a training tool for residents and as a rehearsal and preoperative planning tool for experts. A variety of commercial simulators are nowadays available for laparoscopic, endoscopic, and endovascular procedures.

References

[1] L. Joskowicz, E. Hazan, Computer aided orthopaedic surgery: incremental shift or paradigm change?, Medical Image Analysis 33 (2016) 84–90.

[2] L. Joskowicz, C. Milgrom, A. Simkin, L. Tockus, Z. Yaniv, FRACAS: a system for computer-aided image-guided long bone fracture surgery, Computer-Aided Surgery (formerly J. Image Guided Surgery) 3 (6) (1999) 271–328.

[3] M. Liebergall, L. Joskowicz, R. Mosheiff, Computer-aided orthopaedic surgery in skeletal trauma, in: R. Bucholz, J. Heckman (Eds.), Rockwood and Green's Fractures in Adults, 8th ed., Lippincott Williams and Wilkins, 2015, pp. 575–607.

[4] J. Kurtinaitis, N. Porvaneckas, G. Kvederas, T. Butenas, V. Uvarovas, Revision rates after surgical treatment for femoral neck fractures: results of 2-year follow-up, Medicina (Kaunas) 49 (3) (2013) 138–142.

[5] P. Olsson, F. Nysjö, J.M. Hirsch, I.B. Carlbom, A haptic-assisted cranio-maxillofacial surgery planning system for restoring skeletal anatomy in complex trauma cases, International Journal of Computer Assisted Radiology and Surgery 8 (6) (2013) 887–894.

[6] J. Pettersson, K.L. Palmerius, H. Knutsson, O. Wahlström, B. Tillander, M. Borga, Simulation of patient specific cervical hip fracture surgery with a volume haptic interface, IEEE Transactions on Biomedical Engineering 55 (4) (2008) 1255–1265.

[7] M. Harders, A. Barlit, C. Gerber, J. Hodler, G. Székely, An optimized surgical planning environment for complex proximal humerus fractures, in: Proceedings of MICCAI Workshop on Interaction in Medical Image Analysis and Visualization, vol. 10, 2007, pp. 201–206.

[8] P. Fürnstahl, G. Székely, C. Gerber, J. Hodler, G. Snedeker, M. Harders, Computer assisted reconstruction of complex proximal humerus fractures for preoperative planning, Medical Image Analysis 16 (3) (2010) 704–720.

[9] J. Fornaro, M. Harders, M. Keel, B. Marincek, O. Trentz, G. Székely, T. Frauenfelder, Interactive visuo-haptic surgical planning tool for pelvic and acetabular fractures, Studies in Health Technology and Informatics 132 (2008) 123.

[10] J. Fornaro, M. Keel, M. Harders, B. Marincek, G. Székely, T. Frauenfelder, An interactive surgical planning tool for acetabular fractures: initial results, Journal of Orthopaedic Surgery and Research 5 (1) (2010) 50–55.

[11] A. Willis, D. Anderson, T.P. Thomas, T. Brown, J.L. Marsh, 3D reconstruction of highly fragmented bone fractures, in: Proceedings of SPIE Conference on Medical Imaging, International Society for Optics and Photonics, 2007, pp. 65121–65126.

[12] B. Zhou, A. Willis, Y. Sui, D. Anderson, T.P. Thomas, T. Brown, Improving inter-fragmentary alignment for virtual 3D reconstruction of highly fragmented bone fractures, in: Proc. SPIE Conf. Medical Imaging, Int. Society for Optics and Photonics, 2009, pp. 725934–725939.

[13] B. Zhou, A. Willis, Y. Sui, D. Anderson, T. Brown, T.P. Thomas, Virtual 3D bone fracture reconstruction via inter-fragmentary surface alignment, in: Proc. 12th IEEE International Conference on Computer Vision, 2009, pp. 1809–1816.

[14] T.P. Thomas, D.D. Anderson, A.R. Willis, P. Liu, M.C. Frank, T.D. Brown, A computational/experimental platform for investigating three-dimensional puzzle solving of comminuted articular fractures, Computer Methods in Biomechanics and Biomedical Engineering 14 (3) (2011) 263–270.

[15] T. Okada, Y. Iwasaki, T. Koyama, N. Sugano, Y.W. Chen, K. Yonenobu, Y. Sato, Computer-assisted preoperative planning for reduction of proximal femoral fracture using 3D CT data, IEEE Transactions on Biomedical Engineering 56 (3) (2009) 749–759.

[16] G. Papaioannou, E.A. Karabassi, On the automatic assemblage of arbitrary broken solid artifacts, Image and Vision Computing 21 (5) (2003) 401–412.

[17] M.H. Moghari, P. Abolmaesumi, Global registration of multiple bone fragments using statistical atlas models: feasibility experiments, in: Proceedings of 30th IEEE Conference on Engineering in Medicine and Biology, 2008, pp. 5374–5377.

[18] S. Winkelbach, F. Wahl, Pairwise matching of 3D fragments using cluster trees, International Journal of Computer Vision 78 (1) (2008) 1–13.

[19] S. Winkelbach, M. Rilk, C. Schonfelder, F. Wahl, Fast random sample matching of 3D fragments, in: C.E. Rasmussen, et al. (Eds.), DAGM 2004, in: Lecture Notes in Computer Science, vol. 3175, Springer, Berlin, Heidelberg, 2004, pp. 129–136.

[20] I. Kovler, Haptic Interface for Computer-Assisted Patient-Specific Preoperative Planning in Orthopaedic Fracture Surgery, MSc Thesis, The Hebrew University of Jerusalem, Israel, 2015.

[21] I. Kovler, L. Joskowicz, A. Kronman, Y. Weill, J. Salavarrieta, Haptic computer-assisted patient specific preoperative planning for orthopaedic fracture surgery, International Journal of Computer-Aided Radiology and Surgery 10 (10) (2015) 1535–1546.

[22] L. Joskowicz, Modeling and simulation, in: F.A. Jolesz (Ed.), Intraoperative Imaging and Image-Guided Therapy, Springer Science, 2014, pp. 49–62.

[23] E. Peleg, M. Beek, L. Joskowicz, M. Liebergall, R. Mosheiff, C. Whyne, Patient specific quantitative analysis of fracture fixation in the proximal femur implementing principal strain ratios: method and experimental validation, Journal of Biomechanics 43 (14) (2011) 2684–2688.

[24] Bullet Physics Library, Real-time physics simulation, http://bulletphysics.org/wordpress.

[25] C.B. Zilles, J.K. Salisbury, A constraint-based god-object method for haptic display, in: Proc. IEEE Int. Conf. on Intelligent Robots and Systems, vol. 3, 1995, pp. 146–151.

[26] Haptic Library and Haptic Device Application Program Interfaces, Sensable Inc., http://www.dentsable.com/openhaptics-toolkit-hdapi.htm.

[27] GLUT and OpenGL Utility libraries, https://www.opengl.org/resources/libraries.

[28] A.L. Benabid, P. Pollak, A. Louveau, S. Henry, J. de Rougemont, Combined thalamotomy and stimulation: stereotactic surgery of the VIM thalamic nucleus for bilateral Parkinson disease, Stereotactic and Functional Neurosurgery 50 (1987) 344–346.

[29] A.L. Benabid, P. Pollak, C. Gross, D. Hoffmann, A. Benazzouz, D.M. Gao, et al., Acute and long-term effects of subthalamic nucleus stimulation in Parkinson's disease, Stereotactic and Functional Neurosurgery 62 (1994) 76–84.

[30] G.P. Kratimenos, D.G. Thomas, S.D. Shorvon, D.R. Fish, Stereotactic insertion of intracerebral electrodes in the investigation of epilepsy, British Journal of Neurosurgery 7 (1993) 45–52.

[31] F. Dubeau, R.S. McLachlan, Invasive electrographic recording techniques in temporal lobe epilepsy, Canadian Journal of Neurological Sciences 27 (2000) S29–S34.

[32] Stereotaxy: Stereotactic Planning & Surgery Refined, in: Brainlab [Internet], [cited July 15, 2019]. Available: https://www.brainlab.com/surgery-products/overview-neurosurgery-products/stereotactic-planning-software/.

[33] Neurosurgery navigation: StealthStation Surgical Navigation System, in: Medtronic [Internet], [cited July 15, 2019]. Available: http://www.medtronic.com/us-en/healthcare-professionals/products/neurological/surgical-navigation-systems/stealthstation/cranial-neurosurgery-navigation.html.

[34] J.P. McGahan, V.A. van Raalte, History of ablation, in: Tumor Ablation, 2005, pp. 3–15.

[35] S.N. Goldberg, Radiofrequency tumor ablation: principles and techniques, European Journal of Ultrasound 13 (2001) 129–147.

[36] S.M. Weber, F.T. Lee, Cryoablation: history, mechanism of action, and guidance modalities, in: Tumor Ablation, 2005, pp. 250–265.

[37] T. Butz, S.K. Warfield, K. Tuncali, SG Silverman, E. van Sonnenberg, F.A. Jolesz, et al., Pre- and intra-operative planning and simulation of percutaneous tumor ablation, in: Medical Image Computing and Computer-Assisted Intervention – MICCAI 2000, in: Lecture Notes in Computer Science, vol. 1935, Springer, 2000, pp. 317–326.

[38] C. Villard, L. Soler, N. Papier, V. Agnus, S. Thery, A. Gangi, et al., Virtual radiofrequency ablation of liver tumors, in: International Symposium on Surgery Simulation and Soft Tissue Modeling – IS4TM 2003, in: Lecture Notes in Computer Science, vol. 2673, Springer, 2003, pp. 366–374.

[39] Y.L. Shao, B. Arjun, H.L. Leo, K.J. Chua, A computational theoretical model for radiofrequency ablation of tumor with complex vascularization, Computers in Biology and Medicine 89 (2017) 282–292.

[40] C. Rieder, T. Kroeger, C. Schumann, H.K. Hahn, GPU-based real-time approximation of the ablation zone for radiofrequency ablation, IEEE Transactions on Visualization and Computer Graphics 17 (2011) 1812–1821.

[41] C. Essert-Villard, C. Baegert, P. Schreck, Multi-semantic approach towards a generic formal solver of tool placement for percutaneous surgery, in: Proc. Int. Conf. on Knowledge Engineering and Ontology Development, 2009, pp. 443–446.

[42] C. Essert, C. Haegelen, F. Lalys, A. Abadie, Automatic computation of electrode trajectories for Deep Brain Stimulation: a hybrid symbolic and numerical approach, International Journal of Computer Assisted Radiology and Surgery 7 (2012) 517–532.

[43] C. Baegert, C. Villard, P. Schreck, L. Soler, A. Gangi, Trajectory optimization for the planning of percutaneous radiofrequency ablation of hepatic tumors, Computer Aided Surgery 12 (2007) 82–90.

[44] J.A. Nelder, R. Mead, A simplex method for function minimization, The Computer Journal 7 (1965) 308–313.

[45] A. Jaberzadeh, C. Essert, Pre-operative planning of multiple probes in three dimensions for liver cryosurgery: comparison of different optimization methods, Mathematical Methods in the Applied Sciences 39 (2015) 4764–4772.

[46] N. Hamze, J. Voirin, P. Collet, P. Jannin, C. Haegelen, C. Essert, Pareto front vs. weighted sum for automatic trajectory planning of Deep Brain Stimulation, in: Medical Image Computing and Computer Assisted Intervention – MICCAI 2016, in: Lecture Notes in Computer Science, vol. 9900, 2016, pp. 534–541.

CHAPTER 33

Human–machine interfaces for medical imaging and clinical interventions

Roy Eagleson[a], Sandrine de Ribaupierre[b]
[a]Software Engineering, University of Western Ontario, London, ON, Canada
[b]Clinical Neurological Sciences, University of Western Ontario, London, ON, Canada

Contents

33.1.	HCI for medical imaging vs clinical interventions	817
	33.1.1 HCI for diagnostic queries (using medical imaging)	818
	33.1.2 HCI for planning, guiding, and executing imperative actions (computer-assisted interventions)	819
33.2.	Human–computer interfaces: design and evaluation	820
33.3.	What is an interface?	821
33.4.	Human outputs are computer inputs	822
33.5.	Position inputs (free-space pointing and navigation interactions)	822
33.6.	Direct manipulation vs proxy-based interactions (cursors)	823
33.7.	Control of viewpoint	824
33.8.	Selection (object-based interactions)	824
33.9.	Quantification (object-based position setting)	825
33.10.	User interactions: selection vs position, object-based vs free-space	826
33.11.	Text inputs (strings encoded/parsed as formal and informal language)	828
33.12.	Language-based control (text commands or spoken language)	828
33.13.	Image-based and workspace-based interactions: movement and selection events	830
33.14.	Task representations for image-based and intervention-based interfaces	833
33.15.	Design and evaluation guidelines for human–computer interfaces: human inputs are computer outputs – the system design must respect perceptual capacities and constraints	834
33.16.	Objective evaluation of performance on a task mediated by an interface	836
	References	838

33.1. HCI for medical imaging vs clinical interventions

A broad characterization of the distinction between "Medical Imaging" and "Computer-Assisted Interventions" is that Medical Imaging displays are used for diagnosis, and Computer-Assisted Interventions make use of displays as information for basing actions. The former set of tasks answer queries, while the latter are used for navigation and manipulation: they are actions which are imperative in nature. While systems can support a mix of these two broad use cases, we use this distinction to outline some typical exam-

Handbook of Medical Image Computing and Computer Assisted Intervention
https://doi.org/10.1016/B978-0-12-816176-0.00038-7

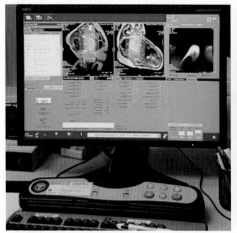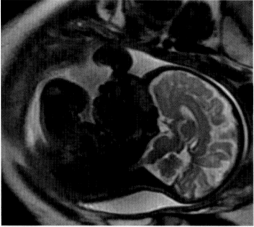

Figure 33.1 (left) MRI console during a fetal MRI acquisition where the parameters can be adjusted; (right) image of a fetal head.

ples from clinical settings. Some refer to this distinction as the "MIC" and the "CAI" of MICCAI (e.g., [9]), and so these task categories are the primary drivers that distinguish two HCI design streams.

33.1.1 HCI for diagnostic queries (using medical imaging)

While "medical image understanding" might seem to be almost synonymous with "Visual Perception", we can identify a fundamental difference between the two: Visual Perception involves the human visual system, which has evolved to "understand" (i.e., derive semantics from) a natural scene. "Medical Image Understanding", on the other hand, makes use of physics-based sensors to produce an array which is perceived as an image. While viewing an X-Ray image may feel like looking at a natural pattern, it is far from natural scene understanding. This is the trap through which many medical imaging innovations fall. The human perceptual system is specialized for natural scenes. When the pipeline involve inputs which are physics-based sensors (e.g., coils in an MRI scanner) and there is a processing flow which, after considering several arbitrary parameters, maps this onto a visual image, then it seems clear that misperceptions of the information are almost inevitable. In the face of recognizing this shortcoming, it has been a common theme in Medical Imaging that the goal is to somehow optimize the mapping to the display so that the speed and accuracy of perceiving "what" or "where" is improved. "Is there a lesion in this sample?" "Is there flow in the vessel?" "Is *that* anatomical structure normal or is it pathological?" (See Fig. 33.1.)

To facilitate such tasks using visual information, the processing pipeline embodies an algorithm which can have several degrees of freedom. These are parameters associated with the displayed image and, accordingly, they can be adjusted interactively at the user interface: (e.g., color lookup tables, contrast adjustments, histogramming, ROI, rotation of the image, translation, zoom, etc.). Quasiautomated tools and algorithms can help with shape estimation, (such as segmentation, 3D rendering of reconstructed volumes, detection, classification, localization, estimation of volumes, or shape parameters). Later we will discuss how this process is not just data-driven, but involves "top-down" processing in addition to the "bottom-up" flow, which is predominant in Medical Imaging (except when humans are involved, using HCI as part of the processing hierarchy). In any case, each of these, in Medical Imaging ("MIC"), can be used as objective metrics for "Diagnosis". Consider next, the "CAI", of MICCAI, in the following section.

33.1.2 HCI for planning, guiding, and executing imperative actions (computer-assisted interventions)

Not only is the human perceptual/cognitive system able to "understand" a natural scene but, critically, it is then able to act within it. This notion of the sensorimotor system completes the concept of the "Perception–Action" loop that connects humans with the world. Certainly, we have evolved to deal within a natural world. Our perceptual–motor system is so adaptive that it is at least feasible that humans (making use of HCI systems) might be able to accomplish tasks which were formerly accomplished using natural vision and hand-held tools. Accordingly, they may be competent to perform similar tasks using medical imaging (within unnatural scenes) with the addition of artificial user-input devices to allow computers to drive effectors to perform medical interventions. In retrospect, it is a pretty bold stance. Yet, there has been some relatively recent progress over the past couple of decades in this regard.

Some of the first examples of Human–Machine Interfaces for Computer-Assisted Interventions have been confined to the domain of Endoscopy/Laparoscopy. Other examples include: Microscopy, Ultrasound Guidance, keyhole robotic surgery (e.g., Computer Motion's Zeus, Intuitive Surgical's da Vinci, Renishaw's Neuromate, and a well-established set of platforms for Neuronavigation [Medtronics, BrainLab, Synaptive, etc.]). (See Fig. 33.2.) These classes of clinical procedures take place within a workspace that is reasonably constrained, making "computer-assistance" more feasible (as contrasted with "open surgery").

Our main caveat, for the whole enterprise, is that this enterprise will be about "System Design" as much as it is about "System Evaluation", which will not be "unit testing". Instead, it will be the empiricism needed to measure the facilitation of the task for which the interface was designed. Later, we will develop an argument for objective evaluations of this "facilitation" in terms of the only performance metric that is relevant to a sensorimotor task − the product of speed and accuracy.

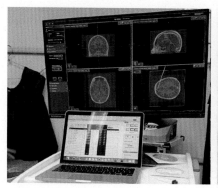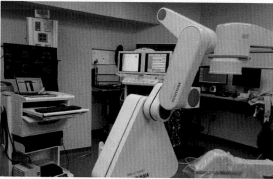

Figure 33.2 Setup during an epilepsy case using a robot for intracranial electrodes insertion: (left) monitor with different views of the brain on which the planning is performed; (right) robotic arm ready for the procedure.

33.2. Human–computer interfaces: design and evaluation

One of the characteristics of the domain of Human–Computer Interfaces that is both exhilarating and challenging is the vast breadth of the subject. There is no shortage of wonder and fascination for students studying this domain. And yet, the seemingly unbridled nature belies a stark simplicity – there are a number of unifying principles that can be identified – and these principles serve to provide a structure for the study of "HCI". The domain is fundamentally about connecting humans to computers/machines (Human–Computer Interfaces are simply restricted instances of Human–Machine Interfaces). Once identified, these fundamental principles can be used to establish "Guidelines for Design", and "Methodologies for Evaluation".

Parenthetically, the processes of "Design and Evaluation" are merely pragmatic forms of a more fundamental pair of endeavors known broadly as "Engineering and Science". Roughly speaking, Engineering is the enterprise where a conceptual representation of a system is transformed into, or "designed as", a physical system implementation. Science is the complementary process, whereby an existing physical system is examined through observation, guided by the "Scientific Method", in an attempt to build conceptual representations, or "theories", of the function or structure of the system. Accordingly, we treat Design and Evaluation as complementary trajectories. They should not be decoupled since, from an epistemological point of view, the two streams are needed to provide the complementary efforts that are needed for the "iterative process of design" (cf. [2,3]). There must be representations for concepts of systems, and there must be representations for implementations of systems. The two must be functionally and structurally equivalent. They must be "semantically equivalent". And so, accordingly, "Design and Evaluation" need to remain entwined though iterations of the overall enterprise.

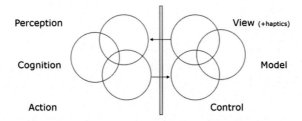

Figure 33.3 Schematic of the information-processing categories in HCI.

33.3. What is an interface?

The "interface" between any two regimes is quite simply, and essentially, the boundary between the two, whether that be a membrane between two volumes, a line that segments two areas, or a set of input and output connections between two agents. The study of the interface itself is restricted to the exchanges that take place between the two. Furthermore, the interface is characterized entirely by capturing the nature of that exchange – whether it be mediated by energy, matter, or abstract information. Let's explore this notion of an "interface," as a central them in this chapter on "Human–Computer Interfaces" for MICCAI.

If you were to ask researchers in Surface Science "what is an interface?", they might talk about a membrane that separates two material phases: perhaps solids, liquids, or gases. This is extremely instructive, since we learn that the study of the interface would be cast in a language relating to the materials and energies exchanged across the interface. The same would be true in Biology, Chemistry, or Physics. Will this be true if the interface passes something more like "view", or "command and control"?

If you were to ask Software Engineers "what is an interface?", they might talk about two Software Objects; essentially, two abstractions which encapsulate information, communicating by passing messages (or invoking methods by passing parameters and returned structures; cf. Alan Kay's development of Object-Oriented programming in 1968). A software API (or "Applications Programming Interface") is simply a list of the names of a set of functions, along with the data types passed and returned. An API deliberately hides the implementations of the functions that receive the input parameters: in other words, the API does not contain the source code for these functions, and therefore, this is NOT a behavioral representation. Furthermore, it has nothing much to say about the programmer's implementation of applications which will make use of the API calls. It exclusively and exhaustively lists only the data flow direction, and the data types. The same principle is true throughout Software Engineering; throughout Computer Engineering for that matter; and by extension, throughout any other discipline of Engineering. Accordingly, so we argue here, the same is true for HCI. (See Fig. 33.3.)

If two entities do not interact across a boundary, there's not much to say about the pair together. A boundary which does not permit an exchange is not particularly interesting. Such an interface would block all interaction – there would be zero flow and not much to discuss. On the other extreme would be an interface so permeable that there is unrestricted flow – to the extent where the two regimes would not be disconnected at all – they would simply be the same regime.

So, indeed, what makes an interface interesting is that it permits a precise characterization of the exchange, cast in terms of a set of constraints that clearly and extensively describe the interface: namely: What is exchanged? What direction does it flow? And what quantitative model can be used to describe the flow, as a function of the processes on either side that produce and consume it. So, to characterize a Human–Computer Interface for Medical Imaging and Computer-Assisted Interventions, we are essentially asking – what are the types of exchanges that can occur across the implicit interface? The answer to this question is surprisingly constrained, and so we explore it here.

33.4. Human outputs are computer inputs

The outputs from a human (which become inputs for the computer or the machine) can only be produced using muscles. Humans, like all other organisms, interact with the physical world exclusively with actions that are caused by muscles producing forces in conjunction with states of position (configuration, kinematics, and dynamics). There are no exceptions; muscles are the only "output" system for interaction and control within a physical world [6,7]. "Language" is a very special form of output, but still makes use of muscle control: whether by text, by voice, or by gestures (cf. [4,5]). This special capacity underpins to the human ability to share "concepts" (declarations), "goals" (action plans to accomplish a task), and "beliefs" (the concepts that arise in the cognitive system of the user, based on their perception of the medical imagery or visual data, cf. [10,11]). This is a guiding constraint for analysis of Medical Imaging displays. But first we can consider a lower-bandwidth channel across the Human–Computer Interface: namely, the computer "inputs" (cf. [18,19]).

All computer "input" devices (receiving human outputs) are sensitive to the relationship between position and force that the human "controls" in order to perform a task. Since this is a very low-bandwidth exchange, compared to the bandwidth of the flow of information from the computer to the human, we will first explore "computer input devices" by examining a cursory but representative set of illustrative examples.

33.5. Position inputs (free-space pointing and navigation interactions)

Let us begin by considering the following list of 2D pointing devices and ask the question – are they all providing the same information?

- Mouse
- Trackball
- Light Pen on Screen
- Finger on Touchpad

To be sure, each physical device is used to indicate a position – in these instances, position on a 2D space. The devices themselves may either present this information in absolute, or relative, coordinates. A touchscreen, for example, is an intrinsic part of a display, and so the position interaction is reported in the absolute coordinate frame of the display (x, y). A mouse, on the other hand, does not report absolute position; a mouse does not know where it is located. Interacting with a mouse does not produce an absolute position, rather, a stream of "changes in position" $(\Delta x, \Delta y)$. The operating system integrates these changes of position over time, thereby updating the position of the cursor on the screen (cf. [13,14]). Gyroscopic-based position devices are the same – they can only report changes in attitude – the system must then integrate those changes over time in order to estimate a position, relative to some initial frame. The feedback provided to the user is a "proxy" in the scene (or "cursor" in 2D).

33.6. Direct manipulation vs proxy-based interactions (cursors)

When you move a position-based input device, you observe the motion of the cursor or proxy. It certainly feels as if, while you are moving your hand, that it is connected mechanically to the proxy – but, of course, it is all mediated by integration, and this is done typically by the operating system or VR API.

The user's experience is that they are directly controlling the proxy (cf. [29,22]), when in fact they are moving their hand and controlling a device which is actually out of the view. Only under very special circumstances is the hand or finger in actual registration with the perceived movement in the scene; indeed, this is very difficult to do in Augmented Reality displays (cf. [1,24]). A "touchscreen" is a 2D example which, on the other hand, works very well – but this is due to the fact that the device itself is a sensor for the direct input, as well as the display itself. In augmented reality, this is not the case – and is precisely what leads to frequent failures in AR for the user experience of "direct manipulation".

The same distinction can be made for position-based computer input devices with higher degrees of freedom. They may report absolute 3D or 6 dof coordinates, but on the other hand if they report "changes" in these 6 parameters, then the system will need to integrate them and update a cursor in the 3D environment, which will serve as a proxy for the absolute position in the workspace. The data type of any position-based device is "tuples". There will be an ordered pair in 2D, a triple for 3D, a 6-tuple for 6 dof; and so on. However, one major difference is that while 2D input devices are exclusively used while in contact with a surface (such as a mousepad, or the sphere of a

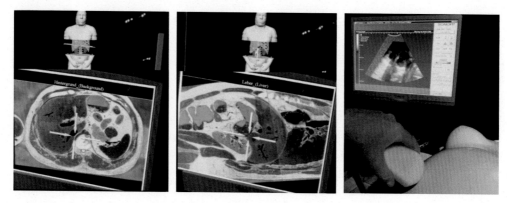

Figure 33.4 In addition to position-based interactions with objects, the user can also control the viewpoint.

trackball), this is not the case for a 3D device (since the surface contact would remove that third degree of freedom). Counterintuitively, the lack of contact with a constrained surface raises problems for 3D input devices; and as we will discuss shortly, this arises from an impaired ability to select virtual objects by interacting with them.

33.7. Control of viewpoint

One very special kind of Position-based interaction is where the interaction is bound to the viewpoint, or "camera", rather than an object in the view. Position-based interactions can also be used to change the position of the viewpoint (such as a virtual camera in 3D, or the view on a 2D plane, image, or pages of text on a document). This distinction corresponds to the dichotomy of space-based motions: Navigation vs Manipulation; object-based vs viewer-based. (See Fig. 33.4.)

33.8. Selection (object-based interactions)

The other form of interaction is object-based, whether that is a mouse button, a switch on a panel, a drop-down menu item, or an interaction signaled by a superposition of a cursor and a target in the workspace. "Selections" can also be mapped onto objects in the display using a focus-traversal mechanism (which is a discrete and coarse method for hopping between existing objects in the display; often by pressing the TAB key), or, less frequently in GUI systems, the traversal could be made directly by somehow naming those objects.

This raises an important distinction: Position-based interactions are posed within free space (they do not necessarily need to map to objects), whereas selection interactions do. And aside from text-based interactions, after these three kinds of interaction, there

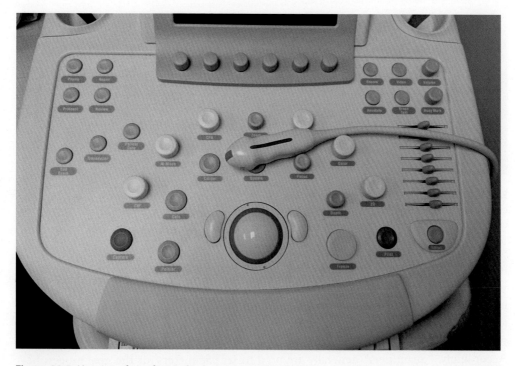

Figure 33.5 User Interfaces for Medical Imaging make good use of the four types of computer inputs: Selection (buttons), Quantification (sliders and knobs), position (trackball and ultrasound probe), and text (optional keyboard not visible in this photograph).

are NO other kinds of interaction that can be transmitted from humans to computers (or to machines in general, for that matter). (See Fig. 33.5 for examples of selection, quantification, and position inputs.)

33.9. Quantification (object-based position setting)

When we consider objects which the user can interact with by setting their position and/or orientation (such as a slider, a lever, a knob, etc.), then we have combined selection and position into a single interaction which we can call "quantification". The data type of the quantifier is, generally, a scalar value along a continuum – which is, in practical terms, sampled from a set of discrete values. But in any case, once the interaction occurs, the device will retain that "state" – it holds the quantity as a value. Any object in the user interface, which can respond to a pointing interaction in a way which changes its state and returns that value as a quantity, will be a kind of quantifier.

It's not trite to point out that quantifiers are simply objects which can support "one degree-of-freedom position". A slider is a 1 dof position input device; same for a knob, except the interaction is rotational rather than translational. So we should note that in-

Figure 33.6 Targeting tasks involve navigating through a space and then interacting with the perceived target can be accomplished using quantifiers (left image), direct pointing (middle image), or changing the position of a proxy or tool.

teractions that return ordered pairs corresponding to the position of the interaction are "Position" interactions, which can include 3D position, 6 dof (position and orientation in 3D), or in general, n–tuples corresponding to the configuration of the input device. (See Fig. 33.6.) However, in the case of quantifiers, the returned n–tuple is associated with the state of an object (i.e., the quantifier), rather than as a position in free space. Accordingly, "quantifiers" generally are used to set parameters for the goal process being controlled, rather than to specify positions in the workspace. Positions within the workspace are set using "proxies", or cursors in the workspace. Objects which, upon interaction with the pointing mechanism, return an event of being selected or deselected, are stateful "switches", and so these are "button events" – they are interactions which lead to a change in state of the way the goal process is being controlled by the user.

33.10. User interactions: selection vs position, object-based vs free-space

So, we are left with the following restricted space of input types: there are either position events (either posed in free space, or mediated by an object in the workspace), or else there are object-based events which are selection events (action events, or one-of-many item events).

This sounds a bit audacious. How can there be only two types of interaction, position and selection? You can either specify a position in n–degrees-of-freedom, or you can select an object by interacting with it. Well, this surprising restriction is actually a function of the space of human "outputs". When you consider the human as a system and ask, what is the set of possible "output devices", it turns out the only way for us to "output" is using muscle. There are no other output channels or interfaces. That's all

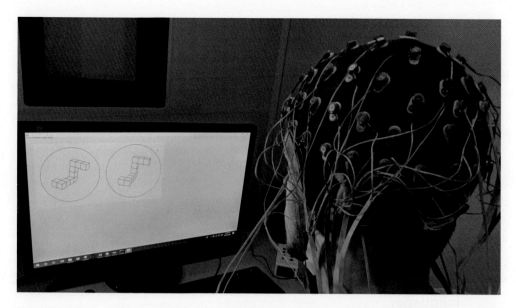

Figure 33.7 Even when interactions are mediated by a Brain–Computer Interface, these are still object-based selections or changes in the position or orientation of the perceived entities.

we've got! And if you think you have a pious hope that brain–computer interfaces will allow us to download our whole "user experience", think again. When we are cogitating, it's all about "entities and relations", formulated in sequences (i.e., "sequential", not "parallel") within the conscious mind. (See Fig. 33.7.)

Humans have goals and beliefs, and in accord with those, to perform tasks, we formulate action plans which are ultimately implemented using movements, which are effected using muscles. And in turn, when our muscles act as effectors that drive the dynamics, kinematics, and configuration of our limbs, these dynamics will evolve in free space, or in interaction with objects in the environment. The resulting behaviors will manifest as an evolution of Forces, in relation to Position states (configuration, kinematics, and dynamics). To take a simple example, if we interact while holding a spring that is connected to a stationary frame, for the "linear range" of the spring, we mean that there will be a linear relationship between force and position.

If we move our fingertip through free space, the characteristic relationship is to observe changes in position, with relatively small changes in force. The technical term for this is "isotonic" (the "tone" of the muscle stays constant). At the other extreme is a force that is exerted on a stationary frame, which resists change in position (i.e., a hard contact with an object). The technical term for this is "isometric" (the position metric stays constant).

On a graph of force versus position (F vs X), behaviors which evolve roughly along horizontal trajectories are "isotonic" and those that evolve along vertical trajectories are "isometric". The former are like "movement through space to new positions", and the latter are "interaction with a stationary object".

When you go to push a button on a console, or to interact with a checkbox on a touchscreen, you move through space until you interact with the object, at which point motion stops but force increases. So the sequence of movement-and-selection begins as a roughly isotonic interaction, followed by the selection phase which is isometric. If you then moved to a slider, the release of the button puts you back in a mode of free-space movement, until you interact with the slider lever, at which point you stop moving perpendicular to the plane of the touchscreen, but you are free to move parallel to the surface, which is a constrained isotonic motion. All interactions with computers, machines, or even surgical tools, will be about movement, selection, movement, selection, etc. Those are the only behaviors which can be measured, as outputs from the human who is performing a task.

33.11. Text inputs (strings encoded/parsed as formal and informal language)

The following itemized list allows us to begin an analysis of "computer input" devices, starting with the earliest and most flexible form (text input):
- Keyboard (physical keys, membrane key panels, keyboards displayed on touchscreens)
- Voice Recognition
- Handwriting Recognition
- QR-code and barcode scanners

In each of these cases, the user provides a string of characters to the computer (even voice recognition modules ultimately pass strings of text to the computer).

33.12. Language-based control (text commands or spoken language)

There is a very special way that humans can communicate – we seem almost singularly capable of this – through the use of "language". This is not just through the use of human languages (informal, spoken, or written), but also through the production and understanding of very formal languages that can be used to control machines or computers.

These can range in complexity, from single-word spoken commands (which are really, once detected by the computer, simply forms of "selection" – they are equivalent to pushing a button which selects a mode), to short phrases (typical noun/verb pairs), all the way to spoken command phrases, or queries. The use of spoken language – or more frequently keyboard-typed as a "command line" or database query – are less frequently used. However, we do not want to omit a discussion here.

Information can be passed to a computer, or passed back from a computer, using character-based strings (sentences), or equivalently, using voice recognition and voice synthesis (and less frequently, using handwriting recognition). But blending these distinctions into "text-based interactions", we must note something important: these interactions are patently not movement-and-selection based on the position of our input devices relative to objects in the workspace – however, semantically they are "about" the entities (objects) in the task-based workspace, and the relationships between these entities.

Put more frankly, "language-based interactions" will make use of symbols that represent "objects and entities" [28], and these symbols will take the form of "nouns and verbs". The nouns will either be labels which can be associated with entities, or else they will be demonstratives (this and that, here and there, "pointers and indexes") which will refer to entities in the domain. The verbs will describe relationships between entities, such as interactions, manipulations, navigations, or command-like expressions (corresponding to the "imperative" sentence types in human languages). As an example of these kinds of imperative-sentence text-based interactions, consider the development of IF-based parsers that followed Weizenbaum's (1966) work [30], to Winograd's [32] (in 1972), and through to interactive text-based interfaces for navigation and manipulation within spaces of 3D objects [8], paving the way for more sophisticated natural language understanding systems that can be directed through imperative sentences to perform actions, when prefaced by "Siri!", or "Hey, Google!". In a very limited sense, these systems can respond to queries, such as "What time is it?", although often by submitting the queries verbatim to web-based search engines. (See Fig. 33.8.)

Other queries (corresponding to the "where", "what", "when", or less frequently, "who"), or for ontology-based knowledge level interactions (such as with medical ontologies), the special verbs correspond to the "existential and possessive" verbs (is-a and has-a) for sentences which would have a declarative type.

Queries posed as "how" interrogatives are seeking to obtain returned expressions which are in the form of imperatives; they are sequences of actions which specify how to perform a task. Queries posed as "why" interrogatives are seeking to obtain returned expressions which are in the form of declaratives; they are lists of existential and possessive relations between entities in the knowledge domain (i.e., the ontological representation of the clinical workspace.)

A good example of this is provided in the work of Jannin's team [20] using the OntoSPM knowledge base, Protégé's Ontology viewer, and B<>COM's "Surgery Workflow Toolbox" software. (See Fig. 33.9.)

These representations, and their interactive software tools, form "interactions" at a higher abstract level, corresponding to the knowledge level. We do foresee a time when human–machine interaction with Medical Imaging systems, or with Computer-Assisted Interventions, will rise more generally to this semantic level – but for now we will

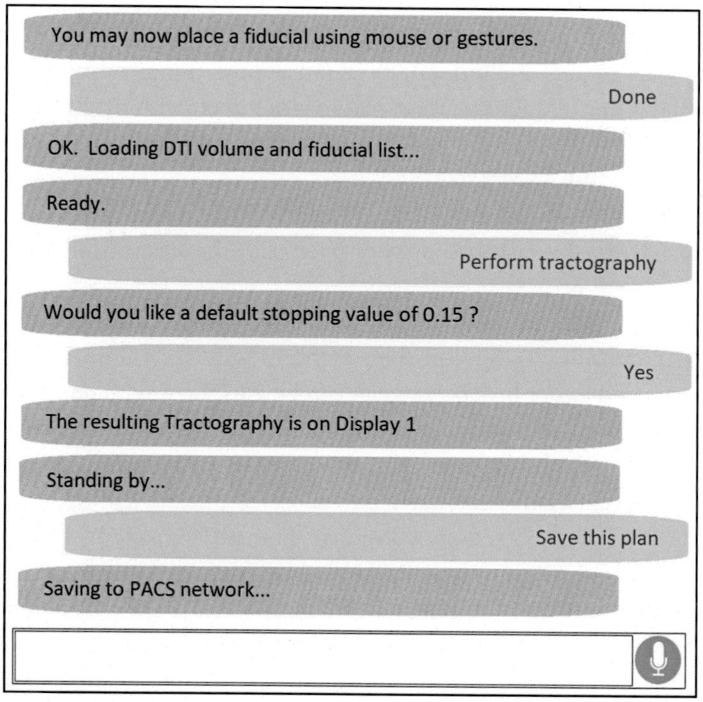

Figure 33.8 Example of a natural-language interface for medical data analysis (adapted from a concept by Fast et al. [15]).

restrict our discussion to lower abstractions corresponding to objects in a medical image or in a clinical workspace, posed in terms of their structural and functional relationships. Accordingly, we return now to movement-and-selection interactions, based on entities and their relationships in the image or in the scene-based display. (See Fig. 33.10.)

Gesture-based interactions are not a new class of interaction. They are either position-based or selection interactions (or alternating combinations of just these two).

33.13. Image-based and workspace-based interactions: movement and selection events

The consequence of this analysis is that it then leads to a very systematic prescription for a general methodology for estimating the performance of a user – an agent who is performing tasks. Objective estimates of task performance will involve estimating the speed and accuracy of each of these sequences of movement-and-selection… movement-and-selection-and-movement-and-selection, etc.

Of course, the other side of the loop-of-control is the perception of the display, the analysis and recognition of the state of the workspace and the task evolution, and sub-

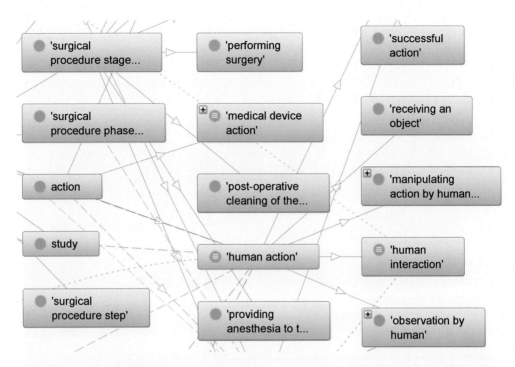

Figure 33.9 Goals and Beliefs of the clinician can be represented as ontologies of domain knowledge.

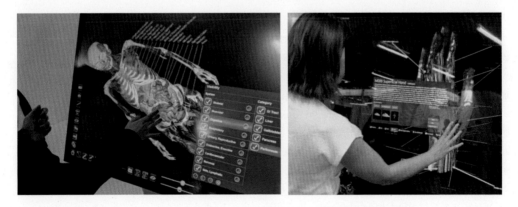

Figure 33.10 Example of an anatomical table showing gesture-based interactions.

sequent planning and execution of the next movement-and-selection interaction. The initial arc of this loop is known as the "evaluation" aspect of HCI, and the descending arc of this loop of control is called the "execution" aspect of HCI. This is what led Don Norman [26] to propose an overarching principle in HCI: reduce the gulf of evaluation, and the gulf of execution. In other words, optimize the display so as to facilitate

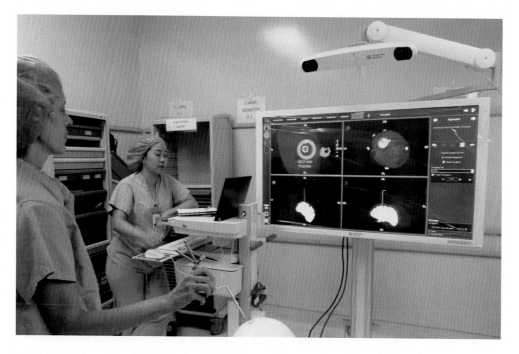

Figure 33.11 Example of the Synaptive Software for planning surgical approaches in neurosurgery.

the user's situational awareness of the progress of their task, as well as optimize the set of interactions provided to the user so that they can map the goals of their task onto interactions that will realize the task. (See Fig. 33.11.)

In Software Engineering, the programming idiom for human–computer interfaces is such that, when a system starts to run, first the view on the display will have been initialized to some visual structure (as specified by the programmer using declarations of the objects that will be contained in the display, along with their relative configuration) and then the computer will rest in an "event-driven" state. It will wait for there to be some interaction from the user. The software contains a set of event callback functions, or more recently, "event listeners" – which will encapsulate the particular behaviors (represented as coded modules which will be invoked for any particular "event") that will be triggered by these events on the user interface.

Since these event-driven behaviors can also depend on the internal system state, this model then generalizes to, exactly, the quintessential set that characterizes general "computation." There is a finite set of inputs/events, a finite set of states that the system can take, a finite set of output symbols or visual displays, and a mapping between them (called the transformation function), but really is the "computer program", whether it be represented as a state table, state diagram, or in a computer language. Accordingly, the "program" that is written and embodied by the behavior of the interface is derived from an information-processing model of the user's task.

33.14. Task representations for image-based and intervention-based interfaces

What remains to be examined is the role that the "task" itself plays when considering the human–computer interface (as shared with Navab's lab in [16] and [27]). Consequently, what gives rise to the behavioral (functional) aspects of the human–computer interface are:

(1) The representation of the task embodied by the computer (in terms of the input–output and state-based behaviors, i.e., the "program" that is embodied by the human–computer interface), and

(2) The representation of the task embodied by the user, in terms of the perceived inputs and planned motor responses (it is the "user's task," which is the goal, and the mapping to planned actions that drives the user's behaviors).

Accordingly, as part of their task goals and their cognitive beliefs about the progression of the task as the interactions evolve over time. For Medical Imaging, or for Clinical or Surgical Interactions, the tasks that the user is performing can be characterized in the same way that spoken sentences are characterized. There are only three types of expressions that can be posed as the basis for representing these tasks:

(1) Declarations about what exists in the displayed data or the experienced workspace are expressions at the knowledge level,

(2) Imperatives posed as part of a planning process that describe the action-based interactions in a workspace, or in the steps for processing the imaging data,

(3) Queries which, in general, are restricted to questions about "where" (localization/segmentation), "what" (detection/classification), and less frequently "when".

These three forms of expression, whether represented at the computer algorithm level or represented in terms of the knowledge-level "goals and beliefs" of the interventionist or the diagnostician, are combined into sequences – in other words, these expressions are sequenced by coordinating conjunctions, ("and", "then", "subsequently", "followed by", etc.) or by subordinating conjunctions ("if", "else", "whenever", "otherwise", "in case", etc.).

The response to a query allows either the human or the computer to change their knowledge of the state of the task, the result of imperatives is an action which will change the state of the workspace or image data, and the declaratives are expressions about the knowledge and beliefs about the problem domain. Complex structured tasks can be represented using hierarchical nesting of the workflow representations. (See Fig. 33.12.)

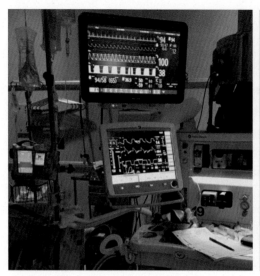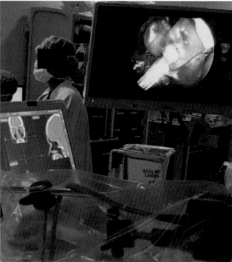

Figure 33.12 Operative Room setting for an endoscopic transphenoidal case: (left) anesthesia monitors to follow the vitals of the patient; (right) endoscopic camera showing the surgical cavity and neuromonitoring using tracked instruments.

33.15. Design and evaluation guidelines for human–computer interfaces: human inputs are computer outputs – the system design must respect perceptual capacities and constraints

By adopting the perspective that HCI design is constrained by the special capacities and constraints of human Perception, Cognition, and Action, we can derive a set of HCI Guidelines for the system's Design and Evaluation.

Consider the following diagram, whose arrows represent the flows within an information-processing model of the human. We note the key stages: the perceptual system processes sensory inputs and extracts descriptions of the entities, and their relations, in the user's domain. These descriptions allow the cognitive system to adopt beliefs about the current state of the user's world, which in the case of HCI is the view of a task that is being conducted by the user. The task itself is embodied by the user, and at the cognitive level this is represented as goals and beliefs about the task being conducted. In order to do so, the user must form action plans which are then executed through the action system which, at its lowest level, operates through control of effectors, with feedback from the sensory system – this completes the loop of perception/cognition/action. (See Fig. 33.13.)

In the boxes within this diagram, we identify Design Principles that are a reflection of the special capacities and constraints of the human (the user of the HCI system).

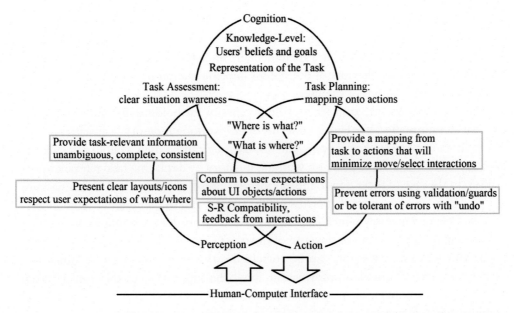

Figure 33.13 User Interface Design Principles result from the special capacities and constraints of the human.

In a very general sense, the design guidelines will revolve around a common theme of facilitating the user's task by regarding the human–computer interface as a tool for the user who is conducting a task. The user's goals and beliefs will include a set of expectations about the world being perceived (the domain entities, and their relations) and about the objects being controlled (again, the entities within the domain, and the changes that can be effected to put them into new relations). Accordingly, the display should be designed to allow the user to effortlessly evaluate the state of the task, and there should be controllable objects (which are selection and quantification entities) which provide functionality that can be used to execute a task in step-by-step fashion (sequences of movement and interaction). The mapping between these interactions (which launch functionalities subsequently executed by the system) should be designed according to the principle that there should be minimal and natural mappings from the goals of the user, to its execution within the world of the problem domain. If done properly, then the system design is able to minimize this "gulf of execution."

In addition to these information-processing capacities of the user, there are also constraints that must be recognized simultaneously. The human action system, constrained to two modes of output (movement and interaction), stands in contrast to the perceptual system, which by comparison has a very high throughput of information. So much sensory information can be made available, yet only a small part of that information is task-relevant. Accordingly, the user must either make use of their attention-based top-down processing to discover the task-relevant information, or else the HCI display can be designed so that this "gulf of evaluation" is minimized. Furthermore, since perceptual–motor control operates incrementally and iteratively as a loop-of-control, the stimulus–response behaviors of the system implementation must be consistent with the low-level expectations of the user.

The cognitive system, with its enormous capacity for holding domain knowledge, can face an information bottleneck in terms of its "working memory" capacity for executing short-term tasks. Accordingly, the display itself can be used to hold information in order to minimize the reliance on working memory by displaying task-relevant information. In the face of these constraints on the perceptual, cognitive, and action systems, a good design will recognize that errors will be made – and so the system should, if possible, be designed in a way which can either prevent errors (by constraining the space of possible inputs as a function of the state of the user's task), or else it should be designed, again, if possible, so that errors can be corrected – that steps taken can be "undone". The system may also provide information about the kinds of steps that can be taken ("tooltips", for example, or by providing online help or task-relevant implementation examples when requested).

These **Design Guidelines** are summarized here (and expanded in [12]):

- Design the system display entities, and interaction behaviors, to match existing user expectations

- The Display should be designed so that the User's Evaluation of the state of the task is effortless

- The UI controls should afford sequences towards the goal execution with minimal steps/effort

- Clear, task-relevant information displayed should not be ambiguous or incomplete (or else these should support queries from the user to resolve them)

- User interaction errors should be prevented or "undoable" if possible

- The interactions that lead to visual feedback should not violate natural stimulus–response expectations

Now, within the domain of Medical Imaging and Computer-Assisted Interventions, there are two broad categories of task, Medical Imaging Displays for Diagnostic Tasks, and Computer-Assisted Interventional Interfaces for surgical or clinical interactions.

33.16. Objective evaluation of performance on a task mediated by an interface

Before the advent of human–computer interfaces, Experimental Psychologists had known that the objective evaluation of performance on a task can be formulated by considering both the time (or speed) and the error rate (or accuracy) of the sequence of actions which make up the overarching task [25,33,31]. They had also known that these are the **only** objective measures that can be made. And more recently, due to the prevalent theories and empirical support of the speed–accuracy trade-off, it has become recognized that these two measures cannot be disentangled. Put succinctly and emphatically, *"**performance of a task is the product of speed and accuracy, relative to that task**".* (Within the HMI literature, this fundamental principle goes back as far as Fitts [17], Hyman [23], Hick [21], or perhaps Woodworth [34].) What we would like to emphasize here is that there are **no other** objective metrics of performance (any other would either be noncausal correlate measures, or worse, be "subjective", and consequently prone to all of the cognitive and methodological biases that make subjective evaluations a very weak hand to play).

There is an easy *Gedankenexperiment* that can be conducted in this regard. Pretend, for the sake of argument, that there might be, say, three objective metrics of performance: "Speed, Accuracy, and Path Length". Well, then, what happens if your data shows that you have improved your speed and decreased your path length, but your accuracy is lower? Presumably that calls your performance into question. And what if you have improved your accuracy and decreased your path length, but you have been much slower? Well, then, have you improved your performance by being much slower while taking a shorter path? Really? But now: what if you have improved your speed and your accuracy, but not your path length? Well, from the perspective of the task – the increase in path length is irrelevant. As long as your speed and accuracy are both better, then, by definition, your performance has improved.

"Path length" would only arise as a metric if it was explicitly made part of the goals of the task. In this case, it would be a dual task, such as when you are asked to "point to a target while at the same time minimizing your path length." Then, in that case, you have *two* tasks – and you can consider the speed and accuracy of both of those tasks, and then consider whether or not there exists a trade-off between accuracy constraints of the two tasks – in which you will need to consider some weighting function if you need to extract a single performance measure from this dual task. Alternately, you can extract performance metrics on the two aspects of the dual task.

This principle of objective performance metrics based on speed and accuracy can be applied hierarchically to any particular subtask of an overarching task; whether they comprised goal-directed movements, or discrete choice-based tasks (where in the discrete case, one considers the reciprocals of the task time and the error rate). While we have tried to provide an encompassing review of a broad area of research, we do hope that this article has been an argument that champions this particular emphatic point about the quantitative evaluation of human–machine interfaces for Medical Imaging, and Computer-Assisted Interventions.

References

[1] K. Abhari, J. Baxter, E. Chen, A. Khan, C. Wedlake, T. Peters, S. de Ribaupierre, R. Eagleson, The role of augmented reality in training the planning of brain tumor resection, in: Augmented reality environments for medical imaging and computer-assisted Interventions (AECAI), 2013.

[2] Fred Brooks, The Mythical Man-Month: Essays on Software Engineering, Addison-Wesley, Reading, MA, 1975.

[3] Fred Brooks, The Design of Design: Essays from a Computer Scientist, Addison-Wesley, Reading, MA, 2010.

[4] W. Buxton, Lexical and pragmatic considerations of input structures, Computer Graphics 17 (1) (1983) 31–37.

[5] W. Buxton, R. Hill, P. Rowley, Issues and techniques in touch-sensitive tablet input, in: Proceedings of SIGGRAPH '85, Computer Graphics 19 (3) (1985) 215–224.

[6] S. Card, W. English, B. Burr, Evaluation of mouse, rate-controlled isometric joystick, step keys and text keys for text selection on a CRT, Ergonomics 21 (8) (1978) 601–613.

[7] S. Card, J.D. Mackinlay, G.G. Robertson, The design space of input devices, in: Proceedings of CHI '90, ACM Conference on Human Factors in Software, 1990.

[8] W. Crowther, D. Woods, WOOD0350 aka. Adventure, computer program; source code; executable online: https://quuxplusone.github.io/Advent/play.html, 1976.

[9] M. Descoteaux, L. Maier-Hein, A. Franz, P. Jannin, L. Collins, S. Duchesne, Introduction: MICCAI 2017, Preface to Proceedings of the 20th International Conference on Medical Imaging and Computer-Assisted Intervention, September 11, 2017, Quebec City.

[10] R. Eagleson, T. Peters, Perceptual capacities and constraints in augmented reality biomedical displays, Australasian Physical & Engineering Sciences in Medicine 31 (4) (2008) 371.

[11] R. Eagleson, S. de Ribaupierre, Visual perception and human–computer interaction in surgical augmented and virtual reality environments, in: Mixed and Augmented Reality in Medicine, 2018, pp. 83–98.

[12] R. Eagleson, G. Hattab, Tutorial on design guidelines for HCI in medical imaging and computer-assisted interventions, in: Conference on Computer-Assisted Radiology and Surgery (CARS 2019), Rennes, June 18, 2019, 2019.

[13] D. Engelbart, Augmenting Human Intellect: A Conceptual Framework, Summary Report, Contract AF 49(638) 1024, SRI Project 3578, October, Stanford Research Institute, Menlo Park, Calif., 1962.

[14] W. English, D. Engelbart, M. Berman, Display-selection techniques for text manipulation, IEEE Transactions on Human Factors in Electronics HFE-8 (1) (March 1967) 5–15.

[15] E. Fast, B. Chen, J. Mendelsohn, J. Bassen, M. Bernstein, IRIS: a conversational agent for complex tasks, in: ACM Conference on Human Factors in Computing Systems (CHI 2018), 2018.

[16] M. Feuerstein, T. Sielhorst, J. Traub, C. Bichlmeier, N. Navab, Action- and workflow-driven augmented reality for computer-aided medical procedures, IEEE Computer Graphics and Applications 2 (September/October 2007) 10–14.

[17] P. Fitts, The information capacity of the human motor system in controlling the amplitude of movement, Journal of Experimental Psychology 47 (1954) 381–391.

[18] J. Foley, A. Van Dam, Fundamentals of Interactive Computer Graphics, Addison-Wesley, Reading, MA, 1982.

[19] J.D. Foley, V.L. Wallace, P. Chan, The human factors of computer graphics interaction techniques, IEEE Computer Graphics and Applications 4 (11) (1984) 13–48.

[20] B. Gibaud, G. Forestier, C. Feldmann, G. Ferrigno, P. Gonçalves, T. Haidegger, C. Julliard, D. Katić, H. Kenngott, L. Maier-Hein, K. März, E. de Momi, D.Á. Nagy, H. Nakawala, J. Neumann, T. Neumuth, J. Rojas Balderrama, S. Speidel, M. Wagner, P. Jannin, Toward a standard ontology of surgical process models, International Journal of Computer Assisted Radiology and Surgery 13 (2018) 1397–1408.

[21] W. Hick, On the rate of gain of information, Quarterly Journal of Experimental Psychology 4 (1952) 11–26.

[22] E. Hutchins, J. Hollan, D. Norman, Direct manipulation interfaces, Human–Computer Interaction 1 (1985) 311–338.

[23] R. Hyman, Stimulus information as a determinant of reaction time, Journal of Experimental Psychology 45 (1953) 188–196.

[24] M. Kramers, R. Armstrong, S. Bakhshmand, A. Fenster, S. de Ribaupierre, R. Eagleson, Evaluation of a mobile augmented reality application for image guidance of neurosurgical interventions, in: MMVR, Medicine Meets Virtual Reality, 2014, pp. 204–208.

[25] L. McLeod, The interrelations of speed, accuracy, and difficulty, Journal of Experimental Psychology 12 (5) (1929) 431–443.

[26] D. Norman, User Centered System Design: New Perspectives on Human–Computer Interaction, CRC Press, ISBN 978-0-89859-872-8, 1986.

[27] B. Preim, HCI in medical visualization, in: Hans Hagen (Ed.), Scientific Visualization: Interactions, Features, Metaphors, Dagstuhl Publishing, 2011, pp. 292–310.

[28] Willard Van Ormon Quine, Word and Object, MIT Press, 1960.

[29] B. Shneiderman, The future of interactive systems and the emergence of direct manipulation, Behaviour & Information Technology 1 (3) (1982) 237–256.

[30] J. Weizenbaum, ELIZA—a computer program for the study of natural language communication between man and machine, Communications of the ACM 9 (1966) 36–45.

[31] A. Wickelgren, Speed-accuracy tradeoff and information processing dynamics, Acta Psychologia 41 (1) (February 1977) 67–85.

[32] T. Winograd, Understanding Natural Language, Academic Press, New York, 1972.

[33] C. Wood, R. Jennings, Speed-accuracy tradeoff functions in choice reaction time: experimental design and computational procedures, Perception and Psychophysics 19 (1) (1976) 92–102.

[34] R. Woodworth, Accuracy of Voluntary Movement, PhD Thesis (Advisor: Cattell), Columbia University, 1899.

CHAPTER 34

Robotic interventions*

Pradipta Biswas, Sakura Sikander, Pankaj Pramod Kulkarni, Marilu Ortiz, Sang-Eun Song
Mechanical and Aerospace Engineering, University of Central Florida, Orlando, FL, United States

Contents

34.1. Introduction	841
34.2. Precision positioning	842
34.3. Master–slave system	844
34.4. Image guided robotic tool guide	846
34.5. Interactive manipulation	848
34.6. Articulated access	850
34.7. Untethered microrobots	852
34.8. Soft robotics	853
34.9. Summary	855
References	855

34.1. Introduction

It has been three decades since the first robot was used for surgery [1]. Since then, rapid advances in the field of engineering have made surgical robotics more accessible for medical use. Over 150 surgical robots have been developed from the early 1990s till 2010 alone [2]. Robot assisted surgical procedures have tripled in the world from 80,000 to 205,000 in between 2007 and 2010 [3]. The da Vinci, RoboDoc, and Mako are among the established surgical robots used for surgery for a longer period. Robotic surgery uses ergonomic interfaces to access surgical sites with higher accuracy and enabling functions.

In recent years, more and more companies and research labs have become interested in medical robotics. Surgical robots have broken out of the traditional realm of multifunctional robotics and have become more focused on surgery-specific robots incorporating various newly available technologies. The recent advancements in medical imaging, haptics, computer vision, and miniaturization technologies are encouraging the development and implementation of new surgical robots in all surgical fields with specialized features.

Research and development of surgical robots requires multidisciplinary collaborative efforts from engineers, scientists, and physicians. The ability to think across disciplines and to understand tradeoffs and interaction between them is crucial. Human factors are

---

* We thank Dr. Yaela Marks for her editorial support.

Handbook of Medical Image Computing and Computer Assisted Intervention
https://doi.org/10.1016/B978-0-12-816176-0.00039-9

841

fundamental in the process, too. The surgical robotic development team must design and build the system in possession of deep understanding of how the user will utilize the aid. Involving physicians from the onset of the development is crucial, particularly if the adaptation of surgical robotics is to move from the first enthusiastic early adopters into widespread use.

This chapter presents an overview of various robotic interventions with fundamental functions and technology utilizations such as precision positioning, master–slave systems, image guided robotic interventions, interactive manipulation, articulated access, and untethered microrobots followed by the latest soft robotics applications in healthcare.

34.2. Precision positioning

In this section we briefly discuss a number of surgical robotic systems, which have been designed to act as fixtures for the positioning of intervention tools. These robotic fixtures permit precise positioning of the end effector at the desired target based on the feedback from various imaging and navigation systems (e.g., drilling or milling tool guides) in orthopedic surgery.

Mazor X Robotic guide system [4] is a spine surgery system from Mazor Robotics (now owned by Medtronic), consisting of a robotic precision guidance system and planning workstation shown in Fig. 34.1. The guidance system consists of a surgical arm, integrated 3D camera, and physician control panel. It generates a 3D model of the vertebrae using proprietary software from CT scans. Mazor X planning software allows the physician to create a spinal alignment plan for simulation of the impact of planned operations. The 3D camera maps the operating area, which has a rigidly attached mount, to create a 3D model of the surgical area that is synced to the preoperative plan using intraoperative fluoroscopic imaging. Intraoperative guidance follows a preoperative plan so that the surgical arm will align tools according to the surgical plan. Mazor X is a monitoring mode robotic system that follows a plan created by the physician before operation. Non-MRI based imaging (CT scan) provides image-based guidance with a 3D model while inserting implants.

ExcelsiusGPS [5], also a spine surgery system, follows a preoperative plan for the placement of pedicle screws in the patient's spine. Excelsius robotic system uses a robotic arm to align the position for surgical screw placement. It does not attach to the patient and is navigated using a 3D camera system. Once the robotic arm is in position, the physician hand turns the tool for screw placement into the patient's vertebrae with depth monitored through fluoroscopic imaging. Excelsius is a monitoring mode robotic system that follows a plan created by the physician before operation. It uses a telemanipulator system but allows for hands-on adjustment of the robotic arm to align with preoperative screw placement. Non-MRI based imaging, through fluoroscopy, provides image-based navigation for screw placement and depth control.

Plaskos et al. developed a bone-mounted robot PRAXITELES to be used as a system to accurately and precisely position a passive guide along different planes of the

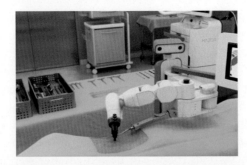

Figure 34.1 The MazorX robotic guidance system to guide sophisticated spine surgery procedures. It consists of a robotic arm and a 3D camera. The arm provides guidance for the operating tool and the 3D camera maps the operating area and matches with the preoperative 3D image. © 2019 Medtronic.

knee bone and enable planar cuts to perform knee arthroplasty [6]. It consists of two motorized degrees of freedom (DOF) for saw guide positioning around the distal femur and two passive DOF to align motorized DOF with the cutting plane for the femoral component of the knee prosthesis. The system enables rotation of the tool along with sliding in cutting plane while maintaining a fixed, minimally invasive, entry point. It is integrated with image-free navigation. The system has a small and portable size with a "universal" feature to align the guide along any plane and depth in the sagittal plane.

ROSA Brain [7] developed by Medtech can perform cranial interventions. The 6-DOF robotic arm on ROSA acts as GPS for the minimally invasive procedure, and the 2-DOF arm is used to support the patients head and can be equipped with a stereotactic frame or a head holder. ROSA utilizes 3D CT scan data from the patient for preoperative planning and the markers mounted on the stereotactic frame are used to sync with the 3D patient model and the ROSA robot. The robot provides precise placement and guidance for neurosurgical interventions.

In [8], a compact, 6-DOF, orthopedic robotic system was presented that can be used to position a tool guide to drive the drilling or milling tools. BRIGIT (Bone Resection Instrument Guidance by Intelligent Telemanipulator) is mounted on a wheeled trolley and has control software. For the surgical planning, the guide position is obtained after the registration procedure that involves collection of anatomical points on the bone. The registration is performed either by force control where the physician grabs the tool tip, or it is done in the teleoperation mode using a master device. To optimize the placement of the robotic system in operating theater and enhance the system performance, the developers devised a method based on interval analysis. This system is small, easy to install and operate, and has been applied to High Tibial Osteotomy.

Other than these, Wu et al. developed an MRI-guided probe positioning device for performing cryoablation procedures for treating tumors in areas such as the kidney, liver, etc. [9]. Chen et al. had initially started development of the system in [10].

Kobler et al. developed a passive robot with parallel configuration that is intended to be used as a guide for drilling, a tool to precisely position a neuroprosthetic device for minimally invasive cochlear implant surgery [11]. It is a bone attached system with redundant and reconfigurable features. The design consists of a Stewart–Gough platform that directly attaches to the bone anchors over the skull and allows rigid fixation of a linear slide, holding the tool. The platform is connected to the base joint using six prismatic joints that contain equipped spherical magnetic bearings. Since the system does not need rigid fixation, the physician can position the bone anchors at the most appropriate skull thickness. This robot can be reused after sterilization, unlike other microstereotactic frames.

Apart from these, other positioning robots include an MR compatible device developed by Mylonas et al. for positioning and guidance of a High Intensity Focused Ultrasound (HIFU) transducer for targeting tumors existing in abdominal and thyroid regions [12]. Similarly, Hata et al. developed an image guided cryotherapy probe guide for precise positioning in the treatment of renal cancer [13].

Positioning robots are plentiful in the surgical field. Robot precision bolsters the physician's activity and reduces errors, post operation complexities, and hospital returns.

34.3. Master–slave system

Teleoperated surgical robots provide superior instrumentation and versatile motion through small incisions controlled by the physician. Typically, the physician manipulates an ergonomic master input device in a visualization environment (physician console) and these inputs are translated into motion by a 3D vision system (endoscope) and wristed laparoscopic surgical instruments. The major advantage over the traditional (hand operated) surgical method is that it can compensate for human hand tremors and can also minimize the hand motion for surgical tasks, thereby reducing procedure time.

da Vinci [14,15] is used in multiple fields of surgery such as head and neck, thoracic, colorectal, gynecology, and urology in the form of laparoscopic surgery. The robot is equipped with 3 or 4 robotic arms. Incisions will be made for each instrument. One of the arms will be equipped with a 3D endoscope that displays on the visual system. In order to reduce trauma, the arms move around a fixed pivot point. Different instruments are designed with a specific purpose. Recent advancements include a single port system shown in Fig. 34.2.

Monarch platform [16,17] by Auris is intended for diagnostic and therapeutic bronchoscopic procedures. The teleoperated endolumenal robot can navigate inside the body, image, and treat conditions without making incisions. Monarch Platform is a neither a haptic feedback nor monitoring tool, as the robot only transmits visual information to the physician. It is not autonomous. Monarch Platform uses a custom

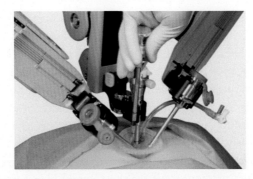

Figure 34.2 da Vinci SP system for single incision (port) robotic surgery. The robot provides three fully-wristed, elbowed instruments through a single 2.5 cm cannula. © 2019 Intuitive Surgical.

controller to allow the physician to directly control the endoscope as the physician navigates the lungs. Visual feedback is given from the endoscope as well as an image display for navigation. The robot is mounted on a stationary platform that controls the feed rate of the endoscope. The feed rate and navigation are all controlled by the physician at the visual platform in a master–slave relationship.

Virtual Incision's miniaturized robot [18] is used for gastrointestinal operations. The Virtual Incision robot is inserted into the abdominal cavity after an incision is made at the belly button. The two-arm manipulator robot, equipped with an HD camera, performs the operation within the abdomen. It is mounted onto the side of the operating table with an adjustable positioning arm. Virtual Incision provides neither haptic feedback nor monitoring. Data is received through a monitor system for arm positioning. Video footage shows physicians controlling the robot with two Geomagic Touch devices and a custom master device. The slave device is a telemanipulator using a wireless connection between the master–slave system. Video is streamed from the HD camera for an endoscope image-based navigation.

Revo-I [19,20] is a laparoscopic surgical robot. Revo-I has been marketed in South Korea to be more cost effective than the da Vinci of Intuitive Surgical. Like da Vinci, Revo-I is a 4-arm robotic platform with one arm equipped with a 3D camera. Different end effector attachments allow customization of the operating procedure. It is currently designed with tactile feedback, which results in decreased grasping strength but improved performance. Haptic feedback will be implemented in future revisions after development of kinesthetic feedback is added. A periscopic control station is used by the physician for the custom master device in the master–slave system with visual imaging used for navigation.

Avatera [21] is based on a 4-arm robot platform design with interchangeable tools. Avatera is still in early development so little is known as to whether haptic feedback or monitoring systems will be used. Imagery shows a control unit with an HD monitor for open display as well as a periscopic side periphery.

ARTAS [22] is a hair restoration robot developed by Restoration Robotics Inc. It restores hair to a patient's head through the transplantation of hair follicles. A dissecting punch removes sections of healthy hair follicles and grafts the hair by inserting the plugs at the transplant location. A robot arm and guidance system determine the angle and location of the operating tool while following the doctor's operative plan. ARTAS operates via a monitoring mode system with a standard master device that allows control through a keyboard or touch interface. The robot arm acts as a telemanipulator and operates semiautonomously.

Canady Hybrid Plasma Scalpel [23] is also a laparoscopic surgical robot. Canady Robotic Surgical System's primary tools are the Canady Flex Lapo Wrist and Canady Hybrid Plasma Scalpel. The Lapo Wrist is a 7 DOF, directly operated surgical instrument with a grasping tool at the end. The Plasma Scalpel delivers a beam that simultaneously cuts and coagulates the operating tissue. Canady Robotic Surgical System is neither haptic nor monitoring, as the physician receives optical feedback from an endoscope. The Canady is a true hands-on system with the physician directly manipulating the instruments.

Overall, master and slave type surgical robots are found in large numbers due to the fact that they combine the performance and precision of a robot while allowing the surgeon, who is skillful in performing that particular surgical activity, to maintain overall control.

34.4. Image guided robotic tool guide

Numerous research groups have designed and developed robotic needle guide systems that improve targeting accuracy by either providing a physical guidance for manual insertion or enabling a complete automated intervention. Most of these systems mainly fall under the category of image guided systems as they use either MRI, CT or Ultrasound modalities or a combination of these for real time image feedback of the intervention. This section reviews some systems that have been reported in last ten years and are limited to straight needle insertions (i.e., not steerable) interventions. Actuation and control technology, along with materials used for construction, are the main aspects that differentiate these systems from each other, and hence, are reviewed here.

The first ultrasound guided transperineal prostate intervention system, developed by Ho et al., was based on the dual-cone concept to ensure full access with minimum incision and without any physical obstruction [24]. It consists of a gantry and gun-holder used to fix a position on an x–y plane and z axis, respectively, and an ultrasound probe holder. It is mounted on a 6-DOF ball joint. The needle insertion depth is fixed by an automatic shifting stopper. Software was built for image modeling, target planning, and positioning the robot interactively. Kobayashi et al. developed a liver intervention system that includes a 3-DOF needle manipulator and a physical model for the organ [25]. The

Figure 34.3 Robopsy designed to help doctors do needle biopsies under CT guide. The robot consists of two hoops that are assembled concentrically to enable needle orientation. Source: MIT Precision Engineering Research Group.

manipulator provides positioning, posture alignment, and insertion motion of needle, all driven by a flexible rack power transmission allowing actuator positioning outside the manipulator for compact design and safety. Mura et al. developed a telemanipulated robotic platform that uses 3D US tracking to perform intravascular procedures [26]. It consists of an endovascular device that is driven by a magnetic unit.

A needle intervention system for the CT-guided abdomen and thoracic regions was developed by Arnolli et al. [27]. It consists of a 2-DOF orientation module, a serial mechanism and a pneumatic–hydraulic locking module used to lock the first module while permitting 6-DOF movement for it. The orientation module has a needle guide mounted on its end segment that can be oriented about the Remote Center of Motion (RCM) point. A Graphical User Interface (GUI) was developed for needle trajectory planning. CT compatibility tests reported only minor artifacts.

Robopsy developed by Walsh et al. [28] is a DC motor actuated, 4-DOF, patient attached, telerobotic system used for lung biopsies. The robot, shown in Fig. 34.3, consists of two concentric hoops that provide 2-DOF for needle compound angles, and a carriage mounted over the hoops that provides another 2-DOF for gripping and insertion. The actuation units were installed outside the scan plane to minimize image degradation. A 4-axis controller and amplifier from Galil Motion Control was used, and a Visual Basic 6 based GUI was developed. Also, since all the metallic parts were installed outside the scan plane, the needle and its trajectory were clearly visible without any hindrance, ensuring CT compatibility. Torabi et al. developed a unique robotic system for steering a percutaneous instrument for targeting multiadjacent points during the procedures such as brachytherapy [29]. In the case of CT compatible robotic needle guide systems, X-ray transparency is one of the requirements which restricts the selection of materials. Therefore, plastics such as Teflon, PEEK, and glass fiber, carbon-reinforced epoxies, ceramics were used in [27] with carbon nanotubes for signal wires.

Under MRI environment, Groenhuis et al. recently developed a compact 4-DOF breast biopsy system, Stormram 4, consisting of stepper motors with pneumatically driven piston-rack mechanisms [30]. It has a serial kinematic design with a cart that can slide over a rack fixed on a base. There are two curved racks which orient a lifter. A needle holder is driven by the platform installed on the lifter. Arduino Mega board controls the valve manifold with a user interface for manual and automatic control. Similar to Stormram, numerous breast intervention robotic systems, designed for operation under MRI [31–38], have been developed.

MrBot, an MR safe robot for manual transperineal prostate biopsy, under development for over a decade now [39] and first MR compatible robot to get FDA approval has a 5-DOF parallel–link construction and 1-DOF needle driver for insertion. The needle driver is a new addition, replacing the original brachytherapy needle driver in [40]. The suction cups and attachment mechanism to the adapter plate are used for height adjustment. The controller includes a PC, motion control card, and other interfaces for electrical, optical, and pneumatic systems. Visual C++ based software was used. Similarly, other MR compatible robotic systems for prostate interventions are [41–56]. There has also been development of MRI compatible intervention robots in the field of neurosurgery [57].

One of the major limitations of designing an MRI compatible robotic intervention system is the type of material that can be used for manufacturing it. This restriction limits material choices such as nonmagnetic, nonconductive, nonferrous metallic materials to achieve structural rigidity of the system. Further, to minimize any image degradation caused by the intervention, the minimum amount of metallic materials is used even though they may be nonferrous. Hence, plastics/polymers become an attractive option. A wide variety of plastics/polymers have been used for manufacturing the structural parts of these systems, which includes silicone [30] and Teflon (PTFE) [39]. Stormram 4, the breast biopsy system was printed using FullCore 720, an amber material.

34.5. Interactive manipulation

This section describes various interactive manipulator robotic systems. This kind of robots provides guidance to the physician while operating and providing feedback in the form of haptics or visual guidance to keep the physician on the desired path or profile. Various control schemes, including force control to optimize cutting speed for orthopedic robots, have been developed to interact with target and user handling.

Song et al. developed an orthopedic robot (HyBAR) to perform interactive bone milling operations [58]. A preoperative path plan is made using the CT scan of the patient. It is active during milling and the physician monitors the action during the operation.

Mako's robotic arm provides guides to physicians in total hip, total knee, and partial knee replacement surgery [59,60]. Its software generates a 3D virtual model from a CT

Figure 34.4 NAVIO Surgical System that controls the tool and tissue contact based on its location. The hand-piece enables accurate removal of bone while the portable cart loaded with software for image free registration and patient specific planning. Source: Smith & Nephew Inc.

scan for a preoperative plan. The physician modifies the plan and syncs the 3D model to points on the patient's bone using the robotic arm before operation. It creates virtual boundaries that provide a haptic feedback to guide the physician through the operation. The robotic arm is a hands-on device used to assist the physician in optimizing tissue removal with a visual display generating a digital image for navigation.

TCAT is an orthopedic robot developed by Think Surgical Inc. [61]. It generates a 3D image from CT scans for a preoperative plan that the physician tailors to the procedure. TCAT is an autonomous robotic milling system that follows the intended procedure with a manual safety override button for physician intervention. TCAT is a monitoring mode robotic system with a standard master device that communicates through telemanipulation. The surgical procedure is performed semiautonomously.

NAVIO Surgical System [62] shown in Fig. 34.4, operates on the knee. The NAVIO Surgical System is capable of generating a 3D virtual model during the operation process, which means no preoperative CT scan of the knee is needed. The NAVIO hand-piece movement is tracked with respect to the patient's bone in operation so computer assistance can navigate the physician to bone tissue in need of removal. A retractable, spherical deburring tool is used to remove bone tissue. NAVIO is also a positioning mode robotic system, as the surgical system is a true hands-on surgical device and provides a virtual image on the monitor device for image-based navigation of the knee.

TiRobot [63] operates on the spine and orthopedic trauma. TiRobot uses 3D and 2D images to allow physicians to construct a plan for screw placement and drill trajectory. The robotic arm guides the physician and assists in stable insertion of the robotic tool with navigation assistance on a monitoring device. TiRobot is also a positioning mode robotic system as the surgical system is a true hands-on surgical device and real-time navigation.

OMNIBotics [64] operates on the knee. This robotic device does not require an MRI or CT scan before surgery as a 3D model of the knee is generated using OMNI Art software and a tool end effector synced to a navigation system. Their Active Spacer robot is used to predict the expected gap between the interacting knee surfaces and plan for needed bone removal. The robot captures quantitative data using force feedback to measure soft tissue tension. The robotic cutting guide is mounted to the knee to assist with precise cutting and validation through measurement of removed material. OMNIBotics is also a positioning mode robotic system, as the surgical system is a true hands-on surgical device. Validating measurements are taken using instruments used in operation and are displayed on a monitoring device. This equates to image free navigation as measurements are taken after cutting bone.

Interactive manipulator robotic systems have been shown to be very helpful to physicians in terms of providing the ability to create a "draft" on the computer of what should take place in reality, allowing the physician to refine their approach prior to subjecting patients to any risks associated with incisions/surgery. While the above examples focused mainly on the spine, knee, or hip region, similar tools can also be used for other body parts.

34.6. Articulated access

Some surgical robotic systems utilize highly articulated access for surgical benefits. When a robot's joint number approaches infinity then it is known as a continuum robot. A traditional surgical robot uses stiff and straight instruments with a functional articulating tip, which limits its access to certain places. A key advantage of having a continuum mechanism over the traditional manipulator is that it is not limited to a certain number of DOF. Having a highly articulated robotic manipulator can be hugely beneficial for navigating through a complex path inside the body (i.e., nonlinear pathways) for interventional surgery. These kinds of robot have the potential to perform neurosurgery, otolaryngology, cardiac surgery, vascular surgery, abdominal intervention, and urology.

Yoon et al. has developed a 4-DOF flexible continuum robotic system [65]. It uses two modules with 2-DOF for each and a spring backbone. The spring back bone is covered with intermittent small aluminum cylinders having four holes to pass strings through it. Adjusting the strings, the robotic manipulator creates a specific curvature by adjusting the spring deflection for a certain shape change. The spring backbone makes it back drivable and flexible at the same time.

Bajo et al. has developed a robot assisted microsurgery robot of the throat using the trans-nasal approach [66]. The surgical manipulator is made of a flexible passive stem and two active segments. Phantom Omni is used to control the endoscopic manipulator. And additional DOF is provided by the base which pushes the endoscope through the orifice and desired path. The arm has three lumens at its tip to provide provision for surgical tools.

Abidi et al. developed a two module robot using a flexible fluidic actuator with the STIFF FLOP manipulator mechanism [67]. This flexible structure is used in conjunc-

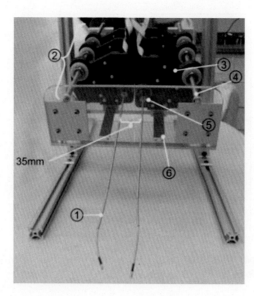

Figure 34.5 Prototype of the telerobotic system designed for transnasal surgery showing (1) active cannula with gripper end effector, (2) actuation module (for the cannula on the left), (3) carrier for one of the tubes, (4) lead screw for translation of the carriers, (5) collet closure for grasping one tube, and (6) guide rail. Source: [69].

tion with the rigid trocar to provide navigational flexibility at the tip, regardless of the insertion orientation. The inside lumen of the flexible structure is used to insert an endoscopic camera. Cianchetti et al. also developed a similar kind of manipulator using a single module for similar purposes [68].

Burgner et al. developed a telerobotic system, shown in Fig. 34.5, for transnasal surgery [69]. The robot uses a three concentric tube mechanism (also known as an active cannula) to provide flexibility. The robot actuates two cannulas. The two endoscopic tools are operated using two Phantom Omni.

Niobe system from Stereotaxis Inc. performs electrophysiology procedures using a remote magnetic field to guide a catheter [70]. With this device, two permanent magnets are on a pivoted arm and are enclosed within stationary housing, keeping the patient in the middle of them. A continuum endoscopic tip is navigated through the desired path using a mouse on a PC.

Other continuum robots include an MR guided 6-DOF robot developed by Su et al. for steering tubes along the curved areas inside the human body actuated using piezoelectric motors [71]. Mitchell et al. developed an endoscopic robotic platform that uses concentric tubes to perform complex end-effector maneuvers in a limited workspace to treat the prostate using the standard HoLEP (Holmium Laser Enucleation of the prostate) procedure [72]. Dwyer et al. developed a robotic mechanism for a 2-DOF concentric tube continuum robot that can be attached to a larger robotic arm

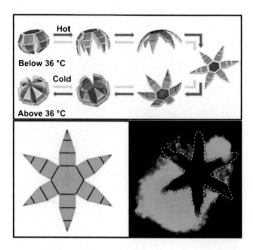

Figure 34.6 A micro-gripper developed by JHU showing temperature-controlled gripping tasks to sample tissue inside boy. Source: ACS Publications.

to perform a fetoscopic surgical procedure to treat twin–twin transfusion syndrome [73]. The 2-DOF robot also has a camera mounted on the distal end for imaging. Ota et al. developed a robotic system, CardioARM, that has high articulation capability to perform a minimally invasive delivery of therapy to the pericardial space [74]. In this system, the catheter is advanced through a series of connected cylindrical links for delivery of camera and therapy.

34.7. Untethered microrobots

Most conventional robots are tethered. One concern about these tethers is that they tend to restrict the movement and access to hard to reach places. Untethered manipulators/robots have advantages over the conventional ones. Typically, they are actuated by using magnetic stimuli, shape memory materials, or stimuli responsive polymers. One of their advantages is their miniaturized size. This has the potential to travel to complex and small paths inside the human body such as blood vessels, inside the liver, gastrointestinal tract, etc. Another concern of the traditional tethered robotic systems is that they can cause damage to the tissues while going through the passage area due to their large force. But the untethered robot maneuver does not have this issue.

Gultepe et al. has developed a micro-gripper tool for biopsy in the bile duct [75]. As shown in Fig. 34.6, the star shape thermo-sensitive microgripper derives mechanical energy from the residual stress powered microactuators and responds to thermal environmental cues. An endoscope carries the microactuator to the bile duct and then the thermal cue actuates the microactuator for the biopsy.

Utilizing another type of cue, Ongaro et al. developed a soft stimuli responsive gripper maneuverable by magnetic gradient [76,77].

Pacchierotti et al. developed a microteleoperation system with haptic feedback for intuitive steering and control. The miniaturized soft polymeric gripper responds to temperature for actuation and weak magnetic force for wirelessly positioning to a certain place [78].

Yim et al. developed a wireless gastrointestinal biopsy tool mounted with a micro gripper to collect tissue samples for the biopsy [79]. The micro-grippers are thermosensitive and folds when certain thermal stimuli are presented to collect the sample.

PillCAM Small Bowel Capsule [80] is a vitamin capsule sized minirobotic camera module. It is a substitute to the traditional endoscopic method. After swallowing the capsule by the patient, it naturally slides through the gastrointestinal tube gradually transmitting videos wirelessly.

Keller et al. developed a magnetically controlled capsule which transmits video wirelessly [81]. Unlike the PillCAM this has a strong neodymium magnet in the capsule which is guided by an external magnetic peddle from the patients back side [81].

Many untethered robots which are not microsized are capsule robots. These miniaturized robots substitute the normal push type endoscopic device. Primarily they all share the same fundamental principle of gradually crawling or sliding through the gastrointestinal tract like the PillCAM or NEMO and transmitting the video. They mainly differ in terms of how they are actuated or travel through the gastrointestinal tract. Various capsule robots have been developed for endoscopic procedures [82–88].

34.8. Soft robotics

The medical robotics field has continued to look for systems with increased flexibility and more compliant for human interactions. Current challenges with conventional rigid robotics systems in medical interventions are related to lack of instrument dexterity, flexibility, modular stiffness, and bending capabilities, as well as lack of materials able to change their shape and squeeze to reach complex and narrow body areas [89]. These challenges have driven the necessity for advancing the soft robotics field. In recent research, promising implantable soft robots and surgical manipulators prototypes have been developed [90,91].

Recent advancements in technology has enabled the use of smart and soft materials, flexible stretchable and miniature actuators, flexible sensors and sources of power capable of being compliant with the soft and flexible environment, making them more suitable to medical interventions. These recent and emerging multidisciplinary developments pose a promising advancement in key health care areas. Some examples of the recent developments in medical interventions are discussed.

Soft surgical manipulators are examples of recent research. In the work of Cianchetti et al. [89], a soft manipulator for surgical operations was developed. Inspired by the bio-

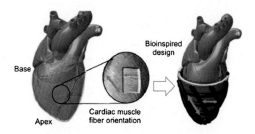

Figure 34.7 A direct cardiac compression device mimicking heart muscle using McKibben mechanism actuated by pneumatic power. Source: [92].

logical octopus' capabilities, the device is flexible and capable of maneuvering inside the body and of adjusting its stiffness as necessary to hold organs in place or to reach complex areas of the body. The device has a modular structure composed of soft and flexible materials and is capable of modulating its stiffness by using the concept of granular jamming, which enables density changes when a flexible membrane with the granular matter is vacuumed. The device is capable of reducing its diameter up to 40%, enabling it to squeeze and reach complex areas of the body. It can bend and elongate and produce forces up to 47.1 N, which makes it suitable for surgical retraction tasks.

Soft robots that can be implanted to provide therapy, devices that can act as artificial muscles or that can navigate inside the body are some of the research areas. One example, developed by researchers at Harvard University, is the Soft Robotic Sleeve to support heart functions [92]. The sleeve is implanted around the heart and compresses and twists to act as a cardiac ventricular assistive device. One of the device benefits is that is not come in contact with blood, thereby reducing risks of infections or clotting. This device was biologically inspired by the orientation of the two outer muscle layers of the mammalian heart. The device was tested in pigs and proven to restore cardiac output after a drug-induced cardiac arrest. An illustrated model of the device is shown in Fig. 34.7. Other interesting applications are being developed with materials and technologies that mimic biological organs or creatures.

In the field of rehabilitation, extensive research is being conducted to develop assistive devices that are soft, flexible, lightweight, and compliant to human interaction. Scientists at the Wyss Institute have developed several soft robots for patients who have suffered various mobility impairments due to a stroke or other conditions. As an example, a soft wearable exoskeleton was developed to assist patients in regaining their gait, and a soft glove to help provide therapy to regain arm mobility. These devices utilize soft materials technologies as the actuation mechanism. The advantages that these systems have over the conventional rigid joints robots are their light weight, therefore, they can be worn without imposing additional fatigue to the patient and will not restrict patient normal motion due their flexibility.

34.9. Summary

Robotic interventions are being introduced and some of them are clinically well-accepted as a smarter alternative to traditional tools in healthcare. The most obvious advantage of robotic precision and fatigueless performance has been widely utilized in various procedures not only increasing accuracy but also reducing time and error. In this area, identifying procedures that can be most beneficial by robotic technologies can be an emerging effort. Technically, clinical and regulation friendly design would be a key component for early implementation.

Master–slave systems continue benefit the advantages of physical separation with enhanced task delivery using well-designed user interfaces. Developments of long-distance operability seem less of interest lately, perhaps because even though it enables remote operation by a particular physician, the limitations of human skill still remain.

With advancements in medical imaging, image guided robotic interventions have been urged in the diagnosis and focal therapy of many diseases. The challenges of deploying a robotic intervention in a high strength magnetic field in MRI have been addressed by researchers and the utilization of piezoelectric and pneumatic actuators with optical sensors is reaching an acceptable tool for MRI environment. The ability to interactively adjust manipulation of robotic interventions has been an important consideration for patient safety. Real time information on physical contact or visual monitoring of target tissue is becoming more a part of robotic intervention control and less as a safety barrier.

Various highly articulated robotic manipulators have been challenging hard-to-reach areas of human body. To that extent, untethered devices can be an ideal approach. However, applicable dimensions that can be located in the human body without diminishing the advantages of utilizing natural access lumens and deliverable functions are still rather limited. In microscale, nevertheless, interesting developments are being carried out.

Robotic interventions utilizing soft robotics technologies have been challenging the limitations of conventional rigid robotics. Soft robotic technologies can be particularly beneficial for soft tissue or human movement related tasks due the nature of compliance. The task-oriented design and control of soft robotic interventions are rapidly growing with enabling technologies especially in composite materials.

References

[1] H.P. Ganapathi, G. Ogaya-Pinies, T. Rogers, V.R. Patel, Surgical robotics: past, present and future, in: V.R. Patel, M. Ramalingam (Eds.), Operative Atlas of Laparoscopic and Robotic Reconstructive Urology, second edition, Springer International Publishing, Cham, 2017, pp. 3–11.

[2] P.P. Pott, H.-p. Scharf, M.L.R. Schwarz, Today's state of the art in surgical robotics, Computer Aided Surgery 10 (2) (2005) 101–132, https://doi.org/10.3109/10929080500228753.

[3] G.I. Barbash, S.A. Glied, New technology and health care costs—the case of robot-assisted surgery, The New England Journal of Medicine 363 (8) (2010) 701–704.

[4] Mazor X Stealth Edition. Retrieved from https://www.medtronic.com/us-en/healthcare-professionals/products/neurological/spine-robotics/mazorx.html, 2019.

[5] ExcelsiusGPS. Retrieved from http://globusmedical.com/ExcelsiusGPS/, 2019.

[6] C. Plaskos, P. Cinquin, S. Lavallée, A.J. Hodgson, Praxiteles: a miniature bone-mounted robot for minimal access total knee arthroplasty, The International Journal of Medical Robotics and Computer Assisted Surgery 1 (4) (2006) 67–79, https://doi.org/10.1002/rcs.59.

[7] Rosa Brain. Retrieved from http://www.medtech.fr/en/rosa-brain, 2019.

[8] P. Maillet, B. Nahum, L. Blondel, P. Poignet, E. Dombre, BRIGIT, a robotized tool guide for orthopedic surgery, in: Proceedings of the 2005 IEEE International Conference on Robotics and Automation, 2005, 18–22 April, 2005.

[9] F.Y. Wu, M. Torabi, A. Yamada, A. Golden, G.S. Fischer, K. Tuncali, D.D. Frey, C. Walsh, An MRI Coil-Mounted Multi-probe robotic positioner for cryoablation, ASME, 2013.

[10] X. Chen, K. Tuncali, A.H. Slocum, C.J. Walsh, Design of an instrument guide for MRI-guided percutaneous interventions, in: ASME Design of Medical Devices Conference, Minneapolis, Minnesota, USA, 10–12 Apr., 2011.

[11] J-P. Kobler, K. Nuelle, G.J. Lexow, T.S. Rau, O. Majdani, L.A. Kahrs, J. Kotlarski, T. Ortmaier, Configuration optimization and experimental accuracy evaluation of a bone-attached, parallel robot for skull surgery, International Journal of Computer Assisted Radiology and Surgery 11 (3) (2016) 421–436, https://doi.org/10.1007/s11548-015-1300-4.

[12] N. Mylonas, C. Damianou, A prototype MR compatible positioning device for guiding a focused ultrasound system for the treatment of abdominal and thyroid cancer, International Journal of Monitoring and Surveillance Technologies Research 1 (4) (2013) 48–60.

[13] N. Hata, S.-E. Song, O. Olubiyi, Y. Arimitsu, K. Fujimoto, T. Kato, K. Tuncali, S. Tani, J. Tokuda, Body-mounted robotic instrument guide for image-guided cryotherapy of renal cancer, Medical Physics 43 (2016) 843–853, PMID: 26843245.

[14] I. Tateya, Y.W. Koh, R.K. Tsang, S.S. Hong, R. Uozumi, Y. Kishimoto, T. Sugimoto, F.C. Holsinger, Flexible next-generation robotic surgical system for transoral endoscopic hypopharyngectomy: a comparative preclinical study, Head Neck 40 (1) (2018) 16–23, PMID: 29130568.

[15] M.E. Hagen, M.K. Jung, F. Ris, J. Fakhro, N.C. Buchs, L. Buehler, P. Morel, Early clinical experience with the da Vinci Xi Surgical System in general surgery, Journal of Robotic Surgery 11 (3) (2017) 347–353, PMID: 28028750.

[16] Auris Monarch Platform. Retrieved from https://www.aurishealth.com/, 2019.

[17] M. Harris, First surgical robot from secretive startup Auris cleared for use, IEEE Spectrum (7 Jun 2016).

[18] Robot Assisted Surgical Technologies. Retrieved from https://www.virtualincision.com/, 2019.

[19] Revo Surgical Solution. Retrieved from http://revosurgical.com/#/main.html, 2019.

[20] D.K. Kim, D.W. Park, K.H. Rha, Robot-assisted partial nephrectomy with the REVO-I robot platform in porcine models, European Urology 69 (3) (2016) 541–542, https://doi.org/10.1016/j.eururo.2015.11.024.

[21] Avatera System. Retrieved from https://www.avatera.eu/1/avatera-system/, 2019.

[22] Artas Robotic Hair Restoration. Retrieved from https://artas.com/physicians/, 2019.

[23] Canady Hybrid Plasma Technology. Retrieved from http://www.usmedinnovations.com/products-technology/canady-hybrid-plasma-technology/, 2019.

[24] H.S.S. Ho, P. Mohan, E.D. Lim, D.L. Li, J.S.P. Yuen, W.S. Ng, W.K.O. Lau, C.W.S. Cheng, Robotic ultrasound-guided prostate intervention device: system description and results from phantom studies, The International Journal of Medical Robotics and Computer Assisted Surgery 5 (2009) 51–58.

[25] Y. Kobayashi, A. Onishi, H. Watanabe, T. Hoshi, K. Kawamura, M. Hashizume, M.G. Fujie, Development of an integrated needle insertion system with image guidance and deformation simulation, Computerized Medical Imaging and Graphics 34 (2010) 9–18.

[26] M. Mura, S. Parrini, G. Ciuti, V. Ferrari, C. Freschi, M. Ferrari, P. Dario, A. Menciassi, A computer-assisted robotic platform for vascular procedures exploiting 3D US-based tracking, Computer Assisted Surgery (Abingdon) 21 (1) (2016) 63–79, https://doi.org/10.1080/24699322.2016.1185467, PMID: 27973966.

[27] M.M. Arnolli, M. Buijze, M. Franken, K.P. de Jong, D.M. Brouwer, I.A.M.J. Broeders, System for CT-guided needle placement in the thorax and abdomen: a design for clinical acceptability, applicability and usability, The International Journal of Medical Robotics and Computer Assisted Surgery 14 (2018) e1877.

[28] C.J. Walsh, N.C. Hanumara, A.H. Slocum, J.-A. Shepard, R. Gupta, A patient-mounted, telerobotic tool for CT-guided percutaneous interventions, Journal of Medical Devices 2 (2008) 011007.

[29] M. Torabi, R. Gupta, C.J. Walsh, Compact robotically steerable image-guided instrument for Multi-Adjacent-Point (MAP) targeting, IEEE Transactions on Robotics 30 (4) (2014) 802–815.

[30] V. Groenhuis, F.J. Siepel, J. Veltman, S. Stramigioli, Design and characterization of Stormram 4: an MRI-compatible robotic system for breast biopsy, IEEE, 2017.

[31] T. Zhang, D. Navarro-Alarcon, K.W. Ng, M.K. Chow, Y.H. Liu, H.L. Chung, A novel palm-shape breast deformation robot for MRI-guided biopsy, in: 2016 IEEE International Conference on Robotics and Biomimetics, ROBIO 2016, 2017, pp. 527–532.

[32] D. Navarro-Alarcon, S. Singh, T. Zhang, H.L. Chung, K.W. Ng, M.K. Chow, Y. Liu, Developing a compact robotic needle driver for MRI-guided breast biopsy in tight environments, IEEE Robotics and Automation Letters 2 (2017) 1648–1655.

[33] S.B. Park, J.G. Kim, K.W. Lim, C.H. Yoon, D.J. Kim, H.S. Kang, Y.H. Jo, A magnetic resonance image-guided breast needle intervention robot system: overview and design considerations, International Journal of Computer Assisted Radiology and Surgery (2017) 1–13.

[34] K.G. Chan, T. Fielding, M. Anvari, An image-guided automated robot for MRI breast biopsy, The International Journal of Medical Robotics and Computer Assisted Surgery 12 (2016) 461–477.

[35] S. Jiang, J. Lou, Z. Yang, J. Dai, Y. Yu, Design, analysis and control of a novel tendon-driven magnetic resonance-guided robotic system for minimally invasive breast surgery, Proceedings of the Institution of Mechanical Engineers, Part H: Journal of Engineering in Medicine 229 (2015) 652–669.

[36] B. Yang, S. Roys, U.-X. Tan, M. Philip, H. Richard, R. Gullapalli, J.P. Desai, Design, development, and evaluation of a master–slave surgical system for breast biopsy under continuous MRI, The International Journal of Robotics Research 33 (2014) 616–630, PMID: 25313266.

[37] B. Yang, U.-X. Tan, A.B. McMillan, R. Gullapalli, J.P. Desai, Design and control of a 1-DOF MRI-compatible pneumatically actuated robot with long transmission lines, IEEE/ASME Transactions on Mechatronics 16 (2011) 1040–1048.

[38] R. Kokes, K. Lister, R. Gullapalli, B. Zhang, A. MacMillan, H. Richard, J.P. Desai, Towards a tele-operated needle driver robot with haptic feedback for RFA of breast tumors under continuous MRI, Medical Image Analysis 13 (2009) 445–455, PMID: 19303805.

[39] D. Stoianovici, C. Kim, D. Petrisor, C. Jun, S. Lim, M.W. Ball, A. Ross, K.J. Macura, M.E. Allaf, MR safe robot, FDA clearance, safety and feasibility of prostate biopsy clinical trial, IEEE/ASME Transactions on Mechatronics 22 (2017) 115–126.

[40] D. Stoianovici, D. Song, D. Petrisor, D. Ursu, D. Mazilu, M. Mutener, M. Schar, A. Patriciu, "MRI Stealth" robot for prostate interventions, Minimally Invasive Therapy & Allied Technologies 16 (2007) 241–248.

[41] H. Su, W. Shang, G. Cole, G. Li, K. Harrington, A. Camilo, J. Tokuda, C.M. Tempany, N. Hata, G.S. Fischer, Piezoelectrically actuated robotic system for MRI-guided prostate percutaneous therapy, IEEE/ASME Transactions on Mechatronics: a joint publication of the IEEE Industrial Electronics Society and the ASME Dynamic Systems and Control Division 20 (2015) 1920–1932, PMID: 26412962.

[42] H. Su, W. Shang, G. Li, N. Patel, G.S. Fischer, An MRI-guided telesurgery system using a Fabry–Perot interferometry force sensor and a pneumatic haptic device, Annals of Biomedical Engineering (2017) 1–12.

[43] S. Eslami, W. Shang, G. Li, N. Patel, G.S. Fischer, J. Tokuda, N. Hata, C.M. Tempany, I. Iorda-chita, In-bore prostate transperineal interventions with an MRI-guided parallel manipulator: system development and preliminary evaluation, The International Journal of Medical Robotics + Computer Assisted Surgery: MRCAS 12 (2016) 199–213, PMID: 26111458.

[44] S.-T. Kim, Y. Kim, J. Kim, Design of an MR-compatible biopsy needle manipulator using pull–pull cable transmission, International Journal of Precision Engineering and Manufacturing 17 (2016) 1129–1137.

[45] L. Chen, T. Paetz, V. Dicken, S. Krass, J.A. Issawi, D. Ojdanic, S. Krass, G. Tigelaar, J. Sabisch, A. van Poelgeest, J. Schaechtele, Design of a dedicated five degree-of-freedom magnetic resonance imaging compatible robot for image guided prostate biopsy, Journal of Medical Devices 9 (2015) 015002.

[46] S.-E. Song, J. Tokuda, K. Tuncali, C.M. Tempany, E. Zhang, N. Hata, Development and prelimi-nary evaluation of a motorized needle guide template for MRI-guided targeted prostate biopsy, IEEE Transactions on Biomedical Engineering 60 (2013) 3019–3027.

[47] S.-E. Song, N.B. Cho, G. Fischer, N. Hata, C. Tempany, G. Fichtinger, I. Iordachita, Development of a pneumatic robot for MRI-guided transperineal prostate biopsy and brachytherapy: new approaches, IEEE, 2010.

[48] G.S. Fischer, I. Iordachita, C. Csoma, J. Tokuda, S.P. DiMaio, C.M. Tempany, N. Hata, G. Fichtinger, MRI-compatible pneumatic robot for transperineal prostate needle placement, IEEE/ASME Transac-tions on Mechatronics 13 (2008) 295–305.

[49] A.A. Goldenberg, J. Trachtenberg, W. Kucharczyk, Y. Yi, M. Haider, L. Ma, R. Weersink, C. Raoufi, Robotic system for closed-bore MRI-guided prostatic interventions, IEEE/ASME Transactions on Mechatronics 13 (2008) 374–379.

[50] D. Stoianovici, C. Kim, G. Srimathveeravalli, P. Sebrecht, D. Petrisor, J. Coleman, S.B. Solomon, H. Hricak, MRI-safe robot for endorectal prostate biopsy, IEEE/ASME Transactions on Mechatronics: a joint publication of the IEEE Industrial Electronics Society and the ASME Dynamic Systems and Control Division 19 (2013) 1289–1299, PMID: 25378897.

[51] A. Squires, S. Xu, R. Seifabadi, Y. Chen, H. Agarwal, M. Bernardo, A. Negussie, P. Pinto, P. Choyke, B. Wood, Z. Tsz Ho Tse, Robot for magnetic resonance imaging guided focal prostate laser ablation, Journal of Medical Devices 10 (2016) 030942.

[52] M.G. Schouten, J. Ansems, W.K.J. Renema, D. Bosboom, T.W.J. Scheenen, J.J. Fütterer, The accuracy and safety aspects of a novel robotic needle guide manipulator to perform transrectal prostate biopsies, Medical Physics 37 (2010) 4744–4750.

[53] S. Jiang, F. Sun, J. Dai, J. Liu, Z. Yang, Design and analysis of a tendon-based MRI-compatible surgery robot for transperineal prostate needle placement, Proceedings of the Institution of Mechanical Engineers, Part C: Journal of Mechanical Engineering Science 229 (2015) 335–348.

[54] H. Elhawary, Z.T.H. Tse, M. Rea, A. Zivanovic, B. Davies, C. Besant, N. de Souza, D. McRobbie, I. Young, M. Lamperth, Robotic system for transrectal biopsy of the prostate: real-time guidance under MRI, IEEE Engineering in Medicine and Biology Magazine 29 (2010) 78–86.

[55] S. Jiang, W. Feng, J. Lou, Z. Yang, J. Liu, J. Yang, Modelling and control of a five-degrees-of-freedom pneumatically actuated magnetic resonance-compatible robot, The International Journal of Medical Robotics and Computer Assisted Surgery 10 (2014) 170–179, PMID: 23893561.

[56] A. Krieger, S.-E. Song, N.B. Cho, I. Iordachita, P. Guion, G. Fichtinger, L.L. Whitcomb, Devel-opment and evaluation of an actuated MRI-compatible robotic system for MRI-guided prostate intervention, IEEE/ASME Transactions on Mechatronics: a joint publication of the IEEE Indus-trial Electronics Society and the ASME Dynamic Systems and Control Division 18 (2012) 273–284, PMID: 23326181.

[57] M. Ho, Y. Kim, S.S. Cheng, R. Gullapalli, J.P. Desai, Design, development, and evaluation of an MRI-guided SMA spring-actuated neurosurgical robot, The International Journal of Robotics Re-search 34 (8) (2015) 1147–1163, https://doi.org/10.1177/0278364915579069, PMID: 26622075.

[58] S. Song, A. Mor, B. Jaramaz, HyBAR: hybrid bone-attached robot for joint arthroplasty, The International Journal of Medical Robotics + Computer Assisted Surgery: MRCAS 5 (2) (2009) 223–231, Available from: http://www.ncbi.nlm.nih.gov/pmc/articles/PMC3672054/.

[59] Mako Technology Overview. Retrieved from https://www.stryker.com/us/en/joint-replacement/systems/mako-robotic-arm-assisted-surgery.html, 2019.

[60] Mako Robotic-Arm Assisted Technology for Joint Replacement. Retrieved from https://www.stryker.com/us/en/joint-replacement/systems/mako-robotic-arm-assisted-surgery.html, 2019.

[61] M.H.L. Liow, P.L. Chin, H.N. Pang, D.K.-J. Tay, S.-J. Yeo, THINK surgical TSolution-One (Robodoc) total knee arthroplasty, SICOT-J. 3 (2017) 63, Available from: http://www.ncbi.nlm.nih.gov/pmc/articles/PMC5663203/.

[62] Navio Surgical System. Retrieved from http://www.smith-nephew.com/professional/microsites/navio/navio-technology/product-overview/, 2019.

[63] Tinavi. Retrieved from http://www.tinavi.com/index.html, 2019.

[64] OMNIBotics Total Knee Replacement. Retrieved from https://www.omnils.com/medical-professionals/omnibotics-overview/, 2019.

[65] Y. Hyun-Soo, Y. Byung-Ju, A 4-DOF flexible continuum robot using a spring backbone, in: 2009 International Conference on Mechatronics and Automation, 2009, 9–12 Aug., 2009.

[66] A. Bajo, L.M. Dharamsi, J.L. Netterville, C.G. Garrett, N. Simaan, Robotic-assisted micro-surgery of the throat: the trans-nasal approach, in: 2013 IEEE International Conference on Robotics and Automation, 2013, 6–10 May, 2013.

[67] H. Abidi, G. Gerboni, M. Brancadoro, J. Fras, A. Diodato, M. Cianchetti, H. Wurdemann, K. Althoefer, A. Menciassi, Highly dexterous 2-module soft robot for intra-organ navigation in minimally invasive surgery, The International Journal of Medical Robotics and Computer Assisted Surgery 14 (1) (2018) e1875.

[68] M. Cianchetti, T. Ranzani, G. Gerboni, I. De Falco, C. Laschi, A. Menciassi, STIFF-FLOP surgical manipulator: mechanical design and experimental characterization of the single module, IEEE, 2013.

[69] J. Burgner, D.C. Rucker, H.B. Gilbert, P.J. Swaney, P.T. Russell, K.D. Weaver, R.J. Webster, A telerobotic system for transnasal surgery, IEEE/ASME Transactions on Mechatronics 19 (3) (2014) 996–1006.

[70] Stereotaxis Niobe. Retrieved from http://www.stereotaxis.com/products/#!/niobe, 2019.

[71] H. Su, G. Li, D.C. Rucker, R.J. Webster III, G.S. Fischer, A concentric tube continuum robot with piezoelectric actuation for MRI-guided closed-loop targeting, Annals of Biomedical Engineering 44 (10) (2016) 2863–2873, https://doi.org/10.1007/s10439-016-1585-7, PMID: 26983842.

[72] C.R. Mitchell, R.J. Hendrick, R.J. Webster, S.D. Herrell, Toward improving transurethral prostate surgery: development and initial experiments with a prototype concentric tube robotic platform, Journal of Endourology (2016) 692–696.

[73] G. Dwyer, F. Chadebecq, M.T. Amo, C. Bergeles, E. Maneas, V. Pawar, E.V. Poorten, J. Deprest, S. Ourselin, P.D. Coppi, T. Vercauteren, D. Stoyanov, A continuum robot and control interface for surgical assist in fetoscopic interventions, IEEE Robotics and Automation Letters 2 (3) (2017) 1656–1663.

[74] T. Ota, A. Degani, D. Schwartzman, B. Zubiate, J. McGarvey, H. Choset, M.A. Zenati, A highly articulated robotic surgical system for minimally invasive surgery, The Annals of Thoracic Surgery 87 (4) (2009) 1253–1256, https://doi.org/10.1016/j.athoracsur.2008.10.026, PMID: 19324161.

[75] E. Gultepe, J.S. Randhawa, S. Kadam, S. Yamanaka, F.M. Selaru, E.J. Shin, A.N. Kalloo, D.H. Gracias, Biopsy with thermally-responsive untethered microtools, Advanced Materials 25 (4) (2012) 514–519, https://doi.org/10.1002/adma.201203348.

[76] F. Ongaro, C. Pacchierotti, C. Yoon, D. Prattichizzo, D.H. Gracias, S. Misra, Evaluation of an electromagnetic system with haptic feedback for control of untethered, soft grippers affected by disturbances, IEEE, 2016.

[77] F. Ongaro, C. Yoon, F. van den Brink, M. Abayazid, S.H. Oh, D.H. Gracias, S. Misra, Control of untethered soft grippers for pick-and-place tasks, IEEE, 2016.

[78] C. Pacchierotti, F. Ongaro, F. van den Brink, C. Yoon, D. Prattichizzo, D.H. Gracias, S. Misra, Steering and control of miniaturized untethered soft magnetic grippers with haptic assistance, IEEE Transactions on Automation Science and Engineering 15 (1) (2018) 290–306.

[79] S. Yim, E. Gultepe, D.H. Gracias, M. Sitti, Biopsy using a magnetic capsule endoscope carrying, releasing, and retrieving untethered microgrippers, IEEE Transactions on Biomedical Engineering 61 (2) (2014) 513–521.

[80] PillCam Colon System. Retrieved from http://pillcamcolon.com/product-details.html, 2019.

[81] J. Keller, C. Fibbe, F. Volke, J. Gerber, A.C. Mosse, M. Reimann-Zawadzki, E. Rabinovitz, P. Layer, P. Swain, Remote magnetic control of a wireless capsule endoscope in the esophagus is safe and feasible: results of a randomized, clinical trial in healthy volunteers, Gastrointestinal Endoscopy 72 (5) (2010) 941–946.

[82] I. De Falco, G. Tortora, P. Dario, A. Menciassi, An integrated system for wireless capsule endoscopy in a liquid-distended stomach, IEEE Transactions on Biomedical Engineering 61 (3) (2014) 794–804.

[83] A. Menciassi, P. Valdastri, K. Harada, P. Dario, Single and multiple robotic capsules for endoluminal diagnosis and surgery, in: Surgical Robotics, Springer, 2011, pp. 313–354.

[84] P. Valdastri, R.J. Webster III, C. Quaglia, M. Quirini, A. Menciassi, P. Dario, A new mechanism for mesoscale legged locomotion in compliant tubular environments, IEEE Transactions on Robotics 25 (5) (2009) 1047–1057.

[85] M. Simi, P. Valdastri, C. Quaglia, A. Menciassi, P. Dario, Design, fabrication, and testing of a capsule with hybrid locomotion for gastrointestinal tract exploration, IEEE/ASME Transactions on Mechatronics 15 (2) (2010) 170–180.

[86] H. Yu, M.N. Huda, S.O. Wane, A novel acceleration profile for the motion control of capsubots, IEEE, 2011.

[87] H. Li, K. Furuta, F.L. Chernousko, Motion generation of the capsubot using internal force and static friction, IEEE, 2006.

[88] L. Kim, S.C. Tang, S. Yoo, Prototype modular capsule robots for capsule endoscopies, in: 2013 13th International Conference on Control, Automation and Systems (ICCAS 2013), 2013, 20–23 Oct., 2013.

[89] M. Cianchetti, T. Ranzani, G. Gerboni, T. Nanayakkara, K. Althoefer, P. Dasgupta, A. Menciassi, Soft robotics technologies to address shortcomings in today's minimally invasive surgery: the STIFF-FLOP approach, Soft Robotics 1 (2) (2014) 122–131.

[90] A. Kim, M. Ochoa, R. Rahimi, B. Ziaie, New and emerging energy sources for implantable wireless microdevices, IEEE Access 3 (2015) 89–98.

[91] C. Pang, C. Lee, K.Y. Suh, Recent advances in flexible sensors for wearable and implantable devices, Journal of Applied Polymer Science 130 (3) (2013) 1429–1441.

[92] E.T. Roche, M.A. Horvath, I. Wamala, A. Alazmani, S.E. Song, W. Whyte, Z. Machaidze, C.J. Payne, J.C. Weaver, G. Fishbein, J. Kuebler, N.V. Vasilyev, D.J. Mooney, F.A. Pigula, C.J. Walsh, Soft robotic sleeve supports heart function, Science Translational Medicine 9 (373) (2017), PMID: 28100834.

CHAPTER 35

System integration

Andras Lasso[a], Peter Kazanzides[b]
[a]School of Computing, Queen's University, Kingston, Ontario, Canada
[b]Computer Science, Johns Hopkins University, Baltimore, MD, United States

Contents

35.1.	Introduction	862
35.2.	System design	862
	35.2.1 Programming language and platform	863
	35.2.2 Design approaches	863
35.3.	Frameworks and middleware	864
	35.3.1 Middleware	864
	35.3.1.1 Networking: UDP and TCP	*865*
	35.3.1.2 Data serialization	*865*
	35.3.1.3 Robot Operating System (ROS)	*866*
	35.3.1.4 OpenIGTLink	*867*
	35.3.2 Application frameworks	867
	35.3.2.1 Requirements	*867*
	35.3.2.2 Overview of existing application frameworks	*869*
35.4.	Development process	871
	35.4.1 Software configuration management	871
	35.4.2 Build systems	873
	35.4.3 Documentation	873
	35.4.4 Testing	874
35.5.	Example integrated systems	875
	35.5.1 Da Vinci Research Kit (dVRK)	875
	35.5.1.1 DVRK system architecture	*875*
	35.5.1.2 dVRK I/O layer	*877*
	35.5.1.3 DVRK real-time control layer	*878*
	35.5.1.4 DVRK ROS interface	*879*
	35.5.1.5 DVRK with image guidance	*881*
	35.5.1.6 DVRK with augmented reality HMD	*881*
	35.5.2 SlicerIGT based interventional and training systems	882
	35.5.2.1 3D Slicer module design	*883*
	35.5.2.2 Surgical navigation system for breast cancer resection	*884*
	35.5.2.3 Virtual/augmented reality applications	*886*
35.6.	Conclusions	888
	References	889

Handbook of Medical Image Computing and Computer Assisted Intervention
https://doi.org/10.1016/B978-0-12-816176-0.00040-5

35.1. Introduction

Many computer assisted intervention (CAI) systems are created by integrating a number of different devices, such as imaging, robotics, visualization, and haptics, to solve a clinical problem. It is therefore important to consider the processes, tools, and best practices in the area of system integration. This chapter focuses on the software aspects pertaining to the integration of CAI systems. First, several design considerations are discussed, such as programming language and platform, followed by a discussion of object-oriented and component-based design approaches. In recent years, component-based design has become the predominant approach for larger systems due to the looser coupling between components as compared to the coupling between objects.

Component-based software generally relies on middleware to handle the communication between components, and so the chapter continues with a review of different middleware options, highlighting two popular choices: Robot Operating System (ROS) [8] and OpenIGTLink [7]. While both packages support a variety of devices, ROS is especially attractive for CAI systems that integrate robots, while OpenIGTLink is widely used with medical imaging.

This is followed by a discussion of frameworks suitable for creating CAI applications, especially for translational research and product prototyping. Many potential frameworks are listed and more details are provided for the two of the largest, most commonly used platforms, 3D Slicer [6] and MITK [23].

The next section discusses the software development process. Although research software is not subject to the strict design controls used for commercial medical device software development, there are several advantages to adopting some good development practices. This section describes best practices in the areas of software configuration management, build systems, documentation, and testing. Following these practices will lead to software that is easier to use, easier to maintain, and better prepared for clinical evaluation or commercialization.

Finally, the chapter concludes with examples of integrated systems that illustrate many of the concepts presented in this chapter. The first is the da Vinci Research Kit (dVRK) [9], which is an open research platform created by integrating open source electronics and software with the mechanical components of a da Vinci Surgical Robot. Additional examples are shown for CAI applications implemented using the 3D Slicer application framework.

35.2. System design

Although system designs vary based on the problem being addressed, there are some key design decisions that are common to all projects. These include the choice of programming language, platform, and design approach. The following sections present a brief overview of these design choices.

35.2.1 Programming language and platform

Most computer-assisted intervention systems require interaction with the physical world and thus require some level of real-time performance. This often leads to the choice of a compiled language, such as C++, due to its faster execution times. On the other hand, compiled languages are not ideal for interactive debugging because it is necessary to recompile the program every time a change is made. In this case, an interpreted language such as Python may be more attractive. It is not unusual for systems to be constructed with a mix of languages to attempt to reap the benefits of each language. One common design is to use C++ for performance-critical modules, with Python scripts to "glue" these modules together. An example of this design is provided by 3D Slicer [6], which consists of Python scripts that utilize a large collection of C++ modules.

The platform choice refers not only to the operating system, but possibly also to an environment or framework. Two popular operating systems are Windows and Linux, though OS X is also used, and mobile operating systems, such as iOS and Android, are becoming more prevalent. Development environments often encapsulate the underlying operating system and thus can provide some amount of portability. Examples of these environments include Matlab,[1] Qt, and 3D Slicer. In other cases, such as Robot Operating System (ROS) [8], the platform may require a specific operating system (e.g., ROS is best supported on Linux).

Typically, decisions about programming language are based on developer familiarity, availability of existing software packages, and performance considerations. The situation is similar for choosing the platform, possibly with an additional constraint regarding the availability of drivers for specific hardware components.

35.2.2 Design approaches

Two popular design approaches are object-oriented design and component-based design. In object-oriented design, the basic software elements are objects that are instances of classes and data exchange occurs by calling methods in these classes. Component-based design consists of components (which may be implemented as objects), but data exchange occurs by passing messages between components. Thus, a component-based design involves a looser coupling between its basic software elements. Both approaches have merits and here too the choice of design approach may depend on developer preference, familiarity, and compatibility with other packages or tools. For example, use of ROS imposes a component-based design approach.

Component-based design is especially useful for larger systems because the message passing paradigm is generally more robust to concurrent execution. Modern software systems often benefit from parallel threads of execution; for example, one thread may wait for user input, another may wait for information from a device, and another

---

[1] MATLAB® is a trademark of The MathWorks.

may perform some computation. Parallel execution may be implemented by multiple executable programs (multiprocessing) or by multiple threads within a single process (multithreading), or some combination of both (e.g., multiple threads in multiple processes). In an object-oriented design, use of multiple threads can lead to data corruption when objects in different threads invoke the same methods or invoke methods that operate on the same data. Programmers can use mutual exclusion primitives, such as semaphores, to guard against these issues, but it is easy to make a mistake. In contrast, message passing is generally implemented using structures, such as queues, that can be systematically protected against mutual exclusion problems. Thus, a component-based design can provide an advantage for concurrent systems.

While some developers define software components to be independent binary executables (i.e., each component is a separate process), we adopt a broader definition that allows multiple components to exist in each process. When multiple components exist in a single process, it is possible to use simple and efficient data exchange mechanisms, based on shared memory, that also provide thread safety (e.g., that one thread is not attempting to read an element from shared memory while another thread is writing that same element); examples include OROCOS [19] and cisst [16,13,17]. In the multiprocessing case, it is common to adopt middleware to provide the communication between processes; this is especially true for component-based designs (such as ROS) where each component is a separate process.

There are two general classes of message-based communication: client/server and publish/subscribe. In the first case, the client initiates communication with the server, often in a manner similar to a *remote procedure call*. Specifically, the client provides input parameters to a routine on the server and receives the results as output parameters. It is also possible for the server to send *events* to the client to indicate asynchronous actions, such as changes of state on the server. In the publish/subscribe model, each component can publish and/or subscribe to data. The component publishing the data does not need to know how many other components (if any) have subscribed to the data. Similarly, the subscribing component does not need to know the identity of the publisher. Additional information about middleware options is given in the following section.

35.3. Frameworks and middleware

35.3.1 Middleware

Middleware refers to a software package that provides communication services between software components or applications in distributed systems. Many middleware solutions attempt to be both platform and language independent, that is, to support a variety of operating systems and programming languages. In most cases, middleware packages rely on the widely-used User Datagram Protocol (UDP) or Transmission Control Protocol (TCP), which both depend on the Internet Protocol (IP). Thus, it is helpful to first review the capabilities and limitations of these two protocols, since the various middleware packages leverage the capabilities, but still suffer from the limitations. Furthermore, in some cases a middleware solution may not be available for a particular platform, or may impose other challenges, leaving direct use of UDP or TCP as the best alternative. In this case, the programmer must create and use *sockets*, which are supported (with minor differences) on all major platforms.

35.3.1.1 Networking: UDP and TCP

UDP is a packet-oriented protocol, where one software component sends a packet and one or more software components may receive it. There is no guarantee that the packet will be delivered and the receiver does not provide an acknowledgment. The advantage of UDP is that, due to its simplicity, it has low overhead and therefore low latency. Although there are no guarantees of delivery, in practice most packets are delivered. UDP is especially useful for real-time data streams (e.g., measurements of a robot's position) where it would be better to transmit the latest value rather than to retransmit an older value that was not delivered.

TCP establishes a virtual connection between a client and server and provides guaranteed delivery of messages. Large messages are split into smaller packets and are guaranteed to be received in the correct order. The disadvantage of TCP is that these guarantees increase the overhead and latency of communication. Thus, TCP is more suitable when high reliability is required, although UDP may also be used if reliability is explicitly provided by the programmer, for example, by sending an acknowledgment packet via UDP.

35.3.1.2 Data serialization

In addition to the networking aspect, it is also necessary to consider the representation of the data, which may differ based on the operating system (including whether 32 or 64 bit), compiler, and programming language. A typical solution is for the sender to *serialize* the data into a standard format before transmitting it and then for the receiver to *deserialize* from the standard format into the correct native representation.

Some packages address only one of the two requirements of networking and data representation. For example, ZeroMQ (http://zeromq.org/) fulfills the networking requirement with a design that its developers call "sockets on steroids", but programmers must either write the serialization/deserialization code by hand or use an additional package, such as Google protocol buffers (Protobufs, https://developers.google.com/protocol-buffers/) or FlatBuffers (https://google.github.io/flatbuffers/). Typically, packages that provide serialization require the programmer to define the data format using a text file; depending on the package, this may be called an Interface Definition Language (IDL), a schema, or similar. The package then provides a "compiler" that processes this text file and generates the appropriate serialization/deserialization code for the particular platform and language.

Other middleware packages provide both networking and data representation. CORBA (www.corba.org) is an early example and it has been used for some computer-assisted intervention systems [4,5]. Internet Communications Engine (ICE) [20] is another example that has been used for robotics [21,13].

35.3.1.3 Robot Operating System (ROS)

Robot Operating System (ROS, www.ros.org) [8] is a more recent package that has become the de facto standard in robotics and provides both networking and data representation (in addition to many other features unrelated to middleware). ROS was initially created by Willow Garage, then transferred to the Open Source Robotics Foundation (OSRF), which has recently created an Open Robotics subsidiary. ROS introduced two methods of communication between components (called *nodes*): *topics* and *services*. *Topics* are implemented using a publish/subscribe paradigm, where the sender publishes a message and any number of nodes may subscribe to it. When a topic is received, ROS invokes a user-supplied callback to process the data. *Services* follow the client/server or remote procedure call (RPC) approach, where the client node fills in the *Request* field of the service data structure, invokes the service, and then waits for the server to provide the results via the *Response* field of the service data structure. Services are implemented using TCP, whereas topics may use either TCP or UDP. In practice, ROS topics are much more commonly used than ROS services, even in cases where services would seem to be a better choice (for example, commands to change the state of the robot or to move to a new location). One limitation of ROS is that it is best supported on Ubuntu Linux and thus is difficult to use in cases where some parts of the system must use a different platform. This was one of the motivations for the development of ROS 2, which uses Data Distribution Service (DDS) as its middleware. DDS has been standardized by the Object Management Group (OMG) and is a popular cross-platform publish/subscribe middleware. At present, a large part of the robotics community still uses the original version of ROS (ROS 1), but this may change as ROS 2 becomes more mature.

Although ROS provides a standard middleware, via topics and services, there currently is little standardization of topic names and payloads (message types). It is not always clear which type to use; for example, ROS *geometry_msgs* provides *Pose* and *Transform* types, as well as the *Stamped* versions of these types. This makes it difficult to "plug and play" different types of robots and developers often must resort to writing small ROS "glue" nodes to translate from one type of message to another when integrating packages. One recent effort to provide standardization of message names and types, at least for the domain of teleoperated and cooperatively-controlled robots, is the Collaborative Robotics Toolkit (CRTK), https://github.com/collaborative-robotics. One aspect of the standardization is to distinguish between different types of motion commands; for example, a *servo* motion command is intended to provide an immediate setpoint (e.g., position, velocity, or effort), whereas a *move* command provides a goal and assumes an underlying trajectory planner. Since CRTK is still evolving, it is best to check the project website for the most up-to-date information. Note that the CRTK standard API is not ROS-specific – it is an abstract definition and CRTK will include implementations for common robotics middleware such as ROS.

35.3.1.4 OpenIGTLink

Although early middleware such as CORBA were used for CAI systems, the complexity and requirement for an IDL led to several efforts to produce a simpler alternative (though with some added functionality compared to UDP or TCP). A notable example is OpenIGTLink [7], which is a very simple and efficient message-based communication protocol over TCP or UDP. Message types are defined for all information objects commonly used in CAI applications, such as position, transform, image, string, sensor data (http://openigtlink.org/developers/spec). Messages have a static "header" that is quick and easy to parse, followed by a message "body". The message body consists of "content" (static structure defined by the OpenIGTLink standard) and an optional "metadata" section (list of key/value pairs). This structure allows customization and extension of the protocol while maintaining basic interoperability with all OpenIGTLink-compliant software. While OpenIGTLink can be used in a completely stateless manner, OpenIGTLink version 2 introduced data query and publish/subscribe mechanisms, and OpenIGTLink version 3 added a generic command message (COMMAND).

OpenIGTLink is directly supported by some commercial products (BrainLab surgical navigation systems, some Siemens MRI scanners, KUKA robots, Waters intraoperative mass spectrometers, etc.) and many CAI tools and applications (3D Slicer, MITK-IGT, CustusX, IBIS, NifTK, ROS, etc.). Since many commercial products do not provide an OpenIGTLink interface out of the box, a common approach is to implement a communication bridge, which translates standard OpenIGTLink messages to proprietary device interfaces. The Plus toolkit [1] implements a communication bridge to a wide range of devices used in CAI systems, such as optical and electromagnetic position tracking devices, ultrasound systems, general imaging devices (webcams, frame grabbers, cameras), inertial measurement units, spectrometers, and serial communication devices. The toolkit also implements various calibration, data synchronization, interpolation, image volume reconstruction, and simulation algorithms.

35.3.2 Application frameworks

35.3.2.1 Requirements

All CAI systems require user interfaces that allow operators to create plans, carry out a procedure, and evaluate results after completion. The majority of user interfaces are implemented as software applications that receive inputs and give feedback to users most commonly using standard computing peripherals, such as mouse, keyboard, display, touchscreen, and increasingly using mobile tablets and virtual/augmented reality headsets and wireless controllers. This section gives guidance for implementing such software applications.

Successful software projects typically do not deliver "perfect" results, just software that is good enough for the specific purpose. Since development time and costs are always limited, it is necessary to make trade-offs between important aspects of the software, such as robustness, flexibility, extensibility, ease of use, performance, or maintainability. These choices then dictate all major software architectural, design, and development process decisions.

Robustness (program behavior is predictable, does not crash or hang) is important for all software that is used during medical interventions. Study protocols are set up in a way that a software crash would not impact patient safety. Still, frequent software errors are typically not tolerated because of time delays and/or extra effort needed from operating room staff to deal with the issue.

Flexibility and extensibility (how easy it is to use existing features in different contexts and add new features) is a key requirement for systems used in *research* projects – where it is expected that the project may go in completely unknown directions as new questions and interesting results emerge. This is in stark contrast with *product development* projects, where the general direction of the project is expected to be known in advance, and significant product modifications are avoided to limit costs, need to retrain users, and risk of breaking existing functionality.

Maintainability (effort required to keep existing features working while dealing with hardware and software obsolescence, fixing issues, and adding new features) is important for long-term projects. These include product and research platform development projects.

Ease of use (ability to use the software without specialized training, requiring very few interactions for performing common tasks) and optimal performance (responsiveness, fast computations) are essential for commercial products but typically not critical for research software.

Platform independence (ability to easily switch between different hardware devices, operating systems, or software versions) is very desirable for research projects. On the other hand, platform independence is often not necessary for product development, since system support on multiple platforms or switch between platforms would be so expensive anyway that it is not even considered.

License compatibility (making sure the resulting software conforms to all licensing requirements specified in its components) is a strong requirement for commercial products. Licenses that put any limitation on how derivative work (software that application developers implemented) may be used, shared, or distributed – such as GPL license –

is typically banned from commercial software. Research software may utilize GPL software without requiring public disclosure of all source code, since the software is not distributed publicly. Still, relying on GPL is too restrictive even in research software because it is not known in advance what the software will be used for later. It is less risky and more future-proof to build on alternative software libraries that come with nonrestrictive licenses, such as BSD, MIT, or Apache.

From the above paragraphs it is clear that there are significant differences between requirements for research software and for commercial product development. In this chapter, we focus on requirements for research software that is suitable to be used during computer aided interventions.

35.3.2.2 Overview of existing application frameworks

In the past 20 years, hundreds of CAI and medical image computing applications have been developed, many of them with the ambition to make them generally usable frameworks [3]. Most of these software have been abandoned when the main developers left the project or project funding stopped; others just remained small, focused efforts, kept alive by a few part-time enthusiasts. As a result, it is not easy to find application frameworks that fulfill most important requirements for research application frameworks.

A number of application frameworks that saw significant investment earlier have been abandoned or their publicly visible development activity is diminished to a minimal level in recent years. Examples include IGSTK (https://www.kitware.com/igstk), deVide (https://github.com/cpbotha/devide/), Gimias (http://www.gimias.org/), medInria (https://med.inria.fr/), and CamiTK (http://camitk.imag.fr/). Since both user and developer numbers are very low (few commits per months, few user questions a month), their survival in a crowded field is questionable and so these application frameworks are probably not good candidates as the basis of new projects.

Relying on closed-source software severely limits reproducibility of research results. Software platforms that require buying expensive licenses reduces availability and flexibility of all applications developed on top of them. Therefore, commercial software frameworks such as MevisLab, Amira-Avizo, OsiriX, Simpleware, Matlab/Simulink, or Labview are not ideal as research software platforms. Open-source applications with restrictive licenses, such as ITKSnap (http://www.itksnap.org) or InVesalius (https://github.com/invesalius/invesalius3), are not well suited as platforms, as they impose severe limitations on how derived software projects may be used or distributed.

There are excellent application frameworks that were originally not intended for medical imaging, but due to their flexibility they may be considered for this purpose. Such frameworks include simulation/technical computing applications, such as Paraview (https://www.paraview.org/), or gaming engines, such as Unity (https://unity3d.com/) or Unreal (https://www.unrealengine.com). The main problem with building on technologies built for a different purpose is that all features that are commonly needed in

CAI software need to be developed from the ground up, which takes many years of development effort and the roadmap and priorities of the platform may diverge from the needs of the application.

Frameworks that only work on a single operating system are not well suited for scientific research, where software may need to be used in a heterogeneous environment. A notable example is Horos (https://horosproject.org/) that only runs on Mac OS. There is growing interest in using the web browser as an operating system for medical image computing applications. Efforts with promising results include OHIF (http://ohif.org/), Cornerstone (https://cornerstonejs.org/), and Kitware's Glance (https://kitware.github.io/paraview-glance/app/) viewers. However, running interactive, high-performance interventional software applications in a web browser is typically suboptimal because the strong isolation from the rest of the system (hardware components and other software components) and the extra abstraction layer on top of the host operating system may decrease software performance.

There are applications targeting very specific clinical use cases. These may be good choices to be used as the basis of software applications that are guaranteed to be used only in a small number of predefined scenarios. Examples include the MITK-diffusion application (http://www.mitk.org/wiki/DiffusionImaging) for diffusion imaging, NifTK for general surgical navigation (http://www.niftk.org/), or CustusX (https://www.custusx.org/) and IBIS (http://ibisneuronav.org/) for ultrasound-guided neuro-navigation. The advantage of applications with reduced scope is that they may be simpler to learn and easier to use than more generic software. However, in research work it is often not known in advance what directions the project will go and there is a high chance that some desirable features are not readily available in the software.

We are only aware of two frameworks with sufficient user and developer community, feature set, and stability that make them solid bases for CAI applications: 3D Slicer (https://www.slicer.org) and MITK (http://mitk.org).

Both frameworks have been continuously developed for about 20 years. Both are designed to be very generic: capable of loading, visualizing, and analyzing almost any kind of medical data sets. They are open-source and come with BSD-type nonrestricted licenses, which allows usage and customization for any purposes without any limitations. They are built on the same foundation libraries: VTK for visualization, ITK for image processing, Qt and CTK for GUI and operating system abstraction, DCMTK for DICOM. They are implemented in C++ and features are also accessible in Python. Both application frameworks are used as a basis of commercial products, some of them with FDA approval or CE marking.

The two frameworks chose different approaches for feature integration. *3D Slicer* makes all features available to end users in a single application. Users download a core application then can choose from over a 100 freely available extensions that add features in specific domains, such as diffusion imaging, image-guided therapy, radiotherapy, chest imaging, or cardiac interventions. *MITK* is accessible to users via applications built from MITK core components by various groups. German Cancer Research Center (DKFZ) provides a generic Workbench and a diffusion imaging application. The Niftk project at University College London (UCL) and King's College London (KCL) provides a collection of applications for registration, segmentation, image analysis, and image-guided therapy [24].

Over time, adoption of 3D Slicer in the research and development community grew significantly larger than MITK (estimated from number of citations, traffic on discussion forums, etc.) but both frameworks are constantly improved as their developers collaborate at many levels. Most notably, they created the CTK toolkit (http://www.commontk.org) to facilitate sharing of source code and there are common efforts in improving DICOM support, web frameworks, and image-guided interventions.

35.4. Development process

Professional software development processes are the subjects of many books and typically involve phases of requirements generation, specification, design, implementation, testing, and maintenance. A well-documented software development process is especially important in regulated industries, including the medical device industry. The focus of this chapter, however, is on development of research software. Nevertheless, there is value in good development practices to enable robust and maintainable research systems, and possibly to facilitate future commercialization. The previous section presented some suggestions for good system design; in this section, we present some "best practices" for the implementation, testing, and maintenance of software.

35.4.1 Software configuration management

Software configuration management is one of the primary concerns during system implementation and maintenance. Fortunately, there are many available tools, beginning with systems such as Revision Control System (RCS) and Concurrent Versions System (CVS), which have been followed by newer tools such as Subversion (SVN), Mercurial (Hg) and Git. The basic approach is to create a software *repository*, usually on a network drive or online, and then to keep a *working copy* of the software on your local hard drive. Software changes are made in the working copy and then *checked in* to the repository. Conversely, software can be *checked out* from the repository to the working copy. This basic approach supports multiple developers, assuming that they all have access to the repository, but is useful even for a single developer because the repository maintains a history of all software that was checked in. For example, if your latest change introduced an error, it is easy to revert back to the previous version or to compare the current version of the software to the previously working version. Generally, it is also possible to

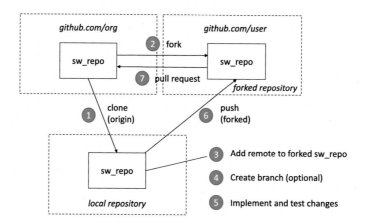

Figure 35.1 Typical Git workflow for open source project on GitHub. User forks original repository and commits changes to forked repository, then issues pull request to original repository.

label, or *tag*, a particular version of the software, for example, to indicate a particular release.

Another common concept is *branches*, which enable parallel development of different versions or features of the software. For example, two programmers can each work on a separate branch, implement different features, and then later *merge* their branches back into the main branch (sometimes called *trunk* or *master*).

One of the most popular software configuration management packages is Git, initially released in 2005. One reason for its popularity is the widespread use of GitHub (www.github.com), which is a code hosting platform that is based on Git. GitHub provides users with free public repositories and many popular open-source packages are hosted there. GitHub offers unlimited free hosting of private repositories for research groups and, for a fee, GitHub also provides private repositories for corporate customers. Many researchers create and use free GitHub repositories, even in cases where there is only a single developer.

For collaborative development in large software projects, it is advantageous to have a well-defined workflow. One popular workflow, that is based on Git and GitHub, is illustrated in Fig. 35.1. This figure shows the scenario where an organization, *org*, maintains a public repository, *sw_repo*, on GitHub. Any researcher can *clone* the repository (Step 1), thereby creating a repository (and working copy) on their computer. For researchers who just wish to use the software, and do not plan to contribute back, this is sufficient. However, researchers who wish to contribute to *sw_repo* must do so indirectly, since write access to the primary repository is generally limited to a few trusted developers. Other researchers can instead create a *forked* copy of the repository on their GitHub account and push their changes to that repository, before issuing a *pull request* to the maintainers of the original repository. This mechanism gives the maintainers a convenient way to review the proposed changes and possibly request modifications, before merging the changes to the original repository. Some steps shown in Fig. 35.1 can be done in a different order (e.g., the repository can be forked before being cloned) and other variations may be necessary. Note that in this workflow, the local repository has two remotes: the original repository and the forked repository. The reason for keeping a remote to the original repository is to enable merges from the original repository to incorporate changes that were done in parallel by other developers.

35.4.2 Build systems

In addition to source code control, it is necessary to consider the build system. For projects that will only ever be built on a specific platform, it is fine to use a native build system, such as Microsoft Visual Studio (on Windows) or Xcode (on OS X), especially since these typically provide an integrated development environment (IDE) that includes source code editors, debuggers, documentation, and other tools. In addition, there are cross-platform IDEs, such as Eclipse and Qt Creator. An alternative approach is to use a build tool such as CMake (www.cmake.org), which takes a text description of the build process (in a file called CMakeLists.txt) and generates the appropriate configuration for the native build tool. For example, CMake can generate Solution files for Microsoft Visual Studio or makefiles for many different compilers (e.g., gcc on Linux). CMake also provides a portable way to configure the build, which includes setting of different options and specifying paths to dependencies. Because the CMakeLists.txt files are plain text, it is also easy to review them and track changes within the source code control system.

35.4.3 Documentation

Documentation is critical for the medical device industry and comes in many forms, including requirements, design, verification and validation, and testing. These documents are tangible products of the development process that is necessary to obtain regulatory approval for medical devices, as well as to enable the company to continue to develop and maintain the software as the engineering team changes. This type of development process is generally too cumbersome for research; in fact, most companies distinguish between research and product development and apply their development process only to the latter. Nevertheless, for research software that is expected to be more widely used, some level of documentation is prudent and could also help if that software is ever considered for commercial release.

Two important forms of documentation are an architectural overview of the design and detailed design descriptions. The former is best represented by block diagrams. While any block diagram is better than nothing, there is some advantage to using a standard format, specifically the Unified Modeling Language (UML). UML has grown in complexity over the years to support many different kinds of diagrams, but there are a few more widely used types of diagrams. Kruchten [22] first defined the "4+1" view of architecture, where the "4" views are logical, physical, process, and development, and the "+1" view is use cases (or scenarios). However, this work predated both UML and the rise of component-based design. UML 2 now defines a component diagram that can be used to document the architecture of a component-based system.

Detailed design documentation is best embedded in the source code because it makes it more likely that developers will update the documentation when they change the software. One popular tool is doxygen (http://www.doxygen.nl/), which embeds documentation in comments, using special syntax. The doxygen tool is able to extract this documentation and format it, including the automatic creation of class inheritance diagrams.

User documentation is often written in text files using markdown or restructured-text markup. These text files are human-readable and so can be created using any text editor. There are a number of authoring tools available for markdown, such as GitHub's web editor or Visual Studio Code (using markdown plugins). Documentation with rich formatting can be published on the web using GitHub, ReadTheDocs, or other online services, or can be uploaded to any web server after converting to HTML files or PDF using Sphinx (http://www.sphinx-doc.org/) or pandoc (https://pandoc.org/).

35.4.4 Testing

In the medical device industry, the terms *verification* and *validation* are often used, but both imply some form of testing. Generally, software verification ensures that specific software components or subsystems meet their design requirements, whereas the goal of validation is to demonstrate that the overall system satisfies the customer requirements under realistic conditions.

Developers of many open source software packages have implemented automated testing; this can generally be considered as software verification since the tests cover operation of specific components in a virtual environment. In other words, automated testing is most practical when there is no interaction with the user or physical environment. Some ideal applications of automated testing include mathematical and image processing functions, where the computed results can be compared to the known, or assumed correct, results. Automated software testing typically includes use of a testing framework (i.e., a standard way to write tests), a tool for executing the tests on as many different platforms as possible, and then a tool to report the results to a *dashboard* (e.g., a web page). Examples of testing frameworks include the *xUnit* family, where *x* refers to the language; e.g., *JUnit* (https://junit.org) for Java and *CppUnit* (https://sourceforge.net/projects/cppunit/) for C++, and similar frameworks such as *Google Test* (https://github.com/google/googletest). The CMake package described earlier includes CTest to compile the software and execute the tests, and CDash to provide the dashboard for visualization testing results. Alternatively, Travis CI (https://travis-ci.org/)

and Appveyor (https://www.appveyor.com/) are conveniently integrated with GitHub to support building, executing, and visualizing the results of automated testing for open source projects hosted on GitHub.

Because automated testing is usually not feasible to verify large integrated systems or to validate the overall application, these tests are generally conducted manually. A typical approach is to first validate the application with a *phantom*, which is an inanimate object that represents the patient anatomy. Subsequently, the system may be validated on animal tissue (grocery store meat), in-vivo (with animals) or with cadavers. In these scenarios, data collection can be critical because there often is not enough time to evaluate the results while the animal is under anesthesia or while the cadaveric procedure is being performed. Thus, it is advantageous to consider the use of frameworks, such as ROS, that provide integrated tools for data collection and replay.

35.5. Example integrated systems

35.5.1 Da Vinci Research Kit (dVRK)

The da Vinci Research Kit (dVRK) is an open source research platform created by integrating open source electronics and software with the mechanical components of the da Vinci Surgical Robot [9], as shown in Fig. 35.2. The mechanical components consist of the Master Tool Manipulator (MTM), Patient Side Manipulator (PSM), Endoscopic Camera Manipulator (ECM), Master Console stereo display, and footpedal tray. Because this chapter is about system integration, we do not delve into the mechanical hardware, electronics, or FPGA firmware of the dVRK, but instead focus on the open source software and its external interfaces (e.g., ROS).

35.5.1.1 DVRK system architecture

As shown in Fig. 35.3 (middle section), the dVRK architecture [11] consists of:

1. One hardware Input/Output (I/O) component, *mtsRobotIO1394* (~3 kHz), handling I/O communication over the FireWire bus,
2. Multiple low-level control components, *mtsPID* (3 kHz, one for each manipulator) providing joint level PID control,
3. Multiple mid-level control components (1 kHz, different components for each type of manipulator, such as da Vinci MTM and PSM) managing forward and inverse kinematics computation, trajectory generation and manipulator level state transition,
4. Teleoperation components *mtsTeleoperation* (1 kHz) connecting MTMs and PSMs,
5. A console component (event-triggered) emulating the master console environment of a da Vinci system.

Fig. 35.3 also shows optional Qt widget components and ROS interface components. The ROS interfaces (bridge components) will be presented later.

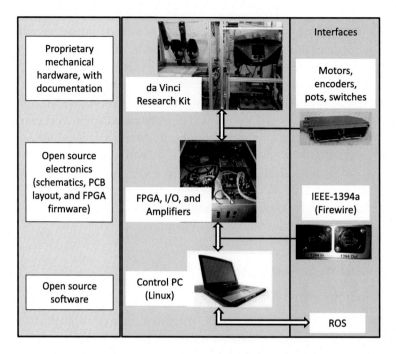

Figure 35.2 Overview of the da Vinci Research Kit (dVRK): Mechanical hardware provided by da Vinci Surgical System, electronics by open-source IEEE-1394 FPGA board coupled with Quad Linear Amplifier (QLA), and software by open-source cisst package with ROS interfaces.

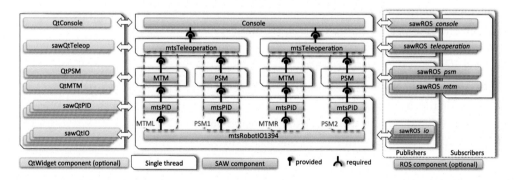

Figure 35.3 Robot teleoperation control architecture with two MTMs and two PSMs, arranged by functional layers and showing thread boundaries [11].

The dVRK component-based software relies on the *cisst* package [16,13,17], which provides a component-based framework to define, deploy, and manage components (*cisstMultiTask*). The cisst package contains other pertinent libraries, such as a linear algebra and spatial transformation library (*cisstVector*) and a robot kinematics, dynamics, and control library (*cisstRobot*). The *cisst* libraries also form the basis of the Surgical Assistant Workstation (SAW) package [15]. SAW is a collection of reusable components, based on *cisst*, with standardized interfaces that enable rapid prototyping of CAI systems. SAW provides diverse application components that range from hardware interface components (e.g., to robots, tracking systems, haptic devices, force sensors) and software components (e.g., controller, simulator, ROS bridge). The dVRK uses a combination of general-purpose SAW components (e.g., *mtsPID*, *mtsRobotIO1394*) and dVRK-specific SAW components (e.g., for the *MTM*, *PSM*), as shown in Fig. 35.3.

The *cisstMultiTask* library was primarily designed to support real-time computing with multiple components in a single process. Each *cisst* component contains *provided* and *required* interfaces and a *state table* that maintains a time-indexed history of the component data (typically, the members of the component class). The state table is implemented as a ring buffer, with a single writer (the component) and potentially multiple readers (other components). Reading of the state table is implemented lock-free to minimize overhead. Correctness of the lock-free implementation has been proven using formal methods [14]. Most *cisst* components contain their own thread and execute either continuously, periodically, or in response to an external event. However, it is also possible to chain execution of multiple components into a single thread, using special component interfaces called *ExecIn* and *ExecOut*. If the *ExecIn* interface of the child component is connected to the *ExecOut* interface of the parent component, the parent executes the child component by issuing a run event; otherwise, separate threads are created for each component.

35.5.1.2 dVRK I/O layer

The dVRK I/O layer is represented by the *mtsRobotIO1394* component and the underlying IEEE 1394 (FireWire) fieldbus. This section presents a brief overview of the fieldbus as background information for the design of the I/O layer software.

One of the most desirable properties of a fieldbus is to provide deterministic performance with low latency. A major source of latency is the software overhead on the control PC. This can be minimized by limiting the number of communication transactions performed by the PC. This motivates use of a fieldbus that supports broadcast, multicast and peer-to-peer transfers. A second desirable property is for the fieldbus to support "daisy chain" connection; that is, where one cable connects from the PC to the first interface board, another cable connects from the first board to the second board, and so on. This enables the bus topology to scale with the number of manipulators and facilitates reconfiguration to support different setups. From the software perspective, this leads to a situation where a single resource (i.e., FireWire port) is shared between multiple robot arms and where, for efficiency, data from multiple arms should be combined into a single packet.

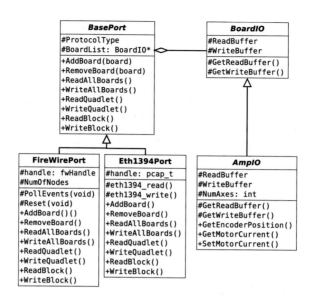

Figure 35.4 UML class diagram of interface software (subset of class members shown): the design can scale and support different fieldbus implementations, such as FireWire and Ethernet.

Fig. 35.4 presents a UML class diagram of the interface software that supports the above design. Two bases classes are defined: (1) *BasePort* represents the physical fieldbus port resource, which, depending on the implementation, can be a Firewire or Ethernet port, and (2) the abstract *BoardIO* class that represents the controller board. Currently, there is one derived class, *AmpIO*, that encapsulates the functionality of the FPGA/QLA board set. For a typical system, one port will connect to multiple FPGA nodes; thus the *BasePort* object maintains a list of *BoardIO* objects. The *BasePort* class contains two methods, *ReadAllBoards* and *WriteAllBoards*, which read all feedback data into local buffers and transmit all output data from local buffers, respectively. This allows the class to implement more efficient communication mechanisms, such as a broadcast write and consolidated read [10]. The *AmpIO* API provides a set of functions to extract feedback data, such as encoder positions, from the read buffer, and to write data, such as desired motor currents, into the write buffer.

35.5.1.3 DVRK real-time control layer

The real-time control layer includes the low-level and mid-level control components. The low-level control implements the joint controllers for the da Vinci manipulators and is typically configured to run at 3 kHz. The mid-level control incorporates the robot kinematics and contains a state machine that manages the robot states (e.g., homing, idle, moving in joint or Cartesian space); it typically runs at 1 kHz.

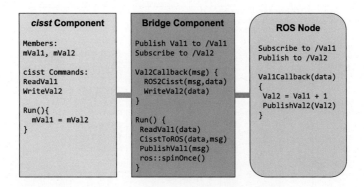

Figure 35.5 *cisst*/ROS bridge example: a *cisst* component interfaces with a ROS node using a bridge component.

The dVRK uses the *ExecIn/ExecOut* feature described above to logically separate the I/O component (*sawRobotIO1394*) from the low-level control components (*sawPID*), while still achieving synchronous communication and minimal latency for maximum control performance. In this case, the *RunEvent* is generated by the *mtsRobotIO1394* component after it receives feedback from the controller boards and before it writes the control output. Thus, the *mtsPID* components receive the freshest feedback data and compute the control output, which is immediately sent to the hardware when the *mtsPID* components return the execution thread to the *mtsRobotIO1394* component. On average, the latency for data transfer between the two components is 21.3 μs, with a maximum value of 115.2 μs.

35.5.1.4 DVRK ROS interface

Robot Operating System (ROS) is used to provide a high level application interface due to its wide acceptance in the research community, large set of utilities and tools for controlling, launching and visualizing robots, and the benefits of a standardized middleware that enables integration with a wide variety of systems and well-documented packages, such as RViz and MoveIt!. ROS also provides a convenient build system.

This section presents the bridge-based design that enables integration of the *cisst* real-time control framework within a ROS environment. The implementation includes a set of conversion functions, a *cisst* publisher and subscriber, and a bridge component. The bridge component is both a periodic component (inherits from *mtsTaskPeriodic*) and a ROS node. As an *mtsTaskPeriodic* component, it is executed periodically at a user specified frequency and connected, via *cisst* interfaces, to the other *cisst* components. The bridge component also functions as a ROS node with a node handle that can publish and subscribe to ROS messages.

To illustrate this design, consider the example in Fig. 35.5, which has one *cisst* component connected to a ROS node via a *cisst*-to-ROS bridge. The *cisst* component has a

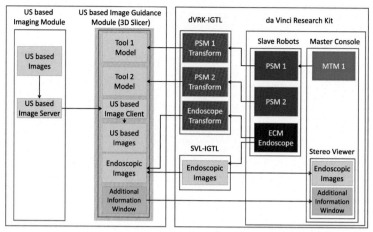

Figure 35.6 System architecture for ultrasound-based, image-guided telerobotic system. The US-based Imaging module can provide ultrasound images to the Image Guidance module (3D Slicer plug-in) for visualization, along with live stereo endoscope video (via SVL-IGTL) and models of the drill, laser, and US transducer that are positioned based on kinematic position feedback from the da Vinci PSMs (via dVRK-IGTL). Visualizations from 3D Slicer are simultaneously presented on a separate screen and on the da Vinci stereo viewer using an additional information window.

periodic *Run* method that assigns *mVal2* to *mVal1*. It also contains a provided interface with two commands: *ReadVal1* and *WriteVal2*. The bridge component connects to the *ReadVal1* command and publishes to the ROS topic */Val1*. Similarly, the bridge subscribes to the ROS topic */Val2* and connects to the *WriteVal2* command. On the ROS side, the node simply subscribes to */Val1*, increments the received value, and publishes to */Val2*. At runtime, the bridge node fetches data through the *cisst* interface, converts it to a ROS message, and then publishes the message to ROS. In the reverse direction, the *ros::spinOnce* function is called at the end of the *Run* method, which calls the subscriber callback function, converts data, and triggers the corresponding *cisst* write command. The bridge always publishes at its specified update rate. If the *cisst* component is faster than the bridge component, the bridge only fetches the latest data at runtime, thus throttling the data flow. If the bridge component updates faster, it publishes the latest data at the bridge's rate. For certain applications that require publishing and subscribing at the exact controller update rate, programmers can either create a separate bridge for each *cisst* controller component or directly initialize a publisher node within the *cisst* component and call *publish* and *ros::spinOnce* manually.

The initial dVRK ROS interface used a somewhat arbitrary collection of topic names and message types, but now conforms to the Collaborative Robotics Toolkit (CRTK) mentioned above and is actively updated as CRTK continues to evolve.

35.5.1.5 DVRK with image guidance

Although most members of the dVRK community use the ROS interface, it is possible to use bridges to other middleware, such as OpenIGTLink. This is especially attractive when it is necessary to interface the dVRK to 3D Slicer for medical image visualization, as was the case when photoacoustic image guidance was integrated with the dVRK [12]. Briefly, a pulsed laser was attached to one da Vinci instrument and an ultrasound probe to another. The energy from the pulsed laser was preferentially absorbed by blood, causing a large photoacoustic effect (ultrasound wave) to emanate from the blood vessel, even when behind other soft tissue or bone. The user interface included visualization of the endoscope video, photoacoustic image, and virtual models of the instrument, ultrasound probe and (diffused) laser beam. The system architecture is shown in Fig. 35.6, where the "US-based" modules are capable of processing conventional (B Mode) ultrasound or photoacoustic images. The *dVRK-IGTL* and *SVL-IGTL* components are the OpenIGTLink bridges, where the first handles transforms (i.e., poses of the robot arms) and the second handles the endoscope images, which are acquired using the *cisstStereoVision* library (hence the *svl* prefix). A sample visualization (with a phantom) is shown in Fig. 35.7.

35.5.1.6 DVRK with augmented reality HMD

The dVRK was integrated with an optical see-through head mounted display (HMD) to provide an application for augmented reality guidance, called ARssist, for the bedside assistant (also called First Assistant) in da Vinci robotic surgery [25,27]. Fig. 35.8 shows the normal (unassisted) view, followed by two different augmented reality views: (1) stereo endoscope video displayed in a virtual stereo monitor, and (2) stereo endoscope video displayed at the base of the virtual endoscope frustum. This system effectively gives the assistant "X-ray vision" to see robotic instruments inside the patient as well as the spatial location of the endoscope field of view with respect to the patient.

The implementation of ARssist required integration of the dVRK with the Unity3D game engine, which drove the Microsoft HoloLens HMD. Fiducial marker tracking, using the HoloLens world camera, is implemented using a port of ARToolKit [26] to HoloLens (https://github.com/qian256/HoloLensARToolKit). The ROS interface to the dVRK was used to obtain the robot kinematic data and the stereo endoscope video. One ROS node (*udp_relay*) was created to receive the joint state ROS topic, serialize to JSON, and then send to the HoloLens via UDP protocol. A second ROS node (*arssist_streamer*) was introduced to fetch the two channels of endoscopy and stream them to the HoloLens via Motion-JPEG protocol. There are two points to note: (1) It would have been a significant effort to create a ROS interface on the HoloLens and thus a UDP socket was used (an alternative would have been OpenIGTLink, as illustrated in the next example in Section 35.5.2.3), and (2) It was more convenient to interface to the dVRK via its standard ROS interface than to modify the dVRK code to add

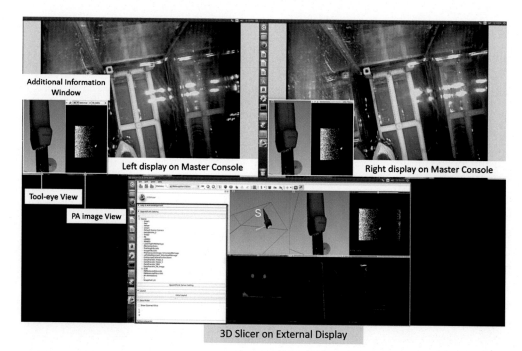

Figure 35.7 Visualization of photoacoustic-guidance for dVRK. Top shows left and right images displayed (in stereo) on dVRK Master Console; these consist of endoscope video with augmented overlay (Additional Information Window). Bottom shows main 3D Slicer display which is displayed on separate monitor.

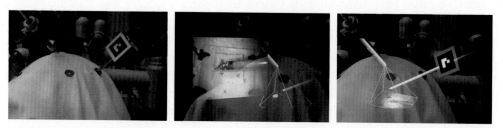

Figure 35.8 (Left) Normal view of surgical field (no assistance); (Middle) Augmented display showing endoscope field of view (frustum), instrument inside body, and endoscope video on virtual monitor; (Right) Augmented display, but with endoscope video rendered at base of frustum [27].

a custom UDP interface. More recently, however, an open source package that uses a UDP interface, with JSON serialization, has been released for mixed reality visualization of the dVRK [28].

35.5.2 SlicerIGT based interventional and training systems

SlicerIGT is a toolset for building medical interventional and training systems, typically using real-time imaging and position tracking, mainly for translational research

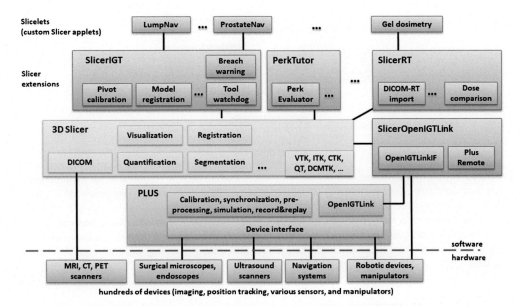

Figure 35.9 Overview of system components that can be combined to build complete medical interventional or training systems.

use. The toolset includes the 3D Slicer application platform for data visualization and interaction, the Plus toolkit (www.plustoolkit.org) for data acquisition and calibration, OpenIGTLink for real-time data transfer, SlicerIGT, PerkTutor, and other 3D Slicer extensions for interventional calibration, registration, surgical navigation, and skill assessment and feedback (Fig. 35.9).

The SlicerIGT toolset allows building custom systems without any programming (just by configuring existing software components) for quick prototyping. These prototypes can be further developed into software highly optimized for specific clinical workflows, most often with minimal effort: only a simplified user interface layer needs to be implemented.

35.5.2.1 3D Slicer module design

Applications that contain many features developed by a diverse group of developers may become very complicated and unstable over time. Significant effort must be invested into designing an architecture that allows implementing highly cohesive and loosely coupled components. 3D Slicer goes through a major refactoring every 3–5 years. Each time the design is improved based on lessons learned and realigned with changes in the software industry, and consistently applied to all software components. Currently, 3D Slicer is just starting its 5th generation.

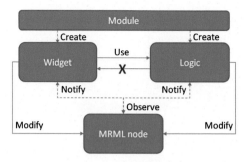

Figure 35.10 Internal structure of a 3D Slicer module. *Module* class is responsible for instantiating other module classes. Data is stored in *MRML node* classes. Data processing is implemented in *Logic* classes (which may observe MRML node changes and perform processing automatically). User interface is implemented in *Widget* classes, which usually modifies data in MRML nodes and calls logic methods for data processing. It is important that *Logic* class must not use (or even be aware of) the *Widget* class to make sure the module can be used for bulk data processing, without requiring a user interface.

The 3D Slicer framework consists of an application core, which is responsible for setting up the main window, standard user interface elements, and creating a central data container, the *MRML scene* and modules that operate on the data. MRML is an acronym for Medical Reality Modeling Language, an extensible software library that can represent data structures (nodes) that are used in medical image computing, such as volumes (images), models (surface meshes), transforms, points sets, or segmentations.

Modules rarely communicate or call each other's methods directly. Instead, they usually observe the scene and react to relevant data changes. This decoupling of modules from each other offers great flexibility, since modules can be combined to implement a complex workflow without any of the modules requiring one to know how the inputs were generated or how its outputs will be used.

The internal design of modules follows a model-view-controller type of separation of data (MRML node), graphical user interface (Widget), and behavior (Logic) as shown in Fig. 35.10. Decoupling of data and behavior is important because it allows adding various processing methods without making data objects overly complex. Separation of user interface from the rest of the module is important because it allows using a module without any user interface (for batch processing, or when used by another module).

35.5.2.2 Surgical navigation system for breast cancer resection

A complete surgical navigation system for a breast cancer resection procedure (lumpectomy) was implemented based on SlicerIGT [2]. The system components are shown in Fig. 35.11. Ultrasound probe, cautery tool, and tumor position are continuously acquired using an electromagnetic tracker. Ultrasound images and tracking information are recorded by Plus toolkit and made available through OpenIGTLink to 3D Slicer.

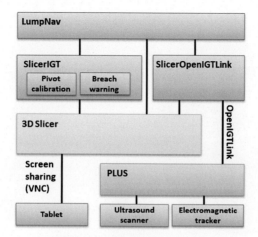

Figure 35.11 Components of surgical navigation system for breast cancer resection. Only a single custom module, *LumpNav*, had to be developed for this clinical application.

Figure 35.12 Clinicians using electromagnetic navigation for breast lumpectomy procedure. Position of tumor relative to cautery is shown on overhead display. The software is implemented using 3D Slicer, SlicerIGT extensions, and a small custom module for providing a simplified user interface optimized to be used in the operating room.

A custom *LumpNav* module replaces the standard 3D Slicer graphical user interface with a simplified touch-screen friendly interface that surgeons can use during the procedure on a tablet. The LumpNav module uses basic visualization features of the Slicer core and specialized calibration and visualization features of the SlicerIGT extension to implement the clinical workflow. The system has been successfully used for tens of patient cases in the operating room (Fig. 35.12). The software was iteratively refined

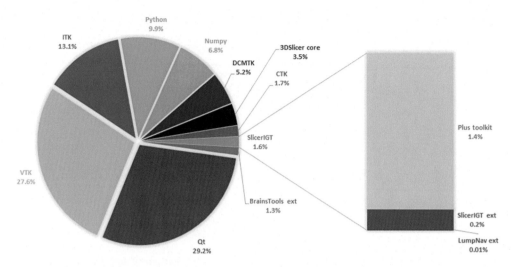

Figure 35.13 Size of software components in term of lines of source code. While size, complexity, or effort to develop or maintain software is not directly measurable by counting source code lines, this example illustrates how a small fraction of custom development was needed to create a new software application (LumpNav) which was robust and capable enough to be used on human patients in the operating room. The amount of custom source code was only 0.01% of the total size of all software components that were used to build the application (operating system and system-level libraries were excluded).

based on feedback received from surgeons. Most of the requested improvements were implemented and tested in about a week, since typically features were already available in the Slicer core or extensions and they only had to be enabled and exposed on the user interface.

The amount of custom software that had to be developed specifically for this clinical procedure was extremely small. In term of lines of source code, the LumpNav module size was 0.01% of the total source code used for building the software (including all software toolkits and libraries, except system libraries), as shown in Fig. 35.13.

35.5.2.3 Virtual/augmented reality applications

Virtual and augmented reality (VR and AR) has been the focus of research for decades, but affordable and practically usable hardware has become available only recently. Therefore, many groups started to explore the application of these technologies for CAI systems. In this section, we present examples of how VR and AR capable systems can be built based on the 3D Slicer application framework.

3D Slicer has direct support for virtual reality applications, via SlicerVirtualReality extension (https://github.com/KitwareMedical/SlicerVirtualReality) [18]. Users can view content of any 3D view in virtual reality by a single click of a button, move around in space and move and interact with objects in the scene. The feature uses VTK

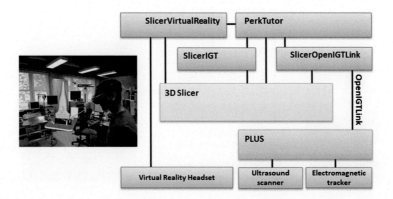

Figure 35.14 Virtual reality was used in ultrasound-guided needle insertion training. Needle and ultrasound probe position and images were recorded and analyzed using PerkTutor extension. Trainees reviewed their own performance in virtual reality in close-up 3D view.

toolkit's OpenVR interface, which is compatible with all commonly-used high-end virtual reality hardware, such as HTC Vive, Windows Mixed Reality, and Oculus Rift headsets. All rendering modes (surface rendering, volume rendering) are available as in regular desktop rendering and the application remains fully responsive while immersive viewing is enabled.

Virtual reality visualization has been evaluated on a number of applications. Medical students used it for reviewing their recorded ultrasound-guided needle insertions practice in close-up 3D view (Fig. 35.14), pediatric cardiologists viewed complex congenital abnormalities in 4D ultrasound images and cardiac implant placement plans in 4D CT data sets, and it showed promising potential in simulating various minimally invasive procedures.

Current augmented reality hardware suffer from issues such as limited field of view, fixed focal distance, tracking instability, too large and heavy headset for prolonged use, and limited computational capacity of untethered devices. Due to these problems, augmented reality cannot yet fulfill its full potential in CAI. However, feasibility studies and a few clinical applications are possible even using current technology. Unfortunately, there is no augmented reality software interface that would give low-level access to a wide range of devices and could be utilized from existing application frameworks. Developers who do not want to be locked into proprietary software development kits can use Unity (https://unity3d.com/) or Unreal (https://www.unrealengine.com) game engines. As mentioned before, a huge limitation of these systems is that existing medical image computing software libraries are not available in these frameworks (especially when deploying applications on standalone headsets, such as Microsoft HoloLens or Magic Leap). To reduce the burden of redeveloping all features, such as DICOM networking, image visualization, segmentation, surgical planning, etc., a promising

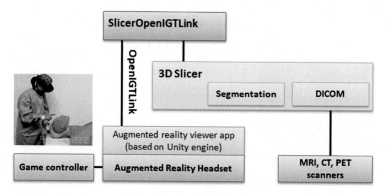

Figure 35.15 Implementing augmented reality system using gaming engine and existing CAI application framework. 3D Slicer is used for image import, visualization, segmentation, procedure planning. Created models are sent for visualization and patient registration to the augmented reality headset via OpenIGTLink.

approach is to use the gaming engine on the headset as a 3D viewer, which visualizes models (and maybe image slices and volumes) sent from existing CAI software through OpenIGTLink (Fig. 35.15). While various network protocols could be used, OpenIGTLink is a good choice because it can already transfer all commonly needed CAI data types, it is a very simple socket-based protocol, therefore it can be easily implemented in any software environment, and it is already implemented in many CAI applications.

35.6. Conclusions

This chapter focused on the design approaches, tools, and development processes that are intended to facilitate integration of various devices in computer assisted intervention (CAI) systems. The choice of programming language and platform generally depends on specific factors, such as development team experience and hardware constraints.

A component-based approach, using a standard middleware to provide the messaging capabilities, is recommended especially for large, complex systems. Two popular middleware choices are Robot Operating System (ROS) and OpenIGTLink. ROS is widely used in robotics and provides a complete development environment, including build system and package management, in addition to middleware, though (at present) is primarily focused on the Linux platform. In contrast, OpenIGTLink provides only a messaging system, but has the advantage of being light-weight, available on multiple platforms, and easy to implement on new platforms. It is widely used in CAI systems, especially when necessary to interface with common CAI devices such as medical imaging systems, visualization software (e.g., 3D Slicer), tracking systems, and some robots.

The chapter also reviewed application frameworks that support the development of CAI systems. The review did not focus on general frameworks, such as Qt, Matlab, and LabView, though many of these are also used. Due to the prevalence of medical images in CAI systems, the two most popular CAI application frameworks, 3D Slicer and MITK, have a central focus on image visualization and user interaction, but also are readily extensible to integrate other CAI devices, such as tracking systems and robots.

Finally, the chapter concluded with a presentation of two different CAI systems, the da Vinci Research Kit (dVRK) and the Slicer IGT environment. These serve to demonstrate many of the system integration concepts presented in this chapter, such as component-based design and use of application frameworks (3D Slicer) and middleware (ROS and OpenIGTLink). The dVRK example demonstrates how to build a complex robotic system, with several manipulators, from the ground up, while also leveraging middleware to facilitate integration with other devices. The Slicer IGT examples demonstrate the value of building on an existing application framework such as 3D Slicer, which enables the creation of CAI applications with a rich set of features, but requiring relatively low development effort. Furthermore, the development process described in this chapter is based on best practices in the community (especially, the open source community), but were also used for large portions of the presented systems. The reader can observe this by visiting the project GitHub pages, which show evidence of the described Git workflow, the use of automated testing (when feasible), and reference manuals generated by doxygen.

References

[1] A. Lasso, T. Heffter, A. Rankin, C. Pinter, T. Ungi, G. Fichtinger, PLUS: open-source toolkit for ultrasound-guided intervention systems, IEEE Transactions on Biomedical Engineering 61 (10) (Oct. 2014) 2527–2537, https://doi.org/10.1109/TBME.2014.2322864.

[2] T. Ungi, G. Gauvin, A. Lasso, C. Yeo, P. Pezeshki, T. Vaughan, K. Carter, J. Rudan, C. Engel, G. Fichtinger, Navigated breast tumor excision using electromagnetically tracked ultrasound and surgical instruments, IEEE Transactions on Biomedical Engineering (2015 Aug.).

[3] Open-source platforms for navigated image-guided interventions, Medical Image Analysis 33 (June 2016), https://doi.org/10.1016/j.media.2016.06.011.

[4] A. Bzostek, R. Kumar, N. Hata, O. Schorr, R. Kikinis, R. Taylor, Distributed modular computer-integrated surgical robotic systems: implementation using modular software and networked systems, in: Proc. Medical Image Computing and Computer Assisted Intervention, MICCAI 2000, Pittsburgh, PA, Oct. 2000, pp. 969–978.

[5] O. Schorr, N. Hata, A. Bzostek, R. Kumar, C. Burghart, R.H. Taylor, R. Kikinis, Distributed modular computer-integrated surgical robotic systems: architecture for intelligent object distribution, in: Proc. Medical Image Computing and Computer Assisted Intervention, MICCAI 2000, Pittsburgh, PA, Oct. 2000.

[6] A. Fedorov, R. Beichel, J. Kalpathy-Cramer, J. Finet, J-C. Fillion-Robin, S. Pujol, C. Bauer, D. Jennings, F.M. Fennessy, M. Sonka, J. Buatti, S.R. Aylward, J.V. Miller, S. Pieper, R. Kikinis, 3D Slicer as an image computing platform for the quantitative imaging network, Magnetic Resonance Imaging 30 (9) (2012 Nov.) 1323–1341, PMID: 22770690, PMCID: PMC3466397.

[7] J. Tokuda, G.S. Fischer, X. Papademetris, Z. Yaniv, L. Ibanez, P. Cheng, H. Liu, J. Blevins, J. Arata, A.J. Golby, T. Kapur, S. Pieper, E.C. Burdette, G. Fichtinger, C.M. Tempany, N. Hata, OpenIGTLink: an open network protocol for image-guided therapy environment, The International Journal of Medical Robotics and Computer Assisted Surgery 5 (4) (2009) 423–434.

[8] M. Quigley, K. Conley, B. Gerkey, J. Faust, T.B. Foote, J. Leibs, R. Wheeler, A.Y. Ng, ROS: an open-source Robot Operating System, in: IEEE Intl. Conf. on Robotics and Automation (ICRA), Workshop on Open Source Software, 2009.

[9] P. Kazanzides, Z. Chen, A. Deguet, G.S. Fischer, R.H. Taylor, S.P. DiMaio, An open-source research kit for the da Vinci ® Surgical System, in: IEEE Intl. Conf. on Robotics and Automation, ICRA, 2014, pp. 6434–6439.

[10] Z. Chen, P. Kazanzides, Multi-kilohertz control of multiple robots via IEEE-1394 (Firewire), in: IEEE Intl. Conf. on Technologies for Practical Robot Applications, TePRA, 2014.

[11] Z. Chen, A. Deguet, R.H. Taylor, P. Kazanzides, Software architecture of the da Vinci Research Kit, in: IEEE Intl. Conf. on Robotic Computing, Taichung, Taiwan, 2017.

[12] S. Kim, Y. Tan, A. Deguet, P. Kazanzides, Real-time image-guided telerobotic system integrating 3D Slicer and the da Vinci Research Kit, in: IEEE Intl. Conf. on Robotic Computing, Taichung, Taiwan, 2017.

[13] M.Y. Jung, A. Deguet, P. Kazanzides, A component-based architecture for flexible integration of robotic systems, in: IEEE/RSJ Intl. Conf. on Intelligent Robots and Systems, IROS, 2010.

[14] P. Kazanzides, Y. Kouskouslas, A. Deguet, Z. Shao, Proving the correctness of concurrent robot software, in: IEEE Intl. Conf. on Robotics and Automation, ICRA, St. Paul, MN, May 2012, pp. 4718–4723.

[15] P. Kazanzides, S. DiMaio, A. Deguet, B. Vagvolgyi, M. Balicki, C. Schneider, R. Kumar, A. Jog, B. Itkowitz, C. Hasser, R. Taylor, The Surgical Assistant Workstation (SAW) in minimally-invasive surgery and microsurgery, in: MICCAI Workshop on Systems and Arch. for Computer Assisted Interventions, Midas Journal (June 2010), http://hdl.handle.net/10380/3179.

[16] A. Kapoor, A. Deguet, P. Kazanzides, Software components and frameworks for medical robot control, in: IEEE Intl. Conf. on Robotics and Automation, ICRA, May 2006, pp. 3813–3818.

[17] M.Y. Jung, M. Balicki, A. Deguet, R.H. Taylor, P. Kazanzides, Lessons learned from the development of component-based medical robot systems, Journal of Software Engineering for Robotics (JOSER) 5 (2) (Sept. 2014) 25–41.

[18] Saleh Choueib, Csaba Pinter, Andras Lasso, Jean-Christophe Fillion-Robin, Jean-Baptiste Vimort, Ken Martin, Gabor Fichtinger, Evaluation of 3D Slicer as a medical virtual reality visualization platform, Proceedings of SPIE Medical Imaging (2019) 1095113-1–1095113-8.

[19] H. Bruyninckx, P. Soetens, B. Koninckx, The real-time motion control core of the Orocos project, in: IEEE Intl. Conf. on Robotics and Automation, ICRA, Sept. 2003, pp. 2766–2771.

[20] M. Henning, A new approach to object-oriented middleware, IEEE Internet Computing 8 (1) (Jan.–Feb. 2004) 66–75.

[21] A. Brooks, T. Kaupp, A. Makarenko, S. Williams, A. Oreback, Towards component-based robotics, in: Intl. Conf. on Intelligent Robots and Systems, IROS, Aug. 2005, pp. 163–168.

[22] P. Kruchten, The 4+1 view model of architecture, IEEE Software 12 (1995) 42–50.

[23] M. Nolden, S. Zelzer, A. Seitel, D. Wald, M. Müller, A.M. Franz, D. Maleike, M. Fangerau, M. Baumhauer, L. Maier-Hein, K.H. Maier-Hein, H.P. Meinzer, I. Wolf, The medical imaging interaction toolkit: challenges and advances: 10 years of open-source development, International Journal of Computer Assisted Radiology and Surgery 8 (4) (2013) 607–620.

[24] M.J. Clarkson, G. Zombori, S. Thompson, J. Totz, Y. Song, M. Espak, S. Johnsen, D. Hawkes, S. Ourselin, The NifTK software platform for image-guided interventions: platform overview and NiftyLink messaging, International Journal of Computer Assisted Radiology and Surgery 10 (3) (2014) 301–316.

[25] L. Qian, A. Deguet, P. Kazanzides, ARssist: augmented reality on a head-mounted display for the first assistant in robotic surgery, Healthcare Technology Letters 5 (5) (2018) 194–200.

[26] H. Kato, M. Billinghurst, Marker tracking and HMD calibration for a video-based augmented reality conferencing system, in: IEEE/ACM Intl. Workshop on Augmented Reality, IWAR, 1999, pp. 85–94.

[27] L. Qian, A. Deguet, Z. Wang, Y.H. Liu, P. Kazanzides, Augmented reality assisted instrument insertion and tool manipulation for the first assistant in robotic surgery, in: IEEE Intl. Conf. on Robotics and Automation, ICRA, 2019, pp. 5173–5179.

[28] L. Qian, A. Deguet, P. Kazanzides, dVRK-XR: mixed reality extension for da Vinci Research Kit, in: Hamlyn Symposium on Medical Robotics, 2019, pp. 93–94.

CHAPTER 36

Clinical translation

Aaron Fenster

Robarts Research Institute, Western University, London, ON, Canada

Contents

36.1. Introduction		893
36.2. Definitions		894
36.3. Useful researcher characteristics for clinical translation		896
	36.3.1 Comfort zone	897
	36.3.2 Team-based approach	898
	36.3.3 Embracing change	898
	36.3.4 Commercialization	899
	36.3.5 Selection of a clinical translatable idea	899
	36.3.6 Clinical trials	900
	36.3.7 Regulatory approval	900
36.4. Example of clinical translation: 3D ultrasound-guided prostate biopsy		901
	36.4.1 Clinical need	901
	36.4.2 Clinical research partners and generation of the hypothesis	901
	36.4.3 Development of basic tools	902
	36.4.4 Applied research	903
	36.4.5 Clinical research	903
	36.4.6 Commercialization	904
	36.4.7 Actions based on lessons learned	904
36.5. Conclusions		905
References		906

36.1. Introduction

The number of innovations and publications focusing on medical image computing and image–guided interventions have increased significantly over the past four decades. Traditional journals in this field are highly respected and new journals are being continuously launched. These journals have described some innovations that have revolutionized diagnostic and therapeutic medicine and other innovations have entered routine clinical use. However, the vast majority of the innovations have not been translated into clinical use to have an impact on healthcare or the provisions of health outcomes. While the ultimate goal of research in our field is clinical translation, i.e., migration of innovations from lab to bedside, not all investigators have the knowledge or capability to participate in the steps involved. Thus, it is important to understand the process, by which clinical translation is realized, best practices in the process, and some lessons.

Handbook of Medical Image Computing and Computer Assisted Intervention
https://doi.org/10.1016/B978-0-12-816176-0.00041-7

Most investigators understand and agree what is meant by clinical research; however, translational research is not well defined and difficult to articulate. Many believe that clinical translation is the final step in a unidirectional process that starts with basic research and end with clinical implementation of the innovation in a clinical setting. While this understanding is workable for many, it misses the complexity of the clinical translation process resulting in suboptimal progression of the innovation from idea to clinical use. It also misses the opportunity to provide our trainees with the experience in the clinical translation process, which may be needed for their future careers. Furthermore, lack of understanding also obscures whether clinical translation stops at first-in-human testing, a clinical trial, commercialization of the innovation or integration into clinical practice.

To accelerate translational research, the NIH in the United States has recognized the importance of clinical translation and lack of training in this type of research through the K30 and Clinical and Translational Science Award (CTSA) programs. However, research in medical image computing and computer assisted intervention is complex, spanning the spectrum from basic research to population research, involving researchers and their collaborators from a wide range of fields [15,18]. Although many articles and documents have described clinical translation, it is appropriate to review some of the terms used in our field and develop a common understanding what "clinical translation" encompasses. This chapter is a step in this discussion by reviewing some definitions, characteristics of a translational researcher, and some lessons learned by the author of this chapter.

36.2. Definitions

While there is general agreement that both basic and applied research are important, there is a tension between basic and applied researchers competing for grants and recognition [6,14,26]. Heated discussions occur between these researchers when grant funding allocation priorities are being considered and established. Clearly, basic research is needed to build a foundation by which applied researchers can base their innovation to solve real-world problems so that clinical researchers can investigate the utility of the solution using human subjects. It is clear that basic, applied, and clinical research are part of the clinical translation process, as none can be removed and all play a critical role in clinical translation. Thus, proper communication between scientists requires agreement on the definitions and how translational research fits into the translational spectrum [20].

Basic research starts with a hypothesis and proceeds with theoretical and/or laboratory experiments to prove or disprove the hypothesis, thereby gaining knowledge about nature and its laws. No consideration is typically given whether the knowledge gained has a practical application or use. It is generally assumed that the knowledge gained may have a short- or long-term impact, or no impact on healthcare at all.

Applied research starts with articulation of a clinical need or a problem affecting patients and the healthcare system. This information is then used to establish a statement of the goal and a method to verify that the goal has been achieved. An applied researcher then proceeds to use basic knowledge generated by basic researchers and multidisciplinary expertise in one's lab and/or through collaborations to develop a solution to solve the clinical need.

Clinical research involves the use of human subjects, tissues from human subjects or cognitive phenomena from human subjects [17]. Thus, clinical researchers are involved in diagnostic methods, therapeutic interventions, epidemiological studies, and clinical service research.

Clinical translation research is less clear, but we expect that it involves the step of getting the laboratory innovative solution to the clinical need to the patient's bedside [25]. Many organizations have attempted to define it, and the NIH – National Center for Advanced Translational Sciences in the United States – provided the following definition:

> *"Translation is the process of turning observations in the laboratory, clinic and community into interventions that improve the health of individuals and the public – from diagnostics and therapeutics to medical procedures and behavioral changes."*
>
> **https://ncats.nih.gov/translation#learn-more**

These research areas may appear to be distinct and involve participants working in silos; however, they are components of the *clinical translation continuum*, in which research findings progress from the lab to patient healthcare and the community [7]. Research in these areas is intertwined and feeding each other, making it difficult for individuals to understand their role, which results in missing components in the progression to clinical translation. Many investigators lack the knowledge and face common barriers in translational research, which hinder advances in diagnostic and therapeutic medicine. To clarify the relationship between roles of researchers focusing on different aspects in the *clinical translation continuum*, it has been divided into four phases with the T0 to T4 classification system [6,10,24–26] as shown in Fig. 36.1, which has been modified slightly here.

T0 refers to the translation of hypotheses or ideas into basic research, which includes theoretical, experimental preclinical, but not involving human subjects, e.g., developing a new image segmentation method and testing it on images in a data bank.

T1 refers to translation to humans including first-in-human test, proof-of-concept studies, feasibility studies, and phase 1 and some phase 2 clinical trials focused on diagnostic, therapeutic, and prevention methods, e.g., testing a new imaging system in a highly controlled setting using a few human subjects, not necessarily patients.

T2 refers to translation to patients involving phase 2 and 3 clinical trials demonstrating efficacy and effectiveness of a new diagnostic or therapeutic method, e.g., demonstration in a randomly controlled trials that ultrasound/MRI fusion biopsy is an effective method to monitor prostate cancer patients on active surveillance.

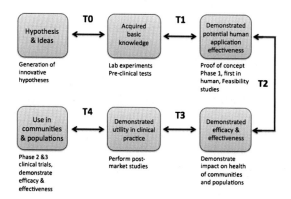

Figure 36.1 Schematic diagram of the clinical translation pathway showing the translation of hypotheses and novel ideas through the various steps leading to adoption by communities and populations. Note that the transitions are bidirectional as knowledge gained in any step can influence other steps in the process.

T3 refers translation to clinical practice involving phase 3 trials focused on comparative effectiveness research and postmarket studies, e.g., demonstration that tomosynthesis is superior to digital mammography for screening women for breast cancer.

T4 refers to translation to communities involving population level outcome and impact on society.

36.3. Useful researcher characteristics for clinical translation

The ultimate goal of researchers in working on MICCAI topics is to improve healthcare. As discussed above, the *clinical translation continuum* has many steps and involves a complex set of skills, significant time, and costs. Thus, individuals often ask how they can move their innovations from their "bench" closer or to the "bedside". Very few researchers have all the skills themselves to do that, yet are convinced that if they do not lead the effort, their innovations may not be translated to clinical use.

It is clear that a complex set of skills is needed to integrate all components from outputs of basic research to methods used by clinical researchers. Basic researchers may develop a new tool and then begin to search for an application by trying to find a clinician to test or use it. Applied researches may recognize the clinical need but may not have the best tools to solve the problem effectively. Clinical researchers may have first-hand knowledge of the clinical need and access to patients, but may not have the best tool or the skills needed to be able to develop the technology to meet the clinical need. While there are some talented researchers who can integrate all aspects, few have the skills to span this broad spectrum.

Researchers have taken various routs to overcome these barriers. Some basic or applied researchers have opted to enter medical school to acquire the skill needed for

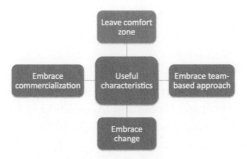

Figure 36.2 Useful characteristics of individuals who pursue clinical translation successfully.

clinical research, and some clinicians have technology-based training (e.g., PhD in an engineering discipline) and are able to apply new concepts in technology to solve clinical problems. However, the majority of researchers must find a different mechanism to span the skills needed to translate their innovations through the *clinical translation continuum* to clinical use. A workable solution for many is to lead an interdisciplinary team that is able to fill the skill gaps needed to overcome the barriers to translation. The following (Fig. 36.2) are some of the characteristics for these researchers that may help to overcome the barriers to clinical translation and may help or accelerate clinical translation by moving innovations from "bed to bedside" more efficiently.

36.3.1 Comfort zone

One of the key barriers is the inability or lack of interest for working outside one's comfort zone. Developing one's career and achieving international prominence requires a focused effort in one's field. Grant funding competition also drives us to stay within a narrow area where we have developed our reputation, yet clinical translation of an innovation is a large positive indicator of success. Thus, the best route for a successful research program with healthcare impact is to encompass clinical translation. However, to be able to integrate a broad range of knowledge needed to leverage basic research finding, applied research methods and clinical translation pathways requires stepping outside one's comfort zone and be conversant in a wide range of subjects. To achieve this working level and acquire the language of other fields requires a substantial effort and commitment to this goal. There are many ways to acquire the comfort to understand and be able to converse effectively with researchers who are to fill the skill gaps. However, first is to acknowledge that one researcher cannot be an expert in all fields, but can acquire sufficient knowledge to understand a wide range of fields. This can be achieved by attending clinical rounds, and applied and basic engineering seminars and sessions at conferences. Many clinical conferences have technology-based sessions, and many engineering conferences have sessions with an emphasis on clinical translation. These are valuable opportunities to acquire the language of other disciplines and to understand the needs of other fields.

36.3.2 Team-based approach

Clinical translation requires individuals to move an innovation through the complete path from basic research to clinical application. Acquisition of a broad range of knowledge and language of other fields is necessary but not sufficient as experts are required the required components at all phases of the process. Thus, a team-based approach is needed with integration of a wide range of skills. This requires integration of trainees (graduate students and postdoctoral fellows) from different university departments, technical staff to perform different skilled tasks and other researchers as partners and/or collaborators to bring key expertise needed for the project. In addition and most importantly, committed clinical partners are needed to interact with the team at all phases, but especially at the project's inception to identify the clinical need and viability of the potential solution, as well as at the testing phase to identify improvements in the technology to optimize outcome and clinical workflow. Frequent meetings of the collaborating researchers and clinical partners are required to ensure that the research program remains on the right track and that the end product is likely to be successful from a clinical translation perspective. For example, development of ultrasound/MRI fusion biopsy system requires computer scientists with expertise in segmentation and registration, software developers for the 3D visualization system, mechanical engineers to design the hardware, electrical engineers to develop the electronics and control subsystem, and an interventional radiologist and/or urologist to help guide the development and perform the clinical tests with patients scheduled for prostate biopsy. Having all this expertise in the lab and with clinical partners who have access to patients is difficult but required for efficient translation. This example of translation from basic research to translation to the community is discussed below in more detail.

36.3.3 Embracing change

Researchers are now facing an accelerated pace in changes in technology, with advances in computer technology and software concepts (e.g., machine learning methods) occurring in unprecedented pace. In addition, health care is also undergoing changes with a shift to personalized and evidence-based medicine as well as patient-centered outcome. Technology is no longer adopted because it is new or has the best specifications. These changes are providing unprecedented opportunities for those who are prepared with the knowledge to adapt to these changes and those who are willing to embrace the changes. Staying current and developing a wide network of colleagues is required, which is best achieved through attendance and participation in leading clinical and technology-based conferences. For example, integrating the latest image processing methods using deep convolutional networks and the latest technical innovations in robotics can result in improved interventional procedures making them more accurate, less variable, and requiring a shorter procedure time. Clearly, incorporating these advances into one's research program requires embracing change and constant learning.

36.3.4 Commercialization

The clinical translation process does not stop at performance of a clinical trial, but can extend to making the innovation available to a wider community through commercialization [12]. The path to commercialization is complex, has many pitfalls, and is the subject of institutional regulations, and in some countries, federal regulations [19]. Much information is available through the technology transfer officers (TTOs) at universities on the topic of commercialization and guidance of the innovation through the commercialization pathway, and is therefore not repeated here. However, a researcher committed to clinical translation and clinical impact should become aware of the possible avenues for commercialization of their innovations, as well as the rights of the researcher and their obligations to their employer, e.g., whether the researcher is required to assign the invention to the university (as in some US universities), or the researcher owns the invention and only needs to disclose it to their university (as in some Canadian universities and institutions). The MICCAI community of researchers has had many successful commercialized innovations through both licenses of technology as well as spin-out of start-up companies. These researchers are rewarded by being active participants in global clinical translation of their innovation as well as having a richer training environment allowing their trainees to experience the commercialization process. Some researchers have had their trainees lead the spin-out companies who have achieved international success.

36.3.5 Selection of a clinical translatable idea

The first and one of the most important steps along the pathway for clinical translation is identifying the clinical need. Clearly, a potential solution that does not solve the clinical need will most likely not be beneficial and certainly not fundable. Furthermore, if the goal for clinical translation includes commercialization for dissemination of the product, then it must have a clinical benefit. The process of assessing the clinical need can take many forms and involves discussions with local or distant experts. The optimal approach to maximize opportunity for translation is to obtain buy-in of the clinical need from one's local clinical partner in the research project, as constant engagement of the physician in the solution will be critical in its success. However, relying only on one's clinical partner is not sufficient as local bias may not be reflected widely. Thus, validation of the clinical need with external clinical experts is needed through discussions and attendance of clinical sessions at international conferences. Conferences such as the Radiological Society of North America (RSNA) are among the best as the clinical sessions cover all aspects of radiology and radiation oncology.

36.3.6 Clinical trials

An important step in the clinical translation pathway is the performance of a clinical trial used to test the developed medical technology. Although the clinical trial world thinks of clinical trials in terms of pharmaceuticals, understanding the issues and aspects of medical device trials is critical. Although there are similarities between clinical trials testing pharmaceuticals and medical devices, there are significant differences. Pharmaceutical trials are divided in phases (phase 1 to phase 4), but medical devices trials are classified as Pilot, Pivotal, and postapproval.

Pilot trials typically involve a small population of 10 to 30 individuals with the disease or condition. These trials are primarily used to determine preliminary safety and device performance information.

Pivotal trials involve larger populations of 150 to 300 individuals with the disease or condition. These trials are primarily used to determine effectiveness of the device and to identify any adverse effects.

Postapproval trials are used to collect long-term information on patients treated with the medical device. This information is also used to identify any long-term adverse effects in the use of the device.

36.3.7 Regulatory approval

In an effort to ensure safety of a medical device, regulatory approval must be obtained prior to clinical use. Different jurisdictions have different rules, but they are generally similar. In the USA, devices are classified into Class I, II or III, each requiring a different path to use with humans. Class I devices pose the minimal risk to the patient, are controlled the least, and are therefore exempt from premarket submission. Class II devices pose a moderate risk and thus require Premarket Notification 510(k) that demonstrates substantial equivalence to an approved device. However, Class III devices pose a high risk of illness or injury to humans and therefor require Premarket Approval (PMA), which is an involved process requiring submission of clinical data to support the claims of the device. Typical class III devices are implantable pacemakers and breast implants.

Unlike the USA classification of devices, which depends of similar (predicate) devices that have been approved by the FDA, Europe uses a rule-based system. In Europe, devices are classified into four basic categories: noninvasive devices, invasive medical devices, active medical devices, and special rules, which include radiological diagnostic devices. These categories are further segmented into four classes, similar to the FDA classification: Class I are low-risk or low/medium risk devices; Class IIa devices present a medium risk; Class IIb present a medium/high risk; and Class III present a high risk.

Medical device classification in China is similar to that of FDA with classification into 3 classes. For more details about medical device approval, see the web sites' references in the citation section.

36.4. Example of clinical translation: 3D ultrasound-guided prostate biopsy

The following is an example of clinical translation from the author's laboratory. The example describes the progression from concept to commercialization and lessons learned.

36.4.1 Clinical need

Recognizing that establishing the clinical need is paramount and that partnership with physicians is critical to success, the author established a close relationship with the Department of Radiology in the adjoining hospital to the research lab. This included attendance in some radiology rounds and having lunch with the radiologists to develop a mechanism to discuss topics and establish trust. In addition, working closely with the Chair of the Department ensured that physics and engineering inputs were welcomed, and that support of research projects involving staff members and resources in the department were also welcomed. Furthermore, understanding that new and young radiologists would be interested in research projects and were still building their CVs for promotion, much effort was made to meet and establish rapport with them.

In one of the discussions with a new radiologist who was performing prostate biopsies, he described his frustration at performing repeated biopsies on some men, and receiving repeated negative results in spite of rising PSA in these men. The discussion led to the challenge from the radiologist whether we can develop a better method to perform prostate biopsies over the conventional 2D ultrasound-guided sextant approach. This conversation established the clinical need **to improve the positive yield of prostate biopsy and reduce the number of repeat biopsies.**

During the discussions of possible solutions, it was hypothesized that a 3D ultrasound image of the prostate would help in planning the biopsy procedure, ensure the biopsy cores would be distributed properly, and that recording of the biopsy core locations would be possible in 3D in case a repeat biopsy were needed to avoid original locations.

36.4.2 Clinical research partners and generation of the hypothesis

Success of the project clearly required a long-term collaborative partnership with a radiologist for insights into the procedure, expertise related to ultrasound imaging of the prostate, and feedback on possible workflow issues with any innovative new approach. This required assembling a prototype 3D ultrasound imaging system and imaging a patient's prostate to demonstrate that the use of 3D ultrasound imaging of the prostate was viable and had the potential to help solve the problem. In addition, preliminary results were also needed for submitted grants.

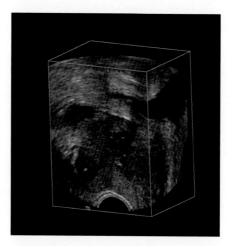

Figure 36.3 3D ultrasound image of the prostate showing the image slices in multiple planes. The prostate tumor is present in the lower right side of the peripheral zone. The image of the prostate was acquired using an end-firing transducer, which was rotated by 180 degrees.

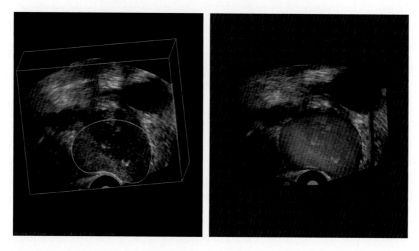

Figure 36.4 3D ultrasound image of the prostate showing the segmented boundary of the prostate in two views.

36.4.3 Development of basic tools

Development of 3D ultrasound guided system for imaging the prostate required multiple basic tools to be assembled into a complete system: mechanism to rotate the end-firing transducer to allow acquisition of the 2D ultrasound images, 3D ultrasound image reconstruction from a series of 2D ultrasound images (Fig. 36.3), segmentation of the prostate boundary (Fig. 36.4) [4,11,13], segmentation of the biopsy needles as the needle is fired into the prostate [3,5], and 3D ultrasound to MR image registration (added

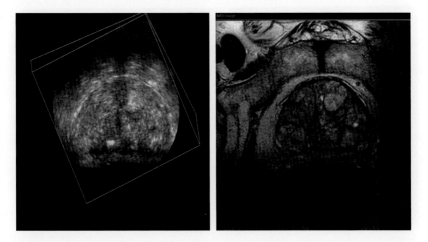

Figure 36.5 (left) 3D ultrasound image which has been registered to the MR image (right) prior to prostate biopsy.

later) [21–23]. Development of these tools required establishing collaborations with other investigators (i.e., prostate segmentation) and hiring engineers and software developers with the appropriate skills.

36.4.4 Applied research

Clearly, developing the complete 3D ultrasound-guided prostate biopsy system required a wide range of expertise [1,9]. Due to potential commercialization of the technology and to maintain a simple IP ownership portfolio, we hired individuals with expertise that was missing in the lab rather that make the IP ownership complex due to many collaborations. Based on the detailed specification and biopsy workflow, all components of the system were developed and integrated. This required a few cycles of modifications based on the system's use with patients scheduled for prostate biopsy.

36.4.5 Clinical research

With the complete system, regulatory and IRB approvals, our clinical collaborators performed clinical trials investigating the utility of this new approach to prostate biopsy (Figs. 36.5 and 36.6). Small Phase I trials were performed as well as a Phase II randomly controlled trial with 200 subjects, which was funded by the Ontario Institute for Cancer Research (Cool et al. [2], Elliot et al. [8], Marks et al. [16]). These trials were aimed at establishing for which men the more complicated 3D ultrasound-guided biopsy was suitable.

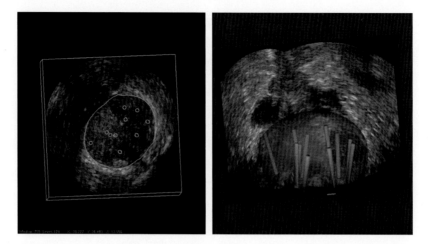

Figure 36.6 Two views of a 3D ultrasound image with the biopsy cores depicted as narrow tubes. The cores were obtained by segmenting the biopsy needle as it was fired into the prostate.

36.4.6 Commercialization

It was clear that clinical translation beyond a local clinical trial would require commercialization of the system [19]. Thus, we adopted an aggressive patenting policy and patents were filed on all modules and tools to be incorporated into the system. Since the potential market size was very large and no similar system was available at the time, the institution was willing to fund the patents, which required assigning the patents to the institution. After developing the prototype system, in which we could demonstrate the approach to acquiring 2D ultrasound images of the prostate and reconstructing them into a 3D ultrasound image, as well as software that allowed viewing the 3D ultrasound image (few other tools were available at the time), we were able to attract a company that licensed the technology and contracted our lab to develop the complete commercializable system, which is distributed globally.

36.4.7 Actions based on lessons learned

- Develop strong partnerships with a clinical departments and physicians.
- Establish a clinical need and validate it with experts from different institutions.
- Embrace change in technology and healthcare system.
- Upgrade knowledge constantly in diverse technology fields.
- Become aware of clinical problems facing physicians in delivering accurate diagnosis and therapy.
- Establish a team of experts in diverse fields through collaborations and/or hiring staff.
- Be aware of path to commercialization at your institution.
- Be aware of the path to obtain IRB and regulatory approval.

36.5. Conclusions

Successful translational research moves in a bidirectional manner between types of research – basic research and applied research, applied research and clinical research, clinical research and population research. Thus, clinical translation involves collaboration between a wide variety of researchers and technical expertise. While it may not be expected that any single researcher's laboratory can accommodate the personnel and expertise for the complete clinical translation pathway, successful translation requires effective collaboration and communication. In addition to translation of the specific innovation, collaborations between researchers from different disciplines generate new insights and ideas. Most importantly for clinical translation is identification of the *clinical need*. Thus, effective collaboration between scientists and physicians is critical. Researchers isolated in engineering, computational or physics laboratories may not interact sufficiently often with clinicians, and therefore must find avenues to interact with them on a regular basis to allow development of trust and common purpose. Researchers embedded in health care centers have a direct access to physicians, clinical fellows and residents, but must interact with basic scientists to allow integration of the latest advances in technology. Clearly, wherever researchers are located, effective clinical translation will require them to be able to speak the language of other disciplines and be comfortable outside their areas of expertise. This approach to research will not only accelerate clinical translations of one's innovation, but will also generate an exciting research program that will stimulate innovations among the researchers and their trainees.

Regulatory information

http://www.fda.gov/MedicalDevices/DeviceRegulationandGuidance/
http://www.pharmasug.org/cd/papers/IB/IB01.pdf
http://eng.sfda.gov.cn/WS03/CL0768/144302.html
http://www.sfda.com/medical-device.html
http://www.fda.gov/downloads/Training/ClinicalInvestigatorTrainingCourse/UCM378265.pdf

Medical device trials

https://premier-research.com/perspectivesmedical-devices-vs-drug-trials/
https://cdn2.hubspot.net/hub/149400/file-646377456-pdf/docs/mc-n-med-dev-trials-compare-with-drug-trials.pdf
https://www.experis.ca/Website-File-Pile/Whitepapers/Experis/IT_Medicial-Device-Clinical-Trials_091912.pdf

Clinical translation continuum

https://ictr.wisc.edu/what-are-the-t0-to-t4-research-classifications/
http://www.ucdenver.edu/research/CCTSI/news-events/CCTSISummit/Documents/CCTSISummitIII_T3-T4Research_Morrato_Aug2015.pdf

References

[1] J. Bax, D. Cool, L. Gardi, K. Knight, D. Smith, J. Montreuil, A. Fenster, Mechanically assisted 3D ultrasound guided prostate biopsy system, Med. Phys. 35 (12) (2008) 5397–5410.

[2] D.W. Cool, C. Romagnoli, J.I. Izawa, J. Chin, L. Gardi, D. Tessier, A. Fenster, Comparison of prostate MRI-3D transrectal ultrasound fusion biopsy for first-time and repeat biopsy patients with previous atypical small acinar proliferation, Can. Urol. Assoc. J. 10 (9–10) (2016) 342–348, https://doi.org/10.5489/cuaj.3831.

[3] M. Ding, H.N. Cardinal, A. Fenster, Automatic needle segmentation in three-dimensional ultrasound images using two orthogonal two-dimensional image projections, Med. Phys. 30 (2) (2003) 222–234.

[4] M. Ding, B. Chiu, I. Gyacskov, X. Yuan, M. Drangova, D.B. Downey, A. Fenster, Fast prostate segmentation in 3D TRUS images based on continuity constraint using an autoregressive model, Med. Phys. 34 (11) (2007) 4109–4125, https://doi.org/10.1118/1.2777005.

[5] M. Ding, A. Fenster, A real-time biopsy needle segmentation technique using Hough transform, Med. Phys. 30 (8) (2003) 2222–2233.

[6] D. Dougherty, P.H. Conway, The "3T's" road map to transform US health care: the "how" of high-quality care, JAMA 299 (19) (2008) 2319–2321, https://doi.org/10.1001/jama.299.19.2319.

[7] B.C. Drolet, N.M. Lorenzi, Translational research: understanding the continuum from bench to bedside, Transl. Res. 157 (1) (2011) 1–5, https://doi.org/10.1016/j.trsl.2010.10.002.

[8] T.L. Elliot, D.B. Downey, S. Tong, C.A. McLean, A. Fenster, Accuracy of prostate volume measurements in vitro using three-dimensional ultrasound, Acad. Radiol. 3 (5) (1996) 401–406.

[9] A. Fenster, D.B. Downey, Three-dimensional ultrasound imaging, Annu. Rev. Biomed. Eng. 02 (2000) 457–475.

[10] F. Gannon, The steps from translatable to translational research, EMBO Rep. 15 (11) (2014) 1107–1108, https://doi.org/10.15252/embr.201439587.

[11] J.D. Gill, H.M. Ladak, D.A. Steinman, A. Fenster, Accuracy and variability assessment of a semiautomatic technique for segmentation of the carotid arteries from three-dimensional ultrasound images, Med. Phys. 27 (6) (2000) 1333–1342.

[12] J.M. Grimshaw, M.P. Eccles, J.N. Lavis, S.J. Hill, J.E. Squires, Knowledge translation of research findings, Implement. Sci. 7 (50) (2012), https://doi.org/10.1186/1748-5908-7-50.

[13] A.C. Hodge, A. Fenster, D.B. Downey, H.M. Ladak, Prostate boundary segmentation from ultrasound images using 2D active shape models: optimisation and extension to 3D, Comput. Methods Programs Biomed. 84 (2–3) (2006) 99–113.

[14] C. Lenfant, Shattuck lecture – clinical research to clinical practice – lost in translation?, N. Engl. J. Med. 349 (9) (2003) 868–874, https://doi.org/10.1056/NEJMsa035507.

[15] F.M. Marincola, The trouble with translational medicine, J. Intern. Med. 270 (2) (2011) 123–127, https://doi.org/10.1111/j.1365-2796.2011.02402.x.

[16] L. Marks, A. Ward, L. Gardi, R. Bentley, D. Kumar, S. Gupta, A. Fenster, Tracking of prostate biopsy sites using a 3D ultrasound device (Artemis), J. Urol. 183 (2010) e832.

[17] D.G. Nathan, The several Cs of translational clinical research, J. Clin. Invest. 115 (4) (2005) 795–797, https://doi.org/10.1172/JCI24753.

[18] R.B. Nussenblatt, F.M. Marincola, A.N. Schechter, Translational medicine – doing it backwards, J. Transl. Med. 8 (2010) 12, https://doi.org/10.1186/1479-5876-8-12.

[19] L.M. Portilla, B. Alving, Reaping the benefits of biomedical research: partnerships required, Sci. Transl. Med. 2 (35) (2010) 35cm17, https://doi.org/10.1126/scitranslmed.3001137.

[20] D.M. Rubio, E.E. Schoenbaum, L.S. Lee, D.E. Schteingart, P.R. Marantz, K.E. Anderson, K. Esposito, Defining translational research: implications for training, Acad. Med. 85 (3) (2010) 470–475, https://doi.org/10.1097/ACM.0b013e3181ccd618.

[21] Y. Sun, W. Qiu, C. Romagnoli, A. Fenster, 3D non-rigid surface-based MR-TRUS registration for image-guided prostate biopsy, in: Medical Imaging 2014: Image-Guided Procedures, Robotic Interventions, and Modeling, vol. 9036, 2014, 90362J.

[22] Y. Sun, W. Qiu, J. Yuan, C. Romagnoli, A. Fenster, Three-dimensional nonrigid landmark-based magnetic resonance to transrectal ultrasound registration for image-guided prostate biopsy, J. Med. Imaging (Bellingham) 2 (2) (2015) 025002, https://doi.org/10.1117/1.JMI.2.2.025002.

[23] Y. Sun, J. Yuan, W. Qiu, M. Rajchl, C. Romagnoli, A. Fenster, Three-dimensional nonrigid MR-TRUS registration using dual optimization, IEEE Trans. Med. Imaging 34 (5) (2015) 1085–1095, https://doi.org/10.1109/Tmi.2014.2375207.

[24] P.G. Szilagyi, Translational research and pediatrics, Acad. Pediatr. 9 (2) (2009) 71–80, https://doi.org/10.1016/j.acap.2008.11.002.

[25] J.M. Westfall, J. Mold, L. Fagnan, Practice-based research – "Blue Highways" on the NIH roadmap, JAMA 297 (4) (2007) 403–406, https://doi.org/10.1001/jama.297.4.403.

[26] S.H. Woolf, The meaning of translational research and why it matters, JAMA 299 (2) (2008) 211–213, https://doi.org/10.1001/jama.2007.26.

CHAPTER 37

Interventional procedures training

Tamas Ungi[a], Matthew Holden[a], Boris Zevin[b], Gabor Fichtinger[a]
[a]School of Computing, Queen's University, Kingston, ON, Canada
[b]Department of Surgery, Queen's University, Kingston, ON, Canada

Contents

37.1. Introduction	909
37.2. Assessment	911
37.2.1 Rating by expert reviewers	912
37.2.2 Real-time spatial tracking	913
37.2.3 Automatic video analysis	915
37.2.4 Crowdsourcing	916
37.3. Feedback	917
37.3.1 Feedback in complex procedures	917
37.3.2 Learning curves and performance benchmarks	918
37.4. Simulated environments	919
37.4.1 Animal models	920
37.4.2 Synthetic models	920
37.4.3 Box trainers	921
37.4.4 Virtual reality	923
37.5. Shared resources	924
37.6. Summary	925
References	925

37.1. Introduction

Medical education and competency assessment have been criticized to overly focus on lexical knowledge and written tests. Investing in better education and evaluation of procedural skills would likely result in better patient care [5]. However, studies suggest that most medical students leave school with insufficient surgical and procedural skills to perform basic procedures without putting patients at risk [9,40]. Although this gap in education has been realized by both practitioners and researchers, implementing a change in the education system is challenging for medical schools. Education could be improved by increasing exposure to practical procedural education sessions in medical schools. But such a change would require fundamental changes in the current curriculum structure, and it would probably require significantly more faculty resources. In fact, the fundamentals of medical education have not changed much in the past centuries. The apprenticeship model and one-on-one training is still the dominant teaching method for procedural medical skills [43]. More practice opportunities for students would require proportionally more supervision by experienced physicians, which is simply not feasible due to the limited time physicians can dedicate to teaching while balancing their main responsibility for patient care. To make a meaningful change in procedural skills education, supervision by experienced physicians need to be at least partially replaced by new technologies. That is why computer-guided medical training could bring the long-awaited transformation in medical education to reality.

Many procedures have been taught and performed for decades without computer-assisted training, but recent changes in social awareness of patient safety and physician liability increased the need for more objective measures in training. Computer-assisted training technology offers many advantages in making the training process more standardized and objective. Increased awareness of patient safety demands that physicians develop means for quality assurance in their training programs. Professional organizations recommend documented proof of skills of medical trainees before they perform those procedures on patients. This is a daunting task for most medical specialties. In many specialties it is hard to put objective measures on the interactions between physicians and patients. But interventional procedures have a great potential to exploit computers and technology to objectively measure and document performance of technical skills.

Computers can help resolve two problematic aspects of skill assessment. First, computers are inherently objective. They ignore potential bias based on, e.g., race and gender by design. Computers always perform skill analysis based on the same preprogrammed metrics. Second, they are more accessible than experienced physician observers. This is important for equity aspects in training. Students can use computer-based training as much as they need. Today, computers are often more accessible for medical students than experienced physician mentors. Especially in remote or underserved regions, physicians may not be available for students because they are overburdened with patient care. Using computer-based simulators and trainers, students can practice procedures until they meet expected benchmarks. Computerized skill assessment can inform them continuously by providing feedback on their progress towards these benchmarks.

Computer-assisted training has yet another potential in medical education besides objective skill assessment and accessibility. Feedback is the most important element of training. Any new technology for training should reinforce good practices and point out mistakes to avoid. Without feedback, progress along the learning curve is not guaranteed. Besides skill assessment and accessibility, algorithm development also needs to focus on giving useful feedback for trainees. This is an especially exciting field of research as new visualization devices supporting augmented and virtual reality have recently become affordable for almost everyone. The learning environment of surgical and other procedural skills can be improved today with virtual reality technology in any medical school with technology that was only available in a few research laboratories just a decade ago.

In addition to improving learning experience for existing procedures, computerized training has another important aspect for researchers of new intervention guidance technologies. Training can be the key to acceptance and success of new technologies. Therefore, development of training methods should be an integral part of all innovation. Computer-assisted intervention guidance procedures are rarely intuitive enough to be performed without specific training. Every new surgical navigation and guidance method needs to eventually be evaluated by clinical practitioners. They will only find them helpful if they can learn to use the new techniques quickly and effortlessly. Researchers of new assisted interventions should keep training in mind from the onset of development of new assistive technologies. Training materials can be updated as the procedure evolves through cycles of testing by clinical users. Medical technology is often criticized to lag behind other technology-intensive application areas like military or aviation. The entertainment industry seems to lead by decades of evolution ahead of medicine when we compare their virtual and augmented reality visualization to radiological and surgical navigation displays. The technology seems to be available for medical applications as well. It is enough to visit a major conference for anyone to see that cutting-edge technology is just waiting for clinical translation. A few clinicians involved in the development process typically have no issues during the first evaluation in patients, but evidence-based clinical research requires multicenter trials for the adoption of new methods. Any new technology will only have a chance to be used at other places, outside where it was invented, if it comes with an excellent training support for effortless reproduction of results.

In this chapter we review four aspects of computer-assisted training technology for medical interventions. The first section discusses various ways to obtain data while trainees practice different procedures, and how this data can be used to assess the skills of trainees. The second section reviews available technology for generating feedback for trainees on their performance and ways to improve their procedures. The third section discusses simulation environments for deployment of training systems. Finally, shared software and data resources are discussed that enable quick entry for new researchers to this field and facilitate collaboration between existing research groups. We end this chapter with a short summary.

37.2. Assessment

Performance assessment is the first task any surgical or interventional training software is required to perform, after simulating the medical procedure. There is a wide variety of sensors available to collect data during practice procedures. Every training system uses one or a combination of these sensors. Some sensors like pupillometry or sweat sensors provide general information on the stress levels of trainees, but in this chapter we focus on devices more specific to the medical procedures. There is no commonly accepted system for data collection. Instrument-heavy procedures like laparoscopic and robotic surgery are often best analyzed by accurate spatial tracking. Freehand and open procedures may require different sensing modalities.

It is beyond the scope of this chapter to generally define what makes physicians good at their profession. We only discuss expertise of procedural skills, so we can refer to features that are easier to define and quantify, like positional accuracy, appropriate force, or timeliness. But often we see the same procedure assessed by different metrics in different published research. A common taxonomy of metrics was proposed by Schmitz et al. [46], as a resource for designing new training systems and methods. It is important to refer to these common definitions to make systems and research results comparable with each other. Without fair comparison between different research prototypes, there is little hope for this area to make significant progress towards translation to users. The next subsections discuss the most commonly used assessment methods such as expert observers, spatial tracking, automatic video analysis, and crowdsourcing.

37.2.1 Rating by expert reviewers

Assessment of surgical or interventional skills by experienced clinicians has been utilized since the introduction of the apprenticeship model in medical education. Historically, assessments of learners in surgery and interventional procedures were primarily subjective in their nature (i.e., did the trainee do a "good job" at a particular task); however, subjective assessments are prone to assessment bias, where trainees can be unfairly penalized on the basis of gender, race, religion, or socioeconomic status. Objective assessment scales for surgical and interventional skills were developed to overcome the limitation of subjective assessment. Objective assessment can (1) aid learning by provision of constructive feedback, (2) determine the level that a trainee has achieved, (3) check whether a trainee has made progress, (4) ensure patient's safety before a trainee performs an unsupervised procedure, and (5) certify completion of training [4]. As these assessment scales are the currently accepted standard of practice, they are important resources and reference points for anyone who is developing computerized training technology.

Currently available objective assessment scales can be grouped into the categories of checklists, global rating scales, procedure-specific assessment scales, and rubrics. Checklists are now available for common surgical procedures such as appendectomy, cholecystectomy, Nissen fundoplication, ventral hernia repair, and others [3]. The main advantages of checklists include objectivity, unambiguous expectations and the opportunity to provide immediate and relevant feedback [42]. The main disadvantage is that a checklist for one procedure cannot be used for assessment of another procedure. A checklist is completed by observing a surgical or interventional procedure and checking off the items on the list that were "completed" and "not-completed". Checklists turn examiners into observers of behavior rather than interpreters of behavior, thereby making the assessment more objective and less subjective.

Global rating scales (GRS) offer another method for objective assessment of surgical and interventional procedural skills. Global rating scales are not procedure-specific, which makes them a convenient tool for educators with results that are comparable to each other. Examples of GRS for assessment of technical skills include Objective Structured Assessment of Technical Skill Global Rating Scale (OSATS GRS) [37], and the Global Operative Assessment of Laparoscopic Skills (GOALS) [54]. The main advantage of global rating scales is their generalizability across different procedures. Global rating scales are designed to assess generic surgical and interventional skills such as tissue handling, knowledge of instruments, use of assistants, etc. These generic skills are transferable from one procedure to the next. Checklists, on the other hand, evaluate whether specific operative steps were completed correctly, making them not transferable from one procedure to the next [18]. The three main disadvantages of global rating scales are (1) the requirement to train the raters in the use of the scale [15], (2) the challenge of using the scores on global rating scales for formative feedback, and (3) the subjectivity introduced during judgment of how a trainee performs on a particular component of the global rating scale.

Procedure-specific checklists form the middle ground between checklists and global rating scales [41]. They are specific enough to provide useful formative feedback to the individual that is being assessed; however, they are not as prescriptive as checklists. They provide formative feedback via identification of specific areas of weakness, while offering some flexibility in regards to the completion of specific operative steps. An example of a procedure specific rating scale is the BOSATS scale [57].

Rubrics are similar to rating scales, but instead of characterizing skill levels with numerical values they provide explicit definitions and criteria for skill levels. In contrast to global rating scales, rubrics with descriptions of skill levels make standards of performance explicit [48]. Advantages of rubrics for surgical and interventional skills include (1) shared frames of reference for raters through the use of a clear assessment framework and scoring guide; (2) improvement in the consistency, reliability, and efficiency of scoring for both single and multiple assessors; (3) providing trainees with immediate feedback on performance; and (4) improvement in trainees' ability to self-assess performance [24]. Example of a rubric for objective assessment of surgical skill is the Surgical Procedure Feedback Rubric developed by Toprak et al. [48].

Rating scales have been validated and used consistently in medical education [37]. These rating scales are trusted tools, therefore computerized assessment methods should be validated against them.

37.2.2 Real-time spatial tracking

Motion analysis by real-time tracking devices have been used to supplement human observer analysis of surgical motions. The first application of tool tracking was in laparoscopic surgery, because laparoscopic instruments are easy to equip with additional motion sensors and they restrict the freedom of motion to make motion analysis simpler. The Imperial College Surgical Assessment Device (ICSAD) has been one of the first systems ever used for motion analysis during surgical training. It was first used in laparoscopic procedures [55], then in open surgical tasks [8,39]. It is still used as an objective and quantitative assessment tool in interventional procedure training [6]. Since the invention of ICSAD, similar systems have been developed to measure procedural skills based on motion analysis.

Hand and instrument motion data can be used in various ways to estimate skill levels of trainees. ICSAD offers motion quantification by total path length and motion count. But other metrics such as idle time (hand velocity under 20 mm/s for over 0.5 s) were also found to correlate with experience level. Novices were found to pause their motions more often than others [7]. Motion metrics are usually computed from the raw motion data directly, and threshold values are applied to either the metrics themselves or a mathematical combination of the metrics. Decisions based on metrics values lead to the classification of expertise levels. A recently developed artificial neural network-based algorithm seem to be a better choice for determining the skill levels compared to simpler machine learning methods [45]. Convolutional neural networks are effective in processing laparoscopic video data, and even classify the operator's skill level at a high accuracy [13]. However, this area needs further research to collect sufficient evidence for acceptance by medical schools.

Hand motion is most commonly tracked by electromagnetic sensors, because their small size enables seamless integration to existing scenarios. Wires to sensors can usually be managed, and they avoid line of sight issues of optical trackers. But a wide variety of devices can also be used to track instrument or hand motions. Active optical markers require line of sight between tracked markers and camera, but they provide very high accuracy and precision [7]. Optical markers can be active LED lights, passive light reflective objects, or even simple printed optical patterns (Fig. 37.1). Accelerometers and gyroscopes are affordable, small, and wireless sensors that provide rotational data, but absolute pose (position and orientation) cannot be measured with such devices. Rotational data may still be enough to recognize and classify surgical skills [32]. Most hand motion tracking systems sense only one or a few points on each hand, but gloves can be equipped with flex sensors to track each joint on the hand [45]. A common issue with all of these tracking devices is that they require an extra device, a sensor or a marker, be added to the existing surgical instruments or the hands of the operator. While this is usually feasible without much interference with the normal procedures, especially in simulated environments, there is a need for automatically tracking and recognizing operator actions without altering the operative field. This is especially important for the study of translation of procedural skills from simulators to clinical environments. The rapid evolution of automatic video processing may take some territory over from optical and electromagnetic tracking devices.

Figure 37.1 Surgical instruments equipped with optical markers for spatial tracking. 3D-printed attachments are designed for minimal interference with normal handling of the instruments.

37.2.3 Automatic video analysis

Video camera technology underwent a staggering innovative improvement in the past decade. Cameras of the smallest size and under-$100 price provide 1080p resolution at 30 fps and beyond. The accessibility of cameras contributed to the renewed attention to computer vision and video processing algorithms. An impressive body of research has been published recently on video-based assessment of medical interventions training. And this may just be the beginning of transformative changes, because automatic video processing is already in a more advanced stage in other industries such as surveillance or autonomous driving. When that level of video-based decision making is adapted to medical training, it may not only enable new procedures to be taught by computers, but also many tracker-based training systems may become obsolete.

Video recordings of learners can also be reviewed by expert practitioners. In fact, this is often used in medical schools today. Trainees and teachers often review video recordings of these procedures to discuss, give feedback, or grade the skills of trainees. The main limitations of this learning method are the cost, availability, and potential subjectivity of expert physicians. To address the problem of limited resources, researchers experimented with rating recorded procedures based on only parts of the full procedures, but they found that the reliability of ratings dropped with shorter video segments [44]. Automatic video processing seems to be the only way to scale up video-based skill assessment to become a universal teaching tool in medical education. While video reviews and feedback by experts is only available a few times for each medical trainee, computerized assessment is virtually unlimited. It could guide the trainee all the way through the learning process, regardless how long it takes to master the necessary skills for each individual.

Standard tools in well-defined environments make video processing easier for algorithms. Therefore, the most popular application of this technology is laparoscopic surgery. It has been shown that motion economy and smoothness is characteristic of skill [17]. While most methods require some user interactions or special markers to identify surgical tools, modern machine learning algorithms are capable of reliably identifying surgical instruments in a fully automated way in real-time video sequences [25].

Automatic video review for rating surgical skills has not only been applied in laparoscopic procedures. It has also been shown that videos from overhead mounted cameras are helpful in rating suturing skills [38]. When practicing periodic motions like running sutures or repeated knot tying, entropy-based webcam video analysis methods seem to perform extremely well in classifying skill level. Organized motions in videos are associated with less entropy of the video image content over time [58]. Videos of eye surgery were classified for skill level using convolutional neural networks on features extracted from the videos [31].

It seems to be clear after about a decade of research in automatic analysis of trainee videos that it is a very promising avenue of research, but it can only be made robust for widespread use if the research community works together on collecting training data for machine learning methods. State-of-the-art machine learning is extremely dependent on the amount of training data. Current efforts are already targeting these wide collaborations. Public databases are created for challenge events at research conferences to productively compete in the analysis of these public datasets. These efforts will hopefully be nurtured and grown into global initiatives, engaging even more researchers and creating large public datasets.

37.2.4 Crowdsourcing

In the past decades a new concept also emerged for accomplishing large tasks that require human observer input. The concept, called *crowdsourcing*, is based on the idea of distributing work in an open community through the Internet. The lack of quality control of individuals in the *crowd* is compensated by aggregating the results from parallel processing by multiple people. Crowd work is managed online through websites designed specifically for these tasks. General sites like Amazon Mechanical Turk can be used to hire volunteers to watch and label video segments, usually for a small financial compensation. It has been shown that a group of 32 random crowd workers provide a more reliable assessment of surgical skills from urethrovesical anastomosis videos than faculty experts [36], and online workers to perform this task were available at any time during the day, unlike most experts. To make the classification of video segments easier, it is recommended to offer a few keywords for reviewers and ask them to pick the ones more characteristic of the video that they are watching [12]. These labels can later be used to classify the video into skill levels.

Crowdsourcing may solve assessment tasks in medical training in the future, but controversies still exist on the feasibility of this method for some procedures. It was found that complications after intracorporeal urinary diversion during robotic radical cystectomy were not predicted by crowd workers after reviewing video recordings [19].

However, experienced surgeons were also unable to predict complications from the same videos. Algorithms and computers can clearly outperform human observers in some video processing tasks already, and the use of machine learning technology in nonmedical applications have also been proven extremely useful. Crowdsourcing may be affordable, but a minimal cost will always remain proportional to the amount of work. Trainees may also be concerned about data protection and privacy issues, when video recordings of their performances are shared with a global network of raters. Therefore, there are plenty of reasons to believe that video processing will play a much more significant role in interventional procedures training in the future.

37.3. Feedback

Feedback is the key element of learning. It gives the trainee hints on how to modify their actions to achieve a better performance, but feedback of training systems can be implemented in many ways. Often, providing a trainee a score as an objective measurement of skill level is insufficient feedback in training [51]. This may be the reason why the apprenticeship model has survived so long even with its known limitations. The verbal feedback from an experienced observer is extremely hard to substitute.

Interventional procedures are often best described with graphical representation, rather than text. Pictures, videos, or real-life demonstrations better illustrate the spatial relationship between anatomy and instruments or the pace of a procedure. One way to provide trainees with graphical feedback on their performance is through augmented reality display. This shows trainees perspectives of the surgical scene that cannot be seen by the naked eye or through traditional medical imaging modalities. While this feedback is not quantitative, it facilitates trainees' understanding of their movements in space relative to the anatomy. Augmented reality graphical feedback has been shown to improve trainee performance when provided in real time, especially for percutaneous interventions [28,30]. With augmented reality technologies becoming increasingly available to consumers, this will make such graphical feedback even more effective and accessible. The next two sections discuss two aspects of performance feedback: first, how to define simple metrics for complex medical procedures, and second, how to establish benchmarks and analyze learning curves.

37.3.1 Feedback in complex procedures

Most surgical and procedural skill assessment systems focus on a single task like suturing or needle placement. But real-life procedures often involve a series of tasks to be performed before and after the actual intervention. These additional tasks include disinfecting the skin, applying anesthesia, or delivering an injection. Failure to perform any procedural step appropriately defeats the purpose of accurate needle placement. Therefore, training systems need to be prepared to handle multistep processes, detect whether they are performed in the correct order, and give feedback to the trainee on procedural mistakes.

Teaching is most effective when learners realize what specific mistakes they have made and how to correct them. Systems that analyze trainee inputs to assess skill levels without domain specific knowledge are helpful in assessing trainee performance, but they are not accelerating the learning process and cannot substitute an experienced trainer person [29]. Domain specific knowledge about each aspect of the intervention may be incorporated into computerized assessment through expert-defined performance metrics. Domain specific knowledge about the workflow of an intervention may be modeled based on expert consultation using Surgical Process Models (SPM) [34].

When expert-defined performance metrics are used for assessment, each metric acts as quality indicator for some aspect of the intervention. As a result, these metrics can be translated into feedback using expert domain knowledge [22]. Of course, these metrics must be interpreted in the context of the expert population. In addition, machine learning methods can be applied to provide specific feedback to trainees via OSATS-like ratings [52].

Given a model of the surgical process, motion analysis or video analysis can be used to recognize individual activities during interventions training in real time. This has been commonly achieved using Hidden Markov Models [11,23] to represent the transitions between activities, but methods using Dynamic Time Warping [1] have also been implemented. In recent years, deep learning-based video assessment has been the most popular method [53,26]. By recognizing the ongoing activity, information on how to best complete the activity can be provided in real time to the trainee. Furthermore, the subsequent activity can be automatically predicted [27,16] to provide information on which activity to perform next. In the case where the sequence of activities is linear, like central line catheterization, information about the ongoing activity can be used in real time to remind the trainee of specific workflow mistakes and how to correct them [21] (Fig. 37.2). Finally, at the end of the intervention, this activity recognition may be combined with expert-defined performance metrics to provide specific feedback on how to improve in each phase of the intervention.

37.3.2 Learning curves and performance benchmarks

It is also important to provide trainees with feedback on their progression towards proficiency. This can be done through monitoring trainees' learning curves over time. This may include both their overall performance learning curves and their learning curves with respect to each aspect of the intervention. This can be done by visual inspection of learning curve plots or quantitatively through cumulative sum analysis [10].

To interpret one's own learning curves, they must be put into perspective of expectations. Proficiency benchmarks must be established so trainees can see how much

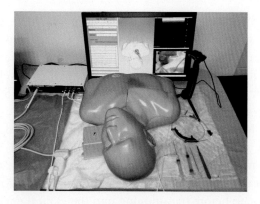

Figure 37.2 Training system for central line catheterization. Electromagnetic tracking sensors are complemented by webcam-based object recognition. Procedure steps are automatically recognized and displayed for trainees to guide through the early stages of learning.

they need to learn before achieving the expected level of skills in a given training environment. It is often a challenging process to establish benchmarks, because the skill levels of novices and experts are usually too diverse and too far from each other. The benchmark may also be dependent on the stage of training and the training environment. While there exist both participant-centered approaches (e.g., contrasting groups method) and item-centered approaches (e.g., Angoff method with domain experts), no standard method for setting performance benchmarks has been established by the community [20]. Regardless of the method for establishing the performance benchmark, it must be justified empirically, and every trainee must meet the benchmark prior to patient encounters. It is a good practice to validate the benchmarks by parallel measurement of trainee performances by an automatic method and an already accepted expert review. Benchmark performance metrics can be adjusted based on what procedures were labeled as proficient by the expert reviewers.

37.4. Simulated environments

When implementing training environments for medical procedures, the first difficult choice for the teachers to make is often how to simulate the patient and the interventional tools. The most realistic environments may be the most expensive, but may not be most effective in training. Animal models are often the first choice when practice on human subjects is not safe or feasible. Synthetic models of various fidelity are also commonly used. Recent developments in virtual and augmented reality provide a new emerging technology that may replace many more animal and synthetic models in the future. In the next sections, we discuss these options for simulation.

37.4.1 Animal models

Just a few decades ago it was considered standard practice that medical students learned their practical skills on patients. Currently that is not an accepted learning method, because it conflicts with patient rights and safety. Animals were chosen as alternative learning models. Most medical schools are currently equipped with animal operating rooms and facilities to conduct research on animals. However, the cost of care, animal rights awareness, and long-term planning requirements impose significant limitations on how much of the procedural training can be performed on animals. It was also shown that synthetic models offer similar value in training [37], therefore today the vast majority of medical interventions training and testing of new methods is done on synthetic phantom models before transitioning into the clinical environment.

37.4.2 Synthetic models

Different kinds of plastic materials are suitable for manufacturing anatomical models for practicing procedures. The most common material in research setting is silicone, because it is simple to handle and does not require special laboratory equipment. Making an entire anatomical region from silicone with realistic visual and tactile properties of different tissues is possible, e.g., for practicing oncoplastic surgery [35].

There are a few cases when silicone cannot be used. These include ultrasound-guided procedures. Ultrasound image is generated with the assumption that echo time is proportional to the depth of tissue boundaries in the body. But the speed of sound in silicone is only around 900 m/s, while it is typically 1540 m/s in human soft tissue. The slow speed of sound delays echoes, causing objects to appear in ultrasound much deeper than they really are. Although some ultrasound machines allow the user to set the speed of sound, but silicone also attenuates ultrasound signal much more than human tissue. Therefore, silicone is only suitable for very superficial ultrasound-guided procedures. Alternatives to silicone for ultrasound-guided procedures include organic materials like gelatine and agar gel, and synthetic materials like polyvinyl chloride and polyvinyl alcohol. Phantom models from organic materials can be made at a lower cost, but they dry out and decay over time. Synthetic plastics typically require more time and special equipment when being prepared, but they last longer, and they are reusable for minimally invasive procedures like needle insertions. Recent improvement in rapid prototyping technology and availability of low-cost 3D printers allow researchers to efficiently design and print mold shapes for soft tissue models. 3D printed bone models are also commonly used, and they can be combined with soft tissue models (Fig. 37.3). The best synthetic models work with multiple modalities like ultrasound and multispectral imaging, while providing realistic tactile feedback.

Creating anatomical models often requires the combination of various software and hardware tools. The rapidly developing field of 3-dimensional design requires contin-

Figure 37.3 3D-printed lumbar spine model that can be filled with soft gel for simulated lumbar puncture procedures. Plastic tube can be filled with water to simulate cerebrospinal fluid.

uous self-teaching from researchers to be able to effectively exploit these new technologies. Fortunately, there is a selection of resources available for design procedures, and often an abundance of community-created training materials on video sharing sites and other websites. Many design software is free, or free for academic use. The design process typically starts with a conventional volumetric medical imaging modality, like a computed tomography (CT) or magnetic resonance imaging (MRI) scan of the region. Volumetric images of anatomical regions are first segmented to create organ shapes. Although automatic segmentation methods are available both in research literature and in open-source and commercial software products, it is best to use manual segmentation methods for creating training models. These models require high accuracy and anatomical correctness. After segmentation the anatomical surface models may be combined with parts designed in mechanical engineering applications, and finally translated to an instruction sets for 3D printers (Fig. 37.4). Manufacturing should be considered from the first step of the design process. Anatomical images are best rotated before segmentation so their main axes align with the directions of the 3D printer axes at the end of the design process. Complex shapes are best prepared in parts that can be printed without much support material. Good models often require many iterations of testing on prototypes, which requires considerable time.

37.4.3 Box trainers

Simplified environments can be built for practicing specific procedures or skills. A popular training environment is the laparoscopic box trainer, a simple design with holes to hold trocars for practicing tasks and skills on various synthetic models (Fig. 37.5).

Similar trainers exist for other specialties, like colonoscopy or ureteroscopy. These trainers typically have low fidelity, and the procedures performed with them have little in common with clinical procedures. But they teach just those skills, like hand–eye coordination, which can be easily complemented by anatomy and pathology knowledge

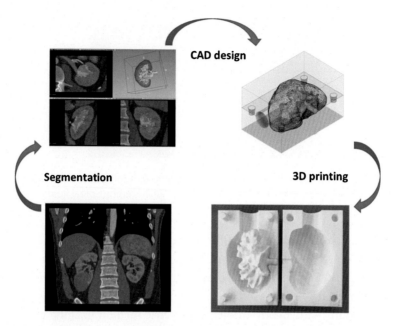

Figure 37.4 Typical design process of anatomical phantom models. Anatomical shapes are segmented, and imported into professional computer-assisted design (CAD) software. Final models are translated to 3D printer instruction sets.

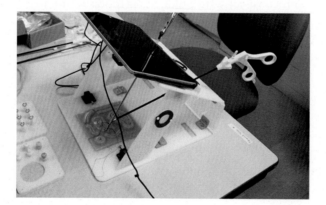

Figure 37.5 Box trainer for laparoscopic surgery skills.

to effectively apply them in clinical procedures later. The popularity of box trainers proves that fidelity is not the most important aspect of medical procedures simulators. It is more important to find critical tasks and challenging features that need the most practice in a procedure. If a simple simulated environment can capture those features, then adding more realism may not improve the effectiveness of the training system.

Figure 37.6 Medical student reviews his procedure using a virtual reality display after practicing ultrasound-guided needle targeting. For the student, only the virtual reality display is visible, while this picture combines virtual reality and a photograph for illustration.

37.4.4 Virtual reality

When the environment is hard to simulate by either biological or synthetic materials, virtual reality environments may help. Virtual reality head-mounted displays have become affordable and feasible for personal computers. Even high-end cell phones come with the capability to render virtual reality scenes. Consumer virtual reality will probably always have its technical limitations. Tactile feedback is often not part of these systems. But head-mounted displays are a great adjunct or alternative to simulated environments in some procedures. Entire operating rooms or emergency scenarios could be shown in virtual reality to improve the realism and simulate the stress factors when practicing on simulated models. Haptic interfaces are also added to high-end simulators, but current haptics technology can only simulate rigid tools like laparoscopic tools and needles. Simulating tactile sensation of the hands would be important for surgical training, and hopefully future technology will make it available.

Virtual reality also offers visualization overlaid with physical models that help understand anatomical relations and hand–eye coordination for trainees. Current consumer augmented reality displays lack the spatial registration accuracy required for guidance of precise surgical tools, but they are already useful for creating a more understandable picture of spatial relationships for trainees than they could ever experience without virtual reality (Fig. 37.6). The rapid development of virtual and augmented reality technologies will inevitably result in a wider use in medical training. Creating virtual reality educational content requires special skills, including artistic components. Hiring professional modelers is often beyond the budget of research projects, but lots of models are already available freely online for fantasy and hobby projects, and hopefully models for medical education will also be shared in larger numbers in the future.

37.5. Shared resources

Shared software is a key to productive collaboration between researchers in computer-assisted intervention training. Training systems typically include components for sensing trainee actions, data processing for performance evaluation, computer graphics for feedback visualization, and other smaller components. Development of such a system takes excessive resources away from research. In addition, independent software tools make the results of different research teams harder to compare. Shared software enables effortless data sharing and reuse of earlier results by other teams.

Open-source initiatives have been the most successful models in creating research software platforms. Visualization of 3-dimensional graphics is almost exclusively performed with the open-source Visualization Toolkit (VTK, www.vtk.org) in both research and commercial projects. It would be inconceivable today that a researcher would have the time to get familiar with computer graphics at the level that is provided by VTK for free. Other components of intervention training systems are also provided by open-source software. Communication with hardware devices such as tracking sensors or imaging systems is another major task that requires significant technical background. The PLUS toolkit (www.PlusToolkit.org) implements communication interfaces with a wide range of devices, even complete surgical navigation systems. Data acquired from devices is stored in a standardized format and provided in real time for user interface applications. Typically, PLUS server is run in the background and applications get real-time data through the OpenIGTLink (www.OpenIgtLink.org) network protocol [47]. Applications implementing graphical user interfaces only need to integrate OpenIGTLink to be able to communicate with hundreds of devices and benefit from the data filtering, synchronization, and calibration features of PLUS. User interface applications are also typically started from an application platform. The most popular open-source application platforms implementing OpenIGTLink are 3D Slicer (www.slicer.org) [14] and (www.mitk.org) MITK [33].

3D Slicer provides an example for incremental development towards specific applications. 3D Slicer was originally developed as an advanced viewer for medical images. Adding OpenIGTLink to 3D Slicer allowed the development of the SlicerIGT extension (www.SlicerIGT.org) for using real-time tracking and imaging data [49]. Algorithms specifically implemented for training medical interventions were added as the Perk Tutor extension (www.PerkTutor.org) [50]. When a new training application is developed for a specific medical intervention, e.g., for central line catheterization, only minimal coding is required due to the multitude of software features already implemented in the underlying software toolkits [21,56]. The proportion of software code amounts in different software architectural layers show that with the proper use of open-source platforms, researchers can focus their time only on the critical part of their applications (Fig. 37.7).

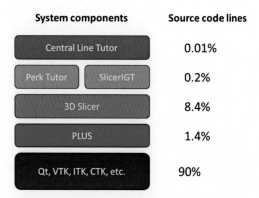

System components   **Source code lines**

Central Line Tutor		0.01%
Perk Tutor	SlicerIGT	0.2%
3D Slicer		8.4%
PLUS		1.4%
Qt, VTK, ITK, CTK, etc.		90%

Figure 37.7 Proportions in lines of software code in a typical training simulator for central line insertion.

Shared software tools are a great step towards productive collaboration between research groups. But data is becoming increasingly important too, especially with the data–demanding machine learning algorithms gaining popularity. Shared data can be used to fairly compare different algorithms with each other, and to create benchmark levels in training [2].

37.6. Summary

There is a high demand for better education in surgical and interventional skills in medicine. Computerized training methods have been developed, but they are often not the standard method of education worldwide, yet. Future research needs more focus on objective measurement of competency, creating and analyzing shared databases, and building shared platforms to facilitate wider dissemination of research outcomes. Only synchronized efforts and multicenter research studies can provide enough evidence to convince medical educators on a global level on the benefit of computer-assisted training methods. These studies require large international trainee cohorts and many years of follow-up. Primary outcomes need to directly focus on the reduction of clinical complications and improvement in patient outcomes. If researchers take advantage of new technologies and collaborate on shared platforms, their work will achieve these ambitious goals. Good research practices and timely dissemination of knowledge will change the daily practice of medical education to the benefit of healthcare on a global scale.

References

[1] S.A. Ahmadi, T. Sielhorst, R. Stauder, M. Horn, H. Feussner, N. Navab, Recovery of surgical workflow without explicit models, in: International Conference on Medical Image Computing and Computer-Assisted Intervention, Springer, Berlin, Heidelberg, Oct. 2006, pp. 420–428.

[2] N. Ahmidi, L. Tao, S. Sefati, Y. Gao, C. Lea, B.B. Haro, L. Zappella, S. Khudanpur, R. Vidal, G.D. Hager, A dataset and benchmarks for segmentation and recognition of gestures in robotic surgery, IEEE Transactions on Biomedical Engineering 64 (9) (Sept. 2017) 2025–2041.

[3] American College of Surgeons, ACS/APDS Surgery Resident Skills Curriculum, retrieved from http://www.facs.org/education/surgicalskills.html, July 2018.

[4] J.D. Beard, Assessment of surgical competence, British Journal of Surgery 94 (11) (Nov. 2007) 1315–1316.

[5] C.H. Bisgaard, S.L.M. Rubak, S.A. Rodt, J.A.K. Petersen, P. Musaeus, The effects of graduate competency-based education and mastery learning on patient care and return on investment: a narrative review of basic anesthetic procedures, BMC Medical Education 18 (1) (June 2018) 154.

[6] M.A. Corvetto, J.C. Pedemonte, D. Varas, C. Fuentes, F.R. Altermatt, Simulation-based training program with deliberate practice for ultrasound-guided jugular central venous catheter placement, Acta Anaesthesiologica Scandinavica 61 (9) (Oct. 2017) 1184–1191.

[7] A.L. D'Angelo, D.N. Rutherford, R.D. Ray, S. Laufer, C. Kwan, E.R. Cohen, A. Mason, C.M. Pugh, Idle time: an underdeveloped performance metric for assessing surgical skill, The American Journal of Surgery 209 (4) (Apr. 2015) 645–651.

[8] V. Datta, S. Mackay, M. Mandalia, A. Darzi, The use of electromagnetic motion tracking analysis to objectively measure open surgical skill in the laboratory-based model, Journal of the American College of Surgeons 193 (5) (Nov. 2001) 479–485.

[9] C.R. Davis, E.C. Toll, A.S. Bates, M.D. Cole, F.C. Smith, Surgical and procedural skills training at medical school–a national review, International Journal of Surgery 12 (8) (Aug. 2014) 877–882.

[10] G.R. de Oliveira Filho, P.E. Helayel, D.B. da Conceição, I.S. Garzel, P. Pavei, M.S. Ceccon, Learning curves and mathematical models for interventional ultrasound basic skills, Anesthesia and Analgesia 106 (2) (Feb. 2008) 568–573.

[11] A. Dosis, F. Bello, D. Gillies, S. Undre, R. Aggarwal, A. Darzi, Laparoscopic task recognition using hidden Markov models, Studies in Health Technology and Informatics 111 (2005) 115–122.

[12] M. Ershad, R. Rege, A.M. Fey, Meaningful assessment of robotic surgical style using the wisdom of crowds, International Journal of Computer Assisted Radiology and Surgery 24 (Mar. 2018) 1–2.

[13] H.I. Fawaz, G. Forestier, J. Weber, L. Idoumghar, P.A. Muller, Evaluating surgical skills from kinematic data using convolutional neural networks, in: A. Frangi, J. Schnabel, C. Davatzikos, C. Alberola-López, G. Fichtinger (Eds.), Medical Image Computing and Computer Assisted Intervention – MICCAI 2018, MICCAI 2018, in: Lecture Notes in Computer Science, vol. 11073, Springer, Cham, 2018, pp. 214–221.

[14] A. Fedorov, R. Beichel, J. Kalpathy-Cramer, J. Finet, J.C. Fillion-Robin, S. Pujol, C. Bauer, D. Jennings, F. Fennessy, M. Sonka, J. Buatti, S. Aylward, J.V. Miller, S. Pieper, R. Kikinis, 3D Slicer as an image computing platform for the Quantitative Imaging Network, Magnetic Resonance Imaging 30 (9) (Nov. 2012) 1323–1341.

[15] M. Feldman, Rater training to support high-stakes simulation-based assessments, Journal of Continuing Education in the Health Professions 32 (4) (2012) 279–286.

[16] G. Forestier, F. Petitjean, L. Riffaud, P. Jannin, Automatic matching of surgeries to predict surgeons' next actions, Artificial Intelligence in Medicine 81 (Sept. 2017) 3–11.

[17] S. Ganni, S.M. Botden, M. Chmarra, R.H. Goossens, J.J. Jakimowicz, A software-based tool for video motion tracking in the surgical skills assessment landscape, Surgical Endoscopy 32 (6) (June 2018) 2994–2999.

[18] I. Ghaderi, F. Manji, Y.S. Park, D. Juul, M. Ott, I. Harris, T.M. Farrell, Technical skills assessment toolbox: a review using the unitary framework of validity, Annals of Surgery 261 (2) (Feb. 2015) 251–262.

[19] M.G. Goldenberg, A. Garbens, P. Szasz, T. Hauer, T.P. Grantcharov, Systematic review to establish absolute standards for technical performance in surgery, British Journal of Surgery 104 (1) (Jan. 2017) 13–21.

[20] M.G. Goldenberg, J. Nabhani, C.J. Wallis, S. Chopra, A.J. Hung, A. Schuckman, H. Djaladat, S. Daneshmand, M.M. Desai, M. Aron, I.S. Gill, Feasibility of expert and crowd-sourced review of intraoperative video for quality improvement of intracorporeal urinary diversion during robotic radical cystectomy, Canadian Urological Association Journal 11 (10) (Oct. 2017) 331.

[21] R. Hisey, T. Ungi, M. Holden, Z. Baum, Z. Keri, C. McCallum, D.W. Howes, G. Fichtinger, Real-time workflow detection using webcam video for providing real-time feedback in central venous catheterization training, in: Medical Imaging 2018: Image-Guided Procedures, Robotic Interventions, and Modeling, vol. 10576, International Society for Optics and Photonics, Mar. 2018, 1057620.

[22] M.S. Holden, Z. Keri, T. Ungi, G. Fichtinger, Overall proficiency assessment in point-of-care ultrasound interventions: the stopwatch is not enough, in: Imaging for Patient-Customized Simulations and Systems for Point-of-Care Ultrasound, vol. 14, Springer, Cham, Sept. 2017, pp. 146–153.

[23] M.S. Holden, T. Ungi, D. Sargent, R.C. McGraw, E.C. Chen, S. Ganapathy, T.M. Peters, G. Fichtinger, Feasibility of real-time workflow segmentation for tracked needle interventions, IEEE Transactions on Biomedical Engineering 61 (6) (June 2014) 1720–1728.

[24] J.J. Isaacson, A.S. Stacy, Rubrics for clinical evaluation: objectifying the subjective experience, Nurse Education in Practice 9 (2) (Mar. 2009) 134–140.

[25] A. Jin, S. Yeung, J. Jopling, J. Krause, D. Azagury, A. Milstein, L. Fei-Fei, Tool detection and operative skill assessment in surgical videos using region-based convolutional neural networks, in: 2018 IEEE Winter Conference on Applications of Computer Vision (WACV), IEEE, Mar. 2018, pp. 691–699.

[26] Y. Jin, Q. Dou, H. Chen, L. Yu, J. Qin, C.W. Fu, P.A. Heng, SV-RCNet: workflow recognition from surgical videos using recurrent convolutional network, IEEE Transactions on Medical Imaging 37 (5) (May 2018) 1114–1126.

[27] D. Katić, A.L. Wekerle, F. Gärtner, H. Kenngott, B.P. Müller-Stich, R. Dillmann, S. Speidel, Ontology-based prediction of surgical events in laparoscopic surgery, in: Medical Imaging 2013: Image-Guided Procedures, Robotic Interventions, and Modeling, vol. 8671, International Society for Optics and Photonics, Mar. 2013, 86711A.

[28] Z. Keri, D. Sydor, T. Ungi, M.S. Holden, R. McGraw, P. Mousavi, D.P. Borschneck, G. Fichtinger, M. Jaeger, Computerized training system for ultrasound-guided lumbar puncture on abnormal spine models: a randomized controlled trial, Canadian Journal of Anesthesia (Journal canadien d'anesthésie) 62 (7) (July 2015) 777–784.

[29] A. Khan, S. Mellor, E. Berlin, R. Thompson, R. McNaney, P. Olivier, T. Plötz, Beyond activity recognition: skill assessment from accelerometer data, in: Proceedings of the 2015 ACM International Joint Conference on Pervasive and Ubiquitous Computing, ACM, Sept. 2015, pp. 1155–1166.

[30] E.J. Kim, J. Min, J. Song, K. Song, J.H. Song, H.J. Byon, The effect of electromagnetic guidance system on early learning curve of ultrasound for novices, Korean Journal of Anesthesiology 69 (1) (Feb. 2016) 15–20.

[31] T.S. Kim, M. O'Brien, S. Zafar, G.D. Hager, S. Sikder, S.S. Vedula, Objective assessment of intraoperative technical skill in capsulorhexis using videos of cataract surgery, International Journal of Computer Assisted Radiology and Surgery 14 (6) (June 2019) 1097–1105, https://doi.org/10.1007/s11548-019-01956-8.

[32] G.S. Kirby, P. Guyver, L. Strickland, A. Alvand, G.Z. Yang, C. Hargrove, B.P. Lo, J.L. Rees, Assessing arthroscopic skills using wireless elbow-worn motion sensors, The Journal of Bone and Joint Surgery 97 (13) (July 2015) 1119–1127.

[33] M. Klemm, T. Kirchner, J. Gröhl, D. Cheray, M. Nolden, A. Seitel, H. Hoppe, L. Maier-Hein, A.M. Franz, MITK-OpenIGTLink for combining open-source toolkits in real-time computer-assisted interventions, International Journal of Computer Assisted Radiology and Surgery 12 (3) (Mar. 2017) 351–361.

[34] F. Lalys, P. Jannin, Surgical process modelling: a review, International Journal of Computer Assisted Radiology and Surgery 9 (3) (May 2014) 495–511.

[35] D.R. Leff, G. Petrou, S. Mavroveli, M. Bersihand, D. Cocker, R. Al-Mufti, D.J. Hadjiminas, A. Darzi, G.B. Hanna, Validation of an oncoplastic breast simulator for assessment of technical skills in wide local excision, British Journal of Surgery 103 (3) (Feb. 2016) 207–217.

[36] T.S. Lendvay, K.R. Ghani, J.O. Peabody, S. Linsell, D.C. Miller, B. Comstock, Is crowdsourcing surgical skill assessment reliable? An analysis of robotic prostatectomies, Journal of Urology 197 (4) (Apr. 2017) E890–E891.

[37] J.A. Martin, G. Regehr, R. Reznick, H. Macrae, J. Murnaghan, C. Hutchison, M. Brown, Objective structured assessment of technical skill (OSATS) for surgical residents, British Journal of Surgery 84 (2) (Feb. 1997) 273–278.

[38] B. Miller, D. Azari, R. Radwin, B. Le, MP01-07 use of computer vision motion analysis to aid in surgical skill assessment of suturing tasks, The Journal of Urology 199 (4) (2018) e4.

[39] K. Moorthy, Y. Munz, S.K. Sarker, A. Darzi, Objective assessment of technical skills in surgery, BMJ 327 (7422) (Nov. 2003) 1032–1037.

[40] M. Morris, A. O'Neill, A. Gillis, S. Charania, J. Fitzpatrick, A. Redmond, S. Rosli, P.F. Ridgway, Prepared for practice? Interns' experiences of undergraduate clinical skills training in Ireland, Journal of Medical Education and Curricular Development 3 (2016), JMECD-S39381.

[41] V.N. Palter, T.P. Grantcharov, A prospective study demonstrating the reliability and validity of two procedure-specific evaluation tools to assess operative competence in laparoscopic colorectal surgery, Surgical Endoscopy 26 (9) (Sep. 2012) 2489–2503.

[42] G. Regehr, H. MacRae, R.K. Reznick, D. Szalay, Comparing the psychometric properties of check-lists and global rating scales for assessing performance on an OSCE-format examination, Academic Medicine 73 (9) (Sept. 1998) 993–997.

[43] R.K. Reznick, H. MacRae, Teaching surgical skills—changes in the wind, The New England Journal of Medicine 355 (25) (Dec. 2006) 2664–2669.

[44] J.M. Sawyer, N.E. Anton, J.R. Korndorffer Jr., C.G. DuCoin, D. Stefanidis, Time crunch: increasing the efficiency of assessment of technical surgical skill via brief video clips, Surgery 163 (4) (Apr. 2018) 933–937.

[45] L. Sbernini, L.R. Quitadamo, F. Riillo, N. Di Lorenzo, A.L. Gaspari, G. Saggio, Sensory-glove-based open surgery skill evaluation, IEEE Transactions on Human-Machine Systems 48 (2) (Apr. 2018) 213–218.

[46] C.C. Schmitz, D. DaRosa, M.E. Sullivan, S. Meyerson, K. Yoshida, J.R. Korndorffer Jr, Development and verification of a taxonomy of assessment metrics for surgical technical skills, Academic Medicine 89 (1) (Jan. 2014) 153–161.

[47] J. Tokuda, G.S. Fischer, X. Papademetris, Z. Yaniv, L. Ibanez, P. Cheng, H. Liu, J. Blevins, J. Arata, A.J. Golby, T. Kapur, OpenIGTLink: an open network protocol for image-guided therapy environment, The International Journal of Medical Robotics and Computer Assisted Surgery 5 (4) (Dec. 2009) 423–434.

[48] A. Toprak, U. Luhanga, S. Jones, A. Winthrop, L. McEwen, Validation of a novel intraoperative assessment tool: the surgical procedure feedback rubric, The American Journal of Surgery 211 (2) (Feb. 2016) 369–376.

[49] T. Ungi, A. Lasso, G. Fichtinger, Open-source platforms for navigated image-guided interventions, Medical Image Analysis 33 (Oct. 2016) 181–186.

[50] T. Ungi, D. Sargent, E. Moult, A. Lasso, C. Pinter, R.C. McGraw, G. Fichtinger, Perk Tutor: an open-source training platform for ultrasound-guided needle insertions, IEEE Transactions on Biomedical Engineering 59 (12) (Dec. 2012) 3475–3481.

[51] M.C. Porte, G. Xeroulis, R.K. Reznick, A. Dubrowski, Verbal feedback from an expert is more effective than self-accessed feedback about motion efficiency in learning new surgical skills, The American Journal of Surgery 193 (1) (Jan. 2007) 105–110.

[52] Y. Sharma, T. Plötz, N. Hammerld, S. Mellor, R. McNaney, P. Olivier, S. Deshmukh, A. McCaskie, I. Essa, Automated surgical OSATS prediction from videos, in: Biomedical Imaging (ISBI), 2014 IEEE 11th International Symposium on, IEEE, Apr. 2014, pp. 461–464.

[53] A.P. Twinanda, S. Shehata, D. Mutter, J. Marescaux, M. De Mathelin, N. Padoy, Endonet: a deep architecture for recognition tasks on laparoscopic videos, IEEE Transactions on Medical Imaging 36 (1) (Jan. 2017) 86–97.

[54] M.C. Vassiliou, L.S. Feldman, C.G. Andrew, S. Bergman, K. Leffondré, D. Stanbridge, G.M. Fried, A global assessment tool for evaluation of intraoperative laparoscopic skills, The American Journal of Surgery 190 (1) (July 2005) 107–113.

[55] J.D. Westwood, H.M. Hoffman, D. Stredney, S.J. Weghorst, Validation of virtual reality to teach and assess psychomotor skills in laparoscopic surgery: results from randomised controlled studies using the MIST VR laparoscopic simulator, in: Medicine Meets Virtual Reality: Art, Science, Technology: Healthcare and Evolution, 1998, p. 124.

[56] S. Xia, Z. Keri, M.S. Holden, R. Hisey, H. Lia, T. Ungi, C.H. Mitchell, G. Fichtinger, A learning curve analysis of ultrasound-guided in-plane and out-of-plane vascular access training with Perk Tutor, in: Medical Imaging 2018: Image-Guided Procedures, Robotic Interventions, and Modeling, vol. 10576, International Society for Optics and Photonics, Mar. 2018, 1057625.

[57] B. Zevin, E.M. Bonrath, R. Aggarwal, N.J. Dedy, N. Ahmed, T.P. Grantcharov, Development, feasibility, validity, and reliability of a scale for objective assessment of operative performance in laparoscopic gastric bypass surgery, Journal of the American College of Surgeons 216 (5) (May 2013) 955–965.

[58] A. Zia, Y. Sharma, V. Bettadapura, E.L. Sarin, I. Essa, Video and accelerometer-based motion analysis for automated surgical skills assessment, International Journal of Computer Assisted Radiology and Surgery 13 (3) (Mar. 2018) 443–455.

CHAPTER 38

Surgical data science

Gregory D. Hager[a]**, Lena Maier-Hein**[b]**, S. Swaroop Vedula**[a]

[a]Johns Hopkins University, Malone Center for Engineering in Healthcare, Baltimore, MD, United States
[b]German Cancer Research Center (DKFZ), Div. Computer Assisted Medical Interventions (CAMI), Heidelberg, Germany

Contents

38.1. Concept of surgical data science (SDS)	931
38.2. Clinical context for SDS and its applications	934
38.3. Technical approaches for SDS	938
38.4. Future challenges for SDS	942
38.5. Conclusion	945
Acknowledgments	945
References	945

38.1. Concept of surgical data science (SDS)

Data science is an interdisciplinary field that focuses on the extraction of knowledge from data. In surgery, it is fueled by advances in sensor technology and surgical techniques, which have led to availability of new types of data, such as instrument motion data, video images, intraoperative radiologic images, and data captured from wearable technologies. To improve patient care through surgical data science, it is necessary to overcome challenges in capturing, handling and analyzing the data, as well as in translating findings into applications for clinical use. These challenges span multiple disciplines and consequently, a multidisciplinary approach through SDS is necessary to solve them. In this context, an international initiative, comprising clinical, computing, and engineering experts, provided the following definition of the emerging field of SDS [1]:

> *Surgical data science aims to improve the quality of interventional healthcare and its value through the capture, organization, analysis, and modeling of data. It encompasses all clinical disciplines in which patient care requires intervention to manipulate anatomical structures with a diagnostic, prognostic or therapeutic goal, such as surgery, interventional radiology, radiotherapy and interventional gastroenterology. Data may pertain to any part of the patient-care process (from initial presentation to long-term outcomes), may concern the patient, caregivers, and/or technology used to deliver care, and is analyzed in the context of generic domain-specific knowledge derived from existing evidence, clinical guidelines, current practice patterns, caregiver experience, and patient preferences. Data may be obtained through medical records, imaging, medical devices, or sensors that may either be positioned on patients or caregivers, or integrated into the instruments and technology used*

Handbook of Medical Image Computing and Computer Assisted Intervention
https://doi.org/10.1016/B978-0-12-816176-0.00043-0

Figure 38.1 *Value in surgical care.* The goal for surgical data science is to maximize incidence of intended outcomes and minimize risk of adverse outcomes, thereby optimizing value in care.

to deliver care. Improvement may result from understanding processes and strategies, predicting events and clinical outcome, assisting physicians in decision-making and planning execution, optimizing ergonomics of systems, controlling devices before, during and after treatment, and from advances in prevention, training, simulation, and assessment. Surgical data science builds on principles and methods from other data-intensive disciplines, such as computer science, engineering, information theory, statistics, mathematics, and epidemiology, and complements other information-enabled technologies such as surgical robotics, smart operating rooms, and electronic patient records.

The overall goal for SDS is to maximize value in surgical care for patients, where value is defined as outcomes achieved per a unit of resources spent [2]. Value in care is maximized when the likelihood of intended or targeted outcomes is high and the incidence of preventable or adverse outcomes is low (Fig. 38.1). In surgical care, this becomes possible when surgical procedures, which are designed to effectively address the target pathology, are safely, skillfully, and efficiently performed (i.e., appropriate "dose"), with support from timely and accurate decision-making followed by effective pre- and postoperative care. In other words, surgical patient care is a process or a pathway that includes assessment of risk of disease, the decision to seek care, diagnosis, surgical decision-making, choice of intervention and its delivery, postinterventional care, outcomes assessment, and recuperative care. All components of this surgical care pathway affect outcomes of care, and are targeted by SDS. However, this necessitates capturing data on all aspects of the patient care process – pre-, intra-, and postoperative care – and enabling analytics to provide relevant caregivers with accurate assistance at the correct time (i.e., the right information to the right person at the right time) [1,3].

Fig. 38.2 illustrates some of the principal technical components and actors involved in surgical support systems based on SDS. The core of an SDS system is the knowledge base which stores *factual* and *practical* knowledge [4]. *Factual knowledge* is explicit knowledge that can be retrieved from canonical sources, for example, textbooks, scientific articles, or clinical guidelines. In contrast, *practical knowledge* relates to information

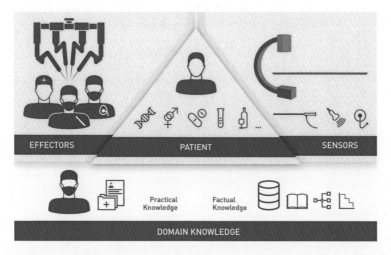

Figure 38.2 *Overview of components in surgical data science (SDS).* SDS systems acquire and process data related to (1) the *patient* getting a diagnosis or treatment (e.g., medical history, lab reports, genetic data), (2) the *effectors*, such as surgeons, nurses, robots, involved in the manipulation of the patient (e.g., kinematic information from a robot) and (3) the *sensors* perceiving patient- and procedure-related data (e.g., intraoperative tracking data, ultrasound/endoscopic image data). The data is holistically processed with (4) domain knowledge including *factual knowledge*, such as previous findings from studies or (hospital-specific) standards related to the clinical workflow, as well as *practical knowledge* from previous procedures.

gained from judgement or experience and it is often implicit and/or fuzzy. It includes case knowledge as well as expert knowledge, opinions, and preferences.

Fig. 38.3 illustrates the data/information flow that supports an ideal SDS system in terms of the following components:

Acquisition of case-specific data.   Data about patients and caregivers is continuously acquired during all aspects of surgical training, diagnosis, treatment planning, plan execution, assessment, and/or follow-up. It includes medical images, clinical data such as lab results, past history, and genomic data, as well as vital signals acquired during an intervention.

Generation of case-specific information.   The acquired raw data is then processed to generate case-specific relevant information (*case-specific information* in Fig. 38.3). For example, morphological or functional information related to the location and size of tumors or tissue perfusion properties may be extracted from raw images using image processing techniques. In this context, domain knowledge, such as prior information on the shape or size of organs, may be used to leverage the performance of image processing algorithms. Also, case knowledge or factual knowledge stored in the knowledge base may be used to infer new information about a pa-

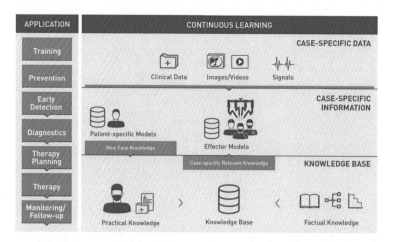

Figure 38.3 *Technical view of SDS demonstrating the process of continuous learning.* Case-specific data about the patient (e.g., images, laboratory test results) are converted into case-specific information (e.g., a representation of the patient anatomy/physiology as part of the patient model or a representation of the surgeon's skill as part of the effector model) using the knowledge base. The latter contains both practical knowledge from previous cases and factual knowledge, extracted from clinical guidelines or studies, for example. The derived case-specific knowledge is then fed into the knowledge base to serve as relevant information for future cases. Figure inspired by [3].

tient (e.g., a prognosis). The generated information (also referred to as *models* in Fig. 38.3) may refer to both, the patient and the effectors.

Application.   The information generated can be used to provide context-aware assistance, such as suggestion of a treatment plan before intervention, or the visualization of critical structures via Augmented Reality (AR) during treatment.

Update of the knowledge base.   New data and information that is generated throughout the patient care process is finally added to the knowledge base. For example, models for predicting intra- or postoperative complications are updated based on the current case.

Thus far we have provided a conceptual narrative on SDS. The next section explores application areas of SDS to illustrate the concept within a clinical context. The subsequent section describes some of the useful technical background specific to SDS. We then close the chapter with a discussion of future directions for the field.

38.2. Clinical context for SDS and its applications

As noted above, the eventual goal for SDS is to improve value in healthcare, which itself derives from many factors along a given surgical care pathway as noted in Fig. 38.3. The clinical context for SDS may be understood from the perspective of its potential contributions to the surgical care pathway. First, SDS yields tools to assist surgeons based upon the context of the care pathway. This includes decision support, visualization, and physical assistance through automated surgical systems. Second, skill and competency of surgical care providers affect patient outcomes [5,6]. SDS facilitates novel analytics and technology to assess provider skill and competency, and support their training through automated feedback. Third, reliable and accurate measurement of outcomes is necessary to improve surgical care. Traditional research methodologies in surgery, such as quality improvement studies, volume-outcome studies, and comparative and noncomparative cohort studies, have been constrained to one or a few outcomes by study design and/or limited ability to measure them. SDS enables both novel measures of outcomes and evaluating outcomes within the overall surgical care pathway, i.e., end-to-end modeling of care pathways. Fourth, SDS holds the promise that its clinical applications will be integrated into care pathways. In what follows, we explore these topics in greater detail.

Automating intelligent surgical assistance

SDS tools for surgical assistance should be accurate, context-aware, and either autonomous or readily accessible to the users through seamless integration with patient care workflows [4]. As shown in Fig. 38.3, context-aware SDS applications provide timely and relevant actionable insights. Context awareness refers specifically to a given patient, as well as to the timepoint in the care pathway. For example, specificity within the operating room may be with respect to the activity in the surgical field or to the stage of the surgical process. Such specificity is possible through data science techniques that automate detection of surgical activity and model the surgical process [7–10].

For decision support, SDS offers new analytical methods and extends traditional methods by enabling the capture of data from new sources and transforming previously unused data, perhaps due to their complexity, into useful representations. A few examples of data science techniques applied to traditional data sources, such as registries and cohort studies, include predicting risk of surgical site infections [11,12], risk of complications and death after surgery [13], hemodynamic instability before patients decompensate [14], risk of reoperation and death after endovascular aneurysm repair [15], outcomes after radiosurgery for cerebral arteriovenous malformations [16,17], predicting survival in patients with burns [18], and treatment planning in radiotherapy for prostate [19,20] and lung cancer [21]. Wearable devices, sensorized surgical instruments or environments, and radiologic and video images are examples of other data sources that can be modeled using data science techniques for surgical decision support. For instance, counting the number of steps taken by patients in the hospital with an accelerometer may be useful to predict the risk of readmission after cardiac surgery [22].

Augmentation of surgical visualization through SDS is data-driven and context-specific as opposed to traditional approaches that simply modify technologies to merge or overlay existing visual data from two or more sources (e.g., integrating intraoperative imaging into the operating microscope [23]). Examples of data-driven augmented visualization include patient-specific virtual reality simulations for preoperative intervention planning [24], augmented reality applications to overlay data-driven reconstructions of anatomy on the endoscopic view of the surgical field [25,26], or patient-specific mathematical simulation driven models to continuously predict tissue deformation during surgery of brain tumors [27].

Techniques for automated surgical systems that can physically assist or guide surgeons in patient care is one of the frontiers for SDS. Examples of preliminary research towards such automated systems include robotic path planning [28,29], intelligent assistance to improve localization of target anatomical structures or surgical instruments within the body [30–32], and collaborative surgical robots [33–37]. In summary, surgical assistance in different forms is feasible through SDS and it is an active area of ongoing research.

Training and assessing providers

Training providers and assessing their skill is a critical aspect of improving value in surgical care. In surgery, providers' skill in delivering interventions is not only an integral aspect of treatment but also determines safety and effectiveness of care [5,6]. In this context, "providers" refers to both the operating surgeon and the remaining surgical team, and "skill" includes technical and nontechnical skills. Previous advances in methods for provider assessment constituted scales to assess skill for use by expert raters. However, constrained resources, limited training opportunities, and the need to efficiently train and assess providers make traditional evaluation methods inefficient to use. Furthermore, increasing amounts of data are now available from multiple sources such as video images and various types of sensors placed either on providers or elsewhere in the operating room environment. These data contain information useful to assess provider skill and to support their training using techniques such as crowdsourcing [38–40] and machine learning [41]. The complexity and magnitude of the data preclude the use of conventional analytical techniques and require a data science approach to model the data and to develop products that can be seemlessly integrated into surgical workflows. In addition, it is essential to determine the association between surgical skill and outcomes of care. Currently there is relatively limited evidence to inform how care may be improved by augmenting provider training [42]. SDS aims to address these limitations by diversifying the data used to assess skill, measures outcomes of care (e.g., patient-reported and functional outcomes), and enabling analytics to determine the effect of training augmented by data-driven assessments on outcomes of care. We refer to Chapter 37 for more discussion of computer-aided training for surgery.

Improving measurement of surgical outcomes

The development life-cycle of SDS applications includes evaluating their impact on outcomes of care. It follows that the outcomes should be clearly defined along with a rationale for how modifying them will improve patient care. Surgical outcomes may reflect intended outcomes (anatomical or physiological), adverse events, processes of care, or patient reported measures including patient satisfaction. Traditionally, surgical research has emphasized measures that manifest in patients as outcomes, e.g., death, readmission, reoperation, duration of hospital stay [5,43]. Others described physiological effects of anatomical manipulation during surgery, e.g., relief from symptoms such as pain and seizures [44,45]. Some outcomes served as measures of quality of care, e.g., prevention of adverse events such as venous thromboembolism [46]. More recently, following an overall trend in healthcare, focus has shifted to patient-centered outcomes, which are typically reported by patients as those that are important to them given patient-specific characteristics and disease status. At the same time, efficiency in surgical care is evaluated through process outcomes, e.g., time to delivery of optimal care [47, 48]. Furthermore, outcomes within surgical care pathways have complex relationships. Certain outcomes are definitive measures of care, for example, major complications or death [13]. On the other hand, process outcomes such as time to optimal care may affect other outcomes downstream in the pathway. Other outcomes may serve as mediators of postoperative events. For example, blood transfusion during surgery, which may be predicted through algorithms [49], may explain risk of certain postoperative adverse events. Finally, data science techniques also enable capture and analysis of data from new sources, such as wearable devices, to develop novel outcomes of care. In summary, outcomes of care are a core aspect of SDS not only because it aims to improve them but also because it drives innovation in measurement of existing outcomes and development of new ones.

Integrating data science into the surgical care pathway

Care for surgical patients, before, during, and after surgery, is a process that sequentially evolves over time. This process may have different patterns based on patient-specific factors as well as individual, local, or regional variations in practice. These variations in practice were conventionally studied at a coarse level of the care pathway, e.g., through volume-outcome relationships, and standardized through community consensus on preferred practice patterns. However, modeling the surgical care pathway at different levels of granularity is essential to understand practice variation, factors affecting it, as well as consequential practice variations, i.e., those affecting outcomes of care. Such complex modeling of the surgical care pathway becomes possible when relevant data can be captured throughout the pathway without interfering with it, as illustrated by the Operating Room Black Box Study [50]. Another role for SDS in modeling the surgical care pathway is to transform unstructured data that may be easily obtained, e.g., video images of the patient care space or data from wearable devices, into a useful representation in addition to uncovering gaps in data and their sources that can lead to informative models. In addition, SDS enables modeling the surgical care pathway in its entirety. Currently, surgical process modeling, an established methodology to quantify the course of intervention or workflow, is focused upon the intraoperative segment of the surgical care pathway [8,51]. While intraoperative care is a major determinant of outcomes, both pre- and postoperative aspects of the pathway can influence efficiency and outcomes in surgical patients. Thus, modeling the overall surgical care pathway is necessary to determine whether and how to intervene to maximize value in care overall [52]. A data science approach to model the entire surgical care pathway enables analytics for local and global optimization [8].

In summary, SDS is not limited to developing algorithms and determining their validity for clinical applications. A value-driven approach to SDS means that the utility of its applications is determined by how they affect outcomes of care. A variety of outcomes may be relevant for SDS applications, and this diversity in outcomes should be addressed in SDS through systematic methodologies to measure them following adequate consultation within multidisciplinary teams. Finally, evaluating the impact of SDS applications on outcomes and value in care may rely upon established study design methods, such as randomized controlled trials and well-designed nonrandomized studies that can allow causal inference.

38.3. Technical approaches for SDS

The previous section reviewed some use cases of SDS. In each of these use cases, it is necessary to translate available data into useful or actionable information. The technical underpinnings of this translation draw on traditional mathematics and statistics, as well as more recent advances in machine learning. In this section, we focus on techniques that have received recent attention or have been of particular interest in surgical data science. In particular, relative to many other areas of medicine, surgery is unique in that it is a time-series process with an overall structure that is preserved across patients, surgeons, and institutions. This process can be analyzed at many levels, from fine-grained analysis of surgeon movement to modeling of the surgical team, to end-to-end analysis of the surgical pathway. Here, we focus largely on modeling surgical activity itself. We break this discussion into several topics: data sources, data labeling and sparsely annotated data, ontologies and semantic models, and time-series modeling inference. Further technical challenges are discussed in [3].

Data sources

At the core of surgical data science is the data available. As noted previously, there are various data sources available for the study and support of surgery. For the purposes of our discussion, it is useful to identify three groups of data sources:

Electronic Health Record (EHR) Data is commonly captured on the patient during the course of patient care. There is extensive literature on the structuring and management of this data that we will not review here. We do note that much of the EHR data that is necessary to support SDS is not in structured form as it takes the form of clinical notes that are in textual form. Thus, clinical natural language processing bears important relevance to SDS [53].

Medical imaging data is often used to diagnose disease that is treated surgically, and is also sometimes (but much less frequently) used to assess the success of surgery. The challenge with much of this data is that the interpretation of the images takes the form of a radiology report which is often not sufficiently specific to support the currently available machine learning methods. Developing methods to extract clinically relevant information from images is an area of very active interest which will bring immediate benefits to surgical data science.

Monitoring and procedure data is generated from medical devices used in the patient management process. Traditionally this includes information on patient vital signs and related patient support systems during the procedure. Looking ahead, there are many ongoing efforts to support acquisition of video recordings of minimally invasive surgery, which provides the fine-grained analysis of the surgical process and work product [8–10, 54,55], and tool movement captured from surgical robots [7,56,57]. This data is not yet routinely captured and stored, but there are now a growing number of initiatives to develop and demonstrate the value of scalable methods to capture and exploit this data [50,54,58].

Creating labeled data and dealing with sparsely annotated data:

Both traditional statistical inference and machine learning techniques will play a key role in future SDS applications [1,3]. The latter are particularly data hungry, and thus the availability of processed data sets is one of the major barriers to progress in the field. In computer assisted minimally-invasive surgery, for example, the amount of publicly available annotated data is steadily increasing. However, it is extremely challenging to capture all the variations (e.g., all medical devices applied in an intervention) that may occur in clinical practice. Furthermore, algorithms trained on data of one specific domain (e.g., the specific hardware in a specific hospital for a specific intervention) typically do not generalize well to new domains [58]. This is an important limitation as processing of (sufficient) training data is extremely labor-intensive and is currently hindering progress in the field. Several different approaches have been introduced to address this issue:

Crowdsourcing. In crowdsourcing-based approaches, annotation tasks are outsourced to masses of anonymous workers in an online community. In the context of SDS, the concept has successfully been applied to instrument segmentation [59], correspondence search [60], and skill assessment [38,39,61], for example. More recent approaches are directed to automatically estimate the skills of a user based on the interaction with the annotation software [62] in order to deal with the high variation in annotation quality. Also, concepts for crowd-algorithm collaboration are being investigated [63,64].

Transfer learning. The concept of transfer learning in general and domain adaptation [65] in particular has successfully been applied in various fields to compensate for the fact that algorithms trained on a specific training domain typically do not generalize well on the target domain. Wirkert et al. [66], for example, used domain adaptation in the context of oxygenation estimation from multispectral imaging data in order to compensate for the fact that no reference labels for oxygenation can be obtained. The approach involves using unlabeled real measurements of the target domain to give different weight to training samples that were generated with a Monte Carlo approach to train the algorithm.

Selfsupervised learning. Another approach is to create methods that exploit natural structure in data to "selfsupervise" their learning. This concept is gaining increasing attention in various communities [67–70]. It holds great potential for the field of SDS as it is often the small amount of annotated medical image data rather than the amount of raw medical data that causes the bottleneck related to training data acquisition. An approach by Ross et al. [58], for example, was based on the hypothesis that unlabeled video data can be used to learn a representation of the target domain (here, the specific hardware setup and surgical procedure that an instrument segmentation algorithm is applied in) to boost the performance of state-of-the-art machine learning algorithms. A core component of this approach is a so-called auxiliary task (here, recolorization) that is used to pretrain a convolutional neural network (CNN) for the target task. Other recent work has exploited ordering in surgery [71] to learn representations that are highly predictive, and then to retarget those representations to other tasks where a small number of labels are available.

Ontologies and semantic models

An important adjunct to analytical techniques to structure data is ontologies that identify and characterize essential concepts in the SDS domain. Ontologies comprise a structured vocabulary of terms that represent distinct entities and their relationships in a given domain. Engineering shared ontologies is necessary for SDS to deliver technology and analytics that improve surgical care. Shared ontologies can ensure standardized design and evaluation of SDS applications, in addition to facilitating collaboration within and across multidisciplinary teams as illustrated by the Gene Ontology (GO) [72] for the human genome project. Many examples of ontologies applicable to SDS can be found in the Open Biological and Biomedical Ontologies (OBO) Foundry project [73], which employs the Basic Formal Ontology (BFO) [74] as a common basis and includes, e.g., the Foundational Model of Anatomy (FMA) [75], the Information Artifact Ontology (IAO) [76], and the Phenotype And Trait Ontology (PATO) [77]. Using ontologies from a common top-level ontology, such as the BFO, facilitates data integration and fosters reusability, but relevant stand-alone ontologies exist as well. Examples include

RadLex [78], an ontology for radiology developed by the Radiological Society of North America (RSNA) and the Systematized Nomenclature of Human and Veterinary Medicine – Clinical Terms (SNOMED CT) [79], an ontology-like nomenclature that covers a wide array of terms used in clinical routine. Nevertheless, SDS poses a complex challenge for developing and implementing standardized ontologies owing to the diversity of clinical contexts and its applications. For example, OntoSPM [80] is one of the earliest ontologies developed to support modeling intraoperative surgical processes, specifically focused upon surgical activities, instruments, and personnel. This ontology has been adapted for laparoscopic surgery as LapOntoSPM [81], and it may be further redesigned for other contexts such as robotic surgery. In summary, we believe that ontologies for SDS applications can be transformative to advance science when developed with inputs from both clinical and engineering disciplines. Their benefit, however, still remains to be demonstrated.

Inference and machine learning

Abstractly, the problem of inference from data is quite easily stated: given observed quantities X (e.g., a surgical recording or a patient history), infer a value Y or distribution over Y (e.g., the skill of a surgeon or the likelihood of positive outcomes for the patient). In some domains, the model relating X and Y can be deduced from known principles, and the inference process can be treated by well-established model-based statistical methods. However, for many areas of surgery this is not the case – for example, what is a model of the relationship between a video of how a surgeon manipulates tissue and the quality of patient outcomes? Thus, much of the recent work on surgical data science has focused on data-driven machine learning to move the field forward. Common approaches include support vector machines [82], random forests [83], and more recently, deep learning [84].

The analysis of tool movement and video data acquired during the performance of surgery is a rapidly emerging topic of research. There are three major problems that have been addressed on this topic so far: (1) surgical phase recognition, (2) surgical skill assessment, and (3) automated assistance. Surgical phase recognition is an extremely active area [7]. Early work focused on the use of Hidden Markov Models and their variants to map tool movement signals to gesture, maneuver, and phase labels [85]. Subsequent work has explored conditional random fields [86,87], hybrid dynamical systems [88], and recurrent neural networks [89,90]. Video analysis has largely made use of increasingly sophisticated spatio-temporal neural networks [91]. Signals from the surrounding surgical environment have also been used to segment the workflow [54]. Reviews of this work include [7,10].

Skill assessment is addressed using similar methods with diverse data representations and features [41]. Early work emphasized generic motion efficiency features computed using instrument motion data, and relied upon techniques such as linear and logistic regression [92,93], nearest neighbor classification [93], support vector machines [94,95], and fuzzy models [96]. Subsequent research used a variety of signal and hand-engineered features, and additional techniques such as Markov models [97], discriminant function analysis [98], linear discriminant analysis [99], and simple neural networks [100]. Recent research is largely focused upon deep learning techniques including sophisticated spatio-temporal neural networks, some examples of which are cited in [101–106].

No matter what technique is used, developing generalizable models requires careful attention to the details of training. First, the data set must be representative of the population of data that the algorithm in question will process in the real-world application. Second, the training process must be carried out on data that is independent of data used to evaluate the performance of the model. This includes tuning any hyperparameters of the method itself – e.g., the number and depth of trees in the random forest. Thus, typically there is a training set used to infer model parameters, a validation set used to assess generalization performance for a given trained model using a set of hyperparameters, and a final test set that is used to assess the performance of the trained model once a good set of hyperparameters is identified. Ideally, benchmarking is performed in a standardized manner, e.g., via shared public data sets or international challenges. As previously noted, the paucity of publicly available data continues to hamper progress. In the context of benchmarking methods, potential biases or pitfalls in performing the ranking must also be considered [107,108].

38.4. Future challenges for SDS

SDS is an area that is still quite new and is rapidly developing. A decade ago there were few, if any, studies that had made use of data captured automatically and at scale, and nearly all analysis was based on manual annotation and classical statistical methods. Today, there are numerous publications that report highly scalable data analysis methods using semi- or fully-automated data capture and/or crowd-sourcing [38,39,59,60,64]. Data sets are now being collected which leverage the growing availability of EHR data to begin shedding light on the relationship between patient state and outcomes post surgery. However, this is just the beginning. In what follows, we articulate several areas where progress is needed and possible.

Pervasive data capture

There are several nascent efforts to develop frameworks for pervasive data capture related to surgery. Recent advances in storage, networking, and data compression have created conditions where fine-grained data on surgery can be captured, streamed, and stored. For example, a single OR streaming HD video requires about 8 Mbps of network bandwidth. Assuming 12 hours of actual operating usage per day, this translates to about 50 GB of video data per day without compression, or roughly 1 TB of data per month.

For archival purposes, this could be compressed by a factor of 10 to 100 or more – this is easily manageable and sustainable with today's technology. Including other time-series data streams will not substantially increase this number.

Given technology is no longer a substantial barrier, what stands in the way of data capture? It is a combination of initial costs, legal and regulatory hurdles, and lack of incentives to initiate this change [1,3]. In this regard, organizing the SDS community to articulate the gains that can be achieved through comprehensive capture and review of data will be essential to convince stakeholders to make the investment, and the surgical community to commit to including data capture in standard surgical practice [50].

Patient models

Surgical outcomes fundamentally depend on the health status and anatomic structure of the patient. In many cases, the relationship between patient health status, patient anatomy and surgical outcomes is not well understood. For example, spine surgery and surgery for nasal obstruction are two procedures that are known to have low success rates [109,110]. Although there have been various hypotheses about why this is the case, none have been found to be explanatory. Given large scale data, there is evidence that it may be possible to develop a far more nuanced statistical model for patients undergoing surgery using a combination of generative modeling [111], nonparametric statistical modeling [112], or a combination of both [113,114]. Developing and deploying these models specific to surgery will create a new lens to identify patient populations that are likely to benefit from surgery (or a specific type or "dose" of surgery) versus those that are not.

Models of surgeon performance

The complement to patient anatomy is surgeon performance. Given millions of performances of major surgeries, it should be possible to create models for the anticipated progress of surgery. The initial research described above is highly under-powered in that it tends to focus on a single institution, a small number of surgeons, and a cohort of patients that consent to have their data recorded. Scaling these models to thousands or millions of surgeries will make it possible to create a quantitative, more fine-grained definition for a "typical" surgery. Together with a statistical model for the patient, it will also begin to inform the complex interrelationship between surgeon performance, patient status, surgical workflow, and outcomes to drive effective "precision medicine" [115]. Creating these models will require new, creative approaches to model time-series at scale as well as ways to quickly identify and address both anomalous performance, and to quality control the models that are extracted from the data.

Surgical augmentation

Given strong models for how surgery "should be" performed, advances in artificial intelligence and machine learning methods offer the opportunity to augment human performance to improve surgery. This includes physical augmentation using currently available or envisioned robotic platforms [33,37], cognitive augmentation using information overlay [116,117], and anticipation or giving advice. Creating these systems will require well-validated models of surgical performance, advanced perception to ground performance to the current patient, and substantial human–factors engineering to understand when and how to augment the surgeon.

Efficient learning

As noted previously, labeled data is far harder to come by in surgery than in many other domains. While innovative approaches such as crowdsourcing offer the possibility of acquiring labeled data relatively cheaply, these methods also have their limits. As mentioned above, methods that are able to learn from data without supervision or leverage the data available from other domains are key. In this context, concepts such as selfsupervised learning [58], multitask learning [118], and embodied learning [119] hold high potential for application in the surgical domain.

Causal analysis of interventional pathways

The end-goal of SDS is to improve value – that is, to create improved outcomes and lower cost. The areas of work described above provide a basis for making decisions as to how to improve care, but these decisions depend on understanding how a given intervention or change is likely to affect outcomes. Historically, providing strong causal conclusions from surgery has been difficult. Every patient is different; every surgeon is different; there are many factors that affect patient outcomes beyond the surgeon and the patient. Furthermore, randomized controlled trials (RCTs) to evaluate surgical interventions are difficult to be performed [120]. Thus, it is hard to provide the same quality of evidence and understanding of surgery as, e.g., a drug for treating a common non-life-threatening condition. Large-scale data will provide a new lens on the relationships among many factors in surgery. However, correlation is not causation. While it may not be possible to entirely replace evidence from RCTs, recent advances in causal analysis [121] promise to make it possible to perform "synthetic" randomized comparisons that can illuminate factors in surgical care that are most consequential to outcomes.

Finding good use cases

Surgery as a field is broad and diverse. As SDS evolves, it is important to choose problems where an impact can be made. Surgeries that are routine and consistently have good outcomes with few side-effects are not as likely to yield as much benefit from SDS as surgeries where outcomes have high variability and/or where the relationship between patient, surgical performance, and outcome is opaque. Good candidates for research on SDS itself will be surgeries that are common enough to provide a large number of examples, where outcomes are variable across patients, surgeons, or institutions, and where it is possible to formulate good hypotheses as to what may lead to improvement. As SDS evolves, we believe methodologies for discovering what to focus on will be as important as the techniques to create improvement for a given use case.

38.5. Conclusion

In conclusion, SDS will pave the way for data-driven interventional healthcare and evolve as a key component to improve the quality and efficiency of care. Exploiting the full potential of the field will require the establishment of a culture of continuous measurement, assessment and improvement using evidence from data as a core component [1].

Acknowledgments

Many thanks to Carolin Feldmann (CAMI, DKFZ) for generation of the figures as well as to Tobias Ross (CAMI, DKFZ) and Keno März (CAMI, DKFZ) for contributing text and references to the chapter. The authors wish to acknowledge the support of the European Research Council (ERC-2015-StG-37960), NIH (R01-DE025265; PI: Dr. Masaru Ishii).

References

[1] L. Maier-Hein, S.S. Vedula, S. Speidel, N. Navab, R. Kikinis, A. Park, et al., Surgical data science for next-generation interventions, Nature Biomedical Engineering 1 (9) (2017) 691.

[2] M.E. Porter, What is value in health care?, The New England Journal of Medicine 363 (26) (2010) 2477–2481.

[3] L. Maier-Hein, M. Eisenmann, C. Feldmann, H. Feussner, G. Forestier, S. Giannarou, et al., Surgical data science: a consensus perspective, arXiv:cs/1806031, 2018, URL: http://arxiv.org/abs/1806.03184.

[4] K. März, M. Hafezi, T. Weller, A. Saffari, M. Nolden, N. Fard, et al., Toward knowledge-based liver surgery: holistic information processing for surgical decision support, International Journal of Computer Assisted Radiology and Surgery 10 (6) (2015) 749–759.

[5] J.D. Birkmeyer, J.F. Finks, A. O'reilly, M. Oerline, A.M. Carlin, A.R. Nunn, et al., Surgical skill and complication rates after bariatric surgery, The New England Journal of Medicine 369 (15) (2013) 1434–1442.

[6] M. Nathan, J.M. Karamichalis, H. Liu, S. Emani, C. Baird, F. Pigula, et al., Surgical technical performance scores are predictors of late mortality and unplanned reinterventions in infants after cardiac surgery, The Journal of Thoracic and Cardiovascular Surgery 144 (5) (2012), https://doi.org/10.1016/j.jtcvs.2012.07.081, 1095–1101.e7.

[7] N. Ahmidi, L. Tao, S. Sefati, Y. Gao, C. Lea, B.B. Haro, et al., A dataset and benchmarks for segmentation and recognition of gestures in robotic surgery, IEEE Transactions on Biomedical Engineering 64 (9) (2017) 2025–2041.

[8] D. Neumuth, F. Loebe, H. Herre, T. Neumuth, Modeling surgical processes: a four-level translational approach, Artificial Intelligence in Medicine 51 (3) (2011) 147–161.

[9] O. Dergachyova, D. Bouget, A. Huaulmé, X. Morandi, P. Jannin, Automatic data-driven real-time segmentation and recognition of surgical workflow, International Journal of Computer Assisted Radiology and Surgery 11 (6) (2016) 1081–1089.

[10] F. Lalys, P. Jannin, Surgical process modelling: a review, International Journal of Computer Assisted Radiology and Surgery 9 (3) (2014) 495–511.

[11] P.C. Sanger, V.V. Simianu, C.E. Gaskill, C.A. Armstrong, A.L. Hartzler, R.J. Lordon, et al., Diagnosing surgical site infection using wound photography: a scenario-based study, Journal of the American College of Surgeons 224 (1) (2017) 8–15.

[12] C. Ke, Y. Jin, H. Evans, B. Lober, X. Qian, J. Liu, et al., Prognostics of surgical site infections using dynamic health data, Journal of Biomedical Informatics 65 (2017) 22–33.

[13] A. Bihorac, T. Ozrazgat-Baslanti, A. Ebadi, A. Motaei, M. Madkour, P.M. Pardalos, et al., Mysurgeryrisk: development and validation of a machine-learning risk algorithm for major complications and death after surgery, Annals of Surgery 269 (4) (2019) 652–662.

[14] H. Kim, S.B. Lee, Y. Son, M. Czosnyka, D.J. Kim, Hemodynamic instability and cardiovascular events after traumatic brain injury predict outcome after artifact removal with deep belief network analysis, Journal of Neurosurgical Anesthesiology 30 (4) (2018) 347–353.

[15] A. Karthikesalingam, O. Attallah, X. Ma, S.S. Bahia, L. Thompson, A. Vidal-Diez, et al., An artificial neural network stratifies the risks of reintervention and mortality after endovascular aneurysm repair, a retrospective observational study, PLoS ONE 10 (7) (2015) e0129024.

[16] E.K. Oermann, A. Rubinsteyn, D. Ding, J. Mascitelli, R.M. Starke, J.B. Bederson, et al., Using a machine learning approach to predict outcomes after radiosurgery for cerebral arteriovenous malformations, Scientific Reports 6 (2016) 21161.

[17] Z.G. Merali, C.D. Witiw, J.H. Badhiwala, J.R. Wilson, M.G. Fehlings, Using a machine learning approach to predict outcome after surgery for degenerative cervical myelopathy, PLoS ONE 14, 4 (2019) e0215133.

[18] A.N. Cobb, W. Daungjaiboon, S.A. Brownlee, A.J. Baldea, A.P. Sanford, M.M. Mosier, et al., Seeing the forest beyond the trees: predicting survival in burn patients with machine learning, American Journal of Surgery 215 (3) (2018) 411–416, https://doi.org/10.1016/j.amjsurg.2017.10.027.

[19] A. Nicolae, G. Morton, H. Chung, A. Loblaw, S. Jain, D. Mitchell, et al., Evaluation of a machine-learning algorithm for treatment planning in prostate low-dose-rate brachytherapy, International Journal of Radiation Oncology, Biology, Physics 97 (4) (2017) 822–829.

[20] H. Wang, P. Dong, H. Liu, L. Xing, Development of an autonomous treatment planning strategy for radiation therapy with effective use of population-based prior data, Medical Physics 44 (2) (2017) 389–396.

[21] G. Valdes, C.B. Simone II, J. Chen, A. Lin, S.S. Yom, A.J. Pattison, et al., Clinical decision support of radiotherapy treatment planning: a data-driven machine learning strategy for patient-specific dosimetric decision making, Radiotherapy and Oncology 125 (3) (2017) 392–397.

[22] T. Takahashi, M. Kumamaru, S. Jenkins, M. Saitoh, T. Morisawa, H. Matsuda, In-patient step count predicts re-hospitalization after cardiac surgery, Journal of Cardiology 66 (4) (2015) 286–291.

[23] J.P. Ehlers, A. Uchida, S.K. Srivastava, The integrative surgical theater: combining intraoperative optical coherence tomography and 3d digital visualization for vitreoretinal surgery in the discover study, Retina 38 (2018) S88–S96.

[24] M. Pfeiffer, H. Kenngott, A. Preukschas, M. Huber, L. Bettscheider, B. Müller-Stich, et al., Imhotep: virtual reality framework for surgical applications, International Journal of Computer Assisted Radiology and Surgery 13 (5) (2018) 741–748, https://doi.org/10.1007/s11548-018-1730-x.

[25] S. Bernhardt, S.A. Nicolau, L. Soler, C. Doignon, The status of augmented reality in laparoscopic surgery as of 2016, Medical Image Analysis 37 (2017) 66–90.

[26] S.I. O'Donoghue, B.F. Baldi, S.J. Clark, A.E. Darling, J.M. Hogan, S. Kaur, et al., Visualization of biomedical data, Annual Review of Biomedical Data Science 1 (1) (2018) 275–304, https://doi.org/10.1146/annurev-biodatasci-080917-013424.

[27] M. Tonutti, G. Gras, G.Z. Yang, A machine learning approach for real-time modelling of tissue deformation in image-guided neurosurgery, Artificial Intelligence in Medicine 80 (2017) 39–47.

[28] N. Ahmidi, G.D. Hager, L. Ishii, G.L. Gallia, M. Ishii, Robotic path planning for surgeon skill evaluation in minimally-invasive sinus surgery, in: International Conference on Medical Image Computing and Computer-Assisted Intervention, Springer, 2012, pp. 471–478.

[29] Y. Kassahun, B. Yu, A.T. Tibebu, D. Stoyanov, S. Giannarou, J.H. Metzen, et al., Surgical robotics beyond enhanced dexterity instrumentation: a survey of machine learning techniques and their role in intelligent and autonomous surgical actions, International Journal of Computer Assisted Radiology and Surgery 11 (4) (2016) 553–568.

[30] L. Zhang, M. Ye, S. Giannarou, P. Pratt, G.Z. Yang, Motion-compensated autonomous scanning for tumour localisation using intraoperative ultrasound, in: International Conference on Medical Image Computing and Computer-Assisted Intervention, Springer, 2017, pp. 619–627.

[31] D. Allman, F. Assis, J. Chrispin, M.A.L. Bell, A deep learning-based approach to identify in vivo catheter tips during photoacoustic-guided cardiac interventions, in: Photons Plus Ultrasound: Imaging and Sensing 2019, vol. 10878, International Society for Optics and Photonics, 2019, 108785E.

[32] M.A.L. Bell, Deep learning the sound of light to guide surgeries, in: Advanced Biomedical and Clinical Diagnostic and Surgical Guidance Systems XVII, vol. 10868, International Society for Optics and Photonics, 2019, 108680G.

[33] N. Padoy, G.D. Hager, Human-machine collaborative surgery using learned models, in: 2011 IEEE International Conference on Robotics and Automation, IEEE, 2011, pp. 5285–5292.

[34] M.A.L. Bell, H.T. Sen, I.I. Iordachita, P. Kazanides, J. Wong, In vivo reproducibility of robotic probe placement for a novel ultrasound-guided radiation therapy system, Journal of Medical Imaging 1 (2) (2014) 025001.

[35] Z. Chen, A. Malpani, P. Chalasani, A. Deguet, S.S. Vedula, P. Kazanides, et al., Virtual fixture assistance for needle passing and knot tying, in: 2016 IEEE/RSJ International Conference on Intelligent Robots and Systems (IROS), IEEE, 2016, pp. 2343–2350.

[36] B.S. Peters, P.R. Armijo, C. Krause, S.A. Choudhury, D. Oleynikov, Review of emerging surgical robotic technology, Surgical Endoscopy 32 (4) (2018) 1636–1655.

[37] A. Shademan, R.S. Decker, J.D. Opfermann, S. Leonard, A. Krieger, P.C. Kim, Supervised autonomous robotic soft tissue surgery, Science Translational Medicine 8 (337) (2016) 337.

[38] A. Malpani, S.S. Vedula, C.C.G. Chen, G.D. Hager, A study of crowdsourced segment-level surgical skill assessment using pairwise rankings, International Journal of Computer Assisted Radiology and Surgery 10 (9) (2015) 1435–1447.

[39] T.S. Lendvay, L. White, T. Kowalewski, Crowdsourcing to assess surgical skill, JAMA Surgery 150 (11) (2015) 1086–1087.

[40] J.C. Dai, T.S. Lendvay, M.D. Sorensen, Crowdsourcing in surgical skills acquisition: a developing technology in surgical education, Journal of Graduate Medical Education 9 (6) (2017) 697–705.

[41] S.S. Vedula, M. Ishii, G.D. Hager, Objective assessment of surgical technical skill and competency in the operating room, Annual Review of Biomedical Engineering 19 (2017) 301–325.

[42] R. Aggarwal, K.M. Brown, P.C. de Groen, A.G. Gallagher, K. Henriksen, L.R. Kavoussi, et al., Simulation research in gastrointestinal and urologic care—challenges and opportunities: summary of a national institute of diabetes and digestive and kidney diseases and national institute of biomedical imaging and bioengineering workshop, Annals of Surgery 267 (1) (2018) 26–34.

[43] J.S. Kim, R.K. Merrill, V. Arvind, D. Kaji, S.D. Pasik, C.C. Nwachukwu, et al., Examining the ability of artificial neural networks machine learning models to accurately predict complications following posterior lumbar spine fusion, Spine 43 (12) (2018) 853.

[44] J. Lötsch, A. Ultsch, E. Kalso, Prediction of persistent post-surgery pain by preoperative cold pain sensitivity: biomarker development with machine-learning-derived analysis, British Journal of Anaesthesia 119 (4) (2017) 821–829.

[45] S. Khor, D. Lavallee, A.M. Cizik, C. Bellabarba, J.R. Chapman, C.R. Howe, et al., Development and validation of a prediction model for pain and functional outcomes after lumbar spine surgery, JAMA Surgery 153 (7) (2018) 634–642.

[46] P. Ferroni, F.M. Zanzotto, N. Scarpato, S. Riondino, U. Nanni, M. Roselli, et al., Risk assessment for venous thromboembolism in chemotherapy-treated ambulatory cancer patients: a machine learning approach, Medical Decision Making 37 (2) (2017) 234–242.

[47] I. Aksamentov, A.P. Twinanda, D. Mutter, J. Marescaux, N. Padoy, Deep neural networks predict remaining surgery duration from cholecystectomy videos, in: International Conference on Medical Image Computing and Computer-Assisted Intervention, Springer, 2017, pp. 586–593.

[48] J.P. Tuwatananurak, S. Zadeh, X. Xu, J.A. Vacanti, W.R. Fulton, J.M. Ehrenfeld, et al., Machine learning can improve estimation of surgical case duration: a pilot study, Journal of Medical Systems 43 (3) (2019) 44.

[49] W.M. Durand, J.M. DePasse, A.H. Daniels, Predictive modeling for blood transfusion after adult spinal deformity surgery: a tree-based machine learning approach, Spine 43 (15) (2018) 1058–1066.

[50] J.J. Jung, P. Jüni, G. Lebovic, T. Grantcharov, First-year analysis of the operating room black box study, Annals of Surgery (2018).

[51] N. Bahou, C. Fenwick, G. Anderson, R. Van Der Meer, T. Vassalos, Modeling the critical care pathway for cardiothoracic surgery, Health Care Management Science (2017) 1–12.

[52] R. Aringhieri, D. Duma, A hybrid model for the analysis of a surgical pathway, in: 2014 4th International Conference on Simulation and Modeling Methodologies, Technologies and Applications (SIMULTECH), IEEE, 2014, pp. 889–900.

[53] K. Kreimeyer, M. Foster, A. Pandey, N. Arya, G. Halford, S.F. Jones, et al., Natural language processing systems for capturing and standardizing unstructured clinical information: a systematic review, Journal of Biomedical Informatics 73 (2017) 14–29.

[54] N. Padoy, T. Blum, S.A. Ahmadi, H. Feussner, M.O. Berger, N. Navab, Statistical modeling and recognition of surgical workflow, Medical Image Analysis 16 (3) (2012) 632–641.

[55] F. Meeuwsen, F. van Luyn, M.D. Blikkendaal, F. Jansen, J. van den Dobbelsteen, Surgical phase modelling in minimal invasive surgery, Surgical Endoscopy (2018) 1–7.

[56] A.J. Hung, J. Chen, A. Jarc, D. Hatcher, H. Djaladat, I.S. Gill, Development and validation of objective performance metrics for robot-assisted radical prostatectomy: a pilot study, The Journal of Urology 199 (1) (2018) 296–304.

[57] A.J. Hung, J. Chen, Z. Che, T. Nilanon, A. Jarc, M. Titus, et al., Utilizing machine learning and automated performance metrics to evaluate robot-assisted radical prostatectomy performance and predict outcomes, Journal of Endourology 32 (5) (2018) 438–444.

[58] T. Ross, D. Zimmerer, A. Vemuri, F. Isensee, M. Wiesenfarth, S. Bodenstedt, et al., Exploiting the potential of unlabeled endoscopic video data with self-supervised learning, International Journal of Computer Assisted Radiology and Surgery 13 (2018) 925–933.

[59] L. Maier-Hein, S. Mersmann, D. Kondermann, S. Bodenstedt, A. Sanchez, C. Stock, et al., Can masses of non-experts train highly accurate image classifiers?, in: International Conference on Medical Image Computing and Computer-Assisted Intervention, Springer, 2014, pp. 438–445.

[60] L. Maier-Hein, D. Kondermann, T. Roß, S. Mersmann, E. Heim, S. Bodenstedt, et al., Crowdtruth validation: a new paradigm for validating algorithms that rely on image correspondences, International Journal of Computer Assisted Radiology and Surgery 10 (8) (2015) 1201–1212.

[61] D. Holst, T.M. Kowalewski, L.W. White, T.C. Brand, J.D. Harper, M.D. Sorenson, et al., Crowdsourced assessment of technical skills: an adjunct to urology resident surgical simulation training, Journal of Endourology 29 (5) (2015) 604–609.

[62] E. Heim, T. Roß, et al., Large-scale medical image annotation with crowd-powered algorithms, Journal of Medical Imaging 5 (3) (2018) 034002, https://doi.org/10.1117/1.JMI.5.3.034002.

[63] L. Maier-Hein, T. Ross, J. Gröhl, B. Glocker, S. Bodenstedt, C. Stock, et al., Crowd-algorithm collaboration for large-scale endoscopic image annotation with confidence, in: International Conference on Medical Image Computing and Computer-Assisted Intervention, Springer, 2016, pp. 616–623.

[64] S. Albarqouni, C. Baur, F. Achilles, V. Belagiannis, S. Demirci, N. Navab, Aggnet: deep learning from crowds for mitosis detection in breast cancer histology images, IEEE Transactions on Medical Imaging 35 (5) (2016) 1313–1321.

[65] X. Glorot, A. Bordes, Y. Bengio, Domain adaptation for large-scale sentiment classification: a deep learning approach, in: Proceedings of the 28th International Conference on Machine Learning (ICML-11), 2011, pp. 513–520.

[66] S.J. Wirkert, A.S. Vemuri, H.G. Kenngott, S. Moccia, M. Götz, B.F. Mayer, et al., Physiological parameter estimation from multispectral images unleashed, in: International Conference on Medical Image Computing and Computer-Assisted Intervention, Springer, 2017, pp. 134–141.

[67] P. Agrawal, J. Carreira, J. Malik, Learning to see by moving, in: Proceedings of the IEEE International Conference on Computer Vision, 2015, pp. 37–45.

[68] R. Zhang, P. Isola, A.A. Efros, Colorful image colorization, in: European Conference on Computer Vision, Springer, 2016, pp. 649–666.

[69] R. Zhang, P. Isola, A.A. Efros, Split-brain autoencoders: unsupervised learning by cross-channel prediction, in: CVPR, vol. 1, 2017, p. 5.

[70] R. DiPietro, G.D. Hager, Unsupervised learning for surgical motion by learning to predict the future, in: International Conference on Medical Image Computing and Computer-Assisted Intervention, Springer, 2018, pp. 281–288.

[71] I. Funke, A. Jenke, S.T. Mees, J. Weitz, S. Speidel, S. Bodenstedt, Temporal coherence-based self-supervised learning for laparoscopic workflow analysis, in: D. Stoyanov, Z. Taylor, D. Sarikaya, J. McLeod, M.A. González Ballester, N.C. Codella, et al. (Eds.), OR 2.0 Context-Aware Operating Theaters, Computer Assisted Robotic Endoscopy, Clinical Image-Based Procedures, and Skin Image Analysis, Springer International Publishing, Cham, ISBN 978-3-030-01201-4, 2018, pp. 85–93.

[72] G.O. Consortium, The gene ontology (go) database and informatics resource, Nucleic Acids Research 32 (suppl_1) (2004) D258–D261.

[73] B. Smith, M. Ashburner, C. Rosse, J. Bard, W. Bug, W. Ceusters, et al., The OBO foundry: coordinated evolution of ontologies to support biomedical data integration, Nature Biotechnology 25 (11) (2007) 1251–1255.

[74] R. Arp, B. Smith, A.D. Spear, Building Ontologies With Basic Formal Ontology, MIT Press, 2015.

[75] C. Rosse, J.L.V. Mejino Jr, A reference ontology for biomedical informatics: the foundational model of anatomy, Journal of Biomedical Informatics 36 (6) (2003) 478–500.

[76] W. Ceusters, An information artifact ontology perspective on data collections and associated representational artifacts, Studies in Health Technology and Informatics 180 (2012) 68–72.

[77] P.M. Mabee, M. Ashburner, Q. Cronk, G.V. Gkoutos, M. Haendel, E. Segerdell, et al., Phenotype ontologies: the bridge between genomics and evolution, Trends in Ecology & Evolution 22 (7) (2007) 345–350.

[78] F. Calderoni, C.D. Mattia, S. Nici, F. Rottoli, M. Sutto, M. Campoleoni, et al., [P025] The use of radlex playbook to manage CT big data: an Italian multicentre study, European Journal of Medical Physics 52 (2018) 106.

[79] K. Donnelly, SNOMED-CT: the advanced terminology and coding system for eHealth, Studies in Health Technology and Informatics 121 (2006) 279.

[80] B. Gibaud, G. Forestier, C. Feldmann, G. Ferrigno, P. Gonçalves, T. Haidegger, et al., Toward a standard ontology of surgical process models, International Journal of Computer Assisted Radiology and Surgery 13 (9) (2018) 1397–1408.

[81] D. Katić, C. Julliard, A.L. Wekerle, H. Kenngott, B.P. Müller-Stich, R. Dillmann, et al., LapOntoSPM: an ontology for laparoscopic surgeries and its application to surgical phase recognition, International Journal of Computer Assisted Radiology and Surgery 10 (9) (2015) 1427–1434.

[82] C. Cortes, V. Vapnik, Support-vector networks, Machine Learning 20 (3) (1995) 273–297.

[83] L. Breiman, Random forests, Machine Learning 45 (1) (2001) 5–32.

[84] J. Schmidhuber, Deep learning in neural networks: an overview, Neural Networks 61 (2015) 85–117.

[85] H.C. Lin, I. Shafran, D. Yuh, G.D. Hager, Towards automatic skill evaluation: detection and segmentation of robot-assisted surgical motions, Computer Aided Surgery 11 (5) (2006) 220–230.

[86] C. Lea, G.D. Hager, R. Vidal, An improved model for segmentation and recognition of fine-grained activities with application to surgical training tasks, in: 2015 IEEE Winter Conference on Applications of Computer Vision, IEEE, 2015, pp. 1123–1129.

[87] C.S. Lea, et al., Multi-Modal Models for Fine-Grained Action Segmentation in Situated Environments, PhD thesis, Johns Hopkins University, 2017.

[88] B.B. Haro, L. Zappella, R. Vidal, Surgical gesture classification from video data, in: International Conference on Medical Image Computing and Computer-Assisted Intervention, Springer, 2012, pp. 34–41.

[89] R. DiPietro, C. Lea, A. Malpani, N. Ahmidi, S.S. Vedula, G.I. Lee, et al., Recognizing surgical activities with recurrent neural networks, in: International Conference on Medical Image Computing and Computer-Assisted Intervention, Springer, 2016, pp. 551–558.

[90] R. DiPietro, N. Ahmidi, A. Malpani, M. Waldram, G.I. Lee, M.R. Lee, et al., Segmenting and classifying activities in robot-assisted surgery with recurrent neural networks, International Journal of Computer Assisted Radiology and Surgery (2019) 1–16.

[91] F. Yu, G.S. Croso, T.S. Kim, Z. Song, F. Parker, G.D. Hager, et al., Assessment of automated identification of phases in videos of cataract surgery using machine learning and deep learning techniques, JAMA Network Open 2 (4) (2019) e191860.

[92] E.D. Gomez, R. Aggarwal, W. McMahan, K. Bark, K.J. Kuchenbecker, Objective assessment of robotic surgical skill using instrument contact vibrations, Surgical Endoscopy 30 (4) (2016) 1419–1431.

[93] M.J. Fard, S. Ameri, R. Darin Ellis, R.B. Chinnam, A.K. Pandya, M.D. Klein, Automated robot-assisted surgical skill evaluation: predictive analytics approach, The International Journal of Medical Robotics and Computer Assisted Surgery 14 (1) (2018) e1850.

[94] R. Kumar, A. Jog, B. Vagvolgyi, H. Nguyen, G. Hager, C.C.G. Chen, et al., Objective measures for longitudinal assessment of robotic surgery training, Journal of Thoracic and Cardiovascular Surgery 143 (3) (2012) 528–534.

[95] N. Ahmidi, P. Poddar, J.D. Jones, S.S. Vedula, L. Ishii, G.D. Hager, et al., Automated objective surgical skill assessment in the operating room from unstructured tool motion in septoplasty, International Journal of Computer Assisted Radiology and Surgery 10 (6) (2015) 981–991.

[96] I. Hajshirmohammadi, Using Fuzzy Set Theory to Objectively Evaluate Performance on Minimally Invasive Surgical Simulators, PhD thesis, School of Engineering Science – Simon Fraser University, 2006.

[97] N. Ahmidi, M. Ishii, G. Fichtinger, G.L. Gallia, G.D. Hager, An objective and automated method for assessing surgical skill in endoscopic sinus surgery using eye-tracking and tool-motion data, in: International Forum of Allergy & Rhinology, vol. 2, Wiley Online Library, 2012, pp. 507–515.

[98] M. Aizuddin, N. Oshima, R. Midorikawa, A. Takanishi, Development of sensor system for effective evaluation of surgical skill, in: The First IEEE/RAS-EMBS International Conference on Biomedical Robotics and Biomechatronics, 2006, BioRob 2006, IEEE, 2006, pp. 678–683.

[99] T. Horeman, J. Dankelman, F.W. Jansen, J.J. van den Dobbelsteen, Assessment of laparoscopic skills based on force and motion parameters, IEEE Transactions on Biomedical Engineering 61 (3) (2013) 805–813.

[100] B.D. Kramer, D.P. Losey, M.K. O'Malley, SOM and LVQ classification of endovascular surgeons using motion-based metrics, in: Advances in Self-Organizing Maps and Learning Vector Quantization, Springer, 2016, pp. 227–237.

[101] T.S. Kim, M. O'Brien, S. Zafar, G.D. Hager, S. Sikder, S.S. Vedula, Objective assessment of intra-operative technical skill in capsulorhexis using videos of cataract surgery, International Journal of Computer Assisted Radiology and Surgery (2019) 1–9.

[102] M. Benmansour, W. Handouzi, A. Malti, Task-specific surgical skill assessment with neural net-works, in: International Conference on Advanced Intelligent Systems for Sustainable Development, Springer, 2018, pp. 159–167.

[103] Z. Wang, A.M. Fey, Deep learning with convolutional neural network for objective skill evaluation in robot-assisted surgery, International Journal of Computer Assisted Radiology and Surgery 13 (12) (2018) 1959–1970.

[104] A. Jin, S. Yeung, J. Jopling, J. Krause, D. Azagury, A. Milstein, et al., Tool detection and operative skill assessment in surgical videos using region-based convolutional neural networks, in: 2018 IEEE Winter Conference on Applications of Computer Vision (WACV), IEEE, 2018, pp. 691–699.

[105] H. Doughty, D. Damen, W. Mayol-Cuevas, Who's better? Who's best? Pairwise deep ranking for skill determination, in: Proceedings of the IEEE Conference on Computer Vision and Pattern Recogni-tion, 2018, pp. 6057–6066.

[106] H.I. Fawaz, G. Forestier, J. Weber, L. Idoumghar, P.A. Muller, Evaluating surgical skills from kine-matic data using convolutional neural networks, in: International Conference on Medical Image Computing and Computer-Assisted Intervention, Springer, 2018, pp. 214–221.

[107] L. Maier-Hein, M. Eisenmann, A. Reinke, S. Onogur, M. Stankovic, P. Scholz, et al., Why rankings of biomedical image analysis competitions should be interpreted with care, Nature Communications 9 (2018) 5217.

[108] A. Reinke, M. Eisenmann, S. Onogur, M. Stankovic, P. Scholz, P.M. Full, et al., How to exploit weaknesses in biomedical challenge design and organization, in: International Conference on Medical Image Computing and Computer-Assisted Intervention, Springer, 2018, pp. 388–395.

[109] R.A. Deyo, S.K. Mirza, B.I. Martin, W. Kreuter, D.C. Goodman, J.G. Jarvik, Trends, major medical complications, and charges associated with surgery for lumbar spinal stenosis in older adults, JAMA 303 (13) (2010) 1259–1265.

[110] E.M. Floyd, S. Ho, P. Patel, R.M. Rosenfeld, E. Gordin, Systematic review and meta-analysis of studies evaluating functional rhinoplasty outcomes with the NOSE score, Otolaryngology–Head and Neck Surgery 156 (5) (2017) 809–815.

[111] C. Xiao, E. Choi, J. Sun, Opportunities and challenges in developing deep learning models using electronic health records data: a systematic review, Journal of the American Medical Informatics Association 25 (10) (2018) 1419–1428.

[112] A. Sinha, S. Leonard, A. Reiter, M. Ishii, R.H. Taylor, G.D. Hager, Automatic segmentation and statistical shape modeling of the paranasal sinuses to estimate natural variations, in: Medical Imaging 2016: Image Processing, vol. 9784, International Society for Optics and Photonics, 2016, 97840D.

[113] R. Vijayan, T. De Silva, R. Han, X. Zhang, A. Uneri, S. Doerr, M.D. Ketcha, A. Perdomo-Pantoja, N. Theodore, J.H. Siewerdsen, Automatic pedicle screw planning using atlas-based registration of anatomy and reference trajectories, Physics in Medicine and Biology (2019).

[114] R.C. Vijayan, T.S. De Silva, R. Han, A. Uneri, S.A. Doerr, M.D. Ketcha, A. Perdomo-Pantoja, N. Theodore, J.H. Siewerdsen, Automatic trajectory and instrument planning for robot-assisted spine surgery, in: Medical Imaging 2019: Image-Guided Procedures, Robotic Interventions, and Modeling, vol. 10951, International Society for Optics and Photonics, 2019, p. 1095102.

[115] A. Rosen, S.L. Zeger, Precision medicine: discovering clinically relevant and mechanistically an-chored disease subgroups at scale, The Journal of Clinical Investigation 129 (3) (2019).

[116] L.M. Su, B.P. Vagvolgyi, R. Agarwal, C.E. Reiley, R.H. Taylor, G.D. Hager, Augmented reality during robot-assisted laparoscopic partial nephrectomy: toward real-time 3D-CT to stereoscopic video registration, Urology 73 (4) (2009) 896–900.

[117] T.M. Peters, Overview of mixed and augmented reality in medicine, in: Mixed and Augmented Reality in Medicine, CRC Press, 2018, pp. 1–13.

[118] Y. Zhang, Q. Yang, A survey on multi-task learning, arXiv preprint, arXiv:1707.08114, 2017.

[119] D. Jayaraman, K. Grauman, Learning image representations tied to ego-motion, in: Proceedings of the IEEE International Conference on Computer Vision, 2015, pp. 1413–1421.

[120] P. McCulloch, I. Taylor, M. Sasako, B. Lovett, D. Griffin, Randomised trials in surgery: problems and possible solutions, BMJ 324 (7351) (2002) 1448–1451.

[121] J. Peters, D. Janzing, B. Schölkopf, Elements of Causal Inference: Foundations and Learning Algorithms, MIT Press, 2017.

CHAPTER 39

Computational biomechanics for medical image analysis

Adam Wittek, Karol Miller

Intelligent Systems for Medicine Laboratory, Department of Mechanical Engineering, The University of Western Australia, Perth, WA, Australia

Contents

39.1. Introduction	953
39.2. Image analysis informs biomechanics: patient-specific computational biomechanics model from medical images	955
39.2.1 Geometry extraction from medical images: segmentation	955
39.2.2 Finite element mesh generation	956
39.2.3 Image as a computational biomechanics model: meshless discretization	958
39.3. Biomechanics informs image analysis: computational biomechanics model as image registration tool	961
39.3.1 Biomechanics-based image registration: problem formulation	963
39.3.2 Biomechanics-based image registration: examples	964
39.3.2.1 *Neuroimage registration*	*964*
39.3.2.2 *Magnetic resonance (MR) image registration for intracranial electrode localization for epilepsy treatment*	*965*
39.3.2.3 *Whole-body computed tomography (CT) image registration*	*969*
39.4. Discussion	969
Acknowledgments	972
References	972

39.1. Introduction

Biomechanics has been traditionally defined as mechanics applied to biology. The quest for understanding the mechanics of living systems has always been regarded as the key subject of biomechanics [31]. Consequently, biomechanics has played an important role in understanding the disease and injury mechanisms. The examples include mechanobiology of tumor growth [20], low pressure hydrocephalus formation [14,27], relationship between loading and femur fracture patterns [91], formulation of traumatic injury criteria for the aorta [5], brain [56,64,82,90], neck [13,65,72,74], and other body parts/organs. The key feature of these studies is that they focus on generic properties and responses of the human body tissues and organs that represent population percentiles and age groups rather than individuals.

At the turn of XXI century it has been envisaged [15,35] that Computer-Integrated Surgery (CIS) systems could extend surgeons' ability to plan and carry out surgical in-

Handbook of Medical Image Computing and Computer Assisted Intervention
https://doi.org/10.1016/B978-0-12-816176-0.00044-2

terventions more accurately and with less trauma. CIS systems rely on biomechanical models to estimate complex deformation fields within the body organs. This requires transition from generic understanding of biomechanical phenomena in a human (or animal) organism to patient-specific solutions that address biomechanics of a particular individual. In practice, medical images acquired using different modalities are the key source of patient-specific information required for computational biomechanics models representing a particular individual. This includes patient-specific geometry, boundary conditions, loads acting on the body organs, and, to limited extent, estimates of the patient-specific material properties. Computational biomechanics models created using such image-derived information can then be applied to predict patient-specific biomechanical responses such as intraoperative deformations for image-guided surgery. Therefore, in this chapter, we view the roles of biomechanics and medical image analysis in computer assisted intervention as complementary and consider the following two synergistic aspects:

1) Image analysis informs biomechanics — we discuss generation of patient-specific computational models from medical images;

2) Biomechanics informs image analysis — we discuss application of computational biomechanics models in nonrigid image registration. We illustrate the key points of this chapter with two examples of intrapatient neuroimage registration and an example of whole body computed tomography (CT) image registration.

Soft tissues exhibit nonlinear stress–strain relationship (material nonlinearity) [31] and undergo large deformations (geometric nonlinearity). This is combined with nonlinear boundary conditions (through contact interactions of soft tissues with other organs, skull, vertebra, and ribs) and discontinuities induced by surgical dissection. Therefore, while noting the studies that rely on linear elasticity and assume infinitesimally small deformations of the body organs and tissues, we discuss only the solutions and examples that utilize and are compatible with methods of nonlinear computational biomechanics that account for geometric and material nonlinearity.

Following main-stream engineering practice, nonlinear finite element (FE) analysis [3,6] remains a method of choice for computational biomechanics models (Fig. 39.1(A)). However, the limitations of the FE analysis (for detailed discussion in the context of biomechanics, see [85,88]), including time consuming generation of computational grids and accuracy and stability deterioration when modeling continua undergoing large deformations, resulted in interest in application of meshless discretization in biomechanics [26,58,67]. Therefore, in our discussion of computational biomechanics in the context of medical image analysis, we include both finite element (Fig. 39.1(A)) and meshless (Fig. 39.1(B)) methods. The discussion in this chapter is, to large extent, based on our previous review of the methods for generating of patient-specific computational biomechanics models [85] and our previous research on computation of brain deformations for image-guided neurosurgery [48,52,58,67,71, 89,93].

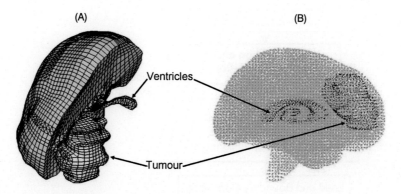

(A)   **(B)**

Ventricles

Tumour

Figure 39.1 Patient-specific computational models of the brain with tumor: (A) Finite element discretization. Adapted from Wittek et al. [87]; (B) Meshless discretization used in Miller et al. [67]. Adapted from Miller et al. [67]. Blue crosses indicate the integration points, and green circles indicate the support nodes.

39.2. Image analysis informs biomechanics: patient-specific computational biomechanics model from medical images[1]

39.2.1 Geometry extraction from medical images: segmentation

The finite element method utilizes a mesh of interconnected hexahedral and/or tetrahedral elements as a computational grid. To generate such grids, enclosed surface that defines the boundary of the analyzed continuum (human body organ) is needed [18,19]. Extracting such a surface from medical images necessitates segmentation (Fig. 39.2). To render patient-specific FE model generation truly applicable to large clinical studies, segmentation (and other stages of model development) would ideally be automated.

Automated image segmentation remains a challenging task due to the complexity of medical images. Consequently, there is no universal algorithm for segmenting every medical image. The techniques available for segmentation are specific to the application, the imaging modality and anatomic structure under consideration [85]. Examples of the techniques that have been used to automate the segmentation of anatomical structures include thresholding [73], region growing, watershed based methods [8], level set approach [80], and edge detection algorithms (such as the contour tracing using the concept of extended boundary [61], Canny edge detection [17], Sobel edge detection and Laplacian edge detection [25]).

To improve the segmentation of medical images, anatomical prior information can be used to help delineate anatomical structures. This often involves statistical methods and, recently, machine learning. Examples include the Expectation–Maximization (EM) segmentation algorithm that has been applied in the segmentation of various anatomical structures, such as the brain [55,76] and long bones (femur and tibia) [78].

---

[1] This section is based on [85].

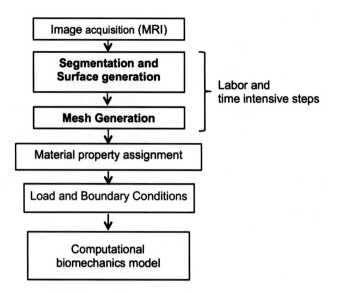

Figure 39.2 From a medical image to patient-specific computational biomechanics model using finite element method (neurosurgery simulation example). Image segmentation, surface generation and finite element mesh generation often require direct involvement of the analyst and, therefore, are labor intensive. Adapted from Wittek et al. [85].

39.2.2 Finite element mesh generation

Today 4-noded tetrahedra and 8-noded hexahedra are the most commonly used types of finite elements. Tetrahedral mesh generators are a standard feature of commonly used Computer-Aided Engineering CAE packages. They use well-established techniques and optimization schemes [21] including Delaunay triangulation method [2], modified-octree technique [63], and advancing front technique [62]. Tetrahedral mesh generators available in commercial CAE packages facilitate automated (with the required analyst's input, typically limited to the parameters determining the element size, mesh density, and element quality) discretization of objects analyzed in engineering applications.

As discussed in section *Geometry extraction from medical images: segmentation* when creating patient-specific biomechanical models, information about geometry of the analyzed continuum must be extracted (through image segmentation) from medical images. Attempts to address this challenge led to commercial (e.g., Mimics® biomedical.materialise.com/mimics) and open-source (e.g., Slicer3D http://www.slicer.org/) software packages that integrate image segmentation and meshing algorithms. Despite promising results, the quest for automated generation of patient-specific tetrahedral meshes from medical images is far from over as segmentation of images of organs with geometry/anatomy distorted by disease and pathology (such as tumors) still remains a challenge [85] and tends to rely on analyst experience and ability to manually outline boundaries of different anatomical structures in the images. Methods for tetrahedral mesh generation are still an active research topic, as indicated by the regularly held Tetrahedron Workshop on Grid Generation for Numerical Computations [34,75]. This includes challenges highlighted in the earlier studies on automated mesh generation, such as variation of element quality according to the mesh generation method employed [41] and element quality control [81,95].

Although numerous automated generators of tetrahedral meshes are available and in many studies such meshes have been used as a method of choice for patient-specific computational grids for biomechanical models, accuracy and robustness of the results obtained using 4-noded tetrahedral elements should not be taken for granted. This is because such elements exhibit artificial stiffening, known as volumetric locking, when applied in modeling of incompressible or nearly incompressible continua such as soft tissues [44]. In the presence of volumetric locking, the results are mesh-dependent. Unfortunately, this fact appears to be often overlooked in a peer reviewed process, leading to many papers with results potentially affected by volumetric locking being published. Two types of methods to address volumetric locking have been used: (1) Improved linear tetrahedral elements employing a range of countermeasures to prevent locking; (2) Higher-order and mixed-formulation elements. The former includes average nodal pressure (ANP) tetrahedral element [12] and its improvement by Joldes et al. [49] that provides much better results for nearly incompressible materials than the standard tetrahedral element with only small increase in the computational cost.

Second-order 10-noded and mixed-formulation (displacement–pressure) tetrahedral elements are readily available in commercial and open-source finite element codes. They are effective in dealing with volumetric locking although they do not eliminate locking completely [79]. However, their computation cost is at least four times higher than that of standard linear 4-noded tetrahedral elements. The cost difference is even higher for finite element analysis using explicit time stepping. This might be a limiting factor as many important applications, including image-guided surgery, require models consisting of over hundred thousand elements to be solved in-real time (in practice tens of seconds [36]) on commodity hardware.

Underintegrated (using the number of Gauss points lower than that required to accurately conduct spatial integration given the order of the interpolating polynomial in the element shape functions) hexahedral elements do not exhibit volumetric locking [24,49] and are by far the most efficient when explicit time integration schemes are used [89,90]. However, despite decades of intense effort, there are no automatic hexahedral meshing algorithms available which would work for complicated shapes routinely encountered when modeling human organs. Hexahedral meshing is particularly challenging when tumor and other pathologies affect the patient's anatomy [87]. The manual or semimanual [37] generation of a three-dimensional hexahedral mesh, although often a highly accurate method, requires significant time and operator effort. Consequently, mesh refinements and convergence studies are rarely reported for this type of mesh.

Various automated hexahedral meshing methods such as plastering [11], whisker weaving [83], centroidal Voronoi tesselation [43], and octree-based [45,63,94,95] techniques have been proposed. Although such methods can produce meshes of high quality, element size control remains a challenge. They require substantial level of technical competency and experience from an analyst constructing patient-specific hexahedral meshes — an important constraint in clinical applications where the users are medical professionals rather than finite element and computer science experts.

39.2.3 Image as a computational biomechanics model: meshless discretization

Mesh generation constitutes the bulk of the setup time for a problem (Fig. 39.2). This is especially true for anatomical hexahedral finite element mesh development. For example, Ateshian et al. [1] stated that the process of generating a patient-specific articular contact FE model from CT arthrography (CTA) image data takes over 100 hours for segmentation and mesh generation. Even when a good quality mesh is created, the FE solution method often fails in the case of large deformations, due to problems such as element inversion. Tissue dissection simulation is also difficult, as small and poorly shaped elements are created during the process of rupture simulation [84].

Meshless methods of computational mechanics have been recognized as one possible solution for some of these challenges [26,42,47,48,53,92]. In meshless methods, the field variable interpolation is constructed over an unstructured "cloud" of nodes scattered within the problem domain and on its boundary with the spatial integration conducted over a grid of background integration cells that do not need to conform to the boundary of the analyzed continuum [42]. Such clouds and grids are incomparably easier to generate than finite element meshes.

To fully utilize the merits of meshless discretization and open path for automated generation of patient-specific models from medical images, we require an approach that would enable us to distinguish between different tissue types depicted in the image while avoiding segmentation. Such an approach has been proposed in the previous studies conducted at The University of Western Australia's Intelligent Systems for Medicine Laboratory in which segmentation was replaced by fuzzy tissue classification (Fig. 39.3, right column). In fuzzy tissue classification, surfaces are not generated as the material properties are assigned based on the image intensity directly at the integration points (Fig. 39.3). The process is described in detail in Zhang et al. [93], Li et al. [57] and Li et al. [58]. Although fuzzy tissue classification may slightly impede the accuracy of stress computation, the verification conducted in Zhang et al. [93] showed that the overall accuracy is little affected, with the differences between the results of meshless and finite element computations of the brain deformations of up to only 0.6 mm. As the intraoperative MRI resolution is typically of an order of 1 mm × 1 mm × 2.5 mm, these differences can be regarded as negligible for practical purposes. Most importantly

(A)   (B)

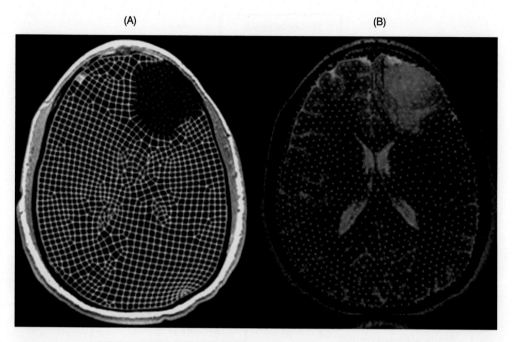

Figure 39.3 (A) Patient-specific finite element model of the brain with the geometry of the parenchyma, tumor (red), and ventricle (blue) obtained through the MRI segmentation. Note clearly defined boundaries between the parenchyma, tumor, and ventricles. (B) The meshless model of the same brain created using fuzzy tissue classification without the surfaces (boundaries) explicitly separating the parenchyma, tumor, and ventricles. The fuzzy membership functions, that describe the probability of a given integration point to belong to the parenchyma, tumor, and ventricles, are indicated by the level of red for tumor and blue for ventricles. The support nodes are shown as green circles. Adapted from Zhang et al. [93].

the meshless computational grids with the material properties assigned using fuzzy tissue classification become more robust and the entire patient-specific modeling workflow is simplified and much easier to automate (Figs. 39.3 and 39.4).

Meshless methods offer a prospect of automated generation of patient-specific computational grids directly from medical images and their robustness in handling of large deformations is superior to the finite element method [7,48,59,60]. However, important deficiencies of meshless methods, that preclude their use by a nonspecialist in the clinical environment, have been highlighted in the literature:

- Inability to create shape functions for arbitrary grids. Only "admissible node distributions" can be used [22]. The user must have sufficient knowledge and experience to understand what constitutes an "admissible" grid, and what modifications are necessary if the grid is not "admissible".
- Lack of theoretical error bounds on numerical integration due to the nonpolynomial nature of integrands. Without rigorously established error bounds, the solution

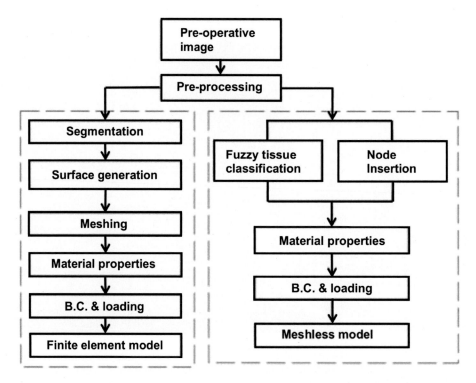

Figure 39.4 Comparison of the conventional construction of patient-specific computational biomechanics model using image segmentation for defining organ geometry and finite element discretization (left hand-side column) and the automated process that uses fuzzy tissue classification and meshless discretization (right hand-side column). "B.C." stands for the boundary conditions. Adapted from Zhang et al. [93].

methods cannot be used in sensitive applications like computational biomechanics for medicine.

Recent developments in meshless algorithms [48], to large extent, have eliminated these deficiencies and made meshless methods even more suitable for patient–specific computational biomechanics applications. They include modified moving least squares approximation which can handle almost arbitrary nodal distributions without loss of accuracy [22], algorithms for efficient and accurate imposition of prescribed displacements on the boundary (a problem referred to in computational mechanics as essential boundary conditions imposition) [51] and adaptive integration that distributes the integration points to achieve the accuracy specified by the user [54]. Although these developments do not eliminate the need for general knowledge of computational mechanics when applying meshless methods in creation of patient–specific computational biomechanics models, they make it possible to use such methods as tools without the requirement for expertise in the specific meshless algorithms.

39.3. Biomechanics informs image analysis: computational biomechanics model as image registration tool

In this section we focus on application of patient-specific computational biomechanics in intrapatient nonrigid registration (that accounts for organ deformations) of medical images. Examples include image-guided surgery, where the high-quality image acquired before the surgery (preoperative image) needs to be aligned (registered) to lower quality image acquired during surgery (intraoperative image), and diagnosis where the images of the abdominal and other organs acquired for different body posture of the patient need to be compared.

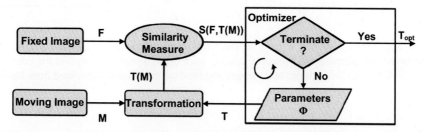

Figure 39.5 Key components of a general image-based registration process. Modified from Mostayed et al. [71].

Image registration has been a subject of extensive research effort and numerous publications. Entering a search term "medical + image + registration" in Web of Science database search engine returns over 2,400 journal articles, books, and book chapters published in years 1989–2019. Other chapters of this book discuss image registration in great detail. Traditionally image registration has relied solely on image processing methods. We refer to such methods as image-based. The basic components of an image-based registration algorithm are shown in Fig. 39.5. The moving image M (preoperative image in image-guided surgery) is transformed using the selected transformation T to obtain the transformed image T(M). The transformed image is then compared with the fixed image F (intraoperative image in image-guided surgery) using a chosen similarity metric S. Then an optimizer is applied to find the parameters of the transform that minimizes the difference between the moving and fixed image in the context of the selected similarity metric. The parameters Φ of the transform are iterated within the optimization loop to achieve the best agreement between the fixed and moving images for the selected metric S. This alone, however, may not ensure plausibility of the predicted deformations as the principles of nonlinear biomechanics governing the deformation behavior of the organ depicted in the image are not taken into account.

The information about the organ deformations/state during surgery acquired using various technologies/modalities is often limited. For instance, the quality of the images acquired during surgery (intraoperative images) may be inferior to that of the images

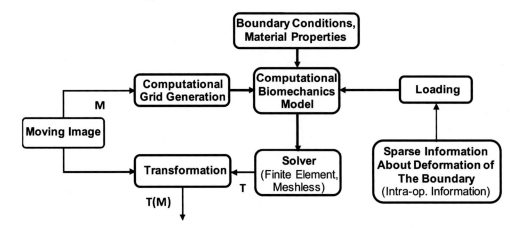

Figure 39.6 Key components of a general biomechanics-based registration process. In this chapter we discuss both finite element and meshless solvers. "Intra-op. Information" indicates the information obtained from intraoperative images (the images acquired during surgery). Modified from Mostayed et al. [71].

acquired before the surgery (preoperative images), the intraoperative images may be acquired only for part of the organ or infrequently due to strict time constraints during surgery, geometry of the organ depicted in the image can be strongly affected by surgical dissection, tumor resection, the moving and fixed image may be acquired in different modalities (preoperative image using MR and intraoperative using CT or ultrasound). These limitations and constraints may pose a challenge for image-based registration methods as determining parameters for the transform that warps the moving image becomes a formidable task if the differences between the images are large and the quality of one of the images is poor.

Unlike the image-based registration, biomechanics-based registration methods do not require a fixed (intraoperative) image to update the moving (preoperative) image, as the transform (deformation field) is computed using a patient-specific computational biomechanics model (see Fig. 39.6). Rather than relying on optimization as in image-based methods, the registration accuracy depends on predictive power of the model. The information about the geometry of anatomical features of interest is extracted from the moving image to create a computational grid for the model. This is completed by defining the boundary conditions (e.g., contacts) and material properties for the tissues depicted in the image. The loading is typically defined from sparse information available in the fixed image (such as deformation of the organ surface due to surgery). A solver is then applied to compute the transform (deformation field) which is then applied to warp the moving image. As soft tissues exhibit nonlinear stress–strain relationship (material nonlinearity) [31] and the body organs tend to undergo large deformations (geometric nonlinearity) combined with discontinuities induced by surgical dissection, solving the governing equations and computing the transform requires application of methods of nonlinear computational mechanics — in practice, nonlinear finite element and meshless solvers (Fig. 39.6). We discussed generating patient-specific computational models for such solvers in the previous section *Image analysis informs biomechanics: patient-specific computational biomechanics models from medical images.*

In this section, we discuss biomechanics-based registration using the examples of neuroimage registration in craniotomy induced brain shift and whole-body computed tomography (CT) registration. We focus on formulation of the problem and robust algorithms for computing the transform (deformation field).

39.3.1 Biomechanics-based image registration: problem formulation

As explained in Fig. 39.6, only sparse information is required to define the loading that drives the deformation computation in biomechanics-based intrapatient image registration. Loading, boundary conditions, and material properties for patient-specific models used in such computations have been discussed in detail in our previous publications [69,70,85,86]. Following this previous work, we advocate defining the load through the prescribed displacement of the organ surface and formulating the problem of computing the organ deformations for image registration (in particular for image-guided surgery) in the following way:

- Known: initial position of the entire domain (as imaged by magnetic resonance MR or computed tomography CT) and current position of some parts of the boundary, e.g., the displacement of the exposed (due to craniotomy) surface of the brain (see Fig. 39.6 and Fig. 39.7). No surface tractions are applied;
- Unknown: deformation field within the domain (the brain), in particular, current position of the tumor, other pathologies, and critical healthy areas.

Problems of this type are referred to as *Dirichlet-type problems* [69] or problems with *Dirichlet boundary conditions* [23]. We showed that for Dirichlet-type problems, the predicted deformations are only very weakly sensitive to the variation in mechanical properties of the analyzed continua [86]. This facilitates accurate patient-specific computational biomechanics modeling without patient-specific information about the tissue mechanical properties. Despite an on-going progress and research effort (for most up-to-date review see [9,10]), that includes ultrasound [28,46], magnetic resonance (MR) [38,40], and optical elastography, there is no reliable noninvasive method to determine constitutive properties of human soft tissues in vivo. Nevertheless, our previous results [32,57,58,71] discussed in the next section, as well as the results by other research groups [16,29], indicate that for medical image registration formulated as a Dirichlet-type problem of computational mechanics, clinically relevant results can be obtained even without the knowledge of patient-specific material properties of soft tissues (see Fig. 39.10).

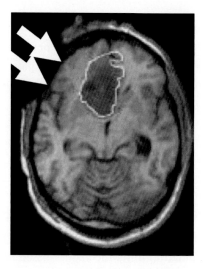

Figure 39.7 Schematic representation of the load defined by prescribing the displacements (white arrow lines) on the organ surface (in the craniotomy area in this figure).

39.3.2 Biomechanics-based image registration: examples

39.3.2.1 Neuroimage registration[2]

As the brain undergoes deformation (known as brain shift) following the craniotomy, intraoperative localization of the tumor boundaries is a well-recognized challenge in neurosurgery. Although such localization in principle can be achieved using intraoperative imaging, acquiring intraoperative MRI is often cumbersome and intraoperative MR scanners are expensive. Hardware limitations of these scanners make it infeasible to achieve frequent whole brain imaging during surgery. An alternative approach is to acquire rapid sparse intraoperative data and use it to predict the deformation for the whole brain. An example is the study by Mostayed et al. [71] in which intrapatient registration of high-quality MRI to intraoperative brain geometry was performed using biomechanics-based and image-based (BSpline interpolation — implementation in 3DSlicer, www.slicer.org, open source software platform for medical image informatics, image processing and three-dimensional visualization [30]) methods for 13 retrospective image-set of patients undergoing glioma resection.

In Mostayed et al. [71], the biomechanics-based registration was performed using fully nonlinear (that accounts for both geometric and material nonlinearity) total-Lagrangian explicit dynamics finite element algorithm previously developed and verified by our research group for computation of soft continua deformations [50,68]. The algorithm was also implemented on a Graphics Processing Unit (GPU) for real-time

---

[2] This section is based on [71].

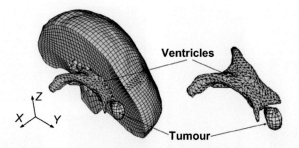

Figure 39.8 Example of the patient-specific finite element mesh created from the segmented preoperative MRI used by Mostayed et al. [71]. Adapted from Mostayed et al. [71].

computations [52], so that the solution of the entire model takes less than 10 s. The patient-specific finite element computational grids (finite element meshes) were created through the image segmentation (Fig. 39.8). Following the formulation of image registration as a Dirichlet-type problem of computational mechanics, the loading was defined by prescribing the displacement in on the brain surface in the craniotomy area. Despite using this very sparse intraoperative information and without patient-specific knowledge of the material properties (Young's modulus of 3000 Pa was used for the parenchyma), the registration accuracy was at least as high as that using BSpline algorithm that used the information from the entire intraoperative image (Figs. 39.9 and 39.10).

39.3.2.2 Magnetic resonance (MR) image registration for intracranial electrode localization for epilepsy treatment[3]

Intracranial EEG (iEEG) is the clinical gold standard for functional localization of the seizure onset zones (SOZ); invasive electrodes are implanted and monitored for several days, and then removed during a second surgery when the resection is performed [4] (Fig. 39.11). Placement of electrodes must be verified to enable clinicians to associate measured data with preoperative images of cortical structures. Electrode grids in the intracranial space, and the body's inflammatory response to the craniotomy, displace and deform the brain from the configuration observed in presurgical MR imaging. This deformation (brain shift) must be accounted for to ensure accurate alignment of electrode placements and correct clinical evaluation of invasive data. This challenging problem has been addressed in the previous studies conducted at the Intelligent Systems for Medicine Laboratory, The University of Western Australia [48,66,77] using the biomechanics-based registration process summarized in Fig. 39.6. These studies employed patient-specific computational biomechanics models to compute the deformation field within the brain and then apply the computed deformations to register

---

[3] This section includes the results from [48].

Figure 39.9 Results for 12 image-sets from Mostayed et al. [71]: qualitative comparison of the registration results obtained using computational biomechanics model (nonlinear finite element analysis) and BSpline algorithm. The figure shows the Canny edges (detected using Canny edge filter [17]) in the intraoperative and registered images. Red color indicates the nonoverlapping pixels of the intraoperative slice and blue color indicates the nonoverlapping pixels of the preoperative slice. Green color indicates the overlapping pixels. The number in each image denotes a particular neurosurgery patient. For each patient (image-set), the left-hand-side image shows edges for the biomechanics-based warping and the right-hand-side image shows edges for the BSpline-based registration. Adapted from Mostayed et al. [71].

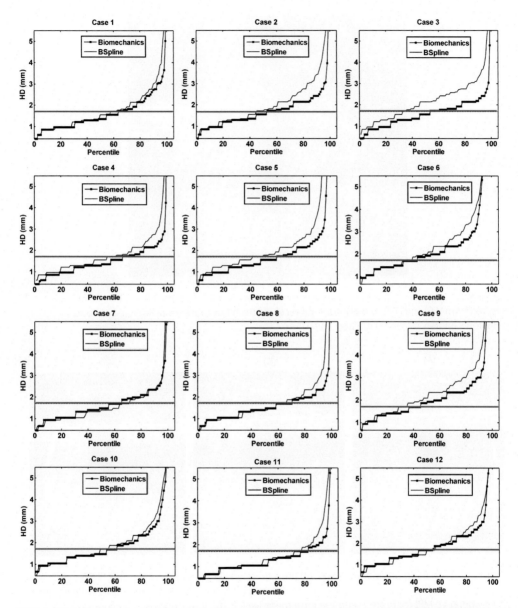

Figure 39.10 Results for 12 image-sets (cases) from Mostayed et al. [71]: quantitative comparison of the registration results obtained using computational biomechanics model (nonlinear finite element analysis) and BSpline algorithm. Each plot shows the Hausdorff distance [39] between the intraoperative and registered preoperative images against the percentile of Canny edges (detected using Canny edge filter [17]) for axial slices. The horizontal line is the 1.7 mm mark which is the two-times in-plane resolution of the intraoperative images used by Mostayed et al. [71]. Note that the accuracy of biomechanics-based registration is at least as high as that of the image-based (BSpline) registration. For detailed discussion of application of the Hausdorff distance as an image similarity metric, see Garlapati et al. [33]. Adapted from Mostayed et al. [71].

Figure 39.11 Brain cortical surface exposed by the craniotomy with intracranial EEG (iEEG) implanted. Adapted from [66] and [77]. The photograph received from Computational Radiology Laboratory (CRL) at Boston Children's Hospital (Boston, MA, USA).

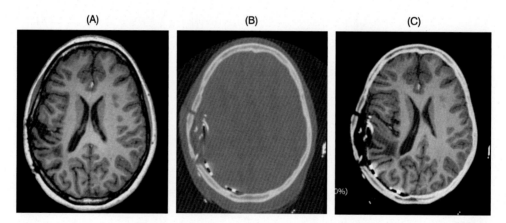

Figure 39.12 (A) Brain preoperative MRI; (B) Intraoperative CT with intracranial EEG (iEEG) electrodes implanted. The electrodes, that define the deformed brain surface, are clearly visible (white points); (C) Preoperative MRI registered onto the intraoperative CT. The figure shows 2D sections of 3D image volumes. Adapted from Joldes et al. [48].

(warp) the preoperative MRI to the intraoperative (after implanting the iEEG electrodes) brain geometry [48] (Fig. 39.12). The patient-specific finite element mesh was constructed from the high resolution preoperative MRI. The load was defined as imposed displacements (determined from the intraoperative CT).

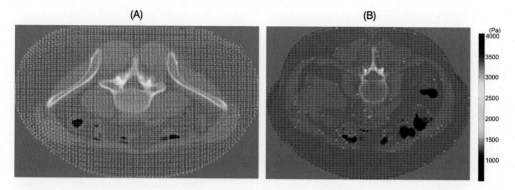

Figure 39.13 Example of meshless discretization used by Li et al. [58] when creating patient-specific computational biomechanics models. (A) Distribution of support nodes and integration points on a selected transverse section. The blue crosses and yellow circles represent the support nodes and integration points, respectively. (B) Assignment of the material properties using fuzzy tissue classification. The shear modulus magnitude is represented by a color scale. Note that the integration points belonging to the same tissue type (indicated by the same color) match the areas where the image intensity is similar. Only local tissue misclassification is present. This can be seen as a local variation in the integration point color (where the adjacent integration points have different color and, consequently, different shear modulus assigned) at the boundaries between different tissue types. Eight tissue types are distinguished: Type 1, 2 and 3 is for lungs and other gas-filled spaces (such as abdominal cavity), Type 4 — fat, Type 5 – muscles and abdominal organs, Type 6 — stomach and intestines, and Type 7 and 8 — bones (treated as rigid). Adapted from Li et al. [58].

39.3.2.3 *Whole-body computed tomography (CT) image registration*[4]

The study using biomechanics-based whole-body CT registration conducted by Li et al. [58] is an example of application of fuzzy tissue classification and meshless discretization to construct patient-specific computational biomechanics models in a semiautomated fashion (Fig. 39.13). The previously verified Meshless Total Lagrangian Explicit Dynamics algorithm [42] was used for solving the governing equations of continuum mechanics. The loading was defined by prescribing the displacements of the vertebrae extracted from the moving and fixed images. Despite using this very sparse information to define the load for computational biomechanics models and distinguishing only eight tissue types when constructing the models (Fig. 39.13(B)), the results by Li et al. [58] indicate successful registration of most image features (Figs. 39.14 and 39.15).

39.4. Discussion

The review and examples presented in this chapter point to complementary roles of image analysis and computational biomechanics. Medical images are in practice the pri-

---

[4] This section is based on [58].

Moving/Fixed Images   Registered/Fixed Image

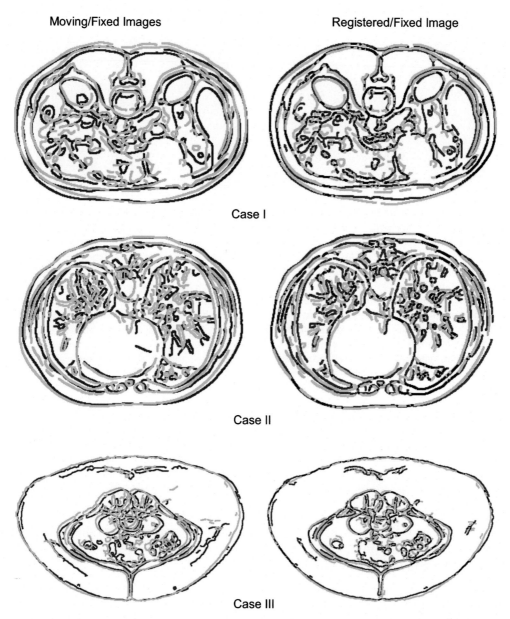

Case I

Case II

Case III

Figure 39.14 Results from Li et al. [58]: qualitative evaluation of biomechanics-based whole body CT image registration. The figure shows the Canny edges (detected using Canny edge filter [17]) in the moving, target (fixed) and registered (i.e., moving image warped using the deformation computed by biomechanical models) images: (Left-hand-side column) Comparison of the edges in the moving and fixed image; (Right-hand-side column) Comparison of the edges in the registered and target images. Edges in the moving image are indicated by red color; edges in target image — by green; and the edges in the registered image — by pink. Good overlap (with some local misalignment) between the edges in registered and target images is evident. Adapted from Li et al. [58].

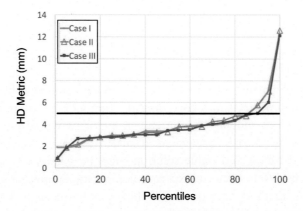

Figure 39.15 The percentile edge-based Hausdorff Distance (HD) metric for three cases/image-sets analyzed in Li et al. [58]. Around 85–95% of edges are accurately registered using the patient-specific nonlinear meshless models created by Li et al. [58]. The percentile HD metric were measured in transverse sections for three image sets. The horizontal line is the 5.0 mm mark which is the two-times in-plane resolution of the intraoperative images used in Li et al. [58]. For detailed discussion of application of the Hausdorff distance as an image similarity metric, see Garlapati el. [33]. Figure created from the results (figures) published in Li et al. [58].

mary (if not the only) source of patient-specific information about the organ geometry and loading acting on the organs when creating computational biomechanics models for surgical simulation. Such models, on the other hand, can inform image analysis by computing deformation fields within organs during surgery. The computed deformations are then used to register (warp) high quality preoperative images to the intraoperative organ geometry in a process known as biomechanics-based image registration. Unlike image-based registration that relies solely on image processing techniques, the biomechanics-based registration using appropriate nonlinear formulation of computational mechanics, that accounts for both material (nonlinear stress–strain relationship) and geometric (large deformations of soft tissues) nonlinearity, not only ensures plausibility of the predicted deformations but also does not require an intraoperative image. It should be noted that this requires also application of hyperelastic (or hyperviscoelastic) material models consistent with such formulation. Some authors choose linear elastic material model with geometrically nonlinear solution procedure. This, however, may lead to erroneous results in the presence of large strain or element rotation [3].

As shown in the examples discussed in sections *Neuroimage registration, Magnetic Resonance (MR) image registration for intracranial electrode localization for epilepsy* treatment, and *Whole body Computed Tomography (CT) image registration* for image registration formulated as a Dirichlet-type problem of computational mechanics (where the loading is defined by prescribing deformations on the boundary of the analyzed object), sparse information about deformations of the organ surface and neo-Hookean material model (the simplest hyperelastic model) are sufficient to facilitate biomechanics-based registration with the accuracy at least as high as that of the image-based registration using the intraoperative image. It is necessary to note that this conclusion is limited to intrapatient image registration as no examples of interpatient registration were discussed in this chapter.

Although formally many different methods can be used to solve the equations of nonlinear continuum mechanics governing the behavior of computational biomechanics models, for such models to be useful in a clinical workflow, patient-specific computational grids need to be generated in automated/semiautomated mode from medical images and robust and stable solution must be guaranteed without the requirement for the user to become an expert in computational mechanics. Traditionally used finite element method does not fulfill these conditions as it necessitates image segmentation to define closed surfaces for creation of patient-specific finite element meshes. Construction of such meshes is time consuming and requires involvement of an experienced analyst and the solution stability and accuracy deteriorate when the analyzed organ undergoes large deformations and fragmentation (discontinuities) due to surgical dissection. Therefore, we recommend meshless methods of computational mechanics that utilize grids in a form of clouds of points (nodes). As shown in the example of biomechanics-based whole body image registration discussed in section *Whole body Computed Tomography (CT) image registration* such methods facilitate generation of patient-specific computational biomechanics models directly from medical image without any need for image segmentation. Recent developments in adaptive integration [54] and shape functions [22] for meshless discretization reduce the requirements for expert knowledge in computational mechanics when creating meshless computational grids as the solution accuracy is guaranteed for almost arbitrary node placement.

Acknowledgments

The funding from the Australian Government through the Australian Research Council ARC (Discovery Project Grants DP160100714, DP1092893, and DP120100402) and National Health and Medical Research Council NHMRC (Project Grants APP1006031 and APP1144519) is gratefully acknowledged.

References

[1] G.A. Ateshian, C.R. Henak, J.A. Weiss, Toward patient-specific articular contact mechanics, Journal of Biomechanics 48 (2015) 779–786.

[2] T.J. Baker, Automatic mesh generation for complex three-dimensional regions using a constrained Delaunay triangulation, Engineering Computations 5 (1989) 161–175.

[3] K.-J. Bathe, Finite Element Procedures, Prentice-Hall, Upper Saddle River, ISBN 0-13-301458-4, 1996.

[4] J.A. Bauman, E. Feoli, P. Romanelli, W.K. Doyle, O. Devinsky, H.L. Weiner, Multistage epilepsy surgery: safety, efficacy, and utility of a novel approach in pediatric extratemporal epilepsy, Neurosurgery 56 (2005) 318–334.

[5] A. Belwadi, K.H. Yang, Mechanism of aortic injury in nearside left lateral automotive crashes: a finite element accident injury reconstruction approach, in: Proc. of 2011 IRCOBI Conference on the Biomechanics of Impact, International Research Council on the Biomechanics of Injury, Krakow, Poland, 14 September 2011, 2011, pp. 169–180.

[6] T. Belytschko, W.K. Liu, B. Moran, K. Elkhodary, Nonlinear Finite Elements for Continua and Structures, 2nd edition, Wiley, Chichester, 2014.

[7] T. Belytschko, T. Rabczuk, A. Huerta, S. Fernández-Méndez, Meshfree methods, in: E. Stein, R. Borst, T.J. Hughes (Eds.), Encyclopedia of Computational Mechanics, Wiley, Chichester, 2004.

[8] S. Beucher, F. Meyer, The morphological approach to segmentation: the watershed transformation, in: E.R. Dougherty (Ed.), Mathematical Morphology in Image Processing, Dekker, New York, 1993, pp. 433–482.

[9] L.E. Bilston, Brain tissue mechanical properties, in: K. Miller (Ed.), Biomechanics of the Brain, 1st edition, Springer, 2011, pp. 69–89.

[10] L.E. Bilston, Brain tissue mechanical properties, in: K. Miller (Ed.), Biomechanics of the Brain, 2nd edition, Springer, ISBN 978-3-030-04995-9, 2019, in press.

[11] T.D. Blacker, R.J. Meyers, Seams and wedges in plastering: a 3-D hexahedral mesh generation algorithm, Engineering with Computers 9 (1993) 83–93.

[12] J. Bonet, A.J. Burton, A simple average nodal pressure tetrahedral element for incompressible and nearly incompressible dynamic explicit applications, Communications in Numerical Methods in Engineering 14 (1998) 437–449.

[13] O. Bostrom, M.Y. Svensson, B. Aldman, H.A. Hansson, Y. Haland, P. Lovsund, T. Seeman, A. Suneson, A. Saljo, T. Ortengren, A new neck injury criterion candidate - based on injury findings in the cervical spinal ganglia after experimental neck extension trauma, in: Proc. of 1996 International IRCOBI Conference on the Biomechanics of Impact. International Research Council on the Biomechanics of Injury, Dublin, Ireland, 1996, pp. 123–136.

[14] S. Bottan, D. Poulikakos, V. Kurtcuoglu, Phantom model of physiologic intracranial pressure and cerebrospinal fluid dynamics, IEEE Transactions on Biomedical Engineering 59 (2012) 1532–1538.

[15] R. Bucholz, W. MacNeil, L. McDurmont, The operating room of the future, Clinical Neurosurgery 51 (2004) 228–237.

[16] M. Bucki, C. Lobos, Y. Payan, A fast and robust patient specific finite element mesh registration technique: application to 60 clinical cases, Medical Image Analysis 14 (2010) 303–317.

[17] J. Canny, A computational approach to edge detection, IEEE Transactions on Pattern Analysis and Machine Intelligence PAMI-8 (1986) 679–698.

[18] G.F. Carey, Computational Grids: Generations, Adaptation & Solution Strategies, CRC Press, 1997.

[19] J.C. Cavendish, D.A. Field, W.H. Frey, An approach to automatic 3-dimensional finite-element mesh generation, International Journal for Numerical Methods in Engineering 21 (1985) 329–347.

[20] P.K. Chaudhuri, B.C. Low, C.T. Lim, Mechanobiology of tumor growth, Chemical Reviews 118 (2018) 6499–6515.

[21] W.Y. Choi, D.Y. Kwak, I.H. Son, Y.T. Im, Tetrahedral mesh generation based on advancing front technique and optimization scheme, International Journal for Numerical Methods in Engineering 58 (2003) 1857–1872.

[22] H.A. Chowdhury, A. Wittek, K. Miller, G.R. Joldes, An element free Galerkin method based on the modified moving least squares approximation, Journal of Scientific Computing 71 (2017) 1197–1211.

[23] P.G. Ciarlet, Mathematical Elasticity, North Holland, The Netherlands, 1988.

[24] Dassault Systèmes Simulia Corporation, ABAQUS Online Documentation, 2014.

[25] L.S. Davis, A survey of edge detection techniques, Computer Graphics and Image Processing 4 (1975) 248–270.

[26] M. Doblare, E. Cueto, B. Calvo, M.A. Martinez, J.M. Garcia, J. Cegonino, On the employ of meshless methods in biomechanics, Computer Methods in Applied Mechanics and Engineering 194 (2005) 801–821.

[27] T. Dutta-Roy, A. Wittek, K. Miller, Biomechanical modelling of normal pressure hydrocephalus, Journal of Biomechanics 41 (2008) 2263–2271.

[28] M. Ertl, N. Raasch, G. Hammel, K. Harter, C. Lang, Transtemporal investigation of brain parenchyma elasticity using 2-d shear wave elastography: definition of age-matched normal values, Ultrasound in Medicine & Biology 44 (2018) 78–84.

[29] X. Fan, D.W. Roberts, T.J. Schaewe, S. Ji, L.H. Holton, D.A. Simon, K.D. Paulsen, Intraoperative image updating for brain shift following dural opening, Journal of Neurosurgery 126 (2017) 1924–1933.

[30] A. Fedorov, R. Beichel, J. Kalpathy-Cramer, J. Finet, J.-C. Fillion-Robin, S. Pujol, C. Bauer, D. Jennings, F. Fennessy, M. Sonka, J. Buatti, S. Aylward, J.V. Miller, S. Pieper, R. Kikinis, 3D Slicer as an image computing platform for the quantitative imaging network, Magnetic Resonance Imaging 30 (2012) 1323–1341.

[31] Y.C. Fung, Biomechanics. Mechanical Properties of Living Tissues, second ed., Springer-Verlag, New York, 1993, pp. 392–426.

[32] R.R. Garlapati, A. Roy, G.R. Joldes, A. Wittek, A. Mostayed, B. Doyle, S.K. Warfield, R. Kikinis, N. Knuckey, S. Bunt, K. Miller, More accurate neuronavigation data provided by biomechanical modeling instead of rigid registration, Journal of Neurosurgery 120 (2014) 1477–1483.

[33] R.R. Garlapati, A. Mostayed, G.R. Joldes, A. Wittek, B. Doyle, K. Miller, Towards measuring neuroimage misalignment, Computers in Biology and Medicine 64 (2015) 12–23.

[34] C. Geuzaine, J.-F. Renacle, Fifth Workshop on Grid Generation for Numerical Computations, Liege, Belgium, 2016, http://tetrahedron.montefiore.ulg.ac.be/.

[35] S. Graham, R. Taylor, M. Vannier, Needs assessment for computer-integrated surgery systems, in: S.L. Delp, A.M. DiGoia, B. Jaramaz (Eds.), Medical Image Computing and Computer-Assisted Intervention MICCAI 2000, in: Lecture Notes in Computer Science, vol. 1935, Springer, Berlin Heidelberg, ISBN 978-3-540-41189-5, 2000, pp. 931–939.

[36] W.E.L. Grimson, M.E. Leventon, G. Ettinger, A. Chabrerie, F. Ozlen, S. Nakajima, H. Atsumi, R. Kikinis, P. Black, Clinical experience with a high precision image-guided neurosurgery system, in: W.M. Wells, A. Colchester, S. Delp (Eds.), Medical Image Computing and Computer-Assisted Intervention – MICCAI'98, MICCAI 1998, in: Lecture Notes in Computer Science, vol. 1496, Springer, Berlin, Heidelberg, 1998, pp. 63–73.

[37] N.M. Grosland, K.H. Shivanna, V.A. Magnotta, N.A. Kallemeyn, N.A. DeVries, S.C. Tadepalli, C. Lisle, IA-FEMesh: an open-source, interactive, multiblock approach to anatomic finite element model development, Computer Methods and Programs in Biomedicine 94 (2009) 96–107.

[38] J. Guo, S. Hirsch, A. Fehlner, S. Papazoglou, M. Scheel, J. Braun, I. Sack, Towards an elastographic atlas of brain anatomy, PLoS ONE 8 (2013) e71807-1-10.

[39] F. Hausdorff, Set Theory, Chelsea Publishing Company, New York, 1957.

[40] L.V. Hiscox, C.L. Johnson, E. Barnhill, M.D.J. McGarry, J. Huston, E.J. van Beek, J.M. Starr, N. Roberts, Magnetic resonance elastography (MRE) of the human brain: technique, findings and clinical applications, Physics in Medicine and Biology 61 (2016) R401–R437.

[41] K. Ho-Le, Finite element mesh generation methods: a review and classification, Computer-Aided Design 20 (1988) 27–38.

[42] A. Horton, A. Wittek, G.R. Joldes, K. Miller, A meshless total Lagrangian explicit dynamics algorithm for surgical simulation, International Journal for Numerical Methods in Biomedical Engineering 26 (2010) 977–998.

[43] K. Hu, Y.J. Zhang, Centroidal Voronoi tessellation based polycube construction for adaptive all-hexahedral mesh generation, Computer Methods in Applied Mechanics and Engineering 305 (2016) 405–421.

[44] T.J.R. Hughes, The Finite Element Method: Linear Static and Dynamic Finite Element Analysis, Dover Publications, Mineola, 2000.

[45] Y. Ito, A.M. Shih, B.K. Soni, Octree-based reasonable-quality hexahedral mesh generation using a new set of refinement templates, International Journal for Numerical Methods in Engineering 77 (2009) 1809–1833.

[46] Y. Jiang, G. Li, L.-X. Qian, S. Liang, M. Destrade, Y. Cao, Measuring the linear and nonlinear elastic properties of brain tissue with shear waves and inverse analysis, Biomechanics and Modeling in Mechanobiology 14 (2015) 1119–1128.

[47] X. Jin, G.R. Joldes, K. Miller, K.H. Yang, A. Wittek, Meshless algorithm for soft tissue cutting in surgical simulation, Computer Methods in Biomechanics and Biomedical Engineering 17 (2014) 800–817.

[48] G. Joldes, G. Bourantas, B. Zwick, H. Chowdhury, A. Wittek, S. Agrawal, K. Mountris, D. Hyde, S.K. Warfield, K. Miller, Suite of meshless algorithms for accurate computation of soft tissue deformation for surgical simulation, Medical Image Analysis 56 (2019) 152–171.

[49] G.R. Joldes, A. Wittek, K. Miller, Non-locking tetrahedral finite element for surgical simulation, Communications in Numerical Methods in Engineering 25 (2009) 827–836.

[50] G.R. Joldes, A. Wittek, K. Miller, Suite of finite element algorithms for accurate computation of soft tissue deformation for surgical simulation, Medical Image Analysis 13 (2009) 912–919.

[51] G.R. Joldes, H. Chowdhury, A. Wittek, K. Miller, A new method for essential boundary conditions imposition in explicit meshless methods, Engineering Analysis with Boundary Elements 80 (2017) 94–104.

[52] G.R. Joldes, A. Wittek, K. Miller, Real-time nonlinear finite element computations on GPU - application to neurosurgical simulation, Computer Methods in Applied Mechanics and Engineering 199 (2010) 3305–3314.

[53] G.R. Joldes, A. Wittek, K. Miller, Stable time step estimates for mesh-free particle methods, International Journal for Numerical Methods in Engineering 91 (2012) 450–456.

[54] G.R. Joldes, A. Wittek, K. Miller, Adaptive numerical integration in element-free Galerkin methods for elliptic boundary value problems, Engineering Analysis with Boundary Elements 51 (2015) 52–63.

[55] T. Kapur, W.E.L. Grimson, W.M. Wells III, R. Kikinis, Segmentation of brain tissue from magnetic resonance images, Medical Image Analysis 1 (1996) 109–127.

[56] T. Kikuchi, A. Togawa, D. Murakami, K. Tatsu, C. Pal, T. Okabe, A study of brain injury mechanisms in vehicle crashes, in: 24th Enhanced Safety of Vehicles ESV Conference, Gothenburg, Sweden, 2015.

[57] M. Li, K. Miller, G.R. Joldes, B. Doyle, R.R. Garlapati, R. Kikinis, A. Wittek, Patient-specific biomechanical model as whole-body CT image registration tool, Medical Image Analysis 22 (2015) 22–34.

[58] M. Li, K. Miller, G.R. Joldes, R. Kikinis, A. Wittek, Biomechanical model for computing deformations for whole-body image registration: a meshless approach, International Journal for Numerical Methods in Biomedical Engineering 32 (2016), e02771-02771-02718.

[59] S. Li, W.K. Liu, Meshfree Particle Methods, Springer-Verlag, Berlin Heidelberg, ISBN 978-3-540-22256-9, 2004.

[60] G.R. Liu, Mesh Free Methods: Moving Beyond the Finite Element Method, CRC Press, Boca Raton, 2003.

[61] Y.-T. Liow, A contour tracing algorithm that preserves common boundaries between regions, CVGIP. Image Understanding 53 (1991) 313–321.

[62] R. Löhner, Progress in grid generation via the advancing front technique, Engineering Computations 12 (1996) 186–210.

[63] L. Marechal, Advances in octree-based all-hexahedral mesh generation: handling sharp features, in: B. Clark (Ed.), Proc. of the 18th International Meshing Roundtable, Springer, Berlin Heidelberg, 2009, pp. 65–84.

[64] S.S. Margulies, L.E. Thibault, An analytical model of traumatic diffuse brain injury, Journal of Biomechanical Engineering – Transactions of the ASME 111 (1989) 241–249.

[65] T. Matsushita, N. Yamazaki, T. Sato, K. Hirabayashi, Biomechanical and medical investigations of human neck injury in low velocity collisions, Neuro-Orthopaedics 21 (1997) 27–45.

[66] L.P.M. Menagé, Computer Simulation of Brain Deformations for the Surgical Treatment of Paediatric Epilepsy, School of Mechanical and Chemical Engineering. MSc (Master of Professional Engineering) Thesis, The University of Western Australia, Perth, Western Australia, Australia, 2017.

[67] K. Miller, A. Horton, G.R. Joldes, A. Wittek, Beyond finite elements: a comprehensive, patient-specific neurosurgical simulation utilizing a meshless method, Journal of Biomechanics 45 (2012) 2698–2701.

[68] K. Miller, G. Joldes, D. Lance, A. Wittek, Total Lagrangian explicit dynamics finite element algorithm for computing soft tissue deformation, Communications in Numerical Methods in Engineering 23 (2007) 121–134.

[69] K. Miller, J. Lu, On the prospect of patient-specific biomechanics without patient-specific properties of tissues, Journal of the Mechanical Behavior of Biomedical Materials 27 (2013) 154–166.

[70] K. Miller, A. Wittek, G. Joldes, Biomechanical modeling of the brain for computer-assisted neurosurgery, in: Biomechanics of the Brain, Springer, New York, 2011, pp. 111–136.

[71] A. Mostayed, R. Garlapati, G. Joldes, A. Wittek, A. Roy, R. Kikinis, S. Warfield, K. Miller, Biomechanical model as a registration tool for image-guided neurosurgery: evaluation against BSpline registration, Annals of Biomedical Engineering 41 (2013) 2409–2425.

[72] K. Ono, K. Kaneoka, A. Wittek, J. Kajzer, Cervical injury mechanism based on the analysis of human cervical vertebral motion and head-neck-torso kinematics during low speed rear impacts, in: Proc. of 41st Stapp Car Crash Conference, Society of Automotive Engineers, Inc., Lake Buena Vista, Florida, USA, 1997, pp. 339–356.

[73] N. Otsu, A threshold selection method from gray-level histograms, IEEE Transactions on Systems, Man and Cybernetics 9 (1979) 62–66.

[74] M.M. Panjabi, S. Ito, P.C. Ivancic, W. Rubin (Eds.), Evaluation of the intervertebral neck injury criterion using simulated rear impacts, Journal of Biomechanics 38 (2005) 1694–1701.

[75] S. Perotto, L. Formaggia, New challenges in grid generation and adaptivity for scientific computing, in: Fourth Tetrahedron Workshop on Grid Generation for Numerical Computations, in: SEMA SIMAI Springer Series, ISBN 978-3-319-35926-7, 2014.

[76] K.M. Pohl, S. Bouix, M. Nakamura, T. Rohlfing, R.W. McCarley, R. Kikinis, W.E.L. Grimson, M.E. Shenton, W.M. Wells, A hierarchical algorithm for MR brain image parcellation, IEEE Transactions on Medical Imaging 26 (2007) 1201–1212.

[77] K. Miller, G.R. Joldes, G. Bourantas, S.K. Warfield, D.E. Hyde, R. Kikinis, A. Wittek, Biomechanical modeling and computer simulation of the brain during neurosurgery, International Journal for Numerical Methods in Biomedical Engineering (2019), e3250-1-24, https://onlinelibrary.wiley.com/doi/epdf/10.1002/cnm.3250.

[78] A.J. Ramme, A.J. Criswell, B.R. Wolf, V.A. Magnotta, N.M. Grosland, EM segmentation of the distal femur and proximal tibia: a high-throughput approach to anatomic surface generation, Annals of Biomedical Engineering 39 (2011) 1555–1562.

[79] P.Y. Rohan, C. Lobos, M.A. Nazari, P. Perrier, Y. Payan, Finite element modelling of nearly incompressible materials and volumetric locking: a case study, Computer Methods in Biomechanics and Biomedical Engineering 17 (2014) 192–193.

[80] J.A. Sethian, Set Methods and Fast Marching Methods: Evolving Interfaces in Computational Geometry, Fluid Mechanics, Computer Vision and Materials Science, Cambridge University Press, 1999, ISBN-13: 9780521645577.

[81] J.R. Shewchuk, Delaunay refinement algorithms for triangular mesh generation, Computational Geometry 22 (2002) 21–74.

[82] E.G. Takhounts, M.J. Craig, K. Moorhouse, J. McFadden, V. Hasija, Development of brain injury criteria (BrIC), Stapp Car Crash Journal 57 (2013) 243–266.

[83] T.J. Tautges, T. Blacker, S.A. Mitchell, The whisker weaving algorithm: a connectivity-based method for constructing all-hexahedralfinite element meshes, International Journal for Numerical Methods in Engineering 39 (1996) 3327–3349.

[84] K. Vemaganti, G.R. Joldes, K. Miller, A. Wittek, Total Lagrangian explicit dynamics-based simulation of tissue tearing, in: A. Wittek, P. Nielsen, K. Miller (Eds.), Computational Biomechanics for Medicine: Soft Tissues and Musculoskeletal Systems, Springer, New York, NY, ISBN 978-1-4419-9618-3, 2011, pp. 63–72.

[85] A. Wittek, N. Grosland, G. Joldes, V. Magnotta, K. Miller, From finite element meshes to clouds of points: a review of methods for generation of computational biomechanics models for patient-specific applications, Annals of Biomedical Engineering 44 (2016) 3–15.

[86] A. Wittek, T. Hawkins, K. Miller, On the unimportance of constitutive models in computing brain deformation for image-guided surgery, Biomechanics and Modeling in Mechanobiology 8 (2009) 77–84.

[87] A. Wittek, G. Joldes, M. Couton, S.K. Warfield, K. Miller, Patient-specific non-linear finite element modelling for predicting soft organ deformation in real-time: application to non-rigid neuroimage registration, Progress in Biophysics and Molecular Biology 103 (2010) 292–303.

[88] A. Wittek, G. Joldes, K. Miller, Algorithms for computational biomechanics of the brain, in: K. Miller (Ed.), Biomechanics of the Brain, 2011, pp. 189–219.

[89] A. Wittek, K. Miller, R. Kikinis, S.K. Warfield, Patient-specific model of brain deformation: application to medical image registration, Journal of Biomechanics 40 (2007) 919–929.

[90] K. Yang, A. King, Modeling of the brain for injury simulation and prevention, in: K. Miller (Ed.), Biomechanics of the Brain, Springer, New York, 2011, pp. 91–110.

[91] K.H. Yang, K.L. Shen, C.K. Demetropoulos, A.I. King, P. Kolodziej, R.S. Levine, R.H. Fitzgerald, The relationship between loading conditions and fracture patterns of the proximal femur, Journal of Biomechanical Engineering – Transactions of the ASME 118 (1996) 575–578.

[92] G.Y. Zhang, A. Wittek, G.R. Joldes, X. Jin, K. Miller, A three-dimensional nonlinear meshfree algorithm for simulating mechanical responses of soft tissue, Engineering Analysis with Boundary Elements 42 (2014) 60–66.

[93] J.Y. Zhang, G.R. Joldes, A. Wittek, K. Miller, Patient-specific computational biomechanics of the brain without segmentation and meshing, International Journal for Numerical Methods in Biomedical Engineering 29 (2012) 293–308.

[94] Y. Zhang, C. Bajaj, Adaptive and quality quadrilateral/hexahedral meshing from volumetric data, Computer Methods in Applied Mechanics and Engineering 195 (2006) 942–960.

[95] Y. Zhang, T.J.R. Hughes, C.L. Bajaj, An automatic 3D mesh generation method for domains with multiple materials, Computer Methods in Applied Mechanics and Engineering 199 (2010) 405–415.

CHAPTER 40

Challenges in Computer Assisted Interventions

Challenges in design, development, evaluation, and clinical deployment of Computer Assisted Intervention solutions

P. Stefan[a], **J. Traub**[a,c], **C. Hennersperger**[a], **M. Esposito**[a], **N. Navab**[a,b]

[a]Technische Universität München, Computer Aided Medical Procedures, Munich, Germany
[b]Johns Hopkins University, Computer Aided Medical Procedures, Baltimore, MD, United States
[c]SurgicEye GmbH, Munich, Germany

Contents

40.1.	Introduction to computer assisted interventions	979
	40.1.1 Requirements and definition	980
	40.1.2 Computer assistance	980
	40.1.3 Application domain for interventions	980
	40.1.3.1 General requirements for the design of computer assisted interventions	*981*
40.2.	Advanced technology in computer assisted interventions	984
	40.2.1 Robotics	984
	40.2.2 Augmented reality and advanced visualization/interaction concepts	988
	40.2.3 Artificial intelligence – data-driven decision support	990
40.3.	Translational challenge	991
40.4.	Simulation	994
40.5.	Summary	1004
	References	1004

40.1. Introduction to computer assisted interventions

Historically, surgery was performed by opening the body to gain visual access to the target of the surgery. It was an entirely invasive procedure. Medical imaging provided less invasive or noninvasive view into the human body by using physical principles such as X-rays, ultrasonic wave propagation, and/or magnetic resonance to image deep seated anatomical targets [1] (see Fig. 40.1).

In the past decades, emerging technologies including advanced computing and image processing have brought major changes to medical disciplines. However, we believe that the major changes are still ahead of us thanks to enabling technologies like robotics, augmented reality, and artificial intelligence (see Sect. 40.2).

Handbook of Medical Image Computing and Computer Assisted Intervention
https://doi.org/10.1016/B978-0-12-816176-0.00045-4

The aim of this chapter is to first present the basic requirements of computer assisted interventions. We will then take exemplary systems and discuss their design and development based on such requirements.

40.1.1 Requirements and definition

The overall goal in the design of computer assisted interventions (CAI) is the improvement of the clinical outcome (see Sect. 40.1.2). In today's interventions, the most prominent stakeholders are medical doctors and nurses. Several requirements are introduced in Sect. 40.1.3.1 in order to design end-to-end solutions with potential clinical significance, simulate their application to predict the intended outcome, and evaluate them with measurable parameters to quantify the intended improvements over state-of-the-art procedures.

40.1.2 Computer assistance

Whether we need to focus on Artificial Intelligence (AI) or Intelligence Augmentation (IA) has been actively discussed within the scientific community in the last decades. The choice of terminology hints for the predominance of IA in computer "assisted" interventions. We believe that at least for the next decade, the focus will be on assistance rather than full automation. We therefore define CAI as the field in which the computer systems and technology, and in particular imaging, robotics, machine learning, and augmented reality continuously support the physician in making the right decisions and executing the right actions. Please note that we will also consider advanced solutions for training of physicians and the surgical team as a full component of any CAI solution.

40.1.3 Application domain for interventions

Computer assisted interventions provide solutions in many application domains and includes both surgery and interventional radiology. Fig. 40.1 illustrates the importance of imaging in modern minimally invasive surgery. The importance of imaging has encouraged radiologists to move more and more into the domain of treatment in addition to diagnostics. This created interventional radiology at the intersection of surgery and radiology. It becomes increasingly difficult to strictly separate these two fields as the advancements in robotics, imaging, and AI enable radiologists to propose new treatment strategies for surgeons to act as both radiologist and surgeon within their operating rooms.

Initial systems for computer assisted surgery targeted the neurosurgery domain [2] with stereotactic frames establishing a common reference between the pre-operative images, the patient, and surgical tools allowing guidance during procedures without direct visual control. Visual control could only be provided in radical open surgery. Within the past 25 years CAI solutions were introduced into many other surgical domains, e.g.,

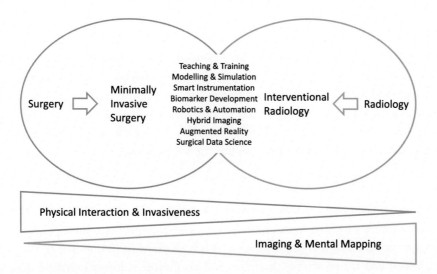

Figure 40.1 Imaging, robotics, advanced visualization, and data science enable patient specific diagnosis and treatment. This shows a continuum in which imaging and radiology meet treatment and surgery. *Own graphic.*

orthopedic, gynecology, urology, and visceral surgery, the later three often in combination with laparoscopic imaging and advanced tools. With these developments open surgery is more and more replaced by minimally invasive surgery.

Interventional radiology started to flourish thanks to a series of pioneering work in angiography. In 1964 the first reported intravascular procedure was performed under angiographic surveillance [3]. Since its early days, in which the focus was only on intraarterial procedures, this field found many new applications, e.g., interventional oncology [4], and bone augmentation. Recently the interventional radiology suites are enhanced and could include smart tools, intelligent catheters, hybrid imaging (MR and/or CT), and robotic systems for imaging and surgical tool manipulation.

40.1.3.1 *General requirements for the design of computer assisted interventions*

With the goal of designing optimal support for clinical procedures, a set of key requirements can be derived in order to ensure that technological solutions provide specific and measurable advances in the clinical domain and thus generate the intended improvement of the clinical outcome.

Relevance

With increasing complexity of procedures and availability of large amounts of heterogeneous diagnostic information, a consistent emphasis on the relevance of information or assistance is key for clinical acceptance. In terms of imaging, one of the major differences between diagnostic and intraoperative imaging is in the fact that during intervention the surgeon only needs the relevant anatomical and physiological information for dynamic monitoring of the surgical process. In fact, in many cases surgeons are overloaded by the amount of information provided by medical imaging modalities, patient monitoring systems, and guidance and navigation solutions. It is therefore important to know the relevance of each information we intend to provide. It is also important to know the phase of procedures in which the information is relevant and the role of the person who is taking advantage of the information within the surgical suite.

Speed

Computational speed has increased substantially over the past years, providing the possibility for computer-assisted solutions to be used not only pre- and postoperatively, but also intraoperatively. For imaging solutions, it is important to notice that in diagnostic imaging speed was for providing sharpness and resolution at lower radiation dose, but was not a strict requirement for the workflow. In CAI, "speed is life", as it is often directly connected to the clinical outcome. Please note that imaging which is not fast enough may not be acceptable in a surgical workflow, even when providing crucial information. This is, of course, not the case for diagnostic imaging.

Flexibility

In contrast to traditional equipment used for diagnostic and surgical procedures, emerging solutions need to be reproducible and reliable, as well as also flexible. One prominent example in this case are the C-arms. While diagnostic X-ray scanners were installed in dedicated rooms and were designed for high resolution and throughput, their flexibility with respect to procedural applications was limited compared to dynamic intraoperative C-arms, providing similar image quality with drastically improved flexibility. Nowadays, such C-arms are considered as not flexible enough and there is more and more interest and products for robotic imaging, e.g., flexible robots holding separately the X-ray source and detector, as well as other imaging modalities including Ultrasound, SPECT, etc. One notices the importance and impact of such flexible solutions when considering that intraoperative imaging needs to quickly capture relevant anatomical or physiological information of patients with different age, sex, and body mass index (BMI). In terms of tomographic reconstruction, a similar trend was followed. First CT machines were used for such 3D reconstructions, in the 1990s stationary C-arms with Cone-beam CT reconstruction capabilities were introduced into the market, and in the early 2000s mobile C-arms with such capabilities also became available. Currently robotic C-arms provide excellent, real-time Cone-Beam CT (CBCT) imaging, providing both flexibility and image quality.

Reproducibility

While fixed settings of diagnostic imaging simplified and guaranteed the reproducibility, the requirement of flexibility brings in clear challenges for guaranteeing the reproducibility of intraoperative solutions. While medical doctors and experts are naturally influenced by their training and expertise, it is the reproducibility of CAI solutions which may guarantee more uniform outcome. For example, for modalities that are currently hand-held, such as ultrasound and Freehand SPECT imaging systems, robotic control could provide more objective and reproducible image acquisitions and therefore clinical measurements and examinations [5,6].

Reliability

Reliability of surgical solutions is critical for certification and translation into practice. Taking the previous requirements of speed, flexibility, and reproducibility into account makes providing reliable CAI solutions a challenging task. However, since this is the key to certification and deployment, CAI researchers need to take this constantly into account. For example, these requirements could be considered as the main reason why marker-based tracking is still the main method used for medical applications. CAI researchers are now trying to use sensor fusion and machine learning to enable marker-less tracking solutions achieving the required level of reliability needed for surgical applications.

Usability

The past years have shown a stronger focus on the usability of novel solutions, especially with respect to the handling of devices, but also interactive visualization of information. In this regard, human factor centered design is now also required for regulated medical devices. In this view, the interaction of medical experts with assisted technologies requires specific and detailed consideration, as classical human–machine interfaces (i.e., mouse, keyboard) are often not appropriate in (sterile) medical settings, and in particular during surgical procedures. Simple solutions like foot pedals with little functionality have been overused and reached their limitations, often requiring delegation of interaction to nonsterile assistants. Though technological advancements have led to robust touchless interaction approaches in the last decade, few have been systematically evaluated in real OR settings [7,8]. We believe that solutions like voice commands have their issues and limitations when used for repetitive commands and could negatively influence team work. Usability in the operating room defines therefore a complex and exciting research direction.

Safety

Safety of medical devices traditionally requires specific attention, but becomes increasingly complex with additional levels of assistance and partial autonomy. In this regard, one not only needs to account for the safe handling of tools and instruments and reducing ionizing radiations, but also consider the impact of automatic information processing, e.g., presenting confidence and uncertainty associated with provided solutions based on machine learning or other advanced techniques. Please note that safety concerns, such as the amount of X-ray radiation, are often dynamic ethical decisions made by the surgeons who try to balance the need for better surgical outcome and the negative side-effects of radiation. This would depend on many factors, including the complexity of the procedure for the specific patient, patient age, and importance of the decision, which requires the image information. CAI systems need to provide additional high level information, such as scattered and accumulated X-ray radiation caused by each dynamic acquisition. Since early 2010s scientists have used advanced 3D computer vision, machine learning, and visualization to enable such solutions [9–11]. Such advanced solutions need to be integrated into CAI systems. One main proposition is to also include ethics and safety education into the biomedical engineering curriculum and train engineers who take such concerns into account in each single step of the design and development of CAI solutions.

40.2. Advanced technology in computer assisted interventions

Every computer assisted intervention is an orchestra of various highly sophisticated technologies, tools, and algorithms [12]. These classically include image analysis, segmentation and registration, real-time tracking, and advanced user interaction and visualization methodologies. In the following we focus on three advanced technologies that have a major impact on the future success of CAI solutions focusing on Intelligence Augmentation and moving towards further integration of automation and artificial intelligence (Fig. 40.2).

40.2.1 Robotics

Robotics could come in as the last link supporting the closure of the Perception–Cognition–Action pipeline in the context of Image-Guided Therapy. Medical Imaging devices (diagnostic as well as intraoperative) provide spatial information about the patient's anatomy. Patient-to-Image Registration allows correlating the position of the image in space to that of the patient within the OR; further objects of interest, such as the surgical tools held by the surgeon, can be added to this digital representation of the world through tracking systems and software. Once the perception of the world is provided, Artificial Intelligence methods can be applied to derive more sophisticated knowledge, or to transform raw sensory data into a format that is useful to the human

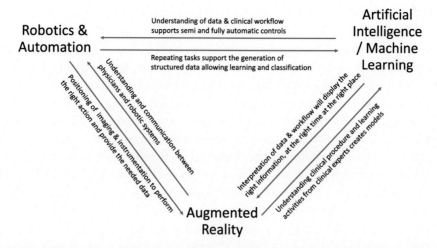

Figure 40.2 *Ecosystem of advanced technology for computer assisted interventions.* The recent advances in augmented reality, artificial intelligence, and robotics are enhancing the applicability and usefulness of CAI solutions in clinical application. *Own graphic.*

operator. A popular approach is to provide spatial surgical navigation, by presenting spatial information about the surgical tool and an anatomical target in a comprehensible and intuitive manner. Alternatively, the surgical action can be taken by the machine itself, in order to execute a plan specified by the surgeon upon the available images, or through an input device directly manipulated by the surgeon.

The first applications of robotics in surgery employed industrial robots, in particular manipulators (or "robot arms") [13,14]. One of these was proposing a robot for autonomous drilling of bones in the context of hip or knee replacement. The robot held the drill, and created place for the prosthetic joint according to a surgical plan specified by the surgeon on preoperative imaging data. The system worked reliably, once accurate registration between the machine and the bone was achieved; this required a careful setup process, which involved a much longer time for the procedure overall. This factor contributed to raising the costs associated with the robotic procedure even further. While some clinical benefits could eventually be proven, further refinements of the system were needed to justify the additional costs in terms of money and time [15]. The recent advancement in collaborative robotics has increased the capabilities of lightweight industrial manipulators. Their employment into autonomous and collaborative robotic imaging schemes promises to automatize screening procedures, or to make real-time multimodal intraoperative imaging feasible [16,17]. However, more work on miniaturized hardware design and autonomous environmental awareness is needed before their deployment in routine procedures.

Shortly after the first autonomous medical robots, shared control solutions started to emerge [18,19]. In this schema, the surgeon and robot hold the surgical tool at the same time. The latter keeps the instrument held by the operator away from sensible regions identified on medical images, or stabilizes the movement to reduce tremor and avoid accidental damage. In addition to ophthalmic surgery, these approaches have been used in orthopedics, neurosurgery, and other surgeries targeting rigid regions of the body or requiring very small motions and delicate interactions [20–22]. In such cases the lack of high variability in the shape of the targeted anatomy made it possible to reliably employ preoperative images to guide open-loop systems. Reliable registration, usability, and setup time represent some of the main challenges for the adoption of these systems. Smaller devices, designed specifically for each procedure and often mounted on the patient, represent much of the expected progress in these areas. These should make registration to the patient more robust and independent of immobilization, and could turn to be easier to use than large generic devices [23].

General and abdominal surgery pose additional challenges due to the complex and unpredictable deformation of soft tissues. The task of keeping track of such deformation over time and identifying the displaced anatomy within preoperative images has not been solved reliably to this point. Consequently, human intelligence is still needed in many steps of such procedures. This fact led to the evolution of human-in-the-loop platforms, such as the da Vinci robot (Intuitive Surgical, Sunnyvale, California). Originally developed for motion compensation during surgery on open heart, it is finding ever wider applications in general surgery, since it can mitigate the burden imposed by minimally invasive laparoscopic surgery on the operator, while retaining the benefits for some of these clinical applications. In conventional laparoscopic surgery, the surgeon must act at the near end of elongated tubular instruments in order to access the internal anatomy of the patient through a reduced access area, i.e., a few small incisions. Visual access is also obtained through a dedicated instrument, i.e., an endoscope, which must be constantly pointed at the operating site by the surgeon itself and/or an assistant, and is often made available on external display monitors. The paradigm of telemanipulated robotic surgery broke the physical coupling between the surgeon's hands and the surgical tools, and proposed a much more convenient setup which has been proven to reduce discomfort on the clinician, and to provide better visualization of the operating site [24,25]. The past decades have therefore brought forward tremendous efforts in this area, resulting in some commercial systems being utilized in daily routine for more than 10 years for different clinical indications. Even if there are different studies and the current robotic systems are still not ideal, recent literature provides evidence of improved efficacy of some of these solutions in comparison to classical surgical approaches [26]. These systems have been presented for different clinical application areas and have focused on different operational settings. Even if most robots aim at minimally invasive surgery, there have also been a series of robotic development of interventional radiology. Note that the adoption of robotic surgery has been slowed down by the difficulty to show sufficient clinical benefits for the patients in order to justify the sensibly increased costs, complexity, and time requirements with respect to conventional interventions, open or laparoscopic surgery. Some authors suggest that the situation might change if robotic platforms manage to make single-port or natural-orifice surgery feasible for a wide range of procedures: such approaches should bring very consistent clinical benefits, and cannot (yet) be performed in a conventional manner. New possibilities could be unlocked on this front by progress in the field of soft and microrobotics, which could allow reaching even more remote target areas without the need for increased invasiveness [27]. Another desired objective to achieve is providing haptic feedback [28]. The lack thereof has been shown to be detrimental in the context of conventional laparoscopic surgery as well [29].

Smooth integration of imaging information with an adequate level of automation and assistance is critical to the success of CAI solutions. Proposed solutions in the literature range from those integrated with scanner technologies [30–32], robotic manipulators utilizing or integrating preinterventional and intraoperative imaging [13,14, 18], as well as robotic systems using mono or stereo vision [33], all the way to robotic imaging systems developed to be integrated with an operating room [34,35] for providing computer-assisted support of procedures. With continuous innovation in this space, these developments support a true integration of physical (tissue) interaction with the required mapping to (image) information. A different categorization of robotic systems is according to their specific level of autonomy, e.g., offering telemanipulation, partial or full autonomy. While initially robotic systems were employed primarily as teleoperated robotic manipulators [36], the improvements to image acquisition, processing, and smooth integration of pre-operative planning have led to partial autonomy both for tissue manipulation [37] and dynamic imaging [38,16].

Robotic surgery as a platform represents a field of opportunity for the progressive introduction of artificial intelligence into the operating room. Video streams can be used for vision-based algorithms. The research trying to exploit resulting video data for scene understanding is abundant [39–41]. Attempts to provide satisfactory AR support by applying pre- or intraoperative data onto the video stream have not yet managed to fully overcome the challenges posed by tissue deformation and depth perception. There are efforts in the direction of partially automating surgical subtasks of increasing complexity. Superhuman performance has been proven possible for tasks such as knot-tying [42]. However, increasing automation must be developed while taking legal and ethical issues into consideration; for example, a 5-tier classification system has been proposed for medical devices in analogy to the existing autonomous driving classification system [43]. Interest is growing into the integration of the surgical robot and the smart OR into a knowledge-based platform. This trend has been named Surgical Data Science [44].

40.2.2 Augmented reality and advanced visualization/interaction concepts

Computer assisted intervention systems have become an integral part of medicine. As mentioned previously, the amount and diversity of patient and procedure related information available to the surgical team has drastically increased [45]. These include basic patient information, dynamic physiologic data from patient monitoring systems, preoperative imaging data such as CT, MRI, and US, and intraoperative data such as optical, X-ray, US, and OCT imaging data. In addition, preoperative planning systems provide detailed and sophisticated treatment plans, tracking systems provide the dynamic pose of surgical instruments, and robotic surgery systems provide a broad range of additional sensory and kinematic data.

With ongoing advances in computing, interventional imaging, and sensor-equipped instruments and robots, the amount of available data will continue to increase rapidly. In order to achieve an optimal surgical outcome, the members of the surgical team must be able to access this information during surgery to recreate a shared mental model of the underlying dynamic surgical scene and make appropriate intraoperative judgments and decisions. The surgical team members need to communicate with each other and interact smoothly with partially autonomous systems, e.g., even when team members are spatially separated from each other within a telemanipulation or telesurgery scenarios.

Augmented reality (AR) has the potential to play an important role in such collaborative environments. AR can provide available information in an intuitive and interactive way in sync with the procedural context and establish the spatial and temporal relation of the information to the surgical scene during different phases of surgery.

In the early days of AR, imprecision of tracking systems, high cost and weight of AR displays, and lack of high computational power, e.g., for real-time depth map reconstruction or realistic rendering, were the major issues the field was concerned with. Only isolated applications were developed in medicine [46]. These proof-of-concept implementations at the time came from highly innovative and strong research laboratories, but the technology was not yet mature and the industry was not yet ready to adapt and implement them.

Today, a few commercial applications exist in the area of image-guidance, i.e., X-ray, US, SPECT, or endoscopic video image guidance, as well as haptic or acoustic guidance [47]. The number of AR laboratory applications is, however, exceedingly larger than the few systems that have found their way into clinical routine [48,47]. The initial technical problems of AR have been largely solved and have given way to problems, such as segmentation, registration, in particular modeling and handling of soft tissue displacements and deformations, and the solution of perceptual issues, e.g., depth perception, in current research. Tracking remains to be an issue.

Major topics that have not yet been sufficiently addressed by the research community are the design of optimal human–computer interfaces and concepts for information dissemination, compatibility with the clinical workflow, and the OR environment, as well as clinical evaluation.

Most often, the display choice is arbitrary [47]. Intuitive system control is in general missing, and often systems are controlled by proxies, e.g., the system developer performing actions based on surgeons' instructions [47]. Unfortunately, common paradigms for user interaction and information manipulation, as used in classical 2D medical displays and input devices, do not translate well for 3D displays [48], and no established design guidelines exist for AR in the CAI context [49].

Additionally, the amount of available data that could be potentially displayed is increasing rapidly. It is obvious, however, that not all of this data can be displayed at the same time, as this would quickly lead to clutter, potentially occlude important information or cognitively overload the user [50].

Furthermore, in addition to the fact that AR environments currently are tailored exclusively to the needs of surgeons, the dissemination of procedure relevant information via AR is usually limited entirely to the surgeon (e.g., when head-mounted-displays are used), completely ignoring the rest of the surgical team. Besides the negative effect on the forming of a shared mental model within the surgical team, this can become a major threat to situational awareness, especially in light of recent findings on the issue of inattentional blindness [51]. Solutions that make the available data accessible for the members of the surgical team are needed.

The research community should therefore focus on the development of intuitive, context-aware information display and interaction paradigms tailored to the context of each stage in the workflow of a specific procedure personalized or at least adapted to each team member's role. In order to identify necessary information, existing procedure workflows have to be studied, recovered, and modeled, e.g., using methods from the field of Surgical Data Science [35,44]. It has to be ensured that this information is attributed to the individual roles of the surgical team in order to be able to develop systems that meet the individual requirements of all team members and support the development and maintenance of a shared mental model over the course of an intervention [52].

The choice of a display device, as well as information visualization and interaction methods, should not be based on subjective criteria, but on the performance of the team on the surgical task, given the specific augmented environment configuration [47]. As a measurable embodiment of the surgical team's performance, clinical accuracy [48] has been proposed. While no formal definition of clinical accuracy exists, it has been described as the maximum error that can be tolerated without compromising patient safety and surgical outcome [48]. However, such tolerances are procedure- and patient-specific, and thus difficult to define.

Calibration and registration algorithms should not be selected based solely on their theoretical accuracy, but also taking into account constraints of the clinical setting and impact on the performance of the team, e.g., intuitiveness, amount of user interaction required, computation time, and reliability [47]. In this context, Yaniv and Linte [47] emphasize that additionally it must be ensured that novel devices do under no circumstances interfere with the function of other devices concurrently used in the OR. An example is the impairment of optical infrared-based tracking by OR lamps and illumination of surgical microscopes [53], as well as the negative effect of the infrared light emitted by the tracking device on the readings of pulse oximeters [54]. As a consequence, a holistic approach should be chosen for the development of AR environments for the clinical setting. Ideally, such an approach provides a robust measure of the clinically imposed accuracy [48], identifies all potential effects of the AR system on other devices and vice versa [47], and leverages usability engineering to optimize integration into the clinical workflow and to optimize the dissemination and perception of information to all members of the surgical team. An approach proposed by Linte et al. [48] involves in vivo experiments where all variables must be closely controlled—"a challenging task" as they put it [48]. In Sect. 40.4 we propose to leverage in vitro experiments towards in vivo conditions using simulation technology and techniques. We discuss this approach as an alternative with the potential to complement in vivo clinical studies or even replace them in earlier stages of development.

40.2.3 Artificial intelligence – data-driven decision support

In order to facilitate methods of artificial intelligence and deep learning in CAI, data needs to be structured, data formats need to be defined, and communication standards need to be established. A move towards establishing these requirements was recently initiated by some of the world's leading research institutions in CAI [44].

Over the past decade, great progress has been made in understanding the workflow of medical procedures and the process of recording it in a structured, user independent manner. Workflow assessment is often performed based on sensor data capturing the procedural configuration, involved team members such as surgeon, assistant surgeon, and nurse, used instrumentation and devices, and changes in the surgical environment [55]. Most approaches rely on vision based systems [56]. This allows the creation of a basis for the design of intelligent solutions and helps identify the phases in an intervention that are subject for supportive devices, automatization and/or visualization based on the workflow [50]. Besides creating an atlas of the intervention, commonly referred to as surgical workflow, patient specific modeling is required to minimize the invasiveness of an intervention. With patient-specific imaging data, planning can be performed based on individual patient case requirements, e.g., defining an optimal needle trajectory or a surgical access path. A structured recording and analysis of surgery with a multitude of different signals and sensors will allow further the identification of the clinical challenges and the modeling and simulation of desired solutions in the form of intelligent CAI systems or smart tools.

In rigid anatomy, many systems have been tested and also established in neurosurgery, trauma surgery, and orthopaedic surgery; however, the major scientific challenges for CAI solution remain in the domain of soft tissue navigation in highly deformable anatomy. Especially in surgical and interventional oncology, the importance of the role of targeted tumor tracers is permanently increasing. The state-of-the-art and routinely used interventional technique to mark suspicious structures is a wire or marker clips. This is getting gradually replaced by functional imaging compounds enabling image guidance during surgical oncology and quality control of the removal of tumor tissue after the intervention [57]. One of the most notable is the prostate-specific membrane antigen (PSMA) ligaments for imaging and therapy of the prostate. Galium 68 (^{68}Ga) ligands allow PET/CT imaging for more specific diagnosis [58]. Technetium 99 (^{99}Tc) and indium 111 (^{111}In) ligands allow for intra-operative guidance using gamma probes and gamma cameras [59,60] and lutetium 177 (^{177}Lu) ligands allow targeting within radioisotope therapy [61].

The widespread use of artificial intelligence and deep learning in medical diagnosis and imaging [62] is already widely discussed and has found its preliminary acceptance in the clinical routine. Similarly in surgery, linking the data to the pathology and patient outcome will ultimately allow the design of data-driven clinical decision support systems within surgical procedures. Some of the leading scientists within the CAI community have also discussed this within their noteworthy article on Surgical Data Science [44].

40.3. Translational challenge

The doubling time of medical knowledge has been estimated to be 7 years in 1980 and 3.5 years in 2010, and is projected to decrease further to 0.2 years in 2020 [63]. With the exponential growth in scientific advancement and resulting technological progress, an explosion in innovation in CAI is expected. However, the translation of innovative medical technology into clinical implementation lags far behind the surge in innovation and research [64].

The process of translation of innovative healthcare technology into clinical use "is long, expensive and prone to high risk, and is characterized by a high long-term failure and a poor adoption rate by end-users" [65]. It "typically lasts more than a decade and is associated with a failure rate of >90%" [65].

The mere availability of a new solution cannot by itself guarantee a successful surgical application. Only very few of the excellent research systems in the CAI domain will make it to clinical routine, and even only a subset of them will define a new clinical standard. More frequently than the success of complete CAI solutions, we find their components becoming part of specific, successful clinical products. The translational challenge is to enable brilliant and working solutions to get introduced into the clinical routine. In research papers the performance parameters considered are in general accuracy, time, or other measures of quality derived from a small, controlled cohort in experimental setups. The clinical key performance indicators, however, are direct and measurable patient outcome, reduction of cost, and therefore offering widespread availability, improved training, learning curve, and ease of use. Such assessment is tedious and time consuming and needs to be summarized in a clinical evaluation report (CER) [66] by qualified domain experts, i.e., surgeons or interventional radiologists. In general there are six major challenges in the translation, i.e., (1) identifying and modeling the real clinical need, patient benefit, and advantage; (2) conducting a sound trial to prove the benefits and their significance; (3) getting the solution certified for clinical use in its target regions; (4) having a reimbursement strategy; (5) providing education and training support; and (6) financing the steps until the solution is profitable. In the following we will provide more details on each of these points.

Clinical need

Most important for the translation from research laboratories to clinical routine is to model the clinical need and provide a specific and efficient solution for it. This is in general done by first carefully observing the application domain to find the current challenges. For medical procedures, this is well described by processes, e.g., in the Stanford Biodesign [67]. More general and not only for medical products and services is the value proposition design that consists of first analyzing the prospect customer to see if the solution provides a core benefit by increasing the desired gains and relieving the pains [68].

Clinical trials

In order to backup the claims for the clinical need and benefit of the product or solution, a clinical study needs to be designed. In general this is performed by a Clinical Research Organization (CRO) with the provided design parameters of the trial. There are guidelines for the conduction of clinical trials from the US Food and Drug Administration (FDA) [69] and EU [70]. All of these are centered around the ethics and the protection of the patient. All clinical trials require IRB/ethical approval. We strongly believe that all biomedical engineers and scientists within the CAI community need to be extensively educated in this regard within their basic education and training pathways.

Certification / regulatory affairs

A CAI solution is a medical product and thus requires certification for clinical use. In order to achieve this, a Device Master Record (DMR) as defined in the Medical Device Quality Management System ISO 13485:2016 [71] is required. This can be at the same time compliant to the FDA 510k [72] or FDA Premarket Approval (PMA) [73] process in USA, as well as the Medical Device Derivative (MDD) [74], i.e., the Council

Directive 93/42/EEC, that will be replaced on May 25, 2020 by the Medical Device Regulation (MDR) [75], i.e., the Council Regulation 2017/745, in EU. Alternative regulations apply in other regions. The most important part of the DMR is the intended use, i.e., a description of the utility of a particular solution. The intended use does not only describe technical features but also the exact application domain, disease, and area of application. A second important component is the clinical evaluation report that needs to compare the solution against the state-of-the-practice, possible substitutes, and alternatives [66]. From the beginning of the development throughout all stages of a medical product development, a risk management system and a risk file need to be maintained [76]. This continues after the product launch in terms of the Post Market Surveillance (PMS).

Reimbursement

One of the major challenges for medical product manufacturers is that the user of a product or service is in general not the payer. In most healthcare systems, the hospital and its clinicians are the provider of healthcare and therefore the users of the product. The payers of the healthcare service are in general insurance companies or private individuals. In order to implement a solution into the clinical routine, a reimbursement needs to be established. This could be defined as part of either existing diagnose related groups (DRG) mainly used for stationary care or part of the International Classification of Procedures in Medicine (ICPM) or its national equivalent, e.g., in Germany the "Operationen- und Prozedurenschlüssel (OPS)".

Service and education

Solutions of CAI are in general solving complex clinical tasks with technical approaches involving a sequence of operations to deliver the desired result. Often manual processing, bulky integration into the clinical infrastructure, and high level technical understanding is required to operate them. While the initial feasibility tests of the research solutions are often conducted by the researcher team itself, a normal clinical team has sometime a hard time using CAI solutions. It is therefore necessary to design and develop intelligent, advanced, and user friendly manuals and training solutions at the same time that the CAI system is designed and developed. Full clinical environment simulations can improve and accelerate this (see Sect. 40.4).

Financing

Finally, the translation of a solution in CAI is an extremely costly procedure. Since the outcome, market, and user acceptance are in general still unknown at the time the investment decision needs to be made, it is a delicate task to gather enough funds to traverse through the entire pathway for clinical introduction. Unfortunately, only few resources are available for nondiluting grants to sponsor parts of the work in the path for clinical integration.

For all the above reasons, it has become utterly difficult to introduce new medical solutions into the clinical workspace. It is interesting to remember that Conrad Roentgen's invention of X-ray imaging was discovered and first demonstrated on December 22, 1895 with an image of the hand of Roentgen's wife. It was then published a few days later [77], and used less than a month later in a clinical procedure [78]. While the benefits of the invention were obvious, it took almost half a century to fully understand the risks. This is just one reason why the process of introduction of new medical solutions needs to follow strict regulatory process allowing fewer inventions to make it into the clinical routine world, carefully weighting the risk–benefit analysis. While it is important to make this process more efficient, one needs to make sure that solutions are only introduced when their risks and benefits are well understood and managed. It is also important that researchers consider not only the business aspects of product developments but also their impact on the society and their availability to greater population around the world.

40.4. Simulation

The translation of healthcare technology is associated with high risk and costs, high long-term failure rates, and poor adaption by end users [65].

Regarding CAI, Linte et al. [48] note: "Mixed reality environments for medical applications have been explored and developed over the past three decades. However, in spite of their reported benefits, few mixed reality environments have been successfully translated into clinical use". Peters and Linte [79] note: "In spite of the development of many sophisticated technologies over the past two decades, other than some isolated examples of successful implementations, minimally invasive therapy is far from enjoying the wide acceptance once envisioned". And although over the last decade, there has been a rapid growth in purchase of commercial surgical robots by healthcare providers, there is little knowledge on how to effectively integrate them into routine practice. As a result, the clinical implementation of robotic systems is still highly variable, and underuse has been reported [80].

Looking at successful translation of innovative healthcare technology into clinical use, Marcus et al. [81] found "the extent of clinical involvement [to be] a significant predictor of a first-in-human study ($p = 0.02$)". "Devices developed with early clinical collaboration were over six times more likely to be translated than those without". "Interestingly, and in contrast to previous studies, industry collaboration was not associated with increased translation" [81].

We believe that simulation has the potential to play a key role in meeting the translational challenges along the innovation pathway, from early clinical collaboration and prototyping to clinical training and product roll-out.

Simulation within the healthcare innovation pathway

Simulation based training and assessment play an increasingly vital role in medical education. Established simulation concepts, methods, and systems from the medical education domain have the potential to make a strong contribution to the translation of healthcare innovation. Simulation provides a high degree of experimental control, and can therefore contribute to reliability and standardization of evaluation scenarios. For many procedures, performance metrics are available that objectively measure clinical performance of medical practitioners and can serve as surrogates for the clinical outcome of the intervention.

Within the healthcare innovation pathway, metrics and outcome surrogates can make a substantial contribution to the evaluation of the efficacy of a novel technology, rating practitioners' performance in assessment scenarios and/or providing personalized feedback within training scenarios. From an ethical and economic point of view, simulation can help reduce or eliminate the need for human cadavers and the use of harmful ionizing radiation for training [82] and/or testing. Furthermore, simulation environments can serve as a reasonable setting for analyzing the clinical workflow, the development of novel ideas, prototyping, and finally for usability evaluation.

In other domains facing similar challenges, e.g., industrial design and product development, simulation has been used for decades, reducing time and effort spent, in particular, in the verification and testing phases [83,84]. There, simulation is considered a key factor that determines successful translation, and the benefits of employing simulation early in the design cycle and consequently throughout the development process have been proven [85,86]. In the medical domain, Jannin and Korb [87] have embedded simulation as an integral element in their framework for technology assessment of systems and procedures in image-guided interventions in form of numerical simulation, as well as simulation of procedures, scenarios, and/or environments, including human-in-the-loop type simulation. While numerical, model-based simulation plays an important role in healthcare technology assessment [88], we focus on human-in-the-loop simulations which are predominant in medical education. Here, simulation has been broadly defined as "a technique—not a technology—to replace or amplify real experiences with guided experiences that evoke or replicate substantial aspects of the real world in a fully interactive manner" [89].

Madani et al. [65] recently investigated the role of simulation in the evaluation and facilitation of the whole product life cycle in healthcare innovation. Through a subject-matter expert panel consisting of physicians, engineers, scientists, and industry leaders, they evaluated the current use and the potential effectiveness of different forms of simulation including "simulated patients (e.g., actor- and patient-based), mannequin-based simulation, and procedural simulation (e.g., synthetic, animal, cadaver, bench-top, and virtual reality simulation), immersive simulation (e.g., simulated ward and simulated operating room), in situ simulation (e.g., simulations performed in the actual clinical environment), and computer-based simulation (e.g., computer modeling, virtual worlds, and serious games)" [65]. They identified high potential utility of simulation throughout all phases of the development cycle but also regretted the fact that currently simulation is often not integrated into the state of practice, especially immersive and in situ simulation. Immersive and in situ simulators, in contrast to procedural simulators, typically reproduce essential parts of the clinical environment and include all actors involved in the procedure. Due to the similarity to the real clinical scenario, their utilization all along the clinical innovation path seems almost inevitable. However, there are currently no examples of the systematic use of such simulation environments.

In the following, we elaborate on how established concepts, methods, and systems from simulation in the medical education domain can support the optimization of the healthcare innovation pathway for CAI.

Simulation-based assessment

The assessment of operative and clinical competency has become a key element of residency training programs in surgical education. The persistence of quality and safety gaps that each year lead to significant morbidity and mortality [90,91] and the acceptance of the premise by medical educators and policymakers that the medical education enterprise bears major responsibility due to an inadequate preparation of trainees have contributed to the global adoption of outcome-based medical education [92].

As a result, assessment phases during residency training are a requirement in many new curricula both to ensure that residents achieve proficiency by the end of their training and to evaluate the training program itself. The American College of Surgeons (ACS) and the Association of Program Directors in Surgery (APDS), for example, designed a simulation-based skills curriculum, with criterion-based goals that have to be reached by residents before proceeding to the operation room. The curriculum consists of 20 basic and 15 advanced surgical skill modules, as well as 10 team-based skill modules [93].

This paradigm shift towards competency-based training, as the predominant model of surgical education, has made assessment an active field of research as it is imperative for the evidence-based verification of the achievement of the educational goals. Therefore, for many surgical procedures, tasks, and skill modules, assessment instruments already exist. For example, Ghaderi et al. [93] have identified and built a toolbox of existing assessment instruments covering 30 of the 45 ACS/APDS modules.

The majority of established assessment tools are observational in the form of global rating scales, checklists, and/or error-based methods that do not require any sensory measurement system and can be readily applied to real surgery as well as simulations. Furthermore, many tools include the task specific components that can be adopted to specific procedures or specific assessment criteria. There is strong evidence for the reliability of these tools and for the validity of scores for the assessment of surgical competency. Notably, regarding observational rating scores, there are strong links between the results of workplace-based assessment (i.e., on the patient) and simulation-based assessment. In a recent metaanalysis Brydges et al. [94] identified a large pooled correlation between simulation-based assessment scores and the behavior of practitioners towards real patients, e.g., in terms of observational ratings on clinical rotations or procedural ratings by instructors. However, observational tools are in general not designed to measure the surgical outcome of a procedure. For example, Anderson et al. [95] could not identify a significant correlation between surgical competency assessed in a simulated procedure using an observational instrument and the surgical outcome of the same simulated procedure. Auerbach et al. [96] only found a weak correlation in a study investigating the relationship between a global rating scale and the real patient outcome in a lumbar puncture procedure. In summary, while the observational assessments capture the skills, attitudes, and behaviors of health practitioners, they do not seem to take patient-outcome well into account.

Many simulation models, however, allow specifically quantifying parameters such as targeting quality, no-go areas or critical structures injured [97], implant placement accuracy, biomechanical strength of a fracture fixation [98], or fracture reduction [95], which could clearly serve as surrogates for patient outcome.

Assessment in healthcare innovation

Concepts from simulation-based competence assessment have the potential to overcome challenges in the health care innovation development pathway in a number of different ways.

Firstly, assessments can be used to determine the proficiency of healthcare practitioners in a specific technique allowing for better candidate selection for a specialized training in the application of novel CAI solutions. Similarly, assessments can be used to determine whether practitioners have reached a level of proficiency, sufficient to include them in a controlled evaluation study or (pre-)clinical evaluations of the novel technology. Finally, assessments can be used to determine whether practitioners after training are proficient enough to use such technology on patients in daily practice.

Secondly, aggregated assessment scores of a larger number of trainees can be used to measure the effectiveness of a product training format and to estimate transferability of the learned techniques into practice.

Thirdly, aggregate assessments can be used as an early preclinical evaluation to estimate the impact of innovative healthcare technology on outcome surrogate parameters under different controlled conditions.

Prototyping

A further application area of simulation in the context of healthcare innovation is prototyping, and in particular virtual prototyping. A major challenge in the development of CAI solutions is the design of intuitive and workflow-compatible systems with minimal intrusion on clinical workflow, low cognitive impositions on the clinical users, and ease of use in general [79,35]. Developers of CAI systems are faced with the substantial question of how such systems should actually be designed to promote these goals. An approach that has been evaluated by Ameri et al. [49] is to use existing interaction metaphors and design guidelines. Their system had already obtained clearance for human trials. However, in a case study using a simulation model they found out that graduate students could obtain significantly better results using the new system compared to the standard one, while experienced physicians could not. A major reason was an unexpected and large degree of variability in the techniques used by the experienced physicians performing the procedure. Their system was, as was revealed in the final evaluation, optimized towards a specific technique used by a collaborating physician and supported in the literature. However, many of the participating experts, over the course of their professional careers, had developed techniques that worked best for them, diverging from what they had been taught and what the best practice guidelines in the literature recommend. Additionally, the system design did not encourage key safety measures and best clinical practices. Even if this is only an isolated case, the findings from this study and implications discussed are of high value for the community: Existing development guidelines cannot be regarded as standard and may not directly apply to novel technology. They therefore need to be completed as the technology advances. Iterative, incremental, and small-scale evaluations involving a representative sample of the intended clinical population are essential in the design and development of innovative CAI solutions.

Gabbard and Swan [99] also recommend this for usability engineering of emerging technologies that have no established design guidelines and often require completely new ways of perceiving and interacting with the technology and the context they are embedded in. They emphasize the importance of iterative design activities in between the "user task analysis phase", where requirements are gathered and user tasks understood, and the "formative user-centered evaluation phase", where an application-level prototype has been developed and is under examination [99]. Furthermore, they recommend to conduct user-based studies in the real environment using the equipment that are most likely used in the final application setting. By striving to match the experimental setting to the application setting as much as possible, results of studies are more likely to transfer smoothly into the final application [99].

It can be argued that this approach to usability engineering, focusing on user-based experiments under application conditions, is applicable to the development of innovative CAI technology as well, and that full-scale simulations of clinical environments are the ideal environment for iterative design and development activities. To broaden the applicability of guidelines, researchers might want to keep simulated user tasks representative, but not so specific such that the findings cannot be applied to the general target procedure or domain [99].

Ideally, an already existing simulation-based assessment environment for the target procedure can be leveraged. On the other hand, newly designing and evaluating such simulation environments promotes understanding of the clinical space and effective design parameters by biomedical engineers [99]. Depending on the progress of prototyping and design or development goals, simple mock-ups, e.g., static images displayed in HMDs [100], up to fully functional prototypes might be employed.

As an interim solution one can also use virtual prototyping [101]. Satava believes that full environment surgical simulators could allow "inventing a new procedure or performing a 'virtual clinical trial', and virtual prototyping of new instruments" [102]. In other areas, e.g., manufacturing [84], immersive simulators allow virtual prototypes to be experienced in their usage context and to gather reliable measurements of man–machine interactions under realistic experimental conditions [103]. Virtual prototyping is particularly useful if the production of a physical prototype is expensive or time-consuming and an iterative approach to development and evaluation, in particular in the absence of established design guidelines or standards, is required. For example, an area within CAI in which development costs are extremely high is robotic surgery. As a result, today's commercially available industrial multipurpose robotic systems used in laboratories and research centers aim at providing general tools for many different tasks, enabling the development of various solutions, and are thus only suited for proof-of-concepts to demonstrate application capabilities. Robotic systems for the clinical implementation need, however, to be specifically designed based on the requirements of each specific clinical application, as soon as the potential benefits and market size justify the cost of their design and development [35]. One way to demonstrate the potential benefits of specific designs before production while keeping cost low is virtual prototyping and evaluation in simulated environments. Fang et al. [104], for example, use AR for virtual prototyping of robots in real environments. Such methods can also support the development and evaluation of functional aspects and interaction design, e.g., for applications where a surgical robot needs to prevent collisions within the OR environment [105], or where the robot aims at collaborating with the surgeon [17] or with another robot [106].

Training

When it comes to the challenges along the development pathway of healthcare innovations, we must not overlook that not only innovators and industry, but also the healthcare practitioners who finally have to use the innovative technologies within their daily practice, face major challenges.

All members of the OR team have to familiarize themselves with a new technology and resulting modification of surgical workflow. Surgeons need to develop or improve their skills when using new technologies in order to safely and efficiently integrate them into their practice. Nurses have to learn to set up systems, to prepare and hand over novel instruments and tools according to the new workflow and adhere to often very strict patient positioning requirements. Anesthesiologists are faced with spatial limitations and special patient positioning that might entail physiological adverse effects or complicated airway management. Additionally, the whole team is potentially faced with the consequences of a steep learning curve, stressed team members, possibly longer duration of the procedure and the potential detrimental impact on communication and teamwork [107].

This becomes most apparent in telemanipulated robotic surgery, which in particular intervenes very strongly in established workflows, places very strict requirements on the positioning of the patient and the devices and equipment surrounding the patient, makes a repositioning of the patient in the case of complications tedious, and physically separates the surgeon from the rest of the team, which in turn impedes the surgeon's situation awareness, makes communication more difficult, and limits the surgeon's ability to use gestures to support communication [80,107]. Some reports of the rapid and largely uncontrolled implementation of robot-assisted surgery reflect and highlight such problems [108–110].

All of this also applies, if perhaps to a lesser extent, to other CAI technologies such as mixed-reality visualization or image-guided interventions. The mere availability of novel technologies cannot by itself guarantee a successful surgical application. Knowledge of the nuances of a technology and the adaptation of communication and teamwork strategies are required to use the full potential of a technology to improve patient outcome, increase efficiency, and reduce surgical and anesthetic complications [107], and should therefore be an aim of the training. Simulation training and in particular multidisciplinary team training have shown to improve patient treatment and reduce or improve the handling of complications while enhancing teamwork [111,112].

To ensure the acquisition of proficiency and adequate training during the introduction of novel CAI solutions, a wider application of proficiency-based surgical simulation training has been proposed [113]. However, to fully use its potential, simulation training has to be provided not only to surgeons, but also to the surgical team. In addition, as Wucherer et al. [114] have proposed, established proficiency-based training approaches such as proficiency-based progression [115] should be extended by a multidisciplinary team training and assessment phase in a full environment simulation. This would allow us to bridge the gap between single profession procedural simulator training and the supervised performance of the OR team in patient care (and likewise in clinical studies evaluating healthcare innovations).

A plethora of skills trainers and procedural simulators is available for training the different professions. Such individual simulators can be effectively linked to create full environment simulations which would allow the introduction of multidisciplinary team scenarios with the capacity to simulate adverse events or complications [114]. In addition to being perceived as realistic, simulator-induced adverse events or complications in

Figure 40.3 Simulation of workflow interruptions, i.e., phone call and patient uttering pain, during a simulated spine surgery procedure [118].

such simulations have been shown to impact intraoperative workload and technical performance, e.g., as demonstrated in the first simulation study on this subject [116–118] (see Fig. 40.3). As surgical systems evolve with new technologies, it is vital both to develop error reporting and prevention strategies and to train and assess surgical teams in the management of technical difficulties, adverse events and complications [128].

In order to create such multidisciplinary simulations, one needs to link individual simulators. This means that changes to the physiology in one simulator need to automatically lead to a corresponding physiologic changes in the other simulators, e.g., a blood loss in a surgical simulator leading to a cardiovascular instability in a anaesthesia mannequin simulator. This requires open interfaces, which are often unfortunately not available [112]. First steps towards open source simulators are, however, being taken by the community [119].

To make effective use of full environment simulations, trainees must first be provided with the level of knowledge and basic skills necessary for the application of a novel CAI solution, e.g., through individual training using task or procedural simulation, and in order to prevent a cognitive overload or expertise reversal [120]. This poses the question of which training modality is best for which learner at different stage of learning [113]. Following the proficiency-based training approach, best-practice guidelines should be translated into training modules of ascending complexity and difficulty, starting with the basic techniques, at first possibly without patient and team related settings, e.g., using gamification methods [121], to teach the basics of altered or novel procedures, then progressing to patient-based settings involving a range of typical patient cases with indications for the application of the novel technology, and finally imparting knowledge of the nuances of the technology applied in complex or rare cases, as well as complication scenarios in multidisciplinary full scale simulation.

Regarding simulation training requirements, Korndorffer et al. [122] argue that "for training use, what needs to be established is whether training improves subjects' ability" and "perhaps even more importantly, simulators need to be evaluated to ensure they avoid training poor technique". This can be established through observation and

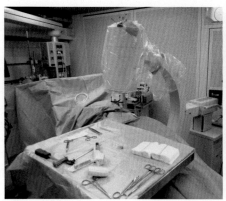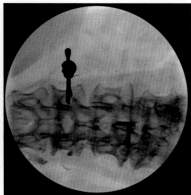

Figure 40.4 Example of a simulated OR environment [118]. C-arm, 3D-printed patient model, and surgical instruments are optically tracked. Simulated X-ray images (DDRs) are generated using the tracking information and patient CT data.

expert opinion or transferability studies [122]. Beyond observation and expert opinion, simulation-based assessments are a suitable method to establish initial evidence for transferability. Furthermore, simulation environments that unobtrusively alter only elements necessary to simulation, e.g., which replace the X-ray images with digitally reconstructed radiographs (DRRs) but keep the physical C-arm or replace the human patient with a 3D-printed anatomy model but keep the original instruments [82,118] (see Fig. 40.4), are inherently more likely to yield a higher degree of transferability.

Replacing old knowledge with new knowledge

A new type of technology may also require one to learn a new technique or adapt to a change of the way the technology is employed [87]. In addition, procedures are taught differently in different institutes and countries. As reported, for example, by Ameri et al. [49], after years of performing a procedure, clinicians often tend to find techniques that work best for them, possibly different from the taught technique or even different from best clinical practices. In all of these cases, in-depth training of the novel technology is needed. Typically, this involves replacing old knowledge (and sometimes misconceptions) with new knowledge. This poses an additional challenge for training, as "in such a case, proactive interference or inhibition (PI) is a possibility, where the new knowledge might be learned initially, but forgetting is accelerated due to the interfering effect of the more stable prior knowledge" [123]. For a successful training in the use of novel technology, the community therefore should develop training strategies that remedy these effects. Literature on PI is vast, and many different approaches have been proposed to handle PI in the context of training [123]. One strategy, which appears to reduce PI and improve learning, is the incorporation of testing phases within learning sessions. Roediger and Karpicke [124] conclude that formative assessment improves such learning and later recall. Their finding supports the concept of proficiency-based progression and underlines the importance of feedback and intermediate assessment strategy to provide effective and persistent training.

Engagement

Another concept which is essential to the learning process and closely related to users' experience with technology is engagement [125]. Recently, Choi et al. [126] have highlighted the importance of this largely understudied concept to simulation training and developed a conceptual framework for engaged learning in simulation based training. In summary, they argue that "optimal engagement occurs when (1) educators deliberately integrate the knowledge, skills, attitudes, and motivations of the learners when creating and facilitating the simulation, and when (2) the fidelity of the simulation is sufficient to allow the learner to suspend disbelief to fully engage in the learning activity, which leads to the desired level of clinical performance" [126]. They propose to establish engagement in three categories, (a) behavioral engagement, through presimulation briefing to suspend disbelief and create a psychologically safe context for learning, (b) emotional engagement, by designing simulations that elicit feelings likely to be encountered in real life, and (c) cognitive engagement, through self-regulated learning, appropriate feedback, and debriefing, e.g., by establishing proficiency-based training. In addition to an improved training effect, an engaging experience with a novel technology during training has, moreover, the potential to increase the of motivation practitioners to use the technology in daily practice and thus improve the long-term adaptation rate [125].

Intraoperative training and assistance

Lastly, educational elements from simulation training might be applicable to intraoperative settings by providing the OR team with intraoperative instructions or guidance in the use of innovative technology. This information should be provided to team members according to their role, the current workflow step, and the devices or instruments used in each workflow step. To support engagement this should happen unobtrusively and provide only information relevant in the current context, much as Azuma had envisioned in a vivid example: "Virtual instructions could remind a novice surgeon of the required steps, without the need to look away from a patient to consult a manual" [127]. The extensive use of optical and auditory sensing and machine learning will soon allow the CAI systems to recognize the workflow and the need for online training or support. Augmented Reality could then provide dynamic and well integrated information to support and train the surgical team during intervention. This could bring another piece of puzzle necessary for smooth transfer of novel CAI technology into routine practice.

40.5. Summary

In this chapter, we aimed at providing the readers with the definition and requirements of computer assisted interventions. We focused in particular on sensing, recognition, action, and the required technologies to enhance these three main components of CAI. Robotics, AI, and AR were presented as some of the main areas of research. The chapter also focused on the importance of research in simulation and training as necessary vehicles for the adaption and transfer of CAI into clinical routine. We did emphasize on this as this is probably the aspect which has been most neglected within the CAI community. We end this chapter by emphasizing on our belief that CAI is an extremely active field of research and with the rise of Robotics, AI, AR, and the evolving field of Surgical Data Science, it promises to enable crucial advancement and impact strongly our healthcare in the years to come.

References

[1] N.B. Smith, A. Webb, Introduction to Medical Imaging: Physics, Engineering and Clinical Applications, Cambridge University Press, Cambridge, ISBN 978-0-521-19065-7, 2010.

[2] A.M. Lozano, P.L. Gildenberg, R.R. Tasker, Textbook of Stereotactic and Functional Neurosurgery, Springer Science & Business Media, ISBN 978-3-540-69959-0, 2009.

[3] S. Athreya, Demystifying Interventional Radiology: A Guide for Medical Students, Springer, ISBN 978-3-319-17238-5, 2015.

[4] R. Gandhi, S. Ganguli, Interventional Oncology, 1st ed., Thieme Publishers New York, New York, ISBN 978-1-62623-081-1, 2016.

[5] P. Matthies, J. Gardiazabal, A. Okur, T. Lasser, N. Navab, Accuracy evaluation of interventional nuclear tomographic reconstruction using mini gamma cameras, in: G.Z. Yang, A. Darzi (Eds.), The Hamlyn Symposium on Medical Robotics, 2014, pp. 31–32.

[6] R. Kojcev, A. Khakzar, B. Fürst, O. Zettinig, C. Fahkry, R. DeJong, et al., On the reproducibility of expert-operated and robotic ultrasound acquisitions, International Journal of Computer Assisted Radiology and Surgery 12 (2017), https://doi.org/10.1007/s11548-017-1561-1.

[7] A. Mewes, B. Hensen, F. Wacker, C. Hansen, Touchless interaction with software in interventional radiology and surgery: a systematic literature review, International Journal of Computer Assisted Radiology and Surgery 12 (2) (2017) 291–305, https://doi.org/10.1007/s11548-016-1480-6.

[8] S. Cronin, G. Doherty, Touchless computer interfaces in hospitals: a review, Health Informatics Journal (2018), https://doi.org/10.1177/1460458217748342.

[9] A. Ladikos, C. Cagniart, R. Ghotbi, M. Reiser, N. Navab, Estimating radiation exposure in interventional environments, in: T. Jiang, N. Navab, J.P.W. Pluim, M.A. Viergever (Eds.), Medical Image Computing and Computer-Assisted Intervention – MICCAI 2010, in: Lecture Notes in Computer Science, Springer, Berlin Heidelberg, ISBN 978-3-642-15711-0, 2010, pp. 237–244.

[10] N.L. Rodas, N. Padoy, Seeing is believing: increasing intraoperative awareness to scattered radiation in interventional procedures by combining augmented reality, Monte Carlo simulations and wireless dosimeters, International Journal of Computer Assisted Radiology and Surgery 10 (8) (2015) 1181–1191.

[11] N. Leucht, S. Habert, P. Wucherer, S. Weidert, N. Navab, P. Fallavollita, Augmented reality for radiation awareness, in: 2015 IEEE International Symposium on Mixed and Augmented Reality, 2015, pp. 60–63.

[12] T. Peters, K. Cleary (Eds.), Image-Guided Interventions: Technology and Applications, Springer US, ISBN 978-0-387-73856-7, 2008.

[13] M. Jakopec, S. Harris, F. Rodriguez y Baena, P. Gomes, J. Cobb, B. Davies, The first clinical application of a "hands-on" robotic knee surgery system, Computer Aided Surgery 6 (6) (2001) 329–339.

[14] G. Brandt, A. Zimolong, L. Carrat, P. Merloz, H.W. Staudte, S. Lavallee, et al., Crigos: a compact robot for image-guided orthopedic surgery, IEEE Transactions on Information Technology in Biomedicine 3 (4) (1999) 252–260.

[15] W.L. Bargar, A. Bauer, M. Börner, Primary and revision total hip replacement using the Robodoc system, Clinical Orthopaedics and Related Research 354 (1998) 82–91, https://doi.org/10.1097/00003086-199809000-00011.

[16] C. Hennersperger, B. Fürst, S. Virga, O. Zettinig, B. Frisch, T. Neff, et al., Towards MRI-based autonomous robotic US acquisitions: a first feasibility study, IEEE Transactions on Medical Imaging 36 (2) (2017) 538–548.

[17] M. Esposito, B. Busam, C. Hennersperger, J. Rackerseder, A. Lu, N. Navab, et al., Cooperative robotic gamma imaging: enhancing US-guided needle biopsy, in: Medical Image Computing and Computer-Assisted Intervention – MICCAI 2015, in: Lecture Notes in Computer Science, Springer, Cham, ISBN 978-3-319-24570-6, 2015, pp. 611–618, ISBN 978-3-319-24571-3.

[18] R. Taylor, P. Jensen, L. Whitcomb, A. Barnes, R. Kumar, D. Stoianovici, et al., A steady-hand robotic system for microsurgical augmentation, The International Journal of Robotics Research 18 (12) (1999) 1201–1210.

[19] C. Song, P.L. Gehlbach, J.U. Kang, Active tremor cancellation by a "smart" handheld vitreoretinal microsurgical tool using swept source optical coherence tomography, Optics Express 20 (21) (2012) 23414, https://doi.org/10.1364/OE.20.023414, URL https://www.osapublishing.org/oe/abstract.cfm?uri=oe-20-21-23414.

[20] J.E. Lang, S. Mannava, A.J. Floyd, M.S. Goddard, B.P. Smith, A. Mofidi, et al., Robotic systems in orthopaedic surgery, Journal of Bone and Joint Surgery. British Volume 93-B (10) (2011) 1296–1299, https://doi.org/10.1302/0301-620X.93B10.27418.

[21] R.A. Beasley, Medical robots: current systems and research directions, Journal of Robotics 2012 (2012) 1–14, https://doi.org/10.1155/2012/401613, 00148, URL http://www.hindawi.com/journals/jr/2012/401613/.

[22] T.A. Mattei, A.H. Rodriguez, D. Sambhara, E. Mendel, Current state-of-the-art and future perspectives of robotic technology in neurosurgery, Neurosurgical Review 37 (3) (2014) 357–366, https://doi.org/10.1007/s10143-014-0540-z, URL http://link.springer.com/10.1007/s10143-014-0540-z.

[23] P. Gomes, Surgical robotics: reviewing the past, analysing the present, imagining the future, Robotics and Computer-Integrated Manufacturing 27 (2) (2011) 261–266, https://doi.org/10.1016/j.rcim.2010.06.009, URL http://linkinghub.elsevier.com/retrieve/pii/S0736584510000608.

[24] R. Berguer, W. Smith, An ergonomic comparison of robotic and laparoscopic technique: the influence of surgeon experience and task complexity, The Journal of Surgical Research 134 (1) (2006) 87–92, https://doi.org/10.1016/j.jss.2005.10.003, URL http://linkinghub.elsevier.com/retrieve/pii/S0022480405005330.

[25] P.C. Giulianotti, F. Sbrana, F.M. Bianco, E.F. Elli, G. Shah, P. Addeo, et al., Robot-assisted laparoscopic pancreatic surgery: single-surgeon experience, Surgical Endoscopy 24 (7) (2010) 1646–1657, https://doi.org/10.1007/s00464-009-0825-4.

[26] S. Maeso, M. Reza, J. Mayol, J. Blasco, M. Guerra, E. Andradas, et al., Efficacy of the da Vinci surgical system in abdominal surgery compared with that of laparoscopy, Annals of Surgery 252 (2) (2010) 254–262, https://doi.org/10.1097/SLA.0b013e3181e6239e.

[27] D. Rattner, A. Kalloo, ASGE/SAGES working group on natural orifice translumenal endoscopic surgery, Surgical Endoscopy and other Interventional Techniques 20 (2) (2006) 329–333, https://doi.org/10.1007/s00464-005-3006-0.

[28] A. Okamura, Haptic feedback in robot-assisted minimally invasive surgery, Current Opinion in Urology 19 (1) (2009) 102–107, https://doi.org/10.1097/MOU.0b013e32831a478c, URL insights.ovid.com.

[29] E.P.W.v.d. Putten, R.H.M. Goossens, J.J. Jakimowicz, J. Dankelman, Haptics in minimally invasive surgery – a review, Minimally Invasive Therapy & Allied Technologies 17 (1) (2008) 3–16, https://doi.org/10.1080/13645700701820242.

[30] R. Monfaredi, K. Cleary, K. Sharma, MRI robots for needle-based interventions: systems and technology, Annals of Biomedical Engineering 46 (10) (2018) 1479–1497, https://doi.org/10.1007/s10439-018-2075-x.

[31] H.B. Gilbert, D.C. Rucker, R.J. Webster III, Concentric tube robots: the state of the art and future directions, in: Robotics Research, Springer, 2016, pp. 253–269.

[32] J. Burgner-Kahrs, D.C. Rucker, H. Choset, Continuum robots for medical applications: a survey, IEEE Transactions on Robotics 31 (6) (2015) 1261–1280.

[33] D. Stoyanov, Surgical vision, Annals of Biomedical Engineering 40 (2) (2012) 332–345.

[34] A.M. Priester, S. Natarajan, M.O. Culjat, Robotic ultrasound systems in medicine, IEEE Transactions on Ultrasonics, Ferroelectrics, and Frequency Control 60 (3) (2013) 507–523.

[35] N. Navab, C. Hennersperger, B. Frisch, B. Fürst Personalized, Relevance-based multimodal robotic imaging and augmented reality for computer assisted interventions, Medical Image Analysis 33 (2016) 64–71, https://doi.org/10.1016/j.media.2016.06.021.

[36] G.H. Ballantyne, Robotic surgery, telerobotic surgery, telepresence, and telementoring, Surgical Endoscopy and Other Interventional Techniques 16 (10) (2002) 1389–1402.

[37] A. Shademan, R.S. Decker, J.D. Opfermann, S. Leonard, A. Krieger, P.C.W. Kim, Supervised autonomous robotic soft tissue surgery, Science Translational Medicine 8 (337) (2016) 337, https://doi.org/10.1126/scitranslmed.aad9398, URL http://stm.sciencemag.org/content/8/337/337ra64.

[38] S. Billings, N. Deshmukh, H.J. Kang, R. Taylor, E.M. Boctor, System for robot-assisted real-time laparoscopic ultrasound elastography, in: Medical Imaging 2012: Image-Guided Procedures, Robotic Interventions, and Modeling, vol. 8316, International Society for Optics and Photonics, 2012, p. 83161W.

[39] F. Lalys, P. Jannin, Surgical process modelling: a review, International Journal of Computer Assisted Radiology and Surgery 9 (3) (2014) 495–511, https://doi.org/10.1007/s11548-013-0940-5.

[40] I. Laina, N. Rieke, C. Rupprecht, J.P. Vizcaíno, A. Eslami, F. Tombari, et al., Concurrent segmentation and localization for tracking of surgical instruments, in: M. Descoteaux, L. Maier-Hein, A. Franz, P. Jannin, D.L. Collins, S. Duchesne (Eds.), Medical Image Computing and Computer-Assisted Intervention – MICCAI 2017, in: Lecture Notes in Computer Science, Springer International Publishing, ISBN 978-3-319-66185-8, 2017, pp. 664–672.

[41] N. Rieke, D.J. Tan, C. Amat di San Filippo, F. Tombari, M. Alsheakhali, V. Belagiannis, et al., Real-time localization of articulated surgical instruments in retinal microsurgery, Medical Image Analysis 34 (2016) 82–100.

[42] J. van den Berg, S. Miller, D. Duckworth, H. Hu, A. Wan, Xiao-Yu Fu, et al., Superhuman performance of surgical tasks by robots using iterative learning from human-guided demonstrations, in: 2010 IEEE International Conference on Robotics and Automation, IEEE, ISBN 978-1-4244-5038-1, 2010, pp. 2074–2081, 00130, URL http://ieeexplore.ieee.org/document/5509621/.

[43] G.Z. Yang, J. Cambias, K. Cleary, E. Daimler, J. Drake, P.E. Dupont, et al., Medical robotics – regulatory, ethical, and legal considerations for increasing levels of autonomy, Science Robotics 2 (4) (2017) eaam8638, https://doi.org/10.1126/scirobotics.aam8638.

[44] L. Maier-Hein, M. Eisenmann, C. Feldmann, H. Feussner, G. Forestier, S. Giannarou, et al., Surgical data science: a consensus perspective, preprint, arXiv:1806.03184, 2018.

[45] H. Müller, A. Hanbury, N.A. Shorbaji, Health information search to deal with the exploding amount of health information produced, Methods of Information in Medicine 51 (06) (2012) 516–518, https://doi.org/10.1055/s-0038-1627049.

[46] T. Sielhorst, M. Feuerstein, N. Navab, Advanced medical displays: a literature review of augmented reality, Journal of Display Technology 4 (4) (2008) 451–467, https://doi.org/10.1109/JDT.2008.2001575.

[47] Z. Yaniv, C.A. Linte, Applications of augmented reality in the operating room, in: Fundamentals of Wearable Computers and Augmented Reality, 2nd ed., CRC Press Taylor & Francis Group, New York, 2016, pp. 485–518.

[48] C.A. Linte, K.P. Davenport, K. Cleary, C. Peters, K.G. Vosburgh, N. Navab, et al., On mixed reality environments for minimally invasive therapy guidance: systems architecture, successes and challenges in their implementation from laboratory to clinic, Computerized Medical Imaging and Graphics 37 (2) (2013) 83–97, https://doi.org/10.1016/j.compmedimag.2012.12.002.

[49] G. Ameri, J.S.H. Baxter, D. Bainbridge, T.M. Peters, E.C.S. Chen, Mixed reality ultrasound guidance system: a case study in system development and a cautionary tale, International Journal of Computer Assisted Radiology and Surgery 13 (4) (2018) 495–505, https://doi.org/10.1007/s11548-017-1665-7.

[50] N. Navab, J. Traub, T. Sielhorst, M. Feuerstein, C. Bichlmeier, Action- and workflow-driven augmented reality for computer-aided medical procedures, IEEE Computer Graphics and Applications 27 (5) (2007) 10–14.

[51] B.J. Dixon, M.J. Daly, H. Chan, A.D. Vescan, I.J. Witterick, J.C. Irish, Surgeons blinded by enhanced navigation: the effect of augmented reality on attention, Surgical Endoscopy 27 (2) (2013) 454–461, https://doi.org/10.1007/s00464-012-2457-3.

[52] A. Bigdelou, T. Sterner, S. Wiesner, T. Wendler, F. Matthes, N. Navab, OR specific domain model for usability evaluations of intra-operative systems, in: R.H. Taylor, G.Z. Yang (Eds.), Information Processing in Computer-Assisted Interventions, Lecture Notes in Computer Science, Springer, Berlin Heidelberg, ISBN 978-3-642-21504-9, 2011, pp. 25–35.

[53] F. Langlotz, Potential pitfalls of computer aided orthopedic surgery, Injury 35 (Suppl. 1) (2004), https://doi.org/10.1016/j.injury.2004.05.006, S–A17–23.

[54] A.M. Mathes, S. Kreuer, S.O. Schneider, S. Ziegeler, U. Grundmann, The performance of six pulse oximeters in the environment of neuronavigation, Anesthesia and Analgesia 107 (2) (2008) 541–544, https://doi.org/10.1213/ane.0b013e31817e6778.

[55] R. Stauder, D. Ostler, T. Vogel, D. Wilhelm, S. Koller, M. Kranzfelder, et al., Surgical data processing for smart intraoperative assistance systems, Innovative Surgical Sciences 2 (3) (2017) 145–152, https://doi.org/10.1515/iss-2017-0035.

[56] D. Bouget, M. Allan, D. Stoyanov, P. Jannin, Vision-based and marker-less surgical tool detection and tracking: a review of the literature, Medical Image Analysis 35 (2017) 633–654.

[57] K. Herrmann, O.E. Nieweg, S.P. Povoski (Eds.), Radioguided Surgery: Current Applications and Innovative Directions in Clinical Practice, Springer International Publishing, Cham, ISBN 978-3-319-26049-5, 2016, ISBN 978-3-319-26051-8.

[58] W.P. Fendler, M. Eiber, M. Beheshti, J. Bomanji, F. Ceci, S. Cho, et al., 68Ga-PSMA PET/CT: joint EANM and SNMMI procedure guideline for prostate cancer imaging: version 1.0, European Journal of Nuclear Medicine and Molecular Imaging 44 (6) (2017) 1014–1024.

[59] S. Robu, M. Schottelius, M. Eiber, T. Maurer, J. Gschwend, M. Schwaiger, et al., Preclinical evaluation and first patient application of 99MTC-PSMA-I&S for SPECT imaging and radioguided surgery in prostate cancer, Journal of Nuclear Medicine 58 (2) (2017) 235–242.

[60] M. Schottelius, M. Wirtz, M. Eiber, T. Maurer, H.J. Wester, [111In]PSMA-I&T: expanding the spectrum of PSMA-I&T applications towards SPECT and radioguided surgery, EJNMMI Research 5 (1) (2015) 68, https://doi.org/10.1186/s13550-015-0147-6.

[61] W.P. Fendler, K. Rahbar, K. Herrmann, C. Kratochwil, M. Eiber, 177Lu-PSMA radioligand therapy for prostate cancer, Journal of Nuclear Medicine 58 (8) (2017) 1196–1200.

[62] G. Litjens, T. Kooi, B.E. Bejnordi, A.A.A. Setio, F. Ciompi, M. Ghafoorian, et al., A survey on deep learning in medical image analysis, Medical Image Analysis 42 (2017) 60–88.

[63] P. Densen, Challenges and opportunities facing medical education, Transactions of the American Clinical and Climatological Association 122 (2011) 48–58.

[64] J.S. Fernandez-Moure, Lost in translation: the gap in scientific advancements and clinical application, Frontiers in Bioengineering and Biotechnology 4 (2016), https://doi.org/10.3389/fbioe.2016.00043.

[65] A. Madani, B. Gallix, C.M. Pugh, D. Azagury, P. Bradley, D. Fowler, et al., Evaluating the role of simulation in healthcare innovation: recommendations of the Simnovate Medical Technologies Domain Group, BMJ Simulation and Technology Enhanced Learning 3 (Suppl. 1) (2017) S8–S14, https://doi.org/10.1136/bmjstel-2016-000178.

[66] Clinical evaluation: a guide for manufacturers and notified bodies under directives 93/42/EEC and 90/385/EEC. MEDDEV 2.7/1 revision 4, European Commission, Health Technology and Cosmetics [Online], available from https://ec.europa.eu/docsroom/documents/17522/attachments/1/translations/en/renditions/native, 2016. (Accessed 11 August 2018).

[67] P.G. Yock, S. Zenios, J. Makower, T.J. Brinton, U.N. Kumar, F.T.J. Watkins, et al., Biodesign: The Process of Innovating Medical Technologies, 2nd ed., Cambridge University Press, 2015.

[68] A. Osterwalder, Y. Pigneur, G. Bernarda, A. Smith, Value Proposition Design: How to Create Products and Services Customers Want, 1st ed., John Wiley & Sons, ISBN 978-1-118-96805-5, 2014.

[69] Clinical trials and human subject protection – regulations: good clinical practice and clinical trials by Food and Drug Administration (FDA) office of the commissioner, [Online], available from: https://www.fda.gov/ScienceResearch/SpecialTopics/RunningClinicalTrials/ucm155713.htm#FDARegulations. (Accessed 12 August 2018).

[70] Guidelines on clinical investigation: a guide for manufacturers and notified bodies. MEDDEV 2.7/4, European Commission, Directorate General for Health and Consumers [Online], available from https://ec.europa.eu/docsroom/documents/10336/attachments/1/translations/en/renditions/native. (Accessed 11 August 2018).

[71] ISO 13485:2016 - medical devices – quality management systems – requirements for regulatory purposes, International Organization for Standardization, URL https://www.iso.org/standard/59752.html, 2016.

[72] 510(k) clearances by Food and Drug Administration (FDA) center for devices and radiological health, [Online], available from: https://www.fda.gov/MedicalDevices/ProductsandMedicalProcedures/DeviceApprovalsandClearances/Clearances/default.htm. (Accessed 13 August 2018).

[73] Premarket approval – PMA by Food and Drug Administration (FDA) center for devices and radiological health, [Online], available from: https://www.fda.gov/MedicalDevices/ProductsandMedicalProcedures/DeviceApprovalsandClearances/PMAApprovals/default.htm. (Accessed 13 August 2018).

[74] Council directive 93/42/EEC of concerning medical devices – MDD – medical device directive, EU Law 93/42/EEC, Council of the European Union, URL https://eur-lex.europa.eu/legal-content/EN/ALL/?uri=CELEX%3A31993L0042, 1993.

[75] Council Regulation 2017/745 – MDR – Medical Device Regulation, Tech. Rep. 2017/745. European Parliament, Council of the European Union, 2017, URL https://eur-lex.europa.eu/legal-content/EN/TXT/?uri=uriserv:OJ.L_.2017.117.01.0001.01.ENG&toc=OJ:L:2017:117:TOC:HTML.

[76] ISO 14971:2007 – medical devices – application of risk management to medical devices, 2nd Ed., Standard, ISO – International Organization for Standardization, URL https://www.iso.org/standard/38193.html, 2007.

[77] A.M.K. Thomas, A.K. Banerjee, The History of Radiology, 1st ed., Oxford Medical Histories, Oxford, United Kingdom, ISBN 978-0-19-963997-7, 2013.

[78] E.H. Burrows, Pioneers and Early Years: History of British Radiology, 1st ed., Colophon, St. Anne, Alderney, Channel Islands, ISBN 978-0-9511676-0-1, 1986.

[79] T.M. Peters, C.A. Linte, Image-guided interventions and computer-integrated therapy: quo vadis?, Medical Image Analysis 33 (2016) 56–63, https://doi.org/10.1016/j.media.2016.06.004.

[80] R. Randell, S. Honey, N. Alvarado, A. Pearman, J. Greenhalgh, A. Long, et al., Embedding robotic surgery into routine practice and impacts on communication and decision making: a review of the experience of surgical teams, Cognition Technology & Work 18 (2) (2016) 423–437, https://doi.org/10.1007/s10111-016-0368-0.

[81] H.J. Marcus, C.J. Payne, A. Hughes-Hallett, G. Gras, K. Leibrandt, D. Nandi, et al., Making the leap: the translation of innovative surgical devices from the laboratory to the operating room, Annals of Surgery 263 (6) (2016) 1077–1078, https://doi.org/10.1097/SLA.0000000000001532.

[82] P. Stefan, S. Habert, A. Winkler, M. Lazarovici, J. Fürmetz, U. Eck, et al., A radiation-free mixed-reality training environment and assessment concept for C-arm-based surgery, International Journal of Computer Assisted Radiology and Surgery (2018), https://doi.org/10.1007/s11548-018-1807-6.

[83] F. Zorriassatine, C. Wykes, R. Parkin, N. Gindy, A survey of virtual prototyping techniques for mechanical product development, in: Proceedings of the Institution of Mechanical Engineers, Part B Journal of Engineering Manufacture 217 (4) (2003) 513–530, https://doi.org/10.1243/095440503321628189.

[84] S. Choi, K. Jung, S.D. Noh, Virtual reality applications in manufacturing industries: past research, present findings, and future directions, Concurrent Engineering 23 (1) (2015) 40–63, https://doi.org/10.1177/1063293X14568814.

[85] C. Jackson, Simulation-Driven Design Benchmark Report: Getting It Right the First Time, Aberdeen Group, 2006.

[86] M. Karlberg, M. Löfstrand, S. Sandberg, M. Lundin, State of the art in simulation-driven design, International Journal of Product Development 18 (1) (2013) 68–87.

[87] P. Jannin, W. Korb, Assessment of image-guided interventions, in: T. Peters, K. Cleary (Eds.), Image-Guided Interventions, Springer US, ISBN 978-0-387-73856-7, 2008, pp. 531–549, ISBN 978-0-387-73858-1.

[88] I.J. Dahabreh, J.A. Chan, A. Earley, D. Moorthy, E.E. Avendano, T.A. Trikalinos, et al., Modeling and Simulation in the Context of Health Technology Assessment: Review of Existing Guidance, Future Research Needs, and Validity Assessment. AHRQ Methods for Effective Health Care, Agency for Healthcare Research and Quality (US), Rockville (MD), 2017, URL http://www.ncbi.nlm.nih.gov/books/NBK424024/.

[89] D. Gaba, The future vision of simulation in health care, Quality and Safety in Health Care 13 (Suppl. 1) (2004) i2–i10, https://doi.org/10.1136/qshc.2004.009878.

[90] Institute of Medicine, To Err Is Human: Building a Safer Health System, The National Academies Press, Washington, DC, ISBN 978-0-309-26174-6, 2000.

[91] D.M. Berwick, K.G. Shojania, Free From Harm: Accelerating Patient Safety Improvement Fifteen Years After to Err Is Human, National Patient Safety Foundation, Boston, MA, 2015.

[92] E.S. Holmboe, O.T. Cate, S.J. Durning, R.E. Hawkins, Assessment challenges in the era of outcomes-based education, in: E.S. Holmboe, S.J. Durning, R.E. Hawkins (Eds.), Practical Guide to the Evaluation of Clinical Competence, Elsevier Health Sciences, ISBN 978-0-323-44894-9, 2017, pp. 1–19, Google-Books-ID: 5fKfDgAAQBAJ.

[93] I. Ghaderi, F. Manji, Y.S. Park, D. Juul, M. Ott, I. Harris, et al., Technical skills assessment toolbox: a review using the unitary framework of validity, Annals of Surgery 261 (2) (2015) 251–262, https://doi.org/10.1097/SLA.0000000000000520.

[94] R. Brydges, R. Hatala, B. Zendejas, P.J. Erwin, D.A. Cook, Linking simulation-based educational assessments and patient-related outcomes: a systematic review and meta-analysis, Academic Medicine 90 (2) (2015) 246, https://doi.org/10.1097/ACM.0000000000000549.

[95] D.D. Anderson, S. Long, G.W. Thomas, M.D. Putnam, J.E. Bechtold, M.D. Karam, Objective structured assessments of technical skills (OSATS) does not assess the quality of the surgical result effectively, Clinical Orthopaedics and Related Research 474 (4) (2016) 874–881, https://doi.org/10.1007/s11999-015-4603-4.

[96] M. Auerbach, D.M. Fein, T.P. Chang, J. Gerard, P. Zaveri, D. Grossman, et al., The correlation of workplace simulation-based assessments with interns' infant lumbar puncture success: a prospective, multicenter, observational study, Simulation in Healthcare 11 (2) (2016) 126, https://doi.org/10.1097/SIH.0000000000000135.

[97] S.J. Johnson, C.M. Hunt, H.M. Woolnough, M. Crawshaw, C. Kilkenny, D.A. Gould, et al., Virtual reality, ultrasound-guided liver biopsy simulator: development and performance discrimination, British Journal of Radiology 85 (1013) (2012) 555–561, https://doi.org/10.1259/bjr/47436030.

[98] M.D. Putnam, E. Kinnucan, J.E. Adams, A.E. Van Heest, D.J. Nuckley, J. Shanedling, On orthopedic surgical skill prediction – the limited value of traditional testing, Journal of Surgical Education 72 (3) (2015) 458–470, https://doi.org/10.1016/j.jsurg.2014.11.001.

[99] J. Gabbard, J. Swan, Usability engineering for augmented reality: employing user-based studies to inform design, IEEE Transactions on Visualization and Computer Graphics 14 (3) (2008) 513–525, https://doi.org/10.1109/TVCG.2008.24.

[100] L. Qian, A. Barthel, A. Johnson, G. Osgood, P. Kazanzides, N. Navab, et al., Comparison of optical see-through head-mounted displays for surgical interventions with object-anchored 2d-display, International Journal of Computer Assisted Radiology and Surgery 12 (6) (2017) 901–910, https://doi.org/10.1007/s11548-017-1564-y.

[101] R.M. Satava, S.B. Jones, Virtual environments for medical training and education, Presence: Teleoperators & Virtual Environments 6 (2) (1997) 139–146, https://doi.org/10.1162/pres.1997.6.2.139.

[102] R.M. Satava, Accomplishments and challenges of surgical simulation, Surgical Endoscopy 15 (3) (2001) 232–241, https://doi.org/10.1007/s004640000369.

[103] J. Frenkel, C. Schubert, G. Kunze, K. Jankov, Using modelica for interactive simulations of technical systems in a virtual reality environment, in: 7th Modelica Conference, 2009, pp. 531–540.

[104] H.C. Fang, S.K. Ong, A.Y.C. Nee, Novel AR-based interface for human–robot interaction and visualization, Advances in Manufacturing 2 (4) (2014) 275–288, https://doi.org/10.1007/s40436-014-0087-9.

[105] A. Ladikos, S. Benhimane, N. Navab, Real-time 3d reconstruction for collision avoidance in interventional environments, in: Medical Image Computing and Computer-Assisted Intervention – MICCAI 2008, in: Lecture Notes in Computer Science, Springer, Berlin, Heidelberg, ISBN 978-3-540-85989-5, 2008, pp. 526–534, ISBN 978-3-540-85990-1.

[106] B. Fürst, J. Sprung, F. Pinto, B. Frisch, T. Wendler, H. Simon, et al., First robotic SPECT for minimally invasive sentinel lymph node mapping, IEEE Transactions on Medical Imaging 35 (3) (2016) 830–838, https://doi.org/10.1109/TMI.2015.2498125.

[107] R.L. Hsu, A.D. Kaye, R.D. Urman, Anesthetic challenges in robotic-assisted urologic surgery, Reviews in Urology 15 (4) (2013) 178–184, URL https://www.ncbi.nlm.nih.gov/pmc/articles/PMC3922322/.

[108] K.C. Zorn, G. Gautam, A.L. Shalhav, R.V. Clayman, T.E. Ahlering, D.M. Albala, et al., Training, credentialing, proctoring and medicolegal risks of robotic urological surgery: recommendations of the society of urologic robotic surgeons, The Journal of Urology 182 (3) (2009) 1126–1132, https://doi.org/10.1016/j.juro.2009.05.042.

[109] Y.L. Lee, G.S. Kilic, J.Y. Phelps, Medicolegal review of liability risks for gynecologists stemming from lack of training in robot-assisted surgery, Journal of Minimally Invasive Gynecology 18 (4) (2011) 512–515, https://doi.org/10.1016/j.jmig.2011.04.002.

[110] M.G. Goldenberg, L. Goldenberg, T.P. Grantcharov, Surgeon performance predicts early continence after robot-assisted radical prostatectomy, Journal of Endourology 31 (9) (2017) 858–863, https://doi.org/10.1089/end.2017.0284.

[111] M.S. Khan, K. Ahmed, A. Gavazzi, R. Gohil, L. Thomas, J. Poulsen, et al., Development and implementation of centralized simulation training evaluation of feasibility, acceptability and construct validity, BJU International 111 (3) (2013) 518–523, https://doi.org/10.1111/j.1464-410X.2012.11204.x.

[112] D. Cumin, M.J. Boyd, C.S. Webster, J.M. Weller, A systematic review of simulation for multidisciplinary team training in operating rooms, Simulation in Healthcare 8 (3) (2013) 171–179, https://doi.org/10.1097/SIH.0b013e31827e2f4c.

[113] D. Stefanidis, N. Sevdalis, J. Paige, B. Zevin, R. Aggarwal, T. Grantcharov, et al., Simulation in surgery: what's needed next?, Annals of Surgery (2014) 1, https://doi.org/10.1097/SLA.0000000000000826, URL http://journals.lww.com/annalsofsurgery/Abstract/publishahead/Simulation_in_Surgery__What_s_Needed_Next__.97671.aspx.

[114] P. Wucherer, P. Stefan, S. Weidert, P. Fallavollita, N. Navab, Task and crisis analysis during surgical training, International Journal of Computer Assisted Radiology and Surgery (2014) 1–10, https://doi.org/10.1007/s11548-013-0970-z.

[115] A.G. Gallagher, Gerald C. O'Sullivan, Fundamentals of Surgical Simulation, Springer, ISBN 978-0-85729-763-1, 2012.

[116] P. Wucherer, P. Stefan, K. Abhari, P. Fallavollita, M. Weigl, M. Lazarovici, et al., Vertebroplasty performance on simulator for 19 surgeons using hierarchical task analysis, IEEE Transactions on Medical Imaging 34 (8) (2015) 1730–1737, https://doi.org/10.1109/TMI.2015.2389033.

[117] M. Weigl, P. Stefan, K. Abhari, P. Wucherer, P. Fallavollita, M. Lazarovici, et al., Intra-operative disruptions, surgeon's mental workload, and technical performance in a full-scale simulated procedure, Surgical Endoscopy 30 (2) (2016) 559–566, https://doi.org/10.1007/s00464-015-4239-1.

[118] P. Stefan, M. Pfandler, P. Wucherer, S. Habert, J. Fürmetz, S. Weidert, et al., Teamtraining und assessment im mixed-reality-basierten simulierten OP, Der Unfallchirurg 121 (4) (2018) 271–277, https://doi.org/10.1007/s00113-018-0467-x.

[119] T. Ungi, D. Sargent, E. Moult, A. Lasso, C. Pinter, R.C. McGraw, et al., Perk tutor: an open-source training platform for ultrasound-guided needle insertions, IEEE Transactions on Biomedical Engineering 59 (12) (2012) 3475–3481, https://doi.org/10.1109/TBME.2012.2219307.

[120] S. Kalyuga, P. Ayres, P. Chandler, J. Sweller, The expertise reversal effect, Educational Psychologist 38 (1) (2003) 23–31, https://doi.org/10.1207/S15326985EP3801_4.

[121] B.P. Kerfoot, N. Kissane, The use of gamification to boost residents' engagement in simulation training, JAMA Surgery 149 (11) (2014) 1208–1209, https://doi.org/10.1001/jamasurg.2014.1779, URL https://jamanetwork.com/journals/jamasurgery/fullarticle/1903020.

[122] J.R. Korndorffer Jr., S.J. Kasten, S.M. Downing, A call for the utilization of consensus standards in the surgical education literature, The American Journal of Surgery 199 (1) (2010) 99–104, https://doi.org/10.1016/j.amjsurg.2009.08.018.

[123] C. Dawson, Towards a conceptual profile: rethinking conceptual mediation in the light of recent cognitive and neuroscientific findings, Research in Science Education 44 (3) (2014) 389–414, https://doi.org/10.1007/s11165-013-9388-4.

[124] H.L. Roediger, J.D. Karpicke, The power of testing memory: basic research and implications for educational practice, Perspectives on Psychological Science: A Journal of the Association for Psychological Science 1 (3) (2006) 181–210, https://doi.org/10.1111/j.1745-6916.2006.00012.x.

[125] H.L. O'Brien, E.G. Toms, What is user engagement? A conceptual framework for defining user engagement with technology, Journal of the American Society for Information Science and Technology 59 (6) (2008) 938–955, https://doi.org/10.1002/asi.20801.

[126] W. Choi, O. Dyens, T. Chan, M. Schijven, S. Lajoie, M.E. Mancini, et al., Engagement and learning in simulation: recommendations of the Simnovate Engaged Learning Domain Group, BMJ Simulation and Technology Enhanced Learning 3 (Suppl. 1) (2017) S23–S32, https://doi.org/10.1136/bmjstel-2016-000177, URL https://stel.bmj.com/content/3/Suppl_1/S23.

[127] R.T. Azuma, A survey of augmented reality, Presence: Teleoperators & Virtual Environments 6 (4) (1997) 355–385, https://doi.org/10.1162/pres.1997.6.4.355.

[128] H. Alemzadeh, J. Raman, N. Leveson, Z. Kalbarczyk, R.K. Iyer, Adverse events in robotic surgery: a retrospective study of 14 years of FDA data, PLoS ONE 11 (4) (2016) e0151470, https://doi.org/10.1371/journal.pone.0151470.

Index

A

Abdominal
  intersubject registration, 308
  interventions, 811, 850
  lesions, 688
  organ segmentation, 142
  surgery, 663, 796, 986
Abnormal anatomy, 605
Abnormal brain tissues, 383
Absorbed energy distribution (AED), 628
Accelerated brain aging, 391
Accuracy, 4, 169, 172, 173, 223–225, 321, 324,
      326, 329, 331, 334, 335, 433, 436, 446,
      538, 590, 594, 595, 782, 785, 790, 791,
      803, 804, 810, 811, 818, 819, 830, 837,
      954, 957, 958, 960
  classification, 472, 475, 538
  clinical, 989
  detection, 475, 733, 751
  heart, 226
  lesions detection, 85
  prediction, 389, 470
  registration, 324, 334, 335, 458, 711, 962, 965
  segmentation, 143–145, 148, 154, 174, 175,
      180, 225, 250, 260
  validation, 785
Acoustic detection, 763
Acquisition, 1, 9, 10, 12, 14, 232, 349, 350, 356,
      362, 489, 636, 653, 658, 678, 685, 898,
      902, 933, 939
  CBCT, 647
  conditions, 2
  equipment, 500
  geometry, 637
  improvement, 349
  interventional, 753
  medical image, 562
  MR, 15, 346, 684, 685
  protocols, 355, 356, 359, 360, 649
  sequences, 345, 349, 362, 635
  strategies, 12
  system, 637
  time, 355
  volumetric, 654

Actionable information, 938
Actionwise objective function, 213
Active appearance models (AAM), 275
Active shape model (ASM), 217, 275
Acute ischemic stroke patients, 657
Adaptive regularization, 313
Advanced
  detection methodology, 78
  neurosurgical instrumentation, 662
  surgical skill, 996
  user interaction, 984
  visualization, 988
Advanced brain aging (ABA), 390
Adversarial
  discriminators, 166
  domain adaptation, 560, 567
  encoder network, 565
  learning, 185, 186
  loss, 166, 170, 177, 178, 185, 186, 191, 192,
      555, 563–565
  network, 166, 174, 177, 179, 548, 555, 556,
      558, 564, 565
  segmentation methods, 564
  training, 172, 188, 337, 548, 555, 558, 563–565,
      568
Aggregated assessment scores, 997
Aggregating predictions, 470
Airway segmentation, 99, 100
Algebraic reconstruction techniques (ART), 644
Aliasing artifacts, 44, 53, 564
Alzheimer disease (AD), 383, 390, 391
Amazon Mechanical Turk (AMT), 112, 113
American Heart Association (AHA), 404
Amyloid pathology, 344, 348
Analysis performance, 264
Anatomical
  labels, 294
  segmentation, 93
  structures, 91–93, 145, 190, 193, 205, 206, 250,
      458, 547, 560, 564, 576, 805, 811, 936,
      955, 956
  structures segmentation, 457, 955
  visualization, 702

Anatomy, 2, 3, 5, 100, 155, 156, 206, 280, 330,
        458, 469, 470, 605, 611, 614, 722, 797,
        798, 805, 806, 917, 921, 936, 940, 957
    brain, 155
    cardiac, 273
    heart, 402
    human, 138, 727
    interest, 782
    liver, 658
    patient, 605, 607, 649, 790, 875, 943
    target, 610
Annotated image datasets, 112
Annotated landmarks, 219, 323
Anomalous performance, 943
Apparent diffusion coefficient (ADC), 390
Application programming interface (API), 791
Architecture, 39, 45, 47, 49, 52–54, 68, 76, 78, 85,
        114, 117, 167, 187, 192, 193, 235, 277,
        288, 416, 418, 481, 487, 493, 495, 497,
        507, 512, 514, 516, 518, 525, 527, 540,
        874, 883
    choice, 494
    convolutional, 169
    design, 175
    details, 192
    FCN, 68–70, 74, 80, 85
    network, 32, 44, 46, 49, 54, 68, 192, 215, 497
    ResNet, 494
    specifications, 81
Arterial spin labeling (ASL), 344
Artifacts, 2, 14, 29, 46, 53, 194, 356, 359, 469,
        470, 560, 570, 639, 644, 674, 680
Artificial Intelligence (AI), 735, 980
Artificial landmarks, 731
Artificial Neural Network (ANN), 483
Assessment, 345, 350, 352, 403, 409, 604–608,
        610, 797, 812, 911–913, 918, 932, 933,
        945, 992, 995–997, 1000
    bias, 912
    computerized, 915, 918
    criteria, 996
    framework, 913
    functional, 355
    instruments, 996
    methods, 912
    performance, 911
    quantitative, 914
    scales, 912
    strategy, 1003

    surgical, 912, 914
    tasks, 916
    tools, 996
Assistant surgeon, 990
Assisted interventions, 911
Atlases, 6, 10, 138–140, 384, 458, 607
    CT image, 5
    images, 5–7, 10, 143, 148, 151, 458
    MR images, 6
    multiple, 140
    patches, 6
    performance, 147
Atrial fibrillation (AF), 175
Atrial segmentation, 276
Augmentation dataset, 195, 238
Augmented network, 233
Augmented reality, 606, 612, 614, 707, 715, 725,
        823, 881, 886, 887, 917, 919, 923, 934,
        936, 979, 980, 988, 1003
    headsets, 868
    HMD, 881
    visualization, 911
Autofluorescence information, 761
Automated
    classification, 388
    detection, 66
    final segmentation, 263
    image segmentation, 955
    intervention, 846
    landmark location, 586
    lesion detection, 78
    liver segmentation, 73
    liver segmentation tool, 85
    pancreas segmentation, 112
    presegmentation, 263
    segmentation, 175, 249, 270, 274, 276, 277,
        288, 405, 406, 413
    surgical systems, 936
    system performance, 70
Automatic
    bone segmentation, 709
    detection, 288
    left atrium segmentation, 175
    liver segmentation, 84, 85, 167, 170, 172
    liver segmentation in CT volumes, 167
    segmentation, 141, 233, 709
    segmentation methods, 435
Automatic brightness control (ABC), 631
Automatic exposure control (AEC), 631

Automatically selected features, 732
Autonomous medical robots, 985
Autonomous robotic, 849
Average nodal pressure (ANP), 957

B

Backbone network, 179
Backbone segmentation network, 197
Backpropagation
    algorithm, 485, 486
    flow, 233
    rule, 486, 487
    standard, 238
Bag classification, 522
Bag label, 522–524, 528, 529, 537, 543
Bag label predictions, 524, 527
Baseline architecture, 70
Beating heart, 702, 704, 712
Benchmark performance metrics, 919
Benign lesions, 83
Bhattacharyya divergence (BD), 329
Bidirectional LSTM, 517, 518
Binary
    classification, 166, 209
    detection, 73
    disease classification, 389
    labels, 525, 540
Biomedical image, 236, 560
    analysis, 548, 559, 565, 568, 570
    segmentation, 231, 233, 237, 244, 560
Biopsy, 533, 543, 653, 662, 685, 687, 757, 759,
        763, 796, 798, 852, 853
    breast, 848
    guns, 677, 678
Bipolar disease, 388
Blood vessel segmentation, 100
Blurred predictions, 563
Body mass index (BMI), 982
Bone
    fracture surgery, 812
    resection instrument guidance, 843
    segmentation, 710
    surface segmentation, 266
    tumor surgery, 798
Boundary segmentation, 277
Boundary shift integral (BSI), 360
Brachytherapy needle driver, 848
Brain, 3, 9, 10, 138, 148, 157, 184, 186, 232, 326,
        347, 348, 357, 381, 382, 385, 386, 389,
        432, 469, 472–474, 576, 796, 805, 955,
        958, 963, 965, 968
    abnormalities, 389
    activity, 348, 380, 472
    age prediction, 381, 389
    aging, 381, 390, 391, 394
    alterations, 383
    anatomical variation, 325
    anatomy, 155
    atlas, 138, 156
    atrophy, 361, 383, 390, 391
    changes, 344, 356, 379, 383, 387, 389, 391
    CT, 331
    CT images, 78
    deformations, 324, 954
    development, 156, 389, 390
    diseases, 393
    extraction, 392
    functional, 380, 394
    functional areas, 138
    functions, 156
    hallucination, 16, 17
    human, 389
    image registration procedure, 320
    images, 322, 381, 382, 440
    imaging, 344, 345, 380, 382, 472
    lesions detection, 392
    mask, 436
    maturation, 389
    metabolism, 347
    MR images registration accuracy, 324
    MRI, 186, 322, 436, 469, 471, 472
    parenchyma, 346
    regions, 348, 386, 387
    registration, 142
    related quantification, 326
    shift, 811, 963–965
    stimulation electrode, 797
    structure, 138, 358, 382, 394
    surface, 965
    tissue, 347
    tumor, 238, 449, 796
    tumor segmentation, 565
    volume, 9, 10
Brain development index (BDI), 389
Breast
    biopsy, 848
    cancer diagnosis, 761
    intervention robotic systems, 848

C

CAI systems, 862, 867, 877, 886, 888, 889, 984, 998, 1003
Camera ego motion, 737
Canady robotic surgical, 846
Cancer
    diagnosis, 605, 767
    interventions, 761
    liver, 657
    lung, 91–94
    patients, 77, 685
Candidate atlases, 141
Candidate detection, 75
Candidate detection lesions, 68
Canonical correlation analysis (CCA), 78
Capsule robots, 853
Cardiac
    anatomy, 273
    dataset, 214
    disease, 568
    motion, 275, 285, 402, 409, 412, 684
    motion modeling, 274
    MRI segmentation, 276, 277, 280
    segmentation, 274, 275, 288
    structures segmentation, 277
    surgery, 703, 850, 935
    ultrasound imaging, 703, 704
    wall motion, 288
    wall segmentation, 274
Cardiac allograft vasculopathy (CAV), 260
Cardiac magnetic resonance (CMR), 273
Cardiac resynchronization therapy (CRT), 288, 411
Cardiovascular
    dataset, 201
    image dataset, 194
Cartilage segmentation, 265
Cartilage segmentation for machine learning, 265
Cascaded deep learning framework, 235
Categorical
    classification, 390
    label, 463
    label prediction, 462
CBCT
    acquisition, 647
    acquisition protocol, 648
    guidance, 651, 661, 662
    image acquisition, 638
Cell segmentation, 533

Cerebral microbleed detection, 112
Cerebrovascular disease, 383
CGAN, 553
    architectures, 79, 81
    network, 81, 86
    training, 82
Challenge dataset, 238
Channel attention block (CAB), 277, 288
Checkerboard artifacts, 193
Chest CT images, 92–94, 96, 97, 101, 102, 336
Chest medical image processing, 93
Chronic obstructive pulmonary disease (COPD), 97
Chronic total occlusions (CTO), 660
Cine acquisitions, 660
Circumferential motion, 410
CisstRobot, 877
Class
    classification, 211
    disease, 119
    labels, 523, 524, 534, 537, 542
    predictions, 535
Classification
    accuracy, 472, 475, 538
    automated, 388
    binary, 166, 209
    capability, 235
    categorical, 390
    class, 211
    clinical, 350
    disease, 111, 113, 114, 122, 123, 276, 381, 392
    error, 72
    for landmark detection, 211
    forests, 470
    hyperplane, 387
    layers, 187, 236, 487, 496
    medical image, 123
    methods, 393
    models, 184
    multilabel, 120
    networks, 86
    performance, 527, 532, 538, 539
    pixelwise, 237
    problem, 392, 469, 471
    results, 99, 472, 544
    RFs, 469, 473
    supervised, 387
    system, 895
    tasks, 126, 184, 186, 464, 471, 491, 498

threshold, 538, 539
voxel, 100
Clinical, 117, 130, 184, 355, 363, 390, 393, 394,
    430, 442, 754, 758, 795, 804, 833, 836,
    894–896, 939, 941, 965, 989, 992, 993,
    997, 999
  acceptance, 981
  accuracy, 989
  analysis, 433
  application, 451, 751, 807, 898, 935, 938, 958,
    986
  application areas, 986
  benefits, 899, 985–987
  center, 114, 130
  challenges, 360, 990
  characteristics, 432
  classification, 350
  competency, 996
  context, 751, 934, 941
  data, 381, 432, 448, 451, 900, 933
  data management, 448
  devices, 750
  diagnosis, 117, 185, 326
  domain, 981
  endpoints, 380
  environment, 959, 993, 996, 998
  evaluation, 357, 965, 989, 992, 997
  evaluation report, 992
  experts, 899
  guidelines, 932
  impact, 899
  implementation, 894, 999
  indications, 986
  information, 113
  infrastructure, 993
  innovation, 996
  integration, 994
  interpretation, 362
  interventions, 817
  involvement, 994
  key, 992
  measurements, 983
  measures, 380
  notes, 939
  outcome, 380, 430, 767, 980–982, 995
  PACS database, 117
  partners, 898, 899
  performance, 995, 1003
  perspective, 115
  practice, 29, 53, 66, 122, 183, 184, 344, 345,
    350, 353, 354, 356, 360, 404, 413, 419,
    432, 473, 561, 570, 712, 757, 894, 896,
    939
  procedure, 432, 819, 981, 994
  relevance, 113, 810
  research, 360, 894, 895, 897, 901, 903, 905
  routine, 109, 805, 941, 988, 991–994, 1004
  service research, 895
  sessions, 899
  setting, 818, 894, 989, 990
  significance, 980
  specialty, 798
  standard, 991
  studies, 750, 955, 992, 1000
  symptoms, 344, 355, 357, 391
  tasks, 993
  team, 993
  tests, 898
  tissue imaging, 748
  training, 994
  translatable idea, 899
  translation, 157, 736, 893, 894, 911
  translation pathway, 900, 905
  trials, 347, 353, 355, 362, 363, 710, 711, 751,
    753, 894, 895, 899, 900, 903, 904, 992,
    999
  ultrasound scanners, 785
  usage, 451
  users, 998
  validation, 810
  validity, 354
  workflow, 602, 613, 685, 898, 972, 989, 990,
    995, 998
  workspace, 829, 830, 994
Clinical evaluation report (CER), 992
Clinical Research Organization (CRO), 992
Clinically
  acceptable, 804
  adequate, 803
  impactful, 452
  informative brain, 383
  irrelevant, 432
  meaningful, 130
  relevant, 963
  relevant dataset, 432
  relevant information, 939
Coarse initial segmentation, 469
Coaxial puncture needles, 678

Cognitive assessments, 353
Coherent point drifting (CPD), 285
Collaborative robotics, 985
Collaborative robotics toolkit, 866
Color information, 730
Combination, 14, 45, 52, 71, 77, 187, 222, 223,
        298, 306, 310, 349, 361–363, 389, 394,
        403, 408, 413, 442, 448, 526, 538, 541,
        555, 564, 586, 627, 635, 654–656, 724,
        732, 911, 914, 920, 943
    features, 441
    linear, 30, 221, 441
    motion, 412
    registration, 5
    segmentation, 564
Comfortable patient positioning, 685
Committed clinical partners, 898
Competency assessment, 909, 997
Complementary metal oxide semiconductor
        (CMOS), 630
Complete dataset, 445
Comprehensive constraints, 177
Computed tomography (CT), 2, 91, 344, 404, 430,
        674, 795, 921, 954, 963, 969, 971, 972
    brain, 331
    datasets, 178
    image
        patches, 560
        resolution, 77
        translation, 186
    imagery, 79
    images, 3–5, 65, 70, 77–79, 95, 96, 98–100,
        178, 180, 195, 297, 331, 459, 469, 470,
        473, 474, 561, 595, 711
    interventions, 674
    liver, 303
    lung, 92, 302, 313
    patch, 6
    registration, 969
    scan slices, 800
    scanners, 70, 77
    segmentation, 197
    volumes, 78, 167, 168, 171, 172, 178, 179, 468,
        610
Computed tomography perfusion (CTP), 311
Computer aided orthopaedic surgery (CAOS), 798
Computer assisted intervention (CAI), 603, 862,
        888, 979–981, 984, 988, 1004

Computer assisted medical interventions (CAMI),
        603
Computer assisted surgery (CAS), 603, 796, 980
Computer vision, 12, 15, 25, 26, 53, 110, 111,
        113, 114, 124, 165, 167, 176, 186, 297,
        303, 308, 310, 313, 386, 392, 460, 468,
        524, 534, 747, 749
Computer vision community, 2
Computer vision tasks, 167
Computerized
    assessment, 915, 918
    assessment methods, 913
    metastatic liver lesion detection, 66
    skill assessment, 910
Concurrent versions system (CVS), 871
Conditional GANs, 553, 554, 562, 567
Conditional random field (CRF), 187
Congenital heart disease, 402, 403, 406, 414, 415
Connected component (CC), 70
Consensus voxels, 153
Constant motion, 417
Contextual
    appearance information, 234
    features, 466, 467
    information, 138, 187, 237, 239, 241
Continuous
    deformation fields, 296
    label space, 462
    motion, 702
    registration, 731, 734
Continuum robot, 851
Contour detection, 187, 278
Contrast information, 764
Control acquisitions, 686
Control motion, 613
Controllable objects, 835
Conventional
    classification networks, 167
    endoscope, 730
    interventions, 987
    laparoscopic surgery, 987
    local regularization, 310
    needles, 677
    registration algorithms, 324, 325
    registration methods, 322, 337
    registration methods accuracy, 336
    robots, 852
    segmentation loss, 170
    voxelwise classification RFs, 476

Convolution layers, 67, 167, 168, 487, 488
Convolutional
    architecture, 169
    layers, 118, 125, 176, 235, 241, 279, 334, 392,
        487, 492–494, 498, 499, 524, 541, 547
    network, 93, 168
Convolutional neural network (CNN), 93, 112,
        122, 126, 155, 185, 187, 189, 191, 211,
        234, 235, 332, 383, 392, 430, 443, 472,
        481, 482, 517, 518, 524, 547, 564, 565,
        587, 590, 710, 732, 733, 914, 916, 940
    architectures, 74, 487, 492, 493
    based segmentation, 188
    features, 499, 734
    layers, 487
    regression, 561, 563
    segmentation network, 169
    training, 126
COPD disease, 97
Coregistration, 658
Coronary
    heart disease, 405, 407
    OCT segmentation, 260
    wall layers segmentation, 261
Coronary artery disease (CAD), 404, 412
Correction network, 335
Correlation ratio (CR), 320
Cranial interventions, 843
Craniofacial surgery, 611, 612
Cross entropy loss, 280
CTO guidance, 653
CVD risk assessment, 404
CycleGAN, 166, 174, 189, 193, 194, 557, 558,
        562
    block, 179

D

Da Vinci
    manipulators, 878
    robot, 986
    robotic surgery, 881
    surgical, 723
    surgical robot, 614, 862, 875
Data augmentation, 81, 85, 185, 192, 238, 277,
        278, 281, 496, 534, 535, 537
Data augmentation approach, 192
Data distribution service (DDS), 866
Data visualization, 250, 268, 883

Dataset
    augmentation, 495
    cardiac, 214
    cardiovascular, 201
    lesions detection, 71
    medical image, 110, 117
    MRI, 180
DCNN architecture, 117, 119
Death after surgery, 935
Decent atlases, 141
Decoder layers, 176
Deconvolutional layers, 235, 279
Deep
    contextual network, 187, 236, 237, 241
    convolutional networks, 898
    fully convolutional neural network architecture,
        167
    layer, 277, 288
    learning, 25, 42, 44, 45, 78, 84, 86, 102,
        110–112, 114, 155, 187, 211, 218, 232,
        235, 239, 274, 276, 277, 321, 332, 392,
        430, 435, 441, 443, 476, 488, 497, 498,
        514, 528, 533, 547, 646, 647, 710, 737,
        941, 990, 991
    algorithms, 109, 174, 276, 392, 524
    approaches, 646
    capabilities, 77
    frameworks, 498
    in biomedical image analysis, 568
    in computer vision, 112
    methods, 66, 241, 277, 332, 381, 534, 639
    paradigm, 737
    perspective, 489
    techniques, 25, 112, 276, 338, 942
    tools, 65
    network, 241, 288, 335
    neural network architectures, 524
    segmentation network, 241
Deep brain stimulation (DBS), 689, 805
Deep convolutional neural network (DCNN), 93,
        117, 233–235, 240
Deep layer aggregation (DLA), 277
Deep neural network (DNN), 47, 48, 93, 109,
        111, 113, 165, 172, 176, 201, 218, 233,
        236, 240, 244, 277, 278, 280, 282, 293,
        381, 392, 523, 524, 526
Deep reinforcement learning (DRL), 211
Deeply supervised network, 167, 187
Defective pixels, 632

Deformable
  image registration, 296, 313, 338
  image registration methods, 313
  multimodal registration, 329, 330
  registration, 5–7, 320, 321, 327, 331, 332, 335,
    336, 662
  registration network, 337
Deformation field, 139, 294, 296, 320, 321, 323,
    585, 962, 963, 965
  gradients, 312
  local, 298
  patterns, 299
Demons registration, 296, 312
Denoising network, 47
DenseNet architecture, 494
DenseNet based architectures, 197
Depth network, 126
Detection, 65, 66, 92, 93, 111, 112, 120, 156, 172,
    184, 223–226, 233, 234, 273, 274, 390,
    457, 458, 468, 628, 636, 660, 662, 727,
    732–734, 747, 749, 754, 756, 757, 819, 833
  accuracy, 475, 733, 751
  algorithm, 93
  approaches, 86
  automated, 66
  automatic, 288
  binary, 73
  challenge, 77
  disease, 113
  efficiency, 628
  landmarks, 167, 205–207, 211, 214, 219, 225,
    227
  lesions, 71, 73, 76, 83–86
  lung cancer, 91, 92
  measures, 86
  methods, 734
  networks, 186, 222
  object, 111, 112, 232, 494, 500, 732
  performance, 68, 73, 74
  performance evaluation, 85
  process, 93
  rate, 85
  results, 76, 85, 222
  software, 83, 84
  strategy, 223
  surgical, 733
  surgical tool, 733
  system, 85
  target, 759
    task, 66, 67, 83, 85, 631
  ultrasound, 761
Detective quantum efficiency (DQE), 628
Device master record (DMR), 992
Device performance information, 900
Diabetic macular edema (DME), 257
Diagnose related groups (DRG), 993
Diagnosis, 51, 54, 65, 66, 77, 87, 96, 97, 326, 350,
    357, 359, 361, 532, 540, 604–606, 747,
    757, 761, 817, 819, 932, 933, 961
  cancer, 605, 767
  clinical, 117, 185, 326
  disease, 112, 387
  interventional, 767
  lung cancer, 91
  medical, 522
  medical image, 113
Diagnostic information, 981
Diagnostic pathology, 113
Dice loss, 170, 176, 281
Dice similarity coefficient (DSC), 280
Dictionary learning, 26, 30, 31, 39, 52, 74
Differential diagnosis, 344, 357
Diffuse lung disease, 92, 93, 96
Diffuse lung disease progresses, 97
Diffuse reflection spectroscopy (DRS), 754
Diffusion tensor imaging (DTI), 347, 385, 418,
    474
Diffusion weighted imaging (DWI), 474
Digitally reconstructed radiographs (DRR), 1002
Discontinuous motion, 295
Discrete registration, 305, 306
Discriminant features, 524
Discriminator, 166, 170, 185, 188, 193, 194, 337,
    548, 549
  domain, 559, 565, 567
  gradient, 551
  layers, 81
  model, 188
  network, 51, 166, 179, 548, 549, 551, 554, 564,
    567
  trained, 81, 166
Disease, 93, 96, 97, 109, 110, 113, 116, 118, 119,
    130, 171, 322, 344–346, 348, 381, 389,
    390, 402, 407, 434, 435, 451, 472, 474,
    533, 562, 565, 570, 582, 689, 747, 750,
    757, 805, 900, 953, 956
  cardiac, 568
  categories, 118

class, 119
classification, 111, 113, 114, 122, 123, 276, 381, 392
decision, 122
detection, 113
diagnosis, 112, 387
evolution, 347, 362
heatmaps, 120
heterogeneity, 381
heterogeneity detection, 381
localization, 110, 113, 120
lung, 93, 97, 102
path, 357
patients, 388
progression, 419
related brain changes, 380
stages, 347, 361
subjects, 347
type, 122
Diseased
    cardiovascular function, 412
    sites, 430
    subjects, 354
    tissue, 416
Disentangled features, 552
Displacement label, 309
Distinctive landmarks, 323
DOF needle manipulator, 846
Domain
    adaptation, 172, 176–178, 180, 185, 186, 548, 558, 565
        methods, 174, 180
        network, 180
        task, 175
    clinical, 981
    discriminator, 559, 565, 567
    specific features, 276
    target, 172–174, 180, 189, 548, 554–558, 564, 567, 569, 570, 940
    voxel, 642
DVRK system architecture, 875
Dyssynchronous motion, 412
Dystonia patients, 689

E

Ejection fraction (EF), 407
Electromagnetic pose sensors, 791
Electron Microscopy (EM), 232
Electronic Health Record (EHR), 604, 938

EM segmentation evaluation, 239
EM segmentation task, 233
Emphysema diagnosis, 97
Emphysema voxels, 97
Encoder layers, 176
Encoder network, 37, 167
Encoder network adversarial, 565
Encountering LSTM, 516
Encourage networks, 190
Encouraging backpropagation, 242
End diastolic (ED), 274
End systolic (ES), 274
Endoscope, 722–725, 731, 747, 759, 844–846, 850
    conventional, 730
    manufacturers, 752
    types, 722
Endoscopic
    robotic platform, 851
    surgery, 613, 798
    ultrasound, 780, 791
Endoscopic camera manipulator (ECM), 875
Endovascular interventions, 681
Engaged learning, 1003
ENT surgery, 612
Erroneous detection, 284
Error backpropagation, 510
Euclidean loss (EL), 119
Evaluation, 4, 116, 120, 126, 172, 233, 238, 242, 244, 274, 281, 433, 444, 445, 800, 803, 806, 808, 819, 820, 831, 995, 999
    clinical, 357, 965, 989, 992, 997
    data, 446
    metrics, 172, 239, 242, 444, 446
    performance, 444, 924
    quantitative, 126, 233, 837
    scenarios, 995
    segmentation, 196
    set, 444–447
    system, 239
Excelsius robotic system, 842
Exhaustive combination search, 361
Expectation maximization (EM), 144, 146
Exponential linear units (ELU), 491
Extensive evaluation, 14
Extracting
    computational features, 437
    features, 440

individual features, 465
lung areas, 102
patches, 540

F

False negative (FN), 537
False positive (FP), 537
False positive rate (FPR), 446
Fast marching method (FMM), 95
FC layers, 492
FCN
    architecture, 68–70, 74, 80, 85
    network architecture, 69
Features, 6, 7, 94, 174, 179, 236, 277, 278, 280,
    323, 327, 330, 430, 431, 434, 436, 459,
    460, 465, 489, 492–494, 523, 524, 537,
    548, 565, 586–589, 730–732, 912, 922, 924
    adversarial loss, 179
    CNNs, 499, 734
    combination, 441
    contextual, 466, 467
    hierarchical, 176
    instance, 523
    intensity, 442
    layer, 168
    learning, 212
    local, 524
    medical image, 430
    predictive, 432
    quantitative, 430
    radiomics, 436, 437, 440
    relevant, 475
    semantic, 437, 733
    tracked, 728
    visualization, 885
Ferromagnetic objects, 782
Fetal heart, 706
Fiber architecture, 418, 419
Fiducial localization error (FLE), 778, 782
Fiducial registration, 778, 780
Fiducial registration error (FRE), 778, 780
Field of view (FOV), 171
Finer scale supervoxels, 471
Fissure curve detection, 103
Flow network, 256
Fluoroscopic guidance, 654, 660
Fluoroscopic visualization, 663
Focal airspace disease, 111
Forest prediction, 461

Formative assessment, 1002
Forward CycleGAN, 562
Foundation model anatomy (FMA), 206
Fourier burst accumulation (FBA), 14
Fractional anisotropy (FA), 354
Fracture surgery, 799
Fracture surgery bone, 812
Fracture visualization, 800
Free form deformation (FFD), 296
Free navigation, 850
Fully connected networks (FCN), 524
Fully convolutional network (FCN), 67, 99, 167,
    185, 218, 235
Functional
    assessment, 355
    brain, 380, 394
    brain changes, 382
    loss, 275
Functional anisotropy (FA), 385, 390
Fuse image labels, 143
Fused information, 609
Fused segmentation, 143, 144

G

Galil motion control, 847
Gastrointestinal biopsy, 853
Gated recurrent units (GRU), 514, 517
Gene ontology (GO), 940
Generative adversarial network (GAN), 78, 80, 81,
    165, 166, 185, 186, 188, 337, 548
Generative networks, 177, 178
Generator, 81, 166, 170, 185, 188, 337, 548, 549,
    781
    in GANs, 188
    learning view, 185
    loss, 170
    model, 188, 553
    network, 166, 170, 548, 558, 564, 569
    outputs, 565
Geographic landmarks, 205
Geometrical information, 749
Gland segmentation, 187
Global rating scales (GRS), 913
Globus pallidus interna (GPI), 805
Gradient information, 592, 709
Gradient vector flow (GVF), 252
Graphical User Interface (GUI), 268, 449, 847
Graphics Processing Unit (GPU), 964

Grasped objects, 801
Gray matter (GM), 3, 325, 389
Green fluorescent protein (GFP), 751
Ground glass opacity (GGO), 95
Ground truth, 116, 121, 167, 168, 170, 186, 191, 196, 215, 238, 239, 278, 280, 283, 336, 352, 355, 433, 474, 737, 803, 810, 811
   segmentation, 281
Groupwise registration, 474
Guidance, 337, 606, 610, 653, 660, 676, 679, 686, 706, 714, 760, 761, 767, 844, 846, 899, 911, 923, 982, 988, 1003
   CBCT, 651, 661, 662
   for neurosurgical interventions, 843
   interventional, 657, 702, 767
   intraoperative, 600, 702, 842
   method, 911
   module, 711
   needle, 653, 659, 685, 763
   surgical, 703, 706, 711, 761, 789
   system, 707, 842, 846
   ultrasound, 660

H

Haar features, 588
HAMMER registration, 334
Handcrafted features, 524
Harmonized acquisitions, 10
Head mounted display (HMD), 881
Healthcare technology assessment, 995
Healthy hearts, 402
Healthy patients, 561, 570
Heart, 94, 194, 223, 225, 226, 273, 275, 276, 281, 283, 402–404, 406, 407, 409, 659, 660, 674, 676, 702, 704, 712, 715
   accuracy, 226
   anatomy, 402
   attack, 273
   beat, 407, 416
   center, 195
   chambers, 214, 411
   cycles, 214, 215
   diseases, 92, 404, 419
   failure, 273, 276, 405, 407, 409, 415
   failure patients, 407
   intraoperative, 714
   model, 275, 285
   muscle, 410
   patient, 419

performance, 407
   segmentation accuracy, 226
   wall, 405, 410
Helical fiber architecture, 410
Hepatic malignant lesions, 78
Hepatic motion, 311
Heterogeneous disease, 393
HFpEF patients, 409
Hidden layers, 74, 482, 483, 531
Hierarchical
   agglomerative segmentation, 234
   features, 176
   layers, 235
Hierarchical Deep Aggregation (HDA), 278
High Intensity Focused Ultrasound (HIFU), 844
High resolution (HR), 95
Hinge Loss (HL), 119
Hippocampal segmentation, 361
Hippocampal volume loss, 358
Hospital information infrastructure, 609
Hounsfield Unit (HU), 66, 79, 631
HR acquisition, 14
Human
   anatomy, 138, 727
   brain, 389
   patient, 1002
Hypodermic needle, 784

I

ImageNet dataset, 123, 496, 498, 570
ImageNet pretrained deep CNN, 113
Impeding ultrasound imaging, 705
Imperfect registration, 144
Imperial College Surgical Assessment Device (ICSAD), 914
Implanted cardioverter defibrillators (ICD), 690
Independent subspace analysis (ISA), 334
Industrial multipurpose robotic systems, 999
Industrial robots, 985
Infant brain images registration, 325
Infant brain MR images, 322, 330
Inferior performance, 140, 234, 241
Information
   assistance, 609
   bottleneck, 836
   clinical, 113
   contextual, 138, 187, 237, 239, 241
   dissemination, 989
   flow, 515, 603, 933

fusion, 608
intensity, 144
interactive visualization, 983
label, 151
local, 188, 235
loss, 187
manipulation, 989
overlay, 944
patient, 982, 988
predictive, 474
processing, 600, 756, 984
relevant, 569, 1003
semantic, 175, 279
system, 608
technology, 607
visualization, 989
Information Artifact Ontology (IAO), 940
Informative features, 441
Initialized deformation field, 322, 323, 326
Inpatient hospitalization, 690
Inspirational network training, 110
Instance
    features, 523
    labels, 523–525, 532
    segmentation, 492, 494
Institutional review board (IRB), 82
Integrated development environment (IDE), 873
Intelligence Augmentation (IA), 980
Intelligent CAI systems, 990
Intensity
    based features, 436
    features, 442
    information, 144
Intensive care units (ICU), 608
Interactive segmentation, 350, 810
Interactive visualization, 797
Interactive visualization information, 983
Interface definition language (IDL), 865
Interferometric detection, 760
Internet Communications Engine (ICE), 866
Internet Protocol (IP), 864
Interpatient registration, 972
Interpretable prediction mechanism, 110
Interslice features, 169
Interstitial lung disease detection, 112
Intersubject abdominal registration, 310
Intervention, 604–607, 610, 615, 674, 675, 678,
    683, 747, 767, 797, 804, 811, 846, 848,

918, 932, 933, 938, 939, 944, 980,
    989–991, 995
    automated, 846
    guidance technologies, 911
    needle, 847
    phase, 606
    physician, 849
    tools, 842
    training, 924
Interventional, 607
    acquisition, 753
    applications, 610, 678, 756
    device guidance tool, 763
    devices, 600, 680, 683, 765
    diagnosis, 767
    environment, 606
    guidance, 657, 702, 767
    imaging, 628, 630, 638, 639, 646, 711, 748,
        749, 754, 988
    imaging systems, 630
    imaging techniques, 761
    instrument, 679, 680, 682
    medicine, 600, 603, 608, 615
    MR, 678, 679
    MRI, 611, 674–677, 684
    oncology, 981, 991
    options, 608
    plan, 606, 609
    platform, 682
    procedural skills, 913
    procedure, 600, 603, 628, 635, 652, 654, 655,
        659, 702, 899, 910, 912, 917
    procedure training, 914
    process, 610
    radiologists, 992
    radiology, 608, 610, 630, 653–655, 980, 981
    radiology procedures, 657
    radiology robotic development, 986
    robots, 613
    rooms, 609, 615
    skills, 912, 913, 925
    stages, 607
    suite, 602, 606
    surgery, 850
    systems, 605, 615
    technique, 991
    tools, 678, 919
    training software, 911
    workflow, 604, 606

Intracranial neurosurgery, 662
Intraoperative
  brain, 964
  cardiac guidance, 703
  CT images, 706
  fluoroscopy guidance, 711
  guidance, 600, 702, 842
  heart, 714
  imaging, 606, 607, 609, 702, 703, 712, 734,
      935, 964, 982, 987
    devices, 606, 731
    modality, 731
    systems, 608
  patient, 705, 714
  registration, 730, 734
  ultrasound, 606, 706, 731
  ultrasound images, 705
Intrapatient
  image registration, 972
  lung motion estimation, 308
  nonrigid registration, 961
  registration, 964
Intraprocedure guidance, 703
Intraslice features, 169
Intravascular ultrasound, 715
Invasive interventions, 676
Irregular motion pattern, 301
Irrelevant features, 475
ISBI EM segmentation, 237
Ischemic heart disease, 407, 412
Isotropic voxel size, 195, 655
Iterative closest point (ICP), 285, 732, 803
Iterative deep aggregation (IDA), 278
Iterative reconstruction (IR), 563

J
Jaccard loss, 170
Joint segmentation, 325

K
Kernel canonical correlation analysis (KCCA), 330
Keyhole neurosurgery, 796, 804, 805
Keyhole robotic surgery, 819
Knee
  MR segmentation, 265
  replacement surgery, 848
  segmentation, 265
KUKA robots, 867

L
Label, 115, 129, 139, 140, 143, 144, 166, 169,
      171, 191, 305–307, 431–433, 460, 461,
      464, 470, 471, 506, 522, 523, 525, 565
  assignment, 304, 305
  atlases, 140
  category, 461
  changes, 305
  data, 433
  decisions, 146
  fusion, 143, 144, 146–148, 158
    community, 147
    strategies, 458
  information, 151
  probabilities, 144
  propagation, 139, 140, 142, 154
  propagation performance, 142
  semantic, 191
  target, 147
  voxelwise, 144
Labeling, 305, 534
  conventions, 156
  multiatlas, 156, 158
  problem, 169
  process, 156
Landmarks, 173, 205–207, 323, 468, 470, 576,
      582, 585, 588, 590, 595, 731, 734, 779
  based approach, 584
  derivation, 212
  detection, 167, 205–207, 211, 214, 219, 225,
      227
  localization, 222
  location, 207, 208, 211–213, 215, 216, 587
  medical, 205
  points, 214, 221, 576, 586, 590
  position, 223, 587, 588, 595
  position in pixels, 215
  positions relative, 224
  regardless, 208
  representation, 207
Laparoscopic surgery, 732, 844, 941, 986, 987
Laparoscopic surgery conventional, 987
Laparoscopic surgical robot, 845, 846
Large deformation diffeomorphic metric mapping
      (LDDMM), 297, 336
Laser interstitial thermal therapy (LITT), 690
Laser speckle contrast imaging (LSCI), 764
Latent target segmentation, 147
Latent true label, 149

Latent true segmentration, 146
Layers, 39, 44, 46, 67, 68, 74, 83, 84, 118, 123,
        178, 194, 235, 260, 263, 278–280, 282,
        337, 482, 483, 485–487, 524, 527, 531, 532
    aggregations, 278
    classification, 187, 236, 487, 496
    CNNs, 487
    convolutional, 118, 125, 176, 235, 241, 279,
        334, 392, 487, 492–494, 498, 499, 524,
        541, 547
    discriminator, 81
    hierarchical, 235
    in classification problems, 492
    motion, 296, 297
    output, 492
Layerwise regularization, 297
Leakage detection process, 99
Learned similarity metric, 329, 330
Learning, 10, 26, 30, 31, 67, 72, 166, 167, 186,
        188, 208, 222, 224, 310, 321–324, 449,
        484, 497, 510, 548, 559, 565, 567, 569,
        899, 1001, 1003
    activity, 1003
    adversarial, 185, 186
    algorithm, 558
    appearance, 331
    appearance mapping models, 325
    approach, 45, 207, 227
    based approaches, 435
    better segmentation, 562
    complexity, 211
    curve, 992
    deep, 25, 42, 44, 45, 78, 84, 86, 102, 110–112,
        114, 155, 187, 211, 218, 232, 235, 239,
        274, 276, 277, 321, 332, 392, 430, 435,
        441, 443, 476, 488, 497, 498, 514, 528,
        533, 547, 646, 647, 710, 737, 941, 990,
        991
    features, 212
    function parametrizations, 35
    generators, 190
    initialized deformation field, 322
    model, 334
    objective, 322, 329
    part, 450
    preliminary, 334
    process, 70, 1003
    rate, 70, 83, 194, 215, 491, 496–498
    regularization term, 310

sessions, 1002
similarity metric, 328, 332
single, 35
strategies, 35, 47
supervised, 26, 29, 31, 32, 168, 207, 310, 313,
        329, 332, 334–336, 380, 387, 389, 390,
        394, 460, 495, 522–524
toolboxes, 448, 450
unsupervised, 30, 31, 166, 332, 336, 337, 380,
        381, 457
Left atrium (LA), 175
Left ventricle (LV), 275, 402
Left ventricular cavity (LVC), 274
Left ventricular myocardium (LVM), 274
LeNet CNN architecture, 492
Lesions, 9, 66, 68–71, 73, 75, 76, 85, 265, 346,
        352, 674, 686, 688, 729, 735
    abdominal, 688
    candidate detection, 68
    detection, 71, 73, 76, 83–86
        accuracy, 85
        dataset, 71
        software, 83, 86
        task, 67
    liver, 65, 66, 77, 82, 86
    multiple, 66
    segmentation, 86, 169, 186
    segmentation masks, 66, 70, 85
    visible, 674
Level accuracy, 522
Leverage annotated datasets, 219
Leveraging multilevel contextual information, 241
Linear
    combination, 30, 221, 441
    predictors, 594
    registration, 321
Liver, 70, 71, 73, 76, 78, 82, 84, 169, 171, 172,
        223, 225, 226, 295, 430, 432, 434, 458,
        459, 653, 657, 682, 684, 686, 687, 843,
        852
    ablations, 688
    anatomy, 658
    biopsies, 686
    blood circulation, 659
    cancer, 657
    CT, 303
    dome, 674, 688
    interventions, 674, 846
    lesion detection, 65, 68, 71, 82, 83, 86

lesion detection task, 67, 84
lesion segmentation, 66
lesions, 65, 66, 77, 82, 86
lesions in CT images, 85
metastases, 68, 69, 83
metastatic lesions, 70, 73
motion, 300
parenchyma, 77, 80
region, 86
segmentation, 73, 76, 85
    algorithm, 73
    network, 76
    results, 76
tissue, 296, 300, 303
tumor segmentation, 67
tumors, 805, 812
Local
    deformation field, 298
    features, 524
    information, 188, 235
    motion, 296
    patch, 6, 50, 329, 330, 467
    regularization, 302
Local binary patterns (LBP), 440
Localization performance, 122
Localized disease, 93
Localized patches, 67
Locating landmarks, 595
Long short-term memory (LSTM), 123, 124, 126,
    507, 514–518
Loopy belief propagation (LBP), 310
Loss, 12, 29, 52, 119, 120, 168, 170, 177, 187,
    191, 236, 280, 337, 345, 347, 506, 511,
    512, 549, 550, 555, 556, 558, 559, 564
    adversarial, 166, 170, 177, 178, 185, 186, 191,
        555, 563–565
    component, 170
    function, 26, 47, 49–51, 54, 67, 79, 82, 86, 119,
        120, 166, 187, 188, 280, 335, 337, 483,
        484, 498, 504, 547, 548, 550, 554, 564,
        570
    generator, 170
    information, 187
    layer, 118, 125
    segmentation, 170, 178, 192, 194
    term, 236, 556, 564
    voxelwise, 561, 564
Low attenuation area (LAA), 97
LSE pooling layer, 119

Lumbar hernia surgery, 715
Lung, 91, 93, 94, 96–98, 100–102, 172, 223, 225,
    226, 295, 297, 299, 300, 311–313
    airway, 98
    area, 94, 97, 98, 101–104
    area extraction, 94, 102
    area segmentation, 102
    boundary, 295
    CAD, 91, 92
    CAD systems, 92, 93
    cancer, 91–94
        detection, 91, 92
        diagnosis, 91
        screening, 93
    CT, 92, 302, 313
    data set, 303
    disease, 93, 97, 102
    disease diagnosis, 312
    fissures, 103, 295
    function, 103
    function assessment, 313
    image, 92
    image processing, 93
    interfaces, 301
    lobe, 97, 103, 104, 295, 312
    lobe classification, 98
    lobe segmentation, 102, 103
    microstructure, 97
    motion, 295, 300, 307, 308
    nodule, 93–95, 101, 560
    nodule detection, 92–94
    nodule detection process, 94, 95
    nodule qualification, 94
    parenchyma, 98, 300
    pleura, 93, 295
    region, 95, 102, 172
    region extraction, 102
    screening, 92
    structure, 92
    tumor, 94
    ventilation, 313
    volume, 313
    volume changes, 313
    volume expansion, 313
Lung Image Database Consortium (LIDC), 92
LV assessment, 411
LV segmentation, 283
LVM assessment, 405, 406

M

Machine learning, 7, 15, 18, 29, 52–54, 99,
        109–111, 140, 142, 143, 154, 155, 165,
        184, 206, 211, 253, 265, 266, 270, 276,
        288, 321–324, 380, 412, 419, 430,
        440–442, 457, 498, 522, 524, 532, 534,
        558, 603, 605, 606, 608, 646, 727, 732,
        898, 914, 916–918, 936, 938, 939, 941,
        944, 980, 983, 984, 1003
    algorithms, 211, 332, 392, 916, 940
    community, 15, 155
    model, 539
    performance, 54
    predictive, 390
    supervised, 387
    techniques, 145, 939
    unsupervised, 165, 387
Macrostructural brain changes, 360
Macrostructural neuronal loss, 344
Magnetic resonance imaging (MRI), 265, 345,
        379, 404, 430, 467, 610, 795, 921
    brain, 186, 322, 436, 469, 471, 472
    compatible intervention robots, 848
    dataset, 180
    interventional, 611, 674–677, 684
    registration, 331
    training images, 180
Magnetic resonance (MR), 2, 78, 344, 674, 963,
        965, 971
    acquisition, 15, 346, 684, 685
    image acquisitions, 4, 684
    images, 5, 17, 44, 78, 148, 331, 388, 561, 562,
        676–678, 684, 685, 702
    interventional, 678, 679
    knee segmentation, 269
    segmentation errors, 351
Magnetic resonance thermal imaging (MRTI), 690
Magnetic transfer ratio (MTR), 347
Malignant lesions, 77, 78, 80, 81, 83, 86
Malignant lesions detection, 78, 86
Malignant liver lesion detection, 77
Malignant liver lesions, 77, 78, 82
Mammalian hearts, 418
Manifold learning, 330
Manual
    labels, 433
    registration, 730, 731
    segmentation, 76, 157, 350, 359, 434, 560, 562,
        568
Manually circumscribed liver, 73, 84, 85
Marginal space learning (MSL), 222, 224
Markov random field (MRF), 145, 470
    labeling, 310
Master tool manipulator (MTM), 875
Maxillofacial surgery, 799
Maximum likelihood estimation (MLE), 144, 149
Mean diffusivity (MD), 385
Mean squared distance (MSD), 319
Meaningful features, 552
Medical
    anatomy education, 138
    anatomy parsing system, 206
    datasets, 197
    diagnosis, 522
    image
        acquisition, 562
        analysis, 112, 165, 184, 201, 205, 206, 250,
            274, 293, 319, 321, 327, 332, 547, 561,
            564, 646, 954
        analysis techniques, 548
        classification, 123
        databases, 113
        dataset, 110, 117
        diagnosis, 113
        features, 430
        informatics, 964
        parsing, 206
        processing, 141
        registration, 293, 294, 306, 307, 310, 313, 963
        segmentation, 67, 155, 187, 188, 197, 206,
            269, 275, 277, 280, 284, 564, 955
        segmentation methods, 187
        segmentation tasks, 185, 188
        synthesis, 186
    interventions, 603, 853, 911, 915, 920, 924
    landmarks, 205
    robotics, 841, 853
    robots, 612, 613
    trainees, 910
    volume segmentation, 185
    volume translation, 185
Medical device derivative (MDD), 992
Medical device regulation (MDR), 993
Memory constraints, 565
Mental diseases, 381, 388
Mental visualization, 653
Metal artifact reduction (MAR), 639
Metallic object, 659

Metastatic liver cancer, 657
Metastatic liver lesions, 66
Methodological development validation, 352
Metric learning, 330
Microrobotics, 987
Microsurgery, 613, 724
Microsurgery applications, 613
MIL pooling, 527–533
MIL pooling layer, 525, 527, 541, 543, 544
Mild cognitive impairment (MCI), 388
Millimeter accuracy, 805
Miniaturized robots, 853
Minimal evaluations, 810
Minimally invasive
    cochlear implant surgery, 844
    procedures, 655, 659, 674, 690, 714, 748, 761,
        843
    surgery, 722, 747, 796, 798, 939, 980, 981, 986
Minimum amount, 550
Minimum mean square error (MMSE), 220
Minimum spanning tree (MST), 302
Mixture of experts (MOE), 394
Modality translation, 189
Model
    atlas performance, 147
    diagnosis uncertainty, 362
    discriminator, 188
    generator, 188, 553
    heart, 275, 285
    learning, 334
    machine learning, 539
    network, 83, 280
    patient, 843
    predictions, 496, 547
    predictive, 389
    registration, 139, 337
    regularization, 297
    segmentation, 174–176
    trained, 126, 336, 337, 569
    training, 175
Monitoring interventional processes, 610
Monomodal registration, 327, 331
Morphological features, 437
Motion, 14, 273, 275, 285, 286, 293–295, 409,
        411, 412, 414, 509, 517, 518, 612, 613,
        682, 683, 702, 712, 729, 732, 736, 749,
        754, 764, 783, 819, 823, 828, 844, 847,
        914
    analysis, 275, 913, 914, 918

    artifacts, 27, 683
    cardiac, 275, 285, 402, 409, 412, 684
    combination, 412
    compensation, 712
    continuous, 702
    control card, 848
    correction, 311
    data, 508, 914
    discontinuities, 293, 301, 313
    economy, 915
    estimation, 294, 409, 729
    field, 297, 298, 310
    in sedated patient, 685
    layers, 296, 297
    liver, 300
    local, 296
    lung, 295, 300, 307, 308
    mask, 300
    needle, 847
    patient, 640, 704, 727
    patterns, 294, 296, 409
    quantification, 914
    reconstruction, 285, 288
    sensors, 914
    surgical, 509, 518, 913
    target, 712
    tracking systems, 914
    vectors, 297
Motionless structures, 764
Multiarray needles, 805
Multiatlas
    label fusion, 469
    labeling, 156, 158
    labeling pipeline, 157
    segmentation, 139, 141, 144–146, 154, 155,
        157, 384
Multiclass classification, 119
Multiconnected domain discriminator, 179
Multiexpert segmentations, 715
Multifunctional robotics, 841
Multilabel, 110
    classification, 120
    classification loss functions, 118
    classification loss layer, 119
    classification problems, 118, 280
    CNN, 117
    CNN architecture, 120
    DCNN classification, 117
    disease classification, 120

image classification network, 119
    problems, 311
Multilayer
    CNN, 170
    perceptron, 124
    segmentation, 261
Multilevel contextual information, 233, 235, 241,
    242, 244
Multimodal
    image registration, 313, 706
    intraoperative imaging, 985
    label fusion, 145
    medical images, 185, 330
    network, 130
    registration, 326, 327, 329–332
    registration performance, 330, 331
    volume segmentation, 191
Multimodality image registration, 206
Multimodality whole heart segmentation, 178
Multiobjective constrained optimization problem,
    797
Multiorgan segmentation, 217–219
Multipatient information, 607
Multiplanar acquisition, 686
Multiple
    atlases, 140
    atlases performance, 148
    cellular layers, 257
    data augmentation, 278
    lesions, 66
    objects, 206
    objects segmentation, 206
    organs, 222, 223
    organs in CT volumes, 223
    registrations, 5
    smaller patches, 534
Multiple instance learning (MIL), 522, 523
Multiple sclerosis (MS), 9
Multiscale features, 176
Multiscale regularization, 176
Multisurface segmentation, 250, 261, 262
Multisurface segmentation tasks, 253
Multiwavelength detection, 751
Mutual information (MI), 142, 143, 148, 176, 327,
    330, 552
Myocardial fiber architecture, 416, 418
Myocardial perfusion reserve (MPR), 413
Myocardial wall motion, 409
Myocardium segmentation, 275

N
Narrow band imaging (NBI), 754
National lung screening trial (NLST), 92
Natural landmarks, 730, 731, 734
Navigation, 654, 661–663, 706, 712, 713, 817,
    824, 829, 845, 849, 982, 991
    assistance, 849
    interactions, 822
    surgical, 661, 662, 777, 790, 911, 985
    system, 660, 842, 849
Navigational guidance, 660
Needle, 675–680, 684, 686, 687, 690, 780, 783,
    791, 796, 805, 806, 811, 812, 847, 902
    advancement, 685
    artifact, 680, 686
    calibration, 785
    driver, 848
    guidance, 653, 659, 685, 763
    guide, 846, 847
    holders, 682, 848
    insertion, 687, 846
    intervention, 847
    length, 690
    line, 806
    material, 680
    motion, 847
    placements, 812
    positioning, 685
    shaft, 686
    tip, 690, 784
    tracked, 784
    trajectory, 685, 686
    trajectory planning, 847
Neighbor voxels, 97
Neighborhood approximation forests (NAF), 266,
    476
Neighboring pixel, 244, 306, 595
Neighboring voxels, 146, 645
Network, 31, 32, 68, 69, 102, 117, 123, 124, 166,
    168, 169, 187, 197, 198, 215, 218,
    234–236, 238, 256, 278, 288, 332, 335,
    348, 354, 362, 443, 444, 482–484, 504,
    524, 531, 534, 548, 549, 898
    adversarial, 166, 174, 177, 179, 548, 555, 556,
        558, 564, 565
    architecture, 32, 44, 46, 49, 54, 68, 192, 215,
        497
    cGAN, 81, 86
    convolutional, 93, 168

deep, 241, 288, 335
designs, 193
discriminator, 51, 166, 179, 548, 549, 551, 554, 564, 567
domain adaptation, 180
generator, 166, 170, 548, 558, 564, 569
input, 69
liver segmentation, 76
model, 83, 280
multimodal, 130
parameters, 553
performance, 179
prediction, 336
registration, 335–337
regression, 335
segmentation, 174, 178, 185, 191, 196, 565
structure, 215
weights, 485
Neural network, 32, 38, 43, 46, 92–94, 110, 122, 123, 130, 165, 176, 238, 240, 278, 281, 329, 435, 443, 450, 481, 482, 524, 527, 535, 548, 549, 552, 553, 588, 732, 734, 942
architectures, 26, 235, 279, 483, 497, 534
for biomedical image segmentation, 244
for prediction, 483
performance, 200
training, 498
Neurodegenerative diseases, 344, 346, 357, 358, 383, 393
Neurodegenerative pathology, 352
Neuroimage registration, 963, 964, 971
Neuroimaging acquisition techniques, 344
Neurological surgery, 724
Neuronal loss, 344, 347, 348, 355
Neuronal loss assessment, 345
Neuronavigation, 819
Neuropsychiatric diseases, 380
Neurosurgery, 603, 613, 662, 715, 779, 796, 798, 811, 850, 964, 986, 991
Neurosurgery applications, 702
Neurosurgical interventions, 675
Nodule detection, 94
Nodule detection lung, 92–94
Nonconvex regularization, 34
Nonlandmark locations, 211
Nonlinear registration, 141, 142, 352
Nonlocal regularization, 310
Nonmotion information, 412

Nonoptimal registration, 308
Nonrigid image registration, 954
Nonrigid registration, 139, 731, 732
Nonrigid registration intrapatient, 961
Nontrainable, 531, 532
Nontrainable elements, 54
Normative brain, 389
Noticeable macrostructural neuronal loss, 358
Novice surgeon, 1003
Nuclear magnetic resonance (NMR), 10
Nuclei segmentation, 234
Nuclei segmentation challenge, 242
Numerical validation, 810

O
Obese patients, 674, 704
Object
    acquisition DAP, 637
    boundaries, 310
    classification accuracy, 239
    detection, 111, 112, 232, 494, 500, 732
    detection performance, 120
    function, 642
    grasping, 800
    instances, 234
    itself, 207, 217, 489, 641
    localization, 492
    shapes, 729
    surface, 801
    target, 586
    type, 803
    visualization challenges, 631
Object Management Group (OMG), 866
Obstetric dataset, 214
Obstructing CNN training, 125
Offline training, 29
Olympus endoscopes, 754
Olympus Lucera flexible endoscope, 750
Oncologic diseases, 676
Oncological patients, 65
Open Source Robotics Foundation (OSRF), 866
Operative assessment, 913
Ophthalmic surgery, 986
Optical coherence tomography (OCT), 257, 260, 660, 724, 748, 760
Optimal segmentation process, 267
Optimized network designs, 196
Optimizers, 496, 499
Ordinary least squares (OLS), 385

Organs, 169, 206, 222, 224–226, 458, 459, 732, 749, 751, 796, 812, 933, 953, 954, 956, 971
Organs motion, 301
Organs motion properties, 297
Organs segmentation, 206, 222
Orthopaedic
    bone fracture surgery, 796, 812
    robot, 848, 849
    robotic system, 843
    spine surgery, 662
    surgery, 715, 796, 798, 803, 842, 991
    trauma surgery, 649, 662, 798, 804
    ultrasound images registration, 711
Outlier detection, 472
Overlapping lesions, 70
Overlay organs, 729

P
Pairwise registration, 139
Pancreas segmentation, 187
Paramount importance, 244
Parenchymal lung disease, 759
Passive robot, 844
Patches
    atlases, 6
    center, 332
    CT image, 560
    dictionary, 7
    extraction, 30
Patchwise
    fashion, 323
    manner, 329
    pixel, 187
Pathological diagnosis, 756
Pathological lung segmentation, 169
Pathology, 10, 102, 113, 117–119, 126, 249, 345, 346, 350–352, 354, 355, 362, 363, 496, 795, 932, 956
    candidate, 121
    classes, 120
    course, 353
    image dataset, 126
    images, 122, 123
    localization, 117, 118
    reports, 122, 124, 126
    subtypes, 357, 362
    thoracic, 113
    vascular, 353

Patient, 9, 10, 70, 73, 85, 96, 112, 126, 172, 178, 382, 383, 387, 402, 406, 432, 504, 505, 556, 561, 562, 603–605, 626, 627, 674–676, 704, 705, 713, 796–798, 842, 846, 847, 875, 881, 895, 896, 898, 909, 910, 933, 934, 957, 961, 980, 984
    access, 675, 678
    age, 984
    anatomical structures, 795
    anatomy, 605, 607, 649, 790, 875, 943
    automatic classification, 388
    benefit, 992
    bone geometry, 796
    care, 599, 600, 612, 615, 909, 910, 931, 932, 934–938, 1000
    collision detection, 652
    condition, 795
    CT scans, 803
    data, 608
    data bases, 609
    discomfort, 561, 562
    entrance dose, 634
    head, 843
    health status, 943
    healthcare, 895
    heart, 419
    history, 941
    human, 1002
    information, 982, 988
    management process, 939
    measurements, 508
    model, 843
    monitoring, 685, 988
    monitoring equipment, 676
    monitoring systems, 982
    motion, 640, 704, 727
    MR images, 565
    normal motion, 854
    outcome, 804, 941, 944, 991, 992, 997, 1000
    populations, 943
    positioning, 685, 1000
    positioning requirements, 1000
    preoperative, 608, 797
    preoperative CT scan, 796
    registration, 779, 780, 790
    safety, 855, 868, 989
    satisfaction, 937
    selection, 411, 432
    setups, 654

skin, 685
skull, 796
specific modeling, 990
state, 615
support, 652
weighing, 652
Patient side manipulator (PSM), 875
Pattern classification, 389
Pelvic surgery, 663
Penalized likelihood (PL), 645
Perceptual loss, 52
Perceptual loss term, 564
Perceptual VGG loss, 52
Percutaneous interventions, 917
Performance
    assessment, 911
    atlases, 147
    benchmarks, 129, 918, 919
    classification, 527, 532, 538, 539
    clinical, 995, 1003
    comparison, 321
    detection, 68, 73, 74
    estimation, 144
    evaluation, 444, 924
    feedback, 917
    gain, 240, 242, 534
    gaps, 111
    heart, 407
    improvement, 111, 120
    level, 143, 144, 148, 151, 153
    level estimation, 158
    machine learning, 54
    measure, 538, 539
    metrics, 537–540, 819, 837
    network, 179
    neural network, 200
    registration, 321, 324–326, 337
    segmentation, 141, 154, 155, 185, 196, 200,
        244, 277, 279, 288
    surgeon, 943
    surgical, 944, 945
Periodic motions, 916
Peristaltic motion, 295
Periventricular lesions, 346
Personalized patient care, 675
PET acquisition, 356
Phase detection, 733, 736
Phase information, 709

Physician, 87, 249, 265, 268, 599, 600, 605, 606,
        655, 656, 841, 842, 844, 899, 901, 904,
        905, 910, 912, 980, 995
    console, 844
    control panel, 842
    intervention, 849
    training, 602
Physiological assessments, 402
Physiological motions, 684, 724
Pixel, 169, 193, 206, 210, 213, 239, 242, 304, 307,
        522, 533–535, 537, 586, 627–629, 631
    aperture, 627
    error, 239, 242
    patchwise, 187
    pitch, 629, 635, 637
    signal, 631
    similarity, 239
    values, 537, 593
Pixelwise, 188
    classification, 237
    classification layer, 167
    classifier, 233, 240
    optimal action, 211
    reconstruction, 189
    reconstruction loss, 189
Plain feedforward architecture, 494
Planned intervention, 605
Planned surgical approach, 606
Pooling layer, 118, 119, 487, 491, 524, 528, 540,
        543, 544
Porcine heart, 713
Pose sensor, 777–781
Pose sensor configuration, 783
Positioning robots, 844
Positron emission tomography (PET), 5, 77, 344,
        404, 413, 430, 473
Post market surveillance (PMS), 993
Postinterventional care, 932
Postoperative CT scan, 812
Preclinical
    imaging studies, 753
    phases, 344
    presentation, 348
Predication layer, 119
Prediction, 5, 110, 114, 122, 123, 125, 129, 169,
        170, 186, 187, 274, 281, 332, 347, 359,
        361, 362, 387, 390, 461, 462, 483, 484,
        496, 499, 508, 513, 537, 548, 549, 555,
        559, 590, 594

accuracy, 389, 470
  for semantic segmentation, 278
  form, 462
  layer, 118–121
  module, 125
  network, 336
  output, 171
  radiomics, 436
  segmentation, 180
  single, 461, 464
  voxel, 176
Predictive
  biomarkers, 381
  features, 432
  function, 558
  information, 474
  machine learning, 390
  model, 389
  power, 475, 962
Predictor, 558
Preempt neuronal loss, 348
Preoperative
  CT images, 706
  CT scan, 849
  images, 795, 797, 806, 807, 811, 962, 965, 971
  patient, 608, 797
  plan, 798, 800, 812, 842, 849
  planning, 796, 799, 812
  planning tool, 812
Presegmentation, 259, 261, 263
Pretrained
  CNN, 498
  convolutional network, 498
  DCNN, 118
  DCNN architectures, 118
  models, 117
  networks, 497, 498
  ResNet, 126
Principal component analysis (PCA), 217, 324, 441, 579
Probabilistic segmentation, 360
Probe motion, 765
Procedural guidance, 660
Procedural skill assessment, 917
Progressive GANs, 560
Prompt biopsy, 757
Prostate cancer patients, 895
Prostate segmentation, 903
Proton resonance frequency shift (PRFS), 683

Public dataset, 113, 116, 130, 233, 237, 244
Pulmonary disease, 403
Pulmonary nodule detection in CT images, 112
Putative clinical utility, 389

Q
Qualitative evaluation, 127, 238, 242
Quality labels, 110
Quantitative
  assessment, 914
  evaluation, 126, 233, 837
  evaluation metrics, 239, 242
  features, 430
  performances, 111, 120
  radiomics features, 431
Quantum detection efficiency (QDE), 628

R
Radiation surgery, 796
Radiology Gamuts Ontology (RGO), 206
Radiomics
  features, 436, 437, 440
  pipeline, 431–434
  prediction, 436
Random forest (RF), 8, 266, 443, 458–460, 476, 524, 588, 710, 732, 941
Random motion, 418
Randomized controlled trials (RCT), 944
Rater performance, 144, 147
Rater performance level, 144, 149
Rater performance model, 157
Rating performance, 150
Raw motion data, 914
Raw pixel values, 529, 587, 592
Receiver operating characteristic (ROC), 430, 446
Receptor labeling, 156
Rectangular patches, 588
Recurrent architecture, 39, 44
Recurrent neural network (RNN), 43, 123, 169, 276, 503, 504, 507, 510, 941
  architecture, 39
Refinement residual block (RRB), 277, 288
Region of interest (ROI), 79, 431, 434, 532
Registered atlases, 143, 147
Registration, 14, 139–141, 206, 293, 294, 303, 307, 320, 321, 324, 325, 351, 352, 360, 469, 605, 606, 611, 631, 646, 658, 661, 662, 711, 714, 725, 726, 730–732, 754, 765, 778, 781, 782, 797, 798, 871, 883, 898, 961, 963, 984, 986, 988

accuracy, 324, 334, 335, 458, 711, 962, 965
algorithms, 146, 294, 295, 304, 319, 321, 329,
    335, 359, 989
approaches, 304, 709
based synthesis, 5
brain, 142
combination, 5
continuous, 731, 734
CT, 969
deformable, 5–7, 320, 321, 327, 331, 332, 335,
    336, 662
error, 139, 309, 313, 778, 804
failures, 140
fiducials, 779, 783
framework, 307
initialization, 338, 706
intraoperative, 730, 734
intrapatient, 964
linear, 321
literature, 778
manual, 730, 731
medical image, 293, 294, 306, 307, 310, 313,
    963
methods, 139, 142, 320, 325, 327, 328, 730
model, 139, 337
MRI, 331
multimodal, 326, 327, 329–332
network, 335–337
parameters for deformable registration, 335
patient, 779, 780, 790
performance, 321, 324–326, 337
philosophy, 139
problem, 306, 322, 325, 778
process, 139, 356, 711
processing, 139
results, 299, 334, 337
steps, 715
target, 778
task, 310, 321, 323, 332, 335, 337
techniques, 308
transformation, 778
Regression
    CNNs, 561, 563
    learning problem, 338
    network, 335
Regularization, 28, 34, 177, 191, 236, 275, 284,
    294–296, 301, 305, 471, 495, 498, 499, 568
    constraint, 36
    counterpart, 301
    energy, 310
    function, 34, 36, 43
    kernels, 298, 299
    local, 302
    method for neural networks, 499
    methods, 300, 301, 303, 498, 499
    model, 297
    part, 28, 42
    scheme, 298
    single iteration, 39
    standard, 294
    techniques, 34
Regulatory information, 905
Reinforcement learning, 35, 211, 212
Relative wall thickness (RWT), 408
Remote procedure call (RPC), 866
Renal tumors, 684, 688, 805
Representation learning, 509
Reproducible classification, 388
ResNet, 93, 95, 118, 123, 167, 188, 197, 494,
    497, 498
    architecture, 494
    architecture variants, 123
    designs, 188
    pretrained, 126
Respiratory motion, 296
Retinal layers, 257, 259, 260
Retinal OCT images, 561
Retinal OCT segmentation, 257
Retinal vein occlusion (RVO), 257
Revision control system (RCS), 871
Revision surgery, 662, 804
RF classification, 472
RF classification algorithm, 472
RF classification model, 472
Right ventricle (RV), 275, 402
Right ventricular cavity (RVC), 274
Ringing artifacts, 15
Risk assessment, 402
RNN architectures, 514
Roadmap fluoroscopic guidance, 655
Robot, 599, 608, 610, 612, 613, 789, 790, 841,
    843, 844, 850, 865, 866, 877, 878, 985,
    986, 988
    arms, 846, 877, 881, 985
    da Vinci, 986
    kinematics, 876, 878, 881
    motions, 613, 614
    orthopaedic, 848, 849

Robot operating system (ROS), 862, 863, 866, 879, 888
Robotic, 611, 613, 788, 855, 862, 866, 888, 980, 984, 985, 1004
  arm, 842–844, 848, 849, 851
  community, 866
  control, 983
  devices, 607, 609, 612, 849
  devices for interventional applications, 612
  devices for microsurgery, 613
  foundation, 866
  imaging, 982
  imaging systems, 987
  instruments, 881
  intervention, 842, 848, 855
  intervention control, 855
  interventional devices, 613
  manipulators, 850, 855, 987
  mechanism, 851
  middleware, 867
  needle guide, 847
  platforms, 987
  precision guidance system, 842
  procedure, 985
  subsidiary, 866
  surgery, 733, 841, 941, 986–988, 999
  systems, 606, 612, 613, 615, 715, 788, 842, 843, 847, 849, 889, 981, 986, 987, 999
    clinical implementation, 994
    for prostate interventions, 848
    in medical interventions, 853
    positioning, 612
  technologies, 855
  tool, 849
  toolkit, 880
ROSA robot, 843

S

Safety assessment, 344
Salient landmarks, 323
Scanner specific atlases, 385
Scene features, 729
Schizophrenia patients classification, 388
Seamless segmentation, 167
SEEG interventions, 805
Segmentation, 66, 92–94, 111, 112, 140, 145, 167, 169, 172, 176, 184–186, 207, 223, 225, 232–234, 250, 253, 257–259, 274, 276, 277, 325, 332, 351, 352, 358, 402, 405, 431, 434, 458, 469, 499, 533, 534, 547, 548, 562, 564, 605, 606, 707, 710, 714, 797, 812, 819, 833, 898, 902, 955, 956, 984, 988
  accuracy, 143–145, 148, 154, 174, 175, 180, 225, 250, 260
  algorithms, 85, 187, 206, 232, 269, 405, 955
  analysis, 352
  anatomical, 93
  approaches, 264, 709
  automated, 175, 249, 270, 274, 276, 277, 288, 405, 406, 413
  automatic, 141, 233, 709
  bone, 710
  cardiac, 274, 275, 288
  challenge, 233, 234, 237–239, 242, 244
  CNN, 192, 548, 565
  combination, 564
  contour, 285
  CT, 197
  deep neural network, 277
  errors, 197, 256, 564
  evaluation, 196
  evaluation metric, 241
  framework, 278, 469
  ground truth, 281
  inaccuracies, 259
  instance, 492, 494
  knee, 265
  lesions, 86, 169, 186
  liver, 73, 76, 85
  loss, 170, 178, 192, 194
  manual, 76, 157, 350, 359, 434, 560, 562, 568
  mapping, 177
  maps, 548
  mask, 66, 73, 85, 173, 187, 560
  mask for brain tumors, 560
  medical image, 67, 155, 187, 188, 197, 206, 269, 275, 277, 280, 284, 564, 955
  methods, 111, 187, 188, 249, 281, 434, 471, 569, 709
  metric, 239
  model, 174–176
  module performs, 269
  multiatlas, 139, 141, 144–146, 154, 155, 157, 384
  multilayer, 261
  network, 174, 178, 185, 191, 196, 565

network for biomedical image segmentation, 233
outcome, 251
performance, 141, 154, 155, 185, 196, 200, 244, 277, 279, 288
pipeline, 140
prediction, 180
problem, 140, 232, 250, 251, 268
process, 86
quality, 252
reproducibility, 350
results, 66, 139, 146, 154, 168, 187, 197, 224, 234, 238, 244, 250, 251, 256, 257, 260, 278, 280, 282, 285, 709
score, 66, 196
semantic, 167, 169, 459, 466, 469
software, 448
tasks, 66, 112, 185, 250, 280, 281, 435, 537, 566
tools, 359
tumor, 169, 564
validation, 715
volumetric, 187, 241
Segmented object, 659
Segmented ultrasound bone, 715
Segmenting brain tumors, 470
Segmentor learning, 185
Seizure onset zones (SOZ), 965
Semantic
features, 437, 733
information, 175, 279
label, 191
pixelwise segmentation, 167
segmentation, 167, 169, 459, 466, 469
Semiautomatic biopsy guns, 678
Semisupervised learning, 335, 393, 471, 560, 567
Semisupervised learning approach, 381
Semisupervised learning methods, 383, 394
Sensorized surgical instruments, 935
Sensory information, 835
Sequence acquisitions, 355
Shallowest layers, 277
Siamese networks, 444
SIFT features, 593
Similarity metric, 294, 303–306, 325, 327–334, 336, 337, 472, 476, 961
Similarity metric for registration task, 329
Similarity metric learning, 328, 332
Simple linear iterative clustering (SLIC), 301

Simultaneous localization and mapping (SLAM), 728
Single
atlas segmentation methods, 139
cadaver brain, 138
cells, 540, 542
class, 437, 446
classification threshold, 539
click, 886
coil, 45
contextual information, 242
convolutional layer, 494
dataset, 445, 446
developer, 872
disease, 432
evaluation, 447
image, 5, 470
instances, 523
label, 142, 522
landmark, 221
learning, 35
measurement vector, 504
nucleus, 243
output, 507
packet, 877
parent, 461
performance measure, 837
point, 577
prediction, 461, 464
rater, 143
resolution, 179
resource, 877
scalar, 526
score, 541
solution, 448
statistic, 464
step, 37, 450
subject prediction, 388
term, 34
thread, 877
writer, 877
WSI, 534
Single photon emission computed tomography (SPECT), 404, 413
Skeletal anatomy, 155
Skill assessment, 736, 910, 939, 941
computerized, 910
for surgical training, 608
surgical, 941

Slicer, 862, 863, 867, 870, 871, 883–886, 888, 889, 924
    application framework, 862, 886
    core, 885, 886
    extensions, 883
    for medical image visualization, 881
    framework, 884
    IGT, 889
    module, 883
SlicerIGT, 882–884
    based interventional, 882
    extension, 885, 924
    toolset, 883
Sliding motion, 294–297
Sliding motion in lung CT, 309
Sliding motion regularization, 313
Sliding organ motion, 297, 303
Small vessel disease (SVD), 391
Softmax classification layer, 235
Softmax loss, 119
Software features, 924
Software objects, 821
Solution accuracy, 972
Sparse combination, 31
Sparse learning, 323
Sparse learning techniques, 323, 325
Sparsity based classification scheme, 85
Spatial transformer network (STN), 337
Specialized surgical suites, 610
Spectral information, 749
Spinal navigation, 662
Spinal neurosurgery, 662
Spine surgery, 612, 662, 798, 842
Spine surgery orthopaedic, 662
Stained pathology, 126
Standard
    backpropagation, 238
    clinical, 991
    GANs, 551, 559
    regularization, 294
Standardized uptake value (SUV), 79
Statistical shape model (SSM), 217, 276
Steadily improving performance, 523
Steep learning curve, 1000
Stereo endoscopes, 723
Stereo visualization, 612
Stereoscopic visualization, 799
Stereotactic neurosurgery, 612, 796
Stochastic gradient descent (SGD), 485

Streak artifacts, 631
Streamlined patient, 654
Structurally correct segmentations, 564
Structure information, 189
Structure segmentation, 233
Subcortical brain, 383
Subdegree accuracy, 777, 780, 782
Subdermal needles, 690
Subjecting patients, 850
Subjective assessments, 912
Subjective evaluations, 837
Subneural networks, 166
Suboptimal surgical, 662
Substantial performance load, 259
Subtle gridline artifacts, 638
Superior performance, 169, 172, 233
Superpixel dictionary learning, 74
Supervised
    action classification, 227
    classification, 387
    learning, 26, 29, 31, 32, 168, 207, 310, 313, 329, 332, 334–336, 380, 387, 389, 390, 394, 460, 495, 522–524
    learning methods, 567
    machine learning, 387
    segmentation method, 568
Supervoxels, 301, 471
Support vector machine (SVM), 234, 387, 390
Support vector regression (SVR), 390
Surface registration, 732
Surface segmentation, 251
Surface segmentation bone, 266
Surgeon, 609, 611–614, 703, 704, 712, 713, 747, 795, 798–800, 802–804, 806–811, 885, 886, 938, 941, 943–945, 980, 982, 984–986, 989, 990, 992, 996, 999, 1000
    expressed satisfaction, 803
    grasps, 802
    interfaces, 608
    movement, 938
    performance, 943
    planning, 811
Surgery, 600, 603, 608, 614, 653, 655, 661, 703, 714, 722, 726, 733, 736, 777, 795–798, 829, 841, 844, 850, 931, 935, 936, 938, 961, 962, 979, 980, 988
    abdominal, 663, 796, 986
    cardiac, 703, 850, 935
    endoscopic, 613, 798

execution, 795
interventional, 850
minimally invasive, 722, 747, 796, 798, 939, 980, 981, 986
orthopaedic, 715, 796, 798, 803, 842, 991
planning, 796, 798, 806
possess grasper joints, 733
robotic, 733, 841, 941, 986–988, 999
simulation, 799
thoracic, 663
time, 736
vascular, 850
Surgical, 509, 612, 652, 663, 734, 736, 783, 796, 806, 812, 836, 910, 912, 913, 931, 935, 938, 941, 987, 989, 991, 1000, 1004
  access, 795
    path, 990
    planning, 797
    point, 797
  action, 985
  activity, 517, 733, 935, 941
  activity recognition, 508
  applications, 778, 804, 983
  approach, 606, 798, 986
  area, 722
  arsenal, 663
  assessment, 912, 914
  assistance, 935, 936
  cameras, 787
  care, 932, 935–937, 940, 944
    for patients, 932
    pathway, 932, 934, 935, 937, 938
    providers, 935
  community, 943
  competency assessment, 997
  constraints, 806
  da Vinci, 723
  data science, 608, 931, 938, 941, 991
  detection, 733
  devices, 600
  discipline, 724
  display, 724
  domains, 944, 980
  education, 996
  environment, 610, 725, 789, 990
  field, 654, 781, 791, 935, 936
  guidance, 703, 706, 711, 761, 789
  guidance systems, 713, 714
  guides, 797

images, 727
instrumentation, 662
instruments, 600, 611, 612, 732, 733, 777, 779, 780, 782, 795, 796, 914, 916, 936, 988
interactions, 833
interventions, 604, 606, 756, 944
intraoperative, 941
microscopes, 611, 726, 990
motion, 509, 518, 913
navigation, 661, 662, 777, 790, 911, 985
navigation accuracy, 779
navigation systems, 603, 606, 611, 614, 782, 924
oncology, 991
outcome, 795, 936, 943, 984, 988, 989, 997
pathway, 938
patient care, 932
patients, 937, 938
performance, 944, 945
phase detection, 733
phase recognition, 941
plan, 985
planning tasks, 797
practice, 943
procedures, 652, 663, 796, 912, 913, 932, 940, 982, 983, 991, 996
process, 918, 935, 939, 982
product, 654, 661
recording, 941
research, 937
resection, 656
robotic systems, 842, 850
robotics, 841, 842
robots, 797, 841, 846, 936, 939, 987, 994, 999
rules, 806, 807
scene, 730, 732, 917, 988
simulations, 606
simulators, 812, 999, 1001
site, 723, 737, 804
site infections, 935
skill assessment, 941
skills, 913, 914, 916, 936
solutions, 983
stylus, 782
suite, 982
support systems, 932
systems, 811, 935
target, 663, 797
target identification, 797
task performance, 608

tasks, 613, 797, 914, 989
team, 936, 938, 980, 988–990, 1000, 1003
team members, 988
techniques, 931
thread, 733
tool, 609, 611–613, 706, 732, 733, 782, 796,
    797, 804, 828, 916, 923, 980, 984–986
  detection, 733
  manipulation, 981
  motions, 612
training, 615, 923, 933
training tool, 736
video, 737, 789
vision, 737
vision algorithms, 737
visualization, 935
workflow, 606, 608, 611, 734, 736, 780, 782,
    789, 936, 943, 982, 990, 999
workflow planning, 797
Surgical Assistant Workstation (SAW), 877
Surgical data science (SDS), 931
Surgical Process Models (SPM), 918
Synthesizing MR images, 78
Synthesizing ultrasound, 331
Synthetic subject images, 5

T
Target
  anatomy, 610
  detection, 759
  domain, 172–174, 940
  intraparenchymatous lesions, 688
  label, 147
  landmark, 211, 212, 215, 595
  landmark location, 211
  motion, 712
  object, 586
  registration, 778
  surgical, 663, 797
  voxel, 152
Target registration error (TRE), 778
Targeted anatomy, 606
Targeted interventions, 615
Tau pathology, 348, 349
Technology transfer officers (TTO), 899
Telemanipulated robotic platform, 847
Telemanipulated robotic surgery, 986, 1000
Teleoperated robotic manipulators, 987
Teleoperated surgical robots, 844

Telerobotic system, 847, 851
Telesurgery scenarios, 988
Temporal registration, 727
Temporal regression network, 276
Textural features, 234
Therapeutic interventions, 674, 685
Thoracic
  disease, 110, 113, 117, 120
  disease detection, 117
  pathology, 113
  surgery, 663
TiRobot, 849
ToF endoscope prototypes, 730
Tongue motion, 14
TPR detection measurements, 74
Tracked
  features, 728
  needle, 784
  surgical instruments, 789, 791
  surgical tools, 614, 706, 707
  ultrasound, 706
Train, 31, 36, 38, 44, 46, 70, 86, 95, 102, 113, 126,
    127, 178, 192, 194, 199, 323, 326, 329,
    335, 337, 433, 435, 443, 444, 468, 500,
    525, 526, 558, 559, 564, 569, 587–589
  adversarial networks, 185
  artificial agents, 595
  classification RFs, 472
  CNNs, 113
  complex deep learning, 110
  GANs, 189
  generators, 194, 196
  models, 49
Trainable
  activation functions, 43
  data, 42
Trained
  classification network, 196
  discriminator, 81, 166
  model, 126, 336, 337, 569
  network, 278
  offline, 37
  pathologist, 533
  regression forest, 323
Trainees, 894, 898, 899, 905, 910–912, 914, 915,
    917, 918, 923, 996, 997, 1001
  medical, 910
  performances, 919
  perspectives, 917

practice, 911
Transferring information, 562
Transition layer, 118–121, 494
Translation, 166, 175, 178, 185, 186, 189, 217, 285, 320, 334, 489, 534, 548, 554, 577, 578, 730, 731, 780, 788, 895–897, 912, 914, 983, 991, 992
  clinical, 157, 736, 893, 894, 911
  CT image, 186
  equivariance, 489
  invariance, 487
  mapping, 189
  parameters, 335, 578
  vector, 287
Translational, 894
  challenge, 991, 994
  perspectives, 736
  research, 894, 895, 905
  researcher, 894
  sciences, 895
  spectrum, 894
Transmission Control Protocol (TCP), 864
Transnasal surgery, 851
Trauma surgery, 798, 991
Trauma surgery orthopaedic, 649, 662, 798, 804
Traumatic brain injuries, 458
True label, 146, 147, 149
True label voxel, 152
True negative (TN), 537
True positive rate (TPR), 446
True positive (TP), 537
True segmentation, 149, 152
Truly model prediction uncertainty, 491
Truncated backpropagation, 513
Truncated backpropagation through time (TBTT), 513
Tubular organs, 766
Tumor, 171, 430, 432, 434, 437, 504, 507, 561, 569, 676, 688, 690, 805, 806, 811, 956, 957, 963
  ablation, 674
  ablation process, 805
  boundaries, 964
  brain, 238, 449, 796
  growth, 953
  lung, 94
  obliteration, 805
  resection, 962

  segmentation, 169, 564
  tissue, 683

U

Ultrasound, 331, 610, 674, 684, 686, 687, 702, 703, 706, 707, 709–711, 714, 715, 731, 785, 787, 795, 812, 895, 898, 902, 962, 982, 983
  bone segmentation, 710
  calibration, 785, 787, 790
  coupling, 785
  coupling medium, 785
  data, 707, 709, 711, 714
  data manipulation, 705
  datasets, 214
  detection, 761
  elastography, 610
  endoscopic, 780, 791
  guidance, 660
  image, 214, 331, 674, 704–706, 786, 884, 887, 902, 904
  image reconstruction, 902
  imagery, 705
  imaging, 702, 706–708, 714, 715, 901
  in orthopaedic surgery, 715
  in spine surgery, 715
  intraoperative, 606, 706, 731
  physics, 706
  probe, 610, 704, 707, 785
  reconstruction, 704
  snapshots, 715
  thermography, 610
  tracked, 706
  transducers, 787
Uncertainty detection, 115
Uncommon features, 437, 440
Unconstrained landmark location, 590
Unconstrained optimization problem, 31
Undertesting machine learning algorithms, 382
Unified modeling language (UML), 873
Universal cardiac introducer (UCI), 712
Universal dependency graph (UDG), 115
Unlabeled
  atlases, 141
  data, 537, 567, 568
  images, 471
  samples, 567
  test image, 140
Unprocessed medical images, 604

Unsupervised
    domain adaptation, 175, 176, 558
    learning, 30, 31, 166, 332, 336, 337, 380, 381,
        457
        algorithms, 166
        for surgical motion, 518
        models, 336
        techniques, 385
    machine learning, 165, 387
Unsupervised domain adaptation (UDA), 558
Untethered
    microrobots, 842, 852
    robot, 853
    robot maneuver, 852
Upsampling features, 277, 279
Upsampling layers, 235, 237, 240
Usability evaluation, 995
User
    acceptance, 993
    commands, 803
    expectations, 836
    experience, 259, 823, 827
    friendly manuals, 993
    inputs, 256, 269
    interaction, 259, 268, 435, 800, 801, 803, 826,
        836, 989
    interface, 250, 804, 819, 825, 832
    interventions, 250
    tasks, 998
User Datagram Protocol (UDP), 864
Utilizes multiple atlases, 140

V
Validation, 82, 83, 87, 195, 263, 347, 348, 350,
        352, 354, 444, 445, 803, 808, 873, 874,
        899
    clinical, 810
    dataset, 497
    segmentation, 715
    set, 444–446
Valvular diseases, 415
Vascular
    brain injury, 390
    pathology, 353
    surgery, 850
VeeDA network, 179
Ventral nerve cord (VNC), 237
Ventricular wall motion, 702
Versatile architecture, 43

Vertebrae landmark localization, 167
Vessel disease, 346, 352, 391
VGG loss, 52
VGG network, 52
Video assessment, 918
Virtual
    incision robot, 845
    model guidance, 713
    objects, 824
    reality visualization, 887
Virtually motionless, 712
Visceral surgery, 732, 981
Visual question answering (VQA), 112
Visualization, 1, 232, 256, 269, 347, 348, 499, 577,
        605–607, 642, 643, 654, 656, 660, 676,
        686, 688, 703, 706, 714, 796, 797, 808,
        862, 870, 881, 898, 924, 934, 935, 984,
        990
    advanced, 988
    anatomical, 702
    augmented reality, 911
    features, 885
    impediment, 703
    information, 989
    methodologies, 984
    requirements, 678
    software, 888
    surgical, 935
    testing results, 874
    volumetric, 797
Visualize anatomy, 600
Visualize lesions, 674
Visualizing anatomy beneath, 785
Visualizing robots, 879
Volume of interest (VOI), 95
Volumetric
    acquisition, 654
    CT images, 468
    CycleGAN block, 174, 175
    domain adaptation method, 174
    segmentation, 187, 241
    visualization, 797
Voxel, 3, 5, 7, 12, 95, 97, 99, 100, 142–144,
        146–152, 191, 223, 225, 237, 260, 266,
        280, 301, 302, 307, 308, 327, 336, 439,
        469–471, 595, 642–644, 787
    classification, 100
    domain, 642
    level, 471

locations, 257
prediction, 176
target, 152
true label, 152
value, 643
Voxelwise
  binary variable, 469
  classification, 470
  label, 144

loss, 561, 564
loss term, 556
semantic segmentation, 458

W

Wasserstein GANs, 551, 552
Weak image labels, 542
White matter (WM), 3, 325, 389
Workflow assessment, 990